Bibliography of Preservation Literature, 1983–1996

Robert E. Schnare, Jr.
and
Susan G. Swartzburg
with
George M. Cunha

The Scarecrow Press, Inc.
Lanham, Maryland, and London
2001

SCARECROW PRESS, INC.

Published in the United States of America
by Scarecrow Press, Inc.
4720 Boston Way, Lanham, Maryland 20706
www.scarecrowpress.com

4 Pleydell Gardens, Folkestone
Kent CT20 2DN, England

British Library Cataloguing in Publication Information Available

Library of Congress Cataloging-in-Publication Data

Schnare, Robert E.
  Bibliography of preservation literature, 1983–1996 / Robert E. Schnare, Jr.
    p. cm.
  Includes index.
  ISBN 0-8108-3712-9 (cloth : alk. paper)
   1. Library materials—Conservation and restoration—Bibliography. 2. Archival
materials— Conservation and restoration—Bibliography. I. Title.
  Z701.2 .S36 2001
  016.0258'4—dc21   99-049600

for
George M. Cunha
and
Susan G. Swartzburg

Contents

Preface   vii
Robert E. Schnare, Jr.

Tribute to George and Susan   ix
Robert H. Patterson

Acknowledgments   xi
Robert E. Schnare, Jr.

Bibliography of Preservation Literature, 1983-1996   1
Robert E. Schnare, Jr.
Susan G. Swartzburg

Bibliography of Preservation Media Literature on the   689
Conservation of Library and Archival Material, 1982-1997
Robert E. Schnare, Jr.

Aspects of Preservation Management in Libraries   723
George M. Cunha
Susan G. Swartzburg
Robert E. Schnare, Jr.

Glossary of Abbreviations and Acronyms   757
Robert E. Schnare, Jr.

Author Index   763

Subject Index   805

About the Authors   825

Preface

This work is dedicated to George M. Cunha and Susan G. Swartzburg. George and Susan's contributions to the field of preservation are many and have been well documented. It was a privilege to have known and worked with both of them. George viewed this work as the third edition of his effort to document the literature of preservation and conservation. Unfortunately, George did not get to take part in this aspect of the project. George, Susan, and I first worked on the Preservation Management Essay, and George died before that was finished. Susan and I worked on the bibliography, and, after her untimely death, I have struggled to finish both the bibliography and the essay.

Compiling a bibliographic survey of Preservation Literature from 1983-1996 has been a monumental task and consumed numerous hours of time. The final project is an attempt at a comprehensive overview of what was published during this time period. The bibliography is divided into two parts. The first part lists print materials published during the 1983-1996 period. Whenever possible, annotations are included to provide information on each work. All periodical citations have had their abbreviations spelled out after the initial citation. A glossary has been created to identify acronyms used in the text and in the annotations. In some cases if the acronym was used in the citation or annotation it may not have been included in the glossary. The extent of the literature is vast, and despite valiant efforts not all citations found could be included, as time and the press of events involved with compiling this bibliography did not allow it. The second part of the bibliographic survey is a compilation of Preservation Media from 1982-1997.

The final piece is an essay on Aspects of Preservation Management. The original project was to have been a major essay on preservation management, but the passing of time and the death of the two main contributors reduced this section to a much shorter work.

Robert E. Schnare, Jr.
August 2000

Tribute to George and Susan

George Cunha and Susan Swartzburg were memorable figures in my professional life and personal friends as well. I feel privileged to have the opportunity to comment on this work, their last collaboration. It is also a humbling experience as they both spoke so well for themselves of their great passion, preservation. They were vigorous and respected colleagues, who, among a handful of others, created a major field of interest in their professions. With their encouragement and support I also came to play a role. To me their absence is a loss of leadership in an area of central importance to my profession, and a loss of individuals for whom I had deep personal affection. It is best that we privately mourn their passing, but in writing about them here, I honor the many abilities they demonstrated. Abilities that shaped the pursuits of a generation of their colleagues who protect our cultural and intellectual patrimony.

If you met them (or read any of their many contributions to the literature of the field), you knew they were on a mission. They were passionate about preservation, and they wanted us to be, too. They wanted us, as information professionals, to assume the responsibility of protecting materials in our care. Most helpfully, they were very clear about what needed to be done, from responsible handling to proper environmental requirements to suitable and responsible hands-on treatment and reformatting. It was indeed the breadth of their vision of preservation that separated them from earlier generations of preservation practitioners, who were trained to deal with individual objects one at a time.

It was that reconceptualization of preservation—from the individual object to whole collections to whole libraries to whole national and international collections—that challenged and ultimately energized librarians and archivists to take action. As firmly entrenched as preservation is today in our professional practice, it may be difficult to believe that their views alarmed many in the traditional conservation community. George and Susan challenged conventional ways of thinking about preservation, and they described a new paradigm.

George in particular. Just who was this retired navy captain anyway? George was trained as a chemist (a fact his critics often overlooked). From the perspective of his own post-retirement, second-career conservatorship experiences, he urged librarians—not just trained conservators—to take on some hands-on protection practices, and limited treatment responsibilities while also initiating sound library-wide practices to protect entire collections. Susan, on the other hand, was a recognized librarian, whose interest was in part based on a life's passion about art. Her strong academic background and professional connections shielded her from some barbs thrown early on at George. Yet they both had occasion to demonstrate that leadership is not for the faint of heart.

Those debates, I want to add quickly, were the exception rather than the rule. The success of preservation emerging into the mainstream of our professions reflected the growing acceptance their message received. The more recent entry into the preservation and access arena is that of information technology. Both George and Susan clearly understood the implications of electronic systems on preservation, and I remember conversations with them on the opportunities and challenges these new technologies presented.

George and Susan were both expert, each in their own distinctive ways, in playing the game—of working within large professional organizations, convincing their listeners and readers of the wisdom of their positions, building strong networks of supporters, and creating successful organizational models that could be emulated by others. Indeed, if one looks for leadership models to emulate, their careers demonstrate the core elements for success.

I am confident that I speak for the many individuals whose professional lives they touched in saying simply that they are missed. There is yet much to be done in the preservation and access fields, of course, and we honor them by continuing to foster preservation goals into the new millennium. But without them to work with, it's not nearly as much fun.

Robert H. Patterson
August 2000

Acknowledgments

There are many people who helped bring this work to publication. I would especially like to thank Sherelyn Ogden for her work in helping to edit the essay. I would also like to thank Bob Patterson who wrote the tribute to George and Susan. Bob offered guidance and suggestions and listened while I struggled to complete this monumental project. I regret that the names of the many individuals who worked to support the efforts of Susan are unknown to me. To these unknown individuals, I thank them for all their efforts on Susan's behalf. Two individuals who helped with my efforts were Laura Moulton and Pamela Wunderlich.

The contributions of the reference staff at the Naval War College Library are gratefully acknowledged. Doris Ottaviano, Alice Juda, Barbara Donnelly, Wayne Rowe, Julie Zecher, and Maggie Rauch of the reference staff helped immensely in tracking down citations to books and periodical articles. Robin Lima, the inter-library loan technician, was also of great assistance in borrowing articles and books. Finally, I would like to especially thank my wife, MaryKay, who offered encouragement and help throughout the project. Her support was greatly appreciated.

Every effort has been made to provide accurate bibliographic citations, and the spelling of names has been verified to the extent possible. Numerous sources were checked and rechecked. However, the literature was often imprecise and the citations incomplete. OCLC was consulted for published monographs and numerous databases were searched to verify periodical citations. In many cases the RLG database was also consulted for citations if an entry could not be found in OCLC. With all the painstaking efforts, errors may still occur and they are regretted. It would be appreciated if these errors were brought to the attention of the author.

Robert E. Schnare, Jr.
August 2000

Bibliography of Preservation Literature
1983-1996

Robert E. Schnare, Jr.
Susan G. Swartzburg

1.   Aarons, John A. "Conservation Activities in Jamaica," COMLA
        Newsletter (Commonwealth Library Association), 62 (December
        1988), 8-9. Describes cooperative preservation initiatives in
        Jamaica.

2.   Aarons, John A. "Contingency and Response Management: Lessons
        from Hurricane Gilbert," Disaster Planning in Jamaica. Kingston,
        Jamaica: Jamaica Library Association, 1989, 39-44. Case study of
        the salvage of materials in an underdeveloped area without
        electricity; preparation and response.

3.   Aarons, John A. "Guidelines for Salvaging Water-Damaged
        Materials," Disaster Planning in Jamaica. Kingston, Jamaica:
        Jamaica Library Association, 1989, 22-25. Reviews drying
        procedures for paper and photographic materials.

4.   Abadie-Maumert, F. A., and N. A. Soteland. "Résistance des CTMP
        au Viellissement", Revue A.T.I.P., 44:6 (1990), 223. Association
        Technique de l'Industrie Papetière (Abstract Bulletin of the Institute
        of Paper Chemistry).

5.   Abbot, Laurie. Final Report of the Archives Preservation Needs
        Assessment Field Test. Mountain View, CA: The Research Libraries
        Group, 1994. 21p. Worksheet and instructions.

6.   Abdullin, R. G. Parmiat'Vremeni: o Sokhrannosti Gazetnykh Fondov
        v Krupneishikh Bibliotekakh. [Memory of Time: About Preserving
        Newspaper Collections in the Largest Libraries], Biblioteka (USSR),
        5 (1983), 27-29.

7.   Abdullin, R. G., and N. N. Bessonova. Gazetnye Fondy Bibliotek:
        Problemy Ucheta i Obespecheni i_a Sokhran Nosti : Sbornik
        Nauchnykh Trudov. Moskva: Gos. Biblioteka (USSR), im. V.I.
        Lenina, 1984. pp. 117-124. Libraries in Soviet Union. Newspapers,
        Conservation and restoration.

8.   Abelson, Philip H. "Brittle Books and Journals," Science, 238:4827
        (October 30, 1987), 595. Editorial on the scope and causes of the
        "Brittle Book" problem.

9.   Abid, Abdelaziz. "Memory of the World - Preserving the
        Documentary Heritage," IFLA Journal (International Federation of
        Library Associations and Institutions), 21:3 (1995), 169-174.
        Outlines the main features of the UNESCO "Memory of the World"
        project to safeguard and provide access to endangered documentary
        heritage. Describes criteria for selection and model projects.
        (Microfilming does not seem to be part of the original project.
        Materials digitized for access, no note on refreshment policies and
        procedures).

10.   Abid, Ann B. "Loss Liability: Risk, Responsibility, Recovery," Art
        Documentation, 10:4 (Winter 1991), 185-187. Issues in security and
        prevention of theft.

11.   Abt, Jeffrey. "Objectifying the Book: The Impact of Science on
        Books and Manuscripts," Library Trends, 36:1 (Summer 1987),
        23-38. Summarizes the history of scientific investigations into the
        physical nature and care of library and archival materials.

12.   Abt, Jeffrey, and Margaret A. Fusco. "A Byzantine Scholar's Letter
        on the Preparation of Manuscript Vellum," Journal of the American
        Institute for Conservation, 28:2 (Fall 1989), 61-66. Illus. Translation
        and commentary on a letter, circa 1295, describing contemporary
        problems and techniques for the preparation of vellum for
        manuscripts.

13.   "Acid Free Becomes Law," Library Journal, 116 (March 1, 1991),
        30.

14.   Acland, Glenda. ed. Electronic Recordkeeping Issues and
        Perspectives - Special Issue of Archives and Manuscript. Canberra,
        Australian Society of Archivists, 1994, 278p. A range of
        perspectives on electronic recordkeeping issues are addressed in a
        special issue of the journal of the Australian Society of Archivists
        (22:1).

15.   "Acme Bookbinding: 175 Years of Preserving the Printed Word
        1821-1996." New Library Scene, 15:5 (October 1996), 5-6.

16.   "Acrylic Controversy," Artfocus, 1:3 (Spring 1993), 5-8. Discussion
        of the permanency of acrylic and synthetic paints used by artists.

17.   Adams, Alton D. "Electric Wire in Buildings," Architects and
        Builders Magazine, (July 1900), 361-363 (September 1900), 421-
        423. Reprinted in Technology and Conservation, 8:1 (1983), 2ff. A
        good discussion of the electro lighting of turn-of-the- century
        buildings.

18. Adams, C. Restauration des Manuscrits et des Livres Anciens. Puteaux, France: Erec, 1984. 166p. Subject heading: Manuscript, Conservation and Restoration.

19. Adams, Dorothy and Douglas. "Profile: Conservation Materials, Ltd.," WAAC Newsletter (Western Association for Art Conservation), 8:1 (January 1986), 12-13. Description of the Adams' mail order conservation materials supply business in Sparks, Nevada.

20. Adams, R. M., et al. "What's New in Occupational Dermatitis?" Patient Care, 21:12 (July 15, 1987), 151-171. Discuss various skin disorders associated with office equipment, such as photocopiers.

21. Adams, Thomas R. "Librarians as Enemies of Books?" College and Research Libraries, 45:3 (May 1984), 196-206.

22. Adams, Virginia M. "Protecting Our Whaling History," Conservation Administration News, 12 (January 1983), 4-5. Description of the new conservation laboratory and the collection management program at the New Bedford Whaling Museum and Library.

23. Adelstein, Peter Z. "Status of Permanence Standards," Journal of Imaging Technology, 12:1 (February 1986), 52-56.

24. Adelstein, Peter Z. "History and Properties of Film Supports," Conservation in Archives. Paris: International Council on Archives, 1989, 89-101. Describes photographic film supports: paper, cellulose, nitrate, cellulose esters, polyester, polycarbonate, and their properties. Paper presented at an International Symposium, Ottawa, Canada, May 1988.

25. Adelstein, Peter Z. "The Latest Word on Storage Conditions," Inform, 5:9 (1991), 6-7. Briefly discusses the new specification IT9.11, which recommends lower temperature and humidity for storage of photographs.

26. Adelstein, Peter Z. "The Latest Word on Archival," Inform, (September 1991), 10-12. Describes the meaning of the "LE" (life expectancy) rating adopted by the ANSI- accredited standards committee to rate life expectancy of photographic, magnetic, and optical media. The LE value replaces the more ambiguous designations of "archival" and "long-term."

27. Adelstein, Peter Z. "Paper Products as Enclosures for Photographic Images," Alkaline Paper Advocate, 8:4 (December 1995), 60.

Reprinted from <u>North American Permanent Papers</u>. ed. Ellen McCrady, Austin, TX: Abbey Publications, 1995, p. 37. Briefly describes the need for and testing of papers that will house photographic materials to ensure that the oxidizing gasses released will not cause serious damage over time.

28.   Adelstein, Peter Z. "The Stability of Optical Disks," <u>Commission on Preservation and Access Newsletter</u>, 58 (July 1993), 3-4. Provides a scientific and standards perspective on the use of optical disks as a storage medium. Notes lack of standards and questions of hardware and format obsolescence.

29.   Adelstein, Peter Z. "Standard Update: Residual Hypo Limits for Microform," <u>Inform</u>, 1:3 (March 1987), 8-10. Discussion of the proposed change in American National Standards Institute (ANSI) PH1.28 and PH1.41 in the use of thiosulfate ion concentration, and its effect on microfilm.

30.   Adelstein, Peter Z. "Status of Permanence Standards of Imaging Materials," <u>Archiving the Audiovisual Heritage</u>. Ottawa, Canada; Northants., England: FIAF,IIC, UNESCO, 1992, 113-123. Discusses work on image permanence standards, through Committee IT9: National Association of Photographic Manufacturers.

31.   Adelstein, Peter Z. "Status of Permanence Standards of Imaging Materials," <u>Journal of Imaging Science and Technology</u>, 36 (January/February 1992), 337-341. An update on the work of Committee IT9 on the permanence of imaging materials for the American National Standards Organization (ANSI).

32.   Adelstein, Peter Z. "Study of Historical Records at the National Archives, Washington DC." <u>Proceedings of Conservation in Archives: International Symposium Ottawa, Canada, May 10-12 1988</u>. Paris: International Council on Archives, 1989. 172-179. Summarizes findings and recommendations of U.S. National Academy of Science committee to investigate options to preserve paper records. Recommended actions include copying to photographic film, electrostatic copying, and environmental control.

33.   Adelstein, Peter Z., and James M. Reilly. "The Image Permanence Institute: New Preservation Resource," <u>Inform</u>, 1:10 (October 1987), 37-39. Creation, purpose and functions of the Institute: research, education, and training.

34.   Adelstein, Peter Z., James M. Reilly, and K. M. Cupriks. "Protection of Microform Images Against Oxidation," <u>Environnement et Conservation de l'Écrit, de l'Image et du Son</u>. Paris: ARSAG, 1994,

31-38. (Actes des Deuxièmes Journées Internationales d'Etudes de l'ARSAG). Describes a polysulfide treatment on freshly processed microfilm to prevent attack by oxidizing agents.

35.   Adelstein, Peter Z., James M. Reilly, D.W. Nishimura, and C. J. Erbland. "Stability of Cellulose Ester Base Photographic Film. Part 1 Laboratory Testing Procedures." SMPTE Journal (Society of Motion Picture and Television Engineers), 101:5 (May 1992), 336-346.

36.   Adelstein, Peter Z., James M. Reilly, D. W. Nishimura, and K. M. Cupriks. "Hydrogen Peroxide Test to Evaluate Redox Blemish Formation on Processed Microfilm," Journal of Imaging Technology, 17:3 (1991), 91-98.

37.   Adelstein, Peter Z., James M. Reilly, D. W. Nishimura, and C. J. Erbland. "Stability of Cellulose Ester Base Photographic Film," SMPTE Journal (Society of Motion Picture and Television Engineers), 101:6 (May 1992), 363-353.

38.   Adelstein, Peter Z., James M. Reilly, and D. W. Nishimura. "Recent Changes in Recommended Storage of Photographic Film," Environnement et Conservation de l'Écrit, de l'Image et du Son. Paris: ARSAG, 1994, 109-113. (Actes des Deuxièmes Journées Internationales d'Etudes de l'ARSAG). Discusses the modifications recently made in the environmental conditions recommended in the ANSI standard for film storage.

39.   Adewoye, Alice Ayanrinda. "Librarian's Attitudes Toward Theft and Mutilation of Library Materials in Academic Libraries in Nigeria," Library Review, 41:1 (1992), 29-36. Study of theft and mutilation in Nigerian libraries; review of literature; lack of concern for the problem by librarians.

40.   Adikwu, C. C. A. "A Survey of University Archives in Five Universities in Nigeria," Library Focus (Nigerian Library Association, Kaduna State Division), 5:1/2 (1987), 24-37. Survey of situation, demonstrating no real archival programs; records housed under appalling conditions with little or no access.

41.   Adkins, Susan A. "Saving Brittle Books: An Annotated Bibliography on Perspective Options," Collection Management, 13:4 (1990), 53-64. Selective bibliography and study outline.

42.   Advisory Committee for the Co-ordination of Information Systems. Electronic Records Guidelines: A Manual for Policy Development and Implementation. Washington, DC: Advisory Committee for the

Coordination of Information Systems, 1989. 122p. Discusses issues, recommendations, and approaches for the development of an electronic records policy. Addresses identification, appraisal, control and use, and disposition. Bibliography.

43.   Aeppel, Timothy. "Stopping Decay of Nation's Books," <u>Friendly Views Newsletter</u>, Los Angeles: Los Angeles Library Association (October 10, 1986). New technology permits the mass deacidification of thousands of books at a time in a process that takes one week.

44.   "Affiliation Affirms Library Preservation and Access Concerns," Commission on Preservation and Access and the Council on Library Resources. <u>Wilson Library Bulletin</u>, 69 (April 1995), 14.

45.   Agaja, James Abayami. "Book Theft and Mutilation: A Case Study," <u>International Library Management</u>, 19 (1987), 119-133. Survey and analysis of the extent of theft and mutilation at Ramat Library, University of Maiduguri, Nigeria, with suggestions for preventive measures.

46.   Agaja, James Aboyomi. "Effects of Harsh Climate on Audiovisual Services in Libraries in Arid Regions," <u>Audiovisual Librarian</u>, 14:3 (August 1988), 126-128. Describes the difficulties of maintaining and providing service for media collections in an extreme environment with an uncertain power supply.

47.   Agarwal, Niraj, and Rick Gustafson. "Effect of Carbohydrate Degradation on Zero-span Tensile Strength," <u>TAPPI Journal</u> (Technical Association of the Pulp and Paper Industry), 78:1 (January 1995), 97-100. Study demonstrating that it is necessary to consider the effect of pulping conditions on each type of carbohydrate degradation in order to better understand the relationship between pulping variable and fiber strength.

48.   Agbabian, M. S., S. F. Masri, and R. L. Negbor. <u>Evaluation of Seismic Mitigation Measures for Art Objects</u>. Manna del Rey, CA: Getty Conservation Scientific Program Report, 1990. 178p.

49.   Agbabian, M.S., W.S. Ginelli, S.F. Masri, and R.L. Negbor. "Evaluation of Earthquake Damage Mitigation Methods for Museum Objects" <u>Studies in Conservation</u>, 36 (1991), 111-120.

50.   Aginsky, Valery N. "Some New Ideas for Dating Ballpoint Inks—A Feasibility Study," <u>Journal of Forensic Sciences</u>, 38:5 (September 1993), 1134-1150. Four techniques are described, all of which are based on the rates of color change in inks as a reaction to chemicals.

51.   Agrawal, Om Prakash. "Conservation of Library Materials:
        Retrospect and Prospect." In Planning Modernization and
        Preservation Programs for South Asian Libraries, ed. Kalpona
        Dasgupta. Calcutta, India: National Library, 1992,
        124-130. Describes library materials found in Indian library
        collections, why they deteriorate; need for more conservation
        facilities.

52.   Agrawal, Om Prakash, ed. Conservation of Manuscripts &
        Documents. Lucknow, India: INTACH, Indian Conservation
        Institute, 1992. 109p. Papers from a seminar held in 1990 to explore
        the problems faced in conserving manuscripts and documents on a
        variety of formats found in Indian libraries. The first section deals
        with specific problems in institutions, the second with technical
        problems and solutions in conservation.

53.   Agrawal, Om Prakash. Conservation of Manuscripts and Paintings of
        South-East Asia. London: Butterworths/International Institute of
        Conservation, 1984. 299p. (Butterworths Series in Conservation
        and Museology). Covers paintings, birch-bark, palm leaf, and paper
        manuscripts. Extensive bibliography.

54.   Agrawal, Om Prakash. "National Seminar on Conservation of
        Manuscripts and Documents: An Introduction." Conservation of
        Manuscripts and Documents, ed. Om Pakash Agrawal. Lucknow,
        India: INTACH, Indian Conservation Institute, 1992, 3-4. An
        introduction to the conservation of manuscripts and documents
        outlining the needs for conservation of these materials in various
        museums and libraries. Points out that manuscripts are not only
        owned by museums and libraries, but also by private collectors,
        temples, research institutes, etc. Some specific problems of
        conservation of birchbark and palm leaf manuscripts are mentioned.

55.   Agrawal, Om Prakash. Preservation of Art Objects and Library
        Materials. New Delhi, India: National Book Trust India, 1993. 100
        p., plates, drawings. Factors of deterioration, such as climate, light,
        insects, microorganisms, pollution, fire, and physical damage are
        discussed. Included are principles of preservation of specific
        materials, namely stone, metal, ceramics, textiles, wood, paper,
        paintings, skin products, photographs, etc.

56.   Agrawal, Om Prakash. "Preserving Photographs," The India
        Magazine of Her People and Culture (October 1990), 94-95.

57.   Agrawal, Om Prakash, and Shashi Dhawan, eds. Biodeterioration of
        Cultural Property: Proceedings of the International Conference on
        Biodeterioration of Cultural Property, February 20-25, 1989. Held at

the National Research Laboratory for Conservation of Cultural
Property. New Delhi, India: ICCROM/INTACH, 1991. 493p.

58.   Agrawal, Usha. "Setting Up a Paper Conservation Laboratory,"
       Journal of Indian Museums, 49-50 (1993-1994), 220-226. Discusses
       requirements for a laboratory for preservation and conservation of
       library and archival materials.

59.   Agresto, John. "Preserving Our Heritage," National Preservation
       News, 5 (July 1986), 10-13. Speech given at the May 15, 1986, New
       York State Conference, "Our Memory at Risk," sponsored by the
       New York State Archives, New York State Library, and the New
       York Document Conservation Advisory Council. {see Conservation
       Administration News, 27 (October 1986), 12.}

60.   "Air Quality Criteria for Storage of Paper Based Archival Records,"
       Technical Notes, American Archivist, 48:1 (Winter 1985), 77.

61.   Aitkin, Susan. "Maintaining the Collection," National Library of
       Australia News (May 1991), 11-13.

62.   Akemann, Sandra P. "Disaster Recovery: The Starting Point,"
       Contingency Journal, (January-March, 1990), 4-7. Reviews elements
       of disaster planning, with emphasis on corporate records.

63.   Akio, Yasue. "pH Surveys of Current Publications in Japan,"
       Conservation Administration News, 50 (July 1992), 1-2, 29.

64.   AKZO Chemicals, Inc. Perspective on Mass Deacidification.
       [prepared for the MARAC Spring 1990 Meeting in New Brunswick,
       NJ, May 17-19], 28p.

65.   Alafiatayo, Benjamin O. "Reader Malpractices in Nigerian
       University Libraries," Library Focus, 4:1/2 (1986), 51-69.

66.   Alafiatayo, Benjamin O. "Students' Attitudes to Book Theft,
       Mutilation in a University Library," Journal of Library and
       Information Science (India), 12:1 (June 1987), 19-37.

67.   "Alaska, Idaho, Montana, Oregon, and Washington," PNLA
       Quarterly (Pacific Northwest Library Association), 51:2 (Winter
       1987), 20-23. Short reports on preservation efforts being taken in
       the five northwestern states.

68.   Albrecht-Kunzeri, I. Gabriella. "Degradation of Archival Materials:
       Report on the Preservation Situation in the National Archives of
       Hungary," Degradácia Archívnych a Kniznicn ch Materiálov vs

Stály a Trvanlivy Papier/Degradation of Archives and Library Materials vs Permanent and Durable Paper for Archives. Bratislava, Slovakia: Slovak National Archives, 1993, 11-15. Review of the causes of deterioration of paper in Europe; outlines preservation initiatives at the National Archives.

69.   Albrecht-Kunzeri, I. Gabriella, and S. Csanyi. "Examination of Paper-adhesive Systems by Accelerated Aging Experiments," Muzeumi Mutargyvedelem, 13 (1984), 97-108. Aging adhesives can change the color of the restored paper. Thirteen kinds of adhesives were examined and compared on hand-made and pulp papers. Results and diagrams are presented. In Hungarian.

70.   Albright, Gary. Duplication of Historical Negatives. Andover, MA: Northeast Document Conservation Center, 1992. 2p. Provides basic advise on preparing collections for duplication; outlines various duplication options.

71.   Albright, Gary. "Flood Aftermath: The Preservation of Water-Damaged Photographs," Topics in Photographic Preservation. Washington, DC: American Institute for Conservation, 3 (1989), 9-11.

72.   Albright, Gary. "Photographs." Conservation in the Library: A Handbook of Use and Care of Traditional and Nontraditional Materials, edited by Susan Swartzburg. Westport, CT: Greenwood Press, 1983, 79-102.

73.   Albright, Gary. "Which Envelope? Selecting Storage Enclosures for Photographs," PictureScope, 31:4 (Winter 1985), 111-113. Description of enclosures available, their pros and cons; cost data.

74.   Albright, V. OCC [Oklahoma Conservation Congress] Basic Book Repair Workshop, Conservation Administration News, 40 (January 1990), 18.

75.   Albro, Sylvia Rodgers. "The Oztoticpac Map: Examination and Conservation Treatment of a 16th-Century Mexican Map on Amate Paper from the Library of Congress," Preprints. ICOM Committee for Conservation, 10th Triennial Meeting, Washington DC, August 22-27, 1993, ed. Janet Bridgland. Washington, DC: International Council of Museums, 1993, 429-434. Examination and conservation treatment are described. Bibliography.

76.   Albro, Sylvia Rodgers, and Thomas C. Albro. "The Examination and Conservation Treatment of the Library of Congress Harkness 1531 Huejotzingo Codex," Journal of the American Institute for

Conservation, 29:2 (Fall 1990), 97-115. The original paper was published in Preprints of Papers. American Institute for Conservation, 16th Annual Meeting, New Orleans, LA:, June 1-8, 1988, 148-160.

77.   Alden, Susan. "Digital Imagery on a Shoestring: A Primer for Librarians," Information Technologies and Libraries (December 1996), 247-250.

78.   Alegbeleye, Bunmi. "A Study of Book Deterioration at the University of Ibadan Library and Its Implications for Preservation and Conservation in African University Libraries," African Journal Library Archives Information Science, 6 (April 1996), 37-45.

79.   Alegbeleye, Bunmi. "Disaster Control Planning in Nigeria," Journal of Librarianship, 22:2 (1990), 91-106. Study of availability of disaster plans in Nigerian libraries, demonstrating need for planning and cooperation.

80.   Alegbeleye, G. O. "The Conservation Scene in Nigeria: A Panoramic View of the Conditions of Bibliographic Resources," Restaurator, 9:1 (1988), 14-26. Presents data from a survey of conditions undertaken in 1908-82, the results of which are typical of conditions in developing countries. Presents suggestions for addressing problems, some of which are specific for tropical climates.

81.   Alegbeleye, G. O. "Newspaper Preservation and Access With Particular Reference to University Libraries in Nigeria," Libri, 38 (September 1988), 191-204.

82.   Alemma, Anaba. "Library Security, Book Theft and Mutilation: A Study of University Libraries in Ghana," Library and Archival Security, 11:2 (1992), 23-35. Report of a study indicating that Ghanaian librarians know little about the extent of theft and mutilation in their collections and have few protective measures in place.

83.   Aleppo, Mario. "Fumigation?" Archives, 19:82 (1989), 74-77. Briefly reviews problems caused by fumigation treatments.

84.   Alexandre, J. L. "Profession Restaurateur" [Profession of Book Restoration], Bulletin Information Association Bibliography France, 152 (1991), 40-1. Presented at the 1991 ABF conference.

85.   Alford, Roger C. "CD-ROM Inside and Out: Here's How CD-ROM Drives Work, How CD-ROM Discs Store Data, and What the Standards Mean," <u>Byte</u>, 18:3 (1993), 197-203.

86.   "Alkaline Imaging Papers Gain Market Share," <u>Alkaline Paper Advocate</u>, 1:4 (October 1988), 41-42. Discusses the conversion to the production of alkaline paper and its effect on the photocopying market.

87.   "Alkaline Papers Gaining Market Share: A Change for All Consumables," <u>Datek Imaging Supplies Monthly</u>, 2:3 (March 1988), 1-4.

88.   "Alkaline Papermaking: PIMA Magazine Round Table." <u>PIMA</u> (Paper Industry Management Association), 72 (May 1990), 23-25. Compares precipitated calcium carbonate filters with ground calcium carbonate. Aspects of paper strength, brightness, and flexibility as well as problems of recycling and sizing systems were discussed by participants from chemical and paper companies.

89.   Allard, Denise, and France Gauthier. "The Continuing Saga of Pressure-Sensitive Adhesives," <u>IIC-CG Bulletin</u> (International Institute for Conservation - Canadian Group), 19:4 (1994), 19-22. Discusses practical ways to remove pressure-sensitive tape residues.

90.   Allen, David Y. "Preserving Maps in Quantity: The Experience of the New York State Historic Map Preservation Project," <u>Meridian</u>, 4 (1990), 29-35. Report on the project, emphasizing the need for bibliographic control and "pragmatic specifications."

91.   Allen, Douglas P. "Optical Disk and the Law - Texas Style," <u>Inform</u>, (April 1988), 43-44.

92.   Allen, John S. "Some New Possibilities in Audio Restoration," <u>ARSC Journal</u> (Association of Recorded Sound Collections), 21:1 (Spring 1990), 39-44. Discussion of the problems and opportunities for the re-recording of sound recordings using digital editing technology.

93.   Allen, Marie. "Analyzing the Data: Summary Findings from Database Inquiries of the 1986 ICA/IFLA Conservation Questionnaire," <u>Politics for the Preservation of the Archival Heritage</u>. Paris: International Council on Archives, 1989, 151-158. Summary of findings; concludes that most repositories lack the basic essentials for preservation.

94.   Allen, Norman S., John H. Appleyard, Michele Edge, David Francis,
        C. Velson Horie, and Terence S. Jewitt. "The Nature of the
        Degradation of Archival Cellulose-ester Base Motion Picture Film:
        The Case for Stabilization," Journal of Photographic Science, 36
        (1988), 34-39. Report of a study of the degradation of a number of
        cellulose acetate/nitrate based 35mm cinematograph films; results
        call into question current standards for storage and suggest
        stabilization as an alternative means of preservation.

95.   Allen, Norman S., Michele Edge, Terence S. Jewitt, and C. Velson
        Horie. "Degradation and Stabilization of Cellulose Triacetate Base
        Motion Picture Film," Journal of Imaging Science and Technology,
        36 (January/February 1992), 4-12. Study of the artificial and natural
        degradation of cellulose triacetate base motion picture film, which
        identifies two degradation processes; implications are discussed.

96.   Allen, Norman S., Michele Edge, John H. Appleyard, Terence S.
        Jewitt, and C. Velson Horie. "Degradation of Historic Cellulose
        Triacetate Cinematograph Film: Influence of Various Film
        Parameters and Prediction of Archival Life," Journal of Photographic
        Science, 36 (1988), 194-198. The natural and artificial degradation of
        cellulose triacetate based cinematographic film has been studied by
        moisture and viscometry.

97.   Allen, Norman S., Michele Edge, John H. Appleyard, Terence S.
        Jewitt, C. Velson Horie, and David Francis. "Degradation of
        Cellulose Triacetate Cinematorgraphic Film: Prediction of Archival
        Life," Polymer Degradation and Stability, 23 (1988), 43-50. Study of
        degradation of reels of cellulose triacetate film with implications for
        the archival storage of cinamatographic film.

98.   Allen, Norman S., Michele Edge, John H. Appleyard, Terence S.
        Jewitt, C. Velson Horie, and David Francis. "Degradation of Historic
        Cellulose Triacetate Cinematographic Film: The Vinegar Syndrome,"
        Polymer Degradation and Stability, 19 (1987), 379-387. Analysis of
        naturally aged films indicate a correlation between moisture, acidity,
        and the degree of degradation.

99.   Allen, Norman S., Michele Edge, C. Velson Horie, Terence S. Jewitt,
        and John H. Appleyard. "The Degradation and Stabilization of
        Historic Cellulose Acetate/Nitrate Base Motion-Picture Film,"
        Journal of Photographic Science, 36:3 (1988), 103-106. Report of a
        study of a number of deteriorated cellulose acetate/nitrate-based
        35mm cinematograph films demonstrating the temperature, moisture
        regain, and pH are important related factors in the degradation
        mechanism.

100. Allen, Norman S., Michele Edge, Terence S. Jewitt, and C.Velson
      Horie. "Initiation of the Degradation of Cellulose Triacetate Base
      Motion Picture Film," Journal of Photographic Science, 38 (1990),
      54-59.

101. Allen, Norman S., Martin Hayes, Michele Edge, Terence S. Jewitt,
      and Karel Brems. "Factors Influencing the Degradation of
      Polyester-Based Cinematographic Film and Audio-Visual Tapes,"
      Archiving the Audio-Visual Heritage. Rushton, England:
      FIAF/UNESCO, 1992, 40-51. Causes and stages of deterioration.

102. Allen, Sue. Decorated Cloth in America, Publishers' Bindings 1840-
      1910. Los Angeles, UCLA Center for 17th and 18th Century Studies,
      William Clark Memorial Library, 1994. 107 p.

103. Allen, Susan M. "The Blumberg Case: A Costly Lesson for
      Librarians!" AB Bookman's Weekly (Antiquarian Bookman), 88
      (Sept. 2, 1991), 769-773.

104. Allen, Susan M. "Theft in Libraries or Archives," College and
      Research Libraries News, 51:10 (November 1990), 939-943. Outline
      of actions to be taken after a theft is discovered: notification of
      appropriate agencies, inventory, and a chronological record of
      events. Emphasizes the need for the inclusion of theft in a disaster
      plan.

105. Allen, Susan M. "Using the Internet to Report Rare Book &
      Manuscript Theft," Rare Books & Manuscripts Librarianship, 10:1
      (1995), 22-37. Report and discussion of a study to determine if
      library security officers would make use of an Internet Listserv to
      communicate information about theft. Concludes that it can be
      effective, concluding "We hope to neutralize the sophistication and
      ruthlessness of criminals by the increasing use of sophisticated
      technologies. The Internet is one of our solutions" (p.34).

106. Allerstrand, Sven. "The Swedish National Archive of Recorded
      Sound and Moving Images - The ARB," Audiovisual Librarian, 14:4
      (November 1988), 182-186. Describes the mission and activities of
      the ARB, established to preserve Swedish audio and video
      recordings.

107. Alley, Brian. "The High Cost of Locking Barn Doors,"
      Technicalities, 7:9 (September 1987), 1. Note on the need for
      security for computer equipment and why libraries should invest in
      it.

108.   Allison, Terry L. "Toward a Shared Enterprise: Western Europe and US Preservation Programs," Collection Management, 15:3/4 (1992), 517-525. Review of preservation problems faced by Western European and U.S. libraries and the need for international cooperation to address them. Paper from a conference, "Shared Resources, Shared Responsibilities," Florence, 1988.

109.   Allsopp, Christine, and Dennis Allsopp. "An Updated Survey of Commercial Products Used to Protect Materials Against Biodeterioration," International Biodeterioration Bulletin, 19:3/4 (Autumn/Winter), 99-146. Information on over 250 products, from 30 manufacturers, on biocides used in the preservation of materials, based upon a survey in 1983.

110.   Allsop Consumer Electronics Division. Compact Disc Care. (Technical Series 4), Bellingham, WA: Allsop, 1985. 3p. Discusses how compact disks store information and how the information is read. Notes that disks must be cleaned regularly and advertises Allsop's cleaning system.

111.   Allsopp, Dennis. "Biology and Growth Requirements of Moulds and Other Deteriogenic Fungi," Journal of the Society of Archivists, 7:8 (October 1985), 530-533. Description of the life requirements of fungi and environmental controls necessary to curtail their growth.

112.   Allsopp, Dennis, and Arthur D. Baynes-Cope. "Small World or the Large World: The Relationship Between Conservators, Curators and Scientists," Biodeterioration of Cultural Property., ed. Om Prakash Agrawal and Shashi Dhawan. New Delhi, India: ICCROM/ INTACH, 1991, 19-27. Explores the reasons for and results of lack of liaison among conservators, curators, and scientists in dealing with objects, with improvements suggested.

113.   Almagro, Bertha R. "The Curse-a-Book Security System," Library and Archival Security, 7:3/4 (Fall/Winter 1985), 49-53. Brief review of the history of theft and mutilation of books; recommendation that libraries return to the medieval approach of placing a curse on those who steal or mutilate books.

114.   Alpert, Gary D., and L. Michael Albert. "Integrated Pest Management: A Program for Museum Environments," A Guide to Museum Pest Control. Washington, DC: Foundation of the American Institute for Conservation of Historic and Artistic Works, and Association of Systematics Collections, 1988, 169-173. Describes a program for managing pests, first by using non-chemical measures, and the use of chemical measures only when absolutely necessary.

115. Alsford, Dennis B. "Fire Safety in Museums," Muse, (Summer 1984), pp. 18-23.

116. Alston, R. C. "Preserving the Record," Archives, 20:88 (October 1992), 181-189. (Bond Memorial Lecture, 2) Addresses questions of preservation and access of records, the need for agreed upon bibliographic records, and digitization, with microfilm as a first step.

117. Alston, Robin. "The Smithsonian Project: Image Capture and Retrieval," Library Conservation News, 9 (January 1985), 6-7. Discusses the digital storage and retrieval project at the Smithsonian Institution. Emphasizes the goal of finding a medium that adequately serves both preservation and access.

118. Alten, Helen. "Caring for Leather, Skin & Furs," The Upper Midwest Collections Care Network, 2:1 (March 1996), 1-7. Describes the preparation of leathers; discusses causes of deterioration, cleaning, storage and display materials.

119. Altenhoner, R. "Neues Forderungsprogramm der Deutschen Forschungsgemeinschaft zur Mikroverfilmung gefahrdeter Bibliotheksbestande" [A new promotional program of the German Research Council for microfilming endangered library holdings], Zeitschrift Feur Bibliotheksuesen und Bibliographie, 40 (May/June 1993), 254-260.

120. Ambacher, Bruce I. "Managing Machine-Readable Archives," Managing Archives and Archival Institutions. ed. James Gregory Bradsher. Chicago, IL: University of Chicago Press, 1988, 121-133. Discusses the management of machine-readable archives, including preservation concerns. Argues that archivists must take part in the creation, maintenance, and use of machine-readable records in order to ensure proper management and preservation.

121. Ambrose, Timothy, and Crispin Paine. Museum Basics. London: ICOM/ Routledge, 1993. 313p. Guide to "best practice," including conservation, facilities management, exhibition, and security.

122. Ambrosino, Leslie. "Disaster Recovery Training at the University of Tulsa," Conservation Administration News, 19 (October 1984), 1.

123. American Association of Law Librarians. Special Committee on Preservation Needs of Law Libraries. Report and Recommendations. Chicago, IL: American Association of Law Librarians, 1992. 100p. (Occasional Papers, 13) Identifies problems and presents a review of initiatives with a five-part program for preservation of legal collections.

124. American Association of Museums. <u>Caring for Collections:</u>
<u>Strategies for Conservation Maintenance and Documentation</u>. A
Report on an American Association of Museums Project.
Washington, DC: American Association of Museums, 1984.
44p. Specific problems in the care of historical, anthropological,
archaeological, and art collections are discussed, with an emphasis on
conservation, maintenance, and documentation.

125. American Association of Museums. Commission on Museums for a
New Century. <u>Museums for a New Century: A Report</u>. Washington,
DC: American Association of Museums, 1984. 144p. Task: "to
study and clarify the role of museums in American society, their
obligations to preserve and interpret our cultural and natural heritage,
and their responsibilities to an everbroadening audience." Chapter 2
deals with conservation issues, emphasizing the need for
conservation in museum and regional centers.

126. American Conference of Governmental Industrial Hygienists.
<u>Industrial Ventilation: A Manual of Recommended Practice</u>. 22nd
ed., Cincinnati, OH: American Conference of Governmental
Industrial Hygienists. 1995. One volume.

127. American Conference of Governmental Industrial Hygienists. <u>Small</u>
<u>Business Health and Safety Guide for Chemical Waste Disposal</u>.
Cincinnati, Ohio: American Conference of Governmental Industrial
Hygienists. 1985. 39p.

128. American Conference of Governmental Industrial Hygienists, Inc.
<u>TLVS:Threshold Limit Values for Chemical Substances and Physical</u>
<u>Agents in the Work Environment and Biological Exposure Indices</u>
<u>with Intended Changes for 1985-86</u>. Cincinnati, OH: ACGIH, Inc.,
1986. Catalog has been issued annually since 1985/1986. Title
varies. Lists over seven hundred toxic substances and physical
agents. These TLVs serve as the basis for many OSHA permissible
limits.

129. American Council of Learned Societies. <u>Technical Scholarship and</u>
<u>the Humanities: The Implications of Electronic Information,</u>
<u>Summary of Proceedings, September 30-October 2, 1992</u>. New
York: American Council of Learned Societies / Getty Trust, 1993,
41p. Conference to address how, and whether, electronic database

systems "will accommodate the contextual and historical information appropriate to scholarship," (5) and to examine proactive strategies for doing so.

130.   American Hospital Association. Resource Center Disaster Plan. Chicago, IL: American Hospital Association, 1987. 16 leaves.

131.   American Institute of Architects Foundation. Towards Standards for Architectural Archives [Conference] February 12-13, 1981. Washington, DC: American Institute of Architects Foundation, 1984. 114p. Proceedings of the Conference Toward Standards for Architectural Archives. Contains a bibliography on the conservation of photographs.

132.   American Institute for Conservation of Historic and Artistic Works. Abstracts of Paper Presented at the 21st Annual Meeting, May 31-June 6, 1993. Washington, DC: American Institute for Conservation of Historic and Artistic Works, 1993. 44p.

133.   American Institute for Conservation of Historic and Artistic Works. "An Account of the Conservation and Preservation Procedures Following a Fire at the Huntington Library and Art Gallery," American Institute of Conservation Journal, 27 (1988), 1-31.

134.   American Institute for Conservation of Historic and Artistic Works. Book and Paper Group Annual. Vol. 2, Washington, DC: American Institute for Conservation of Historic and Artistic Works. 1983. Issued annually, a compilation of papers by members that were presented at AIC Book and Paper Group meetings.

135.   American Institute for Conservation of Historic and Artistic Works. Directory. Washington, DC: American Institute for Conservation of Historic and Artistic Works, 1994. 284p. Includes AIC Bylaws, Code of Ethics. The Directory is published annually.

136.   American Institute for Conservation of Historic and Artistic Works. Final Narrative Report on the Conservation Treatment Records Archive Feasibility and Planning Study. Washington, DC: American Institute for Conservation of Historic and Artistic Works, 1988. 11p.

137.   American Institute for Conservation of Historic and Artistic Works. Fitted Gelatin Materials: Deterioration and Conservation. Postprints of the Photographic Materials Group. Washington, DC: American Institute for Conservation of Historic and Artistic Works. Winter 1984. 9 leaves.

138. American Institute for Conservation of Historic and Artistic Works. Guidelines for Selecting a Conservator. Washington, DC: American Institute for Conservation of Historic and Artistic Works. 1984. Brochure. Explains the role of a conservator, lists information sources, and briefly explains how to select and work with a conservator.

139. American Institute for Conservation of Historic and Artistic Works. Book and Paper Group. Paper Conservation Catalog. Washington, DC: American Institute for Conservation, updates issued periodically. Catalog and inventory of current conservation treatments, "to record common practice."

140. American Institute for Conservation of Historic and Artistic Works. Perspectives on Natural Disaster Mitigation. Washington, DC: Foundation of the American Institute for Conservation of Historic and Artistic Works, 1991. 82p. Papers presented at a 1991 workshop on natural hazards, urban emergencies, safeguarding collections and structures, and human reaction to disaster.

141. American Institute for Conservation of Historic and Artistic Works. Photographic Materials Group. Photographic Materials Conservation Catalog. Washington, DC: Photographic Materials Group, American Institute for Conservation of Historic and Artistic Works. 1994. This is a serial.

142. American Institute for Conservation of Historic and Artistic Works. Preprints of Papers Presented at the Twelfth Annual Meeting 1984. Washington, DC: American Institute for Conservation of Historic and Artistic Works. 1984. 139p. The papers will appear in the Book and Paper Group Annual.

143. American Institute for Conservation of Historic and Artistic Works. Preservation of Collections: Assessment, Evaluation, and Mitigation Strategies. Washington, DC: American Institute for Conservation of Historic and Artistic Works. 1996. 75p. Papers presented at the AIC workshop in Norfolk, VA., June 10-11, 1996.

144. American Institute for Conservation of Historic and Artistic Works. Research Priorities in Art & Architectural Conservation: A Report of the AIC Membership, ed. Eric F. Hansen and Chandra L. Reedy. Washington, DC: American Institute for Conservation of Historic and Artistic Works, 1994. 180 p.

145. American Institute for Conservation of Historic and Artistic Works. Photographic Materials Group. Topics in Photographic Preservation. Washington, DC: American Institute for Conservation of Historic

and Artistic Works. Issued since 1986. Vol. 6 (1995) title is now Topics in Photographic Preservation. 133p. Papers on photographic conservation.

146.   American Insurance Services Group Engineering and Safety Services. Planning for Emergencies. New York: American Insurance Services Group Engineering and Safety Services, 1991. 54p.

147.   [American Library Association]. "ALA: Back to Basics," Wilson Library Bulletin, 65:1 (September 1990), 34-38. American Library Association President Patricia Berger states that literacy and preservation problems have to be solved before the ALA can address the issue of access to information.

148.   [American Library Association]."ALA Books Display Infinity Symbol to Denote Permanent Paper." Technical Services Quarterly, 4:4 (Summer 1987), 80. Announces that ALA has published its first book that carries the ANSI infinity symbol denoting paper permanence.

149.   [American Library Association]. "ALA Preconference [Preservation for Collection Managers, June 1986]," New Library Scene, 5 (August 1986), 19.

150.   [American Library Association]. "ALA on Theft," Conservation Administration News, 19 (October 1984), 20. The ALA Rare Books and Manuscripts Section Security Committee plans to develop an information packet on book theft legislation, prevention, and response.

151.   [American Library Association]. "ALA Urges Use of Permanent Paper," Wilson Library Bulletin, 62 (March 1988), 12.

152.   American Library Association. Basic Preservation Bibliography. Preservation of Library Materials Section. April 1, 1983. Chicago, IL: American Library Association, 1983. 13p.

153.   American Library Association. "Guidelines for Preservation Photocopying," Library Resources and Technical Services, 38:3 (July 1994), 288-292. Guidelines for producing replacement copies, prepared by the Subcommittee on Preservation Photocopying, Reproduction of Library Materials Section.

154.   American Library Association. "Guidelines Regarding Thefts in Libraries, A Draft," College and Research Libraries News, 47:10 (November 1986), 646-649. Includes "Guidelines for What to Do

Before a Library Theft Occurs," Checklist of What to Do After a
Theft Occurs From a Library," and "Draft of Model Legislation:
Theft and Mutilation of Library Materials." The draft statement
emphasizes the need for guidelines for the library system and not
only for the rare book collection.

155.   American Library Association. Preservation Policy. Chicago, IL:
        American Library Association, 1991. 8p. Outlines responsibilities of
        the library profession for the preservation of library materials of all
        types.

156.   American Library Association. "Report of ALA President's
        Committee on Preservation Policy and Proposed ALA Preservation
        Policy," Advances in Preservation and Access. Vol.1. Westport, CT:
        Meckler, 1992, 92-106.

157.   American Library Association. "Standards for Ethical Conduct for
        Rare Book, Manuscript, and Special Collections Librarians, with
        Guidelines for Institutional Practice in Support of the Standards, 2d
        edition, 1992," College and Research Libraries News, 54:4 (April
        1993), 207-215.

158.   American Library Association. Survey of Time Estimates for Simple
        Conservation Procedures. Chicago, IL: The Committee, 1983.
        27p. ALA/RTSD/PLMS Policy and Research Committee.

159.   American Library Association. Association of College and Research
        Libraries. "ACRL Guidelines for the Preparation of Policies on
        Library Access: A Draft," College and Research Libraries News,
        50:5 (May 1989), 386-392. Guidelines include considerations for
        collection management and preservation.

160.   American Library Association. Association of College and Research
        Libraries/ Rare Books and Manuscripts Section. ACRL/RBMS
        Security Committee. "Guidelines Regarding Thefts in Libraries:
        Draft Version," College and Research Libraries News (May 1994),
        289-294. Written by Susan M. Allen, et al. What to do before theft
        occurs and after a theft. Includes directory of agencies that assist in
        protection and recovery; model legislation.

161.   American Library Association. Association of College & Research
        Libraries. "ACRL Guidelines Regarding Thefts in Libraries."
        College and Research Libraries News, 49:3 (March 1988), 159-162.
        Discusses "Guidelines Regarding Thefts in Libraries" developed by
        the Association of College & Research Libraries (ACRL) Rare
        Books and Manuscripts Section's Security Committee. The

guidelines include what to do before and after a library theft occurs, and a draft of model legislation.

162.	American Library Association. Association of College & Research Libraries. <u>Binding Terms: Thesaurus for Use in Rare Books and Special Collections Cataloguing</u>. Chicago, IL: American Library Association, 1988. 37 pp. Prepared by the Rare Books and Manuscripts Sections.

163.	American Library Association. Association of College & Research Libraries. "Guidelines for Borrowing Special Collections Materials for Exhibition," <u>College and Research Libraries News</u> (May 1990), 430-34. Prepared by the Rare Books and Manuscripts Section.

164.	American Library Association. Association for Library Collections and Technical Service. "Guidelines for Cataloging Microform Sets." Chicago, IL: American Library Association, 1989. 2 p. Developed by the Reproduction of Library Materials Section, Bibliographic Control of Microforms Committee.

165.	American Library Association. Association for Library Collections and Technical Service. "Guidelines for Packaging and Shipping Microforms." Chicago, IL: American Library Association, 1989. 2 pp. Developed by the Reproduction of Library Materials Section, Bibliographic Control of Microforms Committee.

166.	American Library Association. Association for Library Collections and Technical Service. "Standard Terminology for USMARC Field 583." Chicago, IL: American Library Association, July 1988. 3 leaves. Prepared by Preservation Program Management Committee, Preservation of Library Materials Section.

167.	American Library Association. Association for Library Collections and Technical Service. Subcommittee on Contract Negotiations for Commercial Reproduction of Library and Archival Materials. "Contract Negotiations for the Commercial Microform Publishing of Library and Archival Materials: Guidelines for Librarians and Archivists," <u>Library Resources and Technical Services</u>, 38:1 (January 1994), 72-85. Guidelines; points for considerations when negotiating with commercial publishers for microfilming of materials for preservation.

168.	American Library Association. Association for Library Collections and Technical Services. Reproduction of Library Materials Section. Subcommittee on Preservation Photocopying Guidelines. "Guidelines for Preservation Photocopying." <u>Library Resources and Technical Services</u>, 38 (July 1994), 288-292.

169.   American Library Association. Association for Library Collections
        and Technical Services. Preservation Microfilming: Planning and
        Production: Papers from the RTSD Preservation Microfilming
        Institute, New Haven, Connecticut, April 21-23, 1988. Chicago, IL:
        Association for Library Collections and Technical Services,
        American Library Association, 1989. 72p. Provides a good
        introduction and overview of principal issues of microfilming. Six
        papers.

170.   American Library Association. Association for Library Collections
        and Technical Services (ALCTS). "Glossary of Selected
        Preservation Terms [draft]," ALCTS Newsletter (Association for
        Library Collections and Technical Service), 1:2 (1990), 14-
        15. Developed by the Preservation of Library Materials Section,
        Library/Vendors Task Force.

171.   American Library Association. Rare Book and Manuscripts Section.
        Security Committee. "Guidelines for the Security of Rare Book,
        Manuscript and Other Special Collections: A Draft," College and
        Research Libraries News, 51:3 (March 1990), 240-244. Prepared by
        Gary Menges.

172.   American Library Association. Rare Book and Manuscripts Section.
        RBMS Ad Hoc Conservators' Collation Committee. "Guidelines for
        Conservators and Curators: Draft III," College & Research Libraries
        News, 49:5 (May 1988), 294-295. Recommendations, and
        comments on collation and marking in special collections are given.

173.   American Library Association. Rare Book and Manuscripts Section.
        RBMS Committee for Developing Guidelines for Borrowing Special
        Collections Materials for Exhibition, "Guidelines for Borrowing
        Special Collections Materials for Exhibition: A Draft," College and
        Research Libraries News (December 1988), 750-754.

174.   American Library Association. Rare Book and Manuscripts Section.
        RBMS Committee for Developing Guidelines for Professional
        Ethics. "Standards for Ethical Conduct for Rare Book, Manuscript,
        and Special Collections Libraries." College and Research Libraries
        News (March 1987), 134-135.

175.   American Library Association. Rare Book and Manuscripts Section.
        RBMS Discussion Group of Curatorial Issues Raised by
        Conservation. "Curator/Conservator Relations: Selected and
        Partially Annotated Bibliography, 1970-1988." Compiled by
        Charlotte B. Brown. Lancaster, PA: Franklin and Marshall College,
        June 1988. 3p.

176.   American Library Association. Rare Book and Manuscripts Section.
        RBMS Ethical Standards Review Committee. "Standards for Ethical
        Conduct for Rare Book, Manuscripts, and Special Collections
        Libraries and Librarians," College and Research Library News,
        (December 1991), 721-727, 729.

177.   American Library Association. Rare Book and Manuscripts Section.
        RBMS Security Committee. "Guidelines Regarding Thefts in
        Libraries: a Draft." College and Research Libraries News, 47:10
        (November 1986), 646-649.

178.   American Library Association. Reference and Adult Services
        Division. History Section. Genealogy Committee. "RASD
        Guidelines for Preservation, Conservation, and Restoration of Local
        History and Local Genealogical Materials [adopted by the RASD
        Board of Directors, June 1992]." Reference Quarterly, 32 (Spring
        1993), 341-344.

179.   American Library Association. Resources and Technical Services
        Division. RTSD Preconference Management Strategies for Disaster
        Preparedness, July 8, 1988 in New Orleans, LA. Chicago, IL:
        American Library Association, 1988. 1v.

180.   American National Standards Institute. American National Standard
        for Imaging Media: Photographic Activity Test. New York: ANSI,
        1994. 13p.

181.   American National Standards Institute. American National Standard
        for Information Sciences - Permanence of Paper for Printed Library
        Materials. New York: ANSI, 1992. ANSI Z39.48-1992. 15p.

182.   American National Standards Institute. American National Standard
        for Information Sciences: Permanence of Paper for Printed Library
        Materials. ANSI Z39.48-1984. New York: ANSI, 1985. 8p.
        Establishes the criteria for permanence of uncoated paper, covering
        specifications for pH, alkaline reserve, and freedom from
        groundwood. Based on work of the CLR Committee on Production
        Guidelines for Book Longevity (published by CLR in 1982).

183.   American National Standards Institute. For Photography (Film)
        Storage of Processed Safety Film. Publication PH1.43. New York:
        ANSI, 1983. 16p.

184.   American National Standards Institute. Processed Diazo Films —
        Specifications for Stability. New York: ANSI, 1985. 22p. ANSI
        PH1.60- 1985, a revision of the 1979 edition.

185.   American National Standards Institute. <u>Processed Vesicular Film —
         Specifications for Stability</u>. New York: ANSI, 1985. ANSI PH1.67-
         1985. 11p.

186.   American National Standards Institute. <u>Standard for Photography
         (Chemicals) — "Residual Thiosulfate and Other Chemicals in Films,
         Plates and Papers- Determination and Measurements</u>. New York:
         ANSI, 1985. ANSI PH4.8-1985. 20p. This is the Methylene Blue
         Test.

187.   American National Standard Institute. <u>Standard for Photography
         (Processing)- "Processed Films, Plates, and Papers - Determination
         and Measurements</u>. New York: ANSI, 1984. ANSI PH1.53-1984.
         11p. Revised ANSI PH1.53-1986. 12p.

188.   American Society for Industrial Security, Standing Committee on
         Museum, Library and Archive Security. <u>Suggested Guidelines in
         Museum Security</u>. Arlington, VA: American Society for Industrial
         Security, 1990. 21p.

189.   American Society for Testing and Materials. Institute for Standards
         Research. <u>Workshop on the Effects of Aging on Printing and
         Writing Papers</u>. Philadelphia, PA: American Society for Testing and
         Materials, 1994. 259p. Proceedings, July 6-8, 1994.

190.   Ames, Anne. "Photocopying of Special Collections Materials,"
         <u>Granite State Libraries</u>, 29:2 (March/April 1993), 5-6. Discusses
         rationale, options, and copyright considerations. The first of a
         continuing series of columns on preservation concerns for New
         Hampshire librarians.

191.   "AMIGOS and Preservation," <u>Conservation Administration News</u>,
         19 (October 1984), 24. Announces creation of a Preservation
         Committee by AMIGOS Bibliographic Council (library network
         serving the Southwest) to assess regional needs, consider
         establishment of a preservation program, and explore cooperation
         with other networks.

192.   Amodeo, Anthony J. "A Debt Unpaid: The Bibliographic Instruction
         Librarian and Library Conservation," <u>College and Research Libraries
         News</u>, 49:9 (October 1988), 601-603. Advocates teaching about the
         care and handling of books within the context of bibliographic
         instruction in academic libraries.

193.   Amodeo, Anthony J. "Photocopying Without (Much) Damage,"
         <u>College and Research Libraries News</u>, 44:10 (November 1983), 365,

368-370. Describes the damage that photocopying can cause materials and discusses current research into the development of machines that are less harmful; offers practical solutions.

194.   Amodeo, Anthony J. "Special Collections Desk Duty: Preventing Damage," College and Research Libraries News, 44:6 (June 1983), 177, 180-182. Instructions for attendants and users on the handling of rare books.

195.   Ampex Corporation. A Guide to Media and Formats, "Care & Handling of Magnetic Tape." Redwood City, CA: Ampex, 1990. n.p.

196.   Ampex Corporation. A Guide to Media and Formats, "Magnetic Tape Glossary." Redwood City, CA: Ampex, 1989. n.p.

197.   Ampex Corporation. A Guide to Media and Formats, "Increasing the Life of Your Audio Tapes." Redwood City, CA: Ampex, May 20, 1987. n.p.

198.   Ampex Corporation. A Guide to Media and Formats, "Maximizing Tape and VTR Reliability." Redwood City, CA: Ampex, April 6, 1984. n.p.

199.   Anderson, David, and Susan Rogers. rev. Document Conservation Guidelines for Restoration-Preservation of Documentary Papers, Maps, Books. Augusta, ME: Maine State Archives, 1996. 23p.

200.   Anderson, Hazel, and John E. McIntyre. Planning Manual for Disaster Control in Scottish Libraries. Edinburgh, Scotland: National Library of Scotland, 1985. 75p. Covers prevention, insurance, response, and recovery, with model disaster control plan. Bibliography.

201.   Anderson, Jennifer, with Pamela Barrios, Cathy Bell, and Robert Espinosa. "Cloth Covered Book Cradles," Abbey Newsletter, 17:7/8 (December 1993), 105-108. Detailed instructions for an elegant cradle.

202.   Anderson, John. "Soft-Spray System Installed at Archives," Texas Libraries, 45 (Fall 1984), 103. Preservation of library materials, equipment, and supplies.

203.   Anderson, Karen. "The Flood of '93 in Iowa," Conservation Administration News, 55 (October 1993), 3. Brief note on how pre-planning and organization ensured the safety of a library's collections.

204.   Anderson, L. E. "Tips on Taping Vertical Records," <u>Sound Box</u> (Sept. 1995), unpaged. Reproduction of vertically cut recordings.

205.   Anderson, Michael. "The Preservation of Machine-Readable Data for Secondary Analysis," <u>Archives</u>, 17:74 (October 1985), 79-93. Review of a seminar on the problems of selection for preservation, format, and usability of machine-readable records. Options are given.

206.   Anderson, Paulene H. <u>Library Media Leadership in Academic Schools</u>. Hamden, CT: Library Professional Publications, 1985. 260pp. This work illustrates how far the "word" of conservation has reached. In chapter 4, "Policies— A Form of Insurance," the author has reprinted, with permission, George Cunha's "What an Institution Can Do to Survey Its Conservation Needs." The book is an excellent overview of library media in secondary schools. If one has questions concerning media, it is well worth consulting.

207.   Anderson, R.G.W. <u>L'Eclisse Delle Memorie</u>. Roma: Laterza 1994. 283pp

208.   Anderson-Smith, Myrtle. "Proposal for a Disaster Control Plan for Aberdeen University Library Special Collection." 26p. in <u>Keeping Our Words</u>. [British Library's] 1988 National Preservation Office Competition, London. 1990.

209.   Anderson, Stanton I. "The History and Natural Aging of Kodak Ektachrome Film," <u>The Imperfect Image: Photographs, Their Past, Present and Future</u>, ed. Ian and Angela Moor. London: Centre for Photographic Conservation, 1992, 268-273.

210.   Anderson, Stanton, and Robert Ellison. "Natural Aging of Photographs," <u>Journal of the American Institute for Conservation</u>, 31:2 (Summer 1992), 213-223. Describes Eastman Kodak's long-term program to monitor photographic image change through accelerated aging by a method of Arrhenius testing.

211.   Anderson, Stanton and Ronald Goetting. "Environmental Effects on the Image Stability of Photographic Products," <u>Journal of Imaging Technology</u>, 14:4 (August 1988), 111-116. Illus. A study to better understand the environmental factors that affect image stability of photographic products; provides information on procedures in processing, handling, and storage.

212.   Anderson, Stanton, and David Kopperl. "Limitations of Accelerated Image Stability," Journal of Imaging Science and Technology, 37 (1993), 363-373. Study documents the danger of using single accelerated aging tests.

213.   Anderson, Stanton, and George Larson. "A Study of Environmental Conditions Associated With Customer Keeping of Photographic Prints," Journal of Imaging Technology, 13 (1987), 49-54. Report of a study to more clearly understand the types of environments that photographic materials are most likely to experience in actual use.

214.   Ando, Masahito, and Shuichi Yasuzawa. "Japanese Archives at the Dawn of a New Age," Information Development, 4:1 (January 1988), 33-36. Initiation of efforts to preserve archival records as part of the national heritage.

215.   Andre, Pamela Q. J., and Nancy L. Eaton. "National Agricultural Text Digitizing Project," Library Hi Tech, 6:3 (1988), 61-66.

216.   Andreae, Christopher. "Preserving Britain's Paper Trail: Mary Goodwin Oversees National Trusts Cache of Paper Objects From Globes to Wallpaper," Christian Science Monitor, 84:233 (1992), 14, col. 2.

217.   Andrews, Christopher. "Mastering The CD-ROM Mastering And Replication Process," CD-ROM Professional (July 1991), 17-18.

218.   Andrews, Harry C. "Redefining Document Management: Whither Electronics, Micrographics?" Inform, 4 (June 1990), 41-43. Compares advantages and disadvantages of electronic document imaging and micrographics. Lack of standards, legal inadmissibility, and uncertain life expectancy are concerns regarding the use of WORM (write once, read many) for permanent records. New flexible systems combine benefits of both technologies— economy of micrographics storage and speed and convenience of electronic imaging for retrieval.

219.   Andrews, Patricia, comp. "Writings on Archives, Historical Manuscripts, and Current Records: 1983," American Archivist, 49:3 (Summer 1986), 277-303. Section IV contains information on preservation, restoration, and storage of records and historical manuscripts.

220.   Andrews, Theresa Meyers, William W. Andrews, and Cathleen Baker. "An Investigation into the Removal of Enzymes from Paper Following Conservation Treatment," American Institute for Conservation Book and Paper Group Annual, 9 (1990), 1-11. Tells

how radioactively labeled enzymes were used to measure the efficiency of rinsing two different alpha-amylases from paper.

221.   Andrews, Theresa Meyers, William W. Andrews, and Cathleen Baker. "An Investigation into the Removal of Enzymes From Paper Following Conservation Treatment," Journal of the American Institute for Conservation, 31:3 (Fall-Winter, 1992), 313-323. 3 figs., 3 tables, materials list, refs. The efficiency of rinsing two different @-amylases out of paper after conservation treatment was measured using radioactively labeled enzymes. The radioactive enzymes were used to treat small samples of Whatman and Japanese papers. The papers were subjected to various rinsing procedures, and the radioactivity remaining in the paper samples was determined.

222.   Andruss, Harvey A. "Tape Cleaner/Evaluators," Technical Service Product Bulletin (3M Company), August 7, 1989. n.p.

223.   Andruss, Harvey A. "Peel Adhesion," Technical Service Product Bulletin (3M Company), October 28, 1988. n.p.

224.   Ang, Soon and Detmar Straub. "Securing CD-ROMs and the Microcomputer Environment," Laserdisc Professional, 2:4 (July 1989), 18-23. Practical approach to establishing a microcomputer security program. Backup and recovery are reviewed; disaster planning is emphasized.

225.   Anglim, Christopher. Special Collections Policies, Procedures and Guidelines (A Model for the Management of Special Legal Collections). Buffalo, NY: William S. Hein, 1993. 556p. Model includes mission, management, and collection development statements. Includes considerable information on preservation management and policies and on the exhibition of fragile materials. Appendixes.

226.   Anglim, Christopher. "Special Collections Programs at the South Texas College of Law Library, Conservation Administration News, 49 (April 1992), 4-5, 25.

227.   Anson, Gordon O. "Art and Light: The Benefits and the Dangers," Picture Framing Magazine, 4:6 (June 1993), 8-12. Review of the causes of light damage to art; recommended measures for curtailment and protection of materials.

228.   Anson, Gordon. "The Light Solution." Museum News, 27 (September/October 1993), 27, 56, 62. An overview of recent developments in lighting technology. Written for museums, but helpful for archives, particularly those with exhibit areas.

229. Anson, Louisa. "Image Compression: Making Multimedia Publishing a Reality," CD-ROM Professional (September 1993), 16-29. This article provides a lengthy overview of the latest issues in image compression. Anson's focus is methods, and she describes the JPEG standard and the basic technology of it. This basic technology is called Discrete Cosine Transform, and it has some disadvantages. Anson describes fractal transform, which is a better method now gaining wider use and interest, even though it is not part of the standard.

230. Anthony, Joseph. "The Art of Art Restoration," US Air (November 1988), 73-75. Explains conservation and the role of conservators to the public.

231. Antwi, I. K. "The Problem of Library Security: The Bauchi Experience," International Library Review, 21:3 (July 1989), 363-372. Describes damage to library collections in Nigeria caused by theft and other causes.

232. Aparac-Gazivoda, Tatjana, and Dragutin Katalenac. Wounded Libraries in Croatia. tr. Vesna Vrgoc. Zagreb, Croatia: Croatian Library Association, 1993. 58p. Illus. (Croatian Library Association, publication 6). Inventory and brief assessment of the damage to Croatian libraries and their collections during the war with the Serbs.

233. Aparecida de Vries, Marsico. "Brazilian National Library's Restoration Laboratory," Conference on Book and Paper Conservation, 1990. Budapest, Hungary: Technical Association of Paper and Printing Industry/National Szechenyi Library, 1992, 347-355. Outlines the process undertaken in the laboratory, established in 1984, and its projects for the preservation of rare books through treatment and microfilming.

234. "An Appeal to Preserve Old Books," New York Times, March 5, 1987, C28.

235. Applebaum, Barbara. "Criteria for Treatment: Reversibility," Journal of the American Institute for Conservation, 26:2 (Fall 1987), 65-73. The principle examined by clarifying its definitions and by examining the variables that make treatment possible.

236. Applebaum, Barbara. Guide to Environmental Protection of Collections. Madison, CT: Sound View Press, 1991. 270p. Basic manual on the physical care of collections; describes physical nature

of objects in collections and how they react to environment. Role of
the conservator is stressed.

237. Applebaum, Barbara, and Paul Himmelstein. "Planning for a
Conservation Survey," Museum News, 64:3 (February 1986),
5-14. Describes the nature of surveys, how to prepare for them, how
to work with the conservator, what is expected, and follow-up.

238. Arai, Hideo. "On the Foxing-Causing Fungi," Papers. International
Council of Museums, Committee on Conservation, 8th Triennial
Meeting, Sydney, Australia, September 6-11, 1988. Los Angeles,
CA: Getty Conservation Institute, 1987, 1165-1167.

239. Arai, Hideo, and Hachiro Mori. "On the Protection of Paper from
Acid Deterioration by Neutralization; Part 1: Preliminary
Experiments on Diethyl Zinc Method," Science for Conservation, 25
(1986), 55-61.

240. Arai, Hideo, N. Matsui, N. Matsumura, and H. Murakita.
"Biochemical Investigations on the Formation Mechanism of
Fixing," The Conservation of Far Eastern Art. London: International
Institute for Conservation, 1988, 11-12. Reports on the components
found in foxing and the formation of foxing by these components.

241. Arai, Hideo, N. Matsumura, and H. Murakita. "Induced Foxing By
Components Found in Foxed Areas," Papers. International Council
on Museums, Committee on Conservation, 9th Triennial Meeting,
Dresden, Germany, August 26-31, 1990. Marina del Rey, CA: Getty
Conservation Institute, 1990, 801-803.

242. Aranyanak, Chiraporn. "Conservation of Ancient Thai Books," The
Conservation of Far Eastern Art. London: International Institute for
Conservation, 1988, 22-24. Describes the production and causes of
deterioration of samut thai handwritten manuscripts. Reviews
conservation treatment and experiments on the effects of insecticides
and fungicides on the growth of insects and fungi in the books.

243. Araujo, Maria Fernanda de Sa Rodrigues Pinho, and Joaquim Marcal
Ferreira de Andrade. "Technical Treatment and Preservation of the
Photographic Collection of the Brazilian National Library," IFLA
Journal (International Federation of Library Associations and
Institutions), 20:3 (1994), 312-20.

244. Arbogast, David. "Architectural Conservation and the Public
Library," Show-Me Libraries, 37 (September 1986), 20-25.
Reprinted from the Iowa Library Quarterly, 1985.

245. "Arcata Improves Its Round-Backing Capability," <u>Publishers Weekly</u> (June 2, 1989), 62.

246. Arceneaux, Pamela D., and Jessica Travis. <u>Books</u>. New Orleans, LA: Historic New Orleans Collection, 1989. 13p. Preservation Guide 5. Basic book care; designed for the book lover whose home collection is worth preserving. Short summaries on storage, handling, cleaning, and rebinding.

247. <u>Archival Administration in the Electronic Information Age: An Advanced Institute For Government Archivists</u>. Pittsburgh, PA: University of Pittsburgh, School of Library and Information Science, 1991. 74pp. Institute held June 2-4, 1991; co-sponsored by the National Association of Government Archives and Records Administrators with support from the Council on Library Resources.

248. "Archival Paper," <u>Conservation Resources Catalogue</u>. Springfield, VA: Conservation Resources, International, L.L.C. 1995, 4-20. A discussion of the chemical structure of papers, how and why they deteriorate, and how to protect them in long-term storage. Includes comprehensive data and technical specification for archival papers and boards.

249. Archivart. Paper and Preservation No. 12, "What Afflicts Some Matboards With Warp, Wave and ? and What Can Be Done About It?" <u>Technology and Conservation</u>, 8:3 (Fall 1983), backcover.

250. "Archives Conserves Damaged Records," <u>OAH Newsletter</u> (Organization of American Historians), 17:4 (November 1989), 11. Case study; salvage of water-damaged early records from the California Supreme Court.

251. <u>Archiving the Audio-Visual Heritage</u>. Rushden, UK: FIAF/UNESCO, 1992. 192p. (Third Joint Technical Symposium, May 3-5, 1990, Ottawa, Canada). Papers address concerns including the handling of film and videotape, preservation of nitrate stock, and the impact of new technologies on preservation.

252. Areal Guerra, Rogelio, Josep Maria Gibert Vives, and Josep Maria Daga Monmany. "Procedure for Simultaneous Deacidification and Sizing of Paper," <u>Restaurator</u>, 16:4 (1995), 175-193.

253. Arfanis, Peter, and Helen Jarvis. "Archives in Cambodia; Neglected Institutions," <u>Archives and Manuscripts</u> (Australian Society of Archivists), 21:2 (November 1993), 252-262. Describes the recent history of the archives and the appalling condition of surviving records.

254. Arfield, J. A. "Theft Detection Systems - Some Practicalities," Security in Academic and Research Libraries. ed. Anthony G. Quinsee and Andrew C. McDonald. Newcastle-upon-Tyne, England: University of Newcastle Library, 1991, 34-37. Practical questions to ask when selecting and implementing detection systems.

255. "Arizona Puts Teeth into Preservation Law," Abbey Newsletter, 9 (Dec. 1985), 109-110. Reports on legislation empowering Arizona's Dept. of Library, Archives and Public Records to set enforceable preservation standards for repositories. Summarizes the provisions of "Standards for Permanent Records Media and Storage," which set storage requirements for paper and microfilms and includes standards for storage containers and environmental specifications.

256. Arizona State Archives. "Preserving Personal Papers and Photographs." Phoenix, AZ: The Archives, 1995. 6p.

257. Arizona State Archives. "Disasters, Preventing and Coping." Phoenix, AZ: The Archives, 1995. 6p.

258. Arlen, Shelly. "Photographs: Interpretive and Instructional Strategies," Special Libraries (Fall 1990), 351-359.

259. Armour, Annie. "Learning from Experience: A Trial-and-Error Approach to Disaster Planning," Southeastern Librarian, 44:2 (Summer 1994), 62-66. Case study. How the University of the South's library learned to deal with moisture problems caused by a defective building; attacking mold; developing a disaster manual.

260. Arney, J. S., and J. Michael Maurer. "Image Analysis and the Documentation of the Condition of Daguerreotypes," Journal of Imaging Science and Technology, 38:2 (1994), 145-153. Describes a diagnostic technique for the conservation of daguerreotypes.

261. Arney, J. S., and D. Stewart. "Surface Topography of Paper from Image Analysis of Reflectance Images," Journal of Imaging Science and Technology, 37 (1993), 504-509. Describes evidence from examination of paper by raking light, and the advantages of digitizing images captured under raking light. Methods are presented for extracting quantitative topographic data from the analysis of these images.

262. Arnold, Richard. Disaster Recovery Plan. Wellesley, MA: QED Information Sciences, Inc., 1988. 133p. Loose-leaf notebook

format. Disaster recovery planning manual for corporate records in electronic or magnetic format.

263. Arnoult, Jean-Marie. "Annual Report 1991-1992 of the PAC [Preservation and Conservation] Core Programme," IFLA Journal (International Federation of Library Associations and Institutions), 19:2 (1993), 213-223.

264. Arnoult, Jean-Marie. "Annual Report of the IFLA PAC Core Programme," IFLA Journal (International Federation of Library Associations and Institutions), 20:2 (1994), 201-208.

265. Arnoult, Jean-Marie. "The Conservation Centre of the Bibliothèque Nationale at the Castle of Sablé," IFLA Journal (International Federation of Library Associations and Institutions), 12:4 (1986), 309-310. Describes the center and its preservation microfilming activities.

266. Arnoult, Jean-Marie. "Environment and Conservation," Le Edizioni Per La Conservazione (February 1989) 101-107.

267. Arnoult, Jean-Marie. "Mass Deacidification at the Bibliothèque Nationale," Preservation of Library Material, ed. Merrily Smith. New York: K.G. Saur, 1987, 129-133. (IFLA Publications, 40). Describes the history, physical plant, and plans related to mass deacidification in France. Discusses other preservation strategies, such as conservation and repair treatments, microfilming, and encouraging publishers to publish books on permanent paper.

268. Arnoult, Jean-Marie. "Mass Deacidification in France," Restaurator, 8:2/3 (1987), 100-105. Report on efforts by the Bibliothèque Nationale to deal with paper deterioration by establishing a treatment center for deacidification with carbonate of methylmagnesium.

269. Arnoult, Jean-Marie. "National and Institutional Approaches to Conservation: Towards International Cooperation," Politics for the Preservation of the Archival Heritage. Paris: International Council on Archives, 1989, 195-203. Reviews the growth and the role of national archives, cooperative initiatives, and takes a look toward the future.

270. Arp, Lori, and Nora J. Quinlan. "Mold at Norlin Library" (may be the first large-scale infestation remedied without the use of fungicides), Colorado Libraries, 17 (March 1991), 35-36.

271. Arps, Mark. "CD-ROM: Archival Considerations," Preservation of Electronic Formats and Electronic Formats for Preservation, ed.

Janice Mohlenrich. Fort Atkinson, WI: Highsmith Press, 1992, 83-107. Overview of optical media; discussion of physical construction, mastering, duplication and life-span of CD-ROMs.

272.   Arrequi, Carmencho. "The Crossed-Structure Binding," New Bookbinder, 14 (1994), 102-107. Illus. Description of a non-adhesive limp binding with a sound sewing structure directly attached to the covering material.

273.   Arruzzolo, G., and E. Veca. "Biological Degradation of Archival Documents: Prevention and Study," Science, Technology and European Cultural Heritage: Proceedings of the European Symposium, Bologna, Italy, June 13-16, 1989. ed. N. S. Baer, C. Sabbioni, and A. I. Sors. Oxford: Butterworth-Heinemann Publishers, 1991. 636-639.

274.   Arson, Patricia, and Thomas E. Brown. "Government Archivists and Government Automation," Government Publications Review, 13 (1986), 561-570.

275.   "Art History/Preservation Needs-Scholarly Resources in Art History: Issues in Preservation," Library Journal, 114:12 (July 1989), 56.

276.   Artim, Nicholas. "An Introduction to Automatic Fire Sprinklers, Part I," WAAC Newsletter (Western Association for Art Conservation), 16:3 (September 1994), 20-27. Presents a detailed overview of fire growth and sprinkler systems, including systems types and components. Enumeration of the advantages and disadvantages of various types of sprinkler heads and common sprinkler piping materials are particularly helpful.

277.   Artim, Nickolas. "An Introduction to Automatic Fire Sprinklers, Part II," WAAC Newsletter (Western Association for Art Conservation), 17:2 (May 1995), 14-22. An overview of sprinkler systems, including systems types, components, operations, and common anxieties.

278.   Artim, Nickolas. "An Update on Micromist Fire Extinguishment Systems," WAAC Newsletter (Western Association for Art Conservation), 17:3 (September 1995), 14. Describes the micromist, a water mist system for extinguishing fires in library stacks, and the further tests that are planned. "This technology represents a potential solution to the protection void left by environmental concerns, and subsequent demise of Halon 1301 gas."

279.   Artim, Nicholas. "Alternatives to Halon 1301ʳ Systems for Cultural Heritage Fire Protection," Focus on Security, 1:2 (January 1994),

4-13. Discusses the options for protection, from retaining the un-modified system, alternative gases, and a variety of sprinkler systems.

280. Artim, Nicholas. "Cultural Heritage Fire Suppression Systems: Alternatives to Halon 1301," WAAC Newsletter (Western Association for Art Conservation), 15:2 (May 1993), 34-36. Outlines fire suppression systems that can be considered for libraries and museums now that Halon 1301 will no longer be available.

281. Artim, Nicholas. "Intellectual Homicide: The Norwich Library Fire," Focus on Security, 1:2 (October 1994), 4-7. Brief description of the Norwich (England) Central Library Fire, August 1994, causes and lack of adequate protection.

282. Artim, Nicholas. "Water Mist Fire-Suppression Systems for Cultural Property Protection," Focus on Security, 3:1 (October 1995), 8-20. Describes system and operation, testing and further development of a system appropriate for museums, archives, and libraries.

283. Artlip, Paul M. "Microform and Optical Disk Formats Co-Exist to Provide End-User Applications Flexibility," Microfilm Review, 16:3 (Summer 1987), 233-236. Describes variety of optical disk formats to 1987 and their relation to library uses and microforms.

284. Aschinger, Erhard, Franz Lechleitner, and Dietrich Schuller. "The Old Phonograms of the Vienna Phonogrammarchiv: Re-recording Principles and Practice," Phonographic Bulletin, 35 (1983), 16-20. Describes the reproduction of the Wiener Archivphonograph from negatives, to replace positive disks destroyed in World War II.

285. Ashcroft, Maggie, and A. Wilson. eds. Theft: The Economic Impact on UK Libraries. Stamford, England: Capital Planning Information, 1992. 42p. These brief proceedings from a seminar held at Stamford, Lincolnshire in November 1992— comprising three papers and record of the subsequent discussion— address the dramatic increase in book theft in British libraries.

286. Ashford, Nicholas A., and Claudia S. Miller. Chemical Exposures: Low Levels and High Stakes. New York: Van Nostrand-Reinhold, 1991. 214p. Based on the landmark New Jersey Department of Health Study.

287. Ashman, John. "Conservation piece [conservation planning]," Scottish Libraries, 20 (March/April 1990), 12.

288.   Ashman, John. "Conservation piece [phase boxes]," Scottish
         Libraries, 22 (July/August 1990), 11. Illustrated.

289.   Ashman, John. "Conservation piece [National Preservation Office
         Annual Seminar held at York]," Scottish Libraries, 24
         (November/December 1990), 7.

290.   Ashman, John. "Conservation piece, (Society of Archivists Annual
         Conference, Newcastle, 1991)," Scottish Libraries, 30
         (November/December 1991), 9.

291.   Ashman, John. "Preventive Care in the Library," Refer (Royal
         Society of Information Science), 5:3 (Spring 1989), 1-2, 4-6. Defines
         terms and discusses environmental concerns, storage, and handling.

292.   Ashpole, Barry R. "Bedazzled ... By Nostalgia or Technology?"
         Antique Phonograph News, 26 (January-February 1993), 3-5,
         13-14. Discusses playback of 78rpm sound recordings: care and
         storage, stylus size and maintenance, playback speeds, and
         "restoration" of sound and quality of performance.

293.   ASHRAE Handbook: Heating, Ventilating, and Air Conditioning
         Applications. Atlanta, GA: American Society of Heating,
         Refrigerating and Air Conditioning Engineers, 1991. One
         volume. The standard setters for HVAC systems devote three pages
         to libraries and museums. Coverage includes heating and cooling
         loads, design concepts and criteria, building contents, temperature
         and humidity, sound and vibration, exhibit cases, and special rooms.
         Issued every four years.

294.   Ashton, Jean. "New Conservation Laboratory at the New York
         Historical Society," Conservation Administration News, 36 (January
         1989), 5, 26.

295.   Association for Information and Image Management. Care and
         Handling of Active Microform Files. Silver Spring, MD: AIIM,
         1988. 6p. Guidance for the storage, handling, care, and use of
         microforms in a working environment.

296.   Association for Information and Image Management. Facsimile and
         Its Role in Electronic Imaging. Sliver Spring, MD: AIIM, 1989,
         36p. (AIIM TR17-1989). Explains facsimile standards; describes
         variety of equipment available, with examples of applications.
         Definitions.

297.   Association for Information and Image Management. Glossary of
        Imaging Technology. 7th ed. Silver Spring, MD: AIIM, 1992. 79p.
        (AIIM TR2-1992).

298.   Association for Information and Image Management. Information
        and Image Management: The State of the Industry. Silver Spring,
        MD: AIIM, 1992. 94p.

299.   Association for Information and Image Management. Microfiche
        Standard for Information and Image Management. (approved as
        Federal Information Processing Standard, FIPS #54-1). ANSI-AIIM
        MS5-1991. Silver Spring, MD: AIIM, 1991, 17p. This Standard
        replaces ANSI-AIIM MS5-1985 and portions of ANSI/AIIM MS2-
        1978.

300.   Association for Information and Image Management. Performance
        Guidelines for the Legal Acceptance of Records Produced by
        Information Technology Systems. Part 1: Performance Guidelines
        for Admissibility of Record Produced by Information Technology
        Systems as Evidence. Silver Spring, MD: AIIM, 1992, 22p.

301.   Association for Information and Image Management. Practice for
        Operational Procedures/ Inspection and Quality Control of First
        Generation Silver Microfilm of Documents. Silver Spring, MD:
        AIIM, 1991. 50p., appendixes. (ANSI/AIIM
        MS23-1991). Describes and recommends test methods and materials
        for measuring the quality of processed, first-generational silver
        microfilms and inspection procedures.

302.   Association for Information and Image Management. Recommended
        Practice for Microfilming Public Records on Silver-Halide Film.
        Silver Spring, MD: AIIM, 1990, 5p. ANSI/AIIM MS48-1990.

303.   Association for Information and Image Management. Recommended
        Practice for the Requirements and Characteristics of Original
        Documents That May Be Microfilmed. Silver Spring, MD: AIIM,
        1990, 3p. ANSI/AIIM35-1990.

304.   Association for Information and Image Management. Resolution as
        It Relates to Photographic and Electronic Imaging. Silver Spring,
        MD: AIIM, 1993. 18p.

305.   Association for Information and Image Management. The Use of
        Optical Disks for Public Records (AIIM TR25-1990). Silver Spring,
        MD: AIIM, 1990, 33p. Discusses electronic storage technology,
        emphasizing optical disks, storage of public records. Addresses

issues in implementing the technology, including preservation for
long term.

306.   Association for Recorded Sound Collections. Associated Audio
         Archives Committee. Audio Preservation, A Planning Study: Final
         Performance Report. Silver Spring, MD: AIIM, 1988. 2 vols., 860p.
         loose-leaf. A review of research and initiatives undertaken to
         preserve audio materials, and an agenda for further research and
         preservation strategies.

307.   Association of British Columbia Archivists. A Manual for Small
         Archives. Vancouver, BC: Association of British Columbia
         Archivists, 1988. 213p., loose-leaf binder. Detailed manual designed
         for people with minimal archival training. Section 6: "Conservation
         and Security," provides basic information on collection management,
         disaster planning, and security.

308.   Association of Forensic Documents Examiners. Post-Symposium
         Report May 3-7, 1990. San Antonio, TX: Association of Forensic
         Documents Examiners, 1990. n.p. Offers information on identifying
         inks and photocopies.

309.   Association of Higher Education Facilities Officers. Preservation of
         Library and Archival Materials. Alexandria, VA: Association of
         Higher Education Facilities Officers, 1991. 66p. Papers from a
         conference co-sponsored by the Commission of Preservation and
         Access. Librarians, archivists, and facilities engineers address the
         issue of the physical maintenance of buildings housing cultural
         property.

310.   Association of Records Managers and Administrators International
         Standards Committee, Vital Records Guidelines. Prairie Village, KS:
         ARMA, 1984. 61p. Guidelines for the selection, protection,
         management, and recovery of vital records; program implementation
         and testing; disaster planning; sample forms; annotated bibliography.

311.   Association of Records Managers and Administrators International.
         Standards Disaster Recovery Sub-Committee. ARMA International
         Guideline for Magnetic Diskettes-Recovery Procedure. Prairie
         Village, KS: Association of Records Managers and Administrators,
         1987, 8p. Practical information focusing on simple recovery
         procedures for magnetic diskettes.

312.   Association of Records Managers and Administrators. Triangle
         Chapter. Guidelines for Disaster Recovery of Records. Raleigh, NC:
         Association of Records Managers and Administrators, 1988.

n.p. Basic guidelines, following closely the Basic Guidelines for Disaster Planning in Oklahoma by Toby Murray.

313.   Association of Reproduction Materials Manufacturers, Inc. Questions and Answers About Ammonia and the Reproduction Industry. Alexandria, VA: Association of Reproduction Materials Manufacturers, Inc. 1988, 14p. Booklet prepared to help insure that diazo equipment is used safely.

314.   [Association of Research Libraries], ARL Committee on Preservation of Research Library Materials. Guidelines for Minimum Preservation Efforts in ARL Libraries. Approved by the ARL Membership on October 25, 1984; revised July 1985. Washington, DC: Association of Research Libraries, 1985. Photocopy, 6p. Stipulates levels of effort that should be achieved by ARL members in the following areas: adoption of a local preservation program statement; compilation, maintenance, and reporting of statistics; participation in national programs to film or otherwise copy materials for preservation; maintenance of acceptable environmental conditions; and budgetary effort (as percentages of acquisitions or of overall budget).

315.   [Association of Research Libraries]. "ARL Committee on Preservation to Gather Statistics," National Preservation News, 2 (October 1985), 3. Describes a pilot survey of ARL libraries to determine the extent of their 1984-85 preservation activity. Questionnaire to gather individual and aggregate information about preservation activity; analysis to determine which statistics are relevant and identifiable.

316.   Association of Research Libraries. Office of Management Studies. Automating Preservation Management in ARL Libraries. Washington DC: Association of Research Libraries, 1993. 175p. (SPEC Kit 198). Compiled by Patricia Brennan and Jutta Reed-Scott. It includes the results of a 1993 ARL survey of libraries on how automation is used in management of preservation activities.

317.   Association of Research Libraries. Office of Management Studies. Binding Operations in ARL Libraries. Washington, DC: Association of Research Libraries, 1985, 105pp. (SPEC Kit 114). A similar compilation on in-house and commercial binding, which reports that in-house binding is usually in the preservation or conservation department.

318.   Association of Research Libraries. Office of Management Studies. Brittle Books Program. Washington, DC: Association of Research Libraries, 1989. 121p. (SPEC Kit 152). Policies and guidelines,

based on a survey of 64 ARL libraries, for dealing with publications
that are so deteriorated that they must be reformatted or lost.

319.   Association of Research Libraries. Office of Management Services.
         The Changing Role of Book Repair in ARL Libraries. Washington,
         DC: Association of Research Libraries, 1993. 127p. (SPEC Kit 190).

320.   Association of Research Libraries. Office of Management Studies.
         Collection Security in ARL Libraries. Washington, DC: Association
         of Research Libraries, 1984. 44p. (SPEC Kit 100). Includes
         questionnaires, forms, policy and procedure statements, and task
         force reports from ARL libraries, with selective bibliography.

321.   Association of Research Libraries. Office of Management Studies.
         Digitizing Technologies for Preservation. Washington, DC:
         Association of Research Libraries, 1996. 173p. (SPEC Kit 214). This
         kit documents the tremendous variety of digital preservation projects
         underway in ARL libraries. Projects are described in terms of size,
         scope, and types of materials being digitized, as well as hardware and
         software issues. Detailed information on project status, materials
         selection, indexing, bibliographic control, staffing, and production
         are included.

322.   Association of Research Libraries. Office of Management Studies.
         Insuring Library Collections and Buildings. Washington, DC:
         Association of Research Libraries, October 1991. 149p. (SPEC Kit
         178). Presents results of a survey of academic library administrators
         planning and insurance needs; examples of insurance policies.

323.   Association of Research Libraries. Office of Management Studies.
         Optical Disks for Storage and Access in ARL Libraries.
         Washington, DC: Association of Research Libraries, 1987. 111p.
         (SPEC Kit 133). Optical systems planning reports and documents
         from assorted research libraries.

324.   Association of Research Libraries. Office of Management Studies.
         Organizing for Preservation. Washington, DC: Association of
         Research Libraries, 1985. 131p. (SPEC Kit 116). Reports results of a
         survey on the place of the preservation department in the library
         administrative structure, and includes related papers from a number
         of member libraries.

325.   Association of Research Libraries. Office of Management Studies.
         Photocopy Services. Washington, DC: Association of Research
         Libraries, 1985. 106p. (SPEC Kit 115). Contains a summary of a
         survey of ARL members on copying practices and administration,
         along with a selection of policy statements, price lists, contracts, etc..

326. Association of Research Libraries. Office of Management Studies. Preservation Guidelines in ARL Libraries. Washington, DC: Association of Research Libraries, 1987. 100p. (SPEC Kit 137). Guidelines, policies, and procedures issued by selected ARL libraries since 1981.

327. Association of Research Libraries. Office of Management Studies. Preservation Education in ARL Libraries. Washington, DC: Association of Research Libraries, 1985. 110p. (SPEC Kit 113). A compilation of materials from member libraries on education of readers, staff, potential donors, and senior administrators, and on management responsibilities.

328. Association of Research Libraries. Preservation. [Research Library Priority for the 1990s: Minutes of the 111th Meeting, October 21-22, 1987, Washington, D.C.]. Washington, DC: Association of Research Libraries, 1987. 125p.

329. Association of Research Libraries. Preservation Planning Conference, May 27-29, 1992, Chicago, Illinois: Summary. Chicago, IL: University of Chicago Library, 1992. 46p., appendices. Representatives from mature preservation programs in research libraries gathered to advance planning for a coordinated North American preservation program for the next decade.

330. Association of Research Libraries. Preservation Statistics. Washington, DC: Association of Research Libraries, 1987/1988. One volume. A serial.

331. Association of Research Libraries. Preserving Knowledge: The Case for Permanent Paper. Rev. ed. Washington, DC: Association of Research Libraries, August 1990. Paged in sections. Compilation of information on the use of alkaline paper "to highlight progress and considerable success in promoting the use of alkaline paper in book production." Other sponsors are Commission on Preservation and Access and National Humanities Alliance.

332. Association pour la Recherche Scientifique sue les Arts Graphiques. Sauvegarde et Conservation des Photographies, Dessins, Imprimbes et Manuscrits: Actes/ des Journées Internationales d'ètudes de l'ARSAG, Paris, France 30 Septembre au 4 Octobre 1991. Paris: Association pour la Recherche Scientifique sur les Arts Graphiques, 1991. 261p. A 1994 edition has also been published.

333.   "Assault on Paper Mountain," History News, 38:4 (April 1983), 21-23. Report on the National Advisory Committee on the Management, Preservation and Use of Local Government Records.

334.   Astle, Deana L. "Preservation Issues and Acquisitions," Library Acquisitions: Practice and Theory, 14:3 (1990), 301-305. Discusses preservation concerns in terms of acquisitions; quality of product, and the purchase of books printed on alkaline paper.

335.   Atkins, Winston, and Ellen Belcher. "Coordinating a Bomb Blast Recovery," Conservation Administration News, 55 (October 1993), 1-2, 24-27. Case study; recovery of research materials following a bombing. Demonstrates need for library preservation staff to be involved in campus emergencies.

336.   Atkinson Ross. "The Acquisitions Librarian as Change Agent in the Transition to the Electronic Library," Library Resources and Technical Services, 36:1 (January 1992), 7-20. Discusses the role of the acquisitions department and how it needs to change/evolve as electronic publishing/resources become more common. Identifies "delivery" and "mediation" as two aspects of information service, and delivery, especially, for acquisitions to address as an evolving task.

337.   Atkinson, Ross W. "Preservation and Collection Development. Toward a Political Synthesis," Journal of Academic Librarianship, 16:2 (May 1990), 98-103. Explains functions and values of preservation from a political perspective.

338.   Atkinson, Ross W. "Selection for Preservation: A Materialistic Approach," Library Resources and Technical Services, 30:4 (October-December 1986), 341-353. Analytical discussion of the "decision cycle" for preservation; presents a methodology for selection for preservation.

339.   Atkinson, Ross. "Text Mutability and Collection Administration," Library Acquisitions: Practice and Theory, 14:4 (1990), 355-358. A cogent description of the librarian's role in the electrically dominated library; a restatement of the Librarian's professional responsibilities.

340.   Atwood, Catherine. "An Exploration of Japanese Books," New Library Scene, 8:3 (June 1989), 1,5-6. A note on the production of Japanese books based upon the author's examination of their structure.

341.   Atwood, Catherine. "Notes on the Preservation of Personnel Health," Book and Paper Group Annual, 9 (1990), 12-16. Creates an

awareness of potential health risks in handling books and documents. Suggestions are made for the safe use of materials.

342.   Atwood, Thomas, and Carol Wall. "A Case Study of Periodical Mutilation in a University Serials Collection," Library and Archival Security, 10:1 (1990), 35-41. Two studies undertaken to assess the extent of mutilation demonstrated that there was little; protective measures were effective.

343.   Aubitz, Shawn, and Gail F. Stern. Developing Archival Exhibitions. Charlottesville, VA: Mid-Atlantic Regional Archives Conference, 1990. 14p. (Technical Leaflet, 5). A brief guide, discussing preservation considerations and suggesting the use of facsimiles whenever possible.

344.   Aubitz, Shawn, and Zorina Siokalo. Disaster Preparedness: A Resource Guide and Manual. 2d ed. Philadelphia, PA: Museum Council of Philadelphia and the Delaware Valley, 1994. 117p. (loose-leaf notebook). Tool to help cultural institutions develop a written disaster preparedness plan. Sections cover preparedness, emergency response, recovery, and "Risk Control Measures for Computers." Model forms.

345.   Aubrey, Rolland. "Specifications and Test Methods Associated with Papers for Permanent Books, Records, and Documents." In Paper Preservation: Current Issues and Recent Developments. Atlanta, GA: TAPPI Press, 1990, 90-93. Reports on the organizations involved in establishing standards and test methods for papers. Paper presented at the Paper Preservation Symposium, Washington, DC, 1988.

346.   Auf der Heide, Erik. Disaster Response: Principles of Preparation and Coordination. St. Louis, MO: C.V. Mosby Co., 1989. 361p.

347.   Austin, D. "Fort Worth Library Builds Preservation Program with Grant [from the Junior League]," Texas Libraries, 53 (Spring/Summer 1992), 11-12.

348.   Australia, National Library. Model for the Recording of Preservation and Conservation Activity. Canberra: National Library of Australia, 1996. 21p.

349.   Australia, National Library. National Preservation Office. Preservation Microfilming: Does It Have a Future? Proceedings of the First National Conference of the National Preservation Office, at

the State Library of South Australia, 4-6 May 1994. convened by Jan
Lyall. Canberra: National Library of Australia, 1995. 198p

350. Australia, National Library. National Preservation Office. "Draft
Statement of Principles of Preservation and Long Term Access to
Australian Digital Objects," AICCM National Newsletter
(Australian Institute for the Conservation of Cultural Materials), 59
(June 1996), 5-7.

351. Australian Archives. Guidelines on Papers for Use by
Commonwealth Agencies. Canberra: Australian Government
Printing Office, 1993. 16p. Provides advice on the types of papers to
be used by Commonwealth agencies when creating records;
discusses properties of papers that affect their performance and
permanence.

352. Australian Archives. Photocopying and Laser Printing Processes —
Their Stability and Permanence. Dickson, ACT, Australia:
Australian Archives, September 1993. 3p. Reviews common
electrophotocopying processes and provides practical advice on
measures to improve durability and stability of photocopies and laser
printed materials.

353. Australian Archives. Thermal Paper — How to Use and Keep
Documents Created On It. Dickson, ACT, Australia: Australian
Archives, August 1994. 3p. Describes properties of thermal papers,
their impermanence; guidelines for preservation of information
and/or original documents.

354. Australian Council of Libraries and Information Service. "The Need
for the Preservation of Australian Created Electronic Information: A
Position Paper," Australian Academic and Research Libraries, 23:4
(1992), 197-205.

355. Australian Society of Archivists. Proceedings of the Australian
Society of Archivists Conference in Townsville, Queensland, May 9-
11, 1994. Canberra: Australian Society of Archivists, 1994. 144
p. Includes papers on conservation.

356. Avallone, S. "LC Agrees to Outside Review of the DEZ Process,"
Library Journal, 112 (February 1, 1987), 20.

357. Avasthi, A. K. "Preserving Microforms Instead of Originals in
Libraries With Special Reference to Publications Like Periodicals
and Newspapers," Planning Modernization and Preservation
Programs of South Asian Libraries. ed. Kalpona Dasgupta. Calcutta,
India: National Library, 1992. 66-90. Thorough review of

microfilming for preservation: formats, advantages, and disadvantages; preservation of microfilm.

358. Avedon, Don M. "All About Optical Disk Systems," Office Systems Management, 2 (1989), 14-15.

359. Avedon, Don M. Introduction to Electronic Imaging. Silver Spring, MD: Association for Information and Image Management, 1992. 53p. Describes the concept and how technologies for electronic image management can be applied to records and information management. Glossary.

360. Avrin, Leila. Scribes, Script and Books: The Book Arts from Antiquity to the Renaissance. Chicago, IL: American Library Association, 1991. 392p. Illustrations, index.

361. Axelrod, Todd M. Collecting Historical Documents: A Guide to Owning History. 2d ed. Neptune City, NJ: T.F.H. Publications, 1986. 237p. Illustrated guide for collectors. Chapter 4: "Maintaining Your Collection," 61-73, describes enemies of papers and reviews protective measures for housing and display. Emphasizes need for conservators to treat damaged materials.

362. Axford, Catherine A. "Museum Pest Management and Control at Getty Conservation Institute," Conservation Administration News, 58-59 (July/October 1994), 34.

363. Ayres, J. Marx, J. Carlos Hand, and Henry Lau. Energy Conservation and Climate Control in Museums. Marina del Rey, CA: Getty Conservation Institute, November 1988. 80p. Illus. (Getty Scientific Program Report). Report of a study using computer simulations to determine energy consumption in museums and the cost of operating HVAC systems in various locations in the United States.

364. Ayres, J. Marx, James Druzik, J. Carlos Hand, Henry Lau, and Steven Weintraub. "Energy Conservation Under Various Outdoor Climates," International Journal of Museum Management and Curatorship, 8 (1989), 299-312. Results of the study, cited above.

365. Aziagba, Philip C. "Deterioration of Library and Archival Materials in the Delta Region of Nigeria," International Library Review, 23 (June 1991), 73-81.

366. Baatz, Wilmer H. "Afro-American Research Material in Microform: A Selected Sampling," Microform Review, 17:4 (October 1988), 190-196. Sampling of what is available; information about the

preservation microfilming at the Schomberg Center for Research in Black Culture, New York Public Library.

367.   Babcock, Philip. "Ready for the Worst," Museum News, 69:3 (May-June 1990), 50-54. Planning for a disaster in a museum.

368.   Babin, Angela. "Celluloid Film Hazards in Conservation," Art Hazards News, 13:8 (1990), 3. Summary of vital facts on the hazards of nitrate film. Reviews the guidelines of NFPA 40: "Standard for Storage and Handling of Cellulose Nitrate Motion Picture Film" (1988).

369.   Bachmann, Konstanze, ed. Conservation Concerns: A Guide for Collectors and Curators. Washington, DC: Smithsonian Institution Press, 1992. 149p. Collection of essays on basic collection care, including works on paper, photographs, and sound recordings. These were originally prepared by conservators for use with the New York Conservation Consultancy program.

370.   Baer, Norbert S. "Air Quality Criteria for Storage of Paper-Based Archival Records," American Archivist, 48:1 (Winter 1985), 77-79. Review of the publication by the National Bureau of Standards, based upon the research undertaken by the National Archives and Records Administration.

371.   Baer, Norbert S., ed. Training in Conservation. New York: New York University Institute of Fine Arts, 1989. 88p. (Proceedings of a symposium, October 1983). Papers that reflect the development of conservation training programs and the role of the conservator.

372.   Baer, Norbert S., and Paul N. Banks. "Conservation Notes: Environmental Standards," International Journal of Museum Management and Curatorship, 6:2 (June 1987), 207-209. Reviews environmental standards for temperature, relative humidity, gaseous pollutants, and particulate matter proposed by Thompson (1986) and the National Research Council (1987) standards.

373.   Baer, Norbert S., and Paul N. Banks. "Indoor Air Pollution: Effects on Cultural and Historic Materials," International Journal of Museum Management and Curatorship, 4:1 (March 1985), 9-20. Reprinted in Care of Collections, ed. Simon Knell. London: Routledge, 1994. 135-146. Discusses pollutants, causes and effects; extensive bibliography.

374.   Baer, Norbert S., and Paul N. Banks. "Particulate Standards for Museums, Libraries, and Archives," Proceedings. 78th Air Pollution Control Association Annual Meeting. Pittsburgh, PA: Air Pollution

Control Association, 1 (1985), 85-88. Sources of indoor particulate pollutants are described, with recommendations for their removal.

375. Baer, Norbert S., and Simeon M. Berman. "An Evaluation of the Statistical Significance of Hudson's Acidity Date for 17th and 18th Century Books in Two Libraries," Restaurator, 7:3 (1986), 119-124. Examination of collections of similar books in urban and rural environments; concludes that atmospheric pollution is a cause of lower pH values, especially on the outer edges, of books in urban libraries.

376. Baer, Norbert S., and Margaret Holben Ellis. "Conservation Notes: On Thymol Fumigation," International Journal of Museum Management and Curatorship, 7:2 (June 1988), 185-188. Discusses effectiveness and toxicity of Thymol, and concludes that the effectiveness of Thymol is not proven.

377. Baer, Norbert S., and Jane Slate Siena. "Conservation: Disaster Planning Initiatives," International Journal of Museum Management and Curatorship, 8:1 (1989), 105-120. A review of the effects of natural disasters and the international initiatives to encourage disaster planning and to assist in recovery.

378. Bagg, Thomas C. "The Dilemma — Preservation Versus Access," Preservation Research & Development: Round Table Proceedings, Sept. 28-29, 1992. Washington, DC: LC Preservation Directorate, June 1993, 57-61.

379. Bagg, Thomas C. "Digitizing Documents: Guidelines for Image Quality," Inform, 1 (November 1987), 6-9.

380. Bagnall, Roger S. Digital Imaging of Papyri: A Report to the Commission on Preservation and Access. Washington, DC: Commission on Preservation and Access, 1995. 8p.

381. Bagnall, Roger S. "Who Will Save the Books? The Case of the Classicists," The New Library Scene, 6:2 (April 1987), 16-18. Also in Humanities, 8:1 (January/February 1987), 21.

382. Bagnall, Roger S., and Carolyn L. Harris. "Involving Scholars in Preservation Decisions: The Case of the Classicists," Journal of Academic Librarianship, 13:3 (July 1987), 140-146. Describes a project that involved scholars in preservation decision making; their education, advantages, and disadvantages.

383.   Bahr, Alice Harrison. "Electronic Collection Security Systems Today: Changes and Choices," Library and Archival Security, 11:1 (1991), 2-22. Reviews security systems and options.

384.   Bahr, Alice Harrison. "Electronic Security for Books," Library Trends, 33:1 (Summer 1984), 29-38. History of electronic security systems, costs, and benefits.

385.   Bahr, Alice Harrison. "The Thief in Our Midst," Library and Archival Security, 9:3/4 (1989), 77-81. Profiles of thieves and discussion.

386.   Baillie, Jeavons. "A Conservation Facility for the Public Record Office of Victoria," AICCM Bulletin (Australian Institute for the Conservation of Cultural Materials), 16:1-2 (1990), 71-73. Development of a preservation program and policies, with guarded optimism for the future of the program.

387.   Baillie, Jeavons. "General Issues in the Production & Management of Microfilms," Preservation Microfilming: Does It Have a Future? Canberra: National Library of Australia, 1995, 132-136. A conservator looks to microfilm for preservation and access; looks to digitization on demand when necessary. Supports established, eye-readable medium, read with easy and minimal technology.

388.   Baird, Brian J. "Commercial Binding as a Preservation Treatment," New Library Scene, 14:5 (October 1995), 5-8, 22. An overview of library binding for preservation and access; managing a binding program and working with the binder.

389.   Baird, Brian J. "The Goals and Objectives of Collections Conservation," Restaurator, 13:4 (1992), 149-161. Describes an effective conservation policy and procedures for collection management.

390.   Baird, Brian J. "A Look at Microenvironments for Books: Strengths and Weaknesses of Various Types of Protective Enclosures," New Library Scene, 13 (April 1994), 8-12.

391.   Baird, Brian J. "Motivating Student Employees: Examples from Collections Conservation," Library Resources & Technical Services, 39:4 (October 1995), 410-416. Management techniques to motivate student employees to strengthen their contribution to a unit, using collection conservation as an example.

392.   Baird, Brian J., and Mick Le Tourneaux. "Treatment 305: A Collections Conservation Approach to Rebinding Laced-on-Board

Binding," Book and Paper Group Annual, 13 (1994), 1-4. Describes a tight joint conservation structure sympathetic to late 18th -and early 19th -century bindings.

393. Baish, Mary Alice. "Special Problems of Preservation in the Tropics," Conservation Administration News, 31 (October 1987), 4-5. Describes environmental factors that accelerate deterioration of paper-based materials in the tropics.

394. Bakal, Carl. "The Quiet Crisis: Are We Losing Our Libraries?" Town and Country (March 1983), 166-169, 251. Overview of problem of deteriorating library collections, written for the public. Emphasis on the low cost for the materials and services available to the public.

395. Baker, Cathleen. "The Role Viscosity Grade Plays When Choosing Methylcellulose as a Sizing Agent," Conference Papers, Manchester 1992. Worcester, England: Institute of Paper Conservation, 1992, 219-221. Discusses how conservators can select viscosity grades of methylcellulose for conservation treatments.

396. Baker, Cathleen A. "Methylcellulose and Sodium Carboxy-methylcellulose: An Evaluation for Use in Paper Conservation Through Accelerated Aging," Adhesives and Consolidents. London: IIC, 1984. (Preprints, Paris: Congress, 2-8 September 1984), 55-59. Describes adhesives and their use, study of their stability over time.

397. Baker, Cathleen, and F. Christopher Tahk. Graduate Education and Training for the Archives Conservator. Buffalo, NY: State University College, Art Conservation Department, 1990. 64p. Report of the Planning Project Panel to investigate graduate education for training archives conservation.

398. Baker, Don. "The Conservation of Jam' al-Tawarikh by Rashid Al-Din (1313)," Arts and the Islamic World (Spring 1991), 32-33. Describes condition before treatment and method used for repair. Discusses paper used, suggesting that it represents an intermediate stage in the divergence of Arab and Persian paper types.

399. Baker, John P. "Conservation and Preservation of Library Materials," ALA World Encyclopedia of Library and Information Services. 2d ed. Chicago, IL: American Library Association, 1986, 219-223. An overview essay.

400. Baker, John P. "Preservation at the New York Public Library." Conservation Administration News, 21 (April 1985), 6-7. Describes

New York Public Library's attempts to find the best way to preserve newsprint and the implementation of preservation microfilming in the 1930s. Describes the formation and activities of the Conservation Division.

401. Baker, John P. "Preserving the Collections of the Science and Technology Research Center of the New York Public Library," Science and Technology Libraries, 7:4 (Summer 1987), 81-95. Describes the Conservation Division at New York Public Library and its role in preserving this material through physical treatment and microfilming.

402. Baker, Mary T., Helen Burgess, Nancy E. Binnie, Michele R. Derrick, and James R. Druzik. "Laboratory Investigation of the Fumigant Vikane," Preprints. International Council of Museums Committee for Conservation, 9th Triennial Meeting, Dresden, Germany, August 26-31, 1990. Vol. 2. Marina del Rey, CA: Getty Conservation Institute, 1990, 804-811.

403. Baker, Richard. "Ark Building Workshop for Worcester Librarians," Conservation Administration News, 21 (April 1985), 1-2, 19-21. Describes a course on disaster planning and recovery with a simulated disaster.

404. Baker, Vicki. "Collection Security: Policies, Procedures, and Technologies," Library Hi-Tech Bibliography, 5:2 (1990), 17-25. Annotated review of the literature on library collection security, 1983-1989.

405. Baldwin, Gordon. Looking at Photographs - A Guide To Terms. Malibu, CA: J. Paul Getty Museum; British Museum Press, 1991. 88p. Concise technical guide to photographic processes and materials, alphabetically arranged.

406. Bales, Erv, and William B. Rose. Bugs, Mold and Rot: Proceedings of the Moisture Control Workshop. Washington, DC: National Institute of Building Sciences, 1992. 71p. Papers from a workshop to explore moisture control in buildings, humidity and moisture, and insect pests, as well as health concerns.

407. Balicki, Alan. Matting and Framing. New Orleans, LA: Historic New Orleans Collection, 1989, 13p. (Preservation Guide 6). Offers suggestions on preserving framed artworks.

408. Balint, Valerie. "A Disaster Preparedness Plan," Chesterwood Pedestal, 10:1 (Fall 1992), 11-2. Brief note on the preparation of a

disaster plan for a house museum and archive, and on the recovery workshop to test the plan.

409. Ballard, Mary W. "Emergency Planning," Conservation Concerns: A Guide for Collectors and Curators. ed. Konstanze Bachmann. Washington, DC: Smithsonian Institution Press, 1992, 11-14. How to assess risks and develop disaster contingency plans; goals and recommendations.

410. Ballard, Mary W., and Norbert S. Baer. "Conservation Notes: Is Fumigation Possible?" International Journal of Museum Management and Curatorship, 6 (1987), 83-86. Reaction to the banning of many fumigants by the Environmental Protection Agency; observes that fumigation is possible and can be appropriate but further research is underway.

411. Ballard, Mary W., and Norbert S. Baer. "Ethylene Oxide Fumigation: Results and Risk Assessment," Restaurator, 7:4 (1986), 143-168. Reviews legislative history of Ethylene Oxide (ETO) and examines it as a fumigant and as a hazard to materials and to people.

412. Ballestrem, Agnes. "High Level, Basic Level and Middle Level Training in Conservation, What Does It Mean?" Preprints. International Council on Museums (ICOM) Committee for Conservation, 7th Triennial Meeting, Copenhagen, September 10-14, 1984. Paris: International Council on Museums, 1984, 84:21:11-2. Argues that anyone responsible for preservation or conservation must have at least a basic knowledge of conservation.

413. Balloffet, Nelly. Library Disaster Handbook: Planning, Resources, Recovery. Highland, NY: Southeastern New York Library Resources Council, 1992. 54p.

414. Balloffet, Nelly, and Jenny Hille. Conservation Techniques for Reference & Research Collections: A Handbook. Elmsford, NY: Lower Hudson Conference of Historical Agencies and Museums, 1996. 47p.

415. Ballou, Hubbard W. "The Micrographic Book Cradle in Retrospect and Replica," Microform Review, 14:3 (Summer 1985), 174-179. History of the cradles that have been developed for microfilming and a description of a cradle being developed by the author.

416. Balon, Brett J., and H. Wayne Gardner. "Disaster Contingency Planning: The Basic Elements," ARMA Records Management Quarterly (Association of Records Managers and Administrators),

21:1 (January 1987), 14-16. Outlines reasons for developing a disaster plan, and discusses how to develop one.

417. Balon, Brett J., and H. Wayne Gardner. "Disaster Planning for Electronic Records," Records Management Quarterly, 22:3 (July 1988), 20-25, 30. Covers major areas of disaster planning: cost benefit analysis, review of options for alternative site selection, action plan, and maintenance.

418. Balon, Brett J. and H. Wayne Gardner. "It'll Never Happen Here: Disaster Contingency Planning in Canadian Urban Municipalities," ARMA Records Management Quarterly (Association of Records Managers and Administrators), 20 (July 1986), 26-28.

419. Bancroft, David J. "Point of View: Pixels and Halide - A Natural Partnership?" SMPTE Journal (Society of Motion Picture and Television Engineers), 103:5 (May 1994), 306-311. Critique and analysis of the proposal by the Technical Council of the motion picture and television industry to define a film digital mastering format.

420. Banik, Gerhard. "Discoloration of Green Copper Pigments in Manuscripts and Works of Graphic Art," Restaurator, 10:2 (1989), 61-73. Conclusions from an investigation into the causes of disintegration of green copper pigments.

421. Banik, Gerhard. "Freeze Drying at the National Library of Austria," International Preservation News, 4 (August 1990), 9-12. Describes the process of freeze-drying documents damaged by flooding using a chamber developed for the mass treatment and strengthening of newspapers.

422. Banik, Gerhard. "Green Copper Pigments and Their Alteration in Manuscripts or Works of Art," Pigments et Colorants de l'Antiquité et du Moyen Age: Teinture, Peinture, Enluminure, Études Historiques et Physico-chemiques. Paris: CNRS, 1990, 89-102. Discusses the composition and use of green pigments and the decomposition mechanisms of support materials; causes of discoloration and loss of mechanical properties of paper, accelerated by an acid environment.

423. Banik, Gerhard. "Paper Splitting," Paper Conservation News, 50 (June 1989), 9-10. Discusses the paper splitting technique developed in Leipzig, Germany, in terms of stability and reversibility.

424. Banik, Gerhard, and Werner K. Sobotka. "Deacidification and Strengthening of Bound Newspapers Through Aqueous Immersion,"

Paper Preservation: Current Issues and Recent Developments. Atlanta, GA: TAPPI Press, 1990, 137-143. (Proceedings of a Paper Preservation Symposium, Washington, DC, 1988). Describes a mass preservation technique used at the Austrian National Library to deacidify, strengthen, and clean embrittled newspapers.

425. Banik, Gerhard, and Werner K. Sobotka. "Standard Specification for Permanent Paper in Austria," Paper Preservation: Current Issues and Recent Developments. Atlanta, GA: TAPPI Press, 1990, 94-95. Describes the Austrian standard for uncoated paperboard.

426. Banik, Gerhard, Werner K. Sobotka, Alfred Vendl, and Stephan Norzicska. "Effects of Atmospheric Pollutants on Deacidified Modern Paper," Preprints, ICOM Committee for Conservation 10th Triennial Meeting. ed. Janet Bridgland. Washington, DC: International Council of Museums, August 1993, 435-441. Presents results of a project investigating the aging behavior of several modern types of paper after deacidification and restrengthening treatment.

427. Banks, Elizabeth. "Preservation and Storage of Oversized and Nonstandard Records," NEA Newsletter (New England Archivists), 19:4 (October 1992), 4-5.

428. Banks, Jennifer. Options for Replacing and Reformatting Deteriorated Materials. Washington, DC: Association of Research Libraries, 1993. 51p. (Preservation Planning Program). Brief discussion of reformatting materials using microfilm and/or electronic technologies; selected readings.

429. Banks, Joyce M. Guidelines for Preventive Conservation/ Directives Regissant la Conservation Preventive. New ed. Ottawa: National Library of Canada, Committee on Conservation/ Preservation of Library Materials, 1987. 45p. Basic principles of preservation and collection management. Bibliography.

430. Banks, Joyce M. "Mass Deacidification at the National Library of Canada," Conservation Administration News, 20 (January 1985), 14-15, 27. Description of the Wei T'o process operating at the Public Archives of Canada.

431. Banks, Paul N. "Carolyn Harris: A Personal Tribute," Conservation Administration News, 57 (April 1994), 4.

432. Banks, Paul N. "Conservation and Preservation," Encyclopedia of Library History, ed. Wayne Wiegand and Donald G. Davis, Jr. New

York: Garland, 1994, 167-169. Short history of preservation and conservation initiatives and activities.

433.   Banks, Paul N. "Environmental Conditions for Storage of Paper-Based Records," Conservation in Archives. Paris: International Council on Archives, 1989, 77-88. (Proceedings of an International Symposium, Ottawa, Canada, May 10-12, 1988). Reviews the environmental factors that affect the longevity of records; comments on the lack of research to determine parameters for the storage of records, and the resultant difficulties in establishing standards.

434.   Banks, Paul N. "ISR/ASTM Workshop on Paper Aging" (Institute for Standards Research Program in Philadelphia, Pa., July 1994), Conservation Administration News, 60 (January 1995), 22.

435.   Banks, Paul N. "A Library Is Not a Museum," Training In Conservation, ed. Norbert S. Baer. New York: New York University Institute of Fine Arts, 1989, 57-65. Outlines the special requirements for the training of library and archives conservators.

436.   Banks, Paul N. "Preservation of Library Collections, and the Concept of Cultural Property," Libraries and Scholarly Communication in the United States: The Historical Dimension, ed. Phyllis Dain and John Y. Cole. New York: Greenwood Press, 1990, 89-110. A reflective essay on the concept of cultural property, national efforts, and legal aspects.

437.   Banks, Paul N. "Training for Preservation Personnel for Archives," Preservation Papers of the 1990 SAA Annual Conference, ed. Karen Garlick. Chicago, IL : Society of American Archivists, 1991, 18-22. Contact and needs for preservation, education for archives conservators and curators. Describes the Columbia Conservation Education Program.

438.   Bansa, Helmut. "The Awareness of Conservation: Reasons for Reorientation in Library Training," Restaurator, 7:1 (1986), 36-47. Stresses the need for education and presents a proposed syllabus for a course for librarians on preservation.

439.   Bansa, Helmut. "Computerized Leafcasting," Restaurator, 11:2 (1990), 69-94. Describes a computer program that executes all calculations necessary for the leafcasting process.

440.   Bansa, Helmut. "The Conservation of Modern Books," IFLA Journal (International Federation of Library Associations and Institutions), 9:2 (1983), 102-113. Defines conservation as a

responsibility of library management; discusses the nature of paper
and urges that librarians press for production of permanent paper.

441.   Bansa, Helmut. "Conservation Treatment of Rare Books,"
        Restaurator, 8:2/3 (1987), 140-150; reprinted in Preservation of
        Library Materials, ed. Merrily Smith. New York: K.G. Sauer, 1987,
        74-82. Covers deacidification, disinfection against mold, and leather
        treatment. Discusses problems in funding conservation and
        variations in policies within the field.

442.   Bansa, Helmut. "How Long Does Paper Last," Edizioni per la
        Conservazione; mensile internationale di prevenzione e
        conservazione cultura e ambiente/ International Monthly Review for
        the Preservation and Conservation Culture and Environment, 1:1
        (1989), 21-33. Discusses the problem of limited permanence of
        contemporary paper products; a plea for the adoption of an
        international standard for the production of durable paper.

443.   Bansa, Helmut. "IFLA Principles on Conservation and
        Preservation," Restaurator, 7:4 (1986), 202-206. History of the
        development of the "Principles" and a critical comparison of the
        1979 and 1985 texts.

444.   Bansa, Helmut. "The New Media: Means for Better Preservation or
        Special Preservation Problems," Restaurator, 12:4 (1991),
        219-233. Predicts a future of an excess of data, much of it in
        unreadable form; discusses reasons for the situation. "The
        preservation of the hardware and software that is necessary to access
        optical databases produced physically in our time might become the
        main problem."

445.   Bansa, Helmut. "Preservation of Library Materials: An International
        Challenge," Books in Peril. Capetown, South Africa: South African
        Library, 1987, 11-25. Review of problems, causes, and solutions.

446.   Bansa, Helmut, and Hans H. Hofer. "Artificial Aging as a Predictor
        of Paper's Future Useful Life," Abbey Newsletter, Monograph
        Supplement 1, 1989. 26p. Argues that natural aging is chemically
        different from artificial aging, thus artificial aging tests on paper are
        not reliable. Translation of "Die Aussagekraft einer Künstlichen
        Alterung von Papier für Progonsen über Seine Künstlige
        Benutzbarkeit," Restaurator, 6:1-2 (1984), 21-60.

447.   Bansa, Helmut, and Harold Schoenung. "Filler for Leafcasting,"
        Restaurator, 10:2 (1989), 74-82. Report of an experiment that tested
        an organic filler in the leafcasting fiber that has resulted in improved
        opacity.

448.   Barber, Giles. "Noah's Ark, or, Thoughts Before and After the
        Flood," Archives, 16:70 (October 1983), 151-160. Discusses disaster
        planning and recovery techniques with some emphasis on rare books.

449.   Barclay, Bob. "CCI: The First Twenty Years," CCI Notes (Canadian
        Conservation Institute), 10 (September 1992), 1-4.
        French/English. History of the accomplishments and activities of the
        Canadian Conservation Institute.

450.   Bard, Charleton C. "Biodeterioration of Photographs,"
        Biodeterioration 6, ed. S. Barry and D.R. Houghton. London: CAB
        International Mycological Institute/Biodeterioration Society, 1986,
        379-382. Examines ways to protect photographic materials from
        fungal attack. Paper presented at the 6th International
        Biodeterioration Symposium, Washington, DC, August 1984.

451.   Bard, Charleton C. "Conservation of Images," Stability and
        Conservation of Photographic Images: Chemical, Electronic and
        Mechanical. Bangkok, Thailand: Society of Photographic Scientists
        and Engineers, 1986, 1-13. Discusses the preservation needs of
        images, noting that silver image is the only acceptable archival image
        among all image types. Notes lack of information on
        non-photographic technologies and recommends that
        "machine-readable records should not be archives, but transferred to
        human-readable microfilm or microfiche."

452.   Bard, Charleton C. "Conservation of Images," Journal of
        Photographic Science, 36 (1988), 99-103. Review of the problems of
        preserving all types of photographic materials; the difference
        between conservation and restoration, need for standardized test
        methods. Transcript of a lecture given at the Royal Photographic
        Society meeting on Stability of Motion Picture Materials.

453.   Barford, Michael. "More Easy Environmental Monitoring," Abbey
        Newsletter, 15:7 (November 1991), 108. Describes small
        microcomputers that can monitor environmental conditions in
        buildings and allow data to be analyzed.

454.   Barger, M. Susan. "Characterization of Corrosion Products on Old
        Protective Glass, Especially Daguerreotype Cover Glasses," Journal
        of Materials Science, 24 (1989), 1343-1356. Study of the protective
        cover glasses used for daguerreotypes and why they cause
        deterioration and corrosion to the images that they are supposed to
        protect.

455. Barger, Susan M. "Daguerreotype Care," PictureScope, 31:1 (Spring 1983), 15-16.

456. Barger, M. Susan, A. P. Giri, William B. White, and Thomas M. Edmondson. "Cleaning Daguerreotypes," Studies in Conservation, 31:1 (February 1986), 15-28. Traditional cleaning methods are discussed. A new method, electrocleaning, is presented and recommendations for care and cleaning of daguerreotypes are given.

457. Barger, M. Susan, A. P. Giri, William B. White, William S. Ginelli, and Frank Preusser. "Protective Surface Coatings for Daguerreotypes," Journal of the American Institute for Conservation, 24:1 (Fall 1984), 40-52. Discusses advantages and disadvantages of protective surface coatings for daguerreotypes.

458. Barger, M. Susan, and Thomas T. Hill. "Thiourea and Ammonium Thiosulfate Treatments for the Removal of 'silvering' from Aged Negative Materials," Journal of Imaging Technology, 14:2 (April 1988), 43-46. Addresses the occurrence of 'silvering' with reference to negative photographic materials; describes the experimental characterization of the phenomenon. Discusses thiourea and ammonium treatments and why they are ill-advised.

459. Barger, M. Susan, Russell Messier, and William B. White. "Daguerreotype Display," PictureScope, 31:2 (Summer 1983), 57-58. Note on how daguerreotypes should be displayed to curtail damage from light.

460. Barger, M. Susan, Russell Messier, and William B. White. "Gilding and Sealing Daguerreotypes," Photographic Science and Engineering, 27 (1983), 141-146. Discussion of the process and its effect on the image.

461. Barger, M. Susan, Russell Messier, and William B. White. "Nondestructive Assessment of Daguerreotype Image Quality by Diffuse Reflectance Spectroscopy," Studies in Conservation, 29:2 (May 1984), 84-86. Describes a non-destructive method for monitoring the changes in appearance in daguerreotypes due to aging or treatment.

462. Barger, M. Susan, and William B. White. The Daguerreotype: 19th Century Technology and Modern Science. Washington, DC: Smithsonian Institution Press, 1991. 252p. Illus. History of the daguerreotype and scientific aspects of the process; examines problems of preservation and conservation.

463. Barger, M. Susan, and William B. White. "How to Enhance Daguerreotype Images," History News, 39:5 (May 1984), 26-28. Discusses enhancement through copying and the use of light.

464. Barger, M. Susan, and William B. White. "Optical Characterization of the Daguerreotype," Photographic Science and Engineering, 28:4 (July-August 1984), 172-174. The proposed physical model for daguerreotypes was tested by quantitative reflectance measurements using a goniophotometer.

465. Barker, Joseph W., et al. "Organizing Out-of-Print and Replacement Acquisitions for Effectiveness, Efficiency, and the Future," Library Acquisitions Practice and Theory, 14:2 (1990),137-163. Traces the theory behind centralized out-of-print searching and acquisitions functions; preservation needs are discussed.

466. Barker, Nicolas. "The Character of a Trimmer: Bibliography and the Conservator," Conservation and Preservation in Small Libraries, ed. Nicholas Hadgraft and Katherine Swift. Cambridge: Parker Library Publications, 1994, 20-22.

467. Barker, Nicolas. "Independent Libraries and National Literary Heritage," Conference on Book and Paper Conservation, 1990. Budapest, Hungary: Technical Association of Paper and Printing Industry/National Szechenyi Library, 1992, 8-12. Discusses the need for cooperation between national, public, and private libraries to preserve the cultural heritage, the need for a European training program in conservation, and cooperative bibliographical and preservation initiatives.

468. [Barker, Nicolas]. "Libraries and the National Literary Heritage: Two Views from Europe," Book Collector, 34:2 (Summer 1985), 145-172. Review of several recent books on the conservation of documentary patrimony through national planning.

469. Barker, Nicolas. "Publishing and Preservation," Library Publishing, ed. David Way. London: British Library, 1985, 57-59. Explains how the "publication" of library collections in microformat can preserve original materials; note for the need to study original bindings. Paper presented at a seminar held at the British Library, April 11-13, 1983. Compare with the next citation.

470. Barker, Nicolas. "Publishing and Preservation," British Library Occasional Papers. No. 2. London: British Library, 1986.

471. [Barker, Nicolas]. "Wither Rare Books?" Book Collector, 41:4 (Winter 1992), 441-445. A discussion of the role of the printed book

in the future, when surrogate copies of text may be readily available on a computer terminal. Summarizes remarks at recent meetings at Oxford, Harvard, and the University of Virginia.

472.   Barlak, Karen. "Emotional Coping Mechanisms in Times of Disaster," New Jersey Libraries, 28:3 (Summer 1995), 13-15. Stages of stress from inception to restoration in a disaster situation. How to recognize emotional stress and post-trauma reactions.

473.   Barlee, George. "Alum Tawed Leather: A Reappraisal," Buchbinder, 1 (1987), 18-20. Notes that alum tawed leathers were among the earliest produced and the effort to have its production reintroduced because of its sturdiness for bookbinding.

474.   Barnard, Bob. "The Way Ahead," Library Conservation News, 26 (January 1990), 1, 7-8. Describes the use of acid-free paper by Her Majesty's Stationery Office for publications of special interest or permanent value.

475.   Barnett, Richard C. "Federal Implementation of Permanent Paper Standards," NAGARA Clearinghouse (National Association of Government Archivists and Records Administrators), Summer 1991, 8-10; Reprinted in Abbey Newsletter, 16:2 (April 1992), 24-25. Discusses levels of papers for government publications and federal records, and requirements for recycled papers.

476.   Barrett, D. "Museums: Brushing the Cobwebs From Forgotten Beginnings," Computer Weekly (August 13, 1987), 14-15. Describes the efforts of the British National Museum of Technology to preserve the documents of the development of information technology. Problems include the rapid obsolescence of computers and related documents.

477.   Barrett, John Paul. How to Make a Book. Astoria, OR: Gaff Press, 1993. 164p. An illustrated guide to making books by hand.

478.   Barrett, Tim. "Old and New Fibers for Fine Papermaking," Counter (University of Iowa Center for the Book), 2 (Spring 1995), 7-9. Briefly describes papermaking process and corruption of pulp by synthetic fibers. Explores techniques for producing pure fibers today.

479.   Barrett, Tim, et al. "Inexpensive Forming of Ultra-Thin Paper Tissues," Abbey Newsletter, 12:8 (December 1988), 134-135. Illus. Describes technique.

480.   Barrett, Timothy. "Early European Papers/Contemporary Preservation Papers: A Report on Research Undertaken from Fall 1984 through Fall 1987," <u>Paper Conservator</u>, 13, 1989. 107p. (entire issue). A major study of papers with implications for librarians and archivists.

481.   Barrett, Timothy. "Evaluating the Effect of Gelatin Sizing With Regard to the Permanence of Paper," <u>Conference Papers, Manchester 1992</u>. Worcester, England: Institute of Paper Conservation, 1992, 228-233. Describes testing on 57 historic papers to determine the effect of gelatin content.

482.   Barrett, Timothy. "Fifteenth-Century Papermaking," <u>Printing History</u>, 15:2; 30 (1993), 33-41. Describes how rags were prepared and paper produced by hand. Notes lack of detailed knowledge of early papermaking and the need for further study of factors of permanence in modern papers.

483.   Barrett, Timothy. "Flax, Fiber Fermentation and Washing During Beating," <u>Friends of Dard Hunter Post-Prints</u>, Chicago, IL: 1 (1992), 9-13. Describes experiments with fermentation and the effect of the process on the permanence of paper thus produced. Suggests how to ensure neutral or alkaline pH.

484.   Barret, Timothy. "Research Into Early Western Papermaking Technology," <u>Oxbow Diary: Paper and Book Intensive 85</u>, ed. Barbara Muriello, Saugatuck, MI: Ox Bow Paper and Book Intensive 85, 1985, 10-15. Discusses his research agenda to investigate how early papers were produced and why they are so durable.

485.   Barrett, Timothy, and Cynthia Mosier. "A Review of Methods for the Identification of Sizing Agents in Paper," <u>Conference Papers, Manchester 1992</u>. Worcester, England: Institute of Paper Conservation, 1992, 207-213. Reviews the literature on tests for sizing in paper with emphasis on those used to detect proteins; describes current testing program.

486.   Barrett, Timothy, and Cynthia Mosier. "The Role of Gelatin in Paper Permanence," <u>Journal of the American Institute of Conservation</u>, 34:3 (Fall/Winter 1995), 173-186. Study of 40 historical paper specimens, analyzed to determine their gelatin content; data indicates that both the appearance and performance of the papers may be affected by their gelatin content.

487.   Barrett, Timothy, and Cynthia Mosier. "The Role of Gelatin in Paper Permanence II," <u>Book and Paper Group Annual</u>, 13 (1994), 5-8. Report of an investigation of older gelatin-sized papers to assess

their permanence; a pilot project for a study of the role of gelatin in paper permanence.

488.   Barrios, Pamela. "Encapsulation as Binding," Abbey Newsletter, 13:3 (June 1989), 47-49. Describes a method for encapsulating two or more folios in a single structure.

489.   Bartell, Blaine M. "Preservation and Restoration of the Hearst Metrotone News Collection at UCLA Film and Television Archive," AMIA Newsletter (Association of Moving Image Archivists), 21 (July 1993), 4-5. Describes a refilming project to provide access and restoration of original film.

490.   Barton, John P., and Johanna G. Wellheiser, eds. An Ounce of Prevention: A Handbook on Disaster Contingency Planning for Archives, Libraries and Record Centers. Toronto, Canada: Toronto Area Archivists Group Education Foundation, 1985. 192p. Covers all aspects of disaster prevention, planning, and recovery. Bibliography.

491.   Baskin, Judith A.D. "The Production and Use of Permanent Paper," COMLA Newsletter (Commonwealth Library Association), 63 (March 1989), 7, 10-11. Report on a seminar held in Sydney, Australia, in 1987 to increase awareness of the problem of impermanent papers and to encourage the use of permanent paper.

492.   Bates, Regis. Disaster Recovery Planning: Networks, Telecommunications, and Data Communications. New York: McGraw-Hill, 1992. 157p.

493.   Batik, Albert L. A Guide to Standards. Silver Spring, MD: Association for Information and Image Management, 1990. 129p.

494.   Battin, Patricia. "Access to Scholarly Materials," Scholars and Research Libraries in the 21st Century. New York: American Council of Learned Societies, 1990, 21-25. (ACLS Occasional Paper, 14).

495.   Battin, Patricia. "'As Far Into the Future as Possible': Choice and Cooperation in the 1990s," Advances in Preservation and Access. Vol. 1. Westport, CT: Meckler, 1992, 41-48. The challenge to preserve information and the role of the Commission on Preservation and Access.

496.   Battin, Patricia. "Battin on Preservation [excerpts from testimony on behalf of increased funding for the National Endowment for the Humanities]," Library Journal, 113 (October 1, 1988), 24.

497.   Battin, Patricia. "Beyond Crumbling Books: Preservation Strategies for the Nineties," Libraries: The Heart of the Matter. Deakin, Australia: Australian Library and Information Association, 1992, 15-18. (ALIA 92: Proceedings of the ALIA 2nd Biennial Conference). Discusses "preservation" in terms of "access," and the challenge to achieve it. Describes the role of CPA as catalyst; potential of digital technology.

498.   Battin, Patricia. "Collection Preservation: The Practical Choices," Paper Preservation: Current Issues and Recent Developments, ed. Philip Luner. Atlanta, GA: TAPPI Press, 1990, 38-39. Paper presented at the TAPPI Paper Preservation Symposium, October 1989.

499.   Battin, Patricia. "Cooperative Preservation in the United States: Progress and Possibilities," Alexandria, 1:2 (August 1989), 7-16.

500.   Battin, Patricia. "Crumbling Books: A Call for Strategies to Preserve Our Cultural Memory," Change, 21:2 (September-October, 1989), 6,56. Discusses the brittle book problem and reformatting for preservation.

501.   Battin, Patricia. "The Electronic Library," Collection Management, 9:2/3 (Summer/Fall 1987), 133-141. Explores the impact of electronically accessible information on traditional library services; a vision of the "electronic scholar."

502.   Battin, Patricia. "Endangered Species and Libraries: Collision, Collusion, or Collaboration?" Scholarly Publishing — An Endangered Species? Washington, DC: Society for Scholarly Publishing, 1989, 22-25. (Proceedings of the Tenth Annual Meeting, June 22-25, 1989, Boston, MA).

503.   Battin, Patricia. "From Preservation to Access: Paradigm for the Nineties," IFLA Journal (International Federation of Library Associations and Institutions), 19:4 (1993), 367-373. Also in the Commission on Preservation and Access Annual Report 1992-1993. Washington, DC: Commission on Preservation and Access, 1993. 1-4. Emphasis on access using new technologies; no concern for preservation of information in electronic formats nor of issue of standards.

504.   Battin, Patricia. "Image Standards and Implications for Preservation," Workshop on Electronic Tests: Proceedings, ed. James Daly. Washington, DC: Library of Congress, 1992, 57-60.

505.   Battin, Patricia. "The Importance of Archives," American Archivist,
         53 (Spring 1990), 188-190. Discusses the evolution of information
         media, differences between library and archival collections, and
         preservation challenges facing the archives community.

506.   Battin, Patricia. "Introduction: Preservation — The National
         Perspective," Issues for a New Decade: Today's Challenge,
         Tomorrow's Opportunity. Boston, MA: G. K. Hall, 1991, 1-9. Scope
         of preservation problems and the role that the Commission on
         Preservation and Access plays to address them.

507.   Battin, Patricia. "Libraries: The Vital Connection," Biblos, 40:4
         (April 1989), 1-12.

508.   Battin, Patricia. "The Primary Role of the Commission on
         Preservation and Access," Research Libraries — Yesterday, Today
         and Tomorrow, ed. William J. Welsh. Westport, CT: Greenwood
         Press, 1993, 319-324. Describes mission and initiatives of the
         Commission: Brittle Books Program; international project;
         establishment of scholarly advisory committees.

509.   Battin, Patricia. "Preservation: The Forgotten Problem," Priorities
         for Academic Libraries, ed. Thomas J. Galvin and Beverly P. Lynch.
         San Francisco, CA: Jossey-Bass, 1983, 61-69. (New Directions for
         Higher Education). Observes that the continuing deterioration of
         research collections printed on unstable paper undermines the
         capacity for productive scholarship; solutions require heightened
         awareness of the problem and cooperative action on a national scale.

510.   Battin, Patricia. "Preservation at the Columbia University Libraries,"
         The Library Preservation Program: Models, Priorities, Possibilities,
         ed. Jan Merrill-Oldham and Merrily Smith. Chicago, IL: American
         Library Association, 1985, 34-40.

511.   Battin, Patricia. "Preservation in the 1990's: New Challenges and
         Opportunities," Rhode Island Library Association Bulletin, 64:1/2
         (January/February 1991), 1-4.

512.   Battin, Patricia. "The Preservation of Knowledge: Strategies for a
         Global Society," Strengthening the US-Japan Library Partnership in
         the Global Information Flow, ed. Theodore F. Welch, Warren M.
         Tsuneishi, and Mary F. Grosch. Chicago IL: American Library
         Association; Tokyo, Japan: Maruzen International, 1991. (Fourth
         US-Japan Conference on Library and Information Science in Higher
         Education).

513.   Battin, Patricia. "Preserving America's National Heritage: The
         Response of the Commission on Preservation and Access." In
         Bowker Annual Library and Book Trade Information. 33d ed. New
         York: Bowker, 1988, 88-91.

514.   Battin, Patricia. "The Primary Role of the Commission on
         Preservation and Access," Research Libraries — Yesterday, Today,
         and Tomorrow: A Selection of Papers Presented at the International
         Seminars, Kanazawa Institute of Technology, Library Center,
         Kanazawa, Japan, 1982-1992, ed. William J. Welsh. Kanazawa,
         Japan: Institute of Technology; Westport, CT: Greenwood Press,
         1993, 319-324.

515.   Battin, Patricia. "The Responsibility of Leadership: Making It
         Happen," Meeting the Preservation Challenge, ed. Jan
         Merrill-Oldham. Washington, DC: Association of Research
         Libraries, 1988, 51-54.

516.   Battin, Patricia. "The Silent Books of the Future: Initiatives to Save
         Yesterday's Literature for Tomorrow," Logos, 2:1 (1991), 11-17;
         reprinted as "Brittle Books," English Today 29, 8:1 (January 1992),
         41-47. Overview of the brittle book problem and initiatives that led
         to the establishment of the Commission on Preservation and Access;
         its activities.

517.   Battin, Patricia, and Maxine K. Sitts. "Institutions Have Moral
         Responsibility to Preserve Great Book Collections," Educational
         Record, 70:2 (Spring 1989), 54-55. Position paper on the ethics of
         book preservation of the human record with all its diversity.

518.   Battista, Carolyn. "Librarians Seek Ways to Safeguard Their
         Crumbling Books," New York Times, Sunday, Nov. 23, 1986,
         XXIII,2:1. Report on the work of Jan Merrill-Oldham and the
         conservation facilities at the University of Connecticut.

519.   Batton, Susan Sayre. "Preservation in Practice," New Jersey
         Libraries, 18:1 (Spring 1985), 5-8. Reviews the components of a
         sound preservation program.

520.   Bauer, R.W., J. L. Baptista, F. J. Ricotta, E. F. Snow, and Z. Bogdan.
         "An Aqueous-Based Motion-Picture Film Cleaner - Final Report,"
         SMPTE Journal (Society of Motion Picture and Television
         Engineers), 102:6 (June 1993), 518-521. Report of a committee
         charged with the development of an environmentally safe film
         cleaner in anticipation of the global phaseout of other
         (ozone-depleting) solvents.

521.   Baughman, Mary. "Book Conservation Training Deep in the Heart
         of Texas," New Library Scene, 5:3 (June 1986), 1, 5-9. Describes the
         Conservation Department and conservation training at the Harry
         Ransom Humanities Research Center, University of Texas.

522.   Bauman, Barry. "Conservation II: The Changing Role of the Private
         Conservator," International Journal of Museum Management and
         Curatorship, 8:1 (1989), 111-113. Describes the role that the
         conservator in private practice can play in the conservation of
         collections.

523.   Baur, Frederick E., Jr. "Preservation and Conservation at the
         American Antiquarian Society," Conservation Administration News,
         20 (January 1985), 1-2, 26. History of preservation at the Society
         from its earliest days; description of the conservation workshop
         established in 1982.

524.   Baynes-Cope, Arthur David. Caring for Books and Documents. 2d
         ed. New York: New Amsterdam Books, 1989. 48p. Handbook for
         the general public.

525.   Baynes-Cope, Arthur David. "Conservation: Why the Scientist Can
         Help," Archives, 16:70 (October 1983), 162-166. A conservation
         scientist talks about care of books and documents, with emphasis on
         environmental controls.

526.   Baynes-Cope, Arthur David. "Deacidification: A Statement from the
         Technical Committee," Journal of the Society of Archivists, 7
         (October 1984), 402-403. Cautionary note, with advice to follow the
         British standard.

527.   Baynes-Cope, Arthur David. "Principles and Ethics in Archival
         Repair and Archival Conservation. Part 1: The Principles of Archival
         Repair and Archival Conservation," Journal of the Society of
         Archivists, 15:1 (1994), 17-26. Restates and discusses the five
         principles first enunciated by Roger Ellis in 1950. Reviews needs
         and sums up with an analysis of the moral qualities required of a
         conservator.

528.   Baynes-Cope, Arthur David. "Standard for Conditions of Display,"
         Veszpr'em, Hungary: National Centre of Museums, 1985. Offprint
         from the Fifth International Restorer Seminar. Veszpr'em, Hungary:
         National Centre of Museums, 1985, 35-39. Covers British Standard
         5454:1977: "Recommendations for the Storage and Display of
         Archival Documents."

529.   Baynes-Cope, Arthur David. The Study and Conservation of Globes.
        Vienna: Internationale Coroelli-Gesellschaft, 1985. 95p. Glossary in
        English and German.

530.   Baynes-Cope, Arthur David. "Thoughts on Ethics in Archival
        Conservation," Restaurator, 9:3 (1988), 136-146. Discusses the
        development of British thinking based on the principles laid down by
        Roger Ellis in the late 1940s; observes that ethics relies on the
        training and understanding of conservators.

531.   Baynes-Cope, Arthur David, and Dennis Allsopp. "Observations on
        Mould Growth in Small Libraries," Biodeterioration 6, ed. S. Barry
        and D. R. Houghton. London: CAB International Mycological
        Institute/Biodeterioration Society, 1986, 382-385. Divides and
        describes mold attack on books into four classes of destruction;
        nature of attack, causes, and remedies. Paper presented at the 6th
        International Biodeterioration Symposium, Washington, DC, August
        1984.

532.   Baynes-Cope, Arthur David, and R. Ellis. "Ethics and the
        Conservation of Archival Documents," Journal of the Society of
        Archivists, 9:4 (1988), 185-187. Discussion of ethics, advocating
        common sense and an understanding of materials.

533.   Beard, John O. "Preservation Problems in Public Libraries,"
        Preserving the Word. London: Library Association, 1987, 46-50.
        Paper presented at the 103rd Library Association Conference,
        Harrogate, England, 1986.

534.   Beardsley, Roger. "A Dub...ious Pleasure," The Record Collector,
        40:3 (July/Sept. 1995), 242-245. Discusses electrical transfers and
        historical examples of dubbing related to reproduction of early
        recordings.

535.   Bearman, David, ed. Archival Management of Electronic Records.
        Pittsburgh, PA: Archives and Museum Informatics, 1991. 56p.
        (Archives and Museum Informatics Technical Report 13). Papers on
        the problems of preserving records in electronic formats, which
        present organizational challenges beyond traditional archival
        methodology.

536.   Bearman, David, ed. Archives and Museum Data Models and
        Dictionaries. Pittsburgh, PA: Archives and Museum Informatics,
        1990. 100p. Archives and Museum Informatics Technical Report 10.

537.   Bearman, David. Electronic Records Guidelines: A Manual for
        Policy Development and Implementation. [Pittsburgh, PA]:

Archives and Museum Informatics, 1989. 122p. Discusses issues, approaches, and recommendations for the development of policies for the management and preservation of electronic records. Bibliography.

538.   Bearman, David. <u>Electronic Evidence: Strategies for Managing Records in Contemporary Organizations</u>. Pittsburgh, PA: Archives & Museum Informatics, 1994. 314p. Collection of papers is accompanied by a new essay exploring the evolution of the concepts of electronic records management, and by a detailed index compiled by Victoria Irons Walch. Papers reprinted were published between 1989 and 1993.

539.   [Bearman, David]. "Introducing the Conservation Information Network," <u>Archival Informatics Newsletter</u>, 2:4 (Winter 1989/1990), 70-73. Describes the conservation databases and how to use CIN effectively.

540.   Bearman, David. <u>Optical Media: Their Implications for Archives and Museums</u>. (Archival Information Technical Report, Vol.1 No.1). Pittsburgh, PA: Archives & Museum Informatics, 1987. 73p. Explains how to decide whether an item of this type is of archival quality.

541.   Bearman, Frederick A. "Nineteenth Century Book Repair Practices: Their Influence on Modern Conservation Ethics," <u>Preprints</u>. International Conference on Conservation and Restoration of Archive and Library Materials. Istituto Centrale per la Patologia del Libro, Rome, Italy: April 22-29, 1996, Vol. 1, 319-325. Investigates the principles of archive repair as established at the Public Records Office, London, C19; how this legacy still forms the cornerstone of modern conservation ethics; their influence on current principles and ethics for repair and conservation of non-archival library collections. (Parts of study originally presented at the International Association for the Conservation of Books, Paper & Archival Material, Tubingen, Germany, 1994).

542.   Beaubien, Denise M., Bruce Emerton, Erich Kesse, Alice L. Primack, and Colleen Seale. "Patron-Use Software in Academic Library Collections," <u>College and Research Libraries News</u>, 49:10 (November 1988), 661-667. University of Florida guidelines for purchasing, circulating, and preserving software, see especially pp. 665-666. Bibliography.

543.   Beaulieu, Ann Hetch, David R. Gehman, and William J. Sparks. "Recent Advances in Acrylic Hot-Melt Pressure-Sensitive Adhesive Technology," <u>TAPPI Journal</u> (Technical Association of the Pulp and

Paper Industry), 67:9 (September 1984), 102-105. Discusses a new patented acrylic hot-melt adhesive technology offering a thermally reversible crosslinking mechanism, which moved this technology into a higher performance category.

544. Beazley, Ken. "Mineral Fillers in Paper," Paper Conservator, 15 (1991), 17-27. Historical introduction; reviews advantages and disadvantages of using mineral fillers in the manufacture of paper. 52 references.

545. Beck, James. Art Restoration: The Culture, the Business, and the Scandal. With Michael Daley. London: John Murray; New York: Norton, 1993. 210p. Strong statement against over-cleaning and invasive restoration or works of art.

546. Bedynski, Maria, and Frida Kalbfleisch. "Conservation Treatment of Rare Atlases at the National Archives of Canada," Archivist, 19:2 (1992), 22-23. Treatment of a collection of rare atlases published between 1548 and 1655. Illus.

547. Behrens, Ulrich. "Deutsche Bucherei: Longer Life for Books," International Preservation News, 10 (July 1995), 10-11. Brief description of the Battelle deacidification process used by the DB.

548. Belcher, Michael. Exhibitions in Museums. Leicester, England: Leicester University Press, 1991. 230p.; Washington, DC: Smithsonian Institution Press, 1992. 248p. Illus. Basic text on museum exhibition; includes practical information on display, security, and conservation.

549. Bell, Mary Margaret. "Preserving Local History in Kentucky Through Microforms," Microform Review, 16:2 (Spring 1987), 126-29. Discusses initiatives by Kentucky institutions to preserve documents of local historical interest.

550. Bell, Nancy. "The Conservation of Bound Paper Manuscripts," Conservation of Historic and Artistic Works on Paper. Ottawa: Canadian Conservation Institute, 1994, 67-69. (Symposium 88). Discusses the nature of bound paper manuscripts and the particular conservation problems they pose.

551. Bell, Nancy. "Considerations When Treating Paper Manuscripts," Conservation and Preservation in the Small Library, ed. Nicholas Hadgraft and Katherine Swift. Cambridge: Parker Library Publications, 1994. 101-106. Selection of material for conservation; evaluating treatment decisions and understanding their results. Case study.

552.   Bell, Nancy. "The Oxford Preservation Survey, 2: A Method for
         Surveying Archives," Paper Conservator, 17 (1993),
         53-55. Describes the method developed for analyzing the physical
         condition of archives with mixed collections.

553.   Bell, Nancy. "Guidelines for Disaster Planning in the Oxford
         Colleges Conservation Consortium: Disaster Prevention." Bulletin of
         the Association of British Theological and Philosophical Libraries,
         2:6 (1989), 78-80.

554.   Bell, Nancy, and Derek Priest. "Fixing Graphite: A Preliminary
         Investigation Into the Conservation of Shelley's Notebooks," Paper
         Conservator, 15 (1991), 53-58. Discusses conservation problems and
         investigation of fixatives commonly used in conservation to find an
         appropriate one.

555.   Bell, Nancy J. "Preservation/Conservation Literature: A Core
         Reference Collection," Library Hi Tech, 1:1 (Summer 1983),
         97-99. Introductory bibliography.

556.   Bell, Nancy J. "Xerography and Preservation: Problems and
         Potential," Library Hi Tech, 1:1 (Summer 1983), 69-73. Concise
         summary of the advantages and disadvantages of photocopying;
         references.

557.   Bellardo, Lew. "Low Energy, Low Technology, Low Toxicity
         Approaches to Preservation," Abbey Newsletter, 19:1 (April 1995),
         9-12. Suggestions for constructing archives that naturally protect
         collections, specifically in regions that lack adequate, affordable
         energy supplies, or access to technology is limited. A modified
         version of a paper originally presented at the ICA Preservation
         Committee Meeting, Oslo; Norway, May 1994.

558.   Bellinger, Meg. "Interview," OCLC Newsletter (Online Computer
         Library Center), 217 (September/October 1995), 21-24. The
         President of Preservation Resources discusses the future of
         preservation.

559.   Bello, Susan. Cooperative Preservation Efforts of Academic
         Libraries. Champaign, IL: University of Illinois, Graduate School of
         Library and Information Science, 1986. 52p. (Occasional Paper,
         174) Analyzes the major national plans for preservation programs in
         the United States from 1954 to 1985; shows the extent to which
         aspects of these plans have been achieved by academic libraries.

560.   Belvin, Robert J. "Crime and Security in New Jersey Libraries,"
        New Jersey Libraries, 27:4 (Fall 1994), 11-14. Report of a survey of
        urban and suburban public libraries to determine extent of use of
        security guards and other security measures.

561.   Belyaeva, Irina. "Phased Conservation at the Library of the USSR
        Academy of Sciences," Conservation Administration News, 46 (July
        1991), 1-2,7. Describes the phased conservation program
        implemented under the direction of Peter Waters, Library of
        Congress, following the disastrous fire in 1988.

562.   Bendror, Jack. "Can Oversewing Make a Comeback?" New Library
        Scene, 11:3 (June 1992), 10-12. Discusses the pros and cons of
        double-fan adhesive binding, which increasingly is replacing
        oversewing as a binding technique. While it offers strength and
        flexibility, the process leaves no margin for error. Suggestions for
        successful adhesive binding are offered.

563.   Benedict, Marjorie A., Michael Knee, and Mina B. La Croix.
        "Finding Space for Periodicals: Weeding, Storage and Microform
        Conversion," Collection Management, 12:3/4 (1990),
        145-154. Describes a controlled growth program, with microforms
        playing an integral role.

564.   Benedikz, Benedikt S. "Conservation: A Personal Viewpoint,"
        Modern Music Librarianship, ed. Alfred Mann. New York:
        Pendragon Press, 1989, 137-141. (Festschrift Series, 8). Considers
        appropriate housing and storage and the tension between
        preservation and use.

565.   Bennett, Richard E. "Paper Preservation Studies at the University of
        Manitoba Libraries," Canadian Library Journal, 49:1 (February
        1992), 41-48. Analysis of a survey to determine the extent of
        embrittlement in the library's collections.

566.   [Bentley-Kemp, Lynne]. "A Visit to NEDCC,"
        Photographi-Conservation, 6:1 (March 1984), 1, 3. Profile of the
        Center; includes reprint of "The Interpositive Method of Copying
        Photographic Negatives," by Robert Alter.

567.   Beöthy-Kozocsa, Ildiko, Teriz Sipos-Richter, and Gyorgyi Szlabey.
        "Parchment Codex Restoration Using Parchment and Cellulose Fiber
        Pulp," Restaurator, 11:2 (1990), 95-109. Describes the procedure for
        the infilling of parchment using a vacuum table.

568.   Berardi, Maria Cristina. "Why Does Parchment Deform? Some
        Observations and Considerations," Leather Conservation News, 8:1

(1992), 12-16. The chemical and physical structures of sheepskins and parchments are examined in relation to causes of deformity in the finished parchment sheets; discusses causes and treatments.

569. Berger, Sidney. "What is so Rare...Issues in Rare Book Librarianship," Library Trends, 36:1 (1987), 9-22. Touches upon preservation theory and physical treatment.

570. Berger, Sidney E. "Special Collections and Security," Focus on Security, 3:2 (Jan. 1996), 8-13. Describes measures that can be taken by librarians to protect collections, including marking, developing procedures for use of materials, need to prosecute. Bibliography.

571. Bergeron, Rosemary. "The Selection of Television Productions for Archival Preservation," Archivaria, 23 (Winter 1986-87), 41-53. Discusses considerations for the preservation for television broadcast videotapes.

572. Bergman, Robert. "Developing a Disaster Plan: The Director's Perspective." In Emergency Preparedness and Response. Washington, DC: National Institute for Conservation, 1991, 17-19.

573. Bering-Jensen, Helle. "A Man With the Right Moves," Insight, (March 19, 1990), 58-60. Profile of John E. Allen and his work in preservation of film, especially nitrate film stock.

574. Berke, Philip. "Hurricane Hazard Mitigation: How Are We Doing?" Natural Hazards Observer, 11:5 (May 1987), 1-2. Discusses environmental efforts and suggestions for action to enact hurricane mitigation measures.

575. Bermane, Daniel. "Influence of Azo-Dye Aggregation on the Dark Stability of "Cibachrome" Images," Journal of Imaging Technology, 11:3 (June 1985), 105-108. Discusses the aging of Cibachrome images for noticeable change.

576. Bernardi, Maria Christina. "Why Does Parchment Deform? Some Observations and Considerations," Leather Conservation News, 8 (1992), 12-16. Examination of the possible relation of thickness of skin and deformation. Because skins differ, it was concluded that "it is risky to join different parchments selected on the basis of species homogeneity, thickness and grain direction." More study is needed. References.

577. Berndt, Harold. "Assessing the Detrimental Effects of Wood and Wood Products on the Environment Inside Display Cases," The American Institute for Conservation of Historic and Artistic Works.

Preprint of Papers Presented at the Fifteenth Annual Meeting. Vancouver, British Columbia, Canada, May 20-24, 1987. 22-23. Detrimental effects of wood-based construction materials used in the museum environment are discussed. Chemistry of wood and wood products is reviewed with regard to emission of formaldehyde and acetic acid, using examples of storage problems reported in the conservation literature. A method for testing wood and wood products for their detrimental effects is presented.

578.   Berndt, Harold. "A Reexamination of Paper Yellowing and the Kubelka-Munk Theory," Historic Textile and Paper Materials II: Conservation and Characterization, ed. Howard L. Needles and S. Haig Zeronian. Washington, DC: American Chemical Society, 1989, 81-91. (ACS Symposium Series, 410). Reexamines the theory and its application to the study of paper yellowing.

579.   Berndt, Harold, and Nancy Love. "What's Wrong With pH? A Conservator and a Scientist Search for Consensus," WAAC Newsletter (Western Association for Art Conservation), 16:2 (May 1994), 14-18. Describes efforts to find an alternative method for pH readings to effectively measure acidity in carbohydrates.

580.   Bernhardt, Alan J. "Charles Zoller and the Autochrome Process," PhotographiConservation, 6:2 (June 1984), 3-4. History and description of the process, with suggestions for preservation.

581.   Berns, Roy S., and Franc Grum. "Exhibiting Artwork: Consider the Illuminating Source," Color Research and Application, 12:2 (April 1987), 63-72. Describe appropriate lighting techniques when exhibiting art.

582.   Bernstein, James. Conservation of Cultural Property: A Basic Reference Shelflist. Washington, DC: National Institute for Conservation of Cultural Property, 1985. 45 leaves. Computerized for frequent updating, designed for use in planning conservation libraries. Jane M. Slate, NIC Program Coordinator.

583.   Berrada, Leyla. "Co-operation in the Area of Preservation of Library & Archival Materials," Proceedings of the Pan-African Conference on the Preservation & Conservation of Library & Archival Materials, Nairobi, Kenya, 21-25 June 1993. The Hague: IFLA, 1995, 163-164. (IFLA Professional Publication 43). Cooperative initiatives in Morocco with UNESCO, government, and nongovernmental agencies.

584.   Berry, Elizabeth. "The West Yorkshire Archive Service: The Development of a Unified Service, 1974-1983 and Its Work to

Bibliography

1986," <u>Journal of the Society of Archivists</u>, 8:4 (October 1987),
247-257. Development and activities of the Service.

585.   Berry, John. "Preservation Priorities, and Politics," <u>Library Journal</u>,
112: 20 (December 1987), 6. Editorial on the urgency of action
regarding the deterioration of library materials.

586.   Bertalan, Sarah. "The Conservation Treatment of the Washington,
DC, Map Collection in the Library of Congress," <u>Conference on
Book and Paper Conservation, 1990</u>. Budapest, Hungary: Technical
Association of Paper and Printing Industry/National Szechenyi
Library, 1992, 356-364. Treatment report, noting damage from
earlier treatment efforts.

587.   Bertalan, Sarah. "Mold: How It Grows and Causes Damage to
Archival Collections," <u>Preservation Papers of the 1991 SAA Annual
Conference</u>, comp. Karen Garlick. Chicago IL: Society of American
Archivists, 1992, 58-62. Describes molds and how they grow;
chemical and non-chemical treatment; recognizing mold and its
damage.

588.   Bertoli, Renato, ed. <u>Micrographic Film Technology</u>. 4th ed. Silver
Spring, MD: Association for Information and Image Management,
1992. 127p. Manual on the basics of microfilm technology,
processes, and films. Reading list; glossary.

589.   Besser, Howard. "The Changing Museum," <u>Information: The
Transformation of Society</u>. Medford, NJ: Learned Information,
1987, 14-19. (ASIS '87: Proceedings of the 50th American Society
of Information Science Annual Meeting, vol. 24). Outlines how high
resolution image digitization is changing the functions of museums;
describes the Berkeley project to digitize objects for access, to
preserve originals. Comments on the possibility that surrogate
copies will be the only ones available.

590.   Besser, Howard. "Getting the Picture on Image Databases: The
Basics," <u>Database</u>, 18:2 (April/May 1995), 12-19. Reviews the basics
of digital imaging, emphasizing the need for careful planning to
ensure ease of access to users.

591.   Besser, Howard. "Images Databases Update: Issues Facing the Field,
Resources and Projects." In <u>Going Digital...</u> Chicago, IL: American
Library Association, 1995, 29-34.

592.   Besser, Howard. "Imaging: Fine Arts," <u>Journal of the American
Society for Information Science</u>, 42:8 (September 1991), 589-596.

593.   Besser, Howard, and Jennifer Trant. <u>Introduction to Imaging: Issues in Constructing an Image Database</u>. Santa Monica, CA: Getty Art History Information Program, 1995. 48p. Describes basic technology and processes involved in creating an image database. Glossary; bibliography.

594.   Best, S., R. Clark, M. Daniels, and R. Withnall. "A Bible Laid Open," <u>Chemistry in Britain</u>, 29:2 (1993), 118-122. Describes construction, development, and textural content of 13th-century bibles produced in Paris, France.

595.   Bevacqua, Joanna and Rafat Ispahany. "Book Repair in the Community College Library," <u>Conservation Administration News</u>, 46 (July 1991)), 8-11. Describes the collection maintenance program at Manhattan Community College (CUNY) Library; includes the conservation directives for staff. Bibliography.

596.   Beyer, Carrie, ed. <u>Preservation Research and Development, Roundtable Proceedings of September 28-29, 1992</u>. Washington, DC: Library of Congress, Preservation Directorate, June 1993. 147p. Contains 31 papers given at the roundtable.

597.   Bicchieri, Marina, Mauro Bartolani, and Eugenio Veca. "Characterization of Low-Molecular Weight Polyvinyl Alcohol for Restoration Purposes," <u>Restaurator</u>, 14:1 (1993), 11-29. Report on the use of polyvinyl alcohol (PVA) for sizing of paper.

598.   Bierbrier, M. L., ed. <u>Papyrus: Structure and Usage</u>. London: British Museum, 1986. 90p. (Occasional Paper, 60). Papers from a symposium on the structure and the use of papyrus, with information about conservation treatments.

599.   Biermann, Christopher. <u>Handbook of Pulping and Papermaking</u>. 2d ed. San Diego, CA: Academic Press, 1996. 754p. A comprehensive reference and educational tool for industry and academia. It offers a concise introduction to the process of papermaking from the production of wood chips to the final testing and use of the paper product.

600.   Bigelow, Susan. "Duels or Dialogues? The Relationship Between Archivists and Conservators," <u>Archivaria</u>, 29 (Winter 1989-90), 51-56. Assesses problems that can arise when relationship between archivist and conservator are undefined.

601.   Bikson, Tora, and E. J. Frinkling. Preserving the Present: Toward Viable Electronic Records. The Hague: Sdu Publication, 1993. 169p. A study of actual and anticipated practices for managing electronic records with the goal of developing policies and procedures to ensure the preservation of electronic records.

602.   Billick, David, comp. "A Selective Bibliography on Library Imaging Technology & Applications," Microform Review, 24:2 (Spring 1995), 69-84. 388 references, arranged by subject. No annotations. Prepared for the 1994 ALA Program "Film to File & Back Again." Section on preservation.

603.   Billings, Harold. "Choices: Inauguration of the Preservation and Conservation Studies Programs at the University of Texas at Austin," Conservation Administration News, 57 (April 1994) 3-4.

604.   Billings, Harold. "The Information Ark: Selection Issues in the Preservation Process," Wilson Library Bulletin, 68:8 (April 1994), 34-37. Voices concern for materials, both printed and published electronically, that escape the acquisition process. Notes need for preservation education.

605.   Billington, James H. The Moral Imperative of Conservation. Chicago, IL: Art Institute of Chicago, June 16, 1987, 18p.; reprinted in Meeting the Preservation Challenge. Washington, DC: Association of Research Libraries, 1988, 5-12. Examines the role of the conservator and selection for preservation.

606.   "Binding It Right: A Survey of American Craft Binders," Bookways, 4 (July 1992), 12-20. Illus. A survey of practices and, to some degree, prices. The binders describe themselves and their operations.

607.   Bird, Alan J. "Permanent Papers — Who Needs Them?" National Library News (Canada), 26:7 (July 1994), 10-11. Discussion of issues and concerns about international and United States standards for permanent papers and a note about the new research program underway by the Canadian government and the paper industry.

608.   Birney, Ann E., and Sara R. Williams. "Mutilation and the Folklore of Academic Librarianship," Library and Archival Security, 7:3/4 (Fall/Winter 1985), 41-47. Notes lack of information and review work that has been done; describes a method for gathering data.

609.   Bisbing, R.E. "Clues in the Dust," American Laboratory, 21:11 (November 1989), 19-24. Application of particle analysis through microscopy to unlock the past.

610.   Bish, Tony. The Care of Business Records. London: Business
        Archives Council, 1986. 8p. (Record Aids, 7). Preservation and
        conservation of business records.

611.   Bish, Tony. "Conservation of the Khalidi Library in the Old City of
        Jerusalem," Conference Papers, Manchester 1992. Worcester,
        England: Institute of Paper Conservation, 1992, 171-181. Describes
        the rebinding and conservation of manuscripts in a private collection.

612.   Biswas, Subhas C. "Acquisitions and Preservation of Indian
        Publications: Problems and Prospects," Planning, Modernization and
        Preservation Programmes for South Asian Libraries, ed. Kalpona
        Dasgupta. Calcutta, India: National Library, 1992. 10-16. Discusses
        the problems of national bibliography due to a lack of preservation,
        leading to strong collections in the United Kingdom and the United
        States, where Indian publications are collected and preserved. Calls
        for a comprehensive preservation initiative in Indian libraries.

613.   Bittner, Nancy, comp. Select Bibliography on Paper Conservation:
        1: 1954-December 1981, ed. Patricia Knittel. Rochester, NY:
        Rochester Institute of Technology, Technical and Educational Center
        of the Graphic Arts, 1983. 20p. Annotated bibliography of 84
        references.

614.   Bjornson, Pamela, and Tom Vincent. "Canadian Serials to 1900:
        CIHM's Micropreservation Project Phase II" (Canadian Institute for
        Historical Microreproductions), The Serials Librarian, 26: 3-4
        (1995), 105-123.

615.   Black, Jeremy. "A British Perspective on the Microfilming of
        Newspapers," Microform Review, 18:1 (Winter 1989),
        41-42. Historian emphasizes the necessity of filming newspapers for
        preservation and access.

616.   Blackman, Kirk. "Disaster Provides Opportunity to Build Bridge
        Between East and West," Disaster Recovery Journal, 4:4
        (October-December 1991), 27-28. Disaster recovery case study by
        BMS-CAT (Blackmon-Mooring-Steamatic Catastrophe) with a
        report on a disaster recovery symposium.

617.   Blackmon-Mooring-Steamatic Catastrophe, Inc. Disaster Plan
        Workbook: Study the Plan, Review the Plan, Practice the Plan, Work
        the Plan: Produced as an Aid in Developing a Disaster Plan. Fort
        Worth, TX: Blackmon-Mooring-Steamatic Catastrophe, Inc., 1992.
        One volume.

618.   Blades, William. The Enemies of Books. rev. ed. London: Stock,
        1988. 155p. Photographic reproduction of the 1902 edition by the
        University of California, Berkeley Photographic Services.

619.   Blais, Louise. "Centenary Snapshots," The Archivist, 110 (1995),
        35-36. Describes how the private sector helped to preserve the
        Canadian film heritage. Issue focuses on the film/sound heritage and
        its preservation. English/French.

620.   Blake, Evelyn G. "Journal Repairs: A Statistical Analysis" (at the
        Medical University of South Carolina), Library Mosaics, 6
        (January/February 1995) 15-17.

621.   Blake, Monica. "Aspects of Electronic Archives," Electronic
        Publishing Review, 6:3 (September, 1986), 151-167. Report on
        research into the feasibility of setting up a national electronic
        archives center in the United Kingdom.

622.   Blanco, Lourdes. "PAC Regional Center: Caracas," International
        Preservation News, 3 (May 1988), 1-4. Description of the regional
        center at the National Library of Venezuela.

623.   Blank, M. G., and S. A. Dobrusina. "Raising of the Book-Paper
        Longevity By Means of Chelates and Ca-Chelate Compound,"
        Preprints. International Council of Museums Committee for
        Conservation 7th Triennial Meeting, Copenhagen, September 10-14,
        1984. Paris: International Council of Museums, 1984.
        84.14.13-16. Investigation of a technique for stabilizing paper.

624.   Blank, Sharon. "An Introduction to Plastics and Rubbers in
        Collections," Studies in Conservation, 35:2 (May 1990),
        53-63. Reviews causes of deterioration in plastics and identifies
        major plastic compounds; chronology of the introduction of plastics.

625.   Blaser, Linda. "The Development of Endpapers," Guild of Book
        Workers Journal, 32:1 (Spring 1994) publication. 1996, 1-28. Traces
        history and use of endpapers; diagrams the structures.

626.   Blaser, Linda A. "Display Cradles for Books: Board Construction,"
        Guild of Book Workers Journal, 30:1 (Spring 1992), 1-16.
        Illus. Instructions for cradles to support books on display.

627.   Blecker, Suzanne. "What's Going On Out There? A Novice
        Librarian's Search for Usable Technology," Conservation
        Administration News, 51 (October 1992), 12-13. Describes the latest
        technology for preserving library materials and of accessing and
        transporting their contents.

628.   Bloom, Beth, and Richard E. Stern. "Mutilation of Library
         Materials: Campus Concern," New Jersey Libraries, 27:4 (Fall 1994),
         15-17. Problem of mutilation in a college library and need to spell
         out policies for acceptable behavior; problems presented by
         electronic media mentioned.

629.   Bloomfield, B. C. "The Librarian as Custodian; Or, A Policeman's
         Lot," Journal of Documentation, 40:2 (June 1984),
         144-151. Addresses issue of what librarians should preserve for the
         future; discusses preservation management and training.

630.   Bloomington (IL) Public Library. Disaster Preparedness Committee.
         Disaster Preparedness Plan. Bloomington, IL: Bloomington Public
         Library, 1991. 64p. Loose-leaf. Step-by-step instructions for
         disaster planning and recovery.

631.   Bluher, Agnes, Ursula Haller, and Gerhard Banik. "The Application
         of Carbopol Poultices on Paper Objects," Restaurator, 16:4 (1995),
         234-47.

632.   Blumenthal, Lyn. "Re:Guarding Video (Preservation)," AfterImage,
         13:7 (February 1986), 11-15. Notes that video is impermanent;
         preservation is short-term, but storage plays an important role in
         longevity.

633.   Boal, Gillian C. "Blast Freezing the Berkeley Law Library
         Infestation," Book and Paper Annual, 9 (1990), 17-28. Information
         of blast-freezing and recovery activities.

634.   Bolhouse, Ann. "Sidebar 4: Microform Preservation and Access
         Today" (at UMI), Library Hi Tech, 12:3 (1994), 97.

635.   Bolnick, Doreen, and Bruce Johnson. "Audiocassette Repair,"
         Library Journal, 114:19 (November 15, 1989), 43-46. Tips on basic
         repair for circulating cassettes.

636.   BonaDea, Artemis. Conservation Book Repair: A Training Manual.
         Juneau: Alaska Dept. of Education, 1995. 190p.

637.   Bond, Elayne. "Generic Letter of Agreement for Microfilming,"
         Abbey Newsletter, 14:4 (July 1990), 70-71. A model to be used as a
         first step in contracting.

638.   Bond, Elayne. "Mass Deacidification at Northwestern University
         Library," Archival Products News, 1:5 (Spring 1993), 3-4. The

library's approach to the project, preparation of materials, and observations about results.

639. Bond, Elayne. "Mass Deacidification: Writing a Contract," The Abbey Newsletter, 17:2 (1993), 18, 20. Contract elements (deacidification process, quantity, specifications, price, period, terms of invoicing, transportation and packing, vendor liability, warrantees and termination) are described based on Northwestern University's experience with vendor provided mass deacidification services.

640. Bond, Randall, Mary De Carlo, Elizabeth Henes, and Eileen Snyder. "Preservation Study at the Syracuse University Libraries," College and Research Libraries, 48:2 (March 1987), 132-147. Report on methodology of a survey of non-rare materials to assess condition.

641. Bonk, Sharon, and Sara Williams. "Stock Revision, Retention and Regulation in US Academic Libraries," Collection Management in Academic Libraries. Aldershot, England; Brookfield, VT: Gower, 1991, 213-234. Examines function of reviewing and discarding materials and discusses how such a program relates to, and can be driven by, preservation concerns.

642. BookLab, Inc. Advantages of Protective Enclosures: The Drop Spine Box. Austin, TX: BookLab, Inc. 1990. 6p. (Booknote #5).

643. BookLab, Inc. BookLab. Austin, TX: BookLab, Inc. 1990. 14p. Describes the preservation services offered by BookLab, including preservation photocopying, binding, and conservation treatments.

644. BookLab, Inc. Collection Maintenance: Repair for Publishers' Cased Books. Austin, TX: BookLab, Inc., 1990. 8p. (Booknote #3).

645. BookLab, Inc. A Glossary for the Structure and Action of Bookbindings. Austin TX: BookLab, Inc., 1990. 6p. (BookLab Booknote #7).

646. BookLab, Inc. Historical Prototypes for Conservation Binding. Austin, TX: BookLab, Inc., 1990. 11p. (BookLab Booknote #9).

647. BookLab, Inc. Leaf Master. Austin, TX: BookLab, Inc., 1993. 8p. (BookLab Booknote #16).

648. BookLab, Inc. Library Collection Conservation, Austin, TX: BookLab, Inc., 1992. 4p. (BookLab Booknote #14).

649.   BookLab, Inc. Millennial Bookbinding, Austin, TX: BookLab, Inc., 1996, 10p. Illus. Discussion of millennial bookbinding by Gary Frost, Philip Smith, Richard Mensky, and Keith Smith.

650.   BookLab, Inc. Polyester Encapsulation and Preservation of Documents. Austin, TX: 1990. 4p. (BookLab Booknote #1).

651.   BookLab, Inc. Preservation Photocopying. Austin, TX: BookLab, Inc., 1990. 7p. (BookLab Booknote #10).

652.   BookLab, Inc. Safe Handling and Exhibition of Books. Austin, TX: BookLab, Inc., 1990. 9p. (BookLab Booknote #4).

653.   BookLab, Inc. Salvage of Library Materials From Water or Insect Damage. Austin, TX: BookLab, Inc., 1990. 7p. (BookLab Booknote #2).

654.   BookLab, Inc. A Sewn Boards Binding for Library & Limited Edition Work. Austin, TX: BookLab, Inc., 1990. 6p. (BookLab Booknote #8).

655.   BookLab, Inc. Survey, Assessment and Planning for Library Cooperation. Austin, TX: BookLab, Inc., 1990. 6p. (BookLab Booknote #6).

656.   BookLab, Inc. Transfer Tape Binding, Austin, TX: BookLab, Inc., 1996, 5p. (BookLab Booknote #24).

657.   BookLab, Inc. Transmitting Library Books, Austin, TX: BookLab, Inc., 1996, 7p. (BookLab Booknote #23).

658.   "Book Repair Pleases Seniors—and Libraries," American Libraries, 18:3 (March 1987), 227. Description of a nonprofit program, Senior Bookbinding Services, that trains retired people in bookbinding and repair.

659.   Books in Peril; Proceedings of the Symposium on the Preservation of Library and Archival Materials in Southern Africa, South African Library, Cape Town, 19-21 November 1986. Cape Town: South African Library, 1987. 196p. Papers presented at a conference to promote awareness of preservation and current activities in South Africa. The need to educate librarians is emphasized.

660.   Boomgaarden, Wesley L. "Case Study: The Benefits of Institutional Preservation Planning in the Context of Statewide Archives and Library Preservation Planning," National Conference on the

Development of Statewide Preservation Programs. Washington, DC: National Conference on the Development of Statewide Preservation Programs, 1991, 62-64.

661. Boomgaarden, Wesley L. "An Edition of One: Xerographic Replacements to Meet Continuing Demand for Brittle Books in Book Format," Archival Products News, 1:3 (Fall 1992), 1-2. Brief note on the need for reformatting as a preservation option; criteria for selection; the role that machine-readable (digitized) reproductions might play in the future.

662. Boomgaarden, Wesley L. "Elements and Interconnections," Preservation Microfilming: Planning and Production. Chicago, IL: American Library Association, 1989, 3-15. Describes elements of a successful preservation microfilming program.

663. Boomgaarden, Wesley L. "Funding," Managing Preservation: A Guidebook. Columbus, OH: State Library of Ohio, 1994, 147-152.

664. Boomgaarden, Wesley L. "Mass Deacidification," Managing Preservation: A Guidebook. Columbus, OH: State Library of Ohio, 1994, 127-132.

665. Boomgaarden, Wesley L. "Options for Replacing and Reformatting Damaged or Deteriorated Library Books and Serials," Managing Preservation: A Guidebook. Columbus, OH: State Library of Ohio, 1994, 117-126.

666. Boomgaarden, Wesley L. "Preserving Our Collections," Preservation Issues (Ohio State Library), 1 (July 1990), 1. Brief, articulate statement on need for preservation.

667. Boomgaarden, Wesley L. "Preservation," Guide to Technical Services Resources, ed. Peggy Johnson. Chicago, IL: American Library Association, 1994, 166-195. Extensive, annotated bibliography selected for "accuracy, currency, availability, and usefulness."

668. Boomgaarden, Wesley L. "Preservation Planning for the Small Special Library," Special Libraries, 76:3 (Summer 1985), 204-211. Covers the basics of preservation, emphasizing that it is a management responsibility.

669. Boomgaarden, Wesley L. "Prospective Preservation," Meeting the Preservation Challenge, ed. Jan Merrill-Oldham. Washington, DC: Association of Research Libraries, 1988, 31-37; published originally in A Research Priority for the 1990s: Minutes of the 111th

Membership Meeting of the Association of Research Libraries. Washington, DC: Association of Research Libraries, October 1987. Discusses the role of storage, environment, and binding in preservation; advocates user education and disaster planning.

670. Boomgaarden, Wesley L. "Selection of Materials," Preservation Microfilming, ed. Nancy E. Gwinn. Chicago, IL: American Library Association, 1987, 26-60. Guidelines, policies, and procedures for selecting materials for preservation microfilming.

671. Boomgaarden, Wesley L., ed. Staff Training and User Awareness in Preservation Management. Washington, DC: Association of Research Libraries, 1993. 89p. (Preservation Planning Resource Guide Series). Briefly defines, outlines, and exemplifies a staff and user education and training program in preservation, with selected documents, including guidelines, manuals, policies, procedures, and hand-outs.

672. Boomgaarden, Wesley L., and Harry Campbell. "Preservation at the Ohio State University Libraries," Conservation Administration News, 25 (April 1986), 6-7, 16. Describes the program at Ohio State and the ARL self-study to help identify needs and priorities.

673. Boomgaarden, Wesley L., and Edward T. O'Neill. "Study of the Magnitude and Characteristics of Book Deterioration in Ohio Libraries," Preservation Issues (Ohio State Library), 6 (December 1991), 1. Results of a survey.

674. Borck, Helga. "Getting Better All the Time: NYPL Begins Collections Improvement Project," New Library Scene, 6:2 (April 1987), 12-13. Summary of the stack cleaning program at the New York Public Library, in which items needing preservation are identified.

675. Borsa, Gedeon. "Preservation of Historic Library Materials in Hungary," Library Conservation News, 15 (April 1987), 4-6. Description of initiatives underway to identify rare books and manuscripts in public and private collections to ensure that the nation's patrimony is preserved.

676. Borshevsky, Mana. "Women' Suffrage Petition of 1893: Documentation and Treatment," AICCM Bulletin (Australian Institute for the Conservation of Cultural Materials), 20:1 (1994), 33-39. Documents the treatment of the petition and what was learned in the process.

677.   Bosch, Stephen, Patricia Promis, and Chris Sugnet. Guide to
        Selecting and Acquiring CD-ROMs, Software, and Other Electronic
        Publications. Chicago, IL: American Library Association, 1994.
        48p. (Acquisition Guidelines, 9). Guide to acquisitions of electronic
        media, noting its impermanence and instability and the need to have
        high user acceptance to be cost-effective.

678.   Boss, Richard W. "Collection Security," Library Trends, 33:1
        (Summer 1984), 39-48. Discusses an administrator's approach to
        security, typical weakness; checklist for a security audit.

679.   Boston, George. "New Technology — Friend or Foe?"
        (Preservation of Digital Information), IFLA Journal (International
        Federation of Library Associations and Institutions), 20:3 (1994),
        331-340.

680.   Boston, George. "The Second Meeting of the International Advisory
        Committee for the UNESCO 'Memory of the World' Programme —
        Rapporteur's Comments," (Paris, France, May 3-5, 1995), IFLA
        Journal (International Federation of Library Associations and
        Institutions), 21:3 (1995), 175-177.

681.   Boston, George, ed. Archiving the Audio-Visual Heritage.
        Northants., England: FIAF/UNESCO, 1992. 192p. Papers from the
        3rd Joint Technical Symposium to address concerns about the
        stability of non-print media, reformatting, and the use of digital
        recording techniques.

682.   Boston, George, ed. Guide to the Basic Technical Equipment
        Required by Audio, Film and Television Archives. Paris: UNESCO,
        1991. 104p. Chapters describe characteristics of each medium,
        copying requirements, and preservation concerns; discusses need for
        technical research and definitions.

683.   Boston Library Consortium. Preservation Committee. Preservation
        Resource Directory. Boston: Boston Library Consortium, 1986. One
        volume. Reference tool that will provide entry into the preservation
        resources available in the Consortium area.

684.   Boston Public Library. Preservation Planning Program: Final Report,
        July 15, 1991. Boston: Boston Public Library, 1991. 25p. ARL
        Preservation Planning Program. Produced by Scot Cornwall, et. al.

685.   Botti, L., G. Impagliazzo, L. Residori, and D. Ruggiero. "Paper
        Packaging for the Long-Term Preservation of Photographic Plates,"
        Restaurator, 15:2 (1994), 79-93. Focuses on housing and storage of

photographic images on glass. Seven papers were tested to
determine stability but only one proved suitable.

686. Boudewijns, Leo. "NVPI, the Dutch Branch of IFPI," <u>Phonographic Bulletin</u>, 48 (May 1987), 10-12. Describes the state of the re-recording industry in the Netherlands, difficulties in establishing the Phonographic Museum, Utrecht, and preserving the sound heritage.

687. Bouley, Raymond J. "The Life and Death of CD-ROM," <u>CD-ROM Librarian</u>, 7:1 (January 1992), 10-17. Discusses results of artificial aging tests of compact disks, and their problems. Cites lack of research and notes the need for libraries to set standards for the media.

688. Boulle, Pierre H. "Use and Preservation: Concerns for France's National Library," <u>Primary Sources and Original Works</u>, 1:1/2 (1991), 237-240. Scholar compares the changes in library serves in the French Revolution and the move of French collection to the Bibliothèque de France; expresses concern about the physical move, unlimited access, and a lack of concern for regional archives.

689. Bourke, Thomas A. "The Anabasis from Analog to Digital Escalates: The Year's Work in the Reproduction of Library Materials," <u>Library Resources and Technical Services</u>, 37:3 (July 1993), 323-334. Review of the literature, 1992, identifying trends in imaging and reformatting. 138 references.

690. Bourke, Thomas A. "The Curse of Acetate: Or, A Base Conundrum Confronted," <u>Microform Review</u>, 23:1 (Winter 1994), 15-17. Describes the problems of cellulose acetate film, and the problem of its durability in the New York Public Library collection.

691. Bourke, Thomas A. "The Microfilming of Newspapers: An Overview," <u>Microform Review</u>, 15:3 (Summer, 1986), 154-157. History of newspaper microfilming at New York Public Library; note on current projects and filming methods.

692. Bourke, Thomas A. "The Reproduction of Library Materials in 1990," <u>Library Resources and Technical Services</u>, 35:3 (July 1991), 307-318. Review essay, with references.

693. Bourke, Thomas A. "Research Libraries Reassess Document Preservation Technologies," <u>Inform</u>, 4:8 (Sept. 1990), 30-34. Discusses the advantages of microforms and the new imaging technologies in the research library setting. Suggests microfilm will continue to serve as the primary preservation medium, but electronic

imaging will serve as an access medium, to some extent market-driven.

694.   Bourke, Thomas A. "Retrospect and Prospect: Micrographics Evolution in Research Libraries," Inform, 1:10 (October 1987), 28-33. History of the use of microfilm and other information technologies in research libraries.

695.   Bourke, Thomas A. "Scholarly Micropublishing, Preservation Microfilming, and the National Preservation Effort in the Last Two Decades of the Twentieth Century: History and Prognosis," Microform Review, 15:3 (Winter 1990), 4-16. Overview of micropublishing, preservation microfilming, and bibliographic control.

696.   Bourke, Thomas A. "Spaulding and Materazzi Revisited: A Ten Year Retrospect," Microform Review, 17:3 (August 1988), 130-136. Review of the debate surrounding questions of archival storage, durability in a working environment, and cost among proponents of silver halide, diazo, and vesicular films.

697.   Bourke, Thomas A. "To Archive or Not To Archive: Is That Really the Question?" Library Journal, 114:17 (October 15, 1989), 52-54. The author's question yields more than one answer. Paradigmatically, research libraries ought to be able to store material archivally so that they be permanently available in perpetuity. Practically, at a minimum level, material that will permit at least long-term storage (100 years) is needed.

698.   Bourke, Thomas A. "Washington Irving's Dialogue with an Unread Book: A Famous Nineteenth Century American Author Deliberates the Relationship Between Preservation and Access, To Which Is Appended a Modern Postscript on the Current State of the Issue," Microform Review, 23:3 (Summer 1994), 130-135. Bourke describes Irving's early 19th-century story of an encounter with a "talking book" in the Westminster Abbey Library, bemoaning the lack of access to itself; the establishment of the Astor Library, of which Irving was president, and the issue of access to its collection; the current situation when "preservation" ensures access to a "virtual" library in electronic formats.

699.   Bowen, Laurel G., and Nan McMurry. "How Firm a Foundation: Getting Cooperative Preservation Off the Ground," (Experimental Approach of the University Center in Georgia), Collection Building, 13:4 (1994) 25-31.

700.   Bower, Peter. "Challenge and Responsibility: Caring for Random Collections of Paper," Paper Conservator, 19 (1995), 63-72. Examination of 22 papers in IPC's collection of discarded materials from conservation labs. Illustrates what information is available from a sheet, and the problems posed by using old papers.

701.   Bowling, Mary B. "The Edison Archives: Adaptation in the Context of Traditional Functions," Science and Technology Libraries, (Summer 1989), 7-21. Organizing the archives, with a section on its preservation problems.

702.   Bowling, Mary B. "Literature on the Preservation of Non-Paper Materials," American Archivist, 53:2 (Spring 1990), 340-348. Bibliographical review of recent literature on preservation of non-paper records: sound recordings, moving images, photographs, microforms, magnetic and optical media.

703.   Bowling, Mary B. "Preservation Management Institute," Conservation Administration News, 31 (October 1987), 16-17. Report on an institute for administrators with preservation responsibilities jointly offered by Simmons College and the Northeast Document Conservation Center. A model for later initiatives.

704.   Bowser, Eileen, and John Kuiper, eds. A Handbook for Film Archivists. New York: Garland, 1991. 194p. and plates. Covers all aspects of film archive management, with emphasis on preservation.

705.   Boyd, Jane, and Don Etherington. Preparation of Archival Copies of Theses and Dissertations. Chicago, IL: American Library Association, 1986. 15p. Earlier version published as Guidelines... in 1985. 8 leaves. Guide prepared by the Physical Quality of Library Materials Committee, Resources and Technical Services Division, ALA.

706.   Boyle, Deirdre. Video Preservation: Securing the Future of the Past. New York: Media Alliance, 1993. 66p. Report of a 1991 symposium, includes a section on preservation activities; list of video preservation resources.

707.   Bozeman, Pat, ed. Forged Documents. New Castle, DE: Oak Knoll Books, 1990. 180p. Papers from a conference to address the impact of forged documents in library and archive collections. Detailed discussion of legal aspects and responsibilities of dealers, curators, and collectors.

708.   Bradley, Susan. "Conservation Recording in the British Museum," Conservator (U.K.), 7 (1983), 9-12. Describes the system for documenting conservation treatments at the British Library.

709.   Bradsher, James Gregory, ed. Managing Archives and Archival Institutions. Chicago, IL: University of Chicago Press, 1989, 304p. Provides a summary of archives management that is both authoritative and sensitive. Includes chapters on preservation, security, and exhibit of materials.

710.   Bradsher, James Gregory, and Mary Lynn Ritzenthaler. "Archival Exhibits," Managing Archives and Archival Institutions. Chicago, IL: University of Chicago Press, 1989, 228-240. Addresses issues of policy, concept, and technical concerns. Bibliography.

711.   Brady, Diane. "Exit Ozone-Destroying Chemicals," Our Planet, 1:213 (1989), 20-21. Representatives from 82 countries and the European Community have stepped up efforts to save the Earth's ozone layer from the depleting effects of chlorofluorocarbons (CFCs). The "Helsinki Declaration..." calls for the phasing out of CFCs by the year 2000.

712.   Brady, Eileen E. "Scandal in the Stacks." Focus on Security, 1:2 (January 1994), 24-27. Discusses the scope of book theft, the Blumberg case, and librarian's reluctance to disclose theft.

713.   Brady, Eileen E., and John F. Guido. "When Is a Disaster Not a Disaster?" Library and Archival Security, 8:3/4 (Fall-Winter 1988), 11-23. Describes the cause of damage and conservation treatment of water-damaged books.

714.   Brahm, Walter. "Conservation as I Remember It: An Undocumented Hindsight," Preservation Issues (Ohio State Library), 11 (March 1993), 2p. Recollections by an early advocate for library preservation programs.

715.   Brandes, Harald. "Are There Alternatives to the Traditional air-conditioned Film Stores?" Archiving the Audio-Visual Heritage. Rushton, England: FIAF/UNESCO, 1992, 23-26. Explores practical measures, containerization and microclimates, for film storage.

716.   Brandes, Harald. "The Uses and Dangers of Solvents in Film Archives," Preserving the Audio-Visual Heritage. Rushton, England: FIAF/UNESCO, 1992, 131-132. Overview of concerns.

717.   Brandis, Leanne. "A Comparison of Methods Used for Measuring the pH of Paper," AICCM Bulletin (Australian Institute for the

Conservation of Cultural Materials), 18:3-4 (1993), 7-17. Study of methods for testing the pH of 5 papers. Results suggest that pH testing solutions provide sufficiently accurate estimations in most cases.

718. Brandis, Leanne. "A Preliminary Investigation Into the Effectiveness of Eucalyptus Oil to Remove Adhesive Material," AICCM Bulletin (Australian Institute for the Conservation of Cultural Material), 18:11/2 (1992), 57-60. A study of the effectiveness of eucalyptus oil in removing adhesives and staining demonstrated that it is not effective and its long-term effect on paper could be harmful.

719. Brandis, Leanne. "Summary and Evaluation of the Testing Sponsored by the Library of Congress of Books Deacidified by the FMC, Akzo, and Wei T'o Mass Deacidification Processes," Restaurator, 15:2 (1994), 109-127. Physical and chemical criteria are discussed; results reveal that none is able to effectively treat all library materials; none always provides uniform treatment; all can adversely affect the condition of books.

720. Brandt, Astrid-Christiane. "Interventions in Libraries & Archives in Which Infections and/or Infestations Have Occurred," Proceedings of the Pan-African Conference on the Preservation & Conservation of Library & Archival Materials, Nairobi, Kenya, 21-25 June 1993. The Hague: IFLA, 1995, 55-59. (IFLA Professional Publication 43). Reviews major pest that infest collections, measures for control and treatment.

721. Brandt, Astrid-Christiane. "A Survey on Mass Deacidification Processes," International Preservation News, 10 (July 1995), 5. Brief review of mass deacidification processes currently available and research at BL and BN to develop a technique that will strengthen as well as deacidify brittle paper.

722. Brandt, Astrid-Christiane. "Conservation Preventative: Grandes Orientations, Strategies et Méthodes," IFLA Journal (International Federation of Library Associations and Institutions), 20:3 (1994), 276-283.

723. Brandt, Astrid-Christiane. La Deacidification de Masse du Papier: Étude Comparative des Procédés Existants/ Mass Deacidification of Paper: A Comparative Study of Existing Processes. tr. Peter Thomas. Paris: Bibliothèque Nationale, 1992. 92p. Describes the causes of paper deterioration and reviews current deacidification processes: Wei T'o and its French and German variants; DEZ (Akzo), Lithco (FMC): strengths, weaknesses, and environmental impact. Includes "Standardized Methods to Test Paper Characteristics." 84 notes.

724.   Brandt, Charles A. E. "Archival Conservation in Canada,"
        Conservation Administration News, 12 (January 1983), 1-3, 5.
        Review of current initiatives.

725.   Brandt, Charles A. E. "Audubon's 'Birds of America,'" The Beaver,
        (Summer 1983), 30-35. Report on the restoration of the book of
        plates.

726.   Brandt, Charles A.E. "Care and Storage of Works on Paper," Library
        and Archival Security, 5:1 (Spring 1983), 1-10. Preservation, care,
        and storage of materials.

727.   Braun, Janice. "Sources for Preservation in Health Science
        Libraries," Watermark (Newsletter of the Association of Librarians in
        the History of Health Sciences), 14:1 (Fall 1990), 1-8.
        Bibliographical essay with sources of advice and assistance.

728.   Bravery, A. F. Mould and Its Control. Aylesbury, England: Building
        Research Establishment, 1985. 4p. (BRE Information U.K.,
        11) Nature of mold in buildings and factors governing its growth;
        remedial and preventive measures are outlined.

729.   Brawner, Lee B., and Norman Nelson. "Improving Security and
        Safety for Libraries," Public Library Quarterly, 5:1 (Spring 1984),
        41-58. Planning for security, from design of facility to planning for
        protection. Bibliography, 1979-1983.

730.   Brederick, Karl, Anna Haberditzl, and Agnes Blueher. "Paper
        Deacidification in a Workshop," Conference on Book and Paper
        Conservation, 1990. Budapest, Hungary: Technical Association of
        Paper and Printing Industry/National Szechenyi Library, 1992,
        545-565. Illus. Charts. Various commercial organic deacidifying
        products and self-prepared aqueous solutions of alkaline earth ions
        were studied for application in the paper conservation workshop.
        Effectiveness was determined analyzing the pH in cold extraction,
        buffer capacity, the benefits of mixing calcium and magnesium
        hydrogen carbonate are discussed. Paper originally presented at the
        9th Triennial Meeting of the International Council of Museums
        Conservation Working Group, Dresden, August 1990; republished in
        Restaurator, 11:3 (1990), 165-178.

731.   Brederick, Karl, and Almut Siller-Grabenstein. "Fixing of Ink Dyes
        as a Basis for Restoration and Preservation Techniques in Archives."
        Restaurator, 9:3 (1988), 113-135. Review of composition of common
        inks demonstrating that water soluble ionic dyes are the

most endangered; discusses the development of fixing agents to strengthen them.

732.   Brennan, Patricia B. M., and Joel S. Silverberg. "Will My Disks Go Floo If I Take Them Through?" College and Research Libraries News, 46:8 (September 1985), 423-424. Discusses the effect of a magnetic security system on magnetic microcomputer disks.

733.   Breslauer, B. H. The Uses of Bookbinding Literature. New York: Books Arts Press, School of Library Service, Columbia University, 1986. 44p. Traces the history of manuals and historical studies in bookbinding.

734.   Bressor, Julie P. Caring for Historical Records: An Introduction. Storrs, CT: University of Connecticut, 1988. 77p.

735.   Brezner, Jerome. "Protecting Books from Living Pests," Paper Preservation: Current Issues and Recent Developments. Atlanta, GA: TAPPI Press, 1988, 65-68.

736.   Brezner, Jerome, and Philip Luner. "Nuke 'em! Library Pest Control Using a Microwave," Library Journal, 114:15 (September 15, 1989), 60-63; response by Sally Roggia, December 1989. Although elements of an integrated pest management program are described, the key for the authors is the microwaving of circulated books. Roggia responds that microwaving is a potentially harmful method that would address a very small problem.

737.   Brezner, Jerome, and Philip Luner. "Preservation of Library Materials by Microwave Radiation," Paper Preservation: Current Issues and Recent Developments. Atlanta, GA: TAPPI Press, 1990, 111-115. Reports favorable results from the use of microwave radiation for destroying insects. Its effect on materials on a molecular level has not been determined.

738.   Brichford, Maynard J. "A Brief History of the Physical Protection of Archives," Conservation Administration News, 31 (October 1987), 10, 21. Brief review of policies and procedures adopted over the centuries that define modern archival practice.

739.   Brichford, Maynard J., and William J. Maher. "Archival Issues in Network Electronic Publications," Library Trends, 43 (Spring 1995), 701-712. Addresses issues in electronic publishing.

740.   Bridgeman, Carleen. "Foolproof Solutions for the Foolhardy," Disaster Recovery Journal, 7:2 (April/June 1994), 77; reprinted in Abbey Newsletter, 18:4/5 (August/September 1994), 51-52.

Practical tips on prevention of loss of data by backing up tapes and using common sense.

741.   Bridgland, Janet. ed. Preprints. ICOM Committee for Conservation 10th Triennial Meeting, Washington DC, August 22-27, 1993, Washington, DC: International Council of Museums, 1993. 2 Vols.

742.   Bridgland, Janet. ed. Preprints. ICOM Committee for Conservation 11th Triennial Meeting, Edinburgh, Scotland, September1-6, 1996. 2 Vols.

743.   Briggs, James R. "Preservation Factors in the Design of New Libraries: A Building Services Engineer's Viewpoint," Conservation and Preservation in the Small Library, ed. Nicholas Hadgraft and Katherine Swift. Cambridge: Parker Library Publications, 1994, 49-69. Considers methods of environmental control and costs, with the goal of designing buildings that provide appropriate environment at low cost. Reviews environmental requirements and environmental control (HVAC) systems, design considerations.

744.   Briggs, James R. "Environmental Control of Modern Records," Conservation of Library and Archive Materials and the Graphic Arts, ed. Guy Petherbridge. London: Butterworths, 1987. 297-305. Discussion of temperature and humidity and methods of control.

745.   Brigham Young University. Harold B. Lee Library. Disaster Preparedness and Salvage Plan. Provo, UT: The Library 1990. 32 leaves. Updated April 1990.

746.   Brimblecombe, Peter, and Brian Ramer. "Museum Display Cases and the Exchange of Water Vapor," Studies in Conservation, 28:4 (November 1983), 179-188. Results of an experiment to examine gas exchange between case and ambient air.

747.   Brinkhus, Gerd. "Conservation and Restoration in State Archives and Scientific Libraries in the Federal Republic of Germany," Restaurator, 9:1 (1988), 3-13. A review of preservation and conservation initiatives in West Germany since World War II.

748.   British Leather Manufacturer's Research Association. The Conservation of Bookbinding Leather. London: British Library, 1984. 78p.; plates. Report by the British Library of a project to investigate the underlying causes of the deterioration of leather due to atmospheric pollution.

749.   British Library. Disposal of Printed Material from Libraries: Capitol Planning Information. London: British Library, 1995. 78p. (British

National Bibliography Research Fund, 72). A study of the rate and methods for the disposal of unwanted materials from British Library Collections, to determine if guidelines are warranted. Results of survey and recommendations.

750. British Library. National Preservation Office. Conservation in Crisis; Proceedings of a Seminar at Loughborough University of Technology, 16-17 July 1986. London: British Library, 1987. 80p.

751. British Library. National Preservation Office. Conservation in Crisis; Proceedings of a Seminar at Loughborough University of Technology, 22-23 July 1987. London: British Library, 1988. 80p.

752. British Library. National Preservation Office. Boxing. London: British Library, 1990. 7p. Discusses the reasons for boxing library materials and the elements of a boxing program.

753. British Library. National Preservation Office. Encapsulation. London: British Library, 1990. 7p. Describes the technique, advantages and disadvantages, materials.

754. British Library. National Preservation Office. Keeping Our Words: 1988. The National Preservation Office Competition. London: British Library, 1989. 66p. Winning entries are abstracted in this bibliography under the names of the winners.

755. British Library. National Preservation Office. Keeping Our Words: 1989. The National Preservation Office Competition. London: British Library, 1990. 72p. Winning entries are abstracted in this bibliography under the names of the winners.

756. British Library. National Preservation Office. Microforms in Libraries: The Untapped Resource? London: British Library. 1993. 93p. Papers given at the National Preservation Office Conference held October13-15, 1992, in Birmingham, England as part of the Mellon Microfilming Project. The papers focused on four areas, the wider view, planning your program, the business, equipment and production, and the users.

757. British Library. National Preservation Office. Mould. London: British Library, 1990. 7p. Provides facts and explains common procedures for combating mold infestation.

758. British Library. National Preservation Office. Preservation and Publications: Proceedings of a Seminar at York University, 17-18 July 1990. London: British Library, 1991. 57p. (National Preservation Office Seminar Papers, No. 5). Papers "move away

from the issues of collection management and preservation addressed at previous seminars to the more specific concerns with the written or published items itself."

759.   British Library. National Preservation Office. Preservation and Technology: Proceedings of a Seminar at York University, 20-21 July 1988. London: British Library, 1989. 80p. (National Preservation Office Seminar Papers, No. 3). These proceedings "reflect informed opinion in the library and archive world on the role of new technology in the preservation of knowledge."

760.   British Library. National Preservation Office. Preservation Microforms. London: British Library, 1988. 19p. Also 1990. 19p.

761.   British Library. National Preservation Office. Preservation Guidelines. London: British Library, 1986. 10p. (typescript).

762.   British Library. National Preservation Office. Preservation Policies— the Choices: Proceedings of a Seminar at York University 28-29 June 1989. London: British Library, 1990. 72p.

763.   British Library. National Preservation Office. Preservation Policies: Glossary. London: British Library, 1990. 10p. Explanations of terms commonly used in library preservation work.

764.   British Library. National Preservation Office. Preservation: A Survival Kit. London: British Library, 1988. 1 portfolio. Information packet for libraries.

765.   British Library. National Preservation Office. Preservation: A Training Pack for Library Staff. London: British Library, 1994. One volume.

766.   British Library. National Preservation Office. Photocopying of Library and Archival Materials. London: British Library, 1995. 7p.

767.   British Library. National Preservation Office. "Security Guidelines," Security in Academic and Research Libraries, ed. Anthony G. Quinsee and Andrew C. McDonald. Newcastle-upon-Type, England: University of Newcastle Library, 1991, 64-66. What a library can do to provide security; sources of assistance.

768.   "British Library to Set Up National Preservation Office," IFLA Journal (International Federation of Library Associations and Institutions), 11:1 (1985), 76-77.

769.   British Records Association. "The Care of Records: Notes for the
         Owner or Custodian," Archives, 16:70 (October 1983), 181-184.
         (British Records Association Memorandum, 22). Basic requirements
         for care of records, issued autumn 1983: accommodation
         (environment); equipment (housing); arrangement; access, and "first
         aid repair."

770.   British Standards Institution. Repair and Allied Processes for the
         Conservation of Documents. 2d ed. London: British Standards
         Institution, 1988. 2 vols. Reflects changes in repair techniques since
         the last standards in 1973.

771.   Broadhurst, Roger N. "The Digitization of Library Material,"
         Information Management and Technology, 26:3 (May 1993), 128-
         132.

772.   Broadhurst, Roger N. "Library Applications for Microfilm
         Digitization," Microform Review, 21 (Fall 1992), 153-155.

773.   Brock-Nannestad, George. "A Comment and Further
         Recommendations on 'International Recording Standards,'" ARSC
         Journal (Association of Recorded Sound Collections), 20:2 (Fall
         1989), 156-161. Author emphasizes that the goal of re-recording is
         first the preservation of the sound as closely as possible to the
         original. However, re-recording for historical purposes and for sound
         are both valid, and standards should reflect this.

774.   Brock-Nannestad, George. "A Knowledge of the Content of
         Material as a Pre-condition for Restoration," Archiving the
         Audio-Visual Heritage. Rushton, England: FIAF/UNESCO, 1992,
         149-154. Discusses ethical and technical concerns in re-recording.

775.   Brockman, James. "Rebacking — An Alternative Approach," New
         Bookbinder, 11 (1991), 36-46. Explains a refined method of
         rebacking books; 40 photographs.

776.   Brockman, James. "A Vellum Over Boards Binding," New
         Bookbinder, 13 (1993), 43-53. Instructions for a technique learned
         from Sydney Cockerell.

777.   BroDart Company. Modern Simplified Book Repair. Williamsport,
         PA: BroDart Co., 1990. 27p. Updated periodically. A repair manual
         using the company's non-archival techniques and products.

778.   Brokerhof, Agnes W. "Icy Insects: Freezing as a Means of Insect
         Control," AICCM Bulletin (Australian Institute for the Conservation

of Cultural Materials), 18:3/4 (1993), 19-23. Study of the lethal effect of cold on the developmental stages of various species.

779.   Brooks, Constance. Disaster Preparedness. Washington, DC: Association of Research Libraries, 1993. 184p. (Preservation Planning Program). Instruction for disaster planning, with selected readings.

780.   Brooks, Connie. Bibliography of Technical Standards for Paper and Paper-Based Library Materials. Chicago, IL: American Library Association, ALCTS, 1988. 10p.

781.   Brooks, Connie, and Joseph F. Schubert. "The New York State Program for the Conservation and Preservation of Library Research Materials," Bookmark, 45:3 (Spring 1987), 140-146.

782.   Broom, Andrew. "The ICA Committee on Conservation and Restoration," IFLA Journal (International Federation of Library Associations and Institutions), 12:4 (1986), 314-316. A brief description of the committee and its activities.

783.   Broughton, Heather. "The Storage of Paper Archives," Dust to Dust? Papers Read at a Conference on the Creation and Care of Excavation Archives Held at Leicestershire Museums and Art Gallery, November 9-11, 1984. Field Archaeology and Museums, Vol. 11, Leicester, England: Society of Museum Archaeologists, 1986, 64-66. Discusses problems related to paper archive storage and the preservation of documents; paper presented at a 1984 conference.

784.   Brown, A. Gilson. "The American Institute for Conservation of Historic and Artistic Works," Conservation Administration News, 28 (January 1987), 8. Describes the goals, objectives, and services of the professional organization for conservators.

785.   Brown, Charlotte. "Deaccessioning for the Greater Good," Wilson Library Bulletin, 61:8 (April 1987), 22-24. Describes the deaccessioning and transfer of a collection of sound recordings from Franklin and Marshall College to the University of Maryland, for preservation and access.

786.   Brown, Charlotte B., and Janet Gertz. "Selection for Preservation: Applications for College Libraries," Building on the 21st Century. Chicago, IL: Association of College and Research Libraries, 1989, 288-294. Study testing the applicability to college libraries of the Atkinson typology for preservation selection. Paper presented at the 5th National Conference of the Association of College and Research Libraries, Cincinnati, OH, April 5-8.

787.   Brown, Charlotte B., and Kathleen Moretto Spencer. "Preservation, a Critical Element of Collection Development in College Libraries," Collection Development in College Libraries. Chicago, IL: American Library Association, 1991, 170-177. Note special collections to be found in college libraries and the need to preserve them. Case Study of Franklin and Marshall College.

788.   Brown, D. W., R. F. Lowry, and L. E. Smith. Prediction of the Long-Term Stability of Polyester-Based Recording Media. Washington, DC: National Bureau of Standards, 1984. 53p. (NSBIR84-2988).

789.   Brown, Frances. "Approaches to Microfilming Case Studies: The Historical Societies' Experience," Preservation Microfilming: Does It Have a Future? Canberra : National Library of Australia, 1995, 66-69. Discusses the poor quality of microfilm produced in in-house operations and the need for improved quality product and records. "A well-produced and presented microform should achieve not only conservation but dissemination in an easy-to-use manner. This is surely the primary aim, otherwise why conserve it?" (69)

790.   Brown, Hyacinth. Disaster Planning in Jamaica: Safeguarding Documents and Vital Data. Kingston, Jamaica: Jamaica Library Association, 1989. 49p. Illus. Papers from a seminar on disaster preparedness, 1986, and report on the effects of Hurricane Gilbert, September 1988.

791.   Brown, J. P. "Putting the 'Museum' Back Into Museum Design," Environmental Monitoring and Control. Dundee, Scotland: Scottish Society for Conservation and Restoration, 1989, 94-104. Discusses the need to restructure organization to ensure that collections are preserved, interpreted, and presented properly.

792.   Brown, Jay Ward. "The Once and Future Book: The Preservation Crisis," Wilson Library Bulletin, 59:9 (May 1985), 591-596. Discusses the crisis of the deterioration of books and ways to combat it. Describes deacidification, microfilming, and digitization and their respective effects and implications.

793.   Brown, K. C., and R. E. Jacobson. "Archival Permanence of Holograms?" Journal of Photographic Science, 33:5 (September-October 1985), 177-182. Review of evidence and discussion of problems, with preliminary recommendations on storage and display.

794.   Brown, Karen E. K. "Mould as a Health Threat," ACA Bulletin (Association of Canadian Archivists) (January 1995), 24-25.

795.   Brown, Karen E. K. "Conservation Concerns: Conservation of the Winslow Papers," ACA Bulletin (Association of Canadian Archivists), 16:2 (1991), 14-16.

796.   Brown, Margaret, comp. Preservation Supply Catalogue, 1996. Washington, DC: Preservation Directorate, Library of Congress, 1996, [17], 38p. Illus. Detailed instructions and specifications for ordering preservation supplies, directed to LC staff but useful for everyone. Options are detailed.

797.   Brown, Meg. "Publishers Bindings & Libraries: An Analysis of Problems and Solutions," New Library Scene, 15:2 (April 1996), 5-6, 10-12, 18-20. Briefly reviews the causes of problems in construction of library bindings, the causes of productions of these bindings. Proposes that librarians work with publishers to have library editions bound by library binders.

798.   Brown, Norman B. "Preservation in the Research Library: Its Past, Present Status, and Encouraging Future," Technical Services Today and Tomorrow, ed. Michael Gorman. Englewood, CO: Libraries Unlimited, 1990, 105-129. History of the development of concern for preservation of research collections from the late 1960s to date, and a review of major issues.

799.   Brown, Rowland C.W. "Mixed Microform and Digital," Inform, 5:9 (October 1991), 10-13. Discusses the activities and goals of the Technology Assessment Advisory Committee (TAAC), Commission on Preservation and Access; summarizes its reports; notes that as technologies evolve, assessment must be continual to ensure access.

800.   Brown, Royston, and Hilary Spiers, eds. Security Systems, Vandalism, and Disaster Planning in Libraries. Stamford, Lincolnshire, England: Capital Planning Information, 1988. 51p. Papers from a seminar held in November 1988 to examine the range of emergencies and incidents in libraries and to provide solutions based on common practice and accumulated wisdom.

801.   Brown, Ruth. "The Library at the Explorers Club," Wilson Library Bulletin, 63:8 (April 1989), 49-51. Description of the library and its collections; preservation and collection maintenance activities.

802.   Brown, Sandford. "Saving Our Heritage," The Lamp (Exxon Corporation), 69:3 (Fall 1987), 18-23. Focuses on the brittle book problem and describes preservation efforts and major institutions.

803.   Browne, Malcolm W. "Nation's Library Calls on Chemists to Stop
        Books From Turning to Dust," New York Times, May 22, 1990, l,
        C11. Library of Congress's plan for a deacidification program.

804.   Browne, Mark. "Early Photographic Albums and Their Contents:
        Conservation and Ethical Problems," Library Conservation News, 43
        (Summer 1994), 4-5. Case study of a treatment of a badly
        deteriorated photo album; emphasizes need to consider ethical and
        financial aspects of physical treatment.

805.   Brownstein, Mark. "One Disk at a Time: Moldy Discs!" CD-Rom
        EndUser, (February 1990), 29. If a CD disk is not protected properly,
        the metallic coating can oxidize and cause deterioration so that the
        disk can no longer be read.

806.   Brückle, Irene. "Aspects of the Use of Alum in Historical
        Papermaking," Conference Papers, Manchester 1992. Worcester,
        England: Institute of Paper Conservation, 1992, 201-206. Reviews
        the role of alum in historical papermaking; history and production
        methods of various aluminum salts and their use. 65 references.

807.   Brückle, Irene. "Historical Manufacture and Use of Blue Paper,"
        Book and Paper Group Annual, 12 (1993), 5-7. Summarizes the
        history, manufacture, and use of blue paper in the West; discusses
        conservation of blue paper.

808.   Brumbaugh, Robert S., and Rulon S. Wells. "Completing Yale's
        Plato Microfilm Project," Yale University Library Gazette, 64:1/2
        (October 1989), 73-75. Report of a project to bring together the
        microfilm copies of all existing manuscripts of Plato's texts to ensure
        their preservation.

809.   Bruno, Michael H. "Stability, Conservation, Preservation and
        Restoration of Graphic Arts Images and Products," Stability and
        Conservation of Photographic Images: Chemical, Electronic and
        Material. Bangkok, Thailand: Society of Photographic Scientists and
        Engineers, 1986, 34-46. Overview of the causes of paper
        deterioration, means of prevention, and methods of treatment.

810.   Bryan, John L. Automatic Sprinkler and Stand-Pipe Systems. 2d ed.
        Boston, MA: National Fire Protection Association, 1990.   568p.
        Illus. Covers the basics of fire suppression systems.

811.   Bryant, Barbara. "Take 2: Restoring Old Films," LC Information
        Bulletin (Library of Congress), 53:10 (May 16, 1994),

196-197. Briefly describes the recopying process at the Library's Motion Picture Conservation Center, Dayton, Ohio.

812.   Buchanan, Sally A. "Administering the Library Conservation Program," Law Library Journal, 77:3 (1984-1985), 569-574. Managing a general collections care and preservation program.

813.   Buchanan, Sally A. "Conservation Needs, Priorities, and Options at Stanford University," The Library Preservation Program: Models, Priorities, Possibilities, ed. Jan Merrill-Oldham and Merrily Smith. Chicago, IL: American Library Association, 1985, 59-62. Preservation and conservation at Stanford University Libraries.

814.   Buchanan, Sally A. Disaster Planning: A Self-Help Guide. Albany, NY: New York State Office of Cultural Education and Division of Library Development, 1988. 34p. Covers disaster planning and recovery, restoration, and conservation; resource materials for disaster planning in New York state institutions.

815.   Buchanan, Sally A. The New York State Disaster Preparedness Pilot Project. Albany, NY: New York Office of Cultural Education Committee and the New York State Division of Library Development, November 1988. 32p. Developed in cooperation with the Northeast Document Conservation Center.

816.   Buchanan, Sally A. "Preservation Perspectives: Disaster Preparedness," Wilson Library Bulletin, 68:4 (December 1993), 59-62. Brief overview of planning, response, and recovery.

817.   Buchanan, Sally A. "Preservation Perspectives: Haiti: An Essential Heritage," Wilson Library Bulletin, 69:8 (April 1995), 68-69. Describes a consulting and training visit to the library of a religious order in Haiti.

818.   Buchanan, Sally A. "Preservation Perspectives: Mass Deacidification," Wilson Library Bulletin, 69:4 (December 1994), 58-59. Discusses mass deacidification processes as a preservation option; describes cause of brittle paper and what treatment might accomplish. How to evaluate the processes.

819.   Buchanan, Sally A. "Preservation Perspectives: Notes on the Care of Collections," Wilson Library Bulletin, 68:8 (April 1994), 67-68. A plea to librarians to stop trying to "repair" books. Reviews how repair can effectively be accomplished.

820. Buchanan, Sally A. "Preservation Perspectives: Saving the Other Stuff," Wilson Library Bulletin, 68:10 (June 1994), 69-70. Preserving special materials: genealogy, local history, legal records, photograph collections. How to assess needs and seek funds. Emphasizes "common sense," good environment, user education, and "an understanding of the place the material has in the life of the library and its users."

821. Buchanan, Sally A. "Preservation Perspectives: The Ties That Bind: Library Collections," Wilson Library Bulletin, 68:6 (February 1994), 52-53. Excellent summary of library binding to preserve collections.

822. Buchanan, Sally A. "Preservation Perspectives: Too Big, Too Expensive, Too Time-Consuming," Wilson Library Bulletin, 68:2 (October 1993), 64. Preservation as asset management; why administrators tend to avoid it.

823. Buchanan, Sally A. Resource Materials for Disaster Planning in New York Institutions. Albany, NY: New York Library Disaster Planning Project, 1988. 29p.

824. Buchanan, Sally A. "The Third Decade: Directions for Preservation Conservation," Conservation Administration News, 33 (April 1988), 3,10.

825. Buchanan, Sally A. "Water Damage: Book Restoration Project Flow Chart," PNLA Quarterly (Pacific Northwest Library Association), 52 (Winter 1988), 20. Reprinted from the Library Disaster Preparedness Handbook, Chicago, IL: American Library Association, 1986.

826. Buchanan, Sally A., and Margaret Domer. "Preservation Perspectives: Writing With Light," (Preservation of Photographs), Wilson Library Bulletin, 69:10 (June 1995) p. 68-70. Brief review of history and process of photographic imaging; basic information on storage, handling, with a note about digital reformatting.

827. Buchanan, Sally A., and Mia Esserman. "Preservation Perspectives: Staff and User Education," Wilson Library Bulletin, 69:2 (October 1994), 63-64. Examples of staff and user education; teaching respect for workplace and materials; public relations for preservation.

828. Buchanan, Sally A., and Kirsten Jensen. "Preservation Perspectives: The Electronic Link" (Preservation of Electronic Formats), Wilson Library Bulletin, 69:6 (February 1995), 53-54. Notes libraries' needs to accept responsibility for selection, care and handling, storage, security and climate control for electronic media. Discusses challenge for preservation, hardware and software concerns.

829.   Buchanan, Sally A., and Toby Murray. Disaster Planning:
        Preparedness and Recovery for Libraries and Archives: A RAMP
        Study With Guidelines. PGI-88/WS6, ERIC ED 297-769. Paris:
        General Information Programme and UNISIST, United Nations
        Educational, Scientific, and Cultural Organization, 1988.
        187p. Covers the planning process, preparation of a disaster plan,
        prevention, and response. Included are forms developed by
        SOLINET and a comprehensive bibliography by Toby Murray.

830.   Buchbauer, G., L. Jirovetz, M. Wasicky, and A. Nikiforov. "On the
        Odour of Old Books," Journal of Pulp & Paper Science, 21:11
        (November 1995), J398-400. Analyzes 4 books published in 1779,
        1922, 1933, 1942 to identify compounds responsible for the musty,
        moldy odor. Two cyclohexanol derivatives and other compounds
        with long-lasting odor effects accounted for much of the complex
        odor of old books. (EMeC).

831.   Buchel, Rudy. "Library's Preservation Lab Saves the Nation's Film
        Heritage," LC Information Bulletin (Library of Congress), 48:21
        (May 22, 1989), 189. Describes the Library's film preservation and
        reformatting activities.

832.   Buck, George. "Halon Update: What Are the Alternatives," Military
        Firefighter, (August 1993), 19.

833.   Buckland, Michael K. "The Roles of Collections and the Scope of
        Collection Development," Journal of Documentation, 45:5
        (September 1989), 213-226. Examines the archival functions of
        collections; the need to preserve materials as one aspect of collection
        development.

834.   Budny, Mildred. "Physical Evidence and Manuscript Conservation:
        A Scholar's Plea," Conservation and Preservation in Small Libraries,
        ed. Nicholas Hadgraft and Katherine Swift. Cambridge: Parker
        Library Publications, 1994. 29-46. Needs for scholars to study book
        as a whole, assessing its physical evidence, which conservators
        should seek to retain. Importance of examining and recording
        physical features.

835.   Bui, Dominic Nghiep Cong. "The Videodisk: Technology,
        Applications, and Some Implications for Archives," American
        Archivist, 47:4 (1984), 418-427. Discusses optical disk technology
        for use in archives. Describes its advantages, but cautions about its
        problems. Reviews the pilot programs of the Public Archives of
        Canada and the Library of Congress.

Bibliography

836. Bulgawicz, Susan L. Disaster Prevention and Recovery: A Planned Approach. Prairie Village, KS: ARMA International, 1988. 79p. Disaster planning and recovery manual; glossary, model forms.

837. Bull, William. "A Photograph Album," Bookbinder (Journal of the Society of Bookbinders and Book Restorers), 2 (1988), 51-62. Instructions for a durable photograph album; photographs are attached without adhesives.

838. Bunch, Antonia J. "Conservation and the Library Community," Library Review, 35 (Spring 1986), 56-61. Describes developing concern for preservation in British libraries.

839. Burchill, Mary D. "Report on Kansas Workshop" (at the Joint Meeting of the Kansas Library Association, Kansas Association of School Libraries, and the Kansas Association for Educational and Communication Technology in Salina in April), New Library Scene, 13 (June 1994), 18.

840. Burdick, Amrita J. "Library Photocopying: The Margin of Caring," New Library Scene, 5:3 (June 1986), 17-18. Illus. Proper ways to photocopy materials from bound volumes.

841. Bureau, William H. "Paper After 30 Years," The Abbey Newsletter, 11:2 (March 1987), 29-30. Changes in paper industry technology have resulted from the impact of changes in the printing industry, the advent of plastics, the computer ages, packaging innovations, and energy and environmental concerns.

842. Burgess, David. Chemical Science and Conservation. London: Macmillan, 1990. 93p. Discusses causes of deterioration of paper, deacidification, cleaning and bleaching, and watermarks; described the role of chemist in conservation.

843. Burgess, Dean. "The Library Has Blown Up!" Library Journal, 114:16 (October 1, 1989), 59-61. Post-mortem of an electrical fire; decisions made and lessons learned.

844. Burgess, Helen D., ed. Conservation of Historic and Artistic Works on Paper. Ottawa: Canadian Conservation Institute, 1994. 304p. (Symposium 88). Proceedings of a symposium; papers concerned with the survey, storage, and display of collections; treatment of books, archival materials, and fine art on paper.

845. Burgess, Helen D. "The Effect of Alkali on Long-Term Stability of Cellulose Fibers," Archivaria, 31 (Winter 1990-91), 218-223.

Discusses the reactions of different fibers and media to alkali.
Reprinted from Book and Paper Annual, 9 (1990).

846.   Burgess, Helen D. "The Effect of Alkali on Long-Term Stability of
        Cellulose Fibers," CCI Newsletter (Canadian Conservation Institute),
        (Autumn/Winter, 1990), 13-14. Note on a research project to address
        the reactions of different fibers, optimum treatment, and how
        differing media are affected.

847.   Burgess, Helen D. "Evaluation and Comparison of Commercial
        Mass-Deacidification Processes; Part 1: Project Planning and
        Selection of Materials," Book and Paper Group Annual, 10 (1991),
        22-42. Describes a testing program developed at the Canadian
        Institute for Conservation to assess several commercial processes.

848.   Burgess, Helen D. "Practical Considerations for Conservation
        Bleaching," Journal of the International Institute for
        Conservation-Canadian Group, 13:2 (1988), 11-26. Comprehensive
        review article incorporating results of several years of research at the
        Canadian Conservation Institute. 48 references.

849.   Burgess, Helen D. "The Use of Chelating Agents in Conservation
        Treatments," Paper Conservator, 15 (1991), 36-44. Provides an
        overview of the chemistry of four common chelating agents;
        discussion of selection of appropriate agents for conservation
        treatment of paper.

850.   Burgess, Helen D., and Nancy E. Binnie. "The Development of a
        Research Approach to the Scientific Study of Cellulose and Ligneous
        Materials," Journal of the American Institute for Conservation, 29:2
        (Fall 1990), 133-152. Describes rationale for project; characteristics
        of 25 papers and textiles selected for the study, and analytical
        procedures that were used. The project investigated the effects of a
        fumigant, sulphuryl fluoride (vikane) on cellulosic and ligneous
        materials.

851.   Burgess, Helen D., and Nancy E. Binnie. "The Effect of
        Vikane[TM] on the Stability of Cellulosic and Ligneous Materials ..
        Measurement of Deterioration by Chemical and Physical Methods,"
        Materials Issues in Art and Archaeology II, ed. Pamela B. Vandiver
        and James Durzik. Pittsburgh, PA: Materials Research Society,
        1991, 791-798. (Materials Research Society Symposium
        Proceedings, 185). Summarizes research at the Canadian
        Conservation Institute with the fumigant Vikane.

852.   Burgess, Helen D., and Aranka Boronyak-Szaplonczay. "Uptake of
        Calcium or Magnesium into Seven Papers During Aqueous

Immersion in Calcium or Magnesium Solutions," Conference Papers: Manchester 1992. Worcester, England: Institute of Paper Conservation, 1992, 264-272. Measures the calcium uptake of seven papers immersed in four chemical solutions; calcium hydroxide gave the greatest uptake in the paper. Appendix.

853.   Burgess, Helen, Stephen Duffy, and Season Tse. "Investigation of the Effect of Alkali on Cellulosic Fibers. Part 1: Rag and Processed Wood Pulp Paper," Paper and Textiles: The Common Ground. Glasgow, Scotland: Scottish Society for Conservation and Restoration, 1991, 29-47. Reports on the first part of a Canadian Conservation Institute study of the effect of washing and alkalization on various cellulosic fibers. Results indicate that various types of paper can react quite differently to the same process.

854.   Burgess, Helen D., and Douglas Goltz. "Effect of Alkali on the Long-Term Stability of Paper Fibers Containing Lignin," Archivaria (Association of Canadian Archivists), 37 (Spring 1994), 190-199. Concludes that lignin may be a contributing factor to alkaline sensitivity, and it is hard to predict which papers will be damaged by alkali.

855.   Burgess, Helen D., and David W. Grattan. "The Conservation of Parylene-Coated Books and Papers," Sauvegarde et Conservation des Photographies, Dessins, Imprimés et Manuscrits. Paris: ARSAG, 1991, 231-242. (Actes des Journeés Internationales d'Études de l'ARSAG, 1991). Testing of parylene papers to determine distribution of parylene in the papers and practicality for preservation.

856.   Burgess, Helen D., Elizbieta M. Kaminska, and Aranka Boronyak-Szaplonczay. Evaluation of Commercial Mass-Deacidification Processes: AKZO-DEZ, WEI T'O and FMC-MG3. Part 1: Naturally Aged Papers. Ottawa: Canadian Conservation Institute, 1992. 55p. Evaluation of the diethyl zinc progress (AKZO), FMC-Lithco, and Wei T'o.

857.   Burgess, Helen D., and Carolyn G. Leckie. "Evaluation of Paper Products with Special Reference to Use With Photographic Materials," Topics in Photographic Preservation, Washington, DC: American Institute for Conservation, Photographic Materials Group, 4 (1991), 96-105. Discusses aspects of the problem of evaluating and selecting appropriate paper materials for photographic collections. Reviews methods of testing paper.

858.   Burke, John. "Current Research Into the Control of Biodeterioration Through the Use of Thermal or Suffocant Conditions," AIC News

(American Institute for Conservation), 18:2 (March 1993), 1-4. A summary of research on pest control methods that are safe and effective. References.

859. Burke, Robert B., and Sam Adeloye. A Manual of Basic Museum Security. Leicester, U.K.: International Council of Museums/Leicestershire Museums, 1986. 125p. General manual for museums around the world.

860. Burn, Margy, and Alan Ventress. "Digitization Projects at the State Library of New South Wales," Preservation Microfilming: Does It Have a Future? Canberra: National Library of Australia, 1995, 111-117. Describes library's "commitment to achieve the mass digitization of the Australian Collections" (112), envisioning the "library without walls." Focus on access. No consideration of preservation issues.

861. Burrow, John, and Diane Cooper. Theft and Loss from U.K. Libraries: A National Survey. London: Home Office Police Department, 1992. 56p. (Crime Prevention Unit Service, 34). Details the findings of the first comprehensive survey of the financial loss borne by the main sectors of the library service; actions that are taken to combat problems; documents scope of loss and mutilation of library materials.

862. Butcher-Younghans, Sherry, and Gretchen E. Anderson. "A Holistic Approach to Museum Pest Management," History News, 45:3 (May-June 1990), 8 p. (Technical Leaflet 171). Discusses problems with traditional chemical pest control methods; describes use of freezing technology.

863. Butler, C. E., C. A. Millington, and David W. G. Clements. "Graft Polymerization: A Means of Strengthening Paper and Increasing the Life Expectancy of Cellulosic Archival Material," Historic Textile and Paper Materials II, ed. Howard L. Needles and S. Haig Zeronian. Washington, DC: American Chemical Society, 1989, 34-53. (ACS Symposium Series, 410). Describes technique and application to whole book treatment; discusses potential for commercial scale operations.

864. Butler, Janet Schecter. Contingency Planning and Disaster Recovery Strategies. Charleston, SC: Computer Technology Research Corp., 1994. 180p. This report explains how modern companies are vulnerable to computer-related disasters and offers practical guidance for establishing an effective disaster recovery plan.

865.   Butler, Meredith. "Electronic Publishing and Its Impact on Libraries: A Literature Review," <u>Library Resources and Technical Services</u>, 28:1 (January 1984), 41-58. Reviews issues in electronic publishing and their impact on libraries. Focuses on the implementation of technology.

866.   Butler, Randall. <u>Disaster at the Los Angeles Central Library: Fire and Recovery</u>. San Marino, CA: Society of California Archivists, 1991. 16p.

867.   Butler, Randall. "Disaster Planning in Nevada," <u>Conservation Administration News</u>, 48 (January 1992), 4-5. Describes a two day disaster recovery workshop focusing on the emergency planning cycle: prevention, preparation, response, and recovery.

868.   Butler, Randall. "Earthquake! The Experience of Two California Libraries," <u>Conservation Administration News</u>, 32 (January 1988), 1-2, 23-24. Describes damage that occurred during the earthquake that struck in October 1987 and the role that structure played in the amount of damage caused.

869.   Butler, Randall. "Grass Valley's Empire Mine: A Conservation Challenge for the Mining Frontier," <u>Conservation Administration News</u>, 34 (July 1988), 1-2.

870.   Butler, Randall. "Here Today ... Gone Tomorrow ... A pH Investigation of Brigham Young University's 1987 Library Acquisitions," <u>College and Research Libraries</u>, 51:6 (November 1990), 539-551. Report of a survey, with survey methodology and statistical model.

871.   Butler, Randall. "IELDRIN Stages Disaster Recovery Workshop." <u>Conservation Administration News</u>, 40 (January 1990), 1-3. Describes the disaster recovery training workshops sponsored by the Inland Empire Libraries Disaster Response Network, California.

872.   Butler, Randall. "LAPNet Holds First Workshop," <u>Conservation Administration News</u>, 35 (October 1988), 8-9.

873.   Butler, Randall. "The Los Angeles Central Library Fire," <u>Conservation Administration News</u>, 27 (October 1986), 1-2, 23-24; 28 (January 1987), 1-2. Description of damage caused and the library's approach to salvage.

874.   Butler, Robert W. <u>Preservation of Library Materials</u>. Beltsville, MD: National Agricultural Library, October 1991. 8p. Bibliography prepared to assist the NAL staff.

875.   Butterfield, Fiona J. "The Potential Long-Term Effects of Gamma
         Irradiation on Paper," Studies in Conservation, 32:4 (November
         1987), 181-191. Results of a study that indicate that some gamma
         irradiation causes an unacceptable level of paper deterioration.

876.   Butterfield, Fiona, and Linda Eaton, comp. Paper and Textiles: The
         Common Ground. Glasgow, Scotland: Scottish Society for
         Conservation and Restoration, 1991. 136p. Papers from a conference
         to address common technical problems and issues.

877.   Byer, Richard J., ed. "Densitomerty: Measuring for Quality
         Control," Inform, 2:1 (January 1988). Defines terms and explains
         how density is measured and interpreted. Edited from an article in
         Encyclopedia of Practical Photography.

878.   Byrne, Sherry. Collection Maintenance and Improvement.
         Washington, DC: Association of Research Libraries, 1993. 195p.
         (Preservation Planning Program). Describes the basic elements of a
         collection maintenance, or preservation, program to extend the useful
         life of library materials, with selected reprints from the library
         literature.

879.   Byrne, Sherry. "Guidelines for Contracting Microfilming Services,"
         Microform Review, 15:4 (Fall 1986), 253-264. Outlines the process
         involved in selecting a vendor for preservation microfilming.
         Sample contract.

880.   Byrne, Sherry, and Mark Roosa. "Microfilm Preserving Brittle Past
         for the Future," Inform, 2:7 (July/August 1988), 6-7. Report on the
         Preservation Microfilming Institute held at Yale University in April
         1988.

881.   Byrne, Sherry, and Barbara Van Deventer. "Preserving the Nation's
         Intellectual Heritage: A Synthesis," College and Research Libraries
         News, 53:5 (May 1992), 313-315. Reviews factors that led to a
         national strategy for preservation and the move toward
         comprehensive collection management programs in the 1990s.

882.   Byrnes, Margaret M. "Issues and Criteria for Comparing In-House
         and Contracted Microfilming," Preservation Microfilming. Chicago,
         IL: American Library Association, 1989, 32-42. Discussion of
         factors to be considered when deciding whether to attempt filming
         in-house or to contract with a preservation microfilming vendor.

883.   Byrnes, Margaret M. "Preservation and Collection Management:
         Some Common Concerns," Collection Building, 9:3/4 (1989),

39-45. Reprinted: The Collection Building Reader, ed. Betty-Carol Sellen and Arthur Curley. New York: Neal Schuman, 1992, 57-63. Describes the relation of preservation to collection development and management, with brief discussion of impact of new imaging technologies.

884.   Byrnes, Margaret M. "Preservation at the University of Michigan," Conservation Administration News, 18 (July 1984), 1-4. Description of program and conservation facility.

885.   Byrnes, Margaret M. "Preservation Microfilming at the National Library of Medicine," Watermark (Newsletter of the Association of Libraries in the History of the Health Sciences), 12:3 (Spring 1989), 14-15. Describes the NLM's preservation microfilming program, begun in 1986.

886.   Byrnes, Margaret M., ed. "Preservation of the Biomedical Literature," Bulletin of the Medical Library Association, 77:3 (July 1989), 257-298. Papers that address the need to preserve bio-medical literature.

887.   Byrnes, Margaret M. "Preservation of the Bio-Medical Literature: An Overview," Bulletin of the Medical Library Association, 77:3 (July 1989), 269-275. Reviews the early conservation and microfilming programs and current preservation activities at the National Library of Medicine.

888.   Byrnes, Margaret M. "Preservation of Library Materials, 1982," Library Resources and Technical Services, 27:3 (July-September 1983), 297-314. Review of the literature and trends of 1982.

889.   Byrnes, Margaret M., and Nancy E. Elkington. "Containing Preservation Microfilming Costs at the University of Michigan Library," Microform Review, 16:1 (Winter 1987), 37-39. Describes efforts to select materials for microfilming more carefully and to manage the preservation microfilming program more efficiently.

890.   Cadoree, Michelle. Computer Crime and Security. Washington, DC: Library of Congress, March 1994. 20p. (LC Science Tracer Bullet, TB 94-1). Annotated bibliography; guide to materials about computer crime and security, including references on viruses, networks, laws, and legislation.

891.   Cady, Susan A. "The Electronic Revolution in Libraries: Microfilm Deja Vu?" College and Research Libraries, 51:4 (July 1990), 374-386. Outlines the history of microfilming; warns that new technological advances may not solve all problems.

892.   Cahill, T. A., R. N. Schwab, B. H Kusko, R. A. Eldred, G. Moller, D. Dutschke, D. L. Wick, and A. S. Pooley. "The Vinland Map, Revisited: New Compositional Evidence on its Inks and Parchment," Analytical Chemistry, 59 (1987), 829-833. The authenticity of the Vinland map, purportedly dating from the mid-15th century, was studied due to previous studies indicating that ink of the map was composed of 20th-century titanium-based pigments containing up to 50% anatase. Therefore, the map ink and parchment were analyzed by PIXE. The analysis indicated that titanium and other medium and heavy elements were present in only trace amounts in the inks, reaching a maximum of 10 ng/cm2. Thus, the previous studies indicating that the map was a forgery must be reevaluated.

893.   Caiaccia, Laura, and Kristen Anderson, eds. Matboard & Glazing Standard Terminology. San Rafael, CA: Guild of Fine Art Care & Treatment Standards, Inc., 1995. 62p. Glossary, prepared to establish an industry standard terminology (includes TAPPI, ASTM).

894.   Cain, Eugene. "The Analysis of Degradation Products Extracted from Selected 19th Century Papers," Book and Paper Annual, 2 (1983), 15-19. Preliminary work to examine deteriorating papers by comparing their chromatographic patterns.

895.   Cains, Anthony. "The Book of Kells: The Exhibition and Transport of an Ancient Manuscript," Science, Technology, and European Cultural Heritage. Boston: Butterworth-Heinemann Publishers, 1991, 338-340. (Proceedings of the European Symposium, Bologna, Italy, 1989, published for the Commission of the European Communities). Describes the special moisture buffered transport and display system devised to travel with the manuscripts as they were exhibited in several museums in the United States.

896.   Cains, Anthony. "The Conservation, Repair and Preservation of Books and Manuscripts in Trinity College, Dublin," First National Conference of Craft Bookbinders — Australia. Kingston, Australia: Australian Craft Bookbinders Guild, November 1984, 1-5. Describes the organization and function of the conservation laboratory; treatment of paper, vellum, and parchment; bookbinding techniques.

897.   Cains, Anthony. "A Facing Method for Leather, Paper and Membrane," Conference Papers, Manchester 1992. Worcester, England: Institute of Paper Conservation, 1992, 153-157. Describes the use of an adhesive coated tissue during conservation treatments.

898.   Cains, Anthony. "In-Site Treatment of Manuscripts and Printed
         Books in Trinity College, Dublin," Conservation and Preservation in
         the Small Library, ed. Nicholas Hadgraft and Katherine Swift.
         Cambridge: Parker Library Publications, 1994, 127-131.
         Illus. Describes phase treatment to stabilize fragile materials, allow
         books to open and undertake a conservation assessment.

899.   Cains, Anthony. "Roger Powell and His Early Irish Manuscripts in
         Dublin," Conservation and Preservation in the Small Library, ed.
         Nicholas Hadgraft and Katherine Swift. Cambridge: Parker Library
         Publications, 1994, 151-156. Illus. Discusses two groups of bindings
         "which together represent the foundation of all present thought and
         methods of non-adhesive binding," (151) and influence of work
         during the Florence Flood, 1966.

900.   Cains, Anthony. "Sidney Morris Cockrell," Conservation and
         Preservation in the Small Library, ed. Nicholas Hadgraft and
         Katherine Swift. Cambridge: Parker Library Publications, 1994,
         157-160. A tribute to a master bookbinder; his concern for
         permanence.

901.   Cains, Anthony, and Paul Sheehan. "Preservation and Conservation
         in the Library of Trinity College, Dublin," International Library
         Review, 18:2 (April 1986), 173-178. The integration of a
         preservation program with a conservation component into the library;
         how this was accomplished at Trinity College, Dublin.

902.   Cains, Anthony, and Katherine Swift. Preserving Our Printed
         Heritage. Dublin, Ireland: Trinity College Library, 1988.
         24p. Illustrated pamphlet describing the preservation and
         conservation of the books in the Long Room, Trinity College
         Library.

903.   Calabro, Giuseppe, Maria Tanasi, and Giancarlo Impagliazzo. "An
         Evaluation Method of Softening Agents for Parchment," Restaurator,
         7:4 (1986), 169-180. Describes research undertaken to evaluate the
         measurement of stiffness in parchment and the effect of softening
         agents.

904.   Caldarano, Niccolo. "The Solander Box: Its Varieties and Its Role as
         an Archival Unit of Storage for Prints and Drawings in a Museum
         Archive or Gallery," Museum Management and Curatorship, 12
         (1993), 387-400. Review of the history, research on protective effect,
         evaluation of materials, design of construction, security aspects,
         costs, and suppliers of Solander boxes and alternative storage
         containers.

905.   Caldararo, Niccolo. "Tests on the Effects of the Use of Ultrasound in the Humidification of Paper," Book and Paper Group Annual, 11 (1992), 1-20. Reviews the use of ultrasound in conservation; compares the effects of humidification of paper by four procedures, including ultrasound humidification.

906.   Caldararo, Niccolo, and R. Ann Sheldon. "The Discovery of Hidden Drawings by Backing Removal: Three Examples Including a Charles Keene Drawing," Restaurator, 13:1 (1992), 1-22. Describes techniques for the removal of poor quality papers and boards from works of art on paper, with examples that uncovered other drawings. 59 references.

907.   Caldwell, Karen. "A Chemical Investigation of PVA Based Adhesives in Book Binding," AICCM Bulletin (Australian Institute for the Conservation of Cultural Materials), 17:1/2 (1991), 21-29. Report of an investigation of PVA and EVA adhesives currently used in commercial bookbinding and conservation; history, chemistry, characteristics.

908.   Calhoun, J. M. "The Physical Properties and Dimensional Behavior of Motion Picture Film," Journal of the Society of Motion Picture Engineers, 43:4 (October 1994), 227-266. A general discussion is given of the physical properties of both nitrate and safety motion picture film and how these properties are influenced by heat, moisture, and other factors.

909.   Cali, Charles L. "A Hidden Enemy: Acidity in Paper," Library and Archival Security, 7:3/4 (Fall/Winter 1985), 33-39. Discusses problems of paper manufacture, techniques of treating paper, and a review of the Wei T'o and DEZ deacidification processes.

910.   California State Library. California Cooperative Preservation Plan: Preliminary Draft. Sacramento: The California State Library, 1992. 34p. Prepared for the California Library and Archival Community and the California Library Networking Task Force.

911.   California State Library. The California Preservation Program. Sacramento, CA: 1995. 34p. A "call to action" to preserve the state's documentary heritage through cooperative initiatives, including a preservation information center, funding programs, identification of materials for preservation, education and training.

912.   Callu, Florence. "A Library in Action," Courier, 5 (May 1989) 10-11. Describes the Bibliothèque Nationale, France, and its collection of manuscripts; some of the new techniques for conservation are discussed.

913.   Calmes, Alan. "Documenting Changes in the Physical Condition of
        the US Declaration of Independence, Constitution, and Bill of
        Rights," Government Publications Review, 15:5 (September/October
        1988), 439-449. Describes the system designed to monitor and
        protect these cultural documents on permanent display in the nation's
        capitol.

914.   Calmes, Alan. "The National Archives' Charters Monitoring
        System," Conservation Administration News, 31 (October 1987),
        6. Describes the $3 million imaging system designed to monitor the
        condition of the Declaration of Independence.

915.   Calmes, Alan. "New Confidence in Microfilm," Library Journal,
        111:15 (September 15, 1986), 38-42. Reviews advances in image
        reproduction technology; reaffirms that microfilm is the most
        practical format for preservation of information.

916.   Calmes, Alan. "New Preservation Concern: Video Recordings,"
        Commission on Preservation and Access Newsletter, 22 (April
        1990), 5-6. Briefly discusses the problems with the preservation of
        video.

917.   Calmes, Alan. "The Paper Preservation Battle," The Record
        (National Archives and Records Administration), 1:4 (March 1995),
        1,8. General overview of brittle paper concerns and solutions,
        including the manufacture of alkaline papers. Notes that NARA will
        issue guidelines on the use of groundwood-containing paper and
        selection of papers that meet retention requirements of federal
        records.

918.   Calmes, Alan. "Plastics Found in Archives," Saving the Twentieth
        Century: The Conservation of Modern Materials, ed. David W.
        Grattan. Ottawa: Canadian Conservation Institute, 1993, 95-102.
        Examines the cycle of development, use, and obsolescence of
        plastics in recording media, aging characteristics, and consequences
        for preservation.

919.   Calmes, Alan. "Practical Aspects of Plastics Found in Archives,"
        Restaurator, 13:1 (1992), 23-36. Describes the variety of plastics
        found in archives, chiefly as information carriers. Notes that their
        composition is continually changing in manufacture and discusses
        storage as a means of retarding deterioration.

920.   Calmes, Alan. "Preservation Administration at the National Archives
        and Records Service," Conservation Administration News, 19
        (October 1984), 4-5.

921.   Calmes, Alan. "Preservation of Video Images," Journal of Imaging
       Science and Technology, 36 (January/February 1992), 1-3.
       Discusses the exponential increase in the use of videotape to
       preserve images and the lack of understanding of its impermanence
       by the public.

922.   Calmes, Alan. "Preservation Planning at the National Archives and
       Records Administration," Infinity (Society of American Archivists
       Preservation Section), 10:2 (Summer 1994), 2-3. Summary of
       proposed initiatives to move beyond the 20-year preservation plan of
       1985.

923.   Calmes, Alan. Preservation Priorities for Textual (Paper) Records at
       the United States National Archives. Washington, DC: NARS,
       1983. Unpublished status report on the National Bureau of
       Standards' survey of the NARS paper holding and on outline for a
       50-year preservation program. (See record for 20-year plan under
       U.S. National Archives and Records Service).

924.   Calmes, Alan. "Relative Longevity of Archival Information on
       Paper, Film, Magneti, and Optical Recording Media," Stability and
       Conservation of Photographic Images: Chemical, Electronic, and
       Material. Bangkok, Thailand: Society of Photographic Scientists and
       Engineers, 1986, 47-65. Describes the composition of paper, film,
       magnetic and optical recording media, with conservative estimates of
       life expectancy of each medium. 21 references.

925.   Calmes, Alan "Relative Longevity of Various Archival Recording
       Media," Conservation in Archives. Paris: International Council on
       Archives, 1989, 207-221. (Proceedings of an International
       Symposium, Ottawa, Canada, May 10-12, 1988). Analyzes the
       longevity of archival recording media, including paper, photographs,
       film, magnetic media, and optical disk, according to physical
       properties, storage environment, and frequency of use. Includes
       discussion of existing media standards and reformatting in response
       to demand for access.

926.   Calmes, Alan. "To Archive and Preserve: A Media Primer," Inform,
       1:5 (May 1987), 14-17. Brief evaluation of each medium for
       preserving permanently valuable archival information: paper,
       photographic film, magnetic tape, magnetic disk, optical digital disk.

927.   Calmes, Alan, and Norbert Baer. "National Archives Advisory
       Committee on Preservation: Science Advice to the Archivist of the
       United States," Restaurator, 10:1 (1989), 16-31. Provides a summary
       of the activities of the Advisory Committee on Preservation,

established in December 1979 as a response to a report concerning the deterioration of public records.

928. Calmes, Alan, Ralph Schofer, and Keith R. Eberhardt. "Theory and Practice of Paper Preservation for Archives," Restaurator, 9:2 (1988), 96-111. Addresses the challenge of preserving huge quantities of paper records by reducing the problem into manageable and efficient subtasks.

929. Calnan, Christopher N. "Aluminum Alkoxide Stabilization of Vegetable Tanned Leather," Environment et Conservation de l'Écrit, de l'Image et du Son. Paris: ARSAG, 1994, 102-105. (Actes des Deuxièmes Journées Internationales d'Etudes de l'ARSAG, 16 au 20 Mai, 1994). Reviews stabilization treatments for leather, including the use of aluminum alkoxides.

930. Calnan, Christopher N. and Betty Haines, eds. Leather: Its Composition and Changes with Time. Northampton, England: Leather Conservation Center, 1991. 90p. Fourteen papers presented at a 1986 conference. Provides a comprehensive scientific background to the structure, properties, and preparation of leather, and insight into various forms of deterioration.

931. Calnan, Christopher N. Fungicides Used on Leather. Northampton, England: Leather Conservation Centre, 1985. 19p. Provides information for the conservator on commercially available fungicides that were evaluated for the prevention of fungal attack on leather. 34 references.

932. Calvini, P., V. Grosso, M. Hey, L. Rossi, and L. Santucci. "Deacidification of Paper: A More Fundamental Approach," Paper Conservator, 12:3 (1988), 35-40. A study of the effects of basic compounds and sodium and lithium carbonates and bicarbonates on pure cellulose paper.

933. Cameron, E. "Various Methods and Standards of Library Binding," Books in Peril. Cape Town, South Africa: South African Library, 1987, 172-181. Discusses the need to define the types of binding needed for library collections and to develop appropriate standards.

934. Cameron, Ross J. National Archives and Records Administration Tape Administration and Preservation Evaluation Systems (TAPES). Washington, DC: National Archives and Records Administration. Center for Electronic Records, 1990. 21p.

935. Camp, John F. "Theft Detection Systems," Library Technology
Reports, 21:2 (March/April 1985), 121-156. Review of available
security equipment for libraries.

936. Campbell, Barbara. "Rare Government Documents: Identification
and Protection," Conservation Administration News, 42 (July 1990),
10-11. How to identify rare government publications and ensure their
protection.

937. Campbell, Gregor R. "Preservation," (Library binding process), New
Library Scene, 13 (October 1994) 5-6.

938. Campbell, Gregor R. "Quality Is Never an Accident," New Library
Scene, 14:2 (April 1995), 5-6. Describes the characteristics of a
quality bindery. For the trade, but useful for librarians.

939. Campbell, Harry. "The Book and Paper Conservator's Professional
Association, the American Institute for Conservation of Historic and
Artistic Works," Preservation Issues (Ohio State Library), 13 (June
1994), 2 leaves. Description of the founding, goals, and initiatives of
the Book and Paper Group and its Library Collections Conservation
Discussion Group (LCCDG).

940. Campbell, Harry H., and Wesley L. Boomgaarden. "The Ohio State
University Libraries Utilization of General Bookbinding Company's
Automated Binding Records System," Serials Review, 12 (Winter
1986), 89-99.

941. Campbell, Nancy, et al. "Through Innovation and Invention, MAPS
Breaks the Mold," OCLC Newsletter (Online Computer Library
Center), 203 (May/June 1993), 24-39. A special report on
MicrogrAphic Preservation Service, Inc., Bethlehem, Pennsylvania,
the non-profit preservation microfilming center that became a part of
OCLC in 1993. (Now called Preservation Resources).

942. Campbell, Robert P. "Disaster Recovery: A Game Plan," Security
Systems Administration, 12:3 (March 1983), 16-19. Contingency
planning and disaster recovery for computer operations.

943. Campion, Susan. "Wallpaper Newspapers of the American Civil
War," Journal of the American Institute of Conservation, 34:2
(Summer 1995), 129-140. Describes history of and treatment of three
Civil War newspapers printed on wallpaper.

944. Canada Emergency Preparedness. Guide to the Preservation of
Essential Records. Ottawa: Emergency Preparedness Canada, 1987.
123p. English/French. Guide for federal, provincial, and municipal

governments, and for industry "to ensure the survival of documents vital to the conduct of government ... in the event of a nuclear attack".

945.   Canada. National Archives. <u>Managing Photographic Records in the Government of Canada</u>. Ottawa: National Archives of Canada, 1993. 37p. English/French.

946.   Canada. National Archives. <u>National Archives of Canada Conservation Policy</u>. Ottawa: National Archives of Canada, November 5, 1987. 11p. English/French. Comprehensive policy statement to provide direction to staff and to communicate the principles that guide the National Archives.

947.   Canada. National Library. <u>Library Disaster Preparedness</u>. Ottawa: National Library of Canada, Federal Libraries Liaison Office, 1984. one portfolio. English/French.

948.   Canada, National Library. <u>Library Binding</u>. Ottawa: National Library of Canada, Federal Libraries Liaison Office, 1986. 2 vols.

949.   Canada, National Library. <u>A National Strategy for Preservation in Canadian Libraries</u>. Ottawa: National Library of Canada, 1992. 27p. English/French. Examines the current Canadian scene, identifies areas of concern, and makes recommendations for a coordinated national effort to preserve the holdings in Canadian libraries.

950.   Canadian Conservation Institute. <u>Computer Technology for Conservators: The Second Wave</u>. Ottawa: CCI, 1995. Papers cover systems analysis and design, database management systems for conservators, and other information for conservators. Proceedings of the 11th Annual 11C-CG Conference Workshop.

951.   Canadian Conservation Institute. <u>Display Methods for Books</u>. Ottawa: Canadian Conservation Institute, 1993, 2p. (English/ French). Special issue of <u>CCI Notes</u>, 11:6 (1993). Discusses considerations for the physical support of books going on display; support methods, materials, suppliers.

952.   Canadian Conservation Institute. "Emergency Preparedness for Cultural Institutions: Introduction." <u>CCI Notes</u> (Canadian Conservation Institute), 14/1 (1995), 2p. Covers need for emergency preparedness.

953. Canadian Conservation Institute. "Emergency Preparedness for Cultural Institutions: Identifying and Reducing Hazards." CCI Notes (Canadian Conservation Institute), 14/2 (1995), 6p.

954. Canadian Conservation Institute. Symposium 88. Conservation of Historic and Artistic Works on Paper. Conservation of Historic and Artistic Works on Paper: Proceedings of a Conference, Ottawa, Canada, October 3-7, 1988. Ottawa: The Institute, 1994. 304p. Edited by Helen D. Burgess.

955. Canadian Cooperative Preservation Project. Guidelines for Preservation Microfilming in Canadian Libraries. Ottawa: National Library of Canada, 1993. 45p. English/French.

956. Canadian Council of Archives. Basic Conservation of Archival Materials: A Guide. Ottawa: Canadian Council on Archives, 1990. 119p + index. English/French. A basic text covering environmental concerns; storage and handling; conservation treatments and repairs. Bibliography.

957. Canadian Council of Archives. Preservation Committee. The Preservation Strategy for Archives in Canada. Ottawa: March 1994. 40p. Bring together current preservation views of the Canadian archival community, and reflects a management approach toward the preservation of archival records. A plan for action.

958. Candee, Mary E., and Richard Casagrande, eds. (PREP, Planning for Response & Emergency Preparedness: a Disaster Preparedness/-Recovery Resource Manual. Austin, TX: Texas Association of Museums, 1993. One volume.

959. Caneva, Giulia, Maria Pia Nugari, and Ornella Salvadori. Biology in the Conservation of Works of Art. Rome: International Centre for the Study of the Preservation and the Restoration of Cultural Property, 1991. 182p. Provides basic information on the problems of biodeterioration; considers paper, parchment, and leather. Bibliographies; glossary.

960. Cardina, Claire A., and George Sedun. "A Solution to Microfilming Oversized Books," Inform, 5:9 (October 1991), 30-31. Describes an inexpensive method for supporting oversize books during microfilming.

961. "Caring for Compact Discs, Videos and Art Prints," Cape Librarian (South Africa), 36:4 (April 1992), 22-23. Brief note on basic care.

962.   Carl, Pauline L. "Crises at Old York: How It Affected the Library," New Jersey Libraries, 28:3 (Summer 1995), 9-11. Case Study: school library fire, and aftermath; efforts to provide service. Lessons learned.

963.   Carlson, Lage. comp. Margaret Brown illus. with Don Etherington and Linda Ogden. Boxes for the Protection of Books: Their Design and Construction. Washington, DC: Preservation Directorate, Collection Services, Library of Congress, 1994. One volume. A comprehensive manual, originally published by the Library of Congress in 1982, which was reprinted by Taurus Bookbindery, Berkeley, CA, 1993. 289p.

964.   Carmack, Noel A. "Post Binding as an Alternative to Leaf Attachment," Archival Products News, 3:3 (Summer 1995), 3-4. Instructions for constructing a post binding to keep fragmented, loose-leaf documents together in consecutive order, for access.

965.   Carmichael, David W. Organizing Archival Records: A Practical Method of Arrangement and Description for Small Archives. Harrisburg, PA: Pennsylvania Historical and Museum Commission, 1993. 53p. Workbook, addressing handling, storage, and preservation concerns.

966.   Carmine, Piero del, Maurice Grange, Franco Lucarelli, and Pier Andrea Mando. "Particle-Induced XRay-Emission with an External Beam: A Non-Destructive Technique for Material Analysis in the Study of Ancient Manuscripts," Ancient & Medieval Book Materials & Techniques. Vatican City: Biblioteca Apostolica Vaticana, 1993, II, 7-27. (Testi & Studi, 358) Proceedings of the ENU Conference, September 1992.

967.   "Carolyn Clark Morrow," OCLC Newsletter (Online Computer Library Center), 186 (July/August 1990), 23-28. Profile; Morrow reflects on preservation in libraries.

968.   Carpenter, Kenneth E., and Jane Carr. "Microform Publishing Contracts," Microform Review, 19:2 (Spring 1990), 83-100. A model contract outline "to help microform publishers and libraries work together effectively" in an option for preservation and access.

969.   Carr, Reg. "Problems of Security in Older Library Buildings," Security in Academic and Research Libraries, ed. Anthony G. Quinsee and Andrew C. McDonald. Newcastle-upon-Tyne, England: University of Newcastle Library, 1991, 6-16. Illus. Reviews problems and offers solutions in a case study of the Brotherton Library, University of Leeds.

970.   Carroll, Carman. "Conservation," <u>Canadian Archives in 1992</u>.
        Ottawa: Canadian Council of Archives, 1992, 114-134. Traces the
        development of preservation programs, education, and training; role
        of the CCA, CCI, National Archives, and Library; concern about
        formats; strategy for the future.

971.   Carroll, Carman U. "A National Conservation Strategy for Canada,"
        <u>SAA Newsletter</u> (Society of American Archivists), (July 1990), 21.

972.   Carroll, J. F., and John M. Calhoun. "Effect of Nitrogen Oxide
        Gasses on Processed Acetate Film," <u>SMPTE Journal</u> (Society of
        Motion Picture and Television Engineers), 5:1/2 (March/June 1983),
        9-15. Report of a study demonstrating that nitrate film should never
        be stored with acetate safety film.

973.   Carter, Henry A. "Chemistry in the Comics: Part 4, The Preservation
        and Deacidification of Comic Books," <u>Journal of Chemical
        Education</u>, 67:1 (January 1990), 3-7. Recommended procedures for
        the storage of comic books, usually printed on highly acidic paper,
        are examined from a chemical standpoint; methods for
        deacidification are discussed.

974.   Carter, Nancy Carol, and Jerry Dupont. "Microforms: Still a Future
        in Law Libraries," <u>Law Library Journal</u>, 76:2 (1983),
        339-344. Discusses the use of microforms as reliable, inexpensive
        preservation media, and argues that newer technologies, though
        promising, are not yet adequate.

975.   Cartier, Georges. "Libraries; Budgets and Budgeting; Repair and
        Maintenance," <u>Courier</u>, 5 (May 1989), 6-8. The role of national
        libraries in the preservation of manuscripts is discussed;
        responsibility of libraries to preserve their national heritage.

976.   Cartier-Bresson, Anne. "Restoring the Reproduction, Reproducing
        the Original," <u>Impact of Science on Society</u>, 42:168 (1992),
        357-365. Examines the levels of restoration of photographs and the
        need to clarify various purposes for treatment.

977.   Carver, Michael. "Lighting Design and Energy Efficiency in
        Museums and Galleries," <u>Museums Environment Energy</u>, ed. Mary
        Cassar. London: Her Majesty's Stationers Office, 1994,
        73-96. Discusses deleterious effects of light; examines how natural
        light and artificial light might effectively be used in museums.

978.   Casey, Mike. "Its Now or Never: A Framework for Making
        Decisions about Sound Recordings," <u>Preservation Papers of the 1991
        SAA Annual Conference</u>, comp. Karen Garlick. Chicago: Society of

American Archivists, 1992, 22-27. Elements include education and structural responsibility, discovering and evaluating holdings, prioritizing, making decisions, long-term development of program.

979.   Cashman , Nadine. ed. Visual Resources Association. Slide Buyer's Guide: An International Directory of Slide Sources for Art and Architecture. 6th ed. Littleton, CO: Libraries Unlimited, 1990. 190p. Provides art slide sources; discusses reproduction techniques, and evaluates quality.

980.   Cass, Glen R., James R. Druzik, Daniel Grosjean, William W. Nazaroff, Paul M. Whitmore, Cynthia L. Whittman. Protection of Works of Art from Atmospheric Ozone. Marina del Rey, CA: Getty Conservation Institute, 1990. 94p. Illus. (Research in Conservation, 5). Assesses the colorfastness of organic colorants and watercolor pigments tested in atmospheric ozone.

981.   Cassar, Mary. "Case Design and Climate Control: A Topological Analysis," Museum, 146 (1985), 104-107. Proposes typologies to standardize terminology for display case design.

982.   Cassar, Mary. "Checklists For the Establishment of a Microclimate," The Conservator, 9 (1985), 14-16. The details needed to produce a microclimate for the display of objects are given.

983.   Cassar, Mary. Environmental Management for Museums & Galleries. London: Routledge, 1995. 165p. Emphasizes need for planning and offers a strategic approach to environmental management; conservation audit; the built environment; environmental control.

984.   Cassar, Mary, ed. Museums Environment Energy. London: Her Majesty's Stationers Office, 1994. 130p. Papers on environmental control and energy efficiency, presenting conventional and alternative solutions.

985.   Cassaro, James P. "Video Formats and the Newest Library Acronyms: DAT and CD/V," Planning and Caring for Library Audio Facilities. Canton, MA: Music Library Association, 1989. 69p. (MLA Technical Report, 17). Discusses the physical nature and preservation challenge of videotape, videodisks, digital audio tape, and CD-video formats.

986.   Caulfield, D. F., and D. E. Gunderson. "Paper Testing and Strength Characteristics," Paper Preservation: Current Issues and Recent Developments. Atlanta, GA: TAPPI Press, 1990, 43-52. Reviews

mechanical and strength properties of paper; strength may serve as an indicator of permanence.

987. Cavasin, Rick. "Parchment vs. Vellum: What's the Difference?" CBBAG Newsletter (Canadian Bookbinders and Book Artist Guild), 14:2 (Summer 1996), 11-13. Discusses the various types of parchment available and their uses.

988. Center for Research Libraries. Final Report of the Preservation Planning Program Study Team. Washington, DC: Association of Research Libraries, Office of Management Studies, 1986. 47p. Describes self-study methodology, makes recommendations, and presents prioritized plans; one of ten final reports from libraries involved in the Association of Research Libraries Office of Management Studies (ARL/OMS) Preservation Planning Program (PPP).

989. Central New York Library Resources Council. Preservation Committee. Preservation Needs Assessment: A Management Tool. Syracuse, NY: Central New York Library Resources Council, 1993. 45p. Describes a project undertaken by 10 libraries to assess preservation needs and priorities using the CALIPR computer-assisted methodology.

990. Centre de Recherche sur la Conservation des Documents Graphiques (CRCDG). Les Documents Graphiques et Photographiques: Analyse et Conservation; Travaux du C.R.C.D.G., 1991-1993. Paris: La Documentation Francaise, 1993. 280p. Contains the results of work carried out at the center; covers study and conservation of autochromes, mirroring on photographs, stain removal on parchment, stability of printer's inks, stability of photocopies.

991. Centre for Photographic Conservation. The Imperfect Image: Photographs; Their Past, Present and Future. London: Centre for Photographic Conservation, 1992. 379. 52 papers by leading photographic conservators, scientists, historians, and curators.

992. Chaback Claudia E. A Performance Comparison Between a Wide-Hinged Endpaper Construction and the Library Binding Institute Standard Endpaper Construction. Rochester, NY: Rochester Institute of Technology, 1987. 93p. Masters thesis.

993. Chace, Myron B. "Preservation Microfiche: A Matter of Standards," Library Resources and Technical Services, 35:2 (April 1991), 186-190. Discusses the standards necessary to ensure the permanence of reformatted preservation copies and describes the standards available for microfiche. Standards for preservation microfiche are

presently (1991) being developed by librarians, archivists, and representatives from corporate and other concerned organizations.

994.   Chace, Myron. "Preservation Microfilming: Standards and Specifications," Preservation Microfilming: Planning and Production. Chicago, IL: American Library Association, 1989, 16-31. A thorough review of the standards and specifications for the microfilming process.

995.   Chadbourne, Robert. "Declaring War on Deterioration: David Magoon Wants to Help," Wilson Library Bulletin, 61:1 (September 1986), 44-48. Profile of David Magoon, President of University Products, supplier of archival quality materials for libraries and archives, and an interview with Ann Russell, Director, Northeast Documents Conservation Center.

996.   Chamberlain, W. R. "A New Approach to Treating Fungus in Small Libraries," Biodeterioration Research I, ed. G. C. Llewellyn and C. E. O'Rear. New York: Plenum Press, 1987, 323-327; updated in Abbey Newsletter, 15:7 (November 1991), 109-111. Basic steps for treating infested areas and discussion of problems that need basic research. Paper originally presented at the First Pan-American Biodeterioration Society Annual Meeting, Washington, DC, July 1986.

997.   Champion, Sandra, and Christine Master. "When Disaster Strikes," School Library Journal, 39:9 (September 1993), 146-149. Assessment of conditions a year after Hurricane Andrew struck Florida.

998.   Chandel, A. S., and R. K. Walia. "Computer-Assisted Stock-Verification System," Libri, 43:2 (1993), 108-122. Describes a system, using dBase III+ and teams of workers to verify that materials are on the shelf, and to establish what is missing

999.   Chaney, Michael, and Alan F. MacDougall, ed. Security and Crime Prevention in Libraries. Aldershot, England: Ashland, 1992. 370p. Provides an assessment of the present situation in the United Kingdom, possible solutions and answers to the problems of vandalism, theft, and violence in the library.

1000.   Chapman, Patricia. "Finance and Policy in Preservation Programs," In Safe Keeping, ed. Jennifer Thorp. Winchester, England: Hampshire County Library/Hampshire Archives Trust, 1988, 36-39. Discusses scope of policies, determining costs of action or inaction.

1001.   Chapman, Patricia. Guidelines on Preservation and Conservation
         Policies in the Archives and Libraries Heritage. Paris: UNESCO,
         1990. 40p. (A RAMP Study; PGI 90/WS/7). Model for helping
         institutions develop their own preservation program.

1002.   Chapman, Patricia. "The National Preservation Office," Archives,
         19:81 (April 1989), 26-29. Describes the establishment and activities
         of the British Library's National Preservation Office.

1003.   Chapman, Patricia. "The National Preservation Office," Assistant
         Librarian, 81:1 (January 1988), 6-8. Describes the goals and
         objectives of the National Preservation Office, established on the
         recommendation of the Radcliffe report.

1004.   Chapman, Patricia, and Stephanie Kenna. "Substitution Microforms:
         A Survey of the Policies and Practices in UK Libraries," Library
         Association Record, 90:5 (May 1988), 282-285. Report of a survey;
         concludes that staff and readers need to be educated about the
         reasons for microfilm substitution.

1005.   Chappas, W. J., and N. McCall. "The Use of Ionizing Radiation in
         Disinfestation of Archival and Manuscript Materials,"
         Biodeterioration 6, ed. S. Barry and D. R. Houghton. London:
         International Mycological Institute/Biodeterioration Society, 1986,
         370-373. (Papers, 6th International Biodeterioration Symposium,
         Washington, DC).

1006.   Charles, Embert. "Breakdown of Sound and Image Carriers in the
         Caribbean," Archiving the Audio-Visual Heritage. Ruston, England:
         FIAF/UNESCO, 1992, 13-16. Discusses the problem of storage and
         protection of magnetic tape in a tropical region with a lack of
         resources.

1007.   Chartand, Robert Lee. "Libraries in Parlous Times: Responsibilities
         and Opportunities: An Introduction," Special Libraries, 78:2 (Spring
         1987), 73-85. Analysis of the planning necessary for emergency
         management (EM) and the role that technology can, and cannot play.
         Describes some of the recently developed EM systems.

1008.   Chavez, Alice M. "Library Crime and Security in Academic
         Libraries in Texas," Library and Archival Security, 12:1 (1993),
         55-78. Overview of theft problem; study of levels of security
         maintained in academic libraries in Texas.

1009.   Cheatham, Bertha M. "A Fight for Rights: A Year in Review,"
         School Library Journal, 35:16 (December 1989), 29-35. Review

article of trends, including the preservation of materials in school library collections.

1010. Chen, Chiou-sen Dora. Serials Management: A Practical Guide. Chicago, American Library Association, 1995. 186p. (Frontiers of Access to Library Materials, 3). Text on all aspects of serials management: acquisition, organization, collection management, and deaccessioning. Ch. 7, pp. 99-106, "Preservation and Bindery": deals clearly and concisely with preservation concerns and the binding process. Clearly written, well-organized text.

1011. Chepesiuk, Ron. " An Anatomy of a Move: The Clemson University Library Special Collections," Wilson Library Bulletin, (June 1991), 32-35, 155.

1012. Chepesiuk, Ron. "Cambodian Libraries in Crisis: The Cornell University Library Preserves a Heritage," Wilson Library Bulletin, 66:5 (January 1992), 3-33. Describes the condition of materials in the Cambodian National Library and National Archives and the efforts of John Dean and colleagues from Cornell University to train staff to preserve them.

1013. Chepesiuk, Ron. "The Conservation Laboratory at Trinity College in Dublin, Ireland," New Library Scene, 5:5 (October 1986), 1, 5. Interview with book conservator Anthony Cains; his philosophy and conservation at the library.

1014. Chepesiuk, Ronald. "Education of an Apprentice: Conservation at Johns Hopkins," Wilson Library Bulletin, 60:1 (September 1985), 43-46. Profile of John Dean and the apprenticeship program he established at Eisenhower Library, Johns Hopkins University.

1015. Chernofsky, Jacob L. "Major Libraries Offered Joint Publishing Role," AB Bookman's Weekly (Antiquarian Bookman), 82:1 (July 4, 1988), 35-38. Profile of Stephen Easton and his company, Archival Facsimiles, Inc., which provides reprints of rare and fragile books; its collaboration with the British Library.

1016. Chernofsky, Jacob L. "The Rocky Road to Electronic Publishing," AB Bookman's Weekly (Antiquarian Bookman), 90:1 (1993), 11. Discusses the fate of the printed book as electronic text becomes more common. Argues that the printed book will not be entirely superseded.

1017. Chicago (IL) Public Library. Special Collections. Preserving Historical Collections. Chicago, IL: Chicago Public Library, 1986. 5p.

1018.   Chickering, F. William. Preservation of Nonprint Materials in Working Collections: A Basic Bibliography. Atlanta: SOLINET, 1985, 9p. (SOLINET Preservation Program Leaflet 3) Covers general works, film media, magnetic tape media, sound recordings. No annotations.

1019.   Chiesa, Adele M. "Identifying the Emergency Management Profession," Special Libraries, 78:2 (Spring 1987), 88-92. How to build an emergency management library collection.

1020.   Child, Bob. "Fumigation and the Rentokil Bubble," Library Conservation News, 32 (July 1991), 1-3. Briefly describes the portable, air-tight bubble that can be deployed to isolate infested collections for treatment.

1021.   Child, Margaret S. "Crystal-Gazes," Research Libraries Group News, 32 (Fall 1993), 9. Talk on libraries, archives, and museums in the 21st century.

1022.   Child, Margaret S., comp. Directory of Information Sources on Scientific Research Related to the Preservation of Sound Recordings, Still and Moving Images and Magnetic Tape. Washington, DC: Commission on Preservation and Access, September 1993. 14p. Provides information about institutions and associations undertaking research and/or providing information about the preservation and restoration of these materials; list of information databases, serials, readings, and proceedings.

1023.   Child, Margaret S. "Further Thoughts on Selection for Preservation: A Materialistic Approach," Library Resources and Technical Services, 30:4 (October/December 1986), 354-362. Amplification of Atkinson approach to selection for preservation, with a strategy for preservation of information through microfilming.

1024.   Child, Margaret S. "The Future of Cooperative Preservation Microfilming," Library Resources and Technical Services, 29:1 (January/March 1985), 94-101. Discussion of initiatives and how librarians can approach cooperative microfilming projects.

1025.   Child, Margaret S. "NEH Support For Special Collections," Library Trends, 36:1 (Summer 1987), 215-228. Discusses programs that supported projects for preservation and access.

1026.   Child, Margaret S. "New Techniques in Preservation," Perspectives, 24:4 (April 1986), 11-12.

1027.   Child, Margaret S. "Preservation Issues for Collection Development
         Staff," Wilson Library Bulletin, 67:3 (November, 1992), 20-21,
         106. Notes need to focus on nature of collections for preservation
         decisions; discusses planning and surveys to identify needs.

1028.   Child, Margaret S. "Preservation Planning," NEDCC News
         (Northeast Documents Conservation Center), 6:2 (Winter 1996), 4-5.

1029.   Child, Margaret S. "Selections for Microfilming," American
         Archivist, 53 (Spring 1990), 250-255. Discusses selection of records
         for preservation in an archival content. Emphasizes the need to
         incorporate preservation considerations into all phases of archives
         administration.

1030.   Child, Margaret S. "Selection for Preservation," Advances in
         Preservation and Access. Vol. 1. Westport, CT: Meckler, 1992,
         147-158. Discussion of criteria for selection of materials for
         preservation and a review of the "great collections" strategy,
         strengths, and weaknesses.

1031.   Childress, Schelley. "Planning for the Worst: Disaster Planning in
         the Library," Southeastern Librarian, 44:2 (Summer 1994), 51-55.
         Outlines the steps in preparing a disaster plan based on St. Andrews
         Presbyterian College Library.

1032.   Chiou-sen, Chen. "New Directions in Library Binding: Life After
         'Class A,'" Conservation Administration News, 39 (October 1989),
         17-18. Report on a binding seminar jointly sponsored by the Library
         Binding Institute and the Preservation of Library Materials Section,
         American Library Association.

1033.   Chisholm, Bill. "Why Electronic Imaging Needs Archive
         Microfilm," Preservation Microfilming: Does It Have a Future?
         Canberra: National Library of Australia, 1995, 128-130. The legal
         reasons for documentation preserved on microfilm, and the role of
         scanning to enhance some images. Advocates hybrid technology.

1034.   Christensen, Carol. "Environmental Standards: Looking Beyond
         Flatlining?" AIC News (American Institute of Conservation), 20:5
         (Sept. 1995) 1, 4-8. Discusses the reception and impacts of the
         Conservation Analytical Laboratory's new guidelines indicating that
         RH between 35% & 65% with fluctuations of 10% as being safe for
         most objects.

1035.   Christensen, John O. "Extended Life for Popular Paperbacks,"
         Library Journal, 114:16 (October 1, 1989), 65-66. Results of a study
         that demonstrated that the covering of mass market paperbacks with

contact paper for circulating collections was the most cost-effective preservation measure.

1036. Christofferson, Lars D. "Resource-Saving Storage of Historical Material," Preprints: ICOM Committee for Conservation 10th Triennial Meeting, ed. Janet Bridgland. Washington DC: International Council of Museums, 1993, 601-604. Describes a collaborative project to map the thermal values and humidity of outdoor climate, building, indoor climate, and storage areas to determine climate control requirements.

1037. Chrzastowski, Tina, David Cobb, Nancy Davis, Jean Geil, and Betsy Kruger. "Library Collection Deterioration: A Study at the University of Illinois at Urbana-Champaign," College and Research Libraries, 50:5 (September 1989), 577-584. Report of a survey of the physical condition of collections; methodology, costs.

1038. Churchville, Lida Holland, and Catherine Hale, comp. Disaster Planning. Washington, DC: National Archives and Records Service Library Information Center, 1990. 23p. (ALIC Bibliography, 1990-1). 228 citations on disaster preparedness and recovery measures.

1039. "Citing No Increased Cost, NISO Urges Use of Acid-Free Paper," Publishers Weekly (February 19, 1988), 16. Librarians and NISO are urging publishers to replace current acid-containing papers with alkaline papers, citing alkaline papers are cheaper to produce and will eliminate one large cause of deteriorating books.

1040. Clack, George. "Preserving Yesterday's News," Humanities, 8:1 (January-February 1987), 24-26; reprinted in New Library Scene, 6:2 (April 1987), 20-21. Note on the U.S. Newspaper Program for preservation and access to all newspapers published in the United States.

1041. Clancy, Elizabeth H. "Practical Procedures for Preserving Photographic Potpourri," Preserving Geoscience Imagery, ed. Louise S. Zipp. Alexandria, VA: Geoscience Information Society, 1993, 13-21. (Proceedings, 23). How to organize, document, and store photographs.

1042. Clapp, Anne F. Curatorial Care of Works of Art on Paper: Basic Procedures for Paper Preservation. New York: Nick Lyons Books, 1987. 191p. Text for conservators and conservation technicians who care for works of art on paper; covers factors potentially harmful to paper and treatments.

1043. Clapperton, John R. Introduction to Bookbinding and Book and Music Repairing. Edinburgh: J. Clapperton, 1995. 12p.

1044. Claremont Colleges. Exhibition Design: Book Supports; Interim Report. Claremont, CA: Claremont Colleges, 1990. 9p. Study and analysis of book supports by students in the Liberal Arts Clinic Program.

1045. Clareson, Thomas F. R., Norman Howden, Kenneth Lavender, and Lisa C. Roberts. AMIGOS Preservation Service Needs Assessment Survey Analysis; Final Report. Dallas, TX: AMIGOS Bibliographic Council, 1992. 80 p., 18 page survey. Discussion of the survey, applicability, clarity, and results.

1046. Clareson, Thomas F.R. "Education, Communication, and Cooperation: OCLC's Preservation Program," OCLC Micro (Online Computer Library Center), 6:6 (December 1990), 10-12. OCLC's role in preservation through bibliographic control, research, programmatic alliances, and education.

1047. Clareson, Thomas F.R.. "The RONDAC Preservation Survey," Conservation Administration News, 47 (October 1991), 14, 27, 29. Discusses the needs assessment survey undertaken by Margaret Child in 1990; summarizes results.

1048. Clareson, Thomas F. R. "'Selling Preservation' Session Attracts Many 'Customers,'" (at the 1994 ALA Conference), Conservation Administration News, 61 (April 1995), 14-15.

1049. Clark, Lenore, ed. Guide to Review of Library Collections: Preservation, Storage, and Withdrawal. Chicago, IL: American Library Association, 1991. 41p. (Collection Management and Development Guide, #5). Prepared to assist librarians responsible for reviewing materials in general collections for preservation; based on a review of the literature, existing policies and practices.

1050. Clark, Tony. Bookbinding with Adhesives. London; New York: McGraw Hill, 1988. 79p. Illus. Basic guide for managers and machine operators on adhesives and their use in commercial binding. Covers adhesive types, how they work, and systems for their use. Glossary.

1051. Clarke, Reginald. "Conservation at the University of West Indies," Conservation Administration News, 58-59 (July/October 1994) p. 25-27.

1052.   Clarke, Reginald. "Construction-Related Threats to Library
        Collections," <u>Library Conservation News</u>, 51 (Summer 1996),
        4-5. Case Study of water damage and mold infestation that occurred
        during a renovation project; salvage, lessons learned.

1053.   Clarkson, Christopher. "Books and Manuscripts," <u>Sotheby's Caring
        for Antiques: A Guide to Handling, Cleaning, Display and
        Restoration</u>, ed. Mette Tang Simpson and Michael Huntley. London:
        Octopus, 1992, 141-147. Briefly discusses the history of
        bookbinding and paper, proper care and conservation of collections.

1054.   Clarkson, Christopher. "Conservation Priorities: A Library
        Conservator's View," <u>Conservation of Library and Archive Materials
        and the Graphic Arts</u>. London: Butterworths, 1987, 235-238.

1055.   Clarkson, Christopher. <u>Limp Vellum Binding and Its Potential as a
        Conservation Type Structure for the Rebinding of Early Printed
        Books: A Break With Nineteenth and Twentieth Century Rebinding
        Attitudes and Practices</u>. Hitchen, Herts., England: Red Gull Press,
        1989. 23p. Reviews the history of this binding technique; provides
        instructions.

1056.   Clarkson, Christopher. "Preservation and Conservation of Library
        and Archive Collections," <u>Paper Conservation News</u>, 74 (June 1995),
        6-7. Notes and thoughts on collection care, with discussion of the
        role of preservation and conservation, and an examination of
        restoration. Emphasizes the need for historical awareness and careful
        documentation of treatments to books. Emphasizes need to consider
        book as artifact.

1057.   Clarkson, Christopher. "Rediscovering Parchment: The Nature of
        the Beast," <u>Conservation and Preservation in the Small Library</u>, ed.
        Nicholas Hadgraft and Katherine Swift. Cambridge: Parker Library
        Publications, 1994, 75-96. Illus. Discusses the physical nature of
        parchment, damage found in the material; storage and proper
        handling. Illus. With Comments on structure and damage. Also in
        <u>Paper Conservator</u>, 16 (1992), 5-26.

1058.   Clarkson, Christopher. "Some Conservation Considerations at
        Oxford and the Bodlian Library," <u>Oxbow Diary: Paper and Book
        Intensive '85</u>, ed. Barbara Mauriello. Saugatuck, MN: Ox Bow Paper
        and Book Intensive, 1985. Gives a history of each of the Oxford
        libraries and discusses the conservation problems in the Bodleian
        collection, with some possible preservation solutions.

1059.   Clarkson, Christopher. "Thoughts on Sewing Frame Design for the
        Book Conservator," <u>Paper Conservator</u>, 19 (1995), 41-54. Brief

history of binding structure; describes the author's attempts to design and make a sewing frame for book conservation.

1060.   Clement, Daniel "The Blistering of Paper During Hydrogen Peroxide Bleaching," Journal of the American Institute for Conservation, 23:1 (Fall 1983), 47-62.

1061.   Clements, David W. G. "The Current Work of the British Library and Its Possible Future Contribution," Journal of Librarianship, 17:2 (April 1985), 91-94. Views preservation needs from the perspective of the British Library and suggests how that library might assist other institutions.

1062.   Clements, David W. G. "Developments in Preservation," British Book News, (April 1988), 260-262. Discusses preservation and use of "long-life-paper."

1063.   Clements, David W. G. "Disaster Preparedness: Why You Should Take Action," Library Association Record, 89:8 (1987), 394. Results of a survey of institutions to determine how many have disaster contingency plans.

1064.   Clements, David W. G. "Emerging Technologies-Paper Strengthening," Restaurator, 8:2/3 (1987), 124-128. Brief report on the British Library project to develop a method for strengthening books without disbinding by impregnation with monomer acrylics that are polymerized by irradiation; research in progress.

1065.   Clements, David W. G. "Graft Copolymerization Techniques for Strengthening Deteriorated Paper: British Library Developments," Paper Preservation: Current Issues and Recent Developments. Atlanta, GA: TAPPI Press, 1990, 149-150. Describes a process that offers promising results for paper strengthening based on graft copolymerization techniques initiated by low-intensity gamma radiation.

1066.   Clements, David W. G. "The National Preservation Office in the British Library," IFLA Journal (International Federation of Library Associations and Institutions), 12:1 (February 1986), 25-32. Describes the National Preservation Program in Great Britain, which developed from the Radcliffe report; emphasis on information provider, through a National Preservation Office.

1067.   Clements, David W. G. "Paper Strengthening at the British Library," Preservation of Library Materials, New York: K. G. Saur, 1987, 152-155. Describes the research underway sponsored by the British Library.

1068.   Clements, David W. G. People's Republic of China: Preservation of
         Library Collections. Paris: UNESCO, 1985. portfolio.
         (FMR/PGI/85/174).

1069.   Clements, David W. G. "Planning for Disaster Control," Security
         Systems, Vandalism and Disaster Planning in Libraries, ed. Royston
         Brown and Hilary Spiers. Stamford, Lincolnshire, England: Capital
         Planning Information, 1988, 1-9. Seminar paper covering need for
         security and response measures, risk assessment, and recovery of
         damaged materials.

1070.   Clements, David W. G. "Policies for Collection and Retention,"
         Managing the Preservation of Serial Literature, ed. Merrily Smith.
         New York: K.G. Saur, 1992. 17-23. IFLA Publication 57.

1071.   Clements, David W. G. "Policy Planning in the UK: From National
         to Local," Preserving the Word. London: Library Association, 1987,
         17-25. (Library Association Conference Proceedings, Harrogate,
         1986). Describes the approach to preservation taken by British
         libraries, reviewing options from accession to use.

1072.   Clements, David W. G., ed. Preservation and Conservation of
         Library and Archival Documents, A UNESCO/IFLA/ICA Enquiry
         Into the Current State of the World's Patrimony. Paris: UNESCO,
         1987. 32p. (RAMP Study, PGI-87/WS/15). Survey indicated that
         there is a strong need for education and training.

1073.   Clements, David W. G. "Preservation and Library School Education
         Programmes," Library Association Record, 88:3 (1986),
         136-137. Report on a survey of education for preservation in British
         library schools following a conference, "Organizing for
         Conservation." Notes inertia toward revision of curricula and
         syllabi.

1074.   Clements, David W. G. "Preservation in Original Format: Policies
         and Options," Preservation of Library Materials, ed. Merrily Smith.
         New York: K.G. Saur, 1987, 43-48. IFLA Publication. 40-41.

1075.   Clements, David W. G. "Preservation Microfilming and Substitution
         Policy in the British Museum," Microform Review, 17:1 (February
         1988), 17-22. Discusses the decision-making process and the role of
         surrogate copies; costs and contracting.

1076.   Clements, David W. G. "Preservation Needs and Trends," Library
         Automation and Networking: New Tools for a New Identity, ed. H.
         Liebaers and M. Walckiers. Munich, Germany: Saur, 1991,

87-91. Describes initiatives to preserve the documentary heritage; emphasizes need for cooperative approaches to selection, collection retention, and preservation. Paper originally presented at the European Foundation for Library Cooperation Conference, May 1990.

1077. Clements, David W. G. "Problems of Cooperative Microfilming," Collection Management, 15:3-4 (1992), 503-507. Discusses the need for resource sharing and the development of cooperative microfilming projects in Europe. Paper from the conference "Shared Resources, Shared Responsibilities," Florence, 1988.

1078. Clements, David W. G. "Problems of the Treatment of Modern Paper Produced Over the Last One Hundred Years," Liber Bulletin, 31 (1988), 25-34. Discusses approaches being taken in the preservation of modern paper.

1079. Clements, David W. G. "The Role of Education and Training in the Preservation of the Archival Heritage," Politics for the Preservation of the Archival Heritage. Paris: International Council on Archives, 1989, 159-173. Notes need to increase awareness of preservation problems as well as to train staff in collection management and preservation. Outlines a program for training conservators, technicians, and managers of collections.

1080. Clements, David W. G. "Seminar on Preservation and Conservation of Library Materials," IFLA Journal (International Federation of Library Associations and Institutions), 14:3 (1988), 281-282.

1081. Clements, David W. G., and Jean-Marie Arnoult. "Preservation Planning in Europe," IFLA Journal (International Federation of Library Associations and Institutions), 14:4 (1988), 354-360. Summary of preservation activities in European countries.

1082. Clements, David W. G., and Jean-Marie Arnoult. "Special Issue on Preservation and Conservation," IFLA Journal (International Federation of Library Associations and Institutions), 20:3 (1994), 260-356.

1083. Clements, David W. G., and George Boston. "Special Issue on the Memory of the World Programme" (new UNESCO PGI initiative), IFLA Journal (International Federation of Library Associations and Institutions), 21:3 (1995), 168-212.

1084. Clements, David W. G., C. E. Butler, and C. A. Millington. "Paper Strengthening at the British Library," Conservation in Archives. Paris: International Council on Archives, 1988, 45-50. Report on the research into strengthening of paper by impregnation with polymers at the British Library; discusses mass treatments by chemical means as an alternative to reformatting. Paper presented at an International Symposium, Ottawa, Canada, May 1988.

1085. Clements, David W. G., J. H. McIlwaine, A.C. Thurston, and S. A. Rudd. Review of Training Needs in Preservation and Conservation. Paris: UNESCO, 1989. 47p. (RAMP study PGI-89\WS\15). Presents the results of a UNESCO-sponsored survey of the provisions made for training conservators internationally; recommendations for further action.

1086. Clements, David W. G., and D. L. Thomas. Guidelines on Best Practices in Basic Collection Management for Non-professional Staff and on the Organization of Training Courses. Paris: UNESCO, June 1992. 27p.

1087. Clements, Jeff. "On Inlaying Techniques," New Bookbinder, 11 (1991), 47-53. Discusses the use of inlaying in bookbinding design; use of experimental materials mentioned.

1088. Clemmer, Dan. "Preservation By All Means," FLICC Newsletter (Federal Library and Information Center Committee), 159 (Winter 1992), 7-8. Discusses rational for rebinding two rare volumes.

1089. Cleveland Area Metropolitan Library System. A Model Plan for Library Disaster Preparation. Cleveland, OH: CAMLS, 1983. 30 leaves.

1090. Cloonan, Michèle Valerie. "ALISE Preservation SIG," Conservation Administration News, 45 (April 1991), 16. Report on the Preservation Special Interest Group (SIG) of the Association for Library and Information Science Education (ALISE) in Chicago, January 10, 1991.

1091. Cloonan, Michèle Valerie. "An Analysis of Dust Cloths for Library Materials," Abbey Newsletter, 7:3 (July 1983), 35.

1092. Cloonan, Michèle Valerie. "Bookbinding, Aesthetics, and Conservation," Libraries & Culture, 30:2 (Spring 1995), 137-152. Review of a century of discussion about what constitutes a sound bookbinding; how and whether books should be rebound, restored, or left untreated. The views of librarians, bibliographers, bookbinders, and conservators are considered in a debate that continues today, a tension between treatment and stabilization, to be sure that bibliographic evidence remains for future scholars.

1093. Cloonan, Michèle Valerie. Early Bindings in Paper: A Brief History of European Hand-Made Paper-Covered Books with a Multilingual Glossary. Boston, MA: GK. Hall, 1991, 146p. Illus. History of paper bookbindings, with glossary of descriptive terms. Bibliography.

1094. Cloonan, Michèle Valerie. Global Perspectives on Preservation Education. Munich, Germany; New Providence, NJ: K.G. Saur, 1994. 109p. (IFLA Publication, 69). A review of trends and direction in education for preservation of library and archival materials, with recommendations for future training, and the role that the International Federation of Library Associations and Institutions (IFLA) can play.

1095. Cloonan, Michèle Valerie. "An Influential 20th Century German-American Bookbinder: Remembering Kathryn (Posy) Gerlach (1908-1993)," Conservation Administration News, 56 (January 1994), 10-11. Profile and remembrance of an influential teacher by a former student.

1096. Cloonan, Michèle Valerie. "Mass Deacidification in the 1990s," Rare Books and Manuscripts Librarianship, 5:2 (1990), 95-103. A review of the development of mass treatments for the preservation of paper-based materials.

1097. Cloonan, Michèle Valerie. Organizing Preservation Activities. Washington, DC: Association of Research Libraries, 1993. 98p. (Preservation Planning Program). Considers staffing, organization, and structure of preservation activities, with selected readings.

1098. Cloonan, Michèle Valerie. "Preservation Education in American Library Schools: Recounting the Ways," Journal of Education for Library and Information Science, 31:3 (Winter 1991), 187-203. Summary of the presentations on programs at the 1989 Association of Library and Information Science Educators Conference, 1989.

1099. Cloonan, Michèle Valerie. "The Preservation of Knowledge," Library Trends (Spring 1993), 594-605. Preservation must look at the "big picture" and also examine the preservation of electronic forms of communication.

1100. Cloonan, Michèle Valerie. "The Preservation of Library Materials and Art on Paper: A Bibliography of Government Publications," Conservation Administration News, 18 (July 1984), 6-8.

1101. Cloonan, Michèle Valerie, ed. Recent Trends in Rare Book Librarianship. Champaign, IL: Graduate School of Library and Information Science, 1987. 256p. Library Trends, 36:1 (Summer 1987), special issue. Highlights various aspects of rare book librarianship and its sub-disciplines, including preservation and conservation.

1102. Cloonan, Michèle Valerie, and Sidney E. Berger. "Recent Trends in Rare Book Librarianship: An Overview," Library Trends, 36:1 (Summer 1987), 3-22. Lists publications from LC, Smithsonian, Dept. of Agriculture, National Bureau of Standards, and UNESCO.

1103. Cloonan, Michèle Valerie,and Patricia C. Norcott. "Evolution of Preservation Librarianship as Reflected in Job Descriptions from 1975 through 1987," College and Research Libraries, 50:6 (November 1989), 646-656. Examines the job content of preservation librarianship as evidenced in job advertisements placed in major publications.

1104. Cluff, E. Dale. "The Role and Responsibility of the Library in Preservation and Conservation," Conserving and Preserving Library Materials, ed. Kathryn L. and William T. Henderson. Urbana-Champaign, IL: University of Illinois Graduate School of Library and Information Service, 1983, 181-196. Summarizes the scope of preservation activities in the library.

1105. Clydesdale, Amanda. Chemicals in Conservation: A Guide to Possible Hazards and Safe Use. 2d ed. Edinburgh: Scottish Society for Conservation and Restoration, 1990. One volume.

1106. Coates, Christine. "Grants for Preservation: 'The Ragged Trousered Philanthropists,'" Library Conservation News, 39 (April 1993), 6-7. Conservation of the novel with funding from the National Manuscripts Conservation Trust.

1107. Coates, Peter. "Planning for Disaster Control," Books in Peril. Cape Town, South Africa: South African Library, 1987, 51-61. Disaster prevention and preparedness.

1108. Coates, Peter. "Preservation in South Africa — The Present Situation," International Preservation News, 6 (June 1993), 9-11. Describes preservation and conservation activities, including physical treatment and reformatting, education and training.

1109. Coates, Peter. "Preservation in South Africa — The Present Situation," Proceedings of the Pan-African Conference on the Preservation & Conservation of Library & Archival Materials,

Nairobi, Kenya, 21-25 June 1993. The Hague: IFLA, 1995, 37-39. (IFLA Professional Publication 43). Overview of activities; lack of funds the greatest concern.

1110. Cochrane, Clive. "The Collection, Preservation and Use of Moving Images in the United Kingdom," Audiovisual Librarian, 20:2 (May 1994), 122-130. Initiatives to encourage the archiving of audiovisual materials; bibliographic control; preservation efforts and concerns, with a note on storage and use.

1111. Cockerell, Douglas. Bookbinding and the Care of Books: A Handbook for Amateurs, Bookbinders and Librarians, intro. Jane Greenfield. New York: Lyons & Burford, 1991. 334p. A reprint of the first edition (1902), which George Cunha calls "the best text on fine binding by an artist/craftsman."

1112. Cockerline, Neil C. "Ethical Considerations for the Conservation of Circus Posters," WAAC Newsletter (Western Association for Art Conservation),17:2 (May 1995), 14-22. History of the production of circus posters, their use; the need to study the techniques of their production and to preserve them.

1113. Coe, Brian, and Mark Haworth-Booth. A Guide to Early Photographic Processes. London: The Victoria and Albert Museum in Association with Hurtwood Press, 1983. 112p.

1114. Cohen, David. "New Books from Old: A Proposal," Serials Librarian, 23: 3/4 (1993), 149-155. Proposes (as a new concept!) that publishers print out-of-print books on demand for libraries as needed, giving publishers responsibility to retain digitized books. Old wine in a somewhat new bottle.

1115. Cohen, Karl. "Preservation of American Video Culture No Easy Task for Archivists," Film/Tape World (San Francisco), 8:5; 89 (June 1995), 20-23. Overview of tape degradation, obsolete formats, new digital technologies, and video restoration efforts at the Bay Area Video Coalition (BAVC); KOFY-TV, UCLA, American Poetry Archive, etc.

1116. Cohen-Stratyner, Barbara and Brigitte Kueppers, eds. Preserving America's Performing Arts. New York: Theater Library Association, 1986. 167p. Contains 33 papers originally presented at a 1982 conference, "Preservation Management for Performing Arts Collections."

1117. Cojocaru, Viorel and Cella Manea. "Neutron Activation Analysis of Pigments Used in the 16th Century Manuscripts From Sucevita."

Restaurator, 8:4 (1987), 189-198. Describes the technique of neutron analysis used to determine the composition of pigments used in miniatures; thus permitting the definition of the nature of most pigments.

1118.   Cole, Susan. Family Papers. New Orleans, LA: Historic New Orleans Collection, 1983. 13p. (Preservation Guide 1). Covers causes of deterioration, storage, organization, and display. Recommended reading and sources of supplies.

1119.   Coleman, Christopher D.G., comp. Preservation Education Directory, 5th ed. Chicago, IL: Association of Library Collections and Technical Services, 1988. 30p.; 7th ed., 1995. 69p. Lists courses offered at accredited library schools; training in conservation; institutions offering courses and workshops; training opportunities abroad. Updated frequently.

1120.   Coleman, Christopher D. G., and Gretchen Karl. "'Text, Lies, and Videotape': A Discussion of Reformatting Technologies," Conservation Administration News, 51 (October 1992), 4-5. Summary of the Los Angeles Preservation Network's Conference on the capabilities of video and digital reformatting and the advantages of the continued use of microfilm. Reformatting procedures, analog videodisk conversion, digitization, and optical scanning are discussed.

1121.   Coles, Laura M. Archival Gold: Managing and Preserving Publishers' Records. Burnaby, BC: Canadian Centre for Studies in Publishing, Simon Fraser University, 1989. 69p. A guide with sound advise about storage and preservation.

1122.   Colleran, Kate, and Marcel Ciantar. "W. Heath: Battle of Trafalger," Conference on Book and Paper Conservation, 1990. Budapest, Hungary: Technical Association of Paper and Printing Industry/National Szechenyi Library, 1992, 271-280. Describes the treatment of a paper panorama in the National Maritime Museum (UK), to prepare it for exhibition. Illus.

1123.   Collier, Mel. "Security Systems: A Case Study," Security Systems, Vandalism and Disaster Planning in Libraries, ed. Royston Brown and Hilary Spiers. Stamford, Lincolnshire, England.: Capital Planning Information, 1988, 23-34. Seminar review of options to ensure security, with copies of Leicester Polytechnic policies; discussion.

1124.   Collings, Thomas J. Archival Care of Still Photographs. London: Society of Archivists, 1983. 11p. (Information Leaflet, 2). Basic information on causes of deterioration, protection of collections, housing and storage.

1125. Collings, Thomas J. The Care and Preservation of Philatelic Materials. London: British Library. 1989. 55p.

1126. Collings, Thomas J., and Derek W. Milner. "A New Chronology of Papermaking Technology," Paper Conservator, 14 (1990), 58-62. Covers papermaking processes and technology from B.C. 3000 to A.D. 1989; an update of the chronology prepared by Dard Hunter.

1127. Collings, Thomas J., and Derek W. Milner. "Paper and Papermaking, Part 1," Library Conservation News, 29 (October 1990), 1,3,6,8. A brief history of paper production.

1128. Collister, Edward A. "Disasters in Documentations Centres: Emergency Actions and Programmes," Documentation et Bibliothèques, 29:3 (July/September 1983), 99-105. (French).

1129. Colorado State University Libraries. A Preservation Program for the Colorado State University Libraries: A Final Report of the ARL/OMS Preservation Planning ARL/OMS Study Team. Washington, DC: Association of Research Libraries, Office of Management Studies, 1985. 19p. The editor of the report was Stephen Green, et al.

1130. Columbia University Libraries. The Preservation of Library Materials: A CUL Handbook. New York: Columbia University Libraries, revised regularly. Binding specifications, guidelines for selection for preservation, preservation microfilming,and the care of microforms; disaster preparedness; general care of collections.

1131. Comfort, Louise K., ed. Managing Disaster: Strategies and Policy Perspectives. Durham, NC: Duke University Press, 1988. 420p. Essays on disaster mitigation, planning, and recovery from a public policy perspective based on a series of meetings organized by the Federal Emergency Management Agency (FEMA).

1132. Commission on Preservation and Access. Annual Report 1 July 1988 - 30 June 1989. Washington, DC: Commission on Preservation and Access. Annual publication; summary of the year's activities.

1133. Commission on Preservation and Access. Books, Paper, and Adhesives. Washington, DC: Commission on Preservation and Access, 1990. 28p.

1134. Commission on Preservation and Access. Commission on Preservation and Access Background Paper. Washington, DC: Commission on Preservation and Access, 1989. 15p. Brochure, describing the mission and activities of the Commission.

1135. Commission on Preservation and Access. The International Program and Its Global Mission: Introduction to Report Series, Washington, DC: Commission on Preservation and Access, January 1995. 4p.

1136. Commission on Preservation and Access. Preservation Priorities in Latin America: A Report From the Sixth IFLA Meeting, Havana, Cuba. Washington, DC: Commission on Preservation and Access, July 1995. 7p.

1137. Commission on Preservation and Access. Preservation and Access. Washington, DC: Commission on Preservation and Access, June 1991. 41p. This study comes down on the side of digital imagery as the medium of the future.

1138. Commission on Preservation and Access. Preserving Digital Information, Report on the Task Force on Archiving of Digital Information. Washington, DC: Commission on Preservation and Access and Research Library Group, May 1, 1996. 64p. Task Force co-chairs Donald Waters, Yale University and John Garrett, Cyber Villages, Corporation. also Draft Report... published August 24, 1995. 48p. Executive Summary... 3p. September 1, 1995.

1139. Commission on Preservation and Access. Preserving Knowledge: The Case for Alkaline Paper. Washington, DC: Commission on Preservation and Access, 1988. 55p.; rev. ed. 1990, 20 pieces. Information packet on alkaline paper.

1140. Commission on Preservation and Access. Preserving the Illustrated Test. Report of the Joint Task Force on Text and Image. Washington, DC: Commission on Preservation and Access, April 1992. 31p. Examines the complex issues involved across a broad spectrum of disciplines in preserving text-cum-image materials.

1141. Commission on Preservation and Access. Preserving the Intellectual Heritage, A Report of the Bellagio Conference Held at the Rockefeller Foundation Study and Conference Center, Bellagio, Italy. Washington, DC: Commission on Preservation and Access, October, 1993. 36p. The conference explored the development of new scholarly linkages in fields heavily dependent on deteriorating literature. Recommendations led to the formation of the European Commission on Preservation and Access, headquartered in Amsterdam.

1142. Commission on Preservation and Access. Report: Review and Assessment Committee. Washington, DC: Commission on Preservation and Access, 1991. 37p. Reviewed first five years of Commission on Preservation and Access.

1143. Commission on Preservation and Access. Scholarly Resources in Art History: Issues in Preservation. Washington, DC: Commission on Preservation and Access, 1989. 48p. Report of the Seminar, Spring Hill, Wayzata, MN, September 29-October 1, 1988, that addressed the technical innovations for preservation and access of text and image for art historians.

1144. Commission on Preservation and Access. Selection for Preservation of Research Library Material. Washington, DC: Commission of Preservation and Access, August 1989. 4p.

1145. Commission on Preservation and Access. Working Paper on the Future. Washington, DC: Commission on Preservation and Access, February, 1994. 6p.

1146. Commission on Preservation and Access. Preservation Science Council. Phase I of Research to Support the Archival Management of Materials Created on Magnetic Media. Washington, DC: Commission on Preservation and Access, 1994. 8p.

1147. Commission on Preservation and Access. Preservation Science Council. Research Project on Temperature and RH Dependence of Paper Deterioration. Washington, DC: Commission on Preservation and Access, 1994. 6p.

1148. Commission on Preservation and Access. Review and Assessment Committee. Final Report. Washington, DC: Committee on Preservation and Access, 1991. 41p. Review of the five-year history of the Commission; assessment of progress in preservation in the nation; discussion of continuing needs; the role of the commission. Also discussed in Microform Review, 21 (Summer 1992), 111-122.

1149.   Commission on Preservation and Access. Scholarly Advisory
          Committee on Art History. Summary of Final Report. Washington,
          DC: Commission on Preservation and Access, August 1994.
          4p. Presents initiatives and strategies for action; journals of
          permanent research value are identified.

1150.   Commission on Preservation and Access. Task Forces on Archival
          Selection. The Preservation of Archival Materials; Report.
          Washington, DC: Commission on Preservation and Access, April
          1993. 7p. Addresses the need to integrate the preservation of records,
          regardless of format into archival management.

1151.   Committee on Institutional Cooperation. Task Force on Mass
          Deacidification. Mass Deacidification: A Report to the Library
          Directors. Champaign, IL: Committee on Institutional Cooperation,
          April 1992. 161p. Assessment of feasibility, problems, and costs,
          recommending further action. Detailed appendixes document the
          preliminary review. Chair was Richard Frieder.

1152.   Committee on Scottish Newspapers. Scottish Newspapers: A
          Programme for Microfilming Scottish Newspapers. Edinburgh,
          Scotland: National Library of Scotland, 1986. 44p. Recommends the
          establishment of a dedicated microfilming unit at the Scottish
          National Library to film endangered newspapers, offer services to
          other libraries, and act as a focus for coordinated newspaper
          microfilming projects.

1153.   Committee on the Records of Government. Report. Washington, DC:
          The Committee, March 1985. 185p. Reprint 1988 by Robert E.
          Krieger Publishers, Malabar, FL. Sponsored by the American
          Council of Learned Societies, Council of Library Resources, Inc. and
          Social Science Research Council. A privately sponsored and funded
          committee organized to identify and propose means by which
          governments at all levels might rid themselves of needless and
          wasteful records while ensuring the preservation of that fraction of
          documents deserving to be kept.

1154.   Commoner, Lucy. "Personnel Protective Equipment for
          Conservators: Gloves and Hand Protection," Journal of the American
          Institute of Conservation, 23:2 (Spring 1984), 153-158. A short
          section covers barrier creams, which "provide less protection than
          gloves and may not be practical in a conservation lab."

1155.   "Companies Making Alkaline or Neutral Paper," Alkaline Paper
          Advocate, 1:2 (March 1988), 1,8,9. List of North American
          companies and trade names of their papers.

1156. Competitive Grade Finder for Paper and Graphic Arts Industries. Exton, PA: Grade Finders, Inc., 1989. 375p., also a 1990-1991 edition published in 1992.

1157. Comstock, Gay Stuart. "Disruptive Behavior: Protecting People, Protecting Rights," Wilson Library Bulletin, 69:6 (February 1995), 33-35. Notes need to develop a code of conduct in the library and enforce it.

1158. Comu, E. and L. Bone. "Seismic Disaster Planning: Preventive Measures Make a Difference," Western Association for Art Conservation, 134:3 (1991), 13-19.

1159. Condon, Garret. "Vanishing Volumes: Librarians Struggle to Save Collections from Disintegrating," Hartford Courant, November 9, 1986, section G pp. 1, 4.

1160. Condrey, Richard, and Faye Phillips. "New Technology: Preservation Through Reformatting: An Update on the LSU Libraries Electronic Imaging Laboratory," Louisiana Library Bulletin, 55 (Spring 1993), 235-237.

1161. Condrey, Richard, and Faye Phillips and Tony Presti. "Historical Ecology: LSU's Electronic Imaging Laboratory," College & Research Library News (September 1993), 440-441, 448. Instructive case study of a pilot project.

1162. Conference des Recteurs et des Principaux des Universités du Quebec. La Gestion des Archives Informatiques. Sainte-Foy: Presses de l'Université du Quebec, 1994. 163p. Subject heading: Archival materials: Conservation and Restoration.

1163. "Conference on Cooperative Preservation Programs," College & Research Libraries News, 47:2 (April 1986), 139-140. The results of a discussion on the role of regional programs in emerging national preservation strategy are outlined. Held at the Northeast Document Conservation Center, October 24-25, 1985.

1164. "Conference on Preservation of Library Materials [Vienna, April 6-11, 1986, special issue]," Restaurator, 8:2-3 (1987), 63-150.

1165. "Conference on the Development of State Preservation Programs [held at the Library of Congress March 1-3]. RTSD Newsletter (Resources and Technical Services Division), 14:3 (1989), 24.

1166. Connecticut State Library. Disaster Recovery Plan for State Agencies and Facilities: Recovery Techniques for Damaged Records. Hartford,

CT: Office of Public Records Administration, Connecticut State
Library, 1990. 8p.

1167.   Connecticut State Librarians Task Force on the Preservation of
         Historical Records. Report and Recommendations to the General
         Assembly from the Committee on Alkaline Paper of the Connecticut
         Preservation Task Force. Connecticut State Library, Hartford, CT:
         1989. 10p.

1168.   Connecticut Preservation Crises: Final Report and Recommendation
         of the Connecticut Preservation Task Force. Hartford, CT:
         Connecticut State Library, 1991. 50p.

1169.   Conrad, Tony. "Old Open-Reel Videotape Restoration," Footage 89:
         North American Film and Video Sources, edited by Richard
         Prelinger and Celeste Hoffman. New York: Prelinger Associates,
         Inc., 1989. n.p. given.

1170.   Conrad, Tony. "Open Reel Videotape Restoration," The Independent
         (October 1987), 12.

1171.   Conroy, Tom. "Informal Observations on 'Leather Burn,' Acidity,
         and Leather Lubricants," Book and Paper Group Annual, 10 (1991),
         43-48. Discusses discoloration and deterioration caused by leather
         bindings that contain contaminants from the tanning process.

1172.   Conroy, Tom. "The Ruined Plough," Binder's Guild Newsletter,
         11:5 (1988), 6-12; reprinted: Abbey Newsletter, 13:3 (June 1989),
         49-54. Illus. Instructions and information on how to best use the
         plough.

1173.   Conroy, Tom. "Pulling for Sewing Through the Fold," New Library
         Scene, 10:5 (October 1991), 13-16. Describes a breaking method for
         the pulling of 19th-and 20th-century books before sewing through the
         fold.

1174.   Conroy, Tom. "Teaching Genealogies of American Hand
         Bookbinders," Guild of Book Workers Journal, 28:1/2 (Spring/Fall
         1990), 64p. and charts; entire issue. Tracing the influence of teachers
         on American bookbinders.

1175.   "Conserving Conservation," Illinois Libraries, 64:5 (May 1983),
         351-364. Four articles on library preservation, covering basic
         information, binding, and disaster planning.

1176. "Conservation Education From Columbia to Texas," ALCTS Newsletter (Association for Library Collections and Technical Services), 3:2 (1992), 16-17.

1177. "Conservation Education Programs Announce Move (from Columbia to University of Texas)," New Library Scene, 11 (February 1992), 7.

1178. "Conservation/Preservation," Bookmark (New York State Library), 45:3 (Spring 1987), 138-191; entire issue. Twelve articles focusing on different aspects of preservation; programs in other states, within New York, and the national preservation agenda.

1179. "Conservation in Ohio [Ohio Cooperative Conservation Information Office] to Serve Multitype Libraries," Library Journal, 108 (November 15, 1983), 2120.

1180. "Conservation of Library Materials," Illinois Libraries, 67:8 (October 1985), 643-770; entire issue. Culmination for a three year project to bring conservation awareness to the state's libraries.

1181. "Conservation Prize" (Riley Dunn & Wilson conservation competition), Public Library Journal, 9 (January/February 1994), 29.

1182. "The Conservator-Restorer: A Definition of the Profession," ICOM News (International Council of Museums), 39:1 (1986), 5-7. Statement on the conservation profession prepared by the ICOM Committee for Conservation Working Group for Training in Conservation and Restoration.

1183. Constance, John A. "Federal Policy on Permanent Papers: First Step, Future Goals," Preservation Papers of the 1991 SAA Annual Conference, comp. Karen Garlick. Chicago: Society of American Archivists, 1992, 119-125. Presents key events leading to the Public Law 101-423, its structure, some concern about lack of standards for permanent papers; a brief note on the chemistry of paper.

1184. Constantinou, Constantina. "Destruction of Knowledge: A Study of Journal Mutilation at a Large University Library," College & Research Libraries, 56:6 (November 1995), 497-507. Examines mutilation by removal of pages; reviews literature and analyzes and interprets result of study; recommendations to help reduce problem, further research.

1185. Conway, Paul, comp. Administration of Preservation Programs in Archives: A Selected Bibliography. Washington, DC: Archives Library Information Center, National Archives and Records

Administration, July 1990. 11p. Introduction, 148 citations; no annotations.

1186. Conway, Paul. "Archival Preservation: Definitions for Improving Education and Training," Restaurator, 10:2 (1989), 47-60. Summarizes the emerging recognition of the need for education and training in preservation; author recommends that leaders in the field cooperate in a variety of initiatives in education. Bibliography.

1187. Conway, Paul. Archival Preservation in the United States and the Role of Information Sources. Ph.D. Dissertation. Ann Arbor, MI, University of Michigan, 1991. 294p.

1188. Conway, Paul. "Archival Preservation Practice in Nationwide Context," American Archivist, 53:2 (Summer 1990), 204-222. Results of a nationwide study of preservation practices.

1189. Conway, Paul. "Are Self-Stick Notes Archival?" SAA Newsletter (Society of American Archivists) (September 1989), 6. A cautionary note on the harm caused by post-it notes.

1190. Conway, Paul. "Digital Imaging and Optical Storage Over the Long Run" Inform, 5:10 (November-December 1991), 31-33. A review of the report, "Digital Image Applications and Optical Media Systems Management Issues, Technical Trends, User Experience: Guidelines for State and Local Government Agencies."

1191. Conway, Paul. "Digitizing Preservation," Library Journal, 119:2 (February 1, 1994), 42-45. Lucid discussion of imaging technology and its potential for access and preservation, and the problems.

1192. Conway, Paul. "The Implications of Digital Imaging for Preservation," NEDCC News (Northeast Documents Conservation Center), 6:1 (Spring 1995), 5-6. Describes the role of digital imaging in a preservation program, noting its goal is "to preserve continuing access to digital data for as long as that data has value."

1193. Conway, Paul. "IPI Reports New Microfilm Permanence Research." SAA Newsletter (Society of American Archivists), September 1988, 7. For a full report see Abbey Newsletter (July 1988), 83-88.

1194. Conway, Paul. Nationwide Strategy for Archival Preservation. Chicago, IL: Society of American Archivists, 1989. 7p.

1195. Conway, Paul, comp. "Preservation Focus," SAA Newsletter (Society of American Archivists), November 1989, 20-23.

Information Storage and Preservation and a Chart of Storage Media, date of origin, shelf life, and storage density.

1196. Conway, Paul. "Preservation in Archives: Survey Outlines Current Needs," SAA Newsletter (Society of American Archivists), September 1989, 7,15. Identified preservation needs through a survey of North American archive repositories.

1197. Conway, Paul. Preservation in the Digital World, Washington, DC: Commission on Preservation and Access, March 1996. 24p. Links the historical context and concepts of preservation practice and management to a new framework for effective leadership in the digital environment.

1198. Conway, Paul. "Preserving History's Future: Developing a National Strategy for Archival Preservation," Advances in Preservation and Access, Vol. 1. Westport, CT: Meckler, 1992, 244-260. Examines national preservation strategy based upon a model developed by the Society of American Archivists. Describes the Society's initiatives and discusses the need for public commitment, education, program development, selection, technical standards, access, and the need for research.

1199. Conway, Paul. "Selecting Microfilm for Digital Preservation: A Case Study from Project Open Book," Library Resources and Technical Services, 40:1 (January 1996), 67-77. Case study of Project Open Book, a "multiyear, multifaceted study exploring the feasibility of converting preservation microfilm to digital imagery" at Yale University Library (67). Explores selection concerns, technical and intellectual. Emphasizes the need for subject indexing to make filmed and/or digitized collections accessible.

1200. Conway, Paul. "TAPPI Meeting on Paper Preservation," SAA Newsletter (Society of American Archivists) (January 1989), 14-15.

1201. Conway, Paul and Shari Weaver. The Setup Phase of Project Open Book. Washington, DC: Commission on Preservation and Access, 1994. 24p.; reprinted in Microform Review, 23:3 (Summer 1994), 107-119. Report on the status of an effort to convert microfilm to digital imagery; methodology and the conversion process.

1202. Cook, L. P. "Stamp Pads and Their Inks," Library Conservation News, 12 (July 1986), 3. An overview of stamping materials in archives, concluding that at present inks do not hasten deterioration of paper.

1203. Cook, Michael. Computer Generated Records. Hampshire, England: Society of Archivists, 1996. 60p. Introduction: the nature and problems of computer generated records.

1204. Cook, Michael. The Management of Information from Archives. Aldershot, England: Gower, 1986. 234p. Text on archives administration. Preservation and conservation concerns mentioned but not addressed in depth.

1205. Cook, Terry. "Easy to Byte, Harder to Chew: The Second Generation of Electronic Records Archives," Archivaria, 33 (Winter 1991-92), 203-216. Discusses the changing nature of technology and the second generation of electronic archives. Eight studies on electronic records are reviewed.

1206. Cook, Virginia. "Safe Keeping: Australian Developments in Document Storage," National Library of Australia News, 5:5 (February 1995), 9-11. Describes the effort to develop Australian-made, low cost, acid-free materials for the storage of documents and books, available since 1994.

1207. Cooke, Donald F. "Map Storage on CD-ROM," Byte, 12:8 (1987), 129-138. Discusses the potential and methods of map storage on CD-ROM, including better access to street maps.

1208. Cooke, George W. "David J. Martinelli: California Craftsman," New Library Scene, 15:3 (June 1996), 5-6, 8-9. Profile of the coordinator of binding services for the nine library University of California system; the UC program, training/background.

1209. Cooke, George W. "Drew University Library: Preservation in Practice," Conservation Administration News, 50 (July 1992), 4-5, 30. Describes the collection management practices and conservation laboratory at the library.

1210. Cooke, George W. "Jane Greenfield: Common Sense in Conservation," Conservation Administration News, 41 (April 1990), 8-9, 31. Profile of the book conservator who established the conservation laboratory at Yale University Library.

1211. Cooke, George W. "Laura S. Young: Hand Bookbinder and Educator," Conservation Administration News, 45 (April 1991), 6-7, 29. Profile of a distinguished binder/conservator who trained many of North America's leading bookbinders and conservators.

1212. Cooke, George W. "Margaret S. Child: Preservation Advocate," Conservation Administration News, 51 (October 1992), 6-7,

31. Profile of leading advocate for the preservation of library and archival materials and her role as a catalyst.

1213.   Cooke, George W. "Marilyn Kemp Weidner: Pioneer Paper Conservator," Conservation Administration News, 50 (July 1992), 8-9, 31. Profile of a distinguished paper conservator and founder of the Conservation Center for Art and Historic Artifacts (CCAHA), Philadelphia; her contributions through development of conservation techniques, education, and training.

1214.   Cooke, George W. "Paul Banks: Profile of an Innovator," Conservation Administration News, 37 (April 1989), 8-9. Profile of a distinguished book conservator and educator.

1215.   Cooke, George W. "Polly Lada-Mocarski: Visionary Conservator," Conservation Administration News, 40 (January 1990), 8-9. Profile of a driving force in the development of conservation education and training in the United States.

1216.   Cooke, George W. "Preservation Group Reaches Out in Bergen County and Beyond," New Jersey Libraries, 26:3 (Summer 1993), 14-18. Describes the initiatives of the Bergen County (NJ) Preservation Committee and an effective page training program.

1217.   Cooke, George W. "Ralph Ocker: A Personal Profile," New Library Scene, 14:4 (August 1995), 7-8, 14. Training in Germany and the establishment of Ocker & Trapp Library Binding in New Jersey.

1218.   Cooke, George W. "Rutherford D. Rogers: A Top-Ranking Administrator Who Said 'Yes' to Conservation and Preservation," Conservation Administration News, 43 (October 1990), 6-7, 30. Profile of a distinguished library administrator and his role in establishing preservation as an integral part of library management.

1219.   Cooke, George W. "Susan Swartzburg, Preservation Advocate," Conservation Administration News, 56 (January 1994), 6-7, 24. Profile of an early preservation librarian.

1220.   Coon, J. Walter. Fire Protection: Design Criteria, Options, Selection. Kingston, MA: R.S. Means, 1991. 319p. Illus. Provides a basic foundation in fire suppression, detection, and alarm systems and equipment.

1221.   Cooper, M. D. "A Cost Comparison of Alternative Book Strategies," Library Quarterly, 59:3 (July 1989), 239-260. Develops a cost methodology to decide location, access, and shelving; collection management and preservation concerns are addressed.

1222.   "Cooperative Grant Helps Preserve Slavic Books," Friendscript (University of Illinois Library Friends at Urbana-Champaign), 10:3 (Fall 1988).

1223.   Coover, James B. "Choosing What Not to Preserve," Music Librarianship in America, ed. Michael Ochs. Cambridge, MA: Harvard University, 1991, 24-36; "Questions and Discussion," 37-42. A look into a future where information is accessed through one databank; an examination of current collection policies and speculation on the materials that are not collected. Advocates cooperative collection development with some consideration for ephemera.

1224.   Copeland, Peter. Sound Recordings. London: British Library, 1991. 80p. Illus. History of sound recording; discussion of sound recording technologies, with emphasis on preservation and archival concerns.

1225.   Copeland, Peter. "Sound Recordings on Optical Discs," Library Conservation News, 38 (January 1993), 7. Describes a process for the storage and retrieval of sound and image on optical disk; questions about permanence and retrieval are raised.

1226.   Corea, Ishvari, and D. M. Thilakaratne. "Conservation and Preservation of Library Materials in Sri Lanka," Planning Modernization and Preservation in South Asian Libraries, ed. Kalpona Dasgupta. Calcutta, India: National Library, 1992, 134-141. Conservation and preservation awareness programs, a pilot project to assess needs, by the National Library Services Board.

1227.   Corfield, Michael. "Conservation Records in the Wiltshire Library and Museum Service," Conservator (U.K.), 7 (1983), 5-8. Describes a computerized record system for conservation examination and treatment.

1228.   Cornish, G. P. "Copyright Issues in Legal Deposit and Preservation," IFLA Journal (International Federation of Library Associations and Institutions), 20:3 (1994) 341-349.

1229.   Cornu, Elisabeth, and Leslie Bone. "Seismic Disaster Planning: Preventive Measures Make a Difference," WAAC Newsletter (Western Association for Art Conservation) (September 1991), 13-19. Systematic guide to minimizing earthquake damage in museums.

1230. Cory, Kenneth A., and David W. Hessler. "Imaging the Archives: Now Is the Time," Library and Archival Security, 12:1 (1993), 7-15. Advocates the imaging of archival collections so that original documents need not be handled, but does not recognize the need to provide back-up on microfilm.

1231. Costain, Charlie. "Framework for Preservation of Museum Collections," CCI Newsletter (Canadian Conservation Institute), 14 (September 1994), 1-4. Discusses the use of a chart to help curators access dangers to collections to help determine guidelines for housing and display. The framework itself is available from CCI.

1232. Cote, William C. "Attacking the Problem — Self Assessment," Library and Archival Security, 11:1 (1991), 125-156. Introduces and reproduced the National Fire Protection Association "Fire Safety Self Inspection Form for Libraries."

1233. Couch, Randall. "Conservation of the Humanities Research Center," Conservation Administration News, 13 (April 1983), 1-3. Description of the facilities and conservation activities at the Harry Ransom Humanities Research Center, University of Texas.

1234. Couch, Randall and Mihaly Turbusz. "Trays for Lining and Partitioning Wooden Storage Drawers," Journal of the American Institute for Conservation, 22:2 (Spring 1983), 92-97. System for lining wooden drawers with acid-free cardboard trays for protection of materials.

1235. Coughlin, Caroline M., and Alice Gertzog. Lyle's Administration of the College Library, 5th ed. Metuchen, NJ: Scarecrow Press, 1992. 603p. Text for college library administrators; notes need for long-range preservation planning.

1236. Coulson, A. J. "Picture Libraries," Audiovisual Librarian, 15:2 (May 1989), 99-102. Describes types of picture collections; briefly discusses status of conservation and laments lack of standards.

1237. Council on Library Resources. Committee on Preservation and Access. Brittle Books. Washington, DC: Council on Library Resources, 1986. 31p. Report of a committee that focused on the problem of brittle books in library collections; advocates a cooperative solution on a national basis.

1238. Council on Library Resources. Committee on Preservation and Access. Interim Report: July 1985. Washington, DC: Council on Library Resources, 1985. 13p. Outlines the committee's progress in considering the nature of the preservation problem, assessing present activity, and identifying needs and solutions. Report focuses on the "brittle book" problem; deems preservation microfilming the most reliable technique for information preservation. Conclusions are offered in the areas of access, funding collaboration, technology, and public understanding.

1239.   Council on Library Resources. Preservation of Government Records. Appendix II of the March 1985 Report of the Committee on the Records of Government. Washington, DC: Council on Library Resources, 1985. 56p+. The Appendix has two parts: Conservation: An Overview. by Judith Fortson-Jones. 27p. and Technology Assessment Report by the National Archives and Records Service, October 1984. (an abridgement of a staff study). 29p.

1240.   Council on Library Resources. Preserving Our Intellectual Heritage: General Directions and Next Steps, Washington, DC: Council on Library Resources, 1984. 13p. Eloquently articles the need and prerequisites for a coherent national strategy for retrospective and prospective preservation.

1241.   Council on Library Resources. "Statement on the Fair Use Doctrine," Washington, DC: Council on Library Resources, February 7, 1996. 4p. Argues that the current principle in copyright law for preservation should be retained in an electronic environment.

1242.   Council on Library Resources. Videodisc and Optical Technologies and Their Applications in Libraries: A Report to the Council on Library Resources. Washington, DC: Council on Library Resources, 1985.

1243.   "Council on Library Resources and Commission on Preservation and Access Affiliate," American Society for Information Science, 21:5 (June 1995), 2. The two groups have agreed to affiliate and Deanna B. Marcum will serve as the President of both groups.

1244.   Courtot, Marilyn E. "Electronic Imaging Standards: A Status Check," Inform, 5:9 (October 1991), 32-36. Discusses the development of standards for optical technology; provides descriptions of different standards.

1245.   Courtot, Marilyn E. "Vaults of Granite and Steel: A Journey Through the Genealogical Storage Complex at the Mormon Church," Inform, 2:7 (July-August 1988), 22-25. Describes the Granite Mountain, Utah, vaults: production of microfilm, environmental controls, security.

1246.   Cowan, Janet. Dry Methods for Surface Cleaning of Paper. Ottawa: Canadian Conservation Institute, 1986. 10p. (Technical Bulletin, 11) Practical instructions for cleaning works on paper.

1247.   Cowan, Wavell F. "Beating," Friends of Dard Hunter Preprints, Chicago, IL: Friends of Dard Hunter, 1 (1992), 19-20. Serial. Describes the effect of beating the pulp in papermaking; the need for collaboration between papermaker and scientist.

1248.   Cox, Lynn. "Preserving Archival Futures," Archives and Museum Informatics Newsletter, 3 (Fall 1989), 9-10. Summary of meeting of archivists and archival educators to plan for preservation initiatives and strategies in the 1990s.

1249.   Cox, Richard J. "Archival Preservation Interests and Issues: An American Perspective," Advances in Preservation and Access, Vol. 1. Westport, CT: Meckler, 1992, 228-243. Preservation issues for the archivist; the move toward collections preservation.

1250.   Cox, Richard J. Archives and Manuscripts Administration: A Basic Annotated Bibliography. Nashville, TN: American Association for State and Local History, Technical Information Service, 1989. 36p. Annotated bibliography of basic literature on archives management, with a section on "Preservation and Security."

1251.   Cox, Richard J. "Collectors and Archival, Manuscript, and Rare Book Security," Focus on Security, 2:3 (April 1995), 19-27. Discusses the threat to collections by collectors, the ACRL Code of Ethics, ethical considerations for librarians.

1252.   Cox, Richard J. "Selecting Historical Records for Microfilming: Some Suggested Procedures for Repositories," Library and Archival Security, 9:2 (1989), 21-41. Case study and model; notes need for priorities and careful evaluation.

1253.   Cox, Richard J., and Lynn W. Cox. "Selecting Information of Enduring Value for Preservation: Contending With the Hydra-Headed Monster," Rethinking the Library in the Information Age, Vol. 2: Issues in Library Research, Proposals for the 1990s. Washington, DC: Government Printing Office, 1988, 115-130. Advocates an activist approach to information appraisal in selection for preservation.

1254.   Cox, Richard J., and Helen W. Samuels. "The Archivist's First Responsibility: A Research Agenda to Improve the Identification and Retention of Records of Enduring Value," American Archivist, 51:1/2 (Winter/Spring 1988), 28-51. Addresses need for the archival profession to develop appraisal theory and practice to cope effectively with modern documentation and to ensure its preservation and future access.

1255. Craddock, Ann Brooke. "Construction Materials for Storage and Exhibition," Conservation Concerns: A Guide for Collectors and Curators, ed. Konstanze Bachmann. Washington, DC: Smithsonian Institution Press, 1992, 23-28. Discusses materials that can, and should not, be used for the storage of materials.

1256. Craddock, Ann Brooke. "Control of Temperature and Humidity in Small Collections," Conservation Concerns: A Guide for Collectors and Curators, Washington, DC: Smithsonian Institution Press, 1992, 15-22. Defines the concepts of relative and absolute humidity and analyzes the relationship between temperature and humidity levels.

1257. Craig, Roger. "Alternative Approaches to the Treatment of Mould Biodeterioration; An International Problem," Paper Conservator, 10 (1986), 27-30. Survey of techniques in British and overseas repositories and discussion of the pros and cons of the various techniques used.

1258. Craiag-Bullen, Catherine. "Searching for a Leaf Caster," Conservation of Historic and Artistic Works on Paper. Ottawa: Canadian Conservation Institute, 1994, 33-37. (Symposium 88). Review of leafcasters on the market.

1259. Crane, Marilyn, and Sheryl Davis. "The Practice of Disaster Response," Conservation Administration News, 55 (October 1993), 8-9. Describes a day-long disaster recovery workshop designed to demonstrate the importance of having a written disaster plan and testing its effectiveness.

1260. Crawford, John C. "The Langholm Library Project," Library Review (Glasgow, Scotland), 44 (1995), 36-44.

1261. Crawford-de Sa, Elizabeth, and Michèle Valerie Cloonan, "The Preservation of Archival and Library Materials; Part I: A Bibliography of Government Publications," Conservation Administration News, 46-47, (July), Part II, (October 1991), 16-17, 30-31; 12-13. Publications issued by government agencies relating to preservation and conservation of library and archival materials.

1262. Creasy, Helen. "A Survey in a Day: Cost-Effective Surveys of Museum Collections in Scotland," Paper Conservator, 17 (1993), 33-38. Discusses survey methodology for a one-day survey and written report undertaken by the Scottish Museum Council.

1263. Creguer, Tina L. "Preserving Our Intellectual Record: An Exercise in Mutability," Research Update (University Microfilms, International) (Winter 1990), 4-5, 46-48. Describes preservation methods, conservation, mass deacidification, microfilming, and archival treatments.

1264. Crespo, Carmen, and Vicente Vinas. The Preservation and Restoration of Paper Records and Books: A RAMP Study with Guidelines. Paris: UNESCO, 1985. 115p. (PGI-84/WS/25). Focuses on paper, ink, causes, effects and prevention of deterioration, and conservation. Bibliography.

1265. Crespo Nogueira, Carmen. Glossary of Basic Archival and Library Conservation Terms. Munich, Germany: Saur, 1988. 151p. (ICA Handbook Series, 4). Terminology commonly found in library and archival conservation literature.

1266. Crespo Nogueira, Carmen. "The Role of ICA's Conservation and Restoration Committee (ICA/CRC)," Politics for the Preservation of the Archival Heritage. Paris: International Council on Archives, 1989, 204-211. Traces the history of the committee and evaluates its accomplishments.

1267. Cressman, Shawne Diaz. "Cornell Workshop on Digital Imaging," Conservation Administration News, 62/63 (Summer/Fall 1995), 9-12. Describes the technology used and Cornell's goal to scan, digitize, produce COM (for preservation), and create hardcopy facsimiles of their brittle books. Excellent summary, raising some good questions about application and cost of the technology for library collections. Notes "creation of paper facsimiles represents a compromise made to satisfy collections curators concerned about quality of digital images." (9)

1268. Crews, Patricia Cox. "A Comparison of Selected UV Filtering Material for the Reduction of Fading," Journal of the American Institute for Conservation, 28:2 (Fall 1989), 117-125. Filters for protecting collections from light are reviewed.

1269. Crews, Patricia Cox. "The Fading Rates of Same Natural Dyes," Studies in Conservation, 32:2 (May 1987), 65-72. Study of the fading rate of natural dyes and implications for museums.

1270. Cribbs, Margaret A. "The Invisible Drip ... How Data Seeps Away in Various Ways," Online, 11:2 (March 1987), 15-26. Discusses the innate impermanence and instability of electronic records; presents three case studies of organizations that invest in their preservation.

1271. Cribbs, Margaret A. "Photographic Conservation: An Update," ARMA Records Management Quarterly (Association of Record Managers and Administrators), 22:3 (July 1988), 17-19. How managers of photographic collections can determine the best environment for storage and use. Distinguishes between archival and heavily consulted research collections.

1272. Crocker, Jane, and Ellen Tiedrich. "Security In the Smaller Academic Library," New Jersey Libraries, 27:4 (Fall 1994), 6-11. Detailed guidelines for security and theft prevention, including emergency planning and staff training.

1273. Croft, Janet Brennan. "Mold Fighting on a Tight Budget," Archival Products News, 4:1 (Winter 1996), 1-2,6. Case study of mold attack on library materials, salvage and cleaning, and plans for prevention of further infestation.

1274. Crole, Sandy. "The Permanence of Paper," Bookbinder (Journal of the Society of Bookbinders and Book Restorers), 2 (1988), 77-88. Brief history of papermaking; production of permanent paper and the use of cotton/linen fibers.

1275. Croll, Michael. "The Life Expectancy of Optical Recordings," Archiving the Audio-Visual Heritage. Rushton, England: FIAF/UNESCO, 1992, 70-77. Explores the potential of optical disk technologies for audio recording.

1276. Crombie, L. ed. Recent Advances in the Chemistry of Insect Control II. Cambridge: Royal Society of Chemistry, 1990. 296p. (Special Publication 79). Focuses on pest control for crop protection, but includes useful information on insecticides and integrated pest management programs. Proceedings of the 2d International Symposium, Oxford, July 17-19, 1989.

1277. Crosbie, Michael J. "Library Science: Planning for Book Conservation, Storage, and Information Retrieval," Architecture (American Institute of Architects), 79:7 (July 1990), 103-105. Environmental control and storage for libraries containing electronic information equipment and media as well as collections of books.

1278. Cross, R. F. Bookbinding Notes: How to Repair and Rebind Paperback Books, Pamphlets and Magazines. Wooster, OH: Booker's, 1988. 105p. Handwritten text on rebinding and repair of paperbacks for the amateur. Xerox produced, hand bound.

1279. Crowe, William J. "Verner Clapp and Preservation of Library Materials: The Years at the Council on Library Resources," Academic Librarianship: Past Present and Future: A Festschrift in Honor of David Kaser, ed. John Richardson Jr. and Jinnie Y. Davis. Englewood, CO: Libraries Unlimited, 1989. The history of Clapp's efforts to arouse concern for preservation and to deal with the problems of brittle paper and poorly made books. Based on a chapter from the author's dissertation, Verner W. Clapp as Opinion Leader and Change Agent in the Preservation of Library Materials, Indiana, 1986.

1280. Crowley, Mary Jo. "Optical Digital Disk Storage: An Application for News Libraries," Special Libraries, 79:1 (Winter 1988), 34-42. Describes technology, equipment, and procedures necessary for converting a clipping collection to optical storage as an alternative to microfilm, microfiche, and/or original material.

1281. Cruse, Larry. "Cartography's Photographic Revolution: Microcartography," Wilson Library Bulletin, 60:2 (October 1985), 17-20. Brief history of the photoreproduction of maps and the need to preserve these collections.

1282. Cruse, Larry. "Design for a Semi-Automatic Map Encapsulator," Western Association of Map Libraries Information Bulletin, 15:1 (November 1983), 1-7. Discussion of concept and instructions for making rolls for encapsulation.

1283. Cruse, Larry. "Storage of Maps on Paper, Microforms, Optical Disks, Digital Disks and Magnetic Memories," Science and Technology Libraries, 5:3 (Spring 1985), 45-57. Special Issue: "Role of Maps in Sci-Tech Libraries," ed. Ellis Mount. Describes the characteristics of and outlook for the application of new technologies to cartography, advantages and disadvantages.

1284. Csaki, Klara. "The Restoration of Dolls and Toys Made from Paper-Based Materials," Conference on Book and Paper Conservation, 1990. Budapest, Hungary: Technical Association of Paper and Printing Industry/National Szechenyi Library, 1992. 228-237. Reviews the history of the objects and materials, testing, and treatments. Illus.

1285. Csenki, Eva. "Metals in Bookbinding," Conference on Book and Paper Conservation, 1990. Budapest: Technical Association of Paper and Printing Industry/National Szechenyi Library, 1992, 188-196. Use of metals in decorative bookbinding.

1286. Cuddihy, Edward F. "Stability and Preservation of Magnetic Tape," Conservation in Archives. Paris: International Council on Archives, 1989, 191-206. Reports on research into the deterioration of magnetic tape with a polyester urethane binder system; evidence that binder failure can be avoided by maintenance of proper storage environment. Paper presented at an International Symposium Ottawa, Canada, May 1989.

1287. Cuddihy, Edward F. "Storage, Preservation and Recovery of Magnetic Tape Recordings," Environnement et Conservation de l'Écrit, de l'Image et du Son. Paris: ARSAG, 1994, 182-186. (Actes des Deuxièmes Journées Internationales d'Etudes de l'ARSAG). Report of a study to identify problems with commercial magnetic tape for spacecraft recorders fabricated with magnetic oxide particles and with oxide and backcoat binders made from polyester urethane.

1288. Cullison, Bonnie Jo. "New Conservation Facilities at the Newberry Library," Conservation Administration News, 22 (July 1985), 8,22-23. Description of the facility.

1289. Cullison, Bonnie Jo. "The Preservation of Archival Material," Researcher's Guide to Archives and Regional History Sources, ed. John C. Larsen. Hamden, CT: Shoe String Press, 1988, 129-140. Outlines preservation strategies, including environmental control, care, and handling.

1290. Cullison, Bonnie Jo, and Jean Donaldson. "Conservators and Curators: A Cooperative Approach to Treatment Specifications," Library Trends, 36:1 (Summer 1987), 229-239. Discusses the role of scholars, curators, and conservators in preserving and conserving historically significant materials.

1291. Cumming, Neil. Security: A Guide to Security System Design and Equipment Selection and Installation. 2d ed. Boston: Butterworth-Heinemann, 1992. 338p. A clear comprehensive presentation of electronic security systems. Each type of security equipment covered (35 categories) is detailed as to its principal operating features, primary uses, suitability for a particular application, and limitations and advantages.

1292. Cummings, Martin M., ed. Influencing Change in Research Librarianship: A Festschrift for Warren J. Haas. Washington, DC: Council on Library Resources, 1988. 108p. Highlights Haas's career and concern for the preservation of library materials.

1293.   Cunha, George M. "Current Trends in Preservation Research and
        Development," American Archivist, 53:2 (Spring 1990),
        192-202. Overview: includes climate control, mold and pest control,
        disaster prevention and recovery, mass deacidification, and paper
        strengthening.

1294.   Cunha, George M. "Disaster Planning: A Guide to Recovery
        Resources," Library Technology Reports, 28:5 (September/October
        1992), 533-624.

1295.   Cunha, George M. "How I Spent My Winter Vacation. (Visit to Saint
        Petersburg and Moscow, December 1991)," Conservation
        Administration News, 50 (July 1992), 11.

1296.   Cunha, George M. "LC's Deacidification Process Leased to
        Chemical Giant," American Libraries, 20:8 (September 1989),
        721. Comment on the role that AKZO might play in the development
        and use of the diethyl zinc (DEZ) deacidification process.

1297.   Cunha, George M. "Mass Deacidification," The Kentucky Archivist,
        5:1 (1983), 5-6. A discussion of the state of the art in 1983 and the
        potential uses for this treatment.

1298.   Cunha, George M. "Mass Deacidification for Libraries," Library
        Technology Reports, 23:3 (May-June 1987), 361-472; "Mass
        Deacidification for Libraries: An Update," Library Technology
        Reports, 25:1 (January-February 1989), 5-81. A review of the
        processes: Diethyl Zinc DEZ) Wei T'o, and the Austrian process; the
        1989 update examines the Bookkeeper, BPA, and Lithco processes,
        as well as recent developments in Europe.

1299.   Cunha, George M. Methods of Evaluation to Determine the
        Preservation Needs in Libraries and Archives: A RAMP Study with
        Guidelines. Paris: UNESCO, September 1988. 76p.
        (PGI-88/WS/16). Outlines the procedure for a preservation survey of
        collections; prepared to assist in the development of basic training
        programs and courses for archives conservation.

1300.   Cunha, George M. "NEDCC: The Original Vision," Conservation
        Administration News, 56 (January 1994), 16-17, 36-38. Describes
        the founding of the New England (now Northeast) Document
        Conservation Center, the first and still the only regional center
        devoted to the treatment of library and archival materials.

1301.   Cunha, George M. "Some Thoughts on Conservation Management,"
        Kentucky Libraries, 54:1 (Spring 1990), 15-18. Overview of

production capabilities, costs, safety, toxicity, effects on books and
paper, impact on library operations, and effect on environment.

1302.   Cunha, George M., and Dorothy G. Library and Archives
        Conservation: 1980s and Beyond. Metuchen, NJ: Scarecrow Press,
        1983. 2 volumes; text and bibliography. The history of library
        preservation and conservation initiatives; identifies trends and
        discusses the future direction of preservation activities.

1303.   Cunha, George M., and Dorothy Cunha G. "When Disaster Strikes"
        In Library and Archives Conservation: 1980s and Beyond.
        Metuchen, NJ: Scarecrow Press, 1983. Vol. 1 pp. 79-96 and Vol. 2
        pp. 304-322.

1304.   Cunha, George M., Howard P. Lowell, and Robert E. Schnare Jr.
        Conservation Survey Manual. Albany, NY: New York Library
        Association, 1982. 64p. A detailed guide for undertaking
        preservation surveys.

1305.   Cunningham, Veronica Calley. "The Preservation of Newspaper
        Clippings," Special Libraries, 78:1 (Winter 1987), 41-46. Problems in
        the preservation of newspapers; preservation microfilming as an
        option for preservation.

1306.   Cunningham-Kruppa, Ellen. "The General Libraries Preservation
        Program: A Preliminary Report," Conservation and Preservation of
        Humanities Research Collections, ed. Dave Oliphant. Austin, TX:
        Harry Ransom Humanities Research Center, University of Texas,
        1989, 156-163. Describes the Libraries' preservation program from
        1980 and future projects.

1307.   Cunningham-Kruppa, Ellen. "The Preservation Officer's Role in
        Collection Development," Wilson Library Bulletin, 67:3 (November
        1992), 27-29, 107. Defines the administrator's role: planning,
        administration, coordinating; discusses programs and projects.

1308.   Curach, Liz. "Palm Leaves & Hot Chips," National Library of
        Australia News, 5:7 (April 1995), 9-11. Report on the state of
        libraries and library collections in Burma, Based on a two-week visit.

1309.   Curran, Charles. "The Secret Page," Library Resources and
        Technical Services, 33:3 (July 1989), 281-283. Parody on ownership
        marking procedures in libraries and archives.

1310.   Curriculum Development for the Training of Personnel in Moving
        Image and Recorded Sound Archives: A RAMP Study. Paris:

UNESCO, 1990. 104p. Focuses on key issues for education and training of archivists specializing in audiovisual materials.

1311.   Currie, Susan, et al. "Cornell University Libraries' Security Checklist," Library and Archival Security, 7:2 (Summer 1985), 3-13. A comprehensive list of questions to be used in the evaluation of library security measures; developed by the library's Conservation Security Subcommittee.

1312.   Curtin, Bonnie Rose. "Archives Preservation: NAGARA GRASPP Project Description," Conservation Administration News, 41 (April 1990), 3-5. Description of the program.

1313.   Curtin, Bonnie Rose. "Is Conservation Ready for Artificial Intelligence?" Abbey Newsletter, 14:1 (Feb. 1990), 1-2. Brief description of the computer driven preservation self-study program being developed by the National Association of Government Archives and Records Administrators (NAGARA).

1314.   Curtin, Bonnie Rose. The NAGARA GRASP: Guide and Resources for Archival Strategic Preservation Planning. Chicago, IL: Society of American Archivists/National Association of Government Archives and Record Administrators, 1990. 2 vols., 3 discs. A computerized tool for preservation planning with considerable printed material.

1315.   Curtin, Bonnie Rose. "Preservation Planning for Archives: Development and Field Testing of the NAGARA GRASPP," American Archivist, 53:2 (Spring 1990), 236-243. Describes the design and field testing of an automated preservation planning system for archives.

1316.   Curtin, Bonnie Rose. "Preservation Planning in Archives," Book and Paper Annual, 9 (1990), 37-40. Discusses archival challenges and the design and field testing of the NAGARA GRASPP automated preservation planning system.

1317.   Cytron, Barry D. Fire! The Library Is Burning. Minneapolis, MN: Lerner Pub. Co., 1988. 56p. Illus. A children's book about the fire and salvage effort at the Jewish Theological Seminary, New York City, in 1966. While salvage technology has evolved considerably since that time, the story reflects the love of the book and the great effort and care devoted to the salvage of the collection by the community.

1318.   Dachs, Karl. "Conservation: The Curator's Point of View," Restaurator, 6:3/4 (1984), 118-126. Discusses the concern for the integrity of the object that must be brought to rare book conservation; the need for reversibility whenever possible, and the need to preserve all historically important characteristics in treatment. Paper presented at the 1983 Congress of the International Federation of Library Associations and Institutions, Munich, Germany.

1319.   Daffner, Lee Ann, Dan Kushel, and John M. Messinger, II. "Investigation of Surface Tarnish Found on 19th Century Daguerreotypes," AIC Bulletin (American Institute of Conservation), 35:1 (Spring 1996), 9-21. Study including preliminary analysis of tarnish found on a collection of daguerreotypes and its rate of occurrence. Describes method of investigation; concludes that the tarnishing may be the result of previous treatment.

1320.   Dahlø, Rolf. "Cold Storage," Library Conservation News, 37 (October 1992), 1-3. Discusses the preservation strategy of housing valuable paper-based library and archival collections in cold storage to retard deterioration. The National Library of Norway will thus preserve its collections.

1321.   Dahlø, Rolf. "Preventing Future Needs for Conservation," Library Conservation News, 25 (October 1989), 1-2. Describes the efforts of the Norwegian National Office for Research and Special Libraries to promote the use of alkaline paper in books.

1322.   Dainton (Lord). "On the Problem of Ploughing ...," Library Association Record, 88:10 (October 1986), 487-492. Notes need for preservation of both "elite" documents and the ephemera of everyday life, and the causes of their destruction. Keynote address at the Library Association Conference on Preservation.

1323.   Dale, Robin. "Selection for Preservation and Access: Notes from the PARS/CMDS Program," ALCTS Newsletter (Association of Library Collections and Technical Services), 6:6 (1995) 79. (1995 ALA Conference).

1324.   Dalley, Jane A. "Pressure-Sensitive Tapes: Their Behavior and Removal, As Illustrated by a Case Study," Conservation of Historic and Artistic Works. Ottawa: Canadian Conservation Institute, 1994, 39-46. (Symposium 88). Report of an investigation into the history, composition, aging characteristics, and behavior of Scotch tape.

1325.   Dalrymple, Helen. "Modern Technology Employed to Store the Original Document," LC Information Bulletin (Library of Congress), 54 (Feb. 6 1995), 42. (Lincoln's Gettysburg address).

1326. Dalton, Susan. "Moving Images: Conservation and Preservation," Conserving and Preserving Materials in Nonbook Formats. Urbana-Champaign, IL: University of Illinois Graduate School of Library and Information Science, 1991, 61-72. (Allerton Park Institute, 30). Reviews initiatives to preserve the moving image, noting that optical disks are not a preservation medium. Emphasizes need for cooperative initiatives.

1327. Daly, James, ed. Workshop on Electronic Texts: Proceedings. Washington, DC: Library of Congress, 1992. 118p. Proceedings of a meeting to explore issues of preservation and access with representatives of projects and interest groups; makes clear that electronic imaging not a preservation medium. Includes papers by Anne Kenney, Pat Battin, Donald Waters, Pamela Andre, Judith Zedar, Michael Lesk, and others.

1328. Dance Heritage Coalition. Beyond Memory: Preserving the Documents of Our Dance Heritage. Pelham, NY: Dance Heritage Coalition, 1994. 12p., appendixes. Discusses the need to document dance, and to organize and preserve archival materials.

1329. D'Angelo, Kathleen T. Mass Treatment Options for the Recovery of Water-Damaged Materials, With Attention to Disaster and Disaster Planning. Chapel Hill, NC: School of Information and Library Science, May 1989. 213 p., typescript. M.D.L.S. thesis. Reviews options then available based on a selective review of the literature.

1330. Dangerfiled, John. "Balancing Safety & Comfort," Heritage Development (U.K.) (May, 1995), 18-19. Renovating and lighting the Bodleian Library's new exhibition space.

1331. Daniel, Floréal, Françoise Flieder, Frédéruque Juchauld, and Carole Yver. "Study of the Homogeneity of Mass Deacidification Treatments Using Atomic Absorption Spectrometry," Preventive Conservation: Practice, Theory and Research, ed. Ashok Roy and Perry Smith. London: International Institute for Conservation, 217-222. (Preprints, Ottawa Congress, September 12-16, 1994). Examines whether homogeneity is in fact a good way to select materials for mass deacidification treatment. Examines concentration levels of magnesium or zinc in different locations on sheets of paper treated by several methods.

1332. Daniel, Floréal, Françoise Flieder, and Francoise Leclerc. "The Behavior of Papers Deacidified Under Pressure by Ethylmagnesium Carbonate as Regards Two Kinds of Accelerated Aging: Wet Heat and Simulated Pollution," Conference on Book and Paper Conservation, 1990. Budapest, Hungary: Technical Association of

Paper and Printing Industry/National Szechenyi Library, 1992, 471-482. Examines the effect of deacidified papers during artificial aging; raises questions that need further study about deacidified papers. Charts.

1333. Daniel, Floréal, Françoise Flieder, and Françoise LeClerc, "The Effects of Pollution on Deacidified Paper," Restaurator, 11:3 (1990), 179-207. Study indicates that some papers might deteriorate more rapidly after deacidification in highly polluted conditions.

1334. Daniel, Vinod, Gordon Hanlon and Shin Maekawa. "Eradication of Insect Pests in Museums Using Nitrogen," WAAC Newsletter (Western Association for Art Conservation), 15:3 (September 1993), 15-19. Describes some of the results of testing several methods of treating infested museum objects by maintaining a low oxygen atmosphere.

1335. Daniel, Vinod, and Shin Maekawa. "Hygromatic Half-Lives of Museum Cases," Restaurator, 14:1 (1993), 30-44. Results of testing for storage boxes for library and archival materials.

1336. Daniel, Vinod, and Shin Maekawa. "The Moisture Buffering Capability of Museum Cases," Issues in Art and Archaeology III. Pittsburgh, PA: Materials Research Society, 1992, 453-458. Examines results of experiments to evaluate the effect of construction and closure characteristics on the moisture buffering capability of solander, portfolio, music, and document boxers used to house materials.

1337. Daniels, Vincent. Early Advances in Conservation. London: British Museum, 1988. 166p. (British Library Occasional Paper, 65). Identifies early conservation practices that have stood the test of time.

1338. Daniels, Vincent. "Factors Influencing the Wash-Fastness of Watercolours," Paper Conservator, 19 (1995), 31-40. Examination suggests that wash-fastness depends on the constituents of the paints and the paper used.

1339. Daniels, Vincent. "Leather Dressing at the BM," Conservation News, 44 (March 1991), 31-32. History of the various formula modifications used since the British Museum leather dressing was introduced in the mid-1930s.

1340. Daniels, Vincent, and Brian Boyd. "The Yellowing of Thymol in the Display of Prints," Studies in Conservation, 31:4 (November 1986),

156-158. Glazed frames that contain Thymol cause discoloration of prints exposed to light.

1341. Daniels, Vincent, and Morven Leese. "The Degradation of Silk by Verdigris," Restaurator 16:1 (1995), 45-63.

1342. Daniels, Vincent, and Ian McIntyre. "An Apparatus for Studying Conservation Light Bleaching," Conservation Science in the UK: Preprints of the Meeting Held in Glasgow, May 1993. ed. Norman H. Tennent. London: James & James Science Publishers, 1993, 122-124. Describes an apparatus for studying conservation light bleaching of paper.

1343. Daniels, Vincent, and Nigel D. Meeks. "Foxing Caused by Copper Alloy Inclusions in Paper," Symposium 88: Conservation of Historic and Artistic Works on Paper; Proceedings of a Conference, Ottawa, Canada, October 3 to 7, 1988. ed. Helen D. Burgess. Ottawa: The Institute, 1994, 229-233. Examination and analysis of foxing of paper caused by brass inclusions.

1344. Daniels, Vincent and Yvonne Shashoua. "Evaluation of Reagents for the Determination of Protein in Solution," Conservation Science in the UK..., ed. Norman H. Tennent. London: James & James Science Publishers , 1993, 99-102. Investigates three solutions for the colorimentric determination of protein ion solution. Paper presented at a conference, Glasgow, May 1993.

1345. Dannelly, Gay. "The Collection Development Officer as Part of the Preservation Team, Or The Y'all Come Approach to Preservation," Wilson Library Bulletin, 67:3 (November 1992), 30-34,107. Discusses cooperation within the context of the Ohio State University Library, with a look toward future concerns.

1346. D'Arienzo, Daria, Anne Ostendorp, and Emily Silverman. "Preservation Microfilming: The Challenge of Saving a Collection at Risk," American Archivist, 57:3 (Summer 1994), 498-513. Case study of the experience and challenge of filming a large collection of papers for preservation and access at a college library; analysis of the outcome of the project.

1347. Darling, Pamela W. "Expanding Preservation Resources: The Corps of Practitioners and the Core of Knowledge," Conserving and Preserving Library Materials, ed. Kathryn L. and William T. Henderson. Urbana-Champaign, IL: University of Illinois Graduate School of Library and Information Science, 1983, 19-36. Describes current projects and programs that inform librarians about preservation needs and management.

1348. Darling, Pamela W. "Planning for the Future," The Library Preservation Program: Models, Priorities, Possibilities, Chicago, IL: American Library Association, 1985, 103-110. Suggests that administrators analyze what has already been done and plan beyond; discusses resource sharing and planning on the national level.

1349. Darling, Pamela W., comp. Preservation Planning Program Resource Notebook, rev. ed. by Wesley L. Boomgaarden. Washington, DC: Association of Research Libraries, Office of Management Studies, 1987, 675p., unbound. Readings on preservation to assist in a self-study.

1350. Darling, Pamela W. Saving the Record: Report on Preserving the Collections of the Smithsonian Institution Libraries. New York: Darling, 1984. 24p.

1351. Darling, Pamela W. "A Slow but Steady Progress: The Search for a National Preservation Strategy," National Preservation News, 1 (July 1985), 12-14. Reviews the history of national planning for the preservation of library materials in the United States.

1352. Darling, Pamela W., and Duane E. Webster. Preservation Planning Program: An Assisted Self-Study Manual for Libraries. expanded ed. Washington, DC: Association of Research Libraries, Office of Management Studies, 1987. 160p.; revised by Jan Merrill-Oldham and Jutta Reed-Scott. Washington, DC: Association of Research Libraries, 1993. 138p. Self-study guide to assess preservation needs.

1353. Darnell, Polly. Managing Our Past to Plan for Our Future: A Five-Year Plan for Cooperative Efforts to Preserve the Documentary Heritage of the Western New York Region. Buffalo: Western New York Documentary Heritage Program, 1990. 24p. Report prepared to ensure the preservation of the region's documentary resources.

1354. Dartmouth College Library. Disaster Manual. 2d ed. Hanover, NH, Dartmouth College Library, 1989. 46 leaves.

1355. Dartnell, Jean. "Library Conservation in the Tropics," Education for Librarianship: Australia, 5:1 (Autumn 1988), 10-17. Identifies issues needing further investigation, including environmental controls, pest control, buildings, and the role of staff and users.

1356. Das, A.C. "Conservation of Some Non-Book Material in the National Library, Calcutta," Conservation of Cultural Property in India, 18-20, New Delhi, Indian Association for the Study of Conservation of Cultural Property (1985-1987), 14-21. Describes the

conservation treatments adopted for non-book materials, including
maps, palm leaf, and illustrated manuscripts.

1357.   Das, Sudhir Kumar. "Repair and Restoration of Parchment and
        Vellum Manuscripts," Conservation of Cultural Property in India.
        New Delhi, Indian Association for the Study of Conservation of
        Cultural Property, 1983, 181-183. Describes methods for cleaning
        and restoring soiled, deteriorated manuscripts and discusses some
        techniques for filling holes in parchment and vellum manuscripts.
        Paper from a seminar, "Conservation of Paintings," 1983.

1358.   Dasgupta, Kalpana, ed. Planning Modernization and Preservation
        Programmes for South Asian Libraries: A Seminar, 1990. Calcutta,
        India: National Library, 1992. 295p. Papers from a conference called
        to encourage the development of regional and national cooperative
        initiatives and programs, with a focus on bibliographic control,
        preservation, and access.

1359.   Daval, Nicola, ed. Collections: Their Development, Management,
        Preservation and Sharing. Washington, DC: Association of Research
        Libraries, 1989. 180p. Papers from the Joint Meeting of the
        Association of Research Libraries and the Standing Conference of
        National and University Libraries, University of York, September 22,
        1988.

1360.   Davies, John. "Guarding and Filing Archives," First National
        Conference of Craft Bookbinders - Australia. Kingston, Australia:
        Craft Bookbinders Guild, November 1984, 6-11. Describes a process
        to guard and then stitch together collections of papers for
        preservation and access.

1361.   Davies, Walter E., "Preserving Magnetic Tape," Broadcast
        Engineering (October 1987), 84-88.

1362.   Davis, Julianna, and Irmgard H. Wolfe. "Preservation Notes,"
        Mississippi Libraries, 58 (Spring 1994) 29.

1363.   Davis, Mary B. "Preservation Using Pesticides: Some Words of
        Caution," Wilson Library Bulletin, 59:6 (February 1985),
        386-388. Discusses the harm that fumigants and pesticides can cause
        humans; suggests alternative pest control techniques, including good
        housekeeping procedures, freezing and other non-toxic treatments.

1364.   Davis, Mary B., Susan Fraser, and Judith Reed. "Preparing for
        Library Emergencies: A Cooperative Approach," Wilson Library
        Bulletin, 66:3 (November 1991), 42-22, 128. Describes the Bronx

(NY) Library Emergency Consortium, established to ensure a cooperative response to a fire or water emergency.

1365. Davis, Nancy. "Hints for Preserving Family Photographs," NEDCC News (Northeast Document Conservation Center), 4:2 (Fall 1992), [4]. Basic tips on handling, housing and storage. Originally published in Handle With Care: Preserving Your Heirlooms (Rochester, NY: Rochester Museum & Science Center 1991).

1366. Davis, Peter. "Preserving China's Past," National Library of Australia News, 5:4 (January 1995), 12-15. Describes preservation initiatives at the Municipal Library of Shanghai and the University Library of Wuhan. Describes briefly the microwave worm killer developed for the Shanghai Library.

1367. Davis, Robert H. "Microform Preservation of Slavic and East European Materials: A Review of Past Activities, Present Conditions, and Future Outlook," Microform Review, 21:3 (Summer 1992), 98-105. Overview of the situation of libraries and archives in Russia, with emphasis on conservation treatment rather than microfilm; suggestions for what can be done.

1368. Davis, Robin J. "Laboratory in the Library: Archival Conservation in Stirling University Library," Library Review, 36:3 (Autumn 1987), 174-178. Briefly describes deacidification and treatment of archival materials.

1369. Davis, Sheryl Jean. "Networking for Disaster Preparedness and Recovery," Building on the First Century. Washington, DC: Association of College and Research Libraries, 1989, 295-297. Proposal that libraries in a regional form networks to provide mutual disaster aid. Paper given at the 5th National Conference of the Association of College and Research Libraries, Cincinnati, OH, April 5-8, 1989.

1370. Davis, Sheryl Jean. "Preservation Intensive Institute: Science for Preservation," Conservation Administration News, 56 (January 1994), 19-20.

1371. Davis, Susan W. "BENCHMARK for Book Repair: A User's Perspective," Library Software Review, 11:4 (July-August 1992), 15-20. Describes and notes strengths and weaknesses of a system designed to track book repair workflow in a workshop.

1372. Dawood, Rosemary. "Preservation of South Asian Language," Illinois Libraries, 72:1 (January 1990), 103-112. Report on a project to acquire, preserve, and make available materials documenting the cultural heritage of Southeast Asian people in the Chicago area.

1373. Dawson, John E. Solving Museum Insect Problems: Chemical Controls, rev. Thomas J. K. Strang. Toronto, Canada: Canadian Conservation Institute, [1993]. 26p. English/French. (Technical Leaflet, 15). Guide to help museum staff understand commercial pest control operations. Describes chemical methods of pest control; safety concerns.

1374. Day, Michael William. Preservation Problems of Electronic Text and Data. Loughborough, U.K.: EMBLA, 1990. 191p. (East Midlands Branch of the Library Association Occasional Papers, 3). Examines issues connected with the problems in preserving information stored in machine-readable form on electronic storage media. Bibliography. Excellent overview.

1375. Day, Rebecca. "Where's the Rot?" Stereo Review, 54:4 (1989), 23-24. Briefly discusses CD longevity and deterioration. Avoids direct answers as to whether CDs can last "forever." Admits that there is no definitive way to predict the life span of a CD. Also discusses industry standards and testing.

1376. Deal, Carl W. "The Latin American Microfilm Project: The First Decade," Microform Review, 15:1 (Winter 1986), 22-27. Summary of activities, primarily the filming of newspapers and journals, to preserve materials in danger of being lost.

1377. Deal, Suzanne. "Conservation Training in Latin America," WAAC Newsletter (Western Association for Art Conservation), 13:2 (May 1991), 19-21. Describes 12 programs of which at least two cover paper conservation.

1378. Dean, John F. "The Complete Repair of Bound Volumes," Serials Review, 13:3 (Fall 1987), 61-67. Description of basic repair techniques that can be done in-house for circulating collections; illustrations by Dean and Jane Dalrymple.

1379. Dean, John F. "Conservation and Collection Management," Journal of Library Administration, 7:2/3 (Fall 1986), 129-141. Reviews essential elements of collection management and relationship to preservation activities and decisions about what is to be preserved, and for how long.

1380. Dean, John F. "Cornell University: A Developing Preservation Program," Conservation Administration News, 39 (October 1989), 4-5, 30-31.

1381.   Dean, John F. "Conservation and Collection Management," Journal of Library Administration, 7:2-3 (Summer/Fall 1986), 129-141. Advocates collection evaluation to identify materials to be preserved and reviews conservation options.

1382.   Dean, John F. "The Preservation of Books and Manuscripts in Cambodia," American Archivist, 53:2 (Spring 1990), 282-293. Report on a program established by Cornell University to help preserve books and manuscripts neglected and damaged during decades of war.

1383.   Dean, John F. "The Self-Destructing Book," Yearbook of Science and the Future, 1989. Chicago, IL: Encyclopedia Britannica, 1988, 212-225. Basic article on the physical nature of paper, the causes of its deterioration, and the potential of deacidification treatments.

1384.   Dean, Susan Thach, and Sara R. Williams. "Renovation for Climate Control," Conservation Administration News, 56 (January 1994), 12-13, 23. Describes a renovation project to stabilize the relative humidity in the Special Collection stacks, University of Colorado Library.

1385.   Dearing, Julie A., and Marie Christine Uginet. "Information Retrieval in ICCROM Library," Terminology for Museums, ed. D. Andrew Roberts. Cambridge, England: Museum Documentation Association, 1990, 493-496. Discusses the organization of the library at the International Centre for the Conservation and Restoration of Cultural Property, Rome, library for access to its collections.

1386.   Dearman, J. Andrew. "On Record-Keeping and the Preservation of Documents in Ancient Israel (1000-587 B. C.)," Libraries and Culture, 24:3 (Summer 1989), 344-356. A note on ancient record-keeping and means of preservation.

1387.   Dearstyne, Bruce. "Preservation of Historical Records," The Archival Enterprise. Chicago, IL: American Library Association, 1993, 151-173. Chapter in a manual on archives management covering sources of problems, preservation administration, reformatting, and conservation.

1388.   DeBakey, Lois. "Book-Burning in Our Medical Libraries: Preservation or Pollution?" American Journal of Cardiology, 6:2 (September 1988), 458-461. Eloquent argument for the use of permanent paper for medical literature; points out that not all scientific literature over three years old is irrelevant.

1389.   DeBakey, Lois D., and Selma DeBakey. "Our Silent Enemy: Ashes
        in Our Libraries," Bulletin of the Medical Library Association, 77:3
        (July 1989), 258-268. A plea for the preservation of the written
        record in the biomedical literature. Notes need for more selection in
        publication in the field so the record can be saved; bibliography.

1390.   Debelius, Elizabeth, Robert Hueber, Elizabeth Napier-Cain, Phillip
        Rogers, and Susan Lee-Bechtold. A Study of Shrink-Wrapped
        Bound Volumes: Initial Findings. Washington, DC: National
        Archives and Records Administration, March 24, 1993. [17p.]
        (Preservation Information Paper, 1). Report of a study to determine
        the effect of shrink-wrapping bound volumes on their appearance and
        longevity.

1391.   DeCandido, GraceAnne Andreassi. "Brazen Overtures: Tool Box,"
        Wilson Library Bulletin, 68 (Jan. 1994), 8. A library school teacher
        discusses her efforts to teach preservation as a tool for librarianship.
        Preservation is used as a theme around which all aspects of
        librarianship are grouped.

1392.   DeCandido, GraceAnne Andreassi. "New Book Deacidification
        Process Prototype Soon to Be Available," Library Journal, 11:3
        (February 15, 1988), 112-114. Brief history of the Bookkeeper
        deacidification process compared with the diethyl zinc and Wei T'o
        processes.

1393.   DeCandido, GraceAnne Andreassi. "Preservation Comes of Age,"
        Library Journal (August 1990), 43. PLMS celebrates a decade of
        preservation activity.

1394.   DeCandido, GraceAnne Andreassi. "Preservation Summit Held at
        LC," Wilson Library Bulletin, 68 (May 1994), 11.

1395.   DeCandido, GraceAnne Andreassi.. "Special Report: Fire at the
        USSR Academy of Sciences Library," Library Journal, 113:11 (June
        15, 1988), 10,12. Brief report on the fire and the reaction by
        Russians, based upon a report to Library Journal by the Novosti
        Press Agency, Moscow.

1396.   DeCandido, GraceAnne Andreassi. "Your Mission Should You
        Choose to Accept It," Wilson Library Bulletin, 69:7 (March 1995),
        6. Preservation is central to the mission of any library, but it can also
        function as a toolbox of ways to think about access, acquisition,
        management, and service in the library.

1397.   DeCandido, GraceAnne Andreassi, and Michael Rogers.
        "Deacidification Not Quite at Warp Speed: LC and CIC Libraries

Search for Solutions," Library Journal, 114:4 (September 1, 1989), 118, 120. Briefly outlines plans for continued testing of available deacidification processes.

1398.   DeCandido, GraceAnne Andreassi, and Janine Stanley-Dunham. "Just an Old (and New) Sweet Song: Fifty Years of New Ideas From PLA," Wilson Library Bulletin, 68:10 (June 1994), 47-50. Report on the 1994 Public Library Association National Convention held in Atlanta, March 22-26, 1994. Topics addresses included library preservation needs.

1399.   DeCandido, Robert. "[Book Conservation]," in Interserevice Resources Management 13-15 October, 1982. West Point, NY: USMA Library, 1984. 30-31. Proceedings of the 26th Military Librarians Workshop. Discusses options for treating damaged books.

1400.   DeCandido, Robert. Collections Conservation. Washington, DC: Association of Research Libraries, 1993. 134p. (Preservation Planning Program). Guide to evaluate present activities and to consider implementation of further activities, such as basic book repair, with selected reprinted materials.

1401.   DeCandido, Robert. "Commission Promotes Levity [Select Berghoff Commission on Access to Humor in Preservation]," Conservation Administration News, 41 (April 1990), 25.

1402.   DeCandido, Robert. "Condition Survey of the United States History, Local History, and Genealogy Collection of the New York Public Library," Library Resources and Technical Services, 33:3 (July 1989), 274-281. Methodology and summary of results.

1403.   DeCandido, Robert. "Considerations in Evaluating Searching for Microform Availability," Microform Review, 19:3 (Summer 1990), 116-118. Presents an approach to cost analysis and discusses the problems of a formulaic approach to preservation decision making.

1404.   DeCandido, Robert. "The Effective Presentation of Statistics," New Library Scene, 14:6 (December 1995), 5-10. Examples of binding statistics.

1405.   DeCandido, Robert. "A Look at the Issue of Ethics [AIC Code]," Conservation Administration News, 58-59 (July/October 1994), 13-15.

1406.   DeCandido, Robert. "A Manifestation of Life: Preservation at the New York Botanical Garden Library," New Library Scene, 14:2

(April 1995), 8-10, 16-17. Describes the creation, history, and activities of the library with its collection of rare books, prints, plans, and mss.

1407. DeCandido, Robert. "Out of the Question," <u>Conservation Administration News</u>, 41 (April 1990), 26-27. Searching to determine whether a title has already been filmed.

1408. DeCandido, Robert. "Out of the Question," <u>Conservation Administration News</u>, 21 (April 1985), 21. Outlines factors to consider in selecting storage enclosures (both paper and plastics) for photographs. Recommends paper.

1409. DeCandido, Robert. "Out of the Question," <u>Conservation Administration News</u>, 22 (July 1985), 10, 24. Discusses (1) photographic storage materials made of polyvinyl chloride and (2) causes and prevention of "foxing."

1410. DeCandido, Robert. "Out of the Question," <u>Conservation Administration News</u>, 23 (October 1985), 17. Discusses the purpose of rounding and backing in library binding and offers tentative guidelines.

1411. DeCandido, Robert. "Out of the Question," <u>Conservation Administration News</u>, 53 (April 1993), 32-33. A reflective essay on the challenge of collection management and selection for preservation.

1412. DeCandido, Robert. "Out of the Question," <u>Conservation Administration News</u>, 47 (October 1991), 16-17,31. Discusses insurance coverage and liability for vendors of preservation-related services.

1413. DeCandido, Robert. "Out of the Question," <u>Conservation Administration News</u>, 28 (January 1987), 17, 27. Discusses digital recording and warns of finite life of compact disks.

1414. DeCandido, Robert. "Out of the Question: Fast Fires," <u>Conservation Administration News</u>, 35 (October 1989), 17.

1415. DeCandido, Robert. "Out of the Question: From the Ridiculous to the Sublimated." (freeze-dry/vacuum-dry world of disaster recovery) <u>Conservation Administration News</u>, 32 (January 1988), 21-22.

1416. DeCandido, Robert. "Out of the Question: How Are Binding Specifications Developed?" <u>Conservation Administration News</u>, 27 (October 1986), 9, 17. A brief and clear discussion on developing specifications using the Library Binding Institute standards, with some comments about the standards.

1417. DeCandido, Robert. "Out of the Question: I'm Searchin', I'm Searchin' Ev'ry Whi-i-ich a-Way, Yay, Yay,'" Conservation Administration News, 40 (January 1990), 20-21. A formula for evaluating the cost-effectiveness of searching prior to microfilming for preservation; concludes that pre-searching appears to be justified.

1418. DeCandido, Robert. "Out of the Question: Packing Books for Transport," Conservation Administration News, 43 (October 1990), 22-23; 44 (January 1991), 22-23.

1419. DeCandido, Robert. "Out of the Question: R-E-S-P-E-C-T," Conservation Administration News, 57 (April 1994), 13-14. Describes workshops in proper care and handling of materials for paging and shelving staff.

1420. DeCandido, Robert. "Out of the Question: Some Nukes," Conservation Administration News, 36 (January 1989), 22. Use of microwave ovens for controlling pests in books.

1421. DeCandido, Robert. "Out of the Question: "Ill Fated Books," Conservation Administration News, 43, 44 (October 1990, January 1991), 22-23 in each volume. Discussion of shipping containers for inter-agency and interlibrary loan, includes cost comparisons for several methods.

1422. DeCandido, Robert. "Out of the Question: "Quis Custodes Iposos Custodiet?" Conservation Administration News, 45 (April 1991), 17-18. Discussion of microform masters, the quality of their production and the security of their storage; with suggestions about possible means of making them more reliable and more secure.

1423. DeCandido, Robert. "Out of the Question: Night Thoughts and Day Musings." Conservation Administration News, 49 (April 1992) 17. Unanswered questions.

1424. DeCandido, Robert. "Out of the Question: Preservation, the INTERNET and You." Conservation Administration News, 53 (April 1993), 32-33. The need for selection in preserving the glut of information available on the INTERNET.

1425. DeCandido, Robert. "Out of the Question: "Scrapbooks, the Smiling Villians." Conservation Administration News, 54 (July 1993), 18-19. A brief and unofficial history of scrapbooks, their value and their immense preservation problems.

1426.   DeCandido, Robert. "A PLMS Perspective on ALCTS
         Restructuring," ALCTS Network News (Association for Library
         Collections and Technical Service), 4 (December 7, 1992), 16.

1427.   DeCandido, Robert. "Preservation Summit Held at LC [3rd Summit,
         March 1994]," Wilson Library Bulletin, 68 (May 1994), 11.

1428.   DeCandido, Robert. "Statistical Methodologies for Preservation,"
         New Library Scene, 14:5 (October 1995), 9-10. Discusses statistical
         methods and their applications for preservation decision making.

1429.   DeCandido, Robert, and GraceAnne Andreassi DeCandido.
         "Micro-Preservation: Conserving the Small Library," Library
         Resources and Technical Services, 29:2 (April-June 1985),
         151-160. Offers suggestions and outlines procedures for the
         preservation of the resources of a small library. Bibliography.

1430.   Robert DeCandido, and GraceAnne Andreassi DeCandido.
         Preservation Tip Sheet-Preservation: A Common Ground, Chicago,
         Il: ALA Graphics, 1991. 4p. Prepared for the Association for Library
         Collections and Technical Services. Discussed two major areas of
         preservation, deteriorating paper and the use and storage of
         collections.

1431.   DeCandido, Robert, and Cheryl Shackelton. Who Ya Gonna Call? A
         Preservation Service Source Book for Libraries and Archives. New
         York: New York Metropolitan Reference and Resource Library
         Agency, 1992. 132p. (METRO Misc. Publ., 42). Alphabetical
         listing of sources of preservation consultation and treatment in the
         New York metropolitan region and beyond. Index; bibliography.

1432.   DeCesare, Kyman B. J. "Safe Nontoxic Pest Control for Books,"
         Abbey Newsletter, 14:1 (February 1990), 16. Describes a technique,
         developed by the author, using argon gas in a sealed container to kill
         pests in books.

1433.   "Declaring War on Deterioration: David Magoon Wants to Help Us,"
         Wilson Library Bulletin, 61:1 (September 1986), 44-48. Profile of
         Magoon and materials developed by University Products for the
         preservation of library and archival collections.

1434.   Deeney, Marion. "Disasters: Are You Ready If One Should Strike
         Your Library?" Southeastern Librarian, 35:2 (Summer 1985),
         42-46. Covers steps necessary to prepare for disaster and recovery.

1435.   DeFelice, Barbara. "Cooperative Collection Development and
Presentation Projects in the Geosciences," Frontiers of Geoscience
Information, 20 (1990), 63-74. (Proceedings of the 24th Meeting of
the Geoscience Information Society, St. Louis, MO, November 6-9,
1989.). Reviews existing and planned cooperative collection
development and preservation programs; describes the Research
Libraries Group Earth Sciences Project.

1436.   Deitch, Joseph. "Portrait: Carolyn Clark Morrow," Wilson Library
Bulletin, 66:5 (January 1992), 65-67. Describes the efforts of
Harvard University Library to preserve its collections and the needs
assessment undertaken under preservation librarian Morrow.

1437.   Deken, Jean Marie. "Recovering from a Major Disaster,"
Midwestern Archivist, 9:1 (1994), 27-34. Practical advice on disaster
response and recovery.

1438.   DeLancie, Philip. "Sticky Shed Syndrome: Tips on Saving Your
Damaged Master Tapes," Mix (May 1990), 148-152. Discusses the
problem of binder and lubricant breakdown on older magnetic tapes;
describes a "baking" treatment to revive them.

1439.   Delaware's Documentary Heritage: The Future of Historical Records
in the First State. Dover, DE: Delaware Historical Records Advisory
Board, 1986. 38p.

1440.   DelCarmine, P., F. Lucarelli, P. A. Mando, and A. Pecchioli. "The
External PIXE Setup for the Analysis of Manuscripts at the Florence
University," Nuclear Instruments and Methods in Physics Research.
Section B: Beam Interactions with Materials and Atoms. B75:1-4
(1993), 480-484. Describes use of the external PIXE beam setup
exclusively used to analyze parchments, rulings, inks, and miniature
temperas in Medieval and Renaissance manuscripts.

1441.   DeLoughry, Thomas J. "Project Aims to Save Visual Images by
Storing Them on Compact Disks," Chronicle of Higher Education,
28 (October 1992), A22. Describes the pilot project between the
University of Southern California, Eastman Kodak, and Cornell
University, in which visual images are stored on compact disk. It is
intended to address the preservation and access aspects of digital
media.

1442.   Demas, Samuel. "National Preservation Planning for Agriculture,"
Agricultural Libraries Information Notes, 17:1/2 (1991),
1-8. Describes the proceedings of a two-day meeting to explore the
application of the Cornell Core Historical Literature project in

Agriculture in a national preservation initiative for agricultural sciences literature.

1443. Demas, Samuel. "Setting Preservation Priorities at the Mann Library: A Disciplinary Approach," Library Hi Tech, 12:3 (1994), 81-88. (Core agricultural literature project).

1444. Demco, Inc. Demco Book Protection and Repair: Quick, Easy Ways to Increase the Life of Your Books, Pamphlets, and Magazines. Madison, WI: Demco, Inc., 1989. 36p. Repair instructions using Demco's products; not recommended for preservation.

1445. Demiller, A. L. "Survey of the Research Collection with Preservation Assessment, Weeding and Inventory Objectives," Kaleidoscope (Mountain Plains Library Association, Academic Library Section, Research Forum), ed. C. Hammond. Emporia, KS: Emporia State University Press., 1991. Describes the inventory process at Colorado State University in which high use items of permanent research value were identified for preservation.

1446. Den Bleyker, Dan. "Disaster Planning for Film and Video Collections," Preservation Papers of the 1990 SAA Annual Conference, comp. Karen Garlick. Chicago: Society of American Archivists, 1991, 67-70. Advice for salvaging film and video.

1447. Densky, Lois R. "CAPES: The New Jersey Experience," Conservation Administration News, 47 (October 1991), 4-5. Describes the Caucus Archival Project Evaluation Service, providing consultation of organization and preservation for access of archival collections.

1448. Densky, Lois R., and Diane Solomon. "A Public Library Preservation Effort," New Jersey Libraries, 18:1 (Spring 1985), 8-12. Description of a program that includes preservation microfilming, phase conservation, and the physical treatment of materials.

1449. Densky-Wolff, Lois R. "CAPES: A Summary of Achievement," New Jersey Libraries, 26:3 (Summer 1993), 7-10. Describes the accomplishments of the Caucus Archival Project Evaluation Service (CAPES) to assist libraries and archives in planning and implementing sound collection management and preservation programs.

1450. D'Entremont, Susan. Disaster Prevention and Preparedness in Archival Facilities. Boston, MA: John Fitzgerald Kennedy Library, 1991. 27p.

1451. DePew, John N. An Investigation of Preservation Service Needs and Options for Florida Libraries. Tallahassee, FL: Florida State University School of Library and Information Studies, 1990. 155p., with appendixes. Report of investigation of needs of Florida libraries, conducted in 1989-90, with options for action.

1452. DePew, John N. "Lessons from Andrew," Southeastern Librarian, 44:2 (Summer 1994), 57-61. Discusses a survey to assess how Florida's libraries were affected by Hurricane Andrew and what effect the 1988 disaster planning and training initiative had on recovery; why the training program's effect was minimal.

1453. DePew, John N. A Library, Media, and Archival Preservation Handbook. Santa Barbara, CA: ABC-CLIO, 1991. 441p. Text on preservation of library and archival materials, with some treatment instructions.

1454. De Pew, John N. "Preservation Planning in Florida," Issues for the New Decade. Boston, MA: GK. Hall, 1991, 13-25. Describes the survey of preservation needs and statewide disaster planning efforts in Florida.

1455. DePew, John N. Statewide Disaster Preparedness and Recovery Program for Florida Libraries. Champaign, IL: Graduate School of Library and Information Studies, University of Illinois Urbana-Champaign, 1989. 51p. (Occasional Papers, 185, February 1989). Report of a statewide project to increase the awareness of the threat of water disasters and to train librarians to prepare for disaster and to respond to it.

1456. DePew, John N. "Time Is Running Out: An Investigation of the LSCA Title III Project Funded by the State Library of Florida," Flash (October 1989), 8-9. Summary of needs assessment survey.

1457. DePew, John, and Santi Basu. "The Application of Bradford's Law in Selecting Periodicals on Conservation and Preservation of Library Materials," Collection Management, 8:1 (Spring 1986), 55-64. A methodology for selection based on common sense.

1458. DePew, John N., with C. Lee Jones. A Library, Media and Archival Preservation Glossary. Santa Barbara, CA: ABC-CLIO, 1992. 192p. Brings together terms used in preservation and conservation of library and archival materials.

1459. DePhilips, Henry A, Jr., and Michele L. Mader. "Identification of Spue on Leather-Bound Library Books in the Watkinson Library of

Trinity College, Hartford, Conn.," Leather Conservation News, 11: 1/2 (Summer/Fall 1995), 8-10. (Issued Summer 1996). Report of analysis of white creamy matter found on books bound in leather; identified and attributed to earlier oiling programs.

1460.   Derben, Peter. "Binding a Collection of Herbarium Specimens," Library Conservation News, 38 (January 1993), 4-5. Describes a technique for conserving specimens by encapsulating each using the ultrasonic welder and placing them in post binders with slipcases.

1461.   Dernovskova, Jana, H. Jirasova, and Jiri Zelinger. "An Investigation of the Hygroscopicity of Parchment Subjected to Different Treatments," Restaurator, 16:1 (1995), 31-44. A study of difference in hygroscopicity between old and new parchments and the effects of conservation treatment, concluding that modern parchments should not be used for substitution in older parchments.

1462.   Derrick, Michele R., Helen D. Burgess, Mary T. Baker, and Nancy E. Binnie. "Sulfuryl Fluoride (Vikane): A Review of Its Use as a Fumigant," Journal of the American Institute for Conservation, 29:1 (Spring 1990), 77-90. Review article to provide conservators with specific, detailed information on the use of Vikane, and a basis for evaluation of sulfuryl fluoride. Includes information on uses, chemical reactivity, physical properties, efficacy, and toxicity. Bibliography.

1463.   Derrick, Michele, Vinod Daniel, and Andrew Parker. "Evaluation of Storage and Display Conditions for Cellulose Nitrate Objects," Preventive Conservation: Practice, Theory and Research, ed. Roy Ashok and Perry Smith. London: International Institute for Conservation, 1994, 207-211. (Preprints of the contributions to the Ottawa Congress, September 12-16, 1994). Study of the changes in elemental composition of old and new cellulose nitrate under controlled environmental conditions.

1464.   DeSantis, F., V. Di Palo, and I. Allegrini. "Determination of Some Atmospheric Pollutants Inside a Museum: Relationship with Concentration Outside," The Science of the Total Environment, 127 (1992), 221-223. Four gasses and two radicals were measured in the Iffizi Gallery, Florence, Italy, to determine what pollutants, and to what extent, entered the museum environment from the outside.

1465.   DeSantis, Pia C. "Some Observations on the Use of Enzymes in Paper Conservation," Journal of the American Institute for Conservation, 23:1 (Fall 1983), 7-27. Use of enzymes to remove adhesives.

1466.   Desmarais, Ellen. "An Update on Mass Deacidification at the
        National Library," National Library News (Canada), 26:7 (July
        1994), 12-13. Mass deacidification is now a major part of collection
        preservation at the National Library; reviews the Wei T'o system in
        use for 12 years and notes its success.

1467.   Desmarais, Ellen. "Conservation at the National Archives of
        Canada," CBBAG Newsletter (Canadian Bookbinders and Book
        Artists Guild), 10:1 (Spring 1992), 3-8; 10:2 (Summer 1992),
        3-6. Describes the development of preservation and conservation
        programs, the organization of the Conservation Unit, its operation
        and techniques used for full treatments.

1468.   Desmarais, Ellen. "An Update on Mass Deacidification at the
        National Library," National Library News (Canada), 26:7 (July
        1994), 12-13. Reviews the effectiveness of the Wei T'o system, in
        operation for 12 years, "a major part of the approach to collection
        preservation."

1469.   De Stefano, Paula. "Use-Based Selection for Preservation
        Microfilming," College & Research Libraries, 56:5 (September
        1995), 409-418. Questions sole reliance on collection-based approach
        to preserve brittle books; argues for development of a more coherent
        strategy for long-term preservation of brittle, circulating materials.

1470.   De Stefano, Paula. "New York State Combines Mass Deacidification
        with Rebinding," Conservation Administration News, 58-59
        (July/October 1994), 22-24. Eleven comprehensive research libraries
        pilot project.

1471.   De Stefano, Paula. "Photograph Preservation: A New Component in
        Preservation Programs," Photograph Preservation and the Research
        Library, ed. J. Porra. Mountain View, CA: Research Library Group,
        1991, 37-43. Discusses need for photographic conservators and
        preservation administrators to collaborate to develop principles for
        decision making.

1472.   "Developments of a National Conservation Treatment Database. A
        Program Report. Preservation Services Branch, National Library of
        Australia," International Journal of Museum Management and
        Curatorship, 4:1 (March 1985), 102-104. The National Library of
        Australia has developed an in-house conservation treatment
        information system and is now preparing controlled vocabulary lists
        and lists of recommended terms for various fields, and designing
        screen and printout formats for data entry and output.

1473. Deventer, Ronald van, John Havermans, and Sandra Berkhout. "A Comparison of Three Durability Standards for Paper," Restaurator, 16:3 (1995), 161-174. Compares three durability standards to find agreements and differences; to determine what paper durability standard is best related to paper. Review: Ellen McCrady, Alkaline Paper Advocate, 8:3 (October 1995) "Despite the inexactitude here, the comparison among the three standards is eye-opening."

1474. De Whitt, Benjamin L. "The Long-Term Preservation of Data on Computer Magnetic Media," Conservation Administration News, 29 (April 1987), 7, 19, 29, and 30 (July 1987), 4, 24. Definition of magnetic tape, problems, and maintenance.

1475. Dhawan, Shashi. Microbial Deterioration of Paper Material: A Literature Review. Lucknow, India: Department of Culture, National Research Library for Conservation of Cultural Property, 1986. 18p. International, technical bibliography.

1476. "Diane Kresh Named Director of Preservation," LC Information Bulletin (Library of Congress), 53 (November 28, 1994) 455-456.

1477. Dick, Ernest J. "Through the Rearview Mirror: Moving Image and Sound Archives in the 1990s," Archivaria, 28 (Summer 1989), 68-73. Reflects on the shifts in communications technologies; emphasizes need for archivists to know the history of these technologies. Notes concern for playback, but considers digitization a promising archival medium.

1478. Dickson, Kathy. "Planning Your Space," Muse News (Oklahoma Museums Association), 16:4 (October 1986), 2-3. Advice on preventing the deterioration of materials from environmental factors.

1479. Diers, Fred V. "Optical and Microfilm Image Digitization," International Journal of Micrographics and Optical Technology, 8:2 (1990), 75-80. Discusses concerns when selecting optical and microfilm digitization systems, including preservation problems and lack of standards.

1480. Dillon, Phyllis. "Conservation Planning: Where Can You Find the Help You Need?" History News, 42:4 (July-August 1987), 10-15. Information on finding specialists and undertaking a conservation survey for planning.

1481. DiMichele, Donna Longo. Archivists and the Preservation of Photographs: Satisfying Information Needs. Thesis, 1994 MSLS, University of North Carolina at Chapel Hill. 31p.

1482. Dirda, Michael. Caring for Your Books. New York: Book-of-the-Month Club, 1990. 67p. Suggestions on how books in private collections can be preserved through proper storage, care, and use.

1483. Dirks, J. Leland. In the Face of Disaster: Preparing for Emergencies in the North Country. Canton, NY: North County Reference and Research Services Council, 1993. 122p. A self-planning disaster prevention, planning, response and recovery manual; text and fill-in-the-blank sheets.

1484. "Disaster-Preparedness and Response," OJO: Connoisseurship and Conservation of Photographs, (Summer/July 1992), 1-8. Entire issue. Basic information for private collectors and small institutions that lack the resources of large, institutional collections.

1485. Disaster Recovery: Contingency Planning and Program Evaluation. Port Jefferson, NY: Chantico, 1985. 108p.

1486. Disaster Recovery Handbook. Blue Ridge Summit, PA: Tab Books (Chantico Publishing Company), 1991. 316p. Presents an essential set of working tools for coping effectively with computer-and communications-related catastrophes. Book jacket lists the editor as Dr. John Buckland.

1487. Ditmitroff, Michael, and James W. Lacksonen. "The Diffusion of Sulphur Dioxide in Air Through Stacked Layers of Paper," Journal of the American Institute of Conservation, 25:1 (Spring 1986), 31-37. A study of the diffusion phenomena in paper to look at the penetration of air pollutants; further research suggested.

1488. Dobrusina, S. A., and E. M. Lotsmanova. "Mechanized Document Restoration by Paper Pulp Filling Process," Preprints: ICOM Committee for Conservation 10th Triennial Meeting, ed. Janet Bridgland. Washington, DC: International Council of Museums, August 1993, 447-449. Discusses equipment for mechanized document restoration of document leaves with mechanical pulp.

1489. Dobrusina, Svetland A., and Vitaliya K. Visotskite. "Chemical Treatment Effects on Parchment Properties in the Course of Aging," Restaurator, 15:4 (1994), 208-219. Describes testing of modern parchment to evaluate the effect of treatments after accelerated aging.

1490. Dodson, Suzanne Cates. "Microfilm - Which Film Type, Which Application?" Microform Review, 14:2 (Spring 1985), 87-98. Discusses the characteristics of the different types of microfilm available; selecting the appropriate one.

1491.   Dodson, Suzanne C. "Microfilm Types: There Really Is a Choice," Library Resources and Technical Services, 30:1 (January-March 1986), 84-90. Discusses the characteristics of silver halide, diazo, and vesicular films and advocates that the purchaser's choice of film should be governed by an understanding of their qualities.

1492.   Dodson, Suzanne Cates. "The Reproduction of Library Materials in 1987: A RLMS Perspective," Library Resources and Technical Services, 32:4 (October 1988), 323-336. Summary of the year's publications, with a note on preservation microfilming and standards; bibliography.

1493.   Dodson, Suzanne Cates. "The Reproduction of Library Materials: 1988 in Review," Library Resources and Technical Services, 33:3 (July 1989), 248-257. Summary of the year's publications with a note on preservation microfilming, micropublishing, photocopying, equipment standards, technical production, and new technology. Bibliography.

1494.   Doinov, D. "Policies for the Preservation of the Archival and Library Heritage in the People's Republic of Bulgaria: Present Condition and Trends for Future Development," Politics for the Preservation of the Archival Heritage. Paris: International Council on Archives, 1989, 182-188. Describes the Bulgarian preservation program.

1495.   Dollar, Charles M. Electronic Records Management and Archives in International Organizations: A RAMP Study. Paris: UNESCO, 1986. 160p. (PGI-86/WS-12).

1496.   Donahue, Mary Kay, Deborah Brown, and Suzanne Gyeszly. "Preservation Techniques to Inhibit Collection Deterioration of New Acquisitions," Academic Libraries: Myths and Realities: Proceedings of the Association of College and Research Libraries Third National Conference, April 4-7, 1984. Chicago, Il: ACRL, 1984, 249-253. Case study; preservation plan to address deterioration caused by high use of materials in open stacks.

1497.   Donnelly, Helene. "Disaster Planning: A Wider Approach," Conservation Administration News, 53 (April 1993), 8-9, 33. A manager's approach to disaster planning, with emphasis on the human factors that come into play during recovery.

1498.   Donnelly, Helene. "Disaster Planning in the '90s: Getting It Right," Conservation Administration News, 52 (January 1993), 10-11.

Reprinted from Law Librarian 23:1 (1992), 19-21. Disaster recovery planning from a risk analysis perspective.

1499.   Donnelly, Helene, and Martin Heaney. "Disaster Planning — A Wider Approach," ASLIB Information (Association for Information Management {United Kingdom}), 21:2 (February 1993), 69-71. Emphasizes the need for attention to both paper and computer files in disaster planning; discusses human factors.

1500.   Donnithorne, Alan. "The Conservation of Papyrus at the British Museum," Papyrus: Structure and Usage, ed. M. L. Bierbriar. London: British Museum, 1986, 1-23. Plates. (Occasional paper, 60). Conservation at the British Museum from mid-19th-century to 1980; describes the collection, deterioration, historical, and current treatment.

1501.   Donovan, Joanne. "Self Preservation," Western Association of Map Libraries Bulletin, 18:1 (November 1986), 66-71. An assortment of preservation tips for map curators.

1502.   D'Ooge, Craig. "Librarian Announces National Film Registry Selections," LC Information Bulletin (Library of Congress), 53 (March 7, 1994), 83-85.

1503.   Dorfman, Harold H. "Microfilm Service Bureaus," International Journal of Micrographics and Optical Technology, 8:2 (1990), 97-100. Advice on choosing and using an outside service bureau to microfilm documents: criteria, standards, and specifications.

1504.   Dorfman, Harold H. "Quality Control of Microfilm," Micrographics and Optical Technology, 8:4 (1990), 217-222. Discusses the elements of quality microfilm; standards cited.

1505.   Dorn, Georgette M. "LC Supports First International Meeting on Preventive Conservation in the Americas," LC Information Bulletin (Library of Congress), 53 (January 10, 1994), 11.

1506.   Dorning, David. "Books and Manuscripts," Treasures on Earth; Good Housekeeping Guide to Churches and Their Contents, ed. Peter Burman. London: Donhead, 1994, 242-258. Discusses causes of damage to books and manuscripts; how to avoid them; safe storage and treatment; working with a conservator.

1507.   Dorrell, Peter G. Photography in Archaeology and Conservation. Cambridge, England: Cambridge University Press, 1989. 262p. A guide for archaeologists to ensure that their records are clear and complete. Includes a chapter on "Photographic Materials, Processing and Printing," and provides sound advice on archival storage.

1508.   Dosunmi, J. A. "Preservation and Conservation of Library Materials in Nigeria: A New Awareness," COMLA Newsletter (Commonwealth Library Association), 64 (June 1989), 3-4. Briefly surveys Nigeria's efforts to preserve library materials.

1509.   Dovey, Bryan. "Displays and Exhibitions," Security in Academic and Research Libraries, ed. Anthony G. Quinsee and Andrew C. McDonald. Newcastle-upon-Tyne, England: University of Newcastle Library, 1991, 28-30. Suggestions for curtailing risk of theft of exhibited materials.

1510.   Dowell, Connie Vinita. "An Award Winner Brings Preservation Out of the Lab," College and Research Libraries News, 54:9 (October 1993), 524-526. Describes the award-winning public relations campaign at the Indiana University Libraries to make the academic community aware of the need to care for and preserve library collections.

1511.   Down, Jane L., Maureen A. MacDonald, Jean Tetreault, R. Scott Williams. Adhesive Testing at the Canadian Conservation Institute — An Evaluation of Selected Poly(vinyl Acetate) and Acrylic Adhesives. Ottawa: Canadian Conservation Institute, 1992. 36p. and tables. (Environmental and Deterioration Report, 1603). Reports on the results of tests, with analysis of data to identify "those adhesives with the most suitable and stable properties for conservation."

1512.   Down, Jane L., and R. Scott Williams. "A Report on the Evaluation of Selected Poly(vinyl acetate) and Acrylic Adhesives for Use in Paper Conservation," Conservation of Historic and Artistic Works on Paper, ed. Helen D. Burgess. Ottawa: Canadian Conservation Institute, 1994, 163-180. (Symposium 88). Discussion of the Canadian Conservation Institute's adhesive testing program to look at stability and aging characteristics; results discussed.

1513.   Downes, Robin N. "Electronic Technology and Access to Information," Journal of Library Administration, 12:3 (1990), 51-61.   Discusses electronic publishing in terms of the long-term effect of information technology. Argues that the library's "potential for loss of control is serious" and that librarians must take a proactive role to ensure access in the future.

1514.   Downing, Alice. "Conservation of Old Cathedral Library," Conservation Administration News, 46 (July 1991), 4-5. Description of the cleaning and refurbishing of the books in the St. Nicholas

Church, Galway, Ireland; unemployed university students assisted in the project.

1515.   Downing, Alice. "Linking Old With New: A Permanent Exhibition of Nineteenth Century Memorabilia in a New Medical Research Unit," Conservation Administration News, 41 (April 1990), 6-7. Preparations for and display of memorabilia, and preservation concerns.

1516.   Downing, Alice. "Some News of Conservation from the West Coast of Ireland," Conservation Administration News, 31 (October 1988), 5, 22. Description of the initiatives of Downing to preserve and conserve collections in her region.

1517.   Downing, Alice. "Work Well Done in Galway," Conservation Administration News, 51 (October 1992), 3. Describes the refurbishment of the Henry Library, St. Nicholas Cathedral, Galway, Ireland.

1518.   Doyle, Robert P., ed. Access to Library Resources Through Technology and Preservation: Proceedings of the 1988 US- USSR Seminar Washington, DC, July 5-8, 1988. Chicago, IL: American Library Association, 1989. 155p.

1519.   Drake, Cindy Steinhoff. "The Weeding of a Historical Society Library," Special Libraries, 83:2 (Spring 1992), 86-91. Case Study of a carefully devised weeding program.

1520.   Dremaite, Grazina. "Restoration of Four Globes from the 17th-18th Centuries," Conference on Book and Paper Conservation, 1990. Budapest, Hungary: Technical Association of Paper and Printing Industry/National Szechenyi Library, 1992, 211-216. Describes treatment undertaken at the University of Vilnius Astronomical Department.

1521.   Drewes, Jeanne M. "Computers: Planning for Disaster," Law Library Journal, 8:1 (Winter 1989), 103-116. Protection of computers: routine back-up, protection of software and hardware, insurance, manufacturer's agreements.

1522.   Drewes, Jeanne M. "A Widening Circle: Preservation Literature Review, 1992," Library Resources and Technical Services, 37:3 (July 1993), 315-322. A review of articles on preservation published in 1992. 123 references.

1523.   Driessen, Karen C., and Sheila A. Smith. A Library Manager's Guide to the Physical Processing of Nonprint Materials. Westport,

CT: Greenwood Press, 1995. 241p. Presents practical methods for the library and the patron, through proper storage, care and handling, and selection of appropriate playback equipment. Covers cartographic materials, sound recordings, film and video, graphics, computer files, realia, kits and interactive media. Clearly written, but dated bibliography.

1524. Drogin, Marc. Biblioclasm: The Mythical Origins, Magic Powers, and Perishability of the Written World. Totowa, NJ: Rowman & Littlefield, 1989. 203p. Compilation of quotations from early manuscripts on the importance and preservation of the written word.

1525. Droguet, A. Kenya: Pilot Project on a National Archival Networking. Serial No. FMR/IPS/UIS/88/120. Paris: UNESCO, 1988. 29p.

1526. Drukker, Leendert. "Make 'em Last: How to Care for Your (Video) Tapes and Gear," Popular Photography, 92:2 (February 1985), 56-64. Basic practical tips on care, handling, and storage of video equipment and tapes.

1527. Druzik, James R., and Paul Banks. "Appropriate Standards for the Indoor Environment," Conservation Administration News, 62/63 (Summer/Fall 1995), 1-8. Summary and discussion of the papers that addressed the standards at the NYU Institute of Fine Arts Conference, June 1995, to address the Smithsonian's relaxation of standards, "an excellent forum for examining conventional wisdom and new findings."

1528. Druzik, James R. "Perspectives of the Scientist: On the Myopia of Science and the Dynamic Range of the Human Mind," Commission on Preservation and Access Newsletter, 57 (June 1993), 3-4. Explains the need to frame questions clearly to assist scientists in finding solutions.

1529. Druzik, James. "A Research Initiative for Preservation in Libraries," Conservation (Newsletter of the Getty Conservation Institute), 8:2 (1994), 14. Summary of the Commission on Preservation and Access research agenda.

1530. Dryden, Donna. "Disaster Plan for a Hospital Library," Biblioteca Media Canadiana, 14:3 (1993), 139-141.

1531. Drysdale, Laura. "Data, Data, Everywhere ...," Museums Journal, 94:6 (June 1994), 19-20. How costly monitoring hardware is replacing careful thought about environmental control.

1532. Dubin, Fred. "Mechanical Systems and Libraries," Library Trends, 36:2 (Fall 1987), 351-360. Practical discussion with a preservation perspective of environmental factors and mechanical design.

1533. Duchemin, Pierre Yves. "Seminar on Preservation of Maps and Other Spatial Information Held at the Russian State Library, 27 September - 1 October 1993," IFLA Journal (International Federation of Library Associations and Institutions), 20:3 (1994) 382-3.

1534. Duchesne, Roddy and Walter W. Griesbrecht. "CD-ROM: An Introduction," Canadian Library Journal, 45:4 (August 1988), 214-223. Descriptions of compact disks and other electronic storage media, advantages and disadvantages; deals with preservation of disks.

1535. Duckett, R.J. "Historic Collections Preservation," Library Association Record, 96 (January 1994) 54. 2d Historic Libraries Forum, November 1993, London.

1536. Dugal, H. S. (Doug), and Salmon Aziz. "Various Causes for the Darkening of Paper," Progress in Paper Recycling, 2:2 (February 1993), 88. Summary of a complex phenomenon in which visible light can bleach rather than darken lignin-containing paper.

1537. Dufour, Frank, and Gilbert Trieb. "The Use of Digital Processing Techniques for the Restoration and Preservation of Sound Recordings," Archiving the Audio-Visual Heritage. Rushton, England: FIAF/UNESCO, 1992, 155-157. Briefly describes research and techniques.

1538. Dunlap, Ellen, and Kathleen Reed. "Borrowing of Special Collections Materials for Exhibition: A Draft," Rare Book and Manuscript Librarianship, 2:1 (Spring 1987), 27-37. Draft guidelines for loans reflecting concern for the physical protection of materials; sample loan agreement.

1539. Dunn, Austin B. "The New Binding Process," Serials, 1:3 (November 1988), 37-39. A commercial library binder discusses how the industry has changed to meet librarians' needs.

1540. Dunn, F. Ian. "The Security Marking of Documentary Materials," Journal of the Society of Archivists, 8:3 (April 1987), 189-191. Discusses good and poor ways of marking, noting that all marking defaces manuscripts and that it should be done for security reasons only after ethical and technical consideration.

1541.   Dupont, Jerry. "Microform Film Stock: A Hobson's Choice. Are Librarians Getting the Worst of Both Worlds?" <u>Library Resources and Technical Services</u>, 30:1 (January/March 1986), 79-83. Addresses the issue of preservation by and of microforms, and access to information on microformat. Points out that silver halide is least suitable in a user environment and is the most expensive type of film stock.

1542.   Duranti, Luciana. "The Odyssey of Record Managers. Part 1: From the Dawn of Civilization to the Fall of the Roman Empire; Part 2: From the Middle Ages to Modern Times," <u>Records Management Quarterly</u>, 23:3 (July 1989), 3-11; 23:4 (October 1989), 3-11. History of records management: collection, housing, preservation.

1543.   Dureau, Jeanne-Marie. "IFLA, France and the USA," <u>Journal of Librarianship</u>, 17:2 (April 1985), 75-85. Describes the tension between the historical and technical approach to preservation and conservation within IFLA; the lack of sound preservation education in French library training, and the situation in the United States, with the Columbia program serving as a model.

1544.   Dureau, Jeanne-Marie, and David W. G. Clements. <u>Principles for the Preservation and Conservation of Library Materials</u>. The Hague, Netherlands: International Federation of Library Associations and Institutions, Section on Conservation, 1986. 25p. (IFLA Professional Report 8). Statement of general guidelines and principles for good practices.

1545.   Durovic, Michel, Jana Dernovskova, and M. Siroky. "Dispersive Glues Used in Preservation," <u>Restaurator</u>, 12:1 (1991), 36-74. Report on the investigation of the physiochemical properties of polycinylacetate, vinyl acetate, and styrene acrylic glues.

1546.   Durovic, Michel, Jana Dernovskora, and M. Siroky. "Dispersive Glues Used for Preservation Purposes," <u>Conference on Book and Paper Conservation, 1990</u>. Budapest, Hungary: Technical Association of Paper and Printing Industry/National Szechenyi Library, 1992, 491-507. Investigation to determine the nature of several synthetic glues. Data tables. References.

1547.   Durovic, Michel, and Jiri Zelinger. "Chemical Processes in the Bleaching of Paper in Library and Archival Collections," <u>Restaurator</u>, 14:2 (1993), 78-101. Bleaching procedures used in Eastern Europe. 61 references.

1548. Dvoriashina, Zinaida P. "Biodamage Protection of Book Collections in the USSR: Some Aspects of Organization of Insect Control," Restaurator, 8:4 (1987), 182-188. Describes an integrated pest management system emphasizing preventive measures; research to study life-cycle and preventive measures.

1549. Dvoriashina, Zinaida P. "The Smirnov Beetle as a Pest in Libraries," Restaurator, 9:2 (1988), 63-81. Study of the life cycle and propagation of a beetle that migrated from Africa to Russia and is increasingly found in libraries and archives, where it eats cellulosic materials.

1550. Dwan, Antoinette. "Paper Complexity and the Interpretation of Conservation Research," Journal of the American Institute for Conservation, 26:1 (Spring 1987), 1-17. Discusses paper variability and its influence on the methods of testing of paper and interpretation of results.

1551. Dwan, Antoinette. "Use of Gortex to Dry Smooth, Calendered, and Modern Papers," Book and Paper Group Annual, 11 (1992), 22-23. Describes the uses of Gortex for drying papers.

1552. Dyer, Victor. "After the Deluge: What Next? A Disaster Planning Workshop," Public Libraries, 26:1 (Spring 1987), 13-15. Report of a workshop simulating disaster, training for salvage and recovery.

1553. Dyson, Brian. "A Little Help Can Go a Long Way," Library Conservation News, 40 (Summer 1993), 4-5. Brief description of the conservation of an important day book at the University of Hull Library with funds from the National Manuscript Conservation Trust.

1554. Eastman Kodak Company. The Book of Film Care. Rochester, NY: Eastman Kodak, 1992. 84p. (H-23) Revised and updated edition of a basic reference on film care and preservation.

1555. Eastman Kodak Company. Conservation of Photographs. Rochester, NY: Eastman Kodak, 1985. 165p. Illus. (Technical Publication F-40). Provides technical information for photographic conservators on the care, treatment, and use of Kodak materials.

1556. Eastman Kodak Company. Copying and Duplicating: In Black-and-White and Color. Rochester, NY: Eastman Kodak Company, 1984. 184p. Handbook on making duplicate copies of photographs, paintings, documents, and other flat reflective originals.

1557. Easton, Roger. "Conservation of Film, Television and Sound Records," Conservation in Archives. Paris: International Council on

Archives, 1989, 163-172. (Proceedings of an International Symposium, Ottawa, Canada, May 10-12, 1988). Summarizes the continuing program at the National Archives of Canada to preserve information in audiovisual formats through proper storage, conversion, and copying.

1558.　　Easton, Roger, and William O'Farrell. "Joint Technical Symposium Focuses on Variety of Preservation Issues," AMIA Newsletter (Association of Moving Images Archivists), 28 (Spring 1995), 5-7. Report of a symposium, sponsored by the Joint Technical Committee, IFLA, ICA, FIAF, FIAT, and IASA, held in London, January 1995, to address concerns about the preservation of audiovisual records in conventional and digital format, including access, technology transfer, copyright, restoration and conservation.

1559.　　Eaton, Fynnette L. Current Practices in the Preservation of Electronic Records at the National Archives. Washington, DC: National Archives, 1991. 10p. Paper presented at the National Archives Sixth Annual Preservation Conference, Washington, DC, March 19, 1991.

1560.　　Eaton, Fynnette L. "The National Archives and Electronic Records for Preservation," Preservation of Electronic Formats and Electronic Formats for Preservation. Fort Atkinson, WI: Highsmith Press, 1992, 41-61. Discusses issues in the preservation of information in electronic formats; standards and guidelines; preservation of federal records at the National Archives; guidelines for storage.

1561.　　Eaton, George T. Conservation of Photographs. Rochester, NY: Eastman Kodak Co., 1985. 156p. Illus. Provides current technical information for the photographic conservator on the care, treatment, and use of Kodak materials.

1562.　　Eaton, George T. Photographic Chemistry in Black and White and Color Photography, 4th ed. rev. Dobbs Ferry, NY: Morgan and Morgan, 1986, 1991. 128p. Intended for those who are active in photography or the photographic industry who have little or no training in chemistry, physics, or photographic theory. Basic text on the photographic process.

1563.　　Eaton, George T. "Photographic Image Oxidation in Processing Black and White Films, Plates and Papers," PhotographiConservation, 7:1 (March 1985), 1,4.

1564.　　Eberhardt, Fritz. "Preserving the Materials of a Heritage," AB Bookman's Weekly (Antiquarian Bookman), 70:15 (October 11, 1982), 2355-2365; reprinted in AB Bookman's Yearbook, 1983.

Clifton, NJ: Antiquarian Bookman, 1983, 74-78. Describes his years as conservator at the Library Company of Philadelphia.

1565. Eden, Paul. "Disaster Management in British Libraries," Library Conservation News, 48 (Autumn 1995), 3. Brief report of results of a survey of libraries with and without disaster plans.

1566. Eden, Paul, John Feather, and Graham Matthews. "Of Special Concern? Preservation in Perspective," Public Library Journal, 9:2 (March/April 1994), 33-38. Results and discussion of a survey to assess preservation awareness and activities in British libraries a decade after the Radcliffe report. Shows people still think of preservation in terms of special collections.

1567. Eden, Paul, John Feather, and Graham Matthews. "Preserving Materials - Saving Resources" Library Conservation News, 40 (Summer 1993), 1-2. Brief description of a survey to assess the impact of the Ratcliffe report on preservation in British Libraries after a decade.

1568. Eden, Paul, John Feather and Graham Matthews. "Preservation and Conservation in British Libraries: A Ten Year Review," Rare Books Newsletter, 46 (March 1994), 49-50. Summary of an assessment of the progress made in preserving library collections in Great Britain in the decade following the Radcliffe report.

1569. Edge, Michele. "The Deterioration of Polymers in Audio-Visual Materials," Archiving the Audio-Visual Heritage. Rushton, England: FIAF/UNESCO, 1992, 29-39. Discusses the problem of instability of polymers in film, when to copy film.

1570. Edge, Michele. "Factors Influencing the Breakdown of Photographic Film: Implications for Archival Storage," Environnement et Conservation de l'Écrit, de l'Image et du Son. Paris: ARSAG, 1994, 114-120. (Actes des Deuxièmes Journées Internationales d'Études de l'ARSAG). Questions the causes of nitrate-base film deterioration, how this can be monitored, and how to determine the best conditions for the storage of nitrate film.

1571. Edge, Michele, Norman S. Allen, Martin Hayes, P. N. K. Riley, C.Velson Horie, and J. Luc-Gardette. "Mechanisms of Deterioration in Cellulose Nitrate Base Archival Cinematograph Film," European Polymer Journal, 26 (1990), 623-630.

1572. Edge, Michele, Norman S. Allen, and Terence S. Jewitt. "The Inhibition of Oxidative and Hydrolytic Degradation Pathways in

Archival Cellulose-Triacetate Base Cinematograph Films," Polymer Degradation and Stability, 29 (1990), 31-48.

1573. Edge, Michele, Norman S. Allen, Terence S. Jewitt, and John H. Appleyard. "Cellulose Acetate: An Archival Polymer Falls Apart," Modern Organic Materials. Edinburgh, Scotland: Scottish Society for Conservation and Restoration, 1988, 67-79. Research to determine the causes of deterioration of cellulose acetate motion picture film; paper presented in April 1988.

1574. Edge, Michele, Norman S. Allen, Terence S. Jewitt, John H. Appleyard, and C.Velson Horie. "The Deterioration Characteristics of Archival Cellulose Triacetate Base Cinematograph Film," Journal of Photographic Science, 36 (1988), 199-203. Discusses the degradation of Triacetate-base cinema film introduced in the 1950s; chemical characteristics of the films; relationship between naturally and artificially aged film.

1575. Edge, Michele, Norman S. Allen, Terence S. Jewitt, and C. Velson Horie. "Fundamental Aspects of the Degradation of Cellulose Triacetate Cinematograph Film," Polymer Degradation and Stability, 25 (1989), 345-362. The effects of photographic processing and metal ion contaminants are examined.

1576. Edge, Michele, Norman S. Allen, D. A. R. Williams, F. Thompson, and C. Velson Horie. "Methods for Predictive Stability Testing of Archival Polymers: A Preliminary Assessment of Cellulose Triacetate Based Motion Picture Film," Polymer Degradation and Stability, 35 (1992), 147-155. Analysis of various physical and chemical methods for predicting the stability of acetate film during archival storage.

1577. Edge, Michele, M. Mohammadian, Martin Hayes, Norman S. Allen, Karel Brems, and K. Jones. "Aspects of Polyester Degradation: Motion Picture Film and Videotape Materials," Journal of Imaging Science and Technology, 36 (January/February 1992), 13-20. Study of the degradation of polyethylene terephthalate as a substrate in motion picture film and videotape.

1578. Edmondson, Ray. "The Building Blocks of Film Archiving," Journal of Film Preservation, 24:50 (March 1995), 55-58. Twelve building blocks: good films, good people, support base, ethics, skills, procedures and principles, facilities, money, policies, information, coordination, intellectual framework.

1579. "Education for Librarianship," Journal of Librarianship, 17:2 (April 1985), 73-105. Papers addressing library education in preservation given at a Library Association Seminar, October 1984, noting the increased emphasis on training in preservation as librarians become aware of the alarming rate of the deterioration in their collections.

1580. Edwards, John D. "Book Losses and Mutilation in Law School Libraries," Law Library Journal, 78:3 (Summer 1986), 443-464. Reports on a survey of law libraries and offers strategies for reducing theft.

1581. Eilers, Delos. "The Work of the Audio Engineering Society Subcommittee for Audio Preservation and Restoration," Archiving the Audio-Visual Heritage. Rushton, England: FIAF/UNESCO, 1992, 124-128. Describes the work of the AES Standards Subcommittee; communication between manufacturers and archivists.

1582. Eisenberg, Daniel. "Problems of the Paperless Book," Scholarly Publishing, 21:1 (October 1989), 11-26. Describes the complexities of converting manuscripts and printed books into electronic texts; what to preserve and how to do it.

1583. Elder, Nelda J., Brice G. Holbrook, Debora L. Madsen, and William H. Wiese. "Collection Development, Selection, and Acquisition of Agricultural Materials," Library Trends, 38:3 (Winter 1990), 442-473. Collection development and preservation, given the fragile nature of materials.

1584. Eldridge, Betsy Palmer. "Sewing Variation," CBBAG Newsletter (Canadian Bookbinders and Book Artists Guild), 12:2 (Summer 1994), 15-16; reprinted Guild of Book Workers Journal, 32:1 (Spring 1994; issued 1996), 29-31. Describes a presentation of sewing variations that were drawn from the AIC/BPG Book Conservation Catalogue at a GBW Standards Seminar, December 1993.

1585. Elkington, Nancy E. "RLG's Collaborative Model for Inter-institutional Preservation," Library Conservation News, 49 (Winter 1995), 4-6. Describes RLG, mission, goals and how it achieves them. Summary of RLG projects and initiatives.

1586. Elkington, Nancy E. "RLMS + PLMS = PARS: Merger of RLMS and PLMS a success!" ALCTS Newsletter (Association for Library Collections and Technical Service), 5:5 (1994) 62-64.

1587. Elkington, Nancy E., and Patricia A. McClung. "Sidebar 10: RLG; A Pioneer in Collaborative Preservation," Library Hi Tech, 12:2 (1994) 30-31.

1588.   Elkington, Nancy E., ed. <u>Digital Imaging Technology for Preservation</u>. Mountain View, CA: Research Libraries Group, 1994. 139p. Proceedings from an RLG Symposium held at Cornell University, Ithaca, NY, March 17-18, 1994; papers provide background on digital imaging technology and options; review projects underway; identify key issues, such as costs, standards, quality control, hardware and software, back-up and migration of data, institutional needs.

1589.   Elkington, Nancy E., ed. <u>RLG Archives Microfilming Handbook</u>. Mountain View, CA: Research Libraries Group, 1994. 208p. This volume addresses the needs of archivists and librarians who are managing projects and programs to preserve microfilm archives and manuscripts.

1590.   Elkington, Nancy E., ed. <u>RLG Preservation Microfilming Handbook</u>. Mountain View, CA: Research Libraries Group, Inc., 1992. 203p. Comprehensive guide to preservation microfilming: definition of the process, terms, and guidelines.

1591.   Ellenberg, Karen T. "The Book Arts and Preservation: An Interview with George M. Cunha," <u>Kentucky Review</u>, 11:3 (Autumn 1992), 58-68. Cunha talks about his life and experiences in conservation and of the people he met.

1592.   Ellenport, Sam. <u>The Future of Hand Bookbinding</u>. Boston, MA: Harcourt Bindery, 1993. 37p.; reprinted in <u>Guild of Book Workers Journal</u>, 31:1/2 (Spring/Fall 1993), 36-49. Also in <u>New Library Scene</u> Part One (October 1992), 5-10, Part Two (December 1992), 6+. Traces trends and developments in edition and conservation hand bookbinding since the late 1950s. Notes lack of mastery of basic bench skills in today's training; sees a more simple structure in the future. Observes that conservation will be slow and costly because of a lack of preservation librarians with a knowledge of book structure and bookbinding techniques.

1593.   Elliott, Lynn. "Disaster Control Planning — A Review and Case Study," <u>The New University Library: Issues for the 1990s and Beyond</u>, ed. Colin Harris. London: Taylor Graham, 1994, 108-119. A review of the literature and a case study of disaster planning at the Manchester Metropolitan University Library; recommendations. 49 ref.

1594.   Ellis, Margaret Holben. <u>The Care of Prints and Drawings</u>. Nashville, TN: American Association of State and Local History Press, 1987. 253p. Reviews the nature of paper and parchment and the media applied to these supports. Offers recommendations for storage and environmental control.

1595.   Ellison, J. Todd. Pointers for Preserving Your Historical Documents. Snow Hill, MD: Worcester County Library, 1987. 10p. Tips on preservation of historical materials.

1596.   Ellison, John, ed. Media Librarianship. New York: Neal-Schuman, 1985. 449p. Basic handbook on non-print media and basic handbook. "Non-Book Storage and Care Self-Evaluation Form," 302-316, can be used as a guide for evaluating the storage and care practices of different non-book materials.

1597.   Ellison, John W., and Patricia Ann Coty, eds. Nonbook Media: Collection Management and User Services. Chicago, IL: American Library Association, 1987. 388p. Discusses a variety of non-print medial, with information on the care, storage, and handling of each.

1598.   Empsucha, Joseph G. "Film/Videotape Fact Sheet," Conservation Administration News, 22 (July 1985), 6, 21. Covers the preservation and storage of nitrate and cellulose acetate film and videotape.

1599.   "Engineering Problems Experienced at Deacidification Test Facility," LC Information Bulletin (Library of Congress), 45:11 (March 17, 1986), 87. The experience of operating a small-scale prototype facility for the deacidification of books using diethyl zinc (DEZ) is recounted.

1600.   England, Claire, and Karen Evans. Disaster Management for Libraries: Planning and Coping. Ottawa: Canadian Library Association, 1988. 207p. Focuses on the economic and time factors involved in preparing for disaster caused by fire, water, or chemicals. Bibliography and a list of helpful Canadian agencies.

1601.   Enright, Brian, Lotte Hellinga, and Beryl Leigh. Selection for Survival: A Review of Acquisition and Retention Policies. London: British Library, 1989. 104p. Report of a management team that undertook an internal review of these policies. Presents Enright's "life cycle" model for library materials.

1602.   Entwistle, R. M., and J. Pearson. "Rentokil Bubble," Conservation News, 38 (March 1989), 7-9; reprinted, Care of Collections, ed. Simon Knell. London: Routledge, 1994, 212-216. The development of the Rentokil Bubble has enabled a safer fumigation method for collections and provides an opportunity for safer alternatives.

1603.   Entwistle, R. M., and J. Pearson. "Workshop Notes — Rentokil Bubble, Results of Test," <u>Conservation News</u>, 38 (1989), 7-9.

1604.   Entwistle, Rosemary. "Of Floods, Fans and Freeze Dryers," <u>Library and Archival Security</u>, 5:1 (Spring 1983), 35-39. Describes the salvage of a small personal collection of water-damaged books, papers, and photographs.

1605.   Epstein, Dena J. "Preserving Our Heritage for the Future," <u>Music Librarianship in America</u>, ed. Michael Ochs. Cambridge, MA: Harvard University, 1991, 18-24. Emphasizes the need to rely on printed material for basic references and means of communication in the foreseeable future because of the impermanence of electronic media. Advocates storage facilities, collection sharing, networks, and consortia.

1606.   Erhardt, David. "Paper Degradation: A Comparison of Industrial and Archival Concerns," <u>Paper Preservation: Current Issues and Recent Developments</u>. Atlanta, GA: TAPPI Press, 1990, 63-68. (Proceedings of the Paper Preservation Symposium, 1988). Compares similarities and differences in the way industry and conservation approach paper science; evaluates how industrial testing may be used for conservation.

1607.   Erhardt, David. "Relationship of Reaction Rates to Room Temperature." <u>Abbey Newsletter</u>, 13:3 (June 1989), 38-39. Examination of the statement that for every 10 degree Celsius rise in temperature, the reaction rate in materials is doubled.

1608.   Erhardt, David, and Judith J. Bischoff. "Temperature and Relative Humidity Effects on the Aging of Cellulose," <u>Preservation Research and Development</u>. Washington, DC: Library of Congress, 1992, 31-34. Proceedings of a Library of Congress Round Table on Preservation Research and Development.

1609.   Erhardt, David, and Marion F. Mecklenburg. "Accelerated vs. Natural Aging: Effect of Aging Conditions on the Aging Process of Cellulose," <u>Materials Issues in Art & Archaeology IV</u>, Pittsburgh, PA: Material Research Society, 1995, 247-270. Graphs. Discusses kinetics of aging and implications for evaluation of changes in the aging process, especially when applied to artificial aging. The problem of comparing accelerated aging conditions is shown to be separate from that of evaluating changes occurring under one specific set of conditions. Criteria for comparing two sets of aging conditions are defined and applied to the problem of evaluating accelerated aging conditions.

1610.   Erhardt, David, and Marion Mecklenburg. "Relative Humidity
         Re-examined," Preventive Conservation: Practice, Theory and
         Research, ed. Ashok Roy and Perry Smith. London: International
         Institute for Conservation, 1994, 32-38. (Preprints, Ottawa Congress,
         September 12-16, 1994). Examines how RH affects the degradation
         process in different materials and the limits of allowable values.
         Concludes that "optimal RH is not a specific value but a range."

1611.   Erhardt, David, David Von Endt, and Walter Hopwood. "The
         Comparison of Accelerated Aging Conditions Through the Analysis
         of Extracts of Artificially Aged Paper," The American Institute for
         Conservation of Historic and Artistic Works (AIC). Preprints of
         Papers Presented at the Fifteenth Annual Meeting. Vancouver,
         British Columbia, Canada, May 20-24, 1987, 43-55. This paper
         presents results from gas chromatographic/-mass spectrometric
         analyses of extracts of artificially aged paper, and compares the types
         and quantities of degradation products that result from different sets
         of aging conditions. The aging of Whatman #1 filter paper at 90°C
         and above 100% relative humidity produces mostly glucose and
         xylose, which result from hydrolysis of the cellulose and xylan in the
         wood pulp-derived paper. Dry oven aging at 90°C and above yields
         product mixtures that contain very little glucose, which indicates that
         hydrolysis of cellulose is at most a minor reaction under these
         conditions. Dry oven aging at 150°C produces a mixture of
         degradation products quite different from those formed at lower
         temperatures.

1612.   Erhardt, David, Marion F. Mecklenburg, Charles S. Tumosa, and
         Mark McCormick. "The Determination of Allowable RH
         Fluctuations," WAAC Newsletter (Western Association for Art
         Conservation), 17:1 (January 1995), 19-23. Deals with the types of
         damage that occur in museum objects that expand and contract as a
         result of changes in humidity, omits consideration effect of high RH
         on degradation of paper, film.

1613.   Erickson, Harold M. "Usage Recommendations for Ox-Amylases:
         Maximizing Enzyme Activity While Minimizing Enzyme-artifact
         Binding Residues," Book and Paper Group Annual, 11 (1991),
         24-33. Reports on investigations of amylases, with specific
         recommendations. References.

1614.   Erickson, Lori. "It's Hands On To Save Books," The Iowan, 36:1
         (Fall 1987), 18-20, 52. Describes William Anthony's preservation
         efforts at the University of Iowa library.

1615.   Ershler, Margaret. "Reel Time: National Film Registry Tour Begins," LC Information Bulletin (Library of Congress), 55 (February 5, 1996), 23-25.

1616.   Espinosa, Robert. "The Limp Vellum Binding: A Modification," The New Bookbinder, 13 (1993), 27-38. A modification of the limp vellum binding structure that allows more flexibility when a book is opened.

1617.   Espinosa, Robert. "Specifications for a Hard-Board Laced-In Conservation Binding," Book and Paper Group Annual, 2 (1983), 25-49. Introduction to problems in conservation binding; specifications.

1618.   Ester, Michael. Digital Image Collections: Issues and Practice. Washington, DC: Commission on Preservation and Access, 1996. 36p. Projects to digitize visual collections present their own unique set of questions and concerns, as well as issues that overlap with digital capture of text.

1619.   Ester, Michael. "Digital Images in the Context of Visual Collections and Scholarship," Visual Resources, 10 (1994), 11-24.

1620.   Ester, Michael. "Image Quality and Viewer Perception," Leonardo: Journal of the International Society for the Arts, Supplemental Issue (1990), 51-63. Reprinted in Visual Resources, 7:4 (1991), 327-352.

1621.   Ester, Michael. "Issues in the Use of Electronic Images for Scholarship in the Arts and Humanities." In Networking in the Humanities, ed. Stephanie Kenna and Seamus Ross. London: Bowker Saur, 1995. 111-125.

1622.   Etherington, Don. "The Constitution Is Back," Conservation Administration News, 52 (January 1993), 13. Describes the design of a system for the display of the Constitution of the Commonwealth of Puerto Rico.

1623.   Etherington, Don. "Disastrous Library Fire in Leningrad, Russia," New Library Scene, 7:3 (June 1988), 1,5-7. Report on author's trip to assist in the salvage and restoration of the books that were damaged in the fire.

1624.   Etherington, Don. "Etherington Reports on Soviet Library Fire," Library Journal (May 15, 1988), 13.

1625.   Etherington, Don. "Japanese Paper Hinge Repair for Loose Boards on Leather Books," Abbey Newsletter, 19:3 (August 1995),

48-49. Instructions for the repair, from a handout prepared for ALA, 1995.

1626.   Etherington, Don. "Looking Toward Developing Standards in Rare Book Conservation," Postprints 1982. Washington, DC: American Institute for Conservation, 1983. Thoughts on the need for standards in book conservation.

1627.   Etherington, Don. "Selected Repair of Joints and Bindings," Guild of Bookworkers Journal, 30:1 (Spring 1992), 24-28. Instruction for several book repair techniques.

1628.   "Ethics of Disbinding Book-Related Artifacts: Panel Discussion," Conservation of Historic and Artistic Works on Paper. Ottawa: Canadian Conservation Institute, 1994, 271-282. (Symposium 88). Joyce Banks, Edward H. Dahl, Don Etheringston, and Debra M. Evetts focus on options for conservators when faced with materials that require major or minor treatment that may change the original condition or form of the item.

1629.   Eulenberg, Julia Niebuhr. "Disaster Planning for Recovery," Taking Control of Your Office Records: A Manager's Guide, ed. Katherine Aschner. White Plains, NY: Knowledge Publications, 1983, 129-151. Basics of disaster planning and recovery; sample forms.

1630.   Eulenberg, Julia Niebuhr. Handbook for the Recovery of Water Damaged Business Records. Prairie Village, KS: Association of Records Managers and Administrators International, 1986, 54p. Covers general principles, applications for salvage of water and fire damaged business records.

1631.   European Register of Microform Masters (EROMM); Workshop - Final Report. [Brussels, Belgium]: May 1990. 19p. Report on a meeting held in December 1989 to discuss the feasibility study, review technologies, and explore cooperative approaches.

1632.   Eusman, Elmer. "Tideline Formation in Paper Objects: Cellulose Degradation at the Wet-Dry Boundary," Conservation Research 1995. Washington, DC: National Gallery, 1995, 11-27. A study of tidelines, causes, and effects on the long-term stability of paper. Suggestions for avoiding them during treatment.

1633.   Evans, Bronwen. "The Duke Humphrey's Library Project: Using an Item-by-Item Survey To Develop a Conservation Programme," Paper Conservator, 17 (1993), 39-44. Describes the objectives of a survey undertaken in 1988; uses of survey; survey form.

1634.   Evans, Debra. "Loss Compensation in Paper," Loss Compensation
        Postprints: Western Association for Art Conservation Annual
        Meeting 1993, ed. Patricia Levengood, Seattle, WA, Patricia
        Levengood, 1994, 225-227. Discusses theoretical issues governing
        loss compensation decisions, with examples of techniques.

1635.   Evans, Frank B. Development and Preservation of the Manuscript
        Collections of the National Diet Library. Paris: UNESCO, 1990.
        48p. (FMR/PGI-84/137). Evaluation of a project by the National Diet
        Library, Japan, to obtain microcopies of war records; provides basic
        information on acquisition, organization, and preservation of the
        material.

1636.   Evans, G. Edward. "Preservation," Developing Library and
        Information Center Collections, 2d ed. Littleton, CO: Libraries
        Unlimited, 1987, 356-369. Covers basics of preservation, with a
        decision flow chart.

1637.   Evetts, Debra M., A. Lockwood, and N. Indicator. "Evaluation of
        Some Impregnating Agents for Use in Paper Conservation,"
        Restaurator, 10:1 (1989), 1-15. Evaluation of five commercial
        impregnation agents for use in paper conservation, studied under
        accelerated aging techniques. 70 references.

1638.   "Examining Insect Infestation," CCI Notes (Canadian Conservation
        Institute), 3/1 (April 1986), 3p. Practical pamphlet on prevention and
        treatment.

1639.   Ezennia, Steve E. "Biological Factors in Paper Deterioration in
        Nigeria," Library and Archival Security, 11:1 (1991),
        103-107. Describes factors that cause damage and measures for
        control.

1640.   Ezennia, Steve E. "Flood, Earthquake, Libraries and Library
        Materials" (in hot, wet climates), Library & Archival Security, 13:1
        (1995), 21-27.

1641.   Ezennia, Steve E. "The Harmattan and Library Resources
        Management in Nigeria: An Appraisal of Effects, Problems, and
        Prospects," Library and Archival Security, 9:2 (1989),
        43-48. Describes the negative effect of this Nigerian wind on library
        resources.

1642.   Ezennia, Steve E. "Problems of Preservation of Library Materials:
        The Nigerian Experience," Library & Archival Security, 12:2 (1994),
        51-62.

1643.   Ezennia, Steve E. "The Struggle to Prevent Micro-organisms from Devouring Library Resources in Nigeria," Library and Archival Security, 12:1 (1993), 23-33. Describes microorganisms that attack collections in Nigeria; preventive methods and chemical treatments are briefly described.

1644.   Ezennia, Steve E., and Emma O. Onwuka. "The Battle for Preservation of Library Materials in Nigeria," Library & Archival Security, 13:1 (1995), 29-39. Focus on audiovisual materials and equipment.

1645.   Fabry, Frank. "Conservation at Case Western Reserve University Library," Conservation Administration News, 16 (January 1984), 5-6. Development and activities of the conservation program.

1646.   Fairbrass, Sheila, ed. Conference Papers: Manchester 1992. Leigh, Worcester, England: Institute of Paper Conservation, 1992. 287p. Forty-six papers on conservation treatments for works of art on paper, library, and archival materials, and reports of scientific research.

1647.   Fairbrass, Sheila. "Dry-Mounting Tissues Used in Conservation: Their Nature and Deterioration Characteristics," Journal of the Society of Archivists, 15:1 (1994), 73-81. Reports the behavior, after light aging, of six commercially available heat set adhesives. The study suggests that the adhesives show only very minor changes when exposed to high amounts of light.

1648.   Fairbrass, Sheila. Learn to Frame. London: William Collins, 1990. 64p. Illus. Basic techniques of picture framing from a conservation perspective. Covers different types of works on paper and their display.

1649.   Fairbrass, Sheila, and Johan Hermans, eds. Modern Art: The Restoration and Techniques of Modern Paper and Prints. London: United Kingdom Institute for Conservation, 1989. 36p. Papers from a conference to address problems caused by new materials and new ways of combining them in contemporary works of art on paper.

1650.   Fairfield, John R. "LBI/NISO and the New Standard," ICI: The Title Page (Information Conservation, Inc.), 9 (June 1996), 1-4. A commercial library binders comments on the testing, analysis, and effort put into the development of a new standard for commercial library binding.

1651.   Falen, Martha. Recovery of Water-Damaged Library Materials. Portland, OR: Library Association of Portland, November 1985.

25p. Disaster recovery manual adapted from Peter Waters. Procedures for Salvage of Water-Damaged Library Materials, Washington, DC: Library of Congress, 1978.

1652.   Fang, Josephine R., and Ann Russell, eds. Education and Training for Preservation and Conservation: Papers of an International Seminar on the Teaching of Preservation Management for Librarians, Archivists, and Information Scientist. New York: Saur, 1991. 113p. (IFLA Publication, 54). Papers addressing education and training needs in preservation and conservation in countries throughout the world.

1653.   Fang, X. "A Study of the Problem of the Aging of Books in University Libraries: Strategies for Countering Its Effects," Journal of Librarianship and Information Science, 43 (1992), 501-505. Study of aging process and an index developed to create an economic benefits index to facilitate cost-effective and optimal approach to preservation.

1654.   Fantaine, Jean-Marc. "The Preservation of Compact Discs — Principles of Analysis," Archiving the Audio-Visual Heritage. Rushton, England: FIAF/UNESCO, 1992, 78-85. Research at the Bibliothèque Nationale, France, into the long-term stability of compact disks.

1655.   Fantel, Hans. "Insuring a Long Life for Compact Disks," New York Times, 20 February 1988, L52. Describes methods and products for cleaning CDs to keep them working properly. Asserts that the longevity of a CD depends on the way that it is kept and treated.

1656.   Farkas, Csilla. "The Problems of Conserving/Restoring a Corvinius Manuscript Covered in Velvet," Conference on Book and Paper Conservation, 1990. Budapest, Hungary: Technical Association of Paper and Printing Industry/National Szechenyi Library, 1992, 164-173. Description of manuscripts, analysis of damage, testing, and treatment procedures are described. Illus.

1657.   [Farr, George F., Jr.] "Interview With George Farr," Research Library Group News, 20 (Fall 1989), 7-8.

1658.   Farr, George F., Jr. "NEH's Program for the Preservation of Brittle Books," Advances in Preservation and Access, Vol. 1. Westport, CT: Meckler, 1992, 49-60. Description of the National Endowment for the Humanities Brittle Books Microfilming Program, how it works and what has been accomplished.

1659.   Farr, George F., Jr. Preservation Strategies and Initiatives New York and the Nation. Albany, NY: New York State Archives, March 23, 1988. 8p. Remarks by George F. Farr, Jr. at the 10th Anniversary of the NY State Archives.

1660.   Farrell, Barbara, and Aileen Debarats. Guide for a Small Map Collection, 2n ed. Ottawa: Association of Canadian Map Librarians, 1984. 101p. Covers the care, handling, and storage of maps.

1661.   Farrell, Roberta. "Biocatalysts Hold Promise of Better Pulp Quality," TAPPI Journal (Technical Association of the Pulp and Paper Industry), 67:10 (October 1985), 31-33. Describes the use of microorganisms for the removal and modification of lignin.

1662.   Farrelly, R.O. "Adhesives," CBBAG Newsletter (Canadian Bookbinders and Book Artists Group); Part 1: "The Basics," 11:2 (Summer 1993), 7-8; Part 2: "Paste and Glue," 11:3 (Autumn 1993), 6-7. Describes how adhesives work and their ingredients. Originally published in the Newsletter of the Association of Book Crafts, New Zealand, September-October 1992.

1663.   Farrington, James. "The Enhancement of Audio Playback in a Library," Planning and Caring for Library Audio Facilities. Canton, MA: Music Library Association, 1989, 21-42. Emphasis on the preservation of audio playback through a regular schedule of cleaning and maintenance. Bibliography; product directory.

1664.   Fasana, Paul J,. and John P. Baker. "Preservation's Place in the Library's Organization and Budget," Advances in Preservation and Access, Vol. 1. Westport, CT: Meckler, 1992, 124-134. Developing and integrating preservation with library operations.

1665.   Fazakas, Karoly, and Zoltan Nagy. "How to Retain All the Information Contained in First World War Photographs," Conference on Book and Paper Conservation, 1990. Budapest, Hungary: Technical Association of Paper and Printing Industry/National Szechenyi Library, 1992. 600-612. Investigation of photographs to determine stability and appropriate preservation methods. Illus.

1666.   Feather, John. "National and International Policies for Preservation," International Library Review, 22:4 (December 1990), 315-327. How national preservation policies have been developed and implemented; their relationship to other preservation initiatives.

1667.   Feather, John. "Preservation and Conservation: A Professional Issue for the 1990s," New Zealand Libraries, 46:2-3 (June-September

1989), 17-25; reprinted in <u>Preservation in Libraries: A Reader</u>, ed. Ross Harvey. London, New York: Bowker-Saur, 1993, 16-29. Basic review of preservation issues and their importance in library management.

1668. Feather, John. <u>Preservation and the Management of Library Collections</u>. London: Library Association, 1991. 122p. Basic text on preservation of library collections.

1669. Feather, John, and A. Lusher A. "Education for Conservation in British Library Schools: Current Practices and Future Prospects," <u>Journal of Librarianship</u>, 21:2 (April 1989), 129-138. Survey reflects the inclusion of preservation in courses at library schools in response to an increased awareness of preservation and conservation needs in British libraries.

1670. Feather, John, and Anne Lusher. <u>The Teaching of Conservation in LIS Schools in Great Britain</u>. London: British Library Research & Development Department, 1988. 49p. (British Library Research Paper, 49). Investigation of the teaching of conservation (preservation) in 15 LIS departments in the UnitedKingdom and evaluate it present and future role in curriculum.

1671. Feather, John, Graham Matthews, and Paul Eden. "Preservation Management in Britain: Present Practice and Future Strategy," <u>Library Conservation News</u>, 49 (Winter 1995), 1-2. Discussion of a survey to investigate the state of preservation policies and practices in British Libraries in the early 1990s, demonstrating concern and activity, and a look to future needs.

1672. Feather, John, Graham Matthews, and Paul Eden. <u>Preservation Management: Policies and Practices in British Libraries</u>. Aldershot, England: Gower, 1996. 174p.

1673. Feilden, Barnard. <u>Between Two Earthquakes: Cultural Property in Seismic Zones</u>. Rome: International Centre for the Conservation and Restoration of Materials; Marina del Rey, CA: Getty Conservation Institute, 1992. 108p. Handbook to provide information on what to do before, during, and following earthquakes that threaten cultural property.

1674. Felker, Aimee M. "Northeast Document Conservation Center." <u>NEA Newsletter</u> (New England Archivists), 16:3 (July 1989), 18-19.

1675. Feller, Robert L. <u>Accelerated Aging in Conservation Science</u>. Santa Monica, CA: Getty Trust Publications, 1994. 300p. (Research in Conservation, 4). Overview of results of research using accelerated aging tests; introduction to reasoning, principles, and limitations of artificial aging.

1676. Feller, Robert L. "Some Factors to Be Considered in Accelerated-Aging Tests," The American Institute for Conservation of Historic and Artistic Works. Preprints of Papers Presented at the Fifteenth Annual Meeting. Vancouver, British Columbia, Canada: May 20-24, 1987, 56-67.

1677. Feller, Robert L., Sang B. Lee, and Mary Curran. "Three Fundamental Aspects of Cellulose Deterioration," Art and Archaeology Technical Abstracts, 22:1, supplement (1985), 277-356. Annotated bibliographies: "The mechanisms by Which Cellulose Tends to Be Degraded in Stages," Hemicelluloses: Their Influence on Paper Permanence," "Hot-Alkali-Soluble Matter as a Measure of Paper Quality and Degradation."

1678. Feller, Robert L., and M. Wilt. Evaluation of Cellulose Ethers for Conservation. Santa Monica, CA: Getty Trust, 1991. 161p. (Research in Conservation, 3). Comprehensive presentation of the properties of cellulose ethers as they relate to conservation; report of a three-year research project.

1679. Fellers, Christer, et al. Aging/Degradation of Paper: A Literature Survey. Stockholm, Sweden: Riksarkivet, September 1989. 139p. English; report also available in Swedish. Review of the literature; summarizes the causes of paper deterioration and suggests avenues for further research.

1680. Fennell, Janice C., ed. Building on the First Century: Proceedings of the Fifth National Conference of the Association of College and Research Libraries. Chicago, IL: American Library Association, 1989. 350p. Contains several papers on preservation topics; each cited separately.

1681. Fennelly, Lawrence. Museum, Archive and Library Security. London; New York: Butterworths, 1983. 912p. Covers security fundamentals: insurance, management, fire protection, and emergency planning, physical security controls, investigating art theft.

1682. Fensterman, Duane W. "Recommendations for the Preservation of Photographic Slides," Conservation Administration News, 31 (October 1987), 7. Advice from published sources.

1683. Fenton-Huie, Shirley. "A Brief History of Papermaking in Australia," Words on Paper, Newsletter of Papermakers of Australia,

11 (November 1986). 1-3. The article traces the development of the craft from 1820 to the present day covering both commercial and handmade mills. It discusses investigations into native plant fibers that were being considered for use as paper pulp for large-scale mills. Historically, a large variety of Australian plant fibers have also been used to supplement rag fibers. The article also discusses the few handmade paper mills that currently serve the artistic community.

1684.   Ferguson, Ann. <u>Conservation Framing for the Professional Picture Framer</u>, 2d ed. Galveston, TX: Windsor Graphics, 1988. 82p. Illus. Covers materials for framing, including wood, paper, glazing materials, adhesives; discusses what materials are appropriate.

1685.   Ferris, Valerie. "Don't Film It If You're Not Recording It," <u>Library Conservation News</u>, 22 (January 1989), 3, 8. Discusses the importance of keeping records of what is filmed; describes the British Library's Register of Preservation Microforms (RPM).

1686.   Ferris, Valerie. "Fire Protection: How Safe Is Your Organization?" <u>Library Conservation News</u>, 51 (Summer 1996), 2. Describes how the Fire Protection Association can assist libraries in fire prevention.

1687.   Ferris, Valerie. "The National Preservation Office," <u>Paper Conservation News</u>, 70 (June 1994), 6. Brief summary of the activities of the British Library's National Preservation Office.

1688.   Ferris, Valerie. "The National Preservation Office: Its Role in the 1990s," <u>ASLIB Information</u> (Association for Information Management {United Kingdom}), 21:2 (February 1993), 63-64. Describes its establishment and role, publications, and activities.

1689.   Ferris, Valerie. "To Boldly Go...A New Look for the National Preservation Office," <u>Library Conservation News</u>, 50 (Spring 1996), 1-2. The future of the NPO, with funding from other legal deposit libraries, to focus more fully on coordination of a national preservation strategy, to provide information and retrieval service, to coordinate and initiate research.

1690.   Fickeissen, Janet L. "Nursing the Nurse's Archives," <u>Conservation Administration News</u>, 57 (April 1994), 14-15. Organizing, preparing a disaster plan, and planning for preservation of New Jersey's Nursing Archives.

1691.   Fidler, Linda M., and William L. Schurk. "Sound Recording Archives," <u>Critical Studies ion Mass Communication</u>, 3:3 (September 1986), 377-379. Overview of the history of sound recording archives; notes that few exist for the preservation of the long-playing disk.

1692.   Field, Jeffrey. "The Goals and Priorities of the NEH Office of Preservation," Conservation Administration News, 25 (April 1986), 4-5, 23-24. Describes the philosophy, funding, and principles of the Office of Preservation.

1693.   Field, Jeffrey. "The NEH Office of Preservation: 1986-1988," Microform Review, 17:4 (October 1988), 187-189. Review of the preservation initiatives supported by NEH.

1694.   Field, Jeffrey. "The Role of the National Endowment for the Humanities Office of Preservation in the National Preservation Effort," Microform Review, 14:2 (Spring 1985), 81-86. Discusses the types of preservation projects that the office expects to support, such as cooperative projects in the national context, problem solving, and humanities documentation.

1695.   Filter, Susan. "Historic Intent: Lodovico Ughi's Topographical Map of Venice (1729); A Large Wall Map as an Historic Document, a Work of Art, and a Material Artifact," Book and Paper Group Annual, 13 (1994), 17-24. A review of extant copies and their current housing and condition to highlight cultural, historical, and artifactual significance, and to make conservators more aware of the significance of their work.

1696.   Fine Arts Trade Guild. Conservation Framing Guide Lines: Works of Art on Paper and Thin Board. London: Fine Arts Trade Guild, c1990. 20p. A small handbook for the general public explaining conservation considerations and options for conservation framing.

1697.   Fineberg, Gail. "Whitman on the Web: Four Recovered Notebooks to Be Digitized," LC Information Bulletin (Library of Congress), 54:7 (April 3, 1995), 139-144. Details of the treatment and preparation of the recently recovered Whitman notebooks for scanning for scholarly access on WWW. Notes need of conservators to be actively involved in digitizing projects using rare and fragile materials. One official continues to maintain that digitizing is also preservation.

1698.   Finlay, Douglas. "Archives: Old Records Meet New Technologies," Administrative Management (December 1986), 37-40. Discusses views on optical disk technology and on the role microfilm can still play.

1699. "First US Meeting Is Held Under New US-USSR Library Agreement," LC Information Bulletin (Library of Congress), 47:30 (July 25, 1988), 309-311. Notes preservation concerns.

1700. Fischer, Audrey. "Optical and Videodisk Technology: A Review of the Literature on Optical Disk and Videodisk Technology, 1985-Mid 1986," Library Hi-Tech, 2:12 (1989), 105-112. An annotated review of the literature.

1701. Fischer, Barbara. "Sewing and Endband in the Islamic Techniques of Binding," Restaurator, 7:4 (1986), 181-201. Classical techniques of the sewing and weaving of the endbands are examined and reconstructed. 23 references.

1702. Fisher, David. "Library Crimes," Library Work, 6 (October 1989), 12-14.

1703. Fisher, Tom. "Impact of Computer Technology on Library Expansions," Library Administration & Management, 9:1 (Winter 1995), 31-36. Examines the impact of information technology on the physical and functional organization of libraries.

1704. Fisher, Steven P. "Preservation via the Internet," Colorado Libraries, 20 (Fall 1994), 52.

1705. Fitzsimons, Eileen. "Limp Vellum Bindings: Their Value as a Conservation Binding," Restaurator, 7:3 (1986), 125-142. Technical and historical description of limp vellum binding and its appropriateness for conservation binding.

1706. Fitzsimmons, Joseph J. "A Realistic Look at the Future of Preservation," Microform Review, 21:1 (Winter 1992), 13-15. Looks toward hybrid systems for preservation and access; emphasizes that such systems must serve users and preserve information for future users.

1707. Flagg, Gordon. "Libraries Dig Out From Bay Area Earthquake," American Libraries, 20:11 (December 1989), 1022-1026. Briefly describes damage to area libraries.

1708. Flagg, Gordon. "Librarians Meet To Fight Book Thieves," American Libraries, 14:10 (November 1983), 648-650. Summary of the proceedings of the "Oberlin" conference on book theft.

1709. Fleischauer, Carol. "Binding Decisions: Criteria and Process," RTSD Newsletter (Resources and Technical Services Division), 13:6,

(1988), 59-60. Note on decision-making regarding the binding of monographs and serials.

1710. Fleischhauer, Carl. "Organizing Digital Archival Collections [computer files]: American Memory's Experiences with Bibliographic Records and Other Finding Aids." Washington, DC: Library of Congress, 1994. Computer file. Presentation given at LC on October 13, 1994.

1711. Fleischauer, Carl. "A Report on the Optical Disk Pilot Program: The Nonprint Project," LC Information Bulletin (Library of Congress), 44:45 (November 11, 1985), 335-339. Discusses the project in detail; reviews the preservation advantages and recognizes actual and potential disadvantages.

1712. Fleischauer, Carl. "Research Access and Use: The Key Facet of the Non-Print Optical Disk Experiment," LC Information Bulletin (Library of Congress), 42:37 (September 12, 1983), 312-316. Explains the non-print optical disk experiment, preservation, and access possibilities.

1713. Flesch, Balint. "The Conservation of Daguerreotypes By Installation and the Types of Installations," Conference on Book and Paper Conservation, 1990. Budapest, Hungary: Technical Association of Paper and Printing Industry/National Szechenyi Library, 1992, 281-294. Discussion of problems presented by European daguerreotypes; reviews early structures.

1714. Fletcher, John M., and Christopher A. Upton. "The Repair of Manuscript Books in Merton College Library 1504," Archives, 17 (April 1986), 138-143. Description of repairs to the books in Merton College Library.

1715. Flieder, Francoise. "Current Research in Paper Conservation," Restoration '92: Conservation, Training, Materials and Techniques: Latest Developments; Preprints ... Amsterdam, 20-22 October, 1992. London: United Kingdom for Conservation, 1992, 85-89. Explains the objectives, activities, and structure of the Centre de Recherches sur la Conservation des Documents Graphiques, Paris, France; presents recent research.

1716. Flieder, Francoise, B. Guineau, C. Laroque, B. Liebard, and P. Richardin. "Analysis and Restoration of Old Transparent Papers," Symposium 88: Conservation of Historic and Artistic Works on Paper; Proceedings of a Conference, Ottawa, Canada, October 3-7, 1988., ed. Helen D. Burgess. Ottawa: The Institute, 1994,

234-244. Study of the manufacture and physical nature of transparent papers with discussion of conservation treatments.

1717. Flora, Nirmolini V. "Some Conservation Problems of Higher Degree Theses in Victorian University Libraries," Australian Academic & Research Libraries, 27 (June 1996), 107-123.

1718. Florentine, Frank A. "The Next Generation of Lights: Electrodless," WAAC Newsletter (Western Association for Art Conservation), 17:3 (September 1995), 12-13. Briefly discusses a new generation of lighting that will produce better lighting using less energy, and reducing maintenance. Case study: Smithsonian National Air and Space Museum.

1719. Flores, Bess. "The Pacific Manuscripts Bureau: An Agent for the Preservation and Distribution of Pacific Island Research Materials," Microform Review, 18:2 (Spring 1989), 103-108. Initiative to preserve and distribute government publications on Pacific Islands culture; describes preservation microfilming program.

1720. Florian, Mary-Lou E. "Conidial Fungi (Mould) Activity on Artifact Materials: A New Look at Prevention, Control, and Eradication," Preprints: ICOM Committee on Conservation 10th Triennial Meeting, ed. Janet Bridgland. Washington, DC: International Council of Museums, 1993, 868-874. Provides a review of the literature on fungus activity to determine what is relevant to its prevention and eradication on cultural property.

1721. Florian, Mary-Lou E. "Ethylene Oxide Fumigation: A Literature Review of the Problems and Interactions with Materials and Substances in Artifacts," A Guide to Museum Pest Control. Washington, DC: Foundation of the American Institute for Conservation of Historic and Artistic Works: Association of Systematics Collections, 1988, 151-158. Discusses the chemistry of ethylene oxide and its reactions with various materials.

1722. Florian, Mary-Lou E. "The Freezing Process — Effects on Insects and Artifact Materials," Leather Conservation News, 3:1 (Fall 1986), 1-13, 17. Literature review and recommended procedures for freezing insect infested artifacts for insect eradication.

1723. Florian, Mary-Lou E. "A Holistic Interpretation of the Deterioration of Vegetable Tanned Leather," Leather Conservation News, 2:1 (Fall 1985), 1-5. Review of the literature; indicates that the decay of leathers comes as much, or more, from inherent vice than from elemental forces, such as exposure to sulphur dioxide.

1724.   Florian, Mary-Lou. "Integrated System Approach to Insect Pest
        Control: An Alternative to Fumigation," Conservation in Archives.
        Paris: International Council on Archives, 1989, 253-262.
        (Proceedings of an International Symposium, Ottawa, Canada, May
        10-12, 1988). Emphasis on prevention of infestation through
        monitoring and environmental controls.

1725.   Florian, Mary-Lou E. "Saga of the Saggy Bag," Leather
        Conservation News, 8 (1992), 1-11. Study of plastic bags used for
        storage of objects, isolation, packing, emergency measures, and
        conservation treatments to determine their effectiveness. References.

1726.   Florida State Historical Records Advisory Board Strategic Plan.
        Tallahassee, FL: Florida State Historical Records Advisory Board,
        1994. 50p.

1727.   Florida State University. The School of Library and Information
        Studies. Florida Library Disaster Preparedness and Recovery Project.
        The Library Disaster Plan Workbook. Tallahassee, FL: Florida Dept.
        of State, Division of Library and Information Services, 1988. One
        volume.

1728.   FMC Corporation-Lithium Division. Evaluation Strategy Paper
        Preservation Systems February 12, 1990. Bessemer City, NC: FMC
        Corporation-Lithium Division, 1990. 96p. An account of the FMC
        corporation deacidification and preservation program.

1729.   Focher, B., A. Marzetti, V. Sarto, P. L. Beltrame, and P. Carniti.
        "Cellulose Materials — Structure and Enzymatic Hydrolysis
        Relationships," Journal of Applied Polymer Science, 29:11
        (November 1984), 3329-3338. The structure and morphology of
        several cellulosic materials were studied by x-ray, CP-MAS nuclear
        magnetic resonance (NMR), water retention, and specific surface
        analysis.

1730.   Fogle, Sonja, ed. Recent Advances in Leather Conservation.
        Washington, DC: Foundation of the American Institute for
        Conservation of Historic and Artistic Works, 1985. 165p. Covers
        fundamental concepts and techniques for leather conservators, new
        developments in treatment; bibliography by Mary Garbin.
        Proceedings of the Leather Refresher Course, June 1984.

1731.   Foldessy, Peter. "The Conservation/Restoration of Different Types
        of Globes," Conference on Book and Paper Conservation, 1990.
        Budapest, Hungary: Technical Association of Paper and Printing
        Industry/National Szechenyi Library, 1992, 217-227. Discussion of

problems in treating globes, especially modern globes made with synthetic materials. Illus.

1732. Fontaine, Jean-Marc. "Preservation of Magnetic Recording Collections Within the Context of Technological Developments," Proceedings of the Pan-African Conference on the Preservation & Conservation of Library & Archival Materials, Nairobi, Kenya, 21-25 June 1993. The Hague: IFLA, 1995, 97-101. (IFLA Professional Publication 43). Brief overview of recording media, causes of damage restoration and research (loose, poor translation.)

1733. Foot, Mirjam. "Aspects of Mass Conservation," IFLA Journal (International Federation of Library Associations and Institutions), 20:3 (1994), 321-330.

1734. Foot, Mirjam. "The Binding Historian and the Book Conservator," Paper Conservator, 8 (1984), 77-83. Binding historian discusses how treatment can distort and obliterate historical evidence about a book's production and history.

1735. Foot, Mirjam M. "Housing Our Collections: Environment & Storage for Libraries & Archives," IFLA Journal (International Federation of Library Associations and Institutions), 22:2 (1996), 110-114. Discusses collection management and strategies for preservation: standards for storage and maintenance; need to understand, security, fire risk, causes of physical deterioration.

1736. Foot, Mirjam M. "Preserving Books and Their History," Bookbinder, 1 (1987), 5-8. Notes that conservation treatment can destroy evidence of the original structure of a book and impede our understanding of its construction.

1737. Foot, Mirjam. "Preservation: Policy, Dilemmas, Needs; a British Library Perspective," Conservation Administration News, Part One, 58-59 (July/October 1994), 1, Part Two (January 1995), 6-10, Part Three (April 1995), 5-8. (Delivered at a conservation forum sponsored by the Harry Ransom Humanities Research Center and the Graduate School of Library and Information Science, University of Texas at Austin, January 1994.)

1738. Foot, Mirjam. "The Reinforcement of Paper by Graft Polymerization," Restoration '92: Conservation, Training, Materials and Techniques: Preprints ... Amsterdam, 20-22 October, 1992. London: United Kingdom Institute for Conservation, 1992, 90-92. Report of the study of a deacidification process developed for the British Library.

1739.   Foot, Mirjam M. Studies in the History of Bookbinding. Aldershot, England: Scolar Press, 1993. 467p. Illus. Essays on the medieval tradition in bookbinding; a collection of previously published articles.

1740.   Ford, Bruce E., Charles F. Cummings, and Gerald Fitzhugh. "Security at Newark Public Library," New Jersey Libraries, 27:4 (Fall 1994), 17-18. Scope of the problem in a large urban library with distinguished collections, protective security measures taken.

1741.   Ford, Jeannette White. Archival Principles and Practice: A Guide for Archives Management. Jefferson, NC: McFarland, 1990. 154p. An illustrated guide to archives management. Chapter 7: "Preservation of Archives" (pp. 117-128) covers environmental concerns, storage and handling, theft and security. Bibliography.

1742.   Forde, Helen. Conservation Department Development at the Malaysian National Library. Paris: UNESCO, 1986. 11p. (FMR/PGI/86/104). Survey report and recommendations for preservation policies and procedures to reduce the need for conservation treatment.

1743.   Forde, Helen. "Conservation Training at the Public Records Office," Journal of Librarianship, 17:2 (April 1985), 95-100. Describes general staff training in preservation and the PRO Conservation Training Program.

1744.   Forde, Helen. "Domesday Bound, 1086 to 1986," The Book Collector, 36:2 (Summer 1987), 201-206. History of the binding and repair of the Domesday Book.

1745.   Forde, Helen. Doomsday Preserved. London: Her Majesty's Stationers Office, 1986. 56p. Illus. Reviews documents and conjectures surrounding the compilation of the volumes, the original and successive bindings. The steps taken to restore and preserve the volume are detailed. References.

1746.   Forde, Helen. The Education of Staff and Users for the Proper Handling of Archival Materials. Paris: UNESCO, 1991. 38p. (RAMP Study, PG!-91/WS/17). Commonsense approach, emphasizing the importance of training and enforcement.

1747.   Forde, Helen. "Loans to Exhibitions: Are They Compatible with Conservation?" Conference on Book and Paper Conservation, 1990. Budapest, Hungary: Technical Association of Paper and Printing Industry/National Szechenyi Library, 1992, 382-387. Discusses the tension between the need to exhibit materials to promote them, resulting stresses on materials, and the need to preserve them.

1748.   Forde, Helen. "Setting Up a Conservation Workshop," Library Conservation News, 35 (April 1992), 3, 6. Describes the elements of a good work space for a small book and paper repair workshop. Diagrams; bibliography.

1749.   Forster, Geoffrey. "A History of Turning Threats Into Opportunities," Library Association Record, 97 (February 1995), 114. Historic Libraries Forum meeting, Birmingham, October 1994.

1750.   Forster, J. P. "Cibachrome Dye Stability and Storage Characteristics," AICCM Bulletin (Australian Institute for the Conservation of Cultural Material), 11:4 (December 1985), 17-31. Discusses characteristics and stability of Cibachrome film.

1751.   Fortson, Judith. "Access to History: Microfilming the Archives of the Communist Party," Conservation Administration News, 60 (January 1995), 1,3-4. Describes the Hoover Institution initiative to microfilm approximately 25,000,000 documents from the archives of the Communist Party, 1917-1991, with assistance from Chadwyck-Healy, in five years.

1752.   Fortson, Judith. Disaster Planning and Recovery; A How-To-Do-It Manual for Librarians and Archivists. New York: Neal-Schuman, 1992. 181p. (How-To-Do-It Manuals for Libraries, 21) Outlines the causes of disasters, preventive measures, recovery techniques. Bibliography; list of vendors and supplies.

1753.   Fortson, Judith. "Disaster Planning: Managing the Financial Risk," Bottom Line, 6:1 (Spring 1992), 26-33. Explores various options for defraying the costs of a disaster, including self-insurance, federal aid, and other kinds of insurance coverage that are available.

1754.   Fortson, Judith. "Earthquake Preparedness," Preservation Papers of the 1990 SAA Annual Conference, comp. Karen Garlick. Chicago: Society of American Archivists, 1991, 62-66. Details structural consideration for buildings located in earthquake zones, disaster preparedness, and a note on response.

1755.   Fortson, Judith. "The Role of the Preservation Administrator," Preservation Papers of the 1991 SAA Annual Conference. comp. Karen Garlick. Chicago: Society of American Archivists, 1992, 6-10. Describes how preservation standards are incorporated into ongoing archival work; what standards are and how they are developed.

1756. Fortson-Jones, Judith. "Conservation: What's an Archivist to Do?" Midwestern Archivist, 9:2 (1984), 83-89. Discusses new technologies for preserving records; basic steps for preserving collections.

1757. Fortson-Jones, Judith. Disaster Prevention and Recovery Plan, State Archives & Research Library, Nebraska State Historical Society. Omaha: Nebraska State Historical Society, 1984. 59 leaves. Revised edition of 1980 plan.

1758. Fortson-Jones, Judith. "How To Develop a Disaster Plan for Book and Record Repositories," History News, 38 (May 1983), 30-31. How a library can develop and implement a disaster plan.

1759. Foster, Clifton D. "Microfilming Activities of the Historical Records Survey 1935-42," American Archivist, 48:1 (Winter 1985), 45-55. Describes the comprehensive microfilming of state records undertaken by the Historical Records Survey in the 1930s. An early preservation initiative that led to several innovations.

1760. Foster, Stephen, et al. Memory of the World: General Guidelines to Safeguard Documentary Heritage. Prepared for UNESCO on behalf of IFLA [Paris]: General Information Programme and UNISIST, United Nations Educational, Scientific and Cultural Organization, 1995. 77p.

1761. Fothergill, Richard, and Ian Butchart. Non-Book Material in Libraries: A Practical Guide. 3d ed. London: Library Association, 1990. 328p. Covers care and maintenance of media and equipment; substantial information on optical storage systems and remote databases.

1762. Fowlstrunker, Skillin Q., and Nouleigh Rhee Furbished. "The Preservation of Librarians," Wilson Library Bulletin, 63:10 (June 1989), 40-41. The preservation of librarians through controlled and monitored environment is humorously discussed.

1763. Fox, Barry. "Tape Life: An Era of Concern," Studio Sound and Broadcast Engineering, 32 (December 1990), 50-54. Describes the causes of tape instability, the sticky tape syndrome, and problems with manufacturers.

1764. Fox, Lisa L. Checklist for Disaster Prevention & Protection. Atlanta: Southeastern Library Network, 1991. n.p.

1765.   Fox, Lisa L. "Conference Examines Climate Control, Compact
         Shelving and Fire Protection," SOLINEWS (Spring 1992), 13-
         14. Reports on the 7th Annual Preservation Meeting at the National
         Archives, March 17, 1992.

1766.   Fox, Lisa L. A Core Collection in Preservation. Chicago, IL:
         Association of Library Collections and Technical Services, 1988.
         15p.; 2d ed., comp. Don K. Thompson and Joan ten Hoor. 1993.
         41p. Annotated bibliography of books, reports, periodicals, and
         articles, covering the entire spectrum of library and archival
         preservation.

1767.   Fox, Lisa L. "Management Strategies for Disaster Preparedness,"
         ALA Yearbook of Library and Information Services 1989, 14.
         Chicago, IL: American Library Association, 1989, 1-6. Outlines
         management strategies that can improve an institution's success in
         disaster planning.

1768.   Fox, Lisa L. "Preservation of Library Materials," ALA Yearbook of
         Library and Information Services 1989, 14. Chicago, IL: American
         Library Association, 1989, 192-194. Also in the 1990 edition, pp.
         192-194. Review of the year in preservation.

1769.   Fox, Lisa L., ed. Preservation Microfilming: A Guide for Librarians
         and Archivists. 2d ed. Chicago, IL: American Library Association,
         1996. 393p.

1770.   Fox, Lisa L. " SOLINET Proposes Conservation Program for the
         Southeast," Conservation Administration News, 17 (April 1984), 20.

1771.   Fox, Lisa L. The SOLINET Preservation Program: Building a
         Preservation Network in the Southeast. Atlanta, GA: Southeast
         Library Network, 1988. 6p.; reprinted in New Library Scene, 7:4
         (August 1988), 1, 5-9. History of the development of the program;
         review of its activities and accomplishments.

1772.   Fox, Lisa L. "A Two-Year Perspective on Library Preservation: An
         Annotated Bibliography," Library Resources and Technical Services,
         30:3 (July/September 1986), 290-318. Review of the literature and
         bibliography.

1773.   Fox, Lisa L. Workbook for Developing a Disaster Plan. Richmond,
         VA: Library of Virginia, Records Management and Imaging Services
         Division, 1996. One volume with disc.

1774.   Fox, Peter. "Legal Processes," Security in Academic and Research
         Libraries, ed. Anthony G. Quinsee and Andrew C. McDonald.

Newcastle-upon-Tyne, England: Newcastle University Library, 1991, 49-53. Actions to be taken when theft is discovered; regulations to deter theft.

1775.   Fragile Harvest: Preserving Iowa's Documentary Heritage: An Action Plan. Jointly authored by Nancy Kraft, Ivan Hanthron, and Robert Strauss. Iowa Cooperative Preservation Consortium, 1995. 30p.

1776.   Frakes, Susan Mackey. "Preservation Internship at St. Bonaventure University," Conservation Administration News, 56 (January 1994), 8-9. Describes an internship for a library school student, including some hands-on repair experience.

1777.   France: Archives Nationales. Les Archives Régionales, la Conservation Pysique des Documents, le Contrôle Scientifique et Technique de L'État (The regional archives, the physical conservation of documents, the state of scientific and technical control). Paris: Archives Nationales, 1990. 77pp. (Proceedings of the 30th National Congress of French Archivists, Saint-Brieuc, October 12-14, 1989).

1778.   France: Archives Nationales. Les Documents Graphiques et Photographiques: Analyse et Conservation (Graphic and Photographic Documents: Analysis and Conservation). Paris: Archives Nationales, La Documentation Francaise, 1988. 211p.

1779.   France: Archives Nationales. Congrès National des Archivistes (29th 1987, Mollins, France. Preservation, Conservation et Conditionnement des Archives avec les Moyens D'Aujourd'hui. Paris: Archives Nationales, 1989. 77p. Proceeding of a conference held October 15, 1987.

1780.   Francis, David. "Film Conservation Center: A Pioneer in Saving Movies," LC Information Bulletin (Library of Congress), 50:1 (January 14, 1991), 3-6. Describes the efforts of the Library of Congress Film Conservation Center to preserve original nitrate films. Discussion of the ethical issues of restoration, preservation, and access.

1781.   Francis, Kathy. "Disaster Prevention, Preparedness and Recovery," Newsletter of the Lower Hudson Conference, 45 (1990), 10p. Addresses concerns specific to textile collections. Covers prevention, planning, options for recovery, supplies, and services.

1782.   Frangakis, Evelyn. "Dropping Acid ... From Paper," Archival Outlook, (July 1993), 20-21. Briefly discusses the causes of acidity in paper and its effect; reviews history and standards for the production of permanent durable paper.

1783.   Frangakis, Evelyn. "Pioneering in Preservation Management," <u>Archival Outlook</u> (January 1985), 8-9. Brief description of the Three-year SAA Preservation Management Training Program, its accomplishments, with consideration for future training.

1784.   Frank, Jerome P. "Binderies Are Going High-Tech," <u>Publishers Weekly</u>, 231:1 (January 9, 1987), 64-68. Describes advances in bindery machinery.

1785.   Frank, Jerome P. "Toward the Totally Acid-Free Book," <u>Publishers Weekly</u>, 336:3 (July 21, 1989), 28-29. Concerns the production of neutral pH end sheets and case bindings.

1786.   Franklin, Phyllis. "Scholars, Librarians, and the Future of Primary Records," <u>College and Research Libraries</u>, 54:5 (September 1993), 397-406. A survey of the members of the Modern Language Association reflects the importance that scholars in the humanities place on original printed records, and that photographic and digitized copies cannot substitute for traditional needs.

1787.   Frase, Robert W. "Permanent Paper: A Progress Report," <u>IFLA Journal</u> (International Federation of Library Associations and Institutions), 17:4 (1991), 366-370. Summary of international movement toward the use of alkaline paper, with recommendations for further action.

1788.   Frase, Robert W. "Permanent Paper: Progress Report II," <u>IFLA Journal</u> (International Federation of Library Associations and Institutions), 21:1 (1995), 44-47. Reports on developments since 1991 in preventive preservation through the use of permanent paper, including publication of ANSI/NISO and ISO standards for coated and uncoated permanent papers; directories and a survey of knowledge and use of permanent papers by European publishers.

1789.   Frazier, Allan. "School Library Destroyed at New Plymouth," <u>PNLA Quarterly</u> (Pacific Northwest Library Association), 52 (Winter 1988), 13. Describes a fire and lessons learned: "greater concern for accurate and complete inventories and more realistic insurance coverage."

1790.   Fredberg, Birgit, and Paulette Pieyns-Rigo. <u>Legal Implications of the Production of Machine-Readable Records by Public Administrations: A RAMP Study</u>. Paris: UNESCO, 1988. 64p.

(PGI-88/WS/15). Survey; data gathered country by country. Identifies weaknesses in legislation.

1791.   Fredericks, Maria. "Recent Trends in Book Conservation and Library Collections Care," Journal of the American Institute for Conservation, 31:1 (Spring 1992), 95-101. Discusses the movement away from full physical treatment and the consequent development of less complex and invasive treatments and increased emphasis on collections management, protective housing, and other preventive measures.

1792.   Fredericks, Maria. "Some Notes on Alum Tawing." Oxbow Diary: Paper and Book Intensive '85, ed. Barbara Muriello, Saugatuck, MN: Ox Bow Paper and Book Intensive, 1985, 77-79. Summary of the process of alum tawing.

1793.   Fredriksson, Berndt. "Collecting Sound Types - A Neglected Activity of the National Archives?" Phonographic Bulletin, 46 (November 1986), 24-28.

1794.   Freedman, Patricia. "Preliminary Care of Sound Archives," Mid-Atlantic Archivist, 12:4 (Fall 1983), 12-13. Practical information on the handling and storage of sound recordings.

1795.   Freunsch, Gail L. "Music Preservation Microfilming Project Marks Its Fifteenth Anniversary," LC Information Bulletin (Library of Congress), 44:24 (June 17, 1985); reprinted in Microform Review, 15:2 (Spring 1986), 103-104. Summary of a Library of Congress Project.

1796.   Frieder, Richard. "Designing a Book Wrapper," Abbey Newsletter, 19:3 (May 1985), 50-52. How to design book wrappers, with an example.

1797.   Frieder, Richard. "Mass Deacidification: Issues for Consideration," Preservation Planning Program: An Assisted Self-Study Manual for Libraries. Rev. 1993 ed. Washington, DC: Association of Research Libraries, 1993, 93-96. Brief review of purpose, processes, and organizational concerns for an institution to determine if it is an appropriate preservation technique.

1798.   Frieder, Richard. "Mass Deacidification: Now That It Is a Reality, What Next?" IFLA Journal (International Federation of Library Associations and Institutions), 17:2 (1991), 142-146. Overview of mass deacidification and guidelines for evaluating processes.

1799.   Frieder, Richard. "The Microfiche Revolution in Libraries," Microform Review, 16:3 (Summer 1987), 214-216. Discusses advantages and disadvantages of microfiche in library preservation.

1800.   Frieder, Richard. "Preservation Activity in the CIC," Conservation Administration News, 39 (October 1989), 11.

1801.   Frieder, Richard. "Preservation at Northwestern University," Conservation Administration News, 28 (January 1987), 5, 24-25. Description of the preservation and conservation activities at Northwestern University Library.

1802.   Friend, F.J. "Theft Detection Systems — Policies," Security in Academic and Research Libraries, ed. Anthony G. Quinsee and Andrew C. McDonald. Newcastle-upon-Tyne, England: Newcastle University Library, 1991, 31-33. Manager's approach to theft prevention; evaluating detection systems.

1803.   Frost, Gary. "Binding Structures for Book Artists," Book Arts Review, 4:1 (January 1985), 1-3. Discussion of early binding structures and how they can be adapted for modern use.

1804.   Frost, Gary. "Conservation Paper Cover and Case Construction Rebinding," Guild of Book Workers Journal, 22:1 (Fall/Winter 1983), 29-38. Describes construction for deteriorated books that must be retained for access in original format.

1805.   Frost, Gary. "Current Methods and Future Standards in the Craft of Hand Bookbinding," Guild of Book Workers Newsletter Extra, (Summer 1984), 5-7. Introduction to an exhibition catalogue; describes the educational work of the Standards Committee, Guild of Book Workers.

1806.   Frost, Gary. Future of the Paper Book. Austin, TX: The BookLab, 1992. 7p. (BookLab BookNote #12).

1807.   Frost, Gary. "Historical Prototypes for Conservation Rebinding," Oxbow Diary: Paper and Book Intensive '85, ed. Barbara Mauriello, Saugatuck, MN: Ox Bow Paper and Book Intensive, 1985, 68-71. Illus. Describes several early binding structures that can serve as prototypes for contemporary conservation binding.

1808.   Frost, Gary. "Meeting Report: BMS CAT [Blackmon-Mooring-Steamatics Catastrophe, Inc.]...Disaster Recovery Services [Training Center and Freeze Drying Facility]," New Library Scene, 7 (October 1988), 14.

1809.   Frost, Gary. Originals and Copies: Duplication and Library
        Preservation. Austin, TX: BookLab, Inc., 1992. 7p. (BookLab
        BookNote #11).

1810.   Frost Gary. Paper Book. Austin, TX: Privately Printed, December
        1993. 5p. (1993 Keepsake). Thoughts on the role of the paper book
        as "leaf master," with access through electronically supplied images.

1811.   Frost, Gary. "Report on the First Annual Books on Demand
        Symposium," Archival Products, 2:2 (Summer 1994), 4.

1812.   Frost, Gary. Three Bookbindings. Austin, TX: BookLab, 1993. 31p.
        Illus. Study of three binding structures: wooden board binding, paper
        case, and sewn board.

1813.   Frost, Gary, and Thomas F. R. Clareson. "Collections Conservation
        Technician Training: The Southwestern Region," Conservation
        Administration News, 58-59 (July/October 1994) 7-12.

1814.   Fu, Paul S. "Handling Water Damage in a Law Library," Law
        Library Journal, 79:4 (Fall 1987), 667-688. Step-by-step discussion
        of disaster recovery and insurance issues.

1815.   Fuchs, Robert, and Doris Oltrogge. "Scientific Analysis of Medieval
        Book-Illumination as a Resource for the Art Historian and
        Conservator," Gazette du Livre Médiéval, 21 (Autumn 1992),
        29-34. Report on studies of original materials, skins, inks, and
        pigments used in medieval book illumination.

1816.   Fujii, Etsuo and Hideko. "Evaluation of the Stability of Thermal Dye
        Transfer Video Prints by Accelerated Fading Tests," Journal of
        Imaging Science and Technology, 36 (January-February 1992),
        29-36. Study of the stability of images printed by a commercial
        videoprinter; numerical and quantitative evaluation of stability
        specified in terms of components of color difference.

1817.   Funston-Mills, Sarah, and William McKinnie. "Archives in the
        School Library Resource Center: Getting Started," Emergency
        Librarian, 15:5 (May-June 1988), 17-23. How schools can develop
        and use archives, with a page of instructions on their care, handling,
        and preservation.

1818.   Fusco, Marilyn. "Acidic Deterioration of Books," Current Studies in
        Librarianship, 12:1/2 (Spring/Fall 1988), 1-11. Basic paper on causes
        of deterioration and remedies.

1819.   Fusonie, Alan. Preservation: Integrity of Our Nation's Records at Risk, Washington, DC: FLICC, 1990. 13p. Paper presented at the Federal Library and Information Center pre-White House Conference, November 26-27, 1990. Updated version presented at the National Library of Medicine.

1820.   Fusonie, Alan, and Richard Myers. "Our Agricultural Landscape: Improving Image Preservation and End-User Image Access Through Laser Disk Technology," Journal of Imaging Science and Technology, 36 (January/February 1992), 60-62. Describes the imaging of valuable historic images using laser disk technology, suggesting that it may be a preservation as well as an access medium.

1821.   "The Future of Conservation," Conservation (Getty Conservation Institute Newsletter), 6 (Fall 1991), 1. Discusses the challenges of the future of conservation, including politics, public awareness, resource allocation, etc.

1822.   Futernick, Robert. "Alternative Techniques in Paper Conservation," Symposium 88: Conservation of Historic and Artistic Works on Paper; Proceedings of a Conference, Ottawa, Canada, October 3 to 7, 1988, ed. Helen D. Burgess. Ottawa: The Institute, 1994, 85-92. Discusses techniques employed at the paper conservation laboratory, Fine Arts Museums of San Francisco.

1823.   Gaba, Theodosia S.A. "Preservation Practices in the University of Cape Coast Library: An Appraisal," ASLIB Proceedings (Association for Information Management {United Kingdom}), 47 (May 1995), 127-129.

1824.   Gage-Babcock and Associates. Fire Protection Study-Mobile Compact Shelving Fire Tests-Archives II. Vienna, VA: Gage-Babcock and Associates, 1990. 17p. Discussion of the challenges facing the conservation community and the issues of resource allocation, politics, and public awareness that will shape the future.

1825.   Galabro, Guiseppe, Maria Teresa Tanasi, and Giancarlo Impagliazzo. "An Evaluation Method of Softening Agents for Parchment," Restaurator, 7:4 (1986), 169-180. Stiffness is the characteristic of choice for the evaluation of the aging of parchment and of the effectiveness of softening agents. Therefore, research was under-taken to evaluate the problems connected with the stiffness measurements on parchment. It involved the development of a sampling method as well as a modification of testing procedures to improve sensitivity. The softening effect of an agent on parchment can be derived from stiffness variations resulting from the treatment of samples. A formula is proposed to appraise the "softening effectiveness index" of an agent, taking into account the quantity absorbed by parchment.

1826.   Gallo, Fausta. Biological Factors in Deterioration of Paper, trans. Susan O'Leary. Rome: International Centre of the Conservation and Restoration of Materials, 1985. 151p. English/French. Provides information necessary in comprehending the threat to books and documents from biological factors and for creating environmental conditions favorable for preservation.

1827.   Gallo, Fausta, and Lorena Botti. "Investigation of the Fungicidal Activity of Sodium Tetraborate and on Its Resistance to the Biological Attacks of a Polyvinyl Alcohol," Restaurator, 6:1/2 (1984), 1-20. Study evaluating the resistance to microbial attack of a commercial product.

1828.   Gallo, Fausta and Margaret Hey. "Foxing, A New Approach," Paper Conservator, 12 (1986), 101-102.

1829.   Gallo, Fausta and G. Pasquariello. "Hypothesis on the Biological Origin of Foxing," Conference on Book and Paper Conservation, 1990. Budapest, Hungary: Technical Association of Paper and Printing Industry/National Szechenyi Library, 1992, 533-544. Describes investigations that have determined that "there are climatic, chemical, and biological factors linked with the appearance of foxing." Illus. Bibliography.

1830.   Galo, Gary A. "Perfect Sound Forever?" ARSC Journal (Association of Recorded Sound Collections), 27:1 (Spring 1996), 104-107. Discusses the disintegration of some CD recordings, and the probable cause, the dye in the color of the disks, including the "bronzing" problem of the Caruso set on the Pearl label. Replacement sets can be obtained from production companies.

1831.   Galvin, Theresa. "The Boston Case of Charles Merrill Mount: The Archivist's Arch Enemy," American Archivist, 53:3 (Summer 1990), 442-450. Discussion and analysis of the Mount case, emphasizing the need for careful record keeping of collections and the people who use them, and the need for surveillance of users.

1832.   Garcia, Debra A. "Recycling Capacity to Increase at Record Rates as Laws Proliferate," Pulp & Paper, May 1990, S1-5,11-16, 25-28. Technology and problems are reviewed; predicts that permanence will suffer because of high mechanical pulp content.

1833.   Garlan, Bonnie. "Peter Fisher: Archival Portfolio Books," <u>Guild of Bookworkers Journal</u>, 29:1 (Spring 1991), 16-26. Summary of a presentation at the 1989 Standards Seminar by a photographer who has developed a variety of book structures to house photographic collections.

1834.   Garlick, Karen. "Planning and Effective Holdings Maintenance Program," <u>American Archivist</u>, 52:3 (Spring 1990), 256-264. The steps that can be taken to improve the storage environment for archival collections.

1835.   Garlick, Karen, comp. <u>Preservation Papers of the 1990 SAA Annual Conference</u>. Chicago, IL: Society of American Archivists, Preservation Section, 1991. 98p. Eighteen papers covering preservation of print and nonprint collections, education and training; disaster planning.

1836.   Garlick, Karen, ed. <u>Preservation Papers of the 1991 SAA Annual Conference</u>. Chicago, IL: Society of American Archivists, 1992. 144p. A collection of 31 preservation papers presented at the 1991 conference.

1837.   Gartner, Richard. "Conservation By the Numbers: Introducing Digital Imaging Into Oxford University," <u>Microform Review</u>, 23:2 (Spring 1994), 49-52. Describes two digitizing projects and the planned central image archive. Attempts to explain advantages and disadvantages of digital imaging.

1838.   Gaskill, Deborah. "Papering the Ravages of Time," <u>Chemistry in Britain</u>, 25:4 (April 1989), 342-343. Reviews current paper conservation processes in the United Kingdom.

1839.   Gast, Monika. "Paper-splitting: A Problematic But Indispensable Method in Paper Restoration," <u>Restaurator</u>, 14:4 (1993), 234-252. Brief discussion of strengthening brittle paper, with detailed description of the technique of paper splitting.

1840.   Gatley, Donald P. "Energy Efficient Dehumidification Technology," <u>Bugs, Mold and Rot II</u>, ed. William B. Rose and Anton Ten Wolde. Washington, DC: National Institute of Building Sciences, 1993, 117-145. Technical overview and evaluation of over 25 devices and systems for reducing RH. 28 figures.

1841.   Gaughan, Thomas M. "Mold Closes Library for Two Weeks" (Saint Petersburg, Fla.), <u>American Libraries</u>, 26 (February 1995), 131-132.

1842.   Gaughan, Thomas M. "Naiveté in High Places," American Libraries, 25 (April 1994), 292. New York times editorial on the disagreement between the Library of Congress and the National Park Service concerning custody and display of handwritten drafts of the Gettysburg address.

1843.   Gavrel, Katherine. "Archives of Canada: Machine-Readable Records Program," Reference Services Review, 15:1/2 (1988), 225-229. Traces historical background and activities of the program, including processing, preservation, and dissemination.

1844.   Gavrel, Katherine. Conceptual Problems Posed by Electronic Records: A RAMP Study. Paris: UNESCO, 1990. 44p. (PGI-90/WS/12). Reviews the impact that the need to preserve electronic records is having on traditional archival practice.

1845.   Gavrel, Katherine. "National Archives of Canada: Machine-Readable Records Program," Reference Service Review, 16:1/2 (1988), 25-29. Describes the acquisition, description, preservation and dissemination of electronic records. Details preservation initiatives and notes that "efforts to find a more stable and cost-effective storage medium are underway."

1846.   Gaylord Bros. An Introduction to Book Repair. Rev. April 1996. Syracuse, NY: Gaylord Bros., 1996. 16p. (Gaylord Preservation Pathfinder, 4).

1847.   Gaylord Bros. An Introduction to Preservation. Rev. ed. 1995, 1996. Syracuse, NY: Gaylord Bros., 1992. 6p. (Gaylord Preservation Pathfinder, 1). Selected bibliography covering preservation basics; environmental control; disaster preparedness and response; preservation of photographs; collections conservation of paper and books; commercial library binding; preservation in public libraries.

1848.   Gaylord Bros. Archival Storage of Paper. rev. ed. 1995. Syracuse, NY: Gaylord Bros., 1993. 17p. Illus. (Gaylord Preservation Pathfinder, 2). Provides information to select appropriate storage systems for flat paper. Storage materials are described, as are effective enclosures for documents, art on paper, pamphlets, magazines, newspapers, and ephemera. Bibliography.

1849.   Gaylord Bros. Archival Storage of Photographic Materials. Syracuse, NY: Gaylord Bros., 1994. 19p. (Gaylord Preservation Pathfinder, 3).

1850.   Gaylord Bros. <u>Bookcraft: Simple Techniques for the Maintenance &</u>
        <u>Repair of Books</u>. Syracuse, NY: Gaylord, 1995. 32p. Illus. Basic
        repair techniques for circulating, non-permanent library materials.
        Clear instructions; helpful preservation tips.

1851.   Geh, Hans-Peter. "Conservation/Preservation: An International
        Approach," <u>Journal of Educational Media and Library Sciences</u>, 23:4
        (Summer 1986), 382-389.

1852.   Geh, Hans-Peter. "Conservation/Preservation: An International
        Approach," <u>Library Resources and Technical Services</u>, 30:1
        (January/March 1986), 31-35. Describes the Preservation and
        Conservation Programme of the International Federation of Library
        Associations and Institutions; emphasizes the importance of
        approaching problems on an international scale.

1853.   Gehl, Paul and Elizabeth Zurawski. "Incunables Bound by Elizabeth
        Kner: The 1950-1951 Project for the Newberry," <u>Guild of Book</u>
        <u>Workers Journal</u>, 31:1/2 (Spring/Fall 1993), 1-35. Illus. Report on
        the rebinding of incunables that lack original binding; aesthetic and
        conservation concerns, and a section from the notebook of the
        conservator.

1854.   Geller, L.D. "In-House Conservation and the General Practice of
        Archival Science," <u>Archivaria</u>, 22 (Summer 1986),
        163-167. Suggests that archivists need to learn basic repair
        techniques to treat collections that do not require full conservation
        treatment.

1855.   Geller, Sidney B. <u>Care and Handling of Computer Magnetic Storage</u>
        <u>Media</u>. Washington, DC: National Bureau of Standards, 1983.
        128p. (NBS Special Publ., 500-101). Guidelines for the care,
        handling, storage, and preservation of computer magnetic storage
        media. Covers transit and disaster recovery.

1856.   Genett, Mary E. "Conservation of Research Library Collections at
        the American Museum of Natural History," <u>Science and Technology</u>
        <u>Libraries</u>, 7:3 (Spring 1987), 15-28; reprinted in <u>Preservation and</u>
        <u>Conservation of Sci-Tech Materials</u>. New York: Haworth Press,
        1987, 15-28. Describes preservation efforts based on a conservation
        survey, policy decisions, and goals.

1857.   Genovese, Robert. <u>Disaster Preparedness Manual</u>. Rev. ed. Buffalo,
        NY: William S. Hein, 1993. 84p. and appendixes. Manual prepared
        for the University of Arizona College of Law Library. The manual
        was first published in 1988 and was further revised in 1998.

1858.   Gent, Megan, and Jacqueline Rees. "A Conservation Treatment to
          Remove Residual Iron from Platinum Prints," V&A Conservation
          Journal (Victorian and Albert Museum), 8 (1993), 18-20, Treatment
          report.

1859.   Gent, Megan, and Jacqueline Rees. "A Conservation Treatment to
          Remove Residual Iron from Platinum Prints," Paper Conservator, 18
          (1994), 90-95. Treatment report.

1860.   George, Gerald. Difficult Choices: How Can Scholars Help Save
          Endangered Research Resources. A Report to the Commission on
          Preservation and Access. Washington, DC: Commission on
          Preservation and Access, July 1, 1995. 28p. The report provides a
          historical view of the work of six advisory committees since 1988
          and, based on their findings, suggests several possibilities for
          consideration. The preferred option is to decide what materials
          should have priority for digitization.

1861.   George, M. "Preservation of Archival and Manuscript Material,"
          Books in Peril. Cape Town, South Africa: South African Library,
          1987, 106-117. Discusses the challenges facing contemporary
          archivists, including a proliferation of documents and a decline of
          physical quality. Discusses preservation decision making and
          actions.

1862.   George, Susan C. "Library Disasters: Are You Prepared?" College &
          Research Libraries News, 56:2 (February 1995), 80-84. How to
          develop and implement a disaster preparedness plan.

1863.   George, Susan C., comp. Emergency Planning and Management in
          Libraries. Chicago, IL: Association of College and Research
          Libraries, American Library Association, 1994. 142p. (Clip Note,
          17). Results of a survey of emergency planning and preparedness at
          261 libraries; model plans selected from survey respondents.

1864.   George, Susan C., and Cheryl T. Naslund. "Library Disasters: A
          Learning Experience," College and Research Libraries News, 47:4
          (April 1986), 251-257. Case study of a series of water leaks; advice
          on disaster planning and salvage.

1865.   George, Thelma H. "International Bookbinding Masterclasses,"
          Conservation Administration News, 37 (April 1989), 15-16.

1866.   Geoscience Information Society. Preserving Geoscience Imagery.
          Alexandria, VA: Geoscience Information Society, 1993. 126p.
          (Proceedings, 23). Nineteen papers on digital imagery, photographic
          collections, strategies for preserving geoscience literature, federal

initiatives to preserve images on laser disk, and basic preservation techniques employed at the U.S. Geological Survey Field Records and Photographic Library.

1867. Gerhardt, Claire. Preventive Conservation in the Tropics: A Bibliography. New York: New York University Institute of Fine Arts Conservation Center, September 1990. 10p. Covers general topics, climate control, micro-climates, mold control and fumigation, security and storage, training, and the museum function in the developing world. Bibliography without annotations.

1868. Gerlach, Gary. "Micrographic Restoration," Plan & Print, 62:2 (February 1989), 6-7. Note on the restoration of archival micrographic images.

1869. Gertz, Janet. "After the Fall," Conservation Administration News, 51 (October 1992), 1-2, 30. Describes the aftermath of the collapse of 12 ranges of shelving in the Columbia University Library Annex, and recovery operation.

1870. Gertz, Janet. Oversize Color Images Project, 1994-1995: A Report to the Commission on Preservation and Access. Washington, DC: Commission on Preservation and Access, 1995. 22p. This report describes a seven-month investigative study to assess the technological possibilities for reformatting brittle maps.

1871. Gertz, Janet E. "Preservation Microfilming for Archives and Manuscripts," American Archivist, 53:2 (Spring 1990), 224-234. Considers the advantages of cooperative microfilming projects; planning a microfilming program.

1872. Gertz, Janet. "Selection for Preservation: A Digital Solution for Illustrated Texts," Library Resources and Technical Services, 40:1 (January 1996), 78-83. Report on the scanning of maps from microfiche; issues of integrity of image, scanning and delivery requirements. Film and digital copies were produced in this project. Questions how these images will be used by scholarly community.

1873. Gertz, Janet. "Ten Years of Preservation in New York State: The Comprehensive Research Libraries," Library Resources and Technical Services, 39:2 (April 1995), 198-208. History and accomplishments of the NY State Program for the Conservation and Preservation of Library Research Material, including its grants programs and initiatives by the comprehensive research libraries.

1874. Gertz, Janet. "The University of Michigan Brittle Book Microfilming Program: A Cost Study and Containing Preservation

Microfilming Costs at the University of Michigan Library,"
Microform Review, 16:1 (Winter 1987), 32-36. Explains the
procedures of the program and describes a cost study that determined
the average time and cost of processing titles through the program.

1875.   Gertz, Janet with Susan Blaine. "Preservation of Printed Music: The
Columbia University Libraries Scores Condition Survey," Fontes
Artis Musicae, 41:3 (1994), 261-269. Report of a condition survey of
music scores with discussion of causes of deterioration, some
solutions, costs.

1876.   Gertz, Janet, Charlotte B. Brown, Jane Beebe, Daria D'Arienzo,
Floyd Merntt, and Lynn Robinson. "Preservation Analysis and the
Brittle Book Problem in College Libraries: The Identification of
Research-Level Collections and Their Implications," College and
Research Libraries, 54:3 (May 1993), 227-239. Examines the extent
of the brittle book problem in college libraries using the Atkinson
methodology.

1877.   Gess, J. M. "Rosin Sizing of Papermaking Fibers," TAPPI Journal
(Technical Association of the Pulp and Papermaking Industry), 72:7
(July 1989), 77-80. Examines the sizing of paper fibers and the
mechanisms involved in the controlled deposition of hydrophobic
material onto cellulose; modifications are proposed.

1878.   Getty Art History Information Program and the American Council of
Learned Societies. Technology, Scholarship and the Humanities: the
Implications of Electronic Information: September 30-October 2,
1992. Santa Monica, CA: The Program, 1993. 43p.

1879.   Getty Conservation Institute. The Conservation Assessment: A Tool
for Planning, Implementing and Fundraising. Marina del Rey, CA:
Getty Conservation Institute/National Institute for Conservation,
1990. 50p. Addresses basic conservation needs and provides
methods for gathering, interpreting, and reporting information
essential for collection care policies and practices.

1880.   Getty Conservation Institute. "Conservation Information Network."
In Computer Technology for Conservators: Proceedings of the 11th
Annual IIC-CG Conference Workshop, May 13-16, 1985, Halifax,
Canada, ed. John Perkins. Halifax, Canada, Atlantic Regional Group
of the International Institute for Conservation of Historic and Artistic
Works, Canadian Group, 1986. 339p. A network of conservation
information is discussed.

1881.   Getty Conservation Institute and National Institute for the
Conservation of Cultural Property. Summary of the Results of the

229

Emergency Response Survey. Washington, DC: Getty Conservation
Institute and National Institute for the Conservation of Cultural
Property, December 1, 1994. 13p.

1882.   Gibb, Ian P., ed. Newspaper Preservation and Access, 2 vols. New
York: Saur, 1988. Volume One, 231p. Volume Two, 449p. (IFLA
Publications, 45, 46). New initiatives, developments, and
technologies for the preservation and access of newspapers.
Proceedings of a 1987 London symposium sponsored by the IFLA
Working Group on Newspapers.

1883.   Gibson, Gerald D. "Audio, Film and Video Survey," IASA Journal,
(International Association of Sound Archives) 4 (November 1994),
53-57.

1884.   Gibson, Gerald D. "Preservation and Conservation of Sound
Recordings," Conserving and Preserving Materials in Nonbook
Formats. Urbana-Champaign: University of Illinois Graduate School
of Library and Information Science, 1991, 27-44. (Allerton Park
Institute, 30). Reviews materials and problems with their
preservation, care, and handling procedures, storage requirements.

1885.   Gibson, Gerald D. "Preservation of Nonpaper Materials,"
Conserving and Preserving Library Materials, ed. Kathryn L. and
William T. Henderson. Urbana-Champaign: University of Illinois
Graduate School of Library and Information Service, 1983,
89-110. Discusses present and future research and developments in
the preservation of film, sound recordings, tapes, computer records,
and other materials. Description of each medium and
recommendations for storage and handling.

1886.   Gibson, Tracy. "Brittle and Bound for Biblioclasm: A Survey of the
Deterioration of Books in a Melbourne College Library," Australian
College Libraries, 6:4 (December 1988), 125-129. Survey to
determine extent of deterioration of paper, bindings, and boards;
notes high percentage of deterioration in recently published items.

1887.   Giese, Diana. "Books at Risk: Mould at a University of Sydney
Library," National Library of Australia News, 4:5 (February 1994),
13-15. Description of a continuing mold outbreak in a storage
repository, the lack of environmental control in the building, and the
inability of the university to provide funds to remedy the situation.

1888.   Giese, Diana. "Meeting Every Challenge: The New Queensland
State Archives Building," National Library of Australia News, 5:5
(February 1995), 12-14. Description of the building design and lay
out, with some emphasis on the Preservation Services Division.

1889.   Giese, Diana. "Preservation in the Tropics," National Library of
         Australia News, 5:8 (May 1995), 12-15. Discussion with conservator
         Guy Petherbridge on strategies for preservation of library and
         archival materials in tropical and subtropical areas, based upon
         Petherbridge's wide experience as a consulting conservator.

1890.   Gilberg, Mark. "The Effects of Low Oxygen Atmospheres on
         Museum Pests," Studies in Conservation, 26:2 (May 1991),
         93-98. Describes research and discusses the possible application of
         low oxygen atmospheres as an alternative to conventional
         commercial fumigation techniques.

1891.   Gilberg, Mark. "Inert Atmosphere Disinfestation of Museum
         Objects Using Ageless Oxygen Absorber," AICCM Bulletin
         (Australian Institute for the Conservation of Cultural Material), 16:3
         (1990), 27-34. Discusses the advantages of using low oxygen
         atmospheres over conventional fumigation techniques; how to
         effectively use this technique.

1892.   Gilberg, Mark. "Pheromone Traps for Monitoring Insect Pests in
         Museums," IIC-CG Bulletin (International Institute for Conservation
         - Canadian Group), 17:2 (1992), 10-14. English/French. Describes
         the use of pheromone traps in museums, libraries, and archives.

1893.   Gilberg, Mark, and Agnes Brokerhof. "The Control of Insect Pests
         in Museum Collections: The Effects of Low Temperature on
         Stegobium Paniceum (Linneas), the Drugstore Beetle," Journal of the
         American Institute for Conservation, 30:2 (Fall 1991),
         197-201. Describes the use of low temperatures as an alternative to
         chemical fumigation to control insect infestation.

1894.   Gilberg, Mark, and C. Garnier. "The Use of Microwaves for Drying
         Flood Damaged Photographic Materials," Topics in Photographic
         Preservation (American Institute for Conservation of Historic and
         Artistic Works, Photographic Materials Group), 3 (1989), 46-51.

1895.   Gilberg, Mark, and John H. A. Grant. "The Conservation of a Birch
         Bark Scroll: A Case Study," Journal of the International Institute for
         Conservation - Canadian Group, 8/9 (1983/84), 23-27. Describes the
         softening and unrolling of birch-bark artifacts with organic solvent
         vapors. Methanol and ethanol vapors work best.

1896.   Gilberg, Mark, and Alex Roach. "The Effects of Low Oxygen
         Atmospheres on the Powderpost Beetle, Lyctus Brunneus
         (Stephens)," Studies in Conservation, 38:2 (May 1993),
         128-132. Test that determined that the exposure of larvae and adult

insects to a low oxygen environment is 100% effective in killing them.

1897.   Gilderson-Duwe, Caroline, comp. Disaster Recovery Supplies & Suppliers. Madison, WI: WISPR, 1995. 24p. Provides information about the statewide emergency government system and disaster response and recovery for librarians. Annotated list of emergency supplies and equipment, vendors, consultants.

1898.   Gillet, Martine, Chantel Garnier, and Françoise Flieder. "Glass Plate Negatives: Preservation and Restoration," Restaurator, 7:2 (1986), 49-80. Review of photographic processes; describes a technique in which the silver image is transferred onto a new base. 67 References.

1899.   Ginn, Ed. "Making the Most of Your Plan," Disaster Recovery, 3:4 (October-December 1990), 11-13. Discusses a "business disruption plan": personnel issues and how to keep operations functioning.

1900.   Ginnell, William S. "Making It Quakeproof," Museum News, 69:3 (May-June 1990), 61-63. Describes the system developed for the Getty Museum.

1901.   Glaser, Mary Todd. "Preservation of Posters," Preserving America's Performing Arts, eds. Barbara Cohen-Stratyner and Brigitte Kueppers. New York: Theater Library Association, 1986, 65-67.

1902.   Glaser, Mary Todd. "Storage Solutions for Oversized Paper," Nashville, TN: American Association for State and Local History, 1994. 5p.; in History News, 49:4 (1994). (Technical Leaflet 188).

1903.   Glaser, Mary Todd, Steven Weintraub, and Ellen Marlatt. "The Bill of Rights Goes to Spain," Book and Paper Group Annual, 12 (1993), 20-23. Describes steps taken to protect the U.S. Bill of Rights when on display at Expo '92 in Spain.

1904.   Glastrup, Jens. "Insecticide Analysis by Gas Chromatography in the Stores of the Danish National Museum's Ethnographic Collection," Studies in Conservation, 32:2 (May 1987), 59-64. Study demonstrating the toxicity of materials in display cases; need for further study of cleaning methods and identification of insecticides in museums.

1905.   Gleaves, Edwin S. "The Document Preservation Imperative in Tennessee," Part 1: "Slow Fires In Our Libraries and Archives"; Part 2: "Preservation Activities in the Tennessee State Library and Archives;" Part 3: "Recommended Preservation Agenda," Tennessee

Librarian, 42:1,2,3 (1990), 17-23; 26-29; 7-18. A summary of the preservation issue, the problem and its causes, and a review of preservation activities and initiatives in Tennessee.

1906. Glenewinkel, Jill. Developing Preservation Awareness for Users of Textual Records. Washington, DC: National Archives, 1990. 3p.

1907. "Glossary of Selected Preservation Terms," ALCTS Newsletter (Association of Library Collections and Technical Services), 1:2 (1990), 14-15. The glossary was developed to help librarians and consumers of Conservation Supplies to choose appropriate materials for use in treating their collections.

1908. Gnirrep, W. K., and J. A. Szirmai. "Spine Reinforced with Metal Rods in Sixteenth-Century Limp Parchment Bindings," Quaerendo, 19:1-2 (1989), 117-140. Describes a method of spine reinforcement based upon examination of 36 exemplars, extant because there had been no attempts to restore them.

1909. Godden, Irene P., and Myra Jo Moon. Organizing for Preservation in ARL Libraries. Washington, DC. Association for Research Libraries, 1985. 131p. (Spec Kit 116). Presents documents of 15 research libraries with active preservation programs.

1910. Goldberg, Martin. "The Never-Ending Saga of Library Theft," Library and Archival Security, 12:1 (1993), 87-100. Profiles of several notorious thieves with suggestions of how librarians might curtail theft.

1911. Goldman, Nancy. "Organization and Management of Film Archives and Libraries," Collection Management, 18:1/2 (1993), 41-48. Overview of general activities, practices, and concerns of film archives; discussion of preservation concerns, including deteriorating film stock and "vinegar syndrome."

1912. Goodair, Christine, and Christopher Jackson. "Developing a Preservation Policy for the Children's Society Library," Library Association Record, 90:10 (October 1988), 570-572. Implementation of a policy and program; received the Duynn & Wilson award for conservation.

1913. Goodrum, Charles, and Helen Dalrymple. "The Electronic Book of the Very Near Future," Books In Our Future. Washington, DC: Library of Congress Center for the Book, 1987, 150-177. Reprinted in Wilson Library Bulletin, 59:9 (May 1985), 587-590. Discusses the future of the book in terms of new technologies; implications for the preservation of deteriorating books.

1914.   Gooes, Roland, and Hans-Evert Bloman. "An Inexpensive Method for Preservation and Long-Term Storage of Color Film," SMPTE Journal (Society of Motion Picture and Television Engineers), 92 (December 1983), 1314-1316. Describes a conditioning apparatus designed by the Swedish Film Institute to save and store all motion picture films produced since the 1950s.

1915.   Gordon, Ann D. Using the Nation's Documentary Heritage: The Report of the Historical Documents Study. Washington, DC: National Historic Publication and Records Commission, 1992. 112p. Addresses needs of researchers, issues of funding, and public policy, with a call for concerted action by users to ensure the collection, preservation, and access to the public record.

1916.   Gordon, Barbara. "Firmitas, Utilitas, and Frugalitas: The Harvard Depository," The Great Divide: Challenges in Remote Storage, ed. James R. Kennedy and Gloria Stockton. Chicago, IL: American Library Association, 1990, 27-36. Discusses planning, shelving, and environmental controls for the Harvard Book Depository.

1917.   Gordon, Ralph W. The Struggle for Permanent Paper. Williamstown, ON, Canada: Published by the author, c1990. 14p. Traces trends in papermaking from the 1950s to the present, including the transition to the production of alkaline paper.

1918.   Goswami, Badri P. Problems of Misplacement, Mutilation and Theft of Books in Libraries. 2d ed. Varanasi, India: Radha Krishna Publications, 1988. 224p. Common sense and social commentary on the values of modern society, in India and the West; will help librarians tighten security systems.

1919.   Gottlieb, Adam. "Chemistry and Conservation of Platinum and Palladium Photographs," Journal of the American Institute of Conservation, 34:1 (Spring 1995), 11-32. Clarifies the chemical composition of platinum and palladium photographs, by reviewing the literature, re-creating the processes according to recipes found, using x-ray spectroscopy to carry out elemental analysis of the metals used in the processes.

1920.   Gould, Constance C., and Karla Pearce. Information Needs in the Sciences: An Assessment. Mountain View, CA: Research Library Group, 1991. 79p. Assessment of needs; preservation of important older materials identified as an "area of opportunity" for RLG.

1921.   Gould, Stephen B. Computer Security Enhancement to Prevent Disasters and Crimes. Washington, DC: Library of Congress,

Congressional Research Service, 1991. 6p. (CRS Report 91-239SPR).

1922. Govan, J. F. "Preservation and Resource Sharing: Conflicting or Complementary?" IFLA Journal (International Federation of Library Associations and Institutions), 2:1 (February 1986), 20-24. Examines the seemingly conflicting needs of preservation and resource sharing; advocates reformatting as a solution.

1923. Gow, Neil A. R., and Geoffrey M. Gadd. The Growing Fungus. London: Chapman & Hall, 1995. 473p. Recent advances in cell biology, physiology, and genetics of growth.

1924. Gracy, David B., II. "Between Muffins and Mercury ... The Elusive Definition of 'Preservation,'" New Library Scene, 9:6 (December 1990), 1,5-7. Discusses what 'Preservation' includes and the difficulty the library profession has in defining it.

1925. Graf, Jace. "The BookLab Story: An Interview with Jace Graf," The Gold Leaf (Hand Bookbinders of California), 12:1 (Spring 1994), 10-17. Describes BookLab, its staff and activities, including edition binding, custom box-making, production of photo-facsimiles, and development of books structures for conservation.

1926. Graf, Jace. "The Persistent Codex: Photocopying and Binding Merge to Preserve the Printed Word," Technicalities, 15 (December 1995), 16-17.

1927. Graff, Michael W. "Avoid Tomorrow's Disaster With Today's Microfilm," Inform, 2:6 (June 1988), 12-13. Emphasizes the need for back-up files for records.

1928. Graham, Crystal. Guidelines for Bibliographic Records for Preservation Microform Masters. Washington, DC: Association of Research Libraries, 1990. 15p.; reprinted in Microform Review, 21:2 (Spring 1992), 67-73. Prepared for use in cataloguing preservation microfilm masters of books and serial publications to achieve the standardization essential for preservation microfilm records.

1929. Graham, Peter S. "Electronic Information and Research Library Technical Services," College and Research Libraries, 51:3 (May 1990), 241-250. Examines the relation of libraries to electronic information and the issue of the preservation of intellectual content in electronic media.

1930.   Graham, Peter S. Intellectual Preservation: Electronic Preservation of the Third Kind. Washington, DC: Commission on Preservation and Access, 1994. 8p. Discusses the need to assure the integrity and authenticity of information as it is originally recorded.

1931.   Graham, Peter S. "Intellectual Preservation in the Electronic Environment," After the Electronic Revolution, Will You Be the First to Go? ed. Arnold Hirshon. Chicago, IL: American Library Association, 1993, 18-38; reprinted in From Catalog to Gateway, 1 (1994), A-D; and as "Preserving the Intellectual Record and the Electronic Environment," Scholarly Communication and the Electronic Environment. Chicago, IL: American Library Association, 1993, 71-101. Also published in After the Electronic Revolution.... Proceedings of the 1992 Association for Library Collections and Technical Services President's Program. Arnold Hirshon ed. Chicago: ALA/ALCTS, 1993. 18-38. Acknowledges the impermanence of electronic information and reviews several encoding systems for identifying primary texts in electronic formats. Paper presented at the 1992 Association of Library Collections and Technical Services Presidents Program.

1932.   Graham, Peter S. "Long-Term Intellectual Preservation," Digital Imaging Technology for Preservation, ed. Nancy E. Elkington. Mountain View, CA: Research Libraries Group, 1994, 41-57. Discusses issues of authenticity and longevity of data; suggests that existing technology might solve the problem of authenticity of text. Notes institutional priorities will need to be shifted to ensure preservation of text in electronic formats.

1933.   Graham, Peter S. "Requirements for the Digital Research Library," College & Research Libraries (July 1995), 331-339.

1934.   Grandinette, Maria, and Randy Silverman. "The Library Collections Conservation Discussion Group: Taking a Comprehensive Look at Book Repair," Library Resources and Technical Services, 38:3 (July 1994), 281-287. Description of the group's efforts to improve the quality of book repair in libraries through expanding treatment selection guidelines, reviewing specifications, defining degree of documentation required, exploring ways to improve training, and identifying further needs.

1935.   Grandinette, Maria, and Randy Silverman. "New Book Repair Methods in Research Libraries," Abbey Newsletter, 19:2 (May 1995), 29-33. A look at the Library Collections Conservation Discussion Group (LCCDG) in AIC, formed to expand book conservation to book repair, address training of paraprofessionals, and review book repair techniques.

1936. Grant, Joan. "Preservation Concerns for Collectors," Manuscripts, 37:3 (Summer 1985), 185-194. Describes causes of deterioration, salvage of damaged materials, and provides advice on storage and handling.

1937. Grant, Sharlane Tyra. "Restoring a Large Collection of Large-Format Mine Maps; Problems, Solutions and Procedures," Conservation of Historic and Artistic Works on Paper. Ottawa: Canadian Conservation Institute, 1994, 47-51. (Symposium 88). Describes a project to restore 1,600 maps in two years, providing a model for funding, planning, and problem solving.

1938. Grantham, Sandra. "A Suction Table/Capillary Matting 'Dry' Lining Technique," Paper Conservation News, 71 (September 1994), 1-3. Description of a reversible lining technique for prints and documents that will not flatten fibers on verso of sheet and will allow visual inspection.

1939. Grattan, David. "The Parylene Project: An Update," CCI Newsletter (Canadian Conservation Institute), 11 (April 1993), 3-4. French/English. Reviews research on application for artifacts, specimens, and paper, as well as the CCI investigation of parylene's aging properties. seven references.

1940. Grattan, David, and Mark Gilberg. "Ageless Oxygen Absorber: Chemical and Physical Properties," Studies in Conservation, 39:3 (August 1994), 210-214. Describes physical and chemical properties, with criteria for museum use. Discussion of problems such as heat generation and hydrogen evolution.

1941. Grauer, Sally. "Bookbinding," Encyclopedia of Library History, ed. Wayne A. Wiegand and Donald G. Davis, Jr. New York: Garland, 1994, 83-85. Brief history of bookbinding and binding materials.

1942. Grauer, Sally. "Jan Merrill-Oldham: The Lady from Connecticut," New Library Scene, 5:6 (December 1986), 16-17. Profile of a preservation specialist.

1943. Grauer, Sally. "Recasing ... A Discussion Between Librarians and Binders," New Library Scene, 8:4 (August 1989), 1, 5-8. A summary of a program given at the 1989 American Library Association Conference. Lyn Jones, University of California - Berkeley, details the decision making and treatment process in her library. Several binders discuss issues from their perspective.

1944.   Grauer, Sally, Barclay Ogden, and Rolland Aubey. "Report on
         ISO/TC46/SC 10/WG4 - Binding," Information Standards Quarterly,
         6:3 (July 1994), 8; reprinted in Abbey Newsletter, 18:4/5
         (August/September 1994), 48-49. Comments on the standards for
         edition binding and for library binding, emphasizing the need for
         them.

1945.   Graves, James S. "Emotional Aftermath of the Northridge
         Earthquake: Lessons for Business," Disaster Recovery Journal, 7:2
         (April/June 1994), 14-20. Summary of the emotional trauma that
         people experience after a disaster and how an organization can help
         personnel recover. Recommends debriefing sessions to deal with
         trauma as soon as possible after disaster.

1946.   Great Britain. Conservation Unit. Conservation Sourcebook.
         London: Her Majesty's Stationers Office, 1991. 122p. List of British
         organizations concerned with the preservation and conservation of
         cultural property.

1947.   Great Britain. Conservation Unit. Directory of Conservation
         Research in the United Kingdom. London: Conservation Unit,
         Museums and Galleries Commission, 1991. 27p.

1948.   Great Britain. Public Record Office. Optical Disc Project Final
         Report. London: Public Record Office, 1989. 32p. An Interim
         Report was issued in 1985 (Library and Information Research Report
         No. 27).

1949.   Greater Northeastern Regional Medical Library Program.
         Preservation Needs Assessment of US Health Sciences Libraries.
         New York: New York Academy of Medicine, 1989. 163p.

1950.   Green, Deidre. "After the Flood: Disaster Response and Recovery
         Planning," Bulletin of the Medical Library Association, 78:3 (July
         1990), 303-305. Case history; describes salvage effort and ensuing
         disaster planning.

1951.   Green, Kevin. "The Case of the Pilkington Technology Center Fire,"
         ASLIB Information (Association for Information Management
         {United Kingdom}), 21:2 (February 1993), 63-64. Case study;
         smoke damage in a library and misadventures with the disaster
         recovery company.

1952.   Green, L. R., and M. Leese. "Nongaseous Deacidification of Paper
         with Methyl Magnesium Carbonate," Restaurator, 12:3 (1991),
         147-162. Experiments indicate that it is effective in a commonly
         available form.

1953.   Green, Paul. "A Comparison of Binding Styles and Usage Levels of
         Engineering Titles at Leeds and Cornell Universities," Collection
         Management, 13:4 (1990), 65-76. Compares binding styles and the
         way bindings wear with use.

1954.   Green, Paul Robert. "The Binding of Periodicals: An Overview,"
         Serials Librarian, 9:2 (Winter 1984), 25-33. Discusses the decision-
         making process in determining with to bind, how to bind it, and what
         not to bind.

1955.   Greenberg, Gerald S. "Books as Disease Carriers, 1880-1920,"
         Libraries and Culture, 23:3 (Summer 1988), 281-294. An
         examination of measures taken by librarians between 1880 and 1920
         to disinfect books that might be contaminated by communicable
         diseases to retain public confidence in libraries.

1956.   Greene, Harlan. "The North Carolina Preservation Consortium,"
         Conservation Administration News, 56 (January 1994),
         4-5. Activities of a consortium that informs, coordinates, and
         provides leverage for preservation initiatives in North Carolina.

1957.   Greene, Harlan. "North Carolina's Preservation Program,"
         Preservation Papers of the 1991 SAA Annual Conference. comp.
         Karen Garlick. Chicago: Society of American Archivists, 1992,
         39-43. Describes statewide preservation needs assessment and
         planning project.

1958.   Greene, Virginia. "Adaptation of Standard Matting Folders,"
         Storage of Natural History Collections. Pittsburgh, PA: Society for
         the Preservation of Natural History Collections, 1992,
         149-152. Describes folders for mounting textiles.

1959.   Greenfield, Jane. Books: Their Care and Repair. New York: H.W.
         Wilson, 1983. 204p. Illus. Manual on the care and repair of books,
         pamphlets, and documents. Covers book structure and basic repairs.

1960.   Greenfield, Jane. The Care of Fine Books. New York: Nick Lyons
         Books, 1988. 160p. Illus. A detailed manual for the preservation and
         physical treatment of rare and fine books.

1961.   Greenfield, Jane, and Jenny Hille. Headbands, How to Work Them.
         New Haven, CT: Edgewood Publ., 1986 80p.; 2d rev. ed. New
         Castle, DE: Oak Knoll Books, 1990. 88p. Illus. Provides
         step-by-step instructions and detailed drawings for twelve
         headbands.

1962.   Greenstein, Shane. "Tape Story Tapestry: Historical Research with Inaccessible Digital Information Technologies," Midwestern Archivist, 15:2 (1990), 77-85. Notes that electronic information technologies make it incredibly easy to destroy records and that control and access mechanisms taken for granted with well-established storage media do not exist for machine-readable data.

1963.   Griffen, Agnes M. "Potential Roles of the Public Library in the Local Emergency Management Program: A Simulation," Special Libraries, 78:2 (Spring 1987), 122-130. Case study; county library and Fire and Rescue Service collaborate in emergency planning.

1964.   Griffin, Marie P. "Preservation at the Institute of Jazz Studies," New Jersey Libraries, 18:1 (Spring 1985), 17-18. Preservation through re-recording and preservation microfilming of related clippings files.

1965.   Griffin, Marie P. "Preservation of Rare and Unique Materials at the Institute of Jazz Studies," Conservation Administration News, 25 (April 1986), 8-9.

1966.   Griffith, J.W. "After the Disaster: Restoring Library Service," Wilson Library Bulletin, 58:4 (December 1983), 258-265. Discusses precautions to be taken to minimize loss and damage from natural disasters; salvage and restoration of collection and facility.

1967.   Grimard, Jacques. "Commentary: The Challenge of the Audio-Visual: Preserving the Evocative Power of the Ephemeral," The Archivist, 110 (1995), 2-4. (French/English) Discusses the need to save the audio-visual heritage in the light of the short life-span of technologies. Issue focuses on the film/sound heritage and its preservation.

1968.   Grimard, Jacques. "Mass Deacidification: Universal Cure or Limited Solution?" American Archivist, 57:4 (Fall 1994), 674-679. Describes the development and operation of the mass deacidification program at the Canadian National Archives and National Library, to treat books; addresses process, limitations, concerns, and the future.

1969.   Grimstad, Kirsten, ed. ICOM Committee for Conservation Preprints. Los Angeles, CA: International Council of Museums, 1990, 2 vols. Proceedings of the 9th Triennial Meeting, Dresden, August 26-31, 1990. Individual papers cited separately.

1970.   Grimwood-Jones, Diana. "Preservation," British Librarianship & Information Work 1981-1985, ed. David W. Bromley and Angela M. Allott. Vol. 2. London: Library Association 1988, 270-284.

Definition of problem, traces history of preservation activities in the United Kingdom and the expanding consciousness of the problem. 65 citations.

1971. Grosjean, Daniel, and Mohamed W. M. Hisham. "A Passive Sampler for Atmospheric Ozone," Journal of the Air Waste Management Association, 42:2 (February 1992), 169-173. Describes the design and testing of a simple, cost-effective passive sampler to determine atmospheric ozone.

1972. Grosjean, Daniel, and Sucha S. Parmar. "Removal of Air Pollutant Mixtures from Museum Display Cases," Studies in Conservation, 36:3 (August 1991), 129-141. Report on studies to investigate the feasibility of removing air pollutants using sorbents such as activated carbon and Purafil.

1973. Grosso, Vilia. "Analysis of Ancient Paper and Ink," International Colloquium on the Role of Chemistry in Archaeology 15-18 November, 1991, ed. M. C. Ganorker and N. Rama Rao. Hyderabad, India: Birlaz Institute of Scientific Research, 1991, 67-75. Six analytical methods were used on several types of ancient paper to find methods of dating them, with encouraging results.

1974. Grover, Mark L. "Paper and Binding Quality of Latin American Books," Abbey Newsletter, 12:5 (July 1988), 90. Results of a study of a random selection of books indicating that while there was some variation from country to country the percentage of groundwood paper is high and the quality of binding is poor.

1975. Gschwind, Rudolf, and Franziska Frey. "Electronic Imaging, a Tool for the Reconstruction of Faded Colored Photographs," The Journal of Imaging Science and Technology, 38:6 (November 1994), 520.

1976. Gschwind, Rudolf, and Franziska Frey. "Reconstruction of Faded Colour Photographs by Digital Imaging," Electronic Imaging and the Visual Arts, ed. Anthony Hamber. Aldershot, England: Brameur, 1992, 4p. [unpaged in one of three volumes] (EVA '92 Proceedings). Describes reconstruction process using a quick, inexpensive technology that does not damage original photographs to restore original colors as accurately as possible; not conservation.

1977. Guay, Louise. "Focus on Preservation: Canadian Audio-Visual Heritage," The Archivist, 110 (1995), 37-38. Briefly describes the work of the National Archives/Canada Task Force on the Preservation and Enhanced Use of Canada's Audio-Visual Heritage, to "identify the problems, define a management and funding frame, work, & develop a joint strategy based on co-operation." (37)

1978.   Gubbins, Donald. "Domesday Rebound 1986," Bookbinder, 1
(1987), 9-17. Illus. Description of the analysis, repair, and rebinding
of the Domesday Book for use and display.

1979.   Guichen, Gael de. Climate in Museums: Measurement. 2d ed.
Rome: Centre for the Study of the Preservation and Restoration of
Cultural Property, 1984. 80p. (English/French). Practical handbook
on the techniques and instruments for measurement of the museum
climate.

1980.   Guichen, Gael de. "How to Make a Rotten Showcase," Museum,
146 (1985), 64-67. Illus. Eleven timely tips.

1981.   Guild of Book Workers. Opportunities for Study in Hand
Bookbinding and Calligraphy. New York: Guild of Book Workers,
updated frequently.

1982.   Guild of Book Workers Journal, 27:1 (Spring 1989), Entire issue. A
tribute to bookbinder, book conservator, and teacher William
Anthony, including a bibliography of his publications, publications
about him, and publications by and about his students.

1983.   Guldbeck, Per E. The Care of Antiques and Historical Collections.
2d ed. rev. by A. Bruce MacLeish. Nashville, TN: American
Association for State and Local History, 1985. 245p. Manual on the
care of "historically significant materials" covering storage, display,
and environmental control.

1984.   Gulick, R. van, and N. E. Kersten-Pampiglione. "A Closer Look at
Iron Gall Ink Burn," Restaurator, 15:3 (1994), 173-187. Reviews
information on the problem of iron gall ink burn from a review of the
literature and inquiries; demonstrates a lack of fundamental
information and the need for closer study and dialogue.

1985.   Gulick, Susan H. "Your Disaster Plan: Does It Cover Everything?"
New Jersey Libraries, 28:3 (Summer 1995), 6-9. Case study of a
library with a disaster plan struck by a plague of disasters, including
winter leaks, serious mold infestation, and an explosion. The need
for communication among staff and in the community is emphasized.

1986.   Gunn, Michael J. Manual of Document Microphotography.
London; Boston: Focal Press, 1985. 232p. Includes a chapter on
care and preservation that discusses problems of library and archival
storage. Glossary.

1987.   Gunn, Michael J. "'Poly' or 'Cell,'" <u>Microform Review</u>, 16:3 (Summer 1987), 231-232. Comparison of cellulose acetate and polyester bas silver halide film; does not note impermanence of cellulose acetate film.

1988.   Gunter, Linda. "Earthquake Recovery at the Libraries of the Claremont Colleges," <u>College and Research Libraries News</u>, 51:10 (November 1990), 935-936. A case study of response and recovery.

1989.   Gurnaguel, Narayr, and Xuejun Zou. "The Effect of Atmospheric Pollutants on Paper Permanence: A Literature Review," <u>TAPPI Journal</u> (Technical Association of the Pulp and Paper Industry), 77:7 (July 1994), 199-204. Review identifies issues for further investigation.

1990.   Gustafson, Ralph A., Ingrid R. Modaresi, Georgia V. Hampton, Ronald J. Chepesiuk, and Gloria A. Kelley. "Fungicidal Efficacy of Selected Chemicals in Thymol Cabinets," <u>Journal of the American Institute for Conservation</u>, 29:2 (Fall 1990), 153-168. Investigation of eight chemicals for possible use in thymol cabinets. None were effective in killing indigenous mold on books; only thymol and paraformaldehyde exhibited fungicidal activity against mold cultures.

1991.   Guttman, Charles M., and Kenneth L. Jewett. "Protection of Archival Materials from Pollutants: Diffusion of Sulphur Dioxide through Boxboard," <u>Journal of the American Institute of Conservation</u>, 32:1 (Spring 1993), 81-92. Report of a study to measure the diffusion of sulphur dioxide through boxboard used to make archival storage boxes. Technical.

1992.   Guttman, Charles M., and Kenneth L. Jewett. "Protection of Archival Records from Pollutants: The Diffusion of S0$\underline{2}$ Through Archival Boxboard," <u>Journal of the American Institute for Conservation</u>, 32:1 (Spring 1993), 81-92; <u>Issues in Art and Archaeology III</u>. Pittsburgh, PA: Materials Research Society, 1992, 447-451. Report of a project to measure the diffusion of sulfur dioxide in boxboard; discusses results in terms of providing micro-environments for archival materials.

1993.   Gwiazda, Henry J. "Preservation Decision-Making and Archival Photocopying: Twentieth-Century Collections at the Kennedy Library," <u>Restaurator</u>, 8:1 (1987), 52-62. Describes photocopying as a preservation measure to protect original documents.

1994.   Gwin, James. E. "Preservation and Environmental Control Issues in the Urban/Metropolitan Academic Library," <u>Academic Libraries in Urban and Metropolitan Areas: A Management Handbook</u>, ed. G. B.

McCabe. Westport, CT: Greenwood, 1992, 187-194. The elements of environmental control: temperature, RH, air pollution, and light, are especially important to monitor in urban libraries, if collections are to be preserved.

1995. Gwinn, Nancy E. "The Fragility of Paper: Can Our Historical Record Be Saved?" Public Historian, 13:3 (Summer 1991), 33-53. Identifies causes of deterioration of library and archival collections, reviews preservation options and costs, and the growth of national and international initiatives to protect and preserve collections.

1996. Gwinn, Nancy E. A National Preservation Program for Agricultural Literature. [Washington, DC: National Agricultural Library], May 1993. 20p. Proposal for a national program to preserve the literature related to agriculture in the United States published prior to 1950, to ensure future access for scholars.

1997. Gwinn, Nancy E. "Politics and Practical Realities: Environmental Issues for the Library Administrator, Advances in Preservation and Access. Vol. 1. Westport, CT: Meckler, 1992, 135-146. Environmental requirements for housing library and archival materials; standards.

1998. Gwinn, Nancy E., ed. Preservation Microfilming: A Guide for Librarians and Archivists. Chicago, IL: American Library Association, 1987. 212p. 2d. ed. by Lisa Fox for the Association of Research Libraries, Chicago, IL, ALA, 1996, 349p. Manual on all aspects of preservation microfilming with chapters by specialists; provides an administrative context for planning and implementing a preservation microfilming project. Papers from a conference for librarians involved in preservation microfilming projects.

1999. Gwinn, Nancy E. "The RTSD Preservation Microfilming Committee: Looking to the 1990s," Library Resources and Technical Services, 34:1 (January 1990), 88-94. A history of the Committee, established in 1980 to collect and disseminate information and to improve communication. The Committee is expanding to address issues concerning preservation microfilming and to facilitate activities.

2000. Gwinn, Nancy E. "The Rise and Fall and Rise of Cooperative Projects," Library Resources and Technical Services, 29:1 (January-March 1985), 80-86. Historical overview of cooperative preservation microfilming projects over the past half-century; discussion of present efforts.

2001. Gwinn, Nancy E. <u>Smithsonian Institution Libraries. Preservation Planning Program; Final Report of the Study Team</u>. Washington, DC: Association of Research Libraries, Office of Management Studies, July 1986. 90p. Report focuses on preservation problems in the general collection, including environment. A strategy for dealing with the Smithsonian's collection is outlined and recommendations are made.

2002. Gwinn, Nancy E. "The Smithsonian Institution Librarians: A Foot in Three Camps," <u>College and Research Libraries</u>, 50:2 (March 1989), 206-214. Discusses the origin and history of the institution and its libraries, the conservation and preservation challenges of preserving library materials.

2003. Gyeszly, Suzanne D., Deborah Brown, and Mary Kay Donahue. "Preservation at Texas A&M University," <u>Conservation Administration News</u>, 15 (October 1983), 5-6,8. Report on preservation planning, policies, and procedures.

2004. Hackman, Larry J. "The United States Needs a National Historical Records Policy!" <u>History News</u> (March-April 1988), 32-37.

2005. Hackney, Stephen. "The Distribution of Gaseous Air Pollution Within Museums," <u>Studies in Conservation</u>, 29:3 (August 1984), 105-116. The significance of air pollution to conservation; assessment of four methods of measuring gaseous air pollution within museums.

2006. Hackney, Stephen. "Framing for Conservation," <u>Environmental Monitoring and Control</u>. Dundee, Scotland: Scottish Society for Conservation and Restoration, 1989, 91-93. Note on creating a cost-effective micro-environment within a frame.

2007. Hadgraft, Nicholas. "Charles Estienne's L'Agriculture et Maison Rustique, 1565: The Plantin Title-Page in a Du Puis Book," <u>The Book Collector</u>, 40:4 (1991), 514-527. Describes the conservation of a unique Plantin edition.

2008. Hadgraft, Nicholas. "Disaster Planning in Small Libraries," <u>Bulletin of the Association of British Theological & Philosophical Libraries</u>, 2:6 (November 1989), 21-33.

2009. Hadgraft, Nicholas. "Maintaining Satisfactory Environments in the Parker Library," <u>Conservation and Preservation in Small Libraries</u>, ed. Nicholas Hadgraft and Katherine Swift. Cambridge: Parker Library Publications, 1994. 47-48. How the RH in the Parker Library was stabilized and is maintained.

2010.   Hadgraft, Nicholas. "The Parker Library Conservation Project 1983-1989," Library Conservation News, 24 (July 1989), 4-7. Describes the conservation project undertaken in the Parker Library, Cambridge University.

2011.   Hadgraft, Nicholas. "Storing and Boxing the Parker Library Manuscripts," Paper Conservator, 18 (1994), 20-20. Discussing the boxing of the collection, the process and problems.

2012.   Hager, Michael, "Saving the Image: The Deterioration of Nitrate Negatives," Image, 26:4 (December 1983), 1-9. Efforts to preserve collections of nitrate negative film of Photographer Nickolas Murray.

2013.   Hahn, Bessie K. "Book Preservation: An International Agenda," International Symposium on New Techniques and Applications in Libraries, Xian Chinese People's Republic, September 8-11 1988. Xian, China: Xian Jiao Tong University Press, 1988, 35-44. Presents an overview of preservation technologies; describes preservation strategies in several U.S. libraries to preserve embrittled collections; advocates national and international policies on cooperative preservation.

2014.   Hahn, Ellen Z. "The Library of Congress Optical Disk Pilot Program: A Report on the Print Project Activities," LC Information Bulletin (Library of Congress), 42:44 (October 31, 1983), 374-376. Report on the print projects designed to test the implementation of optical disk storage for preservation and access.

2015.   Haines, B.M. "The Conservation of Leather Bookbindings," Adhesives and Consolidants. London: International Institute for Conservation, 1984, 50-54. Preprints from a Congress September 2-8, 1984, Paris, France. Report on the development of a treatment for deteriorated leathers and stable bookbinding leather.

2016.   Haines, Betty M., and Christopher Calnan. "The Development of a Stable Binding Leather," Bookbinder (Journal of the Society of Bookbinders and Book Restorers), 2 (1988), 35-50. Reviews the history of deteriorating leather problems and describes new tanning and production techniques that produce archival-quality leathers. Review of research.

2017.   Haines, John H., and Stuart A. Kohler. "An Evaluation of Ortho-phenyl Phenol as a Fungicidal Fumigant for Archives and Libraries," Journal of the American Institute for Conservation, 25:1 (Spring 1986), 49-55. Reports the results of tests using O-phenyl phenol (OPP) and thymol, which demonstrated that neither is totally effective in preventing fungus spores from germinating.

2018.   Haines, Michael. "Physical Hazards and Post-Trauma Problems," New Jersey Libraries, 28:3 (Summer 1995), 11-12. Briefly discusses the "Right to Know" Act to identify hazardous substances; and describes post-traumatic stress and how to help alleviate it.

2019.   Häkkänen, H. J., and J.E.I. Korppi-Tommola. "Laser-induced Fluorescence Imaging of Paper Surfaces," Applied Spectrography, 47:12 (1993), 2122-2125. Study using laser-induced fluorescence imaging to correlate results to predict mottling in various paper brands.

2020.   Hales, Robert. "The Conservation of Books & Documents at Cedric Chivers Limited," In Safe Keeping, ed. Jennifer Thorp. Winchester, U.K.: Hampshire Co. Library / Hampshire Archives Trust, 1988, 29-30. Briefly describes conservation treatment for brittle and / or damaged books.

2021.   Hall, Hal W., and George H. Michaels. "Microform Reader Maintenance," Microform Review, 14:1 (Winter 1985), 24-34. Describe a program and guidelines for regular machine maintenance and repair.

2022.   Hall, Susan. Guidelines for Microfilming Records of Archival Value. Ottawa: National Archives of Canada, 1996. 74+p. (French/English)

2023.   Hallebeek, Pieter B. "The Sulphur Content of New Commercial Leather for Bookbinding," Preprints: ICOM Committee for Conservation 10th Triennial Meeting, ed. Janet Bridgland. Washington, DC: International Council of Museums, 1993, 639-644. Presents analysis of sulphur content in leathers.

2024.   Hamber, Anthony. ed. Electronic Imaging and the Visual Arts. Aldershot, Hants., England: Brameur, 1992. 3 vols. Electronic Imaging and the Visual Arts Conference Proceedings: EVA' 92.

2025.   Hamburg, Doris A. "Library and Archival Collections," Caring for Your Collections. New York: Harry N. Abrams, 1992, 52-63. A summary of collections care, handling, storage, display, and repair for collectors.

2026.   Hamilton, John Maxwell. "Is There a Klepto in the Stacks?" Library and Archival Security, 12:1 (1993), 47-54. Anecdotal discussion of what materials are most often stolen, and why.

2027. Hamilton, Marsha J. Guide to Preservation in Acquisition
       Processing. Chicago: American Library Association, 1993. 34p.
       (Acquisition Guidelines, 8.

2028. Hamilton, Marsha. "Poor Condition: Procedures for Identifying and
       Treating Materials Before Adding to the Collections," RTSD
       Newsletter (Resources and Technical Services Division, American
       Library Association), 13:2 (1988), 19-22. How procedures were
       developed at Ohio State University libraries.

2029. Hamilton, Robert M. "The Library of Parliament Fire," Canadian
       Library Journal, 49:4 (August 1992), 269-270; reprint of an article
       originally published in Canadian Library Bulletin, 9:3 (November
       1952), 75-77. Describes the evaluation and drying of books damaged
       in the fire, August 4, 1952.

2030. Hammer, John H. "On the Political Aspects of Book Preservation in
       the US," Advances in Preservation and Access. Vol. 1. Westport,
       CT: Meckler, 1992, 22-40. Summary of efforts by the scholarly and
       library communities to obtain funding for the nation's "Brittle Book"
       program.

2031. Hammill, Michele E. "Washingtonia II: Conservation of
       Architectural Drawings at the Library of Congress," Book and Paper
       Annual, 12 (1993), 24-31. Describes a multi faceted project with
       collaboration between conservators and curators to preserve and
       make available 4,000 drawings related to Washington, DC.

2032. Hammond, Lorne F. "Historians, Archival Technology and Business
       Ledgers," Archivaria, 28 (Summer 1989), 120-125. Case study
       documenting why an awareness of provenance is important and how
       reformatting of documents into other media can filter out information
       that can be gained from an original object.

2033. Handley, Mhairi. "Digital Archive for the Future — Stability
       Guaranteed," Photographic Materials Group Newsletter (UK), 1
       (January 1996), 4-7. On the production and instability of optical and
       compact disks; why archival information should be stored on
       microfilm.

2034. Hanff, Peter. "Library Theft Protection," College and Research
       Libraries News, 45:6 (June 1984), 289-290. Report on the
       ALA/RBMS Security Committee's informal survey of collection
       security precautions among North American libraries.

2035. Hanff, Peter. "The Story of the Berkeley Library Theft," College and
       Research Libraries News, 45:6 (June 1984), 284-287. Case study:

what went right and what happened when staff encountered the
library's theft plan.

2036.   Hanington, David J. "The Colouring of Pulp for Leaf-Casting,"
Conservation of Historic and Artistic Works on Paper. Ottawa:
Canadian Conservation Institute, 1994, 53-59. (Symposium
88). Describes a technique for the toning of papers that is less costly
and probably more stable than traditional methods.

2037.   Hanington, David, and Claire Titus. "Map of Five Counties," CCI
Newsletter (Canadian Conservation Institute), 8 (October 1991),
1-4. Describes the treatment of a sectioned 19th-century map intended
to be on public display.

2038.   Hankins, Joseph. "Choosing the Right Automatic Sprinkler,"
Disaster Recovery Journal, 5:2 (April-June 1992), 56-60. Practical
review of sprinkler systems on the market and what they can do. The
need to select the appropriate sprinkler system for a facility is
emphasized, and to be sure that the system is approved by a
recognized product certification lab.

2039.   Hanks, Peter. "Conservation or Restoration?" Archives, 19:85 (April
1991), 306-307. Discusses the meaning and scope of conservation,
contrasting it to restoration.

2040.   Hansen, Charles, and Ted Honea. "Shrink-Wrapping for Moving,"
Abbey Newsletter, 14:1 (February 1990), 17-19. Describes the use of
the technique to move the collection of the Sibley Music Library,
Eastmas School of Music, to a new facility. An effective, efficient,
and inexpensive technique.

2041.   Hanson, Carolyn Z. "Electronic Security Has Put a Spotlight On
Theft," Library and Archival Security, 9:3/4 (1989), 63-68. Brief
review of the causes of theft.

2042.   Hanson, Gretchen M. Paper Preservation Within the Academic
Libraries of the Utah College Library Council. Provo, UT: Brigham
Young University School of Library and Information Sciences, 1983.
43p. (Occasional Research Paper, 4). Report of a project undertaken
in the late 1970s to determine the extent of paper preservation
activity among member libraries.

2043.   Hanthron, Ivan. "Tips on Preserving Photographs" Archival Products
News, 3:4 (Fall 1995), 3. Seven tips for the preservation of
photographs: storage, plastic enclosures, paper enclosures, albums,
handling photographs, environment, preservation product

249

sources. Prepared for Iowa libraries and distributed through the Iowa Cooperative Preservation Consortium (ICPC).

2044.   Hanthron, Ivan. "Tips on Preserving Scrapbooks," Archival Product News, 4:2 (Spring 1996), 4. Seven practical suggestions on housing and preserving scrapbooks.

2045.   Hanthron, Ivan. "Water, Water Everywhere: One Iowa Library in the Inland Sea," Conservation Administration News, 57 (April 1994), 9-10. Case study of lessons learned and planning for the future during the floods of 1993 at Iowa State University.

2046.   Hanus, Jozef. "Changes in Brittle Paper During Conservation Treatment," Restaurator, 15:1 (1994), 46-54. Report on the changes in some mechanical properties during conservation treatment of brittle paper.

2047.   Hanus, Jozef. "Gamma Radiation for Use in Archives and Libraries," Abbey Newsletter, 9:2 (April 1985), 34. Report on research underway in Czechoslovakia and Romania.

2048.   Hanus, Jozef. "Recent Situation and Perspectives of Neutral Paper Making in Czech and Slovak Federal Republic," Conference on Book and Paper Conservation, 1990. Budapest, Hungary: Technical Association of Paper and Printing Industry/National Szechenyi Library, 1992, 431-438. Report on papers produced in the Czech and Slovak Republics; notes trend toward alkaline papermaking.

2049.   Hanus, Jozef, and Magda Komornikova. "The Application of Statistical Analysis in Evaluation of Changes in Some Properties of Aged Paper," Archives et Bibliographiques de Belgique, 1/2 (1987), 161-182. Report of a study of the aging resistance of six commercially available writing papers. No references.

2050.   Hanus, Jozef, Magda Komornikova, and Jarmila Minarikova. "Influence of Boxing Materials on the Properties of Different Paper Items Stored Inside," Restaurator, 16:4 (1995), 194-208.

2051.   Hanus, Karen L. "Annotated Bibliography on Electronic Preservation," Preservation of Electronic Formats and Electronic Formats for Preservation, ed. Janice Mohlhenrich. Fort Atkinson, WI: Highsmith Press, 1992, 121-136. Annotated "references to items that examine the issue and problems of protecting machine-readable records for future use and of using machine-readable media to preserve human-readable documents."

2052.   Hanzlova, Jirina. "New Methods of Conservation in the National
         Library of the Czech Socialist Republic, Prague," IFLA Journal
         (International Federation of Library Associations and Institutions),
         14:3 (1988), 247-251. Describes research program in the National
         Library.

2053.   Happoldt, Anita O. Archival Problems in the Preservation of World
         War II Paper. Washington, DC: National Archives, 1983. 31p.
         (CIDS 1983 Happoldt).

2054.   Harmon, James D. Integrated Pest Management in Museum, Library
         and Archival Facilities. Indianapolis, IN: Harmon Preservation Pest
         Management, 1993. 140p. (Loose-leaf notebook). Discusses
         common pests and treatments. Bibliography.

2055.   Harmon, James D., and Christopher Coleman. "Pest Management
         and Disaster Preparedness," Conservation Administration News, 52
         (January 1993), 6-7. Discusses the Integrated Pest Management
         (IPM) approach to pest control and describes the implementation of
         an IPM program at the University of California-Los Angeles Library.

2056.   Harper, James. "Microfilm Reformatting, Linking Past, Present,"
         Inform, 1:10 (October 1987), 14-16. Discussion of reformatting.

2057.   Harriman, Robert. "The World's Biggest Paper Drive," Inform 5:9
         (October 1991), 20-24. Describes the U.S. Newspaper Project.

2058.   Harrington, Gary. "Flood! Or, Disasters Always Happen on a
         Weekend," Southwestern Archivist, 16:4 (Winter 1993),
         1-5. Salvage of materials in the Oklahoma State Archives and
         Library, with assistance from the Oklahoma disaster recovery plan
         and team (O-DRAT).

2059.   Harrington, Richard M., and Brandt S. Braunschweig. "Applying
         Electronic Image Processing to Photostats: The Commonwealth of
         Virginia Has Explored New Technologies for Preserving Endangered
         Data," Inform, 4:5 (May 1990), 31-35. Studies the attempt at the
         Virginia State Library and Archives to capture photostatic
         information before it becomes lost to posterity; no proviso for
         refreshing imaged data.

2060.   Harris, Carolyn. "CAN Moving to UT-Austin," Conservation
         Administration News, 56 (January 1994) 1+.

2061.   Harris, Carolyn. "Cooperative Approaches to Preservation
         Microfilming," Preservation Microfilming, ed. Nancy E. Gwinn.

Chicago, IL: American Library Association, 1989, 55-65. Discusses administration of projects and describes several model projects.

2062. Harris, Carolyn. "Library Binder's Role in Preservation Education," New Library Scene, 9:1 (February 1990), 8-11. How Binders can best serve their customers and more clearly meet their needs. A description of Columbia's Preservation Administration and Conservation Programs.

2063. Harris, Carolyn. "Preservation Considerations in Electronic Security Systems," Library and Archival Security, 11:1 (1991), 35-42. Discusses physical damage to materials caused by security systems; how to limit damage, what to protect, and how.

2064. Harris, Carolyn. "Preservation of Library Materials," ALA Yearbook of Library and Information Sciences. Chicago, IL: American Library Association, 1986, 242-244. Reviews major trends and developments in 1985.

2065. Harris, Carolyn. "Preservation of Paper Based Materials: Mass Deacidification Methods and Projects," Conserving and Preserving Library Materials, ed. Kathryn L. and William T. Henderson. Urbana-Champaign: University of Illinois Graduate School of Library and Information Service, 1983, 57-72. Discussion of mass deacidification techniques.

2066. Harris, Carolyn. "Trends in the Preservation of Rare and Special Materials," Rare Books 1983-84: Trends, Collections, Sources, ed. Alice D. Schreyer. New York: R.R. Bowker, 1983, 121-127. Survey of activities and trends in 1983.

2067. Harris, Carolyn, and Paul N. Banks. "The Library Environment and the Preservation of Library Materials," Facilities Manager, 6:3 (Fall 1990), 21-24. Overview of the causes of deterioration of library materials and the role that the environment plays in preservation. Notes on planning new buildings and disaster preparedness.

2068. Harris, Carolyn, Carol Mandel, and Robert Wolven. "A Cost Model for Preservation: The Columbia University Libraries' Approach," Library Resources and Technical Services, 35:1 (January 1991), 33-54. Presents a comprehensive yet flexible model for identifying the processes involved in preservation activities and their associated costs; provides a methodology for determining unit costs.

2069. Harris, John. "Dry Cleaning: a Billion Old Books Are Disintegrating Because They Were Printed on Paper Treated With Acid. Can They Be Saved?" Forbes, 147:5 (March 4, 1991), 128.

2070. Harris, Kenneth E. "Preservation at the Library of Congress in the 1990s: Success Is a Journey," New Library Scene, 9:6 (December 1990), 8-15. Describes the preservation challenges at the Library of Congress and the past successes upon which the program for the 1990s will build.

2071. Harris, Kenneth E. "A Review of Recent Research Findings on Preservation & Conservation of Library & Archival Materials," Proceedings of the Pan-African Conference on the Preservation & Conservation of Library & Archival Materials, Nairobi, Kenya, 21-25 June 1993. The Hague: IFLA, 1995. 113-127. (IFLA Prof. Publ., 43). Discusses current research and provides information on preservation of paper-based collections. Bibliography.

2072. Harris, Kenneth E., and Chandru J. Shahani. "Library of Congress Mass Deacidification Update," International Preservation News, 10 (July 1995), 6-7. Brief report on results of testing of DEZ and Bookkeeper processes, while continuing evaluation of other techniques.

2073. Harris, Kenneth E., and Chandru J. Shahani. Mass Deacidification: An Initiative to Refine the Diethyl Zinc Process. Washington, DC: Library of Congress Preservation Directorate, October 1994. 31, appendixes, 167p. Detailed report and analysis of the testing of the DEZ process to eliminate odor and to make it more effective.

2074. Harris, Oliver D. "The Drudgery of Stamping: A Physical History of the Records Preservation Section," Archives, 19:81 (April 1989), 3-17. History of the Records Preservation Section, British Records Association.

2075. Harrison, Alice W., Edward A. Collister, and R. Ellen Willis. The Conservation of Archival and Library Materials: A Resource Guide to Audiovisual Aids. Metuchen, NJ: Scarecrow Press, 1982. 202p. Selective, annotated listing of audiovisual material appearing between 1955 and 1980.

2076. Harrison, Helen P. "Conservation and Audiovisual Materials." Audiovisual Librarian, 13:3 (1987), 154-162. Addresses preservation/conservation of and access to audiovisual materials. Touches on discs as storage media. Discusses preservation policy and methods for audiovisual materials drafted by international efforts.

2077. Harrison, Helen P. "International Round Table to Evaluate the Practical Results Emanating From the Approval of the UNESCO

Recommendations for the Safeguarding and Preservation of Moving Images (Belgrade 1980)," Phonographic Bulletin, 52 (November 1988), 30-34. Report of a meeting that focused on the preservation of moving images. Notes technologies of sound and image are converging, so sound should be included in preservation actions. Recommendations.

2078. Harrison, Helen P. "Selection and Audiovisual Collections," IFLA Journal (International Federation of Library Associations and Institutions), 21:3 (1995), 185-190. Describes a-v materials and the particular problems they present. Principles of selection for preservation are discussed.

2079. Harrison, Helen P., and Rolf L. Schursma. The Archival Appraisal of Sound Recordings and Related Materials: A RAMP Study with Guidelines. Paris: UNESCO, 1987. 98p. (PGI-87/WS/1). Discusses the archival character of sound recordings; provides guidelines for their appraisal and preservation. Bibliography.

2080. Harrop, Dorothy A. "Pioneers of Conservation: Roger Powell and Sydney Cockerell," The Book Collector, 35:2 (Summer 1986), 179-190. A tribute to two men who played a leading role in establishing rare book conservation as a discipline.

2081. Hart, Andrew. "The Future of Preservation Education: Notes from the PI Institute," Abbey Newsletter, 17:4 (September 1993), 47-48, 50. Summary of the reactions of participants and an assessment of continuing needs.

2082. Hartley, Jeffery T. Management of Electronic Records. Washington, DC: National Archives and Records Administration, June 1991. 29p. Archives Library Information Center Bibliographies. 276 entries.

2083. "Harvard Tackles Brittle Books," Library Journal, 120 (June 1, 1995), 27.

2084. Harvard University Library. Guidelines for Exhibitions. Cambridge, MA: Harvard University Library, 1987. 27p. Basic guidelines to be amplified by each unit library as necessary.

2085. Harvard University Library. Preservation Office. Mass Deacidification in the Harvard University Library: A Report on the 1991/92 Pilot Operational Program. Cambridge, MA: Harvard University Library, January 1993. 16p. typescript. Review of the AKZO mass deacidification pilot project during its first year: advantages, disadvantages, preliminary cost information, and discussion of concerns for further study.

2086. Harvard University Library. Task Group on Collection Preservation Priorities. Preserving Harvard's Retrospective Collections. Cambridge, MA: Harvard University, 1991; Harvard Library Bulletin, N.S. 2:2 (Summer 1991), 74p. The library's preservation needs assessment and plan for the future of the collections.

2087. Harvey, Christopher. "The Treatment of Flood-Damaged Photographic Material at the Perth Museum & Art Gallery, Scotland," Paper Conservation News, 76 (December 1995), 8-12. Description of treatment of collection of glass plate negatives, lantern slides, roll film, with recommendations for permanent storage.

2088. Harvey, Ross. "The Australian Libraries Summit and Preservation: The View from Victoria," Australian Library Review, 7 (August 1990), 183-188. Discusses reports and describes resolutions for the preservation of Australia's documentary heritage.

2089. Harvey, Ross. "Library and Archives Preservation in Countries of the ASEAN Region" (differences between tropical and temperate zones), Asian Libraries, 4 (December 1995), 42-51.

2090. Harvey, Ross. "Nothing Left to Access? The Problem of Deteriorating Newspapers," Education for Librarianship: Australia, 5:1 (Autumn 1988), 18-26. Discusses the problem of how the provision of information by libraries leads to the deterioration of the physical object, with emphasis on the problem of newspapers. Discusses the proposed Australian newspaper preservation plan and preservation as a part of the library school curriculum.

2091. Harvey, Ross. Preservation in Australian and New Zealand Libraries: Principles, Strategies and Practices for Librarians. Wagga Wagga, Australia: Centre for Information Studies, Charles Stuart University, 1990. (Topics in Australian Library and Information Studies, 30). 1st ed. 373p., 2d ed. 1993, 412p. Reviews causes, nature, and extent of preservation problems; examines causes of deterioration; provides models for integrating preservation into library management.

2092. Harvey, Ross, ed. Preservation in Libraries: A Reader. London; New York: Bowker-Saur, 1993. 483p. (Topics in Library and Information Studies). Practical readings showing how preservation can be integrated into library management; compliments Preservation in Libraries (1993).

2093.   Harvey, Ross. <u>Preservation in Libraries: Principles, Strategies and Practices</u>. New York: R.R. Bowker-Saur, 1993. 269p.; Presents causes, nature, and extent of the preservation problem, discusses measures for prevention; integrating preservation into library management.

2094.   Haserot, Karen E. "The Coloration of Film: Technical, Legal, Historical and Sociocultural Considerations," <u>Techné: Journal of Technology Studies</u>, 3 (Spring 1989), 45-52. Discusses the technology and its legal and moral implications. Bibliography.

2095.   Haskins, Scott M. <u>How to Save Your Stuff From a Disaster: Complete Instructions on How to Protect and Save Your Family History, Heirlooms and Collectibles</u>. Santa Barbara, CA: Preservation Help Publications, 1996. 204p.

2096.   Hasluck, Paul N. <u>Bookbinding, With Numerous Engravings and Diagrams</u>. Wantage, England: The Black Swan Press, 1992. 161p. Reprint of a manual published by Cassell in 1902; represents turn-of-the-century practices.

2097.   Hastings, Carole Marie. "Doin' da Missin' Books Boogie: Thoughts on Axioms, Flexibility, and Attila the Hun," <u>Reference Librarian</u>, 7/8 (Spring/Summer 1983), 111-114. Thoughts on the prevention of book theft by teenagers.

2098.   Hatchfield, Pamela. "Outreach: The Need to Raise Awareness," <u>AIC News</u> (American Institute of Conservation), 20:1 (January 1995), 1-4. Thoughtful essay on developing public awareness of conservation and the role of conservators, to enable the profession to more easily raise funds. Report of several articles and meetings.

2099.   Hatchfield, Pamela and Jane Carpenter. <u>Formaldehyde: How Great Is the Danger to Museum Collections?</u> Cambridge, MA: Harvard University Art Museums, 1987. 44p. Study of the effect of formaldehyde on museum collections, including paper-based materials, specifically on storage and exhibit cases made from plywood and particleboard.

2100.   Hauser, Robert. "Technology Update: Enzymes in Conservation — A Conference Report," <u>Technology & Conservation</u>, 4/93 (Winter 1992-93), 13-14. Summarizes papers at a one-day workshop held in May 1989.

2101.   Hauser, Robert. "Whaling Museum Restores 50 Logbooks," <u>Abbey Newsletter</u>, 11:5 (July 1987), 76-79. Report on a project undertaken at the New Bedford Whaling Museum to evaluate, document, and treat materials and to develop a laboratory manual for the treatment of logbooks.

2102. Havard-Williams, P. "Library and Information Studies," Journal of Librarianship, 17:2 (April 1985), 100-105. Describes the curriculum at Loughborough Polytech and how it is evolving to train librarians about preservation of collections.

2103. Havermans, John. "The Effect of Air Pollutants on the Accelerated Aging of Cellulose Containing Materials," European Cultural Heritage Newsletter on Research, 7:1/4 (December 1993), 13-15. Also in Restaurator, 16:4 (1995), 209-233. Describes a project to determine effects of air pollutants and climate on the stability of celluloseic materials. Describes preliminary data on mass deacidification of paper-based materials. Results of a research project carried out by four European institutions.

2104. Havermans, John "The Effects of Air Pollution on Accelerating Aging of Cellulose Containing Materials; Preliminary Results of the STEP Project," Environnement et Conservation de l'Écrit, de l'Image et du Son. Paris: ARSAG, 1994, 39-47. (Actes des Deuxièmes Jouirnées Internationales d'Études de l'ARSAG, 16 au 20 Mai 1994). See above.

2105. Havermans, John, Ronald van Deventer, and Ted Steemers. "Mass Deacidification of Archival Materials Using Diethyl Zinc," Restaurator, 16:3 (1995), 123-142. By the Dutch State Archives for records dating from 1840 to 1950.

2106. Hayes, Robert Mayo. The Magnitude, Costs, and Benefits of the Preservation of Brittle Books. Washington, DC: Commission on Preservation and Access, 1987. 1 vol., various paging. Three reports commissioned by the Council on Library Resources on the magnitude, costs, and benefits of the preservation of brittle books.

2107. Haynes, Douglas. "Pro-Cite for Library & Archival Condition Surveys," Library Resources & Technical Services, 39:4 (October 1995), 427-433. "Step-by-step guide on how to configure software, enter data, & analyze & interpret results for such surveys," using Pro-Cite 2.02. a "valuable & flexible tool for compiling & analyzing data for library & archival condition & sight surveys" (427/abstr.).

2108. Hazen, Dan C. The Bibliographic Control and Preservation of Latin Americanist Library Resources: A Status Report with Suggestions. Washington, DC: Association of Research Libraries, 1994. 121p. Study of who collections Latin American materials, to what extent there is online bibliographic control, and preservation needs.

2109.   Hazen, Dan C. "Preservation in Poverty and Plenty: Policy Issues
         for the 1990s," Journal of Academic Librarianship, 15:6 (January
         1990), 344-351. Examines and redefines the assumptions underlying
         the approach to preservation and suggests a national collection-based
         program.

2110.   Hazen, Dan C. The Production and Bibliographic Control of Latin
         American Preservation Microforms in the United States.
         Washington, DC: Commission on Preservation and Access, 1991.
         38p.

2111.   Headley, John W. Recipes, Formulas, and Preservation Techniques:
         1273 Record Security. Denver, CO: Bureau of Land Management,
         1988. 94p.

2112.   Heckmann, Harald. "Storage and Handling of Audio and Magnetic
         Materials," Preservation of Library Materials, ed. Merrily Smith.
         New York: Saur, 1987, 67-73. (IFLA Publication, 41). Covers disks,
         magnetic tapes, and videodisks, equipment used for playback; notes
         lack of standards. Advocates reformatting rather than preservation of
         material in original format.

2113.   Hedley, Gerry. "Finding a Structure of Collaboration," CCI
         Newsletter (Canadian Conservation Institute) (Autumn/Winter 1990),
         8-9. Emphasizes the need for collaboration between conservator and
         scientist, a model that works at the Canadian Conservation Institute
         at present.

2114.   Hedlin, Edie, and Thomas E. Weir, Jr., MARC/Life Cycle Tracking
         of Archival Records. Washington, DC: National Archives and
         Records Administration, 1984. (TIP-02, PB87-12656/AS).

2115.   Hedlin, Edie, and Donald F. Harrison. "The National Archives and
         Electronic Data," Reference Services Review, 16:1/2 (1988),
         13-16. Discusses events that led to the National Archives policy of
         preserving magnetic tapes of data generated by federal agencies;
         current methods of preservation and access are described.

2116.   Hedstrom, Margaret. "Optical Disks: Are Archivists Repeating
         Mistakes of the Past?" Archival Informatics Newsletter, 2:3 (1988),
         52-53. Addresses need to develop strategies to preserve data in
         optical formats; notes lack of standards, need to identify archival
         needs when a records management system is designed.

2117.   Hedstrom, Margaret, "Understanding Electronic Incunabula: A
         Framework for Research on Electronic Records," American

Archivist, 54:3 (1991), 334-354. Discusses a research framework that considers the history and interdisciplinary nature of electronic records. Emphasizes that this area of research pertains to all aspects of archival work, in that it is "evolutionizing" the way archives are managed.

2118. Hedstrom, Margaret, and Alan Kowlowitz. "Meeting the Challenge of Machine-Readable Records: A State Archives Perspective," Reference Services Review, 16:1-2 (1988), 31-40. Review of the problems archivists face in identifying and preserving government records in machine-readable formats.

2119. Heidke, Ronald L., Larry H. Feldman, and Charleton C. Bard. "Evolution of Kodak Photographic Color Negative Print Papers," Journal of Imaging Technology, 11:3 (June 1985), 93-97. Eastman Kodak Company has been manufacturing color negative print papers since 1942. Technological breakthroughs in couplers, stabilizers, and ultraviolet absorbers have led to significant gains in image stability.

2120. Heidtmann, Toby. "Help-Net Binding Preparation System at the University of Cincinnati," Serials Review, 15:1 (Spring 1989). 21-26. Description of system and its use in binding preparation.

2121. Heiser, Lois. "Digital Preservation of Yellow Snow," Frontiers of Geoscience Information, 20 (1990), 135-139. Describes the use of an OCR optical scanner to transform embrittled geological reports into digital format; discusses the future for this and other digital storage methods. Paper presented at the 24th Meeting of the Geoscience Information Society, 1990.

2122. Heitshu, Sara. "Preservation as a Cooperative Effort: Intro- and Interinstitutional Activities," Wilson Library Bulletin, 67:3 (November 1992), 22-25, 106-107. Organizing for preservation and organizing staff; cooperative initiatives.

2123. Heller, Jonathan. Photo Preservation Grants: National Historical Publications and Records Commission Records Program; Evaluation, Analysis, Observations, Recommendations. Washington, DC: National Archives, 1985. 72p.

2124. Helliwell, John. "Optical Overview: What's Coming in CD-ROMs and WORMs," CD-ROM EndUser (1986), 149-164. Reviews CD-ROM and WORM technology, highlighting their advantages, and naming particular projects and corporations involved in advancing the technology.

2125.   Helmer, Normandy. "Keeping Scores: Music Preservation at the
        University of Oregon Library," <u>Archival Products News</u>, 3:1 (Winter
        1995), 1-2, 5. Describes problems and methods for binding scores for
        preservation and use.

2126.   Hendee, J. C. "Playing the Silicon Doctor: Preventive Medicine and
        User Awareness in the Computer Virus Age," <u>Focus on Security</u>, 2:2
        (January 1995), 13-31. Discusses computer viruses and methods of
        prevention.

2127.   Henderson, Cathy. "Curator or Conservator: Who Decides on What
        Treatment?" <u>Rare Books and Manuscripts Librarianship</u>, 2:2 (Fall
        1987), 103-107. Describes the concerns of the Committee on
        Curatorial Needs, Rare Books and Manuscripts Section, American
        Library Association, and the need to educate curators about
        conservation.

2128.   Henderson, Harold. "After the Flood (A Restoration Drama),
        <u>Reader: Chicago's Free Weekly</u>, 16:1 (Friday, September 16, 1986),
        1, ff. Description and discussion of treatments of materials damaged
        in the flood from a burst water main at the Chicago Historical
        Society.

2129.   Henderson, Kathryn L. and William T. <u>Conserving and Preserving
        Library Materials</u>. Urbana-Champaign: University of Illinois
        Graduate School of Library and Information Science, 1983. 207p.
        (Allerton Park Institute, 27). Papers presented at the Allerton Park
        Institute, 1981, to assess the current situation and to help set
        objectives for the 1980s.

2130.   Henderson, Kathryn L. and William T., eds. <u>Conserving and
        Preserving Materials in Nonbook Formats</u>. Urbana-Champaign:
        University of Illinois Graduate School of Library and Information
        Science, 1991. 165p. (Allerton Park Institute, 30). Papers from a
        conference to address special needs of non-print collections.

2131.   Henderson, William T. "Preservation and Conservation Decisions in
        the Local Library," <u>Conserving and Preserving Library Materials</u>.
        Urbana-Champaign: University of Illinois Graduate School of
        Library and Information Service, 1983, 111-134. Reviews decision
        making for preservation; case study of the treatment of mold.

2132.   Henderson, William T. "Preservation: A Quarter Century of
        Growth," <u>Technical Services Management, 1965-1990...</u>. New York:
        Haworth Press, 1996, 275-290p.

2133.   Hendley, Tony. The Archival Storage Potential of Microfilm
         Magnetic Media and Optical Data Discs. Hertford, England:
         National Reprographic Centre for Documentation, 1983. 77p. (BNB
         Research Fund Report 10; NRCd Publication, 19). Discusses the
         archival storage potential of microfilm, magnetic media, and optical
         discs with comparison to paper storage; informed discussion of
         preservation issues.

2134.   Hendley, Tony. CD-ROM and Optical Publishing Systems.
         Westport, CT: Meckler Publishing, 1987. 149p. A thorough
         discussion of the role of CD-ROM in optical publishing; comparison
         with paper and microform formats.

2135.   Hendley, Tony. Videodiscs, Compact Discs and Digital Optical
         Discs. Hatfield, England: Cimtech, February 1985. 208p. (Cimtech
         Publication, 23). Introduction to the technologies and the systems;
         their potential for information storage, retrieval, and dissemination.

2136.   Hendricks, Klaus B. "Conservation of Photographs at the Public
         Archives of Canada," Stability and Conservation of Photographic
         Images: Chemical, Electronic and Mechanical. Bangkok, Thailand:
         Society of Photographic Scientists and Engineers, 1986,
         66-77. Describes the collections and the Archives' approach to
         research, preservation, and conservation.

2137.   Hendricks, Klaus B. "Permanence of Paper in Light of Six Centuries
         of Papermaking in Europe," Environnement et Conservation de
         l'Écrit, de l'Image et du Son. Paris: ARSAG, 1994, 132-137. (Actes
         des Deuxièmes Journées Internationales d'Études de l'ARSAG, 16
         au 20 Mai 1994). Reviews the concept of permanence for paper;
         suggesting that permanence be defined in terms of resistance to
         chemical agents. Accelerated aging is also discussed.

2138.   Hendricks, Klaus B. Preservation and Restoration of Photographic
         Materials in Archives and Libraries; A RAMP Study with
         Guidelines. Paris: UNESCO, 1984. 118p. (PGI-84\WS\1). Basic
         study on the nature and problems associated with photographs, with
         recommended measures to help preserve collections. Bibliography.

2139.   Hendriks, Klaus B. "The Preservation, Storage, and Handling of
         Black-and-White Photographic Records," Conserving and Preserving
         Materials in Nonbook Formats. Urbana-Champaign: University of
         Illinois Graduate School of Library and Information Science, 1991,
         91-104. (Allerton Park Institute, 30). Reviews the factors affecting
         stability; offers guidelines for handling and use; covers contingency
         planning.

2140.   Hendriks, Klaus B. "The Stability and Preservation of Recorded Images," Imaging Processes and Materials, Nablette's 8th edition, New York: Van Nostrand Reinhold, 1989, 637-684. Discusses the permanence of photographs, electrostatically produced materials, and electronically stored images, with emphasis on photographic images. Extensive references.

2141.   Hendriks, Klaus B., et al. "The Duplication of Historical Black-and-White Negatives," Journal of Imaging Technology, 12 (1986), 185-199. Compares various negative duplication options for maximum image retention.

2142.   Hendriks, Klaus B., and Diane Hopkins. PHOCUS: A Bibliographic Data Base for the Conservation of Photographic Materials. Ottawa: Public Archives of Canada, 1985. v.p. A technical brochure that offers figures and functional specifications.

2143.   Hendriks, Klaus B., and Brian Lesser. "Disaster Preparedness and Recovery: Photographic Materials," American Archivist, 46:1 (Winter 1983), 52-68. Presents results of experiments involving the immersion of still photographic negatives and prints in tap water and their subsequent drying.

2144.   Hendriks, Klaus B., and Lincoln Ross. "The Restoration of Discolored Black-and-White Photographic Images in Chemical Solutions," American Institute for Conservation of Historic and Artistic Works. Preprints of Papers, 16th Annual Meeting, New Orleans, LA, June 1-5, 1988. Washington, DC: American Institute for Conservation, 1988, 99-117. Examination of the particles of elemental silver and how those that drift away from an image by be converted back to the image silver to yield acceptably restored photographs.

2145.   Hendriks, Klaus B., Douglas R. Madeley, Fred Toll, and Brian Thurgood. "The Duplication of Historical Black-and-White Negatives," Stability and Conservation of Photographic Materials: Chemical, Electronic and Mechanical. Bangkok, Thailand: Society of Photographic Scientists and Engineers, 1986, 109-131. Results of research at the Public Archives of Canada.

2146.   Hendriks, Klaus B., Brian Thurgood, Joe Iraci, Brian Lesser, and Greg Hill. Fundamentals of Photographic Conservation: A Study Guide. Toronto, Canada: Lugus Publications, 1991. 560p. Illus. Comprehensive text on photographic conservation: history, processes, concerns; for training of and use by photographic conservators.

2147. Hendriks, Klaus B., and Anne Whitehurst, comp. Conservation of Photographic Materials: A Basic Reading List. Ottawa: National Archives of Canada, 1988. 32p. (English/French). Bibliography for conservation students, individuals, and institutions; no annotations.

2148. Hendriks, Klaus B., and Anne Whitehurst, comp. "Conservation of Photographic Materials: National Archives of Canada." American Archivist, 52:2 (Spring 1989), 265. Compare with above. Covers references on the preservation of still photographs and some sources for the preservation of microfilms and motion picture films.

2149. Hengemihle, Frank H., Norman Weberg, and Chandru Shahani. Desorption of Residual Ethylene Oxide from Fumigated Library Materials. Washington, DC: Library of Congress, November 1995. 14p. (Preservation Research & Testing Service, 9502). Study addresses hazards for library personnel and readers exposed to high levels of EtO from fumigated materials. Concludes that vigilance needs to be exercised by confining fumigated materials to restricted, well-ventilated area where EtO concentration can be monitored until concentration well below 1ppm. Paper presented at the 1st Pan-American Biodeterioration Society Meeting, Washington DC, July 1986.

2150. Henneberger, Bob. "Preservation and Access of Rare Maps at the University of Georgia Libraries," Microform Review, 23:4 (Fall 1994), 169-171. Discusses the project to scan rare maps and to make them accessible on the Internet. Microfilm is the preservation medium from which the maps were scanned for access.

2151. Henry, J. D., Lars Meyer, and Sharla Richards. "Highlights of the Preservation and Reformatting Section Meeting; ALA Midwinter Meeting, Philadelphia, Pennsylvania," Conservation Administration News, 61 (April 1995), 21.

2152. Henry, Walter. "Electronic Lists, Web Sites & Resource Guides," Abbey Newsletter, 19:4 (September 1995), 67. Directory, for preservation and conservation resources.

2153. Henry, Walter. "Islands in the Net: A Guide to Internet," WAAC Newsletter (Western Association for Art Conservation), 14:3 (September 1992), 19-27. Describes the services that are available through Internet, a global network that ties together a large number of computer networks of different systems. Specialty lists, including the Conservation DistList, and a group of art, physics, and chemistry lists are explained.

2154.   Henry, Walter. "Seismatic Protection for Shelving," WAAC
         Newsletter (Western Association for Art Conservation), 14:3
         (September 1992), 80. Describes the Seismoguard, a device
         developed at Stanford University to prevent books falling off shelves
         during an earthquake.

2155.   Henshaw, Bruce C. "What Paint Formulator Should Know about
         Emulsion Polymerization," JCT/Journal of Coatings Technology,
         57:725 (June 1985), 73-76. A brief discussion of the mechanism of
         emulsion polymerization is presented.

2156.   Henty, Margaret. "Conference Report; Multimedia Preservation:
         Capturing the Rainbow; 2nd National Preservation Office
         Conference, Brisbane, 28-30 November 1995," Australian Academic
         & Research Libraries, 27 (March 1996), 69.

2157.   A Heritage at Risk. Wheaton, IL: Billy Graham Center, Wheaton
         College, 1988. 47p. Proceedings of the Evangelical Archives
         Conference, July 13-16, 1988, to address questions of the
         preservation and promotion of the records of the Evangelical
         movement in the United States.

2158.   Herrick, Roxanna. "Preservation at the State University of New
         York at Stony Brook," Conservation Administration News, 40
         (January 1990), 4-5, 7. Describes the organization and
         implementation of the library's preservation and book repair
         program.

2159.   Herrick, Roxanna. "The Value of Hands-On Experience to the
         Preservation Administrator," Conservation Administration News, 39
         (October 1989), 1-2, 28.

2160.   Herskovitz, Robert. "Use of an Environmental Test Kit in
         Minnesota," Objects Specialty Group Postprints, 1991. Washington,
         DC: American Institute for Conservation, 1992, 31-32. Describes a
         portable kit for testing temperature, humidity, and light levels in
         museums, libraries, and archives.

2161.   Herther, Nancy. "The Silver Disk: Between a Rock and a Hard
         Place: Preservation and Optical Media," Database, 10:2 (April 1987),
         122-124. Summarizes the difficulties in coping with the preservation
         of archival records in new technologies; some potential problems are
         identified.

2162.   Hey, Margaret. "Chinese White — A Potential Source of Trouble on
         Paper?" Wiener uber Naturwissenschaft in der Kunst (1987-1988),

362-369. The nature of the pigment and its possible effect on paper when exposed to light is discussed.

2163.   Hey, Margaret. "Foxing: Some Unanswered Questions," <u>Antiquarian Book Monthly Review</u>, 10:9 (September 1983), 340-343. Discussion of foxing and theories about its causes based upon a review of the literature and author's observations.

2164.   Hey, Margaret. "Foxing Marks on Paper in Books, Prints, Drawings," <u>Conference on Book and Paper Conservation, 1990</u>. Budapest, Hungary: Technical Association of Paper and Printing Industry/National Szechenyi Library, 1992, 244-256. Discusses research on foxing undertaken at the Instituto di Patologia del Libro, Rome. Illus. 40 references.

2165.   Hey, Margaret. "Training of Conservators: The Second Stage," <u>Conference on Book and Paper Conservation, 1990</u>. Budapest, Hungary: Technical Association of Paper and Printing Industry/National Szechenyi Library, 1992, 413-421. Addresses the need for conservators to keep current and fully informed of new preservation/conservation concepts and technologies; addresses issues of ready access to information, translation services.

2166.   Hey, Margaret. "What You Should Know Before Deciding to Deacidify," <u>Paper Conservation News</u>, 75 (September 1995), 6-7. Review of discussions of research on the effect of deacidification on paper underway at the Canadian Conservation Institute.

2167.   Hey, Margaret, G. Pasquariello, F. Gallo, G. Gaudi, and F. Pieridominici. "Paper Analysis in Relation to Foxing," <u>Second International Conference on Non-destructive Testing, Microanalytical Methods and Environmental Evaluation for Study and Conservation of Works of Art, Perugia, Italy, April 1988</u>. Rome: Istituto Centrale per il Restauro, 1988, III/9.1-III/9.10. Deals with the application of scanning electron microscopy and proton-induced x-ray emission analytical techniques to paper showing foxing.

2168.   Heynen, Jeffrey, and Margaret McConnell, comp. <u>Pilot Preservation Statistics Survey, 1984-85: A Compilation of Statistics from a One-Year Pilot Survey of the Members of the Association of Research Libraries</u>. Washington, DC: Association of Research Libraries, 1986. 90p. Statistical data on preservation and conservation activities in ARL libraries.

2169. Hickin, Norman. Bookworms: The Insect Pests of Books. London: Sheppard, 1985. 176p. Description of insect pests that attack books and prevention of infestation.

2170. Hicks, Catherine. "Early Approaches to the Conservation of Works of Art on Paper," Early Advances in Conservation. London British Library, 1988, 7-12. Traces methods of storage of prints, drawings, and watercolors to the 19th century.

2171. Hicks, George. "For the Administrator: Theft and Fraud on the Rise," History News, 43:1 (January-February, 1988), 35-38. Reviewing recent reports of losses from museums, libraries, and archives in the United States. The author stresses accountability and codes of ethics.

2172. Hiebert, Rhonda. Disaster Prevention, Disaster Preparedness, and Disaster Recovery. Hutchinson, KS: South Central Kansas Library System, 1989. 78p.

2173. Higginbotham, Barbra Buckner. "Custodianship to Conservation: Building on the Preservation Foundation of Our Forbears," Building on the First Century. Chicago, IL: American Library Association, 1989, 298-302. An examination of preservation thought and practice in academic and research libraries at the turn of the last century.

2174. Higginbotham, Barbra Buckner. Our Past Preserved: A History of American Library Preservation, 1876 to 1910. Boston: GK. Hall, 1990. 346p. Explores the circumstances and forces that stimulated an awareness of preservation problems in the 19th century; the foundation for contemporary library concerns and activities. Extensive bibliography and notes.

2175. Higginbotham, Barbra Buckner. "To Preserve the Best and Noblest Thoughts of Man ... American Beginnings," Advances in Preservation and Access. Vol. 1. Westport, CT: Meckler, 1992, 2-17. History of cooperative preservation initiatives between 1876 and 1910. Paper originally presented at the 32nd Preconference, Rare Books and Manuscripts Section, American Library Association, 1991.

2176. Higginbotham, Barbra Buckner, and Mary E. Jackson. ed. Advances in Preservation. Vol. 1. Westport, CT: Meckler, 1992, 297p. Addresses contemporary issues in preservation of library and archival materials; activities and issues, management, education, and the role of several organizations are discussed.

2177.   Higgins, Richard. "Racing to Save Decaying Books," New Library Scene, 2:6 (December 1983), 1, 4, 15.General account of the problem and solutions through physical treatment, deacidification, and the use of optical disk technology.

2178.   Hightower, Marvin. "Mapping Out the Library of the Future," New Library Scene, 10:2 (April 1991), 1, 5-7. Discussion of Richard DeGennaro's plans for the future of Harvard's libraries, including the expansion of its off-site storage facilities and the potential for electronic communication, with a note on preservation plans. (Reprinted from the Harvard Gazette).

2179.   Hildesheimer, Françoise. Processing of Architects' Records: A Case-Study. Paris: UNESCO, 1987, 74p. (PGI 86\WS\13). Survey to call attention to the value of architectural records and ensure their preservation.

2180.   Hill, Gregory. "The Conservation of a Photographic Album at the National Archives of Canada," Journal of the American Institute for Conservation, 30:1 (Spring 1991), 75-88. Describes the full conservation treatment of a 19th-century album; discusses treatment options and the decision-making process.

2181.   Hill, Gregory, and Susan North. "A Conservation Survey for the Canadian Centre for Caricature," Conservation of Historic and Artistic Works on Paper. Ottawa: Canadian Conservation Institute, 1994, 11-14. (Symposium 88). Describes a conservation survey of a collection of contemporary works by Canadian cartoonists to determine conservation problems and to estimate resources needed to preserve the material.

2182.   Hill, Thomas. "Conservation of Photographic Materials," AB Bookman's Weekly (Antiquarian Bookman), 71:4 (January 24, 1983), 488-496. Brief history of photographic processes and information on care and storage.

2183.   Hills, Richard L. Papermaking in Britain, 1488-1988: A Short History. London; Atlantic Highlands, NJ: Athelone Press, 1988. 249p. Historical survey with extensive notes, bibliography, glossary.

2184.   Hillyer, Lynda, and Valerie Blythe. "Beating Unwanted Guests," V&A Conservation Journal (Victoria and Albert Museum), 10 (January 1994), 13-15. Report on a meeting of conservation scientists to address the problem of pest control; discussion of a V&A survey of the problem and its active measures for pest control.

2185.   Hincha, Richard. "Crisis in Celluloid: Color Fading and Film Base Deterioration," Archival Issues, 17:2 (1992), 125-135. Discusses causes of film base deterioration and color fading, procedures developed to retard them. Notes "grim prognosis" for film archives.

2186.   Hindbaugh, Nick. "A pH Survey of an Acidic Textbook," Paper Conservator, 14 (1990), 17-22. Presents a procedure for mapping the various pH levels in a badly degraded textblock, using a grid system of readings.

2187.   Hirst, Warwick. "Salvaging Flood Damaged Records," Archives & Manuscripts (Australian Society of Archivists), 13:1 (May 1985), 24-29. Procedures for salvaging water-damaged archival material; case study.

2188.   Hirtle, Peter B. "Historical Note: Atherton Seidell and the Photoduplication of Library," Journal of the American Society for Information Science, 40:6 (November 1990), 424-431. Seidell, a medical researcher, was a pioneer in the use of photoduplication for scholarly communication. While his desire to serve the researcher led to the microfilming programs that have developed, he is unknown today because of his strong belief that such dissemination of information should be free.

2189.   Ho, Elizabeth. "Australian Newspapers, Another Holy Grail: Will Indiana Jones, Alias the Library Manager, Make It?" Preservation Microfilming: Does It Have A Future? Canberra: National Library of Australia, 1995, 17-26. Describes the National Plan for Australian Newspapers (NPLAN). Why they are being preserved; microfilm as a preservation medium.

2190.   Ho, Kathy. Thermal Papers: Their Storability and Permanence. Dickson, ACT, Australia: Australian Archives Custody and Preservation Program, September 1993. 16p.; also published in Archives & Manuscripts (Australian Society of Archivists), 21:2 (November 1993), 236-251.   Report on research on the stability of thermal papers; notes that they are extremely sensitive to environmental changes. Provides suggestions for handling, preservation, and storage.

2191.   Hobbs, Mary. "Books in Crisis at Barchester," Book Collector, 44:1 (Spring 1995), 37-50. Story of the sale of books from the Chichester Cathedral Library in the late 1940s with the excuse that the books were not properly housed and were deteriorating rapidly, practically inaccessible. Discusses current efforts to locate the material, and current measures to preserve and protect these collections, and to make them accessible. "When cathedral libraries, with properly housed & supervised books and changing, well-catalogued exhibitions, can be made available to tourists & the local community, they have now a wider importance than to the scanty band of scholars who actually make use of them." (50).

2192.   Hodge, Stanley P. "The Question of Paperbacks for Academic Libraries: Selection, Treatment, Options, Durability," Academic Libraries: Achieving Excellence in Higher Education. Chicago: Association of College and Research Libraries, 1992, 248-256. Proceedings, Sixth National Conference, Salt Lake City, UT, 1992. Survey of library policies, study of wear on paperback books, demonstrating that their purchase will not present costly preservation problems and will save money.

2193.   Hodges, Anthony. "78s — Preservation or Disposal?" Audiovisual Librarian, 14:1 (February 1988), 29-30. The role regional archives should play in the preservation of sound recordings.

2194.   Hodgson, M. E. "Developments in Water-Based Adhesives," European Adhesives and Sealants, 2:1 (1984), 7-8. The developments, properties, and uses of water-based formulations for contact and pressure-sensitive adhesives are discussed.

2195.   Hoedemaeker, Liesbeth. "Conservation in the Netherlands," Fontes Artis Musicae, 41 (July/September 1994), 251-255.

2196.   Hofenk de Graaff, Judith H. "Research into the Cause of Browning of Paper Mounted in Mats," Contributions of the Central Research Laboratory to the Field of Conservation and Restoration. Amsterdam, Netherlands: Central Research Laboratory, 1994, 21-42. Investigation of the cause of the browning of paper in mats that are stored in boxes in a controlled environment; cause is temperature fluctuation within the micro-environment from the evaporation of water.

2197.   Hofenk de Graaff, Judith H. and Wilma G. Th. Roelofs. "Investigation of the Long-Term Effects of Ethylene Oxide and Gamma Rays on the Aging of Paper," Contributions of the Central Research Laboratory to the Field of Conservation and Restoration. Amsterdam, Netherlands: Central Research Laboratory, 1994. 53-64. Comparison of ethylene oxide (EtO) and gamma radiation in the treatment of mold infestation in paper. EtO does not age paper but gamma radiation had a strong negative effect.

2198.   Hoffman, Ana. "Identifying Nineteenth Century Photographic Processes," Picture Framing Magazine, 5:10 (October 1994),

82-86. Reviews characteristics of photographic images, with identification chart.

2199. Hofmann, C., V. Flamm, G. Banik, and K. Messner. "Bleaching Procedures to Remove Foxing Stains from Paper Objects," Wiener Berichte über Naturwissenschaft in der Kunst, 6/7/8 (1991), 346-365. Illus. Comparison of bleaching procedures for papers damaged by biological infestation; procedures described; results of scientific tests on chemical effects of the bleaches for paper are given.

2200. Hoffmann, Frank, and Lisa McDaniel-Hariston. "Fire in the Library: An Informal Case Study with a Checklist for Minimizing Disastrous Consequences," Southeastern Librarian, 32:2/3 (Summer/Fall 1982), 79-84. Checklist with emphasis on need to know insurance coverage; cultivation of good relationships with public officials and the public; planning for emergencies.

2201. Hoffmann, Hillel L. "A Slow Burn: In Which Cornell's Book Doctors Fight to Save the University Libraries' Collections From Self-Destruction," Cornell Magazine (January-February 1996), 30-35. Describes causes of book deterioration and Cornell's preservation and conservation treatment of books and documents, to reformatting through photocopying, microfilm and digital imaging.

2202. Holden, Jill R. J. Opportunities in the United States for Education in Book and Paper Conservation and Preservation. Alexandria, VA: ERIC Document Reproduction Service, January 1988. 25p. (ED 291 413). Describes opportunities for education in book and paper conservation in the United States.

2203. Holden, Maria. "Principles of Deacidification," Preservation Papers of the 1991 SAA Annual Conference, comp. Karen Garlick. Chicago: Society of American Archivists, 1992, 79-82. Describes deacidification processes, risks and benefits, criteria for deacidification treatment.

2204. Holden, Maria S., and Robert W. Arnold. Basic Preservation of Local Government Records. Nashville, TN: American Association for State and Local History, 1989, 12p. (NICLOG Technical Leaflet 105). Care of paper and photographic records; covers preservation planning, care and handling, environmental concerns, treatment, security, and disaster preparedness. One of a series of technical leaflets prepared to complement The Management of Local Government Records by Bruce W. Dearstyne (1988).

2205. Holder, Carol. "Protecting Your Image: Microform Storage and Security," Inform, 1:10 (October 1988), 18-21. Guidelines for the storage and handling of microforms.

2206. Holford, Pearl. Disaster Plan for the Virginia State Library and Archives. Richmond, VA: Virginia State Library and Archives, 1991. 54p. A plan for libraries and archives in Virginia; instructions, worksheets, sources of assistance.

2207. Holland, Michael E. "Material Selection for Library Conservation," Library and Archival Security, 6:1 (Spring 1984), 7-21. Discusses various conservation selection strategies used by repositories and reported in the literature.

2208. Holland, Michael, and Lawrence Landis. "Records Recovery and Terrorism," Conservation Administration News, 47 (October 1991), 1-3, 15, 22. Case study; recovery of records that were scrambled and soaked in water by vandals.

2209. Holley, Robert P. "Let's Celebrate the Birth of the Preservation and Reformatting Section," ALCTS Newsletter (Association of Library Collections and Technical Services), 5:6 (1994), 74-75.

2210. Holley, Robert P. "The Utah Newspaper Project," Library Resources and Technical Services, 31:2 (April/June 1987), 177-191. Detailed description of one state's project.

2211. Holley, Robert P. "The Preservation Aspects of the United States Newspaper Program: Preliminary Study," Microform Review, 19:3 (Summer 1990), 124-132. Examines the microfilming component of the United State Newspaper Project; descriptions of state projects, with an indication of the success of the program.

2212. Holliday, Paul. A Handbook of Software Development and Operating Procedures for Microcomputers. New York: Macmillan, 1985. 181p. Includes information on maintenance procedures for computers; the preservation of data and equipment is a concern of this book.

2213. Hollinger, William K. "The Chemical Structure and Acid Deterioration of Paper," Library Hi Tech, 1:4 (1984), 51-57. Explains the chemical structure of paper, acid, and its deleterious effect.

2214. Holm, Bill. "Old Photos Might Not Lie, But They Fib A Lot About Color," American Indian Art Magazine (Autumn 1985), 44-49. Anthropologists often have access to old black-and-white photographs of cultural material and use them to draw inference about color of objects that may be misleading.

2215. Holm, Susanne Marie. "A Case History: 'Panoramic View of Sherbrooke ...' by Abbé J.L.H. Roy," Symposium 88: Conservation of Historic and Artistic Works on Paper: Proceedings of a Conference, Ottawa, Canada, 3 to 7 October, 1988. ed. Helen D. Burgess. Ottawa: The Institute, 1994, 93-97. Conservation treatment of a panoramic ink drawing on paper at the Centre du Conservation de Québec.

2216. Holmes, John. "Mass Deacidification of Books at the National Archives and the National Library of Canada," Paper Preservation: Current Issues and Recent Developments. Atlanta, GA: TAPPI Press, 1990, 144-145. Describes the Wei T'o process used in Canada; paper originally presented at the Paper Preservation Symposium, 1988.

2217. Hon, David N.-S. "Critical Evaluation of Mass Deacidification Processes for Book Preservation," Historic Textile and Paper Materials III: Conservation and Characterization, ed. Howard L. Needles and S. Haig Zeronian. Washington, DC: American Chemical Society, 1989, 13-33. Four mass treatment processes: diethyl zinc, Wei T'o, Bookkeepers, and Langwell interleaf vapor phase, are critically evaluated for their chemical characteristics and effectiveness for deacidification.

2218. Honea, Ted. "Conservation and Preservation," Modern Music Librarianship, ed. Alfred Mann. New York: Pendragon Press, 1989, 143-155. (Festschrift Series, 8). Reviews special problems in music libraries: treatment of scores and materials in a variety of sizes and formats.

2219. Honea, Ted. "Music ... A Binding Challenge," New Library Scene, 4:3 (June 1985), 8-10. Discussion of the unique problems presented by music scores, and some appropriate solutions.

2220. Hookham, Francis. "Preservation Factors in the Design of New Libraries: An Architects Viewpoint," Conservation and Preservation in Small Libraries, ed. Nicholas Hadgraft and Katherine Swift. Cambridge: Parker Library Publications, 1994. 70-73. An architects perspective on the adaptation of old buildings for library use and the construction of new library buildings. The planning team, statutory concerns, time and money.

2221. Hopkins, Diane. A Demonstration of PHOCUS: A Bibliographic Database for the Conservation of Photographic Materials. Computer

Technology of Conservators: Proceedings of the 11th Annual
IIC-CG Conference Workshop, May 13-16, 1985, ed. John Perkins.
Halifax, Canada: The Atlantic Regional Group of the International
Institute for Conservation of Historic and Artistic Works, Halifax,
Canada: 1986. 85-100. An online demonstration of PHOCUS is
given.

2222. Horakova, Hana and Frantisek Martinek. "Disinfection of Archive
Documents by Ionizing Radiation," Restaurator, 6:3-4 (1984),
205-216. Report of a study using gamma radiation to eradicate
mildew in archival materials; spores were eradicated but some
deterioration in paper was observed.

2223. Horder, Alan. Guidelines for the Care and Preservation of
Microforms in Tropical Countries. Paris: UNESCO, 1990. 20p.
(PG-90/WS/17). Reviews factors affecting the permanence of
microforms and technical considerations relating to the purchase,
processing, management, protection, and control of a microform
collection.

2224. Horie, C.V. "Industrial Standards of Terminology for
Conservation," Terminology for Museums, ed. D. Andrew Roberts.
Cambridge: Museum Documentation Association, 1990,
473-486. Author argues that terminology in conservation be
developed as has been done in industry, and cites standards.

2225. Horney, Karen. "Digital Technology: Implications for Library
Planning," Advances in Librarianship, 16 (1992), 107-126. Review
of scanning technology and projects. Author views imaging
technology as a preservation medium and does not consider the
problems of preserving information in electronic formats.

2226. Horton, Richard W. "Photo Album Structures," Guild of Book
Workers Journal, 32:1 (Spring 1994, publication 1996),
32-43. Report of a study of the structure and mounting methods in
photo albums, from the 1850s-1950s. Illus.

2227. Horton, Richard W. "Preservation Efforts at the General Libraries,
University of Texas at Austin," Conservation Administration News,
25 (April 1985), 1-3, 21-23. Description of preservation and
conservation efforts in the general libraries, and what is being
accomplished in a few special collections.

2228. Horton, Warren. "Developing a National Strategy for the
Preservation of Australian Library Materials," Libraries: The Heart
of the Matter. Deakin, Australia: Australian Library and Information
Association, 1992, 159-161. (ALIA '92, Proceedings, 2d

Conference, 1992). What has been done, and what should be accomplished in a National Preservation Program; how the National Preservation Office will function.

2229.   Horvath, David G. The Acetate Negative Survey: Final Report. Louisville, KY: University of Louisville, Ekstrom Library Photographic Archives, February 1987. 91p. Survey finds that a substantial number of black-and-white acetate sheet film from 1926-1955 are deteriorated; possible reasons discussed.

2230.   Houston, Penelope. Keepers of the Frame: The Film Archives. London: British Film Institute, 1994. 179p.

2231.   "How to Store Videos," The Unabashed Librarian, 94 (1995), 4.

2232.   Howard, R. C. "The Effects of Recycling on Paper Quality," Paper Technology, 30:4 (April 1991), 20-25; Journal of Pulp and Paper Science, 16:5 (September 1990), J143-149; part of table omitted. Review of research undertaken in the late 1960s. 57 references.

2233.   Howe Lindsay. "The Use of Optical Disc for Archival Image Storage," Archives and Manuscripts (Australian Society of Archivists), 18:1 (May 1990), 89-118. Examines existing and potential use of optical disks as a medium for storing images of archival photographs; notes that its current use of original material but it is not a preservation medium.

2234.   Howe, Michael, Vladimir Zwass, Morris Warren, and Jerry Rhoads. "The Book Preservation Associates (BPA) Mass Deacidification Process," Paper Preservation: Current Issues and Recent Developments. Atlanta, GA: TAPPI Press, 1990, 127-128. Describes the BPA mass deacidification process. Paper presented at the Paper Preservation Symposium, 1988.

2235.   Howell, Alan. "Contracted Microfilming: Case Studies from Australian Libraries," Preservation Microfilming: Does It Have a Future? Canberra: National Library of Australia, 1995, 62-65. Why Australian libraries contract out part or all of their microfilming.

2236.   Howell, Alan G. "Digital Imaging Technology for Preservation and Access: A Cornell University Library Workshop," LASIE (Library Automated Systems Information Exchange), 27 (March 1996), 26-41.

2237.   Howell, Alan G. "Paper Conservation: New Directions," Preserving the Word. London: Library Association, 1987, 63-69. Bibliographic overview of what a conservator believes a librarian should read on preservation and conservation.

2238. Howell, Alan, and Heather Mansell. "Bound To Be Good," Preservation of Library Materials, (Australian Library and Information Association, Special Interest Group for the Preservation of Library Materials), 10 (July 1993), 2. Discusses traditional methods and roles of binding in libraries with details of some alternative techniques. The evolving role of binding in collection management at the State Library of New South Wales is described.

2239. Howington, Tad. "ARMA-Fort Worth Records Project," Conservation Administration News, 47 (October 1991), 6-7. Case study; organizing, cleaning, and rehousing historic records for preservation and access.

2240. Hua, Hai-Yen, W. Fischer, and M. Fath. "Machinery for Paper Restoration," Restaurator, 10:2 (1989), 83-99. Engineering and demonstration of medium-sized machinery used in paper restoration.

2241. Hubbard, William J., and Kathleen W. Langston. "RX for Library Materials: The Holistic Approach," Library and Archival Security, 6:4 (Winter 1984), 17-26. Basic preventive maintenance and preservation of collections, with suggestions for diagnosis, treatment, or referral.

2242. Hudson, F. Lyth, and C. J. Edwards. "Some Direct Observations on the Aging of Paper," Abbey Newsletter, 11:7 (October 1987), 109-110. Report on the condition of a 1909 Everyman volume that was frozen in snow from 1912-1959; testing demonstrates that cold storage does delay the deterioration of books. Originally published in Paper Technology, 7:1 (1966), 27-28.

2243. Humphrey, Bruce J. "The Application of Parylene Conformal Coating Technology to Archival and Artifact Conservation," Studies in Conservation, 26:3 (August 1984), 117-122. Report of a study, discussion of the properties of the polymer, and test results.

2244. Humphrey, Bruce J. "Paper Strengthening with Gas-Phase Parylene Polymers: Practical Considerations," Restaurator, 11:1 (November 1, 1990), 48-68. Describes parylene, its effect on materials, and some tests that have been performed to determine limitations of the process.

2245. Humphrey, Bruce J. "Parylene Gas Phase Consolidation: An Overview," Paper Preservation: Current Issues and Recent Developments. Atlanta, GA: TAPPI Press, 1990, 133-136. Describes the parylene process that can be used to strengthen paper; a gas phase treatment. Paper presented at the Paper Preservation Symposium, 1988.

2246. Humphrey, Bruce J. "Vapor Phase Consolidation of Books With the Parylene Polymers," Journal of the American Institute of Conservation, 25:1 (Spring 1986), 15-29. Discusses the application of parylene technology to the mass conservation of brittle books; results of the author's testing are reviewed and the strengths and weaknesses of the method are discussed.

2247. Humphreys, Betsy L. "Permanence of Paper: Proposed Revision Ready for Ballot," Information Standards Quarterly, 3:1 (January 1991), 2-8. Discussion of the revised standard for the permanence of paper (Z39.48) and the issues that have been considered in its development in the United States; discussion of the development of an international standard.

2248. Hunderman, Harry J., and William B. Rose. "Humidity and Building Materials in the Museum Setting," Construction Specifier, 42:10 (October 1989), 98-104. Deals with the problems created by attempts to maintain relative humidity at 50% in cold climates.

2249. Hunter, John E. "Filing Cabinets and Safes for Protection of Paper Records, Computer Media, and Photographic Records from Fire Damage," CRM Bulletin (Cultural Resources Management), 16:5 (1993), Supplement, 1-8. Cites National Park Service standards for the storage of critical records; discusses criteria for selecting storage cases.

2250. Huntsberry, J. Stephen. "Forged Identification: A Key to Library Archives," Library and Archival Security, 9:3/4 (1989), 69-74. Describes Blumberg's entry to collections using forged identity cards; written when Blumberg was identified but not yet captured.

2251. Huntsberry, J. Stephen. "The Legacy Thief: The Hunt for Stephen Blumberg," Art Documentation, 10:4 (Winter 1991), 181-183. Traces efforts to track down a book thief; how Blumberg managed his thefts and how such thefts might be curtailed.

2252. Huntsberry, J. Stephen. "Library Security: The Blumberg Legacy," Journal of Information Ethics, 1 (Fall 1992), 46-50. Lessons learned about library theft from the Blumberg case.

2253. Huntsberry, J. Stephen. "Product Review: Quorum Security
       Monitor," Focus on Security, 1:1 (October. 1993), 22-23. Brief note
       on a security device that detects airwaves within an enclosed space.

2254. Huntsberry, J. Stephen. "Students Library Security Patrol: A Viable
       Alternative," Conservation Administration News, 49 (April 1992),
       1-2, 26-27. Describes the student security force at Washington State
       University to curtail theft and vandalism, developed from a review of
       the Blumberg theft.

2255. Huntsberry, J. Stephen. "To Catch a Thief," Conservation News,
       12:1 (March 1992), 4-5. Suggestions for improving library/archival
       security, including a review of basic security measures, rights for
       detention, and what to do when theft occurs.

2256. Huntsberry, J. Stephen. "University Library Security: A Militant
       Perspective," Focus on Security, 1:1 (October 1993),
       8-19. Advocates stricter procedures for protection of collections.
       Reprinted from the Proceedings from the National Conference on the
       Protection of Cultural Property, The Security and Protection Alliance
       Among Museums, Libraries, Gardens and Parks, Washington, DC:
       Smithsonian Institution, 1993. 261p.

2257. Hutson, Jennifer. "Disaster Reaction Training at the National Library
       (Or, How Not to Panic if the Library Is Under Water)," National
       Library News (Canada), 26:7 (July 1994), 5-6. A short note on the
       training program for disaster recovery at the National Library of
       Canada.

2258. Hutton, Brian G. "Preservation Policy at the National Library of
       Scotland, Preserving the Word. London: Library Association, 1987,
       26-28. Describes the preservation program at the Scottish National
       Library.

2259. Hutton, Brian G. "Preserving Scotland's Heritage," Library
       Conservation News, 19 (April 1988), 1-3.

2260. Hutton, Brian G. "Reprographic Services in the National Library of
       Scotland," Microform Review, 17:1 (February 1988),
       23-25. Describes the organization of the library's services and its
       cooperative initiatives with the British Library.

2261. Ibrahimah, M. Z. "The Teaching of Preservation and Conservation
       at Bayero University, Keno, Nigeria," Restaurator, 9:1 (1988),
       51-60. Broad outline of a program in its formative stage.

2262. Idsala, Mohamed. "Preservation & Conservation Programmes in North Africa: The Case of Morocco," Proceedings of the Pan-African Conference on the Preservation & Conservation of Library & Archival Materials, Nairobi, Kenya, 21-25 June 1993. The Hague: IFLA, 1995, 45-47. (IFLA Professional Publication 43). Outline of actions taken to preserve written heritage.

2263. Ilbury, Terence James. "Using Microfilm as an Aid to Preservation," Planning Modernization and Preservation Programmes for South Asian Libraries: A Seminar, 1990, ed. Kalpana Dasgupta. Calcutta, India: National Library, 1992, 91-96. Microfilming to preserve information; selections; microfilming in process.

2264. Illinois Library Association. Resources and Technical Services Division. Preservation Committee. Here Tomorrow? A Bibliography of Books and Journals on the Conservation and Preservation of Library Materials. Chicago, IL: Illinois Library Association, 1987. 8p. Bibliography.

2265. Image Permanence Institute. Polysulfide Treatment of Microfilm Using IPI Silverlock (TM) — Some Questions and Answers. Rochester, NY: Image Permanence Institute, 1991. 23p. Discusses in lay language the role of polysulfide toning of silver gelatin microfilm to improve image resistance to fading and red spot formation.

2266. Imhoff, Hans-Christoph von. "Is Conservation Conservative?" ICOM NEWS (International Council of Museums), 39:1 (1986), 2-4. The role and responsibilities of the conservator, and the need for sound training.

2267. Imhoff, Hans-Christoph von. "Training in Conservation and Restoration: A Report on the Interim Meeting of the Working Group, Dresden, September 1983," International Journal of Museum Management and Curatorship, 3 (1984), 71-73.

2268. Inaba, M., and R. Sugista. "Permanence of Washi (Japanese Paper)," The Conservation of Far Eastern Art. London: International Institute for Conservation, 1988, 1-4. Reports on the permanence of Japanese paper and the effect of dosa, a sizing material, on its deterioration through accelerated aging tests.

2269. Inch, Dennis. "The Role of Vendors in Conservation," Conserving and Preserving Library Materials in Nonbook Formats. Urbana-Champaign: University of Illinois Graduate School of Library and Information Science, 1991, 23-26. (Allerton Park Institute, 30). Reviews the vendor's responsibilities ; supplies for preservation of photographic collections.

2270.   Information Systems Consultants, Inc. Videodiscs and Optical
        Digital Disk Technologies and Their Applications in Libraries: A
        Report to the Council on Library Resources. Washington, DC:
        Council on Library Resources, 1985. 19lp. Examines videodisc and
        optical digital disk technologies.

2271.   Inland Marine Underwriters Association. Libraries and Archives: An
        Overview of Risk and Loss Prevention. NY: IMUA/Society of
        American Archivists, 1994. 37p. Discussion of risk management for
        libraries and archives to prevent or curtail risk to collections by fire,
        flood, vandalism, theft; how to work with insurers.

2272.   Institute of Paper Science and Technology. Physical Properties of
        Library Books Deacidified. Atlanta, GA: Institute of Paper Science
        and Technology, June 10, 1991. 1 vol. Technical reports on the
        FMC/Lithco, Akzo, and Wei T'o deacidification processes in
        response to the Library of Congress request; provides testing
        procedures and results.

2273.   International Archival Round Table Conference, 25th, 1987.
        Politique de Preservation du Patrimoine Archivistique/Politics for the
        Preservation of the Archival Heritage. Paris: International Council
        on Archives. 1989. 272p. (English/French). Papers to review needs
        and address an agenda for the future.

2274.   International Association of Sound Archives. Archiving the
        Audio-Visual Heritage: A Joint Technical Symposium, ed. Eva
        Orbanz. West Berlin, Germany: Stiftung Deutsche Kinemathek,
        1988. 169p.

2275.   International Centre for the Study of the Preservation and the
        Restoration of Cultural Property. International Index of Conservation
        Research. Rome: ICCROM, 1988. 60p. (English/French). Various
        editions. 5th ed. 1994. 167p. Briefly summarizes ongoing research
        projects.

2276.   International Centre for the Study of the Preservation and the
        Restoration of Cultural Property (International Index on Training in
        Conservation of Cultural Property. Rome: ICCROM; Malibu, CA:
        Getty Conservation Institute, 1987. 140p. List of worldwide training
        opportunities in conservation.

2277.   International Council of Museums. Committee for Conservation. 8th
        Triennial Meeting, Sydney, Australia, 6-11 September, 1987,
        Preprints. Los Angeles: Getty Conservation Institute, 1987. 3 vols.
        1230p. Papers from 26 working groups.

2278.   International Council of Museums, Committee for Conservation. Abstracts Submitted to the Interim Meeting of the Working Group Graphic Documents, April 3rd-5th 1995, Amsterdam. Amsterdam: Central Research Laboratory for Objects of Art and Science, 1995. v.p., (Abstracts, English/French)

2279.   International Council of Museums. Looting in Africa/Pillage Afrique. Paris: ICOM, 1994. 143p. Illus. (One hundred missing objects). The second in a series to document and publicize objects stolen from their countries. "These publications can be considered reference materials and a means of control while at the same time a way of informing the public" (7). Describes the objects stolen from public collections, with illustrations. Excerpts national legislation regarding stolen art. Describes role of ICOM and Interpol.

2280.   International Federation of Film Archivists. Preservation and Restoration of Moving Images and Sound. Brussels, Belgium: International Federation of Film Archives, 1986, 268p. [66p.], leaves of plates.

2281.   (International Federation of Library Associations and Institutions). IFLA Programme on Preservation and Conservation. IFLA Core Programme, Preservation and Conservation. Paris: Bibliothèque Nationale de France, 1995. 16p.

2282.   Intner, Sheila S. "Preservation Training for Library Users," Technicalities, 14 (September 1994), 7-10.

2283.   Intner, Sheila S. "Training Staff for Preservation," Technicalities, 14 (July 1994), 4-7.

2284.   "Introducing the Conservation Information Network," Archival Information Newsletter, 2:4 (Winter 1988/89), 70-73. A review of the CIN database for conservation and preservation.

2285.   Iowa State University Library. Preservation Planning Program: Final Report. Washington, DC: Association of Research Libraries, 1987. 40p. Self-study to assess the physical condition of the collections and the library environment, and to address preservation needs. 32 recommendations.

2286.   Irblich, Eva, ed. "Seminar on Restoration, Conservation and Reprography of Manuscripts and Rare Books, Vienna and Graz, September 1984," LIBER Bulletin (Ligue des Bibliothèques Européennes de Recherche), 24 (1985), 65p. Entire issue. Proceedings; three treatment reports are in English.

2287. Irwin, John. Preserving Arizona's Historical Records: The Final Report of the Arizona Historical Records Needs and Assessment Project. Phoenix, AZ: Department of Library, Archives and Public Records/Arizona Historical Records Advisory Board, 1983. 71p, appendixes, 36p. Bibliography. Identification of needs with recommendations for future initiatives and action; emphasizes need for cooperative efforts to preserve materials.

2288. Isenberg, Laurie. "Planning for Preservation: A Public Health Library Conditions Survey" (at the University of Michigan), Collection Management, 19:1/2 (1994), 111-119.

2289. Iversen, T. "The Aging of Bleached Kraft Pulps," Environnement et Conservation de l'Écrit, de l'Image et du Son. Paris: ARSAG, 1994, 143-145. (Actes des Deuxièmes Journées Internationales d'Études de l'ARSAG, 16 au 20 Mai, 1994). Study to obtain a preliminary survey of the effects of modern bleaching on the aging stability of commercial kraft pulps.

2290. Iversen, Diann S. "Screams from the Stacks,Conservation for the Small Library," Illinois Libraries, 64:5 (May 1983), 351-354. Basic "consciousness-raising" article with practical tips for planning a preservation program, including disaster planning.

2291. Iversen, Tommy, and Jiri Kolar. Kvavedioxides Effekter pa Papper (Effects of Nitrogen Dioxide of Paper). (FOU-projectct fur papper skonservering, Rapport, 5. Swedish, 3p. summary in English). A pilot project to determine whether normal urban concentrations of NO_2 can affect the aging stability of paper. High gas concentrations, rather than high temperatures, were used for accelerated aging and only brightness of mechanical pulp papers was adversely affected.

2292. Izbicki, Thomas M. "Microform Collections of Medieval and Renaissance Manuscripts in the United States," Collection Management, 15:3-4 (1992), 449-473. Describes individual microform collections; problems of using microforms as a surrogate for original material. Paper presented at "Shared Resources, Shared Responsibilities," Florence, Italy, 1988.

2293. Jackanicz, Donald. "Theft at the National Archives: The Murphy Case, 1962-1975," Library and Archival Security, 10 (1990), 23-50. A theft in the 1960s prompted the National Archives to rethink its approach and philosophy toward security. Considers methods of monitoring researcher access to facilities and documents.

2294.   Jackson, Cheryl. "The Permanence of Thermal Fax Papers," Edizione per la Conservazione, 1 (1990), 11-12. Provides a brief but complete review of the analyses of the durability of thermal paper carried out by the Preservation Services of the Australian Archives.

2295.   Jackson, Cheryl. "A Short Research Project Into the Permanence of Thermal Fax Papers," Abbey Newsletter, 13:8 (December 1989), 133-134, 136. Results of a project to evaluate the permanence of Thermal Fax papers carried out in the Conservation Laboratory, Australian National Archives.

2296.   Jackson, Marie. "A Decade of Achievement: A Review of the NPO," Library Conservation News, 50 (Spring 1996), 4-5. Brief review of accomplishments of the National Preservation Office over its first 12 years.

2297.   Jackson, Marie. "The National Preservation Office," Conservation Administration News, 38 (July 1989), 14. Describes the NPO at the British Library, programs and objectives.

2298.   Jackson, Marie. "Library Security: Facts and Figures," Library Association Record, 93:6 (June 1991), 380-384. Notes lack of solid information on theft from libraries in the U.K.; reviews U.S. studies and case studies of major thefts; recommends full research into the situation in the U.K.

2299.   Jackson, Marie. "Please Can We Have Our Books Back?" Library Association Record, 95:2 (May 1990), 359-363. Discusses the problem of theft and mutilation in British libraries and the National Preservation Office campaign to encourage libraries to deal with security.

2300.   Jackson, Marie. "Preservation," British Librarianship and Information Work, 1986-1990. Vol. 2, ed. by David W. Bromley and Angela M. Allott. London: Library Association, 1993, 275-283. Review of preservation initiatives and activities in the U.K.: conferences, research and development, disaster preparedness, permanent paper, security.

2301.   Jacobs, Donna. "Nineteenth-Century Periodicals: Preservation Decision Making at College Libraries," College and Research Libraries, 52:3 (May 1991), 263-274. Assessment of periodicals to develop a decision-making model for smaller collections; decision tree and a series of questions.

2302.   Jacobsen, Pamela D., and Jerannine Uppgard. "Are Bindery Tours Worthwhile?" New Library Scene, 7:5 (October 1988), 7-9. Study of staff tours demonstrated that those who visited the bindery felt that they learned a great deal.

2303. Jacobson, Bruce F. "The Future of Library Binding — Will It Be Tomorrow's Buggy Whip?" New Library Scene, 4 (February 1985), 1+. A discussion of the effect that the electronic library might have in the library binding industry.

2304. Jacobson, Bruce F. "Librarians and Binders: Toward a Cultural Understanding," New Library Scene, 4:5 (October 1985), 1,13. Notes the need for understanding and laments the lack of education in binding techniques at library schools.

2305. Jagschitz, Gerhard. "Summary and Perspectives," Phonographic Bulletin, 52 (November 1988), 19-21. Calls for the integration of audio and visual archives to ensure the preservation of mass media. Summary of an International Round Table called to examine the UNESCO 1980 Recommendations for the Safeguarding and Preservation of Moving Images.

2306. Jakubs, Deborah. Qualitative Collection Analysis: The Conspectus Methodology. Washington, DC: Association of Research Libraries, Office of Management Studies, February 1989. 119p. (SPEC Kit 151). Results of a survey designed to profile uses of the conspectus and a selection of planning, collection assessment documents, and project reports.

2307. James, Linda. Standing the Test of Time: Quality Assurance for State and Local Government Records Microfilming. St. Paul, MN: Minnesota Historical Society, 1986, 70p. Report documents the situation in state and local government and makes recommendations to correct problems of poor filming.

2308. Januszonok, Teresa. "Conservation in Sheffield," Library Conservation News, 27 (April 1990), 4-5, 8. Describes the conservation services organized for and provided to the public libraries in the Sheffield, England, region.

2309. Januszonok, Teresa. "The Role of the Conservation Unit Within Sheffield City Libraries," Library Review, 36:3 (Autumn, 1987), 186-190. Case study of the development and activities of the Unit.

2310. Jarernporn, Penpan. "Problems of Film Preservation," Archiving the Audio-Visual Heritage. Rushton, England: FIAF/UNESCO, 1992, 21-22. Describes the National Film Archive, Bangkok, Thailand.

2311.   Jefferson, Karen L. "The Role of Private Research Institutions in Cooperative Conservation," Conservation Administration News, 28 (January 1987), 7. Describes the role that private research libraries play in the preservation of collections.

2312.   Jefferson, Melvin. "The Rebinding of CCCC Ms. 280," Conservation and Preservation in the Small Library, ed. Nicholas Hadgraft and Katherine Swift. Cambridge: Parker Library Publications, 1994, 123-126. Illus. Treatment report and photo documentation.

2313.   Jennings, Tom. "The National Archives Bringing America's Past Into the Future," Government Executive, 20:1 (January 1988), 28-31. Describes steps to protect the Constitution and the process of scanning documents, i.e., Civil War records.

2314.   Jenny, Kriss and Tom F. R. Clareson. "OCLC Announces Bibliographic Cooperation for Preservation," OCLC Newsletter (Online Computer Library Network), 186 (July/August 1990), 16-18. Discusses the OCLC guidelines for recording preservation data in cataloging or Union List subsystems to maintain bibliographic control.

2315.   Jensen, Craig W. "Developing a Conservation Policy: The Harold B. Lee Library," Conservation of Library and Archival Materials, ed. Guy Petherbridge. London: Butterworths, 1987, 287-289. What should be included in an institution's preservation policy, including coping with the political climate.

2316.   Jensen, Kirsten, and Andrew Hart. "The Preservation Intensive Institute: State-of-the-Art Education for Preservation Managers," Library Hi Tech News, 107 (November 1993), 1-3. Report of a week-long institute held at Pittsburgh, a collaboration of five universities, to provide advanced continuing education in preservation. Three separate courses offered, briefly described.

2317.   Jerde, Curtis D. "Technical Processing of Popular Music at Tulane University Library's Hogan Jazz Archive: The Rockefeller Project," Technical Services Quarterly, 4:4 (Summer 1987), 49-56. Review of a project to preserve and provide access to the Hogan Jazz Archive, Tulane University.

2318.   Jermann, Peter. "Digital Imaging Basics," Archival Outlook, (January 1995), 8-9. Brief, clear description of digital imaging, how it is done, strengths and weaknesses. Discusses the preservation problems the media presents.

2319.   Jermann, Peter. "Preservation of Electronic Formats," <u>Abbey</u>
        <u>Newsletter</u>, 17:7-8 (December 1993), 100-101. Report on a course
        given by Michael Spring at the University of Pittsburgh, August
        1993, exploring digital technologies as a preservation tool and as
        media that need preservation.

2320.   Jermann, Peter. "Implications of Electronic Formats for Preservation
        Administrators," <u>Commission on Preservation and Access</u>
        <u>Newsletter</u>, XX (November-December 1993), 2 page
        insert. Summary of a talk by Michael Spring, Department of
        Information Science, University of Pittsburgh, on new
        responsibilities for preservation administrators in the evolving digital
        environment. See and compare "Preservation of Electronic Formats,"
        <u>Abbey Newsletter</u>, 17:7-8 (December 1993), 100-101.

2321.   Jessee, W. Scott. "Monks, Monasteries and Manuscripts: Archival
        Sources for Eleventh-Century France," <u>American Archivist</u>, 52:3
        (Summer 1989), 384-390. Collection and preservation of records.

2322.   Jessup, Wendy Claire. <u>Integrated Pest Management: A Selected</u>
        <u>Bibliography for Collections Care</u>. Arlington, VA: Wendy Jessup &
        Assoc., 1995. 29p. Selective, annotated bibliography. Distributed at
        the 23rd Annual Meeting, AIC, Health & Safety Lecture, June 7,
        1995.

2323.   Jett, Maureen Y. "Be a Preservationist," <u>School Library Media</u>
        <u>Activities Monthly</u>, 12 (April 1996), 23-24.

2324.   Jewitt, Crispin. "Conspectus: A Means to Library Conservation,"
        <u>Library Conservation News</u>, 22 (January 1989), 4-6. Discussion of
        the conspectus system to describe collections by subject
        classification.

2325.   Jimenez, Nancy. "ABINIA's Experience in Preserving Rare Books
        in Latin America," <u>IFLA Journal</u> (International Federation of Library
        Associations and Institutions), 21:3 (1995), 195-197. Describes the
        treatment of 218 volumes from 14 Ibero-American countries to
        preserve them, during the Columbus Quincentennial, sponsored by
        the Association of Ibero-American National Libraries (ABINIA).

2326.   Jirat-Wasiutynski, Thea. "Mounting Boards and Adhesives for
        Photographic Prints and Works of Art on Papers," <u>Journal of</u>
        <u>Audiovisual Media in Medicine</u>, 7 (1984), 51-58. Reviews basic
        methods and materials for matting, hinging, and framing photographs
        and works of art on paper to ensure maximum support and
        protection.

2327. Jivendra, (Dr.). "Innovations in Paper Technology for Preservation of Library Materials," Planning, Modernization and Preservation Programmes for South Asian Libraries, ed. Kalpana Dasgupta. Calcutta, India: National Library, 1992, 29-35. Describes elements of permanent paper, effect of ingredients in paper.

2328. Johansson, Eve. "Newsplan," Library Conservation News, 25 (October 1989), 4-5. Describes the activities and accomplishments of the Newsplan Program to promote and coordinate the microfilming and preservation of U.K. local newspapers.

2329. Johns Hopkins University. Milton S. Eisenhower Library. Workshop Manual: Preservation and Conservation. Baltimore, MD: The Library, 1987. 60p.

2330. Johnsen, Jesper Stub. "Image Quality of Chemically Restored Black and White Negatives," Journal of Imaging Science and Technology, 36 (January/February 1992), 46-55. Describes treatment procedures for the reconstruction of faded silver gelatin negative images.

2331. Johnsen, Jesper Stub. "Surveying Large Collections of Photographs for Archival Survival," Preventive Conservation: Practice, Theory and Research, ed. Ashok Roy and Perry Smith. London: International Institute for Conservation, 1994, 202-206. (Preprints of the Contributions to the Ottawa Congress, September 12-16, 1994). Discusses the need for better techniques during surveys of photographic collections and a method being developed to identify breakdown due to instable materials.

2332. Johnson, Arthur W. A Practical Guide to Book Repair and Conservation. London: Thames and Hudson, 1988. 111p. Information on how to curtail deterioration in books, with step-by-step instructions and diagrams; manual for experienced bookbinders.

2333. Johnson, Arthur W. "Paper: Part I, An Introduction for Bookbinders," CBBAG Newsletter (Canadian Bookbinders and Book Artist Guild), 14:2 (Summer 1996), 13-16. Describes the making/manufacture of paper, classifications of paper.

2334. Johnson, Linda B. and Jeff Paul. "Coping With a Quake," College and Research Libraries News, 51:10 (November 1990), 928-933. A review of the responses by area libraries to the Loma Prieta earthquake (October 1989), emphasizing the critical role of communication in disaster response.

2335. Johnson, Peggy. "Depreciation: An Issue for Libraries," Technicalities, 9:5 (May 1989), 5-7. Discusses need to understand the cost of depreciation; quantify preservation decisions to repair or replace.

2336. Johnson, Peggy, ed. Guide to Technical Services Resources. Chicago, IL: American Library Association, 1994. 313p. Bibliographical guide to information sources prepared by experts, including "Preservation," by Wesley Boomgaarden (pp./166-195), and "Reproduction of Library Materials," by Erich Kesse (pp. 196-213).

2337. Johnson, Steve. Appraising Audiovisual Media: A Guide for Attorneys, Trust Officers, Insurance Professionals, and Archivists in Appraising Films, Video, Photographs, Recordings, and Other Audiovisual Assets. Washington, DC: Copyright Information. Services/Assn. for Educational Communication & Technology, 1993. 118p. Provides a basic overview of appraisal, with informative appendices. Brief, accurate summary of condition and conservation concerns, see especially chapter 5: "How to Protect Media Until the Appraiser Arrives," 41-44.

2338. Johnson, William S., ed. Nineteenth-Century Photography, An Annotated Bibliography, 1839-1879. Boston, MA: G. K. Hall, 1990. 962p. Comprehensive bibliography, primarily of English language sources, covering the period 1839-1879.

2339. Johnston, James R. "Born in Fire: Arson, Emergency Actions and Recovery of the Joliet Public Library," Issues for the New Decade. Boston, MA: G. K. Hall, 1991. 27+. Case study of the firebombing of a public library.

2340. Jolliffe, John. "International Cooperation in Preservation," Collection Management, 9:2/3 (Summer/Fall 1987); International Conference on Research Library Cooperation. New York: Haworth Press, 1987, 113-118. Discusses the tension that can arise between "preservation" and "conservation."

2341. Jones, Barclay G. "Litany of Losses," Museum News, 69:3 (May-June 1990), 56-58. A review of disasters and catastrophes; advocates planning beforehand.

2342. Jones, Barclay G., ed. Protecting Historic Architecture and Museum Collections from Natural Disasters. London: Butterworths, 1986. 560p. Handbook, with chapters written by experts; covers all aspects of protection from planning to salvage; bibliographies. Papers originally presented at a seminar in 1982.

2343.   Jones, C. Lee. "Mid-Atlantic Preservation Service (MAPS): New Options for Preservation Microfilming," Microform Review, 18:3 (Summer 1989), 142-144. Describes MAPS' mission, current operations, and goals for the future.

2344.   Jones, Daniel P. "New Jersey Newspaper Project: Microfilming Phase," New Jersey Libraries, 26:3 (Summer 1993), 10-13. Describes the scope of the preservation project and its microfilming phase.

2345.   Jones, David R. "A Stable Future for Suffolk's Archives," Storage, ed. Mark Norman and Victoria Todd. London: United Kingdom Institute for Conservation, 1991, 27-31. Describes the project to construct an environmentally stable archives repository.

2346.   Jones, Fiona. "Five Years Later: The Past, Present and Future of the Records Conservation Training Program of the National Archives of Canada," Conservation of Historic and Artistic Works on Paper. Ottawa: Canadian Conservation Institute, 1994, 61-63. (Symposium 88). Describes the program, levels of training.

2347.   Jones, Fiona, and Kenneth R. Seddon. "The Dunhuang Diamond Sutra: A Study in Scientific Conservation Techniques," Conference on Book and Paper Conservation, 1990. Budapest, Hungary: Technical Association of Paper and Printing Industry, 1992, 238-243. Describes problems caused by earlier attempts at restoration; use of berberine as a solvent, continued research and testing.

2348.   Jones, G. William. "Nitrate Film: Dissolving Images of the Past," Conservation Administration News, 31 (October 1987), 1-3, 12.

2349.   Jones, Helen. "FILM '93: A Visit to BFI/NFTVA J. Paul Getty Conservation Centre, Berhamsted," V&A Conservation Journal, 9 (1993), 21-22. Reports on facilities at the British Film Institute to house the National Film and Television Archive, and research undertaken.

2350.   Jones, Karen. "Colorado Preservation Alliance," Conservation Administration News, 46 (July 1991), 15, 27. Describes statewide preservation efforts in Colorado.

2351.   Jones, Karen. "Is Your Collection Dying on the Shelf?" Unabashed Librarian, 77 (1990), 5. Brief note on how to create a good environment in the library, from the Colorado Preservation Alliance Education Committee.

2352.   Jones, Karen. "Is Your Collection Dying on the Shelf? Tips for Creating a Safe Environment for Your Home Library," Colorado Preservation Alert, 5:2 (Summer 1995), 2p. insert. Briefly describes the hazards of heat, relative humidity, light, pollution, with suggestions.

2353.   Jones, Karen. "Mass Deacidification Technologies," Colorado Libraries, 18 (March 1992), 39-41. Summary of the Diethyl zinc (DEZ), Wei T'o, and Lithco/FMC processes.

2354.   Jones, Karen. "On the Road to Preservation," Colorado Librarian, 19 (Fall 1993), 47-49.

2355.   Jones, Karen. "On the Road: Preservation Education Outreach in Colorado" (Colorado Preservation Alliance), Colorado Libraries, 21 (Fall 1995), 48-49.

2356.   Jones, Karen. "Preservation Outreach in Colorado Libraries," Colorado Librarian, 16 (June 1990), 25-27.

2357.   Jones, Lois Swan, and Sarah Scott Gibson. Art Libraries and Information Services: Development, Organization and Management. New York: Academic Press, 1986. 343p. Covers all aspects of art librarianship including the care and preservation of materials; Preservation concerns are specifically addressed pp. 244-246.

2358.   Jones, Lyn [Maralyn]. "Class A Bindings for Polyester Books," Abbey Newsletter, 8:4 (July 1984), 58-60. How to bind whole books that have been encapsulated based upon the practice at the Avery Architectural and Fine Arts Library, Columbia University.

2359.   Jones, Lyn Maralyn, comp. Collection Conservation Treatment: A Resource Manual for Program Development and Conservation Technician Training. Berkeley, CA: University of California - Berkeley Library, Conservation Department, 1993. [425p]; unpaged loose-leaf notebook. A collection of training instructions from collections conservators who attended a "train the trainers" conference at University of California - Berkeley in 1992.

2360.   Jones, Lyn Maralyn. "More Than Ten Years After: Identify and Direction in Library Preservation," Library Resources and Technical Services, 35:3 (July 1991), 294-306. A review of the literature for 1990, considering preservation in original format; conservation treatments and library binding; pest control; deterioration, deacidification, and strengthening of paper; replacement and reformatting; preservation management and education; state and national initiatives.

2361.   Jones, Lyn [Maralyn]. "Report on the Manufacture of Book Cloth and Buckram," New Library Scene, 7:1 (February 1988), 1, 5-6. Report based upon information presented at the Preservation of Library Materials Library Binding Discussion Group at the American Library Association Mid-winter Meeting.

2362.   Jones, Norvell M. M. Archival Copies of Thermofax, Verifax, and Other Unstable Records. Washington, DC: National Archives and Records Administration, 1990. 17p. (Technical Report. National Archives Technical Information Paper, 5. PB90-171836). Summarizes the results of a study of xerographic copying to determine if it is archivally acceptable. The GPO report on "Electrostatic Copying, Special Development Study for NARA" is included in the appendix.

2363.   Jones, Norvell M. M. "Lamination and Encapsulation for Paper Strengthening," Paper Preservation: Current Issues and Recent Developments. Atlanta, GA: TAPPI Press, 1990, 146-148. Examines the advantages and disadvantages of lamination and encapsulation, two techniques for strengthening deteriorated papers. Paper presented at the 1988 Paper Preservation Symposium.

2364.   Jones, Norvell M. M., and Mary Lynn Ritzenthaler. "Implementing an Archival Preservation Program," Managing Archives and Archival Institutions. Chicago, IL: University of Chicago Press, 1989, 185-206. Presents a basic programmatic approach to preservation for archival collections. Bibliography.

2365.   Jones, P. William. "Nitrate Film: Dissolving Images of the Past," Conservation Administration News, 31 (October 1987), 1-3, 12. Description of the hazard of deteriorating nitrate film, with options for storage and preservation.

2366.   Jones, Roger. "Barrow Lamination: The North Carolina State Archives Experience," American Archivist, 50:3 (Summer 1987), 390-396. After reviewing documentation on the Barrow laminating process, concludes that the process is sound and appropriate for some material. The lack of documentation for the process is lamented.

2367.   Jones-Eddy, Julie, and Ann H. Zwinger. "In-House Preservation of Early US Government Maps," Government Publications Review, 15:1 (January-February 1988), 41-47. Flattening, deacidifying, and rehousing selected maps from a set of 19th-century bound volumes.

2368.   Jordan, Sonja K. Preservation Activities in Bulgaria: The State of Affairs and Possibilities for Cooperation. Washington, DC:

Commission on Preservation and Access, February 1995. 11p. Report of a visit to Bulgarian libraries in March 1994 to assess the extent and physical state of collections, preservation and conservation needs.

2369.   Joshi, Yashodhara. "Protection of Collections from Damage Caused by Pollution," Proceedings of the Pan-African Conference on the Preservation & Conservation of Library & Archival Materials, Nairobi, Kenya, 21-25 June 1993. The Hague: IFLA, 1995, 71-76. (IFLA Professional Publication 43). Discusses the nature of air pollution and its effect on materials; measures for control; need for further research.

2370.   Joynes, Sara, and Graeme Powell. "The Work of the Australian Joint Copying Project in 1989-90," Archives & Manuscripts (Australian Society of Archivists), 19:1 (May 1991), 51-55. Report on a joint microfilming project to preserve and provide access to public records in the State Library of New South Wales, the National Library of Australia, and the British Public Records Office.

2371.   Joynt, Kevin. "Custom Exhibition Mounts for Books," National Library News, 26:7 (July 1994), 20-24. Clearly presented instructions for construction.

2372.   Jueneman, Frederick B. "From Dust to Dust Again," Research and Development, 33 (October 1991), 34. The difficulties in preserving ancient documents, such as cuneiform tablets, are described.

2373.   Jurgens, Jane. "Overcoming 'The Politics of Paper': The Illinois Regional Archives Depository — Chicago," Perspectives, 31:2 (February 1993), 20-21. Describes the process of creating the repository to preserve "all historic records in Cook County."

2374.   Kadoya, Takashi. "On the Degradation of Paper and Printed Matter," Research Libraries — Yesterday, Today and Tomorrow, ed. William J. Welsh. Westport, CT: Greenwood Press, 1993, 334-353. (Contributions in Librarianship and Information Science, 77). A Japanese study of deterioration of Japanese and Western papers and production methods.

2375.   Kaebnick, Gregory E. "In Search of African American History," Inform, 5:9 (October 1991), 28-29. Describes the Moorland-Spingarn Research Center, Howard University, and its preservation microfilming program.

2376.   Kaebnick, Gregory E. "Rediscovering the Age of Discovery,"
         Inform, 6:7 (July-August 1992), 36-38. Describes a non-standard
         system used to record and index images.

2377.   Kaebnick, Gregory E. "Standards Update: The Big Picture," Inform,
         6:10 (November 1992), 16-21. Review of current standards for
         imaging and terminology.

2378.   Kahn, Miriam. "ALA in LA /1993," Conservation Administration
         News, 57 (April 1994), 22-23. 1994 reports from preservation group
         meetings.

2379.   Kahn, Miriam. Disaster Response and Prevention for Computers and
         Data. Columbus, OH: MBK Consulting, 1994, 1995.
         69p. Loose-leaf manual providing basic information for responding
         to a disaster involving water-damaged computers, hardware and
         software. Covers planning, prevention, and response.

2380.   Kahn, Miriam. First Steps for Handling and Drying Water-Damaged
         Materials. Columbus, OH: MBK Consulting, 1994. 31p.
         (loose-leaf). Illustrated guide to be used with a disaster response
         plan.

2381.   Kahn, Miriam. "Fires, Earthquakes and Floods: How to Prepare
         Your Library and Staff," Online, 18:3 (May 1994), 18-24. Need for
         disaster planning and response; components of plan; case studies.

2382.   Kahn, Miriam. "Mastering Disaster: Emergency Planning for
         Libraries," Library Journal, 118:21 (December 1993),
         73-75. Overview of disaster planning and recovery, insurance
         concerns, sources of information and assistance.

2383.   Kalina, Charles R. "Hearing on Implementation of Permanent Paper
         Use," National Library of Medicine News, 46 (November-December
         1991), 4-6. Summary of hearing on the progress of the
         implementation of the use of permanent paper for biomedical
         literature.

2384.   Kalina, Charles R. "Preservation of Biomedical Literature," Greater
         Northern Regional Medical Library Program Newsletter, part 1, 7:3
         (May-June 1989), 6-8; part 2, 7:4 (July-August 1989), 12-13.
         Description of the National Library of Medicine and its mission to
         preserve "books, periodicals, and other library materials pertinent to
         medicine."

2385.   Kalina, Charles R. "A Tale of Two Papers, Now at Last the Best of
         Times," Among Friends, 6:2 (Autumn 1991), 4-5. Describes how the

National Library of Medicine has addressed its brittle book problem by becoming a strong advocate of the use of permanent, alkaline paper by the publishing industry.

2386. Kalina, Charles. R. Use of Permanent Paper for Biomedical Literature. Bethesda, MD: National Library of Medicine, March 1987. 19p. Summarizes the discussion of a group of publishers, editors, paper manufacturers, and distributors to address the need to produce permanent, acid-free paper.

2387. Kaltwasser, Franz Georg. "Old Books Between the Shredder and Conservation," Book Collector, 41:4 (Winter 1992), 456-476. Considers the future of the book, valued, yet sometimes destroyed, often by librarians, in the name of preservation. Notes a lack of attention to selection for preservation and the problems with current preservation technologies.

2388. Kamba, Angeline S. "Archives and National Development in the Third World," Information Development, 3:2 (1987), 108-113. Discusses the National Archives of Zimbabwe and legislation that directs the use on preservation of archival materials documenting the cultural heritage.

2389. Kaminska, Elizbieta M., and Helen D. Burgess. "The Effects of Mass Deacidification Processes on New and Artificially Aged Modern Papers," National Library News (Canada), 26:7 (July 1994), 11-12. Summary of results evaluating three deacidification processes using new and artificially aged papers.

2390. Kamm, Sue. "For Our Next Disaster — Plan Ahead," Unabashed Librarian, 59:2 (1986), 13. Short note on what was learned about disaster preparedness from the Los Angeles Public Library fire.

2391. Kansas City Area Archivists. Keeping Your Past: A Basic Guide to the Care and Preservation of Personal Papers. Kansas City, KA: Kansas City Area Archivists, 1987. 25p. Basic guide prepared for the general public.

2392. Kansas Library Network Board. Saving the Past to Enrich the Future: A Plan for Preserving Information Resources in Kansas. Topeka, KS: Kansas Library Network Board, 1993. 50p. Report of the Kansas Library Network Board's Preservation Committee to the citizens of Kansas.

2393. Kantor, Paul B. Costs of Microfilm Preservation at Research Libraries: A Study of Four Institutions. Washington, DC: Council on Library Resources, November 1986. 35p. Describes the costs of microfilm processing at the libraries of the University of Chicago, Columbia University, the New York Public Library Research Libraries, and the Library of Congress. Kantor found that one-third of the cost of filming is generated by record keeping and administrative activities, and he suggests that costs can be reduced by 10% through refinement of procedures.

2394.   Kaplan, Hilary A., and Brenda S. Banks. "Archival Preservation: The Teaming of the Crew," American Archivist, 53:2 (Spring 1990), 266-273. Reviews the current state of archival preservation; discusses differences between library and archival preservation.

2395.   Kaplan, Hilary A., Maria Holden, and Kathy Ludwig. "Archives Preservation Resource Review," American Archivist, 54:4 (Fall 1991), 502-544. Annotated bibliography of English-language publications and resources published 1986-1990. Covers general works, environmental concerns, disaster planning, security, and conservation treatments.

2396.   Karl, Gretchen. "Los Angeles Preservation Network," WAAC Newsletter (Western Association for Art Conservation), 10:1 (January 1988), 9. Describes LAPNET, the cooperative library preservation program in the Los Angeles, California, area. Two of its major concerns are disaster planning and recovery.

2397.   Karp, Gary. "Calculating Atmospheric Humidity," Studies in Conservation, 28:1 (February 1983), 24-28. Derivations for the functional relationships between psychometric and barometric atmospheric observations.

2398.   Karren, Susan H. Preserving the Record: Federal Agencies and NARA Reference Practices. Washington, DC: National Archives and Records Administration, 1989. 20p.

2399.   Kasinec, E., and R. H. Davis. "Materials for the Study of Russian/Soviet Art and Architecture," Art Documentation, 10:1 (Spring 1991), 19-22. Discusses the problem of the preservation of 20th-century Russian research materials due to their fragility and their scarcity in the West, resulting in high demand. Addresses the need for access through alternative formats.

2400.   Kastaly, Beatrix. "The Composition of Permanent Papers," Conference on Book and Paper Conservation, 1990. Budapest, Hungary: Technical Association of Paper and Printing Industry/National Szechenyi Library, 1992, 444-449. Describes the effort of the National Szechenyi Library, the Hungarian Paper

Research Institute, and the Diosgyor Papermill to produce newsprint for depository copies of newspapers.

2401. Kastaly, Beatrix. "Preservation and Conservation of Library Materials in Hungary," Conservation Administration News, 41, (April 1990), 1-2, 30. Outlines Hungary's approach to preservation, including physical treatment at the National Library, its preservation microfilming program, and the effort to establish a training program for conservators, conservation technicians, and librarians.

2402. Kastaly, Beatrix. "Restoration Training in Hungary," International Preservation News, 4 (August 1990), 4-5. Describes conservation training efforts in Hungary.

2403. Kastaly, Beatrix. "Survey on the Groundwood Content, Acidity, and State of Book-Papers at the National Szechenyi Library: Experiments and Results in the Production of Permanent Printing Papers in Hungary," Degradácia Archivnych a Kniznicnych Materialov vs Stály a Trvanlivy Papier/Degradation of Archives and Library Materials vs Permanent and Durable Paper for Archives. Bratislava, Slovakia: Slovak National Archives, 1993, 43-49. Report on a survey of the state of deterioration of books and newsprint; initiatives to have permanent papers produced in Hungary.

2404. Kathpalia, Yash Pal. A Model Curriculum for the Training of Specialists in Document Preservation and Restoration, A RAMP Study. Paris: UNESCO, 1984. 27p. (PGI 84\WS\2).

2405. Kathpalia, Yash Pal. "Training in Conservation," Archivum, 34 (1988), 105-112. Reviews training facilities worldwide and the need for trained archival conservators.

2406. Kaufman, Diane. "Building Preservation Awareness" (using visual aids and humor in a two-day demonstration given by the Preservation Unit of Virginia Tech Libraries), College & Research Libraries News, 10 (November 1995), 707-78.

2407. Kearsey, Irene. "Fragile Paper — Other Angles, Other Allies?" Archives & Manuscripts (Australian Society of Archivists), 18:1 (May 1990), 75-88. Review of papermaking process, environmental and health concerns. Notes lack of incentive for manufacturers to improve methods, but that some are changing to the production of alkaline papers. 66 references.

2408. Kecskemeti, C. "Financial Support for Preservation Activities," Preservation of Library Materials, ed. Merrily Smith. New York: Saur, 1987, 3-9. (IFLA Professional Publication 41). Strategy for increasing the resources available for preserving library and archival materials.

2409. Keefe, Laurence E., Jr., and Dennis Inch. The Life of a Photograph. Stoneham, MA: Focal Press, 1984; 2d ed. 1990. 384p. Comprehensive coverage of topics relating to the preservation of photographic materials, from processing of negatives to archival storage of the final print.

2410. Keele, Herbert Charles. Preserving Library Book Theft. Suffolk, England: Access Kreleway, Ltd., 1987. 88p. Handbook on security and theft prevention based on sound management practices and common sense.

2411. Keene, James, and Michael Roper. Planning, Equipping and Staffing a Document Reprographic Service: A RAMP Study With Guidelines. Paris: UNESCO, 1984. 84p. (PG1-84/WS/8).

2412. Keene, Suzanne. "Audits of Care: A Framework for Collections Condition Surveys," Storage. London: United Kingdom Institute for Conservation, 1991, 6-16. Reprinted Care of Collections, ed. Simon Knell. London: Routledge, 1994, 60-82. Describes methodology developed by the Museum of London for assessing the condition of museum collections.

2413. Keene, Suzanne, ed. Managing Conservation. London.: United Kingdom Institute for Conservation, 1990. 31p. Papers from a conference on management issues for conservators.

2414. Kehtonen, M., and T. Reponen. "Everyday Activities and Variations of Fungal Spore Concentration in Indoor Air," International Biodeterioration and Biodegradation, 31 (1993), 35-39.

2415. Kellar, Scott. "Binding Structure and Books of Permanent Research Value," New Library Scene, 6:6 (December 1987), 1-8. History of binding practices with emphasis on commercial library binding in the twentieth century.

2416. Kellar, Scott. "Collections Conservation: An Emerging Perspective," Conservation Administration News, 43 (October 1990), 8-9. Explores the emerging role of the collections conservator in libraries and the collections approach to preservation and treatment.

2417. Kellar, Scott. "Conservation for Romania," Conservation Administration News, 56 (January 1994), 14-15, 36. Report of the author's participation in a project initiated by British book and paper conservators to assist Romanian libraries to stabilize and treat collections.

2418. Kellar, Scott. "DEZ Mass Treatment: Testing for Compliance to Specifications," Abbey Newsletter, 16:7-8 (December 1992), 107. Describes the review and testing procedure to ensure that minimum standards for treatment were met.

2419. Keller, Tom. "Teknakul Corner," The Perfect Vision, 1:1 (1986/87), 42-45. Describes "laser rot," a malfunctioning of laser disks.

2420. Kellerman, L. Suzanne. "Moving Fragile Materials: Shrink-Wrapping at Penn State," Collection Management, 18:1/2 (1993), 117-128. Describes the process used to shrink wrap 47,000 brittle books over a six-month period to move to a distant storage site.

2421. Kelser, Marie. "Judging a Book by Its Covers: Academic Institutions Versus Public Libraries: A Preservation Viewpoint," Archival Products News, 4:4 (Fall 1996), 5-6.

2422. Kemp, Toby. "Disaster Assistance Bibliography: Selected References for Cultural/Historic Facilities," Technology and Conservation, 8:2 (Summer 1983), 25-27.

2423. Kemoni, H. N. "Preservation and Conservation of Archival Materials: The Case of Kenya [Kenya National Archives and Documentation Service]," African Journal of Library and Archival Information Science, 6 (April 1996), 46-51.

2424. Kemper, Robert V. "The Potentials and Problems of Computers," Preserving the Anthropological Record, ed. Sydel Silberman and Nancy J. Parezo. New York: Wenner-Gren Foundation, 1992, 105-117. Addresses the appropriate use of computer technology for preserving the anthropological record; case studies.

2425. Kenjo, Toshiko, Hideo Arai, Toshiaki Suzuki. "Application of Scanning Electron Microscope in the Field of Conservation Science of Cultural Properties," JEOL News (Japanese Electron Optics Instrumentation), 25E:1 (1987), 13-17. Research on ancient "urushi" grounding techniques and foxing of paper; analysis of foxing caused by fungi and iron.

2426. Kenkmaa, E. Knige." Dolguiu Zhizn' [Long Life to Books at the State Library of the Estonian SSR]," Bibliotekar' (USSR), 3 (1988), 48-49.

2427.   Kenna, Stephanie. "The National Manuscripts Conservation Trust," Paper Conservation News, 74 (June 1995), 9. Description of the Trust and its role in preserving manuscript/archive collections through its grants program.

2428.   Kennedy, Nora, and Peter Mustardo. "Current Issues in the Preservation of Photographs," AB Bookman's Weekly (Antiquarian Bookman), 83:17 (April 24, 1989), 1773-1783. Summary article on the problems and issues in photographic preservation, with a discussion of training and the role of the Photographic Materials Group, American Institute for Conservation.

2429.   Kennel, Glenn. "Digital Film Scanning and Recording: The Technology and Practice," SMPTE Journal (Society of Motion Picture and Television Engineers), 103:3 (March 1994), 174-181. Uses the example of Kodak's Cincon Digital Film scanner to illustrate key design components and image quality parameters of digital scanning and recording.

2430.   Kennelly, Tamara. "Restoring the Cracked Mirror," Virginia Librarian, 41 (January/February/March 1995), 14-16. Abridged version in NEDCC News (Northeast Documents Conservation Center), 6:2 (Winter 1996), 1-2. Restoring a photograph in the Virginia Tech archives.

2431.   Kenney, Anne R. "Common Problems, Common Solutions: The Preservation Challenge for Librarians and Archivists," Building on the First Century. Chicago, IL: American Library Association, 1989, 303-305. Suggests that librarians and archivists work together to develop collection-level approaches to preservation, commit resources, and develop a plan of action to preserve the documentary heritage. Paper presented at the 5th National Conference of the Association of College and Research Libraries, Cincinnati, OH, April 5-8, 1989.

2432.   Kenney, Anne R. "Digital-to-Microfilm Conversion: An Interim Preservation Solution," Library Resources and Technical Services, 37:4 (October 1993), 388-401; "Erratum." 38:1 (January 1994), 87-95. Illus. Reviews the project at Cornell University to test the feasibility of using digital image technology to improve access to deteriorating materials.

2433.   Kenney, Anne R. "Factors Influencing Development of CXP," Workshop on Electronic Texts: Proceeding, ed. by James Daly. Washington, DC: Library of Congress, 1992, 44-47.

2434.   Kenney, Anne R. "Fighting Back the Flames," Library Mosaics, 2 (March/April 1991), 13. Pilot Project to Record Deteriorating Books as Digital Images and Produce Copies on Demand.

2435.   Kenney, Anne R. "From Analog to Digital: Preservation Reformatting in a Changing World," Preservation Microfilming: Does It Have a Future? Canberra: National Library of Australia, 1995, 90-106. Defines technology, discusses advantages (confusing preservation with access). Describes Cornell and Yale projects. Believes preservation (refreshment) becomes access in the digital world.

2436.   Kenney, Anne R. "The Role of Digital Technology in the Preservation of Research Library Materials," Preservation of Electronic Formats and Electronic Formats for Preservation. Fort Atkinson, WI: Highsmith Press, 1992, 1-22. Describes the Cornell/Xerox project to explore the use of optical media for preservation and access.

2437.   Kenney, Anne R., and Stephen Chapman. Tutorial: Digital Resolution Requirements for Replacing Text-Based Material: Methods for Benchmarking Image Quality. Washington, DC: Commission on Preservation and Access, April 1995. 22p. Guide to estimating the resolution necessary to produce desired image quality in scanned documents; "Quality Index Formulas" to digitize scanning of black-and-white images, which can be modified to produce grayscale scanning.

2438.   Kenney, Anne R., and Paul Conway. "From Analog to Digital: Extending the Preservation Tool Kit," Digital Imaging Technology for Preservation, ed. Nancy E. Elkington. Mountain View, CA: Research Libraries Group, 1994, 11-24. Kenney focuses on technology while Conway focuses on the need to identify users and needs.

2439.   Kenney, Anne R., and Stephen Chapman. Digital Imaging for Libraries and Archives. Ithaca, NY: Cornell University, 1996. 207p.

2440.   Kenney, Anne R., and Stephen Chapman. Digital Resolution Requirements for Replacing Text-Based Materials: Methods for Benchmarking Image Quality. Washington, DC: Commission on Preservation and Access, April 1995. 22p.

2441.   Kenney, Anne R., with Michael A. Friedman and Sue A. Poucher. Preserving Archival Material Through Digital Technology: A Cooperative Demonstration Project (October 1992-March 1993).

Ithaca, NY: Cornell University Library, Department of Preservation
and Conservation, 1993. 19p.

2442. Kenney, Anne R., and Lynne K. Personius. The Cornell/Xerox/
Commission on Preservation and Access Joint Study in Digital
Preservation Report: Phase I (January 1990-December 1991):
Digital Capture, Paper Facsimiles, and Network Access.
Washington, DC: Commission on Preservation and Access, 1992.
47p.; Supplements, individual pagination. Also in Electronic
Library, 10 (July 1992) 155-163. Reports on the Cornell
University/Xerox project investigating the use of digital technology
to preserve deteriorating books. Includes cost studies.

2443. Kenney, Anne R., and Lynne K. Personius. "Digital Imaging for
Library Preservation and Access: Technology Meets a Need,"
IAALD Quarterly (International Association of Agricultural
Information Specialists), 37:1-2 (1992), 91-96. Briefly describes the
joint Cornell/Xerox project to test imaging technology for recording
brittle books to reproduction on demand of high-quality paper
facsimiles, and to allow browsing at a computer terminal.

2444. Kenney, Anne R., and Lynne K. Personius. "Digital Preservation: A
Joint Study," Studies in Multimedia, ed. Susan Stone and Michael
Buckland. Medford, NJ: ASIS/Learned Information, 1992,
47-52. Explores digital technology for reformatting for preservation;
describes Cornell/Xerox pilot project. Paper presented at the 1991
Mid-year Meeting of the American Society for Information Science.

2445. Kenney, Anne R., and Lynne K. Personius. "The Future of Digital
Preservation," Advances in Preservation and Access. Vol. 1.
Westport, CT: Meckler, 1992, 195-212. Describes the project at
Cornell University "to test the feasibility of using digital technology
to preserve and improve access to deteriorating library materials."

2446. Kenney, Anne R., and Lynne K. Personius. A Testbed for Advancing
the Role of Digital Technologies for Library Preservation and
Access. Washington, DC: Commission on Preservation and Access,
October 1993. 113p. A four-page report on the project appeared in
the Commission on Preservation and Access Newsletter 63 (January
1994).

2447. Kenney, Anne R., and Lynne K. Personius. "Update on Digital
Technologies," Commission on Preservation and Access Newsletter,
40 (November/December 1991), 1-6. Also in Microform Review,
21:1 (Winter 1992), 25-29. Reports on the Cornell/Xerox project;
overview of associated technology; preliminary comparisons
between scanning and microfilming in cost and production rate.

2448. Kenny, Geraldine, ed. A Reading Guide to the Preservation of Library Collections. London: Library Association Publishing, 1991. 106p. The introduction by F.W. Ratcliffe presents a succinct history of preservation activities in the United Kingdom.

2449. Kent, Scott. "Binder Breakdown in Back-Coated Tapes," Recording Engineer/Producer, 19 (July 1988), 80-81. Briefly describes the cause of the problem; notes the cure is "time-consuming and somewhat risky for the inexperienced," (81) and is not permanent.

2450. Kenworthy, Mary Anne, Eleanor M. King, Mary Elizabeth Ruwell, and Trudy Van Houton. Preserving Field Records: Archival Techniques for Archaeologists and Anthropologists. Philadelphia, PA: University Museum, University of Pennsylvania, 1985. 102p. Manual for archaeologists and anthropologists on techniques for preserving their field records. Covers paper records, film and video, sound recordings, and machine-readable records.

2451. Ker, Niel. "Gold Toning the Domesday Book Gives Better Than Archival Permanence," Microform Review, 16:4 (Fall 1987), 300-303. Brief description of the preservation microfilming of the Domesday Book.

2452. Kerns, Ruth B. "A Positive Approach to Negatives: Photographs Via Microfilm Technology," American Archivist, 51:1/2 (Winter/Spring 1988), 111-114. Case study of the conversion of deteriorating photo-negatives from the Library of Congress Federal Theater Project into microfilm.

2453. Kesse, Erich J. "Reproduction of Library Materials," Guide to Technical Services Resources, ed. Peggy Johnson. Chicago, IL: American Library Association, 1994, 196-213.

2454. Kesse, Erich J. "The Reproduction of Library Materials in 1989," Library Resources and Technical Services, 34:4 (October 1990), 467-475. Review of the literature.

2455. Kesse, Erich. Survey of Micropublishers: A Report. Washington, DC: Commission on Preservation and Access, October 1992. 78p. with data. Results of a survey to determine how commercial microfilmers produce and store microfilm; recommends that the preservation community take a firm stand about requirements.

2456. Kesse, Erich J. Written Documentation: Forms Used in the Preservation of Archival and Library Materials. Gainesville, FL: University of Florida Libraries, 1989. 137p.

2457. Kesse, Erich, Richard Gilbert, and Michelle Bailey. Written Documentation: Forms Used in the Preservation of Archival and Library Materials. Gainesville, FL: University of Florida Libraries, 1989. 137p. Compilation of forms used in preservation management and conservation by a selection of libraries.

2458. Ketelaar, Eric. "Exploitation of New Archival Materials," Archivum, 35 (1989), 27p. Keynote address, 11th International Congress on Archives, Paris, France, 1988. Addresses the challenge of collecting, organizing, preserving, and "exploiting," or providing access to machine-readable records; notes the difficulty in providing bibliographic control of materials that are impermanent, mutable.

2459. Keyes, Keiko Mizushima. "Some Practical Methods for the Treatment with Moisture of Moisture-Sensitive Works on Paper," Conservation of Historic and Artistic Works on Paper. Ottawa: Canadian Conservation Institute, 1994, 99-107. (Symposium 88). Discusses successful moisture treatments of moisture-sensitive objects, including cleaning, backing removal, and acid reduction.

2460. Khan, M. M. "General Rules for Care and Handling of Library Materials," Lucknow Librarian, 16:2 (1984), 53-57. Rules for staff and users; improved methods for the preservation of library materials.

2461. Khan, Shahabuddin. "Preservation of Library Materials and Training: Situation in Bangladesh," Planning Modernization and Preservation Programmes for South Asia Libraries, ed. Kalpana Dasgupta. Calcutta, India: National Library, 1992, 142-152. Describes the beginning of a preservation program, concerns, objectives.

2462. Khan, Yasmin. "A Treatment of a Publisher's Paste-Up," Paper Conservator, 18 (1994), 71-76. Conservation treatment, requiring that inserts should be made accessible.

2463. Khayundi, Festus E. "An Overview of Preservation & Conservation Programs in Eastern & Southern Africa," Proceedings of the Pan-African Conference on the Preservation & Conservation of Library & Archival Materials, Nairobi, Kenya, 21-25 June 1993. The Hague: IFLA, 1995, 30-36. (IFLA Professional Publication 43). Blames lack of preservation of records on colonial administrations (odd). Presents results of a survey of repositories and conditions; suggests what can be done. Notes need for policy documents, and lack of trained personnel and information.

2464.   Kidd, Harry B. "Micrographics Standards in Libraries," Microform Review, 13:2 (Spring 1994), 93-102. Describes the role of the Association for Information and Image Management in the development and sponsorship of standards applicable to libraries.

2465.   Kidd, Stewart. "First Principles of Disaster Planning for Museums and Galleries," SSCR Journal (Scottish Society for Conservation and Restoration), 3:4 (November 1992), 10-13.

2466.   Kidd, Yvonne. "AIIM Tackles Legality and Performance Standards Issues Affecting Digitally Stored Information," Inform (June 1991), 8-9. Discusses AIIM's attempt to address the issue of legal admissibility of optical disks and other digital media. The task force on legal admissibility was formed to focus on legal admissibility and the development of standards "for the legal acceptance of information storage technology systems."

2467.   Kimball, Margarte. "Broken Promises: What the Disaster Handbooks Don't Tell You," Preservation Papers of the 1990 SAA Annual Conference, comp. Karen Garlick. Chicago: Society of American Archivists, 1991, 71-76. Description of events following the 1989 earthquake at Stanford University. Notes the need to plan how much pace is needed for relocation, if necessary.

2468.   Kimmage, Dennis. "Scholar in USSR Faults 'Upside-Down Glasnost' After Library Fire Destroying 1/2 million Books," American Libraries, 19:5 (May 1988), 332-333. Brief note on Russian scholars' response to the Academy of Sciences fire, Leningrad.

2469.   Kimmage, Dennis A., ed. Russian Libraries in Transition: An Anthology of Glasnost Literature. Jefferson, NC: McFarland, 1992. 214p. Anthology of articles that appeared in Soviet journals and newspapers between 1988 and 1991, drawing attention to the plight of libraries and their collections in a time of transition.

2470.   Kindler, W. A. Jr. "Collection Preservation: The Practical Choices," Paper Preservation: Current Issues and Recent Developments. Atlanta, GA: TAPPI Press, 1990, 35-37. Considers the advantages and problems of paper.

2471.   King, Ed. "British Library Book Preservation Process," Library Conservation News, 35 (April 1992), 1-2. Describes the development of the process, feasibility, and testing studies.

2472.   King, Ed. "New Hope for Decayed Paper: An Update," Library Conservation News, 25 (October 1989), 2-3. Update on the graft copolymerization process to strengthen paper.

2473.   King, Richard G. Jr. "Deterioration of Book Paper: Results of Physical and Chemical Testing of the Paper in 22,800 Monographs from the Collections of the University of California Libraries," Advances in Library Administration and Organization, 2 (1983), 119-149. Reports the results of a system-wide study to test the paper in selected monographs; demonstrates that there is no easy way to identify or predict deterioration in books.

2474.   King, Steve. "Building for Conservation: Appropriate Design for Environmental Control in the Tropics." In Cultural Heritage in Asia and the Pacific: Conservation & Policy: Proceedings of a Symposium, Honolulu, HI, September 1991, ed. Maragret G. H. MacLean. Marina del Rey, CA: Getty Conservation Institute, 1993. 77-93. Includes discussion on passive environmental control strategies in hot and humid regions, suggestions offered for optimizing mechanical air conditioning and dehumidifying display cases.

2475.   Kingsley, Jane, and Linda Warden. "The Mellon Microfilming Project: The James Beort Simonds Collection," Library Conservation News, 48 (Autumn 1995), 4-6. Description of project: materials chosen for filming, preparation, technical aspects of filming, lessons learned. "This project has taught us that it is more realistic to be pessimistic, rather than optimistic, when estimating time schedules." (6)

2476.   Kinsolver, John M. "Illustrated Guide to Common Pests in Museums," A Guide to Museum Pest Control, ed. Lynda A. Zycherman. Washington, DC: Foundation of the American Institute for Conservation of Historic and Artistic Works and Association of Systematics Collections, 1988, 53-81. Describes and illustrated the most common destructive insects found in museums.

2477.   Kireyera, Vilena. "Destruction of the Binding Media of the Green Paint Layer in an Eleventh Century Greek Manuscript," Restaurator, 16:2 (1995), 86-92. Investigation of the cause of a decomposed paint layer in a C11 Byzantine ms., cause was the carbohydrate binder.

2478.   Kirkpatrick, Brett A. "Preservation Activities and Needs in U.S. Biomedical Libraries," Bulletin of the Medical Library Association, 77:3 (July 1989), 276-277. Discusses the result of a survey of biomedical librarians to assess status of preservation activities.

2479. Kirkpatrick, John T. "Explaining Crime and Disorder in Libraries," Library Trends, 33:1 (Summer 1984), 13-28. Discusses the nature of crime, crime in the library, reasons for it, and a behavioral approach to resolving it.

2480. Kirtley, Toby. "Setting Up a Preservation Microfilming Programme," Library Conservation News, 36 (July 1992), 1-2. Describes the implementation of a preservation microfilming program at the Bodleian Library, Oxford.

2481. Kishore, Ranbir. "Need of Creating Awareness for Preservation and Dissemination of Working Knowledge for Conserving Documentary Heritage: Conducting Workshops at Different Locations in India," Planning Modernization and Preservation Programmes for South Asian Libraries. ed. Kalpana Dasgupta. Calcutta, India: National Library, 1992, 121-123. Briefly describes need for training in preservation and conservation and curricula for methodology and treatment.

2482. Kitching, Christopher. Archive Buildings in the United Kingdom, 1977-1992. London: Her Majesty's Stationers Office, 1993. 144p. Prepared by the Royal Commission on Historical Manuscripts to review and promote and assist the proper storage and preservation of manuscripts and records.

2483. Kittle, Paul W. "Effects on Media Materials of Storage in Proximity to a Magnetic Resonance Imaging Scanner," Bulletin of the Medical Library Association, 77:1 (January 1989), 67-69. Brief report of a study of the hazards of magnetic fields to media materials; references.

2484. Kivia, Ivarature. "Preserving Library Materials in the South Pacific," Information Development, 10 (December 1994), 256-262.

2485. Klapproth, Judy. "A Book Cook-Book," Unabashed Librarian, 59:2 (1986), 3-4. How to reglue books using a microwave oven; destructive.

2486. Klasinc, Peter. "The Use of Neutral Paper for the Archive Containers," Degradácia Archivnych a Knizniznych Materialov vs Stály a Trvnalivy Papier/Degradation of Archives and Library Materials vs Permanent and Durable Papers for Archives. Bratislava, Slovakia: Slovak National Archives, 1993, 20-25. Discussion of archival boxes to protect documents.

2487. Klason, C., J. Kubat, A. Mathiasson, M. Qvist, and H. R. Skov. "Embrittlement of Cellulose Using Prehydrolysis," Cellulose

Chemistry and Technology, 23:2 (March/April 1989),
131-148. Experimental study to quantify the degree of embrittlement
imparted to bleached and unbleached cellulose fibers, including
newsprint, by a hydrolytic treatment with aqueous solutions of
mineral and organic acids.

2488. Klee, Eleanore. "Knot-Tack Sewing in the 15th Century," trans.
Didi Dorsey, Binder's Guild Newsletter, 12:6 (September 1989),
7-13. Description of an early binding technique.

2489. Klein, Christine DeBow. Jewelry History: A Core Bibliography in
Support of Preservation. Washington, DC: Commission on
Preservation and Access, February 1992. 41p. Bibliography of
books identified as the core literature of jewelry history, availability,
and condition.

2490. Klein, Larry. "The Care and Storage of Videocassettes," Stereo
Review, 51:8 (August 1986), 100-101. Care of videocassettes in
home collections.

2491. Klein, Larry. "Tape Expectations," High Fidelity, 38:3 (March
1988), 17. Practical discussion of videocassette care, handling, and
storage.

2492. Kleinrichert, Denis. "Personal and Public Aspects of a Disaster."
Disaster Recovery Journal, 9:1 (January-March 1996), 32-36.
Addressing need to have personnel needs and welfare addressed for
effective disaster recovery; reviews elements of personal / home
disaster planning; community factors and recovery.

2493. Klimley, Susan. "Geologic Maps in Books and Serials: A Hidden
Preservation Problem," Proceedings of the Geoscience Information
Society, 17th Meeting, ed. Regina A. Brown. Alexandria, VA:
Geoscience Information Society, 1984, 136-143. Presents the results
of a preservation survey of materials in the Columbia University
Geology Library, noting that inserts present special problems in
rebinding and microfilming.

2494. Kline, Laura S. "The ARL OMS Preservation Self-Study and Its
Implications for Archivists," Preservation Papers of the SAA Annual
Conference, comp. Karen Garlick. Chicago: Society of American
Archives, 1991, 83-85. Discusses the program and its goals;
describes its implementation at Iowa State University in 1984; some
negative impact on the archives.

Bibliography

2495. Knell, Simen, ed. Care of Collections. London: Routledge, 1994. 282p. Reader, collection of articles with a museum focus on collection management environment.

2496. Kniffel, Leonard. "LC, National Park Service Battle Over Gettysburg Address," American Libraries, 25 (April 1994), 296+.

2497. Knight, Nancy H. "Security Systems," American Library Association Yearbook, 1984. Vol. 9. Chicago, IL: American Library Association, 1984, 261-263. Review of security trends: guidelines emerging from the Oberlin Conference on theft, 1983; mutilation studies and data; security systems.

2498. Koch, Janet, and Barbara Irwin. "Conservation at the New Jersey Historical Society," Conservation Administration News, 22 (July 1985), 7, 21-22. Describes the Society's efforts during the past 20 years to preserve its collections through planning for preservation and conservation treatments when needed.

2499. Koch, Mogens S.,et al., eds. Research Techniques in Photographic Conservation: Proceeding of the Conference in Copenhagen, 14-19 May 1995. Copenhagen: Royal Danish Academy of Fine Arts, [1996]. 116p.

2500. Koestler, Robert J. "Practical Application of Nitrogen and Argon Fumigation Procedures for Insect Control in Museum Objects," Preprints, 2d International Conference on Biodeterioration of Cultural Property, Tokyo, Japan, September 1992, 96-98. Discusses the practical implementation of suffocation procedures, including tent enclosures, mini-fumigation bubbles, and pouch or bag systems.

2501. Koestler, Robert J., N. Indicator, and B. Fiske. "Characteristization of Japanese Papers Using Energy-Dispersive X-ray Spectrometry," Restaurator, 13:2 (1992), 58-77. The extent to which analytical results can be used to identify papers.

2502. Koestler, Robert J., and T. M. Mathews. "Application of Anoxic Treatment for Insect Control in Manuscripts of the Library of Megisti Laura, Mount Athos, Greece," Environnement et Conservation de l'Écrit, de l'Image, et de Son. Paris: ARSAG, 1994, 59-62. (Actes des Deuxièmes Journées Internationales d'Études de l'ARSAG, 16 au 20 Mai, 1994). Describes a treatment using argon gas to eradicate insects in parchment and paper manuscripts without causing damage.

2503. Koestler, Robert J., and Edward D. Santoro. "Biodeterioration in Museums - Observations," Biodeterioration Research 3. New York: Plenum Press, 1990, 505-509. Brief overview of the problem of deterioration and a basic approach to solutions; suggestions for further investigation.

2504. Kofler, Brigit. Legal Questions Facing Audiovisual Archives. Paris: United Nations Educational, Scientific and Cultural Organization (UNESCO), 1991. 71p.

2505. Koga, James S. "Security and the PC-Based Public Workstation," Online, 14:5 (September 1990), 63-70. Explores security concerns and preventive measures for PC-based public access workstations.

2506. Koncz, Pal. "The Cleaning and Conservation of Metallic Fittings and Finishes on Bookbindings," Conference on Book and Paper Conservation, 1990. Budapest, Hungary: Technical Association of Paper and Printing Industry/National Szechenyi Library, 1992, 197-202. Description of cleaning techniques.

2507. Koolik, Marilyn Gold. "The Preservation of Israel's Moving-Image Documents: A Look to the Future," Documenting Israel, ed. Charles Berlin. Cambridge, MA: Harvard College Library, 1995, 89-108. A survey of the moving image material being produced in Israel today and its preservation from a legal point of view. Proceedings of a conference held at Harvard, May 10-12, 1995.

2508. Koops, R. L. "Archive Conservation: A Review of Growing Problems and New Solutions," Conservation, Training, Materials and Techniques: Latest Developments. Preprints ... Amsterdam, 1992. Restoration '92: London: United Kingdom Institute for Conservation, 1992, 14-19. Describes the development of archives conservation in the Netherlands, problems and solutions.

2509. Koplowitz, Bradford. "WHC Establishes a Preservation Laboratory," Conservation Administration News, 53 (April 1993), 1-2, 7. Describes the creation of a treatment facility for the Western History Collection, University of Oklahoma, which treats materials from all branches of the library system.

2510. Kopp, Leslie Hansen, ed. Dance Archives: A Practical Manual for Documenting & Preserving the Ephemeral Art. Lee, MA: Preserve, Inc., 1995. Loose-leaf notebook. Includes Afterimage, 1:1 - 2:3. A practical manual on organizing, housing, and preserving dance documentation in all media, including video and film, paper, photographs, oral and video histories. Glossary, bibliography.

2511.   Kopperl, David F., and Thomas J. Huttemann, Jr. "Effect of Residual Thiosulfate Ion on the Image Stability of Microfilms," Journal of Imaging Technology (August 1986), 173-180. Report on accelerated aging tests indicating that even at high residual thiosulfate levels, temperature, and relative humidity, there is no noticeable image deterioration of silver halide microfilm.

2512.   Kopperl, D. F., and C. C. Bard. "Freeze/Thaw Cycling of Motion Picture Film," SMPTE Journal (Society of Motion Picture and Television Engineers), 94:8 (August 1983), 826-827. Experimental results and physical considerations are cited that should alleviate concerns about the freeze/thaw cycling of processed motion-picture film.

2513.   Kopperl, D. F., R. R. Goetting, T. J. Huttemann, Jr., and M. L. Schickling. "Use of Arrhennius Testing to Evaluate the Thiosulfate Tolerance of Black-and-White Aerial Films," Journal of Imaging Science and Technology, 36 (January/February 1992), 42-45. Three experiments to determine the tolerance of black-and-white aerial films to residual thiosulfate ions; separate limits recommended for medium-term, long-term, and archival storage requirements.

2514.   Koretsky, Elaine. "The Coloring of Pulp in Alkaline Papermaking," Alkaline Paper Advocate, 1:4 (October 1988), 34-35. A hand papermaker describes how she identified a technique to stabilize colors in alkaline paper.

2515.   Korey, Marie E. "The Oberlin Conference on Theft," Rare Books 1983-84: Trends, Collections, Sources, ed. Alice Schreyer. New York: R. R. Bowker, 1984, 129-132. A brief summary of the conference.

2516.   Körmendy, Lazos, ed. Manual of Archival Reprography. New York: Saur, 1989. 223p. (ICA Handbook Series, 5). General manual on microfilming for archivists.

2517.   Koster, Chris. "Theft and Loss from U.K. Libraries: A Public Librarian's View," Library Conservation News, 39 (April 1993), 1-2. Reaction to a report prepared by the Home Office Police Research group; notes theft is caused by users and security systems are necessary, with legal enforcement of fines.

2518.   Kotelnikova, Natalia Y. "IFLA Workshop on the Preservation of Maps and Other Spatial Information, Moscow, 26 September - 1 October 1993," IFLA Journal (International Federation of Library Associations and Institutions), 20:1 (1994), 83-85.

2519. Kouris, Michael, ed. The Dictionary of Paper, 5th ed. Atlanta, GA: Tappi Press, 1996. 450p. Defines over 5,300 terms commonly used in the pulp and paper industry.

2520. Kovacic, Ellen Siegel, and Laurel Sturman Wolfson. "Moldbusters!!" Conservation Administration News, 50 (July 1992), 6-7, 28. Describes the outbreak, treatment, and analysis of the cause of an outbreak of mold at the Hebrew Union College, Cincinnati, OH.

2521. Kovacs, Beatrice. "Preservation of Materials in Science and Technology Libraries," Preservation and Conservation of Sci-Tech Materials. New York: Haworth Press, 1987, 3-13. Summary of current preservation activities and a review of the literature.

2522. Kowalik, R. "Microbiodeterioration of Library Materials, Part 2: Chapters 5-9: Microbiodecomposition of Auxiliary Materials," Restaurator, 6:1/2 (1984), 61-115.

2523. Kozak, John J,. and Richard E. Spatz. "Deacidification of Paper by the Bookkeeper Process," Paper Preservation: Current Issues and Recent Developments. Atlanta, GA: TAPPI Press, 1990, 129-132. Describes the process. Paper presented at the 1988 Paper Preservation Symposium.

2524. Kraft, Nancy. "The Iowa Cooperative Preservation Consortium," Archival Products News, 2:1 (Spring 1994), 1, 4. How the Consortium proved its effectiveness in the 1993 floods; initiatives for disaster planning and recovery.

2525. Kraft, Nancy. "Tips on Protective Enclosures for Pamphlets," Archival Product News, 4:2 (Spring 1996), 3. Ten tips for preserving documents and memorabilia.

2526. Kraft, Nancy, and Ivan Hanthron. "Tips on Preserving Your Documents," Archival Product News, 3:4 (Fall 1995), 4. Six helpful tips for preserving documents and memorabilia, including environment, storage, copies. Prepared for Iowa libraries and distributed through the Iowa Cooperative Preservation Consortium (ICPC).

2527. Kraner, Thomas. "Passing the Acid Test," Publishers Weekly, (August 19, 1996), 28-29. Have high paper prices helped the recycled and acid-free markets. One study say yes and no.

2528.   Krause, F.   "Considerations for Interlibrary Loan in the German Democratic Republic," Liber Bulletin (Ligue des Bibliothèques Européennes de Recherche), 34 (1989), 67-70. Discusses what materials should or should not be loaned, from a preservation viewpoint.

2529.   Krause, Peter. "Preservation of Autochrome Plates in the Collection of the National Geographic Society," Journal of Imaging Science, 29:5 (1985), 182. Case study.

2530.   Krause, Peter. "How to Care for Vintage Photos," Historic Preservation, 39:2 (March-April 1987), 14-16. Discusses the instability of albumen prints, storage conditions, and acceptable restoration treatments.

2531.   Krause, Peter. "Properties and Stability of Color Photographs," Conservation in Archives. Paris: International Council on Archives, 1989, 129-135. Overview of the properties of historic and contemporary color photographic materials; how factors such as storage environment, processing procedures, and inherent properties influence stability. Paper presented at Symposium 88, Ottawa, Canada, May 1988.

2532.   Krill, John. "Paper's Presence," Winterthur Newsletter, 29:1 (Spring 1983), 5-7. Traces the technical development of papermaking and the problems caused; suggests how paper degradation can be retarded; discusses repair and conservation.

2533.   Krist, Gabriela, et al. Bibliography: Theses, Dissertations, Research Reports in Conservation. 2d ed. Rome: International Centre for the Study of the Preservation and the Restoration of Cultural Property (ICCROM), 1990. 282p. Compilation of over 3,550 titles from 74 training institutions in 20 countries, arranged by country, institution, date.

2534.   Kruger, Betsy. "Automating Preservation Information in RLIN," Library Resources and Technical Services, 32:2 (April 1988), 116-126. Describes the efforts of the Research Library Group, through the Research Libraries Information Network (RLIN), to support cooperative and individual preservation efforts.

2535.   Krummel, D. F. "Kepler and His Custody: Scholarship and Conservation Policy," Conserving and Preserving Library Materials, ed. Kathryn L. and William T. Henderson. Urbana-Champaign: University of Illinois Graduate School of Library and Information Science, 1983, 165-180. (Allerton Park Institute, 27). Discussion of preservation and access; what is preserved and what will be made available, and to whom.

2536. Kruth, Leslie M. "A Survey of Recent Scientific Research Which Has Caused a Re-evaluation of Commonly Used Practices in Book and Paper Conservation," Book and Paper Annual, 7 (1988), 30-39; reprinted in part, "Paper Conservation Update: Bleaching and Fumigation," Abbey Newsletter, 13:5 (1989), 90-92. Changing and evolving approaches to the question of bleaching and fumigation in conservation.

2537. Kuak, Sim Joo. "The Micrographic Programme at the University of Malaya Library," Kekal Abadi, 8:3 (September 1989), 1-5. Describes the preservation microfilming program at the University of Malaya, including local newspapers, rare books, and Malayan manuscripts.

2538. Kuflic, Louise. "Decisions in Conservation and Preservation in the Conservation Laboratory," Conserving and Preserving Library Materials, ed. Kathryn L. and William T. Henderson. Urbana-Champaign: University of Illinois Graduate School of Library and Information Science, 1983, 135-146. Describes the role of the conservator and relationship with clients.

2539. Kuiper, John B. "Film Preservation at George Eastman House," Image, 26:4 (December 1983), 21-24. Describes the copying of nitrate onto acetate film for preservation, with originals stored in special vaults.

2540. Kuiper, John B. "Preserving Our Moving Image: A Conspiracy of Facts," Conservation Administration News, 44 (January 1991), 4-5, 29-30. Describes efforts to preserve our heritage of film and video and the role that film archivists are playing.

2541. KuKubo, Robert J. "A Review of Areas of Actual & Potential Co-Operation in Preservation & Conservation Efforts in Southern Africa," Proceedings of the Pan-African Conference on the Preservation & Conservation of Library & Archival Materials, Nairobi, Kenya, 21-25 June, 1993. The Hague: IFLA, 1995, 157-162. (IFLA Professional Publication 43). Outlines actual and potential areas of cooperation, constraints, and enhancements.

2542. Kula, Sam. Archival Appraisal of Moving Images: A RAMP Study with Guidelines. Paris: UNESCO, 1983. 134p. (PG1-83/WS/18).

2543. Kula, Sam. "Film Archives at the Centenary of Film," Archivaria, 40 (Fall 1995), 210-225.

2544.   Kulka, Edward. Archival Enclosures: A Guide. Ottawa: Canadian Council of Archives, 1995. 68p. Summarizes and interprets existing standards, specifications, and recommendations for archival storage materials and list of suppliers.

2545.   Kusack, James M. "Facility Evaluation in Libraries: A Strategy and Methodology for Library Managers," Library Administration & Management, 7:2 (Spring 1993), 107-111. Describes the process of post occupancy evaluation (POE) as it can be applied to library buildings, suggests evaluation methods, and provides a planning outline.

2546.   Kwater, Elizabeth. "Preservation Issues: How to Achieve More With Less," Acquisitions 91, ed. David C. Genaway. Canfield, OH: Genaway and Associates, 1991, 169-187. Overview of library preservation within the context of collection management; defines terms; summary of preservation problems and possible solutions.

2547.   Kyle, Hedi. "The Book as Spine," Ampersand, 11:3 (Autumn 1991), 12-15. Illustrated study of book construction with comparison to the human body.

2548.   Kyle, Hedi. "Conservator and Book Artist: Observations and Personal History," New Bookbinder, 11 (1991), 67-77. Discusses importance of book preservation in the face of advancing computer technology; role of the international book conservation community and the author's personal history and role in book conservation.

2549.   Kyle, Hedi, with Nelly Balloffet, Judith Reed, and Virginia Wisniewski-Klett. Library Materials Preservation Manual: Practical Methods for Preserving Books, Pamphlets, and Other Printed Materials. Bronxville, NY: Nicholas T. Smith, 1983. 160p. Manual of basic repairs that can be done in-house with training.

2550.   Kyle, Hedi. "Preservation Enclosures," Guild of Bookworkers Journal, 30:1 (Spring 1992), 17-33. Instructions for protective enclosures for books and documents.

2551.   Laberge, Danielle. "Information, Knowledge and Rights: The Preservation of Archives as a Political and Social Issue," Archivaria, 25 (Winter 1987-88), 44-50. Describes the nature of information, its use and misuse, emphasizing the archivist's need to preserve records for the future.

2552.   LaFleur, Frances. "The Preservation of Chinese Materials at Columbia University," Conservation Administration News, 36 (January 1988), 8-9.

2553. Lafontaine, R. H. "Silica gel/Le gel de Silice," Canadian Conservation Institute Technical Bulletin, 10 (October 1984), 1-17. The purpose of this technical bulletin is to explain the use of silica gel, how it controls relative humidity, and how it is conditioned for use and maintained.

2554. Lal, Avinashi. "Preservation of Library Materials in Original Format: Policy and Perspective," Planning, Modernization and Preservation Programmes for South Asian Libraries, ed. Kalpana Dasgupta. Calcutta, India: National Library, 1992, 22-28. Discusses and defines original format, print and non-print, and importance of their preservation. Describes technologies for preservation: deacidification, restoration, photo copying, electronic formats.

2555. Lamb, Robert S. II, Comprehensive Academic Library Preservation and Conservation Activities Survey for Fiscal Year 1988-1989. Terre Haute, IN: Indiana State University Library, 1989. 95p. (ERIC ED326224). Presents results of a survey designed to obtain information on preservation and conservation policies and procedures of 18 academic libraries in Illinois, Indiana, and Ohio.

2556. Lamb, Robert S. II, "Library Preservation Survey," Conservation Administration News, 45 (April 1991), 4-5. The results of a survey, undertaken in 1988, of preservation and conservation efforts in 18 libraries in Indiana, Illinois, and Ohio.

2557. Lamb, Robert Scott. "Sins of Omission - Indiana's Deteriorating Book Collections," Indiana Libraries, 6:1 (1986), 52-55. Scope of the brittle book problem and implications for the citizens of Indiana; solutions are suggested and a state wide approach to preservation is recommended.

2558. Lambert, Frank L., Vinod Daniel, and Frank D. Preusser. "The Rate of Absorption of Oxygen by Ageless [TM]: The Utility of an Oxygen Scavenger in Sealed Cases," Studies in Conservation, 37:4 (November 1992), 267-274. The kinetics of the reaction of Ageless with oxygen were studied; its usefulness as an oxygen scavenger is discussed.

2559. Lamolinara, Guy. "Conserving History: LC and Antiquities Authority Join on Scroll Project," LC Information Bulletin (Library of Congress), 52:8 (April 19, 1993), 164-166. Description of the preparation by conservators for the exhibition of fragile papyrus fragments.

2560.   Lange, Holley, and Jean B. Winkler. "Preservation and Maintenance of Electronic and Optical Data," Library Hi Tech Bibliography, 6 (1991), 139-150.

2561.   Langlois, Juan C. "A Fragile Heritage," Courier, 5 (May 1989), 5. Notes difficulty and challenge of preserving original manuscripts.

2562.   Lankford, Mary D. "Some Observations on Book Preservation," School Library Journal, 36:11 (November 1990), 27-30. Cites problems in preserving a wide variety of school library materials; offers some solutions for protection and preservation.

2563.   Lape, Laura G. "A Balancing Act: Copyright in the Electronic Network Environment," Safeguarding Electronic Information, ed. Jana Vorleys. Jefferson, NC: McFarland, 1996, 34-52. Explores copyright and the network environment: policies and copyright law; copyright doctrine of fixation as it applies to networks; public access to works; i.e. "fair use."

2564.   LaRose, Michele. "Conservation Planning and Programs," Conservation in Archives. Paris: International Council on Archives, 1989, 297-308. Presents guidelines for developing and implementing an institutional preservation program. Paper presented at an international symposium, Ottawa, Canada, 1988.

2565.   Larsen, A. Dean. "Preservation and Materials Processing," Library Technical Services: Operations and Management, ed. Irene P. Godden. New York: Academic Press, 1984, 195-247. (Library and Information Science Series). Overview of preservation management and responsibilities, with citations from the literature. Covers organization, binding and repairs, physical environment, disasters and disaster planning, insurance, security, photoduplication and microfilming, weeding and storage, good processing and housekeeping procedures, and current activity in the field. Bibliography.

2566.   Larsen, A. Dean. "Preservation at the Brigham Young University Library," The Library Preservation Program: Models, Priorities, Possibilities, ed. Jan Merrill-Oldham and Merrily Smith. Chicago, IL: American Library Association, 1985, 21-26. Case study of a model program.

2567.   Larsen, A. Dean, and Randy S. Silverman. "Preservation," Library Technical Services. 2d ed. New York: Academic Press, 1991, 205-269. Comprehensive overview of preservation management and issues of the 1990s. Bibliography.

2568. Larsen, John C., ed. Museum Librarianship. Hamden, CT: Shoe String Press, 1985. 136p. Includes chapters on collection preservation and maintenance.

2569. Larsen, Rene. "Evaluation of the Correlation Between Natural and Artificial Aging of Vegetable Tanned Leather and Determination of Parameters for Standardization of an Artificial Aging Method: STEP Leather Project," European Cultural Heritage Newsletter on Research (Special Issue), 7:1-4 (December 1993), 19-26. Report on a project to describe leather deterioration and to develop analytical methods using minuscule samples from precious leathers.

2570. Larsen, R. "Review of the Results of the STEP Leather Project," Environnement et Conservation de l'Écrit, de l'Image et du Son. Paris: ARSAG, 1994, 48-55. (Actes des Deuxièmes Journées Internationales d'Études de l'ARSAG. 16-20 Mai, 1994). Review of results and preliminary conclusions from three years of work on a project to describe leather deterioration and to develop analytical methods for analysis

2571. Larsgaard, Mary Lynette. "Conservation of Cartographic Collections," Conserving and Preserving Materials in Nonbook Formats. Urbana-Champaign: University of Illinois Graduate School of Library and Information Science, 1991, 135-145. (Allerton Park Institute, 30). Care, handling, and treatment of paper-based maps.

2572. Larsgaard, Mary. Map Librarianship; An Introduction. 2d ed. Littleton, CO: Libraries Unlimited, 1987, 382p. Text on all aspects of map librarianship with summary of storage, handling, and preservation issues.

2573. LaRue, James. "The Book as Artifact," Illinois Libraries, 67:8 (October 1985), 685-695. Description of a conservation workstation for in-house repairs.

2574. "Laser Rot," The Perfect Vision, 1:1 (Winter 1986-1987), 34-35. Diseases that thrive on laser video disks.

2575. Lateulere, John. The Computer Virus Threat and What You Can Do About It," CD-ROM Professional, 5:5 (September 1992), 105-111. A five-step program for increased security; sampler of anti-virus software.

2576. Latour, Terry. "Mitigating Fate and Acts of God: Why Emergency Preparedness Plans Are Worth the Effort," Mississippi Libraries, 54:4 (Winter 1990), 108-110. Reinforces that plans need to be in place before a disaster strikes.

2577.   Lauder, John. "Digitization of Microfilm: A Scottish Perspective,"
        Microform Review, 24:4 (Fall 1995), 178-181.

2578.   Lauder, John E. "The Scottish Newspapers Microfilming Unit,"
        Microform Review, 24:2 (Spring 1995), 50-54. Describes the
        newspaper unit, filming procedures, with a look to the future, when
        the newspaper project is completed.

2579.   Laughton, Louise W. "Paper Industry Moves into Alkaline Age,"
        New Library Scene, 8:5 (October 1989), 1,5. Discusses the reasons
        for the paper industry's change to the production of alkaline paper,
        the effect on the market, and on libraries and archives.

2580.   Lau-Greig, Deborah. "Determination of Taste Preference of
        Silverfish and Efficacy of Three Bait Recipes," AICCM Bulletin,
        (Australian Institute for the Conservation of Cultural Material),
        18:1/2 (1992), 45-50. Three recipes were evaluated and were not
        effective in killing insects in a six-week period.

2581.   Laursen, Per. "Leaf-Casting Machines," Conference on Book and
        Paper Conservation, 1990. Budapest, Hungary: Technical
        Association of Paper and Printing Industry/National Szechenyi
        Library, 1992, 108-114. Describes the process of leaf-casting and the
        machine that author developed. Illus.

2582.   Lavender, Kenneth, and Scott Stockton. Book Repair: A
        How-To-Do-It Manual for Librarians. New York: Neal Schuman,
        1992. 127p. Conservation advice and repair techniques.

2583.   Lavrencic, Tamara J. "Duplicate Plans, Their Manufacture and
        Treatment," AICCM Bulletin (Australian Institute for the
        Conservation of Cultural Material), 13:3/4 (December 1987),
        139-147. Describes the materials used for producing duplicates of
        maps, architectural and engineering drawings, and the difficulties in
        preserving them.

2584.   Lavrencic, Tamara. "Ink Permanence Testing," AICCM National
        Newsletter (Australian Institute for the Conservation of Cultural
        Material), 30 (March 1989), 11. Testing of lightfastness of 25
        permanent pens; results confirmed that black pens have better
        colorfastness than most colored pens.

2585.   Lavrencic, Tamara. "Mixed (In-House & Contracted) Microfilm
        Production," Preservation Microfilming: Does It Have a Future?
        Canberra: National Library of Australia, 1995, 77-80. Case study:

Bibliography

State Library of Queensland, newspaper microfilming project, from contracted to in-house.

2586. Lavrencic, Tamara. Protective Treatments and Repair of Paper Records. Brisbane: Library Board of Queensland, 1987. 38p. Provides basic information on the nature of deterioration of paper; guide to basic methods of preservation; basic conservation techniques; salvage of water-damaged materials.

2587. Lavrencic, Tamara. Storage and Preservation of Paper Records. Brisbane: Library Board of Queensland, 1987. 60p. Provides basic information on the nature of deterioration of paper; options to prevent further deterioration.

2588. Law, Margaret H., and Bruce Rosen. Framework and Policy Recommendations for the Exchange and Preservation of Electronic Records. Gaithersburg, MD: National Institute of Standards and Technology, National Computer Systems Laboratory for the National Archives and Records Administration, 1989. 48p. Discusses the preservation of electronic records, emphasizing the importance of recognizing the challenges and drafting policies that address them.

2589. Lawrence, Deirdre E., and Susan Swartzburg. "Emergency Plan for Art Libraries," Art Documentation (Summer 1984), 58-60.

2590. Lawrence, Deirdre E. "The Preservation Projects at the Brooklyn Museum Libraries and Archives," Conservation Administration News, 34 (July 1988), 5, 22. Description of preservation initiatives with descriptions of work accomplished with funding from the National Endowment for the Humanities and the New York State Library.

2591. Lawrence, John H. Photographs. New Orleans, LA: Historic New Orleans Collection, 1983. 13p. (Preservation Guide 2). Brief guide for collectors with bibliography, glossary, and list of supplies.

2592. Lawrence, Patricia O'Reilly. Before Disaster Strikes: Prevention, Planning and Recovery, Caring for Your Personal Collections in the Event of a Disaster. New Orleans, LA: Historic New Orleans Collection, 1992. 40p. Illus. Presents information to the public about the dangers that can befall valuable possessions, describes measures to protect property.

2593. Lawson, Peter. "Freezing as a Means of Pest Control," Library Conservation News, 20 (July 1988), 6. Description of the British Library's experiment, placing an infested volume in a blast freeze

318

chamber to eliminate infestation. Concludes that such treatment offers safe, nonchemical control of light, local infestation.

2594. Lawson, Peter. "Palm Leaf Books and Their Conservation," Library Conservation News, 16 (July 1987), 4-7. The first of two articles on the subject; discusses history, botanical structure, makeup, damage, and storage of these kind of books.

2595. Lawson, Peter. "The Preservation of Pre-tenth Century Paper," The Conservation of Far Eastern Art. London: International Institute for Conservation, 1988, 115-118. Describes the problems in a collection of manuscript and printed material that was mounted, prior to 1960, using unstable materials. Notes concern for loss of evidence when elements in the paper are contaminated with modern material, making analysis difficult. Describes the British Library's present policy of preservation for this type of material.

2596. Lawson, Peter. "The Work of the British Library's Oriental Conservation Studio," Conference on Book and Paper Conservation, 1990. Budapest, Hungary: Technical Association of Paper and Printing Industry/National Szechenyi Library, 1992, 365-370. Unit deals primarily with non-paper materials; policy of minimum intervention. 11 References.

2597. Lawton, George. "Alkaline Papermaking at Simpson-Plainwell Paper Company," Alkaline Paper Advocate, 1:4 (October 1988), 36-40. Description of a manufacturer's conversion to alkaline paper production.

2598. Lawton, Stephen. "Being There," Inform, 5:9 (October 1991), 25-27. Discusses the need for the establishment of standards for optical disks. Describes four points of failure in optical media and states that until optical disks are proven to be long-lasting, one should beware.

2599. Layland, Penelope. "Microfilming Newspapers: A Solution to Hand," National Library of Australia News, 4:5 (February 1994), 9-12. Discusses causes of deterioration and the need for preservation microfilming of newspapers. Describes the Australian initiative.

2600. Layne, Stevan P. The Official Library Security Manual. Dillon, CO: Layne Consultants International, 1994. 49p. A "How To" guide for managers administrators that covers numerous items such as protecting rare books.

2601. Lazar, Jon H. "Bidding Library Binding," New Library Scene, 7:5 (October 1988), 1, 5. Advice on the bidding process and how the Library Binding Institute Standards should be used.

2602. Lazar, Wanda. "A Proposed University Specialization in Sound Preservation," ARSC Journal (Association of Recorded Sound Collections), 26:1 (1995), 46-52. Argument for and design of a university course to train sound archivists working in sound preservation. Discusses the nature and complexity of work, with proposed syllabus.

2603. Learn, Larry L. "In the Smoke of the Chicago Fire," Library Hi Tech, 51 (July-August 1988), 4-6. Disaster planning and recovery for telecommunications; addresses issue of liability for loss of service.

2604. Leary, William. The Archival Appraisal of Photographs: A RAMP Study with Guidelines. Paris: UNESCO, 1985. 121p.

2605. Leary, William H. "Preservation Microfilming at the National Archives," Microform Review, 16:4 (Fall 1987), 287-290. Describes efforts at the National archives to film its holdings and to encourage other federal agencies to do so; discussion of costs and benefits.

2606. Lechleitner, Franz. "A Newly Constructed Cylander Replay Machine for 2-inch Diameter Cylinders," Archiving the Audio-Visual Heritage. Rushton, England: FIAF/UNESCO, 1992. 145-148. Describes the development of a machine for the re-recording of cylinders.

2607. Ledden, Larry. Complete Guide to Scanning. Westfield, NY: Family Technologies, 1994. 120p.

2608. Lee, Richard E. Jr., and David L. Denlinger, eds. Insects at Low Temperature. London; New York: Chapman and Hall, 1991. 513p. Study of the reactions of various insects to low temperatures and tolerance of insects. Emphasis is on prolonging the life cycle, not halting it.

2609. Lee, S. B., J. Bogaard, and Robert L. Feller. "Bleaching by Light 1: Effect of pH on the Bleaching or Darkening of Papers in the Dry and in the Immersed Condition Under Visible and Near-Ultraviolet Light," "Bleaching by Light 2: Studies of the Bleaching of Thermally Discolored Sugars and Other 'model' Compounds," Conservation of Historic and Artistic Works on Paper. Ottawa: Canadian Conservation Institute, 1994, 181-190, 191-198. (Symposium 88). Describes an experiment to gain background information on the process of bleaching of discolored papers by light.

2610. Lee, S. B., J. Bogaard, and Robert L. Feller. "Damaging Effects of Visible and Near-Ultraviolet Radiation on Paper," Historic Textile and Paper Materials II: Conservation and Characterization, ed. Howard L. Needles and S. Haig Zeronian. Washington, DC: American Chemical Society, 1989, 54-62. (ACS Symposium 410). Study of papers with little or no lignin content indicated that ultraviolet filters noticeably reduced, but did not prevent, deterioration during exposure and subsequent aging.

2611. Lee, S. B., J. Bogaard, and Robert L. Feller. "Darkening of Paper Following Exposure to Visible and Near-Ultraviolet Radiation," Journal of the American Institute for Conservation, 28:1 (Spring 1989), 1-18. Graphs. Report on experiments using different sources of light, demonstrating that deterioration is chiefly influenced by the content of lignin and the pH of the test sheets.

2612. Lee, S. B., J. Bogaard, and Robert L. Feller. "Relation of Cellulose Chain Scission to Hot-Alkali-Soluble Content During Thermal and Photochemical Degradation of Paper," Journal of Imaging Science, 29:2 (March-April 1985), 61-64. Chain scission, and mild oxidation of the type that leads to the formation of alkali-sensitive groups without scission, can be viewed as the results of two different chemical processes.

2613. Leek, Matthew R. "Will a Good Disc Last Forever?" CD-ROM Professional, 8:11 (November 1995), 102-110. Discusses the production and causes of deterioration of CD-readable disks, through inherent vice, heat, light, mishandling; results of accelerated aging tests. Does not really deal with issue of technological obsolescence. (Excellent process, however).

2614. Legenfelder, Helga. "Illuminated Manuscripts and Colour Microfiche — A Chance for Medieval Research?" Liber Bulletin (Ligue des Bibliothèques Européennes de Recherche), 29 (1987), 51-54. Describes how color microfiche can provide access; briefly describes the technology and projects underway.

2615. Leigh, David. "A Focus for Conservation," Library Conservation News, 22 (January 1989), 1-3. Describes the activities of the Conservation Unit, Museums and Galleries Commission, United Kingdom, established in 1987.

2616. Lemke, Antje B. "Art Archives: A Common Concern of Archivists, Librarians and Museum Professionals," Art Libraries Journal, 14:2 (1989), 5-11. A history, description, and scope of art archives.

2617. Lemley, Brad. "Preserving the Past on Disk," PC Magazine, 4 (1985), 199-212. Describes the digitization project at the Smithsonian Air and Space Museum; advantages for storage, preservation, and access.

2618. Lemmon, Alfred E. "Confronting Man and Nature: The National Archives of El Salvador," American Archivist, 54:3 (Summer 1991), 404-410. Author describes the challenges that he observed during his visit to the Salvadoran archives in 1989. He review the basic needs of the archives and relates examples of improvised solutions to protect materials from war, earthquake, and general neglect.

2619. Lemmon, Alfred E. "Latin American Archives and Preservation and Conservation Institute," SAA Newsletter (Society of American Archivists) (January 1990), 14-15.

2620. Lener, Dewayne J. Paper Preservation: Conservation Techniques and Methodology. Orting, WA: Heritage Quest Press, 1988. 123p. Preservation manual for private collectors; includes hands-on instructions for difficult procedures. No information on collection maintenance nor on conservators.

2621. Leonhirth, Janene. "Administration of Photographic Collections: A Bibliographic Essay," Provenance, 6:1 (Spring 1988), 60-66. Review of literature on photographic preservation.

2622. Leonov, Valery. "Preserving the Collective Memory," Getty Conservation Institute Newsletter, 7:1 (Winter 1992), 8-11. Leonov discusses the recovery effort following the fire at the Academy of Science Library, St. Petersburg, Russia, and needs for the future with Jane Slate Siena.

2623. Lepiney, Lionelle de. "Bibliothèque Nationale de France: The Technical Centre in Marne-la-Vallée," International Preservation News, 10 (July 1995), 4. Brief description of the new conservation facilities for physical treatment, preservation of electronic data, research, education, and training. It is operative in January 1996.

2624. Leroy, Martine, and Françoise Flieder. "The Setting of Modern Inks Before Restoration Treatments," Restaurator, 14:3 (1993), 131-140. Research into fixatives to ensure stability of inks during leafcasting.

2625.   LeRoy, Peter. Library Binding: A Selected and Annotated
        Bibliography. Ottawa: Council on Federal Libraries, 1990. 13
        leaves. Bibliography covering repair and conservation.

2626.   Lesk, Michael. Image Formats for Preservation and Access: A
        Report of the Technology Assessment Advisory Committee to the
        Commission on Preservation and Access. Washington, DC:
        Commission on Preservation and Access, 1990. 10p.; reprinted
        Information Technology and Libraries, 9:4 (December 1990),
        300-308. Also in Microform Review 21:1 (Winter 1992), 17-
        24. Presents digital imagery as a viable alternative that offers long-
        term promise for preservation; compares digital to microform
        imagery.

2627.   Lesk, Michael. Preservation of New Technology. Washington, DC:
        Commission on Preservation and Access, 1992. 19p. Examines
        new technologies for information. Concludes that the survival of
        digital information will depend primarily on regular copying to new
        devises; notes the need for a coordinated approach to the
        preservation of digital information.

2628.   Lesk, Michael. "Special Section: Digital Imagery, Preservation and
        Access," Information Technology and Libraries, 9 (December 1990),
        300-306. The author explains the alternatives of preserving paper-
        based materials in their original form by microfilming and by
        electronic imaging.

2629.   Lesley, Van. "Abandoned in a Field: Librarians Save a Rare Bible;
        During the Final Days of the Former Soviet Union, Lithuanian
        Librarians Rescued a Pillaged Trove of Rare Books," American
        Libraries, 25 (June 1994), 582+.

2630.   Lester, Michael. "Bookbinding Supplies in Australia," First National
        Conference of Craft Bookbinders - Australia. Kingston, Australia:
        Craft Bookbinders Guild, November 1984, 14-15. Note on an
        initiative to develop a directory of suppliers of bookbinding materials
        in Australia.

2631.   Leveque, Margaret A. "The Problem of Formaldehyde: A Case
        Study," American Institute for Conservation Preprints. Washington,
        DC: American Institute for Conservation, 1986, 56-64. Deterioration
        caused by formaldehyde off-gassing in the storage area of the Boston
        Museum, measures taken for correction, treatment, and a note about
        continuing research.

2632.   Levin, Jeffrey. "Conservation at the Crossroads," Conservation
        (Getty Conservation Institute), 10:1 (1995), 4-9. Report on a

gathering of conservators at GCI, November 1994, organized by
Robert Straus and Barclay Ogden, to explore collective approaches to
increase public support for conservation; consensus about selection
for preservation and conservation, and how to increase public
awareness of conservation were addressed.

2633.   Levin, Jeffrey. "Environmental Research at the GCI," Conservation
(Getty Conservation Institute), 8:1 (Winter 1993), 4-9. A review of
the Getty Conservation Institute's research programs, including
indoor and outdoor pollutants, pest control, and air quality in the
museum environment.

2634.   Levin, Jeffrey. "The Preservation of Information," Conservation
(Getty Conservation Institute), 8:2 (1994), 4-7. A review of
preservation challenges and initiatives for libraries and archives.

2635.   Levitt, Alan M., and Karla H. Conford. "Contingency and Disaster
Recovery Planning," Records and Retrieval Report, 7:7 (September
1991), 1-16. Review of disaster planning; emphasis on business
recovery.

2636.   Levitt, Martin L. "A Case Study in Audio Tape Transfer," College
and Research Libraries News, 49:10 (November 1988),
654-657. Case study of the transfer of early tape recordings to newly
developed tape; why and how the project was completed in-house
with appropriate quality control.

2637.   Levy, B. "The 'K-118' Binding Structure: A 500-Year-Old
Experiment for Modern-Day Book Conservation," Library Chronicle
(University of Texas at Austin), 44/45 (1989), 116-133.

2638.   Lewis, David W. "Inventing the Electronic University," College and
Research Libraries, 49:4 (July 1988), 291-304. Calls for a
reinvention of the way information and communication is organized
at the university. Discusses preservation considerations of electronic
information.

2639.   Lewis, Eleanor J., Eric Weltman, and Jonathan Kleinman. "Energy
Efficiency in Libraries," Library Administration and Management,
7:3 (Summer 1993), 153-158. Recommendations, including an
energy audit, retrofitting with newer technologies for heating,
ventilation, and air conditioning,;reducing power usage; and
increasing the role of employees and the community in saving
energy.

2640.   Lewis, Page. "OSU Preservation Administrator Making Past
Accessible to the Future," Research Libraries in OCLC, 18 (Winter

1986), 8-9. Profile of Wesley Boomgaarden, Preservation Librarian, Ohio State University Libraries, the scope of the Preservation Administrator's responsibilities, and his views on the preservation field.

2641.   Lewis, Page. "Optical Disk Pilot Program Supported by Library of Congress," Research Libraries in OCLC, 18 (Winter 1986), 10-11. Describes the development of the pilot program, application of the technology for preservation, preservation needs of optical disks, development of technical standards, problems associated with technology, and longevity of disk players.

2642.   Lewis, Stephen. ed. Disaster Recovery Yellow Pages. 6th edition. Newton, MA: Systems Audit Group, Inc., 1997. 280p. Lists over 2,300 vendors.

2643.   Li, Min Lim. "The Museum of Ravaged Books," Wanted in Rome (October 4, 1995), 11. Popular article in tourist magazine on the Musea della Patalogia del Libro, and its "bizarre collection of ravaged books," and the Istituto della Patalogia del Libro and its conservation work.

2644.   Libengoud, Ronald S., and Bryon J. Perun. "The Key to Good Security: Proprietary Keyways and Electronic Locks," Focus on Security, 2:3 (April 1995), 6-16. Discussion of keying systems appropriate for libraries.

2645.   Liberatore, Anthony M. "Production of Paper for Libraries," Paper Preservation: Current Issues and Recent Developments. Atlanta, GA: TAPPI Press, 1990, 85-89. Places in historic context the switch at Glatfelder Mills from the production of acidic to alkaline paper. Paper presented at Symposium 88, Ottawa, Canada, May 1988.

2646.   "The Library and Courts Annex: Preserving, Protecting and Promoting Our Cultural Heritage [at the California State Library]," California State Library Foundation Bulletin, 43 (April 1993), 32-35.

2647.   Library Applications of Optical Disk Technology, January 1982-October 1989. Springfield, VA: National Technical Information Service (NTIS), November 1989. 122p.

2648.   Library Association of Portland. The Recovery of Water-Damaged Library Materials. Portland, OR: Multnomah County Library, 1985. 37p.

2649.   Library of Congress. "At the Library of Congress, Diane Nester Kresh has been Appointed Director of Preservation and National

Preservation Program Officer," American Libraries, 26 (February 1995), 178.

2650.   Library [of Congress and] Bowdoin College to Preserve Rare Films of the Arctic," LC Information Bulletin (Library of Congress), 48:31 (July 31, 1989), 266-267.

2651.   "Library of Congress and Mass Deacidification RFP," ALCTS Newsletter (Association of Library Collections and Technical Services), 2:8 (1991), 89-90. LC rejects all 3 proposals.

2652.   Library of Congress. "Book Deacidification Program Update," LC Information Bulletin (Library of Congress), 45:36 (September 8, 1986), 310-311.

2653.   Library of Congress. Books in Our Future: Perspectives and Proposals. Washington, DC: Joint Committee on the Library, Congress of the United States, 1987. 49p. Describes electronic publishing and the future of books.

2654.   "Library of Congress. "Announces Completion of Mass Deacidification Test," American Archivist, 46 (Spring 1983), 205.

2655.   "Library of Congress Collections Decimated by Thieves," Transcript of All Things Considered (National Public Radio 4:30 p.m.), November 28, 1995. 4p.

2656.   Library of Congress. "Commissioning of Pilot DEZ Facility Is Complete," LC Information Bulletin (Library of Congress), (March 7, 1988), 86-87.

2657.   "Library [of Congress] Cosponsors Documentary Film About Preservation," LC Information Bulletin (Library of Congress), 45:15 (April 14, 1986), 1. A film being produced for television broadcast intends to raise public awareness about preservation problems.

2658.   Library of Congress. "Deacidification Program Update," LC Information Bulletin (Library of Congress), 45:46 (November 17, 1986), 378-379.

2659.   Library of Congress. "DEZ Update," National Preservation News, 2 (October 1985), 14.

2660.   Library of Congress. "Division on Management and Technology, Section on Conservation," LC Information Bulletin (Library of Congress) (April 11, 1988), 154.

2661. Library of Congress. Film Preservation 1993: A Study of the Current State of American Film Preservation. Washington, DC: Library of Congress, 1993. 4 vols. Describes the current state of preservation in the U.S. film industry and in public and nonprofit archives, gathered from hearings and written comments in response to the National Film Preservation Act (1992).

2662. Library of Congress. "LC and Deacidification," Library Journal, (August 1985), 6. Letter to the editor by Peter Sparks, Director of Preservation, Library of Congress.

2663. Library of Congress. "LC & NYPL [on Microfilm] Preserving U.S. Phone Directories," ALCTS Newsletter (Association of Library Collections and Technical Services), 4:2/3 (1993), 27.

2664. Library of Congress. "LC Launches Management Plan for Optical Disk Project," American Archivist, 46:4 (1983), 474-475.

2665. Library of Congress. "LC's Mass Deacidification Facility Destroyed," Wilson Library Bulletin, 60 (May 1986), 8-9.

2666. Library of Congress. "LC's Mass Deacidification Process," RTSD Newsletter (Resources and Technical Services Division), 9:4 (1984), 37.

2667. Library of Congress. "LC's Mobile Repair Stations," The Abbey Newsletter, 7:6 (1983), 70. Describes the LC Binding Office's mobile binding repair units.

2668. Library of Congress. "LC Reports Flaws in DEZ [diethyl zinc] Process with Contract With Chemical Firm," Library Journal, 111 (August 1986), 22.

2669. Library of Congress. "LC Responds to Deacidification Bids From Industry: All Offers Are Turned Down," LC Information Bulletin (Library of Congress), 50 (September 23, 1991), 347.

2670. Library of Congress. "Librarian Appoints Film Preservation Task Forces: To Assist in Planning National Program" (to work with National Film Preservation Board), LC Information Bulletin (Library of Congress), 53 (February 21, 1994), 63-64.

2671. Library of Congress. "Library Announces Book Preservation Plans: Status of the Mass Deacidification Program," LC Information Bulletin (Library of Congress), 50 (May 6, 1991), 162. Library of Congress hope to contract for mass deacidification on services in summer 1991.

2672.   Library of Congress. "Library Issues Policy Statement on Its Use of Print Materials in Optical Disk Format," LC Information Bulletin (Library of Congress), 45:39 (September 22, 1986), 322-323, 328.

2673.   [Library of Congress]. "Library Receives Reader's Digest Grant to Help Restore Fire-Damaged Leningrad Library," LC Information Bulletin (Library of Congress), 48:35 (August 28, 1989), 297-298.

2674.   Library of Congress. "Library's Book Deacidification Program Moves Forward Following Review of Incidents at Pilot Plant," LC Information Bulletin (Library of Congress), 45:27 (July 7, 1986), 255-256, 260.

2675.   Library of Congress. Making Today's Books Last: Vapor Phase Deacidification at the Library of Congress. Washington, DC: Library of Congress, 1985. 13p. Explains Library of Congress's DEZ deacidification process, why it is needed, and anticipated results. Includes artist's rendering of the planned facilities at Fort Detrick.

2676.   "Library of Congress Plans Deacidification Facility," AB Bookman's Weekly (Antiquarian Bookman), 75 (January 28, 1985), 522.

2677.   Library of Congress. "Restoration Office Uses New Techniques to Complete Brahms Preservation Project," LC Information Bulletin (Library of Congress), 42:45 (November 7, 1983), 376-378.

2678.   Library of Congress. Redefining Film Preservation: A National Plan by Annette Milville and Scott Simmon. Washington, DC: Library of Congress, 1994. 80p. Outlines basic steps that must be taken to save American films and make them accessible to the public; advocates a public-private partnership. Issues include storage, access, partnerships, funding. Thirty recommendations on how to ensure the long-term survival of the American film heritage.

2679.   Library of Congress. "Thanhouser Gift Establishes Funds for Preservation of Silent Films..," LC Information Bulletin (Library of Congress), 48:44 (October 30, 1989), 381-382, 384-385. The Library received $40,000 to restore silent films.

2680.   "Library [of Congress] to Host Symposium on Preserving Serials," LC Information Bulletin (Library of Congress), 48:4 (January 23, 1989), 33-34.

2681.   Library of Congress. Computer Files Steering Committee. Preservation of Computer File Materials. Washington, DC: Library of Congress, 1992. 43p. Reviews actions of other institutions, identifies specific actions necessary to preserve computer file materials, and presents the policies and recommendations made by the committee.

2682. Library of Congress. National Film Preservation Board. The National Film Preservation Plan: An Implementation Strategy. Washington, DC: Library of Congress, June 1995. 12p. Strategies for implementation, including conservation, increasing funding and fostering partnerships, repatriation of American films, expanding public access and outreach. Recognition that electronic media may provide access but cannot be a preservation medium.

2683. Library of Congress. National Preservation Program Office. Audiovisual Resources for Preserving Library and Archival Materials. Washington, DC: Library of Congress, 1983. 8p. (Preservation Leaflet No. 6).

2684. Library of Congress. National Preservation Program Office. Ownership Marking of Paper-Based Materials. rev. ed. Washington, DC: Library of Congress, June 1993. 3p. (Preservation Leaflet No. 4). Briefly discusses methods of marking manuscripts, the damage that it may cause, and a note about the ink that the Library has developed. Previous editions exist.

2685. Library of Congress. National Preservation Program Office. Paper and Its Preservation: Environmental Controls. Rev. ed. Washington, DC: Library of Congress, October 1993. 5p. (Preservation Leaflet No. 2). First published 1983.

2686. Library of Congress. Preservation Directorate. An Evaluation of the Bookkeeper Mass Deacidification Process: Technical Evaluation Team Report. Pittsburgh, PA: Institute of Paper Technology, October 1994. 73p. and appendices. Summary of text results with technical reports by the study team members, and the Institute of Paper Technology in the appendices. Produced by Sally Buchanan, et al.

2687. Library of Congress. Preservation Directorate. Collection Preservation Microfilming Planning: Questions Yielding Information to Draft a Planning Document. Washington, DC: Library of Congress, 1991. 7p.

2688. Library of Congress. Preservation Reference Service. Preservation Microfilming: Bibliography. Washington, DC: Library of Congress, August 1988. 13p.

2689.   Library of Congress. Preservation Reference Service. Magnetic
        Media Preservation: Selected Bibliography: Associations, Agencies,
        and Resources. Washington. DC: Library of Congress, June 1988.
        2p. (Preservation Information Series Fact Sheet).

2690.   Library of Congress. Photoduplication Service. Specifications for the
        Microfilming of Books and Pamphlets in the Library of Congress.
        Silver Spring, MD: National Micrographics Association, 1983.
        16p. Originally published by the Library of Congress in 1973.

2691.   Library of Congress and Ameritech. National Digital Library
        Competition: 1996 Guidelines and Application Instructions.
        Washington, DC: Library of Congress, 1996. 21p.

2692.   "Library Preservation: The Administrative Challenge — A Summary
        Report," RTSD Newsletter (Resources and Technical Services
        Division), 8:4 (July/August 1983), 41-46. A summary of the ALA
        Preservation Conference held in Washington, DC, on April 29, 1983.

2693.   "Library Preservation: Implementing Programs," RTSD Newsletter
        (Resources and Technical Services Division), 9:5 (1984), 45-47.

2694.   "Library to Deacidify Books," Nature, 351:6326 (June 6, 1991), 429.
        Plans at Johns Hopkins University's Eisenhower Library for book
        preservation.

2695.   Lienardy, Anne. "A Bibliographical Survey of Mass Deacidification
        Methods," Restaurator, 12:2 (1991), 75-103. Summarizes the
        bibliographic review undertaken prior to testing the processes.
        Describes treatment processes, consequences for books, advantages
        and disadvantages.

2696.   Lienardy, Anne. "Evaluation of Seven Mass Deacidification
        Treatments," Restaurator, 15:1 (1994), 1-25. Testing methods and
        results are described.

2697.   Lienardy, Anne, and Philippe van Damme. "Paper Washing," Paper
        Conservator, 14 (1990), 23-49. Exploration of the benefits of
        washing a variety of papers prior to deacidification.

2698.   Lienardy, Anne, and Philippe van Damme. "Practical
        Deacidification," Restaurator, 11:1 (1990), 1-21. Seven
        deacidification methods selected after a survey of the literature are
        reviewed, tested, and evaluated. 53 references.

2699. Liers, J., and P. Schwerdt. "The Battelle Mass Deacidification Process Equipment and Technology," Restaurator, 16:1 (1995), 1-9. Description of equipment and technology.

2700. Light Impressions. Mounting Techniques. Rochester, NY: Light Impressions, 1985. 4p.

2701. Ligterink, Frank J., Henk J. Porck, and Wim J. Th. Smit. "Foxing Stains and Discoloration of Leaf Margins and Paper Surrounding Printing Ink: Coherent Phenomena in Books," Abbey Newsletter, 13:4 (December 1989), 146. A study of the foxing phenomenena that demonstrated the need for further study into its cause, which may be influenced by moisture during and following production of paper. A summary of an article that appeared in Restauro, 3 (1989) and De Restautator 1 (1989).

2702. Ligterink, Frank J., Henk J. Porck, and Wim J. Th. Smit. "Foxing Stains and Discolouration of Leaf Margins and Paper Surrounding Printing Ink: Elements of a Complex Phenomenon in Books," Paper Conservator, 15 (1991), 42-52. Proposes a redefinition of the phenomenon of foxing after investigation of paper discoloration in a large number of books.

2703. Likhachev, Dmitrii. Bitter Thoughts After the Fire." In Dennis A. Kimmage, Russian Libraries in Transition: An Anthology of Glasnost Literature. Jefferson, NC: McFarland, 1992, 5-12. Description of the fire at the Academy of Science, fire St. Petersburg, and the events that followed. From Russian History, 15 (Spring 1988), trans. Richard Hellie and Jean Laves Hellie.

2704. Lilly, Roy S., Barbara F. Schlomon, and Wendy Hu. "Rip-off Revisited: Periodical Mutilation in a University Research Library," Library and Archival Security, 11:1 (1991), 43-70. Study of student attitudes toward mutilation of journals; notes need to educate students about the consequences.

2705. Lincoln, Alan J. "Computer Security," Library and Archival Security, 11:1 (1991), 157-171. Basic information on computer security.

2706. Lincoln, Alan Jay. Crime in the Library: A Study of Patterns, Impact and Security. New York: R. R. Bowker, 1984. 179p. Covers theft, vandalism, robberies, and assault, and problem patron behavior; an interdisciplinary approach to help the reader understand the issues and take steps to lessen the effects.

2707.   Lincoln, Alan J. "Library Legislation Related to Crime and Security, Part 3," Library and Archival Security, 11:2 (1992), 23-35. Covers federal legislation on conduct on library premises.

2708.   Lincoln, Alan Jay. "Patterns and Costs of Crime," Library Trends, 33:1 (Summer 1984), 69-76. Describes the Library Crime Research Project, a three-year project to study crime and disruptions in libraries. Examines cost and effect of crime and vandalism.

2709.   Lincoln, Alan Jay, ed. Protecting the Library. Champaign: University of Illinois Graduate School of Library and Information Science, 1984. 94p. Library Trends, 33:1 (Summer 1984), 3-94. Contributors examine issues and concerns related to the protection of the library.

2710.   Lincoln, Alan Jay, and Carol Zall Lincoln. Library Crime and Security: An International Perspective. New York: Haworth Press, 1987. 162p. Analysis of library crime and disruption in Great Britain, Canada and the United States and its impact upon an institution. Bibliography.

2711.   Lindblom, Beth C., and Karen Motylewski. Disaster Planning for Cultural Institutions. Nashville, TN: American Association for State and Local History, 1993. 8p. (Technical Leaflet, 183). Also published in History News, 48:1 (January-February 1993). Basic instructions for smaller institutions: identifying and decreasing risks; developing a plan within an institutional context; identifying resources; writing and maintaining the plan.

2712.   Lindner, Jim. "Confessions of a Videotape Restorer; or, How Come These Tapes All Need to Be Cleaned Differently?" AMIA Newsletter (Association of Moving Image Archivists), 24 (April 1994), 9-10.

2713.   Lindner, Jim. "Digization Reconsidered: A Video Guru Takes on the Technocrats," SAA Business Archives Newsletter (Society of American Archivists), 12:1 (Summer 1995), 1, 12-14.

2714.   Lindner, Jim. "Magnetic Tape Deterioration: Tidal Wave at Our Shores," Video Magazine (February 1996), 7.

2715.   Lindner, Jim. "The Proper Care and Feeding of Videotape," Abbey Newsletter, 18:8 (1994), 114-115. The article includes a list of recommendations for the storage and preservation of videotape. The list includes manufacturers recommendations and those based on the author's experience with old and obsolete tapes.

2716.   Lindner, Jim. "Videotape Restoration — Where Do I Start?" NML Bits (National Media Laboratory), 4:2 (September 1995); reprinted in Abbey Newsletter, 18:6 (October 1994), 75-76. How to prioritize and select videotapes for restoration. Checklist.

2717.   Lindsay, Jen. "A Limp Vellum Binding Sewn on Alum-Tawed Thongs," New Bookbinder, 11 (1991), 3-19. Illus. Brief history of the use of vellum; step-by-step instructions for producing a limp vellum binding. Bibliography.

2718.   Lindsay, Helen, and Christopher Clarkson. "Housing Single-Sheet Material: The Development of the Fascicule System at the Bodleian Library," Paper Conservator, 18 (1994), 40-48. Describes previous housing systems and the decision-making process that led to the introduction of the fascicule system and design specifications.

2719.   Line, Maurice B. "Interlending and Conservation: Friends or Foes?" Interlending and Document Supply, 16:1 (January 1988), 7-11. Conservation is of no benefit unless the items conserved are used in the future, but it should not prevent use. Discusses options.

2720.   Linnean Society of London. Preserving the Archives of Nature: A Guide for the Owners of Papers on Nature Conservation prepared by the Library Committee of the Linnean Society of London. London: The Society, 1994. 8p.

2721.   Lipinski, Barry V. "A Practical Approach to Library Security," New Jersey Libraries, 27:4 (Fall 1994), 19-20. A supervisor provides a commonsense approach to security concerns.

2722.   Lister Hill National Center for Biomedical Communications. Communications Engineering Branch. Document Preservation by Electronic Imaging. Vol. 1: Synopsis. Bethesda, MD: Lister Hill National Center for Biomedical Communications, April 1989, 31p. Synopsis of a program to investigate the application of electronic imaging (EI) to document preservation; brief history and background; list of attributes; summary of findings and conclusion.

2723.   Littman, Marlyn Kemper. "Protecting Electronic Data: A Losing Battle?" Safeguarding Electronic Information, ed. Jona Varlejs. Jefferson, NC: McFarland, 1996, 20-33. Describes typical incursions, outlines protective measures; emphasizes need for constant vigilance and use of multiple protective strategies.

2724.   Livingston, Richard A. "Implementing an Environmental Monitoring Program," Construction Specifier, 43:7 (July 1990),

136-143. Outline for a successful environmental monitoring program, including an overall strategy with clear objectives, the variables to be monitored, desired data quality, and clear data interpretation.

2725. Lochead, Richard. "A Home for Audio-Visual Archives," <u>Archivist</u> (National Archives of Canada) (November-December 1990), 30-33. Description of the National Archives of Canada collection developed to preserve the non-print heritage and to provide access.

2726. Lockhart, Vicki, and Ann Swartzell. "Evaluation of Microfilm Vendors," <u>Microform Review</u>, 19:3 (Summer 1990), 119-123. Discussion of results of a study to evaluate the work of preservation microfilmers.

2727. Logan, Kevin J. "Preserving the Past for the Future," <u>Documentation Newsletter</u>, 15:1 (Spring 1989), 5-9. Briefly describes the preservation survey of the Cornell University Department of Manuscripts and University Archives and its five-year preservation plan which runs 112 pages.

2728. Lombardo, Daniel. "Open Access vs. Preservation: The Amherst Local History Project," <u>Library Journal</u>, 111:4 (March 1, 1986), 66-67. Addresses question of preservation and access to local history collections by students.

2729. Lombardo, Daniel. "The Use of Microform to Support the Amherst Local History Project," <u>Microform Review</u>, 16:2 (Spring 1987), 130-133. Issue of access versus preservation of rare documents is argued and a short-term policy and microfilming project is discussed. Demonstrates that microfilm can provide a satisfactory solution.

2730. London, Jonathan. "The Treaty of Waitangi - Its Preservation," <u>AICCM Bulletin</u> (Australian Institute for the Conservation of Cultural Material), 20:1 (1994), 25-31. Traces the history of the treaty and its preservation over 150 years, to its present housing in the National Archives Constitution Room.

2731. Long, Jane Sennett, ed. <u>Invest in the American Collection: Edited Proceedings from a Regional Forum on the Conservation of Cultural Property</u>. Washington, DC: National Institute for Conservation, 1988. 51p. Includes the remarks of 21 speakers who addressed current issues in conservation and preservation at a forum held June 16-18, 1987, at the Art Institute of Chicago.

2732. Longstreth, Karl E. "The Preservation of Library Materials in 1988: A Review of the Literature," <u>Library Resources and Technical</u>

Services, 33:4 (July 1989), 217-226. Reviews trends in preservation and conservation as reflected in the professional literature published during 1988.

2733. Longstreth, Karl E. "The Preservation of Library Materials in 1989: A Review of the Literature," Library Resources and Technical Services, 34:4 (October 1990), 544-465. Reviews trends in preservation and conservation as reflected in the professional literature published during 1989.

2734. Looms, Peter Olaf. "Long Term Conservation & Dissemination Issues for Large-Scale Electronic Image Databases," Electronic Imaging & the Visual Arts, ed. Anthony Hamber. Aldershot, England: Brameur, 1992. 9 pages (volume unpaged). Discusses imaging technology to preserve images of objects, which are often fragile and make the surrogate images widely accessible, protecting the originals. No discussion of preserving the image database.

2735. Lora, Pat. "AV Frontier: Preservation or Global Delete? What's the Future of Media?" Wilson Library Bulletin, 66:3 (November 1991), 59-60. The impermanence of video, magnetic tapes, and compact disks; suggestions for storage and handling.

2736. Lord, Allyn, Carolyn Reno, and Marie Demeroukas. Steal This Handbook! A Template for Creating a Museum's Emergency Preparedness Plan. Columbia, SC: Southeastern Registrar's Association, 1994. 250p. A sample emergency plan, covering preparedness and recovery based on the work of the Ozarks Group for Emergency Resources (OGER). Bibliography.

2737. Lord, Kenniston W., Jr. The Data Center Disaster Consultant. 2d ed. Englewood Cliffs, NJ: Prentice-Hall, 1983. 215p. Disaster planning manual with model, survey forms, and other examples.

2738. Lord Cultural Resources Planning & Management, Inc. in association with Murray Frost. Feasibility Study for a Mass Deacidification Centre for Libraries and Archives in Metropolitan Toronto. Toronto: LCPRM, 1989. 143p.

2739. Loretto, Chris. "Standards for Preservation Microfilming," Preservation Microfilming: Does It Have a Future? Canberra: National Library of Australia, 1995, 149-156. Discussion of standards for microfilming; thoughts about future needs.

2740. Los Angeles Preservation Network. Disaster Consultants. Los Angeles: The Network, 1996. n.p.

2741. Los Angeles Preservation Network. List of Supplies and Suppliers, Los Angeles: Los Angeles Preservation Network, 1991. one volume. 2d edition. 1996. One volume.

2742. Los Angeles Preservation Network. "LAPNet sponsors first Preservation Workshop," Library Journal, 113 (August 1988), 24.

2743. Los Angeles Preservation Network News. LAPNews. Los Angeles: The Network, 1995. Irregular.

2744. "Los Angeles Public Library Now Drying Books," Wilson Library Bulletin (December 1988), 15-16. The Library is now drying books after water damage during the fire, which occurred in September 1986.

2745. Los Angeles Public Library. Save the Books. Los Angeles, CA: Los Angeles Public Library; ARCO, 1986. 8p. Promotional pamphlet describing the fire of April 29, 1986, and subsequent conservation efforts.

2746. Loughridge, Brendan. "Conservation, Culture and Curriculum," International Library Cooperation, ed. Ahmed H. Helal and Joachim J. Weiss. Essen, Germany: Universitätsbibliothek Essen, 1988, 18-38. (Festschrift in Honor of Prof. Dr. Guenther Pflug). Reviews discussion about the role of education for conservation and preservation in the library school curriculum, with emphasis on the United Kingdom. Papers from the 10th Anniversary Essen Symposium, October 19-22, 1987.

2747. Low, Annette. "The Conservation of Charles Dickens' Manuscripts," V&A Conservation Journal (Victoria and Albert Museum), 9 (October 1993), 4-7. Treatment of previously bound and cockled manuscripts for rehousing and access.

2748. Lowell, Howard P. "Archives Preservation: Onward Toward the 21st Century," Preservation Papers of the 1990 SAA Annual Conference, comp. Karen Garlick. Chicago: Society of American Archivists, 1991, 94-96. Brief overview of SAA initiatives and activities to further efforts to preserve archival materials in the 1980s.

2749. Lowell, Howard P. "Bob Patterson: Preservation Pioneer and Leader," Conservation Administration News, 57 (April 1994) 6.

2750. Lowell, Howard P. A Conservation Plan for New Jersey Libraries: First Steps Toward a State Approach for the Preservation of Library Materials in New Jersey. Andover, MA: Northeast Document

Conservation Center, 1985. 28p. Provides a rational, and plan for action developed for and with the New Jersey State Library Committee on Preservation.

2751. Lowell, Howard P. "Permanent Paper for State Government Records," NAGARA Clearinghouse (National Association of Government Archivists and Record Administrators), 6:2 (Spring 1990), 4-5. Summarizes the legislative picture, national and state, regarding paper for archival records.

2752. Lowell, Howard P. "Preservation Microfilming: An Overview," Management Quarterly, 19:1 (January 1985), 22-24,26, 28-29, 36.

2753. Lowell, Howard P. "Preservation Needs in State Archives," Conservation Administration News, 24 (January 1985), 5, 23. Summary of a two-year study to assess preservation needs undertaken for the National Association of Government Archives and Records Administrators (NAGARA).

2754. Lowell, Howard P. Preservation Needs in State Archives. Albany, NY: National Association of Government Archives and Records Administrators, 1986, 1988. 56p., appendix. Report of a survey to document preservation action and needs in state archives and to make recommendations for the physical preservation of the documentary heritage through state and federal funding for conservation.

2755. Lowell, Howard P. "The Quiet Crisis in State Archives," ARMA Records Management Quarterly (Association of Records Managers and Administrators), 22:2 (April 1988), 23-26, 36. Summary of a study to assess preservation needs, with recommendations for action.

2756. Lowell, Howard. "Preservation Needs in State Archives," Conservation Administration News, 24 (January 1986), 5, 23.

2757. Lowry, Marcia Duncan. Preservation and Conservation in the Small Library. Chicago, IL: American Library Association, Library Administration and Management Association, 1989. 16p. (LAMA Small Libraries Publications Series, 15). Focuses on preservation planning and collection maintenance practices appropriate for circulating collections.

2758. Lowry, Maynard, and Philip M. O'Brien. "Rubble with a Cause: Earthquake Preparedness in California," College and Research Libraries News, 51:3 (March 1990), 192-197. A survey of earthquake damage in academic libraries. Stack failure was the cause of the greatest damage. Only 39 institutions reported that they had disaster plans.

2759.   Ludwig, Kathy. "Factors That Influence Permanence," <u>Preservation Papers of the 1991 SAA Annual Conference</u>, comp. Karen Garlick. Chicago: Society of American Archivists, 1992, 70-78. Traces the history and technology of paper and papermaking, factors affecting its permanence. 21 refs.

2760.   Lull, William P. [Response to] 21 August 1994 Smithsonian Press Release "Work With Scientists Revises Guidelines for Climate Control in Museums and Archivists," Princeton Junction, NJ: Garrison/Lull, Inc., October 7, 1994. 5p.

2761.   Lull, William P. "Selecting Fluorescent Lamps for UV Output," <u>Abbey Newsletter</u>, 16:4 (August 1992), 54-55. Analysis of ultraviolet light output in fluorescent lamps. Chart.

2762.   Lull, William P., with Paul N. Banks. <u>Conservation Environment: Guidelines for Libraries and Archives</u>. Albany, NY: New York State Program for the Conservation and Preservation of Library Research Materials, 1991. 88p. Revised ed. Ottawa: Canadian Council of Archives, 1995. 102p. Discusses environmental concerns, assessment, monitoring, and the establishment of practical solutions, both interim and low-cost measures to improve the environment.

2763.   Lull, William P., and M. A. Garrison. "Planning and Design of Museum Storage Environments," <u>Registrar</u>, 5:2 (Spring 1988), 4-14. Covers pre-design planning, selection of an architect and engineer, and guidelines for a sound storage environment.

2764.   Lunas, Susan. "Bookbinding Restoration Workshop," <u>Conservation Administration News</u>, 39 (October 1989), 14-15. Report on the workshop by Bernard Middleton at the Rochester Institute of Technology, 1989.

2765.   Lunas, Susan. "Repairing Tears Without Tears," <u>Binders' Guild Newsletter</u>, 15:6 (September 1992), 5-7. Illus. Basic instructions.

2766.   Lund, Thomas D. "The Physical Aspects of Newspaper Collection Management: Some Problems and Their Solution," <u>Newspapers in the Library</u>, ed. Lois N. Upham. New York: Haworth Press, 1988, 29-36. Report of a survey of selected repositories to determine how they dealt with the maintenance and preservation of newspaper collections. The urgency to film collections is stressed.

2767.   Lunde, Diane B., and Karen Jones. "Preservation Outreach in Colorado; Update: 1994," Colorado Libraries, 20 (Spring 1994), 46-47.

2768.   Lundeen, Gerald W. "Preservation of Paper Based Materials: Present and Future Research and Development in the Paper Industry," Conserving and Preserving Library Materials, ed. Kathryn L. and William T. Henderson. Urbana-Champaign: University of Illinois Graduate School of Library and Information Science, 1983, 73-88. Discussion of paper and causes of its deterioration; current developments in the paper industry; standards and the need for standards.

2769.   Lundquist, Eric G. Salvage of Water Damaged Books, Documents, Micrographic and Magnetic Media. San Francisco, CA: Document Reprocessors of San Francisco, 1985, 1986. 103p. Overview of disaster planning and salvage procedures, with emphasis on the work of Document Reprocessors.

2770.   Luner, Philip. "Evaluation of Paper Permanence," Wood Science Technology, 22 (1988), 81-97. Evaluation of the thermal stability of papermaking under conditions of artificial aging; overview of the complexities in studying the permanence and durability of papers.

2771.   Luner, Philip, ed. Paper Preservation: Current Issues and Recent Developments. Atlanta, GA: TAPPI Press, 1990. 150p. Papers presented at the TAPPI Paper Preservation symposium, October 1988; librarians, archivists, conservators, paper scientists, and manufacturers address issues of paper permanence, deacidification and strengthening, and the alkaline papermaking process.

2772.   Lushington, Nolan. "Getting It Right: Evaluating Plans in the Library Building Planning Process," Library Administration & Management, 7:3 (Summer 1993), 159-163. Outlines steps in the planning process and provides a framework and guidelines for evaluating the architectural work as it relates to function.

2773.   Lyall, Jan. "Developing and Managing Preservation Programmes in the South-East Asian and Pacific Regions," IFLA Journal (International Federation of Library Associations and Institutions), 20:3 (1994), 262-275.

2774.   Lyall, Jan. "Disaster Planning for Libraries & Archives: Understanding the Essential Issues," Proceedings of the Pan-African Conference on the Preservation & Conservation of Library & Archival Materials, Nairobi, Kenya, 21-25 June 1993. The Hague: IFLA, 1995, 103-112. (IFLA Professional Publication 43). Addresses basic management aspects of disaster planning. Describes what a disaster plan is, the basic elements of the plan, problems. Bibliography.

2775.   Lyall, Jan. "Permanent Paper: To Be Or Not To Be?" AICCM Bulletin (Australian Institute for the Conservation of Cultural Material), 16:4 (1990), 11-21. Describes the causes of deterioration of paper, efforts to remedy the problem, research, and the development of standards for the production of permanent papers.

2776.   Lyall, Jan. Memory of the World: A Survey of Current Library Preservation Activities. Paris: UNESCO, 1996. 59p. Prepared for UNESCO on behalf of IFLA. A total of 916 questionnaires were distributed to at least 155 countries. Only 155 libraries from 58 countries answered and only 36% were national libraries. Only six surveys were returned from North America.

2777.   Lyall, Jan. "Preserving Australia's Documentary Heritage: The Role of the National Preservation Office," Libraries: The Heart of the Matter. Deakin, Australia: Australian Library and Information Association, 1992, 193-194. (ALIA '92; Proceedings, 2d Conference 1992). Describes the methods by which the office will operate and the activities likely to be undertaken during its first three years of existence.

2778.   Lyman, Peter. "What Is a Digital Library? Technology, Intellectual Property and the Public Interest," Daedalus, 125:4 (Fall 1996), 1-33.

2779.   Lynch, Clifford A. Accessibility and Integrity of Networked Information Collections. Washington, DC: United States Congress, Office of Technology Assessment, July 5, 1993. 107p.

2780.   Lynch, Clifford A. Electronic Publishing, Electronic Libraries, and the National Research and Education Network: Policy and Technology Issues (revised draft). Washington, DC: United States Congress, Office of Technology Assessment, August 1990. 41p. Examines the current state of electronic networks and looks at future developments, arguing that the "electronic library" will evolve naturally out of existing computer-based information networks and retrieval systems. Examines technical, organizational, and policy issues relating to electronic information transfer.

2781.   Lynch, Clifford A. "The Integrity of Digital Information: Mechanics and Definitional Issues," Journal of the American Society for Information Science, 45 (December 1994), 737-744.

2782.   Lynch, Clifford A., and Edwin B. Brownrigg, "Conservation, Preservation and Digitization," College and Research Libraries, 47:4 (1986), 379-382. Briefly discusses current preservation/conservation technology, and then discusses the advantages of digitization. Calls for re-thinking of conservation and preservation, utilizing digitization. Outlines ways in which digitization helps.

2783.   Lynch, Clifford A. and Edwin B. Brownrigg. "Library Applications of Electronic Imaging Technology," Information Technology and Libraries, 5:2 (June 1986), 100-105. Examines new technologies in the library environment: storage of data, remote access and preservation, imaging rare and fragile books.

2784.   Lynch, Richard E. Preserving Yesterday While Planning for Tomorrow: A View from the State, 1991. Phoenix, AZ: Council of State Historical Records Coordinators, 1991. 22p. Provides a brief history of the council, a report on its biennial meeting, and recommendations for continued action.

2785.   Lynn, M. Stuart. "Digital Preservation and Access: Liberals and Conservatives," Digital Imaging Technology for Preservation, ed. Nancy E. Elkington. Mountain View, CA: Research Libraries Group, 1994, 1-9. Also in Syllabus, 8:3 (1994), 24,26, 54-56. Considers imaging technology for preservation of scholarly materials to provide worldwide access through global networks; notes need for continuous refreshment of information.

2786.   Lynn, M. Stuart. "Digital Technologies, Preservation and Access," Commission on Preservation and Access Newsletter, 43 (March 1992), 1-3. Discusses the use of analog and digital storage and the role that each can play in preservation and access. Argues that the current limits of digital media must be recognized and that analog forms are not yet obsolete.

2787.   Lynn, M. Stuart, et al. Preservation and Access Technology: The Relationship Between Digital and Other Media Conservation Processes: A Structures Glossary of Technical Terms. Washington, DC: Commission on Preservation and Access, 1990. 68p.; reprinted

Information Technology and Libraries, 9:4 (December 1990),
309-336. Glossary compiled to help clarify technical issues.

2788. McAfee, Melissa. "Letter from London; Conservation Programs in
London, The Roehampton Institute," Conservation Administration
News, 48 (January 1992), 30-31. Describes the course in
bookbinding.

2789. McAfee, Melissa. "Letter from London: Conservation Training
Programs in and Around London," Conservation Administration
News, 49 (April 1992), 30-31. Briefly describes courses in
bookbinding, book and paper conservation at the City Literary
Institute, Guildford College of Technology, West Dean College.

2790. McAfee, Melissa. "Letter from London: Conservation Training
Programs in London: Camberwell College of Arts," Conservation
Administration News, 46 (July 1991), 28-30. Describes the programs
in conservation offered at Comberwell College.

2791. McAfee, Melissa. "Letter from London: Conservation Training
Programs in London: London College of Printing," Conservation
Administration News, 47 (October 1991), 30-31. Describes the
mission and curriculum of the program.

2792. McAusland, Jane. Guide to Conservation Mounting and Framing
of Works of Art on Paper. London: Sotheby, 1988. 6p.Pamphlet
on conservation framing, prepared by the Institute of Paper
Conservation.

2793. McAusland, Jane. "A Short History of the Institute of Paper
Conservation: The First Ten Years," Paper Conservation News, 39
(September 1986), 4-5.

2794. McBain, Janet. "The Scottish Film Archive," Audiovisual Librarian,
13:2 (May 1987), 88-90. Brief description of the archive; preserving
film and history of film on a limited budget.

2795. McBeth, Sue. "Microforms: From Concept to Marketing,"
Preservation Microfilming: Does It Have a Future?. Canberra:

National Library of Australia, 1995. 157-163p. Addresses the publishing and marketing of microforms. How to prepare material, select bureau, marketing.

2796. McCabe, Constance. "Preservation of 19th Century Negatives in the National Archives," Journal of the American Institute for Conservation, 30:1 (Spring 1991), 41-73. Illus. Describes a project to conserve nearly 8,000 collodion glass plate negatives by noted 19th-century photographers. Discusses the physical nature of the negatives and characteristic deterioration related to inherent constitutional factors, and preservation issues relating to duplication, rehousing, and storage. Bibliography.

2797. McCabe, Constance. "Glass Plate Negatives: The Importance of Relative Humidity in Storage," Sauvegarde et Conservation des Photographies, Dessins, Imprimés et Manuscrits. Paris: Association pour la Recherche Scientifique sur les Arts Graphiques, 1991, 38-44. Short history of glass plate negatives; overview of preservation issues; discussion of experiments studying the effect of relative humidity on the stability of the glass and emulsion layers.

2798. McCabe, Constance. "Photographic Preservation: Addressing Complex Institutional Needs," Restaurator, 12:4 (1991), 185-200. The preservation challenge of large archival collection of photographs; options, environmental storage conditions.

2799. McCabe, Constance. "Preservation of 19th Century Negatives in the National Archives," Journal of the American Institute for Conservation, 30:1 (Spring 1991), 41-73. Describes a project to preserve a large collection of glass plate negatives and preservation issues.

2800. McCabe, Gerard B., ed. Operations Handbook for the Small Academic Library. Westport, CT: Greenwood Press, 1989. 349p. Basic hands-on guide; preservation concerns addressed in most chapters, including one chapter on preservation.

2801. McCall, Nancy. "Ionizing Radiation as an Experiment: A Case Study," Conservation Administration News, 23 (October 1985), 1-2,

20-21. Report on a technique used to treat a badly infested archival collection. Although long-range effect is unknown, suggests that the method is warranted when the intellectual value of materials is of greater priority than the physical preservation of the actual items.

2802.   McCarthy, Paul H., ed. Archives Assessment and Planning Workbook. Chicago, IL: Society of American Archives, 1989. 86p. Ten sections covering the fundamental areas of archival work, including one on preservation.

2803.   McCarthy, Paul H. "Photofiching: A Catchy New Technique," Conservation Administration News, 22 (July 1985), 1-2, 18-19. Describes a project to preserve photographic images through the use of circulating images on microfiche, with original materials preserved and available for use only under special circumstances.

2804.   McCarthy, Paul H., and R. Bruce Parham. "Photo-microfiche: A Conservation and Research Tool," Microform Review, 16:2 (Spring 1987), 118-125. Describes the preservation of a rare photograph collection on Alaska, with access provided by microfiche.

2805.   McCausland, Sigrid. "The Keeping Archives Workshops Program," Archives & Manuscripts (Australian Society of Archivists), 17:2 (November 1989), 151-163. Describes "Conservation on the Move," a series of workshops given in New South Wales, Australia, on archival policies and practices.

2806.   McCawley, J. C., and T. G. Stone. "A Mobile Conservation Laboratory Service," Studies in Conservation, 28:3 (August 1983), 97-106. Description of a mobile lab providing basic conservation assistance to museums, galleries, and other cultural institutions across Canada.

2807.   McCay, Lynne. "Notes From a Congressional Informer," Special Libraries, 78:2 (Spring 1987), 112-115. Describes the services provided to Congress on comprehensive emergency management by the Library of Congress Congressional Research Service.

2808. McClary, Andrew. "Beware the Deadly Books: A Forgotten Episode in Library History," Journal of Library History, 20:4 (Fall 1985), 427-432. Review of a scare in the early 1900s that books could carry germs and the disinfection programs undertaken in libraries despite a lack of evidence that books could communicate disease.

2809. McCleary, John. Vacuum Freeze-Drying, A Method Used to Salvage Water-Damaged Archival and Library Materials: A RAMP Study with Guidelines. Paris: UNESCO, 1987. 63p. (PGI-87/WS/7). Summarizes the data on freeze-drying and discusses methods in current practice; case studies; bibliography.

2810. McClintock, T. K. "Observations in Developments in the Treatment of Works on Paper," Journal of the American Institute for Conservation, 31:1 (Spring 1992), 107-115. Notes improved quality and relevance of scientific research, appreciation of variations in treatment.

2811. McClung, Patricia A. "Consortia Action: RLG's Preservation Program," Advances in Preservation and Access. Vol. 1. Westport, CT: Meckler, 1992, 61-70. A summary of the initiatives and activities of the Research Library Group's Preservation Program.

2812. McClung, Patricia A. "Costs Associated with Preservation Microfilming: Results of the Research Libraries Group Study," Library Resources and Technical Services, 30:4 (October/December 1986), 363-374. Reprinted: Preservation Microfilming. Chicago, IL: American Library Association, 1989, 363-374. Results of a study to identify costs; results varied among participating institutions, arguing against the existence of a typical project upon which others can base their own estimation.

2813. McClung, Patricia A. Digital Collections Inventory Report. Washington, DC: Council on Library Resources and Commission on Preservation and Access, 1996. 64p.

2814. McClung, Patricia A. ed., RLG Digital Image Access Project: Proceedings from an RLG Symposium held March 31 and April 1,

1995, Palo Alto, CA. Mountain View, CA: Research Libraries Group, 1995. 104p.

2815.   McClung, Patricia. "RLG Symposium on Preservation of Photograph Collection in Research Libraries," Photograph Preservation and the Research Library, ed. Jennifer Porro. Mountain View, CA: RLG, 1991, 51-54. Attendees recommended that RLG publicize the symposium presentations, develop decision models and appraisal guidelines for photographic material, and sponsor reformatting projects.

2816.   McColgin, Michael. "Of Poultices and Bamboo Knives," Conservation Administration News, 40 (January 1990), 6-7. Treatment of a rare Arizona proclamation that had previously been folded and glued to acidic board.

2817.   McColgin, Michael. "Photocopying on Archival Paper," The Abbey Newsletter, 11:8 (December 1987), 126. Use of normal bond paper in electrostatic copiers can result in an accumulation of "fuzz" on the drum and loss of image. Permanent/durable paper for archival photocopying is being investigated: Archival Bond by Xerox and Technaclear has done well under limited testing conditions. The Government Printing Office is studying electrostatic copiers and toners to identify those that produce archival copies.

2818.   McColgin, Michael. "Preservation in Arizona: The First Decade," Conservation Administration News, 43 (October 1990), 1-2, 28-29. Describes a decade's effort to preserve library and archival collections in Arizona.

2819.   McCombs, Phil. "Library of Congress Books to Be Preserved," Washington Post (May 10, 1984), 9B. Discusses approval to build a plant to mass deacidify library books.

2820.   McCormick, Don, and Seth Winner. "The Toscanini Legacy," ARSC Journal (Association of Recorded Sound Archivists), 20 (1989), 182-190. Describes the approach to the preservation of sound recordings at the Rogers and Hammerstein Archives of Recorded Sound, New York Public Library.

2821.   McCormick, Edith. "Burst Water Pipe Threatens N.Y. State Library
         Again," American Libraries, 23:2 (February 1992), 133-134. Case
         study of problems caused by repeatedly frozen water pipes.

2822.   McCormick-Goodhart, Mark H. ""An Analysis of Image
         Deterioration in Wet-Plate Negatives from the Mathew Brady
         Studios," Journal of Imaging Science and Technology, 36:3 (1992),
         297-305. Investigation of the deterioration of collodian wet-plate
         negatives made in the Brady studios in the 1860s, leading to a further
         study of the glass used.

2823.   McCormick-Goodhart, Mark H. "The Allowable Temperature and
         Relative Humidity Range for the Safe Use and Storage of
         Photographic Materials," Journal Society of Archivists (Canada),
         17:1 (1996), 7-21. The author says that the allowable ranges of
         temperature and relative humidity are the same for old brittle
         materials as they are for new material, because the elastic limits do
         not change with age.

2824.   McCoy, R. W. "Cooperative Preservation Activities of the Research
         Libraries Group (RLG)," Preservation of Library Materials, ed.
         Merrily Smith. New York: Saur, 1987, 83-88. (IFLA Publications,
         40). Reviews the cooperative preservation activities of the Research
         Libraries Group, a partnership of 35 university and research libraries.

2825.   McCrady, Ellen. " The ACS Symposium in LA, September 28-29,
         1988," Abbey Newsletter, 12:8 (December 1988), 130-131. Report
         on the Symposium on Historic Textile and Paper Materials:
         Conservation and Characterization II. Sponsored by the Cellulose,
         Paper and Textile Division of the American Chemical Society.

2826.   McCrady, Ellen. "Accelerated Aging and the Effects of Enclosure,"
         Abbey Newsletter, 8 (April 1984), 28-29. Discusses the results of
         accelerated aging tests in materials enclosed (through encapsulation
         or deacidification), and suggests how deterioration might be further
         slowed.

2827.   [McCrady, Ellen]. "The Abbey Permanent Paper Survey: Interim Report, March 1994," Alkaline Paper Advocate, 6:6 (December 1993), 44-47. Results of a questionnaire sent to paper manufacturers asking which of their papers meet the new ANSI standard for permanent paper.

2828.   [McCrady, Ellen]. "The Advantages of Low RH," Abbey Newsletter, 14:1 (February 1990), 15. Brief discussion of the advantages and disadvantages of storing paper-based materials in low relative humidity, citing the discrepancies in research to date. Notes that determining the appropriate RH for collection storage depends upon a number of related factors.

2829.   McCrady, Ellen. " Albumen Prints, RH and pH," Abbey Newsletter, 8 (April 1984), 40. Reports that research indicates albumen prints should be stored at 30-40% relative humidity and that contact with Alkaline storage materials may hasten deterioration.

2830.   [McCrady, Ellen]. "An Annotated Bibliography on Various pH Measurements," Alkaline Paper Advocate, 4:1 (February 1991), 4-5.

2831.   McCrady, Ellen. "Canadian Government Looks at Alkaline Paper," Alkaline Paper Advocate, 2:5 (November 1989), 47-48, 50-51. Summary of a study, "The Runability of Alkaline Paperstocks within the National Printing Bureau," undertaken by a working group appointed in 1989 by the Canadian Government.

2832.   McCrady, Ellen. "Carbonate Content of Certain Archival Paper," Alkaline Paper Advocate, 1:4 (October 1988), 31-32. A study of calcium content of supposedly permanent papers and the need for testing to determine the exact amount of calcium present when the amount does not reach 3%.

2833.   McCrady, Ellen. "Cleaning the Indoor Air," Abbey Newsletter, 7:5 (1983), 57-58. Brief description of the use of activated alumina filters for removal of gaseous contaminants.

2834.   McCrady, Ellen. "Clinton Mandates Recycled Paper in Executive Branch, Bypassing Permanence Standards," Alkaline Paper

Advocate, 6:4 (1993), 25-26, 28. Discussion of the "Executive Order 12873 of October 20, 1993: Federal Acquisition, Recycling, and Waste Prevention" and its lack of reference to permanence considerations, or, to Public Law 101-423, "Joint Resolution to Establish a National Policy on Permanent Papers."

2835. McCrady, Ellen. "Conference on Book Theft," Abbey Newsletter, 7:5 (1983), 60. Summary of the 1983 Oberlin Conference on Book Theft.

2836. McCrady, Ellen. "Consensus Builds for a National Preservation Strategy," Abbey Newsletter, 16:1 (February 1992), 8.

2837. McCrady, Ellen. "Conservatism in Conservation: A Round-Table Discussion, May 1991," Abbey Newsletter, 15 (1991), 101-103. Describes the perspective toward paper conservation treatment that advocates a conservative approach and minimal intervention.

2838. McCrady, Ellen. "Control Fire in Compact Shelving," Abbey Newsletter, 14 (June 1990), 47. Discusses fire tests conducted on movable shelving for the National Archives and Records Administration's new facility at College Park, MD. Tests were performed by Underwriters Laboratory.

2839. McCrady, Ellen. "Copenhagen, September 1984: ICOM Committee for Conservation," Abbey Newsletter, 8:5 (October 1984), 81-83.

2840. McCrady, Ellen. "Deacidification vs. Microfilming," Abbey Newsletter, 14:6 (October 1990), 112-113. Lucid discussion of the options.

2841. McCrady, Ellen. "Definitions of Permanence and Durability," Alkaline Paper Advocate, 2:4 (October 1989), 42-44. Author quotes standard definitions, notes their "inherent difficulties and ambiguities," and discusses them in the context of use.

2842. McCrady, Ellen. "Diffusion of New Knowledge in Conservation," Preprints. International Conference on Conservation and Restoration of Archive and Library Materials, Erice (Italy), April 22-29, 1996.

Rome: Istituto Centrale per la Patologia del Libro. 2, April 22-29, 1996, 513-516. Notes need for more cooperation, communication, and collaboration between scientists and conservators; how communication might be fostered.

2843.   [McCrady, Ellen]. "The Dilemma of Office Paper Recycling," Alkaline Paper Advocate, 4:4 (August 1991), 36-37. Describes the variety of office waste papers and the problems of attempting to recycle them; inks are the greatest cause of difficulty.

2844.   McCrady, Ellen. "A Few Points from the NARA Conference on Exhibitions," Abbey Newsletter, 14 (June 1990), 43. Discusses exhibition illumination limits in terms of an annual cumulative measurement. Suggestions are made for humidity and gaseous pollution control for items in transit.

2845.   McCrady, Ellen. "From the TAPPI Archives: the 1930 and 1933 Reports of the Permanence/Durability Committee," Alkaline Paper Advocate, 5:5 (November 1992), 37-39. Exerpts from these reports, which identify environment as a factor in deterioration.

2846.   McCrady, Ellen. "The Great Cotton Rag Myth," Alkaline Paper Advocate, 5:5 (November 1992), 33-34. Research proves that the earliest papers were made of linen or hemp; transition to cotton fibers occurred during the industrial revolution of the 19th century.

2847.   McCrady, Ellen. "GPO Takes Affirmative Action," Alkaline Paper Advocate, 3 (March 1990), 1-2. Tells how Congress directed GPO to develop plans to use archival paper.

2848.   [McCrady, Ellen]. "Guide to Drafting of Contracts," Abbey Newsletter, 8:1, part 2: Special Supplement on Library Binding (February 1984), 13-16. Clear discussion by a librarian and former library binder.

2849.   McCrady, Ellen. "Guidelines for Preservation Photocopying of Replacement Pages," Abbey Newsletter, 15 (September 1991), 79-80. Reprinted with permission of the American Library Association, from ALCT's 1990 "Guidelines for Preservation Photocopying of Replacement Pages," ALA 1990.

2850.   McCrady, Ellen. "History of the Abbey Publications," Library Resources and Technical Services, 35:1 (January 1991), 104-108. A leading advocate for the preservation of library and archival materials describes how she became involved, established her newsletters, and developed a research agenda.

2851.   McCrady, Ellen. "The History of Microfilm Blemishes," Restaurator, 6:3 (Fall 1984), 191-204. Describes the discovery in the 1960s of small blemishes on negative microfilm that led to several years of research by Eastman Kodak and the National Bureau of Standards. Cause was identified and recommendations for appropriate storage and housing were developed.

2852.   McCrady, Ellen. "How Leather Dressing May Have Originated," Abbey Newsletter, 14:1 (February 1990), 19-20. Gives some early formulas; notes that there is no evidence that leather dressings help preserve books and a good deal of circumstantial evidence that they may be harmful.

2853.   McCrady, Ellen. "Hurricane Hugo Puts Disaster Plans to Test," Abbey Newsletter, 13:7 (November 1989), 113-114.

2854.   McCrady, Ellen. "The Idea of Whole-Discipline Preservation in Libraries, Archives and Museums," Abbey Newsletter, 18:1 (April 1994), 1-2, 4. Discusses an approach to preservation of collections by discipline, not by medium, using the example of agriculture. Notes need for more emphasis on preserving materials in the natural sciences.

2855.   McCrady, Ellen. "Indoor Environment Standards: A Report on the NYU Symposium," Abbey Newsletter, 19:6/7 (December 1995), 93-94, 96-98. Summary of presentations, review of the published commentary, and editorial discussion; list of recent publications by the speakers. McCrady feels that the controversy has developed because the conditions for good research were wanting, and "good and productive communication between researchers and practitioners is sadly lacking"(96).

2856. McCrady, Ellen. "The ISO April Meeting," Abbey Newsletter, 14 (June 1990), 44. Discusses methods to be used for round robin testing relating to paper permanence.

2857. McCrady, Ellen. "International Seminar on Preservation Research, May 1991," Abbey Newsletter, 15:5 (September 1991), 76-79. Thorough report and discussion of the key papers presented, with the resolution to go forward to the International Council on Archives and the International Federation of Library Associations and Institutions.

2858. McCrady, Ellen. "LA Public Library Burns," Abbey Newsletter, 10:3 (June 1986), 33-34. Carefully researched analysis of the disaster, its causes, and its aftermath.

2859. McCrady, Ellen. "LC Invites Proposals for Deacidification Service," Abbey Newsletter, 14 (October 1990), 97-98, 100-102.

2860. McCrady, Ellen. "Librarians and Paper Permanence," Alkaline Paper Advocate, 6:6 (December 1993), 48-52. Describes librarians' advocacy of permanent paper from support of the work of William Barrow to the Yale University Library survey of the collections.

2861. McCrady, Ellen. "Lignin on Trial: A Report of the ISR Workshop, July 6-8 at ASTM Headquarters," Abbey Newsletter, 18:3 (July 1994), 1-2, 28. Report on a meeting to explore ways of formulating permanence standards, and to establish a research agenda.

2862. McCrady, Ellen. "Lithco Pilot Plant to Open Soon," Abbey Newsletter, 14 (April 1990), 26. Highlights a commercial process said to increase the life of treated paper by tenfold and to strengthen it as well.

2863. McCrady, Ellen. "Mold as a Threat to Human Health," Abbey Newsletter, 18:6 (1994), 65-66. Discussion of possible risks to librarians and archivists from mold and other microorganisms.

2864. McCrady, Ellen. "The Nature of Lignin," Alkaline Paper Advocate, 4:4 (August 1991), 33-34. Descriptions of what lignins are and how they can interact with other materials.

2865. McCrady, Ellen. "Nine Preservation Self-Studies," Abbey Newsletter, 12:2 (February 1988), 32-25. A review and analysis of the reports of the first assisted self-study projects undertaken with the assistance of the ARL/OMS Preservation Planning Program; identifies important concerns.

2866. McCrady, Ellen. "NISO Draft Standard Allows Significantly More Lignin," Alkaline Paper Advocate, 3 (December 1990), 61-62. Update on ANSI Standard Z39.48.

2867. McCrady, Ellen. " NLM Hearing on Permanent Paper," Abbey Newsletter, 11:2 (1987), 19-20. Medical publishers complain of the cost of permanent paper. In the meantime the medical literature is deteriorating rapidly.

2868. McCrady, Ellen. North American Permanent Papers. Austin, TX: Abbey Publications, May 1994. 46p. 2d ed., 1995. 52p. List of permanent papers that meet the ANSI/ISO standard; addresses and telephone numbers of manufacturers. Publication to be updated on a regular basis.

2869. McCrady, Ellen. "Notes from TAPPI Papermakers, 1992: Alkaline Conversion Round Table," Alkaline Paper Advocate, 5:4 (September 1992), 25-27. Informative information on the problems that paper manufacturers have encountered during conversion to alkaline paper production.

2870. McCrady, Ellen. "Offsite Storage at UT (University of Texas) Austin," Abbey Newsletter, 16:7-8 (December 1992), 105-106. Description of a remote storage facility planned for "permanent, important, but little used" library and archival material.

2871. McCrady, Ellen. "An Overview of Occupational Hazards, Excluding Those Hazards Involved with Conservation Treatments and

Fumigation," Conservation Administration News, 20 (January 1985), 4-5. Cites hazards encountered by preservation administrators, including back injuries, dust particles, pollutants, and stress.

2872.   McCrady, Ellen. "Paper Permanence Debate II," Alkaline Paper Advocate, 7:2 (July 1994), 1-2, 12-14. Summary of discussion at a workshop to address issues concerning the permanence of paper and to establish a research agenda.

2873.   McCrady, Ellen. "The Permanent Paper Law," Abbey Newsletter, 14 (December 1990), 133-134. Text of PL 101-423.

2874.   McCrady, Ellen. "Permanent Papers on the Market," Abbey Newsletter, 15:6 (October 1991), 93-95. Summary of the results of a survey of manufacturers undertaken in the summer of 1991.

2875.   McCrady, Ellen. "pH is Hard to Measure," The Abbey Newsletter, 11:8 (December 1987), 131-132. pH measurements of paper taken with distilled water are frequently low. A representative of Orion Research, Inc., explained the choice, use, and maintenance of electrodes and buffer solutions, and how to get a good reading from a properly calibrated meter. Potassium chloride was recommended as an additive. Other peculiarities of distilled water are mentioned.

2876.   McCrady, Ellen. "Production and Use of Long-Lasting Paper in the USA," Conference on Book and Paper Conservation, 1990. Budapest, Hungary: Technical Association of Paper and Printing Industry/National Szechenyi Library, 1992, 422-430. Describes the slow but steady conversion of papermills in the United States to the production of alkaline papers and the development of standards. Proposed and existing standards are cited and a list of standards organizations is provided.

2877.   McCrady, Ellen. "Progress in Preservation," Alkaline Paper Advocate, 4:2 (May 1991), 15-18. Summary of conservation and preservation concerns and developments over the last few years.

2878.   McCrady, Ellen. "Some Permanent Copy Papers," Alkaline Paper Advocate, 5:5 (November 1992), 39-40. A list of permanent copy papers on the market; suggests purchasing by brand name to avoid inflated pricing.

2879. McCrady, Ellen. "Some Permanent Papers for Dissertations," Abbey Newsletter, 19:6 (December 1995), 116. List of papers taken from "North American Permanent Papers," 1995 ed., listed under categories assigned by their mills.

2880. McCrady, Ellen. "Spots and Boxes," Mid-Atlantic Archivist, 12:4 (Fall 1983), 13-14. Discussion of redox blemishes on microfilm and how the problem was resolved.

2881. McCrady, Ellen. "State Laws Concerning Permanent Paper," Abbey Newsletter, 14 (October 1990), 108-109. Text from Arizona, Colorado, Connecticut, Indiana, North Carolina, and Virginia.

2882. [McCrady, Ellen]. "Stephen Blumberg and His Stolen Books," Abbey Newsletter, 15:7 (November 1991), 105-106. Concise summary of the Blumberg theft, causes and effects.

2883. McCrady, Ellen. "Symposium '88, October 3-7, 1988 Ottawa," Abbey Newsletter, 12:8 (December 1988), 144-146. Report on symposium by Canadian Conservation Institute and National Gallery of Canada on conservation of books, archival materials, and works of art on paper.

2884. McCrady, Ellen. "Temperature and RH Guidelines Challenged by the Smithsonian," Abbey Newsletter, 18:4/5 (August/September 1994), 44-47. Reaction to a press release by the Smithsonian's Conservation Analytical Laboratory lessening the recommendations for environmental control limits in museum collections, with press release and responses from CAL scientists and a conservation scientist.

2885. McCrady, Ellen. "Testimony of NIC (National Institute for Conservation) in Favor of H.J. Res. 226 (Permanent Paper)," Alkaline Paper Advocate, 3 (March 1990), 2.

2886.　McCrady, Ellen. "Three Deacidification Methods Compared," <u>Abbey Newsletter</u>, 15:8 (December 1991), 121-122. Careful analysis of the Institute of Paper Science and Technology reports on books deacidified by the Akzo, FMC/Lithco, and Wei T'o processes.

2887.　McCrady, Ellen. "Top Priority Research Projects Chosen by CPA Group," <u>Abbey Newsletter</u>, 17:7/8 (1993), 99. Brief discussion of six preservation science projects that received endorsements by Commission on Preservation and Access.

2888.　McCrady, Ellen. "Toward the Acid-Free Office," <u>Preservation Paper of the 1990 SAA Annual Conference</u>, comp. Karen Garlick. Chicago: Society of American Archivists, 1991, 34-41. Discusses advances in production and use of acid-free papers, what archivists and records managers can do to further their acceptance and use. Lists standards organization, proposed and existing standards, and permanent papers on the market.

2889.　McCrady, Ellen. "Training in Paper Conservation," <u>Abbey Newsletter</u>, 7:2 Supplement (1983), 1-2.

2890.　McCrady, Ellen. "A Treatment for Brittle Flaking Tape Recordings," <u>Abbey Newsletter</u>, 14 (November 1990), 123. Notes how Agfa research labs in Munich and the United States have found a reliable way to rejuvenate deteriorated tapes long enough to transfer them to a digital master.

2891.　McCrady, Ellen. "The Trouble with Alkaline Chemistry," <u>Alkaline Paper Advocate</u>, 5:2 (May 1992), 12.

2892.　McCrady, Ellen. "Weakening Paper in Immersion," <u>Abbey Newsletter</u>, 7:3 (1983), 40. A summary of a paper by A. A. Robertson in <u>Tappi</u> in 1970.

2893.　McCrady, Ellen. "Why Collections Deteriorate: Putting Acidic Paper in Perspective," <u>Alkaline Paper Advocate</u>, 1:4 (October 1988), 31-32; reprinted in <u>Preservation in Libraries; A Reader</u>, ed. Ross Harvey. New York: Bowker-Saur, 1993, 88-91. Discusses contemporary causes of deterioration, and the increased wear on paper; the solution is permanent/durable paper.

2894. McCrady, Ellen. "Wood Is Good," Mid-Atlantic Archivist, 13:2 (Spring 1984), 11-12. Discussion of the reasons for the problems with wood pulp paper and developments that now enable manufacturers to make permanent/durable high quality paper from wood pulp.

2895. McCrady, Ellen, and Michael Koenig. "Columbia Study on Use of Permanent Book Paper," Abbey Newsletter, 8 (February 1984), 2. Preliminary report on a small-scale survey of incoming books at Columbia University. Found that 40% used acid-free paper.

2896. McCrank, Lawrence J. "Integrating Conservation and Collection Management: An Experimental Workshop Report," Library and Archival Security, 6:1 (Spring 1984), 23-48. Describes a workshop to train conservation-minded library and archival administrators at the University of Maryland College and Library and Information Services in 1979-80. Worksheets included.

2897. McCrone, Walter. "Vineland Map," Analytical Chemistry, 60:10 (May 10, 1989), 1009-1081. Reports on the analysis carried out in the authentication of the Vineland map circa 1440, belonging to the Beinecke Library, Yale University. The controversy is a case study in the strengths and weaknesses of chemical analysis and points up the need for careful professional evaluation of object, provenance, and evidence by archivists.

2898. McCue, Peter. "The Complexities of the Conservation Issue: Can We Curb the Crisis?" Education for Librarianship: Australia, 5:1 (Autumn 1988), 27-35. Identifies preservation and conservation as a major issue in librarianship and describes the approach taken in Western Australia; need for a cooperative approach is emphasized.

2899. McDaniel, Danny L. "Fire Suppression Systems: Alternatives to Halon for Cultural and Historic Facilities," Technology & Conservation, 2/94 (Summer 1994), 17-19. Review of fire suppression systems, halon and alternatives. Urges careful evaluation of needs, then "consider the most efficient and cost-effective way to provide the level of protection that is needed" (19).

2900. McDaniel, George. "The Calm Before the Storm," History News, 45:1 (January/February 1990), 22-24. Briefly describes the Charleston (SC) Archives, Libraries and Museums (CALM) plan for disaster and its success after Hurricane Hugo struck.

2901. MacDonald, Chloe Gregg, Joseph K. McGregor, Carol Edwards, and Isabella Hopkins. "Application of Paper Preservation Techniques by the U.S. Geological Survey Field Records and Photographic Libraries," Preserving Geoscience Imagery, ed. Louise S. Zipp. Alexandria, VA: Geoscience Information Society, 1993, 125-126. (Proceedings, 23). Techniques for geoscientists to preserve paper and photographs.

2902. MacDonald, Eric. "Creating a Preservation Department from Existing Staff Resources: The UC Irvine Experience," Conservation Administration News, 55 (October 1993), 6-7, 34-35. Establishing a "viable, focused department" through reorganization of staff.

2903. McDonald, Franklyn. "Emergency Planning for Protection of Records," Disaster Planning in Jamaica. Kingston, Jamaica: Jamaica Library Association, 1989, 7-10. Overview of contingency planning by the Director of the Office of Disaster Preparedness and Emergency Relief Coordination.

2904. McDonald, Peter. "Color Microform: New Possibilities," Microform Review, 17:3 (August 1988), 146-149. Discussion of issues surrounding the use of color microfilm, with a plea for further study of its permanence and stability.

2905. McDonald, Peter. "The Core Agriculture Literature Project: Setting Priorities for Preservation," Abbey Newsletter, 15:2 (April 1991), 17-18. Describes a project at Cornell University to identify the core literature in agriculture and to identify material for preservation.

2906. McDonald, Peter. "Studying the Preservation Needs of Sound Archives in the United States," Conservation Administration News, 36 (January 1989), 4, 19.

2907. McDonnel, Robert J. "Double Dip Your Problem Negatives," Industrial Photography, 33:10 (October 1984), 40-42. Describes an interesting printing technique for improving contrast balance in problematic negatives.

2908. MacDougall, Alan F., and Michael Chaney. Security and Crime Prevention in Libraries. Aldershot, England; Brookfield, VT: Ashgate, 1992. 370p. Summary of the scope of the problem, developments, initiatives, possible solutions, from a British perspective.

2909. MacDougall, Jennifer. Newsplan: Guidelines for the Microfilming of Newspapers. Dublin: National Library of Ireland, 1994. 30p.

2910. McGee, Ann E. "Evaluating and Comparing Mass Deacidification Benefits: Enhanced and Extended Useful Life," Restaurator, 12:2 (1991), 104-109. Testing suggested by FMC Corporation before and after accelerated aging of treated and untreated papers to evaluate deacidification processes.

2911. McGiffen, Robert F., Jr. A Current Status Report on Fumigation in Museums and Historical Agencies. Nashville, TN: American Association for State and Local History, 1985. 16p. (AASLH Technical Report, 4). Review and discussion of problems with fumigants; bibliography.

2912. McGiffen, Robert F. "Health and Safety in the Museum Workplace," Museum News, 64:2 (October 1985), 36-43. Describes problems resulting from careless work habits or improper protection. Bibliography; sources of assistance.

2913. McGing, Angela, and Anne Picot. "The Conservation of Building Plans Project," Archives and Manuscripts, 16:2 (November 1988), 97-118. Describes a project to film all plans from 1909 and to conserve records of permanent value. Discusses successful application of conservation techniques to a large volume of records by unskilled workers.

2914. McGleave, Peter. "Conservation of Library Collections," An Leabharlann, The Irish Library, 4:3 (1987), 79-86. Author suggests that the libraries main strength lies in its staff.

2915. McGovern, Jim. "How Do You Get Ready for a Disaster? Selecting a Restoration Company," Disaster Recovery Journal, 4:4 (October-December), 30-32.

2916. McGuinna, Niamh. "A Method for In Sita Capillary Washing," Paper Conservation News, 74 (June 1995), 13. Treatment of an early Persian parchment manuscript using the capillary washing technique.

2917. McIlwaine, John. "Preservation and Storage," Information Sources in Cartography. New York: Bowker, 1990, 279-294. General review article dealing with storage and preservation concerns.

2918. MacInnes, Andrew N., and Andrew R. Barron. "Spectroscopic Evaluation of the Efficacy of Two Mass Deacidification Processes for Paper," Journal of Materials Chemistry, 2:10 (1992), 1049-1056. Compares paper samples using diethyl zinc and magnesium butoxytriglycolate and analyzes results. Neither chemical process was effective on glossy, kaolin-coated paper.

2919. McIntyre, John E. "Action Planning for Disaster," Refer (Journal of the Information Sciences Group, Library Association, U.K.), 5:4 (Summer 1989), 1-7. Covers prevention, preparedness, salvage, recovery, with discussion of sprinkler systems.

2920. McIntyre, John E. "Disaster Control Planning," Conference on Book and Paper Conservation, 1990. Budapest, Hungary: Technical Association of Paper and Printing Industry/National Szechenyi Library, 1992, 50-61. Outlines the elements of a disaster plan and requirements for salvage.

2921. McIntyre, John E. "National Library of Scotland Preservation Policy," Conference on Book and Paper Conservation, 1990.

Budapest, Hungary: Technical Association of Paper and Printing Industry/National Szechenyi Library, 1992, 79-96.

2922. McIntyre, John E. "Preservation at the National Library of Scotland," Conservation Administration News, 52 (January 1993), 1-3. Describes the development, organization, and activities of the Conservation Division.

2923. McIntyre, John E. "Principles and Applications," Preserving the Word. London: Library Association, 1987, 58-62. Brief discussion of the causes of deterioration of library collections.

2924. McIntyre, Mary. "Custom Phase Boxes for Books," National Library News (Canada), 26:7 (July 1994), 17-19. Clear instruction for construction.

2925. McKay, Richard S. "Risk Management: Weighing the Pros and Cons," Inform, 1:1 (January 1987), 16-18. Defines risk management as the identification, analysis, and evaluation of risk and the selection of the best ways of dealing with it.

2926. McKay, Christine, and Anthony W. Smith. "The Effect of Wetting Agents on the Tensile Strength of Paper," Conservation of Historic and Artistic Works on Paper. Ottawa: Canadian Conservation Institute, 1994, 199-203. (Symposium 88). Investigates the changes that may occur in the tensile strength of paper following treatment with water-containing wetting agents.

2927. McKay, Susan S. "Storage of Machine-Readable Records," Disaster Planning in Jamaica. Kingston, Jamaica: Jamaica Library Association, 1989, 14-18. Strategies for the preservation and protection of electronic data in computer files.

2928. McKenzie, Alex W. "Permanent Papers — From Then to When," AICCM Bulletin (Australian Institute for the Conservation of Cultural Material), 16:4 (1990), special issue, "Conference Proceedings: Permanent Paper;" reprinted in Alkaline Paper Advocate, 5:1 (March 1992), 1-2,4-6. A concise history of papermaking and the problems that each change in the process has

Bibliography

produced. Discusses needs for the present and the future to ensure the survival of printed materials.

2929. MacKenzie, George. "Availability, Affordability and Application of Preservation and Conservation Technologies," Proceedings of the Pan-African Conference on the Preservation and Conservation of Library and Archival Materials, Nairobi, Kenya , 21-25 June 1993. The Hague: IFLA (1995) 129-137. (IFLA Professional Publication 43). Overview of conservation and preservation technologies; protection against insects, fire, floods, security, housing, and handling: physical treatment; repair, deacidification.

2930. MacKenzie, George. "Preservation of Electronic Media," Library Conservation News, 38 (January 1993), 1-3, 7. Describes the problems and challenges of preservation of information in electronic formats available today, with a look toward future technologies. Notes that the greatest long-term problem is accessibility.

2931. McKeon, D. B. "The Conservation Administrator of the Future," Conservation Administration News, 22 (July 1985), 9, 23-24. Presents the results of a survey to determine expert opinion on the developments in preservation and conservation that will occur in the last 15 years of the 20th century.

2932. McKeon, Donald. "Conservation for Libraries and Archives: 1981-2001; Consideration of Future Developments and Personnel," Restaurator, 6:3/4 (1984), 139-146. Author predicts that conservation personnel for libraries will be trained as administrators with library or scientific backgrounds.

2933. McKern, Debra. "Copiers for Bound Volumes: A Survey of Available Equipment," Library Technology Reports, 25:6 (November/December 1989), 863-867. Review of equipment.

2934. McKern, Debra. "Public-Use Copiers in Library Service," Library Resources and Technical Services, 32:2 (April 1989), 160-163. Discusses a survey to determine what features librarians considered essential for public service use of photocopiers.

2935.   McKern, Debra and Sherry Byrne. <u>ALA Target Packet for Use in</u>
        <u>Preservation Microfilming</u>. Chicago, IL: American Library
        Association, 1991. 55p. Contains definitions and descriptions of all
        types of targets that are needed for microfilming including sample
        target sequences, instructions for their use, model forms, and actual
        targets ready for use.

2936.   McKitterick, David. "Evidence in the Printed Book and the
        Avoidance of Damage: A Bibliographer's Viewpoint," <u>Conservation</u>
        <u>and Preservation in Small Libraries</u>, ed. Nicholas Hadgraft and
        Katherine Swift. Cambridge: Parker Library Publications, 1994. 23-
        28. Discusses need to preserve as much physical evidence as possible
        about the construction of a book, with emphasis on preserving old
        bindings.

2937.   McKitterick, David. "The Survival of Books," <u>Book Collector</u>, 43:1
        (Spring 1994), 9-26. Bibliographic essay on the need to preserve
        books as physical objects that tell us about our history.

2938.   McLean, William. "Bloom on Leather," <u>CBBAG Newsletter</u>
        (Canadian Bookbinders and Book Artist Guild), 14:2 (Summer
        1996), 10-11. Discusses "spue," crystalline surface deposits and
        microbial growth on leather bindings, caused by a poor environment
        and by deposits within the leather that rise to the surface under poor
        storage conditions. Describes cleaning methods.

2939.   McNeil, Beth, and Denise J. Johnson, eds. <u>Patron Behavior in</u>
        <u>Libraries: A Handbook of Positive Approaches to Negative</u>
        <u>Situations</u>. Chicago: American Library Association, 1996.
        160p. Overview of problem patrons and how to handle problem
        situations and problem people from legal, psychological
        perspectives.

2940.   MacQueen, Scott. "The Restoration of '20,000 Leagues Under the
        Sea,'" <u>The Perfect Vision</u>, 6:21 (Spring 1994), 38-45. Detailed
        history of the restoration of the 1954 Disney film, the first live-action
        film in color, cinemascope, and stereo sound.

2941.   Mace, Angela. "Grants for Preservation: Conservation of
         Architectural Manuscripts at the British Architectural Library,"
         Library Conservation News, 39 (April 1993), 5-6. Briefly describes
         conservation of an album and collections of manuscripts with
         funding from the National Manuscripts Conservation Trust.

2942.   Macklin, Lisa A., and Martha K. Tarlton. "Emergency Management
         and Disaster Mitigation Periodicals: An Annotated Bibliography,"
         Serials Review, 17:2 (1991), 21-26, 40.

2943.   Madden, Ken. "Technical Aspects of Paper Production/Finishing
         and Converting Processes/Paper Recycling/Archival Paper
         Production," AICCM Bulletin (Australian Institute for the
         Conservation of Cultural Material), 16:4 (1990), 39-51. History of
         paper production and current practices.

2944.   Maddow, Ben. Slow Fires: On the Preservation of the Human
         Record. Washington, DC: Council on Library Resources, 1987.
         24p. Transcript of the one-hour version of the video "Slow Fires,"
         which describes the deterioration and destruction of the world's
         documentary heritage.

2945.   Magenau, Carol. "Spring Conference Report," ACRL/New England
         Chapter News, 49 (June 1988), 3-6. Report of a conference,
         "Preserve or Perish: Will Our Collection Survive?" jointly sponsored
         by the ACRL/New England Chapter and the New England Library
         Association Academic Librarians.

2946.   Maggen, Michael. "Conservation of the Allepo Codex," Restaurator,
         12:2 (1991), 116-130. Physical treatment of a 10th- century codex in
         Hebrew.

2947.   Maggen, Michael. "Constructing a Mini-Vacuum Unit and Using It
         for Philatelic Materials," Restaurator, 14:1 (1993), 45-
         56. Development of a miniature suction unit.

2948.   Maggen, Michael, and Shalom Sabar. "The Conservation of Two
         Kariaite Marriage Contracts," Restaurator, 16:2 (1995), 77-
         85. Treatment of C13 and C18 documents on goatskin.

2949.   Magorrian, Vincent. "Climate Controls," Museum News, 71:4 (July-August 1992), 65-67. Brief outline of practical steps a museum should take when changing its HVAC system, and gives some estimate of the length of time and cost for completing such a project.

2950.   Magrath, Lynn L., and Kenneth E. Dowlin. "The Potential for Development of a Clearinghouse for Emergency Information in the Public Library," Special Libraries, 78:2 (Spring 1987), 131-135. The role that the public library can play in the creation and dissemination of an on-line clearinghouse for emergency information.

2951.   Magrath, Lynn L., and Kenneth E. Dowlin. "The Public Library as a Clearinghouse for Emergency Information," PNLA Quarterly (Pacific Northwest Library Association), 52 (Winter 1988), 22, 26. The role that the library can play as a center for information on risk mitigation preparedness, disaster response, and recovery.

2952.   Maines and Associates. Disaster Plan Template. Ithaca, NY: Rachel P. Maines and Associates, 1990. rev. 1993. (software).

2953.   "Major Database Disasters: Could They Happen Here?" American Libraries, 14:10 (November 1983), 645-647. Interviews with bibliographic utilities on threats to computerized database security, including natural disasters, insider reprogramming, false input data, stolen passwords, altered fields, computer overload, etc.

2954.   Makepeace, Chris E. Ephemera: A Book on Its Collection, Conservation, and Use. Aldershot, England; Brookfield, VT: Gower, 1985. 247p. Discusses the collection, use, storage, preservation, and conservation of ephemeral materials.

2955.   Makes, F. "Damage to Old Bookbindings in the Skolkloster Library," Skolkloster Studies, 17 (1984); Nordisk Tidskrift for Booch Biblioteksvasen, 71 (1984), 33-57. Examination of mold growth on a collection of calf-bound books and their treatment.

2956.   "Making a Clear Case for Protection," Technology and Conservation, 8:2 (Summer 1983), 15-16. The use of Melinex 516, a polyester film manufactured by ICI Americas Inc., for encapsulation using an ultrasonic welding unit is described.

2957. "Making Old Documents Young Again," Du Pont Magazine, 81:6 (December-November 1987), 18-21. The article describes some ways Mylar polyester film is used by paper conservators at the Conservation Center for Artistic and Historic Artifacts in Philadelphia. The article mentions the use of Mylar as a work surface, support during washing, encapsulation material, and for the manufacture of specialized flexible tools.

2958. Malaro, Marie C. "Collection Care and Accountability; Legal and Ethical Standards," Legal Problems of Museum Administration. Philadelphia, PA: American Law Institute, 1989, 381-400. Reviews legal situation regarding accountability of staff and trustees to protect cultural property in collections.

2959. Malaro, Marie C. A Legal Primer on Managing Museum Collections. Washington, DC: Smithsonian Institution Press, 1985, 351p. Focuses on legal concerns of museum administrators. Chapters are devoted to "Care of Collections" and "Insurance."

2960. Mallinson, John C. The Foundations of Magnetic Recording. 2d ed. San Diego, CA; Academic Press, 1993. 217p. Text on the fundamentals of magnetic recording media, science, and technology.

2961. Mallinson, John C. "Magnetic Tape Recording: History, Evolution, and Archival Considerations," Conservation in Archives. Paris: International Council on Archives, 1989, 181-190. (International Symposium, Ottawa, Canada, May 10-12, 1988). Brief history of audio, video, and computer tape recording; discusses deterioration of software; expresses concern about the abilities of hardware.

2962. Mallinson, John C. "The Next Decade in Magnetic Recording," IEEE Transactions on Magnetics (Institute of Electrical and Electronic Engineers), 21:3 (May 1985). n.p.

2963. Mallinson, John C. "On the Preservation of Human and Machine-Readable Records," Information Technology and Libraries, 7:1

(March 1988), 19-23. Discusses why the Committee on Preservation, National Archives and Records Administration, recommended that the majority of the National Archives' holdings be preserved on human-readable microfilm. Describes machine-readable information as impermanent, intended only for ready access.

2964.　Mallinson, J. C. "Preservation of Video Images," Environnement et Conservation de l'Écrit, de l'Image et du Son. Paris: ARSAG, 1994, 177-181. (Actes des Deuxièmes Journées Internationales d'Études d'ARSAG, 16 au 20 Mai 1994). Discusses the physicochemical factors of importance in the deterioration of videotapes and makes recommendations for their proper archival environment. Notes that the problem of playback is a concern after 20 years.

2965.　Mallinson, John C., and Sue Gavrel. "Preserving Machine-Readable Archival Records for the Millennia," Archivaria, 22 (Summer 1986), 147-155.

2966.　Malone, Paul. "Mixed Microfilm Production: The Western Australian Archives Experiment," Preservation Microfilming: Does It Have a Future? Canberra: National Library of Australia, 1995. 81-88. Explores costs and benefits of in-house and contracted microfilming with focus on Western Australia, advantages, disadvantages of each; difficulty of establishing criteria for costs.

2967.　Malone, Paul. "Technology for Libraries," AICCM Bulletin, (Australian Institute for the Conservation of Cultural Material), 12:3/4 (December 1986), 103-112. Note on the use of optical disks and video technology to produce surrogate copies for access to information in fragile, valuable materials.

2968.　Manici, Marilena, and Paola F. Munafò, eds. Ancient and Medieval Book Materials and Techniques. Proceeding of a Symposium Held in Erice, Sicily, September 18-25, 1992. Ettore Majoraná Centre for Scientific Culture, International School for the Study of Written Records. Città del Vaticano: Biblioteca Apostolica Vaticana, 1993. 2 vols.

2969.　Manning, Ralph W. "Canadian Cooperative Preservation," Library Conservation News, 43 (Summer 1994), 1-2. Describes the Canadian

Cooperative Preservation Project, 1991-1993, resulting in a national strategy and the "Guidelines for Preservation Microfilming in Canadian Libraries."

2970. Manning, Ralph W. Canadian Cooperative Preservation Project: Final Summary Report. Ottawa: National Library of Canada, 1994. 29p.

2971. Manning, Ralph W. "Preservation Microfilming: A Canadian Perspective," Preservation Microfilming: Does It Have a Future? Canberra: National Library of Australia, 1995. 2-16p. Describes the Canadian Cooperative Preservation Project, its focus on preservation, microfilming, funding, selection, standards, bibliographic control, storage, legal concerns.

2972. Manns, Basil. "The Electronic Document Image Preservation Format," Preservation of Electronic Formats and Electronic Formats for Preservation, ed. Janice Mohlhenrich. Fort Atkinson, WI: Highsmith Press, 1992, 63-81. Format concerns that affect preservation of, and access to, electronic documents; selection of formats; need for standards.

2973. Manns, Basil, and Tamara Swora. "Books to Bits: Digital Imaging at the Library of Congress." Journal of Information & Image Management, 19:10 (October 1985), 26-32. Discusses the continuing evolution of the library's digital imaging system, describes the development of the data-base, and provides a detailed technical overview of the configuration, input, image processing, compression, and hardware specifications.

2974. Marais, A. "The Development of a Phase-Box Programme," Books in Peril. Cape Town, South Africa: South African Library, 1987, 158-162. Benefits of establishing a phase boxing program for lesser-used library materials; instructions.

2975. Maravel, Martine, and Françoise Flieder. "The Stability of Printing Inks," Restuarator, 14:3 (1993). Report on exhaustive testing of the stability of black and colored printing inks. 35 references.

2976. Marchant, Eric W. "Some Aspects of Fire Safety in Libraries," Library Review, 37:2 (1988), 19-26. Provisions for fire safety to protect people and collections.

2977. Marchbank, A. M. "Raising Staff Awareness," Security in Academic and Research Libraries, eds. Anthony G. Quinsee and Andrew C. McDonald. Newcastle-upon-Tyne, England: Newcastle University Library, 1991, 41-48. Problems in libraries, staff awareness, and response, from a British perspective.

2978. Marcon, Paul. "A Shipping Case Study," CCI Newsletter (Canadian Conservation Institute), 14 (September 1994), 4-5. Experiment, using dataloggers packed in shipping crates, to measure what happens to objects in transit; demonstrates that sound packing does offer some protection.

2979. Marcoux, Yves. Disaster Planning: Introductory Readings. Ottawa: National Archives Library, Canadian Center for Information and Documentation on Archives, 1990. 1p. (CCIDA Bibliographies, 15).

2980. Marcoux, Yves, and Anne Whitehurst. Conservation. Ottawa: National Archives Library, Canadian Center for Information and Documentation on Archives, 1989. 1p. (CCIDA Bibliographies, 9). Bibliography.

2981. Marcum, Deanna B. "CLR Supports National Preservation Planning," National Preservation News, 2 (October 1985), 1-3.

2982. Marcum, Deanna B. Preservation Education Institute: Final Report From School of Library and Information Science, the Catholic University of America. Washington, DC: Commission on Preservation and Access, 1990. 9p. Institute on Preservation Education, Queenstown, MD, August 2-4, 1990.

2983. Marcum, Deanna B. "Preservation Education," Advances in Preservation and Access. Vol. 1. Westport, CT: Meckler, 1992, 115-123. Describes the mission of the Commission on Preservation and

Access Task Force to identify needs and develop strategies for instruction.

2984.   Marcum, Deanna B. "The Preservation of Digital Information," Journal of Academic Librarianship, 22:6 (November 1996), 451-454.

2985.   Mareck, Robert. "Practicum on Preservation Selection," Collection Management for the 1990s..., ed. Joseph J. Branin. Chicago, IL: American Library Association, 1992, 114-126. (ALCTS (Association for Library Collections and Technical Services). Papers on Library Technical Services and Collections, #3). Presents the methodology developed by Ross Atkinson for the selection of materials for preservation, with examples. Paper presented at the Midwest Collection Management Institute, Chicago, 1989.

2986.   Maree, J. "The Conservation of Leather Bindings," Books in Peril. Cape Town, South Africa: South African Library, 1987, 165-171. Outlines problems to be found in collections and offers practical suggestions for caring for leather bindings.

2987.   Margeton, Stephen G., and Willis C. Meredith. Law Library Preservation: Books, Microforms and Electronic Media. Dobbs Ferry, NY: Glanville, 1994. 85p. (Law Library Information Report, 16). A basic manual for beginners; some information out of date.

2988.   Marine, Stephen. "Library Preservation: Fundamental Techniques," RTSD Newsletter (Resources and Technical Services Division), 11:1 (1986), 1-2. Report on a basic conservation treatments workshop held at Stanford University, August 1985.

2989.   Markham, Robert. "Religion Converted to Microformat," Microform Review, 16:3 (Summer 1987), 217-223. Report on the Association of Theological Libraries' on-going preservation microfilming project; discusses history and background of the program, goals and objectives, and issues for consideration.

2990.   Marrelli, Nancy. "Fire and Flood at Concordia University Archives," Archiavaria, 17 (Winter 1983-84), 266-274. Describes salvage preparation and operations, drying methods, sterilization, restoration; recommendations to facilitate salvage operations.

2991. Marrelli, Nancy, ed. Implementing Preservation Management: A How-To-Manual for Archives. Montreal: National Library of Quebec and National Library of Canada, 1996, 106p. Provides a practical approach to preservation.

2992. Marrelli, Nancy. La Gestion de la Preservation: Un manuel Pratique pour les Services d'Archives. Montreal: Reseau des Archives du Québec, 1996. 107p.

2993. Marshall, Mary E. "Compact Disc's 'Indestructibility': Myth and Maybe," OCLC Micro (Online Computer Library Center), 7:1 (February 1991), 20-23. Considers some current studies of maximum expected disk life. Discusses production, problems, and suggests measures for preservation through care and handling.

2994. Martin, Elizabeth. Collecting and Preserving Old Photographs. London: Collins, 1988. 160p. Illus. Written for collectors, covers history and photographic processes; storage, handling, and care; conservation.

2995. Martin, Graham, and David Ford. "Data From the Ether," V&A Conservation Journal (Victoria and Albert), 1:4 (July 1992), 7-8. Describes the Meaco Museum Monitor, now in use at the museum, the first radio telemetry system for RH and temperature data collection. It is wire-free and movable, making it useful for temporary exhibition areas.

2996. Martin, Mike. "Compact Disc Media Evaluation: What We Now Know About Compact Discs," CD-ROM Professional, 6:2 (March 1993), 74-77. Technical report on a study of CD-ROM permanence and error loss. Concludes that the media is permanent, but does not discuss reformatting or the issue of playback.

2997. Martin, Murray S. "Binding, Mending, and Preservation: Value Maintenance Tools," Technicalities, 15 (December 1995), 8-9.

2998.   Martin, Robert S., and Faye Phillips. "Scanning Historical
        Documents: The Electronic Imaging Laboratory at Louisiana State
        University," Journal of Education for Library and Information
        Science, 34:4 (Fall 1993), 298-301. Describes a pilot project to
        digitize and provide access to scarce materials while preserving them;
        how rare documents are preserved is not made clear in this article.

2999.   Martin, Susan K. "Polyester Film Book Supports," Abbey
        Newsletter, 14:3 (June 1990), 55. Instructions for making book
        cradles of flexible polyester film.

3000.   Martin, Susan K. "Security in Libraries, Part III: Disaster
        Prevention," Library Issues, 7:6 (July 1987), 1-2. Brief overview of
        concerns: fire and water damage, theft, and prevention.

3001.   Martinez, Ed. "Hurricane Iwa Revisited," Library Mosaics, 3:6
        (November-December 1992), 14-16. Case study of evacuation,
        freezing, then air drying a college library collection following a
        devastating storm.

3002.   Marwick, Charles, "Will This Page Still Exist Sometime in the Future
        When You Want to Read About Deteriorating Paper in Medical
        Journals, Other Scientific Literature?" Journal of the American
        Medical Association, 257:21 (June 5, 1987), 2877-2882. A summary
        of the National Library of Medicine hearings on the brittle book
        problem.

3003.   Maryland. Task Force to Initiate Preservation Planning in Maryland.
        Treasures of the Past: Resources of the Future, a Preservation Plan
        for Maryland's Library and Archival Collections. [Baltimore]: The
        Task Force, 1994. 32p.

3004.   Mason, Pamela R. "Imaging System Components and Standards,"
        Digital Imaging Technology for Preservation, ed. Nancy E.
        Elkington. Mountain View, CA: Research Libraries Group, 1994,
        25-40. Contrasts preservation needs with commercial needs for which
        imaging technologies were designed. Describes equipment and
        functions.

3005.   Mason, Robert M. "All About Diskettes," Library Journal, 109:5 (March 1984), 558-559. Describes how disks are made and how they should be handled and protected from harmful environments.

3006.   Massachusetts. Supreme Judicial Court. Archives and Records Preservation. Boston, MA: Supreme Judicial Court, 1988. 7p.

3007.   Massachusetts. Supreme Judicial Court. Emergency Disaster Contingency Plan for the Division of Archives and Records Preservation. Boston, MA: Massachusetts Supreme Judicial Court, May 1988. 75p. Revised Draft.

3008.   Massachusetts. Task Force on Preservation and Access. Preserved to Serve: The Massachusetts Preservation Agenda. Boston, MA: February, 1992. 36p. Review and needs assessment of the documentary resources in Massachusetts; strategies to ensure their preservation for future access.

3009.   Massachusetts Committee for the Preservation of Architectural Records. Proceedings of the Symposium on the Appraisal of Architectural Records. Cambridge. MA: Massachusetts Committee for the Preservation of Architectural Records, 1987. 106p.

3010.   Masschelein-Kleiner, Liliana. Ancient Binding Media, Varnishes and Adhesives, trans. Janet Bridgland, Sue Walston, and A. E. Werner. Rome: International Center for the Preservation and Restoration of Cultural Property, 1985. 115p. Discusses the physical and chemical properties of film-forming materials; bibliography.

3011.   Mast, Sharon. "Ripping Off and Ripping Out: Book Theft and Mutilation from Academic Libraries," Shades of Deviance, eds. Michael Hill, Sharon Mast, Richard Bowman, and Charlotte Care. Palmerston, NZ: Dunmore Press, 1983, 80-98; reprinted in Library and Archival Security, 5:4 (Winter 1983), 31-51. Examines mutilation of materials in terms of theft; notes need to provide a culture that discourages deviant behavior.

3012.   Masters, Ian G. "New Life for Old Recordings," Stereo Review, 50:11 (November 1985), 81-83, 132-133. Author describes his techniques for home re-recording of old disks onto tape cassettes.

3013.   Matero, Frank G. "The Conservation of Immovable Cultural Property: Ethical & Practical Dilemmas," Journal of the American Institute of Conservation, 32:1 (Spring 1993), 15-21. Discussion of the conservation of cultural property, including sites, monuments, and buildings, and the establishment of standards for the examination, documentation, and treatment of traditional historic and artistic works.

3014.   Matheson, Ann. "Scottish Newspapers," Library Review, 36 (Autumn 1987), 179-185. Describes the condition of Scottish newspapers, and preservation and microfilming efforts to preserve them.

3015.   Matheson, Arden, and Georgina Lewis. "Disaster Planning in Alberta Public Libraries," PNLA Quarterly (Pacific Northwest Library Association), 52 (Winter 1988), 12-13. Discusses disasters that damaged library collections in Alberta, Canada, and notes needs for disaster plans; University of Alberta completed its disaster planning and recovery manual.

3016.   Mathews, Anne J., ed. Rethinking the Library in the Information Age. A Summary of Issues in Library Research. Volume 1. Alexandria, VA: Microfilm International Corporation, October 1988. 41p. ED 301 226

3017.   Mathews, Anne J., ed. Rethinking the Library in the Information Age. Issues in Library Research: Proposals For the 1990s. Volume 2. Washington, DC: US Govt. Print. Off., 1988. 226p. ED 301 227

3018.   Mathews, Anne J., ed. Rethinking the Library in the Information Age. Volume 3. Washington, DC: Office of Educational Research and Improvement, 1988. 75p. ED 307 898

3019.   Mathews, John. "Conservation of Electronic Imaging on Class CDs," Electronic Imaging and the Visual Arts, Proceedings of the

1993 Conference. Aldershot, England: Bramen, 1993, 134-138. Describes the impermanence of current information media and makes a care for glass-tempered compact disks that could be permanent and durable. Does not mention technical obsolescence.

3020.   Matthews, Fred W. "Dalhousie Fire," Canadian Library Journal, 43:4 (August 1986), 221-226. Description of the salvage and drying operation.

3021.   Matthews, Fred W. "Sorting a Mountain of Books," Library Resources and Technical Services, 31:1 (January/March 1987), 88-94. Description of a system using mini-computers to sort and reassemble books that were dried following the Dalhousie Law School Library fires.

3022.   Matthews, Graham. "Fire and Water: Damage at the USSR Academy of Sciences Library," Library Association Record, 90:5 (May 1988), 279-281. An early report on the fire based upon reports in the Soviet and Western literature.

3023.   Matthews, Graham. Preservation of Russian and Soviet Materials in British Libraries: Report to the British Library Research and Development Department on Project SI/SG/014. Liverpool: Liverpool Polytechnic Press, 1991. 63p.

3024.   Matthews, Graham. "Preservation of Russian and Soviet Materials in British Libraries," Library Conservation News, 33 (October 1991), 1-3. Presents results of a survey to determine condition of materials; further condition surveys are recommended.

3025.   Matthews, Graham. "Surveying Collection: The Importance of Condition Assessment for Preservation Management," Journal of Librarianship and Information Science, 27 (December 1995), 227-236.

3026.   Matthews, Graham, and Paul Eden. Disaster Management in British Libraries: Project Report With Guidelines for Library Managers. London: British Library, 1996. 176p. (Library and Information Research Report 109). A report on a research project "to achieve an

overview of current disaster management practices in British
Libraries and to produce guidelines."

3027. Matthews, Graham, and Paul Eden. "Guidelines on Disaster
Management," Library Conservation News, 51 (Summer 1996), 1-
2. Briefly describes a study and report on disaster planning in British
libraries, resulting in the publication of guidelines for planning,
salvage and recovery.

3028. Matthews, Ian. "The Issue Life of Bookstock," Public Library
Journal 9 (September/October 1994), 123-125.

3029. Mattsson, Irene. Rescuing Pictures: The Care and Restoration of
Early Photographic Material/ Bilden räddas: Tillvaratagande och
restaurering av äldere fotomaterial. Stockholm, Sweden: Nordiske
Museet, 1985. 132p. Illus. Swedish/English text, pp. 105-128. How
to preserve and treat nitrate and glass plate negatives with original
emulsion; identification, documentation, and storage of materials.

3030. Matwale, Gideon Mukro. "A Review of Problems Related to the
Establishment of Effective Conservation Programmes for Library
and Archives Materials in Kenya," Proceedings of the Pan-African
Conference on the Preservation and Conservation of Library and
Archival Materials, Nairobi, Kenya, 21-25 June1993. The Hague:
IFLA, (1995), 49-54. (IFLA Professional Publication 43). Considers
administrative and technical problems; a clear articulation of the
problems in Africa overall.

3031. Maver, Ian. "Conserving the Records of the First Astronomer
Royal," Paper Conservator, 14 (1990), 31-45. Describes the cleaning,
housing, and treatment of a collection of letters and manuscripts that
had previously been treated in 1835.

3032. Maxson, Holly. "The Delamination of the Washington and Lee
Ledger: Part 2: The Treatment Case History," Early Advances in
Conservation. London: British Library, 1988. 41-50. Describes a
treatment of delamination and stabilization of ledger leaves.

3033. Mayfield, David M. "Using Micrographics Technology to Preserve and Make Accessible Records of Permanent Value," Library Resources and Technical Services, 29:4 (October/December 1985), 360-366. Describes the use of microfilm technology by the Genealogical Library, Church of Jesus Christ of Latter-Day Saints, including filming of records, processing and storing film, cataloguing, and use.

3034. Mayhew, Frances Whitaker, and Ira Block. "Changes in the Infrared Absorbance and Color of Aged Cellulose Film," Issues in Art and Archaeology III. Pittsburgh, PA: Materials Research Society, 1992, 459-469.

3035. Maylone, R. Russell. "A Case Study in Disaster: The Memorial Day Steam Cleaning," Illinois Libraries, 64:5 (May 1983), 354-357. Report of a pipe malfunction that caused steam to enter the Special Collections Department, Northwestern University Library. Originally published in the Association of Research Libraries SPEC Kit 69, November-December 1980.

3036. Maynor, Catherine I. "Publications of the Book and Paper Group," Journal of the American Institute for Conservation, 31:1 (Spring 1992), 103-106. Overview of its three publication efforts and their products.

3037. Mazal, Otto. "Interlibrary Lending of Precious Books and Manuscripts," LIBER Bulletin (Ligue des Bibliothèques Européennes de Recherche), 34 (1989), 78-81. Includes rules of lending precious materials to exhibitions.

3038. Mazikana, Peter C. "An Evaluation of Preservation and Conservation Programs and Facilities in Africa," Proceedings of the Pan-African Conference on the Preservation and Conservation of Library and Archival Materials, Nairobi, Kenya, 21-25 June 1993. The Hague: IFLA, (1995), 21-29. (IFLA Professional Publication 43). Notes lack of trained personnel, especially lack of conservators, lack of equipment and ability to obtain it; lack of defined and articulated programs for the preservation of materials.

3039. Mazikana, Peter C. "A Strategy for the Preservation of Audiovisual Materials," Audiovisual Librarian, 14:1 (February 1988), 24-28. Addresses problems of preserving audiovisual collections, especially in underdeveloped countries; seeks a multipronged approach to the problems of storage and access, with national and international cooperation.

3040. Mbaye, Saliou. "Problems of Preservation and Conservation in Libraries and Archives of Black Africa." Proceedings of the Pan-African Conference on the Preservation and Conservation of Library and Archival Materials, Nairobi, Kenya, 21-25 June 1993. The Hague: IFLA, (1995), 41-44. (IFLA Professional Publication 43). Notes environmental problems, lack of training or understanding of conservation and preservation. Need for appropriate buildings, training of specialists and staff. Looks to UNESCO, etc. for assistance.

3041. Mead, Melissa and Barbara Lilly. As Perfect a State of Preservation as Any Vigilance Can Secure: A Celebration of Ten Years of New York State Program for the Conservation and Preservation of Library Research Materials. Albany, NY: Comprehensive Research Libraries of New York State, 1996. 16p.

3042. Meadows, Jack. "Preservation Training for Librarians," In Safe Keeping, ed. Jennifer Thorp. Winchester, England: Hampshire Co. Library / Hampshire Archives Trust, 1988, 13-14. Discusses need for librarians to know what needs to be preserved and how materials can be preserved; not how to do treatments; outlines what should be included in the L. S. curriculum.

3043. Mecklenburg, Marion F., Charles S. Tumosa, and Mark H. McCormick-Goodhart. "A General Model Relating Externally Applied Forces to Environmentally Induced Stresses in Materials," Materials Research Society Symposium Proceedings, 352 (1995), 285-292.

3044. Meierhusby, Barbara, Jesse Munn, Terry Wallis, and Mary Wootton. "Quality Materials: Handmade Paper, Taking a Closer Look," Book and Paper Annual, 12 (1993), 61-65. Describes the endpaper project at the Library of Congress to develop appropriate papers for conservation.

3045.   Meigs, James B. "How Long Will Videotape Really Last?" Video Review, 4 (July 1984), 24-26. Briefly explains the problems with videotape that cause instability and suggests how to preserve videotape for as long as possible.

3046.   Meister, Pamela, ed. 1991 Disaster Preparedness Seminar Proceedings. Baton Rouge, LA: Southeastern Museums Conference with the support of the Institute of Museum Services, 1991. 156p.

3047.   Melin, Nancy. "The Book on Library Uses." CD-ROM Review, 1:1 (September 1986), 36-38. Discusses the applications of optical disk technology to the preservation problem. Lists vendors. While the article is positive about the medium, author does note libraries skepticism, due to compatibility problems. Highlights advantages of using CD-ROMs in libraries. Discusses reasons for hesitancy of some to accept CD-ROMs as solution for too many library problems.

3048.   Melville, Annette, and Simmon Scott. Coordinators. Film Preservation 1993: A Study of the Current State of American Film Preservation. Washington, DC: Library of Congress, 1993. 748p. Four volumes.

3049.   Melville, Annette, and Simmon Scott. Coordinators. Redefining Film Preservation: A National Plan. Washington, DC: Library of Congress, 1994. 80p. Both documents were prepared and submitted to Congress as mandated by PL 102-73, the National Film Preservation Act of 1992.

3050.   Melville, Annette, and Simmon Scott. Redefing Film Preservation: A National Plan: Recommendations of the Librarian of Congress in Consultation with the National Film Preservation Board. [Washington, D.C.]: Library of Congress, 1994. 79p.

3051.   Menne-Haritz, Angelika, ed. Information Handling in Offices and Archives. Munich, Germany: Saur, 1993. 197p. Papers from a 1991 symposium on the consequences of information technologies for archives and records management. Preservation concerns addressed, including impermanence of data and problems of playback.

3052. Menzies, Richard, Robyn Tamblyn, Jean-Pierre Farant, James Hanley, Fatima Nunes, and Robert Tamblyn. "The Effect of Varying Levels of Outdoor-Air Supply on the Symptoms of Sick Building Syndrome," New England Journal of Medicine, 323:12 (March 25, 1993), 821-827. Report of a study to determine the effect of increased air circulation in buildings.

3053. Meredith, Willis C., and Naomi Ronen. "American Association of Law Libraries Research Libraries Group Microform Master Survey: Report on the Survey Form Presented to the Commission on Preservation and Access," Microform Review, 21:1 (Winter 1992), 33-41. Summarizes the results of the survey to determine what differences exist between industry and preservation standards.

3054. Merrill-Oldham, Jan. "Binding for Research Libraries," New Library Scene, 3:4 (August 1984), 1, 4-6; flow chart, 22. Describes the alternatives and the decision process for selecting appropriate library bindings.

3055. Merrill-Oldham, Jan. Conservation and Preservation of Library Materials: A Program for the University of Connecticut Libraries. Storrs, CT: University of Connecticut, 1984. 65p. Comprehensive, detailed study of care and handling problems in a mid-sized research library.

3056. Merrill-Oldham, Jan. "Finding Your Way Around ALA," The Endpaper: Newsletter of the Library Binding Institute (May/June 1986), 8-11.

3057. Merrill-Oldham, Jan. "Getting Educated: A Librarian's View," New Library Scene, 3:3 (June 1984), 1, 6, 13. Discussion of changes in library binding techniques and how the librarian can become familiar with them.

3058. Merrill-Oldham, Jan. "Guide to Drafting of Contracts," Abbey Newsletter, 8:1 (February 1984), 41-46.

Bibliography

3059. Merrill-Oldham, Jan. "Library Preservation: The Administrative Challenge — A Summary Report," RTSD Newsletter (Resources and Technical Services Division), 8:4 (July/August 1983), 41-46. Summary of papers presented at a 1983 Conference, Washington, DC, sponsored by the Resources and Technical Services Division of the American Library Association and the Library of Congress National Preservation Program Office.

3060. Merrill-Oldham, Jan. Managing a Library Binding Program. Washington, DC: Association of Research Libraries, 1993. 160p. (Preservation Planning Program). Guide to a review of a library's commercial binding activities from a preservation perspective. Selection of reading on library binding.

3061. Merrill-Oldham, Jan, ed. Meeting the Preservation Challenge. Washington, DC: Association of Research Libraries, 1989. 70p. A collection of papers that focus on preservation concerns presented at the 111th Membership Meeting of the Association of Research Libraries, October 1987. Includes remarks by Librarian of Congress James Billington and many university librarians.

3062. Merrill-Oldham, Jan. "Method of Leaf Attachment: A Decision Tree for Library Binding," New Library Scene, 4:4 (August 1985), 16.

3063. Merrill-Oldham, Jan. "Postcards: Navigating the Preservation Options." In Postcards in the Library: Invaluable Visual Resources, ed. Norman D. Stevens, New York: Haworth Press, 1996. 199-213. A basic popular guide, covering all the forms of deterioration and principal means of preventing or slowing it: housing, cleaning, repair, and climate control.

3064. Merrill-Oldham, Jan. "Preservation Comes of Age: An Action Agenda for the 80s and Beyond," American Libraries, 16:11 (December 1985), 770-772. Cites goals of preservation administration, programs in libraries, education and training, reformatting projects, binding and environmental concerns.

381

3065. Merrill-Oldham, Jan. Preservation Education in ARL Libraries. Washington, DC: Association of Research Libraries, Office of Management Studies, 1985. 173p. (SPEC Kit 113). Documents include preservation policy statements, staff training materials, treatment procedures, library newsletters, and information about hands-on workshops.

3066. Merrill-Oldham, Jan. "Preservation in Research Libraries: A New Approach to Caretaking," New Library Scene, 5:6 (December 1986), 1,5-6. Describes preservation librarianship, scope, and responsibilities.

3067. Merrill-Oldham, Jan. "Preservation of Library Materials," ALA Yearbook of Library and Information Services '84: A Review of Library Events in 1983. Vol. 9. Chicago, Il.: American Library Association, 1984, 224-226. Summary of activities in 1983: conferences, publications, grants, regional conservation centers, professional organizations, education and training, research.

3068. Merrill-Oldham, Jan. "The Preservation Program Defined," Meeting the Preservation Challenge. Washington, DC: Association of Research Libraries, 1988, 19-25. Discusses elements of a sound preservation program in libraries.

3069. Merrill-Oldham, Jan. "Staff and User Education," Chapter IXA Phase II, Task Force F. In Preservation Planning Program: An Assisted Self-Study Manual for Libraries. Expanded 1987 ed. Washington, DC: Association of Research Libraries. pp. IX.A1-A18.

3070. Merrill-Oldham, Jan. "State of Connecticut Library Binding Contract, as Applied to the University of Connecticut Libraries in Preservation Planning Program: An Assisted Self-Study Manual for Libraries. Washington, DC: Association of Research Libraries, 1987. 589-601.

3071. Merrill-Oldham, Jan, Carolyn Clark Morrow, and Mark Roosa. Preservation Program Models: A Study Project and Report. Washington, DC: Association of Research Libraries, 1991. 54p. Prepared to assist administrators of research libraries in the shaping of programs to preserve the nation's research collections. Provides an outline of the components of a preservation program. Case histories: UC-Berkeley, University of Delaware, and Ohio State University.

3072.   Merrill-Oldham, Jan, and Paul Parisi. Guide to the Library Binding Institute Standard for Library Binding. Chicago, IL: American Library Association, 1990. 62p. Supplement and compliment to the Library Binding Institute Standards; translates the technical language for librarians.

3073.   Merrill-Oldham, Jan, and Jutta Reed-Scott. eds. Preservation Planning Program: An Assisted Self-Study Manual for Libraries. Rev. ed. Washington, DC: ARL Office of Management Services, 1993. 138p.

3074.   Merrill-Oldham, Jan, and Merrily Smith, eds. Library Preservation Program: Models, Priorities, Possibilities. Chicago, IL: American Library Association, 1985. 117p. Papers from a conference for library administrators held in 1983; emphasis on organization and planning, assessment of needs and priorities, programs, and fiscal support.

3075.   Merrill-Oldham, Jan, and Gay Walker, eds. Brittle Books Programs. Washington, DC: Association of Research Libraries, March 1989. 121p. (SPEC Kit, 152).   Results of a survey of 64 ARL libraries on brittle book activities at their institutions; includes policies and procedural forms from selected libraries; selected reading list.

3076.   Mertz, Gregory A. "Light Levels Lowered in Exhibit Cases," CRM Bulletin (Cultural Resources Management), 11:2 (April 1988), 15-17. A technique for lowering light on vulnerable objects on display.

3077.   Messier, Paul, and Timothy Vitale. "Cracking in Albumen Photographs: An ESEM Investigation," Microscopy Research and Technique, 25:5/6 (1993), 374-383. Study of the interaction of water with albumen photographs.

3078. Messner, K. L. Alberighi, G. Banik, etal.. "Comparison of Possible Chemical and Microbial Factors Influencing Paper Decay by Iron-gall Inks," Biodeterioration 7, (1988), 449-454.

3079. Metcalf, Keyes D. Planning Academic and Research Library Buildings. 2d ed. rev. by Philip D. Leighton and David C. Weber. Chicago, IL: American Library Association, 1986. 630p. Updated edition of the classic text on planning, design, and construction of library buildings; preservation of materials remains a concern in the 2d edition.

3080. "Methods of Affixing Leaves: Options and Implications," New Library Scene, 2:5 (October 1983), 9-12. Pros and cons of several methods are described and illustrated; based upon a report by Paul Parisi given at an Institute on Library Binding.

3081. Meyer, Duane G. "The Vital Role of Local Records for the Study and Understanding of State and Local History," Show-Me Libraries, 38:1/2 (October/November 1986), 7-10. Emphasizes the importance of publicizing the need to preserve local history records and to see that they are copied.

3082. Michaels, Jan. "The Condition Survey of Sound Recordings at the National Library of Canada: Implications for Conservation," Saving the Twentieth Century: The Conservation of Modern Materials, ed. David Grattan. Ottawa: Canadian Conservation Institute, 1993, 13-23. (Symposium 91). Reviews the survey, discusses results, and describes actions to be taken by the library to preserve the material. Notes lack of planned and coordinated research into the problem of the preservation of audio materials.

3083. Michaels, Jan. "A Meeting in the Field: Workshop on the Effects of Aging on Printing and Writing Papers," Infinity (Society of American Archivists Preservation Section), 10:2 (Summer 1994), 5-7. Report on the American Society for Testing Materials meeting to develop research proposals to address important questions concerning permanent paper.

3084.   Michaels, Jan. "Preservation at the National Library of Canada," COMLA Newsletter (Commonwealth Library Association), 65 (September 1989), 3-4. Describes the library's mission and activities, including its mass deacidification process, establishment of the Preservation Collection of Canadiana, and preservation planning efforts.

3085.   Michaels, Jan. "Standing on the Shoulders of Giants," National Library News (Canada), 26:7 (July 1994), 1-4. Description of the preservation program at the National Library of Canada, including disaster recovery, cooperative microfilming programs, and advocacy.

3086.   Michaels, Jan. "Textblocks and Printers' Errors: Some Bibliographical Considerations for Book Conservators," Conservation of Historic and Artistic Works on Paper. Ottawa: Canada: Canadian Conservation Institute, 1994, 73-77. (Symposium 88). Discusses some types of printers' errors as they pertain to bibliography and conservation; how a book conservator can guard against destruction or alteration of bibliographic evidence.

3087.   Michalski, Stefan. "Leakage Predictions for Buildings, Cases, Bags and Bottles," Studies in Conservation, 39:3 (August 1994), 169-186. Presents a summary of equations for leakage, including vapor diffusion through still air in openings and infiltration of air/vapor/particulate mixture.

3088.   Michalski, Stefan. "New Lamps for Museum Lighting," CCI Newsletter (Canadian Conservation Institute), 17 (March 1996), 7-8. Briefly reviews the effect of new energy efficiency regulations in Canadian museum/exhibition lighting; notes where change is needed, and effect.

3089.   Michalski, Stefan. "Relative Humidity: A Discussion of Correct/Incorrect Values," Preprints: ICOM Committee on Conservation 10th Triennial Meeting, ed. Janet Bridgland. Washington, DC: International Council of Museums, 1993, 624-629. Reviews current data on control of relative humidity for collections.

3090.   Michalski, Stefan. "Relative Humidity and Temperature Guidelines: What's Happening," CCI Newsletter (Canadian Conservation Institute), 14 (September 1994), 6-8. Summarizes CCI's current approach to temperature and relative humidity. Advocates a broader range of fluctuation, to be determined by the physical nature of the objects to be protected.

3091.   Michalski, Stefan. "Relative Humidity Control Module Construction and Assembly Manual. Ottawa: Canadian Conservation Institute, 1985. 43 leaves. 25 technical drawings.

3092.   Michigan Archival Association. The Photograph Primer, eds. Mark Coir etal. Michigan Archival Association. Printed by Elite Printing Services, St. Clair Shores, MI, 1994. 20p.

3093.   Michigan State Historical Records Advisory Board. Strategies to Preserve Michigan's Historical Records. Lansing, MI: MSHRAB, 1994, 32.

3094.   Mickelson, Meredith. "A Note on the Treatment of Two Gelatin Silver Photographs by Harold Edgerton from the Portfolio 'Seeing the Unseen,'" Journal of the American Institute for Conservation, 27:1 (Spring 1988), 38-39. Technical information about Filmoplast-P is discussed and a procedure for removal of the yellowed tape is described.

3095.   "Micrographic TM - A State of the Art Color Microfiche System," Paper Conservation News, 63 (September 1992), 6-8. Describes a system that is stable and accessible to a reader with a magnifying glass and can be transferred to digital format.

3096.   Mid-Atlantic Preservation Service (MAPS) Technical Issues Density Reading Frequency, 1 (May 5, 1987), n.p.

3097.   Middleton, Bernard. "A Century of Developments in Restoration Binding," New Bookbinder, 14 (1994), 66-69. Reflections on the changes in bookbinding practices, materials, and techniques.

3098.   Middleton, Bernard C. A History of English Craft Bookbinding Technique. 3d ed. London: Scholar Press, 1988. 307p. 4th ed. New

Castle, DE: Oak Knoll Press, 1996, 372p. The basic text on craft binding practices.

3099.   Middleton, Bernard C. The Restoration of Leather Bindings. Rev. ed. Chicago, IL: American Library Association, 1984. 201p. (Library Technology Program, 20). Manual for librarians on the techniques of restoring leather bindings, with a statement about the conservator's role.

3100.   Mielke, Gerald P. "Hot Melts for Bookbinding: Past, Present, and Projected," TAPPI Journal (Technical Association for the Pulp and Paper Industry), 72:12 (December 1989), 85-89. An historical summary and overview of current problems. Describes hot melt adhesives that can be recycled easily, that will not give way in the presence of solvents from the ink, and that will last longer.

3101.   Mielke, Gerald P. "Keeping Book Covers on the Straight and Narrow," New Library Scene, 2:5 (October 1983), 1,6. Discusses causes of cover warp on commercially bound books, attributed to "hygroexpansivity" of the materials comprising the cover.

3102.   Mihram, Danielle. "Online Databases and Book Preservation," College and Research Libraries News, 49:3 (March 1988), 152-155. Report on a meeting at the Modern Language Association conference, December 1987, to explore ways in which scholars might contribute to the preservation of books.

3103.   Mihram, Danielle. "Paper Deacidification: A Bibliographic Survey," Restaurator, 7:2/3 (1986), 81-98, 99-118. Bibliographic survey, limited to publications in the English language through 1982.

3104.   Mijland, H. J. M., F. F.M. Ector, and K. van der Hoeven. "The Eindhoven Variant: A Method to Survey the Deterioration of Archival Collections," Restaurator, 12:3 (1991), 163-182. Survey and analysis record series dating from 1800 to circa 1900-1920.

3105.   Miles, Gwyn. "Conservation Terminology," Terminology for Museums, ed. D. Andrew Roberts. Cambridge, England: Museum Documentation Association, 1990, 469-472. Notes need for a language for documentation, and systems for recording that encompass all fields of conservation.

3106. Milevski, Robert J. "Book Repair and Care in a Big Way: Stanford Conference Sells Out," New Library Scene, 4:6 (December 1985), 1, 5, 8, 15. Report on a 5-day training institute in August 1985 on care and repair techniques.

3107. Milevski, Robert J. Book Repair Manual. Carbondale, IL: Illinois Cooperative Conservation Program, 1984, 1986, 1987, 1988; Springfield, IL: Illinois State Library, 1992. 71p. Illustrated manual on basic book repair treatments. The manual originally appeared in Illinois Libraries, 67:8 (October 1985), 648-684; 77:2 (Spring 1995), 76-112. A manual for basic book repair developed for the ICCP workshops. Covers descriptions of book repair problems, instructions for repair techniques, list of supplies and suppliers, glossary, and reading list. The manual also appeared in Illinois Libraries, 77:2 (Spring 1995), 76-112. Carbondale: ICCP, 1984. 36p. Well illustrated, easy to follow step-by-step instructions for performing basic book repairs, including recasing a textblock in its original cover, replacing a worn spine, and repairing loose hinges.

3108. Milevski, Robert J. "Library Preservation: Implementing Programs — A Summary Report," New Library Scene, 4:2 (April 1985), 1, 5, 7-8. Report of the Conservation Conference held on March 8-9, 1985 in Alexandria. Sponsors were Resources and Technical Services Division of the American Library Association and the Library of Congress.

3109. Milevski, Robert J. "Recasing a Textblock into Its Original Cover, and Replacing a Worn Spine With a New Buckram Spine," Book Repair Manual. Carbondale, IL: Illinois Cooperative Conservation Program, July 1984, 25-30.

3110. Milevski, Robert J., and Linda Nainis. "Implementing a Book Repair and Treatment Program," Library Resources and Technical Services, 31:2 (April/June 1987), 159-176. Design for an in-house repair unit; costs of equipment, supplies, and selection of materials and personnel are discussed.

3111.   Milkovic, Milan. "The Binding of Periodicals: Basic Concepts and Procedures," Serials Librarian, 11:2 (October 1986), 93-118. Outlines methods and techniques for managing a serials binding unit with emphasis on preservation of materials. Bibliography.

3112.   Miller, Bruce F., and William Root. "Long-Term Storage of Wheat Starch Paste," Studies in Conservation, 36:2 (May 1991), 85-92. Describes two methods for storing wheat starch paste that will allow it to remain mold-free for up to six months at room temperature without fungicides.

3113.   Miller, Elizabeth, and Alison Richmond. "Conservation Liaison: A Case Study," V&A Conservation Journal (Victoria and Albert Museum), 7 (1993), 4-7. Discussion of collaboration between curator and conservator in conditioning and treatment of hand-colored lithograph.

3114.   Miller, J. Hillis. Preserving the Literary Heritage. Washington, DC: Commission on Preservation and Access, 1991. 7p. Final report of the Scholarly Advisory Committee on Modern Language and Literature, Commission on Preservation and Access, emphasizing need to educate academics about the magnitude of the brittle book problem.

3115.   Miller, John W. "The Microfilming of Newspapers: The Indiana Historical Society Newspaper Microfilm Project," Newspapers in the Library, ed. Lois N. Upham. New York: Haworth Press, 1988, 37-41. Description of an in-house microfilming project.

3116.   Miller, Michael. Ideas for Preservation Fund Raising: A Support Package for Libraries and Archives. Washington, DC: Commission on Preservation and Access, 1990. 1 portfolio. Information packet.

3117.   Miller, Michael, comp. Supporting Preservation and Access. Washington, DC: Commission on Preservation and Access, 1990. 1 portfolio. Ideas to gain financial support for libraries.

3118.   Miller, Page P. "Insuring the Preservation of Electronic Records," Chronicle of Higher Education, February 3, 1993, A44. Discusses the need for "scholars, public-interest groups, and citizens to push for a comprehensive, national information policy that will ensure the preservation of all records of historical value."

3119.   Miller, R. Bruce. "Libraries and Computers: Disaster Prevention and Recovery," Information Technology and Libraries, 7:4 (December 1988), 349-358. Surveys areas of vulnerability for databases, provide guidelines to minimize threat of disaster, and outlines recovery procedures.

3120.   Miller, Richard F. "The DEZ Mass Deacidification Process," Conference on Book and Paper Conservation, 1990. Budapest, Hungary: Technical Association of Paper and Printing Industry/National Szechenyi Library, 1992, 126-133; "The DEZ Process of Mass Deacidification," Restoration '92: Conservation, Training, Materials and Techniques: Latest Developments. Preprints ... Amsterdam, 20-22 October 1992. Amsterdam, Netherlands: RAI, 1992, 80-84, with illus. Describes the diethyl zinc process for deacidification of books and papers.

3121.   Miller, Sally McIntosh. "North Bennet Street School," New Library Scene, 7:2 (April 1988), 1, 5-6. Description of a bookbinding and book conservation training program in Boston, MA.

3122.   Miller, Sheila. "Partnership in Preservation," Archival Products News, 4:2 (Spring 1996), 5. Describes the public-private collaboration between a public library and a private historical society in a rural area to build new quarters, hire an archivist, and preserve and make accessible its resources.

3123.   Mills, John S., and Raymond White. The Organic Chemistry of Museum Objects. London: Butterworth-Heinemann, 1994. 206p.; 1987 edition, 165p. Reviews the composition, chemistry, and analysis of organic materials in the structure of objects in museum collections for conservators and students.

3124. Mills, Roger. "Presents from the Past," Classic CD (June 1992), 16-18. Describes the reformatting of early sound recordings to compact disk using computer technology to recover sound quality.

3125. Minkler, Whitney S., and Robert W. Starbird. "Determination of Harmful Residual Chemicals on Archival Film - An Important Aspect of Micrographic File Management," ARMA Records Management Quarterly (Association of Records Managers and Administrators), 19:1 (January 1985), 30-36. Describes the testing procedures that ensure permanence of silver halide microfilm.

3126. Minneapolis Institute of Arts Library. Silent Fires. Minneapolis, MN: Minneapolis Institute of Arts, 1990. [10p.] Catalog for an exhibition on the deterioration of books, including a reprint of the essay, "Millions of Books are Turning to Dust - Can They Be Saved?" by Eric Stange, and a glossary of "Terms and Techniques of Book Preservation."

3127. Minnesota. Department of Administration, Data, and Records Management. Information Pursuit: Promoting a Better Understanding of Information and Records Management. St. Paul, MN: Department of Administration, Data and Records Management Division, 1985. 89p.

3128. Mironov, Boris. "Priceless Manuscripts Turn to Dust," Russian Libraries in Transition: An Anthology of Glasnost Literature. Jefferson, NC: McFarland, 1992, 17-18. Editorial citing the appalling conditions in the Lenin Library from the Moscow News, February 1989.

3129. Mishra, Anupama, and Shashi Dhawan. "Fungicides and Their Application in Conservation of Cultural Property," Journal of Indian Museums, 63 (1987), 155-162. The problem of Biodeterioration caused by fungi is acute in tropical countries like India. Fungicides are the chemicals used to inhibit or destroy fungal growth. The types of fungicides in general use are listed. Selected fungicides and their field of application are indicated.

3130.   Mitchell, Ann M. "On the Preservation of Dufaycolor
        Transparencies at Sydney Hospital," Archives and Manuscripts, 14:1
        (May 1986), 61-65. Briefly describes process and short-term
        methods to stabilize and preserve the images.

3131.   Mitchell, John. "Restoration of Cloth Bindings," Society of
        Bookbinders Newsletter, 5 (March 1992), 6-9; 6 (June 1992), 6-
        10. Instructions for the treatment of case bindings.

3132.   Mitchell, Michael. "Victorian Movable Toy Books," Library
        Conservation News, 35 (April 1992), 4-5. Describes the repair of
        several late 19th-century movable books.

3133.   Mitchell, Peter. "Inside the Compact Disc System," High Fidelity,
        33:7 (1983), 39-44. Describes how compact disks are made, "from
        disc mastering and pressing to final playback."

3134.   Mobbs, Leslie. "Handle With Care: Archives, Users and Original
        Documents," Preservation Papers of the 1991, SAA Annual
        Conference, ed. Karen Garlick. Chicago: Society of American
        Archives, 1992, 136-139. Training staff and public to handle original
        materials properly, with care. Need for finding aids, use of surrogate
        copies.

3135.   Modern Manuscripts: A Fragile Heritage. Paris: UNESCO, 1989.
        25p. From the Courier, May 1989. An attempt to show how modern
        scholarship and technology are using original manuscripts to shed
        light on the complex gestation of works of modern literature.

3136.   Moffett, William A. "The Oberlin Conference on Theft," ALA
        Yearbook of Library and Information Services '84. Vol. 9. Chicago,
        IL: American Library Association, 1984, 275-276. Summary of
        papers and discussion at the conference.

3137.   Mohlhenrich, Janice, ed. Preservation of Electronic Formats and
        Electronic Formats for Preservation. Fort Atkinson, WI: Highsmith
        Press, 1993. 144p. Papers from a conference to address research and
        development in the preservation of electronically stored information,

and the potential for electronic technologies as a preservation medium.

3138. Mokretsova, Inna. "Principles of Conservation of Byzantine Binding," Restaurator, 15:3 (1994), 142-172. Concerns regarding the conservation of Byzantine bindings; need to conserve details of early bindings and repair methods.

3139. Mokretsova, Inna. "Russian Medieval Book Binding," Restaurator, 16:2 (1995), 100-122.

3140. Moltke-Hansen, David. "Preservation Planning in South Carolina: Prospects in Perspective," South Carolina Librarian, 30 (Fall 1986), 10-13. Describes the state's PALMCOP Program and discusses need for planning for preservation in institutional, local, regional, and national bases.

3141. Moltke-Hansen, David. "South Carolina and the Preservation Revolution," Preservation Papers of the 1990 SAA Annual Conference. Chicago: Society of American Archivists, 1991, 51-57. Discusses the nature of "revolution," or change, how preservation initiatives took root in South Carolina's institutions.

3142. Monforte, John. "The Digital Reproduction of Sound," Scientific American, 251:6 (June 1984), 78-84. Describes the digitization process of analog recordings; advantages and problems encountered.

3143. Montague, Robert. "A Nation's Printed Heritage on Microfiche," Conservation Administration News, 24 (January 1986), 7, 24. Describes the activities of the Canadian Institute for Historical Microreproduction and its goal to preserve and make available Canada's printed heritage.

3144. Monteith, Basil. "Insurance as It Relates to the Protection of Documents and Vital Records," Disaster Planning in Jamaica. Kingston, Jamaica: Jamaica Library Association, 1989, 26-27. Short overview of requirements and policies available.

3145. Montevecchi, U., T. Bonisoli, and M. Filippi. "Equipping and Conservation in Museums, Libraries and Archives: Surveys and Feasibility Studies," Science, Technology and European Cultural Heritage. Oxford; Boston: Published for the Commission of the European Communities by Butterworth-Heinemann Publishers, 1991, 727-730. Proceedings of the European Symposium, Bologna, Italy, June 1989. Describes a research project to investigate conservation conditions and employment possibilities in the Piedmont, Italy, region; proposed design modification for environmental improvement as well as physical function of buildings.

3146. Montori, Carla J. "Library Preservation in 1986: An Annotated Bibliography," Library Resources and Technical Services, 31:4 (October/December 1987), 365-385. Summary of the year's trends with annotated bibliography arranged by topic.

3147. Montori, Carla. "Managing the Library's Commercial Library Binding Program," Technical Services Quarterly, 5:3 (1988), 21-25. Describes the management of a commercial library binding program.

3148. Montori, Carla J. "Preservation Planning: The Vital First Step," Conserving and Preserving Materials in Nonbook Formats. Urbana-Champaign: University of Illinois Graduate School of Library and Information Science, 1991, 147-156. (Allerton Park Institute, 30). Initiating programs through condition surveys, policy statements. Describes retrospective and prospective preservation through collection maintenance.

3149. Montori, Carla J., and James R. Canary. "Preservation at Indiana University Libraries," Conservation Administration News, 27 (October 1986), 8, 27. Description of the preservation program, established in 1984.

3150. Montori, Carla J., and Karl E. Longstreth. "The Preservation of Library Materials, 1987: A Review of the Literature," Library Resources and Technical Services, 31:3 (July 1988), 235-

247. Summary of the year's trends with annotated bibliography arranged by topic.

3151. Moon, Myra Jo. "A Preservation Internship at Johns Hopkins," Conservation Administration News, 17 (April 1984), 5-6. Description of the internship and its benefits.

3152. Moor, Ian. "The Conservation and Restoration of Photographic Images," AICCM Bulletin (Australia Institute for the Conservation of Cultural Material), 10:1 (June 1984), 83-89. Demonstrates safe, practical techniques for the preservation of photographic images; discussion of standards and ethics.

3153. Moor, Ian and Angela. "Atlantic Silversafe Photostore: A Suitable Paper for Photographic Conservation?" Library Conservation News, 30 (January 1991), 4-6. Describes need for correct storage of sensitive photographic materials and the Atlantis Silversafe paper developed for this purpose; provides its specifications.

3154. Moor, Ian L. and Angela. "Exhibiting Photographs: The Effect of the Exhibition Environment on Photographs," Conference on Book and Paper Conservation, 1990. Budapest, Hungary: Technical Association of Paper and Printing Industry/National Szechenyi Library, 1992, 388-392. Describes the threat to photographic materials because of their sensitivity to the environment, especially light; emphasizes need to understand photographic processes to curtail damage.

3155. Moor, Ian L. and Angela. "Fire and Flood: Criteria for the Conservation and Analysis of Artifacts," Recent Advances in the Conservation and Analysis of Artifacts, ed. James Black. London: University of London Institute of Archaeology; Summer School Press, 1987, 319-322. Describes the basic points of an effective Disaster Contingency and Recovery Plan for photographic materials, emphasizing the need to understand the diverse nature and characteristics of these materials.

3156. Moor, Ian L. and Angela. "Photographs, Images or Artifacts," Journal of Photographic Science, 36 (1988), 120-121. Discussion of the relationship between the visual, chemical, and physical properties that constitute a photograph; need for professional agreement on ethics and standards for preserving photographic materials.

3157.   Moore, Pete. "Why Fires Go to Blazes," New Scientist 148 (3 June 1995), 26-30. Describes research on how small fires can erupt into infernos, which can lead to safer building design and construction and improved firefighting techniques.

3158.   Moran, Barbara B. Academic Libraries: The Changing Knowledge Center of Colleges and Universities. Washington, DC: Association for the Study of Higher Education, 1984. 97p. Concerns for preservation of research materials are included in this statement of problems and challenges facing academic libraries at the end of the century.

3159.   Moran, Barbara B., Thomas T. Surprenant, and Merrily E. Taylor. "The Electronic Campus: The Impact of the Scholar's Workstation Project on the Library at Brown," College and Research Libraries, (January 1987), 5-16. A research project conducted at the Brown University Library system intended to gauge the effects of campuswide computerization on the libraries. Describes library's role in computerization and makes recommendations.

3160.   Moreau, Michael. "Putting It Back Together: Los Angeles Central Library," Wilson Library Bulletin, 61:7 (March 1987), 35-39. Describes efforts to rebuild building and collections and to repair damaged collections.

3161.   Morentz, James W. "Computerizing Libraries for Emergency Planning," Special Libraries, 78:2 (Spring 1987), 100-104. Describes inexpensive computer programs that can provide guidelines for emergency planning.

3162.   Morgan, John. Conservation of Plastics: An Introduction to Their History, Manufacture, Deterioration, Identification, and Care. London: Conservation Unit, Museums and Galleries Commission/Plastics Historical Society, 1991. 55p. Introduction to the technology and history of plastics; practical measures to deal with them, some controversial.

3163.   Moroz, Richard, and Eva Roever. "A New Approach to Systematic Dry Cleaning with Technical Devices," Restaurator, 14:3 (1993), 172-187. Examines new dry cleaning techniques for works on paper.

3164.   Morozova, I. "Flood, Fire - Now What? Talking About a Sore Subject: The Fate of Libraries," Russian Libraries in Transition: An Anthology of Glasnost Literature. Jefferson, NC: McFarland, 1992, 13-16. Describes the appalling physical condition of the Lenin Library. From Pravda, August 8, 1988, and translated in the Current Digest of the Soviet Press.

3165.   Morris, John. "Fire Protection in the Library," Construction Specifier, 42:10 (October 1989), 133-141. Traces the history of library fires and policies of fire protection; bookstack construction and its effect on spread of fire; elements of a fire protection plan in library construction; types of automatic suppressant systems and descriptions of new buildings with such systems.

3166.   Morris, John. The Library Disaster Preparedness Handbook. Chicago, IL: American Library Association, 1986. 129p. Review of preventive measures and recovery plans for libraries.

3167.   Morris, John. "The Los Angeles Central Library Fire," Library Association Record, 88:9 (September 1986), 441-443. Report on the fire; cites inadequacy of building and commends Eric Lundquist for his innovative salvage operation.

3168.   Morris, John. "Los Angeles Library Fire - Learning the Hard Way," Canadian Library Journal, 44:4 (August 1987), 217-221. Analysis of the fire and lessons learned.

3169.   Morris, John. "Mopping Up After Library Fires," Fire Prevention, 230 (June 1989), 33-35. Describes the drying process used for the recovery of water-damaged books following the Los Angeles Public Library fire.

3170. Morris, John. "Planning and Design for Safety and Security," PNLA Quarterly (Pacific Northwest Library Association) (Summer 1988), 22-24.

3171. Morris, John. "Protecting the Library from Fire," Fire Journal, (March 1986). Causes of fires and prevention; discussion of sprinklers and suppressant systems. Reprinted in Library Trends, 33:1 (Summer 1984), 49-56.

3172. Morris, John William. "The Long Term Protection of Private Map Collections," Map Collector (March 1985), 16-19. Written for private collectors and librarians, covers environment, storage, viewing, as well as problems with paper and adhesives.

3173. Morris, Patricia A. "Educational Options for Preservation Administrators: An Afterward on the Preservation Management Institute," American Archivist, 53:2 (Spring 1990), 244-248. Review the effectiveness of a training institute developed by the Society of American Archivists and the Northeast Document Conservation Center held at NEDCC in 1987.

3174. Morris, Patricia A. Environmental Controls for Local Government Records. Nashville, TN: American Association for State and Local History, 1989. 11p. (NICLOG Technical Leaflet 111). Basic, non-technical recommendations for local government archivists and records managers; compliments The Management of Local Government Records. Bruce W. Dearstyne (1988).

3175. Morris, Patricia A. "Mold Spores [sic]: South Carolina Archives into Defensive Action," NAGARA Clearinghouse (National Association of Government Archivists and Records Administrators), 10:1 (Winter 1994), 1, 6-7. Describes mold outbreaks at the archives, housed in an inadequate building that cannot offer protection for the collections.

3176. Morris, Patricia A. "PALMCOP: A Statewide Preservation Effort in South Carolina," Conservation Administration News, 40 (January 1990), 10-11, 30. Describes a statewide preservation effort organized for museums, libraries, archives, and public record offices.

3177.   Morrow, Carolyn Clark. "Developing Preservation Programs in Libraries," Issues in Library Management: A Reader for the Professional Librarian. White Plains, NY: Knowledge Industries, 1984, 97-127; reprinted from The Preservation Challenge (White Plains, NY: Knowledge Industries, 1983), 61-91. Covers planning, environmental considerations, disaster planning, treatment options.

3178.   Morrow, Carolyn Clark., "Illinois Cooperative Conservation Program," Conservation Administration News, 16 (January 1984), 1-4. Description of the establishment of a statewide preservation and conservation program, goals, and accomplishments.

3179.   Morrow, Carolyn Clark. "Library Bindings and Conservation," Illinois Libraries, 64:5 (May 1983), 357-360. Library binding procedures and options for libraries.

3180.   Morrow, Carolyn Clark, ed. National Conference on the Development of Statewide Preservation Programs. Washington, DC: National Conference on the Development of Statewide Preservation Programs. 1991. 107p. Report of a conference held in Washington, DC, March 1-3, 1989, on the development of statewide preservation programs, their current status, and future direction.

3181.   Morrow, Carolyn Clark. "National Preservation Planning and Regional Cooperative Conservation Efforts," Conserving and Preserving Library Materials, eds. Kathryn L. and William T. Henderson. Urbana-Champaign: University of Illinois Graduate School of Library and Information Service, 1983, 37-56. Chronology of national planning initiatives; discussion of services needed.

3182.   Morrow, Carolyn Clark, ed. The Preservation Challenge: A Guide to Conserving Library Materials, with Gay Walker, intro. Pamela W. Darling. White Plains, NY: Knowledge Industries, 1983. 231p. A collection of papers presenting an overview of preservation, including case studies, options for care.

3183.   Morrow, Carolyn Clark. "Preservation Comes of Age," Library and Book Trade Almanac, 34th ed., 1989-90. New York: Bowker, 1989, 71-76. Reviews success in preserving brittle books; identifies areas of concern: persuading publishers to use alkaline paper, defining national strategies and standards to preserve non-print collections, addressing needs of smaller institutions.

3184. Morrow, Carolyn Clark. "Staffing the Preservation Program," Meeting the Preservation Challenge. Washington, DC: Association of Research Libraries, 1988, 26-30. Discusses the role and rank of a preservation librarian; distinguishes it from the role of the collections conservator.

3185. Morrow, Carolyn C., and Carole Dyal. Conservation Treatment Procedures: A Manual of Step-by-Step Procedures for the Maintenance and Repair of Library Materials. 2d ed. Littleton, CO: Libraries Unlimited, 1986. 225p. Illustrated treatment manual; glossary, list of supplies, bibliography.

3186. Morse, Elizabeth. Enzyme Treatment: The Science and the Applications in Conserving Artistic and Historic Works: A Selected Bibliography 1940-1990. Provo, UT: Abbey Publications, 1990. 17p. Bibliography from a seminar sponsored by Technology & Conservation. See full bibliography, following.

3187. Morse, Elizabeth. "Enzyme Treatments for Conserving Artistic/Historic Works," Technology & Conservation, 11:1 (Spring 1992), 20-24. Bibliography citing general works, objects, paintings, paper, photographic materials, textile conservation, and desizing. No annotations.

3188. Morton, Bernard W. Humidification Handbook: What, Why and How. Hopkins, MN: Dri-Steam Humidifier Company, 1986. 108p.

3189. Moses, Kathy S. "Conservation, Preservation and Automation of the Frederick Douglass Home," Conservation Administration News, 58-59 (July/October 1994), 27-28.

3190. Mosher, Paul H. "Book Production Quality: A Librarian's View; Or, The Self-Destructing Library," Library Resources and Technical Services, 28:1 (January-March 1984), 15-19. Discussion of the importance of book production guidelines for publishers so that libraries can be sure that permanent and durable books will be added to collections.

3191. Mosher, Paul H. "Collaborative Interdependence: The Human Dimension of the Conspectus," IFLA Journal (International Federation of Library Associations and Institutions), 16:3 (1990), 327-331. A consideration of the human factors in cooperative initiatives; the results of a study demonstrating bibliographer's willingness to cooperate in selection for acquisition and preservation.

3192. Mosher, Paul H. "Reviewing for Preservation, Storage and Weeding," Collection Management, 26, eds. Charles B. Osborn and Ross Atkinson. Greenwich, CT: JAI Press, 1991, 373-391. Covers benefits and problems of weeding collections; provides historical context and methods.

3193. Motylewski, Karen. "A Checklist of Construction Concerns," NEDCC News (Northeast Documents Conservation Center), 2 (Spring 1990), 4. Pinpoints problems that arise from construction and that result in fire dangers, water hazards, security lapses, and collection damage.

3194. Motylewski, Karen. "A Matter of Control," Museum News, 69:2 (April 1990), 64-67. Discussion of appropriate climate control for the protection of collections in museums. Emphasizes the need for a stable environment and a monitoring program.

3195. Motylewski, Karen. "Parsimonious Preservation," Northeast Document Conservation Center News (Winter 1989), 2. Brief introductory paragraph, followed by six practical recommendations for improving a storage environment without spending a lot of money. Recommendations are from William Lull. This article was later turned into a technical leaflet "Low Cost? No Cost Improvements in Climate Control," 1991. 1p.

3196. Motylewski, Karen. Protecting Collections During Renovation. Andover, MA: Northeast Document Conservation Center, 1994. 7p.

3197.   Motylewski, Karen. What an Institution Can Do to Survey Its Own Conservation Needs. Andover, MA: Northeast Document Conservation Center, 1989. 36p. Presents survey methodology and procedures.

3198.   Motylewski, Karen, and Mary Elizabeth Ruwell. "Preservation and Conservation: Complimentary Needs for Libraries and Archives," Advances in Preservation and Access. Vol. 1. Westport, CT: Meckler, 1992, 213-226. Planning, phased preservation, selection of treatments, options.

3199.   Mount, Barbara L. "Save the Books," Columbia, 13:3 (December 1987), 14-19. Discussion of the problem of deteriorating library collections and Columbia University's efforts to deal with it to ensure access for the future.

3200.   Mount, Ellis, ed. Preservation and Conservation of Sci-Tech Materials. New York: Haworth Press, 1987. 79p. Special issue of Science and Technology Libraries, 7:3 (Spring 1987). Problems of preservation of science and technology collections; case studies.

3201.   Mount Angel Abbey. Book Conservation at Mount Angel Abbey. St. Benedict, OR: Benedictine Press, 1985. 14p. Describes the conservation of the collection of pre-19th century books in the Abbey library, and materials used. Exhibition catalog.

3202.   Moving Images: Final Report of the International Roundtable to Evaluate the Practical Results of the UNESCO Recommendation for the Safeguarding and Preservation of Moving Images. Paris: UNESCO, 1989. 27p. Report of a survey undertaken for the International Federation of Film Archives and the International Federation of Television Archives to assess the preservation of film and television archives; discussion of results, with recommendations.

3203.   Mowat, Ian M. "Preservation Problems in Academic Libraries," Preserving the Word. London: Library Association, 1987, 37-43. Summary of results of a questionnaire sent to academic and polytechnic libraries in the United Kingdom to determine the strength of their preservation and conservation activities; the lack of concern and implications for collections are discussed.

3204.   Mowery, J. Franklin. "Clasps, Schliessen, Clausuren: A Guide to the Manufacture and the Literature of Clasps," Guild of Bookworkers Journal, 29:2 (Fall 1991), 1-58. Illus. History of the use of clasps in bookbinding, with instructions for making reproductions.

3205.   Mowery, J. Franklin. "Conservation Decisions at the Folger Library," Conservation of Historic and Artistic Works on Paper. Ottawa: Canadian Conservation Institute, 1994, 79-82. (Symposium 88). Describes which and how conservation decisions are made; emphasizes functional properties of the book to provide stable textblocks with historically compatible bindings for scholarly access.

3206.   Mowery, J. Franklin. "Leafcasting: 'Filling the Holes': The Current Status of Leafcasting Techniques," Conservation in Archives. Paris: International Council on Archives, 1989, 337-343. (Proceedings of an international symposium, Ottawa, Canada, 1988). Overview of the leafcasting process; discussion of equipment needs and effectiveness.

3207.   Mowery, J. Franklin. "The Logic and Techniques of German Bookbinding," Guild of Book Workers Journal, 29:1 (Spring 1991), 1-15. Details the characteristics of German bookbinding; covers textblock preparation, preparing leather, and covering.

3208.   Mowery, J. Franklin. "Parchment: Historical Overview and Conservation of Books," summary by Jim Dorssey in 'Binder's' Guild Newsletter, 18:3 (April 1995). Summary with diagrams.

3209.   Mowery, J. Franklin. "A Stand-Alone Imaging System to Assist in Leafcasting Developed at the Folger Shakespeare Library, Washington, DC," Restaurator, 12:2 (1991), 110-115. Describes a system that performs automatic and accurate measurements to ensure the proper amount of pulp will be used to fill losses.

3210.   Mroz, Terry. "The Phased Box at CCA: A Revised Model,"
        Conservation Administration News, 31 (Winter 1988), 6-
        7. Modification of the Library of Congress models; illustrated.

3211.   Mroz, Terry Rempel. "Technique: The 'Livre de Raison,'" Le
        Journal (Association des Relieurs du Québec), 7:3 (1989), 47-
        54. Describes the construction of 16th-and 17th-century limp vellum
        bound books with tacketing.

3212.   Msuya, Jangawe. "Serials Mutilation Hazard at the University of Dar
        es Salaam Library in Tanzania," Library and Archival Security, 11:1
        (1993), 109-116. Results of a survey to assess mutilation, with
        suggested remedial actions.

3213.   Mulhern, Brian J. "Fifty Years of the Library Binding Institute,"
        Managing a Library Binding Program, ed. Jan Merrill-Oldham.
        Washington, DC: Association of Research Libraries, 1993, 95-104.
        (Preservation Planning Program). History of the Library Binding
        Institute, reprinted from a souvenir program, April 1985.

3214.   Mullock, Hilary. "Xuan Paper," Paper Conservator, 19 (1995), 23-
        30. Describes contemporary production of xuan handmade paper, and
        illustrates its practical use.

3215.   Munn, Jesse. "Alum Tawing Goat and Calf Vellum: Current
        Experiments," Guild of Book Workers Journal, 22:2 (Spring/Summer
        1984), 17-20. An attempt at the Library of Congress to alum taw a
        piece of goat vellum and a piece of calf vellum as a method in
        conservation.

3216.   Munoff, Gerald J., Mary Lynn Ritzenthaler, and Marjery Long. A
        Select Bibliography for the Administration of Photographic
        Collections. Chicago, IL: Society of American Archivists, 1983.
        4p. Basic, annotated bibliography prepared as a part of the Society of
        American Archivists Basic Archival Conservation Program.

3217.   Munoz-Sola, Haydee. "Preservation of Library Materials in a
        Tropical Climate: The Puerto Rican Experience," Preservation and
        Conservation of Sci-Tech Materials, ed. Ellis Mount. New York:

Haworth Press, 1987, 41-47. Describes efforts to preserve the Health Science Collection against ravages of a tropical climate; sees need for further study of preservation needs in tropics.

3218.   Munoz Vinas, Salvador, and Eugene Farrell. "Technical Analysis of Illuminated Manuscripts from the Library of the University of Valencia, Spain," Conservation of the Iberian and Latin American Cultural Heritage, eds. H.W.M. Hodges, John S. Mills, and Perry Smith. London: International Institute for Conservation, 1992, 99-103. (Preprints: Contributions to the Madrid Congress, September 1992). Report on the physical nature of the collection compared with early records and receipts for the production or purchase of manuscripts; emphasis on pigment analysis.

3219.   Murowanyj, Una, comp. "Conservation," Select Bibliography of Archives Management and Administration Literature. Edmonton, Canada: Provincial Archives of Alberta, 1990, 20-25. Bibliography; no annotations.

3220.   Murphy, Jack. "Preserving a National Treasure," Du Pont Magazine, 83:1 (January-February 1989), 23-25. Describes the preservation of an archival collection of drawings, correspondence, manuscripts, and photographs belonging to Frank Lloyd Wright.

3221.   Murphy, William T. Cold Storage of Color Film Materials. Washington, DC: National Archives and Records Administration, 1987. 12 leaves. (TIP-03, PB87 125225/AS).

3222.   Murphy, William T. "Storage of Acetate Film Materials: A Discussion at the National Archives and Records Administration," Journal of Film Preservation, 23:48 (April 1994), 51-53. Summary of the National Archives and Records Administration Advisory Committee on Preservation meeting, September 1993; includes a list of consensus recommendations regarding acetate degradation and storage.

3223.   Murray, Toby. "Basic Guidelines for Disaster Planning," Issues for a New Decade: Today's Challenge, Tomorrow's Opportunity. Boston, MA: G. K. Hall, 1991, 143-167. First published by the author in

1984, 1986, and republished by the Oklahoma Conservation Congress in 1994. Outline to assist in the preparation of a disaster plan and organization of salvage procedures.

3224. Murray, Toby. "BCPM Emergency Planning Seminar," Conservation Administration News, 20 (January 1985), 16-18. Seminar at the British Columbia Provincial Museum.

3225. Murray, Toby. Bibliography on Disasters, Disaster Preparedness and Disaster Recovery. Tulsa, OK: University of Tulsa, 1987. 43p.; 1994. Updated regularly. Comprehensive bibliography, no annotations.

3226. Murray, Toby. "BMS CAT (Blackmon-Mooring-Steamatic Catastrophe, Inc.) Seminar/Reception for Leningrad Librarians," Conservation Administration News, 46 (July 1991), 18.

3227. Murray, Toby. "Conservare '93," Conservation Administration News 56 (January 1994) 18. (European Heritage Forum, October, Ostend, Belgium).

3228. Murray, Toby. "Don't Get Caught With Your Plans Down," Records Management Quarterly, 21:2 (April 1987), 12-14, 16-21, 26-30, 41. Step-by-step guidance on recovery operations; bibliography.

3229. Murray, Toby. "Flood Recovery in Tulsa," Conservation Administration News, 22 (July 1985), 4-5, 20. Case study. Reprinted in Illinois Libraries, 67:8 (October 1985), 717-719.

3230. Murray, Toby. "Hacksaws, Hard Hats, and Headaches," Conservation Administration News, 38 (July 1989), 10-11, 25. Case study of the planning, design, and conservation of a conservation workshop.

3231. Murray, Toby. "O-DRAT! The Oklahoma Disaster Recovery Assistance Team," Conservation Administration News, 37 (April 1989), 4-5, 29. Description of O-DRAT, creation, operation, and problems.

3232. Murray, Toby. "Planning for the Unexpected," Muse News, 17:2 (April 1987), 2-3. Note on how to prepare and write a disaster plan.

3233. Murray, Toby. "Preservation Awareness Quiz," Conservation Administration News, 23 (October 1985), 22-23.

3234. Murray, Toby. Recovery of Water-Damaged Library Materials: A Workshop. Carbondale, IL: The Program, 1986. One volume. Sponsored by the Illinois Cooperative Conservation Program, Morris Library, Southern Illinois University at Carbondale.

3235. Murray, Toby. "SMU Symposium [Preservation Policies]," Conservation Administration News, 54 (July 1993), 16-18.

3236. Musembi, Musila. "Archives Development in Kenya," Information Development, 2:4 (October 1986), 218-222. Describes the establishment of the National Archives of Kenya following a history of mismanagement, destruction, and poor advice from foreign consultants.

3237. Musembi, Musila. "Preservation of Audio-Visual Archives in Eastern Africa," Archiving the Audio-Visual Heritage. Rushton, England: FIAF/UNESCO, 1992, 17-20. Describes the lack of interest and resources for the preservation of new media by librarians and archivists in Africa.

3238. Musson, Melvyn, and Humphrey L. Crook, Jr. "Earthquake Preparedness Planning," Disaster Recovery Journal, 4:3 (July-September 1991), 30-33. Development of a plan for corporate recovery, flowchart.

3239. Mustardo, Peter. Photograph Preservation: Basic Methods of Safeguarding Your Collection. [Washington, DC]: Mid-Atlantic Regional Archives Conference, 1994. 36p.

3240. Mustardo, Peter J. "Protective Enclosures for the Care of Books," AB Bookman's Weekly (Antiquarian Bookman), 83:25 (June 19, 1989), 2730-2733. Discussion of protective enclosures and the styles that can be adapted for collections.

3241.   Muya, E. M. "The Problems and Conservation of Library Materials," Librarianship and Documentation Studies: A Handbook of Teaching and Learning Materials, ed. Lutz Hütteman. Vol. 2. Bonn, Germany: Deutsche Stiftung für Internationale Entwicklung, 1986, 61-68. Basic review of preservation problems in libraries, ranging from poor production of materials, to poor environment; Notes need to include preservation in the library school curriculum and to train more conservators.

3242.   Myers, Richard. "Effective Image Management: Exploring the Possibilities Offered by Laser Disc and Electronic Imaging," Preserving Geoscience Imagery, ed. Louise S. Zipp. Alexandria, VA: Geoscience Information Society, 1993, 31-32. (Proceedings, 23). Use of optical disk technology to reproduce images for access, thus protecting original fragile materials from unnecessary handling.

3243.   Nadeau, Luis. Encyclopedia of Printing, Photographic and Photomechanical Processes. Fredericton, NB: Atelier L. Nadeau, 1989. 542p. two volumes. Distinguishes among reproduction technologies. Reference tool that contains an exhaustive listing of historical and modern, rare and common photographic and photomechanical processes.

3244.   Nadeau, Luis. History and Practice of Platinum Printing. Fredericton, NB: Atelier L. Nadeau, 1986. 96p.

3245.   Nainis, Linda. "Description of Cooperative Preservation Photocopying Project," Abbey Newsletter, 15:2 (April 1991), 26-28. Also in Archival Products, 1:2 (Summer 1992), 1, 3. Case study.

3246.   Nainis, Linda, and Laura A. Bedard. "Preservation Book Survey in an Academic Law Library," Law Library Journal, 78:2 (Spring 1986), 243-259. Describes methodology and results of a survey of the collection at Georgetown University Law Library, with recommendations for preservation and treatment.

3247.   Nainis, Linda, Charles Kalina, Carolyn Morrow Manns, and Jan Merrill-Oldham. "Why GPO Should Use Alkaline Paper," Alkaline

Paper Advocate, 1:2 (March 1988), 13-16. Background paper; describes the problem of acid paper and the benefits of using alkaline paper for all government publications.

3248. Nainis, Linda, and Robert J. Milevski. "Book Repair: One Component of an Overall Preservation Program," New Library Scene, 6:2 (April 1987), 1, 5-10. Overview of components of a preservation program, noting that many libraries fail to do routine book maintenance. Describes the program at the Georgetown University Law Library and how it compliments the library's collection maintenance program.

3249. Nakamura, Tokio, A. Hatai, and K. Okamoto. "Archival Stability of Metal Video Tape as Used for Beta-CAM SP," Archiving the Audio-Visual Heritage. Rushton, England: FIAF/UNESCO, 1992, 61-69. Describes the medium that came on the market in 1985, its advantages, and recommends storage conditions for a life of 10 years.

3250. Nash, John C., and Mary M. Nash. "Matching Risk to Cost in Computer File Back-up Strategies," Canadian Journal of Information Science, 17:2 (July 1992), 1-15. Considers the issue of back-up versus cost of loss and presents a model for risk analysis.

3251. Nasland, Cheryl Terrass. "Preservation Programs in Small Academic Libraries," Operations Handbook for the Small Academic Library, ed. Gerard B. McCabe. Westport, CT: Greenwood Press, 1989, 153-162. Discusses the importance of preservation as an inherent library function; describes the elements of a preservation program and how it can be implemented.

3252. National Academy of Public Administration. The Archives of the Future: Archival Strategies for the Treatment of Electronic Databases. Washington, DC: National Academy of Public Administration, 1992. 40p. and appendices. A study concerning major federal automated databases that leave longterm historical and research value to the nation.

3253.   National Academy of Public Administration. Effects of Electronic
        Recordkeeping on the Historical Record of the U.S. Government: A
        Report for the National Archives and Records Administration/
        National Academy of Public Administration. Washington, DC:
        National Academy of Public Administration, 1989. 69p. technical
        appendices. (PB89-152219). Investigates how electronic technology
        affects the recordkeeping practices of the Federal government, and
        examines the question of retention and loss.

3254.   National Association of Government Archives and Records
        Administrators. A New Age: Electronic Information Systems, State
        Governments, and the Preservation of the Archival Record.
        Lexington, KY: Council on State Governments, 1991. 11p.

3255.   National Association of Government Archives and Records
        Administrators. Guide and Resources for Archival Strategic
        Preservation Planning (GRASPP), Albany, NY: NAGARA, 1990.
        Two volumes A computer-assisted self-study based on an expert
        system; a manual offering specific preservation strategies, and a
        resource bibliography of over 600 citations.

3256.   National Association of Government Archives and Records
        Administrators. Preservation Needs in State Archives. Albany, NY:
        NAGARA, 1986, 1988. 56p. Identifies the preservation problems
        facing state archives and outlines steps to be taken to foster
        preservation activities.

3257.   National Association of Government Archives and Records
        Administrators. State Government Records and the Public Interest.
        Albany, NY: NAGARA, February 1986, 72p. Presents an important
        message concerning the valuable nature of state government records
        as both an information and a cultural resource, and the need to
        preserve them.

3258.   National Center for Film and Video Preservation. Moving Image
        Preservation: A Basic Bibliography. Washington, DC: National
        Center for Film and Video Preservation [1992]. 4p. Covers general
        references, film preservation, videotape, technical data; no
        annotations.

3259. National Conference on Cultural Property Protection. The Security and Protection Alliance Among Museums, Libraries, Gardens and Parks. Washington, DC: Smithsonian Institution, 1993. 261p. A Conference on the Protection of Cultural Property, February 21-25, 1993 sponsored by the Smithsonian Institution.

3260. "National Conference on the Development of Statewide Preservation Programs Is Held," LC Information Bulletin (Library of Congress) (March 6, 1989), 90-91. Summary of meeting.

3261. "National Digital Library Federation Agreement," IAC(SM) Newsletter (International Association of Computer Service Managers), 13 (June 1995), 7.

3262. "National Digital Library Federation (NDFL) Constituted as Charter Organization, Adopts Three Part Agenda," Commission on Preservation and Access Newsletter, 92 (September 1996), 1, 3. also in IAC(SM) Newsletter (International Association of Computer Service Managers), 14 (October 1, 1996), 10. The three points are: a. Discovery and Retrieval, b. Intellectual Property Rights and Economic Models, c. Archiving of Digital Information.

3263. "National Digital Library Program," LC Information Bulletin (Library of Congress), 55 (June 24-July 8, 1996), 234-261, 55 (June 12, 1996), 251-274. Articles on the National Digital Library.

3264. "National Digital Library Program Awards Contract for Digital Conversion to Preservation Resources," OCLC Newsletter, 224 (November-December 1996), 6.

3265. National Endowment for the Humanities, Office of Preservation. Preservation, a Selective Program to Save Books, Journals, Newspapers, Manuscripts, Documents, Maps, Drawings, Plans, Photographs, Film, and Tapes of Significance for Humanities Research Now and in the Future. Washington, DC: National Endowment for the Humanities, Office of Preservation, 1986. 6pp.

3266.   National Fire Protection Association. Automatic Sprinkler System
         Handbook. 2d ed. Quincy, MA: NFPA, 1985. 477p. Text for those
         who design, install, or inspect automatic sprinkler systems.

3267.   National Fire Protection Association. Recommended Practice for
         Disaster Management. Quincy, MA: NFPA, 1995. 16p. (NFPA
         publ.1600). Minimum criteria for disaster management and
         development of a program for effective disaster mitigation,
         preparedness, response, and recovery. Bibliography, definition of
         terms, list of disaster management and related organizations.

3268.   National Fire Protection Association. Recommended Practice for the
         Protection of Libraries and Library Collections. Boston: NFPA,
         1991. 48p. (NFPA Publ. 910). Guidelines for libraries that are
         updated on a regular basis.

3269.   National Fire Protection Association. Recommended Practice for the
         Protection of Archives. Boston, MA: National Fire Protection
         Association, 1991. (NFPA Publ. 911).

3270.   National Fire Protection Association. Recommended Practice for the
         Protection of Museums. Boston, MA: National Fire Protection
         Association, 1991 (NFPA Publ. 912).

3271.   National Fire Protection Association. Standard on Clean Agent Fire
         Extinguishing Systems. NFPA #2001. Quincy, MA: National Fire
         Protection Association, 1994. 51p. Provides an overview of
         Minimum requirements for total flooding, clean agent fire
         extinguishing systems, including components, system design,
         inspection, and maintenance. Covers agents introduced in response to
         restrictions on production of halon.

3272.   National Governors Association. Executive Chamber Records: A
         Guide for Governors. Washington, DC: Office of State Services,
         National Governors Association, 1989. 52p. Describes and outlines
         a record management program for governors and their staff to
         "ensure proper preservation of essential records for subsequent
         administrations," and "to provide for proper preservation of historical
         records."

3273. National Historical Publications and Records Commission.
Electronic Records Issues. Washington, DC: National Archives and
Records Administration, 1990. 37p. (Its Report, 4). Identifies
system dependency, fragility of the records, and ease of change/loss
of information as issues of importance. Suggests archivists'
participation in designing information systems, the development of
standards, and interdisciplinary cooperation as to resolving the
problems.

3274. National Historical Publications and Records Commission. Research
Issues in Electronic Records. Washington, DC: NHPRC, 1991.
37p. Report to identify and analyze issues and initiate a course of
action for the preservation of electronic records.

3275. National Historical Publications and Records Commission. To
Protect a Priceless Legacy: The Preservation and Use of America's
Historical Records. Washington, DC: NHPRC, 1992. 90p.

3276. National Institute for the Conservation of Cultural Property.
Collections Care: Catalyst for Funds. Washington, DC: National
Institute for Conservation, 1994. 20p. Concerns Fund Raising.

3277. National Institute for the Conservation of Cultural Property.
Emergency Preparedness and Response: Federal Aid for Cultural
Institutions During an Emergency. Washington, DC: National
Institute for Conservation, 1991. 16p. Outlines the types of federal
assistance available to libraries, archives, museums, historical
societies, historic preservation organizations, and conservation
organizations during an emergency.

3278. National Institute for the Conservation of Cultural Property.
Emergency Preparedness and Response: Materials Developed from
the NIC Seminar, October 19, 1990, Washington, DC. Washington,
DC: National Institute for Conservation, 1991. 47p. Covers all
aspects of contingency planning; bibliography.

3279. National Institute for the Conservation of Cultural Property. Training
for Collection Care and Maintenance: A Suggested Curriculum.
Washington, DC: National Institute for the Conservation of Cultural

Property, 1996. 115p. Based on a pilot program of the Northeast Document Conservation Center, Andover, MA.

3280.   "National Library Pioneers Vacuum Packaging of Library Materials," Australian Map Circule Newsletter, 32 (September 1984), 6-7. Describes how the National Library of Australia uses vacuum packaging to store low-use materials such as newspapers, magazines, and loose-leaf items.

3281.   National Research Council. Committee on Preservation of Historical Records. Preservation of Historical Records. Washington, DC: National Academy Press, 1986. 108p. Report; various methods for preserving paper records are examined and alternative actions for preserving original documents and/or the information in them are assessed.

3282.   National Research Council. Computers at Risk: Safe Computing in the Information Age, by the System Security Study Committee, Computer Science and Telecommunications Board, Commission on Physical Sciences, Mathematics, and Applications, National Research Council. Washington, DC: National Academy Press, 1990. 301p. Report of a study to address security and trustworthiness of U.S. computing and communications systems. Assessment of key issues; recommendations for enhancing the security of the computer communications infrastructure.

3283.   Nazaroff, W. W., M. P. Ligocki, L. G. Salmon, G. R. Cass, T. Fall, M. C. Jones, H. I. H. Liu, and T. Ma. Airborne Particles in Museums. Marina del Rey, CA: Getty Conservation Institute, 1993. 144p. 65 charts. (Research in Conservation, 6). Assesses the intrusion of airborne particles into museum buildings; suggests measures to substantially reduce the rate of soiling.

3284.   Nazhad, Mousa M., and Laszlo Paszner. "Fundamentals of Strength Loss in Recycled Paper," TAPPI Journal (Technical Association of the Pulp and Paper Industry), 77:9 (September 1994), 171-179. Discusses the problem of lost fiber bonding ability when chemical pulp papers dry. Review of previous research; directions for further research. 120 citations.

3285. Nazhad M., and L. Paszner. "Temperature Effect on Paper Recycling," Progress in Paper Recycling, 3:3 (May 1994), 22-28. Drying and heating after drying weaken paper and increase its brittleness; literature review.

3286. Nebraska. Documents Preservation Advisory Council. A Preservation Action Agenda for Nebraska: Report and Recommendations to Preserve Nebraska's Documentary Collections. Lincoln, NE: Documents Preservation Advisory Council, 1991. 39p.

3287. Needles, Howard L., and S. Haig Zeronian, eds. Historic Textile and Paper Materials Conservation and Characterization. Washington, DC: American Chemical Society, 1986. 464p. (Advances in Chemistry Series, No. 212).

3288. Neeval, Johan G. "Exposure of Objects of Art and Science to Light from Electric Flash-Guns and Photocopiers," Contributions of the Central Research Laboratory to the Field of Conservation and Restoration. Amsterdam, Netherlands: Central Research Laboratory, 1994, 77-87. Discusses potential problems and hazards from exposure to light from flashguns and photocopiers, identifying equipment with higher UV exposure.

3289. Neeval, Johan G. "Phytate: A Potential Conservation Agent for the Treatment of Ink Corrosion Caused by Irongall Inks," Restaurator, 16:3 (1995), 143-160. Discusses the causes of deterioration of irongall inks. Describes treatment of endangered paper samples with an aqueous solution of the complexing agent phytate.

3290. Nelb, Tawny Ryan. "Reformatting Oversize Records: What Smaller Institutions Can Do," Preservation Papers of the 1990 SAA Annual Conference, comp. Karen Garlick. Chicago: Society of American Archivists, 1991, 46-50. Discusses reformatting options, preservation and conservation, for 35mm film, aperture cards, electrostatic copying, film, and scanning.

3291. Nelb, Tawny Ryan. "Will Your Drawings Be There When You Need Them?" Plan and Print Magazine, N64:12 (December 1991); corrected text, March 1992. 5p. Offprint. Discusses the need to preserve drawings, appropriate media for permanence, storage conditions, documentation, and legal issues. Electronic data problems are also discussed.

3292. NELINET Preservation Advisory Committee. Living Through Loans: Guidelines for Preserving ILL Material. Newton, MA: NELINET, March 1996. 8p.

3293. Nelson, Anna Kasten. "The 1985 Report of the Committee on the Records of Government: An Assessment," Government Information Quarterly, 4:2 (1987), 143-150. Describes the formation of a committee to examine policy and practices regarding the preservation of federal records and the impact of computer technologies of federal recordkeeping.

3294. Nelson, Carl L. Protecting the Past from Natural Disasters. Washington, DC: Preservation Press, 1991. 182p. Illus. Basic text outlining procedures for protecting cultural property and weathering natural disasters. Bibliography.

3295. Nelson, Milo. "An Acidic Change," Wilson Library Bulletin, 63:3 (November 1988), 4. Editorial and brief summary of discussion about production and use of acid-free paper at the 1988 TAPPI Symposium, which brought papermakers, librarians, archivists, government officials, and paper scientists together to address concerns.

3296. Nelson, Milo. "Strong Conservation on a Brittle Subject - TAPPI Meets in Washington," Wilson Library Bulletin, 63:4 (December 1988), 66-67, 20. Full report of the 1988 TAPPI Symposium, cited above.

3297. Nelson, Nancy Melin. "Preservation Matters," Information Today, 6:10 (November 1989), 9-11. Discusses current preservation initiatives, including the brittle book microfilming project guided by the Research Libraries Group.

3298. Nelson, Nancy Melin. "Preservation Microfilming Services," News from Research Publications, 8:1 (1990), 1,6. Describes the development of preservation microfilming efforts in the United States and the role that Research Publications, a commercial microfilmer, can play.

3299. Nelson, Norman L. "Reducing Theft, Mutilation and Defacement of Library Materials," Conservation Administration News, 17 (April 1984), 1-4, 6. Guidelines for libraries; bibliography covering 1979-83.

3300. Nelson-Strauss, Brenda. "Preserving Chicago Symphony Orchestra Broadcast Tapes," Midwestern Archivist, 16:1 (1993), 21-30. Case study of audio preservation project; clear description of problems inherent in early recording media, with guidelines for storage and handling.

3301. Nelson-Strauss, Brenda. "Preservation Policies and Priorities for Recorded Sound Collections," Notes (Music Library Association), 48 (December 1991), 425-436. Originally in Preservation Paper of the 1990 SAA Annual Conference, comp. Karen Garlick. Chicago: Society of American Archivists, 1991, 11-17. Covers assessment of collections, determining priorities, strategies; emphasizes the need for comprehensive preservation policies.

3302. Nemeyer, Sheldon. "Historical Note: Color News Film, 1965-1975," SMPTE Journal (Society of Motion Picture and Television Engineers), 103:2 (February 1994), 112-113. Technical aspects and historical problems during the decade when television news program production shifted from black-and-white to color film.

3303. Nesheim, Kenneth. "Yale Non-Toxic Method of Eradication Book-eating Insects by Deep-Freezing," Restaurator, 6:3/4 (1984), 147-164. Presents the reasons behind the choice of deep-freezing over alternative methods; describes the program over the initial two-year period of its operation.

3304. Netherlands. Coordinatiepunt Nationaal Conserversengbeleid. Expert Meeting on Conservation of Acid Paper Material and the Use of Permanent Paper. The Hague: CNC, 1992, 115p. (French/English). Proceedings of a meeting December 17-19, 1991.

3305. Netherlands. Coordinatiepunt Nationaal Conserversengbeleid. Endangered Books and Documents, edited by R.C. Hol and L. Voogt. The Hague: CNC, 1991. 217p + appendices. (Dutch/English). A damage survey of post-1800 archive and library material held by the General Archives of the Netherlands and the National Library of the Netherlands.

3306. Netherlands. Coordinatiepunt Nationaal Conserveringsbeleid. The Future of Our Past: Final Report of the National Preservation Office of the Netherlands (CNC) on the Mass Conservation Trial Programme. The Hague: CNC, 1993. 32p.

3307. Netherlands. Ministry of Welfare, Health and Cultural Affairs. Factsheet: Delta Plan for the Preservation of Cultural Heritage. The Hague: Ministry of Welfare, Health and Cultural Affairs, 1992, 10p. (C-11-E-1992). Scope of the plan to address preservation and conservation needs in Dutch museums, libraries, and archives.

3308. Netsky, Ron. "Saving Traces of the Past," Sunday Democrat and Chronicle. Rochester, NY, December 18, 1988, 4-6. Conservators at the Margaret Woodbury Strong Museum employ both art and chemistry to preserve artifacts.

3309. Neuemeier, Paul J. "The 2010: An Integrated Optical Mass Memory System," Journal of Imaging Technology, 10:4 (August 1984), 162-165. Describes 2010, an optical system that uses scanning and digitizing.

3310. "New Deacidification Process Testing in North Carolina," Library Journal, (April 15, 1990), 15. The article discusses the lithium process which deacidifies and strengthens acidic paper.

3311. New Jersey Records Control and Preservation Training Workbook. Trenton, NJ: New Jersey Division of Archives and Records Management, 1990. 2 vols. and 27 minute videotape.

3312. "New Listserv and WWW Sites for Preservation Educators: (PRESED-L and PRESED-X)," ALCTS Newsletter (Association for Library Collections and Technical Services), 6:3 (1995), 40p.

3313. "New Process Saves Books," New York Times, May 17, 1988, p. C5.

3314. New South Wales State Library. Counter-Disaster Manual. Sydney, Australia: State Library of New South Wales, 1992. 191p. Covers disaster prevention, reaction, and recovery procedures.

3315. New York Document Conservation Advisory Council. Our Memory at Risk: Preserving New York's Unique Research Resources. Albany, NY: New York State Education Dept. (1988), 56p. Provides an overview of the preservation problems in the state's libraries and records repositories; recommends actions to ensure survival of the state's documentary heritage.

3316. New York Historical Records Program Development Project. Microfilming Historical Records in New York: Questions and Issues for Statewide Planning. Albany, NY: New York Historical Records Program Development Project, 1988. 11p.

3317. New York Historical Records Program Development Project. Microfilming Local Government Archival Records in New York: Questions and Issues for Statewide Planning. Albany, NY: New York Historical Records Program Development Project, 1988. 11p.

3318. New York Metropolitan Library Agency (METRO). Analysis of Conservation Resources Survey Questionnaires. New York: METRO, 1985. n.p. Responses to a questionnaire sent to METRO member institutions to identify conservation resources.

3319. New York Metropolitan Library Agency (METRO). Hold Everything! A Storage and Housing Information Sourcebook for Libraries and Archives. New York: METRO, 1990. 63p.

3320. New York State Archives and Records Administration. Computer and Audiovisual Records in the State Government: Preliminary Report of the Special Media Records Project. Albany: Governor's Office of Management and Productivity, April 1986. 69p.

3321.   New York State Archives and Records Administration. Managing
         Records in E-Mail Systems. Albany, NY: New York State Archives
         and Records Administration, 1995. 43p.

3322.   New York State Archives and Records Administration. Local
         Government Records Services. Producing High Quality Microfilm.
         Albany, NY: University of the State of New York, State Education
         Department, New York State Archives and Records Administration,
         1994. 52p.

3323.   New York State Archives and Records Administration. Selecting
         Historical Records for Microfilming: Procedures for New York's
         Repositories. Albany, NY: New York State Archives and Records
         Administration, 1989. 31 leaves.

3324.   New York State Archives and Records Administration. A Strategic
         Plan for Managing and Preserving Electronic Records in New York
         State Government: Final Report. Albany, NY: State University of
         New York, 1988. 44p. Discusses issues of preservation and access
         that electronic records create; offers suggestions and specific
         activities to address concerns.

3325.   New York State Archives and Records Administration.
         Strengthening New York's Historical Records Program: A Self-
         Study Guide. Albany, NY: New York State Archives and Records
         Administration, 1989, 157p. Workbook on collection management
         with attention to issues of preservation and access, and fund-raising.

3326.   New York State Archives and Records Administration. Local
         Government Records Services. Targeting Information Packet.
         [Albany, NY]: New York State Archives and Records
         Administration, Local Government Records Services, Publications
         and Educational Resources Unit, [1995], [25]p.

3327.   New York State Program for the Conservation and Preservation of
         Library Research Materials. Discretionary Grant Program
         Application Workbook. Albany, NY: New York State Division of
         Library Development, 1990. 100p. Workbook to aid in the

preparation of applications to the program, contains hints on grant writing, sample forms, and examples.

3328. New York State Program for the Conservation and Preservation of Research Materials. Disaster Preparedness: Planning Resource Packet. Albany, NY: University of the State of New York, State Education Department and New York State Library, 1988. One packet of nine pieces.

3329. New York State Program for the Conservation and Preservation of Research Materials. Environmental Controls Resource Packet. Albany, NY: New York State Program for the Conservation and Preservation of Library Research Materials, 1990. 4 pieces. See also LULL, William P.

3330. New York State Program for the Conservation and Preservation of Library Research Materials Coordinated Preservation Project. Pre-Pilot Test of the Akzo Mass Deacidification Process: Final Report May 1994. New York: Columbia University Libraries, 1994. 10p.

3331. New York State Program for the Conservation and Preservation of Library Research Materials. Selected Press Clippings about Projects Funded by the Discretionary Grant Program 1988/89 and 1989/90. Albany, NY: New York State Division of Library Development, 1990. 75p.

3332. New York State Seminar on Mass Deacidification. Proceedings of the New York State Seminar on Mass Deacidification, Albany, New York, October 15-16, 1992. New York: Columbia University Libraries, 1993. 133p.

3333. New York University Libraries. Preservation Committee. Disaster Plan Workbook. New York: New York University Libraries, 1984. 75p. Loose-leaf. A fill-in-the-blanks disaster plan with basic information on emergency procedures and resources.

3334. Newberry Library. Conservation at the Newberry Library: Case History. Chicago IL: Newberry Library, 1984. 8p.

3335. Newborg, Gerald G. "Collection Snapshot: North Dakota Television Newsfilm Preservation Project," Views (Visual Resources Section, Society of American Archivists), 8:3 (August 1994), 4-5. Report on a project to preserve the Historical Society's television newsfilm collection.

3336.   Newman, Linda P. "Color Photocopying to Reproduce/Preserve Geologic Maps in Literature," Geoscience Information Society, 19 (1989), 205-208.

3337.   Newmark, Anne, ed. Guidelines for Conservation Framing of Works of Art on Paper. Leigh, Worcester, U.K.: Institute of Paper Conservation, 1992. 6p. Outlines processes and materials involved in conservation framing.

3338.   Nickerson, Matthew. "pH: Only a Piece of the Preservation Puzzle: A Comparison of the Preservation Studies at Brigham Young, Yale and Syracuse Universities," Library Resources and Technical Services, 36:1 (January 1992), 105-112. A comparison and analysis. The three collections showed similar percentage of deteriorated books, but brittleness percentages varied widely, indicating that environmental conditions can also affect brittleness.

3339.   Niederberger, Mary. "Acid Test Libraries in Bind to Keep Books from Crumbling," Pittsburgh Press, April 3, 1989, B1, B3.

3340.   Niederer, Karl J. "Collection Care and the Microenvironment," Library Conservation News, 20 (July 1988), 2-3.

3341.   Niknam, Mehrdad. "Conservation of Library Materials in Iran," Conservation Administration News, 46 (July 1991), 6-7. Describes the measures to preserve library and archival materials in Iran and at the National Library.

3342.   Niknam, Mehrdad. "A New Horizon in the Future of the Conservation of Library Materials in Iran," Conference on Book and Paper Conservation, 1990. Budapest, Hungary: Technical Association of Paper and Printing Industry/National Szechenyi Library, 1992, 343-346p. Preservation initiatives in Iran; conservation training.

3343. Nikolova, D. P., J. P. Tevetkova, and Tz. Iv. Pishmanova. "Bleaching of Paper Materials with Hydrogen Peroxide for the Purpose of Conservation Using an Enzyme Modification of the Method," Communications, Department of Chemistry, Bulgarian Academy of Sciences, 24:3 (1991), 383-390. Describes a modification of the traditional method of bleaching paper, with good results.

3344. Nizette, Mark. "The Conservation of an Alethoscope Image," AICCM Bulletin (Australia Institute for the Conservation of Cultural Material), 11:1/2 (June 1985), 3-15. Describes the treatment of the image so it could still be used in a viewing device.

3345. Nizette, Mark. "On the State of Photographic Conservation in Australia: 1985 and the Future," AICCM Bulletin (Australian Institute for the Conservation of Cultural Material), 12:3/4 (December 1986), 103-112. Outlines the history of photographic conservation, the state of photographic conservation around the world, and the discipline in Australia, with suggestions for improving practices.

3346. Nizette, Mark. "The Permanence of Photographs," AICCM Bulletin (Australian Institute for the Conservation of Cultural Material), 11:4 (December 1985), 31-46. Discussion of the physical nature of photographs and causes of their deterioration. Emphasizes need to select appropriate papers and films for photographic images that are to be preserved.

3347. Nizette, Mark. "The Role of the Silver Image in Determining Colour Potential of Finlay Plates: Preliminary Investigations," AICCM Bulletin (Australian Institute for the Conservation of Cultural Material), 9:1 (1983), 21-41. A study of an early (c1916-18) color photographic technique; how the colors were recorded.

3348. N'jie, S. P. C. "Collecting Policies and Preservation: The Gambia," Preservation of Library Materials, ed. Merrily Smith. New York: Saur, 1987, 24-30. (IFLA Publications. No. 40). Reviews collecting and preservation policies under development in Gambia; stresses

Bibliography

need for nation to develop a more defined collection development policy on a national scale.

3349.   Nogueira, Carmen C., ed. Glossary of Basic Archival and Library Conservation Terms: English with Equivalents in Spanish, German, Italian, French, and Russian. New York: Saur, 1988, 151p. (International Council on Archives Handbook Series, 4).

3350.   Nol, Lea, Y. Hennis, and R. G. Kenneth. "Biological Factors of Foxing in Postage Stamp Paper," International Biodeterioration Bulletin, 19 (1983), 19-25. Identification of seven species of fungus and their effect upon colors.

3351.   Noll, William. "Cylinders Kiev: Folklife Center Restores Ukrainian Minstrelsy (Wax cylinders from the Rylsky Institute)," LC Information Bulletin (Library of Congress) 54 (February 20, 1995), 78-80.

3352.   Noonan, Mary. "Book Preservation and Conservation in the Latin American Collection," Caribbean Collections: Recession Management Strategies for Libraries, ed. Mina Jane Grothey. Madison, WI: Seminar on the Acquisition of Latin American Library Materials, 1988, 143-156. Report of a "study that examined paper quality and binding strength of a representative sample of recently published Latin American monographs"; greatest problem is acid paper.

3353.   Nordstrand, Ove K. "The Conservation Treatment of Paper," Restaurator, 8:2/3 (1987), 133-139. Survey of frequently used procedures for paper conservation: disinfection, cleaning, deacidification, resizing, mending, etc., with discussion of special conservation problems.

3354.   Norman, Daniel. "The Mounting of Single Leaf Parchment and Vellum Objects for Display," V&A Conservation Journal (Victoria and Albert), 9 (October 1993), 10-13. Addresses problem of displaying and storing single leaf parchment items; describes a method of mounting parchment.

424

3355. Norman, Joanna. "Florida's Quest for Alkaline Paper Legislation," Preservation Papers of the 1990 SAA Annual Conference, comp. Karen Garlick. Chicago: Society of American Archivists (1991), 42-45. Efforts to develop legislation and questions about standards raised by officials.

3356. Norman, Mark, and Victoria Todd. Storage. London: United Kingdom Institute for Conservation, 1991. 32p. Papers from a conference exploring concerns about the storage of collections.

3357. Norris, Debbie Hess. Inpainting Outline. Washington, DC: American Institute for Conservation of Historic and Artistic Works, Photographic Materials Group, 1994. 27p.

3358. Norris, Debbie Hess. "Platinum Photographs: Deterioration and Preservation," Photographic Conservation, 7:2 (June 1985), 1. How to identify platinum images, store them, and recognize deterioration.

3359. Norris, Debbie Hess. "Preservation Planning For Diverse Photographic Holdings," Photograph Conservation and the Research Library. Mountain View, CA: Research Libraries Group, 1991. 19-27. Planning, including assessment of environmental requirements, establishment of handling procedures and disaster plans, duplication of deteriorating negative, rehousing, evaluation of future preservation strategies.

3360. Norris, Debbie Hess. "The Proper Storage and Display of a Photograph Collection," Book and Paper Group Annual, 2 (1983), 66-81. Discusses types of materials found in collections and the problems each presents. Provides information on proper storage, matting and mounting. Bibliography.

3361. Norris, Terry O. "Preservation Photocopying Conference: Introductory Remarks and Historical Perspective," Restaurator, 8:1 (1987), 3-8.

3362. Norris, Thomas D. "Not Such Strange Bedfellows: Appraisal and Preservation in Practice," Preservation Papers of the 1991 SAA Annual Conference, comp. Karen Garlick. Chicago: Society of

American Archivists, 1992, 1-5. Discusses the need to identify preservation needs during the appraisal process.

3363. North Carolina Preservation Consortium. Preservation Issues: A Periodic Publication of the North Carolina Preservation Consortium. Durham, NC: The Consortium, 1994-.

3364. North Dakota Library Association. Disaster Preparedness Planning for North Dakota Libraries. [Bismark, ND]: North Dakota Library Association, 1987. 52p. Introductory planning manual; outline, bibliography.

3365. North Dakota State Historical Records Advisory Board. 1994-1995 Planning Project Study Issue: Documentary Publishing and Preservation Microfilming. Bismark, ND: The Board, 1995, 1p.

3366. Northeast Document Conservation Center. "Care of Photographs," Archival Products News, 2:2 (Summer 1994), 1-2, reprinted from Preservation of Library and Archival Materials: A Manual. Andover, MA: NEDCC, 1994. Note on environmental considerations, storage materials, enclosures.

3367. Northeast Document Conservation Center. "NEDCC Offers Helpful Hints for Preserving Family Collections," Northeast Document Conservation Center News, (Summer 1989), 2.

3368. Northeast Document Conservation Center. Integrated Pest Management. Andover, MA: Northeast Document Conservation Center, 1994. 7p. (Technical Leaflet). Brief overview of approaches to pest control in libraries and archives.

3369. Northeast Document Conservation Center. It Can Happen Here! Disaster Planning for Connecticut Towns and Municipalities. Andover, MA: NEDCC, 1991. one volume.

3370. Northeast Document Conservation Center. Protecting Books and Paper Against Mold. Andover, MA: Northeast Document Conservation Center, 1994. 6 p. (Technical Leaflet). Basic information for libraries and archives.

3371.	Northeast Document Conservation Center. Protecting Books and Paper During Exhibition. Andover, MA: Northeast Document Conservation Center, 1994. 9p. (Technical Leaflet). Presents five simple rules for display of books and paper documents.

3372.	Northeast Document Conservation Center. Protection from Light Damage. Andover, MA: Northeast Document Conservation Center, 1994. 8p. (Technical Leaflet). Guidelines for the protection of collections from damage from light.

3373.	Northeast Document Conservation Center. Protecting Books and Paper Against Mold. Andover, MA: Northeast Document Conservation Center, [1994]. 6p. Technical leaflet. Much of the information in this leaflet comes from a course taught by Mary-Lou Florian at the Campbell Center for Historic Preservation Studies, in September 1993.

3374.	Northeast Document Conservation Center. Tips for Low-Cost Environmental Control. Andover, MA: Northeast Document Conservation Center, 1990. Reprinted College and Research Libraries News (May 1990), 408.

3375.	Northwestern University Library. Preservation Planning Program Study Team. Final Report. Washington, DC: Office of Management Studies, Association of Research Libraries, 1986. 45p. Result of a year-long study designed to establish a five-year plan for preserving the library's collections.

3376.	Novikova, G. M. "Mycodestruction of Drawings, Conference on Book and Paper Conservation, 1990. Budapest, Hungary: Technical Association of Paper and Printing Industry/National Szechenyi Library, 1992, 515-532. Discussion of fungi that can affect drawings; methods of control. Illus. 10 references.

3377.	Nowicke, Carole Elizabeth. "Managing Tomorrow's Records Today: An Experiment in Archival Preservation of Electronic Mail," Midwestern Archivist, 13:2 (1988), 67-75. Describes an experiment within the Naval Laboratory community to examine use of e-mail and to attempt to manage and preserve important messages.

3378. Nugent, William R. "Applications of Digital Optical Disks in Library Preservation and Reference," International Journal of Micrographics and Video Technology, 3:1 (1984), 59-61. Discusses the potential use of optical storage for preservation as well as reference services. Describes the Library of Congress's Optical Disk Pilot Program, and briefly discusses the future of optical disk applications in libraries.

3379. Nugent, William R. "Issues in Optical Disk Longevity, From Trithemius to Arrhenius Testing," Archiving the Audio-Visual Heritage. Rushton, England: FIAF/UNESCO, 1992, 89-95. Describes the parameters of testing materials for longevity and deterioration.

3380. Nugent, William R. "Optical Discs: An Emerging Technology for Libraries," IFLA Journal (International Federation of Library Associations and Institutions), 12:3 (1986), 175-181. Describes optical disk technology, applications in a library setting, and preservation challenges.

3381. Nugent, William R. "The Role of National Standards in Information Preservation on Optical Digital Disk," National Preservation News, 4 (April 1986), 11-13. Discusses the rewriting of digital information onto new disks as deterioration sets in and its use as a preservation medium. Describes Error Detection and Correction (EDAC) systems, which provide "flawless duplication."

3382. Nunberg, Geoffrey. "The Places of Books in the Age of Electronic Reproduction," Representations, 42 (Spring 1993), 13-37. Discusses the role of the printed text, past, present, and future, and its relationship to information in electronic formats.

3383. Nyberg, Sandra. "The Case of the Flourishing Fungi," SOLINEWS, (Spring 1991), 10. Steps to control fungi.

3384. Nyberg, Sandra. "The Invasion of the Giant Spore," Atlanta, GA: Southeast Library Network, 1987. 20p. (SOLINET Preservation Program Leaflet No. 5). Outlines the causes of mold, mildew, and fungi; chemical treatments are described but maintenance of a good environment is considered the critical factor in control. Bibliography.

3385. Nyberg, Sandra. "Out of the Question: How Effective Is Orthophenyl Phenol?" Conservation Administration News, 33 (April 1988), 14-15, 23.

3386. Nye, James. "Toward a Sociology of South Asian Book Preservation," Planning Modernization and Preservation Programs for South Asian Libraries, ed. Kalpana Dasgupta. Calcutta, India: National Library, 1992, 106-112. Addresses issues of the production of microfilm surrogate copies for preservation, and their use.

3387. Nyren, Karl. "The DEZ Process and the Library of Congress," Library Journal, 111:5 (15 September 1986), 33-35. A review of the Library of Congress's development and dissemination of information about its diethyl zinc (DEZ) deacidification process to the public. See also editorial, p. 4.

3388. Nyuksha, Y. P. "Conservation of Library Collections: A Concept Based on Experience in the Former Soviet Union," Restaurator, 15:1 (1994), 55-63. Discusses the impact of conservator's work and responsibility in the library system.

3389. Nyuksha, Y. P. Biodeterioration of Paper and Books. St. Petersburg, Russia: Russian Academy of Sciences, 1993. 250p. Russian/English. Summary of the author's investigations into the preservation of library and archival materials; examination of microorganisms in paper-based collections.

3390. Nyuksha, Y. P., and L. A. Karpenko. "Investigation of Fermentative Cleaning Processes in Book Restoration," Restaurator, 7:1 (1986), 22-35. Discusses the application of fermentative reactions in chemicals to the cleaning of library and archival materials.

3391. Nyuksha, Y. P. "Some Special Cases of Biological Deterioration in
       Books," Restaurator, 5:3/4 (1983), 177-1182. Describes nine species
       of fungus in the Aspergillis Flavus group, which consume plastic,
       metal, and library materials.

3392. Nyuksha, Y. P., O. A. Gromov, J. V. Pokrovskaja, and M. E.
       Saltykov. "Mass Processing of Documents for Fungi Contamination
       Control," Preprints. International Council of Museums, Committee
       for Conservation, 9th Triennial Meeting, Dresden, Germany, August
       26-31, Los Angeles: ICOM Committee for Conservation, 1990, Vol.
       2, 478-481.

3393. Oakland Library Consortium. Preserving Library Resources: A
       Guide for Staff. Pittsburgh, PA: Oakland Library Consortium, 1990.
       24p. Provides basic information on preservation and conservation for
       staff training. List of supplies and suppliers; bibliography.

3394. Oakley, Robert L. Copyright and Preservation: A Serious Problem in
       Need of a Thoughtful Solution. Washington, DC: Commission on
       Preservation and Access, 1990. 58p. Law and legislation regarding
       copyright and reformatting of library materials.

3395. O'Connell, Mildred. "Disaster Planning: Writing and Implementing
       Plans for Collections-Holding Institutions," Technology &
       Conservation, 8:2 (Summer 1983), 18-24. Thorough introduction to
       key issues in disaster planning.

3396. O'Connell, Mildred. "Disaster Planning for Libraries," AB
       Bookman's Weekly (Antiquarian Bookman), 71:25 (June 1983),
       4693-4701. General information on disaster planning with practical
       tips.

3397. O'Connell, Mildred. "The New Museum Climate Standards &
       Technologies," Abbey Newsletter, 20:4/5 (September 1996), 58-
       60. NEDCC's Conference at the Museum of Fine Arts, Boston, April
       25-26, 1996.

3398. O'Connell, Mildred. "Northeast Document Conservation Center at
       21," Wilson Library Bulletin, 69:4 (December 1994), 44-46,

119. Brief history and review of NEDCC's activities and future initiatives.

3399.   O'Connell, Mildred. "Obituary: George Cunha" Abbey Newsletter, 18:7 (November 1994), 81.

3400.   O'Connor, B.C. "Preservation and Repacking of Lantern Slides Within a Desktop Digital Imaging Environment," Microcomputing Information Management, 9:4 (1992), 209-224. Project at Emporia State University.

3401.   O'Connor, Gail M. "Care and Preservation of Videotapes," New Jersey Libraries, 18:1 (Spring 1985), 18-19. Tips on the care, storage, and handling of videotapes.

3402.   O'Connor, Joan L. "Conservation of Documents in an Exhibit," American Archivist, 47:2 (Spring 1984), 156-163. Case study of the planning for exhibits at the John F. Kennedy Library, Boston, MA.

3403.   Odegaard, Nancy. "Insect Monitoring in Museums," WAAC Newsletter (Western Association for Art Conservation), 13 (January 1991), 19-20. Discusses integrated pest management and provides guidelines for monitoring using sticky traps to identify insects.

3404.   Odlyha, M., R. M. Walker, and W. H. Liddell. "A Study of the Effects of Conservation Treatment on the Fanshawe Archive," Conservation of the Iberian and Latin American Cultural Heritage, eds. H. W. H. Hodges, John S. Mills, and Perry Smith. London: International Institute for Conservation, 1992, 104-111. (Preprints: Contributions to the Madrid Congress, September 1992); Journal of Thermal Analysis, 40:1 (1993), 285-302. Treatment of three documents, 1665-66, to test the effects of three deacidification treatments.

3405.   O'Donnell, Francis J. "From Negative to Positive Images," Humanities, 7:4 (August 1986), 30-31. Case study. Preservation of photographic archives at the Southwest Museum.

3406. Ogden, Barclay W. "Determining Conservation Options at the University of California at Berkeley," The Library Preservation Program: Models, Priorities, Possibilities, eds. Jan Merrill-Oldham and Merrily Smith. Chicago, IL: American Library Association, 1985, 63-68. Case study.

3407. Ogden, Barclay W. "NEH Supports Conference on Training in Collection Conservation," ALCTS Newsletter (Association for Library Collections and Technical Services), 3:6 (1992), 60-61. Report on Conference held at UC Berkeley, April 28-May 2nd 1992.

3408. Ogden, Barclay W. On the Preservation of Books and Documents in Original Form. Washington, DC: Commission on Preservation and Access, October 1989. 6p. Also in Abbey Newsletter, 14 (July 1990), 62-64. Discusses issues relevant to the preservation of scholarly materials as artifacts.

3409. Ogden, Barclay W. "Preservation Selection and Treatment Options," Meeting the Preservation Challenge. Washington, DC: Association of Research Libraries, 1988, 38-42. Methodology for selection for preservation and treatment.

3410. Ogden, Barclay W., and Maralyn Jones. CALIPR: An Automated Tool to Assess Preservation Needs of Book and Document Collections for Institutional or Statewide Planning. Berkeley: University of California, 1992. 70p. Four diskettes.

3411. Ogden, Barclay W., and Robert Strauss. Performance Measures for Library Binding: Final Report. Edina, MN: Library Binding Institute, September 22, 1995. 17p. Project to identify performance criteria for library binding.

3412. Ogden, Sherelyn. "Book Conservation at Northeast Document Conservation Center," Northeast Document Conservation Center News (Summer 1989), 4. Similar article in Guild of Book Workers Journal, 19:1/2 1980-1981 (1985), 37-41.

3413. Ogden, Sherelyn. "Helen Burgess Lectures at NEDCC," Conservation Administration News, 23 (October 1985), 9.

3414. Ogden, Sherelyn. "NEDCC in Nigeria: A Personal Report," Conservation Administration News, 45 (April 1991), 1-3, 30. Report on Odgen's survey of conservation needs in Nigerian libraries, indicating the need to teach preservation measures, including handling and storage of materials. Expanded from Northeast Document Conservation Center News, 2:2 (Winter 1990).

3415. Ogden, Sherelyn, ed. Preservation of Library and Archival Materials: A Manual. Andover, MA: Northeast Document Conservation Center, 1992; 2d ed., revised, 1994. Sections separately paged. A compilation of NEDCC's technical leaflets providing basic information on preservation and conservation of library and archival materials. Bibliographies; resource lists.

3416. Ogden, Sherelyn. "Preservation Options for Scrapbook and Album Formats," The Book and Paper Group Annual, 10 (1991), 149-163. Among items discussed are treatment selection criteria such as artifactual value, informational value, condition, level of use, cost and security needs.

3417. Ogden, Sherelyn. "A Regional Perspective on Preservation: The NEDCC Experience," Libraries and Culture, 27:1 (Winter 1992), 49-58. A history of the Northeast Document Conservation Center.

3418. Ogden, Sherelyn. "Security From Loss: Water and Fire Damage, Biological Agents, Theft, and Vandalism," Rare Books & Manuscripts Librarian, 11:1 (1996), 43-47. Reprinted from Preservation of Library & Archival Materials, NEDCC, 1994.

3419. Ogden, Sherelyn. "Treatment of Wooden Shelving for Books," Conservation Administration News, 27 (October 1986), 6. How to protect books from acids exuded from wood. Available also as a hand-out from the Northeast Document Conservation Center.

3420.   Ogden, Stanley Lee. "Magna Carta: Journey from Philadelphia to
         Washington," New Library Scene, 7:1 (February 1988), 8-9. Brief
         description of the inspection, packing, and transport of the document.

3421.   Ohio Academic Libraries. Progress Through Collaboration, Storage
         and Technology. Columbus, OH: Ohio Board of Regents, September
         1987. 70p.

3422.   Ohio Cooperative Conservation Information Office. Library
         Preservation Repair Kits Realia. Columbus: Ohio Cooperative
         Conservation Information Office, 1984. One repair kit with manuals.

3423.   Ohio State Library. Managing Preservation: A Guidebook: A
         Cooperative Publication of the State Library of Ohio and the Ohio
         Preservation Council. Columbus: State Library of Ohio, 1995. 176p.

3424.   Ohio State University Libraries. Preservation Planning Program
         Study Report; Final Report. Washington, DC: Association of
         Research Libraries, October 1986. 95p. Report of an 11-month
         study, see following.

3425.   Ohio State University Libraries. Preserving the Ohio State
         University Libraries' Collections: The OSUL Preservation Planning
         Program. Washington, DC: Office of Management Studies,
         Association of Research Libraries, 1986. 74p. Result of an 11-month
         study that confirms the poor condition of the library's collections and
         offers detailed recommendations designed to enhance their longevity.

3426.   Ojo-Igbinoba, M. E. "Conservation, Preservation and Restoration in
         Nigerian Libraries," Information Development, 7:1 (January 1991),
         39-44. Addresses problems, including pest and environmental
         control, vandalism, poor quality paper, need for trained personnel for
         repair and conservation.

3427.   Oklahoma Historical Records Advisory Board. Preserving Today's
         Records for Tomorrow's Use: A Mandate for Action. Oklahoma
         City, OK: Oklahoma Historical Records Advisory Board, January
         1985. 103p. Report to provide leadership and planning for the
         protection of the states records.

3428.   Oklahoma State University Library. A Preservation Program for the Oklahoma State University Library: Final Report of the Preservation Program Planning Study. Washington, DC: Association of Research Libraries Office of Management Studies, 1990. 42 leaves.

3429.   Okula, Susan. "Disintegrating Books: Libraries Seek to Preserve Fragile Volumes," Boston Sunday Globe, October 12, 1986, 81.

3430.   Oliphant, David, ed. Conservation and Preservation of Humanities Research Collections: Essays on Treatment and Care of Rare Books, Manuscripts, Photography and Art on Paper and Canvas. Austin, TX: Harry Ransom Humanities Research Center, University of Texas, 1989. 166p. Special issue of Library Chronicle, 44/45 (1989). Ten essays by the Conservation staff, focusing on programs and treatments.

3431.   Olkowski, William and Helga. Contracting for Pest Control Services; Cockroaches, Mice, Rats and Flies in Public and Private Buildings: A Consumer's Guide. Berkeley, CA: Bio-Integral Resource Center, n.d. 39p. Written for the lay person who is planning to hire a professional pest control service. Describes the tasks required of a professional, safe methods of pest control, and the role of building occupants in reducing the problem. Bibliography.

3432.   Olkowski, William, and Helga. "Pests That Damage Paper: Silverfish, Firebrats and Booklice," Common Sense Pest Control, 3:1 (Winter 1987), 1-5. Describes the insects, their habitat, and the damage they can cause. Methods of control are described.

3433.   Olkowski, William, Helga Olkowski and Sheila Daar. "IPM for the German Cockroach," The IPM Practitioner, 6:3 (Summer 1990), 7-10. Briefly describes the biology of the cockroach, monitoring programs, methods of inhibiting roaches, and use of insecticides.

3434.   Olkowski, William, Helga Olkowski, and Sheila Daar. Integrated Pest Management for the German Cockroach. Berkeley, CA: Bio-Integral Resource Center, 1984. 22p. (BIRC Technical Review). Describes the biology and habitat of the cockroach; methods of roach control. Bibliography.

3435.   Olkowski, William, Helga Olkowski, and Sheila Daar. "What Is
         IPM?" Common Sense Pest Control, 4:3 (Summer 1989), 9-
         16. Discusses the concept of integrated pest management (IPM), a
         combination of strategies to eliminate pests.

3436.   Olley, Lorraine. "Fundraising for Preservation," Preservation
         Planning Program: An Assisted Self-Study Manual for Libraries.
         Washington, DC: Association of Research Libraries (1993), 125-
         129. Overview of strategies for raising funds for preservation
         projects; sources of funding.

3437.   Olley, Lorraine. "Indiana University Libraries Presents Preservation
         Awareness Week," Conservation Administration News, 53 (April
         1993), 10-11. Describes events focusing on the preservation of
         library materials.

3438.   Olson, David J. Are We Losing Our Past? Records Preservation in
         the North Carolina State Archives. Raleigh, NC: The Friends of the
         Archives, 1989. 16p. Assessment of strengths and weakness of NC's
         program of records management and preservation. Causes of
         deterioration, action needed.

3439.   Olson, David J. "North Carolina and Paper Preservation: Ninety
         Years of Leadership," North Carolina Libraries, 52 (Spring 1994)
         10-12p.

3440.   Olson, Nancy B. "Hanging Your Software Up to Dry," College and
         Research Libraries News, 47:10 (November 1986), 634-636.
         Description of the salvage of a water-damaged audiovisual
         collection, including computer software, at Mankato (MN) State
         University Library, June 1986. Disks were salvaged, techniques
         explained.

3441.   Olson, Nancy B., and Edward Swanson. "The Year's Work in
         Nonbook Processing, 1987," Library Resources and Technical
         Services, 32:4 (October 1988), 391-398. Review of the literature on
         cataloguing and preservation concerns for computer files, music and

sound recordings, film and video, graphic materials, and three
dimensional objects. 80 references.

3442.   Olson, Nancy B., and Edward Swanson. "The Year's Work in
Nonbook Processing, 1988," Library Resources and Technical
Services, 33:4 (October 1989), 335-343. Preservation of nonbook
materials is briefly noted, pp. 339-340, with several citations.

3443.   Olson, Robert A. "Earthquake Protection for Data Systems,"
Disaster Recovery Journal, 5:2 (April-June 1992), 35-42. Discusses
design considerations and non-structural elements that will offer
protection; testing and analysis of effect on media and computers.

3444.   Olszewski, Ann. "Malevolent Mold," Preservation Issues, Ohio
State Library, 17 (October 1995) 2p. How to control mold and to
deal with an outbreak; summary of a workshop given by Lisa Fox.

3445.   Olszewski, Ann. "Protecting Collections from Insects and Pests,"
Preservation Issues, Ohio State Library, 18 (February 1996) 2p. How
to establish and manage an integrated pest management program in
the library; based on a workshop by Tom Parker.

3446.   Onadiran, G. T. "Book Theft in University Libraries in Nigeria,"
Library and Archival Security, 8:3/4 (Fall/Winter 1988), 37-48. An
examination of the extent of book theft; suggestions for prevention
or reduction of theft.

3447.   Onadiran, G. T. "Library Users as Security Problems in Africa,"
International Library Movement, 8:1 (1986), 37-43. Discusses causes
of theft in libraries and preventive measures: security controls,
sanctions, availability of photocopiers, policies, and staff attitude.

3448.   O'Neill, Edward T., and Wesley L. Boomgaarden. "Book
Deterioration in Ohio Libraries," Annual Review of OCLC Research,
July 1992-June 1993. Dublin, OH: Online Computer Library Center,
Inc., 1993, 42-46. Survey of the physical condition of a random
sample of books in Ohio libraries published between 1851 and 1939
to provide a framework for the measurement of at-risk books against
national efforts.

3449. O'Neill, Edward T., and Wesley L. Boomgaarden. Book
       Deterioration and Loss: Magnitude and Characteristics in Ohio
       Libraries. Dublin, OH: OCLC Office of Research and the Ohio State
       University Libraries' Preservation Office, 1994/ 1995. 33 leaves.
       Also in Library Resources and Technical Services, 39:4 (October
       1995), 394-408. Survey of conditions of books in Ohio libraries
       published between 1851-1939, concluding with the estimation of
       50,000 titles that were unusable, most of which were missing or lost.
       Fewer that 5,000 titles were unusable due to damage; 6,000 unusable
       due to extreme deterioration methodology.

3450. O'Neill, Edward T., and Eric Jul. "OSU and OCLC to Study Book
       Deterioration in Ohio Libraries," OCLC Newsletter (Online
       Computer Library Center, Inc.), 191 (May/June 1991), 10-
       11. Describes methodology of a survey to provide data for statewide
       preservation programs.

3451. Online Computer Library Center, Inc. The OCLC Guide to
       Preservation Data. Dublin, OH: Online Computer Library Center,
       1991 and 1995, 33p. Describes how libraries can use OCLC's
       central registry to record and provide access to preservation
       information to avoid duplication and assist in cooperative efforts.

3452. Ontario Museum Association and Toronto Area Archivists Group.
       Museum and Archival Supplies Handbook. 2d ed., 1985. 174p. Lists
       over 600 North American suppliers of conservation and archival
       materials, nearly half of which are in the United States.

3453. Oosten, Th. B. van. "Characterization of Parchments and Animal
       Glues from Different Kinds of Animals by Thin Layer Isoelectric
       Focusing," Leather Conservation News, 5:2 (1989), 1-6. Describes a
       method that characterizes specific animal proteins, which can
       facilitate the identification of leathers prior to conservation treatment.

3454. Opela, Vladimir. "Fungal and Bacterial Attack on Motion Picture
       Film," Archiving the Audio-Visual Heritage. Rushton, England:
       FIAF/UNESCO, 1992, 139-144. Describes research at Charles

University, Prague, Czech Republic, into causes and prevention of damage by micro organisms.

3455.   Orange, Rosanna. "Conservation Repair Standards for Paper Records at National Archives," Artifacts (Bulletin of the Archives and Records Association of New Zealand) (December 1985), 9-12. Abbreviated list for paper and photograph repair, based upon Kathpalia's UNESCO manual and other national and international standards.

3456.   Orbanz, Eva, Helen P. Harrison, and Henning Schou. Archiving the Audio-Visual Heritage. Berlin, Germany: Stiftung Deutsche Kinemathek, 1988. 192p. Anthology of papers on film, video, sound recording. Addresses issues relating to the preservation of modern audiovisual media. Papers from a joint technical symposium.

3457.   Orcutt, Joyce. "The Care and Preservation of Photographic Materials," AB Bookman's Weekly (Antiquarian Bookman), 80:16 (November 2, 1987), 1681-1689. Briefly reviews the history of photography and the physical nature of the photographic image, with advice on the care, housing, and handling of photographic images.

3458.   Oregon State Archives. Handbook of Recommended Environmental Conditions and Handling Procedures for Magnetic Tape. Portland, OR: State Archives, 1984. 21p. Provides optimal recommended standards for storage and use of reel-to-reel magnetic tape.

3459.   O'Reilly, Susan. "Romania," Conservation News (United Kingdom Institute for Conservation of Historic and Artistic Works), 46 (November 1991), 27-29. An update on projects of the Conservation for Romania Trust for the National Library and monastic collections.

3460.   Organ, Robert, and Brian Ramer. "Some Hard Truths [Interview]," Museum, 146 (1985), 68-70. Discussion of cases and their role in protecting objects from vibrations, pollutants, and ultraviolet rays. Proper lighting methods and climate control are recommended.

3461.   Orkiszewski, Lea. "Electronic Imaging Provides New Look at History," LLA Bulletin (Louisiana Library Association), 54 (Winter

1992), 197-199. Storing rare materials electronically at Louisiana State University Library.

3462. Orr, Bonnie, Thomas F. R. Clareson, and Ivan Hanthron. "Money Talks in Miami, ALA Preconference Institute on Developing the Midas Touch, June 1994" Conservation Administration News, 60 (January 1995), 20-21.

3463. Orr, Gloria J. "Preservation Photocopying of Bound Volumes: An Increasingly Viable Option," Library Resources and Technical Services, 34:4 (October 1990), 445-454. An evaluation of photocopying equipment for preservation photocopying and information on how to select a photocopier; tables of comparison.

3464. Orraca, Jose. "Developing Treatment Criteria in the Conservation of Photographs," Topics in Photographic Preservation, 4 (1991), 150-155. Describes the development of photographic conservation as a specialty and discusses connoisseurship involved.

3465. Orraca, Jose. "Glossary of Terms Used in the Conservation of Photographs," OJO: Connoisseurship and Conservation of Photographs, Part 1, 4 (Spring 1993), 3-7. Glossary of general, condition, and treatment terms used in photographic conservation.

3466. Osborne, Larry N. "Those (In)destructible Disks; or, Another Myth Exploded," Library Hi Tech, 7:3; 27 (1989), 7-10, 28. Characteristics of 5 1/2 inch floppy disks; how to salvage disks damaged by spilled substances.

3467. Osorio, Fernando. A Conservation Plan for the Juan Mandez Photographic Collection. Thesis. Rochester, NY, Rochester Institute of Technology. 1996. 39p.

3468. Ostendorp, Anne. "The Preservation and Processing Analysis: The Dwight Morrow Papers at Amherst College," Preservation Papers of the 1991 SAA Annual Conference, comp. Karen Garlick. Chicago: Society of American Archivists, 1992, 11-15. Describes a project to organize and preserve a collection of papers within a NEH grant time frame.

3469.   Ostroff, Eugene, ed. Pioneers of Photography: Their Achievements in Science and Technology. Springfield, VA: Society for Imaging Science and Technology, 1987. 285p. Includes relevant chapters on the history, technology, and stability of photographic materials.

3470.   Otness, H. M. "'Going Plating' — Stealing Maps From Libraries," Western Association of Map Libraries Information Bulletin, 19:4 (August 1988), 206-210..

3471.   O'Toole, James M. "On the Idea of Permanence," American Archivist, 52:1 (Winter 1989), 10-25. The essay explores the changing understanding archivists have had of the idea of permanence as it applies to the records in their custody, noting shift from an emphasis on permanence of intellectual content to permanence of original material, and the trend toward more careful appraisal.

3472.   Otto, Henrik. "Paper Splitting: An Old Skilled Technology Becoming Industrialized," International Preservation News, 10 (July 1995) 12. Briefly describes the paper-splitting techniques for the strengthening of paper and the machine developed for the process at the Deutsche Bücherei.

3473.   Oudard, Denis. "Long-Term Archiving on Optical Disc - A Market Response Approach," Archiving the Audio-Visual Heritage. Rushton, England: FIAF/UNESCO, 1992, 96-102. Describes the century disk, with an anticipated longevity of 100 years; briefly notes playback concerns.

3474.   Overman, Linda. "Deacidification Update," The Primary Source (Society of Mississippi Archivists), 9:3 (Fall 1987), 20-23. Bibliography on "the mass deacidification controversy."

3475.   Overman, Linda. "Disaster Preparedness," Mississippi Libraries, 50:3 (Fall 1986), 62-64. Reviews need for and basic elements of a good disaster plan.

3476. Overman, Linda. "The Effects of the Environment on Paper," Mississippi Libraries, 49:2 (Summer 1985), 27-29. Discusses causes of deterioration; effect of temperature and humidity, light, and pollution on materials.

3477. Overman, Linda, and Terry Latour. "Easy Steps for the Preservation of Bound Volumes," Mississippi Libraries, 49 (Winter 1985), 88-90. Basic steps to preserve library materials: cleanliness, prevention of mold, shelving; presents directions for treatment of leather bindings with the TALAS formula.

3478. Overman, Linda. "Managing the Archival Environment: Environmental and Security Issues," Mississippi Libraries, 59 (Summer 1995) 38-40.

3479. Overmire, Rozell. "Functional Requirements for Exhibit Management Systems," Archival Informatics Technical Report, 2:4 (Winter 1988-1989), 1-127.

3480. Owen, Linda, Julia D. Ree, and Judith Medlin-Smith. "Earthquake: Coping With Disaster," Library Mosaics, 3:6 (November-December 1992), 7-11. Case study of the damage and recovery at the University of California-Riverside in June 1992.

3481. Owens, Sheryl. "Proactive Problem Patron Preparedness," Library and Archival Security, 12:2 (1994), 11-24. Provides a practical proactive approach to handling problem patrons in libraries.

3482. Oye, Raysabro. "The Significance of Deacidification on Paper Properties," Paper Preservation: Current Issues and Recent Developments. Atlanta, GA: TAPPI Press, 1990, 122-126. (Proceedings, Paper Preservation Symposium). Discusses degradation of paper and the effect of deacidification on the process from a technical perspective.

3483. Pacey, Antony. "Alkaline 'Permanent' Paper," Canadian Library Journal, 48:6 (December 1991), 412-414. Discussion of paper manufacturing processes and their effects on library materials.

Standards are explained and advantages of alkaline paper are described.

3484. Pacey, Antony. "Canadian Libraries and Mass Deacidification," Canadian Library Journal, 49:2 (April 1992), 115-120. Causes of deterioration and a review of the various deacidification systems on the market.

3485. Pacey, Antony. "Library Preservation: The Approach at the National Museums of Canada," Canadian Library Journal, 47:1 (February 1990), 27-33. Describes the responsibilities of the library's preservation officer, a position established after a 1983 survey of the collections indicated that they were in poor condition.

3486. Padfield, Timothy. "Climate Control in Libraries and Archives," Preservation of Library Materials. Vol. 2. Munich, Germany; New York: Saur, 1987, 124-138. (IFLA Publication, 41). Describes mechanical environmental control systems, collection needs, and how these can be met; discusses passive climate control.

3487. Padfield, Tim. "Climate Control in Museums," In Conference Proceedings of the 1986 National Conference on Museum Security: Cultural Institution Protection. Washington, DC: Smithsonian Institution, 1986. 3p. Emphasizes need for climate control in museums and suggests that range of temperature and humidity gradually fluctuate between seasons.

3488. Padfield, Tim. "A Cooled Display Case," Museum, 146 (1985), 102-103. Construction of a cooled case for a vellum document.

3489. Page, Joanne. "Profile: Margaret Lecky," WAAC Newsletter (Western Association for Art Conservation), 8:2 (May 1986), 9-10. Interview with Los Angeles bookbinder and conservator Margaret Lecky.

3490. Page, Julie A., and George J. Soete. "Preservation Orientation for Library Staff," College and Research Libraries News, 55:6 (June 1994), 358-360. Describes a program designed to educate all library staff about the care and handling of library materials.

3491.   Page, R. L. "The Conservator and the Scholar," Conservation and
         Preservation in Small Libraries, eds. Nicholas Hadgraft and
         Katherine Swift. Cambridge: Paker Library Publications, 1994, 15-
         19. The need for conservators to supply physical evidence
         information to scholars, and their own scholarly contribution through
         examination of physical evidence relating to production and further
         treatment of books and manuscripts.

3492.   Page, Susan. "Machine-Made Oriental Papers in Western Paper
         Conservation," Conservation of Historic and Artistic Works on
         Paper: Proceedings of a Conference, Ottawa, Canada, 3 to 7 October,
         1988, ed. Helen D. Burgess. Ottawa: 1994, 251-254. Describes
         advantages of using Japanese machine-made papers in conservation;
         three conservation treatments.

3493.   Page, Susan, and Diane S. Nixon. "Storing and Handling Oversized
         Documents, General Considerations and a Case Study at the US
         National Archives-Pacific Southwest Region; Presented at the 1993
         NARA Conference," Restaurator, 15:3 (1994), 129-141. Reviews
         considerations for storage, housing, use, and management of
         collections of large documents. Case study.

3494.   Paine, Shelley Reisman. Basic Principles for Controlling
         Environmental Conditions in Historical Agencies and Museums.
         Nashville, TN: American Association for State and Local History,
         1985. 16p. (AASLH Technical Report, 3). Reviews causes of
         deterioration and offers suggestions for curtailing effects.
         Bibliography.

3495.   Paliouras, Eleni, and Susan Richards, comp. Photographic
         Conservation: A Selected Bibliography. Vol. 2, 1981-1985, ed.
         Richard Schmidle. Rochester, NY: Technical and Education Center,
         Graphic Arts and Photography, Rochester Institute of Technology,
         1986. 18p. 78 annotated references to major articles.

3496.   Palm, Jonas. Deteriorating Paper in Sweden: A Deterioration Survey
         of the Royal Library, Gothenburg University Library, Uppsala

University Library and the National Archives. Stockholm: Riksarkivet, 1988. 30p. (Fou-projektet för papperskonservering, 3).

3497. Palm, Jonas. "The Effects of Deacidification on Different Types of Paper Exposed to Air-Pollution and Accelerated Aging," Conference on Book and Paper Conservation, 1990. Budapest, Hungary: Technical Association of Paper and Printing Industry/National Szechenyi Library, 1992, 483-490. Report of a study to determine if books should be deacidified as published or retroactively, as needed; found the retroactive approach to be more effective.

3498. Palm, Jonas. "Preservation and Conservation of Non-Book Materials in Libraries and Archives," Proceedings of the Pan-African Conference on the Preservation and Conservation of Library and Archival Materials, Nairobi, Kenya, 21-25 June 1993. The Hague: IFLA, 1995, 89-96. (IFLA Professional Publication 43). Discusses problem of permanence, need to understand materials, problems, handling, and storage.

3499. Palmer, Joseph W. Audiovisual Programs Related to Preservation: A Mediagraphy. Buffalo, NY: School of Information and Library Studies, State University of New York, 1991. 26p. Bibliography. Typescript.

3500. Palmer, Joseph W. "Saving Those Historic Videotapes: It May Already Be Too Late," Public Libraries, 33:2 (March/April 1994), 99-101. Notes the value of historic videotapes, the need to identify and catalog them, and to house them under environmentally safe conditions.

3501. Palmer, Pat. "What Is a Bookbinder?" The Abbey Newsletter, 11:1 (January 1987), 7-8. Summarizes the discussion of panelists Bill Anthony, Betsy Eldridge, Bill Minter, and Sylvia Rennie moderated by Robert Kerns and sponsored by the Art Institute of Chicago.

3502. Palmer, R. E., ed. Preserving the Word. London: Library Association, 1987. 147p. Papers presented at the Library Association Conference, Harrogate 1986, which focused on the preservation of library materials.

3503. Palmetto Archives, Libraries and Museum Council on Preservation. Hope for the Future: A Report on the Preservation of South Carolina's Paper-Based Records. Columbia, SC: Palmetto Archives, Libraries and Museums Council on Preservation, 1989. 35p.

3504. Pamplona, Denise, and Marcia Couri. "Bibliophagous Insects: Enemies of Documents and Collections," International Symposium and First World Congress on the Preservation and Conservation of Natural History Collections. Vol. 2. Rio de Janeiro, Brazil: Museu Nacional, 1992, 367-372. Describes the damage that bibliophlagous organisms, fungi, bacteria, insects, rodents, and humans, which eat books and other objects.

3505. Pan, Jixing. "On the Origin of Papermaking in the Light of Scientific Research on Recent Archaeological Discoveries," Friends of the Dard Hunter Paper Museum Newsletter, 6:1 (June 1987), 2-5. The article describes new information brought to light by modern archaeological excavations in various parts of China and discusses the conclusions reached from numerous microscopic and chemical analyses of the excavated paper samples.

3506. Panone, Carolyn. "In the Face of Adversity," Library Conservation News, 51 (Summer 1996), 3. Briefly describes the recovery process for a small public library following a fire set by a vandal.

3507. "Paper Deterioration: A Report on the Causes, the Extent of the Problem, Effects and Consequences of Paper Deterioration in Libraries and Archives...Including Recommendations, June 15, 1992," Federal-State Task Group, Federal Republic of Germany, Microform Review, 23 (Winter 1994), 29-37.

3508. "Paper for Government Publications: Not Up to Standard?" Bernan Associates' Government Publications News, 1:3 (March 1988), 1,4.

3509. Paris, Jan. Choosing and Working With a Conservator. Atlanta, GA: Southeast Library Network, 1990. 24p. Explores the issues surrounding the selection of a conservator, the nature of conservation, and the role of the conservator. Brief bibliography; information resources.

3510. Parisi, David Harlan. A Performance Evaluation of Rounded and Backed Books vs. Square Backed Books. Rochester, NY: Library Binding Institute, 1983. 75p. Illus. Describes the testing of two binding structures to compare their effectiveness. Master's thesis.

3511. Parisi, Paul A. "Advanced Bindery/Library Exchange: Ready, Willing, and ABLE," Library Acquisitions: Practice and Theory, 12:1 (1988), 81-86. Describes advantages and disadvantages of hardware/software developed by Mekatronics/Bendror that enables a library to prepare and ship materials to the bindery.

3512. Parisi, Paul A. "Binding Software Interface-A Top Priority," New Library Scene, 11 (August 1992), 1, 5-6.

3513. Parisi, Paul A. "Certified Library Binding - Is It Worth the Trouble?" New Library Scene, 10:5 (October 1991), 11,16. Traces the history of the Library Binding Institute inspection and certification process; proposes a new review and evaluation program.

3514. Parisi, Paul A. "The Eighth Edition of the Library Binding Institute Standard for Library Binding: A Cooperative Effort," New Library Scene, 5:1 (February 1986), 1, 5-6.

3515. Parisi, Paul A. "Library Binding in North America," New Library Scene, 12:5 (October 1993), 8-10.

3516. Parisi, Paul A. "Library Binding — Much More Than Class A," New Library Scene, (October 1992), 14-17.

3517. Parisi, Paul A. "Methods of Affixing Leaves: Options and Implications," New Library Scene, 5:5 (October 1986), 9-12. Also in New Library Scene, 13 (February 1994), 8-11. Earlier version in Library Scene, 2:5 (1983), 9-13. Discussion of methods that can be used, and when each is appropriate. Covers methods of commercial library binding.

3518.   Parisi, Paul A. "A Multi-Product Standard - RX for Fair
        Competition," New Library Scene, 12:1 (February 1993), 14-
        15. Discussion of the Library Binding Institute standards for library
        binding; why flatback, double-fan adhesive bindings with a single
        lining do not meet the standard and are not sturdy.

3519.   Parisi, Paul A. "New Directions in Library Binding - Life After
        Class A; Technical Considerations: 1986 LBI Standard," New
        Library Scene, 11:3 (June 1992), 6-9. Discusses several options for
        binding and concludes with a series of thought-provoking questions
        about commercial library binding.

3520.   Parisi, Paul A. "An Overview of Library Binding: Where We Are,
        How We Got Here, What We Do," New Library Scene (February
        1993), 5-9.

3521.   Parisi, Paul A., and Jan Merrill-Oldham. "The LBI Standard for
        Library Binding: The Glossary," School Library Journal, 33:2
        (October 1986), 96-98. Glossary of 33 terms for book preservation, to
        be used with the 8th edition of the LBI Standard for Library Binding.

3522.   Parisi, Paul A., and Jan Merrill-Oldham, eds. Library Binding
        Institute Standard for Library Binding. 8th ed. Rochester, NY:
        Library Binding Institute, 1986. 17p.

3523.   Parker, A. E. "Flexible Light Guides," Library Conservation News,
        15 (April 1987), 1-3, 7. Discussion of the use of fiber optic lighting in
        exhibition cases; use in British Library described.

3524.   Parker, A. E. "Freeze-Drying of Vellum," Library Conservation
        News, 33 (October 1991), 4-6. Describes experiments to determine if
        the process could be applied to vellum; while vellum can be frozen,
        further testing is necessary.

3525.   Parker, A. E. "The Freeze-Drying Process: Some Conclusions,"
        Library Conservation News, 23 (April 1989), 4-6, 8. Explains the
        general principles of the process, evaluates its usefulness for treating
        a wide range of materials.

3526.   Parker, A. E. "Freeze-Drying Vellum Archival Materials," Journal of the Society of Archivists, 14:2 (1993), 175-188. Describes experiments and concludes that vellum can be freeze-dried, but illuminated vellum sheets could suffer.

3527.   Parker, Peter J. "Statutory Protection of Library Materials," Library Trends, 33:1 (Summer 1984), 77-94. Examines and discusses statutory and legal remedies available to administrators for the protection of their institutions, employees, and collections.

3528.   Parker, Thomas A. "Integrated Pest Management for Libraries," Preservation of Library Materials, ed. Merrily A. Smith. New York: Saur, 1987, 103-123. Review of the common pests found in libraries and archives, with discussion of the advantages and disadvantages of fumigation. A common-sense approach to pest control is recommended. Bibliography.

3529.   Parker, Thomas A. An Integrated Pest Management Program for the Library of Congress. Lansdowne, PA: Pest Control Services, 1987. 46p. and appendices . Presents results of a survey of LC facilities and an outline for an integrated pest control program. Bibliography.

3530.   Parker, Thomas A. "Pesticide Terminology," A Guide to Museum Pest Control. Washington, DC: Foundation of the American Institute for Conservation of Historic and Artistic Works and Association of Systematics Collections, 1988, 123-126. Pesticide types are listed.

3531.   Parker, Thomas A. Study on Integrated Pest Management for Libraries and Archives. Paris: UNESCO, 1988. 119p. (PGI-88/WS/20); reissued as How to Recognize and Eliminate Silverfish, Beetles, Cockroaches, Moths, Termites, Rats and Mildew in Libraries and Archives. Upland, PA: Diane Publication Co, 1988. 119p. Addresses problems caused by the major insect and rodent pests and molds and mildews in libraries; measures and costs for control.

3532.   Parks, E. J., C. M. Guttman, K. L. Jewett, and F. E. Brinckman. Studies on the Degradation Products of Paper With and Without

Bibliography

Pollutants in a Closed Environment; I: Preliminary Results. Washington, DC: National Archives and Records Administration, May 1990. 36p. (NISTAR 4456). Report on a search of autocatylitic degradation products and those mobile enough to affect adjacent papers.

3533. Parliament, Robert. "The Conservation Services Program at Princeton University Library," New Jersey Libraries, 18:1 (Spring 1985), 12-17. Description of structure and activities, including commercial library binding program.

3534. Parliament, Robert A. "Construction and Start-Up of the Deacidification Unit at Princeton University Library," Book and Paper Group Annual, 12 (1983), 82-85. Description of the project, equipment, and procedures.

3535. Parsons, M. J. Binding Services Handbook. Leeds, UK: Northern Library Services, 1987. 16p.

3536. Partridge, Sharon. "Book Bugs in Colorado," Colorado Preservation Alert, 4:4 (Winter 1994), [4-5]. Describes common pests and measures for control.

3537. Partridge, Sharon, and Karen Jones. Annotated Bibliography: Myra Jo Moon Memorial Preservation Reference Collection. Denver, CO: Colorado Preservation Alliance, 1994. [14p.]

3538. Pascoe, M.W. Impact of Environmental Pollution on the Preservation of Archives and Records: A RAMP Study. Paris: UNESCO, 1988. 44p. (PGI-88/WS/18). Describes the chemical and physical structure of paper documents and examines how pollutants can damage them; strategies for dealing with pollutants.

3539. Passaglia, Elio. The Characterization of Microenvironments and the Degradation of Archival Records: A Research Program. Gaithersburg, MD: U.S. Dept. of Commerce, National Bureau of Standards, 1987. Various paging. (NBSIR 87-3635). Study of problems of microenvironments in containers holding archival materials; mathematical models for the study of phenomena.

450

3540.   Passaglia, Elio. "The Characterization of Microenvironments and the Degradation of Archival Records," Restaurator, 10:3/4 (1989), 123-150. Summary of report, cited above.

3541.   Pastine, Maureen. "Library Theft: How to Start a Multi-Million Dollar Business," Focus On Security, 1:3 (April 1994), 19-27. Discussion of book theft in libraries, Southern Methodist University, problems, and the need to announce theft when it occurs. Select bibliography.

3542.   Pate, Michael B. "The Marquette Electronic Archive," Preservation of Electronic Formats and Electronic Formats for Preservation. Fort Atkinson, WI: Highsmith Press, 1992, 23-40. Describes a project to preserve rare books and manuscripts in electronic format.

3543.   Patkus, Beth. "Light Protection for Books and Paper," NEDCC News (Northeast Documents Conservation Center), 5:2 (Summer 1994), 4-5.

3544.   Paton, Christopher Ann. "Annotated Selected Bibliography of Works Relating to Sound Recordings and Magnetic and Optical Media," Midwestern Archivist, 16:1 (1991), 31-47. 81 citations selected for their insights into the special nature and needs of sound recordings.

3545.   Paton, Christopher Ann. "A Bibliography for Recorded Sound Archives Management," SAA Muse (Society of American Archivists) (Autumn 1992), 2-4. Annotated bibliography.

3546.   Paton, Christopher Ann. "Preservation of Acetate Disc Sound Recordings at Georgia State University," Midwestern Archivist, 16:1 (1993), 11-20. Case study of how an archivist learned to care for recordings, developed procedures for producing archival preservation copies, and located a lab to handle re-recording. Recommendations that archivists should follow.

3547.   Paton, Christopher Ann. "Whispers in the Stacks: The Problem of Sound Recordings in Archives," American Archivist, 53:2 (Spring

1990), 274-280. Discusses status of sound recordings in archival collections; recommends actions to improve their control and preservation, including establishment of national or regional recording facilities.

3548. Patterson, Diana. "Coffee Stains Tell a Tale?" CBBAG Newsletter (Canadian Bookbinders and Book Arts Guild), 14:2 (Summer 1996), 23-24. Study of physical evidence in a Welsh manuscript of the Book of Aneirin, c. 1250 by two scribes; a small manuscript, rebound in 1986 by Julian Thomas, retaining its structural evidence.

3549. Patterson, Diana. "Too Nice to Throw Out," CBBAG Newsletter (Canadian Bookbinders and Book Artists Guild), 8:2 (Summer 1990), 23-24. A plea to the binder/conservator to save essential structural evidence, such as endpapers, and other bibliographical evidence, for bibliographers and scholars of the book.

3550. Patterson, Brad. "The Anatomy of an Interest Group," Artifacts, 2 (June 1986), 1-5.

3551. Patterson, Elizabeth L. "Pornography, Publishing, and Preservation: A Womanist View," Microform Review, 19:1 (Winter 1990), 20-23. Overview of concerns surrounding the production, collection, and preservation of sexually graphic materials; notes that most libraries do not have formed policies.

3552. Patterson, Robert H. "Conservation: What We Should Do Until the Conservator and the 21st Century Arrive," Conserving and Preserving Library Materials, eds. Kathryn L. and William T. Henderson, Champaign-Urbana: University of Illinois Graduate School of Library and Information Science, 1983, 9-18. Discussion of preservation and what librarians can do to prolong the usefulness of their collections.

3553. Patterson, Robert H. "CAN Moving to UT-Austin," Conservation Administration News 56 (January 1994) 1-2.

3554. Patterson, Robert H. "Conservation and Preservation in Japan and the US: A Report of the Fourth US-Japan Conference on Libraries and Information Science in Higher Education," Conservation Administration News, 36 (January 1989), 15. Report on a conference in which the use of optical disks and CD-ROMs for preservation purposes is discussed, along with ways of strengthening the potential for their use in preservation.

3555. Patterson, Robert H. "George Martin Cunha: A Tribute," Conservation Administration News, 61 (April 1995), 9.

3556. Patterson, Robert H. "Our Debt to George Cunha," Conservation Administration News, 39 (October 1989), 3, 32. reprinted in Kentucky Librarian, 54 (Winter/Spring 1990), 26-27.

3557. Pattison, Todd A. "The Conservation Treatment of the Davenport Manuscript," Conservation Administration News, 49 (April 1992), 3, 27. Describes the physical treatment of a diary written between 1730 and 1770.

3558. Patton, Mary. "Care and Preservation of Film and Microforms: Bibliography," Conservation Oklahoma Now, 4:1 (January 1985), 8-10. Annotated bibliography, 1970-1982.

3559. Pauk, Stephen. "The Bookeeper Mass Deacidification Process: Some Effects on 20th Century Library Materials," Abbey Newsletter, 20:4/5 (September 1996), 50-52.

3560. Paul, Karen Dawley. Records Management Handbook for United States Senators and Their Archival Repositories. Washington, DC: Government Printing Office, 1992. 179p. Guidelines for staff who administer senator's records and information resources, with a focus on preservation of both print and non-print records.

3561. Paulson, Barbara A. "Developing a Preservation Policy and Procedure Statement for a Health Sciences Library," Bulletin of the Medical Library Association, 77:3 (July 1989), 293-298. The Health Sciences Library, Columbia University, preservation policy with a note on its development.

3562.   Pavelka, Karen. "Establishing a Treatment Archive to Extend the
         Documentation of Conservation Treatments," Restaurator, 11:3
         (1990), 156-164. Describes treatment archives created to study
         treatments to naturally aged paper to determine long-term effects.
         Paper originally presented at the Working Group on Graphic
         Documents, International Council of Museums Committee for
         Conservation, 9th Triennial Meeting, Dresden, Germany, August 31,
         1990, and at the Conference on Book and Paper Conservation,
         Budapest, Hungary, September 1990. It is reprinted in its
         proceedings as "The Establishment of a Treatment Archives as an
         Extension of the Documentation of Conservation Treatments,"
         Conference on Book and Paper Conservation, 1990. Budapest,
         Hungary: Technical Association of Paper and Printing
         Industry/National Szechenyi Library, 1992, 508-514.

3563.   Pavelka, Karen L. "Treating Manuscripts from the William Faulkner
         Collection," Book and Paper Group Annual, 13 (1994), 31-34. A
         review of decision-making processes to conserve and to make
         manuscripts available for research; collaboration between scholar,
         curator, and conservator.

3564.   Payton, Rob, and Kate Starling. "The Use of Carbon Dioxide for
         Fumigation at the Museum of London," Conservation News, 53
         (March 1994), 16-17. Report on the use of the Rentokil bubble to
         fumigate natural history objects; concerns are noted.

3565.   Peacock, Richard W., et al. Technical Reference Guide for the
         HAZARD I Fire Hazard Assessment Method. Vol. II. Gaithersburg,
         MD: National Institute of Standards and Technology, Center for Fire
         Research, 1991. 271p.

3566.   Peacock, Richard W., et al. Software User's Guide for the HAZARD
         I Fire Hazard Assessment Method. Vol. 1, ver. 1.1. Gaithersburg,
         MD: National Institute of Standards and Technology, Center for Fire
         Research, 1991. 286p.

3567.   Pearce, Michael, ed. Non-Standard Collection Management.
         Brookfield, VT: Ashgate Publishing, 1992. 250p. Discussion of
         conservation and preservation practices.

3568. Pearson, Colin. "Building Out Pests," AICCM Bulletin (Australian
       Institute for the Conservation of Cultural Material), 19:1/2 (1993),
       41-55. Discusses the building as the first barrier to pest control.

3569. Pearson, Colin. "Crisis Facing Conservation Teaching Profession,"
       Abbey Newsletter, 18:3 (July 1994), 36-39. Looks at the crisis
       caused by the need for cost controls in higher education; provides
       some data and makes suggestions to increase effectiveness.

3570. Pearson, Colin, and Wendy Smith. "Your Future in Their Hands-
       Preservation Training and Development: Preservation of Library and
       Archival Materials at the University of Canberra," Preservation of
       Library Materials (Australia Library and Information Association
       Special Interest Group for the Preservation of Library Materials) 13
       (November 1995), 3-14. Describes the Conservation of Cultural
       Materials (CCM) program at the University of Canberra, which trains
       conservators to work in libraries and archives throughout Australia.

3571. Pearson, Glenda J. "The Reproduction of Library Materials in
       1991," Library Resources and Technical Services, 36:3 (July 1992),
       339-359. A bibliographic review of major concerns, including
       bibliographic control, copyright, document delivery, equipment,
       technical aspects, publishing, and standards. New technologies for
       reformatting are emphasized.

3572. Pedersen, Terri L. "Theft and Mutilation of Library Materials,"
       College and Research Libraries, 51:2 (March 1990), 120-
       128. Discussion of the problem and previous attempts to study and
       address theft and mutilation of collections. A survey at Emporia State
       University indicated that users are not aware of the expense of theft
       and that clearly stated penalties are necessary; further study is
       needed.

3573. Pederson, Ann. "Deciding What Is Worth Saving - New Directions
       in Archival Selection and Appraisal," Preservation of Library
       Materials (Australian Library and Information Association Special
       Interest Group for the Preservation of Library Materials), 11

(November 1993), 3-12. Decision making and selection for preservation of archival materials.

3574. Pederson, Ann, ed. Keeping Archives. Sydney, Australia: Australian Society of Archivists, 1987. 374p. Introductory manual for archivists with practical guidelines. Preservation and conservation concerns are emphasized throughout the text.

3575. Pedley, Avril. "A Proposal for a Binding/Conservation Survey, St. Catharine's College, Cambridge," 19p. Keeping Our Word. [British Library's] 1989 National Preservation Office Competition. London, 1990.

3576. Pegg, R. K., and G. Norris. "Temperature and Humidity Variations in Map Storage Areas," Cartographic Journal, 22 (June 1985), 20-22. Examines the Microclimate characteristics in a collection when climate controls were shut down for a weekend.

3577. Pelz, Perri, and Monona Rossol. Safe Pest Control Procedures for Museum Collections. New York: Center for Occupational Hazards, 1983. 8p. Discussion of the problem of using fumigants in museums; summary of the June 1983 Fumigations Hazards Conference.

3578. Pelzman, Frankie, and Mary Jo Goodwin. "The White House Conference on Libraries and Information Services: Agenda for the Nineties," Wilson Library Bulletin, 66:2 (October 1991), 46-49. Summarizes the proceedings for the 1991 White House Conference on Libraries and Information Services (WHCLIS 2), at which concerns for preservation and access were discussed.

3579. Pence, Cheryl. "Audiovisual Resources on Preservation Topics," American Archivist, 53:2 (Spring 1990), 350-354. Lists and reviews audiovisual productions.

3580. Pence, Cheryl. "It Was Worth Buying, But Is It Worth Keeping? Preservation, Selection, and Collection Development," Illinois Libraries, 71:1 (January 1989), 52-53. Discusses the Atkinson model for selection for preservation and the need for a coordinated structure between acquisition and preservation.

3581. Pence, Cheryl. "Preservation in Illinois: Activities and Plans," Illinois Libraries, 72:1 (Jan. 1990), 69-71. Describes the development and activities of the Illinois Cooperative Conservation Program at the Illinois State Library and its emphasis on disaster planning and recovery.

3582. Penn, Ira A., Anne Morddel, Gail Pennix, and Kelvin Smith. Records Management Handbook. Aldershot, Hants., UK; Brookfield, VT: Gower, 1989. 249p.; 2d ed. by Ira A. Penn, Gail Pennix, and Jim Coulson, 1994. 303p. Basic text for records managers, with emphasis on organization and preservation. Chapter on "Disaster Planning and Recovery," provides a basic outline for a disaster plan.

3583. Pennsylvania Historical and Museum Commission. Vital Records Disaster Planning. [Harrisburg]: Governor's Office, 1995. 24p.

3584. Pennsylvania Preservation Advisory Committee. Our Commonwealth: Preserving Pennsylvania's Documentary Heritage. Harrisburg, PA: Pennsylvania Preservation Advisory Committee, 1996. 34p.

3585. Pennsylvania State University Libraries, Preservation Committee. "Guaranteeing a Library for the Future: The Final Report of the Preservation Committee of the Pennsylvania State University Libraries," Restaurator, 8:4 (1987), 151-178. The report, elaborated by an eight-person committee between May 1984 and September 1985, gives thorough information on the condition of a 2.8-million-volume library system with respect to preservation. Acquisition and bindery, environmental and storage conditions, disaster prevention and preparedness, and brittle and damaged materials are discussed as well as education for preservation and the need for a preservation librarian. The results of the report's findings are summarized in recommendations (a total of 34) at the end of every section.

3586.   Peppiatt, Michael. "Treasury of France: The Bibliothèque Nationale Is Much More Than a Library," Connoisseur (January 1986), 59-67. Description of the library, including mention of conservation of books and prints.

3587.   Percy, Theresa Rini, and Sherelyn Ogden. "A Technical Assist," Museum News, 72:2 (March/April 1993), 68-72. Describes a program to train a conservation technician to undertake book and paper treatments at the Old Sturbridge Village (MA) Research Library through the Northeast Document Conservation Center.

3588.   Perdue, Lewis. "Blanket Security," PC World (Personnel Computer), 7:2 (February 1989), 164-167. General introductory article about PC security.

3589.   Perkins, John, ed. with Candace Boyer and Edward T. Paterson, asst. eds. Computer Technology for Conservators. Halifax, Canada: Atlantic Regional Group, International Institute for Conservation - Canadian Group, 1986. 339p. Papers on the application of computers to conservation, from recordkeeping to analysis and treatment. Suggested readings and glossary. Papers from the 11th Annual IIC-CG Conference Workshop, May 1986.

3590.   Perkins, John W. "To Mend or Not To Mend ... That Is the Question, But What Is the Answer?" New Library Scene, 2:2 (April 1983), 1,16. Examines the cost of repairing books in-house and the cost of commercial library binding.

3591.   "Permanence of Magnetic Materials and Optical Disks," Abbey Newsletter, 14:2 (April 1990), 25-26. Announces the formation of a joint technical commission between the Audio Engineering Society and the American National Standards Institute to develop standards and "promote communication" between those in the field and to address the issue of the permanence of magnetic and optical material.

3592.   Permanent Paper. London: Library Association; National Preservation Office; Publishers Association, 1986. 8p.

3593. Perminova, O. I. "The Preservation of Leather Bindings of Cartographic Atlases, at the Russian State Library; Presented at a Seminar on Preservation of Maps, Moscow, October 1993," IFLA Journal (International Federation of Library Associations and Institutions 20:3 (1994), 306-11.

3594. Perry, Alan, F. "All Mashed Up: Library and Archives Recovery from Hurricane Hugo in St. Croix," Preservation Papers of the 1990 SAA Annual Conference, comp. Karen Garlick. Chicago: Society of American Archivists, 1991, 77-82. Case study; recovery of records from badly damaged archives repository; lessons learned.

3595. Perry, Alan F. "Preservation of Local Records," Show-Me Libraries, 38:1/2 (October/November 1986), 16-20.

3596. Perry, Alan F. "The Role of Federal Agencies in Cooperative Conservation," Conservation Administration News, 28 (January 1987), 6, 25. Describes the role that federal agencies play in assisting other agencies in funding, providing technical advice and assistance, and training of conservation interns.

3597. Perry, Joanne M. "Map Storage Methods: A Bibliography," Bulletin (Geography and Map Division, Special Libraries Association), 131 (March 1983), 14-15. Brief bibliography; no annotations.

3598. Perry, Lawrence G. "Preparing for an Emergency: A Step-by Step Approach," Disaster Recovery Journal, 7:4 (October-December 1994), 36-38. Basic steps for preparing and implementing a disaster plan.

3599. Pershey, Edward Jay. Management of Photographic Collections in Historical Agencies and Museums. 5. Nashville: Technical Information Service of the American Association for State and Local History, 1986. 16p. Discusses the curatorial decisions necessary in the proper management of photographic collections.

3600. Persky, Gail, "The Mellon Microform Master Project at the New York Public Library," Microform Review, 13:1 (Winter 1984), 11-16. Describes project goals and its methodology.

3601.　Perti, R. K. "Problems and Studies in the Conservation of the Archival Heritage in Tropical Countries," Politics for the Preservation of the Archival Heritage. Paris: International Council on Archives, 1989, 189-194. Brief review of preservation problems in Southeast Asia; notes need for basic guidelines for preservation management.

3602.　Peters, D. "Training of Restorers," Books in Peril. Cape Town, South Africa: South African Library, 1987, 129-135.

3603.　Peterson, Keith C. Preserving Idaho's Documentary Heritage: A Report to the Government and People of Idaho. Boise, ID: Idaho State Historical Records Advisory Board, 1989. 60p. Report on the condition of the state's public and private records, with recommendation for preservation and access.

3604.　Peterson, Kenneth G. "Challenge or Dilemma: The Impact of Collection Development, Reference Services, and Preservation on Access to Library Resources," Access to Scholarly Information, ed. Sul H. Lee. Ann Arbor, MI: Pierian Press, 1985, 25-41. Examines major issues of access; summary of preservation issues.

3605.　Peterson, Kenneth G. "Incorporating Preservation into Library Organization: The Southern Illinois University of Carbondale Model," Illinois Libraries, 67:8 (October 1985), 723-725. Reprinted: "Preservation at the Morris Library, Southern Illinois University," The Library Preservation Program: Models, Priorities, Possibilities, ed. Jan Merrill-Oldham and Merrily Smith. Chicago, IL: American Library Association, 1985, 41-50. Description of the development of the program.

3606.　Peterson, Trudy. "From the Acting Archivist of the United States," Archival Outlook (November 1993), 16. Discusses the use of optical media by the National Archives.

3607.　Petherbridge, Guy, ed. Conservation of Library and Archive Materials and the Graphic Arts. Boston, MA: Butterworths, 1987. 328p. Papers by leading conservators on the conservation of paper, vellum and parchment, books and bindings, and modern records; proceedings of the 1980 Conference on Library and Archival Materials and the Graphic Arts.

3608. Pfingstag, Gerhard. "Colorants in Inks for Writing, Drawing, and Marking," International Paper History, 4:2 (1994), 22-26. Review of ink composition; discussion of requirements for effective writing, drawing, and marking inks and identifies major colorants used.

3609. Pflieger, Fran, ed. Preservation of Library and Archival Materials. Alexandria, VA: The Association of Higher Education Facilities Officers, 1991. 66p.

3610. Phelps, Douglas. "Preparations for Binding ... Things Library School Never Taught Us," New Library Scene, 3:5 (October 1984), 1, 5, 7-8. Discusses what library binding is, and various techniques, and dealing with the bindery.

3611. Phibbs, Hugh. "Advanced Frame Sealing," Picture Framing Magazine, 5:10 (October 1994), 22-26. Describes a protective sealed frame package for works of art.

3612. Phibbs, Hugh, and Paula Volent. Preservation Hinging, supplement, Picture Framing Magazine, 5:2 (February 1994), 28p. Covers selection of adhesives, the hinge and hinge placement, hinging oversize materials, and art handling. Library of Congress Specification for Mat/Mounting Board is tipped in.

3613. Phillips, Charles. "To Educate or Conserve: Can Historical Organizations Afford to Make a Choice?" History News, 40:6 (January 1985), 6-10. Addresses issues of preservation and access; views conservation and preservation as opposed to access.

3614. Phillips, Charles, and Patricia Hogan. A Culture at Risk: Who Cares for America's Heritage? Nashville, TN: American Association for State and Local History, 1984. 95p. Historical overview and statistical report on the current state of local history collections.

3615.   Phillips, Faye, and Richard Condrey. "Louisiana State University Libraries' Electronic Imaging Laboratory," Microform Review, 23:1 (Winter 1994), 26-28. Describes a project to reformat rare books for access through electronic image to be accessible on CD-ROM, not through printed text.

3616.   Phillips, Morgan W. "Notes on a Method for Consolidating Leather," American Institute for Conservation Journal, 24:1 (Fall 1984), 53-56. Describes an experimental method.

3617.   Phillips, Rodney, and John P. Baker. "The 'Great War' Preserved for Modern Memory: Preserving the World War I Collections at the New York Public Library," Microform Review, 17:5 (December 1988), 279-285. Case study; describes the collection and efforts to preserve it.

3618.   Phippen, William, and Gregor Trinkaus-Randall. "Conservation at the Peabody Museum of Salem," Conservation Administration News, 21 (April 1985), 4-5, 21-22. History of the collection, preservation and conservation initiatives developed through careful planning.

3619.   "Photocopiers," Library Technology Reports, 20:3 (May-June 1984), 287-422. Reports on 19 photocopiers; longevity of products not addressed. Glossary.

3620.   Photograph Collection Management: Brass Tacks Workshops, Basic Training for Historical Societies. [Columbus, OH]: Ohio Association of Historical Societies and Museums, 1995. 56p.

3621.   "Physical Planning Guidelines for Housing Library Systems," Library Systems Newsletter, 4:1 (January 1984), 4-8. Stresses necessity for appropriate storage conditions for materials, which are described.

3622.   Piccolo, Cecila M. "Resources and Technical Services News: New Developments in Preservation and Reproduction," Library Resources and Technical Services, 33:3 (July 1989), 297-302. Summary of new equipment marketed for preservation.

3623.   Pickard, Kim. "Conservation, Preservation and Restoration of Paper," New England Printer and Publisher (June 1985), 38-41. Describes the Northeast Document Conservation Center and its services.

3624.   Pickett, A. G., and M. M. Lemcoe. Preservation and Storage of Sound Recordings. Silver Spring, MD: Association of Recorded Sound Archivists, 1991. 74p. Reissue of the basic student prepared by the Library of Congress in 1959; issues are yet to be addressed.

3625.   [Pickwoad, Nicholas]. "Books and Documents," National Trust Manual of Good Housekeeping, comp. Hermoine Sandwith and Sheila Stainton. London: National Trust/Penguin, 1984, 1985, 26-47. Care, handling, and display of books and documents in historic buildings and/or private collections.

3626.   Pickwoad, Nicholas. "The Conservation of CCCC Ms. 197B," Conservation and Preservation in the Small Library, eds. Nicholas Hadgraft and Katherine Sift. Cambridge: Parker Library Publications, 1994, 114-122. Illus. Conservation report on the treatment and rebinding of a manuscript; analysis of physical evidence of production and previous treatments.

3627.   Pickwoad, Nicholas. "Determining How Best to Conserve Books in Special Collections," Book and Paper Group Annual, 13 (1994), 35-41. Presents a framework for decision making for conservation treatment.

3628.   Pickwoad, Nicholas. "Distinguishing Between the Good and Bad Repair of Books," Conservation and Preservation in the Small Library, eds. Nicholas Hadgraft and Katherine Swift. Cambridge: Parker Library Publications (1994), 141-149. How to evaluate conservation and repair treatments; how successfully did treatment meet desired goals? Questions to be asked prior to treatment; materials, structures, and evaluation. Emphasizes need to have trained conservators undertake treatment.

3629.   Pickwoad, Nicholas. "'Give Me Your Tired, Your Poor...The Wretched Refuse of Your Teeming Shore...'; The Problems

Presented by the Jewish Books of the 18th and Early 19th Centuries," Preprints, International Conference on Conservation and Restoration of Archive and Library Materials, Erice, Italy, (22-23 April, 1996), Rome: Istituto Centrale per la Patologia del Libro, 275-281. Report of the examination of 650 exemplars of Widener Library, Harvard, the varieties of binding structures that reflect the difficult circumstances of their manufacturing; why it is important to preserve these artifacts as they are, making surrogate copies for research of content.

3630.   Picot, Anne. "Waste Paper and Other Stories," Archives and Manuscripts, 17:2 (November 1989), 235-237. Commentary on the need to determine standards for permanence if recycled paper is to be used for records of permanent value.

3631.   Picture Elements, Inc. Guidelines for Electronic Preservation of Visual Materials. Part 1, submitted to the Library of Congress. March, 1995. 23p. + 12p. appendices. Revision 1.1 Report distinguishes an "archival" or "preservation" copy of originals to digital copies made at a lower spatial resolution or compressed for storage. Key issues for preservation are image quality choices, processing, and compression.

3632.   Piechota, Dennis. "Relative Humidity in Cases: Buffered Silica Gel Versus Saturated Salt Solutions," WAAC Newsletter (Western Association for Art Conservation), 15:1 (January 1993), 19-21. Explains the means by which buffered sicilia gel and saturated salt solutions regulate relative humidity within a closed exhibition case. Air circulation and air pollution from salt solutions are discussed.

3633.   Pietila, Anna-Maaija. "Microfilming in the Helsinki University Library," Microform Review, 23:1 (Winter 1994), 6-9. Describes the preservation microfilming program to preserve Finnish literature, newspapers, and periodicals; describes collections.

3634.   Piggott, Michael. "Conservation," Keeping Archives, ed. Ann Pederson. Sydney, Australia: Australian Society of Archivists; 1987,

219-252. Thoroughly reviews preservation and conservation concerns for archivists.

3635.   Pilette, Roberta. "A Report on the AIC Meeting in Nashville, (June 1994)," Conservation Administration News, 58-59 (July/October 1994), 34-35.

3636.   Pilette, Roberta, and Carolyn Harris. "It Takes Two to Tango: A Conservator's View of Curator/Conservator Relations," Rare Book and Manuscript Librarianship, 4:2 (Fall 1989), 103-111. Discusses the information necessary for an intelligent conservation decision and how it can be obtained.

3637.   Pinion, Catherine F. "The National Collection of Audiovisual Materials: Some Problems and Practices," IFLA Journal (International Federation of Library Associations and Institutions), 15:2 (1989), 112-117. Notes the need for national libraries to collect, or coordinate, the collection and preservation of audiovisual materials, as they do printed materials.

3638.   Pinion, Catherine F. "Preservation of Audiovisual Materials: UNESCO Seminar, Berlin, 23-24 May 1987," Audiovisual Librarian, 13:1 (August 1987) 177-178. Report of a seminar to address training needs for curators of audiovisual collections, with emphasis on third world countries; recommendations to UNESCO.

3639.   Pinniger, David. Insect Pests in Museums. London: Institute of Archaeology Publication, 1989. 45p. Causes of infestation are explained and recommendations given for prevention and treatment. The benefits and limits of insecticides and the integrated use of physical and chemical methods are discussed.

3640.   Pinzelik, Barbara P. "Monitoring Book Losses in an Academic Library," Library and Archival Security, 6:4 (Winter 1984), 1-12. Describes methods used at Purdue University Library.

3641.   Pirio, Pamela. "The Problem of Conservation in Small Libraries and a Practical Solution," Archival Products News, 3:3 (Summer 1995), 1-2, 5. Survey of libraries in the St. Louis Regional Library Network in 1992 indicated that preservation is important in small libraries, but they often lack knowledge, skill, and budget for this function. Practical information and measures to care for collections.

3642. Pitschmann, Louis. "Library Preservation: The Fiske Icelandic Collection at Cornell," Medieval Academy News (February 1992), 2. Discusses the need to set preservation priorities in medieval studies; explains why the Icelandic Collection at Cornell University is a likely candidate for reformatting.

3643. Pitti, Daniel V. "Access to Digital Representations of Archival Materials: The Berkeley Finding Aid Project," RLG Digital Image Access Project. Palo Alto, CA: Proceedings from an RLG Symposium held March 31 and April 1, 1995. 73-81.

3644. Plane, Robert A. "Books, Libraries, Scholarship, and the Future," Priorities for Academic Libraries, eds. Thomas J. Galvin and Beverly P. Lynch. San Francisco, CA: Jossey Bass, 1982, 89-96. How to deal with exponential increase in library material; "our only chance to avoid being buried in paper is through utilization of computer technology" (91). Discusses selection and preservation concerns.

3645. Plotnik, Arthur. "Can Bill Welsh Conquer Time and Space for Libraries?" American Libraries, 15:11 (December 1984): 765-769. Views optical disk storage as inevitable due to space constraints. Also argues that the mass-deacidification project is necessary.

3646. Plotnik, Art. "18 Million LAPL Fire: Salvaged Hopes - If It Had to Happen, This Was the Best Time," American Libraries, 17:6 (June 1986), 384-386. Critique of the Los Angeles Public Library fire and salvage operation.

3647. Plumbe, Wilfred J. "Climate as a Factor in the Planning of University Library Buildings," Tropical Librarianship. Metuchen, NJ: Scarecrow Press, 1987, 18-28. Describes climate and its effect on the preservation of library materials; emphasizes the importance of roofing, windows, and walls. Reprint of article that originally appeared in UNESCO Bulletin for Libraries, 17:6 (November-December 1963), 316-325, and still timely.

3648.   Plumbe, Wilfred J. "The Preservation of Books in Guyana," Tropical Librarianship. Metuchen NJ: Scarecrow Press, 1987, 236-240. Basic discussion of enemies of library and archival materials in the tropics. Provides simple, practical solutions.

3649.   Podany, Jerry C. "Emergency Preparedness: Facing the Inevitable," Emergency Preparedness and Response. National Institute for Conservation, 1991. 20-21.

3650.   Podany, Jerry C. "Emergency Preparedness Plan: Developing One and Practicing It," paper presented at the AIC Workshop, Albuquerque, NM, 1991. Perspectives on Natural Mitigation. Washington, DC: Foundation of the American Institute for Conservation, 1991. 69-73.

3651.   Podany, Jerry C. "Safeguarding a Collection and Building From Natural Hazards," paper presented at the AIC Workshop, Albuquerque, NM, 1991. Perspectives on Natural Mitigation. Washington, DC: Foundation for the American Institute of Conservation, 1991. 51-67.

3652.   Podany, Jerry C., and B. Metro. "Survey of Artificat Damage in the Aby Area Museums," Earthquake Spectra. Supplement to Volume 6 (May 1990), 352-358.

3653.   Podany, Jerry C., and Susan Lansing Maish. "Can the Complex Be Made Simple — Informing the Public About Conservation Through Museum Exhibits," American Institute for Conservation Journal, 32:2 (Summer 1993), 101-108. Describes the efforts to establish realistic and accessible approaches to presenting a complex subject to the public.

3654.   Podmore, Hazel. "A Layby on the Super Highway: An Account of a Pilot Project to Digitize from Microfilm," Library Conservation News, 47 (Summer 1995), 4-5. Description of a project to produce digitized material for access: challenges and questions.

3655.   Polaroid Corporation. Storing, Handling and Preserving Polaroid
         Photographs: A Guide. Norwood, MA: Polaroid, 1984. 48p.
         Illus. Covers storage, handling, and use; environmental protection;
         matting, framing, and exhibition; conservation.

3656.   Pollack, Andrew. "Storing Images and Not Paper." New York
         Times (September 1986), D2. Discusses the use of optical disk
         technology to cut down on labor and paper-work in work in a
         corporate setting. Image processing systems can be used not only for
         storage but for dual manipulation as well.

3657.   Pollock, Michael, "Conservation of the Sind Government Archives,"
         Library Conservation News, 21 (October 1988), 6, 8. Meeting at the
         National Museum of Pakistan in Karachi.

3658.   Pollock, Michael. "Surveying the Collections," Library Conservation
         News, 21 (October 1988), 4-6. Report on a survey of the British
         Library's monographic and periodical collections to determine
         binding condition and paper strength. Survey methods are described
         and implications are noted.

3659.   Polloni, Diana. "Picking Up the Pieces, Document SOS Salvage and
         Restoration Experts," The Law Librarian, 26 (September 1995) 409-
         411.

3660.   Pols, Robert. Dating Old Photographs. Birmingham: Federation of
         Family History Societies, 1995. 91p.

3661.   Ponsonby, S. "Visnews Film Archive," Audiovisual Librarian, 14:3
         (August 1988), 142-146. Describes the operations of Visnews,
         focusing on its cataloguing system, its storage facilities, and
         preservation functions.

3662.   Poprady, Geza. "Preservation Microfilming at the National Library
         of Hungary," International Preservation News, 4 (August 1990), 6-
         8. Describes national project to film Hungarian newspapers,
         periodicals, and special collections.

3663.   Poprady, Geza. "Preservation Strategy for Library Holdings,"
         Conference on Book and Paper Conservation, 1990. Budapest:
         Hungary: Technical Association of Paper and Printing
         Industry/National Szechenyi Library, 1992, 1-7. Basic needs for
         preservation and conservation: storage conditions, surrogate copies,
         mass treatments, research.

3664.   Porck, Henk J. Mass Deacidification : An Update on Possibilities
         and Limitations. Amsterdam: European Commission on
         Preservation and Access; Washington, DC: Commission on
         Preservation and Access, 1996. 54p.

3665.   Porck, Henk J., and L. Voogt. "Paper Conservation in the
         Netherlands: The Joint Approach," International Paper History, 3:3
         (1993), 33-37. Describes research projects into the effect of air
         pollution and deterioration on collections to identify preventive
         measures.

3666.   Porck, Henk J., Wim J. Th. Smit, Jacob van Heijst, and Idelette van
         Leewen. "Research on Mass Conservation of Archival and Library
         Materials," Paper Preservation: Current Trends and Recent
         Developments. Atlanta, GA: TAPPI Press, 1990, 69-73. Describes a
         project to determine the relationship between air pollutants and the
         rate of deterioration of paper and other cellulosic materials.

3667.   Porro, Jennifer, ed. Photograph Preservation and the Research
         Library. Mountain View, CA: The Research Libraries Group, 1991.
         56p. Papers from a RLG Symposium, October 1990, describing
         methods and problems associated with the preservation of
         photographic collections.

3668.   Porter, Bruce. "The Gregorian Age," Connoisseur, 214:864
         (February 1984), 88-95. Describes the revitalization of New York
         Public Library under the presidency of Vartan Gregorian, including
         the conservation of books and documents.

3669.   Porter, Cheryl. "Some Considerations in Regard to the Need for
         Pigment Identification and Some Methods Suggested," Conservation
         and Preservation in the Small Library, eds. Nicholas Hadgraft and

Katherine Swift. Cambridge: Parker Library Publications, 1994, 97-100. Methods for analysis of painting materials, including those used on illuminated manuscripts.

3670. Postlewaite, A.W. "Fumigation, Choice of Fumigant and Design of Facility," Preprints. International Council of Museums Committee on Conservation, 8th Triennial Meeting, Sydney, Australia, 6-11 September 1987, vol. 3. Marina del Rey, CA: Getty Conservation Institute, 1987, 1189-1196.

3671. Potter, Constance. "To Preserve and Make Available": Conflicts in Reference. Washington, DC: National Archives, 1987. 12p. (CIDS 1987 Potter).

3672. Poulin, Steve. "Spend Your Conservation Dollar Wisely," Museum Quarterly, 13:1 (March 1984), 27-30. Practical suggestions for small museums advocating UV filters for lighting, the use of acid-free materials for storage and display; recommends monitoring of collections.

3673. Powell, Graeme. "Australian Joint Copying Project," Archives & Manuscripts (Australian Society of Archivists) 13:2 (November 1985), 181-188. Extracts from the project's annual report, 1985-1985.

3674. Powell, Graeme. "The 35th Year of the Australian Joint Copying Project," Archives & Manuscripts (Australian Society of Archivists), 12:2 (November 1984), 147-151. Insight into a typical year's activities.

3675. Powell-Froissard, Lily. "French Group Works to Save Documents of the Past and Future," Abbey Newsletter, 19:4 (September 1995), 65-66. Describes the purpose of the association, Sauver les Documents en Peril des Bibliothèques Francaises (Save the Endangered Documents in French Libraries), and its initiatives to date. Reprinted in Alkaline Paper Advocate, 8:3 (October 1995), 40-41.

3676. Preiss, Lydia. "Adhesives in Bookbinding," First National Conference of Craft Bookbinders - Australia. Kingston, Australia:

Craft Bookbinders Guild, November 1984, 31-34. Review of traditional and modern synthetic bookbinding adhesives: glue, paste, PVAs, with recommendations for EVA copolymer adhesives. Manufacturer's product data.

3677. Preiss, Lydia. "Preservation of the Anson Logs," AICCM Bulletin (Australian Institute for the Conservation of Cultural Material), 12:3-4 (December 1986), 95-101. Describes the minimal conservation treatment of four log books, 1740-44, and conversion to microfilm with close collaboration between curator and conservator.

3678. Preiss, Lydia, and Brian Hawke. "A Comparison of the Fastness of Two Types of Leather Dyes," AICCM Bulletin (Australian Institute for the Conservation of Cultural Material), 9:3-4 (1983), 79-83. Study of two leather dyes for color fastness, indicating the superiority of Ironbark basic water dye over Aniline spirit dye.

3679. "Preservation: The Battle to Save the Nation's Libraries," Research Libraries Group News, 11 (September 1986), 11-16. Describes the Research Library Group's Preservation Program and the projects that it has supported.

3680. "Preservation Efforts Attract Federal Funds for Regional Use," FEDLINK Technical Notes (Federal Library Network), 6:11 (November 1989), 1,7.

3681. "Preservation Guidelines: General Hints on the Care of Books and Documents," An Leabharlann; The Irish Library, 3:3 (1986), 85-88. Basic preservation information, with tips reprinted from the British Library National Preservation Office's Preservation Guidelines.

3682. "Preservation in the 90s," OCLC Newsletter (Online Computer Library Center), 186 (July/August 1990), 16-22. Issue on preservation initiatives, with emphasis on OCLC's involvement.

3683. "Preservation Photocopying in Libraries and Archives." Restaurator, 8:1 (1987), 1-62. Entire issue. Proceedings of NARA Conference.

3684. "A Preservation Primer and Resource Guide for North Carolina Libraries," North Carolina Libraries, 52 (Spring 1994), 17-20.

3685. "Preservation Project Turns Tattered Papers into Digitized Documents," Wilson Library Bulletin, 69 (May 1995) 14.

3686. "The Preservation Research and Testing Office," National Preservation News, 3 (January 1986), 9-11. Describes the research program at the Library of Congress Conservation Unit and its contribution to conservation.

3687. "Preservation Science Council Frames New Research Agenda," Commission on Preservation and Access Newsletter, 92 (September 1996), 1, 3. Economics of information preservation and management of storage environments were the top agenda items.

3688. "Preservation Treatment Options for Law Libraries," Law Library Journal, 84:2 (Spring 1992), 259-279. Recommendations from the American Association of Law Librarians Committee on Preservation Needs of Law Libraries for the preservation of collections of permanent value.

3689. "Preserving Art Serials," The Research Libraries Group News, 41 (Fall 1996), 5.

3690. "Preserving the National Collections," Incite (Australian Library Association), 8 (May 1989), 6-7. Brief description of the preservation activities at the National Library of Australia and the upgrading of its facilities for the preservation and restoration of sound recordings.

3691. "Preserving the National Collections," Incite (Australian Library Association), 8 (May 1989), 6-7. Describes the preservation activities at the National Library of Australia.

3692. "Preserving the Digital Archive," Online and CD-ROM Review, 19 (October 1995), 289-291.

3693. Presley, Roger L., and Christina Landram. "The Life Expectancy of Paperback Books in Academic Libraries," Technical Services Quarterly, 4:3 (Spring 1987), 21-32. Report of a study to monitor the use of unbound paperback books in an academic library; demonstrates that there is no need to bind such books.

3694. Presley, Roger L., and Christina Landram. "The Life Expectancy of Paperback Books in Academic Libraries: A Follow-Up Study," Technical Services Quarterly, 7:4 (1990), 1-10. Review of a policy to add unbound paperback books to a circulating collection; found binding unnecessary.

3695. Preslock, Karen. "Pest Control in Museums (1986): A Partially Annotated Bibliography," A Guide to Museum Pest Control. Washington, DC: Association of Systematics Collections, 1988, 177-198. Detailed bibliography.

3696. Preusser, Frank, and James R. Druzik. " Environmental Research at the Getty Conservation Institute," Restaurator, 10:3/4 (1989), 160-196. Examines pollutant concentrations in museum buildings, assessment of damage to materials, and control strategies. 117 references.

3697. "Preventive Conservation," Conservation (Newsletter of the Getty Conservation Institute), 7:1 (Winter 1992), 4-7. Discusses the need for preventive preservation to slow deterioration of cultural property; describes scientific research and management considerations.

3698. Price, Bennett J. "Computer Room Air Conditioning," Library Hi Tech, 7:3 (1989), 27, 29-47. Basics of computer room air conditioning, from construction to maintenance.

3699. Price, Bennett J. "Computer Room Fire Protection," Library Hi Tech, 8:8 (1990), 29, 43-55. Discusses emergency planning, fire detection and suppression systems, and options.

3700. Price, Helen. Stopping the Rot: A Handbook of Preventive Conservation for Local Studies Collections. Sydney, Australia: Library Association of Australia, 1988, 48p. (Occasional Paper, 10);

2d ed., 1989. 69p. (Occasional Paper, 11). Practical guidelines for preservation for library staff and volunteers caring for historic records. Covers causes of deterioration, prevention and treatment, storage, reformatting, and disaster awareness.

3701. Price, Joseph. "The Optical Disk Pilot Program at the Library of Congress," Videodisc and Optical Disk, 4:6 (1984), 424-432.

3702. Price, Lois Olcott. "Line Shade and Shadow: The Role of Ink in American Architectural Drawings Prior to 1860," Book and Paper Group Annual, 13 (1994), 42-46. A review of inks used in American architectural drawings prior to 1860, characteristics and implications for conservation.

3703. Price, Lois Olcott. Managing a Mold Invasion: Guidelines for Disaster Response. Philadelphia: Conservation Center for Art and Historic Artifacts, 1994. 6p. Technical series No. 1. Covers health concerns, first response, inactivation procedures, fungicides, cleaning and disinfecting, follow-up, and prevention planning. Plus references on specific topics and list of service providers for mold disaster recovery.

3704. Price, Lois Olcott. Mold. Philadelphia, PA: Conservation Center for Art and Historic Artifacts, 1994. 6 leaf pamphlet. (CCAHA Technical Series, 1). Rev. ed. 1996. Causes of mold; how to respond and treat infested materials. Bibliography; sources of assistance.

3705. Price, Lois Olcott. "The Spore Invades and Begins to Grow. Now What? Preservation Papers of the 1991 SAA Annual Conference. Comp, Karen Garlick. Chicago: Society of American Archivists, 1992, 63-67. Discusses ways to identify and treat mold; cleaning.

3706. Price, Robin. "Preparing for Disaster," Journal of the Society of Archivists, 7:3 (April 1983), 167-172. Discusses need for planning; brief bibliography and plan for action.

3707. Price, Robin Murray. "Preservation, Conservation, and Disaster Control in the Wellcome Institute for the History of Medicine," Caribbean Collections: Recession Management Strategies for

Libraries, eds. Mina Jane Grothy. Madison, WI: SALALM (Seminar on the Acquisition of Latin American Library Materials), 1988, 157-166. Describes the Wellcome Institute collection and measures for its preservation: environmental control; emergency planning; reformatting; conservation treatment.

3708. Priest, Derek J. "Modern Paper," Modern Art. London: United Kingdom Institute for Conservation, 1989, 5-7. Discusses the basics of papermaking and the complexity of the process.

3709. Priest, Derek J. "Paper and Its Problems," Library Review, 36 (Autumn 1987), 164-173. Describes papermaking processes and the additives that go into the final product; causes of paper deterioration are reviewed.

3710. Priest, Derek J. "Paper Conservation: Some Polymeric Aspects," Polymers in Conservation. London: Royal Society of Chemistry, 1992, 159-183. (Proceedings of an International Conference, 1991). Describes the nature of paper from a polymeric standpoint and discusses reasons for its deterioration. Outlines current developments in the area of mass treatments for books.

3711. Priest, Derek J. "Permanence and Alkaline-Neutral Papermaking," Historic Textile and Paper Materials II: Conservation and Characterization, eds. Howard L. Needles and S. Haig Zeronian. Washington, DC: American Chemical Society, 1989, 2-12. (ACS Symposium Series, 410). Describes the technicalities and economic advantage in making neutral/alkaline papers, and how this leads to the production of permanent papers.

3712. Priest, Derek J., and Mark Farrar. "The Effect of Aluminum Salts on the Degradation of Paper," Conservation of Historic and Artistic Works on Paper; Proceedings of a Conference, Ottawa, Canada, 3 to 7 October, 1988. ed. Helen D. Burgess. Ottawa: 1994, 255-262. Describes a technique for preparing noncomplex "model" papers with controlled aging behavior; recent results.

3713. Priest, Derek J., Juntai Lau, and R. Prosser. "Pigment Coated Paper: Experiments on Permanence," Conference on Book and Paper

Conservation, 1990. Budapest, Hungary: Technical Association of
Paper and Printing Industry/National Szechenyi Library, 1992, 450-
470. Experiments to assess the permanence of coated paper conclude
that "conventional clay and carbonate coatings are unlikely to worsen
longevity and may even improve it under certain circumstances."

3714.   Priest, Derek J., and J. Stanley. "The Ageing of Paper Containing
Chemithermomechanical Pulp," Environnement et Conservation de
l'Écrit, de l'Image, et du Son. Paris: ARSAG, 1994, 154-160.
(Actes des Deuxièmes Journées Internationales d'Études de
l'ARSAG). Discusses the results of accelerated aging tests on papers
containing high lignin content, and the need for further assessment of
results.

3715.   A Primer on Disaster Preparedness, Management, and Response.
Washington, DC: The Smithsonian Institution, October 1993. One
volume. Contains selected reprints issued by the Smithsonian
Institution, National Archives and Records Administration, Library
of Congress, and National Park Service. Includes revised text of
Peter Waters publication Procedures for Salvage of Water Damaged
Library Materials.

3716.   Proceedings Pan-African Conference on the Preservation and
Conservation of Library and Archival Materials, Nairobi, Kenya,
21-25 June 1993, eds. Jean-Marie Arnoult, Virginia Kemp, and
Musila Musumbi. The Hague: IFLA, 1995. 211p. (IFLA
Professional Publication 43). Conference to foster cooperation
between African nations and to access preservation /conservation
activities. It also sought to create understanding, to compare
experiences, and to establish an agenda for the next decade.

3717.   "Procurement of Writing, Copying and Printing Paper for the Federal
Records," NARA Bulletin (National Archives and Records
Administration), 95-97 (September 8, 1995), 6p. Advises Federal
Agencies to procure permanent alkaline paper. Recommends
compliance with PL 101-423, EO 12873 and EPA guidelines.

3718.   Proffitt, Kevin. "The Micrographics Program of the American
Jewish Archives," Microform Review, 15:2 (Spring 1986), 87-

90. Describes the history of the micrographics program at the American Jewish Archives, Hebrew Union College-Jewish Institute of Religion, Cincinnati, OH.

3719. "Project Archon," Conservation Administration News, 14 (1983), 5-6. The examination and encoding of the physical condition of the paper and binding of rare books carried out at New York University.

3720. Promenschenkel, George. "Conference on Research Library Directors Focuses on Archiving Digital Information," OCLC Newsletter (Online Computer Library Collection), 220 (March/April 1996), 14-15.

3721. Prosperi, Cecilia. "Archival Bindings in Italian Archives," Conference on Book and Paper Conservation, 1990. Budapest, Hungary: Technical Association of Paper and Printing Industry/National Szechenyi Library, 1992, 33-37. Emphasizes the need to preserve original structural elements in conservation treatments; describes basic treatments.

3722. Prosser, Ruth. "Pigment Coated Printing Papers," Modern Art. London: United Kingdom Institute for Conservation, 1989, 8-12. Describes the production and ingredients in pigment-coated papers.

3723. Proulx, E. Annie. "A Library Rebounds," Horticulture, 69:3 (March 1991), 26-35. Describes the rehabilitation of the library of the Massachusetts Horticultural Society. The causes of preservation problems and the efforts to preserve the collection are discussed.

3724. "Public Drive for Alkaline Paper Inspires New Action in the Mills." Publishers Weekly (July 21, 1989), pp. 30-37.

3725. Puglia, Steven T. The Care and Duplication of Historical Negative Collections. Nashville, TN: American Association for State and Local History, 1989. 64p. Discusses deterioration of black-and-white negatives, proper storage, and duplication options. Bibliography.

3726. Puglia, Steven T. "Cost-Benefit Analysis for Black and White Acetate: Cool/Cold Storage vs. Duplication," Abbey Newsletter, 19:4 (September 1995), 71-72. Basic guidance and a framework to conduct a cost-benefit analysis comparing duplication with cool/cold storage. Paper originally presented at the 1995 NARA Conference, "Cellulose Acetate Films: Magnitude and Nature of the Preservation Concerns." Complete cost-benefit analysis in Topics in Photographic Preservation, 6 (1995).

3727. Puglia, Steven T. "Duplication Options for Deteriorating Photo Collections," Photographic Preservation and the Research Library, ed. Jennifer Porro. Mountain View, CA: RLG, 1991, 29-35. Includes electrophotographic copying, electronic imaging, contact photographic methods; photographic methods recommended for preservation because of impermanence of electronic media.

3728. Puglia, Steven T. "Negative Duplication: Evaluating the Reproduction and Preservation Needs of Collections," Conservation Administration News, 38 (July 1989), 8-9. Guidelines for evaluating collections for duplication options. Condensed from a paper presented at the Photographic Materials Group meeting, 1989.

3729. Puglia, Steven T. A Short Guide to Nitrate Negatives: History, Care, and Duplication. Andover, MA: Northeast Document Conservation Center, 1986. 8p. This leaflet was revised in 1991 by NEDCC and is now 5p.

3730. Puissant, Maria J. "Experiences in the Conservation and Restoration of Water-Sensitive Bookbinding Leather," Environnement et Conservation de l'Écrit, de l'Image et du Son. Paris: ARSAG, 1994, 197-200. (Actes des Deuxièmes Journées Internationales d'Études de l'ARSAG). Describes the irreversible reaction when vegetable-tanned leathers are exposed to water, with preventive measures in treatment.

3731. Puissant, Maria J. "The School for Book Restoration at the Centro del Bel Libro, Ascona, Switzerland," Restaurator, 9:1 (1988), 37-50. Describes the history, goals, and curriculum of the school to train bookbinders and book conservators.

3732. Purinton, Nancy, and Susan Filter. "Gore-Tex: An Introduction to the Material and Treatments," Book and Paper Group Annual, 11 (1992), 141-155. Describes the material and its applications for conservation.

3733. Pyatt, T. D. "Preservation Programming in Major Research Libraries," Library and Archival Security, 7:3/4 (Fall/Winter 1985), 23-32. Presents results of a 1985 survey of research library directors, noting that they wanted more literature on how to do preservation and conservation, which was already available; looking for direction on a national level.

3734. Pymm, Bob, and Dina Junkermann. "Photograph Archives: An Approach to Access and Preservation," Audiovisual Librarian, 14:4 (November 1988), 187-194. Case study; development of a database for the Australian War Memorial.

3735. Quainton, (Baron). "The Doomsday Debate," Preserving the Word. London: Library Association, (1987), 1-9. Paper presented at a conference on book preservation, Harrogate, 1986.

3736. Quant, Abigail. "Notes from the Field: Tanning and Leather Research in England," Leather Conservation News, 2:1 (Fall 1985), 14-15.

3737. Quant, Abigail. "The Use of Computers in Surveying the Manuscript Collection of the Walters Art Gallery," Proceedings of the Institute of Paper Conservation 10th Anniversary Conference, Oxford, England, 14-18 April 1986. Leigh, Worcester., England: Institute of Paper Conservation, 1986, C1-C2. Describes an effective way of surveying a collection and recording data on condition for analysis and to establish priorities for treatment.

3738. Quinsee, Anthony G., and Andrew C. McDonald, eds. Security in Academic and Research Libraries. Newcastle-upon-Tyne, England: University of Newcastle Library, 1991. 79p. Proceedings of three seminars held in 1989 and 1990 to foster heightened awareness of

security and to encourage managers to address policies and
procedures.

3739.   Quinn, Judy, and Michael Rogers. "Akzo Chemicals, Inc. Has Signed
         an Agreement With Harvard University Library to use Akzo's DEZ
         Vapor Deacification Process to Preserve Part of Its Collection. Johns
         Hopkins Will Also Use the Process, Which Was Rejected by the
         Library of Congress," Library Journal, 117:2 (February 1, 1992), 15.

3740.   Quinn, Judy, and Michael Rogers. [Library of Congress]. "LC Turns
         Down All Deacidification Preservation Bids," Library Journal,
         116:16 (October 1, 1991), 14.

3741.   Racelis, Fernando. "The Composition of Inks," Conservation
         Administration News, 29 (April 1987), 6,10,13. Description of
         composition of inks and effect upon media.

3742.   Ragsdale, Kate W., and Janice Simpson. "Bring on the Safe Side,"
         College and Research Libraries News, 57:6 (June 1996), 351-
         354. Emergency procedures for disabled users and staff;
         incorporation into disaster plan.

3743.   Raitt, Mildred D. "Standards in Binding," Scholarly Publishing,
         14:2 (February 1983), 187-189. Requests to publishers in designing
         scholarly publications so that they can be properly bound and
         preserved.

3744.   Rajer, Tony. Preventive Conservation: Principles and Practices for
         Paintings, Prints, and Books, a Common Sense Approach to Caring
         for Your Collections in Barbados. Bridetown, Barbados: Barbados
         Gallery of Art, 1995. 44p.

3745.   Raloff, Janet. "Halting Untimely Book Ends," Science News, 123:10
         (March 5, 1983), 154-156; reprinted in New Library Scene, 2:3 (June
         1983), 1,4,13-14; Library and Archival Security, 7:2 (Summer 1985),
         21-26. Summary of deacidification processes developed by the
         Library of Congress and Richard Smith of Wei T'o.

3746.   Ram, A. T., and J. L. McCrea. "Ability of Processed Cellulose Ester Photographic Films," Journal of the Society of Motion Picture and Television Engineers, 97 (June 1988), 474-483.

3747.   Ram, Tulsi. "Archival Preservation of Photographic Films: A Perspective," Polymer Degradation and Stability, 29 (1990), 3-29.

3748.   Ram, Tulsi. "Molecular Sieves: Antidote to Vinegar Syndrome," AMIA Newsletter (Association of Motion Picture Archivists), 19 (March 1993), 1. Discusses a technology that will absorb moisture, acetic acid, and methylene chloride, which should lessen or prevent "vinegar syndrome," the deterioration in cellulose triacetate film that occurs when the acetate ion reacts with moisture to form acetic acid.

3749.   Ram, Tulsi, S. Masaryk-Morris, David Kopperl, and Richard W. Bauer. "Simulated Ageing of Processed Cellulose Triacetate Motion Picture Films," Archiving the Audio-Visual Heritage. Rushton, England: FIAF/UNESCO, (1992), 52-60. Report on research on the vinegar syndrome, the stability of cellulose triacetate, and to determine effective storage procedures.

3750.   Ram, Tulsi, S. Masaryk-Morris, David Kopperl, and Richard W. Bauer. "Simulated Aging of Processed Cellulose Triacetate Motion Picture Films," Journal of Imaging Science and Technology, 36 (January/February 1992), 21-28. See above.

3751.   Ram, Tulsi, J. P. Pytlak, H. D. Heuer, D. F. Kopperl, and D. C. Carroll. "Molecular Sieves: An Aid to Film Preservation," Environnement et Conservation de l'Écrit, de l'Image et du Son. Paris: ARSAG, 1944, 121-127. (Actes des Deuxièmes Journées Internationales d'Études de l'ARSAG, 16 au 20 Mai 1994). Describes current and ongoing research into the causes and effects of vinegar syndrome in film and proposes a new methodology to help minimize its rate.

3752.   Ram, A. Tulsi, et al. "The Effects and Prevention of Vinegar Syndrome," Journal of Imaging Science and Technology, 38:3 (June 1994), 249-261.

3753.   Ramer, Brian. A Conservation Survey of Museum Collections in
        Scotland. Edinburgh, Scotland: Scottish Museums Council, 1989.
        160p. Report on a major two-year project carried out by the Scottish
        Museums Council on conservation in the museums of Scotland. The
        recommendations it makes, both in remedial and preventive terms,
        can be applied to museums nationwide.

3754.   Ramer, Brian. "The Development of a Local Humidity Control
        System," International Journal of Museum Management and
        Curatorship, 3:2 (June 1984), 183-191. Description of a system using
        silica gel for exhibition cases. Abridged version: "Show-Cases
        Modified for Climate Control," Museum (UNESCO), 37:2 (1985),
        91-94.

3755.   Ranada, David. "The Care and Feeding of a CD Player," Stereo
        Review, 49:12 (December 1984), 59-61. Describes the care of a CD
        player and compact disks; discusses potential sound quality
        improvement with the introduction of CDs.

3756.   Ranada, David. "Digital Debut: First Impressions of the Compact
        Disc System," Stereo Review, 47:12 (December 1982), 61-
        70. Positively reviews the new CD media; discusses the advantages
        over other audio media, and briefly mentions shortcomings.

3757.   Ranade, Sanjay., ed. Jukebox and Robotic Libraries for Mass
        Storage. Westport, CT: Meckler, 1992. 128p. Describes different
        uses of storage media in a hierarchy.

3758.   Ranade, Sanjay. Mass Storage Techniques. Westport, CT: Meckler,
        1991. 145p. Extensive technical description of the working of mass
        storage systems, with some discussion of optical media. Focuses on
        networked systems.

3759.   Randall, Thea. "Preservation and Conservation," Local Studies
        Collection: A Manual, ed. Michael Dewe. Aldershot, Hants., UK;
        Brookfield, VT: Gower, 1991, 140-172. Overview of preservation
        concerns with focus on special collections. References and
        bibliography.

3760. Randall, Thea, and Pauline Thomson. " A proposal for a Preservation Survey of the Collections at the William Salt Library Stafford. 29p. Keeping Our Words. 1989 [British Library]. National Preservation Office Competition, London: NPO, 1990.

3761. Randolph, Pamela Young. "Museum Housekeeping: Developing a Collection Maintenance Program," Technical Information (Virginia Association of Museums) (Winter/Spring 1987), 3-4, 7-8. Organization and implementation of maintenance procedures to ensure a clean and safe environment for materials.

3762. Rankin, Keith. "A Plea for the Preservation of New Zealand's Business Archives," Archifacts, 4 (1988/89), 33-35.

3763. Rao, N. Rama, and N. Jagadish Kumar. "Aqueous Deacidification of Manuscripts by a Physiologically Active Reagent," Journal of Archaeological Chemistry, 4 (December 1986), 39-41. Aqueous deacidification of manuscripts dating 1948 has been carried out by using 1% sodium dehydroacetate (SDHA). The deacidification papers were conditioned at 65% relative humidity and 27 degrees C, and physical parameters such as brightness, MIT-folding endurance, tensile strength, tearing strength, etc. were determined. It was observed that the strength of the deacidified paper improved as the pH and the other physical parameters were increased.

3764. Rao, Y. Rajeshwar, and P. K. Saiprakash. "Effect of Combinations of Some Fumigants on Paper in Conservation Studies," Journal of Archaeological Chemistry, 4 (December 1986), 23-26. This paper highlights the use of combined fumigant systems such as para-dichlorobenzenes thymol, naphthalene thymol, and para-dichlorobenzene naphthelene in conservation studies. The combined system causes no damage to paper. The insecticidal properties seem to depend on the nature of the combinations. The para-dichlorobenzene naphthalene system was found to be most effective while the naphthalene thymol system was found least effective.

3765. Raper, Diane. "Having a Flood? Law Librarian, 19:3 (December 1988), 85-88. Coping with water damage at the Law Society Library.

3766.   Raphael, Toby J. "Airtight Humidity Stabilized Display Cases: The Practical Design and Fabrication of Sealed Exhibit Cases," Objects Specialty Group Postprints, 1991. Washington, DC: American Institute for Conservation, 1992, 78-87. Describes exhibition cases specially designed by the National Park Service to provide a microclimate for objects displayed in facilities where overall humidity control cannot be achieved.

3767.   Raphael, Toby J. "The Care of Leather and Skin Products: A Curator's Guide," Leather Conservation News, 9 (1993), 1-15. Summarizes practices for the care of objects made of leather and skin materials.

3768.   Raphael, Toby J. "Ethnographic Skin and Leather Products: A Call for Conservation Treatment," Symposium 86: The Care and Conservation of Ethnographic Materials. Ottawa: Canadian Conservation Institute, (1988), 68-73.

3769.   Raphael, Toby J., and Ellen McCrady. "Leather Dressing: To Dress or Not to Dress," Leather Conservation News, 1:1 (Spring 1983), 9-10. A brief review of research on leather dressing concluding that it is an irreversible procedure in most cases with little or no preservative effect and many potentially dangerous side effects.

3770.   Rapson, Howard W., C. Bertil Anderson, and Aida Magued. "Natural Aging of Laboratory Bleached Pulps," Paper Preservation: Current Issues and Recent Developments. Atlanta, GA: TAPPI Press, 1990, 58-62. Explores yellowing or bleached pulps as they age to identify causes of yellowing.

3771.   Ratcliffe, F.W. "The Current Situation in the United Kingdom," Journal of Librarianship, 17:2 (April 1985), 85-91. Notes past and present that ignorance about preservation among British librarians, the need to train staff and users, and the role that the book trade could play by producing permanent/durable products.

3772.   Ratcliffe, Frederick W. "National Cooperation in Preservation and Conservation," Alexandria, 1:3 (December 1989), 31-41. Reviews the causes for increased interest in preservation, the Cambridge

Preservation Project resulting in the Ratcliffe report (1984), and the role that the National Preservation Office, the British Library, plays in addressing the preservation concerns of libraries in Great Britain.

3773.   Ratcliffe, F.W. "Preservation: A Decade of Progress," Library Review, 36 (Winter 1987), 228-236. Summary of preservation activities that have taken place in British libraries and archives.

3774.   Ratcliffe, Frederick W. "Preservation and Scholarship in Libraries," Library Review (Glasgow, Scotland, 40:2/3 (1991), 62-71.

3775.   Ratcliffe, Frederick W., and D. Patterson. Preservation Policies and Conservation in British Libraries. London: British Library, 1984. 131p. (Library and Information Research Report, 25). Report of the Cambridge University Library Conservation project to determine preservation policies and practices in British libraries and to identify training facilities.

3776.   Raub, Wolfard. "The Preservation of Old and Precious Books at the Munster University Library," Conservation Administration News, 51 (October 1992), 10-11. Discusses the decision-making process between curator and conservator.

3777.   Ravines, Patrick, and Annari Faurie. "The Impregnation and Absorption Behaviour of Methyl Cellulose on Two Modern Papers," Preprints: ICOM Committee for Conservation 10th Triennial Meeting, ed. Janet Bridgland. Washington, DC: International Council of Museums, 1993, 462-468. Investigation of the impregnation and absorption behavior of commercially available methylcellulose.

3778.   Ravines, P., N. Indicator, and Debra M. Evetts. "Methyl Cellulose as an Impregnating Agent for Use In Paper Conservation," Restaurator, 10:1 (1989), 32-36. Effects of accelerated aging of paper treated with methylcellulose are reported.

3779.   Ray, Joyce M., Sharon R. Crutchfield, and Fred W. Todd. Disaster Manual for San Antonio Area Libraries and Other Collection-

Holding Institutions. San Antonio, TX: Council of Research and Academic Libraries, 1984. 12 leaves in portfolio.

3780. Rayer, Nina. "Proper Care of Paper Collections," Conservation News (Rocky Mountain Regional Conservation Center), 1:4 (Spring 1984), 4-5; 2:1 (Summer 1984), 4-5. Framing of paper objects for storage and display; considers the elements of the frame package.

3781. Raynes, Patricia. "Insects and Their Control in the Library," Conservation Administration News, 27 (October 1986), 4, 24-25. Describes measures through the centuries to protect collections from damage; discusses current methods of treatment and problems with fumigation.

3782. Rebrikova, N. L., and N. V. Manturovskaya. "Study of Factors Facilitating the Loss of Stability of Microscopic Fungi in Library and Museum Collections," Preprints: ICOM Committee for Conservation 10th Triennial Meeting, ed. Janet Bridgland. Washington, DC: International Council of Museums, (1993), 887-890. Study of insatiability of fungal cells; includes mycological investigation of water-damaged books.

3783. Rebsamen, Werner. "Acid-PHree Binders Board: A Reality," New Library Scene, 3:6 (December 1984), 13-17. Describes how binders' board is made and why acid-free boards are necessary.

3784. Rebsamen, Werner. "Binding Quality: LBI's Ultimate Goal," New Library Scene, 2:6 (December 1983), 13-15. Discusses the Library Binding Institute's standards and their enforcement.

3785. Rebsamen, Werner. "C-1 Book Cloth vs. Group F Buckram," New Library Scene, 8:6 (December 1989), 6-9. Testing results for this lighter weight buckram book covering demonstrate that it is appropriate for small, light-weight volumes.

3786. Rebsamen, Werner. "Cutting and Trimming," New Library Scene, 7:4 (August 1988), 13-16. Describes the operations of cutting and trimming in book production and in the library bindery.

3787.   Rebsamen, Werner. "Economics of Library Binding," New Library Scene, 8:4 (August 1989), 1, 5-8. An examination of the hypothesis that prebinding is more cost-effective than using standard publisher's bindings, concluding that it is more cost-effective to pre-bind. Summary of a Rochester Institute of Technology Masters thesis.

3788.   Rebsamen, Werner. "Endpaper Construction for Recasing," New Library Scene, 4:3 (June 1985), 15-18. Describes when recasing is appropriate and how it is done.

3789.   Rebsamen, Werner. "The Future of Printing and Publishing," New Library Scene, 4:2 (April 1985), 16-19. Discussion of the impact of electronic technologies on printing and publishing. Author believes there will be an increase in printed material that will need to be bound.

3790.   Rebsamen, Werner. "Gebrochener Ruecken (Shaped Spine Case-Binding Techniques)," Abbey Newsletter, 11:3 (April 1987), 47-48.

3791.   Rebsamen, Werner. "Guidelines to Library Bindings," New Library Scene, 2:3 (June 1983), 7-8. Guidelines and definitions for commercial library binding.

3792.   Rebsamen, Werner. "A Library Binding Performance Evaluation," New Library Scene, 2:5 (October 1983), 7, 14-15. Discusses the research of David Parisi on the evaluation of rounded and backed and squarebacked books; determines that problems occur when the text block is poorly made.

3793.   Rebsamen, Werner. "Library Binding Quality ... Do You Get What You Pay For?" New Library Scene, 7:2 (April 1988), 13-16. Discusses the causes of poor quality library binding and how the American Library Association and the Library Binding Institute have dealt with the problem.

3794.   Rebsamen, Werner, Long-Term Service Life and Performance Characteristics of PVA Emulsion Adhesives Used for the Double Fabbing Process in Library Binding; Are Adhesives a Viable Alternative? Rochester, NY: Rochester Institute of Technology,

1991. 85p. (LBI Technology Committee Research Report). Discusses the Library Binding Institute standard for adhesive bindings and the adhesives that do not meet the standard; new adhesive formulations are reviewed.

3795. Rebsamen, Werner. "Mekanotch: An Adhesive Binding Method With a Future, If ...' New Library Scene, 3:2 (April 1984), 19-21. Description of the Mekanotch technique.

3796. Rebsamen, Werner. "New Cover Only — How Much Can We Save?" New Library Scene, 6:1 (February 1987), 15-19. Discusses binding options for libraries. The current practice of recasing books is described.

3797. Rebsamen, Werner. "New Softcover Binding Technology OTABIND Is Coming to North America," New Library Scene, 7:1 (February 1988), 11-15. Describes a softcover binding using a hot melt technique that produces a flexible, durable book.

3798. Rebsamen, Werner. "Otabind - A New Lay-Flat Paperback Binding," Publishers Weekly (March 4, 1988), 83-88.

3799. Rebsamen, Werner. "Oversew or Adhesive Bind?" New Library Scene, 5:6 (December 1986), 12-15. Discusses oversewing and adhesive binding, noting that adhesive binding is usually more satisfactory.

3800. Rebsamen, Werner. "Paper Grain," New Library Scene, 4:1 (February 1985), 13-16. Illus. Explains how paper grain affects book function and binding.

3801. Rebsamen, Werner. "Performance Testing With the Universal Book Tester," New Library Scene, 6:5 (October 1987), 13-18. Describes the development and applications of the Universal Book Tester, developed by William Barrow.

3802. Rebsamen, Werner. "Rounding and Backing ... Fact and Fiction," New Library Scene, 3:4 (August 1984), 18-21. Discusses the necessity of this process in binding.

3803. Rebsamen, Werner. "Sewing Threads Used in Bookbinding," New Library Scene, 3:3 (June 1984), 15-16. Describes the various threads used for binding.

3804. Rebsamen, Werner. "Spine Preparation Techniques Used on Adhesive Bound Books," New Library Scene, 8:2 (April 1989), 7-13. Describes the problems that a binder faces when doing adhesive bindings and the techniques for doing it.

3805. Rebsamen, Werner. "Technically Speaking: Book Testing at Rochester Institute of Technology," New Library Scene, 6:3 (June 1987), 16-19. A history of the Dudley A. Weiss Book Testing Laboratory.

3806. Rebsamen, Werner. Technically Speaking: Articles on Library Binding. Edina, MN: Library Binding Institute, 1992. Compilation of 50 articles from author's "Technically Speaking" column in New Library Scene, 1975-1989. Covers a wide range of topics relating to library and publishers bindings.

3807. Rebsamen, Werner. "Technically Speaking: Book Tumble Test," New Library Scene, 3:5 (October 1984), 14-17. Describes a procedure to test the durability of library bindings.

3808. Rebsamen, Werner A. "Technically Speaking: Hot-Stamping Foils," New Library Scene, 5:1 (February 1986), 14-15.

3809. Rebsamen, Werner. "Technically Speaking: Joint Adhesion," New Library Scene, 2:4 (August 1983), 7, 16, 18. Construction of the library-bound book and problems with glues.

3810. "Recent Film Research at IPI," AMIA Newsletter (Association of Moving Image Archivists), 26 (October 1994), 8, 19. Summary of research on the permanence of film recently completed and currently underway at the Image Permanence Institute.

3811. "Recommendations for Storing and Handling Machine-Readable Data Carriers," Restaurator, 12:4 (1991), 233. Eight recommendations for storage and playback.

3812. Reed, Judith A. "Preservation: No Beginning and No End in Sight," The Public Garden, 4:2 (April 1989), 20-21. How to care for collections of books and where to turn for assistance.

3813. Reed, Judith A., and Bernadette Callery. "Conservation Survey Databases: Computer Based Tools for Evaluating and Monitoring Collection Condition," The Gold Leaf, 12:1 (Spring 1994), 3-5. Note on the philosophy behind the design of a collection condition survey database for the New York Botanical Garden Library; emphasizes importance of involving conservators and curators in the design of the database.

3814. Reed, Marcia. "To Catch These Thieves: The Librarian as Protector of the Books," Art Documentation, 10:4 (Winter 1991), 175-177.

3815. Reed-Scott, Jutta, comp. Preservation Organization and Staffing. Washington, DC: Association of Research Libraries, 1990. 135p. (SPEC Kit, 160). Examines changes in organization and staffing in Association of Research Libraries members since 1985, with organization charts and mission statements from selected institutions.

3816. Reed-Scott, Jutta, and Nicola Daval. ARL Preservation Statistics, 1988-89: A Compilation of Statistics From the Members of the Association of Research Libraries. Washington, DC: Association of Research Libraries, 1990. 62p.

3817. Reedy, Terry, and Chandra Reedy. Statistical Analysis in Art Conservation Research. Marina del Rey, CA: Getty Conservation Institute, 1988. 108p.

3818. Rees, Eiluned. "Conservation Conversation Piece: A Valedictory Address," Library Conservation News, 34 (January 1992), 6-7. Describes experience in establishing a conservation unit at the National Library of Wales; reflections on library preservation.

3819. Rees, Eiluned. "Wales and the Preservation Problem," Library Conservation News, 18 (January 1988), 1,3. Efforts to preserve materials and the National Library's preservation and outreach programs are described.

3820. Rees, Eiluned. "Wales and the Preservation Problems," Preserving the Word. London: Library Association, (1987), 29-32. Paper presented at a conference on preservation, Harrogate, 1986.

3821. Reeser, Cheryl V. "Libraries in Disaster: Idaho," PNLA Quarterly (Pacific Northwest Library Association), 52 (Winter 1988), 16-17. Describes the salvage of the collection when a library was destroyed by floodwater from a break in the Teton Dam.

3822. Reeves, Sally K. "A Case Study in Rehousing an Oversized Collection at the New Orleans Notarial Archives," comp. Karen Galick. Preservation Papers of the 1991 SAA Annual Conference. Chicago: Society of American Archivists, (1992), 44-48. The rehousing of a collection of architectural drawings, water-color with ink notations that have been repaired and rebound by WPA Workers c.1940. Collection disbound and rehoused in steel drawers after cleaning, flattening, and further repair.

3823. Regnault, Pacale. "Academic Conservation Courses in German-Speaking Countries," Paper Conservation News, 73 (March 1995), 10-11. Briefly describes the new programs for professional training in book and paper conservation.

3824. Reich, Victoria Ann, Connie Brooks, Willy Comwell, and Schott Wicles. "Electronic Discussion Lists and Journals: A Guide for Technical Services Staff," Library Resources and Technical Services, 39:3 (July 1995), 303-319. Recommended electronic discussion groups "which allows us to make professional contacts, deepen technical knowledge and take the opportunity to learn about new areas" (303). "Preservation," (316-319): AMIA-L; Conservation DistList; ERECS-L (Management and Preservation of Electronic Records); Imagelib.

3825. Reich, Victoria Ann, and Melissa Ann Betcher. "Library of Congress Staff Test Optical Disk System," College and Research Libraries, 47:4 (July 1986), 385-391. Discusses advantages and disadvantages identified during testing of the optical disk system; concludes that further discussion and testing can lead to successful use of the technology.

3826. Reid, Marion T., and Marsha J. Hamilton. "Technical Services Management," RTSD Newsletter (Resources and Technical Services Division), 13:2 (1988), 19-23. Describes how procedures were developed at Ohio State University Libraries for technical services staff to identify materials in process that need to be considered for preservation treatment before they are added to the collection.

3827. Reilly, James M. Albumen & Salted Paper Book. Rochester, NY: Rochester Institute of Technology, 1985. 133p.

3828. Reilly, James M. Care and Identification of 19th-Century Photographic Prints. Rochester, NY: Eastman Kodak, 1986. 116p. Analysis of 19th-century photographic and photomechanical print processes. Discusses causes of deterioration; recommendations for care, storage, and display.

3829. Reilly, James M. IPI Storage Guide for Acetate Film. Rochester, NY: Image Permanence Institute, 1993. 22p., graphs, tables, wheel. Overview of environmental specifications for film storage to assist managers in the evaluation of the storage conditions of their collections of film.

3830. Reilly, James M. "The Image Permanence Institute: A New Resource for the Photographic Preservation Community," PictureScope, 32:4 (Winter 1987), 146-147, 156. Description of the Institute and its mission of research and training in photographic conservation.

3831. Reilly, James M. "Preserving Photograph Collections in Research Libraries: A Perspective," Photograph Preservation and the Research Library. Mountain View, CA: Research Libraries Group, (1991), 7-

17. Questions that must be answered before determining preservation strategies.

3832.   Reilly, James M. "Research on Paper Ageing," Commission on Preservation and Access Newsletter, 71 (September 1994), 3-4.

3833.   Reilly, James M. "Stability of Black-and-White Photographic Images, With Special Reference to Microfilm," Abbey Newsletter, 12 (July 1988), 83-88; Microform Review, 17 (December 1988), 270-278.

3834.   Reilly, James M., et al. "When Clouds Obscure Silver Film's Lining IPI [Image Permanence Institute] Research Points to New Care and Handling for Silver Film," Inform, 2 (September 1988), 16-20. Presentation to the Conservation in Archives Symposium at the National Archives of Canada, May 1988.

3835.   Reilly, James M., Peter Z. Adelstein, and Douglas W. Nishimura. Preservation of Safety Film. Rochester: Rochester Institute of Technology, Image Permanence Institute, 1991. 103p. Final Report to the Office of Preservation, National Endowment for the Humanities; discusses the results of a long-term research project investigating deterioration processes of cellulose acetate film.

3836.   Reilly, James M., and Kaspars M. Cupriks. Sulfiding Protection for Silver Images. Rochester, NY: Image Permanence Institute, Rochester Institute of Technology, March 28, 1991. 176p.

3837.   Reilly, James M., and Dr. Franziska Frey. Recommendations for the Evaluation of Digital Images Produced From the Photographic, Microphotographic, and Various Paper Formats. Washington, DC: Library of Congress, American Memory Technical Document, June 1996. n.p.

3838.   Reilly, James M., Nora Kennedy, Donald Black, and Theodore Van Dam. "Image Structure and Deterioration in Albumen Prints," Photographic Science and Engineering, 28:4 (July-August 1984). The image structure and changes in image structure during deterioration of albumen prints were investigated by use of transmission electron microscopy.

3839.   Reilly, James M., Douglas W. Nishimura, and Edward Zinn. New
        Tools for Preservation: Assessing Long-Term Environmental Effects
        on Library and Archives Collections. Washington, DC:
        Commission on Preservation and Access, November 1995.
        35p. Introduces the concept of the Time Weighted Preservation
        Index (TWPI), which provides a new way to measure and quantify
        how temperature and humidity changes effect the preservation
        quality of storage environments for paper, photographic, and
        magnetic tape materials. Describes plans for a new preservation
        environment monitor instrument.

3840.   Reilly, James M., Douglas W. Nishimura, Kaspars M. Cupriks, and
        Peter Z. Adelstein. "Stability of Black-and-White Photographic
        Images, with Special Reference to Microfilm," Conservation in
        Archives. Paris: International Council on Archives, 1989, 117-127;
        reprinted in Abbey Newsletter, 12:5 (July 1988), 83-88; Microform
        Review, 17:5 (December 1988), 270-278; and as "When Clouds
        Obscure Silver Film's Lining: IPI Research Points to New Care and
        Handling for Silver Film," Inform, 2:8 (September 1988), 116-20,
        37-38. Discusses intrinsic causes of deterioration and describes the
        research conducted at the Image Permanence Institute, Rochester
        Institute of Technology, into protecting microfilm from oxidative
        attack through sulfiding. Paper originally presented at an
        International Symposium, Ottawa, Canada, May 1988.

3841.   Reilly, James M., Douglas W. Nishimura, Luis Pavao, and Peter Z.
        Adelstein. "Photographic Enclosures: Research and Specifications,"
        Restaurator, 10:3/4 (1989), 102-111. Reviews potentially harmful
        effects of storage enclosure materials and adhesives.

3842.   Reimer, Chris, and Milton Shefter. Fire Suppression Update: Paper
        Presented at the 135th SMPTE Technical Conference October 29-
        November 2, 1993, Los Angeles Convention Center, Los Angeles,
        CA., White Plains, NY: Society of Motion Picture and Television
        Engineers, Inc. 1993. 19 columns. Preprint No. 135-91.

3843.   Reimer, Derek. "Report on an Operational Test of the DRYPUR Film Cleaner," American Archivist, 48:1 (Winter 1985), 79-82. Review of a non-aqueous, frictionless film cleaning system.

3844.   Reinsch, Mary. "Library Disasters and Effective Staff Management," Conservation Administration News, 55 (October 1993), 4-5, 31-33. Reviews factors and steps to ensure effective disaster recovery. Bibliography.

3845.   Rempel, Siegfried. The Care of Photographs. Wheatley, England: Conservation Resources, 1987; New York: Nick Lyons, 1988, 192p. Test covering the preservation and conservation treatment of photographs. Bibliography.

3846.   Rempel, Siegfried. "Cold and Cool Vault Environments for the Storage of Historic Photographic Materials," Conservation Administration News, 38 (July 1989), 6-7,9. Description of the design of the cold storage facility for the photographic collection at the Canadian Centre for Architecture, Montreal.

3847.   Rempel, Siegfried. "Efficient Storage of Loose Photographic Prints," Conservation Notes, 10 (November 1984) 1-4. Describes a simple storage holder for photographic prints that will minimize damage during storage and handling.

3848.   Rempel, Siegfried. "Zcolite Molecular Traps and Their Use in Preventive Conservation," WAAC Newsletter (Western Association for Art Conservation), 18:1 (January 1996), 12-18. Discusses zcolites, naturally occurring alumninosilicote minerals and their ability to trap chemical pollutants; their use as molecular sieves to trap pollutants, especially with storage boxes for books and manuscripts, to create a fairly safe microenvironment. Preliminary research findings.

3849.   Rempel-Mroz, Terry. "The Book Snake," CBBAG Newsletter (Canadian Bookbinders and Book Artists Guild), (Autumn 1991), 16-17. Instructions for making a pliant tube, filled with granular material, to gently hold books open.

3850.   Rendell, Kenneth W. History Comes to Life: Collecting Historical Letters and Documents. Norman, OK: University of Oklahoma Press, 1995. 279p. Illus. General text for collectors with excellent brief information on the market, forgeries, and a brief note on preservation.

3851.   Rendell, Kenneth W. "Latter Day Taints: The Mark Hoffmann Case," Manuscripts, 40 (Winter 1988), 5-14. Expert discusses Hoffmann, his forgeries, and his undoing.

3852.   "Rep. Rose Holds Hearing on Security, Access to Stacks," LC Information Bulletin (Library of Congress), 52:13 (June 28, 1993), 269-275. Summary of congressional hearing on the closing of the Library of Congress stacks to the public following a series of thefts.

3853.   "Rescuing the Orphans: National Film Preservation Act Signed Into Law," LC Information Bulletin (Library of Congress), (October 7, 1996), 356,368. HR 1734 National Film Preservation Act of 1996.

3854.   Research Libraries Group, Inc. Final Report of the Archives Preservation Needs Assessment Field Test Conducted by Members of the Research Libraries Group, Inc. Mountain View, CA: The Group, 1994. 25p. Compiled by Laurie Abbott. Tool developed by the Commission on Preservation and Access and field tested by RLG.

3855.   Research Libraries Group, Inc. "RLG Brings Together National Experts to Revise Preservation Microfilming Guidelines," Research Libraries Group Newsletter, (April 13, 1990), 2p.

3856.   Research Libraries Group, Inc. "RLG Contributes to National Preservation Effort" Research Libraries Group Newsletter, 20 (Fall 1989), 3-6. Review of RLG's role in a national effort to microfilm brittle books, and an agenda for the future.

3857.   Research Libraries Group, Inc. "RLG Contributes to National Preservation Effort," RLG News, 20 (Summer/Fall 1986), 3-8. Summary of purpose, accomplishments, and plans for the

Research Libraries Group, with an interview with George Farr, National Endowment for the Humanities Preservation Office.

3858.   Research Libraries Group, Inc. RLG Preservation Manual, 2d ed. Stanford, CA: Research Libraries Group, 1986. Loose-leaf workbook. 1st ed. 1983. 141p. Manual on preservation of library materials with emphasis on preservation microfilming.

3859.   Research Libraries Group, Inc. RLG Preservation Union List, 3d ed. Stanford, CA: Research Libraries Group, October 1986. 16 microfiche; RLIN Register of Microform Masters. 4th ed. Mountain View, CA: Research Libraries Group, 1988. 46 microfiche. List of materials in microform as held by members of the Research Libraries Group.

3860.   Research Libraries Group, Inc. "RLG Taskforce Publishes Report on Preserving Digital Data," Information Today, 13:7 (July 1996), 35. Conclusions of the Taskforce on Archiving of Digital Information.

3861.   Research Libraries Group, Inc. Selecting Library and Archive Collections for Digital Reformatting: Proceedings from an RLG Symposium Held November 5-6, 1995 in Washington, DC, hosted by the Smithsonian Institution Libraries and the National Gallery of Art. Mountain View, CA: Research Libraries Group, 1996. 170p.

3862.   "Restorers in Massachusetts Give History a Future," New York Times, December 28, 1986, Sec. 1, page 34, Col. 1. Describes the work of the Northeast Documents Conservation Center.

3863.   Reyes, Patricia. "Conservation at the Pierpont Morgan Library," Conservation Administration News, 52 (January 1993), 12,28. Describes the library's conservation efforts and its new conservation facility.

3864.   Reynolds, Anne L. "Breaking Ground: Building Statewide Preservation Planning," n.p. June 28, 1992. 7p. Paper given by the Director of Wesley Free Public Library at ALA, June 28, 1992 entitled: "The Food Chain of Statewide Planning: Preservation in Massachusetts."

3865.   Reynolds, Anne L., Nancy C. Schrock, and Joanna Walsh. "Preservation: The Public Library Response," Library Journal, 114:3 (February 15, 1989), 128-132. Describes how the Wesley (MA) Public Library undertook a detailed survey of the condition of its collections and is using the information to obtain funding for repair and treatment, and a continuing collection maintenance program.

3866.   Rhode Island Council for the Preservation of Research Resources. Bricks and Mortar for the Mind: Statewide Preservation Program for Rhode Island. Providence, RI: Department of State Library Services, September 1992. 23p. A survey of state needs and recommendations for achieving a statewide preservation program.

3867.   Rhode Island Historical Records Advisory Board. Heritage 2001: A Strategic Plan. Providence, RI: Rhode Island Historical Records Advisory Board, 1996. 24p. Emphasis is on preserving the state's historical records.

3868.   "Rhode Island Preservation Conference News Brief," Newsletter of the RI Chapter of SLA, 14:1 (Fall 1990), 6-8. Conference held October 1, 1990, featured speakers Ann Russell and Pat Batten.

3869.   Rhode Island. Department of State Library Services. Disaster Readiness, Response and Recovery Manual. [Providence, RI, 1992], sections, with disk. Workbook with text on planning and recovery to assist individual institutions; list of services.

3870.   Rhodes, Barbara. "The Columbia Conservator Internship," Conservation Administration News, 28 (January 1987), 9, 28. Description of the Columbia internship program and the author's experience working with Nicholas Pickwood in England.

3871.   Rhodes, Barbara J. "Consolidation of Leather Book Bindings with Praline "N": Some Observations," Leather Conservation News, 10:1 (1994), 31-34. Describes theory, process, and rationale for consolidating fragile, deteriorating leather bookbindings using praline-N, and advantages and disadvantages.

3872.   Rhodes, Barbara J., comp. Hell & High-Water: A Disaster Information Sourcebook. New York: New York Metropolitan Reference and Research Agency, 1988. 58p. Compiled for a series of workshops on disaster planning and coping sponsored by METRO for its members. This sourcebook is not limited to the New York Metropolitan area. The text, by preservation specialists, provides basic information for the preparation of a disaster plan.

3873.   Rhodes, Barbara. "Hell's Own Brew: Home Book Renovation from 19th Century Receipts to Today's Kitchen Chemistry, Its Legacy for Preservation," Paper Conservator, 15 (1991), 59-70. Survey of the book care information available in domestic encyclopedias, bibliophilic handbooks, and library manuals, with implications for preservation. Bibliography.

3874.   Rhodes, Barbara J., comp. Hold Everything! A Storage and Housing Information Sourcebook for Libraries and Archives. New York: New York Metropolitan Reference and Research Agency, 1990. 63p. Provides considerable information on the housing and storage of library and archival materials; covers environmental control and monitoring; shelving and other storage furniture; protective enclosures; cleaning and moving of collections. List of suppliers and services.

3875.   Rhodes, Barbara J. "Preservation at the AMNH Library," Conservation Administration News, 44 (January 1991), 3, 27-29. Describes the program to preserve library and archival collections at the American Museum of Natural History, New York, and its book and paper conservation laboratory.

3876.   Rhodes, James B. "Conservation of Cartographic Materials," Information Bulletin (Western Association of Map Librarians), 23:3 (June 1992), 163-167. Describes the evolution in treatment of maps since the author joined the National Archives in the 1950s; notes problems that will be faced in dealing with electronic formats.

3877. Rhyne, Charles S. Computer Images for Research, Teaching and
Publication in Art History and Related Disciplines. Washington, DC:
Commission on Preservation and Access, January 1996. 12p. A
shorten version appears in Visual Resources, An International
Journal of Documentation, 11:3 (1995).

3878. Rhys-Lewis, Jonathan. "Re-Structuring and Reform: The Coming of
Age of Conservation in Berkshire," Journal of the Society of
Archivists, 13 (1992), 42-45. Transformation of an antiquated
country bindery into a modern conservation unit, performing services
from surveys to treatment of local records.

3879. Rice, James. "Managing Bibliographic Information with Personal
Desktop Technology." Academe, 75:4 (July-August 1989) 18-
21. Discusses the capabilities of online bibliographic tools, CD-
ROMs, online public access catalogs, and the electronic management
of all of these.

3880. Richards, Daniel T., and Lucretia W. McClure. "Selection for
Preservation: Considerations for the Health Sciences," Bulletin of the
Medical Library Association, 77:3 (July 1989), 284-292. Summary
of the literature on selection for preservation; describes the scholarly
record for biomedicine and presents criteria for selection for
preservation.

3881. Richards, David, and Edmund DiGiulio. "Film to Video Transfers:
Time for Change," SMPTE Journal (Society of Motion Picture and
Television Engineers), 103:2 (February 1994), 85-93. Reexamines
the process of converting motion-picture film images to television.

3882. Richardson, Bill. As the Book Crumbles. Montreal, Canada: CBC
Enterprises, 1990. 9 leaves. Brochure to accompany television
video.

3883. Richmond, Alison, ed. Modern Works, Modern Problems?
Conference Papers. [London]: Institute of Paper Conservation,
1994. 180p. Papers presented to the Institute of Paper Conservation
held at the Tate Gallery March 3-5, 1994.

3884.   Rieke, Judith. "Keepers of Maps: Some Advice on Preservation," Wilson Library Bulletin, 60:2 (October 1985), 25-27. Covers handling, storage, preservation, and lamination or encapsulation.

3885.   Rieke, Judith L., Suzanne Gyeszly, and Leslie Steele. "Preservation of Sheet Maps: Lamination or Encapsulation, A Durability Study," Bulletin. Geography and Map Division, Special Libraries Association, 138 (December 1984), 2-10. Results of a study indicating that encapsulation is a better option in high-use collections.

3886.   Rieken, Henry. "The Agony of Choice: Strategies for Preservation and Scholarship," Annual Report July 1, 1990-June 30, 1991. Washington, DC: Commission on Preservation and Access, 1991. 7-13.

3887.   Riemer, Janet T. "Preservation Internship at Cornell University," Conservation Administration News, 53 (April 1993), 6-7. Describes a six-month Mellon internship, rotating through the units of the Conservation Division.

3888.   Riemer, John J. "A Rising Sense of Urgency: The Years' Work in Serials, 1991," Library Resources and Technical Services, 26:3 (July 1992), 361-373. Review of the critical issues in serials librarianship during a time of evolving technology and escalating costs. Cites preservation concerns of theft, mutilation, and selection.

3889.   Riess, Hanley L. "Records Management in the Engineering and Construction Department of the New York City Transit Authority," International Journal of Micrographics and Optical Technology, 8:2 (1990), 91-96. Adoption of microfilm, rather than original drawings, ultimately making use of optical disk for the most frequently used drawings in conjunction with computerized records management.

3890.   Rightmeyer, Sandra P. "Disaster Planning or, the 'What Next' Attitude," New Jersey Libraries, 28:3 (Summer 1995), 3-5. Introduction to disaster planning. "Planning for disasters of any level can expedite the recovery and preserve the people involved"(5).

3891.   Riley, Gordon. "Managing Microcomputer Security: Policy and
         Practice Considerations for CD-ROM and Public Access
         Workstations," Library and Archival Security, 11:2 (1992), 1-
         22. Focus on computer viruses and preventive measures to be taken
         by librarians; urges that librarians play a more active role in planning
         for the introduction of computer technology.

3892.   Riley, Martha. "Archives: What to Save and How to Save It," The
         Public Garden, 4:2 (April 1989), 14-17. Organizing and preserving
         records and documentation.

3893.   Ringrose, Jayne. "Making Things Available," Book Collector, 39:1
         (Spring 1990), 55-73. Describes the collections and the function of
         the Manuscript Department at Cambridge University Library.
         Discusses the problems presented when researchers use original
         manuscripts, and the threat of photocopying.

3894.   Rising, Marsha H. "Local Records as a Resource for Genealogists,"
         Show-Me Libraries, 38:1/2 (October/November 1986), 11-15.

3895.   Ritzenthaler, Mary Lynn. "Archival Conservation in Local History
         Collections," Illinois Libraries, 64:5 (May 1983), 360-364. Strategies
         and priorities for preservation of local history collections in all
         media.

3896.   Ritzenthaler, Mary Lynn. Archives and Manuscripts: Conservation.
         Chicago, IL: Society of American Archivists, 1983. 144p. (Basic
         Manual Series). Practical text on archives preservation and
         conservation including definitions and philosophy, causes of
         deterioration, proper environment and storage, and treatment
         procedures. Bibliography; glossary.

3897.   Ritzenthaler, Mary Lynn. "The Challenge of Archival Preservation,"
         Conserving and Preserving Materials in Nonbook Formats. Urbana-
         Champaign: University of Illinois Graduate School of Library and
         Information Science (1991), 127-134. (Allerton Park Institute,
         30). Preservation of archival records through holdings maintenance,

appropriate storage environment and systems, and treatment to stabilize materials.

3898. Ritzenthaler, M. L. Preservation of Archival Records: Holdings Maintenance at the National Archives. Washington, DC: National Archives and Records Administration, 1990. 29p. (Technical Information Paper, 6; NTIS PB 90-168733/AS).

3899. Ritzenthaler, Mary Lynn. "Holdings Maintenance at the National Archives of the United States," Restaurator, 10:3/4 (1989), 151-159. Describes the program and its emphasis on staff training.

3900. Ritzenthaler, Mary Lynn. Preserving Archives and Manuscripts. Chicago, IL: Society of American Archivists, 1993. 225p. A basic text that describes safe, low technology, and inexpensive approaches to the handling, housing, and storage of archival collections.

3901. Ritzenthaler, Mary L. "Preserving Family Records," Prologue, (22:2) (Summer 1990), 204-207.

3902. Ritzenthaler, Mary Lynn. "Preservation of Photographic" (SAA Basic Archival Conservation Program Leaflet). Chicago, IL: Society of American Archivists, March 1984. 4 p. Covers causes of deterioration, environmental controls, references.

3903. Ritzenthaler, Mary L. "Storage Enclosures for Photographic Materials" (SAA Basic Archival Conservation Program Leaflet). Chicago, IL: Society of American Archivists, November 1984. 4 p. Outlines factors to consider, describes uses of paper and plastic enclosures, and provides storage guidelines and a suppliers list.

3904. Ritzenthaler, Mary Lynn, Gerald J. Munoff, and Margery S. Long. Archives and Manuscripts: Administration of Photographic Collections. Chicago, IL: Society of American Archivists, 1984. 173p. (SAA Basic Archival Series). Manual covering all aspects of management and conservation of historical photograph collections. Glossary; bibliography. Developed from a series of workshops.

3905.   Roads, Christopher. H. "Archivist's View of the Desiderata for Long Term Image Permanence," Journal of Photographic Science, 36 (1988), 118-119. Review of problems and hopes for laser disk technology for optical and audio recording.

3906.   Roads, Christopher H. Radio and Television Recordings as Archival Materials. Paris: The Congress, 1988. 10p. The 11th International Congress on Archives.

3907.   Roads, Christopher H., and Lloyd Stickells. "New Digital Processing Desk at the British Library National Sound Archive," Phonographic Bulletin, 45 (June 1986), 39-44.

3908.   Robbins, Louise S. Model Preservation Program for a Small University Library. Ada, OK: East Central University, 1990. 24 leaves. (Available from ERIC: ED 311912). Earlier Edition 1988 (Available from ERIC: ED 055143). Model preservation program for a university library serving less than 5,000 students, with disaster plan.

3909.   Robbins, Louise S. "Preservation in the Trenches," Conservation Administration News, 37 (April 1989), 1-2, 28-29. Case study dealing with a mold and fungal infestation of a library collection.

3910.   Roberts, Barbara O., et. al "An Account of the Conservation and Preservation Procedures Following a Fire at the Huntington Library and Art Gallery," Journal of the American Institute for Conservation, 27:1 (Spring 1988), 1-31. Report by the members of the conservation team on the actions taken in the aftermath of an electrical fire. Ron Tanks reports on the treatment of damaged books, p. 26.

3911.   Roberts, Barbara O. "Establishing a Disaster Prevention/Response Plan: An International Perspective and Assessment," Technology & Conservation, 4:3 (Winter 1992-93), 15-17, 35-36. Discusses current approaches to risk management and hazard mitigation. Review of the situation in the United States

3912.   Roberts, Barbara O. "Fire Suppression and Life Without Halon," WAAC Newsletter (Western Association for Art Conservation), 15:2

(May 1993), 31-33. Reports on the phase-out of halons used for fire suppression and problems that will need to be resolved.

3913.   Roberts, Brian A. "Herstellung der Einbanddecke," Newsletter of the Canadian Bookbinders and Artists Guild, 10:2 (Summer 1992), 10-14. Describes a technique used at the Lipposche Landesbibliothek, Detmold, for a case binding for books in general collections.

3914.   Roberts, F. X. "Bookmarks and the Abuse of Books," AB Bookman's Weekly (Antiquarian Bookman), 93:11 (March 14, 1994), 1125-1133. Discussion of early and contemporary bookmarks and how those objects can harm books.

3915.   Roberts, F.X. "Bookmarks and the Abuse of Books," AB 1996 Bookman's Yearbook (Antiquarian Bookman). 1996. 25-28p.

3916.   Roberts, Susanne F. Medieval Academy of America. Committee on Library Preservation. Summary Report, October 1990 - February 1994. Washington, DC, Commission on Preservation and Access, August 1994. 2p. Report on activities, including the raising of awareness of need for preservation and the location of collections and recommendations.

3917.   Roberts, Susanne F., compiler. Preservation Programs in Progress Covering Medieval Studies Material. New Haven, CT: Yale University Libraries, November, 1991. 31p.

3918.   Robertson, Guy. "Hoping for the Best, Preparing for the Worst: A Disaster Planner's Experience," Feliciter (Canadian Library Association), 41:2 (February 1995), 20-25. A consultant reviews disaster planning, risk analysis, and guidelines for response.

3919.   Robertson, Linda. "Microbial Growth in Starch," PIMA Magazine (Paper Industry Management Association), 76:6 (June 1994), 74-75. Explores cause and mechanism of starch degradation and how to control it.

3920.   Robin, Eleanor F. "Preservation Notes; Our Aging Microforms:
        Preservation and Maintenance," Mississippi Libraries, 59 (Spring
        1995), 12.

3921.   Robinson, James H., et al. Accident Investigation Board Report of
        Mishaps at the Deacidificaiton Pilot Plant. Greenbelt, MD: National
        Aeronautics and Space Administration, Goddard Space Flight
        Center, 1986. 167p.

3922.   Robinson, Lawrence S. "Establishing a Preservation Microfilming
        Program: The Library of Congress Experience," Microform Review,
        13:4 (Fall 1984), 239-244. Examines the Library's approach to
        selection and review of material for microfilming.

3923.   Robinson, Peter. The Digitization of Primary Textual Sources.
        Oxford: Office for Humanities Communication, 1993. 104p.

3924.   Robinson, Peter. The Transcription of Primary Textual Sources
        Using SGML. Oxford: Office for Humanities Communication, 1994.
        136p.

3925.   Roe, Kathleen. Statewide Access to Historical Records in New York
        State: Planning for the Future. Albany, NY: Division of External
        Programs, New York State Archives and Records Administration,
        State Education Department, 1995. 26p.

3926.   Rogers, Michael. "Chemicals in Deacidification Process Face Ban
        From EPA," Library Journal, 117:19 (November 15, 1992), 15. The
        EPA may ban the chemicals used in the Wei T'o method of paper
        deacidification.

3927.   Rogers, Michael. "RLG Task Force Will Study the Preservation of
        Digital Info," Library Journal, 120 (1 April 1995), 35.

3928.   Rogers, Rutherford D. "Library Preservation: Its Scope, History, and
        Importance," The Library Preservation Program: Models, Priorities,
        Possibilities, eds. Jan Merrill-Oldham and Merrily Smith. Chicago,
        IL: American Library Association, 1985, 7-18. History of the library
        profession's handling of the preservation problem and a look toward
        actions that are needed.

3929.   Romao, Paula, Adalio Alarcao, and Cesar Viana. "Human Saliva as
        a Cleaning Agent for Dirty Surfaces," Studies in Conservation, 35:3
        (August 1990), 153-155. Concludes that the alpha-amylase in saliva

accounts for its good cleaning ability. Discusses comparisons with other cleaning solvents.

3930.   Romer, Grant B. "Can We Afford to Exhibit Our Valued Photographs?" PictureScope, 32:4 (Winter 1987), 136-137. Cautionary note, urging monitoring programs and a change in the philosophy of exhibition.

3931.   Romer, Grant B. "Guidelines for the Administration and Care of Daguerreotype Collections," Conservation Administration News, 38 (July 1989), 4-5. Emphasizes need for protective housing and storage.

3932.   "Roof Leak Stirs Town to Action," Kemp Public Library, Wichita Falls, Texas, American Libraries, 26 (November 1995), 1000.

3933.   Rooks, Dana. "The Virtual Library, Pitfalls, Promises and Potential," Public Access Computer Systems Review, 4:4 (1993), 22-29.

3934.   Roosa, Mark S. " Audio Tape Transfer," College & Research Library News, 50 (February 1989), 312-313. Response to Levitt, Martin L. "A Case Study in Audio Tape Transfer," College & Research Library News, 49 (November 1988), 654-657. Points out the potential problems in using the new digital technology (RDAT) Rotary Digital Audio Tape) format for the audio preservation project Levitt describes at the Library of Congress.

3935.   Roosa, Mark. Care, Handling and Storage of Photographs. Washington, DC: Library of Congress, National Preservation Office, 1992. 8p. Compiled for the IFLA Core Programme: Preservation and Conservation.

3936.   Roosa, Mark. "Motion Picture Film Preservation 1970-1989: Selected Bibliography," Washington, DC: Library of Congress Preservation Office, January 1989. Fact Sheet from the Preservation Information Series.

3937.   Roosa, Mark. "Preservation and Reformatting Issues for Sound Recordings," Preservation Papers of the 1991 SAA Annual Conference, comp. Karen Garlick. Chicago: Society of American Archivists, 1992, 16-21. Reviews sound recording formats: cylinders, disks, and magnetic tape, physical nature and how each medium can be preserved.

3938. Roosa, Mark. "U.S. Promotes the Manufacture and Use of Permanent Paper," International Preservation News, 2 (January 1988), 1-3. Summary of actions taken in the United States to foster the use of permanent/durable papers.

3939. Roosa, Mark and Jane Gottlieb. Knowing the Score: Preserving Collections of Music. Canton, MA: Music Library Association, 1994. 92p.

3940. Roosens, Laurent. History of Photography: Bibliography of Books. London: Mansell, 1989-1999. Vol. 1 pages unknown, Vol. 2, 389p, Vol. 3, 464p. Vol. 4 is not yet published.

3941. Root, Nina J. "Decision Making for Collection Management," Collection Management, 7:1 (Spring 1985), 93-101. Advocates clear policies for selection, retention, preserving, or discarding materials.

3942. Root, Nina J. "Preserving and Maintaining Museum Library Collections," Museum Librarianship, ed. John C. Larson. Hamden, CT: Shoestring Press/Library Professional Publication, 1985. 51-66p. Covers housing and storage, environment, housekeeping, and security; processing, binding, mending, and restoration; stresses the need for a written preservation policy that is an integral part of the museum policy.

3943. Roper, Michael. "Advanced Technical Media: The Conservation and Storage of Audio-Visual and Machine-Readable Records," Journal of the Society of Archivists, 7:2 (October 1982), 106-112. Discusses methods for addressing the preservation of "modern media" and its uses for preserving and storing older materials.

3944. Roper, Michael. "Application of Microforms in the Management of Libraries and Archives," Proceedings of the Pan-African Conference on the Preservation and Conservation of Library an Archival Materials, Nairobi, Kenya, 21-25 June 1993. The Hague: IFLA (1995), 139-149. (IFLA Professional Publication 43). Microfilming for preservation; preparation, filming and processing, care and use, films; note on imaging technologies.

3945.   Roper, Michael. Directory of National Standards Relating to Archives Administration and Records Management: A RAMP Study. Paris: UNESCO, 1986. 59p. (PGI-86/WS/16). A guide to existing standards including those for security, collection management, and preservation.

3946.   Roper, Michael. Guidelines for the Preservation of Microforms. Paris: International Council on Archives, 1986. 18p. (ICA Studies, 2). Storage, handling, care of microfilm, from filming through access.

3947.   Roper, Michael. Planning, Equipping and Staffing an Archival Preservation and Conservation Service: A RAMP Study With Guidelines. Paris: UNESCO, 1989. 78p. (PGI-89/WS/4). Outlines principles of archival preservation and provides summaries of treatment options and planning considerations; for developing countries in tropical areas.

3948.   Roper, Michael. "Preservation Training for Non-Professional Staff & Users," In Safe Keeping, ed. Jennifer Thorp. Winchester, England, Hampshire Co. Library / Hampshire Archives Trust, (1988), 15-17. Care and handling of circulating collections; clear rules and good work habits.

3949.   Rose, Carolyn L., and Amparo R. de Torres, eds. Storage of Natural History Collections: Ideas and Practical Solutions. Pittsburgh, PA: Society for the Preservation of Natural History Collections, 1992. 346p. "A sampling of methods used for storage ... by professionals and volunteers." A useful collection of published materials.

3950.   Rose, Cordelia. Courier Speak: A Phrase Book for Couriers of Museum Objects. Washington, DC: Smithsonian Press, 1993. 271p. A book of terms in French, German, Spanish, Russian, Japanese, and English relating to all aspects of the transport of art objects, with discussion of the responsibilities of the courier. Only problem: Japanese characters and Cyrillic alphabet used, which would be a problem for those not familiar with them — a phonetic interpretation would have been helpful.

3951.   Rose, Ingrid, Yvonne Efremov, and Mihai Lupu. "Microscopic
         Examination of Works of Art on Paper During Solvent Treatments in
         Order to Determine Their Effects on Fibers and Pigments: A Joint
         American-Romanian Research Project," Preprints; ICOM Committee
         for Conservation 10th Triennial Meeting, ed. Janet Bridgland.
         Washington, DC: International Council of Museums, 1993, 469-
         473. Explores the effects of solvent treatment methods on fibers and
         pigments, and their behavior when paper is floated or immersed in
         water.

3952.   Rosenber, Diana. "Everyday Care of Books in Libraries,"
         Proceedings of the Pan-African Conference on the Preservation and
         Conservation of Library and Archival Materials, Nairobi, Kenya, 21-
         25 June 1993. The Hague: IFLA (1995), 77-87. (IFLA Professional
         Publication 43). Emphasizes collection maintenance in preservation;
         need to keep materials as long as possible. "Rules for handling
         books" included (85).

3953.   Rosenthal, Joseph A. "Preservation at the University of California
         Libraries at Berkeley," The Library Preservation Program: Models,
         Priorities, Possibilities, eds. Jan Merrill-Oldham and Merrily Smith.
         Chicago, IL: American Library Association, (1985), 27-33.

3954.   Ross, Lincoln. "Chemical Restoration of Albumen and Gelatin
         Printing-Out-Paper Prints," Journal of Imaging Science and
         Technology, 36 (January/February 1992), 56-59. Discusses a process
         that employs a gold chloride as a bleach, with experimental results.

3955.   Ross, Lincoln, "Experiments on the Image Stability of Resin-Coated
         Black and White Photographic Papers," PictureScope, 32:4 (Winter
         1987), 138-145. Results of an investigation to determine the long-
         term stability of these papers; demonstrates that resin-coated papers
         deteriorate.

3956.   Roth, Stacy. "The Care and Preservation of Sound Recordings,"
         Conservation Administration News, 23 (October 1985), 4-5, 24.
         Covers wax cylinders, phonodisks, magnetic tape, and compact disks.
         Bibliography.

510

3957. Rothenberg, Jeff. "Ensuring the Longevity of Digital Documents," Scientific American, 272:1 (January 1995), 42-47. Discusses the challenge of preserving information in impermanent electronic formats. Urges complete documentation of systems used. "The programs used to generate our digital documents, as well as all the systems software" (47).

3958. Rothstein, Edward. "The Distinction Between Copies and Originals Is Becoming Meaningless on the Web," New York Times (January 6, 1997. D5. In technology column.

3959. Rountree, Nancy C. Preservation of Books in Libraries. East Carolina University Department of Library and Information Studies, 1987. 29 leaves

3960. Rouyer, Philippe. "Humidity Control and the Preservation of Silver Gelatin Microfilm," Microform Review, 21:2 (Spring 1992), 74-76. Discusses the revised ANSI Standard IT9.11-1991: "Image Media-Processed Safety Film," covering long-term storage requirements for proper humidity controls for silver gelatin film.

3961. Rouyer, Philippe. "Micrographics Coming of Age: The Pre-War Period," Microform Review, 23:1 (Winter 1994), 12-14. A brief technical history of films used and early processing practices.

3962. Rouyer, Philippe. "Report on the Deuxièmes Journées Internationales d'Étude de l'ARSAG: Environnement et Conservation de l'Écrit, de l'Image et du Son, Paris, 16-20 Mai 1994," Microform Review, 23 (Fall 1994), 172-177.

3963. Rowe, Judith. "United States/National Archives and Records Administration Management, Preservation and Access from Electronic Records With Enduring Value: Response to Recommendations; 1991," Government Publications Review, 19 (May/June 1992), 304-306.

3964. Rowley, Gordon, and Ivan Hanthron. "Designing a Conservation Treatment Facility: Charting a Course into a Less Familiar Region of Planning for Libraries, (at Iowa State University)," The Journal of Academic Librarianship, 22 (March 1996), 97-104.

3965.   Rowoldt, Sandra. "The Greening of Archive Buildings: Natural Air-Conditioning in the Southern African Context," Janus; Revue Archivistique: Archival Review, 2 (1993), 36-41. Discussion of air-conditioning and how the thermodynamic equilibrium of medieval thick stone wall buildings might be replicated for energy-efficient environmental control.

3966.   Roy, Gillian. "The Camberwell Paper Conservation Degrees," Library Conservation News, 36 (July 1992), 2-3. Brief description of the structure, goals, and objectives of the BA (Honors) and MA courses.

3967.   Royal Geographical Society. The Storage and Conservation of Maps. London: Royal Geographical Society, 1984. 8p. Considers storage for heavily used and archival maps; emphasizes need for a good environment.

3968.   Rozsondai, Marianne. "The Preservation of Historical Evidence: The Need for Cooperation Between Librarians and Conservators," Conference on Book and Paper Conservation, 1990. Budapest, Hungary: Technical Association of Paper and Printing Industry/National Szechenyi Library, (1992), 42-47. Scholar's argument for retaining books as closely as possible to original condition.

3969.   Rude, Renee, and Robert Hauptman. "Theft, Dissimulation and Trespass: Some Observations on Security," Library and Archival Security, 12 (1993), 17-22. Review of literature; concludes that theft is inevitable but that librarians must take measures to curtail it.

3970.   Rule, Amy. "Security in Libraries, Archives, and Museums: A Selective Bibliography of Recent Titles," Conservation News, 13:23 (June-September 1993), 3-5. 51 citations; no annotations.

3971.   Rusch, Stacy J., and Robert F. Strohm. "To Preserve and Hand
         Down: Conservation at the Virginia Historical Society," Virginia
         Librarian, 41 (April/May/June 1995), 11-13.

3972.   Russell, Ann. "Comments on the Dedication of NEDCC's George
         Cunha Library," Conservation Administration News, 45 (April
         1991), 11, 24.

3973.   Russell, Ann. "Current Assets for Preservation: Remarks." In Invest
         in the American Collection, ed. Jane Sennett Long. Washington, DC:
         National Committee to Save America's Collections, 1987. 28-29.

3974.   Russell, Ann. "Effective Response by a Regional Conservation
         Center," Emergency Preparedness and Response, Washington, DC:
         National Institute for the Conservation of Cultural Property, 1991.
         10-13.

3975.   Russell, Ann. "Funding," National Conference on the Development
         of State-wide Preservation Programs, ed. Carolyn Clark Morrow.
         Washington, DC: Library of Congress, 1991. 75-76.

3976.   Russell, Ann. "Glasnost Meets Conservation," Museum News,
         (March/April 1996), 30-32, 73.

3977.   Russell, Ann. "If You Need to Ask What It Costs." In The Library
         Preservation Programs: Models, Priorities, Possibilities, eds. Jan
         Merrill-Oldham and Merrily Smith. Chicago, IL: American Library
         Association, 1985. 84-88.

3978.   Russell, Ann. "In My Opinion: Regional Conservation Centers Need
         Your Support," History News, 38:5 (May 1983), 28-29. Description
         of the activities at the Northeast Document Conservation Center and
         the need for more such centers.

3979.   Russell, Ann. "International Conference on Preservation Education
         for Librarians [Held at Austrian National Library]," IFLA Journal
         (International Federation of Library Associations and
         Institutions),12:3 (1986), 242-244.

3980.   Russell, Ann. "Introduction to Disaster Planning and Recovery,"
        The Book and Paper Annual 4, (1986), 129-138.

3981.   Russell, Ann. "The NEH and NEA Strengthen Culture," Boston
        Herald (July 31, 1995), 20.

3982.   Russell, Ann. "The Northeast Document Conservation Center,"
        CRIARL Newsletter (Consortium of Rhode Island Academic and
        Research Libraries), 2:1 (March 1983), 3-4.

3983.   Russell, Ann. "The Northeast Document Conservation Center:
        Cooperative Solutions to Preservation Problems of New Jersey
        Libraries," New Jersey Libraries, 18:1 (Spring 1985), 4-5. Describes
        the services offered to New Jersey libraries by NEDCC.

3984.   Russell, Ann. "An Ounce of Prevention: Preservation of Library
        Collections," Interservice Resources Management 13-15 October,
        1982. West Point, NY: USMA Library, 1984. 25-29. Proceedings of
        the 26th Military Librarians Workshop.

3985.   Russell, Ann. "Planning Guidelines for New Regional Conservation
        Centers," RTSD Newsletter (Resources and Technical Services
        Division), 12:4 (Fall 1987), 42-43.

3986.   Russell, Ann. "Preservation: A National Problem," Rhode Island
        Library Association Bulletin, 64:9 (September 1991), 1-2.

3987.   Russell, Ann. "Preservation Education for Librarians," Conservation
        Administration News, 26 (July 1986), 11-12.

3988.   Russell, Ann. "A Race Against Time: Preserving the Past,"
        Humanities, 12:2 (March/April1991), 34-37.

3989.   Russell, Ann. "Regional Conservation Centers Need Your Support,"
        History News (May 1983), 28-29.

3990.   Russell, Ann. "Regional Support to State-Wide Preservation
        Planning Programs," Preservation Papers of the 1990 SAA Annual
        Conference, comp. Karen Garlick. Chicago: Society of American

Archivists, 1991, 58-61. Describes regional centers, their relationships with state library agencies; how NEDCC has assisted in state wide planning, with emphasis on New York State.

3991. Russell, Ann. "Try, Try, Again With DEZ," Library Journal, 111:21 (January 1987), 8.

3992. Russell, Ann, Karen Motylewski, and Gay Tracy. "Northeast Document Conservation Center: A Leader in Preservation," Library Resources and Technical Services, 32:1 (January 1988), 43-47. History and mission of the regional center, with description of its services.

3993. Russell, Ann, and Mildred O'Connell. "A Regional Approach to Disaster Coping," Protecting Historic Architecture and Museum Collections from Natural Disasters, ed. Barclay G. Jones. London: Butterworths (1986), 369-389. Describes the services offered by the Northeast Document Conservation Center with advice on the salvage of damaged materials. Case study of the flooding of the Philips Academy, Andover, MA, library. Bibliography.

3994. Rust, Michael K., and Janice M. Kennedy. The Feasibility of Using Modified Atmospheres to Control Insect Pests in Museums. Marina del Rey, CA: Getty Conservation Institute, 1991. 136p. Final report of a study to test the life stages of 10 museum pests to determine when they reach 100% mortality in a humidified nitrogen environment.

3995. Rutherford, Christine. "Disaster: Planning, Preparation, Prevention," Public Libraries, 29:5 (September/October 1990), 271-276. Discusses need for contingency planning, causes of disasters, and preparing and implementing a plan.

3996. Rutherford, L. D. "Cryobibliotherapy," New Library Scene, 6:3 (June 1987), 1-10.

3997. Rutimann, Hans. "An International Perspective," Commission on Preservation and Access Annual Report for 1991-1992. Washington, DC: Commission on Preservation and Access, 1992. 9-17.

3998. Rutimann, Hans. The International Project. Washington, DC: Commission on Preservation and Access, 1989. 7p.

3999. Rutimann, Hans. The International Project 1992 Update: Including Microfilming Projects Abroad. Washington, DC: Commission on Preservation and Access, 1993. 23p.

4000. Rutimann, Hans. "Saving the Memory of Humanity: A Crisis in the World's Libraries," Logos, The Professional Journal for the Book World, 5:4 (January 1995), n.p.

4001. Rutimann, Hans. "New Technologies for Preservation: A Leap of Faith," Library Automation and Networking: New Tools for a New Identity, eds. H. Liebaers and M. Walakiers. Munich, Germany: Saur, (1991), 81-86. Recognizes the impermanence of electronic media; advocates continued conversion of materials into human-readable microfilm, and the creation and maintenance of the European Register of Microfilm Masters.

4002. Rutimann, Hans. Preservation and Access in China: Possibilities for Cooperation. Washington, DC: Commission on Preservation and Access, 1992. 19p. Summary of a visit by library and information specialists to China in 1991 to explore the feasibility of a project to enhance the quality of and access to select materials in Chinese libraries.

4003. Rutimann, Hans. "Saving the Memory of Humanity: A Crisis in the World's Libraries (Activities of organizations involved in preservation of printed materials)," Logos, 5:4 (1994), 166-171.

4004. Rutimann, Hans and Stuart Lynn. Computerization Project of the Archivo General de Indias, Seville, Spain. Washington, DC: Commission on Preservation and Access, 1993. 20p. Considers the technical and operational implications of large-scale image scanning by the means of the Seville Archives's massive project to reformat and make accessible the contents of 45 million documents and 7,000 maps and blueprints comprising the written heritage of Spain's 400 years in power in the Americas.

4005.   Rutimann, Hans, John Swan, Michael K. Tamada, Duane E. Webster,
         and William White. "Technologies for Preserving Library
         Collections" [Letters to the Editor]. The Chronicle of Higher
         Education (15 August 1990), B3-B4. Responses to an article's
         discussion of the use of microfilm versus newer, electronic media as
         a method for preserving research-library collections.

4006.   Rutledge, John and Willy Owen. "Changes in the Quality of Paper in
         French Books, 1860-1914: A Study of Selected Holdings at the
         Wilson Library, University of North Carolina," Library Resources
         and Technical Services, 27:2 (April/June 1983), 177-187. Results of a
         study to help predict the paper quality of French books in advance of
         publication.

4007.   Ruwell, Mary Elizabeth. "The Physical Preservation of
         Anthropological Records," Preserving the Anthropological Record.
         2d ed. Sydel Silverman and Nancy J. Parezo. NY: Wenner-Gren
         Foundation for Anthropological Research, (1995), 197-204.
         Challenge of preserving significant records in a variety of formats.
         Notes problem of paper, audiovisual materials, and especially
         computer-generated information. Guidelines for preservation.

4008.   Ruzicka, Glen. "Rare Book Conservation at the Library of
         Congress," Recent Advances in Leather Conservation, ed. Sonja
         Fogle. Washington, DC: Foundation of the American Institute for
         Conservation (1985), 84-86.

4009.   Ryckman, Pat. "Taming the Chimera: Preservation in a Public
         Library (in Charlotte and Mecklenburg County)," North Carolina
         Libraries, 52 (Spring 1994), 8-9.

4010.   Ryder, Sharon Lee. "Jacob's Pillow," Historic Preservation, 45:2
         (March-April 1993), 34-41, 96. Features the work of Preserve, Inc., a
         nonprofit organization run by Leslie Hansen Kopp, that educates and
         provides dance groups with guidance in preserving the
         documentation of their art.

Bibliography

4011.   Sable, Martin H. The Protection of the Library and Archive: An
        International Bibliography. New York: Haworth Press, 1984.
        183p. Includes sections on protection, disasters, security systems,
        legal concerns.

4012.   Sable, Martin H. "Warfare and the Library: An International
        Bibliography," Library and Archival Security, 7:1 (Spring 1985), 25-
        97. Annotated bibliography of materials an all aspects of the situation
        of libraries during and following armed conflict.

4013.   "A Safe Good Riddance ... To Protect Holdings from Pest Attack,"
        Technology & Conservation, 9:1 (Spring 1985), 5-11. Describes the
        protection program at the Shelburne (VT) Museum.

4014.   "Safeguarding the Nation's Scrapbook," DuPont Magazine, 79:5
        (September/October 1985), 1-3. Protection methods for government
        documents, encapsulation methods, and DuPont's Halon 1301 for
        fire suppression.

4015.   Saffady, William. Computer Storage Technologies: A Guide for
        Electronic Recordkeeping. Prairie Village, KS: ARMA International,
        1996. 108p.

4016.   Saffady, William. Digital Library Concepts and Technologies for the
        Management of Collections: An Analysis of Methods and Costs.
        Chicago, IL: American Library Association, 1995. 219-383. (Library
        Technology Reports 31:3).

4017.   Saffady, William. "Document Scanners for Microcomputers,"
        [Special Issue]. Library Computer Systems and Equipment Review,
        13 (January-June 1992), 2-78.

4018.   Saffady, William. "Electronic Document Imaging vs. CAR Systems,"
        Micrographics and Optical Equipment Review, 17 (1992), 3-75.

4019.   Saffady, William. Electronic Document Imaging: A State of the Art
        Report. Prairie Village, KS: ARMA International, 1996. 198p.

4020.   Saffady, William. Managing Electronic Records. Prairie Village, KS: ARMA International, 1992. 184p. Records management concepts and methodologies applied to electronic records. Emphasizes the impermanence of the media; advocates identification of information of permanent value, development of retention, and reformatting schedules.

4021.   Saffady, William. "Microcomputer-based Electronic Document Imaging Systems: a Survey of Characteristics and Capabilities," Micrographics and Optical Equipment Review, 17 (1992), 86-87.

4022.   Saffady, William. Micrographic Systems. 3d ed. Washington, DC: Association of Image and Information Managers, 1990. 242p. Covers basics of micrographic technology.

4023.   Saffady, William. Optical Disks Versus Magnetic Storage. Westport, CT: Meckler, 1990. 122p. Emphasizes similarities and differences in recording technology, storage capacity, performance characteristics and costs.

4024.   Saffady, William. Optical Disks for Data and Document Storage. Westport, CT: Meckler, 1986. 94p. Review of equipment and applications; physical characteristics of disks. Bibliography.

4025.   Saffady, William. Optical Disks vs. Micrographics. 2d ed., rev. Westport, CT: Meckler, 1993. 104p.; revision of Optical Disks vs. Micrographics as Document Storage and Retrieval Technologies, 1988. 106p. Comparative analysis of optical disk and micrographic technologies for document storage and retrieval.

4026.   Saffady, William. Optical Storage Technology: A State of the Art Review. Westport, CT: Meckler, 1989.

4027.   Saffady, William. Optical Storage Technology 1990-91: A State of the Art Review. Westport, CT: Meckler, 1990. 230p. State of the art survey of optical storage technology, concepts, product development and applications. Extensive bibliography.

4028.   Saffady, William. Optical Storage Technology 1992: A State of the Art Review. Westport, CT: Meckler, 1992. 219p.

4029.   Saffady, William. Optical Disks Systems for Record Management. 2d ed. Oxon Hill, MD: NISO Press, 1995. 48p. Designed as an introduction to optical storage technology, products, and applications. Discusses both storage technology and imaging systems.

4030.   Saffady, William. Stability, Care and Handling of Microforms, Magnetic Media and Optical Disks. Chicago, IL: American Library Association, 1991. 125p. (Library Technology Reports, 27:1). Survey of information (1990) on preservation; describes physical characteristics of each medium, recording technologies, scientific information about the stability of each medium, guidelines for care and handling. Bibliography, p. 89-116.

4031.   Saffady, William. Text Storage and Retrieval Systems: A Technology Survey and Product Directory. Westport, CT: Meckler, 1989. 131p. In three parts, discusses the history of electronic storage technology (including definitions, applications, advantages, and disadvantages); provides a survey of "features and functions" of storage and retrieval systems; and contains a directory of storage retrieval products. Extensive bibliography.

4032.   Safford, Herbert D., and Katherine F. Martin. "Collection Management: The Collection Development Alternative," Collection Development in College Libraries. Chicago, IL: American Library Association (1991), 97-103. Argues that collection development is driven by collection management and preservation decisions.

4033.   Safran, Franciska, and Barbara Vaughan. "The Charting of the Western New York Disaster Preparedness Network," Conservation Administration News, 61 (April 1995), 10-13. Describes an over ambitious attempt to develop a disaster recovery network, paid for by subscription by member libraries. Concludes that sufficient funds can make such plans a reality.

4034.   Sagraves, Barbara, and Jane Welsh. "The Acid-Free Paper Pledge
         Six Years Later," Abbey Newsletter, 19:4 (September 1995), 64;
         Alkaline Paper Advocate, 8:3 (October 1995) 39. Results of survey
         to determine what percentage of new acquisitions were printed on
         acid-free paper. Suggests that soft cover books are more likely to be
         printed on acidic paper.

4035.   Sagraves, Barbara. A Preservation Guide: Saving the Past and the
         Present for the Future. Salt Lake City, UT: Ancestry, 1995. 42p.

4036.   Sahli, Nancy. "Archival Preservation: A Current Perspective,"
         Perspectives (American Historical Association.), 29:2 (February
         1991), 22-23. Outlines the critical role played by the archivist in the
         preservation of the historical record, funding, and the problems
         presented by non-print media.

4037.   St. Laurent, Gilles. The Care and Handling of Recorded Sound
         Materials. Washington, DC: Commission on Preservation and
         Access, 1991. 14p.

4038.   St. Laurent, Gilles. "Cleaning and Storage of 78s and Cylinders,"
         Antique Phonograph News, 25 (September 1993), 3-6, 11-
         12. Describes the composition of various types of disks and
         cylinders, the best ways to clean and preserve them.

4039.   St. Laurent, Gilles. The Preservation of Recorded Sound Materials.
         Washington, DC: Commission on Preservation and Access, 1990.
         12p. Reprinted," ARSC Journal (Association of Recorded Sound
         Collections), 23:2 (Fall 1992), 144-156. Describes the physical
         nature of sound recordings and how they work. Discusses causes of
         deterioration and how to preserve them through proper storage and
         handling. Bibliography.

4040.   Saint Louis Regional Network. Preservation Committee. Saint Louis
         Area Resources for Library Conservation and Disaster Preparedness;
         A Bibliography and Checklist. Saint Louis, MO: Saint Louis
         Regional Network, 1986. 31p. Bibliography and area union list;
         model disaster preparedness plan.

4041.   Sakar, N. N. "Preservation of Material in Original Formats:
        Techniques and Methods," Planning Modernization and Preservation
        Programs for South Asian Libraries, ed. Kalpana Dasgupta. Calcutta,
        India: National Library, (1992), 56-65. Describes scientific methods
        for preservation and conservation, preventive and curative,
        commonly used in Indian libraries and archives.

4042.   Salmon, Lynn G., and Glen R. Cass. "The Fading of Artists'
        Colorants by Exposure to Atmospheric Nitric Acid," Studies in
        Conservation, 38:2 (May 1993), 73-91. Charts. Report of a study to
        assess the fading of works of art when exposed to nitric acid in the
        indoor atmosphere.

4043.   Salter, Charles A., and Jeffrey L. Salter. On the Frontlines: Coping
        With the Library's Problem Patrons. Englewood, CO: Libraries
        Unlimited, 1988. 170p. Describes types and causes of patron mental
        illness likely to disrupt the library; offers tactics and resources for
        help for librarians.

4044.   Salter, David. Pulp and Paper Primer. Atlanta, GA: TAPPI Press,
        1983. 50p. Useful introduction to the paper industry.

4045.   Salter, Laurie. "Requirements for Preservation Storage of Microform
        Masters and Development of a National Strategy," Preservation
        Microfilming: Does It Have a Future? Canberra: National Library
        of Australia (1995), 164-169. Focus on proper storage; standards,
        bibliographic control. Need for a national strategy for the
        preservation of microfilm masters.

4046.   Samuel, John G. "Preservation of Palm-Leaf Manuscripts in Tamil,"
        IFLA Journal (International Federation of Library Associations and
        Institutions), 20:3 (1994), 294-305.

4047.   Samulski, Peter. "The 1981 Flooding of the Muenster University
        Library," Conservation Administration News, 17 (April 1984), 7-
        8,11. Discusses cause, salvage procedures, and consequences of the
        flood.

4048.   Sanders, Howard J. "Hazardous Wastes in Academic Labs," Chemical and Engineering News (February 3, 1986), 21-31. Examines current practices of disposing of hazardous wastes, including organic solvent waste routinely generated in conservation labs.

4049.   Sanders, Jennifer A. An Evaluation of Photo CD's Resolving Power in Scanning Various-Speed Films for Archival Purposes. Thesis, Rochester, NY, Rochester Institute of Technology, 1996. 36 leaves.

4050.   Sanders, S. "Effects of CO2 Fumigation on pH," Preprints. International Council of Museums Committee on Conservation, 8th Triennial Meeting, Sydney, Australia, 6-11 September 1987, Vol. 3. Marina del Rey, CA: Getty Conservation Institute (1987), 945-946.

4051.   Sandwith, Hermoine and Sheila Stainton, comps. The National Trust Manual of Housekeeping. London: National Trust/Penguin, 1984, 1985. 273p. A practical guide with a focus on preventive preservation and environmental controls. Chapter 2 deals specifically with books and documents.

4052.   Saretzky, Gary. "Additional Research on the Effects of Electrostatic Copying in Photographs," Conservation Administration News, 23 (October 1985), 8. Concludes that electrostatic copiers produce minimal, if any density changes, and offers cautionary guidance pending further results.

4053.   Saretzky, Gary. "Bibliographies and Databases for Research on the Preservation of Aural and Graphic Records," PictureScope, 31:4 (Winter 1985), 119-121.

4054.   Saretzky, Gary. "Conservation of Photographs," Conservation Administration News, 24 (January 1986), 19.

4055.   Saretzky, Gary. "The Effects of Electrostatic Copying on Modern Photographs," Book and Paper Annual, 4 (1986), reprinted in PictureScope, 32:2 (Spring 1986), 64-65.

4056.   Saretzky, Gary. "The Nikety Split Method to Repair Record Album Jackets," Abbey Newsletter, 19:2 (May 1995), 44; reprinted with corrections, 19:3 (August 1995), 59. A repair technique for circulating collections.

4057.   Saretzky, Gary. "In Pursuit of the Permanent Print: Recent Developments in Archival Processing," Industrial Photography, 34:4 (April 1985), 33-34; reprinted with correction in Cable Release, 24:5 (January 1986). A cursory update defining "archival print" and recommending fiber-based paper over resin coated, double weight over single, and specific darkroom processing procedures for proper fixing, washing, toning, and drying.

4058.   Saretzky, Gary. "Photographic Conservation," Conservation Administration News, 33 (April 1988), 4-5; 34 (July 1988), 4, 9; 35 (October 1988), 4-5.

4059.   Saretzky, Gary D. "Recent Photographic Conservation and Preservation Literature," PictureScope, 32:4 (Winter 1987), 117-132. Selective review of the literature, with emphasis on publications of 1982-1984.

4060.   Saretzky, Gary. "The Region V Preservation Committee, 1988-1992," New Jersey Libraries, 26:3 (Summer 1993), 13-14. Describes a region's initiatives to promote preservation awareness in libraries.

4061.   Saretzky, Gary. "Research on the Effects of Electrostatic Copying on Photographs," Conservation Administration News, 19 (October 1984), 21.

4062.   Sarkar, N. N. "A New Sterilization Process and Standardization of Lethal Doses for Insect Eggs by Vacuum Fumigation Chamber," Conservation of Cultural Property in India, 18-20 (1985-1987), 86-89. Describes process and experiments to ascertain the lethal does of ethylene oxide and carbon dioxide for different stages of the insect life cycle.

4063.   Sasamori, Katsunosuke. "Preservation and Conservation of Microform Collections and Audiovisual Materials," Research

Libraries - Yesterday, Today and Tomorrow, ed. William J. Welsh. Westport, CT: Greenwood Press, 1993, 325-333. (Contributions in Librarianship and Information Science, 77). Preservation concerns; causes of damage and deterioration of film; storage; restoration treatments.

4064.   Satchell, Stephen. "Protecting Your Data from Fire, Flood, and Pestilence," Info World (September 5, 1988), 57-66.

4065.   Saulmon, Sharon A. "Book Security System Use and Costs in Southwest Public Libraries," Library and Archival Security, 8:3/4 (Fall/Winter 1988), 25-35. Survey of large public libraries to determine use of security systems; results indicate that libraries need individually tailored security programs to meet local needs.

4066.   Saulter, R. Disaster Planning and Recovery for Archival Materials in Rhode Island. Providence, RI: Brown University, 1984. 34p. Developed for Rhode Island institutions for the protection of their materials.

4067.   Saunders, David. "Environmental Monitoring: An Expensive Luxury," Environmental Monitoring and Control. Dundee, Scotland: Scottish Society for Conservation and Restoration, (1989), 1-5. Reviews systems for environmental monitoring.

4068.   Saunders, David. "Ultra-Violet Absorbing Films," Conservation News (UK Institute for Conservation), 47 (March 1992), 40-41. Describes and evaluates self-adhesive films to protect against ultraviolet light.

4069.   Saunders, Margaret. "How a Library Picked Up the Pieces After IRA Blast," Library Association Record, 95:2 (February 1993), 100-101. Case study of salvage and recovery of computers and computerized data; emphasizes importance of regular back-up of data.

4070.   Saurs, Laura. "Preservation of U.S. Government Documents: The 1909 Checklist and Beyond," Proceedings of the 4th Annual Federal Depository Library Conference, 11-14 April 1995, Arlington, VA.

Washington, DC: GPO, (1995), 20-26. How to preserve government publications through a program of boxing, cleaning, and basic collections care, such as proper shelving and handling by staff and patrons, good housekeeping practices, and emergency planning. Newark Public Library's program, begun with a grant from the NJSL.

4071. Savage, Noelle. "Facing Up To Library Security," Wilson Library Bulletin, 58:8 (April 1984), 562-564. Report on a planning seminar held by the New York Metropolitan Reference and Resource Agency (METRO) in 1984, which led to the publication of Hell and High Water. Summary of security, including legal issues and general recommendations.

4072. Sawka, Barbara. "Audio Preservation in the United States: A Report on the ARSC/AAA Planning Study," Midwestern Archivist, 16:1 (1991), 5-10. Summarizes the current state of audio preservation in the United States; discusses how the Association of Sound Recording Archivists is addressing the issues.

4073. Sawicki, Malgorzata. "Picture Frame Conservation or ... Repairing," AICCM Bull. (Australia Institute for the Conservation of Cultural Material), 20:2 (1995), 17-25. Addresses concerns at the art gallery of New South Wales regarding picture frame preservation; case studies address philosophy addressed by conservator, curator, and artist's intent.

4074. Sayre, Edward V., et al., eds. Materials Issues in Art and Archaeology: Symposium Held April 6-8, 1988, Reno, Nevada, USA. Pittsburgh, PA: Materials Research Society, 1988. 321p. Sponsored by the Getty Conservation Institute and co-sponsored by the Conservation Analytical Laboratory of the Smithsonian.

4075. Scaggs, Samuel B. "The U.S. Government Printing Office Perspective on the Use of Alkaline Paper," Paper Preservation: Current Issues and Recent Developments. Atlanta, GA: TAPPI Press, (1990), 96-100. Describes the papers used by the Government Printing Office; and their different uses; paper presented at the Paper Preservation Symposium, Washington, DC, 1988.

4076.   Schachter, June. "Conservation in British Libraries: Impressions of a
         Recent Visitor from Canada," Library Conservation News, 41/42
         (Winter 1993 / Spring 1994), 4-5. Report on NPD activities and
         training, and activities at Oxford.

4077.   Schaefer, Karl R. "The Great Foxing Debate," Conservation
         Administration News, 53 (April 1993), 4-5, 31. Traces discussion of
         the foxing phenomenon and research into its causes. Bibliography.

4078.   Schaeffer, Terry Trosper, Mary T. Baker, Victoria Blythe-Hill, and
         Dianne van der Reyden. "Effects of Aqueous Light Bleaching on the
         Subsequent Aging of Paper," Journal of the American Institute of
         Conservation, 31:3 (Fall-Winter 1992), 289-311.

4079.   Schaeffer, Terry T., and Victoria Blythe-Hill. "Preparation of
         Reproducibly Stained Paper Samples for Conservation Research,"
         Book and Paper Group Annual, 12 (1993), 44-49. Describes the
         production of reducibly stained papers for research in paper
         conservation.

4080.   Schaeffer, Terry T. "A Semiquantitive Essay Based on the TAPPI
         Method for Monitoring Changes in Gelatin Content of Paper due to
         Treatments," Journal of the American Institute of Conservation, 34:2
         (Summer 1995), 95-105. Uses a procedure somewhat differently
         from the TAPPI method to determine if it can be used to determined
         gelatin loss in paper when it is washed. Notes implications of loss
         for conservation.

4081.   Schaub, George. "Protection and Preservation . . . How to Make
         Your Images Outlast You," Darkroom Photography, 7:7 (November
         1985), 54-55. Discussed are factors effecting photographs, including
         environmental concerns, processing methods, and storage methods.

4082.   Schenck, Thomas. "Magnetic Tape Care, Storage and Error
         Recovery," Library Hi Tech, 2:4 (1984), 51-54. Discusses the
         technology of magnetic tape and its physical problems, with
         suggestions for preservation.

4083.   Schene, Michael G., ed. "Preservation Technology," Public Historian, 13:3 (Summer 1991), 180p. (entire issue). Issue focuses on methodologies, techniques, and materials utilized to survey, evaluate, preserve, and manage cultural resources.

4084.   Scherdin, Mary Jane. "The Halo Effect: Psychological Deterrence of Electronic Security Systems," Information Technology and Libraries, 5:3 (September 1986), 232-235.

4085.   Scherdin, Mary Jane. "Security Systems Protect Audiovisual Materials," Library and Archival Security, 11:1 (1991), 23-34. Describes security systems that will not damage audiovisual materials.

4086.   Schewe, Donald B. "The Jimmy Carter Library," Government Information Quarterly, 6:3 (1989), 237-246. Reviews past approaches to the preservation of presidential papers and the development of presidential libraries.

4087.   Schilling, Michael R., and William S. Ginelli. "The Effects of Relative Humidity Changes on Dead Sea Scrolls Parchment Samples," Preprints. ICOM Committee on Conservation, 10th Triennial Meeting, ed. Janet Bridgland. Washington, DC: International Council of Museums, (1993), 50-56. Studies the dimensional response of the parchment to changes in relative humidity.

4088.   Schiro, Joseph. "Preservation at the National Library of Malta," COMLA Newsletter (Commonwealth Library Association), 61 (September 1988), 2-3.

4089.   Schlefer, Elaine. "The 1991 Guild of Book Workers Standards Seminar," Guild of Book Workers Newsletter, 80 (February 1992), 5-9. Report and summary of presentations: Hedi Kyle, "Special Enclosures;" David Bourbeau, "Mastering the Refinements of Case Bookbindings;" Don Glaister, "Building Design and Unusual Materials;" Don Etherington, "Conservation Treatments."

4090. Schlefer, Elaine Reidy. "One-Piece Post Binding with Interior Hinges," Book and Paper Group Annual, 13 (1994), 47-48. Post-binding structure suitable for encapsulated texts.

4091. Schlefer, Elaine. "Wrappers with Magnetic Closures," Abbey Newsletter, 10:5 (October 1986), 74-76.

4092. Schmeisser, Jorg. "Printed to Last?" AICCM Bulletin (Australian Institute for the Conservation of Cultural Material), 11:4 (December 1985), 5-16. Discusses the impermanence of materials with emphasis on printed matter; how to select it for use and preserve it.

4093. Schmidt, J. David. "Freeze Drying of Historic/Cultural Properties: A Valuable Process in Restoration and Documentation," Technology & Conservation, 9:1 (Spring 1985), 20-26. Describes the development of the technique and discusses factors to be considered when purchasing a system for freeze-drying.

4094. Schmude, Karl G. "Can Library Collections Survive? The Problem of Paper Deterioration," Australian Library Journal, 33:1 (February 1984), 15-22. Reviews the problem of the physical deterioration of library collections and the efforts to resolve them in U.S. institutions. Discusses Australia's needs and efforts.

4095. Schmude, Karl G. "Conservation Developments in Australia," Conservation Administration News, 27 (October 1986), 5-6. Discusses current developments, including disaster planning and the establishment of a State Conservation Centre in Adelaide.

4096. Schmude, Karl G. "The Politics and Management of Preservation Planning," IFLA Journal (International Federation of Library Associations and Institutions), 16:3 (1990), 332-225. Discusses reasons why preservation has not been a more critical component in library management and outlines goals to heighten the profile of preservation.

4097. Schmude, Karl. "Why We Need Permanent Paper," Australian Lithographer, Printer and Packager, 18:106 (April-May 1987), 32-33. Reviews the brittle book problem and how it can be addressed worldwide; excerpted as "Facing Collective Amnesia," Incite 8:12 (July 17, 1987), 9.

4098.   Schnare, Robert E. Jr. "Incendiary Gilt: When Your Labels Go Up in Smoke," Conservation Administration News, 36 (January 1989), 1-2. Describes the procedure used to save bound volumes that lost their spine labels due to the removal of soot after a fire.

4099.   Schnare, Robert E. Jr. "Library Preservation Activities in Russia, the Ukraine, and Hungary," Conservation Administration News, 54 (July 1993), 1-3, 9, 13, 29. Report about preservation activities in Eastern Europe.

4100.   Schnare, Robert E. Jr. "Preservation and White House Conference on Library and Information Services," Conservation Administration News, 48 (January 1992), 6-7, 26. Report on the strategies, pre-planning, and efforts of the conference, resulting in the recommendation that Congress articulate and implement policies for the preservation of the nation's information resources.

4101.   Schnare, Robert. E. Jr. "Preservation Legislation in the Federal Sector Since the White House Conference in 1991," White House Conference on Library and Information Science Taskforce Report on Legislation Since the White House Conference in 1991. WHCLIST, 1997. 40p.

4102.   Schnare, Robert. E. Jr. "A Selected Resource List for Preservation," Washington, DC: FLICC, 1990. 2p. Compiled for the Federal Library and Information Center pre-White House Conference, November 26-27, 1990.

4103.   Schnare, Robert E. Jr., and Marilyn D. Curtis. "Fire Aftermath and the Recovery Process," Conservation Administration News, 35 (October 1988), 1-2, 22. Describes the recovery process used after a fire at the Naval War College on October 5, 1986. Emphasizes the need to define terminology in writing a contract for cleaning after the fire.

4104.   Schoenthaler, Jean and Masato Okinaka. "Report: Mass Deacidification for Paper-Based Collections," New Jersey Library Association Preservation Section Newsletter, 12:2 (Winter 1996), 7-9. This is a report of the two-hour video conference in October 1996 from Pittsburgh, sponsored by William Morris College and the Pittsburgh Regional Library Center.

4105.   Schofer, R. E. Cost Comparison of Selected Alternatives for Preserving Historic Pension Files. Gaithersburg, MD: National Bureau of Standards, Center for Applied Mathematics, 1986. 59p. (NBSIR 86-3335) Cost-benefit study of microfilming of records versus storing original paper in environmentally sound conditions.

4106.   "Scholars Fear Millions of Books Will Turn to Dust," Christian Science Monitor (January 4, 1995), 2A.

4107.   Scholtz, James C. Developing and Maintaining Video Collections in Libraries. Santa Barbara, CA: ABC-Clio, 1989. 196p. Text on organization and management of collections in the public library; discusses physical nature of videotapes and their care, storage, and handling.

4108.   Scholtz, James C. Video Acquisitions and Cataloging: A Handbook. Westport, CT: Greenwood, 1995. 184p. Conservation and Preservation issues are included in the chapter on information services (chapter 5).

4109.   Schoolly-West, R. F. ""It's Time for a Revolution," The American Philatelist, 101:3 (March 1987), 246-249. The author urges protection of stamp collections from the ravages of chemical and physical damage.

4110.   Schoolly-West, R. F. "Philatelic Conservation; Part l: Historical Background and Nature of the Materials; Part 2: Hazards to Materials: Prevention and Care," Library Conservation News, 13 (October l986), 4-5,8; 14 (January 1987), 4-5,9. Part l describes the different materials and processes used to "stamp" mail and their problems for the conservator. Part 2 discusses physical and atmospheric damage, chemical effects, and adhesives.

4111.　Schoonmaker, Dina B. "Oberlin College Libraries: A History of Preservation," Preservation Issues (Ohio State Library), 3 (January 1991), 1. Describes the development of the preservation program at Oberlin College library, its outreach program, and, briefly, conservation.

4112.　Schoonmaker, Dina B. "Preservation and Conservation at the Oberlin College Library," Proceedings of the Association of College and Research Libraries Third National Conference. Chicago, IL: American Library Association (1984), 286-289. Case study of a program run by a paraprofessional.

4113.　Schorzman, Terri A., ed. A Practical Introduction to Videohistory: The Smithsonian Institution and Alfred P. Sloan Foundation Experiment. Malabar, FL: Krieger Publications, 1993. 243p. Report of a program to create videohistories of leaders in science and technology. Archival requirements and preservation concerns are addressed, with some cost data.

4114.　Schou, Henning, and Mark Nizette. "The Effects of Temperature and Humidity on Motion Picture Film," Archiving the Audio-Visual Heritage. Rushton, England: FIAF/UNESCO, (1992), 133-138. Preliminary report on research at the National Film and Sound Archive, Australia, to address problems and causes of film deterioration.

4115.　Schrock, Nancy Carlson. "Preservation Factors in the Appraisal of Architectural Records," American Archivist, 59 (Spring 1996), 206-213.

4116.　Schrock, John Richard. "List of Insect Pests by Material or Apparent Damage," AS Guide to Museum Pest Control. Washington, DC: Association of Systematics Collections (1988), 99-107. Includes pests that attack books.

4117.　Schrock, Nancy Carlson. "AIC Initiates Archives Effort," Conservation Administration News, 39 (October 1989), 10,

32. Describes the initiative by the American Institute for Conservation to preserve conservator's treatment records.

4118. Schrock, Nancy Carlson. "Images of New England: Documenting the Built Environment," American Archivist, 50:4 (Fall 1987), 474-498. Review of this history of architecture in New England and its documentation. Differing approaches to the preservation of the documentation are discussed and regional efforts to preserve architectural documentation are suggested.

4119. Schrock, Nancy Carlson. "The Peabody & Stearns Architectural Collection: Assessing Conservation Needs," Conservation of Historic and Artistic Works on Paper. Ottawa: Canadian Conservation Institute, 1994, 3-9. (Symposium 88). Discusses survey methodology and findings. A goal of the project was to define criteria for linking knowledge of condition and costs of treatment with an assessment of intellectual value.

4120. Schrock, Nancy Carlson. "Preservation in the MIT Libraries: A Collection Management Approach," Preservation and Conservation of Sci-Tech Materials. New York: Haworth Press, 1987, 49-68. Describes the integration of preservation into collection management at the MIT libraries.

4121. Schrock, Nancy Carlson. "Preserving Conservator's Records," Art Documentation, 8 (Winter 1989), 195-196. Describes the initiative by the American Institute for Conservation to serve as a clearinghouse for the preservation of conservator's treatment records.

4122. Schrock, Nancy Carlson, and Mary Campbell Cooper. Records in Architectural Offices: Suggestions for the Organization, Storage, and Conservation of Architectural Office Records. 3d rev. ed. Cambridge, MA: Massachusetts Committee for the Preservation of Architectural Records, June 1992. 31p. and appendices. Introduction to records management and preservation for architectural firms, with guidelines for implementing programs.

4123. Schroeder, Don, and Gary Lare. Audiovisual Equipment and Materials: A Basic Repair and Maintenance Manual. Vol. 2.

Metuchen, NJ: Scarecrow Press, 1989. 133p. Illus. Reviews basic
service concepts and covers the repair of equipment found in
libraries. Provides information on the causes of damage and
instructions for simple repairs.

4124.   Schueller, Dietrich. "The Ethics of Preservation, Restoration, and
Re-Issues of Historical Sound Recordings," Journal of the Audio
Engineering Society, 39:12 (December 1991), 1014-1017. Reviews
considerations for re-recording historical materials, problems, and
questions.

4125.   Schueller, Dietrich. "Format-Specific Preservation Costs: A First
Attempt," Phonographic Bulletin, 54 (July 1989), 15-19.

4126.   Schueller, Dietrich. "Handling, Storage and Preservation of Sound
Recordings Under Tropical and Subtropical Climatic Conditions,"
Restaurator, 7:1 (1986), 14-21. Discusses the preservation of sound
recordings and the potential of the compact disk as a storage
medium. Cautions against blind application of new technology.

4127.   Schueller, Dietrich. "Sound Tapes and the 'Vinegar Syndrome,'"
Phonographic Bulletin, 54 (July 1989), 29-31. Describes a syndrome
that affects motion picture films with a cellulose triacetate base and
may also affect acetate-based audio tapes. Recommends procedures
for examining tapes, handling damaged tapes, and preventing future
damage.

4128.   Schueller, Dietrich. "Towards the Automated 'Eternal' Sound
Archive," Archiving the Audio-Visual Heritage. Rushton, England:
FIAF/UNESCO, (1992), 106-110. Observes that it is possible to
develop a permanent sound archive if everyone will agree on this
goal and how best to achieve it.

4129.   Schuff, Fred. "Automated Backup: Intelligent Selection Reduces
Risk and Resources," Disaster Recovery Journal, 3:3 (July-
September 1990), 6-7, 32. Disaster planning should include constant
back-up of computerized data; management needs to determine how
to achieve this.

Bibliography

4130. Schultz, Constance B. "Like a Fireball in the Night..." Perspectives, (January 1989), 5-8. Details a disaster in a faculty office and provides suggestions on how to avoid similar problems in the future.

4131. Schumm, Robert W. "Patterns of Periodical Mutilation at Three Academic Libraries," Serials Librarian, 21:4 (1992), 147-156. Results of a survey indicating that popular journals are more likely to be mutilated.

4132. Schur, Susan E. "Conservation Technology: A Review of Past and Current Nomenclature of Materials," Technology & Conservation, 9:1 (Spring 1985), 34-40. Compilation to provide information on changes that have occurred in the names of commonly referred to materials use in art and conservation.

4133. Schur, Susan E. "Disaster Prevention, Response and Recovery: A Selected Bibliography," Technology and Conservation, 2:4 (Summer 1994), 21-31; 3:5 (Fall 1995), 23-34. References from 1965-1992. No annotations.

4134. Schur, Susan E. Disaster, Response and Recovery: Principles and Procedures for Protecting and Preserving Historic/Cultural Properties and Collections: A Select Bibliography. Boston, MA: Technology & Conservation, 1992. 33p. Comprehensive bibliography, English language; no annotations.

4135. Schuyler, Michael. "Systems Librarians and Automation Review," Computers in Libraries, 10:3 (March 1990), 47-51. Discusses computer and printer obsolescence, and the restoration of damaged computer records.

4136. Schwab, Richard N. "The History of the Book and the Proton Milliprobe: An Application of the PIXE Technique of Analysis," Library Trends, 36:1 (Summer 1987), 53-84. Describes the proton milliprobe as a tool to help analyze pigments, papers, and parchments.

4137. Schwalberg, Bob, Henry Wilhelm, and Carol Brower. "Going, Going, Gone!" Popular Photography, 97:6 (June 1990), 37-49, 60. A summary of the research undertaken by Henry Wilhelm to identify the problems that cause color film to fade and deteriorate. Wilhelm is profiled.

4138.   Schwanke, Harriet. "Hurricane Andrew: Community Information Service Disaster Relief - CIS to the Rescue," Southeastern Librarian, 44:2 (Summer 1994), 69-71. How Dade County, FL, handled the crisis when many of its libraries were destroyed or damaged by Hurricane Andrew; notes how people turned to the library when in crisis.

4139.   Schwartz, Candy, and Peter Hernon. Records Management and the Library: Issues and Practices. Norwood, NJ: Ablex, 1993. 313p. Reviews standard records management practice, storage, and preservation. Chapter 8, "Vital Records and Disaster Management," deals specifically with disaster planning.

4140.   Schwartz, Stanley. Electronic Document and Optical Storage Systems for Local Governments: An Introduction. Albany: University of the State of New York, State Education Department, State Archives and Records Administration, Local Government Records Services, 1993. 19p.

4141.   Schwartz, Stanley. Optical Storage Systems for Records and Information Management: An Overview, Recommendations and Guidelines for Local Governments. Albany: University of the State of New York, State Education Department, State Archives and Records Administration, Local Government Records Services, 1993. 11p.

4142.   Schwartz, Werner. The European Register of Microfilm Masters: Supporting International Cooperation. Washington, DC: Commission on Preservation and Access, May 1995. 8p.; reprinted in Microform Review, 24:4 (Fall 1995), 173-177. Briefly presents EROMM's history and operations, and discusses its role in preserving documents.

4143.   Schwartz, Werner. Preservation by Reformatting: Microfilming and Alternative Technology, Göottingen: SUB, 1995. 208p. Papers presented at a conference held in Hannover, Germany, 1993, in German, English, and French.

4144. Schwerdt, Peter. "The German Mass Deacidification Process: Recent Developments and the Realization at Die Deutsche Bibliothek," Preprints: ICOM Committee for Conservation 10th Triennial Meeting, ed. Janet Bridgland. Washington, DC: International Council of Museums (1993), 479-484. Describes the new mass deacidification system developed in Germany. Bibliography.

4145. Schwerdt, Peter. Mass Deacidification Procedures for Libraries and Archives: State of Development and Perspectives for Implementation in the Federal Republic of Germany. Washington, DC: Commission on Preservation and Access, September 1989. 11p. Summarizes the research on deacidification conducted by the Battelle Institute, Frankfurt, Germany. Commission on Preservation and Access. The study is a translation of an article originally published in German based upon a study done by the Battelle Institute for the West German Library. DEZ, Wei T'o, and the French magnesium methyl carbonate process are studied (News, Library Journal, September 1, p. 118).

4146. Schwerdt, Peter. "A New Pilot Plant for Mass Deacidification in Germany," Conference on Book and Paper Conservation, 1990. Budapest, Hungary: Technical Association of Paper and Printing Industry/National Szechenyi Library, (1992), 115-125. Describes the DB-Battelle system and compares it to other systems. Illus.

4147. Schwirthlich, Anne-Marie. "Arsenals of Democratic Accountability and Continuity: Microfilming Archives," Preservation Microfilming: Does It Have a Future? Canberra: National Library of Australia, (1995), 107-110. Places microfilming in the context of the archival record, preserving information and making it accessible.

4148. Schwirthlich, Anne-Marie. "The Australian War Memorials 1914-1918 War Unit War Diaries Project," Preservation Microfilming: Does It Have a Future? Canberra: National Library of Australia, (1995), 70-76. Describes microfilming project, funding, management, quality control, storage. Case study.

4149.   Scott, Marianne. "Mass Deacidification at the National Library of
        Canada," <u>Library and Archival Security</u>, 8:3/4 (Fall/Winter 1988),
        49-52. Describes the use of Wei T'o mass deacidification system for
        preservation of books; discusses benefits and limitations of system.

4150.   Scott, Marianne. "Mass Deacidification at the National Library of
        Canada," <u>Restaurator</u>, 8:2/3 (1987), 94-98. Report on the first four
        year experience with the Wei T'o Nonacqueous Book
        Deacidification System; describes pre-selection that is necessary.

4151.   Scott, Marianne. "Preservation of the Past for the Future," <u>National
        Library News</u> (Canada), 27:2 (February 1995), 5-6.
        English/French. Overview of the National Library's efforts to
        develop a national strategy and implement preservation activities in
        Canada. (Adopted from keynote address at the National Meeting of
        Canadian Preservation Specialists, October 31-November 1, 1994).

4152.   Scott, Mary W. "Digital Imagery: Here Today, But What About
        Tomorrow?" <u>Preserving Geoscience Imagery</u>, ed. Louise S. Zipp.
        Alexandria, VA: Geoscience Information Society, (1993), 1-4.
        (Proceedings, 23). Summarizes the various problems and presents an
        overview of current status of preservation of cartographic digital
        data.

4153.   Scott, Sally J. "Method for Evaluating Preservation Needs of
        Oversized Illustrations in Geology Theses," <u>Geological Societies and
        Information Transfer</u>, ed. Marie Dvorzak. Alexandria, VA:
        Geoscience Information Society, 1991, 137-146. Discusses the
        findings of a study to determine the extent and nature of the problem.
        Discusses suggestions for the preservation of this material, including
        physical treatment and digitization.

4154.   Scott, Sally J. "Preservation Needs of Oversized Illustrations in
        Geology Master's Theses." <u>Library Resources and Technical
        Services</u>, 37:1 (January 1993), 73-85. Study to determine the extent
        and nature of preservation needs. Use was a primary factor in
        deterioration; quality of paper was not measured. Some suggestions

for preservation are discussed, including physical treatment and digitization. Reformatting of materials recommended.

4155.	Scott, Vicky, ed. Scottish Conservation Directory, 1987-1988: A General Guide to Business in Scotland Specializing in the Care, Maintenance, Repair, Consolidation and Restoration of ... Books and Paper .... Edinburgh, Scotland: Conservation Bureau, 1987. 208p. Includes sources for preservation and conservation of library and archival materials.

4156.	Scott, William E. "The Future of Paper: The U.S. Paper Industry Returns to Alkaline Papermaking as It Enters Its 4th Century," Preservation Issues (State Library of Ohio), 8 (June 1992), 2. Traces the history of papermaking and the acid paper problem. Discusses issues surrounding conversion to alkaline papermaking.

4157.	Scott, William E. Properties of Paper: An Introduction. Atlanta, GA: TAPPI Press, 1989. 170p. Basic text on the characteristics of paper.

4158.	Scottish Society for Conservation and Restoration. Exhibitions and Conservation: Pre-Prints of the Conference Held at the Royal College of Physicians, Edinburgh, 21st-22nd April 1994. Edinburgh: Scottish Society for Conservation and Restoration, 1994. 136p.

4159.	Scottish Society for Conservation and Restoration. Environmental Monitoring and Control. Dundee, Scotland: Scottish Society for Conservation and Restoration, 1989. 104p. Preprints of the papers presented at a conference jointly sponsored by SSCR and the Museums Association to highlight recent developments in monitoring and controlling the museum environment. A variety of systems and their applications are described.

4160.	Scriber, B.W. "Perishable Newsprint as Peril to Record of Current Events," Alkaline Paper Advocate, 7:4 (November 1994), 34-35.

4161.	Seal, Robert A. "Insurance for Libraries," Conservation Administration News, 19 (October 1984), 8-9; 20; (January 1985),

10-11, 26. Overview of the subject of insurance for library collections, with a selective bibliography.

4162.   Seal, Robert A. "Risk Management for Libraries," American Library Association Yearbook, 1989. Chicago, IL: American Library Association (1989), 218-221. Outlines elements of risk management: insurance, disaster planning, theft and security, health and safety, liability, and personnel matters.

4163.   Seaton, D. G. "Conservation in High-Use Collections," Interlending and Document Supply, 11:1 (January 1983), 7-11. Describes the chemical characteristics of books; causes of deterioration; proper housing. Notes need for careful management of circulating collections, including interlibrary loans.

4164.   Sebera, Donald K. "The Effects of Strengthening and Deacidification on Paper Permanence; Part 1: Some Fundamental Considerations," Book and Paper Annual, 9 (1990), 65-117. Examines the efficacy of strengthening and deacidification processes on the permanence and durability of paper.

4165.   Sebera, Donald K. "A Graphical Representation of the Relationship of Environmental Conditions to the Permanence of Hygroscopic Materials and Composites," Conservation in Archives. Paris: International Council on Archives, (1989), 51-75. Describes the isoperm method to graph the relationship of environmental factors to the permanence of hygroscopic materials, such as paper. Paper presented at an international symposium, Ottawa, Canada, May 1988.

4166.   Sebera, Donald K. Isoperms: An Environmental Management Tool. Washington, DC: Commission on Preservation and Access, June 1994. 16p. Describes a technique that quantifies the effect of temperature and humidity on anticipated life expectancy of paper-based collections.

4167.   Sebera, Donald K., and Peter G. Sparks. "The Library of Congress DEZ Gas Diffusion Deacidification Process," Paper Preservation: Current Issues and Recent Developments. Atlanta, GA: TAPPI Press, 1990, 116-126. Describes the diethyl zinc mass deacidification process developed by the Library of Congress highlighting the objectives it was designed to meet.

4168.   Sedar Senghor, Leopold. "The Written Word..." Courier, 5 (May 1989), 4. The fragility of the material on which manuscripts are written, the inadequacy of the resources allocated to national libraries, and lack of facilities for training specialists are all problems of modern civilization. The problems of preservation are discussed.

4169.   Sedinger, Theresa. "Preservation and Conservation in the School Library," Book Report, 10 (January-February 1992), 34. Note on preserving collections; retarding deterioration through environmental controls.

4170.   Segal, Judith. "New Techniques for the Application of Enzymes," Conservation of Historic and Artistic Works on Paper. Ottawa: Canadian Conservation Institute, 1994, 205-208. (Symposium 88). Discusses choice of enzymes, methods of application, sources of heat, inhibitors, and poisons, and the possibility of using enzymes in a partially aqueous medium.

4171.   Seiler, Lauren H. "The Concept of the Book in the Age of Digital Electronic Medium," Library Software Review (January/February 1992) 19-29. Discusses the impact of the digital electronic medium (D.E.M.) on our concept of the book and how the role of the book will change over time. Also discusses databases, reactive media, interactive media, virtual reality in terms of where technology is going.

4172.   Seip, John T. "Laser Rot," The Perfect Vision, 1:1 (1986/87), 35-42. Discusses the controversy over laser rot, a proposed cause of laser failure, and the reactions of consumers and manufacturers.

4173.   Selth, Jeff. "The Object of His Devotion," College and Research Libraries News, 52:11 (December 1991), 712-715. Tale of a theft of books from University of California-Riverside over a 20 year period by a perpetual graduate student well known to the staff.

4174. Selwitz, Charles. Cellulose Nitrate in Conservation. Marina del Rey, CA: Getty Conservation Institute, 1988. 108p. Examines the chemistry of deterioration of cellulose nitrate, and describes circumstances in which there is sufficient stability to permit its use.

4175. "Seminar Examines Preservation, Disaster Planning." FLICC Newsletter (Federal Library Information Center Committee) (Spring 1990), p. 6-7,11. See also FEDLINK Technical Notes (Federal Library Network), (May 1990), 4-5.

4176. Seminar on Preventive Conservation in Latin America, August 19-20, 1993, in Washington, DC. Washington, DC: APOYO, 1993. 43 leaves. Title also in Spanish.

4177. Semke, L. K. "Effects of Juvenile Pine Fibers on Craft Paper Properties," Proceedings of the Symposium on Utilization of the Changing Wood Resources in the Southern United States. June 12-14 1984. Raleigh: North Carolina State University (1984), 160-177. The review of data on non-bleachable and bleachable craft pulps of loblolly and slash pine from geographically distinct areas, and of the properties of papers prepared from these pulps, showed that replacement of mature fibers by juvenile fibers increased burst strength, tensile strength, fold endurance, and apparent density but reduced tear strength. Increasing the density of juvenile wood tended to reverse these trends, reflecting the increased fiber wall thickness with increased density.

4178. Senadeera, N. T. S. A. "Microfilming for the Safety of Library Materials," Information Development, 7:4 (October 1991), 208-212. Microfilming to preserve deteriorated academic library materials; the activities at the University of Peradeniya, Sri Lanca, initiated to preserve materials in case of terrorist attack.

4179. "Senator [Claiborne] Pell Seeks Legislation on Acid-Free Paper," Abbey Newsletter, 12:8 (December 1988), 126-127, 129. Pell's statement and resolution, reprinted from the Congressional Record, October 11, p. S15477, "to establish a national policy on permanent papers," with editorial comment by Ellen McCrady urging standards and the use of alkaline paper.

4180. Seton, Rosemary. The Preservation and Administration of Private Archives: A RAMP Study. Paris: UNESCO, (1984), 68p. Recommends, on the basis of an international survey of nongovernmental archives, a program of action on national, regional, and international levels to promote both preservation and access.

4181. Setos, Andrew G. "Electronic Recapture of Past Sights ... To Preserve the Reel Record," Technology and Conservation, 4:93 (Winter 1992-93), 5-10. Describes the effort by Fox News to preserve its film archive by transferring images by high resolution digitizing of the film.

4182. Severson, Douglas G. "Alfred Stieglitz's Palladium Photographs and Their Treatment by Edward Steichen," Journal of the American Institute of Conservation, 34:1 (Spring 1995), 1-10. Describes historical and experimental investigations to examine the nature of the treatments by Steichen between 1946-1950 to refresh the prints of Stieglitz. Observed effects of the treatments are described and the possible nature of Steichen's procedures is hypothesized.

4183. Shackelton, Cheryl Ann. Preserving African-American Religious Documents: A Guide for Churches and Other Religious Institutions. New York: Schomberg Center for Research in Black Culture, 1990. 6p. Basic guide covering environment, storage, and disaster planning.

4184. Shackelton, Cheryl Ann. "Preserving Black Culture at the Schomberg Center," New York Public Library Research Library Notes, 3:2 (Spring 1991), 17-19. Describes a project to reformat books in the general collection and deacidify rare books, and to survey the collection to oversee conservation treatment.

4185. Shahani, Chandru J. " Preservation Research at the Library of Congress: Recent Progress and Future Trends," Directory: Information Sources on Scientific Research Related to the Preservation of Books, Paper and Adhesives. Washington, DC: Commission on Preservation and Access, 1990, 17-28. Describes the status of several preservation projects, recent progress in the diethyl zinc deacidification program, and other projects.

4186. Shahani, Chandru J., and Robert E. McComb. "A Clarification of Specifications for Archival Paper," TAPPI Journal (Technical Association for the Pulp and Paper Industry), 70:9 (September 1987), 128. Demonstrates that alkaline sized and coated paper loses fold endurance as a result of aging much faster than tear resistance or tensile strength.

4187. Shahani, Chandru J., Frank H. Hengemihle, and Norman Weberg. "The Effect of Fluctuations in Relative Humidity on Library and Archival Materials and Their Aging within Contained Environments," Proceedings of the Pan-African Conference on the Preservation and Conservation of Library and Archival Materials, Nairobi, Kenya, 21-25 June 1993. The Hague: IFLA, (1995), 61-70. (IFLA Professional Publication 43). Notes need for appropriate storage environment as first requirement for preservation. Reviews research at LC.

4188. Shahani, Chandru, and Frank H. Hengemihle. "Effect of Some Deacidification Agents on Copper-Catalyzed Deacidification of Paper," Conservation of Historic and Artistic Works on Paper; Proceedings of a Conference, Ottawa, Canada, 3 to 7 October, 1988, ed. Helen D. Burgess. Ottawa: 1994, 263-268. Report in a continuing investigation of deacidification processes of the degradative effect of trace concentrations of metal contaminants commonly found in paper.

4189. Shahani, Chandru J., Frank H. Hengemihle, and Norman Weberg. "The Effect of Variation in Relative Humidity on the Accelerated Aging of Paper," Historic Textile and Paper Materials II: Conservation and Characterization, eds. Howard L. Needles and S. Haig Zeronian. Washington, DC: American Chemical society, (1989), 63-80. (ACS Symposium Series, 410). Study of the effect of fluctuations in RH on the degradation of paper-based materials under accelerated aging conditions. Demonstrates that cycling does cause deterioration, but the book structure itself may offer some protection.

4190.   Shahani, Chandru J., Frank Hengemihle, and Norman Weberg.
         "Options in Preservation of Library and Archive Collections,"
         Planning Modernization and Preservation Programs for South Asian
         Libraries. Calcutta, India: National Library, 1992, 36-55. Discusses
         the effects of environmental conditions on paper-based collections,
         with emphasis on cycling of RH and the use of micro environments.

4191.   Shahani, Chandru J., and William K. Wilson. "Preservation of
         Libraries and Archives," American Scientist, 75:3 (May/June 1987),
         240-251. Brief history of papermaking; discussion of the problem
         with paper and causes of its deterioration; conservator's role in
         preservation and treatments. Bibliography.

4192.   Shapkina, Larissa B., et al. "New Technologies From the USSR:
         Restoring Book Paper and Drying Water Wetted Books." Book and
         Paper Group Annual, 10 (1991), 216-224.

4193.   Shapkina, Larissa B., et al. "Restoring Book Paper and Drying
         Books After a Disaster," Restaurator, 13:2 (1992), 47-57. Describes
         the treatment of fire and smoke-damaged books from the 1988 fire at
         the Academy of Science, St. Petersburg, including dry leaf-casting
         and manual freeze drying.

4194.   Sharpe, Jerry. "Work at Library Adding Volumes to Her Forte,
         Preserving Documents," Pittsburgh Press (March 2, 1990),
         A2. Describes the book preservation techniques of Sally Buchanan,
         the assistant director for Preservation Services and Cooperative
         Planning at the University of Pittsburgh's Hillman Library.

4195.   Sharpe, John Lawrence. "The Earliest Bindings with Wooden Board
         Covers: The Coptic Contribution to Binding Construction,"
         Preprints. International Conference on Conservation and Restoration
         of Archive and Library Materials, Erice, Italy, April 22-29, 1996,
         Rome: Istituto Centrale per la Patologia del Libro, 2, 1996, 381-400.
         Illus. of bad quality. Survey of extant multi-quiro codexes from
         Egypt, especially those without boards. "The techniques examined in
         these volumes become the foundation of construction techniques seen
         in later Coptic bindings of the C8+9, Byzantine Islamic

construction in the Middle Ages, and the structures preserved in the latest Ethiopic mss" (381-abstr.).

4196. Shaw, Felicity. "The National Library of Bhutan: Development and Conservation of a Specialist Himalayan Collection," Microform Review, 23:4 (Fall 1994), 161-168. Discusses preservation initiatives including the inventorying and selective microfilming of rare materials; the preparation and carving of wood blocks for printing, and conservation measures taken, including fumigation of both manuscripts and printing blocks in the collection.

4197. Shaw, Susan D., and Monona Rossol. Overexposure: Health Hazards in Photography. Rev. ed. New York: Allworth Press, 1991. 320p. Reviews photographic process and materials, current research, laws and regulations affecting the use of and disposal of darkroom chemicals.

4198. Sheehan, Paul. "A Condition Survey of Books in Trinity College Library Dublin," Libri, 40:4 (1990), 306-317. Report on the methods and results of a survey of book papers, 1840-1939.

4199. Sheehy, Carolyn A., ed. Managing Performing Arts Collections in Academic and Public Libraries. Westport, CT: Greenwood, 1994. 225p. Chapters, written by specialists, deal with preservation and conservation concerns.

4200. Sheldon, Ted P., and Gordon O. Hendrickson. "Emergency Management and Academic Library Resources," Special Libraries, 72:2 (Spring 1987), 93-99. Describes the role that academic and research libraries can play when disaster strikes.

4201. Shelly, Marjorie. The Care and Handling of Art Objects Practices in The Metropolitan Museum of Art. New York: Metropolitan Museum of Art/Harry N. Abrams, 1987. 102p. Illus. Simple instructions for dealing with the entire spectrum of museum objects, including works on paper, books, and photographs. Glossary and reading list.

4202. Shelton, Deborah. "The Big Chill," Conservation News (Arizona Paper and Photograph Conservation Group), 14:3 (September 1994), 1,4. Description of a project to identify and store nitrate negative film, bagged in a freezer.

4203. Shenton, Helen. "Book Conservation at the Victoria & Albert Museum, London," Preservation of Library Materials (Australian Library and Information Association Special Interest Group on the Preservation of Library Materials), 11 (November 1993), 13-23. Describes the book conservation program and activities; survey needs, 1985, and institutional response.

4204. Shenton, Helen. "The Conservation of the Heal Textile Sample Books at the Victoria and Albert Museum," Paper Conservator, 14 (1990), 5-16; reprinted in Paper and Textiles: The Common Ground. Glasgow, Scotland: Scottish Society for Conservation and Restoration, (1991), 71-82. Case study of conservation of six volumes of textiles on embrittled sheets of paper.

4205. Shenton, Helen. "The History and Conservation of Tortoiseshell Bookbindings," Conference on Book and Paper Conservation, 1990. Budapest, Hungary: Technical Association of Paper and Printing Industry/National Szechenyi Library (1992), 174-187. Brief history of properties and use. Causes and types of damage are described; treatment report on one volume. Illus.

4206. Shenton, Helen. "The Use of Vacuum Packing in Australia," V&A Conservation Journal (Victoria and Albert Museum), 9 (October 1993), 14-17. Describes the shrink-wrapping of newspapers after microfilming to preserve the originals; shrink-wrapping of rare books for storage; other potential applications.

4207. Shep, Robert L. Cleaning, Repairing and Caring for Books: A Practical Manual. 4th ed. Guildford, UK: Robert Joseph, 1991. 148p. A manual for amateurs; treatments not recommended for valuable collections.

4208. Shepard, Elizabeth., ed. Electronic Records in the New Millennium: Managing Documents for Business and Government. A Window to the Future: Papers From a Conference on Managing Electronic Information 20-24 June 1994. London: School of Library, Archive and Information Studies, University College, London, 1995. 66p. Examines the nature of electronic records, the central role these have come to play in modern life, and what records professionals and their administrative superiors must do to ensure the usefulness of these records into the indefinite future.

4209.   Shepard, Jocelyn. comp. Disaster Resources Information Directory for Pennsylvania Libraries and Archives. Pittsburgh, PA: Pittsburgh Regional Library Center, 1994. 47p.

4210.   Shepard, Richard F. "Expanding Archives: Library of Congress Is Not Just Books." New York Times, The Arts, (September 3, 1990), 11, 14. Describes the Motion Picture, Broadcast and Recorded Sound Division and its preservation efforts.

4211.   Shepilova, Irina G. "Aspects of the Policies and Technologies for Ensuring the Preservation of Documents," Restaurator, 10:3/4 (1989), 112-122. Construction norms and standards for the preservation of materials in archive repositories in the USSR.

4212.   Shepilova, Irina G., and Adrienne G. Thomas, eds. Main Principles of Fire Protection in Libraries and Archives. Paris: UNESCO, 1992. (PGI-92/WS/14). Analysis of fire hazards in libraries and archives; highlighting the most effective methods of extinguishing fires, with a minimum of damage to materials.

4213.   Sherbine, Karen. Libraries and Archives: An Overview of Risk and Loss Prevention. Chicago, IL: Society of American Archivists and Inland Marine Underwriters Association, 1994. 35p. Designed to help archivists and librarians better understand the fundamental issues involved in insuring their collections.

4214.   Sherrington, Jo. "From Here to Posterity: The Scottish Film Archive," Scottish Libraries, 48 (November/December 1994), 16-17.

4215. Sherwood, Arlyn. "Map Preservation: An Overview," Illinois Libraries, 67:8 (October 1985), 705-711. Care and storage of maps; preservation and conservation options.

4216. Shipp, E. R. "At Risk: Treasures of the Law," New York Times, (September 9, 1988), B1, B5. An article on the deteriorating collection in the Library of the Bar of the City of New York, and the need to microfilm its collection for preservation.

4217. Shoaf, Eric C. "Preservation: Meeting a Need," CRIARL Newsletter (Consortium of Rhode Island Academic and Research Libraries), 13:3 (November 1994), 1-2, 6. Discusses brittle books and reformatting options used at Brown University.

4218. Shoumatoff, Alex. "A Reporter at Large: The Mountain of Names," New Yorker, 61:12 (May 13, 1985), 51-101. Describes the Mormon genealogy preservation project and the storage facility for microfilm at Granite Mountain, Utah.

4219. Shrinath, A., J. T. Szewczak, and I. Jerry Bowen. "A Review of Ink-Removal Techniques in Current Deinking Technology," TAPPI Journal (Technical Association for the Pulp and Paper Industry), 74:7 (July 1991), 85-93. Description of nine deinking methods, their chemicals and characteristics; description of principle printing and imaging methods; section on ink-removal strategies.

4220. Shults, Charlene H. "Preservation and Access Through Imaging Technologies: The MIMS 3000," New Jersey Libraries, 27:4 (Summer 1994), 20-22. Describes explorations of the potential of the MIMS 3000 imaging system for access and to see if it could be used to reformat brittle books.

4221. Shults, Terrance G. "Library Security: A Selected Bibliography," New Jersey Libraries, 27:4 (Fall 1994), 20-22. Selection of current (1990+) articles, including computer security and vendors.

4222. Silberman, Richard M. "A Mandate for Change in the Library Environment," Library Administration and Management, 7:3 (Summer 1993), 145-152. Identifies indoor pollutants in the library

Bibliography

environment that endanger humans and collections; presents a
strategy for managing the situation.

4223. Silcox, Tinsley. "Reading About Preservation: Bibliographic
Essay," Fontes Artis Musicae, 41 (July/September 1994), 300-302.

4224. Silver, Jeremy and Lloyd Stickells. "Preserving Sound Recordings at
the British Library National Sound Archive," Library Conservation
News, 13 (October 1986), 1-3. Describes preservation efforts and
technologies.

4225. Silverman, Randy. "Connoisseurship of 19th and Early 20th Century
Publishers' Bookbindings," Preprints. International Conference on
Conservation and Restoration of Archive and Library Materials,
Erice, Italy, April 22-29, 1996, Rome: Istituto Centrale per la
Patologia del Libro, 1, 1996, 249-264. Traces the development of
19th-and 20th-century publishers' binding styles and demonstrates the
rapid loss of these books from U.S. libraries.

4226. Silverman, Randy. "Pamphlet Binders and Their Use in Research
Libraries," Archival Products News, 1:1 (Spring 1992), 2-
3. Describes the damage caused by traditional pamphlet binders and
offers criteria for durable, non-destructive binders.

4227. Silverman, Randy, and Maria Grandinette. The Changing Role of
Book Repair in ARL Libraries. Washington, DC: Association of
Research Libraries, Office of Management Studies, April 1993.
127p. (SPEC KIT 190).

4228. Silverman, Randy and Robert Speiser. "Buying Publishers' Trade
Paperbacks Versus Hardbacks: A Preventive Conservation Strategy
for Research Libraries," Advances in Librarianship, 16 (1992), 127-
151. Review of book and binding production; analysis of cost-
benefits when purchasing books in paper covers.

4229. Silverman, Sydel and Nancy J. Parezo, ed. Preserving the
Anthropological Record. New York: Wenner-Gren Foundation,
1992. 140p., 2d edition, 1995. 254p. Basic guide covering
disposition and preservation of field records in all media. Problems

550

of preservation and access of electronic records are thoroughly discussed.

4230.   Simmons, Alan. "On the Job: Los Angeles," Firehouse (August 1986), 33-35, 67. Describes the 1986 Los Angeles Public Library fire and the factors that contributed to its spread and control.

4231.   Simmons, Peter. "CD-ROM: New Papyrus or Passing Fad?" Microcomputers for Information Management, 6:4 (December 1989), 293-301; reprinted, with addenda, in Canadian CD-ROM News, 5:2 1990), 1-3. Reviews advantages and disadvantages of CD-ROM, noting lack of standards for the media and uncertainty about its role in the future. Addenda notes continued lack of standardization and stability.

4232.   Simon, Barry. "How Lossy Compression Shrinks Image Files," PC Magazine (Personnel Computer) (July 1993), 371-382.

4233.   Simon, Imola. "The Conservation of 16th to 18th Century Paper Bindings," Conference on Book and Paper Conservation, 1990. Budapest, Hungary: Technical Association of Paper and Printing Industry/National Szechenyi Library (1992), 338-342. Describes paper bindings and problems that arise in conservation; emphasizes the renewal or reuse of original materials whenever possible.

4234.   Simon, Imola. "The Most Recent Hungarian Book Conservation Workshop," Conference on Book and Paper Conservation, 1990. Budapest, Hungary: Technical Association of Paper and Printing Industry/National Szechenyi Library (1992), 17-19. Describes the traditional approach to conservation, treatment of the best works, and the new approach of less physical intervention.

4235.   Simon, Lisa. "Building Design and Preservation," Conservation Administration News, 40 (April 1990), 12-14.

4236.   Simon, Matthew J. "The Sick (Library) Building Syndrome," Library Administration and Management, 4:2 (Spring, 1990), 87-91. A lucid discussion of the syndrome in libraries, its causes, effects and potential remedies. While the article deals with hazards to people, the causes also affect collections. Extensive notes.

4237. "A Simple Workstation for the Conservation of Library Materials," Conservation Correspondence (Illinois Cooperative Conservation Program), 4 (September 1984), 10p. Design plan, list of equipment needed, sources of supplies.

4238. Simpson, Bill. "Theft and Loss from U.K. Libraries: An Academic Librarian's View," Library Conservation News, 39 (April 1993), 1-3. Reaction to a report by the Home Office Police Research group; means of prevention.

4239. Simpson, Charles W. "Technical Services Research, 1988-1991," Library Resources and Technical Services, 36:4 (October 1992), 383-408. A review of issues and concerns including preservation, p. 395-397.

4240. Simpson, Edward. "Anthony Cains: Director of Conservation at Trinity College, Dublin." Paper Conservation News, 74 (June 1995), 1-4. Profile of Cains, his approach to conservation and his concern that librarians are not trained for curatorial responsibilities and lack proper training. "I don't really relish the thought of being replaced by a 'Preservation Officer' who talks in a language librarians understand but who has no real understanding of what a book conservator is and does" (4).

4241. Simpson, Edward. "Board Rehitching: A Case-History," Paper Conservation News, 74 (June 1995), 14-15. Treatment report on the repair and reattachment of original boards on a 17th-century book.

4242. Simpson, Edward. "Ian Jones: Conservation Officer at the National Library of Wales," Paper Conservation News, 72 (December 1994), 1-3. Interview, describing the structure of the conservation program, activities, policies, and procedures.

4243. Simpson, Edward. "John McIntyre: Head of Preservation at the National Library of Scotland," Paper Conservation News, 71 (September 1994), 1-3. Interview; McIntyre discusses his background as a bookbinder and the development of the Preservation Department at the National Library of Scotland.

4244. Simpson, Edward. "Jonathan Ashley-Smith: Head of Conservation at the Victoria and Albert Museum," Paper Conservation News, 73 (March 1995), 1-5. Profile; discussion of conservation and training of conservators at the V & A. Preservation of the National Art Library Collections; risk management in conservation and preservation.

4245. Simpson, Edward. "Michael Turner: Head of Conservation at the Boolean Library," Paper Conservation News, 69 (March 1994), 1-3. Interview; profile of Turner and the development of system wide preservation and conservation programs at Oxford.

4246. Simpson, Edward. "Miriam Foot: Director of Collections and Preservation at the British Library," Paper Conservation News, 70 (June 1994), 1-3. Interview; Foot's background as a binding historian and her role at the British Library.

4247. Simpson, Edward. "Setting Up a Board-Slotting Program," Paper Conservator, 18 (1994), 77-89. Describes the program at the Boolean Library, Oxford University; selection of material, with detailed noted on using the technique to reattach boards in books with hollow tubes.

4248. Simpson, Edward. "Strengthening a Weak and Worn Board Attachment: A Case History," Paper Conservation News, 76 (December 1995), 14. Treatment report.

4249. Simpson, Floyd B. Care and Repair of Books. Nashville, TN: Convention Press, 1994. 24p.

4250. Sinclair, Jim, ed. State Library of New South Wales Counter-Disaster Manual. Sydney: State Library of New South Wales, 1992. 192p. Manual in outline form, originally published in 1985. Bibliography.

4251. Sinclair, Regina A. "Continuing a Tradition of Training: New Hands-on Workshops at Johns Hopkins University," Conservation

Administration News, 62/63 (Summer/Fall 1995), 13-15. Describes the NEH-funded workshops for smaller libraries, archives, and historical societies.

4252.   Sinclair, Regina A. "Mellon Internships in Preservation Administration: An Under Appreciated Resource?" Conservation Administration News, 48 (January 1992), 8-11. Informal study of the internships and role the program played in the training of preservation administrators.

4253.   Singh, G.M. "Study on Preservation of Infested Books by Anobium Species," Conservation of Cultural Property in India. 1984-1984, 113-114. Describes the Anobium infestation among books in a Nepal repository and mentions the results shown by using fumigants.

4254.   Singh, Karambir. "Restoration of a Badly Damaged Paper Document," Restoration of Indian Art; Some Case Studies, 1 (1988), 21-25. Describes the treatment and further stabilization measures for an important Mogul document on paper.

4255.   Singh, R. S. Conservation of Documents in Libraries, Archives and Museums. New Delhi, India: Aditya Prakashan, 1993. 159p. Explains the physical nature of paper, causes of its deterioration, and methods of conservation. Bibliography.

4256.   Sinha, S. N. "Training of Conservation Personnel for Archives and Libraries," Conservation of Cultural Property in India; 1983 Seminar, New Delhi, Indian Association for the Study of Conservation of Cultural Property, 16-17 (1983-1984), 124-126. Discusses the necessity of training personnel for conservation in the nation's archival institutions; factors to consider in planning a training program.

4257.   Sinnette, Elinor des Verney, W. Paul Coates, and Thomas C. Battle, eds. Black Bibliophiles and Collectors: Preservers of Black History. Washington, DC: Howard University Press, 1990. 236p. Describes collectors, collections, and the organization and description of Black Studies materials, with a note on their preservation.

Bibliography

4258. Siripant, Sakda. "Conservation of Photographic Images," SPAFA
        Digest (Special Projects in Archeology and Fine Arts, Thailand),
        11:2 (1990), 59-63. Reviews the conservation of photographic
        images and ways of preserving them.

4259. Siripant, Sakda. "Light Stability of Colour Prints," Stability and
        Conservation of Photographic Materials: Chemical, Electronic and
        Mechanical. Bangkok, Thailand: Society of Photographic Scientists
        and Engineers (1988), 194-202. Report on tests of the resistance of
        recent color photographic papers.

4260. Sistach, Maria Carme, and Ignazi Espadaler. "Organic and Inorganic
        Compounds of Iron Gall Inks," Preprints: ICOM Committee on
        Conservation 10th Triennial Meeting, ed. Janet Bridgland.
        Washington, DC: International Council of Museums, 1993, 485-490.
        Analysis of manuscript samples with iron gall inks.

4261. Sitterle, Karen A., and John E. Deleray. "Facing Employee
        Trauma," Disaster Recovery Journal, 7:2 (April/June 1994), 44-
        46. Addresses the issue of employee trauma immediately following a
        disaster, emphasizing the need to provide "swift professional
        intervention."

4262. Sitts, Maxine K. "Commission on Preservation and Access," The
        Bowker Annual Library and Book Trade Almanac, 41st ed., Bowker,
        (1996), 296-301.

4263. Sitts, Maxine K. "Library Practices. Preservation Issues in Technical
        Services: Discoveries of PPP Participants," RTSD Newsletter
        (Resources and Technical Services Division), 11:3 (1986) 25-
        26. Report on the Office of Management Studies Preservation
        Planning Program (PPP). The study of a library and an analysis of its
        technical services practices as they relate to preservation issues.

4264. Sitts, Maxine K. A Practical Guide to Preservation in School and
        Public Libraries. Syracuse, NY: ERIC Clearinghouse on
        Information Resources, 1990. 55p. ED 340 391. How public and
        school libraries can undertake preservation activities, noting essential
        ingredients of awareness, judgment, and advocacy.

4265.   Sitts, Maxine K. "Preservation: Whose Job Is Anyway?"
        Conservation Administration News, 42 (July 1990), 4-6+. Paper
        presented at the Rutgers University Library School on February 7,
        1990.

4266.   Sitts, Maxine K. "Taming Technology for Preservation and Access:
        Strategies for Managing Constant Change." In Library and
        Information Technology Association (US) National Conference (3rd:
        1992: Denver, Colo.) Information Technology. Chicago, Il:
        American Library Association, 1992. 60-62.

4267.   Sitts, Maxine K., and Chandru J. Shahani, comp. Directory,
        Information Sources on Scientific Research Related to the
        Preservation of Books, Paper, and Adhesives. Washington, DC:
        Commission on Preservation and Access, 1990. 28p. Central
        resource for information on scientific research related to the needs of
        librarians and archivists involved in preservation activities; includes
        report on preservation research at the Library of Congress by
        Shahani.

4268.   Skepastianu, Maria, with Jean I. Whiffen. Library Disaster Planning.
        The Hague: IFLA Section on Conservation, 1995. 8p. Leaflet
        outlining causes and effects of disaster; prevention, preparedness,
        response, and recovery. Bibliography.

4269.   Skepastianu, Maria. "Preservation and Conservation Education in
        Greece," Conservation Administration News, 51 (October 1992), 8-
        9, 26-27. Describes programs to train library and archival
        preservation administrators and book conservators.

4270.   Skupsky, Donald S. "Legal Requirements for Microfilm, Computer
        and Optical Disk Records — International Perspectives." Records
        Management Quarterly, 25:1 (January 1991), 32-37. Review the
        regulations for recordkeeping under the common law and civil law
        systems and the difficulties they present in attempting to keep
        records in electronic format by multi national corporations.

4271. Slate, Jane. "Caring for the Nation's Wealth: A National Study Assesses Collection Management, Maintenance and Conservation," Museum News, 64:2 (October 1985), 39-45. Report of a study of current condition of collections; provides an overview of resources available for collections care.

4272. Slavin, John, and Jim Hanlin. "An Investigation of Some Environmental Factors Affecting Migration-Induced Degradation in Paper," Restaurator, 13:2 (1992), 78-94. Study of the effect of selected environmental factors on deterioration caused by acid migration.

4273. Sleep, Esther L. "Rejuvenating an Aging Microfilm Collection," Serials Review, 16:1 (Spring 1990), 81-84. Case study of treatment of a collection that deteriorated because of low humidity.

4274. Slide, Anthony. Nitrate Won't Wait: A History of Film Preservation in the United States. Jefferson City, NC: McFarland, 1992. 240p. Examines preservation issues for newsreel, television, and color film; discusses the role of major institutions in the effort to preserve the motion picture heritage.

4275. Sly, Margaret N. "Legislating Longevity: The Massachusetts Library Theft and Mutilation Law," Preservation Papers of the 1991 SAA Annual Conference, comp. Karen Garlick. Chicago: Society of American Archivists, 1992, 114-118. Describes the process of drafting the law and seeing it through the legislative process. Problems with the public's misinterpretation of the law.

4276. Smeeton, Robin. "The Durable Word: Some British Progress Towards Acid-Free Paper and the Conservation of the National Archive," British Book News (August 1990), 504-505.

4277. Smethurst, J.M. "Library Security: An Overview," Security in Academic and Research Libraries, eds. Anthony G. Quinsee and Andrew C. McDonald. Newcastle-upon-Tyne, England: University of Newcastle Library, 1991, 25-27. Examines problem of theft in libraries and librarians' reluctance to deal with it; notes the United States is ahead of the United Kingdom in dealing with the problem.

4278.   Smith, Anthony W. "The New Degree Courses at Camberwell
         College of Art," Conference on Book and Paper Conservation, 1990.
         Budapest: Technical Association of Paper and Printing
         Industry/National Szechenyi Library (1992), 407-412. Describes the
         conservation training programs at Camberwell.

4279.   Smith, Beryl K., ed. Space Planning for the Art Library. Tucson,
         AZ: Art Libraries Society of North America, 1991. 32p.
         (Occasional Paper, 9).

4280.   Smith, Brian S. "Archives and Government Policy," Journal of the
         Society of Archivists, 9:4 (October 1988), 181-184. Reports on the
         Society of American Archivists effort to promote more government
         intervention to protect the nation's historical records.

4281.   Smith, Brian S. "Record Repositories in 1984," Journal of the
         Society of Archivists, 8:1 (April 1986), 1-16. The result of a 1984
         U.K. survey of publicly funded record repositories are presented.
         Information sought was: staffing levels, storage, holdings and
         acquisitions, finding aids, conservation, and searchroom statistics.

4282.   Smith, Clive. "Starting a Conservation Programme," Archives &
         Manuscripts (Australian Society of Archivists), 15:1 (May 1987), 41-
         47. Caring for collections; photocopying, physical treatments,
         surveying collections to determine needs.

4283.   Smith, Demaris C. Preserving Your Paper Collectibles. White Hall,
         VA: Betterway Publications, 1989. 184p. Covers storage, handling of
         a variety of paper-based materials.

4284.   Smith, Eldred. "Why Microfilm Research Library Collections When
         Electronic Data Bases Could Be Used?" Microform Review, 20:1
         (Winter 1991), 27-29. Advocates preservation in electronic format as
         more useful and cost-efficient and that present microfilming
         technology is flawed. Reprinted from Chronicle of Higher
         Education, July 18, 1990, A44, with an appended note. Replies to
         Smith's article can be found in the August 15, 1990, issue, B3-B4.
         Smith's response can be found in the September 19, 1990, issue, B5.

4285. Smith, Eldred, and Peggy Johnson. "How to Survive the Present While Preparing for the Future: A Research Library Strategy," College and Research Libraries, 54:5 (September 1993), 389-396. Considers preservation as a shared responsibility among libraries, with emphasis in the future on access and document delivery.

4286. Smith, Elizabeth H. "The First Hundred Days," Conservation Administration News, 57 (April 1994), 11-12. Developing a preservation and conservation program at Joyner Library, East Carolina University.

4287. Smith, Elizabeth H. "Library Binding Is a Service," New Library Scene, 14:6 (December 1995), 13-14, 16. Discusses the need for commercial binders to attend to clients' needs and for charts to know the standards and binding techniques appropriate for their collections.

4288. Smith, Elizabeth H. "Preservation Programs at East Carolina University, April 1995 Workshop," Conservation Administration News, 60 (January 1995), 14.

4289. Smith, Ellen. "Archives and Preservation: Clearing the Cobwebs," Pitt/Carnegie Library and Information Science Alumni Association Newsletter (Spring 1989), 4-5.

4290. Smith, Frederick E. "Door Checkers: An Unacceptable Security Alternative," Library and Archival Security, 7:1 (Spring 1985), 7-13. Judges electronic systems to be more effective and cost-effective than human inspectors.

4291. Smith, Frederick E. "Questionable Strategies in Library Security Studies," Library and Archival Security, 6:4 (Winter 1984), 43-53. Examines three strategies.

4292. Smith, Joan C. "National Policy on Permanent Papers," Michigan Alliance for the Conservation of Cultural Heritage Newsletter, 1:1

(Spring 1989), 5-7. Discussion of legislation to establish a national policy on permanent papers.

4293. Smith, John David. "The Conservation Crisis in British Libraries and Archives," Conservation Administration News, 37 (April 1989), 10-11, 32. Summary of the Ratcliffe report identifying preservation problems and needs in British libraries and archives.

4294. Smith, Keith A. Structure of the Visual Book: Book 95. Rev. and expanded ed. Rochester, NY: Keith A. Smith, 1992. 239p. Describes how each inherent part of a book can be used to communicate. Provocative commentary on perception and visual communication.

4295. Smith, Kelvin. "The Preservation of Railway Records," Archives, 17:75 (April 1986), 153-159. Appraisal of records and selection for preservation.

4296. Smith, Leslie. Factors Governing the Long-Term Stability of Polyester-Based Recording Media. Washington, DC: National Institute of Standards and Technology, 1987. 21p.; Restaurator, 12:4 (1991), 201-218. Translates the results of National Archives and National Institute of Science and Technology tests on the longevity of microfilm and magnetic tape into practical terms. Recommendations for storage and handling are given.

4297. Smith, Leslie F., and Barry J. Bauer. "Properties of PET Films," Conservation in Archives. Paris: International Council on Archives, 1989, 103-115. Discusses the manufacture, properties, and relative stability of polyester films; paper presented at an international symposium, Ottawa, Canada, May 1988.

4298. Smith, Margit J. "Handle with Care, the Proper Way to Treat Books," Archival Products News, 3:2 (Spring 1995), 1-2,5. An overview on how staff and patrons should handle and care for books.

4299. Smith Margit J. "Special Collections — Special Treatment: The Treatment of Books Destined for Special Collections for the Rare Book Room," Archival Products News, 4:1 (Winter 1996), 3-

4. Care, handling, and preservation of books in special collection. "The handling and treatment of books for special collections follows mainly common sense guidelines and the application of general principles for dealing with printed materials" (4).

4300. Smith, Merrily A. "Care and Handling of Bound Materials," Preservation of Library Materials. New York: Saur, 1987, 45-54. (IFLA Publications, 41). Discusses various aspects of care, including the library environment, shelving, stack maintenance, rehousing vulnerable materials, and proper exhibition procedures.

4301. Smith, Merrily A., ed. Managing the Preservation of Serial Literature: An International Symposium. New York: Saur, 1992, 292p. (IFLA Publication, 57). Twenty-six papers presented at a conference in 1989 deal with issues of acquisition, organization, and preservation of serial publication: costs, information needs, bibliographic developments, and resource sharing.

4302. Smith, Merrily A., ed. Preservation of Library Materials. Two volumes. New York: Saur, 1987. 323p. (IFLA Publications, 41-42). Papers presented at a Conference of Directors of National Libraries sponsored by IFLA and UNESCO, Vienna, 1986. Specialists and representatives from libraries around the world reviewed the preservation challenge and activities around the world, discussed the physical nature of library collections and the need to provide a foundation for further action.

4303. Smith, Merrily A. "Preservation on the International Front," Meeting the Preservation Challenge. Washington, DC: Association of Research Libraries, 1988, 59-66. Describes cooperative initiatives in the United States, the Americas, Europe, and Asia, and their relevance for ARL libraries.

4304. Smith, Merrily A., and Karen Garlick. "Surveying Library Collections: A Suggested Approach," Technical Services Quarterly, 5:2 (1987), 3-18. Describes the elements of a successful collection survey.

4305. Smith, Merrily A., Norvell M. M. Jones, Susan L. Page, and Marion Peck Dirda. "Pressure-Sensitive Tape and Techniques for Its Removal from Paper," American Institute for Conservation Journal, 23:2 (Spring 1984), 101-113. History of the development of pressure-sensitive tape from its invention in 1845 to the present. Aging properties of tapes are described; testing of solvents and methods for tape removal are discussed. Also published in the Book and Paper Group Annual, 2 (1983), 95-113.

4306. Smith, Michael Clay, and Richard Fossey. Crime on Campus: Legal Issues and Campus Administration. Phoenix, AZ: American Council on Education/Oryx Press, 1995. 251p. Comprehensive discussion of issues related to campus crime and analysis of the law. Suggestions for administrators to deal with crime, with checklists that can be used to evaluate current procedures and defuse potential problems.

4307. Smith, Richard D. "Background, Use and Benefits of Blast Freezers in Prevention and Extermination of Insects," Biodeterioration 6, eds. S. Barry and D. R. Houghton. London: CAB International Mycological Institute/Biodeterioration Society, 1985, 374-379. Reviews existing data on temperature required to kill insects and application for a nonhazardous extermination technique using a commercial freezer. The technique may also be used for the salvage of wet materials. Paper presented at the 6th International Biodeterioration Symposium, Washington, DC, August 1984.

4308. Smith, Richard D. "Deacidification Technologies: State of the Art," Paper Preservation: Current Issues and Recent Developments. Atlanta, GA: TAPPI Press, 1990, 103-110. Outlines the causes of paper acidity; provides a synopsis of existing mass deacidification methods. 41 references.

4309. Smith, Richard D. "Deacidifying Library Collections: Myths and Realities," Restaurator, 8:2/3 (1987), 69-88. Describes the loss of brittle books in collections as a loss of national wealth. Discusses mass deacidification approaches to preservation and compares the Wei T'o process with the diethyl zinc process, with a detailed account of the DEZ mishap in 1986 and the political consequences.

4310.   Smith, Richard D. "Fumigation Dilemma: More Overkill or
         Common Sense," New Library Scene, 3:6 (1984), 1, 5-6. Discussion
         of fumigation in the light of new safety standards; alternative
         treatments to curtail infestation of pests and molds.

4311.   Smith, Richard D. "Fumigation Quandary: More Overkill or
         Common Sense?" Paper Conservator, 10 (1986), 46-
         48. Consideration of pest control methods that are non-toxic. Paper
         presented at the 1986 Institute for Paper Conservation Conference.

4312.   Smith, Richard D. "It's Not Too Late to Save the Books," American
         Libraries, 19:11 (December 1988), 992-994. Review of the 1988
         TAPPI Symposium and its impact on communication and cross-
         fertilization of ideas about the production of permanent paper.

4313.   Smith, Richard D. "Mass Deacidification: The Wei T'o
         Understanding," College and Research Libraries News, 48:1 (January
         1987), 2-10. Review of the brittle book problem and its impact on
         library collections. Discussion of deacidification processes, costs,
         and funding.

4314.   Smith, Richard D. "Mass Deacidification: The Wei T'o Way,"
         College and Research Libraries News, 45:11 (December 1984), 588-
         592. Discussion in 46:1 (January 1985), 9-11. Discusses
         development of the Wei T'o method in use at the Public Archives of
         Canada and mass deacidification methods in general.

4315.   Smith, Richard D. "Mass Deacidification at the Public Archives of
         Canada," Conservation of Library and Archive Materials and the
         Graphic Arts. Boston, MA: Butterworths, 1987, 125-134.

4316.   Smith, Richard D. "Mass Deacidification Cost Comparisons,"
         College and Research Libraries News, 46:3 (March 1985), 122-
         123. Comparison of the Wei T'o and Diethyl Zinc mass
         deacidification processes, with costs based on the Wei T'o system at
         the Public Archives of Canada.

4317. Smith, Richard D. "Non-Aqueous Deacidification: Its Philosophies, Origin, Development and Status," Paper Conservator, 12 (1988), 31-34. Describes deacidification processes and non-aqueous methods, with discussion of the Wei T'o method. Paper originally presented at the "New Directions in Paper Conservation" Conference, Oxford, England, 1986. 115p.

4318. Smith, Richard D. "Paper in Archives, Libraries, and Museums Worldwide," Paper Preservation: Current Issues and Recent Developments. Atlanta, GA: TAPPI Press, 1990, 15-18. Overview of the preservation problem due to acidic collections; the need for preservation.

4319. Smith, Richard D. "Reversibility: A Questionable Philosophy," Restaurator, 9:1 (1988), 199-207. Discusses the concept of reversibility in conservation; notes treatment will change the nature of an object to some degree and questions the need for reversibility in treatment.

4320. Smith, Richard D. "The Use of Redesigned and Mechanically Modified Commercial Freezers to Dry Water-Wetted Books and Exterminate Insects," Restaurator, 6:3/4 (1984), 165-190. Report on the modification and use of a supermarket freezer to dry water-wetted books and to exterminate insects.

4321. Smith, Richard D., and Terry O. Norris. "The Basis and Blight of Scholarly Communication," TAPPI Journal (Technical Association for the Pulp and Paper Industry) (August 1988), 1-2. Note on the Symposium on Paper Preservation sponsored by the Technical Association of the Pulp and Paper Industry.

4322. Smith, Stephanie. Paperwork Management in the Federal Government. Washington, DC: Library of Congress, Congressional Research Service, 1990. 19p.

4323. Smith, Wendy. "Acid Transfer Between Adjacent Paper Sheets." AICCM Bulletin (Australia Institute for the Conservation of Cultural Material), 11:1/2 (June 1985), 38-42. Study of acid transfer from acidic paper to alkaline test papers.

4324.   Smith, Wendy. "Bangkok, April 1992: Developing a Preservation Management Policy," International Preservation News, 5 (December 1992), 11-12. Describes a workshop for Southeast Asian librarians to help them develop preservation policies and procedures for their institutions.

4325.   Smith, Wendy. "Education for Preservation," International Preservation News, 7 (December 1993), 8-9. Describes the process of developing interactive training materials in preservation management for use in Southeast Asia and the Pacific Rim countries.

4326.   Smith, Wendy. "The Ferguson Slipcase," Abbey Newsletter, 13:5 (September 1989), 95-96. Instructions for constructing a protective slipcase for rare and valuable materials developed at the National Library of Australia.

4327.   Smith, Wendy. "A Policy for Preservation at the National Library of Australia," Libraries: The Heart of the Matter. Deakin, Australia: Australian Library and Information Association, 1992, 341-343. (ALIA '92; proceedings, 2d Biennial Conference). Discusses historical developments within Preservation Services at the National Library of Australia, which led to the acceptance of a formal preservation policy for the collections.

4328.   Smith, Wendy, and Jan Lyall. "Routine Testing of Conservation Materials," AICCM Bulletin (Australian Institute for the Conservation of Cultural Material), 9:3-4 (1983), 114-115. Describes results of testing of acid-free glassine paper and heat-set tissue; notes need for testing and sharing of results.

4329.   Smithsonian Institution Libraries. SIL Preservation Planning Program, June 4, 1985-May 1, 1986: Final Report of the Study Team. Washington, DC: Association of Research Libraries, Office of Management Studies, 1986. 78p. in various paging. Authored by Ann Juneau, et al., Nancy E. Gwinn, Chair.

4330.   Smithsonian Institution News. "Work of Smithsonian Scientists Revise Guidelines for Climate Control in Museums and Archives,"

The Abbey Newsletter, 18:4/5 (1994) 45. A transcription of the press release from the Smithsonian researchers who claim that museum objects can safely tolerate a wider range of temperature and relative humidity than previously believed.

4331. Smook, Gary A. Handbook of Pulp and Paper Terminology: A Guide to Industrial and Technological Usage. Vancouver, Canada; Bellingham, WA: Angus Wilde Pub., 1990. 447p. Comprehensive collection of technical and operational terms for pulping, papermaking, and related operations. Definitions are compatible with standard vocabulary when applicable.

4332. Snider, Mike. "History Comes Alive Bit by Bit," USA Today (April 17, 1996), D 1-2. Describes efforts at the Library of Congress to establish the National Digital Library and the preservation concerns.

4333. Snow, Michael R., and Tony J. Zammit. "The Chemical Detection of Iron Used in Inks," AICCM Bulletin (Australian Institute for the Conservation of Cultural Material), 13:3/4 (December 1987), 149-154. Describes a method for the identification of irongall ink in documents.

4334. Sobota, Jan. "The Background and History of a Deck of Late Gothic Playing Cards," Yale University Gazette, 67:1-2 (October 1992), 27-31. Traces history and describes the discovery and conservation of playing cards found in the binding of a book published circa 1520 during its conservation.

4335. Sobota, Jan. "Reflections of a Book Artist," New Bookbinder, 10 (1990), 3-12. A distinguished bookbinder/conservator talks about his philosophy, which reflects his respect for the book and its structure, and the influences on his career.

4336. Society of American Archivists. Preserving History's Future: Nationwide Goals for the Preservation and Use of the Archival Record. Chicago, IL: Society of American Archivists, 1993. 4p.

4337. Society of Mississippi Archivists Conservation Committee. Pictures That Last: Archival Processing Techniques for Black and White

Materials. Hattiesburg, MI: Society of Mississippi Archivists, 1984.
3p. Reprinted: CBBAG Newsletter (Canadian Bookbinders and
Book Artists Guild), 3:2 (Summer 1985), 7-9.

4338. Society of Motion Picture and Television Engineers. "Proposed
Recommended Practice: Care, Storage, Operation, Handling, and
Shipping of Magnetic Recording Tape for Television (RP103),"
SMPTE Journal (Society of Motion Picture and Television
Engineers), 103:10 (October 1994), 692-695. Provides guidance for
technical managers, archivists, and technicians to help maximize life
expectancy and interchange for television (video) magnetic recording
tape.

4339. Society of Motion Picture and Television Engineers. "Proposed
SMPTE Recommended Practice RP131: Storage of Motion Picture
Film," SMPTE Journal (Society of Motion Picture and Television
Engineers), 103:3 (March 1994), 201-205. Provides recommended
environmental conditions for "active working storage," "medium-
term storage," and "extended term storage."

4340. Soest, H. A. B. Van, T. Stambulov, and P.B. Hallebeek.
"Conservation of Leather," Studies in Conservation, 29:1 (February
1984), 21-31. Instructions for analyzing leather; information on
environment; methods of cleaning and restoring leathers.

4341. Soled, E. H., E. A. Veverka, J. Krieg, J. Barrett, and R. J. Allen.
"Information Technology Utilization in Emergency Management at
Exxon Research and Engineering Company," Special Libraries, 78:2
(Spring 1987), 116-121. Describes the safety measures established by
the company's Information Services Division.

4342. Solley, Thomas T., Joan Williams, and Linda Baden. Planning for
Emergencies: A Guide for Museums. Washington, DC: Association
of Art Museum Directors, 1987. 72p. Provides a framework for a
museum to address its needs. Bibliography.

4343. Soloviev, Andrei Yu. "Computerization of the Phased Conservation
Project at the Library of the USSR Academy of Sciences,"
Conservation Administration News, 46 (July 1991), 3, 26.

Describes the databases for collection and treatment information and records implemented at the library following the 1988 fire.

4344. Some Suggestions for the Protection of Books and Manuscripts in a Home Library. Charlottesville, VA: University of Virginia Library, 1986. 8p.

4345. Sommer, Susan T. "Knowing the Score: Preserving Collections of Music, Presented at the 1991 ALA Conference," Fontes Artis Musicae, 41 (July/September 1994), 256-260.

4346. Sonnet-Azize, Rene G. "Preservation and Conservation Measures in Central Africa: Proposals for Training Programmes," Proceedings of the Pan-African Conference on the Preservation and Conservation of Library and Archival Materials, Nairobi, Kenya, 21-25 June 1993. The Hague: International Federation of Library Associations, 1995, 165-168. (IFLA Profess. Publication 43). Current status and strategies for cooperation in Central Africa.

4347. Soon, Ang. "Securing CD-ROMs and the Microcomputer Environment," Laserdisk Professional, 2: 4 (July 1989), p. 18-23.

4348. South Australia, State Library. Preservation Microfilming: Does It Have a Future? Proceedings of the First National Conference. National Preservation Office, State Library of South Australia May 4-6, 1994. Canberra: National Library of Australia, 1995. 198p. Papers that explore preservation and access through microfilm, an established preservation medium, and through digital electronic technologies that are rapidly evolving. Most presenters distinguish between preservation and access, advocating the hybrid approach and the use of new technology for improved access to information.

4349. South Carolina. Department of Archives and History. How to Take Care of Your Papers, Books and Photographs. Columbia, SC: South Carolina Department of Archives & History, 1988. 1 sheet.

4350. South Carolina Historical Records Advisory Board. Preserve or Perish: On the Future of Historical Records in the Palmetto State. Columbia, SC: South Carolina Department of Archives and History,

1988. 69p. Report of a survey of the state's public records, identifying problems, proposing solutions, and presenting an agenda for action.

4351. Southeast Library Network (SOLINET). Environmental Specifications for the Storage of Library and Archival Materials. Atlanta, GA: SOLINET, 1985, 5p. (SOLINET Preservation Program Leaflet 1). Covers temperature, relative humidity, air pollution, and light. Adapted from a document prepared by the Midwest Cooperative Conservation Program.

4352. Southeast Library Network (SOLINET). Preservation Program: Audio-Visual Loan Service. April 1, 1988, 6p. List of audiovisual materials available for loan.

4353. Southeast Library Network (SOLINET) Some Sources of Conservation/Preservation Supplies and Equipment. Atlanta, GA: SOLINET, 1985, 6p. (SOLINET Preservation Program Leaflet 2.). Brief list, including conservation supplies and equipment, disaster recovery services, storage items, and even a poster designer.

4354. Southeast Library Network (SOLINET). Some Sources of Custom Fit Book Boxes. Atlanta, GA: SOLINET, 1986. 1 sheet.

4355. Spadoni, Carl. "The Contribution of Librarianship to Medical Archives," Bibliotheca Medica Canadiana, 9:1 (1987), 53-66.

4356. Sparks, Peter G. "The Library of Congress Preservation Program," The Library Preservation Program: Models, Priorities, Possibilities, eds. Jan Merrill-Oldham and Merrily Smith. Chicago, IL: American Library Association, 1985. 69-72p.

4357. Sparks, Peter G. "Marketing for Preservation," The Library Preservation Program: Models, Priorities, Possibilities. Chicago, IL: American Library Association, 1985. 75-79p. Brief discussion of the marketing approach to fundraising.

4358. Sparks, Peter G. "Mass Deacidification at the Library of Congress," Restaurator, 8:2/3 (1987), 106-110. Review of the causes of the deterioration of cellulose, the effectiveness of the diethyl zinc (DEZ) process developed at the Library of Congress, and discussion of the engineering problems that delayed its production.

4359.   Sparks, Peter G., ed. A Roundtable on Mass Deacidification. Washington, DC: Association of Research Libraries, 1992. 115p. Report of a meeting held in September 1991 to examine issues of cost and priorities, pros and cons of mass deacidification processes, with case studies and reports on research projects.

4360.   Sparks, Peter G. "Some Properties of Polymers and Their Relevance to Double-Fan Adhesive Binding," New Library Scene, 9:4 (August 1990), 1, 5-8. Describes polymers, their action and interaction with other molecules, and how a knowledge of polymers is useful in conservation treatment, including adhesive binding. Discusses the problems with PVA adhesives and the need for further evaluation and performance standards.

4361.   Sparks, Peter G. Technical Considerations in Choosing Mass Deacidification Processes. Washington, DC: Commission on Preservation and Access, 1990. 22p. Summary of technical and logistical factors to be considered when contemplating a commitment to a mass deacidification program.

4362.   Sparks, Peter G. "Technology in Support of Preservation," Preservation of Library Materials, ed. Merrily Smith. New York: Saur, 1987, 126-128. (IFLA Publications, No. 40). Also in Restaurator, 8:2/3 (1987), 65-68.

4363.   Sparks, Peter G., and Richard D. Smith. "Deacidification Dialogue," College and Research Libraries News, 46:1 (January 1985), 9-11. Response to Richard Smith's article, "Mass Deacidification: The Wei T'o Way," College and Research Libraries News, 45:6 (December 1984), with further comments by Smith.

4364.   Spawn, Carol M. "The Megafile Project," Conservation Administration News, 61 (April 1995), 1-4. Description of a project to rehouse the serials in the Academy of Natural Sciences Library, Philadelphia.

4365. Special Libraries Association. <u>Disaster Planning and Recovery; An SLA Information Kit</u>. Washington, DC: Special Libraries Association, 1989. Spiral bound, separately paged. Collection of articles from the library literature on planning and recovery from fire, flood, mold, and other emergencies.

4366. Speller, Benjamin F. "Reconceptualizing Preservation, for North Carolina Repositories," <u>North Carolina Libraries</u>, 52 (Spring 1994), 3-5.

4367. Spence, John. "Mould: A Growing Problem Too Big to Ignore," <u>Phonographic Bulletin</u>, 55 (November 1989), 21-25. Describes conditions that created a mold outbreak in the Radio Archives of the Australian Broadcasting Organization; remedies to solve the problem and clean affected tapes.

4368. Spindler, Robert P. "Dancing Around the Archival Box Revisited," <u>Conservation News</u> (Arizona Paper and Photographic Conservation Group), 11:2 (June 1991), 1-3. Considers preservation as management rather than the treatment of special items; discusses management issues, including security and facilities.

4369. Sprehe, J. Timothy. "Archiving Electronic Databases: The NAPA Report," <u>Inform</u>, 6:3 (March 1992), 28-31. Report of a study by the National Academy of Public Administration examining the federal database environment and identifying databases worthy of preservation.

4370. Spreitzer, Francis, ed. <u>Microforms in Libraries: A Manual for Evaluation and Management</u>. Chicago, IL: American Library Association, 1985. 63p.

4371. Sprod, Dan. "Paper and the Book Publishing Industry," <u>AICCM Bulletin</u> (Australian Institute for the Conservation of Cultural Material), 16:4 (1990), 33-37. Report on the use, or lack thereof, of permanent paper in books published in Australia.

4372.   Srivastava, D. N. "Preservation of Some Rare Materials on Paper at the Intach Indian Conservation Institute, Lucknow," Conservation of Manuscripts and Documents, ed. Om Prakash Agrawal. Lucknow, India: INTACH, Indian Conservation Institute, 1992, 81-84.

4373.   Stability and Conservation of Photographic Images: Chemical, Electronic and Mechanical. Bangkok, Thailand: Society of Photographic Scientists and Engineers, 1986. 210p. Twenty-five papers covering all aspects of photographic and electronic images presented at an international symposium, November 1986. Clear and simple summaries of the state of the art.

4374.   Stagnitto, Janice. "The Shrink Wrap Project at Rutgers University Special Collections and Archives," Book and Paper Group Annual, 12 (1993), 56-60; reprinted in Abbey Newsletter, 18:4/5 (August/September 1994), 56-59. Describes a project to shrink wrap books for protection during construction; costs, cautions.

4375.   Stam, David. "Finding Funds to Support Preservation," The Library Preservation Program: Models, Priorities, Possibilities, eds. Jan Merrill-Oldham and Merrily Smith. Chicago, IL: American Library Association, 1985. 80-83p. Discusses several strategies for fundraising.

4376.   Stam, David. "International Programmes in Preservation," Preserving the Word. London: Library Association, 1987, 10-16. Outlines factors and considerations that influence the development of international cooperative efforts in preservation. Paper presented at a preservation conference, Harrogate, England, 1986.

4377.   Stam, David H. "The Question of Preservation," Research Libraries - Yesterday, Today and Tomorrow, ed. William J. Welsh. Westport, CT: Greenwood Press, 1993, 303-318. (Contributions in Librarianship and Information Science, 77). Overview of preservation concerns and solutions. Emphasizes need for bibliographic control and cooperative resource sharing. Paper presented at the Third International Seminar, Kanazawa Institute of Technology Library Center, Kanazawa, Japan, 1984.

4378. Standiforth, Sarah. "Benefits vs. Costs in Environmental Control," Managing Conservation, ed. Suzanne Keene. London: United Kingdom Institute for Conservation, 1990, 28-30. On assessing costs for preservation.

4379. Stanfill, Nancy E., Scott Devine, and Erika Lindensmith. "The Annual Conference of the Association of Graduate Training Programs in Conservation: A Report from Washington," Conservation Administration News, 58-59 (July/October 1994), 32-33.

4380. Stange, Eric. "Millions of Books Are Turning to Dust - Can They Be Saved?" New York Times Book Review (March 29, 1987), 3, 38. An essay on the deterioration of books, reprinted in Silent Fires: Book Conservation for the 1990s. Minneapolis Institute of Arts Library, 1991.

4381. Stanley, Judith. "Buying Time: A Commentary on the Fiscal Realities of Implementing Library Preservation Programmes," Library Association Record, 93:8 (August 1991), 523-526. Looks at the perception of the cost of preservation promulgated between 1970-1990; progress made in methodology and technologies, and the need to assess needs to ensure proper care and handling of materials, and to learn how to seek funding for special needs.

4382. Stanley, Judith. "The Role of the Original Paper Document in a Changing Information Environment," Canadian Journal of Information & Library Science, 19:1 (April 1994), 18-30. Discusses the role of paper documents in the context of future information environments, offering justification for the preservation of original paper documents.

4383. Stanley, Ted. "The Fraktur: Its History and a Conservation Case Study," Journal of the American Institute for Conservation, 33:1 (Spring 1994), 33-45. Short history on the fraktur in America, with treatment report.

4384. Stanley, Ted. "Papyrus Storage at Princeton University," Book and Paper Group Annual, 13 (1994), 49-55. Describes two safe and reliable storage systems providing protection and ease of access to frequently used papyri.

4385. Stansfield, G. "Pest Control - A Collection Management Problem," Museums Journal, 85:2 (September 1985), 97-99. Review of current pest control practices in U.K. museums; basic information on treatment strategies, including non-chemical approaches.

4386. Stark, Alan. ed. "Obsolete Videotape Formats: Converting to Current Standards," Film Technology News (May 1991), 11.

4387. Starr, Mary Jane. "The Preservation of Canadian Newspapers," Microform Review, 15:3 (Summer 1986), 162-164. Describes the National Library of Canada's Decentralized Program for Canadian Newspapers, in which the National Library coordinates efforts and provides financial assistance.

4388. State University of New York at Stony Brook. Preservation at Stony Brook: Preservation Planning Program Study Report, comp. Donald C. Cook, et al. Washington, DC: Association of Research Libraries, Office of Management Studies, 1985. 40p.

4389. Stazicker, Elizabeth. "Climatic Control: A Hopeless Bewilderment?" Journal of the Society of Archivists, 8:3 (April 1987), 171-173. Raises questions about the lack of understanding of climate control requirements for library and archival collections.

4390. Steckman, Elizabeth. "The Giant Spore vs. The New Jersey State Library," New Jersey Libraries, 26:3 (Summer 1993), 19-21. Case study of an outbreak of mold in the collections.

4391. Steckman, Elizabeth. "Preservation Program Thrives in New Jersey," Conservation Administration News, 48 (January 1992), 1-2, 26. Report on the Maintenance and Preservation of Library Collections grant program, administered by the State Library and its impact on the preservation of the state's documentary heritage.

4392.   Stehkaemper, Hugo. "'Natural' Air Conditioning of Stacks," Restaurator, 9:4 (1988), 163-177. The importance of room and building climate to preservation; how natural air conditioning can be achieved by structural means.

4393.   Sterlini, Philippa. "Surface Cleaning Products and Their Effects on Paper," Paper Conservation News, 76 (December 1995), 3-7. Study to identify characteristics of different products; examination of residues and effect of humidification and immersion.

4394.   Stevard, Bradley W. "Preservation Microfilming, A Joint Venture," Microform Review, 19:2 (Spring 1990), 73-75. Describes the preservation microfilming program at the Genealogical Library Division, State Library, and the American Genealogical Lending Library, Utah.

4395.   Stevens, Norman D. "Humor and Creativity: Preservation," College and Research Libraries News (March 1989), 203-212. Examples from the author's collection of the humorous approach taken by preservation librarians to educate staff and users.

4396.   Stevens, Norman D. "Preservation - A Concern of Every Library and Every Librarian," Library Administration and Management, 4:3 (Summer 1990), 123-126. Notes that the preservation of collections should be the responsibility of every librarian, yet preservation programs have yet to become a reality in most libraries.

4397.   Stevens, Norman D. "A Robotic Book Return," Abbey Newsletter, 12:1 (January 1988), 18-19. Discusses the application of robotics to the book return problem.

4398.   Stevenson, Condit Gaye. Working Together: Case Studies in Preservation. Washington, DC: Commission on Preservation and Access, September 1991. 36p. Summary of statewide and regional cooperative preservation initiatives.

4399.   Stevenson, Mark. "The Treatment of Prints: A History," Conservation of Historic and Artistic Works on Paper; Proceedings of a Conference, Ottawa, Canada, 3 to 7 October, 1988, ed. Helen D.

Burgess. Ottawa: 1994, 133-142. History of the care, handling, and treatment of prints until the 1930s.

4400. Stevenson, Rob, ed. Computer Technology for Conservators — the 2nd Wave. Dartmouth, Nova Scotia: Atlantic Regional Group of International Institute for Conservation-Canadian Group, 1994. n.p. Based on the 19th annual IIC-CG Conference Workshop.

4401. Stewart, Deborah. "CCI's Emergency Service," CCI Newsletter (Canadian Conservation Institute), 11 (April 1993), 1-2. French/English. Describes the scope of the Canadian Conservation Institute's disaster recovery service, with a case study of the recovery process following a fire at the Billings Estate Museum, Ottawa.

4402. Stewart, Eleanore, and Kathleen Orlenko. "A Conservator's Perspective on the Processes and Materials Used in the Production of Computer-Generated Documents," Preprints. International Conference on the Conservation and Restoration of Archive and Library Materials, Erice, Italy, April 22-28, 1996, Rome: Istituto Centrale per la Patologia del Libro, 1, 265-273. Brief history and development of computer desktop printing processes that are described; components of inks and toners, paper quality requirements, and archival properties are detailed.

4403. Stewart, Eleanore. "Freeze Disinfection of the McWilliams Collection," Conservation Administration News, 31 (Winter 1988), 10-11, 25. Case study of the treatment of books from Puerto Rico infested with dry wood termites.

4404. Stewart, Robert W. "Does This Project Deserve the Erasmus Prize? Some Troubling Thoughts About a Large Electronic Imaging Project," Conservation Administration News, 54 (July 1993), 4-5, 33-35. A critique of the project to capture early records in the Archivio Generaal de Indias, Seville, Spain, in electronic format for preservation and access. Author questions the appropriateness of the technology and questions why microfilm was not considered.

4405. Stiber, Linda. "The Delamination of the Washington and Lee Ledger; Part 1: An Overview of Cellulose Acetate Lamination,"

Early Advances in Conservation. London: British Library, 1988, 27-40. Addresses the variable quality of the lamination process, used on archival materials from the 1940s to the 1960s and the factors that cause deterioration. Bibliography.

4406.   Stielow, Frederick J. "Archival Security," Managing Archives and Archival Institutions, ed. J. Gregory Bradsher. Chicago, IL: University of Chicago Press, 1992, 207-217. A review of security needs and implementation. Bibliography.

4407.   Stielow, Frederick J. "Archival Theory and the Preservation of Electronic Media: Opportunities and Standards Below the Cutting Edge," American Archivist, 55:2 (Spring 1992), 332-343. Emphasizes the need for standards and common sense in embracing new technologies for the organization and storage of information. Describes several specific magnetic and optical media and discusses how archivists should adjust to ensure their preservation.

4408.   Stielow, Frederick J. "Biting the Worm: Theory and Tales of Electronic Media Preservation," Conservation Administration News, 47 (October 1991), 10. Discusses the dangers of using electronic media for preservation. Offers advice for those doing so.

4409.   Stielow, Frederick J. "Ducking the Cutting Edge: Archival Theory and the Preservation of Electronic Media," The Ohio Archivist, 22:2 (Fall 1991), 3-7. The author covers the basic elements of the preservation of electronic media.

4410.   Stielow, Frederick J. The Management of Oral History Sound Archives. Westport, CT: Greenwood Press, 1986. 192p. Covers the organization and preservation of sound recordings.

4411.   Stielow, Frederick J. "New Archival and Preservation Scholarship: Communication and Literature in Transition: A Review Article," The Library Quarterly, 63:1 (January 1993), 92-101.

4412.   Stinson, Stephen, "Deterioration of Polymer Materials in Museums Challenges Chemists," Chemical and Engineering News, 70:36

(September 7, 1992), 27-30. Describes problems presented by objects made all or in part of plastics, primarily those containing cellulose nitrate.

4413.   Stirling, Isabel A. "UO Science Library Freeze-Dries a Flood," PNLA Quarterly (Pacific Northwest Library Association), 52 (Winter 1988), 21. Salvage of water-damaged materials at the Science Library, University of Oregon.

4414.   Stobie, Ian. "You Can Take It With You," Practical Computing, 9:9 (September 1986), 97-100. Discusses hard disk/floppy systems for preserving information.

4415.   Stockton, Scott A. Organized Programs in Library Preservation and Conservation Education Since 1975. Denton, TX: Texas Woman's University, 1989. 70 leaves. (MA Thesis).

4416.   Stokes, Daniel A. Will Our Past Be in Our Future? Exploring Videotape as an Archival Medium. Washington, DC: National Archives and Records Administration, 1990. 17p. Explores videotape's potential as an archival medium; notes that it is not a permanent medium. Discusses standards and the need to develop standards for the preservation of videotape.

4417.   Stolow, Nathan. Conservation and Exhibitions: Packing, Transport, Storage and Environmental Conditions. London: Butterworths, 1987, 266p. (Butterworths Series in Conservation and Museology). Practical and detailed manual covering all aspects of the exhibition of valuable materials.

4418.   Stone, Janet L., and Elizabeth A. Morse. "A Method for Storing Additive-Free Wheat Starch Paste," Abbey Newsletter, 13:8 (December 1989), 147-148. A recipe, and its advantages.

4419.   Storack, M. Speranza, and Paola F. Munafò. "A Work in Progress: The Census of Medieval Bookbindings," Preprints. International Conference on Conservation and Restoration of Archive and Library Materials, Erice, Italy, April 22-29, 1996, Rome: Istituto Centrale per la Patologia del Libro, 1996, 401. Describes the census undertaken by the Istituto Central per la Patalogia del Libro, with preliminary results.

4420.   Storch, Paul S. "A Brief Look at Applications of Instrumental Analysis in Conservation," Conservation Administration News, 27 (October 1986), 25-26. Describes instruments used in conservation.

4421.   Storey, Richard, A. M. Wherry, and J. F. Wilson. "Three Views on Security," Journal of the Society of Archivists, 10 (1989), 108-114. Addresses security issues in United Kingdom repositories.

4422.   Storm, William D. "Audio Equipment Considerations for Sound Archives," Phonographic Bulletin, 57 (November 1990), 38-46. Describes the role and function of the sound archive engineer and equipment needed for accurate sound reformatting. Bibliography.

4423.   Storm, William D. "A Proposal for the Establishment of International Re-recording Standards," ARSC Journal (Association of Recorded Sound Archivists), 15:2/3 (1983), 26-37. Preservation of sound recordings through re-recording, ensuring that the product is as close as possible to the original; recommends recording standards and documentation.

4424.   Story, Keith C. Approaches to Pest Management in Museums. Washington, DC: Conservation Analytical Laboratory, Smithsonian Institution, 1985. 165p. Emphasizes low-toxicity and nonchemical methods; describes the Integrated Pest Management (IPM) approach.

4425.   Stover, Mark. "Issues in CD-ROM Security," CD-ROM Librarian, 4:6 (June 1989), 16-20. Discussion about the security of the CD-ROM disk itself.

4426.   Strang, Thomas J. K., and John E. Dawson. Controlling Museum Fungal Problems. Ottawa: Canadian Conservation Institute, 1991. 8p. (CCI Technical Bulletin, 12). French/English. Describes causes of fungal attack and methods of control. Bibliography.

4427.   Strang, Thomas J. K., and John E. Dawson. Controlling Vertebrate Pests in Museums. Ottawa: Canadian Conservation Institute, 1991.

9p. (CCI Technical Bulletin, 13). Describes damage rodents and other vertebrates can cause in museums, describes methods to control them. Bibliography

4428.   Strang, [Thomas J. K.]. "Reducing the Risk to Collections from Pests," CCI Newsletter (Canadian Conservation Institute), 14 (September 1994), 8-10. Discusses methods of passive pest control in lieu of fumigants and pesticides.

4429.   Strang, Thomas J. K. "A Review of Published Temperatures for the Control of Pest Insects in Museums," Collection Forum, 8:2 (Fall 1992), 41-67. Reported temperatures for the extermination and control of 46 museum insect pests are tabulated and graphed with comparisons to mortality data from entomological literature.

4430.   Stranger, Carolla, and Leanne Brandis. "Insect Pests and Their Eradication," Australian Library Journal, 41:3 (August 1992), 180-183. Outline of non chemical methods for controlling insect pests in libraries.

4431.   Strassberg, Richard. Conservation, Safety, Security, and Disaster Considerations in Designing New or Renovated Library Facilities at Cornell University Libraries. Ithaca, NY: Cornell University Library, 1984. 10p.

4432.   Strauss, Robert J., and Barclay W. Ogden. Polyvinyl Acetate Adhesives for Double-Fan Adhesive Binding: Report of a Review and Specification Study. Edina, MN: Library Binding Institute, April 17, 1992. 32p. Reviews information on adhesive bindings in the literature and in discussion with adhesive experts; suggests need for further study.

4433.   Streit, Samual Allen. The Higher Education Act, Title IIC Program: Strengthening Research Library Resources. A Ten Year Profile and an Assessment of the Program's Effects upon the Nation's Scholarship: Executive Summary. Washington, DC: Association of Research Libraries, April 1991. 30p. Data on the number and size of grants with representative case studies demonstrating the program's

Bibliography

effectiveness in developing, preserving, and sharing library resources.

4434. Streit, Samual Allen. "Transfer of Materials From General Stacks to Special Collections," Collection Management, 7:2 (Summer 1985), 33-46.

4435. Strnadova, Jirina, and Michel Durovic. "The Cellulose Ethers in Paper Conservation," Restaurator, 15:4 (1994), 220-241. Examination of cellulose ethers to determine their physical properties and changes that occur under artificial aging.

4436. Ströffer-Hua, Eckhard. "Chemicals: Interactions in Art, Humans and Nature," Restaurator, 14:2 (1993), 57-77. Discusses the mutual influences and cycles of chemical compounds in nature, art, and humans, protective measures and relevant rules for conservation labs.

4437. Ströffer-Hua, Eckhard. "Classical Methods of Bleaching in the Restoration Workshop: The Role of the OH Radical," Restaurator, 12:3 (1991), 131-136. As hazardous gases are to be avoided in conservation, author discusses reactions and chemical kinetics of other processes.

4438. Ströffer-Hua, Eckhard. "New Trends in Science and Their Impact on Conservation and Art - An Excursion Around Restorer's Island," Restaurator, 15:2 (1994), 94-108. Examines the evolving nature of science, the nature of the world, and the art and materials that the conservator handles. He considers the fractural dimension of objects as essence of their physical being, and concludes that a digitized copy of a work of art can result in complete visual restoration.

4439. Strong, Gary E. "Rats! Oh No, Not Rats!" Special Libraries, 78:2 (Spring 1987), 105-111. Describes the California State Library's preservation problems and the activities of its Preservation Office.

4440. Stroud, James. "The HRHRC Diethyl Zinc Mass Deacidification Project," Paper Conservator, 18 (1994), 57-70. Describes a two-year project to study the application of the Akzo diethyl zinc mass deacidification process to archive and manuscript collections.

581

Bibliography

4441.   Stroud, James. "The HRHRC Diethyl Zinc Mass Deacidification
         Project: A Brief Report," Conservation Administration News, 57
         (April 1994), 7-8. Describes tests of the DEZ process on library and
         archival materials, and the protocols developed for effective
         treatment of archival materials.

4442.   Stroud, James. "History and Composition of Manuscript and
         Document Inks," Paper Preservation: Conservation Techniques and
         Methodology, by Dewayne J. Lener. Orting, WA: Heritage Quest
         Press, 1988, 31-51. History and description of inks: use,
         characteristics, problems, conservation solutions.

4443.   Strzelczyk, Alieja B., Joanna Kuroczkin, and Wolfgang E. Krumbein.
         "Studies on the Microbial Degradation of Ancient Leather
         Bookbindings," International Biodeterioration. Part 1, 23 (1987),
         Part 2,25 (1989), 339-347. Study of the role of microorganisms on
         the decomposition of ancient vegetable tanned leathers.

4444.   Strzelczyk, Alieja B., and J. Rozanski. "The Effect of Disinfection
         with Quaternary Ammonium Salt Solution on Paper," Restaurator,
         7:1 (1986), 3-13. Describes a simple chemical treatment for
         disinfection of papers.

4445.   "Study of Book Deterioration in Ohio Libraries," OCLC Newsletter
         (Online Library Consortium), 191 (May-June 1991), 10-
         11. Methodology of the surveys to provide data for statewide
         preservation planning.

4446.   Sturge, John, Vivian Walworth, and Allan Shepp. Imaging Processes
         and Materials, Neblette's 8th edition. New York: Van Nostrand,
         1989, 712p. Text; provides overview of traditional and contemporary
         imaging technologies, their effectiveness and permanence.

4447.   Sturges, Paul. "Archival Problems of Electronic Publications," New
         Horizons for the Information Profession: Meeting the Challenge of
         Change. London: Taylor-Graham, 1988, 158-168. Discusses the

need for data archives, standards, and policies if information in electronic formats is to be preserved.

4448.   Sturges, Paul. Preservation of Electronic Archives. Wellington, NZ: Victoria University Department of Library and Information Studies, 1991. 39p. (Occasional Papers in Bibliography and Librarianship, 16); bibliography by Michael William Day. Describes electronic media and reasons why they are not permanent, archival. Suggests an approach to archiving through proper storage of data and regular refreshment.

4449.   Sturman, Shelly G. "Obtaining Professional Conservation Services," Caring for Your Collections. New York: Harry N. Abrams, 1992, 195-201. Advice on choosing a conservator; outlines the documentation and treatment steps that one can expect from a professional conservator.

4450.   Styka, Wanda Magdaleine. "Care of Photographs: Hints to Create an Enduring Collection," Chesterwood Pedistal, 4:1 (Summer 1986), 5-6. Practical article for general public on care, storage, and handling of family photographs.

4451.   Subt, Sylvia S. Y. "Archival Quality of Xerographic Copies," Restaurator, 8:1 (1987), 29-39. Report of an evaluation of electrostatic copying machines and their performance for "archival" photocopying undertaken at the National Archives.

4452.   Subt, Sylvia S. Y. "Xerographic Quality Control," Inform, 1:7 (July 1987), 10-11,47. Discussion of the testing undertaken at the National Archives and conclusions.

4453.   Subt, Sylvia S. Y., and John G. Koloski. Archival Xerographic Copying: Special Development Study for the National Archives and Records Administration. Washington, DC: U.S. Govt. Printing Office, 1987. 17 leaves. GPO jacket no. 484-988. Results of tests of photocopying machines to develop ways of monitoring xerographic image quality.

4454. Sugarman, Jane E., and Timothy J. Vitale. "Observations on the Drying of Paper: Five Drying Methods and the Drying Process," Journal of the American Institute for Conservation, 31:2 (Summer 1992), 175-197. Describes three experiments to observe the drying of paper; notes some papers change more than others when wet.

4455. Sugaya, Hiroshi. "The Past Quarter Century and the Next Decade of Videotape Recording," SMPTE Journal (Society of Motion Picture and Television Engineers), 101:1 (January 1992), 10-13. Short technical history of the videotape recorder, the future predicted from a trend chart, and technical motivating force of development.

4456. Sullivan, John, and Jennifer Johnson. "The Preservation Directorate: Saving the Library's Legacy," LC Information Bulletin (Library of Congress), 50:13 (July 1, 1991), 247-253; reprinted in New Library Scene, 10:5 (October 1991), 1, 5-10. Describes the Library of Congress preservation and conservation services: the binding, conservation, preservation microfilming, research, and testing, and also the National Preservation Program Office.

4457. Sullivan, Larry E. "United States Newspaper Program: Progress and Prospects," Microform Review, 15:3 (Summer 1986), 158-161. A history of newspaper publishing in the United States, the factors leading to the U.S. Newspaper Project, present status, and future of the program.

4458. Sullivan, Mark. "Cleaning up History in Andover," Boston Globe, (February 11, 1996), 1 Information on Northeast Document Conservation Center.

4459. Sullivan, Peggy. "Preservation and Judgment," School Library Journal, 36:7 (July 1990), 16-19. The need for the preservation of books from a children's librarian's perspective. Text of talk given at the President's Program, American Library Association, January 1990.

4460. Sun, Marjorie. "The Big Problem of Brittle Books," Science, 240 (April 1988), 598-600. Describes high-tech and low-tech measures to deal with acid paper and brittle books, history of the diethyl zinc and other deacidification processes.

4461. Sun, Marjorie. "Rare Treatment for Rare Items," Science, 240: 4852 (April 29, 1988), 599. Describes manuscript preservation efforts at the Library of Congress and the National Archives. The monitoring of the Declaration of Independence, the Bill of Rights, and the Constitution is discussed.

4462. Sun, Marjorie. "Severe Fire Devastates Soviet Science Library," Science, 240:4850 (April 8, 1988), 138-139. Brief report on the Academy of Sciences Library, Leningrad, fire in February 1988.

4463. Sundt, Christine L. Conservation Practices for Slide and Photograph Collections. Austin, TX: Visual Resource Association, 1989. 78p. (VRA Special Bulletin No. 3, 1989). A collection of the author's columns on slide and photograph preservation and conservation, originally published in the International Bulletin for Photographic Documentation of the Visual Arts, 1979-1987.

4464. Sundt, Christine L. "Conservation Transparencies in Paper Mounts," International Bulletin for Photographic Documentation of the Visual Arts, 11:4 (Winter 1984), 20-22. Discusses paper versus glass mounting, storage, and cleaning.

4465. Sung, Carolyn Hoover, Valerii Pavlovich Leonov, and Peter Waters. "Fire Recovery at the Academy of Sciences of the USSR," American Archivist, 53:2 (Spring 1990), 298-312. Describes the recovery efforts following the devastating fire in February 1988.

4466. Suryawanshi, D. G., P. M. Sinha, and Om Prakash Agarawal. "Basic Studies on the Properties of Palm Leaf," Restaurator, 15:2 (1994), 65-78. Report of a study to determine the extent of deterioration caused by internal factors, with suggestions for prolonging the life of palm leaf manuscripts.

4467. Suryawanshi, D. G., and Om Prakash Agrawal. "Evaluation of Hand-Made Nepalese Paper for Lining Paintings," Restaurator 16:2 (1995), 65-76.

4468.   Sutcliffe, Charles. "A Model for the Financial Appraisal of Electronic Book Security Systems with an Application to Berkshire County Libraries," Library and Archival Security, 6:4 (Winter 1984), 27-42. Model for evaluation of book security systems.

4469.   Sutcliffe, Gary. Slide Collection Management in Libraries and Information Units. Brookfield, UT: Ashgate Publishing, 1995. 219p. Contains a chapter on optical disk systems.

4470.   Suthard, K. Peter. Scanning and Digitization. Alexandria, VA: Defense Technical Information Center, 1995. 49p. Discusses and offers suggestions to different methodologies used at DTIC.

4471.   Swan, Christopher. "Preserving Paper Records: Experts Use Modern and Medieval Techniques," Christian Science Monitor (January 20, 1987), 23-24. Conservation at Northeast Documents Conservation Center.

4472.   Swartzburg, Susan G. "ALA Midwinter," Conservation Administration News, 45 (April 1991), 15-16.

4473.   Swartzburg, Susan G. "Audiovisual Aids on the Preservation and Conservation of Library and Archival Materials," Conservation Administration News, 49 (April 1992), 8-13. A selective, annotated bibliography.

4474.   Swartzburg, Susan G. "Basic Preservation Bibliography," Conservation Administration News, 44 (January 1991), 10-12. Bibliography of basic books in print on preservation and conservation of library and archival materials.

4475.   Swartzburg, Susan G. "Conference Report: New Directions in Paper Conservation," Mid-Atlantic Archivist, 15:3 (Summer 1986), 12-13. Report on Institute for Paper Conservation held in Oxford, England, April 14-18, 1986.

4476.   Swartzburg, Susan G., ed. Conservation in the Library: A Handbook of Use and Care of Traditional and Non-Traditional Materials.

Westport, CT: Greenwood Press, 1983. 234p. Chapters by specialists on the care and conservation of library materials, with emphasis on non-print media.

4477. Swartzburg, Susan G. "Continuing Education in Preservation: Challenge for the '90s," Continuing Professional Education and IFLA: Past, Present, and a Vision for the Future. Munich, Germany: Saur, 1993, 247-252. (IFLA Publication 66/67). Discusses the renewed interest in courses on the physical nature of library materials, their care and repair. Describes the Professional Development Program in Preservation at Rutgers University.

4478. Swartzburg, Susan G. "A German Bindery," New Library Scene, 11:3 (June 1992), 1,5. Describes a small, family-run commercial and hand bindery that emphasizes quality and durability.

4479. Swartzburg, Susan G. "IFLA 1989," Conservation Administration News, 40 (January 1990), 15-16.

4480. Swartzburg, Susan G. "IFLA 1990," Conservation Administration News, 44 (January 1991), 15-16.

4481. Swartzburg, Susan G. "IFLA '91 Moscow: Conference and Coup," New Library Scene, 11:2 (April 1992), 7-8. Reaction to the coup in the Soviet Union and reflections on its impact on libraries and its people.

4482. Swartzburg, Susan G. "IFLA 1993: Barcelona," Conservation Administration News, 56 (January 1994), 20-21.

4483. Swartzburg, Susan G. "IFLA 1995: Budapest/ Istanbul Conservation and Preservation," New Library Scene, 15:1 (February 1996), 5-13. Summary of the IFLA Preconference on Conservation held in Budapest, Hungary, and of papers relating to preservation and conservation of the IFLA Conference in Istanbul, 1995.

4484. Swartzburg, Susan G. "NARA Preservation Conference," Conservation Administration News, 50 (July 1992), 16-17. Topic: Designing for Preservation: Planning Archival Storage.

4485.   Swartzburg, Susan G. "NEDCC Celebrates Its 20th Anniversary," Conservation Administration News, 56 (January 1994) 18-19. Reprinted from New Jersey Library Association Preservation Section Newsletter 56 (Spring/Summer 1993).

4486.   Swartzburg, Susan G. "New Conservation Emphasis for the Venerable Oxford University," Conservation Administration News, 12 (January 1983), 6.

4487.   Swartzburg, Susan G. "On Preservation. Bibliography," Art Documentation, 8 (Spring 1989), 29, (Summer 1989), 86-87.

4488.   Swartzburg, Susan G. "Preservation and Access: New Jersey's Documentary Heritage," New Jersey Libraries, 26 (Summer 1993), 3-21.

4489.   Swartzburg, Susan G. "Preservation Education at ALISE," Conservation Administration News, 23 (October 1985), 9-10. Reports on a program at the annual conference of the Association for Library and Information Science Education (in January 1985), which focused on the need to integrate preservation into all areas of library school curricula.

4490.   Swartzburg, Susan G. Preservation Education Directory. Chicago, IL: American Library Association, 1990. 30p. 6th ed. Directory of programs and courses on the preservation and conservation of library and archival materials at accredited library schools in North America; sources of further training.

4491.   Swartzburg, Susan G. "The Preservation of Library and Archival Materials: A Cultural Responsibility," in Théorie et Pratique dans L'Enseignement des Sciences de l'Information. Montreal, Quebec: Université de Montreal. École de Bibliothéconomie et des Sciences de l'Information, 1988. 51-59.

4492.   Swartzburg, Susan G. "Preservation of Sound Recordings," Encyclopedia of Recorded Sound in the United States. ed. Guy A. Marco. New York: Garland, 1993. 542-546. An overview of preservation issues and concerns for phonograph records, magnetic recordings, compact disks.

4493. Swartzburg, Susan G. "Preserving the Cultural Patrimony," À la Recherche de la Mémoire le Patrimoine Culturel, ed. Huguette Rouit and Jean-Marcel Humbert. Munich: K.G. Saur, 1992, 88-96. (IFLA Publication 62) A brief history of the efforts to preserve the cultural heritage; discussion of the problem preservationists face in determining what will be preserved for future generations. A list of agencies is appended. A shorter version of this paper was published in Art Libraries Journal, 15:1, 1990.

4494. Swartzburg, Susan G. Preserving Library Materials: A Manual. Metuchen, NJ: Scarecrow Press, 1995. 503p. 2d. ed. A complete revision of the 1980 edition. A comprehensive overview of preservation in libraries and archives.

4495. Swartzburg, Susan G. "Preserving Newspaper: National and International Cooperative Efforts," Conserving and Preserving Materials in Nonbook Formats. Urbana-Champaign: University of Illinois Graduate School of Library and Information Science, 1991, 73-89. (Allerton Park Institute, 30). Traces the history of the U.S. Newspaper Project, the national program to preserve all U.S. newspapers, and international cooperative initiatives. Discusses microfilm and requirements for its use as a preservation medium.

4496. Swartzburg, Susan G. "A Question of Referrals," Conservation Administration News, 37 (April 1989), 3. Discusses the issue of referrals and recommendations for conservation treatments and services.

4497. Swartzburg, Susan G. (reporter). Report on Electronic Document Imaging, by William Saffady. ARMA Northern NJ Chapter, 1994. 8p.

4498. Swartzburg, Susan G. "Resources for the Conservation of Southeast Asian Art," Art Libraries Journal, 18:2 (1993), 39-43. A brief overview of problems with focus on Cambodia; agencies that can provide assistance.

4499.   Swartzburg, Susan G. "Rutgers Preservation Workshop," Conservation Administration News, 54 (July 1993), 15.

4500.   Swartzburg, Susan G. "Sources of Advice and Assistance," Conservation Administration News, 51 (October 1992), 14-15. On Preservation.

4501.   Swartzburg, Susan G., and Holley Bussey. Libraries and Archives: Design and Renovation With a Preservation Perspective. Metuchen, NJ: Scarecrow Press, Inc., 1991. 235p. Text and annotated bibliography on the planning and designing of library and archive buildings for the preservation of materials and the comfort of people.

4502.   Swartzburg, Susan G., and Robert E. Schnare Jr. "Programs and Issues in Preservation for the 1990s: A Bibliographic Overview," Advances in Preservation and Access. Vol. 1. Westport, CT: Meckler, 1992, 262-282. Bibliographic essay covering concerns such as cooperative efforts, paper deterioration and preservation, mass deacidification and paper strengthening, disaster planning and recovery, environment, theft and security, exhibition, pest control, management, and conservation.

4503.   Swartzburg, Susan, and Neha Weinstein. "Preservation," New Jersey Libraries, 18:1 (Spring 1987), 19p. A special issue devoted to preservation planning and activities in New Jersey libraries.

4504.   Swartzell, Ann. "Library Binding Information," RTSD Newsletter (Resources and Technical Services Division), 12:1 (Winter 1987), 6-8.

4505.   Swartzell, Ann. "Preservation," RTSD Newsletter (Resources and Technical Services Division), 9:3 (1984), 2-4. Discusses preservation surveys at Yale, Harvard, New York Public, Columbia, LC, Stanford, and the Nebraska Historical Society.

4506.   Swartzell, Ann. "Preservation," RTSD Newsletter (Resources and Technical Services Division), 9:4 (1984), 51-52. Discusses photocopying and photocopiers for preservation.

4507.   Swartzell, Ann. "Preservation," RTSD Newsletter (Resources and Technical Services Division), 9:6 (1984), 71-73. Deacidification is the topic of this column.

4508.   Swartzell, Ann. "Preservation," RTSD Newsletter (Resources and Technical Services Division), 9:8 (1984), 98-99. Discussion of the Ox Bow Conference.

4509.   Swartzell, Ann. "Preservation," RTSD Newsletter (Resources and Technical Services Division), 10:4 (1985), 40-42. Preservation Efforts of the ARL Office of Management Studies.

4510.   Swartzell, Ann. "Preservation," RTSD Newsletter (Resources and Technical Services Division), 10:7 (1985), 88-90. Discussion of cleaning projects and programs in libraries.

4511.   Swartzell, Ann. "Preservation," RTSD Newsletter (Resources and Technical Services Division), 11:1 (1986), 6-7. Discussion of the different approaches to preservation administration and the reporting structures of preservation departments, programs, and policies.

4512.   Swartzell, Ann. "Preservation," RTSD Newsletter (Resources and Technical Services Division), 11:4 (1986), 40-41. Preservation: New Standards and Guidelines.

4513.   Swartzell, Ann. "Preservation: Book Repair," RTSD Newsletter (Resources and Technical Services Division), 10:2 (1985), 12-14. Review of manuals on book repair; how to evaluate and select them.

4514.   Swartzell, Ann. "Preservation: Library Binding Information," RTSD Newsletter (Resources and Technical Services Division), 12:1 (Winter 1987), 6-8. Discussion of the application of automated serials control and other systems of commercial library binding.

4515.   Swartzell, Ann. "Preservation Efforts of the ARL Office of Management Studies," RTSD Newsletter (Resources and Technical Services Division), 10:4 (1985), 40-42. Describes their studies and

SPEC (Systems and Procedure Exchange Center) kits on preservation topics.

4516. Swartzell, Ann. "Preservation Microfilming: In-House Initiated Microforms," Conservation Administration News, 34 (July 1988), 6-7. How to organize and implement a preservation microfilming program that is appropriate for an institution.

4517. Swartzell, Ann. "Preservation of Library Materials," ALA Yearbook of Library and Information Services, Chicago, IL: American Library Association, 12, 1987, 235-237, 13, 1988, 245-248, 14, 1989, 183-185. Summary of preservation activities and concerns for the year.

4518. Swieszkowski, Linda. "The Skeleton in Our Closet: Public Library Art Collections Suffer Appalling Loses," Art Documentation, 5:1 (Spring 1986), 22-23. Discusses the problem of theft and mutilation of materials that are difficult and expensive to replace.

4519. Swift, Katherine. "The Oxford Preservation Survey. 1: The Main Survey," Paper Conservator, 17 (1993), 45-52. Describes the surveys undertaken in 1991 and 1993 to assess environmental conditions, conservation and preservation policies, followed by a physical assessment of collections.

4520. Swora, Tamara. "Optical Digital Scanning and Storage Technology: Write-Once and Erasable Media," Library High Tech Bibliography, 2:13 (1987), 113-121. Specialized bibliography of technical developments, 1985-1986, covering digital image processing, equipment and associated software, and systems built around them.

4521. "Syllabus for Serials Collection Management, Records Systems and Preservation Unit," ALCTS Newsletter (Association for Library Collections and Technical Services), 4:1 (1993), 8-9. An outline for instructors in the M.L.S. program.

4522. Sylvestre, Guy. Guidelines for National Libraries. Paris: UNESCO, September 1987. 108p. (PGI-87/WS/17). Report designed to give practical assistance to officials involved in the establishment of national libraries, especially in developing nations; preservation and conservation concerns are addressed.

4523. Sylvestre, Guy "Preserving Canada's Printed Word," National Libraries: Some South African and International Perspectives on Challenges and Opportunities; Tribute to H.J. Aschenborn at Sixty-Five. Pretoria, South Africa: South African State Library, 1986, 239-245. Describes the program and activities of the Canadian Institute for Historical Microreproduction, an initiative to preserve Canada's printed heritage in microformat.

4524. Szczepanowska, Hanna. "Assessing the Activity of Fungal Growth on Art Objects with a View to Possible Fumigation," Conservation Administration News, 37 (April 1989), 12. Instructions for identifying fungi.

4525. Szczepanowska, Hanna. "Biodeterioration of Art Objects on Paper," Paper Conservator, 10 (1986), 31-39.

4526. Szczepanowska, Hanna, and Charles M. Lovett, Jr. "Fungal Stains on Paper: Their Removal and Prevention," The Conservation of Far Eastern Art. London: International Institute for Conservation, 1988, 13-14. Describes treatment for the four fungal stains most frequently found on works on paper.

4527. Szczepanowska, Hanna, and Charles M. Lovett, Jr. "A Study of the Removal and Prevention of Fungal Stains on Paper," Journal of the American Institute for Conservation, 31:2 (Summer 1992), 147-160. Describes a method developed for the study of the removal of fungal stains on paper.

4528. Szczepanowska, Hanna Maria, and William R. Moomaw. "Laser Stain Removal of Fungus-Induced Stains from Paper," Journal of the American Institute for Conservation, 33:1 (Spring 1994), 25-32. Report of a treatment using intense light from a laser and its potential, if used carefully.

4529. Szermai, J. A. "Evolution of the Structure of the Medieval Codex: Consequences for Conservation and Restoration," Conference on

Book and Paper Conservation, 1990. Budapest, Hungary: Technical Association of Paper and Printing Industry/National Szechenyi Library, 1992, 20-31. Research on the physical structure of early books: sewing structures, spine shapes and function, board attachment.

4530. Szewezyk, David M. "Chronology of a Rare Book Sting Operation," AB Bookman's Weekly (Antiquarian Bookman), 90:10 (September 7, 1992), 753-755. Chronology of an operation to catch a thief.

4531. Szlabey, Gyorgyi. "Restoration of Corvina Cod. Lat. 3," Conference on Book and Paper Conservation, 1990. Budapest, Hungary: Technical Association of Paper and Printing Industry, 1992, 596-599. Illus. Describes the treatment of a heavily damaged manuscript.

4532. Szyonczak, Ralph, comp. Preserving the Past and Looking to the Future: Selected References. Bibliography. Compiled by Ralph Szyonczak for GPLNE (Government Publication Librarians of New England) Spring Conference University of Connecticut, Storrs, March 28, 1988. 5p.

4533. Talley, M. Kirby Jr. "Viewpoints: A Nation Mobilizes for Conservation," ICCROM Newsletter (International Center for the Conservation and Restoration of Materials), 19 (June 1993), 6-8. Briefly describes the Netherlands' study to determine the extent of conservation needs in the nation's museums.

4534. Talwar, V.V. "A Stitch in Time," Conservation of Cultural Property in India, New Delhi, Indian Association for the Study of Conservation of Cultural Property, 1983, 84-86. Briefly reviews the causes for the early decay of books and documents and describes steps that could ensure their safety.

4535. Tannenberg, Dieter. "Combination Systems: The Next Generation in Image Management," IMC Journal (International Micrographic Congress), 29:1 (January/February 1993), 7-10. Well-informed discussion of the advantage of combining digitization and microfilming for preservation and access.

4536.   Tanselle, G. Thomas. "The Latest Form of Book-Burning," Common Knowledge, 2:3 (1993), 172-177. Describes the role of the physical book in society and the inadvertent destruction of it by attempts to preserve intellectual content in microfilm or digital formats.

4537.   Tanselle, G. Thomas. Libraries, Museums, and Reading. New York: Columbia University School of Library Service, 1991. 31p. Reprinted in Raritan, 12:1 (Summer 1992), 62-82. Reflections on books, reading, and the role of the original physical object as transmitter of information.

4538.   Tanselle, G. Thomas. "Reproductions and Scholarship," Studies in Bibliography, 42 (September 29, 1989), 25-54. Traces the history of the use of facsimiles in historical research, their acceptance and the difficulties. Expresses concern that facsimiles are not carefully inspected and that original materials are too frequently discarded.

4539.   Taylor, Hugh A. "The Collective Memory: Archives and Libraries as Heritage," Archivaria, 15 (Winter 1982/83), 118-130. Reflections on preserving the written word as a reflection of daily life, not as a record of the elite.

4540.   Taylor, Hugh A. "Strategies for the Future: The Preservation of Archival Materials in Canada," Conservation Administration News, 29 (April 1987), 1-3. Describes the objectives of the Conservation Committee, Canadian Council of Archives.

4541.   Taylor, J. M. "Detecting Art Fraud: Sometimes Scientific Examination Can Help," CCI Newsletter (Canadian Conservation Institute), 12 (September 1993), 12-14. Discusses tests that can be undertaken, with examples, noting limitations of such scientific examination.

4542.   Taylor, Thomas O. "Not All Mylar Is Archival," Abbey Newsletter, 13:5 (September 1989), 81. Describes history of fabrication of Mylar and range of types. Uses of coated and uncoated versions for archival purposes are discussed; Mylar suitable for conservation is identified.

4543.   Taylor, Thomas O. "Preventive Films in Philately: How Do We Find 'The Right Stuff?'" American Philatelist, (March 1988), 234-236. Brief history of plastic films and problems caused by chemical additives; testing discussed and author's product is recommended.

4544.   Technical Association of the Pulp and Paper Industry (TAPPI). Glossary of Reprography and Non-Impact Printing Terms for the Paper and Printing Industries. Atlanta, GA: TAPPI Press, 1989. 54p. Terms reflecting new technologies in printing, including dot-matric printing, reprography, and other non-impacting techniques.

4545.   Teller, Alan. "How Good Pictures Go Bad," Journal of American Photography, 1:1 (January 1983), 24-26. Discusses how improper processing and fixing cause photographs to deteriorate; tips to photographers to preserve their work.

4546.   Templer, Julian. "Systems for Protecting Records," Disaster Planning in Jamaica. Kingston, Jamaica: Jamaica Library Association, 1989, 11-13. Fire protection for paper and electronic records.

4547.   Tending, Antoine. "Architectural Protection of Library Materials in Western Africa," International Preservation News, 6 (June 1993), 7-9. Brief discussion of the environmental factors for the protection and preservation of library and archival materials in the region.

4548.   Tending, Antoine. "Proposals for Training Programmes in Conservation and Preservation," Proceedings of the Pan-African Conference on the Preservation and Conservation of Library and Archival Materials, Nairobi, Kenya, 21-25 June 1993. The Hague: IFLA, 1995, 151-155. (IFLA Professional Publication 43). Outline of a three-week course for scientific and technical staff. Bibliography.

4549.   Tennent, Norman H., ed. Conservation Science in the U.K. London: James & James Science Publishers, 1993. 128p. A representative picture of the breadth of current British conservation research.

Papers presented at the Conservation Science Meeting, Glasgow, Scotland, May 1993.

4550. Tennessee State Library and Archives. The Volunteer Challenge: Final Report of the Statewide Assessment of Historical Records in Tennessee. Nashville, TN: Tennessee State Library and Archives, 1993. 72p. Preservation recommendation centers on getting control of the state's records by developing a comprehensive records management program.

4551. TenWolde, Anton. "Indoor Humidity and the Building Envelope," Bugs, Mold & Rot II, eds. William B. Rose and Anton TenWolde. Washington, DC: National Institute of Building Sciences, 1993, 37-41. Includes practical guidance and knowledgeable discussion of factors that influence growth of mold and deterioration of outer wall, floor, and roof in buildings.

4552. Teo, Elizabeth A. "Conservation of Library Materials and the Environment: A Case Study With Recommendations," Illinois Libraries, 67:8 (October 1985), 711-717. Notes the importance of environmental control for general collections.

4553. Teoman, Elizabeth Gay, and Jane Slate Siena. "Rising from the Ashes: The Los Angeles Public Library," Conservation (Newsletter of the Getty Conservation Institute), 8:2 (1994), 8-11. Describes the library's recovery following the devastating fires in 1986, and the renovation of its historic structure.

4554. Terris, Olwen. "John Paul Getty Jr. Conservation Centre." Audiovisual Librarian, 16:1 (February 1990), 33-34. Brief description of the Centre, its activities, and preservation procedures.

4555. Terry, R. J. "Organizing a Contingency Plan for Success," Disaster Recovery Journal, 8:2 (April-June 1995), 43-46. The basics of emergency planning and preparing a disaster plan.

4556. "Testing of Two Methods for the Recovery of Bibliographic Material Damaged by Bookworms," Revista de Biblioteconomia de Brasilia, 16:2 (July-December 1988), 145-155.

Bibliography

4557.   Texas Association of Museums. PREP Planning for Response and
         Emergency Preparedness: A Disaster Preparedness/Recovery
         Resource Manual, eds. Mary E. Candee and Richard Casagrande.
         Austin, TX: Texas Association of Museums, 1993. Loose-leaf
         notebook. Guide for the preparation of site-specific plans. Provides
         overview of disaster planning and recovery, sample forms and plans,
         resource information, and bibliography.

4558.   Teygeler, Rene, and Henk Porck. "Technical Analysis and
         Conservation of a Bark Manuscript in the Dutch Royal Library,"
         Paper Conservator, 19 (1995), 55-62. Technical examination and
         conservation of a tree bark manuscript.

4559.   Thackery, David, and Edward Meachen. Local History in the
         Library: A Manual for Assessment and Preservation. Bloomington,
         IL: Bloomington Public Library, 1989. 42p. How to collect and
         preserve local history materials.

4560.   Thakre, R. P., and M. N. Bhajbhuje. "Biodeterioration of Books and
         Journals," Biodeterioration of Cultural Property, eds. Om Prakash
         Agrawal and Shashi Dhawan. New Delhi, India: ICCROM/
         INTACH, 1991, 139-147. Discussion of survey to isolate and identify
         the fungal organisms responsible for the degradation of books and
         journals in a library.

4561.   Thibodeau, Kenneth. The Preservation of Electronic Records.
         Washington, DC: National Archives, 1991. 9p. Keynote address
         presented at the National Archives Sixth annual Preservation
         Conference, Washington, DC, March 19, 1991.

4562.   Thoma, George R., and Frank L. Walker. "Archiving the Biomedical
         Literature by Electronic Imaging Methods," ASIS '88: Information
         Technology: Planning for the Next Fifty Years, Proceedings, 25
         (October 1988), 132-136. (51st Annual Meeting of the American
         Society for Information Science). The conclusions of a committee
         that investigated microfilming, mass deacidification, and digital
         imaging for the preservation of biomedical literature at the National
         Library of Medicine.

4563.   Thoma, George R., F. L. Walker, S. Hauser, and M. Gill. Document Preservation by Electronic Imaging. Three volumes. Bethesda, MD: Lister Hill, MD: National Center for Biomedical Communications, April 1989. 32p., 182p., 54p. Report on a research and development program to investigate the applicability of digital electronic imaging (EI) and storage of digital optical WORM disks to the problem of document preservation.

4564.   Thomas, Bill. "Archival Quality: The Test for Methylene Blue," Inform, 1:5 (May 1987), 6-7,46-47. Discussion of regular Methylene Blue testing and its advantages.

4565.   Thomas, David L. Study on Control of Security and Storage of Holdings. Paris: UNESCO, 1987. 62p. (RAMP Study with Guidelines). Provides general guidelines for building design and for the protection of records against specific hazards.

4566.   Thomas, David L. "Architectural Design and Technical Equipment for the Physical Protection and Conservation of Documents," Mitteilungen des Österreichischen Staatsarchivs, 39 (1986), 233-251. (Festschrift fur Rudolf Neck). Discusses the concept of passive conservation: environmental considerations in storage and use of materials.

4567.   Thomas, David L. "Conservation: New Techniques and New Attitudes," Archives, 16:70 (October 1983), 167-177. Traces history of preservation and conservation technologies and looks at current and potential ones.

4568.   Thomas, David L. "Security at the New Public Record Office," Janus, 1 (1992), 110-115. Describes security arrangements planned for the new Public Records Office at Kew; fire protection, design, and internal measures.

4569.   Thomas, David L. Study on Control of Security and Storage of Holdings: A RAMP Study With Guidelines. Paris: UNESCO, February 1987, 47p. (PGI-86/WS/23). Provides general guidelines for building design and for the protection of records against specific hazards; written for developing countries.

4570. Thomas, David L. Survey on National Standards of Paper and Ink to Be Used by the Administration for Records Creation. Paris: UNESCO, 1986. 47p. (PGI-86\WS\22). Review of standards for permanent and non-archival papers in National Archives.

4571. Thomas, James. "Paper and People: An Historical Perspective [1]," In Safe Keeping, ed. Jennifer Thorp. Winchester, England: Hampshire Co. Library / Hampshire Archives Trust, 1988, 1-2. History of papermaking in England. 87 references.

4572. Thomas, John B., III. "The Necessity of Standards in an Automated Environment," Library Trends (Summer 1987), 125-139.

4573. Thomas, Julian. "Basic Bookbinding for Trainees at the National Library of Wales," Conference on Book and Paper Conservation, 1990. Budapest, Hungary: Technical Association of Paper and Printing Industry/National Szechenyi Library, 1992, 402-406. Description of an in-house training program for binding and conservation staff.

4574. Thomas, Julian. "Mass Fumigation at the National Library of Wales," Paper Conservation News, 35 (September 1985), 2-3. Description of the treatment of mold-infested materials by thymol fumigation.

4575. Thomas, Mark, et al. "Security and Preservation of the U.S. Congressional Serial Set," Journal of Government Information, 21 (July/August 1994), 351-366.

4576. Thomas, Sylvia. "The Wakefield Court Rolls," Library Conservation News, 37 (October 1992), 4-5. Brief description of a conservation project supported by the National Manuscripts Conservation Trust (U.K.).

4577.   Thomas, Wendy. "Report on ALA's 1994 Annual Conference in Miami, Imaging, Microform, and New Technology Programs," Microform Review, 23 (Summer 1994), 120-124.

4578.   Thomasset, Annie. "Conservation of a Hand-Colored Albumen Photograph," OJO: Connoisseurship and Conservation of Photographs, 4 (Spring 1993), 8. Treatment: humidification, washing, alkalization, remounting.

4579.   Thompson, Anthony Hugh. Storage, Handling and Preservation of Audiovisual Materials. The Hague, Netherlands: Nederlands Bibliotheek en Lectuur Centrum, 1983. 28p. (AV in Action 3). Basic guide on the care, handling, and housing of circulating collections.

4580.   Thompson, Claudia G. Recycled Papers: The Essential Guide. Cambridge, MA: MIT Press, 1992. 162p. Concise overview of issues surrounding the recycling of paper products; strongly advocates standards for paper production and recycling.

4581.   Thompson, Frank. "Fade Out," American Film, 16:8 (August 1991), 34-38, 46. Discusses the loss of film heritage and efforts to preserve early films.

4582.   Thompson, Jack C. "Building a Medieval Papermill," Conservation Administration News, 53 (April 1993), 13. Brief description and photograph of the papermill, designed to explore the relationship between fiber and the machinery that reduces it to pulp.

4583.   Thompson, Jack C. Manuscript Inks: Being a Personnel Exploration of the Materials and Modes of Production With an Appendix on Ink Sticks by Claes G. Lindblad. Portland, OR: Caber Press, 1996. 65p.

4584.   Thompson, Jack C. "Mass Deacidification: Thoughts on the Cunha Report," Restaurator, 9:3 (1988), 147-162. Review of Cunha's study of mass deacidification systems, 1987; faulting the lack of peer review of the systems and poor quality control that have hampered development efforts.

Bibliography

4585.   Thompson, Jack C.. "Preservation: State of the Art Techniques Available in Northwest," PNLA Quarterly (Pacific Northwest Library Association), 51:2 (Winter 1987), 18-19. Describes the activities of the Thompson Conservation Laboratory, Portland, OR: treatments, education, and training.

4586.   Thompson, John A. Manual of Curatorship: A Guide to Museum Practice. London: Butterworth, 1987, 553p.   Covers museum conservation.

4587.   Thompson, Lawrence S. "Biblioclasm in Norway," Library and Archival Security, 6:4 (Winter 1984), 13-16. Describes the thefts of rare books and manuscripts by a Norwegian civil servant.

4588.   Thompson, Lawrence S. "Library Pests," Library and Archival Security, 9:1 (Spring 1985), 15-24. Humorous look at people as pests, and remedies for the problems they can cause.

4589.   Thomson, Garry. The Museum Environment. 2d ed.   London: Butterworths, 1986. 308p. Text for conservators and collection managers; covers light, humidity, air pollution.

4590.   Thomson, Garry. "Specifications and Logging of the Museum Environment," International Journal of Museum Management and Curatorship, 3:4 (December 1984), 317-326. Discusses specifications for an appropriate museum environment; methods of monitoring with computerized programs.

4591.   Thomson, Garry, and Sarah Staniforth. Conservation and Museum Lighting. 4th ed. London: Museums Association, 1985, 6p. (Museum Information Sheet, 6). Useful for planning storage and exhibition areas.

4592.   Thorburn, Georgine. "Library Fire and Flood - Successful Salvage, but Beware of the Cowboy," ASLIB Information, 21:2 (February 1993), 76-78. Describes the work of a firm specializing in the recovery of books and documents following a disaster.

4593.   Thorburn, Karen J. "Disaster Manual: Save the Horses!" New Jersey Libraries, 28:3 (Summer 1985), 16-18. Preparation of a disaster manual.

4594.   Thorp, Valerie. "Imitation Leather: Structure, Composition, and Conservation," Leather Conservation News, 6:2 (Spring 1990), 7-15. Describes the types of imitation leather, with some emphasis on those made of cellulose nitrate compositions; discusses methods of preservation and conservation. Bibliography.

4595.   Thorp, Jennifer. "Fire, Flood and Pestilence: Disaster Planning," In Safe Keeping. Winchester, England: Hampshire Co. Library / Hampshire Archives Trust, 1988, 18-23. Reviews causes of disasters with examples, and outlines elements of disaster planning and recovery.

4596.   Thorp, Jennifer, ed. In Safe Keeping: The Preservation of Rare Books and Archives. Winchester, England: Hampshire Archives Trust and Hampshire County Library, 1988. 39p. Proceedings of a Regional Conference organized by the South-Western Branch of the Library Association and the Hampshire Archives Trust at the Guildhall, Winchester, November 3,1987.

4597.   Thurston, Anne. "The Zanzibar Archives Project," Information Development, 2:4 (October 1986), 223-226. Describes a project in the summers of 1985 and 1986 to organize and preserve archival materials and to train staff in basic archival management and conservation practices.

4598.   Tibbits, Edie. "Binding Conventions for Music Materials," Library Resources and Technical Services, 40:1 (January 1996), 33-40. Discusses special concerns in the binding of music scores. Presents results of a survey of binding procedures for scores in a small sample and academic libraries indicating that current practices are not sound. Notes need for "carefully established binding procedures...if a music collection is to serve the public...for an extended period of time" (33).

4599. Tibbo, Helen R. "Information Systems, Services, and Technology for the Humanities," Annual Review of Information Science and Technology, 26 (1991), 287-346. Review of the literature, 1981-1990, with a section that specifically addresses preservation concerns.

4600. Tigelaar, Mary Peelen, and Marcia Duncan Lowry. "The Conservator in the Library: Two Perspectives," Library Administration and Management, 3:3 (Summer 1989), 122-130. Tigelaar describes the range of skills displayed by conservators and conservation technicians and how they can be integrated into a library's preservation program; Lowry advocates the professional librarian as preservation officer.

4601. Tilbrooke, David R. W. "Structure, Production and Conservation of Leather and Parchment: A Guide for Bookbinders," First National Conference of Craft Bookbinders - Australia. Kingston, Australia: Craft Bookbinders Guild, November 1984, 35-40. Discussion of skins and their preparation for binding, with a note on preservation of leather.

4602. Tisch, Thomas. "Cleaning Solutions for a Clean Environment: Developments in Motion Picture Film-Cleaning Technology," SMPTE Journal (Society of Motion Picture and Television Engineers), 104:8 (August 1995), 528-533. Article describes the search for an effective film-cleaning alternative, safe to film, lab operator, and environment, with discontinuance of methyl chloroform used for the past 37 years.

4603. Tisch, Thomas. "Film Cleaners to Be Phased Out," AMIA Newsletter (Association of Moving Image Archivists), 21 (July 1993), 1-2. Discussion of options for film cleaning with the phasing out of substances containing chloroflorocarbons (CFCs).

4604. Tissing, Robert W. "Audiovisual Archives in the LBJ Presidential Library," Conservation Administration News, 44 (January 1991), 1-2, 24-25. Describes the scope of the collection and the problems it presents, with preservation guidelines and activities.

4605. Toigo, Jon William. Disaster Recovery Planning: Managing Risk and Catastrophe in Information Systems. Englewood Cliffs, NJ: Yourdon Press, 1989. 267p. Text on disaster planning for recovery of information in electronic formats.

4606. Tomaiuolo, Nicholas. "Deterring Book Theft Our Common Responsibility," Wilson Library Bulletin, 63:5 (January 1989), 58-59. Elements of library security; review of security systems and need for staff awareness.

4607. Tomazello, Maria, Guiomar Carneiro, and Frederico Maximiliano Wiendl. "The Applicability of Gamma Radiation to the Control of Fungi in Naturally Contaminated Papers," Restaurator, 16:2 (1995), 93-99. Investigation of the effectiveness of treatments using gamma radiation for the disinfection of papers naturally contaminated by fungi and bacteria.

4608. Tomer, Christinger. "Developing Financial Support for Library Preservation: An Alternate Approach," Journal of Academic Librarianship, 11:3 (July 1985), 133-135. Examines basis and prospects for cooperative arrangements to preserve documents in digital format, to be reproduced in various formats upon demand.

4609. Tomer, Christinger. "Selecting Library Materials for Preservation," Library and Archival Security, 7:1 (Spring 1985), 1-6. Use as a factor in selection for preservation.

4610. Torraca, Giorgio. Solubility and Solvents for Conservation Problems. Rome: ICCROM, 1990. 64p.

4611. Torres, Amparo R. de, ed. Collections Care: A Basic Reference Shelflist. Washington, DC: National Institute for the Conservation of Cultural Property, 1990. 183p.

4612. Torres, Amparo R. de, ed. Collections Care: A Selected Bibliography. Washington, DC: National Institute for the Conservation of Cultural Property, 1990. 119p.

4613.   Torres, Amparo R. de, ed. The Conservation Assessment: Bibliography. Washington, DC: National Institute for the Conservation of Cultural Property; Marina del Rey, CA: Getty Conservation Institute, 1990. 45p. Citations without annotations.

4614.   Totka, Vincent A. Jr. "Preventing Patron Theft in the Archives," American Archivist, 56:4 (Fall 1993), 664-672. Reports results of a survey to determine security awareness among selected Wisconsin repositories; reflects lack of security, knowledge of the law, and how to manage security.

4615.   Tottie, Thomas. "The Need of Conservation in European Research Libraries: Introduction," LIBER Bulletin, 31 (1988), 9-13. Outlines continuing concern for preservation of library materials from the Middle Ages; suggests the cooperative role Europeans can take to address the problem.

4616.   Toulet, Jean. "The Restoration of Books: A French Perspective," Library Conservation News, 11 (April 1986), 4-6,8. Describes the current state of conservation in France and the conservator's approach to library conservation. Translation of paper originally published in Conservation et Mise en Valeur des Fonds Anciens Rares et Précieux des Bibliothéques Francaises. Villeurbanne: Presse de L.E.N.S.3., 1983. 233p.

4617.   Towner, Lawrence W. "An End to Innocence," American Libraries, 19:3 (March 1988), 210-213. Examines the emergence of theft of library materials, focusing on the Newberry Library experience. Revision of keynote paper presented at the Oberlin Conference on Theft, 1983.

4618.   Townsend, John. Southeastern Library Network. The SOLINET Preservation Planning and Evaluation Project: Final Report. Atlanta, GA: SOLINET Preservation Service, 1994. One volume, various paging.

4619.   Townsend, Joyce H., and Norman H. Tennent. "Color Transparencies: Studies in Light Fading and Storage Stability," Preprints: Committee on Conservation 10th Triennial Meeting, ed.

Janet Bridgland. Washington, DC: International Council of
Museums, 1993, 281-286. Discusses stability of four types of color
transparencies for storage conditions and accelerated light aging.

4620.   Townsend, John, and Norman H. Tennent. "The Photochemical and
Thermal Stability of Colour Transparencies," Color Imaging
Systems. London: Royal Photographic Society, 1988, 117-
123. Report of a study of accelerated light aging test on selected
films.

4621.   Townsend, John. Preservation of Library, Archival and Other Paper-
Based Materials at the Research and Development Centre for
Biology. Richmond, NY: The Author, 1995. 62p.

4622.   Tozo-Waldmann, Suada. "What Happened in the East? Sarajevo:
The National and University Library of Bosnia/Herzegovina,"
International Preservation News, 8 (June 1994), 8. Short report on
the destruction of the library and its collections, reprinted in
translation from Bulletin des Bibliothèques, 2 (1994), 58-62.

4623.   Tracy, Gay S. "After Hurricane Andrew NEDCC Helps Save
Damaged Collections," Conservation Administration News, 53
(April 1993), 3. Illus. Brief description of on-site assistance by
conservators from the Northeast Document Conservation Center
immediately following the disaster.

4624.   Tracy, Gay S. "Treatment Profile: NEDCC's Bindery Conserves an
Important Legal Document," Conservation Administration News, 40
(January 1990), 12. Illus. Describes the conservation of a rare book
from Harvard University Law School.

4625.   Trader, Margaret. "Preservation Technologies: Photocopies,
Microforms, and Digital Imaging, Pros and Cons," Microform
Review, 22:3 (Summer 1993), 127-134. Examines each reformatting
technology and suggests that no one technology will gain complete
acceptance over others as a preservation medium.

4626.   Trainor, Julia. "Standards for Cataloguing Preservation Microform
Masters: Development and Implementation in the Australian

Bibliographic Network," Preservation Microfilming: Does It Have a Future? Canberra: National Library of Australia, 1995, 170-177. Use of the National Bibliographic Database to share information about preservation.

4627. Traister, Daniel. "Book Theft Is Focus of Two-Day Conference," AB Bookman's Weekly (Antiquarian Bookman), 76:16 (October 17, 1983), 2443-2446. Report on the Oberlin Conference, where librarians and dealers gathered to address the issue of theft from libraries.

4628. Traister, Daniel. "Seduction and Betrayal: An Insider's View of Insider Theft of Rare Materials," Wilson Library Bulletin, 69:1 (September 1994), 30-33. Case study of theft by a trusted employee; consequences and lessons for the library community.

4629. Traue, J. E. "The Alexander Turnbull Library: Present Trends and Future Policies," Archifacts (New Zealand), 2 (June 1986), 37-41. Describes the library's mission to ensure the preservation of the documentary history of New Zealand for present and future research through microfilm and the production of indexes and other reference tools.

4630. "Treatment of Leather," Conservation News (Rocky Mountain Regional Conservation Center), 2:2 (Fall 1984), 4-5. Description of the nature of leather and its preservation.

4631. Trechsel, Heinz R. Moisture Control in Buildings. Philadelphia, PA: American Society for Testing and Measurements, 1994. 485p.

4632. Tregarthen Jenkin, Ian. Disaster Planning and Preparedness: An Outline Disaster Control Plan. London: British Library Research and Development Department, 1987. 88p. (British Library Information Guide, 5). Guide for institutions preparing disaster plans; focus on water damage.

4633. Tremain, Brian. "Housing the Photographic Archive - Dust to Dust - Not Necessarily," Dust to Dust? Field Archaeology in Museums. Leicester, England: 1986. Page cites unknown. Considers the protection, care, and storage of photographic negatives and prints; paper presented at a conference in 1984.

4634. Tremain, David. "CCI Assists Dryden Air Crash Investigation," CCI Newsletter (Canadian Conservation Institute), 6 (September 1990), 15-16. English/French. Describes how conservators stabilized aircraft logbooks following a crash, enabling investigators to recover evidence useful for the investigation of the crash. First the records were freeze-dried, then they were strengthened with parylene.

4635. Tremain, David. "Conservation Assists Accident Investigations," Conference on Book and Paper Conservation, 1990. Budapest: Technical Association of Paper and Printing Industry/National Szechenyi Library, 1992, 62-71. Case study of freeze-drying logbooks from a crashed airplane, its recovery and restoration using parylene as a coating.

4636. Trevitt, John. "Permanent Paper - Progress in the U.S. and the U.K.," Logos, 1:1 (1990), 50-53. Discussion of the permanent paper issue, placing responsibility upon publishers; does not see mass deacidification as a solution.

4637. Trevitt, John. "Why We Should Change to Permanent Paper," Library Association Record, 86:11 (November 1984), 469. Chairman of the Publishers Association Production Committee (UK) argues that the British book trade should use permanent paper for all publications of value.

4638. Trezza, Alphonse F., ed. Issues for a New Decade: Today's Challenge, Tomorrow's Opportunity. Boston, MA: G.K. Hall, 1991. 177p. Preservation issues are addressed in papers presented at the 8th annual library conference, Florida State University School of Library and Information Service.

4639. Trinkaus-Randall, Gregor. "After the Deluge, What Next? Or How ECCL Ran a Disaster Workshop," Conservation Administration News, 24 (January 1986), 6, 17, 21. Describes a recovery workshop run by the Essex County (MA) Cooperative Libraries, resulting in personnel in the immediate region trained for salvage.

4640. Trinkaus-Randall, Gregor. "Library Binding as a Preservation Option," Archival Products News, 4:3 (Summer 1996), 3-4.

4641. Trinkhaus-Randall, Gregor. The Massachusetts Preservation Needs Assessment: Ban Analysis. Boston: Massachusetts Board of Library Commissioners, 1993. One volume.

4642. Trinkaus-Randall, Gregor. Preliminary Analysis of Massachusetts Preservation Needs Assessment Survey. Boston, MA: Massachusetts Board of Library Commissioners, November 1990. 56p. Review of a survey to obtain information about the preservation of library and archival materials in the state. Describes survey instrument and results.

4643. Trinkaus-Randall, Gregor. "Preservation Activities," Libraries and Information Services Today. 1991 edition. ed. by June Lester. Chicago, IL: American Library Association, 1991, 200-205. Review of concerns, including permanent paper, archival activities, deacidification, cooperative programs, and the activities of the National Endowment for the Humanities, the Research Libraries Group, and the Commission on Preservation and Access.

4644. Trinkaus-Randall, Gregor. Preserving Library Materials: Statewide Preservation Programs Growing: Massachusetts Joins In. Boston: Massachusetts Board of Library Commissioners, [1989]. 4p.

4645. Trinkaus-Randall, Gregor. "Preserving Special Collections Through Internal Security," College and Research Libraries, 50:4 (July 1989), 448-454. Discussion of methods of security in special collections.

4646. Trinkaus-Randall, Gregor. Protecting Your Collections: A Manual of Archival Security, Chicago, IL: Society of American Archivists, 1995. 92p. Overview of security as an integral part of archival management. Includes disaster preparedness, environmental concerns, staff training, public awareness, crisis management. Discussion of physical security systems.

4647. Trinkaus-Randall, Gregor. "Security and Collections," Archival Outlook, (July 1995), 18-19.

4648. Trinkaus-Randall, Gregor. "Security Issues for Special Collections," Archival Products News, 4:2 (Spring 1996), 1-2. Covers collection care; environmental protection, fire protection, careful cataloging and record keeping, surveillance, and the need to have readers use photo IDs.

4649. Trinkaus-Randall, Gregor. "The Spirit of Massachusetts: Preservation in the 90s," Preservation Papers of the 1991 SAA Annual Conference. Chicago, IL: Society of American Archivists, 1992, 34-38. Statewide planning for preservation of documentary materials in Massachusetts, approach and challenges.

4650. Trinkaus-Randall, Gregor. "Statewide Preservation Planning in Massachusetts," Conservation Administration News, 44 (January 1991), 8-9. Describes the author's first year as conservation consultant for the Massachusetts Board of Library Commissioners and goals for the future.

4651. Trinkaus-Randall, Gregor, and Patience Kennedy Jackson. "Limiting the Use of Bookdrops: A Preservation Necessity," New Library Scene, 10:1 (February 1991), 1, 5. Describes the hazards of bookdrops; how libraries can deal with them.

4652. Trinkley, Michael. Can You Stand the Heat? A Fire Safety Primer for Libraries, Archives and Museums. Atlanta, GA: Southeast Library Network (SOLINET) 1991. 60p. Introduction to fire safety, with description of detection and suppression devises. Outlines elements of a fire safety program for institutions.

4653. Trinkley, Michael. "Critters in the Collection: Integrated Pest Management," Florida Libraries 37 (October 1994), 354-355.

4654. Trinkley, Michael. Hurricane! Surviving the Big One: A Primer for Libraries, Museums and Archives. Columbia, SC: Chicora Foundation; Atlanta, GA: SOLINET, 1993. 76p. Covers disaster planning, storm-proofing a facility, recovery, insurance, and sources of assistance.

4655.　Trinkley, Michael. Preservation Concerns in Construction and Remodeling of Libraries: Planning for Preservation. Columbia, SC: Chicora Foundation, South Carolina State Library, 1992. 96p.

4656.　Truelson, Stanley D. Jr. "Health Science Library Materials: Preservation," Handbook of Medical Library Practice. 4th ed., Vol. 2. Chicago, IL: Medical Library Association, 1983, 139-181. Summary of collection management concerns, with emphasis on decision making for preservation at point of accession; library binding, book repair, environmental concerns. 93 references.

4657.　Trujillo, Rosanne. "Are You a Preservation Saint or Sinner? Report of the PARS Education Committee Program at the 1995 ALA Conference," ALCTS Newsletter (Association for Library Collections and Technical Services), 6 (1995), 80. Reprinted from Cognotes 26 (June 28, 1995), 11.

4658.　Truman, Carol. "Binding With a Flow Chart: The View of a Library Binder," New Library Scene, 8:1 (February 1989), 1,5. Binding supervisor's perspective; critique of a flow chart designed by Jan Merrill-Oldham, University of Connecticut.

4659.　Trumpp, Thomas. "Some Aspects of Communication of Audio-Visual Media From the View of State Archives," Phonographic Bulletin, 53 (March 1989), 11-16. Describes the organization and preservation of audiovisual materials in archives, challenges and problems of impermanent materials.

4660.　Tsang, W. T. "The C^3 Laser." Scientific America, 251:5 (November 1984), 149-161. Describes the C^3 laser, which "promises great improvements in the information-carrying capacity of optical communication systems." Discusses the potential uses of this laser.

4661.　Tse, Season, and Helen D. Burgess. "Degradation of Paper by Commercial Amylase and Protease Enzymes," Conservation of Historic and Artistic Works on Paper; Proceedings of a Conference,

Ottawa, Canada 3 to 7 October, 1988, ed. Helen D. Burgess. Ottawa: Canadian Conservation Institute, 1994, 215-226. Discusses the Canadian Conservation Institute's project to investigate the possible degradative effect of enzyme treatments on seven papers.

4662.   Tse, Season, "Evaluating Commercial Mass Deacidification Processes," CCI Newsletter (Canadian Conservation Institute), 15 (March 1995), 7-8. Brief summary of assessments to date of DEZ, Wei T'o, and FMC-Litheo processes on a variety of library materials.

4663.   Tuck, D. H. Oils and Lubricants Used on Leather. Northampton, England: Leather Conservation Centre, 1983. 22p. Provides insight into the materials used in the manufacture of leather.

4664.   Tuffin, Brian. "In-House Microfilm Production: The State Library of South Australia," Preservation Microfilming: Does It Have a Future? Canberra: National Library of Australia, 1995, 58-61. Describes the evolution of the microfilming program at the State Library of South Australia; current operation.

4665.   Turko, Karen. Mass Deacidification Systems: Planning and Managerial Decision Making. Washington, DC: Association of Research Libraries, 1990. 24p. Identifies issues that library administrators must consider when making decisions on the selection, implementation, and operation of a mass deacidification system. Bibliography.

4666.   Turko, Karen. Preservation Activities in Canada: A Unifying Theme in a Decentralized Country. Washington, DC: Commission on Preservation and Access, February 1996. 16p.

4667.   Turko, Karen. "Toronto Group on Mass Deacidification," Conservation Administration News, 45 (April 1991), 12-13, 23. Creation of the group, results of their survey, and the establishment of the Committee for Preserving Documentary Heritage to collect information and evaluate mass deacidification systems.

4668.   Tukovic-Kiseljev, Dubravka. "Rescuing Water-Damaged Textiles
        During the Los Angeles Riots," Journal of the American Institute of
        Conservation, 34:1 (Spring 1995), 77-83. Case study demonstrating
        how even the best laid plans can go awry in catastrophic situations;
        how well trained conservators handled the situation; why damage
        was limited because of great care in storing objects. "The combined
        effort of conservators, collection manager, curators, curatorial
        assistants and volunteers was fundamental to the successful
        completion of this rescue operation. Teamwork was critical and
        teamwork made it possible to save the artifacts. Each person who
        was part of the team was clear about his or her responsibilities in a
        chain of command that had been clearly defined before the
        emergency" (82).

4669.   Turner, Anne M. It Comes With the Territory: Handling Problem
        Situations in Libraries. Jefferson, NC: McFarland, 1993.
        197p. Commonsense approach to establish fair and appropriate
        behavior rules and training staff to implement them.

4670.   Turner, Eric. "Specific Problems in Tropical Countries," Archivum,
        35 (1989), 153-157. Paper presented at the International Congress
        on Archives, 1988.

4671.   Turner, Jeffrey H. "The Suitability of Diazo Film for Long Term
        Storage," Microform Review, 17:3 (August 1988), 142-
        145. Discusses advantages of diazo film.

4672.   Turner, John. "Binding Arbitration: A Comparison of the Durability
        of Various Hardback and Paperback Bindings," Library Association
        Record, 88:5 (May 1986), 233-235. Results of a three-year
        experiment to test the life of various styles of bookbinding.

4673.   Turner, John. "Conservation Where?" Library Conservation News,
        34 (January 1992), 1-3. Describes the Conservation Department,
        University of Tartu Library, Estonia.

4674.   Turner, John R. "Teaching Conservation," Education for
        Information, 6:2 (June 1988), 145-151. Discusses an "ideal" syllabus

for instruction in conservation and preservation in library schools and more realistic approaches.

4675. Turner, Judith A. "At Work in the Restoration Rooms of the Library of Congress," The Chronicle of Higher Education (March 9, 1988), A3. Describes the Conservation Laboratory at the Library of Congress and the work of Karen Garlick.

4676. Turner, Judith A. "Library of Congress Displays Process to Prevent Books from Crumbling," The Chronicle of Higher Education, (January 20, 1988), A7.

4677. Turner, Judith A. "Technology Unit Likely to Accept Chemical Process Designed to Save Books at Library of Congress," Chronicle of Higher Education (February 10, 1988), 5,7.

4678. Turner, Nancy. "The Conservation of Medieval Manuscript Illuminations and the Question of Compensation," WAAC Newsletter (Western Association for Art Conservation), 16:1 (January 1994), 21-22. Note on treatments, emphasizing the need to know options, old and new, to select appropriate treatment method. Bibliography.

4679. Turner, Patrick. "The Integration of Microfilm into Electronic Imaging Systems," Preservation Microfilming: Does It Have a Future? Canberra: National Library of Australia, 1995, 118-122. Discusses use of microfilm and electronics, looking to the business sectors concern for long-term storage of data. Discusses "information risk" and long-term strategies for image migration.

4680. Turner, Sandra. "Mold ... The Silent Enemy," New Library Scene, 4:4 (August 1985), 1, 6-8, 21. Report on a mold disaster and clean-up efforts.

4681. Tuttle, Craig A. An Ounce of Preservation: A Guide to the Care of Paper and Photographs. Highland City, FL: Rainbow Press, 1995. 111p. Basic overview on paper and photographs, causes of deterioration, storage and repair. For public.

4682. "Two Decades of TV Film to Be Preserved," Northeast Historic Film Moving Image Review (Winter 1988), 1-2. Describes the cooperative initiative of WABI-TV, the Bangor Historical Society, and NHF to save and make accessible an estimated 300 hours (roughly 650,000 feet) of unique 16mm film containing news, sports and commercials shot between 1953-1974.

4683. Twomey, James E. "Descriptive Analysis of a Conservation Awareness Program," Journal of Education for Library and Information Science, 29:3 (Winter 1989), 197-208. Description and analysis of a project with a hands-on component to assess if such training significantly increases student's awareness of conservation.

4684. "UC/Berkeley Library Averts Disaster," American Libraries, 27 (February 1996), 16.

4685. "Ultraviolet Filters for Fluorescent Lamps," CCI Notes (Canadian Conservation Institute), 2/1 (June 1983), 1 leaf. A brief statement about the problem with solutions suppliers.

4686. Underhill, Karen, and Randall Butler. "'Twas the Day After Christmas The Northern Arizona University Cline Library Flood," Conservation Administration News, 46 (July 1991), 12-14. Describes the recovery effort and the lessons learned.

4687. Ungarelli, Donald L. "Are Our Libraries Safe From Losses?" Library and Archival Security, 9:1 (1989), 45-48. Planning and implementing an insurance program.

4688. Ungarelli, Donald L. "Are Our Libraries Safe from Losses? National Fire Statistics, 1989," Library and Archival Security, 11:1 (1991), 117-123. Reviews statistics and advocates sprinkler systems.

4689. Ungarelli, Donald L. "Insurance and Prevention: Why and How," Library Trends, 33:1 (Summer 1984), 57-68. Stresses need for preventive evaluation and life safety procedures; covers appraisal and insurance options.

4690. "Union Carbide Signs Agreement with Wei T'o Associates," College & Research Library News, 1 (January 1990), 28.

4691. "Union Carbide to Market Wei T'o Deacidification Process," Library Journal, 114 (November 15, 1989), 25.

4692. United Kingdom. Public Records Office. Optical Disk Project: Interim Evaluation Report. London: Public Records Office, May 1988. 7p.

4693. United Nations. Advisory Committee for the Co-ordination of Information Systems. Management of Electronic Records: Issues and Guidelines. New York: United Nations, 1990. 189p. Analyzes the management of electronic records in organizations; full of recommendations for how records managers and archivists can administer such records. Contains numerous references to the "preservation" of electronic records, primarily defined as the provision of access and functionality of such records through internal institutional policies and practices and the technical standards-setting arena. Very important report that should be read by all concerned with the preservation of archival records.

4694. United Nations Educational, Scientific and Cultural Organization (UNESCO). Moving Images: Final Report International Roundtable to Evaluate the Practical Results of the UNESCO Recommendation for the Safeguarding and Preservation of Moving Images. Paris: UNESCO, 1989. 27p.

4695. United Nations Educational, Scientific and Cultural Organization, General Information Programme and UNISIST. Curriculum Development for the Training of Personnel in Moving Image and Recorded Sound Archives Paris: UNESCO, 1990. 104p.

4696. United States Advisory Committee on the Records of Congress. First Report: December 31, 1991, Prepared under the Direction of Walter J. Stewart, Chairman, by the Center for Legislative Archives, National Archives and Records Administration, Michel L. Gillette, Director. Washington, DC: The Center, 1992. 40p.

4697. United States Advisory Council of Historic Preservation and the General Services Administration. Fire Safety Retrofitting in Historic Buildings. Washington, DC: Government Printing Office, 1989. 24p.

4698.   United States Army Corps of Engineers. Safety and Health
        Requirements Manual. Washington, DC: Government Printing
        Office, 1984. 393p. Manual prescribes the general safety
        requirements for activities and operations.

4699.   "[United States] Congress Approves Book Deacidification Plan,"
        (Bookkeeper Mass Deacidification Process), LC Information
        Bulletin (Library of Congress), 54 (April 17, 1995), 176+.

4700.   United States. Congress. House. Committee on Education and
        Labor. Subcommittee on Postsecondary Education. Oversight
        Hearing on the Problem of "Brittle Books" in Our Nation's Libraries.
        Washington, DC: Government Printing Office, 1988, 144p. Hearing
        to solicit opinion from experts to determine federal, state, and private
        sector roles in preserving brittle books in the nation's libraries.

4701.   United States. Congress. House. Committee on Education and
        Labor. Use and Control of Ethylene Oxide (EtO): A Hearing Before
        the Subcommittee on Labor Standards of the Committee on
        Education and Labor, House of Representatives, Ninety-eighth
        Congress, First Session, Hearing Held in Washington, DC, on
        November 1, 1983. Washington, DC: Government Printing Office,
        1984. 386p.

4702.   United States. Congress. House. Committee on Science, Space, and
        Technology. Subcommittee on Energy Development and
        Applications. Indoor Air Quality Research: Hearings ... Ninety-
        eighth Congress First Session, August 2, 3, 1983. Washington, DC:
        Government Printing Office, 1984. 508p.

4703.   United States. Congress. House. Committee on Science and
        Technology. Subcommittee on Science, Research, and Technology.
        Preservation of Print. Washington, DC: Government Printing Office,
        1989. 156p.   Hearing to discuss use of alkaline and permanent
        papers.

4704.   United States. Congress. House. Committee on Public Works and
        Transportation. Library of Congress Mass Book Deacidification
        Facility (Microform Report to (Accompany H.R. 5607) (Including

Cost Estimates of the Congressional Budget Office). Washington, DC: Government Printing Office, 1984. 6p.

4705. United States. Congress. House. Government Operations Committee. Archives and Records Service Film-Vault Fire, Suitland, Maryland, December, 7, 1978. Washington, DC: Government Printing Office, 1979. 38p. (96th Congress, 1st Session, 1979. House Report 96-574).

4706. United States. Congress. House. Government Operations Committee. Establishing a National Policy on Permanent Papers. Washington, DC: Government Printing Office, 1990. 9p. Text of a report accompanying the joint resolution establishing a national policy on permanent paper.

4707. United States. Congress. House. Government Operations Committee. Taking a Byte Out of History: The Archival Preservation of Federal Computer Records. Washington, DC: Government Printing Office, 1990. 30p. (101st Congress 2d Session, Report 101-978). Discusses the need to standardize technology for future access. Emphasizes that "preservation" must include ensuring continued access to electronic information.

4708. United States. Congress. House. Government Operations Committee. Government Information, Justice, and Agriculture Subcommittee. To Establish a National Policy on Permanent Papers. Washington, DC: Government Printing Office, 1990. 174p.

4709. United States. Congress. House. Judiciary Committee. Review of the Newspaper Preservation Act of 1970. Washington, DC: Government Printing Office, 1990. 196p. (Hearing before the Subcommittee on Economic and Commercial Law, December 8, 1990).

4710. United States. Congress. House. Office of Technology Assessment. Book Preservation Technologies. Washington, DC: Government Printing Office, May 1988. 124p.; Summary, 14p. Independent assessment by the OTA of the mass deacidification program using the diethyl zinc process underway at the Library of Congress.

4711.   United States. Congress. House. Office of Technology Assessment. Federal Government Information Technology: Electronic Records Systems and Individual Privacy. Washington, DC: Office of Technology Assessment, 1986. 152p.

4712.   United States. Congress. House. Office of Technology Assessment. Federal Government Information Technology: Management, Security, and Congressional Oversight. Washington, DC: Office of Technology Assessment, 1986. 190p.

4713.   United States. Congress. House. Office of Technology Assessment. Informing the Nation: Federal Information Dissemination in an Electronic Age. Washington, DC: Government Printing Office, 1988. 333p.

4714.   United States. Congress. Joint Committee on Printing. Management Practices of the United States Government Printing Office. Washington, DC: Government Printing Office, 1990. 58p.

4715.   United States. Congress. Joint Committee on the Library. Report on Progress in Implementing the National Policy on Acid-Free Paper, February 28, 1992. Washington, DC: Government Printing Office, 1992. 21p.

4716.   United States. Congress. Joint Committee on the Library. Second Report to Congress on the Joint Resolution to Establish a National Policy on Permanent Papers. Washington, DC: Government Printing Office, 1994. 10p. (103rd Congress, 2d Session). Report on steps toward establishing government-wide alkaline paper standards, including purchasing guidelines, education, and addressing the concerns of recycled paper.

4717.   United States. Congress. Joint Committee on the Library. Final Report to Congress on the Joint Resolution to Establish a National Policy on Permanent Papers. Washington, DC: Government Printing Office, 1996. 31p.

4718.   United States. Congress. Senate. Joint Resolution to Establish a
         National Policy on Permanent Paper. Washington, DC: Government
         Printing Office, October 11, 1988. 5p. (Joint Resolution
         394). Recommends the use of permanent paper for federal
         publications of "enduring value."

4719.   United States. Congress. Senate. Committee on Rules and
         Administration. Authorizing and Directing the Librarian of Congress,
         Subject to the Supervision and Authority of a Federal, Civilian, or
         Military Agency, to Proceed With the Construction of the Library of
         Congress Mass Book Deacidification Facility, and for other
         Purposes: Report (to accompany S. 2418). Washington, DC:
         Government Printing Office, 1984. 5p.

4720.   United States. Congress. Senate. Committee on Rules and
         Administration. Library of Congress Mass Book Deacidification
         Facility; Hearing ... On S.2418, Providing for Library of Congress
         Mass Book Facility. Washington, DC: Government Printing Office,
         1984. 41p. Testimony to support the creation of a facility to
         neutralize acid in books.

4721.   United States. Congress. Senate. Commerce, Science and
         Transportation Committee. New Developments in Computer
         Technology: Virtual Reality. Washington, DC: Government Printing
         Office, 1992. 65p.

4722.   United States. Environmental Protection Agency, et. al. Building Air
         Quality: A Guide for Building Owners and Facility Managers.
         Washington, DC: Government Printing Office, 1991. 229p. A video
         is also available. Provides clear guidelines for preventing indoor air
         quality problems and resolving them if they occur.

4723.   United States. Environmental Protection Agency. Office of Air and
         Radiation, Office of Air Quality Planning and Standards. Locating
         and Estimating Air Emissions From Sources of Ethylene Oxide.
         Research Triangle Park, NC: United States. Environmental
         Protection Agency, 1986. 71p.

4724. United States. Environmental Protection Agency. Office of Air Quality Planning and Standards. Sources of Ethylene Oxide Emissions. Research Triangle Park, NC: United States. Environmental Protection Agency, 1985. One volume.

4725. United States. Department of Housing and Urban Development. Safeguard Vital Records: Vital Records and Records Disaster Mitigation and Recovery, Authorized Personnel Only. Washington, DC: U.S. Department of Housing and Urban Development, 1996. One volume. Reprinted from United States National Archives and Records Administration. Vital Records and Records Disaster Mitigation and Recovery. College Park, MD: National Archives and Records Administration, 1996. One volume.

4726. United States. General Accounting Office. The Gettysburg Address [Microform]: Issues Related to Display and Preservation, Report to Congressional Requesters. Washington, DC: The General Accounting Office; Gaithersburg, MD: The Office, 1994. 26p.

4727. United States. General Accounting Office. Space Operations: NASA Is Not Archiving All Potentially Valuable Data. Washington, DC: General Accounting Office, 1990. 51p.

4728. United States. General Accounting Office. Space Operations: NASA Is Not Properly Safeguarding Our Valuable Data From Past Missions. Washington, DC: Government Printing Office, 1990. 76p. Report to the Chairman, Committee on Science, Space and Technology, House.

4729. United States. General Services Administration. Breathing Easy: What You Should Know About Indoor Air Quality. Washington, DC: General Services Administration, Public Building Service, 1992. 11p. A video is also available.

4730. United States. General Services Administration. "Electronic Record Keeping," FIRMR Bulletin (Federal Information Resources Management) (June 18, 1985), 23.

4731. United States. General Services Administration. Electronic Record Keeping. Washington, DC: Information Resources Management Service, 1990. 37p.

4732. United States. Government Printing Office. Use of Alkaline Paper in Government Printing. Washington, DC: Government Printing Office, April 1990. 18p. (Report and Plan Prepared at the Direction of the Committee on Appropriations, House of Representatives).

4733. United States. National Agricultural Library. A Preservation Plan for the National Agricultural Library. Beltsville, MD: The Library, 1991. 41p.

4734. United States. National Archives and Records Administration. The Archives of the Future: Archival Strategies for the Treatment of Electronic Databases. Washington, DC: National Archives and Records Administration, 1992. v.p. Study to provide NARA with better knowledge of the electronic database environment in federal agencies to help build an electronic archive of the nation's history.

4735. United States. National Archives and Records Administration. Effects of Electronic Recordkeeping on Historical Records of the U.S. Government. Washington, DC: National Archives and Records Administration, 1989. 80p. Study to examine the influence of electronic technology and determine how these practices affect the retention or loss of records.

4736. United States. National Archives and Records Administration. Electronic Records Issues: A Report to the National Historical Publications and Records Commission. Washington, DC: NHPRC, 1990. 11p. Looks at the pertinent issues in electronic recordkeeping for the archival community.

4737. United States. National Archives and Records Administration. Expert Systems Technology and Its Implication for Archives. Washington, DC: National Archives and Records Administration, 1991. 47p. TIP NO. 9.

4738.   United States. National Archives and Records Administration. Initial Findings: A Study of Shrink Wrapped, Simulated Bound Volumes. Washington, DC: National Archives and Records Administration, March 24, 1993. 15p.; charts. (Preservation Information Paper, 1). Report on a study of the effect of shrink wrapping on paper; found decreased brightness of paper.

4739.   United States. National Archives and Records Administration. The Management of Audiovisual Records in Federal Agencies: A General Report. Washington, DC: National Archives and Records Administration, 1991. 41p. Provides useful information, applicable to a variety of institutions, on preserving audiovisual records.

4740.   United States. National Archives and Records Administration. Management of Electronic Records in the 1990's: A Report of a Conference Held June 21-23, 1989, Easton, MD. Washington, DC: National Archives and Records Administration, August 1990. 34p.

4741.   United States. National Archives and Records Administration. Management, Preservation and Access for Electronic Records With Enduring Value: Response to Recommendations. Washington, DC: National Archives and Records Administration, July 1991. 20p. NARA's typescript response to above report.

4742.   United States. National Archives and Records Administration. Managing Electronic Records. Washington, DC: National Archives and Records Administration, 1990. 32p.; appendixes. Previous version 1986. 13p. A guide for government officials in managing electronic records. Carefully explains the different responsibilities involved in managing electronic records.

4743.   United States. National Archives and Records Administration. Military Records in the National Archives: A Plan for Their Preservation. Washington, DC: National Archives and Records Administration, 1986. 31p.

4744.   United States. National Archives and Records Administration. National Archives Preservation Research Priorities, Past and Present. Washington, DC: National Archives and Records Administration,

1990. 14 leaves. (Tip O7). By the staffs of the Preservation Policy
and Services Division, Kenneth E. Harris...[et al.] and the Archival
Research and Evaluation Staff, William M. Holems, Alan R. Calmes.

4745.   United States. National Archives and Records Administration. A
National Archives Strategy for the Development and Implementation
of Standards for the Creation, Transfer, Access, and Long-Term
Storage of Electronic Records of the Federal Government. (TIP 8).
Washington, DC: Government Printing Office, June 1990.
22p. Emphasizes the need to identify archival requirements for
electronic records and then work towards the development of
standards.

4746.   United States. National Archives and Records Administration.
Personnel Papers of Executive Officials: A Management Guide.
Washington, DC: National Archives and Records Administration,
1992. 16p.

4747.   United States. National Archives and Records Administration. Select
Bibliography on Electronic Records. Washington, DC: National
Archives and Records Administration, 1991. n.p. Distributed at
NARA's Preservation of Electronic Records Conference.
Bibliography addresses the archival management of electronic
records.

4748.   United States. National Archives and Records Administration.
Strategic Plan for Information Systems and Technology, Fiscal Years
1992-1995. Washington, DC: National Archives and Records
Administration, 1990. 1 vol. updated 1993-1997, 1992. One
volume.

4749.   United States. National Archives and Records Administration.
Technology Assessment Report: Speech Pattern Recognition, Optical
Character Recognition, Digital Roster Scanning. (TIP 10).
Washington, DC: National Archives and Records Administration,
1984. 139p. A discussion of the history, principles, and general
applications of these technologies, including an assessment of each
as it relates to archival problems. The bulk of the report is devoted to

digital roaster scanning and its potential. Further investigation of the technology is recommended.

4750. United States. National Archives and Records Administration. 20-Year Record Preservation Plan. Washington, DC: National Archives and Records Administration. May 1984. 5p.

4751. United States. National Archives and Records Administration. National Archives and Records Administration Twenty Year Preservation Plan. Gaithersburg, MD: National Bureau of Standards, 1985. 67p. (NBSIR 85-2999). Prepared by Alan Calmes. Reports on the results of an extensive collection survey and presents a comprehensive plan for preservation of National Archives holdings.

4752. United States. National Archives and Records Administration. Vital Records and Records Disaster Mitigation and Recovery. College Park, MD: National Archives and Records Administration, 1996. 22p. with appendices.

4753. United States. National Archives and Records Administration. Unpublished Minutes of Meetings, Advisory Committee on Preservation 1980-1986: Executive Secretary of the Advisory Committee on Preservation. Washington, DC: National Archives and Records Administration. [1986]. n.p.

4754. United States. National Archives and Records Administration. Archival Research and Evaluation Staff. Optical Digital Image Storage System: Project Report. Washington, DC: National Archives and Records Administration, March 1991. 378p. Documents all project activities over the five-year period, including preparation work leading up to the pilot project and details of the actual system operations, comparisons to microfilm storage and retrieval, cost and time analysis. Provides basic information on digital imaging and optical disk technologies that are clearly written for the lay person. Glossary.

4755. United States. National Archives and Records Administration. Committee on Authorities and Program Alternatives. NARA and the Disposition of Federal Records: Laws and Authorities and Their

Implementation, a Report. Washington, DC: National Archives and
Records Administration, 1989. 134p. Study to examine the
legislative authorities upon the National Archives; apprises records to
determine which should be preserved and which should be destroyed,
to recommend areas that would increase the effectiveness of the
program.

4756.   United States. National Archives and Records Administration.
Subcommittee C of the Committee on Preservation for the National
Archives and Records Service. Strategic Technology Considerations
Relative to the Preservation and Storage of Human and Machine-
Readable Records. (White Paper). Washington, DC: National
Archives and Records Service, July 1984. 12p. Brief, old, but clear
and readable examination of the (still applicable) issues governing
the choice of digitized vs. microform technology for preservation.
Concludes in favor of microforms.

4757.   United States. National Archives and Records Administration.
Technical Research Staff. Digital Imaging and Optical Digital Data
Disk Storage Systems: Long Term Access Strategies for Federal
Agencies. College Park, MD: National Archives and Records
Administration, July 1994. 295p. (Tech. Info. Paper 12).

4758.   United States. National Archives and Records Administration and
the National Association of Government Archives and Records
Administrators. Digital Imaging and Optical Media Storage Systems
Guidelines for State and Local Government Agencies. Albany, NY:
NAGARA, 1991. 70p. Appendices. Report on a project undertaken
by the NARA Archival Research and Evaluation staff to assess the
experience of 60 state and local governments with digital imaging
and optical media storage systems. Guidelines identify management
issues relating to existing technology and use of digital imaging and
optical disk systems.

4759.   United States. National Bureau of Standards. Air Quality Criteria for
Storage of Paper-Based Archival Records. Washington, DC: U.S.
Dept. of Commerce, National Bureau of Standards, 1983. Three
volumes in one. Prepared for the Public Buildings Service, General

Services Administration and the National Archives and Records Administration by Robert G. Mathey, et al.

4760.   United States. National Commission on Libraries and Information Science. Panel on the Information Policy Implications of Archiving Satellite Data, to Preserve a Sense of Earth From Space. Washington, DC: Government Printing Office, 1984. 47p.

4761.   United States. National Information Standards Organization. Durable Hardcover Bindings for Books, Approved February 28, 1992 by the American National Standards Institute. Bethesda, MD.: NISO Press, 1995. 10p. ANSI/NISO Z39.66-1992.

4762.   United States National Information Standards Organization. Permanence of Paper for Printed Publication and Documents in Libraries and Archives. Bethesda, MD: NISO Press, 1992. 7p. (ANSI/NISO Z39.48-1992).

4763.   United States National Information Standards Organization. Single-tier Steel Bracket Library Shelving. Bethesda, MD: NISO Press, 1995. 20p.(ANSI/NISO Z39.73-1994).

4764.   United States. National Library of Medicine. Going -- Going -- Gone: Preserving Our Medical Heritage. Bethesda, MD: National Library of Medicine, Department. of Health and Human Services, Public Health Service, National Institutes of Health, 1989. 10p. Brochure to alert the medical community to the problem of deteriorating documentary materials.

4765.   United States. National Library of Medicine. Preservation of the Biomedical Literature: A Plan for the National Library of Medicine, comp. Betsy L. Humphreys. Bethesda, MD: National Library of Medicine, 1985. 131p. Results of a self-study to analyze the state of the NML collections, environment, and use, and to present available options for preservation.

4766.   United States. National Park Service. Conserve O Gram Series. Washington, DC: National Park Service. 1993. One volume. A series of more than 50 pamphlets that spotlight must-know supplemental technical information for curators and conservators.

4767.   United States. National Park Service. Museum Handbook. Rev. ed.
        Washington, DC: United States Department of the Interior,
        September 1990. Unpaged notebook. Provides guidance to park staff
        on the scope of collections, handling objects, environmental
        monitoring and control, pest management, museum collections
        storage, packing and shipping, conservation treatment, security, fire
        protection, emergency planning, curatorial health and safety,
        planning and programming for museum collections management, and
        museum ethics.

4768.   United States. National Park Service and Northeast Document
        Conservation Center. School for Scanning. Andover, MA: NEDCC,
        September, 1996. One volume. Notebook given to participants in the
        seminar containing background papers and papers given at the
        seminar held in Washington, DC.

4769.   United States-USSR Seminar on Access to Library Resources
        Through Technology and Preservation, 5-8 July 1988. Papers,
        prepared by U.S. participants. Washington, DC: American Council
        of Learned Societies, 1988. 104p. Twenty-six papers address
        preservation and access concerns from a regional, national, and
        international perspective.

4770.   University of Arizona. College of Law Library. Preservation
        Committee. Disaster Preparedness Manual. Buffalo, NY: William S.
        Hein, 1989. 60p. Model plan for law libraries, and other institutions,
        including emergency and salvage procedures and lists of equipment,
        supplies and services.

4771.   University of California - Los Angeles Libraries. Problem Patron
        Task Force. Patron Relations: A Manual for Library Staff. Los
        Angeles, CA: University of California - Los Angeles Libraries, 1987.
        48p. Covers protocols for dealing with all types of disruptive,
        aberrant, or criminal behavior.

4772.   University of California - San Diego. UCSD Library Disaster
        Prevention and Disaster Preparedness Guidelines. San Diego, CA:
        UCSD Library, 1983. 13p. Prepared by Preservation Team, Barbara
        Begg , et al.

4773. University of Georgia. Final Report: University of Georgia Libraries, Preservation Planning Task Force on Condition of the Collection. Athens, GA: The Task Force, 1990. One volume.

4774. University of Georgia. Report From the Task Force on Education for Preservation. Athens, GA: The Task Force, 1990. 26 leaves. At the head of the title: Preservation Planning Project.

4775. University of Georgia. Report to the Preservation Planning Study Team by the Disaster Management Task Force. Athens, GA: The Task Force, 1990. One volume.

4776. University of Georgia Libraries Preservation Planning Program: Final Report. Athens, GA: The Task Force, 1991. 29 leaves.

4777. University of Georgia Libraries Preservation Planning Program. Background Paper. Athens, GA: The Task Force, 1990. 28 leaves.

4778. University of Glasgow Library. The Past Preserved: Conservation in Glasgow University Library: Catalogue of an Exhibition of Work Funded by the Clydesdale Bank, the Pilgrim Trust and the Radcliffe Trust, Glasgow University Library 13 March-17 May 1984. Glasgow: University of Glasgow, 1984. 24p. Work by Ian Maver.

4779. University of Kansas Libraries Draft Specifications for a State Contract for Preservation Photocopying. [Lawrence, KS: The Libraries, 1995]. 7, 3, [3] leaves.

4780. University of Kentucky Libraries. Preservation Planning Program: Final Report and Implementation Plan. Lexington, KY: University of Kentucky, May 1991. 68p. Submitted by Preservation Planning Program Study Team, Judy Sackett, Chair. An ARL Preservation Planning Program final report.

4781. University of Missouri — Columbia Libraries. Preservation Planning Program Background Paper. Columbia, MO: University of Missouri — Columbia Libraries, January 15, 1986. 20 leaves.

4782.   University of Missouri - Columbia Libraries. Preservation Planning Program Study Team. Preservation at the University of Missouri — Columbia Libraries Columbia, MO: University of Missouri-Columbia Libraries, 1 August 1986. 55 leaves.

4783.   University of Oregon Library. Preservation Program for the University of Oregon Library: the Final Report of The Preservation Planning Program. William Schenck, et al. Washington, DC: Association of Research Libraries, Office of Management Studies, 1986. 44p.

4784.   University of Oxford Libraries Board Preservation Committee. Preservation Report: Part I: Report on the Extent and Condition of Oxford Library Holdings. Oxford: University of Oxford Libraries, November 1994. 111p.

4785.   University of Pennsylvania. Report on the Preservation Planning Project: University of Pennsylvania Libraries. Washington, DC: Commission on Preservation and Access, 1991. 25p. Study to explore the planning and operation of a preservation program for the library's collections.

4786.   University of Pittsburgh. University Libraries. Preservation Planning Project Study Team, Final Report. Pittsburgh, PA: University of Pittsburgh Libraries, 1987. 98p.

4787.   University of Rochester Library. Library Disaster Manual. Rochester, NY: University of Rochester, Rush Rhees Library, 1988. One volume.

4788.   University of Southern California. University Libraries. Preservation Planning Program Final Report: University of Southern California, May 1989. Barbara Robinson, chair. Los Angeles: University of Southern California, University Libraries, 1989, 165p.

4789.   University of Tennessee. Preservation Planning Program Final Report. University of Tennessee, Knoxville Library. Betty Bengston, et al. Washington, DC: Association of Research Libraries, Office of Management Studies, 1986. 28p.

4790. University of Toronto Library. Collection Preservation Committee. Preservation of Library Material; A Report. Toronto, Canada: University of Toronto Library, 1984. 36p. Report presenting concrete recommendations following a careful survey of needs. A useful model.

4791. University of Waterloo Library. University of Waterloo Library Emergency Procedures Manual and Disaster Plan. Waterloo, Ontario: University of Waterloo, 1986. 35p.

4792. University of Western Ontario. University Library System. Committee on Conservation and Preservation. Books on Borrowed Time: The Report. London, Canada: University of Western Ontario, University Library System, 1989. 42p.

4793. Unomah, J. I. "Deterioration and Restoration of Library Materials: The Nigerian Situation," Nigerian Library and Information Science Review (Journal of the Oyo State Division, Nigerian Library Association), 3:1/2 (May/November 1985), 23-28. Examination of "devastating effects" of tropical climate on library materials; causes of deterioration; preventive measures through environmental control; conservation treatments, recommendations.

4794. Upham, Lois N., ed. Newspapers in the Library: New Approaches to Management and Reference Work. New York: Haworth Press, 1988. 167p. (Serials Librarian, supplement 4, vol. 14, 1988). Collection of papers on management and preservation of newspaper collections and the U.S. Newspaper Project.

4795. "Using Gamma Rays to Save Old Books," New York Times, December 27, 1989, D5.

4796. Usmani, Muhamman Adil. "Manuscripts: The Need for Their Search and Preservation," Pakistan Library Bulletin, 17:1 (March 1986), i-viii. Addresses need for the Islamic world to preserve its documentary heritage. Notes that much as been lost to the West and recommends a study to determine what collections exist in Pakistan, their physical condition, and options for access.

4797. Vagarov, Feodor M. "Conservation of New Archival Materials," Archivum, 35 (1989), 135-152. Review of Russian experience in storing archival materials in non-print format; results of a study of practices elsewhere. Covers storage, inspection, preservation, reformatting, education, and training. Keynote paper presented at 2d plenary session, 11th International Congress on Archives, Paris, France, 1988.

4798. Vagarov, Feodor M. "The Impact of Scientific and Technical Progress of Records Storage," Politics for the Preservation of the Archival Heritage. Paris: International Council on Archives, 1989, 174-181.

4799. Vaisey, David. "Archivists, Conservators, and Scientists: The Preservation of the Nation's Heritage," Archives, 18, 79 (April 1988), 131-143. (Maurice Bond Memorial Lecture, 1987). Reflection on the development of the concern for conservation and preservation and discussion of current issues.

4800. Valauskas, Edward J. "Computer Currents: CPR for PCs," Library Journals, 119 (October 1, 1994), 108.

4801. Valauskas, Edward J. "Digital Images Over the Internet," Database, (April 1994), 57-60. Use of JPEG.

4802. Valauskas, Edward J. "Preservation by Computer: The Biblioteka Akademii Nauk Preservation Database," Database, 15:1 (February 1992), 82-84. Describes the database designed by Andrei Soloview for preservation data.

4803. Valentin, Nieves. "Biodeterioration of Library Materials; Disinfection Methods and New Alternatives," Paper Conservator, 10 (1986), 40-45. Results of a study of samples of paper, parchment, and various types of microfilm were treated with products commonly used in paper conservation treatments, in disinfection, and in parchment restoration.

4804.   Valentin, Nieves. "Insect Eradication in Museums and Archives by Oxygen Replacement: A Pilot Project," Preprints. International Council of Museums Committee on Conservation, 9th Triennial Meeting, Dresden, Germany, August 26-31. Marina del Rey, CA: Getty Conservation Institute, 1990, 821-823.

4805.   Valentin, Nieves, et al. "Nitrogen Atmospheres for Insect Eradication on Archival Materials," Conference on Book and Paper Conservation, 1990. Budapest, Hungary: Technical Association of Paper and Printing Industry/National Szechenyi Library, 1992, 326-330. Research on nontoxic methods to eradicate pest infestation, indicating that a modified atmosphere using nitrogen at a low RH has been found effective.

4806.   Valentin, Nieves, Mary Lidstrom, and Frank Preusser. "Microbial Control by Low Oxygen and Low Relative Humidity Environment," Studies in Conservation, 53 (November 1990), 222-230. Describes a straightforward method of controlling mold growth on a contaminated object without having to use toxic compounds or identify the microorganisms involved.

4807.   Valentin, Nieves, and Frank Preusser. "Insect Control by Inert Gases in Museums, Archives and Libraries," Restaurator, 11:1 (1990), 22-33. Study indicates that a nitrogen atmosphere is effective in controlling certain insects.

4808.   Valentin, Nieves, and Frank Preusser. "Nitrogen for Biodeterioration Control in Museum Collections," Biodeterioration Research 3. New York: Plenum Press, 1990, 511-523. Report on a study to determine the optimum relative humidity, temperature, and oxygen concentration required to control infestation of art materials.

4809.   Vallas, Philippe. "Mass Deacidification at the Bibliothèque Nationale (Sable-sur-Sarthe Center): Assessment After Two Years of Operation (Late 1992)," Restaurator, 14:1 (1993), 1-10. Provides a generally positive assessment, although there are some problems with the system that are not considered critical.

4810.   Vallejo, Rosa M. Preservation and Conservation and Their
         Teaching: The Methodology of Vienna '86. The Hague, Netherlands:
         International Federation of Library Associations and Institutions,
         1987. 16p. (ED 299-984,7). Describes the seminar on the teaching
         of conservation and preservation management for librarians,
         archivists, and information scientists held in Vienna, 1986.

4811.   Van Artsdalen, Martha J. "Winterthur: A Museum With Its Own
         Brand of Fire Fighting," Conservation Administration News, 24
         (January 1986), 1-4. Describes the Museum Fire Department and its
         responsibilities.

4812.   Van Bogart, John. Magnetic Tape Storage and Handling: A Guide
         for Libraries and Archives. Washington, DC: Commission on
         Preservation and Access, June 1995. 34p. Helps clarify long-term
         storage requirements for magnetic media and provides guidance on
         how to care for these media to maximize their life expectancies.

4813.   Van Bogart, John. Media Stability Studies: Final Report. St. Paul,
         MN: National Media Lab, July 1994. 86p. In this technical study,
         magnetic tape coupons, reels, and recorded cassettes were aged in
         various temperature/humidity and pollutant environments in an effort
         to understand the long-term stability of various commercial magnetic
         tape media.

4814.   Van Bogart, John. Modeling the Archival Stability of Advances
         Magnetic Media-Metal Particulate and Barium Ferrite. St Paul, MN:
         National Media Lab, June 11, 1992. 8p.

4815.   Van Buskirk, James E. "Disaster in San Francisco," AAL Newsletter
         (Association of Architectural Librarians), 9:1 (January 1990), 3-
         5. Description of the damage following the earthquake and the
         salvage of materials at the San Francisco Academy of Art.

4816.   Van der Hoevan, Hans. Memory of the World: Lost Memory-
         Libraries and Archives Destroyed in the Twentieth Century. Paris:
         UNESCO, 1996. 76p. Prepared on behalf of IFLA and Joan van
         Albada. Lists all libraries destroyed since 1900. It is far from
         exhaustive.

4817.   Van der Reyden, Dianne. "Delta Plan: A Report on the Netherlands
        National Preservation Initiative," Infinity (Society of American
        Archivists Preservation Section), 8:3 (Fall 1992), 5-6. Excerpts from
        the report by the Netherlands Ministry of Welfare, Health and
        Cultural Affairs on the preservation of the Dutch cultural heritage.

4818.   Van der Reyden, Dianne. "Preservation Responsibilities: Material
        Care and Materials Science for Paper-Based Research Collections,"
        Materials Issues in Art and Archeology IV. Pittsburgh, PA:
        Materials Research Society, 1995. 63-69p. (Materials Research
        Society Symposium Proceedings, 352). Emphasizes why original
        materials are important and must be preserved; presents strategies
        and tactics through preservation administration, preservation
        duplication, environmental control, collections maintenance,
        conservation treatment, conservation research, preservation
        education, in table form with action steps, options, and targets or
        goals.

4819.   Van der Reyden, Dianne. "Recent Scientific Research in Paper
        Conservation," Journal of the American Institute for Conservation,
        31:1 (Spring 1992), 117-138. Traces research since 1988 into the
        chemical, physical, and optical properties of paper, aging, and recent
        findings concerned with washing, bleaching, solvents, enzymes, and
        sizing.

4820.   Van der Reyden, Dianne, Christa Hofmann, and Mary Baker.
        "Effects of Aging and Solvent Treatments on Some Properties of
        Contemporary Tracing Papers," American Institute for Conservation
        Journal, 32:2 (Summer 1993), 177-206. Reviews of project, with
        preliminary results. References.

4821.   Van der Reyden, Dianne, et al. "Modern Transparent Papers:
        Materials, Degradation and the Effects of Some Conservation
        Treatments," Materials Issues in Art and Archaeology III.
        Pittsburgh, PA: Materials Research Society, 1992, 379-
        395. Evaluates the effect of water and solvents on transparent papers;
        summarizes findings on materials characterization, degrative effects

of aging, and the effect of solvents used for stain reduction, humidification, and flattening. 48 references.

4822. van der Reyden, Dianne, Erika Mosier, and Mary Baker. "Pigment-Coated Papers. 1. History and Technology; 2. The Effects of Some Solvents Applications Techniques on Selected Examples," Preprints; ICOM Committee on Conservation 10th Triennial Meeting, ed. Janet Bridgland. Washington, DC: International Council of Museums, 1993, 491-506. Provides a chronology of the history and use of coating materials and techniques with emphasis on the roles that pigment properties play in influencing the final coating properties. An investigation of the effects of various treatments on selected examples of pigment-coated papers.

4823. Van der Wateren, Jan. F. "Archival Resources in the Victoria and Albert Museum," Art Libraries Journal, 14:2 (1989), 16-27.

4824. Van Emden, H. F. Pest Control. 2d. ed. London: Edword Arnold, 1989, 117p. Text on pest control management that addresses need to reduce chemical dependence.

4825. Van Gulik, R., and N. E. Kersten-Pampiglione. "A Closer Look at Iron Gall Ink," Restaurator, 15:3 (1994), 173-187. Review of information currently available on iron gall ink burn; emphasizes need for further research. 21 references.

4826. Van Haaften, Julia. "Challenges of Access and Bibliographic Control for Large Photographic Collections," Photographic Preservation and the Research Library, ed. Jennifer Porro. Mountain View, CA: Research Library Group, 1991, 45-49. How detailed descriptive cataloguing can provide access to photographic collections, curtailing unnecessary handling of original materials.

4827. Van Hovweling, Douglas E., and Michael J. McGill. The Evolving National Information Network: Background and Challenges. Washington, DC: Commission on Preservation and Access, June 1993. 32p. Discusses the rapidly developing regional, national, and global communications networks ands the impact on remote access to information.

4828.   Van Zelst, Lambertus. "Needs and Potential Solutions in
         Conservation," Conserving and Preserving Materials in Nonbook
         Formats. Urbana-Champaign: University of Illinois Graduate School
         of Library and Information Science, 1991, 7-22. (Allerton Park
         Institute, 30). Discusses the current state of conservation: public
         awareness, information, training, research, analytical services,
         professional organizations.

4829.   Vance, Jack. "Halons — What Are the Alternatives for the Military,"
         Military Firefighter (May 1993), 36, 38-39. Discusses alternatives to
         Halon.

4830.   Vandiver, Frank. "A Tribute to Those Who Preserve Original
         Sources," Abbey Newsletter, 20:4/5 (September 1996), 49-50.

4831.   Vandiver Pamela B., James R. Druzik, George Segan Wheeler, and
         Iasn C. Freestone, eds. Materials Issues in Art and Archaeology III.
         Pittsburgh, PA: Materials Research Society, 1992. 1101p. (Materials
         Research Association Symposium Proceedings, 267). Presents
         current research in materials, technologies, and the science
         underlying deterioration, preservation, and conservation, p. 337-474.
         "Properties of Materials Used by the Artist, Artisan and
         Conservator," deals with paper-based materials.

4832.   Varlamoff, Marie-Therese. "Annual Report 1994 of the IFLA PAC
         Core Programme," IFLA Journal (International Federation of Library
         Associations and Institutions), 21:2 (1995), 135-141.

4833.   Varlamoff, Marie-Therese. "About the PAC Core Programme,"
         IFLA Journal (International Federation of Library Associations and
         Institutions), 21:3 (1995), 227-228.

4834.   Varlamoff, Marie-Therese. "The Involvement of the IFLA Core
         Programme for Preservation and Conservation (PAC) in UNESCO's
         'Memory of the World' Programme," IFLA Journal (International
         Federation of Library Associations and Institutions), 21:3 (1995),
         183-184. Describes the role of the PAC and the survey of needs and

guidelines developing by Jan Lyall, procedures for selection, funding, etc.

4835.   Varlejs, Jana. "Preservation Education: A Call for Cooperation," Art Documentation, 9:4 (Winter 1990), 193-194. Notes need for cooperative initiatives in preservation and continuing education; describes the Rutgers University Professional Development Certificate Program in Preservation.

4836.   Varlejs, Jana, ed. Safeguarding Electronic Information. Jefferson, NC: McFarland, 1996. 96p. Proceedings of the 32nd Symposium, Graduate, Alumni and Faculty, SCILS, 1995. Papers that encompass technical aspects of security and "ethical issues of personal privacy, intellectual property, protection and censorship" (10).

4837.   Vaughan, Barbara, et al. E.H. Butler Library Disaster Preparedness Plan. Buffalo, NY: State University of New York, Buffalo University Libraries, 1989. 42p.

4838.   Verheyen, Peter S. "Basic Paper Treatments for Printed Book Materials," Guild of Bookworkers Journal, 29:1 (Spring 1991), 1-15. Reviews the methods of conservator Betsy Palmer Eldridge for dealing with common conservation problems; synthesis and discussion of her presentation at the 1989 Standards Seminar.

4839.   Verschoor, Hugo and Jaap Mosk, ed. Contributions of the Central Research Laboratory to the Field of Conservation and Restoration. Amsterdam, Netherlands: Central Research Laboratory, 1994. 124p. (English). Reports of research undertaken in 1992-1993, with full reports from two projects.

4840.   Videnich, Jean. "Library Disaster Recovery Planning," Disaster Recovery (July-September 1989), 22, 28, 56.

4841.   Villas, Philippe. "Mass Deacidification at the Bibliothèque National (Sable-sur-Sarthe Center): Assessment After Two Years of Operation (Late 1992)," Restaurator, 14:1 (1993), 1-10. Assessment of the plant from a librarian's perspective.

4842.   Viñas, Vincente, and Ruth Vinas. <u>Traditional Restoration Techniques; A RAMP Study</u>. Paris: UNESCO, 1988, 80p. (PGI-88/WS/17). Preservation manual with basic testing and conservation treatments described. Covers cellulosic and leather materials.

4843.   Vincent-Daviss, Diana. "Preservation Needs of Law Libraries," <u>Abbey Newsletter</u>, 14:2 (April 1990), 21-22. Describes the goals and activities of the American Association of Law Libraries (AALL) Special Committee on the Preservation Needs of Law Libraries. The committee is establishing priorities to ensure the preservation of legal materials.

4844.   Vine, Mark. "Archival Storage Materials," <u>In Safe Keeping</u>, ed. Jennifer Thorp. Winchester, England: Hampshire Co. Library/ Hampshire Archives Trust, 1985, 27-28. Briefly describes some materials for housing and storage. "Storage and preservation costs need to be put into a firm perspective and compared against the cost (if possible) of replacement, refurbishment and repair" (28).

4845.   Vine, Mark G., and William Hollinger. "Active Archival Housing," <u>Restaurator</u>, 14:3 (1993), 123-130. An explanation of the structure and chemical components of MicroChamber paper and board materials.

4846.   Vinod, Daniel, and Shin Maekawa. "Hygrometic Half-lives of Museum Cases," <u>Restaurator</u>, 14:1 (1993), 30-44. Examines the moisture-buffering capabilities of four archival storage boxes based on construction materials and design within high and low RH conditions.

4847.   Virando, Jacqueline A., comp. <u>Disaster Recovery Planning for Records Managers and Librarians</u>. Silver Spring, MD: Association for Information and Image Management, 1991. 54p. (AIIM Reference Report). Planning manual with bibliography.

4848.   Visscher, William. "Parchment, Vellum and William Cowley," <u>Bookbinder</u>, 1 (1987), 51-54. Describes the manufacture of parchment and vellum for bookbinding.

4849. Vitale, Cammie. "The Blumberg Case and Its Implications for Library Security at the Central University Libraries, Southern Methodist University," Library and Archival Security, 12:1 (1993), 79-85. The impact of the Blumberg thefts on a research library.

4850. Vitale, Timothy. "Effects of Water on the Mechanical Properties of Paper and Their Relationship to the Treatment of Paper," Materials Issues in Art and Archaeology III. Pittsburgh, PA: Materials Research Society, 1992, 397-427. Examines the mechanical properties of paper and the effect of water and organic solvents on paper fiber bonding.

4851. Vitale, Timothy. "Effects of Drying on the Mechanical Properties of Paper and Their Relationship to the Treatment of Paper," Materials Issues in Art and Archaeology III. Pittsburgh, PA: Materials Research Society, 1992, 429-445. Explores the effects of drying of paper after immersion in water.

4852. Vitale, Timothy, and David Erhardt. "Changes in Paper Color Due to Artificial Aging and the Effects of Washing on Color Removal," Preprints: ICOM Committee on Conservation 10th Triennial Meeting, ed. Janet Bridgland. Washington, DC: International Council of Museums, 1993, 507-515. Study of the color change of paper aged under various conditions and the effectiveness of washing for removing colored degradation products.

4853. Vitiello, Giuseppe, "European Register of Microfilm Masters (EROMM)," International Preservation News, 4 (August 1990), 3-4. Describes European Community initiatives for preservation and access, and the effort to create the register.

4854. Vnoucek, Jiri. "Books in Jeopardy - Can We Manage to Restore Medieval Books Without Any Loss of Information?" Conference on Book and Paper Conservation, 1990. Budapest, Hungary: Technical Association of Paper and Printing Industry/National Szechenyi Library, 1992, 48-49. Plea to preserve the physical evidence in early books to aid in their present and future conservation.

Bibliography

4855. Vober, John J. Acid Deterioration of Paper. St. Cloud University, 1986. 40 leaves. MS dissertation.

4856. Vodopivec, Jedert. "Conservation of Manuscripts Written With Iron-Gall Ink," Conference on Book and Paper Conservation, 1990. Budapest, Hungary: Technical Association of Paper and Printing Industry/National Szechenyi Library, 1992, 331-337. Case study of analysis and treatment of a manuscript; notes the need for more research on treatments and the need to store treated materials under environmentally stable conditions.

4857. Vodopivec, Jedert, and Meta Cernic-Letnar. "Applying Synthetic Polymers to Conserve Cultural Property on Paper," Restaurator, 11:1 (1990), 34-47. Presents results of testing synthetic polymers on a variety of papers during treatment and as a strengthening agent following treatment.

4858. Vodopivec, Jedert, and Meta Cernic-Letnar. "Behavior of Different Papers and Synthetic Polymers in the Conservation of Cultural Property on Paper," Conference on Book and Paper Conservation, 1990. Budapest, Hungary: Technical Association of Paper and Printing Industry/National Szechenyi Library, 1992, 566-575. Presents results of a study of synthetic polymers; their use in books and paper and their permanence.

4859. Vodopivec, Jedert and Meta Cernic-Letnar. "Cultural Heritage on Paper: Situation in Slovenia," Degradácua a Archivnych a Kniznicnych Materialov vs Stály a Trvanlivy Papier/Degradation of Archives and Library Materials vs. Permanent and Durable Paper for Archives. Bratislava, Slovakia: Slovak National Archives, 1993, 16-18. Background; discussion of standards; initiatives to promote production and use of permanent paper in Slovenia.

4860. Vogelgesang, Peter. "Optical Digital Recording," Conservation in Archives. Paris: International Council on Archives, 1989, 223-232. (Proceedings of an International Symposium, May 10-12, 1988). Reviews optical recording, including principles and issues of information access and systems obsolescence. Provides a good comparison between optical and magnetic recording.

642

4861. Volgyi, Peter. "Acidfree Papermaking in Hungary," Conference on Book and Paper Conservation, 1990. Budapest, Hungary: Technical Association of Paper and Printing Industry/National Szechenyi Library, 1992, 439-443. Traces the history of efforts and the difficulties of producing acid-free paper on a broad scale; notes continued increase in production.

4862. Vossler, Janet L. "The Human Element of Disaster Recovery," ARMA: International Records Management Quarterly (Association of Records Managers and Administrators), 21:1 (January 1987), 10-12. Discussion of human elements in disaster recovery.

4863. Waechter, Otto. "Paper Strengthening at the National Library of Austria," Preservation of Library Materials, ed. Merrily Smith. New York: Saur, 1987, 141-151. (IFLA Publication 40). Describes treatment for the preservation of newspapers at the Austrian National Library, involving the impregnation of the text block in a vacuum, then freeze drying.

4864. Waechter, Otto. "Tour of the Conservation Laboratory, National Library of Austria," Preservation of Library Materials, ed. Merrily Smith. New York: Saur, 1987, 92-97. IFLA Publication, 41). Describes some of the conservation activities and treatments undertaken at the Conservation Laboratory, Austrian National Library.

4865. Waechter, Otto. "Paper Strengthening; Mass Conservation of Unbound and Bound Newspapers," Restaurator, 8:2-3 (1987), 111-121. Introduced by a history of the efforts undertaken by libraries that are confronted with the poor durability of newsprint and by a survey on newsprint chemistry, a new system for deacidifying and strengthening is described. It consists by first impregnating the volumes with an aqueous solution (or emulsion resp.) of methyl cellulose, a little bit of PVAC and magnesium carbonate in a vacuum chamber and subsequently freeze-drying them to prevent the sheet from sticking together during the drying process. Most important for good success is choosing an appropriate type of methyl cellulose and carrying out freeze-drying in a suitable manner.

4866. Waechter, Wolfgang. "Activities of the Leipzig Regional Centre on Conservation of IFLA," Conference on Book and Paper Conservation, 1990. Budapest, Hungary: Technical Association of Paper and Printing Industry/National Szechenyi Library, 1992, 134-137. Describes the mission of the center, its plan to preserve the cultural heritage, deacidification, and paper-splitting technologies.

4867. Waechter, Wolfgang. "Mechanizing Restoration Work: The Deutsche Bücherei, Leipzig, and Its Role as a Regional Centre for IFLA," IFLA Journal (International Federation of Library Associations and Institutions), 12:4 (1986), 307-309; reprinted Restaurator, 8:2/3 (1987), 129-132. Describes the expansion and activities of the regional center.

4868. Waechter, Wolfgang. "Preservation Activities of the Regional Centre of "PAC of the IFLA at Leipzig," Library Automation and Networking: New Tools for a New Identity, ed. H. Liebaers and M. Walckiers. Munich, Germany: Saur, 1991, 92-95. Brief report on the initiatives and activities of the regional center for conservation.

4869. Waechter, Wolfgang, ed. Study on Mass Conservation Techniques for Treatment of Library and Archives Material. Paris: UNESCO, 1989. 49p. (RAMP Study, PGI-89/WS/14). also reported in Information Reports and Bibliographies, 20:1 (1991), 2-17.

4870. Wagner, Sarah and Doris A. Hamburg. Caring for Your Treasures: Books to Help You. Washington, DC: American Institute for Conservation of Historic and Artistic Works, 1994. One folded sheet ([8]p.)

4871. Wagner, Sarah. "Enclosures for Glass and Film Negatives and Lantern Slides," Storage of Natural History Collections. Pittsburgh, PA: Society for the Preservation of Natural History Collections, 1992, 141-1143. How to construct storage wrappers.

4872. Wagner, Sarah. "Report on Photographic Materials," Infinity, 8:1 (Spring 1992), 6-7. A summary of advances in preservation of photographic materials made by the Image Permanence Institute, Rochester (NY) Institute of Technology.

4873. Wagner, Sarah. "Some Recent Photographic Preservation Activities at the Library of Congress," Topics in Photographic Preservation, 4 (1991), 136-149. Describes the optical disk project, making images accessible, and the physical treatments necessitated by the project, as well as other treatments undertaken and techniques developed.

4874. Wakeling, Ian. "Conserving Children's Social History," Library Conservation News, 41/42 (Winter 1993 / Spring 1994), 6-7. Briefly describes the conservation of the Children's Society, 1881-1928, through a grant from the National Manuscripts Conservation Trust.

4875. Wakeman, Geoffrey. Nineteenth Century Trade Binding. Kidlington, England: Plough Press, 1983. 2 vols., text and samples. Illus. Brief history of the trade.

4876. Walch, Victoria I. "Checklist of Standards Applicable to the Preservation of Archives and Manuscripts," American Archivist, 53:2 (Spring 1990), 324-338. Comprehensive checklist and discussion of standards relating to the preservation of library and archival materials.

4877. Walch, Victoria Irons. Recognizing Leadership and Partnership: A Report on the Condition of Historical Records in the States and Efforts to Ensure Their Preservation and Use. Des Moines, IA: Council of State Historical Records Coordinators, 1993. 166p. Review of the status of archival and records management programs throughout the nation.

4878. Walkden, Stephen A. "New Momentum for Alkaline Papermakers," TAPPI Journal (Technical Association for the Pulp and Paper Industry), 72:11 (November 1989), 8. Describes how alkaline papermaking is meeting the challenge of new printing technologies. Estimates that by 1993, 52% of uncoated freshsheet production will be alkaline.

4879.   Walkden, Stephen A. "An Overview of European Alkaline
        Papermaking and a Comparison with Current USA Position," TAPPI
        Proceedings, 1988 Coating Conference. Atlanta, GA: TAPPI Press,
        1988, 13-17. Reviews the advantages of alkaline paper production.

4880.   Walkden, Stephen. "Permanence and Durability of Paper," Paper
        Preservation: Current Issues and Recent Developments. Atlanta,
        GA: TAPPI Press, 1990, 81-84. Summarizes the problem of acidic
        paper; outlines six areas of improvement in the papermaking process
        by alkaline papermaking.

4881.   Walker, Frank L., and George R. Thoma. "Techniques for Creating
        and Accessing a Document Image Archive," National Online
        Meeting, Proceedings 1989. Medford, NJ: Learned Information,
        1989, 453-462.

4882.   Walker Franklin N. Jr. "The Hattiesburg 'Five-Hundred-Year-
        Flood,' Recovery from a Disaster," Conservation Administration
        News, 16 (January 1984), 7-8. Brief description of the salvage of the
        Hattiesburg Municipal Archive following a major flood.

4883.   Walker, Gay. "Advanced Preservation Planning at Yale,"
        Microform Review, 18:1 (Winter 1989), 20-28. Planning for
        preservation following the Association of Research Libraries Office
        of Management Studies methodology.

4884.   Walker, Gay. "The Evolution of Yale University's Preservation
        Program," The Library Preservation Program: Models, Priorities,
        Possibilities, ed. Jan Merrill-Oldham and Merrily Smith. Chicago,
        IL: American Library Association, 1985, 53-58. Case study.

4885.   Walker, Gay. "One Step Beyond: The Future of Preservation
        Microfilming," Preservation Microfilming. Chicago, IL: American
        Library Association, 1989, 66-72. The role of microfilm in
        preservation and access and the impact of new digitizing
        technologies.

4886.   Walker, Gay. "Preservation Decision-Making and Archival
        Photocopying," Restaurator, 8:1 (1987), 40-51.

4887.   Walker, Gay, ed. Preservation Microfilming: Planning and
         Production. Chicago, IL: Association for Library Collections and
         Technical Services, 1989. 72p. Papers from a conference held in
         April 1988 that address standards and specifications, criteria for
         comparing in-house and contracted microfilming, costs, and
         cooperative approaches.

4888.   Walker, Gay. "Preservation Planning and Perspective," Meeting the
         Preservation Challenge. Washington, DC: Association of Research
         Libraries, 1988, 43-47. Describes the planning process, its elements,
         and how to do it.

4889.   Walker, Gay. "Preservation Planning and the Conspectus at Yale
         University," Conservation Administration News, 31 (October 1987),
         8-9. Describes the use of the National Collections Inventory Project
         Conspectus to identify subjects that are most important in
         preservation and for developing a preservation strategy.

4890.   Walker, Gay, Jane Greenfield, John Fox, and Jeffrey S. Simonoff.
         "The Yale Survey: A Large-Scale Study of Book Deterioration in the
         Yale University Library," College and Research Libraries, 46:2
         (March 1985), 111-132. Discusses the methodology of the survey
         and the nature of the collections in the Yale University Library
         system.

4891.   Wall, Carol. "Inventory: What You Might Expect to Be Missing,"
         Library and Archival Security, 7:2 (Summer 1985), 27-31. Report of
         a sample inventory led to a survey of 143 library collections to
         determine loss rate; no relation between loss rate and security
         measures established.

4892.   Wallace, Jim. "Electronic Imaging in a Comprehensive Program of
         Photographic Preservation," Preserving Geoscience Imaging, ed.
         Louise S. Zipp. Alexandria, VA: Geoscience Information Center,
         1993, 39-40. (Proceedings, 23). Imaging to provide access while
         preserving original materials as part of an overall photographic
         preservation program.

4893. Wallace, Patricia E., Jo Ann Lee, and Dexter R. Schubert. Records Management: Integrated Information Systems. 3d ed. Englewood Cliffs, NJ: Prentice Hall, 1992. 542p. Text on administrative management of records. Includes disaster recovery concepts and care of records in electronic formats.

4894. Wallis, Terry Boone. "Conservation Treatment of Objects for Library of Congress Exhibit," Conservation Administration News, 53 (April 1993), 12-13. Describes some of the physical treatments to prepare rare books and maps for display for the exhibition, "1492: An Ongoing Voyage."

4895. Walne, Peter. Modern Archives Administration and Records Management: A RAMP Reading. Paris: UNESCO, 1985, 587p. (PGI-85/WS/32). Basic reader; reprints three papers on preservation and conservation originally published in the preceding decade.

4896. Walne, Peter. Selected Guidelines for the Management of Records and Archives: A RAMP Reader. Paris: UNESCO, 1990. 214p. (PGI-90/WS/6). Bibliography.

4897. Walsell Leather Museum. Leather Bibliography. Walsell, England: Walsell Leather Museum, 1992. [18p]. Selective bibliography of useful works concerning leather and its history; no annotations. Section on bookbinding and repair, history of bookbinding.

4898. Walsh, Betty. "Salvage Operations for Water-Damaged Collections," WAAC Newsletter (Western Association for Art Conservation), 10:2 (May 1988), 2-4; chart. Basic instructions on how to salvage paper, books, paintings, floppy disks, sound and video recordings, photographs.

4899. Walsh, Judith C. "Protecting Works of Art on Paper from the Effects of Light," Drawing, 9:2 (July-August 1987), 33-34. Describes damage that light can cause to paper-based items and measures for protection and exhibition conditions; directed at the private collector.

4900. Walter, Gerry. "Optical Data Storage Technology: Promise of a New Digital Mass Memory," International Journal of Micrographics and

Video Technology, 1:2/3 (1982), 61-85. Presents an evolution of optical disk technology. Briefly presents a description of its workings. Briefly discusses permanence.

4901. Walter, Katherine L. "State Preservation Planning in Nebraska," Preservation Papers of the 1991 SAA Annual Conference, comp. Karen Garlick. Chicago: Society of American Archivists, 1992, 29-33. Describes a state-wide planning project, what worked and what did not.

4902. Walters, Tyler O. "Breaking New Ground Fostering Preservation: The Society of American Archivists' Preservation Management Training Program," Library Resources and Technical Services, 39:4 (October 1995), 417-426. Overview of preservation education opportunities for librarians and archivists and an examination of the contribution of the SAA three year project to train archivists to establish and maintain comprehensive archival preservation management programs. "A benchmark for future training in both fields" (417).

4903. Walters, Tyler O. "SAA's Preservation Management Training Program Is a Huge Success," College & Research Libraries News, 3 (March 1995), 139.

4904. Walton, Bruce. "National Archives Preservation Services to the National Library," National Library News, 26:7 (July 1994), 7-8. Treatment, photographic, microfilming, and digital imaging services offered.

4905. Walworth, Vivian K. "On the Preservation and Conservation of Instant Photographs," Stability and Conservation of Photographic Images: Chemical, Electronic and Mechanical. Bangkok, Thailand: Society of Photographic Scientists and Engineers, 1986, 79-83. Brief discussion about production and exhibition requirements.

4906. Wang, Kathryn H. Conservation and Preservation of Paper Records and Photographs: A Selected Bibliography of Items Available at the Washington State Library. Olympia, WA: Washington State Library, 1988. 4p.

4907.   Wang, Kathryn H. "Preserving Books: Acid Wars and Other
         Battles," AB Bookman's Weekly (Antiquarian Bookman), 82:5
         (August 1, 1988), 311-316. Care and preservation of collections,
         written for the collector.

4908.   Ward, Alan. A Manual of Sound Archive Administration.
         Aldershot, Hants, England and Brookfield, VT: Gower Publishing,
         1990. 288p. Basic text, covering all aspects of management and
         collections care and preservation.

4909.   Ward, Alan, and Peter Copeland. "Freeze-Drying of Tapes," Library
         Conservation News, 34 (January 1992), 4-5. Describes experiments
         on the freeze-drying of magnetic tapes carrying audio materials.

4910.   Ward, Christine W. "Preservation at the New York State Archives,"
         Conservation Administration News, 26 (July 1986), 4-5, 23-24.

4911.   Ward, Christine W. "What a Difference a Grant Makes: Preserving
         New York's Documentary Heritage," Preservation Papers of the
         1991 SAA Annual Conference, comp. Karen Garlick. Chicago:
         Society of American Archivists, 1992, 49-52. Preservation of
         collections through grant-funded projects, planning and obtaining
         grants.

4912.   Ward, Philip R. Getting the Bugs Out. Victoria, Canada: British
         Columbia Provincial Museum, 1987. 20p. Describes and illustrates
         common pests that attack books and textiles; discusses fumigation
         and extermination.

4913.   Ward, Philip R. The Nature of Conservation: A Race Against Time.
         Marina del Rey, CA: Getty Conservation Institute, 1986, 70p. The
         nature of conservation, written for the public to acquaint it with the
         philosophy behind efforts to preserve the cultural heritage.

4914.   Ward, Philip. "Reflections," CCI Newsletter (Canadian
         Conservation Institute), 6 (September 1990), 11-13.
         (English/French). Reflections on the development of the field of

Bibliography

conservation, the role of the conservator, and the need for more training for curators in materials science and conservation.

4915. Warden, Linda, and Jane Kingsley. "A Stitch in Time: Preservation on a Shoestring," Library Conservation News, 36 (July 1992), 4-5, 8. Describes preservation activities at the Archives and Historical Collection, Royal Veterinary College, London.

4916. Ware, Coral Mary. "What Price Permanence? Why Australia Uses So Little Permanent Paper," AICCM Bulletin (Australian Institute for the Conservation of Cultural Material), 16:4 (1990), 59-68. Review of the use of permanent paper for book production in Australia; cites lack of interest; suggestions for action to promote production of permanent paper.

4917. Ware, Mike. Mechanisms of Image Deterioration in Early Photographs: The Sensitivity to Light of W.H.F. Talbot's Halide Fixed Images, 1834-1844. London: Science Museum/National Museum of Photography, Film and Television, 1994. 92p. Explains early photographic processes and chemistry; implications for storage of prints. Relationship between light levels and length of exposure. Introduces "qualitative concepts of damage."

4918. Warner, Glen. "The Care and Framing of Original Prints," Building a Print Collection: A Guide to Buying Original Prints and Photographs. Toronto, Canada: Key Porter Books, 1984, 159-174. Provides sound advice on housing, storing, and transporting prints, with discussion of conservation and restoration. Glossary.

4919. Warnow-Blewett, Joan. "Saving the Records of Science and Technology: The Role of a Discipline History Center," Preservation and Conservation of Sci-Tech Materials. New York: Haworth Press, 1987, 29-40. Describes the American Institute for Physics planning for the long-term retention of critical materials documenting the history of modern physics.

4920. Warren, Richard Jr. "Handling of Sound Recordings," ARSC Journal (Association of Recorded Sound Archivists), 25:2 (Fall 1994), 139-162. Handling and storage of sound recordings to ensure

651

their preservation and future access. Describes types of materials used as sound carriers.

4921. Warren, Richard Jr. "Storage of Sound Recordings," <u>ARSC Journal</u> (Association of Recorded Sound Collections), 24:2 (Fall 1993), 130-175. Detailed review of standards for the storage and preservation of sound recordings. Includes a comprehensive "Bibliography of Materials on the Planning and Construction of Library Buildings," by Linda Blair, originally published in the 1987 Associated Audio Archives report.

4922. Warren, S. D., Company. <u>Paper Permanence: Preserving the Written Word</u>, rev. ed. Boston, MA: S.D. Warren Company, 1983. 83p Illus. Illustrated history of paper manufacture; discussion of problems in producing permanent-durable paper.

4923. Warren, S. D., Company. <u>Preservation in Original Format; The Role of Paper Quality</u>. Boston, MA: S.D. Warren, 1986. 12p. Pamphlet by a paper company on how permanent and durable papers can be produced.

4924. Washington Research Library Consortium. <u>Books Condition Survey</u>. Washington, DC: Washington Research Library Consortium, 1990. 17p.

4925. Wassell, J. L. "Illini Fighting Redox," <u>Inform</u>, 4:5 (May 1990), 26-30. Describes an effort to salvage microfilm with redox blemishes and the procedure that operates in a specially designed facility at the Illinois State Library.

4926. Waterer, John. <u>John Waterer's Guide to Leather Conservation and Restoration</u>, rev. & abr. Northhampton, England: Museum of Leathercraft, 1986. 52p. A guide to the nature and properties of a variety of leathers, and imitation leathers. Shortened version of <u>A Guide to the Conservation & Restoration of Objects Made Wholly or in Part of Leather</u>. London: G. Bell, 1972.

4927. Waterhouse, John F. "Monitoring the Aging of Paper," <u>Paper Preservation: Current Issues and Recent Developments</u>. Atlanta,

GA: TAPPI Press, 1990), 53-57. Reviews degradation mechanisms and environmental factors that influence the aging of paper. Examines destructive and non-destructive testing methods.

4928.   Waters, Donald J. From Microform to Digital Imagery. Washington, DC: Commission on Preservation and Access, June 1991. 41p. Explores the feasibility of a project at Yale University Library to study the means, costs, and benefits of converting large quantities of preserved library materials from microform to digital images, for enhanced access. Also reported in Inform 5 (October 1991), 14-19+.

4929.   Waters, Donald J. Realizing Benefits from Inter-Institutional Agreements: The Implications of the Draft Report of the Task Force of Digital Information. Washington, DC: Commission on Preservation and Access, January 1996. 4p. Insert in CPA Newsletter (Commission on Preservation and Access), 85, January 1995.

4930.   Waters, Donald J. "Transforming Libraries Through Digital Preservation," Digital Imaging Technology for Preservation, ed. Nancy E. Elkington. Mountain View, CA: Research Libraries Group, 1994, 115-1127. Addresses preservationists' need to preserve scholarly communication in electronic formats; envisions cost savings in terms of storage and ease of access.

4931.   Waters, Donald, and John Garrett. Preserving Digital Information: Report of the Task Force on Archiving of Digital Information. Washington, DC: Commission on Preservation and Access, May 1996. 59p. This is the final report of the joint Commission on Preservation and Access and Research Libraries Group Task Force on Digital Archiving. The Task Force, which was created in December 1994, issued a draft report in August 1995 and this final report in May 1996.

4932.   Waters, Donald J., and Shari Weaver. The Organization Phase of Project Open Book: A Report to the Commission on Preservation and Access. Washington, DC: Commission on Preservation and Access, 1992. 11p. Reprinted Microform Review, 22:4 (Fall 1993), 152-159. Narrates the organizational phase of the university's effort

4933. to convert 10,000 volumes in microfilm format into digital image form and to explore the effects of scale on emerging preservation imaging systems.

4934. Waters, Peter. "Phased Preservation: A Philosophical Concept and Practical Approach to Preservation," Special Libraries, 81:1 (Winter 1990), 35-43. Discusses the evolution of the concept of phased preservation as an extension of collection maintenance and as an alternative to restoration. Describes phased preservation at the Library of Congress and the point system for allocating staff time and resources. The system is to be implemented at the Academy of Sciences Library (BAN), St. Petersburg, Russia.

4935. Waters, Peter. "Phased Conservation Revisited," Conservation (Newsletter of the Getty Conservation Institute), 8:2 (1994), 12-13. Reflections on phased conservation and conservation for library and archival materials.

4936. Waters, Peter. "A Unique Library 'Preventive' Preservation Technology," International Preservation News, 10 (July 1995), 8-9. Describes the use of an automated machine to make custom-fitted archival book boxes for the protection of collections at BAN and LC. Notes that such protection offers the best preservation.

4937. Watkin, Alan. "Library Rebinding - A Suitable Case for Attention," Library Conservation News, 41/42 (Winter 1993/Spring 1994), 3. Short report on library binding practices in Britain.

4938. Watkin, Alan. The Role of Rebinding in Modern Stock Management: A Research Report. Clwyd, Wales, U.K.: Clwyd County Council Library and Information Service, Summer 1992. 43p. Investigation of the impact and benefits of commercial library binding on public library bookstock.

4939. Watkins, Stephanie. "Chemical Watermarking of Paper," Journal of the American Institute for Conservation, 29:2 (Fall 1990), 117-131. Investigation of 20th-century custom watermarks: identification; exploration of the effect of various conservation treatments on the watermarks.

4939.   Watkins, Christine. "Disaster Planning Makes Dollars and Sense: Disaster Planning for Libraries," American Libraries, 27:8 (September 1996), 9+

4940.   Watsky, Lance Ross. The Preservation and Restoration of Sound Recording and Motion Pictures. Chico, CA: California State University, Fall 1995. 53p. MA Thesis.

4941.   Watson, Adele L. "Quake, Rattle, and Roll: Or the Day the Coalinga Library Stood Still and Everything Else Moved," Library and Archival Security, 6:1 (Spring 1984), 1-5. Description of the earthquake and damage to the district library, with comments on disaster preparedness and actions that should be taken when earthquake strikes.

4942.   Watson, Aldren A. Hand Bookbinding: A Manual of Instruction. New York: Macmillan, 1987. 160p. Illus. Describes methods used in traditional bookbinding.

4943.   Watson, Caroline F. A Performance Comparison of Oversewn, PVA Double Fanned, and Cleat-Laced Bindings. Rochester, NY: Rochester Institute of Technology, 1985. 114p. (Masters Thesis).

4944.   Watson, Duane A. "The Divine Library Function: Preservation." School Library Journal, 33:3 (November 1986), 41-45. Basic article on preservation for school librarians, including teaching students how to handle materials.

4945.   Watson, Tom. "After the Fire: Everett Community College Library Is Back in Business," Wilson Library Bulletin, (November 1988), 63-65. Case study of a fire and rebuilding of a library; coping.

4946.   Watson, Tom. "Out of the Ashes: The Los Angeles Public Library," Wilson Library Bulletin, 64:4 (December 1989), 34-39. Reconstruction of the LAPL, reorganization of collections, and funding.

4947.   Watstein, Sarah Barbara. "Book Mutilation: An Unwelcome By-Product of Electronic Security Systems," Library and Archival Security, 5:1 (Spring 1983), 11-33. Review of electronic security systems and results of a survey of research libraries to assess what damage they cause to books. Urges further investigation and study of costs.

4948.   Watt, Marcia A. and Lisa Bible. "CD-ROM Longevity: A Select Bibliography," Conservation Administration News, 60 (January 1995), 11-13. Selected articles that address the issue of longevity and stability of compact disks.

4949.   Watt, Marcia A. "The Preservation of Library Materials in 1991: A Review of the Literature," Library Resources and Technical Services, 36:3 (July 1992), 333-338. Bibliographic essay and review of trends.

4950.   Watt, Marcia A. "2200 Gallons of Water," Southeastern Librarian, 44:2 (Summer 1994), 67-68. Case study; salvage of a water-damaged collection of rare pamphlets.

4951.   Wayne, John J. "LC Puts New Security Measures in Place: Third Arrest Since May 1991 Stirs Media Interest," LC Information Bulletin (Library of Congress), 51:8 (April 20, 1992), 161-162. Describes the security measures that the library has put in place to protect the collections from theft and mutilation.

4952.   Wayne, John J. "Paper Preservation Update: What the Library Is Doing," LC Information Bulletin (Library of Congress), 51:7 (April 6, 1992), 135-136. Brief review of the "Report on Progress in Implementing National Policy on Acid-Free Paper" (December 1991).

4953.   Weaver, Barbara. "Planning for Preservation in New Jersey," New Jersey Libraries, 18:1 (Spring 1985), 2-4. Description of the planning process for a cooperative preservation program for libraries and other cultural institutions in New Jersey.

4954.   Weaver, Chuck. "In Search of the Perfect (+/- 1.5%) Hygrometer .. Slings and Other Errors and the Covey and the Haar," Society of

California Archivists Newsletter, 44 (January 1985), 5-6. Review of several portable, inexpensive sling hygrometers, with caviats.

4955. Weaver, Martin E., with F. G. Matero. Conserving Buildings: Guide to Techniques and Materials. NY: John Wiley, 1993. 270p. A basic text on building conservation, with emphasis on assessing old and new technologies to integrate them effectively.

4956. Weaver, Shari L. "Quality Control," Digital Imaging Technology for Preservation, ed. Nancy E. Elkington. Mountain View, CA: Research Libraries Group, 1994, 81-97. Discusses the effect of source materials, scanning equipment, and other factors on the faithful reproduction of images. Outlines quality control procedures developed for the Cornell and Yale imaging projects.

4957. Weaver-Meyers, Pat L., and Stephen D. Ramsey. "Fines for Food: A Citation System to Control Food and Drink Consumption in the Library," College and Research Libraries News, 51:6 (June 1990), 536-538. A successful effort to curtail food and drink in the library through coordination with the Office of Student Affairs, the University Police, and the library.

4958. Webb, Colin. "Some Insights into Australian Library and Archives Microfilming Experience," Preservation Microfilming: Does It Have a Future? Canberra: National Library of Australia, 1995, 27-44. Preservation microfilming at both institutions from a manager's perspective. Selection of facilities, establishments of procedures, setting priorities, selection issues, discusses some concerns about the Australian Distributed National Collection concept.

4959. Weber, David C. "Brittle Books in Our Nation's Libraries," College and Research Libraries News, 48:5 (May 1987), 238-244. Statement submitted by the Association of Research Libraries and American Library Association before the House Committee on Education and Labor, Subcommittee on Postsecondary Education, March 3, 1987. Presents the national plan for preservation of library materials and a request for a federal policy of commitment and financial support.

4960.   Weber, David C. Library Buildings and the Loma Prieta Earthquake
        Experience of October 1989. Sacramento, CA: State Library
        Foundation, 1990. 66p. Survey of the damage at Stanford
        University, area libraries, and bookshops.

4961.   Weber, Harmut. "Cooperation, Coordination and Unification of
        Resources: A Concept of the Federal State of Baden-Württenberg,
        FRG, for the Preservation of Books and Records," Conference on
        Book and Paper Conservation, 1990. Budapest, Hungary: Technical
        Association of Paper and Printing Industry/National Szechenyi
        Library, 1992, 73-77. Description of the Special Programme for the
        Preservation of Threatened Library and Archival Material, including
        a conservation laboratory, reformatting, and research.

4962.   Weber, Harmut. "Paper Splitting Tested in Germany," Commission
        on Preservation and Access Newsletter, 79 (May 1995) 2;   reprinted
        New Library Scene, 14:3 (June 1995), 6,9. Describes the paper-
        splitting techniques of strengthening brittle paper practiced in
        Leipzig and elsewhere in Germany and the machine developed to
        facilitate the process. Trans. from Archiv-Nachrichten, 9 (December
        1994).

4963.   Weber, Harmut. Opto-Electronic Storage - An Alternative to
        Filming? Washington, DC: Commission on Preservation and Access,
        February 1993. 6p. Explores optical disk technology, concluding
        that it is an access, not a preservation medium.

4964.   Weber, Lisa. "Electronic Records: Too Ephemeral?" Inform, 6:2
        (February 1992), 32-36. Report on a working conference to develop
        a research agenda to ensure that records of enduring value are
        preserved.

4965.   Weber, Mark. "Electrophotography and Archiving," Restaurator, 8:1
        (1987), 9-17. A basis survey of electrophotography is presented
        using different Kodak photocopiers as examples. Identifies the
        advantages of various photocopier types. Closes with remarks on
        future development in data storage and document duplication.

4966. Webster, Duane E. "Technologies for Preserving Library Collections," Chronicle of Higher Education, 36:48 (August 15, 1990), B3-B4.

4967. Wedinger, Robert S. "FMC Mass Paper Preservation System," Conference on Book and Paper Conservation, 1990. Budapest, Hungary: Technical Association of Paper and Printing Industry/National Szechenyi Library, 1992, 152-163. Describes the FMC/Lithco deacidification system and reviews data from independent testing to demonstrate its effectiveness.

4968. Wedinger, Robert S. "The FMC Mass Preservation System," Restaurator, 12:1 (1991), 1-17. Describes the FMC/Lithco deacidification system, its evaluation, and the results of independent laboratory testing.

4969. Wedinger, Robert S. "The FMC Mass Preservation System: Enhancement and Extension of Useful Life," Restaurator, 14:2 (1993), 102-122. Presents some modifications in the FMC/Lithco mass deacidification system, with test data.

4970. Wedinger, Robert S. "Lithco Develops Deacidification/ Strengthening Process," Alkaline Paper Advocate, 2:4 (October 1989), 39-40; reprinted in Abbey Newsletter, 13:7 (November 1989), 126. Description of the process for mass treatment of library and archival materials developed by the Lithium Corporation of America.

4971. Wedinger, Robert S. "Preserving Our Written Heritage," Chemistry in Britain, 28:10 (1992), 898-900. Overview of the technologies being developed for bulk paper deacidification.

4972. Weeks, Linton. "The Washington Post Looks at the Library," LC Information Bulletin (Library of Congress), 50:17 (September 9, 1991), 325-338. A look at the work of Tom Albro, rare book conservator, and Chandru Shahani, Preservation Laboratory director as a part of this in-depth profile of the Library of Congress, originally published in Washington Post Magazine, May 26, 1991.

4973.   Wehrkamp, Tim. A Survey of Description and Preservation of National Archives Textual and Cartographic Records Relating to Major Corps of Topographical Engineers Expeditions in the Trans-Mississippi West, 1819-1863. Washington, DC: National Archives and Records Administration, 1991. 102p.

4974.   Weidner, Marilyn Kemp. "Treatment of Water Sensitive and Friable Media Using Suction and Ultrasonic Mist," Book and Paper Group Annual, 12 (1993), 75-84. Summarizes the history of the suction table, invented by the author, and discusses various treatments, ways of avoiding problems.

4975.   Weidner, Marilyn, and Shannon Zachary. "The System Moisture Chamber/Suction Table/Ultrasonic Humidifier/Air Filter," Conservation of Historic and Artistic Works on Paper; Proceedings of a Conference, Ottawa, Canada, 3 to 7 October, 1988, ed. Helen D. Burgess. Ottawa: 1994, 109-115. Describes treatments for difficult works on paper using the system.

4976.   Weihs, Jean. Accessible Storage of Nonbook Materials. Phoenix, AZ: Oryx Press, 1984. 101p. Text on care and handling of materials in circulating collections; advice on education of patrons in the handling of nonbook materials.

4977.   Weihs, Jean. The Integrated Library: Encouraging Access to Multimedia Materials. 2d ed. Phoenix, AZ: Oryx Press, 1991. 142p. A basic, carefully written and illustrated text on the storage and handling of sound recordings, magnetic media, film, paper-based objects, 3-dimensional objects (realia), computer and optical disks. Bibliographies.

4978.   Weinberg, Gerhard L. "The End of Ranke's History?" Syracuse Scholar, 9:1 (1988), 51-60; reprinted in Germany, Hitler and World War II: Essays in Modern German and World History. Cambridge, U.K.: Cambridge University Press, 1995, 325-336. A distinguished historian discusses the threat to traditional historical research by policies that restrict access to records until they have deteriorated; lack of schedules for their reproduction on microfilm; and the use of

computers that produce machine-readable records that cannot be
reproduced after a brief period of time.

4979.   Weinstein, Frances Ruth. "A Psocid by Any Other Name ... (Is Still
a Pest)," Library and Archival Security, 6:1 (Spring 1984), 57-
63. Identifies common insects common to libraries and discusses
preventive measures.

4980.   Weintraub, Steven. "Creating and Maintaining the Right
Environment," Caring for Your Collections. New York: Harry N.
Abrams, 1992, 19-29. Discussion of proper environment for
collections.

4981.   Weir, Thomas E., Jr. 3480 Class Tape Cartridge Drives and Archival
Data Storage: Technology Assessment Report. Washington, DC:
National Archives and Records Administration, 1988. (TIP-04,
NTIS, PB88-233135), 36p.

4982.   Weiskel, Timothy. "The Electronic Library and the Challenge of
Information Planning," Academe, 75:4 (July-August 1989) 8-
12. Discusses the increasing technology used in libraries and
academia and how the library can / should continue to play a major
role in shaping it; however librarians should make more informed
decisions so that the library remains a place to look for information.
Librarians and academics should work together.

4983.   Weisman, Brenda. "Preservation Planning at the Brooklyn Botanic
Garden Library," Science and Technology Libraries, 7:3 (Spring
1987), 69-79; reprinted Preservation and Conservation of Sci-Tech
Materials. New York: Haworth Press, 1987. Describes the collection
survey and conservation project undertaken at the Book
Conservation Center.

4984.   Weiss, Carla, and David Maine. "Disaster at Rhode Island College: a
Case Study," CRIARL Newsletter (Consortium of Rhode Island
Research and Academic Libraries), 13:3 (November 1994), 3-4. On
July 7, 1993, a pipe burst and leaked over two floors of stacks.

4985.   Weiss, Dudley A. "A Checklist for Buying Library Binding," New Library Scene, 3:2 (April 1984), 16,18. Covers obligations of the library and the binder and urges constant communication between them.

4986.   Weiss, Dudley A. "An Industry Forecast: Library Binders and the Maintenance of Library Materials in the Decade Ahead," New Library Scene, 2:1 (January/February 1983), 1, 4, 6, 8. Predicts that "the challenge to libraries will be how to maintain their vast repository of materials." Discusses curatorial responsibilities of librarians and the effect that new technologies will have on collections and library binding needs.

4987.   Weiss, Dudley A. "LBI at 50 ... Achievements and Principles," New Library Scene, 4:2 (April 1985), 11-14. History of the Library Binding Institute and a look at the future of the industry.

4988.   Weiss, D. A. "The Library Binding Industry: Today and Tomorrow," New Library Scene, 6:5 (October 1987), 1-10. Reflections on the past and future of the industry.

4989.   Weiss, Philip. "The Book Thief: A True Tale of Bibliomania," Harpers, 288:1724 (January 1994), 37-56. Profile of Stephen Blumberg and his thefts of rare books from American libraries.

4990.   Weiss, R. "Staying One Step Ahead of Their Six," Science News, 134 (July 9, 1988), 22. Note on two potential approaches to pest control: modified atmosphere and gamma radiation.

4991.   Welch, Theodore F., Warren M. Tsuneshi, and Mary F. Grosch. Strengthening the U.S.-Japan Library Partnership in the Global Information Flow: Fourth U.S.-Japan Conference on Library and Information Science in Higher Education. Chicago, IL: American Library Association, 1990. 320p.

4992.   "A Well-Documented Solution," DuPont Magazine, 7:6 (November/December 1983), 17-19. Describes the Wei T'o deacidification process at the National Library of Canada.

Bibliography

4993. Wellheiser, Johanna G. Nonchemical Treatment Processes for Disinfection of Insects and Fungi in Library Collections. Munich; New York: K. G. Saur, 1992. 118p. (IFLA Publication, 60). Review of comparative costs, benefits, risks, and areas for more research on processes available for treatment of books and paper.

4994. Wellheiser, Johanna G., ed. Proceedings of the 14th Annual IIC-CG Conference, May 27-30, 1988. Toronto: Toronto Area Conservation Group/International Institute for Conservation - Canadian Group, 1989. 179p. French/English. Sessions dealt with ethics and the role of the non-conservator in conservation; science in conservation; pest control; paper, and textiles; etc. Bibliographies.

4995. Wells, Ellen B., and Renata Rutledge. Book Collecting and Care of Books. Washington, DC: Smithsonian Institution Libraries, 1985., 1987. 24p. Pamphlet for the general public, with half dealing with basic collection care, including the oiling of bindings.

4996. Wells, Rosemary. "The Newsplan Project," In Safe Keeping. ed. Jennifer Thorp. Winchester, U.K.: Hampshire Co. Library / Hampshire Archives Trust, 1988 24-26. Briefly describes project to microfilm local newspapers for preservation and access.

4997. Wells, Rosemary. Newsplan: Report of the Pilot Project in the South-West. London: British Library, 1986. 218p.; 2 microfiche. (Library and Information Research Report, 0263-1709; 38). Report on a pilot project to examine the state of preservation of the region's newspapers.

4998. Welsh, Elizabeth C. "CooL Breeze," WAAC Newsletter (Western Association for Art Conservation), 15:2 (May 1993), 5. Overview of Conservation Online, a Wide Area Information Server (WAIS) that provides access to full-text databases of conservation information.

4999. Welsh, William J. "In Defense of DEZ: LC's Perspective," Library Journal, 112:1 (January 1987), 62-63. Response of the Deputy Librarian of Congress to an LJ article on the development of the diethyl zinc process; discusses safety issues, decision making, progress of the project.

5000.   Welsh, William J. "International Cooperation in Preservation of Library Materials," Collection Management, 9:2/3 (Spring/Summer 1987); International Conference on Research Library Cooperation, New York: Haworth Press, 1987, 119-131. Discusses international cooperation for preservation concerns, including the sharing of preservation methods and a universal preservation program. The Library of Congress's efforts, including its Optical Disk Pilot Program, are discussed.

5001.   Welsh, William J. "The Library of Congress: A More-Than-Equal Partner," Library Resources and Technical Services, 29:1 (January-March, 1985), 87-93. The Library's role and contribution to cooperative microfilming efforts.

5002.   Welsh, William J. "Preserving Through Cooperative Microfilming - The U.S. Approach," National Libraries: Some South African and International Perspectives on Challenges and Opportunities; Tribute to H. J. Aschenborn at 65. Pretoria, South Africa: State Library, 1986, 231-238. Describes the history of preservation microfilming at the Library of Congress and its current activities.

5003.   Welsh, William J., ed. Research Libraries - Yesterday, Today and Tomorrow. Westport, CT: Greenwood Press, 1993. 469p. (Contributions in Librarianship and Information Science, 77). Selection of papers presented between 1982 and 1992 in Japan, some of which focus on preservation.

5004.   West, Tim. "Preserving the Southern Historical Collection," Preservation Papers of the 1991 SAA Annual Conference. comp. Karen Garlick. Chicago: Society of American Archivists, 1992, 53-57. Planning, assessing needs, and obtaining grants to preserve collections and better provide access.

5005.   Westbrook, Lynn. "Developing an In-House Preservation Program: A Survey of Experts," Library and Archival Security, 7:3/4 (Fall/Winter 1985), 1-21. Summarizes the advice and opinions about preservation by 10 preservation librarians.

Bibliography

5006.   Westbrook, Lynn. Paper Preservation: Nature, Extent, and Recommendations. Urbana, IL: University of Illinois. Graduate School of Library and Information Science, 1985. 79p. (Its Occasional Papers, 171) A survey of the preservation problem and approaches to the problem.

5007.   Westcott, David. "New Images from an Old Master: Guidelines for Converting from Micrographic to Electronic Imaging," Inform, 6:5 (May 1992), 36-40, 51. Guidelines and standards for the selection of appropriate microfilm for future conversion to digital format.

5008.   Westcott, David H. "Response to the Final Report on Preservation Microfiche," Inform, 4:4 (April 1990), 16-18. Suggestions for efficient and cost-effective microfiche filming.

5009.   Western New York Library Resource Council. Western New York Disaster Preparedness and Recovery Manual for Libraries and Archives. Buffalo, NY: Western New York Library Resource Council, 1992. One volume. "Barbara Rhodes provided the basic test"

5010.   Westra, Pieter E. "Preservation in Southern Africa: The Current Situation," Books In Peril. Cape Town, South Africa: South African Library, 1987, 26-38. Review of activities, facilities, and training.

5011.   Weststrate, David F. "Warning: Your Collection May Be Bugged," American Philatelist, 98:9 (September 1984), 929-932. Describes the damage that insects, vermin, molds, and fungi can do to stamp collections and how infestation can be prevented.

5012.   Wettasingh, Saroja. "Archive Conservation in South Asia," SALG Newsletter (Southeast Asian Library Group), 34 (June 1989), 9-14. Describes conservation and preservation activities in Afghanistan, Bangladesh, India, the Maldives, Pakistan, and Sri Lanka.

5013.   Weyde, E. "On the Possibility of Improving the Permanence of Photographic Prints," The British Journal of Photography (1935). 1p. One page of practical advice on how to treat photographic prints.

665

5014.   Wharram, Polly. "Eating in the Library: A Modest and Effective
        Solution, Or, HELP! That's Mayonnaise on the Domesday Disc,"
        College and Undergraduate Libraries, 1:1 (1994), 95-97. Describes
        method, a memo to faculty, to curtail eating and drinking in the
        library.

5015.   Whealen, R. E. "Microfilmed Records in the JFK Library,"
        Microform Review, 17:1 (October 1988), 197-200.

5016.   Wheeler, Daniel G. Investments in Brittle Books: Limited Surveys
        of Three ARL Libraries. Chapel Hill, NC: Wheeler, 1987. 71p.

5017.   Wheeler, David L. "After Much Neglect, Cambodia's Library Gets
        American Aid to Save Its Meager Collection of Books and
        Manuscripts," Chronicle of Higher Education, 36:47 (August 8,
        1990), A32.

5018.   Wheeler, James. "Increasing the Life of Your Audio Tape," Journal
        of the Audio Engineering Society, 36:4 (April 1988), 232-
        236. Describes factors necessary for long-term storage of audio
        tapes; measures for prolonging life and recovering data when tapes
        are damaged.

5019.   Wheeler, James. "An Overview of the D1 and D2 Digital Video
        Tape Format; or D1, D2, Which One for You?" Archiving the
        Audio-Visual Heritage. Rushton, England: FIAF/UNESCO, 1992,
        103-105. Briefly discusses digital tape recording formats noting that
        copy quality is excellent.

5020.   Wheeler, James. "Videotape Preservation," Environment et
        Conservation de l'Écrit, de l'Image et du Son. Paris: ARSAG, 1994,
        172-176. (Actes des Deuxième Journées Internationales d'Études de
        l'ARSAG, 16 au 20 Mai, 1994). Discusses the rapid advancement in
        video recording technology. Describes the digital, analog,
        composite, and component video formats, advantages and
        disadvantages.

5021.   Wheeler, Tony. "The Future of Microfilming and Digitization
        Techniques," Preservation Microfilming: Does It Have a Future?
        Canberra: National Library of Australia, 1995, 123-127 Discusses
        microfilm as a preservation medium and describes the new system
        for preservation of color material on microfilm "But in the end the
        future is still about microfilm." (123)

5022.   Whiffin, Jean. "IFLA 1994: Havana Reported" Conservation
        Administration News, 60 (January 1995) 23.

5023.   Whitaker, Albert H., Jr. "Conservators in Archives: The Experience
        of the Massachusetts Archives," Preservation Papers of the 1990
        SAA Annual Conference, comp. Karen Garlick. Chicago: Society of
        American Archivists, 1991, 31-33. Discusses stresses and tensions
        between conservators and archivists, disparate goals, poor
        communication.

5024.   White, David. "Conservation," Handbook of Library Training
        Practice, ed. Ray Prytherch. Brookfield, VT: Gower, 1986, 322-
        340. Reviews essentials of a preservation program in the library;
        provides information on training.

5025.   White, John R. An Introduction to the Preservation of Information
        on Paper-Film-Magnetic and Optical Media. Silver Spring, MD:
        Association for Information and Image Management [1985],
        51p. Practical discussion of the component parts of paper, common
        film types, magnetic tapes, and optical digital disks. Bibliography.

5026.   White, Kris A., and Glenn S. Cook. "Round 'Em Up, Move 'Em
        Out: How to Move and Preserve Archival Materials," Conservation
        Administration News, 57 (April 1994), 16-17. Moving an archive of
        rare and fragile materials; methodology and solutions.

5027.   White, Robert M. "Disc Storage Technology," Scientific American,
        243:2 (August 1980), 138-148. A description of optical disk
        technology, which enables data to be digitized and stored, then
        retrieved and read by laser.

5028. Whitfield, Susan, and Frances Wood, eds. <u>Dunhuang and Turfan: Contents and Conservation of Ancient Documents From Central Asia</u>. London: British Library, 1996. 98p.

5029. Whitmore, Paul M., and John Bogaard. "Determination of the Cellulose Scission Route in the Hydrolytic and Oxidative Degradation of Paper," <u>Restaurator</u>, 15:1 (1994), 26-45. Analysis of cotton linter filter paper under a variety of conditions; results and implications.

5030. Whitmore, Paul M., and John Bogaard. "The Effect of Oxidation on Subsequent Oven Aging of Filter Paper," <u>Restaurator</u>, 16:1 (1995), 10-30. Explores the effect of oxidation that usually occurs during aging; notes that degree of oxidation of cellulose in paper may be an important determinant of the overall degradation rate.

5031. <u>The Whole Art of Bookbinding/ The Whole Process of Marbling Paper</u>. Forward by Bernard Middleton. Austin, TX: W. Thomas Taylor, 1987. 89p. Reprint of the first bookbinding manual to be printed in English.

5032. Wick, Constance S. "Image-Related Aspects of Preserving High-Use Geoscience Literature by Deacidification," <u>Preserving Geoscience Imagery</u>, ed. Louise S. Zipp. Alexandria, VA: Geoscience Information Society, 1993, 5-9 (Proceedings, 23). Describes a project at Harvard to deacidify oversize illustrations, theses, photographs, and cartographic materials, demonstrating where deacidification is effective and identifying areas needing more research.

5033. WiederKehr, Robert R.V.. <u>The Design and Analysis of a Sample Survey of the Condition of Books in the Library of Congress</u>. Rockville, MD: King Research, 1984. 35 leaves. Report submitted to the Library of Congress, Preservation Research Services.

5034. Wiesner, Julius. <u>Mikroskopische Untersuchung der Papiere von El-Faijum (Microscopic Examination of the Faijum Papers)</u>, ed. Jack C. Thompson, trans. Gudrun Aurand. Portland, OR: Caber Press, 1986. 13p. Paper proving that the earliest papers produced in Egypt were made of linen rag fibers with little cotton, and sized with paste to make them appear whiter.

5035. Wilcox, Annie Tremmel. <u>A Degree of Mastery: A Journey Through Craft Apprenticeship</u>. Ames, Iowa: University of Iowa, 1994. 179 leaves. Ph.D. Thesis.

5036. Wilcox, Michael. "Merchant Navy Book of Remembrance: A Method for Binding Vellum Leaves," <u>CBBAG Newsletter</u> (Canadian Bookbinders and Book Artist Guild), 13:2 (Summer 1995), 3-13. A structure devised for a thick volume of inflexible vellum leaves to be on permanent display with a different page shown each day.

5037. Wilhelm, Henry. "Color Photographs and Color Motion Pictures in the Library: For Preservation or Destruction?" <u>Conserving and Preserving Materials in Nonbook Formats</u>. Urbana-Champaign: University of Illinois Graduate School of Library and Information Science, 1991, 105-111. (Allerton Park Institute, 30). Describes the problem of instability of color films; discusses current research; recommends that librarians keep current on the topic.

5038. Wilhelm, Henry. "Going, Going, Going, Gone," <u>Popular Photography</u>, 97 (June 1990), 37. Discusses image stability of modern commercially available color photographic products.

5039. Wilhelm, Henry, and Carol Brower. <u>The Permanence and Care of Color Photographs: Traditional and Digital Color Prints, Color Negatives, Slides and Motion Pictures</u>. Grinell, IA: Preservation Publishing Co., 1993. 744p. 543 illus. Basic text on the preservation of color photographic images; result of years of testing and research into film stability.

5040. Wiliam, Aled Rhys. "Restoration of the Book of Cynog," <u>National Library of Wales Journal</u>, 225:3 (Summer 1988), 245-256. Reconstruction of the 12th-century manuscript.

5041. Wilkinson, Frances C. "What's in a Name? American Library Association Report on Preservation Committee Changes," <u>Against the Grain</u>, 7 (April 1995) 60.

5042.   Willard, Louis Charles. "Brittle Books: What Order of
         Preservation?" <u>Microform Review</u>, 20:1 (Winter 1991), 24-26. A
         critical examination of current practice in the national effort to
         microfilm endangered texts, with a suggestion for alternative
         approaches.

5043.   Willard, Vickie. "Forensic Document Examination," <u>McKay Lodge
         Conservation Report</u>, 6 (Spring 1993), 4,11. Professional forensic
         document examiners use the same tools as conservators, and turn to
         them for technical assistance. Reviews analytical process.

5044.   Williams, Bernard. "Document Delivery and Reproduction Survey,
         October, 1990," <u>FID News Bulletin</u> (Fédération Internationale
         d'Information), 40:10 (1990), 143-147. Discusses multimedia as a
         new trend in information manipulation and dissemination and
         describes two preservation projects combining microform and optical
         disk technology. Discusses the importance of using digital
         technology to enhance, not preclude, microform.

5045.   Williams, Bernard. "The Newer Information Media &
         Conservation," <u>In Safe Keeping</u>, ed. Jennifer Thorp. Winchester,
         U.K.: Hampshire Co. Library / Hampshire Archives Trust, 1988, 31-
         35. Briefly describes media: microforms, magnetic media, online
         electronic publications, optical and compact disks, and their
         preservation problems including obsolescence of technology and
         integrity of text.

5046.   Williams, Bernard. "Optical Disks at the Public Record Office."
         <u>Information Media and Technology</u>, 20:5 (September 1987), 204-
         205. Increasing use of computers in government during the past three
         decades has confronted the Public Records Office with the problem
         of preserving essential data in electronic format.

5047.   Williams, E. A. "The Vulnerable Library," <u>Security Systems,
         Vandalism and Disaster Planning in Libraries</u>, eds. Royston Brown
         and Hilary Spiers. Stamford, Lincolnshire, England.: Capital
         Planning Information, 1988, 10-11. Reviews vulnerability of library

materials, staff, and users; and authors discuss measures for curtailment of theft, vandalism and personal harassment.

5048.   Williams, Edwin L., and Daniel Grosjean. "Exposure of Deacidified and Untreated Paper to Ambient Levels of Sulphur Dioxide and Nitrogen Dioxide: Nature and Yields of Reaction Products," Journal of the American Institute for Conservation, 31:2 (Summer 1992), 199-212. Results of a study using white wove paper and newsprint to study the nature and reaction of deacidified and untreated paper to ambient levels of sulphur dioxide and nitrogen dioxide. The study indicated that pollution from nitrogen dioxide remains a threat to both untreated and treated papers.

5049.   Williams, Edwin L., and Daniel Grosjean. Exposure of Deacidified Paper to Ambient Levels of SO2 and NO2. Marina del Rey, CA: Getty Conservation Institute, 1990. 27p. and data. (Getty Scientific Program Report). Study of the uptake process in deacidification.

5050.   Williams, Edwin L., Eric Grosjean, and Daniel Grosjean. "Exposure of Artists' Colorants to Airborne Formaldehyde," Studies in Conservation, 37:3 (August 1992), 201-210. Report of a study, concluding that formaldehyde is not a major threat to colorants.

5051.   Williams, Gene. "Taking Care of the Small Computer," Wilson Library Bulletin, 61:4 (December 1986), 14-16. Care and maintenance; stresses need for a sound prevention program.

5052.   Williams, Gene. "The VCR In the Library: Tips on Care and Maintenance," Wilson Library Bulletin, 61:2 (October 1986), 14-17. Describes how a VCR works; provides information on how to solve problems and suggestions on maintenance and cleaning.

5053.   Williams, Karen. "Preservation and Conservation in the Elementary Schools," Conservation Administration News, 52 (January 1993), 4-5, 7, 13. A policy statement implemented at the Westwood School, Stillwater, OK.

5054.   Williams, John C. "Permanence of Paper: Novel Aspects," Encyclopedia of Materials Science and Engineering. Oxford, U.K.:

Pergamon, 1988; Supplement, 377-380. Briefly outlines solutions to the problem of paper permanence.

5055. Williams, Lisa B. "Selecting Rare Books for Physical Conservation: Guidelines for Decision Making," College and Research Libraries, 46:2 (March 1985), 153-159. Discussion of knowledgeable decisions and criteria used at the University of Chicago.

5056. Williams, Norman H. "Microform Publishing: Alive and Well in the Electronic Age," Logos, 6:3 (1995), 5p.

5057. Williams, Richard S., Jr., Thomas R. Lyons, Jane G, Ferrigno and Michael C. Quinn. "Evaluation of the National Archives Program to Convert Nitrate Aerial Photographs of the United States to a Stable-Base Safety Film," Photogrammetric Engineering and Remote Sensing, 50:10 (October 1984), 1437-1441. The five principal stages of decomposition of nitrate film are reviewed.

5058. Williamson, C. J. "150 Years of Plastics Degradation," Polymers in Chemistry. Cambridge, U.K.: Royal Society of Chemistry, 1992, 1-13. (Special Publication 105). Notes that all early semi-synthetic plastics are unstable, film being the most obvious example.

5059. Willis, Deborah. "Conservation of the Parker Roll," Conservation and Preservation in the Small Library, eds. Nicholas Hadgraft and Katherine Swift. Cambridge: Parker Library Publications, 1994, 107-113. Case study of treatment of about 20 sheets comprising three documents.

5060. Willis, Don. A Hybrid Systems Approach to Preservation of Printed Material. Washington, DC: Commission on Preservation and Access, 1992. 72p. Reprinted Microform Review, Part 2:, 23:1 (Winter 1994), 18-25.

5061. Willis, Don. "The Resolution Factor in Preserving Page-Based Materials," Preservation of Electronic Formats and Electronic Formats for Preservation, ed. Janice Mohlhenrich. Fort Atkinson, WI: Highsmith Press, 1992, 109-118. Discusses the possibility of creating a hybrid technology combining scanning and high-resolution microfilm for preservation and access; discussion.

5062. Wilman, Hugh. "Copying Books Without Damage," Library Conservation News, 18 (January 1988), 4-6. Describes the development of the overhead photocopier, which can copy books with little or no damage.

5063. Wilman, Hugh. "Copying Without Damage: The British Library Strategy," Archives, 18:79 (1987), 85-88. Describes methods and equipment used at the British Library.

5064. Wilman, Hugh. "Document Delivery Without Damage," Interlending and Document Supply, 13:4 (1985), 112-115. Describes new copiers and image digitizers that can reproduce, even enhance, documents for access.

5065. Wilson, Alexander. Library Policy for Preservation and Conservation in the European Community: Principles, Practices and the Contribution of New Information Technologies. New York: K. G. Saur, 1988. 144p. Study, derived from the IFLA Conference in Vienna, 1986, provides an overview of preservation issues in the member countries of the Common Market, and presents possible cooperative approaches to addressing preservation needs.

5066. Wilson, David L. "Electronic Versions of Public-Domain Texts Draw Praise and Fire." Chronicle of Higher Education (August 12, 1992), a15-a16. Discusses Project Gutenberg and the controversy surrounding electronic text.

5067. Wilson, J. Andrew. "Fire Fighters: An Automatic Fire Suppression System Is Among Your Museum's Best and Safest Forms of Insurance," Museum News, 68:6 (November/December 1989), 68-72. Explains the need for suppressant systems. Sprinkler systems are described; the hazard of Halon is discussed.

5068. Wilson, J. Andrew. "Fire Fighter," Museum News (November-December, 1989), 68-72. Facts on the efficacy of sprinkler systems, including cases of fires in buildings with and without them.

5069.   Wilson, Paul. "Historical Perspective on the Use of Microfilm in Libraries and Archives," Preservation Microfilming: Does It Have a Future? Canberra: National Library of Australia, 1995, 46-57. Describes important developments in microfilm technology in the 1920s and 1930s, use of technology, preservation initiatives.

5070.   Wilson, Paul. "An Overview of the Columbia/Texas Programs in Preservation and Conservation Studies," Preservation of Library Materials (Australia Library and Information Association Special Interest Group for the Preservation of Library Materials.) 13 (November 1995), 15-24. Brief history of the programs; course descriptions.

5071.   Wilson, William K. "Effect of Relative Humidity on Storage and Use of Records," Abbey Newsletter, 17:7-8 (December 1993), 94-95. Demonstrates the advantages of storing paper-based records at a lower (30%) RH.

5072.   Wilson, William K. Environmental Guidelines for the Storage of Paper Records. Bethesda, MD: NISO Press, 1995. 29p. (NISO Technical Report 1; NISO-TROI- 1995). Suggests environmental parameters that influence the preservation of paper-based records in libraries and archives, including temperature, RH, light, air pollutants; values recommended. (AA abridged). Appendix provides background information. Bibliography poorly prepared.

5073.   Wilson, William K. "Remarks on House Resolution 226 to Establish a National Policy on Permanent Paper," Alkaline Paper Advocate, 3:1 (March 1990) 6-8. A statement of the problems and issues involved; a history of the development of standards for production and use of permanent/durable paper.

5074.   Wilson, William K. "Some Happenings on the Way to the Development of Permanent Record Materials," Preservation Research and Development: RoundTable Proceedings, September 28-29, 1992. Washington, DC: Library of Congress, Preservation Directorate, June 1993, 51-56. Condensed: "Some Happenings on the Way to the Development of Permanent Record Materials," North

American Permanent Papers, May 1994. Austin, TX: Abbey Publications, 1994, 27-31.

5075.   Wilson, William K., and Susan Lee-Bechtold. "Standards for Archival Materials," Historic Textile and Paper Materials: Conservation and Characterization, eds. Howard L. Needles and S. Haig Zeronian. Washington, DC: American Chemical Society, 1986, 291-315. (Advances in Chemistry, 212). Suggested program for developing standards for the preservation of library and archival materials.

5076.   Wilson, William K. and Edwin J. Parks. "Historical Survey of Research at the National Bureau of Standards on Materials for Archival Records," Restaurator, 5:3/4 (1983), 191-241. Historical survey of the NBS research on the conservation of archival materials, including acidic inks, predictive value of accelerated aging data, effect of light on paper, lamination, redox blemishes, etc. 178 references.

5077.   Wilthew, Paul. "Bugs, or Beating Unwanted Guests," SCCR Journal (Scottish Society for Conservation and Restoration), 5:1 (February 1994), 18-19. Summary of reports and discussion at a meeting of museum conservation scientists to address the problem of pest control.

5078.   Winkle, Becky. "A Guide for Small Libraries: Preservation on a Shoestring, Low and No-Budget Options to Get a Preservation Program Off the Ground," American Libraries, 16:11 (December 1985), 778-779. Examples of what libraries can accomplish with no special funds.

5079.   Winners, Karen. "Software to Save Your Skin: Using Software to Back Up and Recover Your Company's Data," Disaster Recovery Journal, 7:4 (October-December 1994), 50-52. Practical approaches to the back-up of computer data; considerations when planning a system.

5080.   Winsor, Peter. "The Conservation Information Network," Library Conservation News, 31 (April 1991), 1-3, 6. A description of a cooperative bibliographic database providing international access to conservation literature, with a note on smaller databases.

5081.   Winsor, Peter. Theses and Dissertations in Conservation from United Kingdom Training Institutions. London: British Museum, Department of Conservation, 1985. 16p.

5082.   Winsor, Peter, and Robyn Greenblatt. "On the Record with the Conservation Register," Library Conservation News, 27 (April 1990), 1,3,6. Discusses the organization and use of the register of conservators and conservation services developed by the Conservation Unit, Museums Council (U.K.). The register has over 400 entries; those listed have been recommended by five clients, although none are endorsed by the Unit.

5083.   Winston, Iris. "Hans Rutimann: Preservation Ambassador," National Library News (Canada), 27:2 (February 1995), 1, 5 (English/French). Profile of international preservation consultant for the commission on preservation and access.

5084.   Winston, Iris. "Lignin-Permanent Problem or Manufacturing Solution?" Paper Conservation News, 75 (September 1995), 5 and Conservation Administration News, 62/63 (Summer/Fall), 5. Describes a cooperative research project with Canadian Conservation Institute, National Archives of Canada, National Library of Canada, and members of the pulp and paper industry to support research to determine the impact and importance of lignin on paper permanence. "It is a catalyst for a major cooperative research effort between government and industry and a stepping stone to the finalization of a Canadian standard for paper permanence...."

5085.   Winterble, Peter G. "The Commission on Preservation and Access," Conservation Administration News, 26 (April 1987), 11. Describes the goals and activities of the Commission.

5086.   Winterble, Peter G. "In Pursuit of Preservation," Influencing Change in Research Librarianship: A Festschrift for Warren J. Haas. Washington, DC: Council on Library Resources, 1988. 53-58. Summarizes Haas's accomplishments in addressing the need to preserve collections.

5087.   Wisconsin, State Historical Society of. Division of Archives and Research Services. Electronic Information Project: Final Report. Madison, WI: State Historical Society of Wisconsin, Division of Archives and Research Services, 1994. 48p.

5088.   Wise, Christine. "The Flood and Afterwards: A New Beginning for the Fawcett Library," Library Conservation News, 48 (Autumn 1995), 1-2. Salvage and recovery; lessons learned.

5089.   Wisniewski, Ginny. "The Book - A Critical Part of the Library Infrastructure," Preservation Issues (State Library of Ohio), 4 (May 1991), 2p. Brief illustrated note on the development of book structures and problems from the late 18th-century to date.

5090.   Wittekind, Jürgen. "The Battelle Mass Deacidification Process: A New Method for Deacidifying Books and Archival Materials," Restaurator, 15:4 (1994), 189-207. Describes the process and the plant designed to treat 150,000 books at the Deutsche Bucherei, Leipzig, Germany.

5091.   Wodetzki, Jamie. "Copyright: Decaying Law for Decayed Documents," Preservation Microfilming: Does It Have a Future? Canberra: National Library of Australia, 1995, 137-48. Address the threat that digital storage and delivery of information poses to the interest of copyright owners, and the need to articulate needs and perspectives of the preservation community. Reviews Australian copyright law, problems, and limitations.

5092.   Wojtczak, Miroslawa. "Conservation and Restoration of Early Wallpapers from Krakow," Conference on Book and Paper Conservation, 1990. Budapest, Hungary: Technical Association of Paper and Printing Industry/National Szechenyi Library, 1992, 257-270. Review of history and treatment procedures. Illus.

5093.   Wold, Geoffrey H., and Joseph C. Roicheleau. "Selecting PC-Based Disaster Recovery Planning Software," Disaster Recovery Journal, 5:4 (October-December 1992), 24-28. Discusses how to evaluate and select systems and to use them effectively.

5094.   Wolfe, Irmgard H., and Julianna Davis. "Preservation Notes, Part 1,"
        Mississippi Libraries, 59 (Summer 1995) 43.

5095.   Wolff, Robin. "Preservation Information in the USMARC Format,"
        National Preservation News (October 1987), 506.

5096.   Wolfinger, Matthew. "Micrographics and the Environment,"
        Microform Review, 23 (Summer 1994) 125-129.

5097.   Wood, Daniel B. "Industrial-Strength Drying for Wet Buildings,"
        Christian Science Monitor, Tuesday, May 13, 1989, 13. Profiles
        Solex Technology's process for drying of water-damaged library and
        archival materials.

5098.   Wood, Larry. "How and When to Start a Restoration Project,"
        Conservation Administration News, 56 (January 1994), 3, 11. Note
        on the recovery of fire-and flood-damaged materials; options, by a
        vendor.

5099.   Wood, Mary Lee. Prevention and Treatment of Mold in Library
        Collections With an Emphasis on Tropical Climates: A RAMP
        Study. Paris: UNESCO, 1988. 81p. (PGI-88/WS/9). Reviews the
        structure and nature of molds, with implications for library materials.
        Covers prevention and methods of dealing with infestation.

5100.   Wood, Mary Lee. Selected Bibliography From Prevention and
        Treatment of Mold in Library Collections With an Emphasis on
        Tropical Climates: A RAMP Study. Paris: UNESCO, 1988, and
        Information Reports Bibliographies, 18:5 (1989), 19-21.

5101.   Wood, Steven L. "The Microfilm Service Bureau and Library
        Preservation," Microform Review, 17:1 (February 1988), 32-
        37. How to establish a preservation microfilming program, select a
        vendor; discusses copying methods and equipment.

5102.   Woodhouse, Mark. "Preserving Mark Twain," Archival Products
        News, 2:3 (Fall 1994), 3. Describes the repair and preservation of the

Mark Twain materials housed in a special room at Elmira (NY)
College, leading to an increase of gifts to the collection.

5103.   Woodman, Neville. Report on the Runability of Alkaline
Paperstocks Within the National Printing Bureau. Hull, Quebec:
Canadian Government Printing Services, 1990. 31p.
(English/French) Report on the runability of alkaline paperstocks
within the National Printing Bureau, prepared for the Working Group
on the Possible Use of Alkaline Paper for the Printing of Government
Publications.

5104.   Woods, Chris. "Designing a Conservation Room: An Example from
Dorset," Journal of the Society of Archivists, 13:2 (Autumn 1992),
132-135. Description of workspace designed to meet the needs of a
workshop, studio, and laboratory to treat documents.

5105.   Woods, Chris. "Conservation Forum - The Treatment of Cellulose
Diacetate Negatives," Journal of the Society of Archivists, 13 (1992),
46-47. Technical note on the treatment of cellulose diacetate
negatives to curtail distortion from deterioration due to shrinkage and
disintegration of support.

5106.   Woods, Elaine W. "Newspapers - Toward Preserving a National
Resource," Newspapers in the Library, ed. Lois N. Upham. New
York: Haworth Press, 1988, 1-11. History of the difficulties libraries
have faced in preserving and providing access to newspaper
collections; description of the U.S. Newspaper Project.

5107.   Woods, Jennifer. "Conservation at the Library Company of
Philadelphia," Conservation Administration News, 20 (January
1985), 13, 26. Describes its new conservation workshop.

5108.   Woodward, David. "The Analysis of Paper and Ink in Early Maps,"
Library Trends, 36:1 (Summer 1987), 85-107. Discussion of
techniques to analyze the physical and chemical structure of
historical artifacts, and their value for the analysis of early maps.

5109.   Woodward, Hazel, and J. Eric Davies. "Battered Books and
Shredded Serials," Serials, 1:1 (March 1988), 5-9.

5110.   Woolgar, Chris, Elizabeth Gray, and Anne-Marie Steel. "The Peninsular War Refought," Library Conservation News, 37 (October 1992), 5-7. Describes initiatives by the University of Southampton, England, to conserve the Duke of Wellington's papers.

5111.   "The World's Great Libraries: Arks from the Deluge," Economist, 313:7634/7635 (December 23, 1989), 41-47. The great libraries of the world, such as the British Library and the Library of Congress, are discussed. Many of them are facing a crisis in the preservation of old books.

5112.   Worman, Eugene C. Jr. "Print Collecting and the Problem of Breaking," AB Bookman's Weekly (Antiquarian Bookman), 81:16 (April 18, 1988), 1609-1619. Addresses problem of acid paper and of breaking books for the sale of individual prints.

5113.   Wortman, William A. Collection Management: Background and Principles. Chicago, IL: American Library Association, 1989. 243p. Basic text; chapter 8: "Preservation, Weeding and Removal," p. 179-210, discusses scope of preservation problem and elements of an effective preservation program.

5114.   Wouters, Jan, An Peckstadt, and Lieve Watteeuw. "Leafcasting with Dermal Tissue Preparations: A New Method for Repairing Fragile Parchment and Its Application to the Codex Eyckckensis," Paper Conservator, 19 (1995), 5-22. Describes a new method for repair of badly degraded parchment (C8) by leafcasting with material consisting of hide powder, partially pretanned with formaldehyde, and calcium carbonate added as a filler.

5115.   Wouters, Jan, Gely Gancedo, An Peckstadt, and Lieve Watteeuw. "Parchment Leafcasting with Dermal Tissue Preparations," Preprints: ICOM Committee on Conservation 10th Triennial Meeting, ed. Janet Bridgland. Washington, DC: International Council of Museums, 1993, 524-528. Describes the treatment to preserve an 8th-century illuminated manuscript on parchment.

5116.   Wray, Nick. "When Dinosaurs Ruled the Earth," Audiovisual Librarian, 21 (February 1995), 37-9. Preserving the new technology for future generations.

5117.   Wright, Dorothy W. "Selecting a Preservation Photocopy Machine," College and Research Libraries News, 55:1 (January 1994), 14-19. Practical information on how to evaluate and test equipment; notes need for frequent maintenance.

5118.   Wright, Dorothy, Samuel Demas, and Walter Sybulski. "Cooperative Preservation of State-Level Publications: Preserving the Literature of New York State Agriculture and Rural Life," Library Resources and Technical Services, 37:4 (October 1993), 434-443. Describes a cooperative pilot project to preserve a state's heritage by identifying a core bibliography and undertaking preservation measures on a priority basis.

5119.   Wright, Dorothy, and Peter McDonald. "The Core Literature Approach to Setting Preservation Priorities," Conservation Administration News, 47 (October 1991), 8-9, 29. Describes an analytical approach to determining the critical literature in a discipline so it can be given priority for preservation.

5120.   Wright, Gordon H. "Disaster Management for Libraries: A Management Perspective on Disaster Planning," Emergency Preparedness Digest/Revue de la Protection Civale, 15 (January-March 1989), 14-18. English/French. A review of the factors that come into play when managing disaster recovery; emphasis on communications. An excerpt from Disaster Management for Libraries, by Claire England and Karen Evans (Ottawa: Canadian Library Association, 1988).

5121.   Wright, Logan S. "Phillips Graduate Seminary Library: A Preliminary Assessment," Conservation Administration News, 52 (January 1993), 8-9, 26-27. Conservation survey of a library collection analyzing data with a computer.

5122.   Wright, Sandra. "Conservation Program Planning at the National Archives of Canada," American Archivist, 53:2 (Spring 1990), 314-

322. Describes the development and implementation of the NAC conservation policy; integrating preservation with all archival functions.

5123. Wright, Sandra. "Disaster Planning: A Management Success Story," Conservation in Archives. Paris: International Council on Archives, 1989, 281-290. (Proceedings of an International Symposium, May 1988). Offers practical guidelines toward developing and implementing a disaster plan.

5124. Wright, Sandra, and Peter Yurkiw. "The Collections Survey in the Federal Archives and Management Divisions of the Public Archives of Canada: A Progress Report on Conservation Planning," Archivaria, 22 (Summer 1986), 58-74. Describes methodology, findings, implications, conclusion, and has many charts.

5125. Wurzberger, Marilyn. "Current Security Practices in College and University Special Collections," Rare Book and Manuscript Librarianship, 3:1 (Spring 1988), 43-57. The results of a survey sent to 121 academic libraries in January 1987. While it indicated that security measures could be improved, the incidence of theft was low.

5126. Wust, Ruth. The Optical Disk Project at the Library of Congress: A Case Study in the Use of New Technology in a Library Environment. Berlin: Freie Universität Berlin, Fachbereich Kommunikationswissenschaften, 1990. 313 leaves.

5127. Wyly, Mary. "Bonnie Jo Cullison: The Newberry's Preservation Conscience," American Libraries, 16:11 (December 1985), 766, 784. Profile of a conservator with a strong background for preservation administration.

5128. Wyly, Mary P. "Special Collections Security: Problems, Trends, and Consciousness," Library Trends, 36:1 (Summer 1987), 241-256. Discusses theft; the role that the ALA Rare Books and Manuscripts Section is playing to increase awareness and to seek stiffer penalties for thieves.

5129.   Wynen, Nancy. "The Big One: Staff Survival After a Disaster," Library Administration and Management, 7:2 (Spring 1993), 103-105. Reviews symptoms of stress and suggests assistance that can help staff return to normal.

5130.   Wyoming University, Laramie University Libraries. Report of the Task Force on Preservation Practices. Hanscom, Martha et al. Laramie, Wyoming: Wyoming University, Laramie University Libraries, 1985, 35p. (ERIC 259 757)

5131.   Yaekel, Elizabeth. "Institutionalizing and Archives: Developing Historical Records Programs in Organizations," American Archivist, 52:2 (Spring 1989), 202-207.

5132.   "Yale Part of Battle to Preserve Nation's Books," Library and Archival Security, 8:3/4 (Fall/Winter 1988), 53-57. Description of Yale's preservation microfilming program.

5133.   Yamamoto, Nobuo. "Microfilming Meiji Imprints at the Waseda University Library, Japan," Microform Review, 23 (Spring 1994), 61-63.

5134.   Yasue, Akio. "pH Surveys of Current Publications in Japan," Conservation Administration News, 50 (July 1992), 1-2, 29. Describes an annual pH survey of current monographs that began in 1986. Demonstrates that there is an increase in materials published on alkaline paper.

5135.   Yax, Maggie. "Artist's Books: Good News About the future of the Book," New Library Scene, 10:4 (August 1991), 1, 5-8. Describes artists books, their history and role in cultural history and in library collections.

5136.   Yee, Martha M. "Manifestations and Near-Equivalents of Moving Image Works: A Research Project," Library Resources and Technical Services, 38:4 (October 1994), 355-372. A study of the occurrence of differing versions of films and the lack of visible indicators of these differences; implications for preservation and for scholarly access to the motion picture heritage.

5137. Yerburgh, Mark R. "Studying All Those 'Tiny Little Tea Leaves': The Future of Microforms in a Complex Technological Environment," Microform Review, 16:1 (Winter 1987), 14-20. Considers the future of microforms by surveying the history of their use in libraries and comparing them to other, newer media. Concludes that microforms will continue to be the primary providers of significant but rarely used retrospective materials.

5138. Yetter, George H. "Evolution of a Successful Application by the Colonial Williamsburg Foundation Library for an Institute of Museum Services Grant," Conservation Administration News, 58-59 (July/October 1994), 20-22.

5139. Yorke, Stephen, ed. Playing for Keeps; The Proceedings of an Electronic Records Management Conference hosted by the Australian Archives, Canberra, Australia, 8-10 November, 1994. Dickson, ACT: Australian Archives, 1995. 356p. Papers that address issues of management, preservation and access, presenting an excellent overview of the challenges that records managers and archivists face in preserving and providing access to an impermanent medium.

5140. Young, Christine. "Nitrate Films in the Public Institution," History News, 44:4 (July/August 1989), 8 p. insert. (American Association for State and Local History, Technical Leaflet, 189). The problem of nitrate film, its deterioration, detection, and options for dealing with it.

5141. Young, Laura S. Bookbinding and Conservation by Hand: A Working Guide. NY: RR Bowker, 1981. Rev. by Jerilyn Glenn Davis. New Castle, DE: Oak Knoll Press, 1995. 273p. A detailed and not always clear book of instructions for the advanced binder. The book contains much helpful information on preservation.

5142. Young, Patrick. "Ask the Photographer: Archival Processing of Fiber Base Paper," International Bulletin for Photographic Documentation of the Visual Arts, 13:2 (Summer 1986), 13-14. Instructions about archival processing.

5143.   Young, Philip H. "Perfect Preservation: A Lesson From the Past?"
        College and Research Libraries News (March 1988), 147. and
        Indiana Library, 9:1 (1990), 50-51.

5144.   Young, Raymond, and Roger M. Rowell. Cellulose: Structure,
        Modification and Hydrolysis. Somerset, NJ: John Wiley, 1986,
        379p. Covers structure and nature of cellulose and new methods for
        fiber production.

5145.   Young, Richard F. "Advise and Consent; Conservation in the United
        States Senate," Conservation Administration News, 28 (January
        1987), 4, 16, 21. Outlines the activities of the Senate Library
        Conservation Office.

5146.   Young, Richard F. "The Advisory Committee on the Records of the
        Congress," Conservation Administration News, 47 (October 1991),
        11. Describes the mission of the Committee and its immediate goal
        of a report.

5147.   Young, Richard F. Library and Archival Disaster-Preparedness and
        Recovery: A Manual Workbook. Oakton, VA: BiblioTech, 1995.
        16 leaves. A workbook to accompany a video.

5148.   Young, Richard F. United States Senate Library Disaster
        Preparedness and Recovery Plan. Washington, DC: U.S. Senate
        Library, 1987. 38 leaves. The Senate's disaster manual.

5149.   Zappala, Antonio. "Instruction in 'Book Restoration' in the
        Graduate Course in Conservation of Cultural Property at the
        University of Udine, Udine, Italy," Restaurator, 9:1 (1988), 27-
        36. Describes the goals of the course, with outline of subjects
        covered.

5150.   Zappala, Antonio. "An International Survey of Standardizing Art
        Papers and Others Intended for Conservation," Restaurator, 12:1
        (1991), 18-35. Summary of a questionnaire on durable papers sent to
        selected experts.

5151. Zappala, Antonio. "Problems in Standardizing the Quality of Paper for Permanent Records," Restaurator, 12:3 (1991), 137-146. Reviews worldwide efforts during the 1980s to develop a standard for permanent papers.

5152. Zarubin, Michael Ya, and Sergey M. Shevchenko. "Soviet Wood Chemistry Today," TAPPI Journal (Technical Association for the Pulp and Paper Industry), 72:5 (May 1989), 211-215; 72:6 (June 1989), 183-185. Report on the research and standards of Soviet wood science.

5153. Zeidberg, David S. Collection Security in ARL Libraries. Washington, DC: Association of Research Libraries, 1984. 94p. (SPEC Kit 100). The introduction notes the importance of detailed security policies and procedures and observes that too little attention is paid to prevention of theft.

5154. Zeidberg, David S. "'We Have Met the Enemy ...' Collection Security in Libraries," Rare Book and Manuscript Librarianship, 2:1 (Spring 1987), 19-26. Statement concerning the problem of theft in libraries and the inadequacies in dealing with it.

5155. Zeier, Franz. Books, Boxes and Portfolios: Binding, Construction and Design Step-by-Step. New York: Design Press, 1990. 304p. Instructional text on bookbinding with clear, illustrated instructions.

5156. Zeitschik, Marc. "Archival Survival: The Making of a Preservation Microfilmer," Microform Review, 21:3 (Summer 1992), 107-110. Author describes his experiences creating and developing a company devoted to preservation microfilming; provides advice on how to contract for preservation microfilming.

5157. Zeronian, S. H., and H. L. Needles, eds. Historic Textile and Paper Materials II: Conservation and Characterization. Washington, DC: American Chemical Society, 1989, 260p. (ACS Symposium Series, 410). 1st volume, 1986, 462p. Papers from a symposium to address problems relating to the conservation of paper since 1850.

5158.   Zimmerman, Carole. Bibliography on Mass Deacidification.
         Washington, DC: Library of Congress Preservation Office, 1991.
         32p. 259 citations arranged in chronological blocks; no annotations.

5159.   Zimmerman, Carole. Material Published by Members of the Library
         of Congress Preservation Directorate: A Bibliography. Washington,
         DC: Library of Congress Preservation Directorate, 1994. 37p.

5160.   Zimmerman, Robert. "Shelf Life and Video Tape: Now They Tell
         Us: Memories Recorded on VHS Tape May Not Last More Than a
         Decade," Fortune (October 18, 1993), 99. Article from the
         September/October issues of Sciences.

5161.   Zinn, Edward, James M. Reilly, Peter Z. Adelstein, and Douglas W.
         Nishimura. "Air Pollution Effects on Library Microforms,"
         Preventive Conservation: Practice, Theory and Research, eds. Ashok
         Roy and Perry Smith. London: International Institute for
         Conservation, 1994, 195-201. (Preprints of the contributions to the
         Ottawa Congress, 12-16 September, 1994). See abstract below.

5162.   Zinn, E., J. M. Reilly, P. Z. Adelstein, and D. W. Nishimura.
         "Preservation of Color Photographs: The Danger of Atmospheric
         Oxidants in the Storage Environment," Environnement et
         Conservation de l'Écrit, de l'Image et du Son. Paris: ARSAG, 1994,
         25-30. (Actes des Deuxièmes Journées Internationales d'Études de
         l'ARSAG, 16 au 20 Mai, 1994). Describes research by the Image
         Permanence Institute between 1989 and 1993 to identify and measure
         the threat to microfilm of common air pollutants.

5163.   Zipkowitz, Fay. "Saving Paper Treasures: The Northeast Document
         Conservation Center," Library and Archival Security, 7:2 (Summer
         1985), 15-20. Description of the Northeast Document Conservation
         Center and its services.

5164.   Zipp, Louise S., ed. Preserving Geoscience Imagery. Alexandria,
         VA: Geoscience Information Society, 1993. 126p. (Proceedings,
         23). Papers presented at the October 1992 conference to address new
         technologies that preserve and need to be preserved; approaches and
         strategies for preservation.

5165. Zizhi, Feng. Technological Options for Developing Countries. Paris: International Congress on Archives, 1988. 4p.; reprinted in Archivum, 35 (1989), 159-161. Brief review of problems facing developing countries in the preservation of new archival materials; notes need for technical assistance. Paper originally presented at the International Council on Archives Congress, Paris, France 1988.

5166. Zou, X and N. Gurnagul. "The Role of Lignin in the Mechanical Permanence of Paper," Environnement et Conservation de l'Écrit, de l'Image et du Son. Paris: ARSAG, 1994, 161-165. (Actes des Deuxièmes Journées Internationales d'Études de l'ARSAG). Study of the effects of sulfuric acid groups on the mechanical permanence of paper by accelerated aging of thermomechanical pulp.

5167. Zucker, Barbara. "Photographs: Their Care and Conservation," Illinois Libraries, 67:8 (October 1985), 699-705; reprinted by the Illinois Cooperative Conservation Program, Carbondale, 1984. 6p. Brief history and advice about caring for collections.

5168. Zucker, Barbara. Preservation of Scrapbooks and Albums. Washington, DC: National Cooperative Preservation Project, 1991. (Preservation Basics, Leaflet 1); reprint of "Scrapbooks and Albums," Illinois Libraries, 67:8 (October 1985), 695-699. Note on storage, handling, and options for conservation treatment. Bibliography.

5169. Zycherman, Lynda A. "Pesticide Use Checklist," A Guide to Museum Pest Control. Washington, DC: Association of Systematics Collections, 1988, 127-128. Summarizes steps to take when contemplating the application of a pesticide.

5170. Zycherman, Lynda A., and John R. Schrock, eds. A Guide to Museum Pest Control. Washington, DC: Association of Systematics Collections, 1988. 205p. Covers policy, law and liability, pests and pest identification, treatments. Bibliography by Karen Preslock.

Bibliography of Preservation Media on the Conservation of Library and Archival Material 1982-1997

Robert E. Schnare, Jr.

5171. Acid Free Paper (1990)
Format: Sound Recording
Time: 1 cassette (7 minutes)
Producer/Distributor: National Public Radio, Custom Tape Service, Audience Services, 2025 M Street, NW, Washington, DC 20036
Summary: Recorded on National Public Radio on March 1, 1990. Discussion with several experts on the present deterioration of book paper and the future of acid-free or permanent paper.

American Association of Law Libraries
Format: Sound Recordings
Producer/Distributor: Mobiltape, Valencia, CA.

5172. (1). Administering the Law Library Preservation Program
Time: 4 cassettes
Summary: Recorded at the AALL 84th Annual Meeting, July 21-24, 1991, New Orleans, LA.

5173. (2). Administrating the Library Preservation Program
Time: 1 cassette (60 minutes)
Summary: Recorded at the AALL 77th Annual Meeting, July 1-4, 1984, San Diego, CA.

5174. (3). Disaster Planning for the Law Library
Time: 1 cassette
Summary: Recorded at the AALL 85th Annual Meeting, July 18-23, 1992, San Francisco, CA.

5175. (4). Writing a Preservation Policy
Time: 1 cassette
Summary: Recorded at the AALL 87th Annual Meeting, July 9-13, 1994, Seattle, WA. Sponsored by the Preservation Committee, Academic Law Libraries Special Interest Section and Technical Services Special Interest Section Preservation Committee. Speaker Patricia K. Denham.

5176. The Anatomy of a Book: Format in the Hand-Press Period (1991)
Format: VHS
Time: Approximately 30 minutes
Producer/Distributor: Book Arts Press, 114 Alderman Library, University of Virginia, Charlottesville, VA 22903

Summary: Produced by Terry Belanger and Peter Herdrich. Discusses the book format identification in regard to books printed on the hand-press on hand-made paper. Describes physical construction of pre-1800 printed books. Prepared for individual study and review with accompanying workbook.

5177. Basic Book Repair with Jane Greenfield (1988)
Format: VHS plus guide
Time: 30 minutes
Producer/Distributor: Visual Education for the H.W. Wilson Company, Bronx, NY 10452
Summary: Jane Greenfield demonstrates the repair of a torn page, a cut page, a broken hinge, a shaken hinge, and a flapping spine. Archivally sound techniques and materials are used.

5178. Basic Conservation Procedures (1989)
    also known as Basic Preservation for Libraries and Archives.
Format: VHS
Time: 35 minutes
Producer/Distributor: Nebraska State Historical Society, Lincoln, Nebraska 68501.
Summary: Judith Fortson-Jones first produced these programs as slide presentations. They describe methods to store and handle paper documents and the methods are aimed at the viewer with little experience in conservation techniques.

5179. Basic Deterioration and Preventive Measures for Museum Collections (1985)
Format: VHS
Time: 60 minutes
Producer/Distributor: American Association for State and Local History, Nashville, TN. 37201
Summary: By Shelley Reisman Paine. Why objects in collections deteriorate and how to protect collections. Practical advice for non-specialists.

5180. Be Prepared: Security and Your Library (1994)
Format: VHS
Time: 35 Minutes
Producer: American Library Association Video/Library Video Network, 320 York Road, Towson, MD. 21204-5179
Summary: Overview of security issues directed to all library employees. Useful hints about how to handle potential problem situations and outlines the steps involved in establishing a successful security program.

5181. Book Repair for Circulating Collections (1987)
Format: VHS, Beta, U-Matic
Time: 18 minutes

Producer/Distributor: Istor Productions, 7549 N. Fenwick, Portland, OR 97217.
Summary: Demonstrates easily performed repair techniques for circulating collections, including hinge tightening, and shows some alternatives to rebinding.

5182. Bookbinding with Simple Equipment (1985)
Format: 50 Slides with cassette
Time: 30 minutes
Producer/Distributor: Crystal Productions, Box 12317, Aspen, CO 81612.
Summary: Step-by-step demonstrations show how to make basic soft cover and hard cover books; script included.

5183. Books Are Not for Bashing (1990)
Format: VHS
Time: 10 minutes
Producer/Distributor: Brown University Preservation Office, Providence, RI 02914
Summary: Shows the ways in which library patrons mishandle library materials.

5184. Breathing Easy: What You Should Know About Indoor Air Quality. (1993)
Format: VHS
Time: 13 minutes
Producer/Distributor: Safety and Environmental Management Division, Public Building Services, General Services Administration, Washington, DC.
Summary: Indoor air quality as it relates to federal agencies.

5185. Building Air Quality for Building Owners and Facility Managers, Training Kit — An Introduction to Building Air Quality. (1993)
Format: 121 Color Slides, 108 page instructor book, and 19 page handout.
Producer/Distributor: Office of Air and Radiation, Indoor Air Division, U.S. Environmental Protection Agency, Washington, DC.
Summary: Designed to address the needs of building owners and facility managers and others who work to resolve indoor air pollution problems.

5186. Building a Medieval Papermill (1991)
Time: 30 minutes
Producer/Distributor: Istor Productions, 7549 N. Fenwick, Portland, OR 97217
Summary: Describes the steps in building a medieval papermill in south Idaho in 1991. Also a Public Broadcasting System documentary about paper making in Japan.

Canadian Conservation Institute, Centre de Conservation du Québec and the Audio-Visual Services of the Université du Québec à Montréal, Tape Series. (1995)

Format: VHS, other formats available
Producer/Distributor: Université du Québec à Montréal, Audiovisual
Department, Product Services, Box 8888, Station Centre-ville Montréal
(Québec) H3C 3PB Canada.

5187. Tape 1: Introduction to Preventive Conservation
Time: 10 minutes
Summary: Introduces the series and the concept of preventive conservation in
museums that incorporates all actions and procedures that aim to prolong the
life of an object or specimen by slowing its natural or accidental deterioration
as much as possible. Addresses the responsibilities of the various museum
workers.

5188. Tape 2: Light and Lighting
Time: 15 minutes
Summary: Discusses light and lighting in museums, the damage it can cause to
museum to materials, and what can be done to prevent the damage.

5189. Tape 3: Relative Humidity and Temperature
Time: 17 minutes
Summary: Discusses the effects of humidity and temperature on museums and
their collections and suggests limiting fluctuations of RH and temperature,
avoiding extremes (RH below 35% in winter and above 65% in summer), and
making sure that your museum has at least one hygrothermograph.

5190. Tape 4: Pollutants
Time: 17 minutes
Summary: Discusses different pollutants, both internal and external, that can be
harmful to museum materials. Makes recommendations on how to deal with
them and protect the collections.

5191. Tape 5: Integrated Pest Management
Time: 24 minutes
Summary: Describes the insects that attack museum objects, the damage they
can do, and what museums can do to control them.

5192. Tape 6: Packing and Transportation of Museums Objects
Time: 22 minutes
Summary: Discusses the different protection requirements for the varying
museum artifacts when transporting. Talks about proper packing crates,
security, modes of transportation, condition of artifacts, and loan policies.

5193. Tape 7: Storage
Time: 12 minutes
Summary: Discusses the location and arrangement of museum storage, placing
and protecting objects, environmental conditions, and safety.

5194. Tape 8: Protecting Objects on Exhibitions
Time: 23 minutes
Summary: Discusses the factors to consider when exhibiting museum pieces, such as dust and pollutants, handling by staff, mounts and supports, theft and vandalism, shock and vibration, lighting, temperature and relative humidity, and construction of a display case.

5195. Tape 9: Preventive Conservation in Museums: Disaster Contingency Planning
Time: 21 minutes
Summary: Focuses on disaster planning, prevention, and recovery for museum collections. The video provides the framework from which to begin disaster planning and concisely covers the methods of drying water damaged artifacts.

5196. Tape 10: Closing a Seasonal Museum
Time 15 minutes
Summary: Describes the various tasks involved in closing a museum for some part of the year: cleaning the building, storing the collections, environmental controls, interior and exterior maintenance, pest control, and security.

5197. Tape 11: The Condition Report
Time: 12 minutes
Summary: Describes the condition report, an important tool in preventive conservation that describes the physical state of each item from the moment it enters the museum collection and tracks its condition through the years.

5198. Tape 12: Handling Museum Objects
Time: 9 minutes
Summary: Presents ways in which human error can cause damage to museum objects and makes recommendations for proper handling.

5199. Tape 13: The Care of Paintings
Time: 26 minutes
Summary: Discusses various issues to consider in caring for paintings: structure of a painting, physical characteristics of the materials, examination of paintings, framing, the backing board, hanging methods, lighting levels, controlling relative humidity, handling paintings, dusting, storing, stretcher keys, accession numbers, loan policies, packing crates and restoring paintings.

5200. Tape 14: Care of Works on Paper
Time: 25 minutes
Summary: Discusses factors of paper deterioration and ways they can be controlled: proper environment and light levels, good housekeeping and storage procedures, and proper care and handling. Mounting and framing paper artifacts according to conservation standards is an excellent protective measure.

5201. Tape 15: <u>The Care of Sculptures</u>
Time: 23 minutes
Summary: Deals primarily with the care of wooden and plaster sculptures.
Discusses preventive measures that can reduce deterioration caused by
improper environment, handling, and maintenance.

5202. Tape 16: <u>The Care of Metal Objects</u>
Time: 20 minutes
Summary: Discusses preventive conservation of metal objects that is aimed at
slowing the unavoidable corrosion process and at preventing other damage to
which metals are exposed by their very nature.

5203. Tape 17: <u>The Care of Furniture</u>
Time: 22 minutes
Summary: To preserve the integrity of furniture in museum collections, good
preventive conservation practices are described, such as control of humidity
and temperature variations, regular inspections, and proper methods of
handling and transport.

5204. Tape 18: <u>The Care of Textiles</u>
Time: 20 minutes
Summary: Describes the various agents of deterioration for textiles, i.e., light,
humidity, water, mold, and insects, and suggests appropriate storage practices
and controlled environmental conditions in museums that help prevent
deterioration.

5205. Tape 19: <u>The Care of Museum Objects</u>
Time: 29 minutes
Summary: Describes the factors to consider in the care of museum objects,
such as what materials the objects are made of, the way the objects are made,
the way an object's various components interact, and an object's dimensions,
history, and condition. Suggests proper environment, lighting, pest control,
handling, and supports and handling.

5206. <u>Caring for Your Microform Collection</u> (1991)
Format: VHS
Time: 12 minutes
Producer/Distributor: University Microfilms Preservation Division, Ann
Arbor, MI 48106
Summary: Basic information on the care and handling of preservation
microforms; the effects of the environment; proper cleaning, storage, and the
use of archival containers.

5207. <u>Casting a Font of Metal Type</u> (1986)
Format: VHS
Time: 66 minutes

Producer/Distributor: Distributed by Hill & Dale Press and Typefoundry, PO
Box 263, Terra Alta, WV 26764.
Summary: A detailed explanation of the use of Monotype and Thompson type
casters. Shot in Richard Hopkins' shop in Terra Alta. A fine piece of work,
though too detailed for most persons.

5208. The Changemasters (1986)
Format: 2 VHS tapes
Time: 30 minutes each
Producer/Distributor: Encyclopaedia Britannica Educational Corporation, 310
South Michigan Ave., Chicago, IL 60604.
Summary: The information in these tapes and her book and talk is quite
relevant for preservation administrators. The tapes are subtitled Understanding
Theory and Putting Theory into Action, respectively.

5209. Commercial Library Binding: The Librarian's View (1982)
Format: 76 slides w/cassette, script included
Time: 19 minutes
Producer/Distributor: Yale University Libraries, New Haven, CT 06520.
Summary: Practical and useful discussion of a good conservationally sound,
commercial binding program in a library. Illustrates available binding styles,
how to evaluate binder's performance, and a useful binding contract.

5210. Conservation Bookbinding (1982)
Format: VHS, 3/4 U-Matic + script
Time: 57 minutes
Producer/Distributor: Office of Museum Programs, Smithsonian Institution,
Washington, DC 20560
Summary: A demonstration of the millimeter technique.

5211. Conservation Framing (1989)
Format: VHS
Time: 60 minutes
Producer/Distributor: Columbia Publishing, Akron, Ohio
Summary: Vivian C. Kistler explains the methods, materials, and techniques
available to the professional picture framer. Describes framing procedures and
materials that prevent deterioration and help preserve the piece.

5212. "Culture Shock: Fire Protection for Historic and Cultural Property"
(1996)
Format: VHS
Time: 23 minutes
Producer/Distributor: Cinebar Productions, Inc., 693 J. Clyde Morris Blvd.,
Newport News, VA 23606 with Boston University
Summary: Fire detection and suppression is a technically challenging subject to
present clearly and concisely, but this video manages it well. The central
theme is to encourage custodians to implement the use of fire safety equipment.

5213. Dave's Pond
Time: 25 minutes
Producer/Distributor: Istor Publications, 7549 N. Fenwick, Portland, OR 97217
Summary: Mounting an oversize watercolor.

5214. Disaster Preparedness Planning for Museums (1989)
Format: VHS
Time: 30 minutes
Producer/Distributor: Smith College Museum of Art, Northampton, MA 01060
Summary: This is a fast-paced presentation of how to prepare your institution
and train staff to rescue collections in the event of a disaster.

5215. Easy Techniques for Lasting Book Repair (1991)
Format: VHS
Time: 29 minutes
Producer/Distributor: Demco Video Productions, Madison, WI 53707.
Summary: Joy Andrew, a book repair expert from the University of Wisconsin,
Madison, demonstrates practical ways to quickly and economically repair
damaged hardcover books.

5216. Ebru: Paper Making in the Turkish Tradition (1984)
Format: VHS, U-Matic
Time: 25 minutes
Producer/Distributor: Istor Productions, 7549 N. Fenwick, Portland, OR 97217.
Summary: Don Guyot, master of Turkish paper marbling, demonstrates how to
prepare materials used in this rare art, and how to execute eleven different
patterns.

5217. The Electric Library (1990)
Format: VHS
Time: 13 minutes
Producer/Distributor: OCLC, Dublin, OH 43017
Summary: Ben Franklin show viewers how computers are helping modern
libraries improve their services to patrons, through a whirlwind tour of modern
library from the mailroom to cataloguing, circulation, preservation, electronic
publishing.

5218. Electronic Records Management in the New Millennium: Managing
Documents for Business (1995)
Format: VHS (two tapes with instructional materials)
Time: 75 minutes
Producer/Distributor: London, SLAIS, University College.
Summary: World authorities speak on the subject, the issues involved and
there implications for managers and professionals. Written by Richard Barry
and Anne Thurston.

5219. Elements of Book Conservation (1987)

Format: VHS
Time: 79 minutes
Producer/Distributor: Istor Publications, 7549 N. Fenwick, Portland, OR 97209.
Summary: Combines on one tape three shorter tapes, Manuscript Books, 16th- and 17th-Century Books and 19th- and 20th-Century Books.

5220. Elements of Book Conservation: 16th and 17th Century Books (1982)
Format: VHS, U-Matic
Time: 40 minutes
Producer/Distributor: Jack C. Thompson, Istor Productions, 7549 N. Fenwick, Portland, OR 97217
Summary: The restoration of two early printed books is documented. Basic techniques, such as overcasting cords, rebacking, skiving and paring leather, and tool sharpening are shown.

5221. Elements of Book Conservation: 19th and 20th Century Books (1987)
Format: VHS, U-Matic
Time: 16 minutes
Producer/Distributor: Jack C. Thompson, Istor Productions, 7549 N. Fenwick, Portland, OR 97217
Summary: Reviews how changes in technology have conferred benefits and problems on modern library collections; shows how simple protective enclosures may be made.

5222. Elements of Book Conservation: Manuscript Books (1984)
Format: VHS, U-Matic
Time: 23 minutes
Producer/Distributor: Jack C. Thompson, Istor Productions, 7549 N. Fenwick, Portland, OR 97217
Summary: A Book of Hours is rebound in a style consistent with its original 15th-century binding, after repairing the damage caused by an unsympathetic 19th-century rebinding.

5223. Farewell ETAOIN SHRDLU (1982)
Format: 16mm film, color
Time:
Producer/Distributor: William Sloan, the Museum of Modern Art, 11 West 53rd Street, NY, NY 10019
Summary: Depiction of the last night on which the New York Times was set on Linotype machines, and the introduction of computer-based typesetting at the Times. Narrated by Carl Schlesinger.

5224. Fighting Slow Fires (1988)
Format: VHS
Time: 60 minutes
Producer/Distributor: New York State Library, Albany, NY 12230.

Summary: A teleconference with Connie Brooks, of the New York State Library Conservation and Preservation Program, and David Stam, Syracuse University Librarian, to inform the public about the importance of preserving our intellectual and cultural heritage as recorded in library and archival materials.

5225. Fire Extinguishers: Fight or Flight? (1988)
Format: VHS
Time: 17 minutes
Producer/Distributor: National Fire Protection Association, Quincy, MA 02269
Summary: An educational program designed to teach the general public how to operate portable fire extinguishers safely and effectively, to know the different types of extinguishers, and to evaluate whether to use one. The tape shows the experience of untrained people who try to out small training fires.

5226. Fire Power (1986)
Format: VHS
Time: 18 minutes
Producer/Distributor: National Fire Protection Association, Quincy, MA 02269
Summary: Documents the progression of a fire started in a two-story, frame construction home. Stresses the necessity for quick evacuation in the event of a fire. Shows how a residential sprinkler system can prevent the spread of a fire and minimize damage.

5227. The Fragile Record: Preserving Our Documentary Heritage (1982)
Format: 140 Slides, audiocassette and script
Time: unknown
Producer/Distributor: Archives Division, State Historical Society of Wisconsin, Madison, WI 53706
Summary: Overview of the preservation challenge in libraries and archives and some basic conservation techniques.

5228. From Punch to Printing Type: The Art and Craft of Hand Punchcutting and Typecasting (1985)
Format: VHS
Time: 46 minutes
Producer/Distributor: Book Arts Press Video Productions, Terry Stevik, media coordinator of the School of Library Service, Columbia University. Executive editor: Terry Belanger. Directed by Peter Herdrich. Distributed by Book Arts Press, 114 Alderman Library, University of Virginia, Charlottesville, VA 22903
Summary: A detailed description of cutting a counterpunch and then a punch by hand, preparing it for use, making a strike and justifying it, and casting type using a hand mold. Featuring Stan Nelson, of the Division of Graphic Arts, The National Museum of American History, Smithsonian Institution.

5229. Gerard Cherriere: The Art of Bookbinding (1988)

Format: 16mm film, VHS (17 minutes)
Time: 16 minutes
Producer/Distributor: New York, Produced and directed by Nina Ryan, executive producer, Jane W. Pearce. OCLC bibliographic record (36238930) notes that videotape copy was made in 1996 with the permission of the University of Delaware.
Summary: Gerard Cherriere demonstrates how he designs artistic book covers from first inspirational drawings to the actual selections of leathers and final stitching of the binding.

5230. The Guardians of the Public Record (1985)
Format: VHS
Time: 13 minutes
Producer/Distributor: American Association for State and Local History, Nashville, TN 37201
Summary: Warns of deterioration of historical records due to poor storage. Urges local officials to improve the management of records in their care and describes the basic steps. This program is also available in 63 slides and one sound cassette.

Guild of Book Workers Videotapes
Format: VHS
Time: unknown. Some known videotapes are listed in the bibliography
Producer/Distributor: Istor Publications, 7549 N. Fenwick, Portland, OR 97217.

Pittsburgh 1984

5231. Preparation
Time: unknown
Summary: Featuring Don Etherington.

5232. Paring of Leather Covers and Board Preparation
Time: approximately 2 hours
Summary: Demonstration by Don Etherington.

5233. Edge Gilding and Gauffering
Time: unknown
Summary: Featuring Hugo Peller.

5234. Covering Techniques Using Vellum over Stiff Boards
Time: unknown
Summary: Demonstration of the technique by Heinke Pensky-Adam.

5235. Gold Tooling (Using Gold Leaf)
Time: unknown, one videocassette

Summary: Design Bookbinders Michael Wilcox and Don Glaister demonstrate their craft.

San Francisco 1985

5236. Gold Tooling
Time: unknown
Summary: Demonstrations by Gerard Cherriere and Michael Wilcox.

5237. Half Vellum over Stiff Boards
Time: unknown
Summary: Featuring Silvia Rennie.

5238. Paper Cover, Case Construction, Conservation Rebinding.
Time: 117 minutes
Summary: Gary Frost discussed historical models for conservation rebinding specifications, conservation facilities, and various types of conservation methods.

Philadelphia 1985

5239. Rebacking Cloth Bindings
Time: approximately 2 hours
Summary: Jerilyn Davis discusses and demonstrates various methods of rebacking cloth bound books.

5240. Expandable Piano Hinge Album
Time: approximately 2 hours
Summary: Demonstration of her technique by Hedi Kyle.

5241. Tool Sharpening, featuring David Brock
Time: 115 minutes
Summary: David Brock talks about different types of cutting edges and sharpening methods and demonstrates the sharpening of an English paring knife.

5242. Covering Fine Bindings in Full Leather
Time: 105 minutes
Summary: Featuring William Anthony talking about various types of bindings, including English binding and French binding.

Iowa: 1986

5243. Doublures, Enpapers i.e. Endpapers and Leather hinges
Time: unknown
Summary: William Anthony demonstrates his bookbinding skills.

5244. Turkish Marbling
Time: unknown
Summary: Featuring Paula Gourley.

Austin 1987

5245. Endbands
Time: unknown
Summary: Featuring Jenny Hille.

5246. Tools and Techniques of Paper Repair
Time: unknown
Summary: Featuring Barbara L. Meierjames.

5247. Collaboration Between Binder and Printer
Time: unknown
Summary: Featuring Craig Jensen and Richard-Gabriel Rummonds.

5248. Rebacking Leather Bound Books
Time: 138 minutes
Summary: Featuring Bruce Levy.

Chicago 1988

5249. Sewing Through the Folds
Time: unknown
Summary: Featuring Pamela Spitmueller.

5250. Gougless Onlays
Time: unknown
Summary: Featuring Silvia Rennie.

5251. Japanese Side-Sewn Bindings
Time: unknown
Summary: Featuring Catherine Atwood.

5252. Letterspacing
Time: unknown
Summary: Featuring Kay Amhert.

Portland 1989

5253. Sominagashi
Time: unknown
Summary: Featuring Don Guyot.

5254. Basic Paper Treatment for Book Materials

Time: unknown
Summary: Featuring Betsy Palmer Eldridge.

Washington, DC 1990

5255. Techniques & Logic in German Bookbinding
Time: unknown
Summary: Featuring J. Franklin Mowery.

5256. Edge-to-Edge Doublures
Time: unknown
Summary: Featuring Monique Lallier.

5257. French Onlays
Time: unknown
Summary: Featuring Kristin Tina Miura.

Bloomington 1991

5258. Conservation Treatments
Time: 147 minutes
Summary: Don Etherington demonstrates methods of book repair, including the repair of leather books and the restoration of original bindings.

5259. Special Enclosures
Time: unknown
Summary: Featuring Hedi Kyle.

5260. Case Bindings
Time: 150 minutes
Summary: David Bourbeau explains and demonstrates various methods of case bindings.

5261. Design Binding
Time: unknown
Summary: Featuring Donald Glaister.

San Francisco 1992

5262. Rebacking Leather Bound Books
Time: 80 minutes
Summary: Bernard Middleton demonstrates how to repair a leather bound volume.

5263. Boxmaking for Artists' Books
Time: unknown
Summary: Featuring Daniel Kelm

5264. The Making of a Book
Time: unknown
Summary: Featuring Claire Van Vliet.

5265. Sculptural Binding
Time: unknown
Summary: Featuring Jan Stokes.

5266. Handle with Care (1987)
Format: VHS
Time: 13 minutes
Producer/Distributor: Connexions, with help from the staff of the Bodleian Library, other Oxford College Libraries, the Public Record Office, and the Hampshire Record Office. Commissioned by the Society of Archivists. Distributed by Connexions, 6 Tan-yr-Elgwys, Tregynon, Newtown, Powys SY16 3EZ.
Summary: Handling and transport cause a great deal of damage to books and documents, and the prevention is almost always possible if library and archive staff are trained to handle the material safely and to instruct readers to do likewise. This training package is designed to alert staff and readers to potential dangers and to teach them the best techniques; includes a 30-page information package.

5267. Handle with Care (1988)
Format: VHS
Time: 4 minutes
Producer/Distributor: New York University Library, New York, NY 10012.
Summary: A short, humorous file for students, and other library users on how to care for library materials.

5268. Handle with Care: Library Materials (1990)
Format: VHS
Time: 19 minutes
Producer/Distributor: Case Western Reserve University, University Libraries, Conservation Department, Cleveland, OH 44106.
Summary: Explains the proper way to handle and care for various library materials, and the function of the Conservation Department.

5269. Handling Books in the General Collections: Guidelines for Readers and Library Staff Members (1984)
Format: 84 slides with cassettes
Time: 20 minutes
Producer/Distributor: Library of Congress, Washington, DC 20540.
Summary: A thorough discussion of the proper techniques in handling, shelving, using, and photocopying books with examples of the kind of damage caused by improper techniques.

5270. Handling Printed Books (1989)
Format: VHS
Time: 18 minutes
Producer/Distributor: British Library National Preservation Office, London WC1B 3DG.
Summary: After a brief overview of the structure of books, the video offers a step-by-step guide to desirable staff and patron book handling practices.

5271. The Heckman Bindery (1989)
Format: VHS
Time: 12 minutes
Producer/Distributor: USA Teleproductions, 1440 North Meridean St., Indianapolis, IN 46202.
Summary: A video tour of the Heckman Bindery showing the binding techniques and processes utilized. Also highlights various customer services, including online order processing and traditional and microform preservation.

5272. The Hill Monastic Manuscript Library (1985?)
Format: VHS
Time: 15 minutes
Producer/Distributor: Produced and written by Lucy Cook for the Hill Monastic Manuscript Library and distributed by the Library, Bush Center, Saint John's University, Collegeville, MN 56321.
Summary: Describes the massive microform project of over 20 million pages at St. John's University, copied mostly from European sources. Derived from 35 mm slides.

5273. Hot Times in the Courthouse (1983)
Format: VHS, U-Matic
Time: 15 minutes
Producer/Distributor: Nebraska State Archives Records Management Division, Lincoln, NE 68509.
Summary: Explains how local government agencies can embark on and benefit from a microfilming program with guidelines for insuring microfilm quality.

5274. How to Operate a Book (1986)
Format: VHS, U-Matic
Time: 30 minutes
Producer/Distributor: Books Arts Press Video Productions. Directed by Peter Herdrich (Associated with Viking Productions in New York City). Distributed by Book Arts Press, 114 Alderman Library, University of Virginia, Charlottesville, VA 22903
Summary: An overview of the history of the codex form; the fragility of modern books; librarians' and conservators' obligation to preserve physical evidence. Uses the extensive collection of early bindings at Princeton University. Written by Gary Frost and Terry Belanger; narrated by Gary Frost.

5275. If Disaster Strikes (1988)
Format: VHS
Time: 20 minutes
Producer/Distributor: National Preservation Office, British Library, London
WC1B 3DG
Summary: Intended to help librarians identify potential dangers to collections
and to prepare a contingency plan, this introductory video also describes
procedures for salvaging damaged items. Complements the videos The Inside
Track to Disaster Recovery and Library and Archival Disaster Preparedness
and Recovery.

5276. Ingenious Glutinosity! Unique Self-adhesive, Self Stick Book Repair
and Preservation Materials Presented on Instructional Videotape (1995)
Format: VHS
Time: 23 minutes
Producer/Distributor: Kapco Library Products, PO Box 626, Kent, OH 44240-
0626
Summary: Demonstrations of book repair procedures using Kapco products.

5277. The Inside Track of Disaster Recovery (1986)
Format: VHS
Time: 13 minutes
Producer/Distributor: Association of Records Managers and Administrators
(ARMA) International's Standards Committee, 4200 Somerset Drive, Suite
215, Prairie Village, KS 66208.
Summary: This film stresses that professional assistance is available for
recovery efforts, and emphasizes that utilization of technologies to recover
paper documents, books, microfilm, and magnetic media. The video draws on
recovery activities used after four separate disasters occurring in 1985, in
which "the techniques and methodology were effectively implemented to
achieve a 90% recovery of all damaged records."

5278. An Interview with Miriam de Arteni, Schomburg Center for Research in
Black Culture (1983)
Format: U-matic (5 tapes)
Time: 104 minutes
Producer/Distributor: Schomburg Center for Research in Black Culture, New
York Public Library, 515 Malcolm Boulevard, New York, NY 10037.
Summary: Miriam de Arteni was the conservation office at the Schomburg for
five years beginning in 1978. She talks about her education and work at the
Schomburg. Demonstrates preservation and conservation techniques.

5279. Into the Future: On the Preservation of Knowledge in the Electronic
Age (1997)
Format: VHS
Time: 30 minute or 60 minute version

Producer/Distributor: Council on Library and Information Resources, 1755
Massachusetts Avenue, NW Suite 500. Washington, DC 20036-2188.
Summary: This video is about the hidden crisis of the digital information age.
It asks if digitally stored information and knowledge will survive in the future.
Will humans twenty, fifty, one hundred years from now have access to the
electronically recorded history of our time? What happened to reel to reel?
Can we still read those magnetic tapes from early Voyager probes into space?
What about CD-ROMs? and Windows 2.2? A sequel to Slow Fires.

5280. The Iron Range Research Center (1982)
Format: Two carousels with slides and a cassette tape
Time: 10 minutes
Producer/Distributor: Iron Range Research Center, Box 392, Chisholm, MN
55719
Summary: The program stresses the importance of preserving local heritage
and illustrates the Iron Range Research Center's role in this work. The
Center's holdings and the process of preserving archival materials are also
described.

5281. Japanese Handmade Paper (1987?)
Format: film
Time: 14 minutes
Producer/Distributor: Japan National Tourist Organization, 360 Post St., Suite
401, San Francisco 94108
Summary: no information found.

5282. Japanese Style Papermaking I: Simple Equipment and Techniques
(1994)
Format: VHS
Time: 70 minutes
Producer/Distributor: University of Iowa Center for the Book, Iowa City, Iowa
52242.
Summary: Students and teacher work together using small-scale homemade
tools and least expensive equipment to demonstrate the entire process of
making Japanese style sheets.

5283. Japanese Style Papermaking II: Traditional Equipment and Techniques
(1994)
Time: 35 minutes
Producer/Distributor: University of Iowa Center for the Book, Iowa City, Iowa
52242.
Summary: A professionally made Japanese mould is used in sheet-forming,
permitting thinner and more delicate sheets. Fiber preparation and advanced
actions at the vat are also emphasized.

5284. Japanese Style Papermaking III: Professional Equipment and
Techniques (1994)

Format: VHS
Time: 38 minutes
Producer/Distributor: University of Iowa Center for the Book, Iowa City, Iowa
52242.
Summary: Large 60 by 90 centimeter sheets of conservation quality mending
tissue are produced from high quality kozo (paper mulberry fiber). Highlights
include preparing the plants for making paper.

5285. Keeping House (1990)
Format: VHS
Time: 60 minutes
Producer/Distributor: National Trust Post Shopping Service, PO Box 101,
Melkelsham, Wiltshire, SN12-8EA, England.
Summary: Six sections deal with basic principles of care for ceramics, books,
furniture, metalwork, and floors. An introduction discusses environment and
housekeeping tools. Intended for the staffs of historic houses.

5286. Keeping Your Words (1984)
Format: VHS
Time: 43 minutes
Producer/Distributor: British Library, available from Films for the Humanities
and Sciences, Princeton, NJ 08543.
Summary: Shows how the British Library and other U.K. libraries preserve
books and manuscripts. Describes causes of book destruction, deciding
whether a book is worth keeping and options for restoring. Shows restoration
of a 17th-century leather bound book and rescue and care of fire damaged
volumes.

5287. Leaf Casting System for the Repair of Books and Manuscripts (1986)
Format: VHS, U-Matic
Time: 14 minutes
Producer/Distributor: Esther Boyd-Alkalay. Distributed by Film Officer,
National Maritime Museum, Greenwich, London SE10 9NF
Summary: Clearly details the process of recasting the leaves of a 17th-century
book. Work on fragile manuscripts is also depicted, as well as the use of the
Recurator.

5288. The Lessons of History and Experience in the Design of Conservation
Bindings (1988)
Format: VHS
Time: 130 minutes
Producer/Distributor: Library Binding Services and Archival Products, PO Box
1413, Des Moines, IA 50305.
Summary: Panel discussion held at Drake University, August 8, 1987,
preceding a conference sponsored by LBS Archival Services.

5289. Let the Record Show: Practical Uses for Historical Documents (1989)

Format: VHS
Time: 16 minutes
Producer/Distributor: New York State Archives and Records Administration, Albany, NY 12230.
Summary: Designed to help New Yorkers understand the importance of preserving historical records by showing examples of how they can be used.

5290. Let Us Save What Remains (1991)
Format: VHS
Time: 14 Minutes
Producer/Distributor: Archives Division, Virginia State Library & Archives, 11th St. at Capitol Square, Richmond, VA 32319-3491
Summary: Powerful program designed to inspire and inform Virginia court clerks of the preservation program. Focusing on the link between preservation and history, explains the necessity of preservation activities and outlines available solutions.

5291.. Library and Archival Disaster: Preparedness and Recovery (1986)
Format: VHS
Time: 25 minutes
Producer/Distributor: Biblio Tech Films, 11420 Vale Road, Suite D, Oakton, VA 22124.
Summary: By Richard F. Young and David J. Tinsley, designed to help librarians formulate disaster plans, describes the best ways to deal with catastrophes once they have struck. The film addresses sources of assistance, insurance coverage, the recommended extent of recovery attempts, handling and air-drying of wet books and papers, salvaging microfilm and microfiche, and various recovery methods. Planning tips are intended to ameliorate fire and flood damage. 15 page workbook.

5292. Library Binding: A Shared Responsibility, A Collaborative Process (1990)
Format: VHS
Time: 26 minutes
Producer/Distributor: Library of Congress National Preservation Program Office 20540.
Summary: An overview of commercial library binding, clearly presenting the operations of a bindery and outlining the responsibilities of both librarian and binder to ensure that materials are bound approximately and well.

5293. Library Preservation: Fundamental Techniques (1986)
Format: VHS
Time: 60 minutes each
Producer/Distributor: Produced at the ALA Preservation Institute, August 1985; distributed by the Library of Congress, Washington DC 20540.
Summary: These six videotapes are intended to supplement training offered by qualified instructors teaching basic conservation procedures for general

collections materials. Each tape features a leading authority in the field. The borrower may copy supplementary handouts, accompanying each videotape.

5294. <u>Books in General Collections: Recasing</u>
<u>Summary:</u> Don Etherington demonstrates procedure for reattaching a textblock into its original case.

5295.   <u>Books in General Collections: Paper Repair and Pockets</u>
<u>Summary:</u> Robert Milevski demonstrates paste-making, determining grain direction, mending with Japanese paper and with heat-set tissue, making pockets for maps, and other loose inserts.

5296.   <u>Pamphlet Binding</u>
<u>Summary:</u> Jan Merrill-Oldham demonstrates several different pamphlet binding styles for different kinds of pamphlets (e.g. single signature, adhesive bound).

5297.   <u>Protective Enclosure: Portfolios and Boxes</u>
Time: 120 minutes
<u>Summary:</u> Robert Espinosa demonstrates the construction of phase and clamshell (double-tray) boxes.

5298.   <u>Protective Enclosure: Simple Wrappers</u>
<u>Summary:</u> Lynn Jones demonstrates the construction of light weight enclosures.

5299.   <u>Surface Cleaning, Encapsulations, and Jacket-Making</u>
<u>Summary:</u> Judith Fortson-Jones demonstrates techniques for dry cleaning flat paper, polyester encapsulation of single sheets, and making polyester book jackets.

5300. <u>Library Security</u> (1990)
Format: VHS
Time: 22 minutes
Producer/Distributor: British Library, National Preservation Office.
<u>Summary:</u> The U.K. library community probably loses 963 million each year through theft or mutilation of library stock. Who steals from libraries? Can we stop them? What motivates those who tear out pages? This video aims to raise awareness of the issue of library security.

5301. <u>The Making of a Fine Bound Bible</u> (1984)
Format: VHS
Time: 14 minutes
Producer/Distributor: Oxford University Press by the Church of Scotland Video. Directed by Ian Gull. Narrated by Nick Page. Distributed by Oxford University Press, Walton street, Oxford, England OX2 6DP.

Summary: A promo on the binding of modern Oxford University Press Bibles. Useful primarily for showing the economies of scale of a large extra bindery.

5302 Manufacture of Goldbeater's Skin (1983)
Format: VHS
Time: 15 minutes
Producer/Distributor: Istor Productions, 7549 N. Fenwick, Portland, OR 97217.
Summary: Goldbeater's skin is the outer membrane of ox intestine. It has been used for centuries to separate gold leaf during the final stages of manufacture; it has also been used to repair papyrus and vellum. This videotape shows how this material is made and applied.

5303. Manuscript Illumination: Methods and Materials (1986)
Format: VHS, U-Matic
Time: 15 minutes
Producer/Distributor: Istor Productions, 7549 N. Fenwick, Portland, OR 97217.
Summary: Featuring Joyce Grafe, author of Secreta, this videotape show how to make gesso sottile, lay it on a ground, apply gold, and burnish it.

5304. MAPS: The Future of Preservation Microfilming (1993)
Format: VHS
Time: 16 minutes
Producer/Distributor: OCLC, Dublin, OH 43017
Summary: Focuses on the strengths of the MicrogrAphic Preservation Service as a center for preservation microfilming. Through the presentation of MAPS' services, views also receive an introduction to the process of microfilming for preservation.

5305. Marbling Made Easy (1993)
Format: VHS
Time 35 minutes
Producer/Distributor: Gail Mackenzie, San Mateo, CA 94404.
Summary: Gail Mackenzie is a professional marbler whose work is featured in numerous galleries across the country as well as Tokyo and Frankfurt. She is a 1993 Niche Award designer finalist.

5306. The Mark of the Maker (1991)
Format: VHS
Time: 28 minutes
Producer/Distributor: McGowan Film and Video Inc., 4926 North Wolcott, Chicago, IL 60640
Summary: The story of hand-made paper producers Kathryn and Howard Clark, and the steps and art to making paper. This documentary was also nominated for an Oscar.

5307. <u>Mass Deacidification for Paper Based Collections Video Conference</u> (1995)
Type: VHS
Time: 2 hours
Producer/Distributor: Robert Morris College, Academic Media Center, Narrows Run road, Coraopolis, PA 15108-1189
<u>Summary</u>: We have all witnessed brittle materials in our library and archive collections and have heard of the various options available to respond to this brittleness problem. This video conference provides a forum of discussion of one of these options, mass deacidification. The discussion focuses on the history of the process, research, selection, criteria, and funding.

5308. <u>Materials at Risk: The Preservation Challenge</u> (1990)
Format: slide and audiocassette
Time:
Producer/Distributor: National Audio Visual Center, Washington, DC 20409.
<u>Summary</u>: Archives and libraries contain the documentary heirlooms of our history. Yet any of these documents are inherently unstable, and are further threatened by environmental conditions and disasters. This presentation urges librarians and archivists to provide leadership in mobilizing support for efforts to preserve this heritage.

5309. <u>Mending: A Practical Guide to Book Repair</u> (1987)
Format: VHS
Time: 20 minutes
Producer/Distributor: American Library Association Video, Chicago, IL 60611.
<u>Summary</u>: Presents simple book repair techniques - mending a torn page, reinforcing a weak page, and repairing worn corners. Aimed at school libraries and small public libraries. Techniques and materials used are not archival. A similar title was produced in 1986 by the Orange County Dept. of Education, Costa Mesa, CA.

5310. <u>A Million Pound Book: Audubon's Birds of America</u> (1985)
Format: VHS
Time: 6 minutes
Producer/Distributor: American Museum of Natural History/Alecto Historical Editions. Distributed by Alecto Editions, 46 Kelso Place, London W8 5QG, England.
<u>Summary</u>: Gives descriptions of the restrike edition of six plates from the first edition of Audubon's Birds of America, done in cooperation with the American Museum of Natural History which owns the plates. There are good descriptions of the aquatint process and inking a plate for coloring <u>a lo poupee</u>.

5311. <u>Murder in the Stacks</u> (1987)
Format: VHS
Time: 15 minutes

Producer/Distributor: Columbia University, Library Preservation Department, New York, NY 10027.
Summary: Conceived and written by staff members of Columbia University's Library Preservation Department, with an award of $20,000 from the New York State Education Department's Division of Library Development. Starring Sherlock Holmes and Watson, this educational videotape is aimed at library workers and users. The two sleuths stalk the "murderer" of library books, discovering in the end that the deadly killer is, inescapably, "Everyone, Watson." The people who work in the library and the people who use the library. All the people who come in contact with books but fail to give sufficient thought to the consequences of their actions." Holmes and Watson explain the destructive consequences of common situations like overcrowded shelves and dog-eared pages. The detectives also discuss more unusual problems like poor paper quality in books from Third World and some smaller presses.

5312. Museum Mounting Techniques: A Primer
Time: 15 minutes
Producer/Distributor: Istor Productions, 7549 N. Fenwick, Portland, OR 97217
Summary: An instructional film.

5313. New Jersey Records Control & Preservation Training Workbook (1990)
Format: VHS & 2 vols.
Time: 27 minutes
Producer/Distributor: New Jersey Department of State, Division of Archives & Records Management, Trenton, NJ 08625.
Summary: A training video for records management and preservation with a two-volume workbook.

5314. The Omaha Project: A Rare Book Adventure (1990)
Format: VHS
Time: 12 minutes
Producer/Distributor: OCLC, Dublin, OH 43017.
Summary: Describes the efforts of four OCLC staff members and 40 volunteers to help the FBI inventory more than 20,000 stolen rare books and manuscripts, and help locate their owners.

5315. Operation Book Care (1988)
Format: VHS
Time: 30 minutes
Producer/Distributor: University of Wales, School of Librarianship and Information Studies, Aberystwth, Wales.
Summary: Describes the conservation and restoration of books.

5316. Paper Cleaning: Archival Materials (1987)
Format: VHS, U-Matic
Time: 19 minutes

Producer/Distributor: Istor Productions, 7549 N. Fenwick, Portland, OR 97217.
Summary: Reviews storage options and the importance of environmental monitoring and cleanliness; shows how to safely remove paper clips, clean and mend paper, mylar encapsulate, and how to manufacture an easily made enclosure.

5317. Paper Cleaning: Wet and Dry Methods (1985)
Format: VHS, U-Matic
Time: 10 minutes
Producer/Distributor: Istor Productions, 7549 N. Fenwick, Portland, OR 97217.
Summary: Demonstrates what may be done on the curatorial level to slow deterioration using readily available materials and easily learned techniques.

5318. Papermaking at Ogawamachi (198)
Format: VHS
Time: 35 minutes
Producer/Distributor: Available from Richard Flavin, Jionji Press, 218 Kibem Ogawamachi, Hiki-gun, Saitama 355-03 Japan.
Summary: Japanese hand-made paper uses the inner bark of the Kozo, Mitsumata, and Gampi trees. These fibers, formed into sheets by the "Nagashizuki" technique, create the most elegant and durable of all papers. This video gives details of the process, from harvesting the Kozo trees to drying the finished sheets.

5319. Papermaking USA (1982)
Format: 51 slides
Time:
Producer/Distributor: American Craft Council, Slide\Film Service, 40 West 53 Street, NY, NY 10019.
Summary: Documents work shown at the American Craft Museum II, May 20 to October 1, 1982, in an exhibition entitled "Making Paper." Shows works by thirty-four artists who approach papermaking from varied perspectives.

5320. Paperworks: Stabilizing Archival Collections (1989)
Format: VHS
Time: 23 minutes
Producer/Distributor: American Association for State and Local History, Nashville, TN 37201
Summary: This informative video takes the viewer from the arrival of a collection at an institution through the steps of opening the boxes, preparing the supplies, tools, and work area for initial processing. Demonstrations of sample techniques for a variety of materials, proper storage environments, finding aids, and detailed recordkeeping are provided.

5321 Pen Ruling: A Vanishing Industrial Craft (1985)

713

Format: VHS
Time: 13 minutes
Producer/Distributor: Mirror Productions, 335 Greenwich Street #7B, New
York, NY 10013. Directed by Pauline Spiegel.
Summary: An excellent documentary showing the pen-ruling operations of
Bill Caputo in Lower Manhattan, one of the last pen-rulers in New York City.

5322. Photographic Negatives in the Juley Collection: Their Care and
Preservation (1986)
Format: 109 slides and audiocassette
Time: 23 minutes
Producer/Distributor: Smithsonian Institution, Washington, DC 20560.
Summary: Discusses the different types of photographic negatives found in the
Juley collections and the various methods of care and preservation.

5323. Planning a Preservation Program (1982)
Format: Slide tape in two parts
Time: 30 minutes
Producer/Distributor: Library of Congress, Washington, DC 20450.
Summary: Basic elements of a preservation program, for people who know
nothing about preservation. Part one is for administrators; Part two is more
practical and specific.

5324. Planning Conversion to Micrographic Systems (1987)
Format: 51 slides and script
Time: unknown
Producer/Distributor: Association of Record Managers and Administrators,
Prairie Village, KS 66208.
Summary: Describes microfilm, microfiche, aperture cards, and other
microforms, and basic hardware. Discusses factors to consider when planning
to convert a paper system to a micrographic system, and describes possible
pitfalls.

5325. Preservation: An Investment for the Future (1982)
Format: 16mm color film; VHS
Time: 14 minutes
Producer/Distributor: National Preservation Program Office, Library of
Congress, Washington DC 20450.
Summary: A comprehensive overview of preservation activities at the Library
of Congress.

5326. Preservation and Conservation: Basic Preservation Techniques for
Libraries and Archives (1987)
Format: VHS
Time: 70 minutes
Producer/Distributor: Milton S. Eisenhower Library, Johns Hopkins
University, Baltimore, MD, 21218

Summary: Provides background on preservation, explaining the principles behind the development of conservation techniques, demonstrates such specific techniques as surface cleaning, mending, paperback reinforcement, and pamphlet binding. A detailed depiction of how to reconstruct damaged case bindings for both sewn and glued text blocks is also provided.

5327. Preservation Not! (1993)
Format: VHS
Time: 30 Minutes
Producer/Distributor: E.G. Swem Library, College of William and Mary, Williamsburg, VA 23187.
Summary: Demonstrates proper book handling and shelving, along with common actions that damage books. Intended for use in library staff training, specifically for student library employees. Written and presented by Ethel Hellman and Laura Turner.

5328. Preservation Technology-1980s (1983)
Format: VHS
Time: 52 minutes
Producer/Distributor: Library of Congress, Washington, DC 20450.
Summary: Presents advances made in new preservation technologies and their application at the Library of Congress. Presenters include: William J. Welsh, Deputy Librarian of Congress; Peter Sparks, Director of Preservation; William R. Nugent, Assistant Director, Automated Systems Office; and David G. Remington, Chief, Cataloging Distribution Service.

5329. Preserving the Past, Insuring the Future (1984)
Format: VHS
Time: 14 minutes
Producer/Distributor: Produced for Parks Library by Media Resource Center, Iowa State University, Iowa City, Iowa 52242.
Summary: Videocassette of slide/tape presentation. Identifies pests and mold as agents of library destruction. Focuses on the fumigation projects undertaken by Ivan Hanthorn.

5330. Preserving Our Heritage (1990)
Format: VHS and guides
Time: 79 minutes
Producer/Distributor: Australian Library and Information Association, Artarmon, New South Wales 2064.
Summary: Aims to promote awareness of the need to preserve the documentary heritage.

5331. Presswork and Bindery (1986)
Format: 51 slides, one sound cassette, one instructor's guide.
Time: unknown

Producer/Distributor: Graphic Arts Technical Foundation, Pittsburgh, PA 15213.
Summary: Presswork, binding and finishing, and delivery to the customer are presented.

5332. Printmaking, Papermaking, and Bookbinding Program (1984)
Format: 5 filmstrips and 5 sound cassettes
Time: unknown
Producer/Distributor: Communacad, The Communications Academy, Wilton, CT 06897
Summary: Handmade Paper by Sandy Kinnee and Loretta Woodworth, 80 frames, Paper Techniques by Sandy Kinnee and Loretta Woodworth, 80 frames, Introduction to Printmaking by Sandy Kinnee and Lorry Hubbard, 80 frames, Printmaking with Basic Equipment by Sandy Kinnee and Lorry Hubbard, 79 frames, and Bookbinding with Simple Equipment by Mollie Favour and Loretta Hubbard, 80 frames.

5333. Protecting Library Materials From Wear & Tear (1991)
Format: VHS
Time: 23 minutes
Producer/Distributor: Demco Video Productions, Madison, WI 53707.
Summary: Demonstrates the use of modern materials and adhesives to economically extend the useful life of magazines, paperbacks books, and paper book jackets.

5334. Providing a Future for the Past (1989)
Format: VHS
Time: 13 minutes
Producer/Distributor: University Microfilms Preservation Division, Ann Arbor, MI 48106.
Summary: A basic film on preservation microfilming.

5335. The Recovery of Water-Damaged Library Materials (1986)
Format: 75 slides, audiocassette, study guide
Time: 23 minutes
Producer/Distributor: Illinois Cooperative Conservation Program, Morris Library, Southern Illinois University, Carbondale, IL 62901.
Summary: Stresses disaster planning; describes recovery team procedures and training techniques for recovering water-damaged books and other library materials, including audiovisual materials and catalog cards.

5336. Recovery of Water Damaged Library Materials (1985)
Format: 75 slides with cassette
Time: 23 minutes
Producer/Distributor: Illinois Cooperative Conservation Program, Morris Library, Southern Illinois University, Carbondale, IL 62901.

Summary: Designed to meet the need for planning and preparedness on the part of library staff in meeting water-related emergencies. Offers step-by-step instructions for salvaging a wide range of library materials; script included.

5337. St. Louis Collection: Preserving Our Past (1982)
Format: Slides and script
Time: 10 minutes
Producer/Distributor: Western Historical Manuscript Collection- St. Louis, Thomas Jefferson Library, University of Missouri-St. Louis, 8001 Natural Bridge Road, St. Louis, MO 63121.
Summary: Describes the St. Louis collection and the archives facility. Also included is information concerning archival processing and conservation of historical resources.

5338. Selling Preservation: What to Say to the Customer (1994)
Format: Sound Recordings
Time: 2 cassettes
Producer/Distributor: American Library Association, Chicago, IL 60611. Recorded by Teach'em, Inc. Chicago, IL.
Summary: Four addresses offering practical ideas for preservation education in all types of libraries — school, public, special and academic. Learn tactics to teach "kinder and gentler" use in bibliographic instruction. Speakers: Peggy Sullivan, Anne L. Reynolds, Cheryl Holland, and Lorraine Olley. Recorded at the 113th Annual American Library Association Conference in Miami Beach, FL.

5339. Shedding Light on the Case (1991)
Format: VHS
Time: 15 minutes
Producer/Distributor: Columbia University Libraries, Gifts & Exchange, Room 104 Butler Library, Columbia University, 535 West 114th Street, New York, NY 10027.
Summary: Discusses appropriate exhibition practices for library materials; accompanied by a pamphlet of step-by-step instructions.

5340. Shifu (1987)
Format: VHS
Time: unknown
Producer/Distributor: Cannabis Press, 431 Fukuhara Kasama-shi, Ibarai-ken 309-15 Japan.
Summary: Explains the art of Shifu, on cloth woven from thin strips of Japanese paper.

5341. Simple Conservation Techniques (1984)
Format: 8 slide/tape sets (573 slides, 8 audiocassettes, 8 scripts, and 8 manuals)
Time: unknown

Producer/Distributor: Associations for Higher Education of North Texas, PO Box 688, Richardson, TX 75080.
Summary: Eight sets for the training of library staff to perform simple conservation procedures.

      Part 1 Basic Techniques (63 slides)
      Part 2 Paper Repair (138 slides)
      Part 3 Treatments for Leather books (59 slides)
      Part 4 Protective Housing: Polyethylene and
           Polyester Book Jackets and Encapsulation
           (77 slides)
      Part 5 Protective Housing: Phase Box (47 slides)
      Part 6 Protective Housing: Clamshell Box (70 slides)
      Part 7 Simple Binding: Paperback to Hardback (59 slides)
      Part 8 Print Cleaning and Display Cradles (60 slides)

5342. Slow Fires: On the Preservation of the Human Record (1988)
Format: VHS, 16mm film
Time: 60 or 30 minute versions
Producer/Distributor: Terry Sanders; American Film Foundation, Santa Monica, CA 90406.
Summary: Describes the deterioration of books and other printed materials recorded on acidic paper and argues for the preservation ad conservation of film, maps, and other library and archival materials. The film places sobering emphasis on the loss of the "ordinary" human record through "planned deterioration," the result of insufficient money and time for librarians to deacidify every record. Bound transcript available.

5343. Stopping the Rot (1990)
Format: VHS
Time: 48 minutes
Producer/Distributor: Australian Library and Information Association, Artarmon, New South Wales 2064.
Summary: Aims at promoting awareness of the need to preserve documentary heritage.

5344. Technology of the Medieval Book (1988)
Format: VHS, U-Matic
Time: 15 minutes
Producer/Distributor: Istor Productions, 7549 N. Fenwick, Portland, OR 97217.
Summary: How the materials used in the fabrication of the medieval book were manufactured. Included are thread making; quarter-splitting oak boards; parchment making, threading a bristle needle for sewing the book; and the manufacture of fore edge clasps.

5345. Ticonderoga Mill (1990)
Format: VHS

Time: 17 minutes
Producer/Distributor: International Paper Corporation, 1000 Shore Airport
Rd., Ticonderoga, NY 12883.
Summary: An excellent overview of modern papermaking.

5346. Tosa Tenugo-shi (1987)
Format: VHS
Time: unknown
Producer/Distributor: Cannabis Press, 431 Fukuhara Kasama-shi, Ibarai-ken
309-15 Japan.
Summary: Hand papermaking of this Japanese Press.

5347. Turning to Dust (1990)
Format: VHS
Time: 60 minutes
Producer/Distributor: Canadian Broadcast Corporation, Box 500 Station A,
Toronto, Canada M5W 1E6.
Summary: Discusses the preservation challenge; shows ways of coping with
deteriorating paper and books and ways of preventing deterioration.

5348. Use or Abuse: The role of Staff and Patrons in Maintaining General
Library Collections (1986)
Format: VHS
Time: 23 minutes
Producer/Distributor: Illinois Cooperative Conservation Program, Morris
Library, Southern Illinois University, Carbondale, IL 62901.
Summary: Illustrates typical mishandling procedures, shows the damage they
cause, and describes correct practices for care and handling. A lively and
entertaining program for library staff.

5349. A Useable Past (1987?)
Format: VHS
Time: 20 minutes
Producer/Distributor: New York State Archives, Albany, NY 12230.
Summary: Overview of the New York State Archives - its resources, history,
and challenges; describes need to preserve records and how they are used for
research by scholars, business people, schools.

5350. Washi: Hand-Made Japanese Paper (1986?)
Format: film
Time: unknown
Producer/Distributor: Nikki Visual Images, Inc. 2-1-2, Uchikanda, Chiyoda-
Ku, Tokyo, Japan 101.
Summary: No information available.

5351. Wei T'o: Nonacqueous Deacidification of Art on Paper (1987) also
known as Wei T'o Spray Can System

Format: VHS, U-Matic
Time: 6 minutes
Producer/Distributor: Istor Productions, 7549 N. Fenwick, Portland, OR 97217
Summary: Features Richard D. Smith, the developer of the process, demonstrating the proper use of Wei T'o in aerosol spray can form to deacidify paper. Included is a demonstration of how to measure the pH of paper and for sensitivity of inks and mediums.

5352. Wei T'o: Soft Spray System (1987)
Format: VHS, U-Matic
Time: 11 minutes
Producer/Distributor: Istor Productions, 7549 N. Fenwick, Portland, OR 97217.
Summary: Features the inventor, Richard D. Smith, demonstrating a complete Wei T'o Soft Spray system is uncrated, set up, and placed into service to rapidly deacidify books, documents and works of art on paper; includes instructions for routine system maintenance.

5353. The Well-Built Book — Art and Technology (1991, revised 1998)
Format: VHS or 16mm Film
Time: 28 minutes
Producer/Distributor: BMI, 65 Williams St., Wellesley, MA 02841.
Summary: The tape explains the basics of book manufacturing in simple and accurate terms.

5354. Western Papermaking I: Classroom Equipment and Techniques (1994)
Format: VHS
Time: 30 minutes
Producer/Distributor: University of Iowa Center for the Book, Iowa City, Iowa 52242.
Summary: Key features include: discussion of fiber selection, making beater test sheets, formation of 50 by 60 centimeter paper, drying methods and gelatin sizing.

5355. Western Papermaking II: Professional Equipment and Techniques (1994)
Format: VHS
Time: 25 minutes
Producer/Distributor: University of Iowa Center for the Book, Iowa City, Iowa 52242.
Summary: Production of book paper from fermented flax fiber 7, the making of heavyweight sheets for papercased bindings from lime-cooked flax fiber.

5356. Workshops on Hand Bookbinding (1984)
Format 12 U-matic videocassettes
Time: unknown

Producer/Distributor: Guild of Book Workers, 521 5th Avenue, New York, NY 10175.
Summary: Gold Tooling (3 cassettes), Board Preparation (3 cassettes), Edge Gilding (3 cassettes), and Vellum Binding (3 cassettes).

5357. The World of Letterforms (1986)
Format: VHS
Time: 50 minutes
Producer/Distributor: Purup Electronics by Columbia Films. Written by Paul Soegren; directed by Steen Herdel. Distributed by Purup North America, 1326 Energy Park Drive, St. Paul, MN 55108.
Summary: A leisurely look at the history of letterforms, from the Phoenicians to digitized type design. The pace is rather slow, but the photography of this high-budget production is excellent, and there are some good views of various historical punches.

5358. You Always Hurt the Ones You Love (1983)
Format: 4 VHS tapes
Time: see below
Producer/Distributor: Arizona Department of Libraries, Phoenix, AZ 85007.
Summary: Five Programs designed to give instruction in simple repair techniques for circulating book collections.
    Part 1 Introduction (15 minutes)
    Part 2 Repairing Corners (11 minutes)
    Part 3 Grains of Paper and Repairing Hinges (23 minutes)
    Part 4 Methods of Tipping In (22 minutes)
    Part 5 Rebacking (part 1 33 minutes, part 3 39 minutes)

Aspects of Preservation Management in Libraries

George M. Cunha
Susan G. Swartzburg
Robert E. Schnare, Jr.

During the past thirty years book and paper conservation has shifted from skilled craftsmanship, passed on from generation to generation by rigorous apprenticeship training, to today's concept, where technical skills are considered to be only part of a much broader concept of information preservation. Today, preservation encompasses both the prevention of damage and conservation—the physical treatment of damaged objects. Preservation and conservation of cultural property have become professions dominated, if not controlled, by graduates of training programs in degree-granting institutions. In general, this is a positive movement. However, some ardent advocates of this scientific and technical orientation forget that commonsense approaches to everyday problems in preservation management, as in all professions, often get the best results.

Whenever there is technological innovation there will be those who emphatically proclaim a new era, insisting that the latest developments have made all that has gone before obsolete. The advent of home radio in the 1920s is one example. Radio enthusiasts announced with glee that the phonograph, with its moderately expensive, easily breakable, 78-rpm shellac disks, were a thing of the past. To them, the phonograph industry was doomed. They were wrong. After a very brief setback, the recording industry came back with even greater strength since sound recordings could be played on the radio as well as on home phonograph players. There were new disk formats (45 and 33 1/3 rpm), unbreakable disks, and vastly improved sound quality. Today compact disks and their players, direct descendants of the early hand-wound phonograph players, abound in home entertainment centers. These, too, are considered a transitional technology. On the horizon are even more impressive sound recording media that meet an increasing demand for sound recordings of both music and the spoken word.

The advent of electronic information management has been no different. New information technologies have, in some instances, solved information retrieval bottlenecks and storage problems. Optical disks are capable of storing vast amounts of information that are almost instantly retrievable. These access technologies, especially those on the World Wide Web, are seductive to library and archive managers. However, regardless of the exuberance of some easily influenced collection managers and the hyperbole of some vendors of the new technologies that suddenly appear and then disappear, electronic information did not, and never will, totally displace traditional library and archival management procedures and techniques for book and paper records.

A number of scholars and librarians have expressed their concern about the "out with the old and in with the new" philosophy regarding preservation and access of the written word. They urge librarians and archivists to employ a hybrid approach to preservation and access, incorporating new technologies selectively with already existing tools for the organization, preservation, and retrieval of collections. Their presumption is that it is the responsibility of librarians and archivists to avoid being overwhelmed and swept away by the new technologies. Librarians and archivists should employ the new tools selectively in concert with already existing tools and procedures in the performance of their work.

Libraries and archives contain materials ranging from treasured incunabula, book and paper records, art on paper, and photographs, to magnetic media and machine-readable electronic records. The emphasis in libraries, archives, and even museums today is on the care of collections in their entirety rather than the treatment of single objects. A mass treatment approach to preservation is the only way that we can even begin to solve distressing preservation problems. This mass treatment approach has been developed to address the deterioration of hundreds of millions of book and paper records in the nation's—indeed, the world's—libraries that were published between 1870 and the 1980s, printed on acidic paper with the ingredients of their own destruction within them. Many books and documents have already been lost; others are so fragile that they can no longer circulate.

The new electronic media, which can produce surrogate copies of original books and documents for scholarly use, is itself impermanent. The hardware and software for these media have not been designed and manufactured with permanence as a consideration. These media will become obsolete technologies; this can occur in as short a period of time as a year or two.

Although preservation is an important aspect of the overall management of collections, it is only one of dozens of concerns that constantly confront librarians and archivists. They are also responsible for the organization and the dissemination of their collections in the everyday operation of their establishments. Both conservators and librarians should understand that in order to make significant progress in collections care and preservation, collections management requires proper building maintenance and appropriate housing and storage for a variety of information media. Appropriate housing requires the control of temperature, relative humidity, and light; good housekeeping practices; and protection from mold and insect infestation. In addition, collections will require physical treatment, individually or though mass treatment procedures, such as deacidification, and conversion to other formats. A major problem facing administrators is how to find the money to pay for treatment and/or conversion of deteriorating materials into another medium for preservation and/or access.

The Development of Conservation in Libraries

Thirty years ago conservation and preservation, as we think of them now, did not exist. There were, however, excellent bookbinders and paper restorers who did skilled work on valued library and archival materials. Some worked in libraries while others were in private practice. William J. Barrow, at the W. J. Barrow Research Laboratory, and James Gear, at the National Archives, had undertaken their important research on the deacidification of paper. Carolyn Horton, in private practice in New York City, had begun to stress the importance of methodological treatment for collections instead of concentrating on the salvage of severely damaged books. Harold Tribolet, at the Lakeside Press in Chicago, was emphasizing the need for quality control of materials and high standards for workmanship.

Concurrently, librarians and archivists began to realize the importance of good housekeeping, building maintenance, enhanced security and fire protection. They began to recognize the importance of air conditioning as a form of climate control. Techniques such as vacuum fumigation and sterilization of infested materials were being used in a few major research libraries to control pest and mold infestation. Conservators and some librarians were becoming aware that sunlight and light from fluorescent tubes were doing damaging things to paper. But most custodians of collections—librarians, archivists, and public records managers—even those who were knowledgeable about conservation, were all too often severely limited in their preservation efforts by lack of money and the demands on their time by other aspects of their work. Such was the state of preservation in the 1960s. It would be untrue to say that there was no progress; there certainly was, but it was frightfully slow.

The flooding of the Arno River in Florence, Italy, in the winter of 1966 served as a catalyst for book and paper conservation. The collections in the Laurentian Library and other valuable collections were severely damaged by the floodwaters and mud. Conservators from around the world gathered to salvage this material and in the process they learned a great deal about the physical nature of early books and documents. In addition, the world at large realized the value—and the impermanence—of its documentary heritage. The young conservators who worked in Florence in the months and years following the flood have gone forth to build upon their observations and to develop a greater understanding of the composition of paper and books and the causes of their deterioration. They have developed new methods of repair and preservation. Today they are leaders in the specialties of book and paper conservation and library and archival preservation.

By 1970 enlightened librarians and archivists began to accept the fact that something had to be done about the major problem of book and paper deterioration. They collaborated with conservators in the study of the problem. They published articles on preservation management in the technical and professional literature. Workshops and meetings on preservation and conservation were included in the regular meetings of state and regional library associations. Groups that addressed preservation concerns formed within the American Library Association and the Society of American Archivists. By the end of the decade, the American Institute for Conservation of Historic and Artistic Works (AIC), the professional association for conservators, established its Book and Paper Group. Librarians and archivists who were interested in preservation joined the AIC as associate members and became active in this group.

In July 1973 the New England Library Board (NELB) established the New England Document Conservation Center

(NEDCC). The NELB consisted of the state librarians of the six New England states—Maine, New Hampshire, Vermont, Massachusetts, Rhode Island, and Connecticut—who were authorized by their separate legislatures to act collectively on matters of concern to libraries. The original objective of NEDCC was to make workshop facilities and skilled conservators and technicians available to all libraries in the Northeast. Today it is the Northeast Document Conservation Center, an independent, self-supporting establishment with over thirty employees serving libraries and archives around the country.

Since the 1970s there has been steady progress in the efforts to preserve library and archival collections, although there are still many problems to be solved. Today most librarians accept preservation as one of their major responsibilities. They have found ways to pay for it through federal and state sources as well as support from private foundations. Courses on preservation management are offered at most graduate library schools, and these courses are well attended. More libraries are hiring professional conservators. Many others are creating positions for preservation librarians who have been educated in preservation management as well as librarianship. Care of collections in their entirety rather than the treatment of individual objects is becoming the general practice. Librarians now discuss climate control, housekeeping, storage practices, building maintenance, and preservation technologies as readily as the scholastic and administrative aspects of their work.

The Scope of the Problem

The problem of deteriorating books has increased at a phenomenal rate since paper made from acidic wood pulp was first widely used about 1870. The enormity of the problem has overwhelmed caretakers of paper-based collections. They wondered how they could even begin to take care of the vast number of books that already had brittle pages, and the even greater number of acidic, but not yet brittle, books that appeared to be doomed to self-destruction. By the 1960s it was apparent that well over forty percent of the books that had been printed in the preceding eighty years were already so deteriorated that they could not be used. Dr. Richard Smith, a scientist and librarian, concluded from his research into the problem that between thirty and fifty percent of the 300,000,000 books in North American research libraries were already unusable and that this number was increasing at a rate of 4.8 percent annually. Thus calculated, at the Library of Congress, with a collection of more than 20,000,000 shelved books, 4.8 percent, or at least 960,000 volumes, become unusable every year, although they are still on the shelves, supposedly available to readers. If we assume that the replacement cost (purchase and processing) is $100 a volume, it means that the cost per day for deteriorating books at the Library of Congress is more than a quarter of a million dollars.

Applying Smith's figures to the 300,000,000 books in the nation's research libraries, the combined annual costs for the replacement of deteriorated books is one billion and four hundred forty million dollars ($1,440,000,000), about four times the combined annual book budgets for those libraries. This also means that the value of the books in the nation's research libraries is actually decreasing at a steady rate.

Because our documentary heritage reflects who, what, and why we are, preservation management must always be a vital part of the professional activity of librarians, archivists, and record managers. In addition to attention to the physical treatment of books and documents, preservation managers deal with concerns such as:

- what to preserve;
- what preservation method(s) are required for the collections;
- environmental control;
- building maintenance;
- housekeeping and storage;
- security from theft and vandalism;
- disaster planning and recovery.

Preservation is a tripartite concept: a relationship between collections management, conservation, and the scientist. It is the scientist who provides the knowledge from which new technologies are developed. Professional conservators provide expert assistance in the form of manual skills and expertise in the use of new technologies for the protection and physical treatment of collections. It is, however, the librarians and archivists who must be the decision-makers, who decide what to preserve and how to preserve it, because only they have the professional skills and awareness of the legal, aesthetic, humanistic, and historical ramifications that need to be taken into consideration when making crucial preservation management decisions. And, most important, they pay the bills.

Every library and archives must develop its own preservation program. This means that librarians and archivists, as a part of their professional education and training, should become well informed with regard to:

- the nature of materials;
- the agents of destruction and how they affect books and paper records, photographic materials, magnetic media, and other machine-readable records;
- how damage can be curtailed or prevented;
- what can be done in-house to protect and repair materials, and when to seek expert assistance;
- the importance of long-range planning;
- the advantage of cooperation in preservation initiatives.

The preservation of books and paper records, microforms, and magnetic and electronic media is no longer overwhelming, because today's policymakers, administrators, and curators in libraries and archives have learned to work together to establish priorities and to share resources to accomplish the task. The challenges of negativism, disinterest, and lack of funding do not daunt most librarians and archivists in the 1990s.

There are numerous sources to which librarians and archivists can turn for information, advice, and assistance in preservation management. These include professional associations such as the American Library Association, the Society of American Archivists, the Association of Records Managers and Administrators, the National Association of Government Archivists and Records Administrators, the American Association for State and Local History, the American Institute for Conservation, the Guild of Book Workers, the Association of Sound Recording Archivists, and the Association of Moving Image Archivists. The Getty Conservation Institute in California, regional conservation centers, and, of course, the Northeast Document Conservation Center, the first and still the only conservation center devoted exclusively to the conservation of library and archival

729

materials, all can provide expert assistance. The Council on Library and Information Resources serves as an advocate for the preservation of documentary heritage, encouraging preservation initiatives on a national, indeed, an international scale. State and regional organizations also provide solid training as well as advice and assistance for preservation planning and coordinating cooperative preservation projects.

Financial assistance for preservation initiatives has been generously provided by the National Endowments for the Humanities and the Arts as well as state and local government agencies and private foundations. As federal and state funding decreases, corporate and foundation funding should help to fill the gap, but librarians and archivists must become more skilled in making a strong case for the preservation of the documentary record. They ensure that the records of our past will be available for the future, and they can be extremely effective in making the case for preservation.

The Needs Assessment Survey

When the nonprofit Northeast Document Conservation Center was established in 1973, it was intended to provide only book and paper repair services for libraries. It was to be a conservation facility employing bookbinders and paper conservators who had the knowledge and skills, the tools and equipment, to provide treatments of the highest level. Within a short time, however, it became clear that the Center's rapidly growing clientele, including librarians, archivists, public records managers, historical society and museum directors, wanted more. They sought advice and guidance on preservation measures they could do for themselves, technical training for their employees, and assistance in times of emergency. The Center's response was to provide timely and skilled disaster assistance, to schedule frequent workshops for technicians and other personnel, and to place an increasing emphasis on long-range collections management and preservation training for administrators. These services were developed at the Center and offered in addition to the quality conservation treatment of books and paper objects.

There is nothing mysterious about preservation planning. It is the intelligent application of information about collections care and management that is readily available in a voluminous body of literature on the subject.

Preservation management is common sense. It is a part of the overall management of an institution in which information is selected for retention, processed for easy identification and retrieval, and housed and cared for so that it can be accessed quickly when needed. To concentrate only on selection and processing is to lose sight of the many factors in the life cycle of library and archival materials and the way that they are used. The close relationship between selection, organization, preservation, and access must never be forgotten.

Many administrators agree that collections management and preservation are important, but they need to know how to get started on a comprehensive preservation program in their institutions. One solution is to have a professional preservation specialist come to the institution to undertake a preservation survey. The consultant takes a close look at an institution's organization, its physical plant, and how its collections are cared for. A preservation survey usually takes at least one day, and the institution is scrutinized from top to bottom. The consultant then provides a written report about the conditions as they are and makes recommendations for corrective actions, both short and long term. The Northeast Document Conservation Center was a pioneer in providing such consulting service. Today preservation and conservation surveys, which bring a conservator to an institution to take a close look at the physical condition of specific materials in a collection, are offered by other regional centers, and by consultants who can be hired for the purpose. The costs for most of the surveys by the regional centers are underwritten to some degree. For years, the National Endowment for the Humanities has provided considerable support for such surveys, believing that they are the first step in a sound collections management program in an institution and essential before any funds are allotted for conservation treatments. The intent is that treated objects should not be returned to conditions that caused their deterioration in the first place. Today much support for these surveys comes from several foundations that recognize the need for collections care to preserve our cultural heritage.

New Jersey, with funding from its Historical Commission, developed a special program, the Collection Assessment and Preservation Evaluation Service (CAPES), which is managed by the New Jersey Chapter of the Mid-Atlantic Regional Archives Conference

(MARAC). The Commission was receiving grant applications for conservation treatment when it became clear that the requesting institutions had no idea of collections organization and management. The Commission approached the New Jersey Caucus to develop a consultation project and provided funding for a small honorarium to volunteer archivists to undertake surveys for libraries, archives, and historical societies and help these organizations evaluate their needs. The program has been highly successful, reaching a wide range of organizations. It provides a service that is very much needed within a relatively small geographic region and has done much to raise the awareness of institutions about collections management, and to preserve the state's documentary heritage. MARAC would like to expand CAPES into other states, but part of the success of CAPES is that it draws upon about fourteen talented and dedicated volunteers who live in a relatively compact geographic area. Nevertheless, it is a grass-roots initiative that merits study and consideration in other regions.

Another option is for an organization to undertake its own preservation survey in-house before developing short and long-range plans. In the early 1980s the Association of Research Libraries (ARL) developed a methodology and program for such in-house surveys, the Preservation Planning Program (PPP), and developed a collection of supplementary readings, which has been updated several times over the years. The PPP is intended for research libraries. The process is lengthy and time-consuming, requiring considerable staff involvement and time, but it can be implemented in a less complex way by an institution that uses the process to build support for preservation as well as to establish a program. Even then, the process takes time, and for many institutions it may be easier to bring in a consultant to facilitate, even direct, the process. The most effective way to undertake a preservation survey to assess needs is, at bottom, a management decision.

Over the years the Northeast Document Conservation Center developed a checklist to be followed during a survey; it has been modified to meet the times, not only by NEDCC but also by other regional centers and conservators. Survey methodology is taught in preservation courses in library schools and in continuing education workshops. The survey is the focus of the three-day Preservation Management Institute, offered periodically in the Preservation Program, School of Communication, Information, and Library Studies,

Rutgers University, in New Jersey. Participants spend two days learning how to do their surveys, return home to complete them, then gather together to review their results and to explore what actions their institutions can take, both short and long term. This approach was also the basis for the three-year Society of American Archivists initiative, which trained more than forty archivists in North America in preservation management. These archivists are now able to serve as consultants for preservation planning and management at other institutions.

No two libraries or archives are alike. While librarians and archivists can learn from one another, they must be clearly aware of the circumstances in their own institutions before they begin a focused preservation program. First, administrators need to keep clearly in mind how their institution functions. What are the chains of command? The preservation function must fit into this chain at the appropriate place and level. Then they must look at the environment in which their collections are housed, and the physical condition of their collections. Finally, they need to examine their mission; what clientele do they serve? The survey addresses these matters and provides information for planning.

A general survey can identify problem areas in the collections, which can lead to a survey of the condition of a specific collection by a professional conservator. The appearance of shelved books will give some idea of their general condition. Faded spines are a sign of light damage. Making a random selection from the shelves, a preservation specialist will check for further damage, including page discoloration and brittleness, or worm holes revealing the presence of insects. Dilapidated book covers indicate that housekeeping and storage conditions are not satisfactory.

Review and analysis of the data collected on the survey forms make it possible to draw some conclusions about the condition of the building and its suitability as a repository for materials, the general condition of the materials within, and the potential sources of trouble. It is a good idea to review the data and findings with members of the staff from different departments to help determine priorities from their perspective.

A written survey report, whether prepared by a consultant or by an in-house survey team, makes recommendations for short-middle- and long-term initiatives to help preserve and protect collections. The written report is a planning document to be shared with boards of directors and trustees. It lays the foundation for future activities. Today a number of funding agencies require a written preservation survey when an institution is applying for funds for preservation-related activities, which can include the conservation of rare documents, the purchasing of boxes for protecting collections, the continuing education and training of staff, and even the installation of a new HVAC system. Some agencies will grant funds for preservation surveys as the first step in preservation planning.

As the implementation of a preservation program gets underway, certain points should be kept in mind:

- preservation is mandatory;
- preservation is expensive;
- an effective preservation program focuses on prevention;
- preservation means maintaining materials in a collection so they can be used in the present and in the future;
- institutions cannot justify the indefinite storage of unusable materials;
- the selection of materials for physical conservation treatment should be made by curators, not conservators.

The survey is the first and essential step in the planning process. Careful planning leads to the development of a comprehensive preservation program, meeting short-term goals and establishing realistic long-term ones. While many institutions today have preservation administrators in charge of departments with several units, such as commercial binding, book repair, exhibition preparation, facility and/or stack maintenance, etc., this is not necessary. Preservation is every staff member's responsibility and a staff person who coordinates activities may be all that is needed. Today preservation is, in reality, collections management, managing the resources, print and non-print, that have been selected and organized by the institution, so that they are preserved and will be accessible to present and future users.

Preservation Management

Library and archives preservation includes both prevention and conservation. Prevention of damage means keeping books, documents, and other materials from harm; that responsibility is known as collections maintenance. Conservation refers to the repair and physical treatment of materials that have been damaged by natural aging or by other enemies of books. Preservation is the umbrella term, encompassing both preventive care, collections maintenance, and conservation treatment. Obviously it is more sensible to spend money for prevention than to ignore the need for general care of collections and then spend money for the repair of materials that have been needlessly damaged by neglect.

Prevention is expensive. If collection managers think otherwise they are deceived. Annual budgeting for preventive preservation is essential, however, if materials are to be preserved for present and future users. And, over the long term, it is cheaper than attempting to repair materials that have been damaged by neglect. Custodians of the records of documentary heritage have a moral responsibility to pass on their collections to their successors in as good, or better, condition than when they assumed responsibility for them. Even custodians of collections that are meant to last for only a short time, such as popular reading, sound recordings, or video cassettes, should ensure that these collections are kept under conditions that will extend their life as long as they are wanted by readers. Public librarians owe that to the taxpayers who pay for their collections.

With so much information about collections care and preservation now available, there is little excuse for allowing continuing deterioration, other than by natural aging, of library and archival materials. Collections managers need not be professional conservators to start preservation programs, but they must be sufficiently well informed about the nature of materials and the fundamentals of preservation management to make informed decisions on collections care and preservation.

A number of libraries and archives have established preservation departments within Technical Services or Collections Development/Management Departments. These units are managed by preservation librarians/archivists, who may also be known as preservation administrators. The function of these people is to supervise collections maintenance. Preservation administrators oversee the housing and storage of materials, a library binding program, or book and paper repair workshops. They work closely with physical plant and facilities managers to ensure that buildings and collections are environmentally safe. They work closely with curators of special collections in the preparation of materials for exhibition. They are involved in plans for the reformatting of collections, using various technologies, to provide access to information and, as a by-product, to lessen demand for the use of fragile original research materials.

During the early 1970s individuals such as George Cunha, Paul Banks, Carolyn Horton, and Richard D. Smith became involved in the training of preservation librarians through workshops and seminars. Although preservation entered the library school curriculum of some library schools in the 1970s, it was not until 1980, following a successful seminar run by Banks and Pamela Darling, that a formal post graduate program to train preservation administrators was established at Columbia University's School of Library Service. A conservation program was also established at Columbia, with affiliation with New York University's graduate conservation program, to train book conservators to work in libraries. With the demise of Columbia's library school, both programs relocated to the University of Texas at Austin. In addition to meeting requirements for a degree in library science, the programs provide extensive training in all aspects of preservation management and conservation. Today the graduates of the preservation administration and conservation programs are managing preservation departments and programs throughout the country.

In many institutions responsibility for preservation has been assigned to professionals who have other responsibilities. Today, these professionals can easily receive additional training by attending professional development programs. One example is the Preservation Program at Rutgers University. This program awards a certificate in preservation after a participant earns 100 Continuing Education Unit credits by attending a broad selection of short, intensive courses on the preservation of print and non-print materials, preservation administration, bibliographic control, and information technologies.

Regardless of who does the job, and how that person is trained, the scope of the position of preservation manager or administrator is:

- to be well informed in the theory and practice of preservation management;
- to be well informed about the physical condition and preservation needs of the collections;
- to instruct the staff in collection maintenance from the perspective of access as well as preservation;
- to oversee the preparation of a disaster plan;
- to work with physical plant personnel to ensure effective environmental controls;
- to regularly inspect the interior and exterior of the building; for potential hazards to the collection and to initiate corrective action
- to see that patrons are informed about the proper handling of books, documents, and other information media.

In addition, the preservation administrator may supervise a commercial library binding program, a repair workshop, or a basic repair or conservation unit. The preservation administrator may help select and review materials, such as wrappers, book pockets, microfilm boxes, etc., to ensure that they are suitable for the housing of library and archival materials.

Many of these tasks are mass treatments in the broadest sense. Climate control is mass treatment. So are collections maintenance, housing, and storage. Funds are being utilized for the benefit of the collections in their entirety rather than for the treatment of individual objects. While the importance of binding and basic repair work, even conservation treatment of significant materials, cannot be denied, this is, in effect, treatment of individual objects individually selected. Investment in mass treatment, such as basic collections maintenance, is far more profitable.

The best and unquestionably the most cost-effective way to ensure the preservation of library and archival materials is to keep them in an environment in which the enemies of these materials cannot exist. This requires the control of temperature, relative humidity, air pollution, and light; proper housing and storage of materials; excellent building maintenance and meticulous housekeeping; security from theft

737

and vandalism and careful planning for emergencies. It is easier to list what should be done than to pay for it, but to neglect basic collections care and management is, in reality, ignoring the basic responsibility of a library or archives. In the long run, neglecting the needs of the collections can result in significant expense to an institution, even loss of valuable, sometimes unique, materials.

BASIC REPAIR AND CONSERVATION

Only professionally trained book and paper conservators should be engaged in the physical treatment of incunables and rare books, works of art on paper, and other materials in collections that are unique, or of special importance or value. Professional conservators have the education and training, skills, and experience as well as the tools and equipment necessary for treatments.

Most professional conservators today have been trained in rigorous, highly selective postgraduate programs and have served a minimum of a year's internship before entering the profession. They are trained in art history, materials science, chemistry, and biology. The conservators trained at the University of Texas Conservation Program specialize in the treatment of library and archival materials, graduating with a Masters Degree in Library Science and a certificate in Conservation. They are specifically trained to manage library and archives conservation units. After five years, a conservator may become a Professional Associate of the AIC. In their maturity, they may be elected a Fellow of AIC, or of the International Institute for Conservation of Historic and Artistic Works (IIC). Because the post-graduate educational programs are relatively new, a number of the nation's leading conservators were trained in the more traditional apprenticeship model. In a fairly recent development, some conservators who work exclusively with library and archival materials are returning to library schools to take courses, or to earn the M.L.S. to be able to work more effectively in libraries, or with librarians.

In-House Repair

In-house repair is a controversial subject. There are two schools of thought: the never-nevers and the do-it-yourselfers. The never-nevers proclaim that never, under any circumstance, should anyone other than a professional conservator or bookbinder, or a highly trained conservation technician, be allowed to do any repairs on materials normally found in libraries and archives. The do-it-yourselfers are those who contend that because of the overwhelming amount of repair that always has to be done on collections, and the cost, it is sensible to do as much as possible in a workshop on the premises, with student or volunteer assistance.

The never-never approach simply is not realistic. There will never be enough money to pay professionals for the basic repairs that are continually required for library and archival materials. Even if money were to become available, there are not enough professionals to do all the work. On the other hand, the do-it-yourselfers must accept the fact that there are some things in the collections that, because of their rarity or importance, should be treated only by a skilled conservator. Some conservators are suspicious, if not openly antagonistic, to in-house repair units, for they have seen considerable damage to materials caused by insensitive and poorly trained hands.

Librarians and archivists are already fully occupied by their professional responsibilities and have little time to roll up their sleeves to do basic book and paper repairs. However, they must be well informed about what can and cannot be done in their institutions, and the costs. They need to understand the treatments that will be done in order to be able to supervise those who do the basic repairs. There are many workshops on basic repairs given throughout the country that enable librarians and archivists to understand what basic repairs are, how they are done, the level of training needed for a person to do them, the cost of supplies and equipment, and whether they are feasible. Librarians and archivists who want to learn a technique to understand what is involved—not to do it on library or archives property—can sometimes work individually with a conservator for a day or two at a nominal cost. Today there are centers for book arts in many parts of North America where librarians can, and do, take basic bookbinding courses to understand the construction of the book and the physical nature of paper. How-to information, of varying quality, is widely available; repair information is even exchanged on electronic chat listserves, although some of that information (the Conservation Distlist, managed by conservator Walter Henry, excepted) is singularly wrongheaded and destructive. Caveat emptor.

The preservation administrator, with the curators of

collections, should decide what treatments can safely and cost-effectively be done by in-house staff, students, or volunteers and what materials must be treated by a conservator. Thus, a preservation administrator must:

- be well informed about the physical condition of the materials in various collections;
- understand what treatments are necessary to restore damaged materials to usable condition, as well as the cost;
- be able to determine if fragile or damaged materials can be transferred to a surrogate format, such as a paper facsimile, microfilm, or digital image;
- know what can be accomplished in-house and what must be sent out for treatment;
- establish priorities;
- seek and find funds to pay for treatments.

One of the most important preservation measures for paper records is to rehouse them into archival folders and boxes. During this process, extraneous materials such as pins, staples, and other metal fasteners can be removed. Surface soil can be removed by dry cleaning the paper with a soft eraser. Even dry cleaning, however, must be done carefully. After one workshop, an overzealous staffer returned to his institution and began to dry clean documents too vigorously, rubbing holes in them.

In-house treatment of paper records should be limited to black-and-white materials, and can include manuscript and typescript items, prints, broadsides, maps, or posters. Materials with colored media should never be treated by non-professionals because the media can be unstable.

Tears in paper can be mended using heat-set tissue and a tacking iron, a skill that can be mastered after a little practice on scrap paper. With a little more experience, one can master the use of wheat starch paste, carefully applied along the edges of the tear with a brush, which makes a better repair. The wheat starch paste, however, must be made fresh and does not keep very long. Experienced paper conservators find it quicker to use this latter technique for mending tears, but the part-time worker may not.

Another important task that can be done in-house is to encapsulate fragile documents in polyester film. This task requires only a little training, but the person doing the task must do it properly. At one institution, the student worker placed the documents too close to the adhesive tape used in the procedure; eventually, the adhesive oozed and the encapsulation had to be redone. There are machines available that weld through polyester ultrasonically or by heat thus avoiding the use of tape. They are expensive, but the purchase is worthwhile for institutions with significant collections of valuable documents that can justify the cost of the equipment. Some commercial library binders also do encapsulation for their customers at a reasonable cost.

Protective wrappers or boxes for fragile or rare books and documents can be made in-house. There are a variety of structures, all easy to make, that meet the needs of collections, and it is a rewarding task for students and volunteers. There are numerous instructions available and these techniques are often taught at workshops. The advantages of wrapping or boxing materials are:

- it is inexpensive;
- it can easily be done in-house;
- it protects books and documents from soil, air pollution, pests, fungi, and water damage;
- it protects books with loose covers;
- it offers protection for books with brittle pages until they can be reformatted;
- it preserves and protects the covers and text of books important for their artifactual value.

Protective wrappers and boxes are sometimes called microenvironments or microclimates because they create a stable microenvironment for the object. Making boxes or wrappers for valuable materials housed in buildings where the environment cannot be easily controlled, offers considerable protection from unstable conditions.

If inks are not soluble, deacidification, the removal of many of the harmful acids in the paper, may be done in-house using spray solutions developed by Bookkeepers or Wei T'o. This process requires a workspace with proper ventilation, and a conservator should train the people who do it.

The removal of adhesive tapes should not be done in-house. Adhesives are singularly difficult to remove from paper; often the stains they have made can never be removed. Professional conservators working with masks under fume hoods to loosen the adhesives and remove the tape carefully use powerful and toxic solvents. Because of the toxicity of the process, a number of conservators with fume hoods in their workshops have stopped doing this treatment because of its danger.

Damaged books often require only minor cover and page repair to make them serviceable. These repairs can be done in-house by non-professional staff, students, and volunteers after some basic training and practice on materials intended to be discarded. Suitable quality repair materials must be used, however, or even more damage will be caused.

Adhesive tapes and Elmers Glue are wonderful for a variety of household tasks, but not for the repair of paper and books! Several library supply companies offer acceptable products for treatment at reasonable prices and they also offer instructions and advice, backed by conservators. One caveat: some libraries use adhesive tapes to hold books on reserve together until the end of term when they are discarded. The problem is that the readers don't realize that this is a short-term measure. If the library tapes its books together, they suppose that this is a proper, simple, and inexpensive repair technique that they can use on their own books. How many times have libraries received valuable books, carefully taped together, from conscientious donors, or conservators been asked to work on books in this condition! Think of the possible consequence when you tape together a book or document.

An efficient in-house workshop for the repair of books and documents can be as small as a workbench with only a few simple tools located in a corner of a technical services area, or it might be a separate room with a broad array of equipment. The size and scope of the in-house workshop will be determined by the nature of the materials in the collection and the extent that an institution wants to get involved in mending and physical treatment of its materials. What is cost-effective for one institution may not be for another, so the decision to build and equip a workshop must be made carefully with the needs of the collection and the finances of the institution clearly in mind. There are a number of excellent publications, to be found in the bibliography, on setting up and managing an in-house treatment unit.

In some parts of the United States, regional conservation centers, conservators in private practice, and other treatment facilities are readily available. Most treatments can be done quickly and at far less expense than it would cost an institution to equip a workshop and hire a person to do them in-house. In other parts of the country, help is not so close, and it is often more cost-effective to develop a fairly extensive repair or conservation facility in-house. For a time in the 1980s, having an in-house repair facility gave administrators a certain cachet, and grants were available to enable an institution to establish one. Unfortunately, the money to sustain these workshops was, and is, not readily available today and these workshops languish, with sophisticated equipment left idle because there are no funds for personnel to operate them and no funds for supplies. Perhaps some will convert to regional repair and conservation facilities, supported by a group of institutions to make operations cost-effective. There is, at present, some movement toward that end.

Commercial Library Binding

Managing an institution's library binding program is a major responsibility that requires far more than gathering worn books together to be sent out for rebinding. Binding takes a significant amount of a library's budget. There is a variety of binding techniques available, enabling a library to choose the most effective book structures for its collections. The preservation administrator and the commercial library binder must work closely together, but it is the library's responsibility to prepare specifications to meet its needs. In negotiating contracts, it is wise to remember that cost savings are realized when large quantities of books go through the binding operation routinely; every step that requires removal from the assembly line for a special treatment will cost a little more. Commercial library binding, even though its operations are mechanized to some extent, is a small and labor-intensive industry, dedicated to meeting libraries' needs, but librarians must articulate them clearly. Every librarian responsible for commercial library binding, indeed, every librarian, should visit a commercial library bindery.

743

The preservation administrator responsible for an institution's commercial binding program needs the following qualifications to do an effective job:

- knowledge of the physical construction of books;
- understanding of the difference between hand bookbinding, trade binding, edition binding, machine-sewn library binding, adhesive binding, as well as special binding techniques for materials such as music scores or children's books,
- understanding of sewing techniques;
- familiarity with the Library Binding Institute's Standard for Library Binding,
- knowledge of the strength, durability, and suitability of materials used for the rebinding of books, and their costs;
- ability to recognize different repair requirements and to identify materials that are not suitable for commercial library binding;
- understanding of options and costs of replacement volumes and surrogate copies, produced in facsimile and bound, microfilmed, or digitized.

Every book that leaves the library for rebinding should have inserted between its pages a job order that identifies the book and describes in detail the type of binding required and what materials to use. Much of this binding preparation is computerized today, making control by the library and the binder far easier. When books are returned from the binder, each volume should be examined carefully to be sure that the requirements stipulated for its binding have been met. Problems should be reported to the binder immediately. If mistakes continue, another binder should be used.

DISASTERS AND DISASTER RECOVERY

"Disaster: an event whose timing is unexpected and
the consequences of which are seriously destructive."
University of California Task Force on
Disaster Planning, 1978

"Disaster happens when you are not ready for it."
Common remark

Unquestionably one of the most satisfying developments in preservation management in the 1980s is the realization by librarians and archivists that although disasters occur with distressing frequency, the effects of these misfortunes can often be contained and recovery can be expedited by sensible advance planning. Indeed, a number of funding agencies now require a written disaster plan from a library, archives, or museum before funds will be given for other preservation activities or conservation treatment. Disaster planning and recovery workshops are offered frequently all over the country. Today most administrators recognize that planning for emergencies and potential disasters and seeing that their staff is trained in recovery is their responsibility, and it is good management.

Walter Brahm, former State Librarian of Connecticut and Ohio, in a survey undertaken for Case Western Reserve University, determined that in the state of Ohio alone during any given five-year period there might be fifty major disasters. If that figure is true for each of the fifty states, the threat to library and archival collections, and cost, is significant indeed. Every librarian and archivist is going to have to deal with emergency situations and disaster in the course of his or her professional career. Whether an emergency situation becomes a disaster depends, all too often, on the pre-planning that has taken place in an institution.

The list of library disasters since the Florence Flood of 1966, which brought the attention of the world to the threat to cultural property by natural disaster, is awesome. The record includes:

1973 The St. Louis Federal Records Center fire;
1986 Los Angeles Public Library fire;
1988 Academy of Science Library fire, St. Petersburg,
      Russia;
1992 Hurricane Andrew, South Florida;
1994 Northridge Earthquake, southern California;
1993 Floods of the Mississippi, the Missouri and other
      rivers in the mid-western United States.

Librarians and archivists have learned valuable lessons from each of these disasters, and they have heightened the awareness of the vulnerability of our documentary heritage to the public at large.

Disasters can be categorized as natural events, accidents, vandalism, or the result of human error. Natural events include earthquakes, such as the Northridge quake in 1994, which was followed by raging fires; hurricanes, such as Hugo, that struck Charleston, South Carolina, in 1990, and Andrew that leveled much of south Florida in 1992; tornados and cyclones with their violently destructive winds; flooding, such as occurred in the Midwest in the spring of 1993. Both Hugo and the floods of '93 demonstrated the advantages of careful disaster planning. South Carolina had recently completed a statewide planning initiative by those responsible for cultural property, so they knew what to do when Hugo struck, and they quickly sprang into action. Losses were limited and recovery was prompt, even though the devastation caused by the hurricane was terrible. Again, many librarians whose institutions were threatened by the floods of '93 knew how to protect their collections before water struck, saving many thousands of books and other library materials. When flooding struck, trained recovery teams sprang into action and knew what to do to return the libraries back to normal operation.

Disastrous fires have resulted from accidents in furnace rooms or defective wiring. The destruction from combustion, soot, and smoke from even a minor blaze is bad enough, but all too frequently the water from the firemen's hoses causes more damage than the flames. Wet, sooty materials are unpleasant and costly to salvage. Plumbing failures are frequently the cause of flooding that requires extensive salvage of water-damaged materials. The damage from a malfunctioning air conditioner or sprinkler head can also be serious. Basement storage areas have been filled by ground water entering a building through porous foundation walls, or from ruptured pipes in the above ground levels. Melting snow and ice in the winter and spring and water from torrential rains, which can occur any time of the year, penetrate aging roofs and cause serious water damage to materials in the stacks below.

Buildings are especially vulnerable when construction is underway. Workmen, digging with earth-moving equipment during the construction of additions to libraries in Texas and California, ruptured water mains from which tens of thousands of gallons of water rushed into basement book storage areas in adjacent buildings. Preparing a disaster plan before construction begins is essential, because there will be disasters during the construction period that can be quickly and easily dealt with if the staff is prepared.

Accidents happen all too frequently and some appear ridiculous at first glance. A skunk got into the public library in a small Massachusetts city and was found sitting placidly in the center of the reading room when the staff came to work. When an intrepid librarian, with the aid of a broom, attempted to drive the skunk out of the building, the skunk reacted naturally. That caused a disaster in the library. Another time, a zealous but inexperienced maintenance helper, when attempting to repair a leaking faucet in the library's second floor lavatory, ripped it from the pipe to which it was attached. Because he, and most of the staff, didn't know where the building's main water shut-off valve was located, the reference room received considerable water damage before someone finally managed to find it and stop the flow of water. Disaster planning and preparedness would have prevented both disasters.

The ingenuity of vandals is often demonstrated by their tampering with plumbing facilities, air conditioning systems, or fire sprinklers; their destructive actions can cause serious water damage to library and archival materials. Small fires may be set in remote areas of the stacks, in waste baskets, or in book return boxes thus setting off sprinkler systems. While homeless people do not purposely vandalize, they can cause damage to plumbing or even accidentally start fires. Incidents have occurred that have forced librarians to think more seriously about the problem of homeless people in public spaces and the threat they can cause to public property.

No building, regardless of where it is located and how well it is constructed and secured, is safe from unwanted natural or man-made disasters. The key to keeping emergency situations from becoming disasters, with loss of property, sometimes loss of life, is disaster planning. Thorough contingency planning and a well-trained staff familiar with the plan, results in prompt action, lessening the extent and time necessary for recovery of services.

A major calamity may require millions of dollars for the repair and restoration of materials and the rehabilitation or reconstruction of a building. That is why it is important that library and archives administrators, boards of trustees, and others who are responsible for the care and preservation of cultural property, need to work closely with insurers. The insurance company needs to understand the library's priorities to ensure that operations are returned to normal as quickly as possible and that restoration procedures are begun as promptly as possible, lessening the losses.

Disaster Planning and Prevention

Every library, archive, public records office, historical society, and museum needs to have a contingency, or disaster plan. Most administrators recognize that disasters will occur, and it is best to be prepared for them. Also, such planning can result in reduced insurance premiums.

A disaster prevention plan anticipates possible problem areas, evaluates the effect of a disaster on the building and its contents, and devises ways to minimize damage and loss. The goal is to restore the institution to normal service as rapidly as possible. A basic premise in disaster planning is that every repository is unique and requires its own disaster plan. It is foolhardy to adopt another institution's disaster plan with no review and revision, although much can be gained from reviewing the plans of other institutions and working with some of the model plans that have been prepared for regions around the country. An institution's plan is based on the probable external threats in its geographic area and its particular vulnerabilities due to age and construction features of the building; its physical location relative to seacoast, riverbeds, or other potential natural hazards; the character and size of the collections; the number of staff and its experience.

Disaster Recovery Planning

The objective of disaster recovery planning is to provide guidance for the disaster recovery action teams, whose members will probably not be the same people who are a part of the disaster planning and prevention team. The disaster planning team will have established priorities for the salvage of specific items of value or various categories of materials. The disaster recovery plans are prepared to be implemented by well-organized and trained disaster recovery teams. These people are thoroughly familiar with the disaster plan as well as the recovery document to be used during the salvage and recovery operations. They should be trained in the salvage of fire and water-

748

damaged materials. The disaster recovery document should be understood and approved by the highest levels of administration so that it can be implemented promptly. Much information that has been gathered in the disaster planning document will be used in the disaster recovery document. This is the document that people will take in hand when disaster strikes. It will tell people under stress what to do. It should provide brief, clearly written instructions for action with no extraneous material.

The first page of the document should contain the telephone numbers of the police and fire departments and both the office and home telephone numbers of key personnel, such as the senior administrator, facilities manager, and the members of the disaster recovery action team. Many institutions find it helpful, even if they are not located in the Northeast, to include the telephone number of the Northeast Document Conservation Center, for its staff is available 24 hours a day, seven days a week, and can provide considerable practical and emotional support in an emergency. Their conservators often go to a site to assist in salvage and recovery operations.

The purpose of this document is to serve as a guidebook for the recovery team at the emergency, so copies of it should be kept at the home of key recovery personnel, as well as in their offices. Many institutions now also keep the information in a computer file for easy editing and updating. However, printed copies should always be available in key locations; one cannot count on computers being available and operational when disaster strikes.

Companies that specialize in disaster recovery provide an array of services. They can remove, freeze dry, and sterilize large quantities of materials that have been water-damaged and contaminated. They will even clean them for an institution. If a space is contaminated by hazardous—waste something that every institution should be concerned about—they can provide specially trained and equipped personnel to decontaminate spaces and recover materials. Librarians and archivists should become familiar with these companies and work with them during the disaster planning process, so the vendor selected can respond quickly to an emergency situation, ensuring that the emergency does not become a disaster.

With what appears to be an increase in significant disasters in

749

recent years, far more attention is paid to disaster planning and recovery by federal, state, and regional bodies, making the librarians' and archivists' task much easier. The Federal Emergency Management Agency (FEMA) is available to help with disaster planning and is responsive to needs in catastrophic situations. While human life and safety are the priority, FEMA's staff is aware of the need to rescue cultural property as quickly as possible and is prepared to assist. Many states and regions have prepared lists of agencies and individuals that can provide assistance and supplies in an emergency situation or in a disaster. These documents accompany an institution's disaster plan to be accompanied by a list of local resources.

Because librarians, archivists, and museum personnel are working together in states and regions to develop disaster plans and to provide assistance to one another in an emergency, catastrophic situations are not as disastrous as they used to be. This has become quite clear from the experiences following Hurricane Hugo in South Carolina and in the Midwest during the floods of 1993. Less fortunate was Florida, where statewide disaster planning was not taken seriously by library administrators, who were helpless to act in the early aftermath of the devastation caused by Hurricane Andrew. While salvage companies and conservators came in and did what they could to help, the obvious lack of pre-planning at a time when people were in shock because of personal losses was a serious detriment to effective salvage and recovery.

The key factors in recovery are:

- speed, especially in the summer when there is a high probability of mold growth;
- knowing what to do because there will be no time to search for answers;
- knowing where important materials are located so they can be recovered as quickly as possible;
- knowing where, and to whom, to turn for assistance.

Restoring service may be a simple matter if only minor damage from a leak or an isolated blaze occurs. However, a building can become completely unstable, requiring the use of temporary buildings for days, weeks, or months. It is important to restore at least some service to the public as rapidly as possible or an institution stands a good chance of losing its patrons.

Library, archives, and public records administrators can learn from the business world about the need to get businesses up and running as quickly as possible after a disaster, and especially about the recovery of machine-readable records. A business does not have the luxury of time. Even a short interval of time with no service and loss of records can result in bankruptcy. Thus the business world invests heavily in disaster planning and recovery, staff training, and in the off-site storage of machine-readable records. The corporate record of recovery of information and of reestablishment of service after often-calamitous experiences is impressive. Cultural institutions may not have such financial pressures, or the financial resources, but there is much that the managers of cultural property can learn from the corporate world.

Some thought should be given to the provision of long-term repair and restoration of valuable materials that have been damaged by fire or water. The repair of collections damaged in the Florence flood of 1966 continues today, thirty years later. The Los Angeles Public Library hopes that its collections will be repaired by the end of this decade. The repairs to the collection in the Academy of Sciences Library, St. Petersburg, Russia, will continue well into the twenty-first century. Identifying what materials should receive such treatment with some consideration of the cost involved is important in the planning process and should be discussed frankly with insurers. Books and documents, however, need not, nor should they, be restored to resemble their original appearance. The goal of recovery is to stabilize materials so they can be available to readers in the future; thus they can be cleaned and boxed, not rebound in the manner of their original bindings. Often this is the time to microfilm rare materials for additional access and to ensure that the damaged and fragile originals are less frequently handled.

Magnetic media are especially vulnerable to heat and moisture. Their combustion temperature is much lower than most other materials, and they burn more rapidly. Magnetic images can be distorted or obliterated by levels of heat and moisture that would not cause great damage to paper records. Water alone rarely damages magnetic media and the hardware necessary for playback. Rather, it is the damage that occurs from contamination by dirt and the chemicals in the water that causes the destruction. Thus, even if magnetic media are recovered and cleaned, they should never be run in machines until the hardware has been professionally cleaned. Specialists can often recover data on damaged tapes, but the process is very costly.

Digital and optical electronic media are impermanent, although the technology that produces them may be more permanent than the equipment that will play them back. However, recovery of data is critical in business and industry; it may not be as critical for a library or archive.

To prevent loss of magnetic and electronic data, back up the data and store it off-site, or hire the services of a computer security firm, which is very costly, but effective. The necessity for back up of magnetic and electronic files seems obvious, yet it remains an area where libraries, archives, even public records offices, can be lax. Back-ups are not made as frequently as they should be. Sometimes they are not made at all. Back-ups are frequently kept in the same building, sometimes in the same room, as master copies. Often back-up copies are not checked against the original for accuracy. All too often the back-up copies, and the originals, are not frequently checked for evidence of chemical, physical, or informational deterioration. Today, contingency planning for magnetic and electronic media should be a priority in libraries and archives. Preserving such media is the challenge of the twenty-first century.

There are companies that specialize in the recovery of computer data. If their technicians can gain access to wet and damaged computers quickly enough, they can recover the files in a computer. For libraries and archives that cannot afford the expense of data security services, this service is invaluable. Often a computer will still work after it has dried out and data can be recovered from it without resorting to a recovery service. However, once fire and water have damaged a computer, it should not be retained unless a company that specializes in this work has rehabilitated it.

In Retrospect: Librarians and Archivists as Preservation Managers

The advent of new technologies for information management, which enter the market regularly and often depart as regularly, has led to considerable change in libraries and archives. Because of the variety of information technologies and the speed with which they are evolving, their impact on information management is far greater than the impact Gutenberg's printing press had on society and scholarship in the sixteenth century.

It is difficult today to conceive how librarians at major institutions functioned without recourse to the information technologies of the late twentieth century. Innovations in information management now make it possible to store vast quantities of information and retrieve it almost instantaneously. Networks, such as the World Wide Web, make it possible to communicate and distribute enormous amounts of information worldwide. We have, indeed, become a global village. Today's librarians are well informed and adept in the use of these information technologies. This, however, does not mean that the book- and paper-oriented library will become obsolete, as some predict, with books and documents relegated to museums as curiosities. The new information technologies are tools that librarians and archivists use along with other resources for the gathering, organization, storage, and ready retrieval of the record of the human sojourn on this planet.

The problem of the deterioration of books and paper records, considered alarming only a few decades ago, is now well under control because most librarians and archivists have accepted preservation as one of their major responsibilities. They recognize that the preservation of their collections is too important to leave in the hands of conservators, who cannot make decisions about the nature and use of an institution's collections. Scientists and conservators have identified the causes of paper deterioration. Today, librarians and archivists deal with the preservation of paper-based collections with a hybrid approach of proper storage, conservation treatment, and reformatting.

The critical period for paper dates from about the 1870s through the 1980s, when the industrial age made possible the mass production of paper that carried within it the seeds of its destruction. Today, paper produced for books and documents is far more stable and permanent. The conversion of papermills to the production of alkaline paper using technology that preserves the environment as well as the paper itself, and the increasing availability of high-quality recycled paper for book production and recordkeeping, ensures that the paper documents produced today will not vanish tomorrow. Most scholarly books today are published on permanent and durable alkaline paper, with the number increasing annually.

While the mass deacidification processes that were developed in the past two decades have not turned out to be the uncomplicated and inexpensive mass treatments that librarians and archivists hoped for twenty years ago, these processes do offer a means to extend the life of deteriorating papers for a considerable length of time. Research continues on these processes, but it is unrealistic to believe, as we have learned, that any one of them will be the solution for the treatment of all acidic paper-based materials in a collection. In order to make good use of mass treatment processes, librarians and archivists need to understand the physical nature of their collections and their intended use. Only then can they make informed decisions and select the processes that are appropriate for the treatment of certain materials. Selecting treatment processes is time-consuming and somewhat costly, but the more the institution understands what a mass treatment process will and will not do, and the physical and intellectual nature of its own collections, the less this selection will cost in time and effort. Librarians and archivists need to keep informed about mass treatment technologies, learn a little chemistry, and then make informed decisions. It should be remembered that any physical treatment will change the physical nature of the object being treated and will thus destroy physical evidence for the scholar or bibliographer who may, in the future, need it. Thus, materials with significant artifactual value should not be treated.

Librarians and archivists now understand the critical need to provide a good environment for both print and non-print materials, whether or not they are of permanent research value. Non-print materials react even more unfavorably to poor environmental conditions than do paper-based materials. A proper environment can significantly extend the life of even badly deteriorated paper-based materials. With engineers who specialize in the library and museum environment now available to help, librarians and archivists are learning how to stabilize the environment effectively, often cost-effectively. Architects are learning to design library and archives facilities that are efficient, effective, and attractive, but it is the librarian's and the archivist's responsibility to make clear the requirements for housing collections; the architect then provides a suitable and attractive design to meet those needs.

Through microfilm, the intellectual content of critical books and documents can be preserved for centuries, providing ready access. Although researchers may complain about the awkwardness of microfilm, once they work with it they quickly become adept at handling it. Original materials, while they need to be preserved as the primary record, need only be consulted occasionally by scholars if such surrogate copies are widely available for everyday research use. Microfilmed material can now be reformatted into electronic format to facilitate scholarly communication and research. Studies are underway to determine how best this can be accomplished, and the standards necessary to produce microfilm that can be easily digitized.

Today materials can be put into an electronic format then transferred to microfilm for long-term preservation. At this time, electronic information belongs to the producer, along with the responsibility to refresh it into a current format for as long as the material is needed in an electronic format. Thus, material outside of copyright will belong to the institution or the individual who produces it. Because many books today are produced in electronic format, then printed for distribution, the preservation of much of our present documentary record is in the hands of publishers. There are complicated issues of copyright, royalties, and access that have yet to be resolved; librarians, authors, and publishers need to work together to ensure both preservation and access in the future. Librarians will develop pathways and procedures for dealing with bibliographic control and access to information and will play a leading role in the preservation of information in electronic formats.

As has been stated previously, preservation is expensive. The acquisition of materials, the organization of them, even the technologies that provide access to many of them are also expensive. There will never be enough money to preserve everything, so librarians and archivists have to make choices about what will survive and what will not. Few libraries today can afford the services of a full-time professional conservator, or even a preservation administrator. It has been demonstrated in the past two decades that it is possible to reduce costs for preservation, as well as collections development, through collaboration with other institutions.

The emerging electronic information technologies have already had a profound effect on information management. Because they are not eye-readable, but rather are hardware and software dependent, these information technologies must be carefully documented. As their software and hardware become obsolete, the information must be refreshed into a current technology. Reformatting from one technology to the next is costly and is subject to error. Today's critical electronic records must be identified and microfilmed, to be transformed into hardcopy or into the digital technology of the day when these records are again needed for research.

Once great libraries strived to own as many books as possible and gained stature by their size. Today the emphasis in librarianship is on resource sharing. It is recognized that no library can strive to own and manage everything; the goal is to provide access for as much of the world's written and visual record as possible. Through wise preservation management this goal can be achieved.

Glossary of Abbreviations and Acronyms

Robert E. Schnare, Jr.

AASLH	American Association of State and Local History
ACLIS	Australian Council of Libraries and Information Service
ACRL	Association of College and Research Libraries
ACS	American Chemical Society
AIC	American Institute for Conservation of Historical and Artistic Works
AICCM	Australian Institute for the Conservation of Cultural Materials
AIIM	Association for Information and Image Management
AIMA	Association of Moving Images Archivists
ALA	American Library Association
ALCTS	Association for Library Collections and Technical Services of the American Library Association
ALIC	Archives Library Information Center, National Archives and Records Administration
ALISE	Association for Library and Information Science Education
AMIGOS	Bibliographic Utility for the Southwest
ANSI	American National Standards Institute
APA	Alkaline Paper Advocate
ARB	Arbete (Work) Swedish (Swedish National Archive of Recorded Sound and Moving Images)
ARMA	Association of Records Managers and Administrators
ARSAG	Association pour la Recherche Scientifique sur les Arts Graphiques
ARSC	Association of Recorded Sound Collections
ASC	Association of Systematics Collections
ASHRAE	American Society of Heating, Refrigerating and Air Conditioning Engineers
ASIS	American Society of Information Science
ASLIB	Association for Information Management (United Kingdom)
ASTM	American Society for Testing and Materials

BAN	Academy of Sciences Library, St. Petersburg, Russia
BCPM	British Columbia Provincial Museum
BMS CAT	Blackmon Mooring-Steamatics Catastrophe
BPG	Book and Paper Group of the American Institute for Conservation of Historic and Artistic Works
CAPES	Caucus Archival Project Evaluation Service
CAR	Computer Assisted Research
CBBAG	Canadian Bookbinders and Book Artists Group
CCA	Canadian Council of Archives
CCI	Canadian Conservation Institute
CD/|V	Compact Disc-Video
CIC	Committee on Institutional Cooperation
CIDS	Career Intern Development System (Center for Electronic Records of the National Archives and Records Administration)
CIHM	Canadian Institute for Historical Microproductions
CLR	Council of Library Resources
CMDS	Collection Management and Dissemination Section of the American Library Association
CNRS	Conseil National de Recherche Scientifique (International Council of Scientific Unions)
CPA	Commission on Preservation and Access
CRCDG	Centre de Recherche sur la Conservation des Documents Graphiques
DAT	Digital Audio Tape
EROMM	European Register of Microfilm Masters
EVA	Electronic Imaging and the Visual Arts or Ethylene Vinyl Acetate
FAIC	Foundation for the American Institute for Conservation of Historical and Artistic Works
FIAF	Fédération Internationale des Archives du Film (International Federation of Film Archives)
FIAT	Fédération Internationale des Archives de Télévision (International Federation of Television Archives)

FEDLINK	Federal Library Network
FLICC	Federal Library and Information Center Committee
GBW	Guild of Book Workers
GCI	Getty Conservation Institute
GRASSP	Guide and Resources for Archival Strategic Preservation Planning
HRHRC	Harry Ransom Humanities Research Center, University of Texas at Austin
IASA	International Association of Sound Archives
IASCCP	Indian Association for the Study of Conservation of Cultural Property
ICA	International Council on Archives
ICCROM	International Centre for the Conservation and Restoration of Materials
ICI	Information Conservation, Inc.
IFLA	International Federation of Library Associations and Institutions
IFPI	International Federation of Phonographic Industry
IFPI	International Federation of Photographic Industry
IIC	International Institute for Conservation
INTACH	Indian National Trust for Art and Cultural Heritage
IPI	Image Permanence Institute
IPM	Integrated Pest Management
ISO	International Standards Organization
ISR	Institute for Standards Research
JPEG	Joint Photographic Experts Group (International Standard for Video)
LAPL	Los Angeles Public Library
LBI	Library Bindery Institute
LC	Library of Congress

LCCDG	Library Collection Conservation Discussion Group of the American Institute for the Conservation of Historical and Artistic Works
LSU	Louisiana State University
MARAC	Mid-Atlantic Regional Archives Conference
NAGARA	National Association of Government Archives and Records Administrators
NAPA	National Academy of Public Administration
NARA	National Archives and Records Administration
NARS	National Archives and Records Service
NEA	New England Archivists
NEDCC	Northeast Document Conservation Center, Inc.
NEH	National Endowment for the Humanities
NELINET	New England Library Network
NICLOG	National Information Center for Local Government Records
NISO	National Institute of Standards Organization
NLM	National Library of Medicine
NPO	National Preservation Office of the British Library
NTIS	National Technical Information Service
NVPI	Nederlandse Vereniging van de Platen Industrie (International Federation of Phonographic Industry, Dutch version)
OCLC	Online Computer Library Center
OSHA	Occupational Safety and Health Administration
PALMCOP	Palmetto Archives, Libraries and Museum Council on Preservation
PARS	Preservation and Reformatting Section of the American Library Association
PLMS	Preservation of Library Materials Section of the American Library Association
PPP	Preservation Planning Program of the Association of Research Libraries
PVA	Poly (vinyl) Acetate

RAMP   Records and Archival Management Programme
(United Nations)
RASD   Reference and Adult Services Division of the
American Library Association
RBMS   Rare Book and Manuscript Section of the
American Library Association
RLG   Research Libraries Group
RLMS   Reproduction of Library Materials Section of the
American Library Association
RONDAC   Regional OCLC Network Directors Advisory
Committee
RTSD   Resources and Technical Services Division of
the American Library Association

SAA   Society of American Archivists
SIG   Preservation Special Interest Group of
Association for Library and Information Science
Education
SMPTE   Society of Motion Picture and Television
Engineers
SOLINET   Southeast Library Network
SSCR   Scottish Society for Conservation and
Restoration

TAPPI   Technical Association of Paper and Printing
Industry

UNESCO   United Nations Educational, Scientific and
Cultural Organization
UNISIST   United Nations Intergovernmental Programme
for Cooperation in the Field of Scientific and
Technical Information

WAAC   Western Association for Art Conservation
WISPR   Wisconsin Preservation Program
WORM   Write once, read many (CD-ROM)

Author Index

Aarons, John A., 1, 2, 3
Abadie-Maumert, F. A., 4
Abbot, Laurie, 5, 3854
Abdullin, R. G., 6, 7
Abelson, Philip H., 8
Abid, Abdelaziz, 9
Abid, Ann B., 10
Abt, Jeffrey, 11, 12
Acland, Glenda, 14
Acme Bookbinding, 15
Adams, Alton D., 17
Adams, C., 18
Adams, Dorothy, 19
Adams, Douglas, 19
Adams, R. M., 20
Adams, Thomas R., 21
Adams, Virginia M., 22
Adeloye, Sam, 859
Adelstein, Peter Z., 23, 24, 25, 26, 27,
    28, 29, 30, 31, 32, 33, 34, 35, 36,
    37, 38, 3835, 3840, 3841, 5161,
    5162
Adewoye, Alice Ayanrinda, 39
Adikwu, C. C. A., 40
Adkins, Susan A., 41
Advisory Committee for the
    Coordination of Information
    Systems, 42
Aeppel, Timothy, 43
Agaja, James Abayami, 45, 46
Agarwal, Niraj, 47
Agbabian, M. S., 48, 49
Aginsky, Valery N., 50
Agrawal, Om Prakash, 51, 52, 53, 54,
    55, 56, 57, 112, 4372, 4467, 4560
Agrawal, Usha, 58
Agresto, John, 59
Aitkin, Susan, 61
Akemann, Sandra P., 62
Akio, Yasue, 63
AKZO Chemicals, Inc., 64
Alafiatayo, Benjamin O., 65, 66
Alarcao, Adalio, 3929
Albada, Joan van, 4816
Albert, Michael L., 114
Albrecht-Kunzeri, I. Gabriella, 68, 69
Albright, Gary, 70, 71, 72, 73
Albright, V., 74
Albro, Sylvia Rodgers, 75, 76
Albro, Thomas C., 76, 4972

Alden, Susan, 77
Alecto Historical Editions, 5310
Alegbeleye, Bunmi, 78, 79
Alegbeleye, G. O., 80, 81
Alemma, Anaba, 82
Aleppo, Mario, 83
Alexandre, J. L., 84
Alford, Roger C., 85
Allard, Denise, 89
Allegrini, I., 1464
Allen, David Y., 90
Allen, Douglas P., 91
Allen, John S., 92
Allen, Marie, 93
Allen, Norman S., 94, 95, 96, 97, 98,
    99, 100, 101, 1571, 1572, 1573,
    1574, 1575, 1577
Allen, R. J., 4341
Allen, Susan M., 103, 104, 105, 160,
    1055
Allen, Susan, 102
Allerstrand, Sven, 106
Alley, Brian, 107
Allison, Terry L., 108
Allott, Angela M., 1970, 2300
Allsop Consumer Electronics Division,
    110
Allsopp, Christine, 109
Allsopp, Dennis, 109, 111, 112, 531
Almagro, Bertha R., 113
Alpert, Gary D., 114
Alsford, Dennis B., 115
Alston, R. C., 116
Alston, Robin, 117
Alten, Helen, 118
Altenhoner, R., 119
Ambacher, Bruce I., 120
Ambrose, Timothy, 121
Ambrosino, Leslie, 122
American Association of Law
    Libraries, 123, 3688, 5172, 5173,
    5174, 5175
American Association of Museums,
    124, 125
American Association of State and
    Local History, 5179, 5230, 5320
American Conference of
    Governmental Industrial
    Hygienists, Inc., 126, 127, 128
American Council of Learned

Societies, 129, 1878, 4769
American Craft Council, 5319
American Film Foundation, 5342
American Hospital Association, 130
American Institute for Conservation of
    Historic and Artistic Works, 132,
    133, 134, 135, 136, 137, 138,
    139, 140, 141, 142, 143, 144, 145
American Institute of Architects
    Foundation, 131
American Insurance Services Group
    and Engineering and Safety
    Services, 146
American Library Association, 147,
    148, 149, 150, 151, 152, 153,
    154, 155 156, 157, 158, 178, 179,
    2692, 5180, 5293, 5294, 5295,
    5338, 5296, 5297, 5298, 5299,
    5309
American Library Association,
    Association for Library
    Collections and Technical
    Services, 164, 165, 166, 167,
    168, 169, 170
American Library Association,
    Association of College and
    Research Libraries, 159, 160,
    161, 162, 163,
American Library Association, Rare
    Book and Manuscript Section,
    171, 172, 173, 174, 175, 176, 177
American Museum of Natural History,
    5310
American National Standards Institute,
    180, 181, 182, 183, 184, 185,
    186, 187
American Society for Industrial
    Security, 188
American Society for Testing and
    Materials, 189
American Society of Heating,
    Refrigerating and Air
    Conditioning Engineers, 293
Ames, Anne, 190
Amhert, Kay, 5252
AMIGOS, 191
Amodeo, Anthony J., 192, 193, 194
Ampex Corporation, 195, 196, 197,
    198
Anderson, C. Bertil, 3770
Anderson, David, 199
Anderson, Gretchen E., 862
Anderson, Hazel, 200
Anderson, Jennifer, 201

Anderson, John, 202
Anderson, Karen, 203
Anderson, Kristen, 893
Anderson, L. E., 204
Anderson, Michael, 205
Anderson, Paulene H., 206
Anderson, R. G. W., 207
Anderson, Stanton, 209, 210, 211, 212,
    213
Anderson-Smith, Myrtle, 208
Ando, Masahito, 214
Andre, Pamela Q. J., 215, 1327
Andreae, Christopher, 216
Andrew, Joy, 5214
Andrews, Christopher, 217
Andrews, Harry C., 218
Andrews, Patricia, 219
Andrews, Theresa Meyers, 220, 221
Andrews, William W., 220, 221
Andruss, Harvey A., 222, 223
Ang, Soon, 224
Anglim, Christopher, 225, 226
Anson, Gordon O., 227, 228
Anson, Louisa, 229
Anthony, Joseph, 230
Anthony, William, 5242, 5243
Antwi, I. K., 231
Aparac-Gazivoda, Tatjana, 232
Aparecida de Vries, Marsico, 233
APOYO, 4176
Applebaum, Barbara, 235, 236, 237
Appleyard, John H., 94, 96, 97, 98, 99,
    1573, 1574
Arai, Hideo, 238, 239, 240, 241, 2425
Aranyanak, Chiraporn, 242
Araujo, Maria Fernanda de Sa
    Rodrigues Pinho, 243
Arbogast, David, 244
Arceneaux, Pamela D., 246
Areal Guerra, Rogelio, 252
Arfanis, Peter, 253
Arfield, J. A., 254
Arizona Department of Libraries, 5358
Arizona State Archives, 256, 257
Arlen, Shelly, 258
Armour, Annie, 259
Arney, J. S., 260, 261
Arnold, Richard, 262
Arnold, Robert W., 2204
Arnoult, Jean-Marie, 263, 264, 265,
    266, 267, 268, 269, 1081, 1082,
    3716
Arp, Lori, 270
Arps, Mark, 271

Arrequi, Carmencho, 272
Arruzzolo, G., 273
Arson, Patricia, 274
Arteni, Miriam de, 5278
Artim, Nicholas, 276, 277, 278, 279, 280, 281, 282
Artlip, Paul M., 283
Aschinger, Erhard, 284
Aschner, Katherine, 1629
Ashcroft, Maggie, 285
Ashford, Nicholas A., 286
Ashman, John, 287, 288, 289, 290, 291
Ashok, Roy, 1463
Ashpole, Barry R., 292
Ashton, Jean, 294
Association for Information and Image Management, 295, 296, 297, 298, 299, 300, 301, 302, 303, 304, 305
Association for Recorded Sound Collections, 306
Association of British Columbia Archivists, 307
Association of Forensic Documents Examiners, 308
Association of Higher Education Facilities Officers, 309
Association of Moving Image Archivists, 3810
Association of Records Managers and Administrators, 312, 5277
Association of Records Managers and Administrators International, 310, 311
Association of Reproduction Materials Manufacturers, Inc., 313
Association of Research Libraries, 314, 315, 328, 329, 330, 331, 3815, 3816
Association of Research Libraries, Office of Management Studies, 316, 317, 318, 319, 320, 321, 322, 323, 324, 325, 326, 327
Association pour la Recherche Scientifique sue les Arts Graphique, 332
Astle, Deana L., 334
Atkins, Winston, 335
Atkinson, Ross W., 336, 337, 338, 339
Atwood, Catherine, 340, 341
Atwood, Thomas, 342
Aubey, Rolland, 1944
Aubitz, Shawn, 343, 344
Aubrey, Rolland, 345
Auf der Heide, Erik, 346

Aurand, Gudrun, 5034
Austin, D., 347
Australian Archives, 351, 352, 353, 5139
Australian Council of Libraries and Information Service, 354
Australian Library and Information Association, 3690, 3691, 5330, 5343
Australian National Library, 348, 349, 350, 1472, 3280
Australian Society of Archivists, 355
Avallone, S., 356
Avasthi, A. K., 357
Avedon, Don M., 358, 359
Avrin, Leila, 360
Axelrod, Todd M., 361
Axford, Catherine A., 362
Ayres, J. Mar, 363, 364
Aziagba, Philip C., 365

Baatz, Wilmer H., 366
Babcock, Philip, 367
Babin, Angela, 368
Bachmann, Konstanze, 369, 409, 1255
Baden, Linda, 4342
Baer, Norbert S., 273, 370, 371, 372, 373, 374, 375, 376, 377, 410, 411, 435, 927
Bagg, Thomas C., 378, 379
Bagnall, Roger S., 380, 381, 382
Bahr, Alice Harrison, 383, 384, 385
Bailey, Michelle, 2457
Baillie, Jeavons, 386, 387
Baird, Brian J., 388, 389, 390, 391, 392
Baish, Mary Alice, 393
Bakal, Carl, 394
Baker, Cathleen A., 220, 221, 395, 396, 397
Baker, Don, 398
Baker, John P., 399, 400, 401, 1664, 3617
Baker, Mary T., 402, 1462, 4078, 4820, 4822
Baker, Richard, 403
Baker, Vicki, 404
Baldwin, Gordon, 405
Bales, Erv, 406
Balicki, Alan, 407
Balint, Valerie, 408
Ballard, Mary W., 409, 410, 411
Ballestrem, Agnes, 412
Balloffet, Nelly, 413, 414, 2549

Ballou, Hubbard W., 415
Balon, Brett J., 416, 417, 418
Bancroft, David J., 419
Bangor (ME) Historical Society, 4682
Banik, Gerhard, 420, 421, 422, 423,
    424, 425, 426, 631, 2199, 3078
Banks, Brenda S., 2394
Banks, Elizabeth, 427
Banks, Jennifer, 428
Banks, Joyce M., 429, 430
Banks, Paul N., 372, 373, 374, 431,
    432, 433, 434, 435, 436, 437,
    1214, 1527, 2067, 2762
Bansa, Helmut, 438, 439, 440, 441,
    442, 443, 444, 445, 446, 447
Baptista, J. L., 520
Barber, Giles, 448
Barclay, Bob, 449
Bard, Charleton C., 450, 451, 452,
    2119, 2512
Barford, Michael, 453
Barger, M. Susan, 454, 455, 456, 457,
    458, 459, 460, 461, 462, 463, 464
Barker, Joseph W., 465
Barker, Nicolas, 466, 467, 468, 469,
    470, 471
Barlak, Karen, 472
Barlee, George, 473
Barnard, Bob, 474
Barnett, Richard C., 475
Barrett, D., 476
Barrett, J., 4341
Barrett, John Paul, 477
Barrett, Timothy, 478, 479, 480, 481,
    482, 483, 484, 485, 486, 487
Barrios, Pamela, 201, 488
Barron, Andrew R., 2918
Barry, Richard, 5218
Bartell, Blaine M., 489
Bartolani, Mauro, 597
Barton, John P., 490
Baskin, Judith A. D., 491
Basu, Santi, 1457
Bates, Regis, 492
Batik, Albert L., 493
Battin, Patricia, 494, 495, 496, 497,
    498, 499, 500, 501, 502, 503,
    504, 505, 506, 507, 508, 509,
    510, 511, 512, 513, 514, 515,
    516, 517, 1327
Battista, Carolyn, 518
Battle, Thomas C., 4257
Batton, Susan Sayre, 519
Bauer, Barry J., 4297

Bauer, Richard W., 520, 3749, 3750
Baughman, Mary, 521
Bauman, Barry, 522
Baur, Frederick E., 523
Baynes-Cope, Arthur David, 112, 524,
    525, 526, 527, 528, 529, 530,
    531, 532
Beard, John O., 533
Beardsley, Roger, 534
Bearman, David, 535, 536, 537, 538,
    539, 540
Bearman, Frederick A., 541
Beaubien, Denise M., 542
Beaulieu, Ann Hetch, 543
Beazley, Ken, 544
Beck, James, 545
Bedard, Laura A., 3246
Bedynski, Maria, 546
Behrens, Ulrich, 547
Belanger, Terry, 5176, 5228, 5274
Belcher, Ellen, 335
Belcher, Michael, 548
Bell, Cathy, 201
Bell, Mary Margaret, 549
Bell, Nancy J., 550, 551, 552, 553,
    554, 555, 556
Bellardo, Lew, 557
Bellinger, Meg, 558
Bello, Susan, 559
Beltrame, P. L., 1729
Belvin, Robert J., 560
Belyaeva, Irina, 561
Bendror, Jack, 562
Benedict, Marjorie A., 563
Benedikz, Benedikt S., 564
Bengston, Betty, 4789
Bennett, Richard E., 565
Bentley-Kemp, Lynne, 566
Beöthy-Kozocsa, Ildiko, 567
Berardi, Maria Cristina, 568
Berger, Sidney E., 569, 570, 1102
Bergeron, Rosemary, 571
Bergman, Robert, 572
Bering-Jensen, Helle, 573
Berke, Philip, 574
Berkhout, Sandra, 1473
Berman, Simeon M., 375
Bermane, Daniel, 575
Bernardi, Maria Christina, 576
Berndt, Harold, 577, 578, 579
Bernhardt, Alan J., 580
Berns, Roy S., 581
Bernstein, James, 582
Berrada, Leyla, 583

Berry, Elizabeth, 584
Berry, John, 585
Bertalan, Sarah, 586, 587
Bertoli, Renato, 588
Besser, Howard, 589, 590, 591, 592, 593
Bessonova, N. N., 7
Best, S., 594
Betcher, Melissa Ann, 3825
Bevacqua, Joanna, 595
Beyer, Carrie, 596
Bhajbhuje, M. N., 4560
Bible, Lisa, 4948
Biblio Tech Films, 5291
Bicchieri, Marina, 597
Bierbrier, M. L., 598
Biermann, Christopher, 599
Bigelow, Susan, 600
Bikson, Tora, 601
Billick, David, 602
Billings, Harold, 603, 604
Billington, James H., 605
Binnie, Nancy E., 402, 850, 851, 1462
Bird, Alan J., 607
Birney, Ann E., 608
Bisbing, R. E., 609
Bischoff, Judith J., 1608
Bish, Tony, 610, 611
Biswas, Subhas C., 612
Bittner, Nancy, 613
Bjornson, Pamela, 614
Black, Donald, 3838
Black, James, 3155
Black, Jeremy, 615
Blackman, Kirk, 616
Blades, William, 618
Blaine, Susan, 1875
Blais, Louise, 619
Blake, Evelyn G., 620
Blake, Monica, 621
Blanco, Lourdes, 622
Blank, M. G., 623
Blank, Sharon, 624
Blaser, Linda A., 625, 626
Blecker, Suzanne, 627
Block, Ira, 3034
Bloman, Hans-Evert, 1914
Bloom, Beth, 628
Bloomfield, B. C., 629
Bloomington (IL) Public Library, 630
Bluher, Agnes, 631
Blumenthal, Lyn, 632
Blythe, Valerie, 2184
Blythe-Hill, Victoria, 4078, 4079

Boal, Gillian C., 633
Bodleian Library, 5266
Bogaard, John, 2609, 2610, 2611, 2612, 5029, 5030
Bogdan, Z., 520
Bolhouse, Ann, 634
Bolnick, Doreen, 635
BonaDea, Artemis, 636
Bond, Elayne, 637, 638, 639
Bond, Randall, 640
Bone, Leslie, 1158, 1229
Bonisoli, T., 3145
Bonk, Sharon, 641
Book Manufacturers Institute, 5353
BookLab, Inc., 644, 645, 646, 647, 648, 649, 650, 651, 652, 653, 654, 655, 656, 657, 658
Books Arts Press, 5176, 5228, 5274
Boomgaarden, Wesley L., 660, 661, 662, 663, 664, 665, 666, 667, 668, 669, 670, 671, 672, 673, 940, 1349, 2336, 3448, 3449
Borck, Helga, 674
Boronyak-Szaplonczay, Aranka, 852, 856
Borsa, Gedeon, 675
Borshevsky, Mana, 676
Bosch, Stephen, 677
Boss, Richard W., 678
Boston Library Consortium, 683
Boston Public Library, 684
Boston, George, 679, 680, 681, 682, 1083
Botti, Lorena, 685, 1827
Boudewijns, Leo, 686
Bouley, Raymond J., 687
Bourbeau, David, 5260
Boulle, Pierre H., 688
Bourke, Thomas A., 689, 690, 691, 692, 693, 694, 695, 696, 697, 698
Bowen, Laurel G., 699
Bower, Peter, 700
Bowling, Mary B., 701, 702, 703
Bowser, Eileen, 704
Boyd, Brian, 1340
Boyd, Jane, 705
Boyd-Alkalay, Ester, 5287
Boyer, Candace, 3589
Boyle, Deirdre, 706
Bozeman, Pat, 707
Bradley, Susan, 708
Bradsher, James Gregory, 709, 710
Brady, Diane, 711
Brady, Eileen E., 712, 713

Brahm, Walter, 714
Brandes, Harald, 715, 716
Brandis, Leanne, 717, 718, 719, 4430
Brandt, Astrid-Christiane, 720, 721, 722, 723
Brandt, Charles A. E., 724, 725, 726
Braun, Janice, 727
Braunschweig, Brandt S., 2059
Bravery, A. F., 728
Brawner, Lee B., 729
Brederick, Karl, 730, 731
Brems, Karel, 101, 1577
Brennan, Patricia B. M., 316, 732
Breslauer, B. H., 733
Bressor, Julie P., 734
Brezner, Jerome, 735, 736, 737
Brichford, Maynard J., 738, 739
Bridgeman, Carleen, 740
Bridgland, Janet, 75, 426, 741, 742, 1036, 1488, 1720, 2023, 3010, 3089, 3777, 3782, 3951, 4087, 4144, 4260, 4619, 4822, 4852, 5115
Briggs, James R., 743, 744
Brimblecombe, Peter, 746
Brinckman, F. E., 3532
Brinkhus, Gerd, 747
British Leather Manufacturer's Research Association, 748
British Library National Preservation Office, 750, 751, 752, 753, 754, 755, 756, 757, 758, 759, 760, 761, 762, 763, 764, 765, 766, 767, 3592, 3681, 5270, 5275, 5300
British Library, 749, 768, 5111, 5286
British Museum, Department of Conservation, 5081
British Records Association, 769
British Standards Institution, 770
Broadhurst, Roger N., 771, 772
Brock, David, 5241
Brockman, James, 775, 776
Brock-Nannestad, George, 773, 774
BroDart Company, 777
Brokerhof, Agnes W., 778, 1893
Bromley, David W., 1970, 2300
Brooks, Constance, 779, 780, 781, 3824
Broom, Andrew, 782
Broughton, Heather, 783
Brower, Carol, 4137, 5039
Brown University, 5183
Brown, A. Gilson, 784

Brown, Charlotte B., 175, 785, 786, 787, 1876
Brown, D. W., 788
Brown, Deborah, 1496, 2003
Brown, Frances, 789
Brown, Hyacinth, 790
Brown, J. P., 791
Brown, Jay Ward, 792
Brown, K. C., 793
Brown, Karen E. K., 794, 795
Brown, Margaret, 796
Brown, Meg, 797, 963
Brown, Norman B., 798
Brown, Regina A., 2493
Brown, Rowland C. W., 799
Brown, Royston, 800, 1069, 1123, 5047
Brown, Ruth, 801
Brown, Sandford, 802
Brown, Thomas E., 274
Browne, Malcolm W., 803
Browne, Mark, 804
Brownrigg, Edwin B., 2782, 2783
Brownstein, Mark, 805
Brückle, Irene, 806, 807
Brumbaugh, Robert S., 808
Bruno, Michael H., 809
Bryan, John L., 810
Bryant, Barbara, 811
Buchanan, Sally A., 812, 813, 814, 815, 816, 817, 818, 819, 820, 821, 822, 823, 824, 825, 826, 827, 828, 829
Buchbauer, G., 830
Buchel, Rudy, 831
Buck, George, 832
Buckland, John, 1486
Buckland, Michael K., 833, 2444
Budny, Mildred, 834
Bui, Dominic Nghiep Cong, 835
Bulgawicz, Susan L., 836
Bull, William, 837
Bunch, Antonia J., 838
Burchill, Mary D., 839
Burdick, Amrita J., 840
Bureau, William H., 841
Burgess, David, 842
Burgess, Dean, 843
Burgess, Helen D., 402, 844, 845, 846, 847, 848, 849, 850, 851, 852, 853, 854, 855, 856, 857, 954, 1343, 1462, 1512, 1716, 1822, 2215, 2389, 3492, 3712, 4188, 4399, 4661, 4975

Burke, John, 858
Burke, Robert B., 859
Burn, Margy, 860
Burrow, John, 861
Bussey, Holley, 4501
Butchart, Ian, 1761
Butcher-Younghans, Sherry, 862
Butler, C. E., 863, 1084
Butler, Janet Schecter, 864
Butler, Meredith, 865
Butler, Randall, 866, 867, 868, 869,
    870, 871, 872, 873, 4686
Butler, Robert W., 874
Butterfield, Fiona J., 875, 876
Byer, Richard J., 877
Byrne, Sherry, 878, 879, 880, 881,
    2935
Byrnes, Margaret M., 882, 883, 884,
    885, 886, 887, 888, 889

Cadoree, Michelle, 890
Cady, Susan A., 891
Cahill, T. A., 892
Caiaccia, Laura, 893
Cain, Eugene, 894
Cains, Anthony, 895, 896, 897, 898,
    900, 901, 902
Calabro, Giuseppe, 903
Caldararo, Niccolo, 904, 905, 906
Caldwell, Karen, 907
Calhoun, John M., 908, 972
Cali, Charles L., 909
California State Library, 910, 911
Callery, Bernadette, 3813
Callu, Florence, 912
Calmes, Alan R., 913, 914, 915, 916,
    917, 918, 919, 920, 921, 922,
    923, 924, 925, 926, 927, 928,
    4744, 4751
Calnan, Christopher N., 929, 930, 931,
    2016
Calvini, P., 932
Cameron, E., 933
Cameron, Ross J., 934
Camp, John F., 935
Campbell, Barbara, 936
Campbell, Gregor R., 937, 938
Campbell, Harry H., 939, 940
Campbell, Nancy, 941
Campbell, Robert P., 942
Campion, Susan, 943
Canada Emergency Preparedness, 944
Canada National Archives, 945, 946
Canada National Library, 947, 948,

949, 2646
Canadian Broadcast Corporation, 5347
Canadian Conservation Institute, 950,
    951, 952, 953, 954, 1628, 5187,
    5188, 5190, 5191, 5192, 5193,
    5194, 5195, 5196, 5197, 5198,
    5199, 51200, 5201, 5202, 5203,
    5204, 5205
Canadian Cooperative Preservation
    Project, 955
Canadian Council of Archives, 956,
    957
Canary, James R., 3149
Candee, Mary E., 958, 4557
Caneva, Giulia, 959
Cannabis Press, 5340, 5346
Caputo, Bill, 5321
Cardina, Claire A., 960
Carl, Pauline L., 962
Carlson, Lage, 963
Carmack, Noel A., 964
Carmichael, David W., 965
Carmine, Piero del, 966
Carneiro, Guiomar, 4607
Carniti, P., 1729
Carpenter, Jane, 2099
Carpenter, Kenneth E., 968
Carr, Jane, 968
Carr, Reg, 969
Carroll, Carman U., 970, 971
Carroll, D. C., 3751
Carter, Henry A., 973
Carter, Nancy Carol, 974
Cartier, Georges, 975
Cartier-Bresson, Anne, 976
Carver, Michael, 977
Casagrande, Richard, 958, 4557
Case Western Reserve University,
    5268
Casey, Mike, 978
Cashman, Nadine, 979
Cass, Glen R., 980, 3283, 4042
Cassar, Mary, 977, 981, 982, 983, 984
Cassaro, James P., 985
Caulfield, D. F., 986
Cavasin, Rick, 987
Center for Research Libraries, 988
Central New York Library Resources
    Council, 989
Centre de Conservation du Québec,
    5187, 5188, 5190, 5191, 5192,
    5193, 5194, 5195, 5196, 5197,
    5198, 5199, 51200, 5201, 5202,
    5203, 5204, 5205

Centre de Recherche sur la
  Conservation des
  DocumentsGraphiques, 990
Centre for Photographic Conservation,
  991
Cernic-Letnar, Meta, 4857, 4858, 4859
Chaback, Claudia E., 992
Chace, Myron B., 993, 994
Chadbourne, Robert, 995
Chamberlain, W. R., 996
Champion, Sandra, 997
Chandel, A. S., 998
Chaney, Michael, 999, 2908
Chapman, Patricia, 1000, 1001, 1002,
  1003, 1004
Chapman, Stephen, 2437, 2439, 2440
Chappas, W. J., 1005
Charles, Embert, 1006
Chartand, Robert Lee, 1007
Chavez, Alice M., 1008
Cheatham, Bertha M., 1009
Chen, Chiou-sen Dora, 1010
Chepesiuk, Ronald J., 1011, 1012,
  1013, 1014, 1990
Chernofsky, Jacob L., 1015, 1016
Cherriere, Gerald, 5229, 5236
Chicago Public Library, 1017
Chickering, F. William, 1018
Chiesa, Adele M., 1019
Child, Bob, 1020
Child, Margaret S., 1021, 1022, 1023,
  1024, 1025, 1026, 1027, 1028,
  1029, 1030
Childress, Schelley, 1031
Chiou-sen, Chen, 1032
Chisholm, Bill, 1033
Christensen, Carol, 1034
Christensen, John O., 1035
Christofferson, Lars D., 1036
Chrzastowski, Tina, 1037
Churchville, Lida Holland, 1038
Ciantar, Marcel, 1122
Clack, George, 1040
Clancy, Elizabeth H., 1041
Clapp, Anne F., 1042
Clapperton, John R., 1043
Clareson, Thomas F. R., 1045, 1046,
  1047, 1048, 1813, 2314, 3462
Clark, Lenore, 1049
Clark, Tony, 1050
Clarke, Reginald, 1051, 1052
Clarkson, Christopher, 1053, 1054,
  1055, 1056, 1057, 1058, 1059,
  2718

Clement, Daniel, 1060
Clements, David W. G., 863, 1061,
  1062, 1063, 1064, 1065, 1066,
  1067, 1068, 1069, 1070, 1071,
  1072, 1073, 1074, 1075, 1076,
  1077, 1078, 1079, 1080, 1081,
  1082, 1083, 1084, 1085, 1086,
  1544
Clements, Jeff, 1087
Clemmer, Dan, 1088
Cleveland Area Metropolitian Library
  System, 1089
Cloonan, Michèle Valerie, 1090, 1091,
  1092, 1093, 1094, 1095, 1096,
  1097, 1098, 1099, 1100, 1101,
  1102, 1103, 1261
Cluff, E. Dale, 1104
Clydesdale, Amanda, 1105
Coates, Christine, 1106
Coates, Peter, 1107, 1108, 1109
Coates, W. Paul, 4257
Cobb, David, 1037
Cochrane, Clive, 1110
Cockerell, Douglas, 1111
Cockerline, Neil C., 1112
Coe, Brian, 1113
Cohen, David, 1114
Cohen, Karl, 1115
Cohen-Stratyner, Barbara, 1116
Cojocaru, Viorel, 1117
Cole, Susan, 1118
Coleman, Christopher D. G., 1119,
  1120, 2055
Coles, Laura M., 1121
College of William & Mary, E.G.
  Swem Library, 5327
Colleran, Kate, 1122
Collier, Mel, 1123
Collings, Thomas J., 1124, 1125,
  1126, 1127
Collister, Edward A., 1128, 2075
Colorado State University Libraries,
  1129
Columbia Films, 5357
Columbia Publishing, 5211
Columbia University Libraries, 1130,
  3332, 5339
Columbia University Library, 5311,
Comfort, Louise K., 1131
Commission on Preservation and
  Access, 1132, 1133, 1134, 1135,
  1136, 1137, 1138, 1139, 1140,
  1141, 1142, 1143, 1144, 1145,
  1146, 1147, 1148, 1149, 1150

Committee on Institutional Cooperation, 1151
Committee on Scotish Newspapers, 1152
Committee on the Records of Government, 1153
Commoner, Lucy, 1154
Communacad, The Communications Academy, 5332
Comstock, Gay Stuart, 1157
Comu, E., 1158
Comwell, Willy, 3824
Condon, Garret, 1159
Condrey, Richard, 1160, 1161, 3615
Conference des Recteurs et des Principaux des Universités Québec, 1162
Conford, Karla H., 2635
Connecticut State Librarians Task Force on Preservation of Historical Records, 1167
Connecticut State Library, 1166, 1168
Conrad, Tony, 1169, 1170
Conroy, Tom, 1171, 1172, 1173, 1174
Constance, John A., 1183
Constantinou, Constantina, 1184
Conway, Paul, 1185, 1186, 1187, 1188, 1189, 1190, 1191, 1192, 1193, 1194, 1195, 1196, 1197, 1198, 1199, 1200, 1201, 2438
Cook, Donald C., 4388
Cook, Glenn S., 5026
Cook, L. P., 1202
Cook, Lucy, 5272
Cook, Michael, 1203, 1204
Cook, Terry, 1205
Cook, Virginia, 1206
Cooke, Donald F., 1207
Cooke, George W., 1208, 1209, 1210, 1211, 1212, 1213, 1214, 1215, 1216, 1217, 1218, 1219
Coon, J. Walter, 1220
Cooper, Diane, 861
Cooper, M. D., 1221
Cooper, Mary Campbell, 4122
Coover, James B., 1223
Copeland, Peter, 1224, 1225
Corea, Ishvari, 1226
Corfield, Michael, 1227
Cornish, G. P., 1228
Cornu, Elisabeth, 1229
Cory, Kenneth A., 1230
Costain, Charlie, 1231
Cote, William C., 1232

Coty, Patricia Ann, 1597
Couch, Randall, 1233, 1234
Coughlin, Caroline M., 1235
Coulson, A. J., 1236
Council on Library and Information Resources, 5279
Council on Library Resources, 1237, 1238, 1239, 1240, 1241, 1242, 1243
Couri, Marcia, 3504
Courtot, Marilyn E., 1244, 1245
Cowan, Janet, 1246
Cowan, Wavell F., 1247
Cox, Lynn W., 1248, 1253
Cox, Richard J., 1249, 1250, 1251, 1252, 1253, 1254
Craddock, Ann Brooke, 1255, 1256
Craiag-Bullen, Catherine, 1258
Craig, Roger, 1257
Crane, Marilyn, 1259
Crawford, John C., 1260
Crawford-de Sa, Elizabeth, 1261
Creasy, Helen, 1262
Creguer, Tina L., 1263
Crespo Nogueira, Carmen, 1264, 1265, 1266
Cressman, Shawne Diaz, 1267
Crews, Patricia Cox, 1268, 1269
Cribbs, Margaret A., 1270, 1271
Crocker, Jane, 1272
Croft, Janet Brennan, 1273
Crole, Sandy, 1274
Croll, Michael, 1275
Crombie, L., 1276
Crook, Humphrey L., Jr., 3238
Crosbie, Michael J., 1277
Cross, R. F., 1278
Crowe, William J., 1279
Crowley, Mary Jo, 1280
Cruse, Larry, 1281, 1282, 1283
Crutchfield, Sharon R., 3779
Crystal Productions, 5182
Csaki, Klara, 1284
Csanyi, S, 69
Csenki, Eva, 1285
Cuddihy, Edward F., 1286, 1287
Cullison, Bonnie Jo, 1288, 1289, 1290
Cumming, Neil, 1291
Cummings, Charles F., 1740
Cummings, Martin M., 1292
Cunha, George M., 1293, 1294, 1295, 1296, 1297, 1298, 1299, 1300, 1301, 1302, 1303, 1304
Cunningham, Veronica Calley, 1305

Cunningham-Kruppa, Ellen, 1306, 1307
Cupriks, Kaspars M., 34, 36, 3836, 3840
Curach, Liz, 1308
Curran, Charles, 1309
Curran, Mary, 1677
Currie, Susan, 1311
Curtin, Bonnie Rose, 1312, 1313, 1314, 1315, 1316
Curtis, Marilyn D., 4103
Cytron, Barry D., 1317

D'Angelo, Kathleen T., 1329
D'Arienzo, Daria, 1346
D'Entremont, Susan, 1450
D'Ooge, Craig, 1502
Daar, Sheila, 3433, 3434, 3435
Dachs, Karl, 1318
Daffner, Lee Ann, 1319
Daga Monmany, Josep Maria, 252
Dahlø, Rolf, 1320, 1321
Dainton, Lord, 1322
Dale, Robin, 1323
Dalley, Jane A., 1324
Dalrymple, Helen, 1325, 1913
Dalton, Susan, 1326
Daly, James, 1327
Damme, Philippe van, 2697, 2698
Dance Heritage Coalition, 1328
Dangerfiled, John, 1330
Daniel, Floréal, 1331, 1332, 1333
Daniel, Vinod, 1334, 1335, 1336, 1463, 2558
Daniels, M., 594
Daniels, Vincent, 1337, 1338, 1339, 1340, 1341, 1342, 1343, 1344
Dannelly, Gay, 1345
Darling, Pamela W., 1347, 1348, 1349, 1350, 1351, 1352
Darnell, Polly, 1353
Dartmouth College Library, 1354
Dartnell, Jean, 1355
Das, A. C., 1356
Das, Sudhir Kumar, 1357
Dasgupta, Kalpana, 51, 357, 612, 1226, 1358, 2263, 2327, 2461, 2481, 2554, 3386, 4041
Daval, Nicola, 1359, 3816
Davies, J. Eric, 5109
Davies, John, 1360
Davies, Walter E., 1361
Davis, Donald G., Jr., 432, 1941
Davis, Jerilyn Glenn, 5141

Davis, Jinnie Y., 1279
Davis, Julianna, 1362, 5094
Davis, Mary B., 1363, 1364
Davis, Nancy, 1037, 1365
Davis, Peter, 1366
Davis, R. H., 2399
Davis, Robert H., 1367
Davis, Robin J., 1368
Davis, Sheryl Jean, 1259, 1369, 1370
Davis, Susan W., 1371
Dawood, Rosemary, 1372
Dawson, John E., 1373, 4426, 4427
Day, Michael William, 1374
Day, Rebecca, 1375
de Sa Rodrigues Pinho, Fernanda, 243
De Stefano, Paula, 1469, 1470, 1471
De Whitt, Benjamin L., 1474
Deal, Carl W., 1376
Deal, Suzanne, 1377
Dean, John F., 1378, 1379, 1380, 1381, 1382, 1383
Dean, Susan Thach, 1384
Dearing, Julie A., 1385
Dearman, J. Andrew, 1386
Dearstyne, Bruce, 1387
DeBakey, Lois D., 1388, 1389
DeBakey, Selma, 1389
Debelius, Elizabeth, 1390
DeCandido, GraceAnne Andreassi, 1391, 1392, 1393, 1394, 1395, 1396, 1397, 1398
DeCandido, Robert, 1399, 1400, 1401, 1402, 1403, 1404, 1405, 1406, 1407, 1408, 1409, 1410, 1411, 1412, 1413, 1414, 1415, 1416, 1417, 1418, 1419, 1420, 1421, 1422, 1423, 1424, 1425, 1426, 1427, 1428, 1429, 1430, 1431
DeCesare, Kyman B. J., 1432
Deeney, Marion, 1434
DeFelice, Barbara, 1435
Deitch, Joseph, 1436
Deken, Jean Marie, 1437
DeLancie, Philip, 1438
Delaware Historical Records Advisory Board, 1439
DelCarmine, P., 1440
Deleray, John E., 4261
DeLoughry, Thomas J., 1441
Demas, Samuel, 1442, 1443, 5118
Demco, 1444, 5215, 5333
Demeroukas, Marie, 2736
Demiller, A. L., 1445
Den Bleyker, Dan, 1446

Denham, Patricia K., 5175
Denlinger, David L., 2608
Densky, Lois R., 1447
Densky-Wolff, Lois R., 1448, 1449
DePew, John N., 1451, 1452, 1453,
    1454, 1455, 1456, 1457, 1458
DePhilips, Henry A., Jr., 1459
Derben, Peter, 1460
Dernovskova, Jana, 1461, 1545, 1546
Derrick, Michele R., 402, 1462, 1463
DeSantis, F., 1464
DeSantis, Pia C., 1465
Desmarais, Ellen, 1466, 1467, 1468
Deventer, Ronald Van, 1473, 2105
Devine, Scott, 4379
Dhawan, Shashi, 57, 112, 1475, 3129,
    4560
Di Palo, V., 1464
Dick, Ernest J., 1477
Dickson, Kathy, 1478
Diers, Fred V., 1479
DiGiulio, Edmund, 3881
Dillon, Phyllis, 1480
DiMichele, Donna Longo, 1481
Dirda, Marion Peck, 4305
Dirda, Michael, 1482
Dirks, J. Leland, 1483
Ditmitroff, Michael, 1487
Dobrusina, S. A., 623
Dobrusina, Svetland A., 1488, 1489
Dodson, Suzanne Cates, 1490, 1491,
    1492, 1493
Doinov, D., 1494
Dollar, Charles M., 1495
Domer, Margaret, 826
Donahue, Mary Kay, 1496, 2003
Donaldson, Jean, 1290
Donnelly, Helene, 1497, 1498, 1499
Donnithorne, Alan, 1500
Donovan, Joanne, 1501
Dorfman, Harold H., 1503, 1504
Dorn, Georgette M., 1505
Dorning, David, 1506
Dorrell, Peter G., 1507
Dosunmi, J. A., 1508
Dovey, Bryan, 1509
Dowell, Connie Vinita, 1510
Dowlin, Kenneth E., 2950, 2951
Down, Jane L., 1511, 1512
Downes, Robin N., 1513
Downing, Alice, 1514, 1515, 1516,
    1517
Doyle, Robert P., 1518
Drake, Cindy Steinhoff, 1519

Dremaite, Grazina, 1520
Drewes, Jeanne M., 1521, 1522
Driessen, Karen C., 1523
Drogin, Marc, 1524
Droguet, A., 1525
Drukker, Leendert, 1526
Druzik, James R., 364, 402, 980, 1527,
    1528, 1529, 4831
Dryden, Donna, 1530
Drysdale, Laura, 1531
Dubin, Fred, 1532
Duchemin, Pierre Yves, 1533
Duchesne, Roddy, 1534
Duckett, R. J., 1535
Duffy, Stephen, 853
Dufour, Frank, 1537
Dugal, H. S., 1536
Dunlap, Ellen, 1538
Dunn, Austin B., 1539
Dunn, F. Ian, 1540
Dupont, Jerry, 974, 1541
Duranti, Luciana, 1542
Dureau, Jeanne-Marie, 1543, 1544
Durovic, Michel, 1545, 1546, 1547,
    4435
Dutschke, D., 892
Dvoriashina, Zinaida P., 1548, 1549
Dvorzak, Marie, 4153
Dwan, Antoinette, 1550, 1551
Dyal, Carole, 3185
Dyer, Victor, 1552
Dyson, Brian, 1553

Eastman Kodak Company, 1554, 1555,
    1556
Easton, Roger, 1557, 1558
Eaton, Fynnette L., 1559, 1560
Eaton, George T., 1561, 1562, 1563
Eaton, Linda, 876
Eaton, Nancy L., 215
Eberhardt, Fritz, 1564
Eberhardt, Keith R., 928
Ector, F. F. M., 3104
Eden, Paul, 1565, 1566, 1567, 1568,
    1671, 1672, 3026, 3027
Edge, Michele, 94, 95, 96, 97, 98, 99,
    100, 101, 1569, 1570, 1571,
    1572, 1573, 1574, 1575, 1576,
    1577
Edmondson, Ray, 1578
Edmondson, Thomas M., 456
Edwards, C. J., 2242
Edwards, Carol, 2901
Edwards, John D., 1580

Efremov, Yvonne, 3951
Eilers, Delos, 1581
Eisenberg, Daniel, 1582
Elder, Nelda J., 1583
Eldred, R. A., 892
Eldridge, Betsy Palmer, 1584
Elkington, Nancy E., 889, 1585, 1586, 1587, 1588, 1589, 1590, 2785, 3004, 4930, 4956
Ellenberg, Karen T., 1591
Ellenport, Sam, 1592
Elliott, Lynn, 1593
Ellis, Margaret Holben, 376, 1594
Ellis, Roger, 527, 530, 532
Ellison, J. Todd, 1595
Ellison, John W., 1596, 1597
Ellison, Robert, 210
Emerton, Bruce, 542
Empsucha, Joseph G., 1598
Encyclopedia Britannia, 5208
England, Claire, 1600
Enright, Brian, 1601
Entwistle, Rosemary M., 1602, 1603, 1604
Epstein, Dena J., 1605
Erhardt, David, 1606, 1607, 1608, 1609, 1610, 1611, 1612, 4852
Erickson, Harold M., 1613
Erickson, Lori, 1614
Ershler, Margaret, 1615
Espadaler, Ignazi, 4260
Espinosa, Robert, 201, 1616, 1617
Esserman, Mia, 827
Ester, Michael, 1618, 1619, 1620, 1621
Etherington, Don, 705, 963, 1622, 1623, 1624, 1625, 1626, 1627, 4089
Eulenberg, Julia Niebuhr, 1629, 1630
European Register of Microfilm Masters, 1631
Eusman, Elmer, 1632
Evans, Bronwen, 1633
Evans, Debra, 1634
Evans, Frank B., 1635
Evans, G. Edward, 1636
Evans, Karen, 1600, 5120
Evetts, Debra M., 1628, 1637, 3778
Ezennia, Steve E., 1639, 1640, 1641, 1642, 1643, 1644

Fabry, Frank, 1645
Fairbrass, Sheila, 1646, 1647, 1648, 1649

Fairfield, John R., 1650
Falen, Martha, 1651
Fall, T., 3283
Fang, Josephine R., 1652
Fang, X., 1653
Fantaine, Jean-Marc, 1654
Fantel, Hans, 1655
Farant, Jean-Pierre, 3052
Farkas, Csilla, 1656
Farr, George F., 1657, 1658, 1659
Farrar, Mark, 3712
Farrell, Barbara, 1660
Farrell, Eugene, 3218
Farrell, Roberta, 1661
Farrelly, R. O., 1662
Farrington, James, 1663
Fasana, Paul J., 1664
Fath, M., 2240
Faurie, Annari, 3777
Fazakas, Karoly, 1665
Feather, John, 1566, 1567, 1568, 1666, 1667, 1668, 1669, 1670, 1671, 1672
FEDLINK, 3680, 4175
Feilden, Barnard, 1673
Feldman, Larry H., 2119
Felker, Aimee M., 1674
Feller, Robert L., 1675, 1676, 1677, 1678, 2609, 2610, 2611, 2612
Fellers, Christer, 1679
Fennell, Janice C., 1680
Fennelly, Lawrence, 1681
Fensterman, Duane W., 1682
Fenton-Huie, Shirley, 1683
Ferguson, Ann, 1684
Ferreira de Andrade, Joaquim Marcal, 243
Ferrigno, Jane G., 5057
Ferris, Valerie, 1685, 1686, 1687, 1688, 1689
Fickeissen, Janet L., 1690
Fidler, Linda M., 1691
Field, Jeffrey, 1692, 1693, 1694
Filippi, M., 3145
Film for the Humanities and Sciences, 5286
Filter, Susan, 1695
Fine Arts Trade Guild, 1696
Fineberg, Gail, 1697
Finlay, Douglas, 1698
Fischer, Audrey, 1700
Fischer, Barbara, 1701
Fisher, David, 1702
Fisher, Steven P., 1704

Fisher, Tom, 1703
Fiske, B., 2501
Fitzhugh, Gerald, 1740
Fitzsimmons, Joseph J., 1706
Fitzsimons, Eileen, 1705
Flagg, Gordon, 1707, 1708
Flamm, V., 2199
Flavin, Richard, 5318
Fleischauer, Carl, 1709, 1710, 1711,
    1712
Flesch, Balint, 1713
Fletcher, John M., 1714
Flieder, Françoise, 1331, 1332, 1333,
    1715, 1716, 1898, 2624, 2975
Flora, Nirmolini V., 1717
Florentine, Frank A., 1718
Flores, Bess, 1719
Florian, Mary-Lou E., 1720, 1721,
    1722, 1723, 1724, 1725
Florida State Historical Records
    Advisory Board, 1726
Florida State University, 1727
FMC Corporation-Lithium Division,
    1728
Focher, B., 1729
Fogle, Sonja, 1730, 4008
Foldessy, Peter, 1731
Fontaine, Jean-Marc, 1732
Foot, Mirjam M., 1733, 1734, 1735,
    1736, 1737, 1738, 1739
Ford, Bruce E., 1740
Ford, David, 2995
Ford, Jeannette White, 1741
Forde, Helen, 1742, 1743, 1744, 1745,
    1746, 1747, 1748
Forster, Geoffrey, 1749
Forster, J. P., 1750
Fortson, Judith, 1751, 1752, 1753,
    1754, 1755
Fortson-Jones, Judith, 1756, 1757,
    1758
Fossey, Richard, 4306
Foster, Clifton D., 1759
Foster, Stephen, 1760
Fothergill, Richard, 1761
Fowlstrunker, Skillin Q., 1762
Fox, Barry, 1763
Fox, John, 4890
Fox, Lisa L., 1764, 1765, 1766, 1767,
    1768, 1769, 1770, 1771, 1772,
    1773
Fox, Peter, 1774
Frakes, Susan Mackey, 1776
France: Archives Nationales, 1777,
    1778, 1779
Francis, David, 94, 97, 98, 1780
Francis, Kathy, 1781
Frangakis, Evelyn, 1782, 1783
Frank, Jerome P., 1784, 1785
Franklin, Ben, 5217
Franklin, Phyllis, 1786
Frase, Robert W., 1787, 1788
Fraser, Susan, 1364
Frazier, Allan, 1789
Fredberg, Birgit, 1790
Fredericks, Maria, 1791, 1792
Fredriksson, Berndt, 1793
Freedman, Patricia, 1794
Freestone, Iasn C., 4831
Freunsch, Gail L., 1795
Frey, Franziska, 1975, 1976, 3837
Frieder, Richard, 1151, 1796, 1797,
    1798, 1799, 1800, 1801
Friedman, Michael A., 2441
Friend, F. J., 1802
Frinkling, E. J., 601
Frost, Gary, 1803, 1804, 1805, 1806,
    1807, 1808, 1809, 1810, 1811,
    1812, 1813
Fu, Paul S., 1814
Fuchs, Robert, 1815
Fujii, Etsuo, 1816
Funston-Mills, Sarah, 1817
Furbished, Nouleigh Rhee, 1762
Fusco, Margaret A., 12
Fusco, Marilyn, 1818
Fusonie, Alan, 1819, 1820
Futernick, Robert, 1822

Gaba, Theodosia S. A., 1823
Gadd, Geoffrey M., 1923
Galabro, Guiseppe, 1825
Gallo, Fausta, 1826, 1827, 1828, 1829
Galo, Gary A., 1830
Galvin, Theresa, 1831
Galvin, Thomas J., 3644
Gancedo, Gely, 5115
Ganorker, M. C., 1973
Garcia, Debra A., 1832
Gardner, H. Wayne, 416, 417, 418
Garlan, Bonnie, 1833
Garlick, Karen, 437, 587, 978, 1183,
    1446, 1754, 1755, 1834, 1835,
    1836, 1957, 2203, 2467, 2494,
    2748, 2759, 2888, 3134, 3290,
    3301, 3354, 3355, 3362, 3467,
    3468, 3594, 3705, 3937, 3990,

4275, 4304, 4675, 4901, 4911, 5004, 5023
Garnier, Chantel, 1894, 1898
Garrett, John, 4931
Garrison, M. A., 2763
Gartner, Richard, 1837
Gaskill, Deborah, 1838
Gast, Monika, 1839
Gatley, Donald P., 1840
Gaughan, Thomas M., 1841, 1842
Gauthier, France, 89
Gavrel, Katherine, 1843, 1844, 1845
Gavrel, Sue, 2965
Gaylord Bros., 1846, 1847, 1848, 1849, 1850
Geh, Hans-Peter, 1851, 1852
Gehl, Paul, 1853
Gehman, David R., 543
Geil, Jean, 1037
Geller, L. D., 1854
Geller, Sidney B., 1855
Genett, Mary E., 1856
Genovese, Robert, 1857
Gent, Megan, 1858, 1859
George, Gerald, 1860
George, M., 1861
George, Susan C., 1862, 1863, 1864
George, Thelma H., 1865
Gerhardt, Claire, 1867
Gerlach, Gary, 1868
Gertz, Janet E., 786, 1869, 1870, 1871, 1872, 1873, 1874, 1875, 1876
Gertzog, Alice, 1235
Gess, J. M., 1877
Getty Art History Information Program, 1878
Getty Conservation Institute, 1879, 1880, 1881, 3697
Gibb, Ian P., 1882
Gibert Vives, Josep Maria, 252
Gibson, Gerald D., 1883, 1884, 1885
Gibson, Sarah Scott, 2357
Gibson, Tracy, 1886
Giese, Diana, 1887, 1888, 1889
Gilberg, Mark, 1890, 1891, 1892, 1893, 1894, 1895, 1896, 1940
Gilbert, Richard, 2457
Gilderson-Duwe, Caroline, 1897
Gill, M., 4563
Gillet, Martine, 1898
Ginelli, William S., 49, 457, 4087
Ginn, Ed, 1899
Ginnelli, William S., 1900
Giri, A. P., 456, 457

Glaister, Donald, 5235, 5261
Glaser, Mary Todd, 1901, 1902, 1903
Glastrup, Jens, 1904
Gleaves, Edwin S., 1905
Glenewinkel, Jill, 1906
Gnirrep, W. K., 1908
Godden, Irene P., 1909
Goetting, Ronald R., 211, 2513
Goldberg, Martin, 1910
Goldman, Nancy, 1911
Goltz, Douglas, 854
Goodair, Christine, 1912
Goodrum, Charles, 1913
Goodwin, Mary Jo, 216, 3578
Gooes, Roland, 1914
Gordon, Ann D., 1915
Gordon, Barbara, 1916
Gordon, Ralph W., 1917
Goswami, Badri P., 1918
Gottlieb, Adam, 1919
Gottlieb, Jane, 3939
Gould, Constance C., 1920
Gould, Stephen B., 1921
Gourley, Paula, 5244
Govan, J. F., 1922
Gow, Neil A. R., 1923
Gracy, David B., 1924
Grade Finders, Inc., 1156
Graf, Jace, 1925, 1926
Grafe, Joyce, 5303
Graff, Michael W., 1927
Graham, Crystal, 1928
Graham, Peter S., 1929, 1930, 1931, 1932, 1933
Grandinette, Maria, 1934, 1935
Grange, Maurice, 966
Grant, Joan, 1936
Grant, John H. A., 1895
Grant, Sharlane Tyra, 1937
Grantham, Sandra, 1938
Graphic Arts Technical Foundation, 5331
Grattan, David W., 855, 918, 1939, 1940
Grauer, Sally, 1941, 1942, 1943, 1944
Graves, James S., 1945
Gray, Elizabeth, 5110
Great Britain: Conservation Unit, 1946, 1947
Great Britain Public Record Office, 1948
Greater Northeastern Regional Medical Program, 1949
Green, Deidre, 1950

Green, Kevin, 1951
Green, L. R., 1952
Green, Paul Robert, 1953, 1954
Greenberg, Gerald S., 1955
Greenblatt, Robyn, 5082
Greene, Harlan, 1956, 1957
Greene, Virginia, 1958
Greenfield, Jane, 1111, 1959, 1960, 1961, 4890
Greenstein, Shane, 1962
Griesbrecht, Walter W., 1534
Griffen, Agnes M., 1963
Griffin, Marie P., 1964, 1965
Griffith, J. W., 1966
Grimard, Jacques, 1967, 1968
Grimstad, Kirsten, 1969
Grimwood-Jones, Diana, 1970
Gromov, O. A., 3392
Grosch, Mary F., 512, 4991
Grosjean, Daniel, 980, 1971, 1972, 5048, 5049, 5050
Grosjean, Eric, 5050
Grosso, Vilia, 932, 1973
Grothy, Mina Jane, 3707
Grover, Mark L., 1974
Grum, Franc, 581
Gschwind, Rudolf, 1975, 1976
Guay, Louise, 1977
Gubbins, Donald, 1978
Guichen, Gael de, 1979, 1980
Guido, John F., 713
Guild of Book Workers, 1981, 1982, 5231, 5232, 5233, 5234, 5235, 5236, 5237, 5238, 5239, 5240, 5241, 5242, 5243, 5244, 5245, 5246, 5247, 5248, 5249, 5250, 5251, 5252, 5253, 5254, 5255, 5256, 5257, 5258, 5259, 5260, 5261, 5262, 5263, 5264, 5265, 5356
Guineau, B., 1716
Guldbeck, Per E., 1983
Gulick, R. van, 1984
Gulick, Susan H., 1985
Gull, Ian, 5301
Gunderson, D. E., 986
Gunn, Michael J., 1986, 1987
Gunter, Linda, 1988
Gurnaguel, Narayr, 1989
Gustafson, Ralph A., 1990
Guttman, Charles M., 1991, 1992, 3532
Guyot, Don, 5216, 5253
Gwiazda, Henry J., 1993

Gwin, James.E, 1994
Gwinn, Nancy E., 1995, 1996, 1997, 1998, 1999, 2000, 2001, 2002
Gyeszly, Suzanne D., 1496, 2003, 3885

H.W. Wilson Company, 5177
Haberditzl, Anna, 730
Hackman, Larry J., 2004
Hackney, Stephen, 2005, 2006
Hadgraft, Nicholas, 466, 551, 743, 824, 833, 898, 899, 900, 1057, 2007, 2008, 2009, 2010, 2011, 2020, 2312, 2936, 3491, 3626, 3628, 3669, 5059
Hager, Michael, 2012
Hahn, Bessie K., 2013
Hahn, Ellen Z., 2014
Haines, Betty M., 930, 2015, 2016
Haines, John H., 2017
Haines, Michael, 2018
Häkkänen, H. J., 2019
Hale, Catherine, 1038
Hales, Robert, 2020
Hall, Hal W., 2021
Hall, Susan, 2022
Hallebeek, Pieter B., 2023, 4340
Haller, Ursula, 631
Hamber, Anthony, 1976, 2024, 2734
Hamburg, Doris A., 2025
Hamilton, John Maxwell, 2026
Hamilton, Marsha J., 2027, 3826
Hamilton, Robert M., 2029
Hammer, John H., 2030
Hammill, Michele E., 2031
Hammond, Lorne F., 2032
Hampton, Georgia V., 1990
Hand, J. Carlos, 363, 364
Handley, Mhairi, 2033
Hanff, Peter, 2034, 2035
Hanington, David J., 2036, 2037
Hankins, Joseph, 2038
Hanks, Peter, 2039
Hanley, James, 3052
Hanlin, Jim, 4272
Hanlon, Gordon, 1334
Hansen, Charles, 2040
Hansen, Eric F., 144
Hanson, Carolyn Z., 2041
Hanson, Gretchen M., 2042
Hanthron, Ivan, 1775, 2043, 2044, 2045, 2526, 3462, 3964
Hanus, Jozef, 2046, 2047, 2048, 2049, 2050

Hanus, Karen L., 2051
Hanzlova, Jirina, 2052
Happoldt, Anita O., 2053
Harmon, James D., 2054, 2055
Harper, James, 2056
Harriman, Robert, 2057
Harrington, Gary, 2058
Harrington, Richard M., 2059
Harris, Carolyn L., 382, 2060, 2061,
     2062, 2063, 2064, 2065, 2066,
     2067, 2068
Harris, John, 2069
Harris, Kenneth E., 2070, 2071, 2072,
     2073
Harris, Oliver D., 2074
Harrison, Alice W., 2075
Harrison, Donald F., 2115
Harrison, Helen P., 2076, 2077, 2078,
     2079, 3456
Harrop, Dorothy A., 2080
Hart, Andrew, 2081, 2316
Hartley, Jeffery T., 2082
Harvard University Library, 2084,
     2085, 2086
Harvey, Christopher, 2087
Harvey, Ross, 2088, 2089, 2090, 2091,
     2092, 2093
Haserot, Karen E., 2094
Haskins, Scott M., 2095
Hasluck, Paul N., 2096
Hastings, Carole Marie, 2097
Hatai, A., 3249
Hatchfield, Pamela, 2098, 2099
Hauptman, Robert, 3969
Hauser, Robert, 2100, 2101
Hauser, S., 4563
Havard-Williams, P., 2102
Havermans, John, 1473, 2103, 2104,
     2105
Hawke, Brian, 3678
Haworth-Booth, Mark, 1113
Hayes, Martin, 101, 1571, 1577
Hayes, Robert Mayo, 2106
Haynes, Douglas, 2107
Hazen, Dan C., 2108, 2109, 2110
Headley, John W., 2111
Heaney, Martin, 1499
Heckmann, Harald, 2112
Hedley, Gerry, 2113
Hedlin, Edie, 2114, 2115
Hedstrom, Margaret, 2116, 2117, 2118
Heidke, Ronald L., 2119
Heidtmann, Toby, 2120
Heijst, Jacob van, 3666

Heiser, Lois, 2121
Heitshu, Sara, 2122
Heller, Jonathan, 2123
Hellinga, Lotte, 1601
Helliwell, John, 2124
Hellman, Ethel, 5327
Helmer, Normandy, 2125
Hendee, J. C., 2126
Henderson, Cathy, 2127
Henderson, Harold, 2128
Henderson, Kathryn L., 2129, 2130
Henderson, William T., 2131, 2132
Hendley, Tony, 2133, 2134, 2135
Hendrickson, Gordon O., 4200
Hendriks, Klaus B., 2136, 2137, 2138,
     2139, 2140, 2141, 2142, 2143,
     2144, 2145, 2146, 2147, 2148
Hengemihle, Frank H., 2149, 4187,
     4188, 4189, 4190
Henneberger, Bob, 2150
Hennis, Y., 3350
Henry, J. D., 2151
Henry, Walter, 2152, 2153, 2154
Henshaw, Bruce C., 2155
Henty, Margaret, 2156
Hermans, Johan, 1649
Hernon, Peter, 4139
Herdal, Steen, 5357
Herdrich, Peter, 5176, 528, 5274
Herrick, Roxanna, 2158, 2159
Herskovitz, Robert, 2160
Herther, Nancy, 2161
Hessler, David W., 1230
Heuer, H. D., 3751
Hey, Margaret, 932, 1828, 2162, 2163,
     2164, 2165, 2166, 2167
Heynen, Jeffrey, 2168
Hickin, Norman, 2169
Hicks, Catherine, 2170
Hicks, George, 2171
Hiebert, Rhonda, 2172
Higginbotham, Barbra Buckner, 2173,
     2174, 2175, 2176
Higgins, Richard, 2177
Hightower, Marvin, 2178
Hildesheimer, Françoise, 2179
Hill & Dale Press and Typefoundry,
     5207
Hill, Gregory, 2146, 2180, 2181
Hill Monastic Manuscript Library,
     5272
Hill, Thomas T., 458, 2182
Hille, Jenny, 414, 1961
Hills, Richard L., 2183

Hillyer, Lynda, 2184
Himmelstein, Paul, 237
Hincha, Richard, 2185
Hindbaugh, Nick, 2186
Hirshon, Arnold, 1931
Hirst, Warwick, 2187
Hirtle, Peter B., 2188
Hisham, Mohamed W. M., 1971
Ho, Elizabeth, 2189
Ho, Kathy, 2190
Hobbs, Mary, 2191
Hodge, Stanley P., 2192
Hodges, Anthony, 2193
Hodgson, M. E., 2194
Hoedemaeker, Liesbeth, 2195
Hoeven, K. van der, 3104
Hofenk de Graaff, Judith H., 2196, 2197
Hofer, Hans H., 446
Hoffman, Ana, 2198
Hoffmann, Frank, 2200
Hoffmann, Hillel L., 2201
Hofmann, C., 2199
Hofmann, Christa, 4820
Hogan, Patricia, 3614
Holbrook, Brice G., 1583
Holden, Jill R. J., 2202
Holden, Maria S., 2203, 2204, 2395
Holder, Carol, 2205
Holems, William M., 4744
Holford, Pearl, 2206
Holland, Cheryl, 5388
Holland, Michael E., 2207, 2208
Holley, Robert P., 2209, 2210, 2211
Holliday, Paul, 2212
Hollinger, William K., 2213, 4845
Holm, Bill, 2214
Holm, Susanne Marie, 2215
Holmes, John, 2216
Hon, David N.-S, 2217
Honea, Ted, 2040, 2218, 2219
Hookham, Francis, 2220
Hopkins, Diane, 2142, 2221
Hopkins, Isabella, 2901
Hopkins, Richard, 5207
Hopwood, Walter, 1611
Horakova, Hana, 2222
Horder, Alan, 2223
Horie, C. Velson, 94, 95, 96, 97, 98, 99, 100, 1571, 1574, 1575, 2224
Horney, Karen, 2225
Horton, Richard W., 2226, 2227
Horton, Warren, 2228
Horvath, David G., 2229

Houston, Penelope, 2230
Howard, R. C., 2232
Howden, Norman, 1045
Howe, Lindsay, 2233
Howe, Michael, 2234
Howell, Alan G., 2235, 2236, 2237, 2238
Howington, Tad, 2239
Hu, Wendy, 2704
Hua, Hai-Yen, 2240
Hubbard, Lorry, 5332
Hubbard, William J., 2241
Hudson, F. Lyth, 2242
Huebe, Robert, 1390
Humbert, Jean-Marcel, 4493
Humphrey, Bruce J., 2243, 2244, 2245, 2246
Humphreys, Betsy L., 2247, 4765
Hunderman, Harry J., 2248
Hunter, Dard, 1126, 1247
Hunter, John E., 2249
Huntley, Michael, 1053
Huntsberry, J. Stephen, 2250, 2251, 2252, 2253, 2254, 2255, 2256
Hutson, Jennifer, 2257
Huttemann, Thomas J., Jr., 2511, 2513
Hutton, Brian G., 2258, 2259, 2260

Ibrahimah, M. Z., 2261
Idsala, Mohamed, 2262
Ilbury, Terence James, 2263
Illinois Cooperative Conservation Program, 4237, 5335, 5336, 5348
Illinois Library Association, 2264
Image Permanence Institute, 2265
Imhoff, Hans-Christoph von, 2266, 2267
Impagliazzo, Giancarlo, 685, 903, 1825
Inaba, M., 2268
Inch, Dennis, 2269
Indicator, N., 1637, 2501, 3778
Information Systems Consultants, Inc., 2270
Inland Marine Underwriters Association, 2271
Institute of Paper Science and Technology, 2272
International Archival Round Table Conference, 2273
International Association of Sound Archives, 2274
International Council of Museums, 2277, 2278, 2279

International Federation of Film
    Archivists, 2280
International Federation of Library
    Associations and Institutions,
    2281, 3716
International Paper Corporation, 5345
Intner, Sheila S., 2282, 2283
Iowa Cooperation Preservation
    Consortium, 1725
Iowa State University, 2285, 5329
Iraci, Joe, 2146
Irblich, Eva, 2286
Iron Range Research Center, 5280
Irwin, Barbara, 2498
Irwin, John, 2287
Isenberg, Laurie, 2288
Ispahany, Rafat, 595
Istor Publications, 5213, 5216, 5181,
    5186, 5219, 5220, 5221, 5222,
    5302, 5303, 5312, 5316, 5317,
    5344, 5351, 5352
Iverson, Diann S., 2290
Iverson, Tommy, 2289, 2291
Izbicki, Thomas M., 2292

Jackanicz, Donald, 2293
Jackson, Cheryl, 2294, 2295
Jackson, Christopher, 1912
Jackson, Marie, 2296, 2297, 2298,
    2299, 2300
Jacobs, Donna, 2301
Jacobsen, Pamela D., 2302
Jacobson, Bruce F., 2303, 2304
Jacobson, R. E., 793
Jagschitz, Gerhard, 2305
Jakubs, Deborah, 2306
James, Linda, 2307
Januszonok, Teresa, 2308, 2309
Japan National Tourist Organization,
    5281
Jarernporn, Penpan, 2310
Jarvis, Helen, 253
Jefferson, Karen L., 2311
Jefferson, Melvin, 2312
Jennings, Tom, 2313
Jenny, Kriss, 2314
Jensen, Craig W., 2315, 5247
Jensen, Kirsten, 828, 2316
Jerde, Curtis D., 2317
Jermann, Peter, 2318, 2319, 2320
Jerry Bowen, I., 4219
Jessee, W. Scott, 2321
Jessup, Wendy Claire, 2322
Jett, Maureen Y., 2323

Jewett, Kenneth L., 1991, 1992, 3532
Jewitt, Crispin, 2324
Jewitt, Terence S., 94, 95, 96, 97, 98,
    99, 100, 101, 1572, 1573, 1574,
    1575
Jimenez, Nancy, 2325
Jionji Press, 5318
Jirasova, H., 1461
Jirat-Wasiutynski, Thea, 2326
Jirovetz, L., 830
Jivendra, Dr., 2327
Johansson, Eve, 2328
Johns Hopkins University, Milton S.
    Eisenhower Library, 2329, 2694
    5326
Johnsen, Jesper Stub, 2330, 2331
Johnson, Arthur W., 2332, 2333
Johnson, Bruce, 635
Johnson, Denise J., 2939
Johnson, Jennifer, 4456
Johnson, Linda B., 2334
Johnson, Peggy, 667, 2335, 2336,
    2453, 4285
Johnson, Steve, 2337
Johnson, William S., 2338
Johnston, James R., 2339
Jolliffe, John, 2340
Jones, Barclay G., 2341, 2342
Jones, C. Lee, 1458, 2343
Jones, Daniel P., 2344
Jones, David R., 2345
Jones, Fiona, 2346, 2347
Jones, G. William, 2348
Jones, Helen, 2349
Jones, Karen, 1577, 2350, 2351, 2352,
    2353, 2354, 2355, 2356, 2767,
    3537
Jones, Lois Swan, 2357
Jones, Lyn Maralyn, 2358, 2359, 2360,
    2361, 3410
Jones, Lyn, 1943
Jones, Michael C., 3283
Jones, Norvell M. M., 2362, 2363,
    2364, 4305
Jones, P. William, 2365
Jones, Roger, 2366
Jones-Eddy, Julie, 2367
Jordan, Sonja K., 2368
Joshi, Yashodhara, 2369
Joynes, Sara, 2370
Joynt, Kevin, 2371
Juchauld, Frédéruque, 1331
Jueneman, Frederick B., 2372
Jul, Eric, 3450

Juneau, Ann, 4329
Junkermann, Dina, 3734
Jurgens, Jane, 2373

Kadoya, Takashi, 2374
Kaebnick, Gregory E., 2375, 2376, 2377
Kahn, Miriam, 2378, 2379, 2380, 2381, 2382
Kalbfleisch, Frida, 546
Kalina, Charles R., 2383, 2384, 2385, 2386, 3247
Kaltwasser, Franz Georg, 2387
Kamba, Angeline S., 2388
Kaminska, Elizbieta M., 856, 2389
Kamm, Sue, 2390
Kansas City Area Archivists, 2391
Kansas Library Network Board, 2392
Kantor, Paul B., 2393
Kapco Library Products, 5276
Kaplan, Hilary A., 2394, 2395
Karl, Gretchen, 2396
Karp, Gary, 2397
Karpenko, L. A., 3390
Karren, Susan H., 2398
Kasinec, E., 2399
Kastaly, Beatrix, 2400, 2401, 2402, 2403
Katalenac, Dragutin, 232
Kathpalia, Yash Pal, 2404, 2405
Kaufman, Diane, 2406
Kearsey, Irene, 2407
Kecskemeti, C., 2408
Keefe, Laurence E., 2409
Keele, Herbert Charles, 2410
Keene, James, 2411
Keene, Suzanne, 2412, 2413
Kehtonen, M., 2414
Kellar, Scott, 2415, 2416, 2417, 2418
Keller, Tom, 2419
Kellerman, L. Suzanne, 2420
Kelley, Gloria A., 1990
Kelser, Marie, 2421
Kemoni, H. N., 2423
Kemp, Toby, 2422
Kemp, Virginia, 3716
Kemper, Robert V., 2424
Kenjo, Toshiko, 2425
Kenkmaa, E. Knige, 2426
Kenna, Stephanie, 1004, 1621, 2427
Kennedy, Nora, 2428, 3838
Kennel, Glenn, 2429
Kennelly, Tamara, 2430
Kenneth, R. G., 3350

Kenney, Anne R., 1327, 2431, 2432, 2433, 2434, 2435, 2436, 2437, 2438, 2439, 2440, 2441, 2442, 2443, 2444, 2445, 2446, 2447
Kenny, Geraldine, 2448
Kent, Scott, 2449
Kenworthy, Mary Anne, 2450
Ker, Niel, 2451
Kerns, Ruth B., 2452
Kersten-Pampiglione, N. E., 1984, 4825
Kesse, Erich J., 542, 2336, 2453, 2454, 2455, 2456, 2457
Ketelaar, Eric, 2458
Keyes, Keiko Mizushima, 2459
Khan, M. M., 2460
Khan, Shahabuddin, 2461
Khan, Yasmin, 2462
Khayundi, Festus E., 2463
Kidd, Harry B., 2464
Kidd, Stewart, 2465
Kidd, Yvonne, 2466
Kimball, Margarte, 2467
Kimmage, Dennis A., 2468, 2469
Kindler, W. A., Jr., 2470
King, Ed, 2471, 2472
King, Eleanor M., 2450
King, Richard G., Jr., 2473
Kingsley, Jane, 2475, 4915
Kinnee, Sandy, 5332
Kinsolver, John M., 2476
Kireyera, Vilena, 2477
Kirkpatrick, Brett A., 2478
Kirkpatrick, John T., 2479
Kirtley, Toby, 2480
Kishore, Ranbir, 2481
Kistler, Vivian C., 5211
Kitching, Christopher, 2482
Kittle, Paul W., 2483
Kivia, Ivarature, 2484
Klapproth, Judy, 2485
Klasinc, Peter, 2486
Klason, C., 2487
Klee, Eleanore, 2488
Klein, Christine DeBow, 2489
Klein, Larry, 2490, 2491
Kleinman, Jonathan, 2639
Kleinrichert, Denis, 2492
Klem, Daniel, 5263
Klimley, Susan, 2493
Kline, Laura S., 2494
Knee, Michael, 563
Knell, Simen, 2495
Kniffel, Leonard, 2496

Knight, Nancy H., 2497
Koch, Janet, 2498
Koch, Mogens S., 2499
Koenig, Michael, 2895
Koestler, Robert J., 2500, 2501, 2502, 2503
Kofler, Brigit, 2504
Koga, James S., 2505
Kohler, Stuart A., 2017
Kolar, Jiri, 2291
Koloski, John G., 4453
Komornikova, Magda, 2049, 2050
Koncz, Pal, 2506
Koolik, Marilyn Gold, 2507
Koops, R. L., 2508
Koplowitz, Bradford, 2509
Kopp, Leslie Hansen, 2510
Kopperl, David F., 212, 2511, 2512, 2513, 3749, 3750, 3751
Koretsky, Elaine, 2514
Korey, Marie E., 2515
Körmendy, Lazos, 2516
Korppi-Tommola, J.E.I., 2019
Koster, Chris, 2517
Kotelnikova, Natalia Y., 2518
Kouris, Michael, 2519
Kovacic, Ellen Siegel, 2520
Kovacs, Beatrice, 2521
Kowalik, R., 2522
Kowlowitz, Alan, 2118
Kozak, John J., 2523
Kraft, Nancy, 1775, 2524, 2525, 2526
Kraner, Thomas, 2527
Krause, F., 2528
Krause, Peter, 2529, 2530, 2531
Krieg, J., 4341
Krill, John, 2532
Krist, Gabriela, 2533
Kruger, Betsy, 1037, 2534
Krumbein, Wolfgang E., 4443
Krummel, D. F., 2535
Kruth, Leslie M., 2536
Kuak, Sim Joo, 2537
Kueppers, Brigitte, 1116, 1901
Kuflic, Louise, 2538
Kuiper, John B., 704, 2539, 2540
KuKubo, Robert J., 2541
Kula, Sam, 2542, 2543
Kulka, Edward, 2544
Kumar, N. Jagadish, 3763
Kuroczkin, Joanna, 4443
Kusack, James M., 2545
Kushel, Dan, 1319
Kusko, B. H., 892

Kwater, Elizabeth, 2546
Kyle, Hedi, 2547, 2548, 2549, 2550

La Croix, Mina B., 563
Laberge, Danielle, 2551
Lacksonen, James W., 1487
LaFleur, Frances, 2552
Lafontaine, R. H., 2553
Lal, Avinashi, 2554
Lallier, Monique, 5256
Lamb, Robert S., II, 2555, 2556
Lamb, Robert Scott, 2557
Lambert, Frank L., 2558
Lamolinara, Guy, 2559
Landis, Lawrence, 2208
Landram, Christina, 3693, 3694
Lange, Holley, 2560
Langlois, Juan C., 2561
Langston, Kathleen W., 2241
Lankford, Mary D., 2562
Lape, Laura G., 2563
Lare, Gary, 4123
Laroque, C., 1716
LaRose, Michele, 2564
Larsen, A. Dean, 2565, 2566, 2567
Larsen, John C., 2568
Larsen, Rene, 2569, 2570
Larsgaard, Mary Lynette, 2571, 2572
Larson, George, 213
LaRue, James, 2573
Lateulere, John, 2575
Latour, Terry, 2576, 3477
Lau, Henry, 363
Lau, Juntai, 3713
Lauder, John E., 2577, 2578
Laughton, Louise W., 2579
Lau-Greig, Deborah, 2580
Laursen, Per, 2581
Lavender, Kenneth, 1045, 2582
Lavrencic, Tamara J., 2583, 2584, 2585, 2586, 2587
Law, Margaret H., 2588
Lawrence, Deirdre E., 2589, 2590
Lawrence, John H., 2591
Lawrence, Patricia O'Reilly, 2592
Lawson, Peter, 2593, 2594, 2595, 2596
Lawton, George, 2597
Lawton, Stephen, 2598
Layland, Penelope, 2599
Layne, Stevan P., 2600
Lazar, Jon H., 2601
Lazar, Wanda, 2602
Le Tourneaux, Mick, 392
Learn, Larry L., 2603

Leary, William H., 2604, 2605
Lechleitner, Franz, 284, 2606
Leckie, Carolyn G., 857
Leclerc, Françoise, 1332, 1333
Ledden, Larry, 2607
Lee, Jo Ann, 4893
Lee, Richard E., Jr., 2608
Lee, Sang B., 1677, 2609, 2610, 2611, 2612
Lee-Bechtold, Susan, 1390, 5075
Leek, Matthew R., 2613
Leese, Morven, 1341, 1952
Leewen, Idelette van, 3666
Legenfelder, Helga, 2614
Leigh, Beryl, 1601
Leigh, David, 2615
Lemcoe, M. M., 3624
Lemke, Antje B., 2616
Lemley, Brad, 2617
Lemmon, Alfred E., 2618, 2619
Lener, Dewayne J., 2620, 4442
Leonhirth, Janene, 2621
Leonov, Valerii Pavlovich, 4465
Leonov, Valery, 2622
Lepiney, Lionelle de, 2623
Leroy, Martine, 2624
LeRoy, Peter, 2625
Lesk, Michael, 1327, 2626, 2627, 2628
Lesley, Van, 2629
Lesser, Brian, 2143, 2146
Lester, Michael, 2630
Levengood, Patricia, 1634
Leveque, Margaret A., 2631
Levin, Jeffrey, 2632, 2633, 2634
Levitt, Alan M., 2635
Levitt, Martin L., 2636
Levy, B., 2637
Levy, Bruce, 5248
Lewis, David W., 2638
Lewis, Eleanor J., 2639
Lewis, Georgina, 3015
Lewis, Page, 2640, 2641
Lewis, Stephen, 2642
Li, Min Lim, 2643
Libengoud, Ronald S., 2644
Liberatore, Anthony M., 2645
Library Association of Portland (OR), 2648
Library Binding and Archival Products, 5288
Library of Congress, 2649, 2650, 2651, 2652, 2653, 2654, 2655, 2656, 2657, 2658, 2659, 2660, 2661, 2662, 2663, 2664, 2665, 2666, 2667, 2668, 2669, 2670, 2671, 2672, 2673, 2674, 2675, 2676, 2677, 2678, 2679, 2680, 2681, 2682, 2688, 2689, 2690, 2691, 5111, 5269, 5293, 5294, 5295, 5296, 5297, 5298, 5299, 5323, 5328
Library of Congress National Preservation Program, 2683, 2684, 2685, 5292, 5325
Library of Congress Preservation Directorate, 2686, 2687, 3686
Liddell, W. H., 3404
Lidstrom, Mary, 1076
Liebaers, H., 1076, 4001, 4868
Liebard, B., 1716
Lienardy, Anne, 2695, 2696, 2697, 2698
Liers, J., 2699
Ligocki, M. P., 3283
Ligterink, Frank J., 2701, 2702
Likhachev, Dmitrii, 2703
Lilly, Barbara, 3041
Lilly, Roy S., 2704
Lincoln, Alan Jay, 2705, 2706, 2707, 2708, 2709, 2710
Lincoln, Carol Zall, 2710
Lindblom, Beth C., 2711
Lindensmith, Erika, 4379
Lindner, Jim, 2712, 2713, 2714, 2715, 2716
Lindsay, Helen, 2718
Lindsay, Jen, 2717
Line, Maurice B., 2719
Linnean Society of London, 2720
Lipinski, Barry V., 2721
Lister Hill National Center for Biomedical Communications, 2722
Littman, Marlyn Kemper, 2723
Liu, H. I. H., 3283
Livingston, Richard A., 2724
Llewellyn, G. C., 996
Lochead, Richard, 2725
Lockhart, Vicki, 2726
Logan, Kevin J., 2727
Lombardo, Daniel, 2728, 2729
London, Jonathan, 2730
Long, Jane Sennett, 2731, 3973
Long, Margery S., 3216, 3904
Longstreth, Karl E., 2732, 2733, 3150
Looms, Peter Olaf, 2734
Lora, Pat, 2735
Lord Cultural Resources Planning &

Management, 2738
Lord, Allyn, 2736
Lord, Kenniston W., 2737
Loretto, Chris, 2739
Los Angeles Preservation Network, 2740, 2741, 2742, 2743
Los Angeles Public Library, 2744, 2745
Lotsmanova, E. M., 1488
Loughridge, Brendan, 2746
Love, Nancy, 579
Lovett, Charles M., Jr., 4526, 4527
Low, Annette, 2747
Lowell, Howard P., 1304, 2748, 2749, 2750, 2751, 2752, 2753, 2754, 2755, 2756
Lowry, Marcia Duncan, 2757, 4600
Lowry, Maynard, 2758
Lowry, R. F., 788
Lucarelli, Franco, 966, 1440
Luc-Gardette, J., 1571
Ludwig, Kathy, 2395, 2759
Lull, William P., 2760, 2761, 2762, 2763
Lunas, Susan, 2764, 2765
Lund, Thomas D., 2766
Lunde, Diane B., 2767
Lundeen, Gerald W., 2768
Lundquist, Eric G., 2769
Luner, Philip, 488, 736, 737, 2770, 2771
Lupu, Mihai, 3951
Lusher, Anne, 1669, 1670
Lushington, Nolan, 2772
Lyall, Jan, 349, 2773, 2774, 2775, 2776, 2777, 4328, 4834
Lyman, Peter, 2778
Lynch, Beverly P., 509, 3644
Lynch, Clifford A., 2779, 2780, 2781, 2782, 2783
Lynch, Richard E., 2784
Lynn, M. Stuart, 2785, 2786, 2787, 4004
Lyons, Thomas R., 5057

Ma, T., 3283
MacDonald, Chloe Gregg, 2901
MacDonald, Eric, 2902
MacDonald, Maureen A., 1511
MacDougall, Alan F., 999, 2908
MacDougall, Jennifer, 2909
Mace, Angela, 2941
MacInnes, Andrew N., 2918
MacKenzie, George, 2929, 2930

Mackenzie, Gail, 5305
Macklin, Lisa A., 2942
MacLean, Maragret G. H., 2474
MacLeish, A. Bruce, 1983
MacQueen, Scott, 2940
Madden, Ken, 2943
Maddow, Ben, 2944
Madeley, Douglas R., 2145
Madsen, Debora L., 1583
Maekawa, Shin, 1334, 1335, 1336, 4846
Magenau, Carol, 2945
Maggen, Michael, 2946, 2947, 2948
Magoon, David, 995, 1433
Magorrian, Vincent, 2949
Magrath, Lynn L., 2950, 2951
Magued, Aida, 3770
Maher, William J., 739
Maines and Associates, 2952
Maish, Susan Lansing, 3653
Makepeace, Chris E., 2954
Makes, F., 2955
Malaro, Marie C., 2958, 2959
Mallinson, John C., 2960, 2961, 2962, 2963, 2964, 2965
Malone, Paul, 2966, 2967
Mandel, Carol, 2068
Mando, Pier Andrea, 966, 1440
Manea, Cella, 1117
Manici, Marilena, 2968
Manning, Ralph W., 2969, 2970, 2971
Manns, Basil, 2972, 2973
Manns, Carolyn Morrow, 3247
Mansell, Heather, 2238
Manturovskaya, N. V., 3782
Marais, A., 2974
Maravel, Martine, 2975
Marchant, Eric W., 2976
Marchbank, A. M., 2977
Marcon, Paul, 2978
Marcoux, Yves, 2979, 2980
Marcum, Deanna B., 1243, 2981, 2982, 2983, 2984
Mareck, Robert, 2985
Maree, J., 2986
Margeton, Stephen G., 2987
Marine, Stephen, 2988
Markham, Robert, 2989
Marlatt, Ellen, 1903
Marrelli, Nancy, 2990, 2991, 2992
Marshall, Mary E., 2993
Martin, Elizabeth, 2994
Martin, Graham, 2995
Martin, Katherine F., 4032

Martin, Mike, 2996
Martin, Murray S., 2997
Martin, Robert S., 2998
Martin, Susan K., 2999, 3000
Martinek, Frantisek, 2222
Martinez, Ed, 3001
Marwick, Charles, 3002
Maryland Task Force to Initiate
    Preservation Planning, 3003
Marzetti, A., 1729
Masaryk-Morris, S., 3749, 3750
Mason, Pamela R., 3004
Mason, Robert M., 3005
Masri, S. F., 48, 49
Massachusetts Committee for the
    Preservation of Architectural
    Records, 3009
Massachusetts Supreme Judicial Court,
    3006, 3007
Massachusetts Task Force on
    Preservation and Access, 3008
Masschelein-Kleiner, Liliana, 3010
Mast, Sharon, 3011
Master, Christine, 997
Masters, Ian G., 3012
Matero, Frank G., 3013, 4955
Matheson, Ann, 3014
Matheson, Arden, 3015
Mathews, Anne J., 3016, 3017, 3018
Mathews, John, 3019
Mathews, T. M., 2502
Mathey, Robert G., 4759
Mathiasson, A., 2487
Matsui, N., 240
Matsumura, N., 240, 241
Matthews, Fred W., 3020, 3021
Matthews, Graham, 1566, 1567, 1568,
    1671, 1672, 3022, 3023, 3024,
    3025, 3026, 3027
Matthews, Ian, 3028
Mattsson, Irene, 3029
Matwale, Gideon Mukro, 3030
Maurer, J. Michael, 260
Mauriello, Barbara, 1058, 1807
Maver, Ian, 3031
Maxson, Holly, 3032
Mayfield, David M., 3033
Mayhew, Frances Whitaker, 3034
Maylone, R. Russell, 3035
Maynor, Catherine I., 3036
Mazal, Otto, 3037
Mazikana, Peter C., 3038, 3039
Mbaye, Saliou, 3040
McAfee, Melissa, 2788, 2790, 2791

McAusland, Jane, 2792, 2793
McBain, Janet, 2794
McBeth, Sue, 2795
McCabe, Constance, 2796, 2797, 2798
McCabe, Gerard B., 2800
McCall, Nancy, 1005, 2801
McCarthy, Paul H., 2802, 2803, 2804
McCausland, Sigrid, 2805
McCawley, J. C., 2806
McCay, Lynne, 2807
McClary, Andrew, 2808
McCleary, John, 2809
McClintock, T. K., 2810
McClung, Patricia A., 1587, 2811,
    2812, 2813, 2814, 2815
McClure, Lucretia W., 3880
McColgin, Michael, 2816, 2817, 2818
McComb, Robert E., 4186
McCombs, Phil, 2819
McConnell, Margaret, 2168
McCormick, Don, 2820
McCormick, Edith, 2821
McCormick-Goodhart, Mark H., 1612,
    2822, 2823, 3043
McCoy, R. W., 2824
McCrady, Ellen, 27, 1473, 2825, 2826,
    2827, 2828, 2829, 2830, 2831,
    2832, 2833, 2834, 2835, 2836,
    2837, 2838, 2839, 2840, 2841,
    2842, 2843, 2844, 2845, 2846,
    2847, 2848, 2849, 2850, 2851,
    2852, 2853, 2854, 2855, 2856,
    2857, 2858, 2859, 2860, 2861,
    2862, 2863, 2864, 2865, 2866,
    2867, 2868, 2869, 2870, 2871,
    2872, 2873, 2874, 2875, 2876,
    2877, 2878, 2879, 2880, 2881,
    2882, 2883, 2884, 2885, 2886,
    2887, 2888, 2889, 2890, 2891,
    2892, 2893, 2894, 2895, 3769,
    4179
McCrank, Lawrence J., 2896
McCrea, J. L., 3746
McCrone, Walter, 2897
McCue, Peter, 2898
McDaniel, Danny L., 2899
McDaniel, George, 2900
McDaniel-Hariston, Lisa, 2200
McDonald, Andrew C., 254, 767, 969,
    1509, 1774, 1802, 2977, 3738,
    4277
McDonald, Franklyn, 2903
McDonald, Peter, 2904, 2905, 2906,
    5119

McDonnel, Robert J., 2907
McGee, Ann E., 2910
McGiffen, Robert F., 2911, 2912
McGill, Michael J., 4827
McGing, Angela, 2913
McGleave, Peter, 2914
McGovern, Jim, 2915
McGown Film and Video, Inc., 5306
McGregor, Joseph K., 2901
McGuinna, Niamh, 2916
McIlwaine, John H., 1085, 2917
McIntyre, Ian, 1342
McIntyre, John E., 200, 2919, 2920, 2921, 2922, 2923
McIntyre, Mary, 2924
McKay, Christine, 2926
McKay, Richard S., 2925
McKay, Susan S., 2927
McKenzie, Alex W., 2928
McKeon, Donald B., 2931, 2932
McKern, Debra, 2933, 2934, 2935
McKinnie, William, 1817
McKitterick, David, 2936, 2937
McLean, William, 2938
McMurry, Nan, 699
McNeil, Beth, 2939
Meachen, Edward, 4559
Mead, Melissa, 3041
Meadows, Jack, 3042
Mecklenburg, Marion F., 1609, 1610, 1612, 3043
Medlin-Smith, Judith, 3480
Meeks, Nigel D., 1343
Meierhusby, Barbara, 3044
Meigs, James B., 3045
Meirejames, Barbara L., 5246
Meister, Pamela, 3046
Melin, Nancy, 3047
Melville, Annette, 3048, 3049, 3050
Menne-Haritz, Angelika, 3051
Menzies, Richard, 3052
Meredith, Willis C., 2987, 3053
Merrill-Oldham, Jan, 3054, 3055, 3056, 3057, 3058, 3059, 3060, 3061, 3062, 3063, 3064, 3065, 3066, 3067, 3068, 3069, 3070, 3071, 3072, 3073, 3074, 3075, 3247, 3521, 3522, 3605, 3953, 3977, 4356, 4375, 4884, 5296
Mertz, Gregory A., 3076
Messier, Paul, 3077
Messier, Russell, 459, 460, 461
Messinger, John M., II, 1319
Messner, K., 2199, 3078

Metcalf, Keyes D., 3079
Meyer, Duane G., 3081
Meyer, Lars, 2151
Michaels, George H., 2021
Michaels, Jan, 3082, 3083, 3084, 3085, 3086
Michalski, Stefan, 3087, 3088, 3089, 3090, 3091
Michigan Archival Association, 3092
Michigan State Historical Records Advisory Board, 3093
Mickelson, Meredith, 3094
Micrographic Preservation Service, 5304
Mid-Atlantic Preservation Service, 3096
Middleton, Bernard C., 3097, 3098, 3099, 5031, 5262
Mielke, Gerald P., 3100, 3101
Mihram, Danielle, 3102, 3103
Mijland, H. J. M., 3104
Miles, Gwyn, 3105
Milevski, Robert J., 3106, 3107, 3108, 3109, 3110, 3248, 5295
Milkovic, Milan, 3111
Miller, Bruce F., 3112
Miller, Claudia S., 286
Miller, Elizabeth, 3113
Miller, J. Hillis, 3114
Miller, John W., 3115
Miller, Michael, 3116, 3117
Miller, Page P., 3118
Miller, R. Bruce, 3119
Miller, Richard F., 3120
Miller, Sally McIntosh, 3121
Miller, Sheila, 3122
Millington, C. A., 1084
Mills, John S., 3123
Mills, Roger, 3124
Milner, Derek W., 1126, 1127
Minarikova, Jarmila, 2050
Minkler, Whitney S., 3125
Minneapolis Institute of Arts Library, 3126
Minnesota Department of Administration, Data and Records Management, 3127
Mironov, Boris, 3128
Mirror Productions, 5321
Mishra, Anupama, 3129
Mitchell, Ann M., 3130
Mitchell, John, 3131
Mitchell, Michael, 3132
Mitchell, Peter, 3133

Miura, Kristin Tina, 5257
Mobbs, Leslie, 3134
Modaresi, Ingrid R., 1990
Moffett, William A., 3136
Mohammadian, M., 1577
Mohlhenrich, Janice, 2972, 3137, 5061
Mokretsova, Inna, 3138, 3139
Moller, G., 892
Moltke-Hansen, David, 3140, 3141
Monforte, John, 3142
Montague, Robert, 3143
Monteith, Basil, 3144
Montevecchi, U., 3145
Montori, Carla J., 3146, 3147, 3148,
    3149, 3150
Moomaw, William R., 4528
Moon, Myra Jo, 1909, 3151
Moor, Ian L., 3152, 3153, 3154, 3155,
    3156
Moore, Pete, 3157
Moran, Barbara B., 3158, 3159
Morddel, Anne, 3582
Moreau, Michael, 3160
Morentz, James W., 3161
Morgan, John, 3162
Mori, Hachiro, 239
Moroz, Richard, 3163
Morozova, I., 3164
Morris, John William, 3172
Morris, John, 3165, 3166, 3167, 3168,
    3169, 3170, 3171
Morris, Patricia A., 3173, 3174, 3175,
    3176
Morrow, Carolyn Clark, 3071, 3177,
    3178, 3179, 3180, 3181, 3182,
    3183, 3184, 3185
Morse, Elizabeth, 3186, 3187
Morton, Bernard W., 3188
Moses, Kathy S., 3189
Mosher, Paul H., 3190, 3191, 3192
Mosier, Cynthia, 485, 486, 487
Mosier, Erika, 4822
Mosk, Jaap, 4839
Motylewski, Karen, 2711, 3193, 3194,
    3195, 3196, 3197, 3198, 3992
Mount, Barbara L., 3199
Mount, Ellis, 1283, 3200, 3217
Mowat, Ian M., 3203
Mowery, J. Franklin, 3204, 3205,
    3206, 3207, 3208, 3209, 5255
Mroz, Terry Rempel, 3210, 3211
Msuya, Jangawe, 3212
Mulhern, Brian J., 3213
Mullock, Hilary, 3214

Munafò, Paola F., 2968, 4420
Munn, Jesse, 3044, 3215
Munoff, Gerald J., 3216, 3904
Munoz Vinas, Salvador, 3218
Munoz-Sola, Haydee, 3217
Murakita, H., 240, 241
Murowanyj, Una, 3219
Murphy, Jack, 3220
Murphy, William T., 3221, 3222
Murray, Toby, 829, 3223, 3224, 3225,
    3226, 3227, 3228, 3229, 3230,
    3231, 3232, 3233, 3234, 3235
Musembi, Musila, 3236, 3237
Museum of Modern Art, 5223
Musson, Melvyn, 3238
Mustardo, Peter J., 2428, 3239, 3240
Musumbi, Musila, 3716
Muya, E. M., 3241
Myers, Richard, 1820, 3242

N'jie, S. P. C., 3348
Nadeau, Luis, 3243, 3244
Nagy, Zoltan, 1665
Nainis, Linda, 3110, 3245, 3246, 3247,
    3248
Nakamura, Tokio, 3249
Napier-Cain, Elizabeth, 1390
Nash, John C., 3250
Nash, Mary M., 3250
Nasland, Cheryl Terrass, 1864, 3251
National Academy of Public
    Administration, 3252, 3253
National Association of Government
    Archives and Records
    Administrators, 1314, 3254,
    3255, 3256, 3257, 4758
National Audio Visual Center, 5308
National Center for Film and Video
    Preservation, 3258
National Conference on Cultural
    Property Protection, 3259
National Digital Library Federation,
    3261, 3262
National Endowment for the
    Humanities, Office of
    Preservation, 3265
National Fire Protection Association,
    3266, 3267, 3268, 3269, 3270,
    3271, 5225, 5226
National Governors Association, 3272
National Historical Publications and
    Records Commission, 3273,
    3274, 3275
National Institute for the Conservation

of Cultural Property, 3276, 3277, 3278, 3279,
National Institute Standards Organization, 1039
National Maritime Museum, Greenwich, 5287
National Public Radio, 5171
National Research Council, 3281, 3282,
National Technical Information Service, 2647
National Trust Post Shopping Service, England, 5285
Nazaroff, William W., 980, 3283
Nazhad, Mousa M., 3284, 3285
Nebraska Document Preservation Advisory Council, 3286
Nebraska State Archives Records Management Division, 5273
Nebraska State Historical Society, 5178
Needles, Howard L., 2217, 3287, 3711, 4189, 5075, 5157
Neeval, Johan G., 3288, 3289
Negbor, R. L., 48, 49
Nelb, Tawny Ryan, 3290, 3291
NELINET Preservation Advisory Committee, 3292
Nelson, Anna Kasten, 3293
Nelson, Carl L., 3294
Nelson, Milo, 3295, 3296
Nelson, Nancy Melin, 3297, 3298
Nelson, Norman L., 729, 3299
Nelson, Sam, 5228
Nelson-Strauss, Brenda, 3300, 3301
Nemeyer, Sheldon, 3302
Nesheim, Kenneth, 3303
Netherlands, 3304, 3305, 3306, 3307
Netsky, Ron, 3308
Neuemeier, Paul J., 3309
New Jersey Department of State, Division of Archives & Records Management, 3311, 5313
New South Wales Library, 3314
New York Document Advisory Council, 3315
New York Historical Records Program, 3316, 3317
New York Metropolitan Library Agency, 3318, 3319
New York State Archives and Records Administration, 3320, 3321, 3322, 3323, 3324, 3325, 3326, 3327, 5289, 5349

New York State Library, 5224
New York State Program for the Conservation and Preservation of Library Research Materials, 3327, 3328, 3329, 3330, 3331
New York University Library, 3333, 3719, 5267
Newberry Library, 3334
Newborg, Gerald G., 3335
Newman, Linda P., 3336
Newmark, Anne, 3337
Nickerson, Matthew, 3338
Niederberger, Mary, 3339
Niederer, Karl J., 3340
Nikiforov, A., 830
Nikki Visual Images, 5350
Niknam, Mehrdad, 3341, 3342
Nikolova, D. P., 3343
Nishimura, Douglas W., 36, 38, 3835, 3839, 3840, 3841, 5161, 5162
Nixon, Diane S., 3493
Nizette, Mark, 3344, 3345, 3346, 3347, 4114
Nogueira, Carmen C., 3349
Nol, Lea, 3350
Noll, William, 3351
Noonan, Mary, 3352
Norcott, Patricia C., 1103
Nordstrand, Ove K., 3353
Norman, Daniel, 3354
Norman, Joanna, 3355
Norman, Mark, 3356
Norris, Debbie Hess, 3357, 3358, 3359, 3360
Norris, G., 3576
Norris, Terry O., 3361, 4321
Norris, Thomas D., 3362
North Carolina Preservation Consortium, 3363
North Dakota Library Association, 3364
North Dakota State Historical Records Advisory Board, 3365
North, Susan, 2181
Northeast Documents Conservation Center (NEDCC), 3366, 3367, 3368, 3369, 3370, 3371, 3372, 3373, 3374
Northeast Historic Film, 4682
Northwestern University Library, 3375
Norzicska, Stephan, 426
Novikova, G. M., 3376
Nowicke, Carole Elizabeth, 3377
Nugari, Maria Pia, 959

Nugent, William R., 3378, 3379, 3380, 3381, 5328
Nunberg, Geoffrey, 3382
Nunes, Fatima, 3052
Nyberg, Sandra, 3383, 3384, 3385
Nye, James, 3386
Nyren, Karl, 3387
Nyuksha, Y. P., 3388, 3389, 3390, 3391, 3392

O'Connell, Mildred, 3395, 3396, 3397, 3398, 3399
O'Connor, B. C., 3400
O'Connor, Gail M., 3401
O'Connor, Joan L., 3402
O'Donnell, Francis J., 3405
O'Farrell, William, 1558
O'Neill, Edward T., 3448, 3449, 3450
O'Rear, C. E., 996
O'Reilly, Susan, 3459
O'Toole, James M., 3471
Oakland Library Consortium, 3393
Oakley, Robert L., 3394
Odegaard, Nancy, 3403
Odlyha, M., 3404
Ogden, Barclay W., 1944, 3406, 3407, 3408, 3409, 3410, 3411, 4432
Ogden, Linda, 963
Ogden, Sherelyn, 3412, 3413, 3414, 3415, 3416, 3417, 3418, 3419, 3587
Ogden, Stanley Lee, 3420
Ohio Academic Libraries, 3241
Ohio Association of Historical Societies and Museums, 3620
Ohio Cooperative Conservation Information Office, 3422
Ohio State Library, 3423
Ohio State Universities Libraries, 3424, 3425
Ojo-Igbinoba, M. E., 3426
Okamoto, K., 3249
Okinaka, Masato, 4104
Oklahoma Historical Records Advisory Board, 3427
Oklahoma State University Library, 3428
Okula, Susan, 3429
Oliphant, David, 1306, 3430
Olkowski, Helga, 3433, 3434, 3435
Olkowski, William, 3431, 3432, 3433, 3434, 3435
Olley, Lorraine, 3436, 3437, 5388
Olson, David J., 3438, 3439

Olson, Nancy B., 3440, 3441, 3442
Olson, Robert A., 3443
Olszewski, Ann, 3444, 3445
Oltrogge, Doris, 1815
Onadiran, G. T., 3446, 3447
Online Computer Library Center (OCLC), 3451, 3682, 5217, 5304, 5314
Ontario Museum Association, 3452
Onwuka, Emma O., 1644
Oosten, Th. B. van, 3453
Opela, Vladimir, 3454
Orange County Dept. of Education, 5309
Orange, Rosanna, 3455
Orbanz, Eva, 3456
Orcutt, Joyce, 3457
Oregon State Archives, 3458
Organ, Robert, 3460
Orkiszewski, Lea, 3461
Orlenko, Kathleen, 4402
Orr, Bonnie, 3462
Orr, Gloria J., 3463
Orraca, Jose, 3464, 3465
Osborne, Larry N., 3466
Osorio, Fernando, 3467
Ostendorp, Anne, 1346, 3468
Ostroff, Eugene, 3469
Otness, H. M., 3470
Otto, Henrik, 3472
Oudard, Denis, 3473
Overman, Linda, 3474, 3475, 3476, 3477, 3478
Overmire, Rozell, 3479
Owen, Linda, 3480
Owen, Willy, 4006
Owens, Sheryl, 3481
Oxford University Press, 5301
Oye, Raysabro, 3482

Pacey, Antony, 3483, 3484, 3485
Padfield, Timothy, 3486, 3487, 3488
Page, Joanne, 3489
Page, Julie A., 3490
Page, Nick, 5301
Page, R. L., 3491
Page, Susan L., 3492, 3493, 4305
Paine, Crispin, 121
Paine, Shelly Reisman, 3494, 5179
Paliouras, Eleni, 3495
Palm, Jonas, 3496, 3497, 3498
Palmer, Joseph W., 3499, 3500
Palmer, Pat, 3501
Palmer, R. E., 3502

Palmetto Archives, Libraries and
 Museum Council on
 Preservation, 3503
Pamplona, Denise, 3504
Pan, Jixing, 3505
Panone, Carolyn, 3506
Parek, Henk J., 2701
Parezo, Nancy J., 2424, 4007, 4229
Parham, R. Bruce, 2804
Paris, Jan, 3509
Parisi, David Harlan, 3510
Parisi, Paul A., 3072, 3511, 3512,
 3513, 3514, 3515, 3516, 3517,
 3518, 3519, 3520, 3521, 3522
Parker, A. E., 3523, 3524, 3525, 3526
Parker, Andrew, 1463
Parker, Peter J., 3527
Parker, Thomas A., 3528, 3529, 3530,
 3531
Parks, E. J., 3532
Parliament, Robert A., 3533, 3534
Parmar, Sucha S., 1972
Parsons, M. J., 3535
Partridge, Sharon, 3536, 3537
Pascoe, M. W., 3538
Pasquariello, G., 1829
Passaglia, Elio, 3539, 3540
Pastine, Maureen, 3541
Paszner, Laszlo, 3284, 3285
Pate, Michael B., 3542
Paterson, Edward T., 3598
Patkus, Beth, 3543
Paton, Christopher Ann, 3544, 3545,
 3546, 3547
Patterson, Brad, 3550
Patterson, Diana, 3548, 3549
Patterson, Elizabeth L., 3551
Patterson, Robert H., 3552, 3553,
 3554, 3555, 3556
Pattison, Todd A., 3557
Patton, Mary, 3558
Pauk, Stephen, 3559
Paul, Jeff, 2334
Paul, Karen Dawley, 3560
Paulson, Barbara A., 3561
Pavao, Luis, 3841
Pavelka, Karen L., 3562, 3563
Payton, Rob, 3564
Peacock, Richard W., 3565, 3566
Pearce, Jane W., 5229
Pearce, Karla, 1920
Pearce, Michael, 3567
Pearson, Colin, 3568, 3569, 3570
Pearson, Glenda J., 3571

Pearson, J., 1602, 1603
Pecchioli, A., 1440
Peckstadt, An, 5114, 5115
Pedersen, Terri L., 3572
Pederson, Ann, 3573, 3574, 3634
Pedley, Avril, 3575
Pegg, R. K., 3576
Peller, Hugo, 5233
Pelz, Perri, 3577
Pelzman, Frankie, 3578
Pence, Cheryl, 3579, 3580, 3581
Penn, Ira A., 3582
Pennix, Gail, 3582
Pennsylvania Historical and Museum
 Commission, 3583
Pennsylvania Preservation Advisory
 Committee, 3584
Pennsylvania State University
 Libraries, Preservation
 Committee, 3585
Pensky-Adam, Heinke, 5234
Peppiatt, Michael, 3586
Percy, Theresa Rini, 3587
Perdue, Lewis, 3588
Perkins, John W., 3589, 3590
Perminova, O. I., 3593
Perry, Alan F., 3594, 3595, 3596
Perry, Joanne M., 3597
Perry, Lawrence G., 3598
Pershey, Edward Jay, 3599
Persky, Gail, 3600
Personius, Lynne K., 2442, 2443,
 2444, 2445, 2446, 2447
Perti, R. K., 3601
Perun, Bryon J., 2644
Peters, D., 3602
Peterson, Keith C., 3603
Peterson, Kenneth G., 3604, 3605
Peterson, Trudy, 3606
Petherbridge, Guy, 3607
Pfingstag, Gerhard, 3608
Pflieger, Fran, 3609
Phelps, Douglas, 3610
Phibbs, Hugh, 3611, 3612
Phillips, Charles, 3613, 3614
Phillips, Faye, 1160, 1161, 2998, 3615
Phillips, Morgan W., 3616
Phillips, Rodney, 3617
Phippen, William, 3618
Piccolo, Cecila M., 3622
Pickard, Kim, 3623
Pickett, A. G., 3624
Pickwoad, Nicholas, 3625, 3626, 3627,
 3628, 3629

Picot, Anne, 2913, 3630
Piechota, Dennis, 3632
Pietila, Anna-Maaija, 3633
Pieyns-Rigo, Paulette, 1790
Piggott, Michael, 3634
Pilette, Roberta, 3635, 3636
Pinion, Catherine F., 3637, 3638
Pinniger, David, 3639
Pinzelik, Barbara P., 3640
Pirio, Pamela, 3641
Pishmanova, Tz. Iv., 3343
Pitschmann, Louis, 3642
Pitti, Daniel V., 3643
Plane, Robert A., 3644
Plotnik, Art, 3645, 3646
Plumbe, Wilfred J., 3647, 3648
Podany, Jerry C., 3649, 3650, 3651,
     3652, 3653
Podmore, Hazel, 3654
Pokrovskaja, J. V., 3392
Polaroid Corporation, 3655
Pollack, Andrew, 3656
Pollock, Michael, 3657, 3658
Polloni, Diana, 3659
Pols, Robert, 3660
Ponsonby, S., 3661
Pooley, A. S., 892
Poprady, Geza, 3662, 3663
Porck, Henk J., 2703, 3664, 3665,
     3666, 4558
Porro, Jennifer, 3667
Porter, Bruce, 3668
Porter, Cheryl, 3669
Postlewaite, A. W., 3670
Potter, Constance, 3671
Poucher, Sue A., 2441
Poulin, Steve, 3672
Powell, Graeme, 2370, 3673, 3674
Powell-Froissard, Lily, 3675
Preiss, Lydia, 3676, 3677, 3678
Presley, Roger L., 3693, 3694
Preslock, Karen, 3695
Presti, Tony, 1161
Preusser, Frank D., 457, 2558, 3696,
     4804, 4806, 4807, 4808
Price, Bennett J., 3698, 3699
Price, Helen, 3700
Price, Joseph, 3701
Price, Lois Olcott, 3702, 3703, 3704,
     3705
Price, Robin Murray, 3706, 3707
Priest, Derek J., 554, 3708, 3709,
     3710, 3711, 3712, 3713, 3714
Primack, Alice L., 542

Proffitt, Kevin, 3718
Promenschenkel, George, 3720
Promis, Patricia, 677
Prosperi, Cecilia, 3721
Prosser, Ruth, 3713, 3722
Proulx, E. Annie, 3723
Prytherch, Ray, 5024
Puglia, Steven T., 3725, 3726, 3727,
     3728, 3729
Puissant, Maria J., 3730, 3731
Purinton, Nancy, 3732
Pyatt, T. D., 3733
Pymm, Bob, 3734
Pytlak, J. P., 3751

Quainton, Baron, 3735
Quant, Abigail, 3736, 3737
Quinlan, Nora J., 270
Quinn, Judy, 3739, 3740
Quinn, Michael C., 5057
Quinsee, Anthony G., 1509, 2977,
     3738, 4277
Qvist, M., 2487

Racelis, Fernando, 3741
Ragsdale, Kate W., 3742
Raitt, Mildred D., 3743
Rajer, Tony, 3744
Raloff, Janet, 3745
Ram, A. Tulsi, 3746, 3747, 3748,
     3749, 3750, 3751, 3752
Rama, N. Rao, 1973
Ramer, Brian, 746, 3460, 3753, 3754
Ramsey, Stephen D., 4957
Ranada, David, 3755, 3756
Ranade, Sanjay, 3757, 3758
Randall, Thea, 3759, 3760
Randolph, Pamela Young, 3761
Rankin, Keith, 3762
Rao, N. Rama, 3763
Rao, Y. Rajeshwar, 3764
Raper, Diane, 3765
Raphael, Toby J., 3766, 3767, 3768,
     3769
Rapson, Howard W., 3770
Ratcliffe, Frederick W., 3771, 3772,
     3773, 3774, 3775
Raub, Wolfard, 3776
Ravines, Patrick, 3777, 3778
Ray, Joyce M., 3779
Rayer, Nina, 3780
Raynes, Patricia, 3781
Rebrikova, N. L., 3782

Rebsamen, Werner A., 3783, 3784, 3785, 3786, 3787, 3788, 3789, 3790, 3791, 3792, 3793, 3794, 3795, 3796, 3797, 3798, 3799, 3800, 3801, 3802, 3803, 3804, 3805, 3806, 3807, 3808, 3809
Ree, Julia D., 3480
Reed, Judith A., 1364, 2549, 3812, 3813
Reed, Kathleen, 1538
Reed, Marcia, 3814
Reed-Scott, Jutta, 316, 3073, 3815, 3816
Reedy, Chandra L., 144, 3817
Reedy, Terry, 3817
Rees, Eiluned, 3818, 3819, 3820
Rees, Jacqueline, 1858, 1859
Reeser, Cheryl V., 3821
Reeves, Sally K., 3822
Regnault, Pacale, 3823
Reich, Victoria Ann, 3824, 3825
Reid, Marion T., 3826
Reilly, James M., 25, 33, 34, 36, 37, 38, 3827, 3828, 3829, 3830, 3831, 3832, 3833, 3834, 3835, 3837, 3838, 3839, 3840, 3841, 5161, 5162
Reimer, Chris, 3842
Reimer, Derek, 3843
Reinsch, Mary, 3844
Remington, David G., 5328
Rempel, Siegfried, 3845, 3846, 3847, 3848
Rempel-Mroz, Terry, 3849
Rendell, Kenneth W., 3850, 3851
Rennie, Silvia, 5237, 5250
Reno, Carolyn, 2736
Reponen, T., 2414
Research Libraries Group, Inc., 3689, 3854, 3855, 3856, 3857, 3858, 3859, 3860, 3861
Residori, L, 685
Reyden, Dianne van der, 4078
Reyes, Patricia, 3863
Reynolds, Anne L., 3864, 3865, 5338
Rhoads, Jerry, 2234
Rhode Island Council for the Preservation of Research Resources, 3866, 3868
Rhode Island Department of State Library Services, 3869
Rhode Island Historical Records Advisory Board, 3867

Rhodes, Barbara J., 3870, 3871, 3872, 3873, 3874, 3875
Rhodes, James B., 3876
Rhyne, Charles S., 3877
Rhys-Lewis, Jonathan, 3878
Rice, James, 3879
Richardin, P., 1716
Richards, Daniel T., 3880
Richards, David, 3881
Richards, Sharla, 2151
Richards, Susan, 3495
Richardson, Bill, 3882
Richardson, John, Jr., 1279
Richmond, Alison, 3113, 3883
Rick, Gustafson, 47
Ricotta, F. J., 520
Rieke, Judith L., 3884, 3885
Rieken, Henry, 3886
Riemer, Janet T., 3887
Riemer, John J., 3888
Riess, Hanley L., 3889
Rightmeyer, Sandra P., 3890
Riley, Gordon, 3891
Riley, Martha, 3892
Riley, P. N. K., 1571
Ringrose, Jayne, 3893
Rising, Marsha H., 3894
Ritzenthaler, Mary Lynn, 710, 2364, 3216, 3895, 3896, 3897, 3898, 3899, 3900, 3901, 3902, 3903, 3904
Roach, Alex, 1896
Roads, Christopher H., 3905, 3906, 3907
Robbins, Louise S., 3908, 3909
Robert Morris College, 5307
Roberts, Barbara O., 3910, 3911, 3912
Roberts, Brian A., 3913
Roberts, F. X., 3914, 3915
Roberts, Lisa C., 1045
Roberts, Susanne F., 3916, 3917
Robertson, Guy, 3918
Robertson, Linda, 3919
Robin, Eleanor F., 3920
Robinson, James H., 3921
Robinson, Lawrence S., 3922
Robinson, Peter, 3923, 3924
Rocky Mountain Regional Conservation Center, 4630
Roe, Kathleen, 3925
Roelofs, Wilma G. Th., 2197
Roever, Eva, 3163
Rogers, Michael, 3739, 3740, 3926, 3927

Rogers, Phillip, 1390
Rogers, Rutherford D., 3928
Rogers, Susan, 199
Roicheleau, Joseph C., 5093
Romao, Paula, 3929
Romer, Grant B., 3930, 3931
Ronen, Naomi, 3053
Rooks, Dana, 3933
Roosa, Mark S., 880, 3071, 3934, 3935, 3936, 3937, 3938, 3939
Roosens, Laurent, 3940
Root, Nina J., 3941, 3942
Root, William, 3112
Roper, Michael, 2411, 3943, 3944, 3945, 3946, 3947, 3948
Rose, Carolyn L., 3949
Rose, Cordelia, 3950
Rose, Ingrid, 3951
Rose, William B., 406, 1840, 2248, 4551
Rosen, Bruce, 2588
Rosenber, Diana, 3952
Rosenthal, Joseph A., 3953
Ross, Lincoln, 2144, 3954, 3955
Rossi, L., 932
Rossol, Monona, 3577, 4197
Roth, Stacy, 3956
Rothenberg, Jeff, 3957
Rothstein, Edward, 3958
Rouit, Huguette, 4493
Rountree, Nancy C., 3959
Rouyer, Philippe, 3960, 3961, 3962
Rowe, Judith, 3963
Rowell, Roger M., 5144
Rowley, Gordon, 3964
Rowoldt, Sandra, 3965
Roy, Ashok, 1331, 2331, 5161
Roy, Gillian, 3966
Royal Geographical Society, 3967
Rozanski, J., 4444
Rozsondai, Marianne, 3968
Rudd, S. A., 1085
Rude, Renee, 3969
Ruggiero, D, 685
Rule, Amy, 3970
Rummonds, Richard-Gabriel, 5247
Rusch, Stacy J., 3971
Russell, Ann, 995, 1652, 3972, 3973, 3974, 3975, 3976, 3977, 3978, 3979, 3980, 3981, 3982, 3983, 3984, 3985, 3986, 3987, 3988, 3989, 3990, 3991, 3992, 3993
Rust, Michael K., 3994
Rutherford, Christine, 3995

Rutherford, L. D., 3996
Rutimann, Hans, 3997, 3998, 3999, 4000, 4001, 4002, 4003, 4004, 4005
Rutledge, John, 4006
Rutledge, Renata, 4995
Ruwell, Mary Elizabeth, 2450, 3198, 4007
Ruzicka, Glen, 4008
Ryan, Nina, 5229
Ryckman, Pat, 4009
Ryder, Sharon Lee, 4010

Sabar, Shalom, 2948
Sable, Martin H., 4011, 4012
Sackett, Judy, 4780
Saffady, William, 4015, 4016, 4017, 4018, 4019, 4020, 4021, 4022, 4023, 4024, 4025, 4026, 4027, 4028, 4029, 4030, 4031, 4497
Safford, Herbert D., 4032
Safran, Franciska, 4033
Sagraves, Barbara, 4034, 4035
Sahli, Nancy, 4036
Saint Johns University, 5272
Saint Louis Regional Network, 4040
Saiprakash, P. K., 3764
Sakar, N. N., 4041
Salmon, Lynn G., 3283, 4042
Salter, Charles A., 4043
Salter, David, 4044
Salter, Jeffrey L., 4043
Salter, Laurie, 4045
Saltykov, M. E., 3392
Salvadori, Ornella, 959
Samuel, John G., 4046
Samuels, Helen W., 1254
Samulski, Peter, 4047
Sanders, Howard J., 4048
Sanders, Jennifer A., 4049
Sanders, S., 4050
Sanders, Terry, 5342
Sandwith, Hermoine, 3625, 4051
Santoro, Edward D., 2503
Santucci, L., 932
Saretzky, Gary D., 4052, 4053, 4054, 4055, 4056, 4057, 4058, 4059, 4060, 4061
Sarkar, N. N., 4062
Sarto, V., 1729
Sasamori, Katsunosuke, 4063
Satchell, Stephen, 4064
Saulmon, Sharon A., 4065
Saulter, R., 4066

Saunders, David, 4067, 4068
Saunders, Margaret, 4069
Saurs, Laura, 4070
Savage, Noelle, 4071
Sawicki, Malgorzata, 4073
Sawka, Barbara, 4072
Sayre, Edward V., 4074
Scaggs, Samuel B., 4075
Schachter, June, 4076
Schaefer, Karl R., 4077
Schaeffer, Terry Trosper, 4078, 4079, 4080
Schaub, George, 4081
Schenck, Thomas, 4082
Schenck, William, 4783
Schene, Michael G., 4083
Scherdin, Mary Jane, 4084, 4085
Schewe, Donald B., 4086
Schickling, M. L., 2513
Schilling, Michael R., 4087
Schiro, Joseph, 4088
Schlefer, Elaine Reidy, 4089, 4090, 4091
Schlesinger, Carl, 5223
Schlomon, Barbara F., 2704
Schmeisser, Jorg, 4092
Schmidt, J. David, 4093
Schmude, Karl G., 4094, 4095, 4096, 4097
Schnare, Robert E., Jr., 1304, 4098, 4099, 4100, 4101, 4102, 4103, 4502
Schoenthaler, Jean, 4104
Schoenung, Harold, 447
Schofer, Ralph E., 928, 4105
Scholtz, James C., 4107, 4108
Schomburg Center for Research in Black Culture, 5278
Schoolly-West, R. F., 4109, 4110
Schoonmaker, Dina B., 4111, 4112
Schorzman, Terri A., 4113
Schou, Henning, 3456, 4114
Schrock, John Richard, 4116, 5170
Schrock, Nancy Carlson, 3865, 4115, 4117, 4118, 4119, 4120, 4121, 4122
Schroeder, Don, 4123
Schubert, Dexter R., 4893
Schubert, Joseph F., 781
Schueller, Dietrich, 4124, 4125, 4126, 4127, 4128
Schuff, Fred, 4129
Schuller, Dietrich, 284
Schultz, Constance B., 4130

Schumm, Robert W., 4131
Schur, Susan E., 4132, 4133, 4134
Schurk, William L., 1691
Schursma, Rolf L., 2079
Schuyler, Michael, 4135
Schwab, Richard N., 892, 4136
Schwalberg, Bob, 4137
Schwanke, Harriet, 4138
Schwartz, Candy, 4139
Schwartz, Stanley, 4141, 4142
Schwartz, Werner, 4140, 4143
Schwerdt, Peter, 2699, 4144, 4145, 4146
Schwirthlich, Anne-Marie, 4147, 4148
Scott, Marianne, 4149, 4150, 4151
Scott, Mary W., 4152
Scott, Sally J., 4153, 4154
Scott, Simmon, 3048, 3049, 3050
Scott, Vicky, 4155
Scott, William E., 4156, 4157
Scottish Society for Conservation and Restoration, 4158, 4159
Scriber, B. W., 4160
Seal, Robert A., 4161, 4162
Seale, Colleen, 542
Seaton, D. G., 4163
Sebera, Donald K., 4164, 4165, 4166, 4167
Sedar Senghor, Leopold, 4168
Seddon, Kenneth R., 2347
Sedinger, Theresa, 4169
Sedun, George, 960
Segal, Judith, 4170
Seiler, Lauren H., 4171
Seip, John T., 4172
Selth, Jeff, 4173
Selwitz, Charles, 4174
Semke, L. K., 4177
Senadeera, N. T. S. A., 4178
Seton, Rosemary, 4180
Setos, Andrew G., 4181
Severson, Douglas G., 4182
Shackelton, Cheryl Ann, 1431, 4183, 4184
Shahani, Chandru J., 2072, 2073, 2149, 4185, 4186, 4187, 4188, 4189, 4190, 4191, 4267
Shapkina, Larissa B., 4192, 4193
Sharpe, Jerry, 4194
Sharpe, John Lawrence, 4195
Shashoua, Yvonne, 1344
Shaw, Felicity, 4196
Shaw, Susan D., 4197
Sheehan, Paul, 901, 4198

Sheehy, Carolyn A., 4199
Shefter, Milton, 3842
Shelburne (VT) Museum, 4013
Sheldon, Ann R., 906
Sheldon, Ted P., 4200
Shelly, Marjorie, 4201
Shelton, Deborah, 4202
Shenton, Helen, 4203, 4204, 4205, 4206
Shep, Robert L., 4207
Shepard, Elizabeth, 4208
Shepard, Jocelyn, 4209
Shepard, Richard F., 4210
Shepilova, Irina G., 4211, 4212
Shepp, Allan, 4446
Sherbine, Karen, 4213
Sherrington, Jo, 4214
Sherwood, Arlyn, 4215
Shevchenko, Sergey M., 5152
Shipp, E. R., 4216
Shoaf, Eric C., 4217
Shoumatoff, Alex, 4218
Shrinath, A., 4219
Shults, Charlene H., 4220
Shults, Terrance G., 4221
Siena, Jane Slate, 377, 2622, 4553
Sift, Katherine, 3626
Silberman, Richard M., 4222
Silberman, Sydel, 2424
Silcox, Tinsley, 4223
Siller-Grabenstein, Almut, 731
Silver, Jeremy, 4224
Silverberg, Joel S., 732
Silverman, Emily, 1346
Silverman, Randy S., 1934, 1935, 2567, 4225, 4226, 4227, 4228
Silverman, Sydel, 4007, 4229
Simmons, Alan, 4230
Simmons, Peter, 4231
Simon, Barry, 4232
Simon, Imola, 4233, 4234
Simon, Lisa, 4235
Simon, Matthew J., 4236
Simonoff, Jeffrey S., 4890
Simpson, Bill, 4238
Simpson, Charles W., 4239
Simpson, Edward, 4240, 4241, 4242, 4243, 4244, 4245, 4246, 4247, 4248
Simpson, Floyd B., 4249
Simpson, Janice, 3742
Simpson, Mette Tang, 1053
Sinclair, Jim, 4250
Sinclair, Regina A., 4251, 4252

Singh, G. M., 4253
Singh, Karambir, 4254
Singh, R. S., 4255
Sinha, S. N., 4256
Sinnette, Elinor des Verney, 4257
Siokalo, Zorina, 344
Sipos-Richter, Teriz, 567
Siripant, Sakda, 4258, 4259
Siroky, M., 1545, 1546
Sistach, Maria Carme, 4260
Sitterle, Karen A., 4261
Sitts, Maxine K., 517, 4262, 4263, 4264, 4265, 4266, 4267
Skepastianu, Maria, 4268, 4269
Skov, H. R., 2487
Skupsky, Donald S., 4270
Slate, Jane, 4271
Slavin, John, 4272
Sleep, Esther L., 4273
Slide, Anthony, 4274
Sly, Margaret N., 4275
Smeeton, Robin, 4276
Smethurst, J. M., 4277
Smit, Wim J. Th., 2701, 2703, 3666
Smith College Museum of Art, 5214
Smith, Anthony W., 2926, 4278
Smith, Beryl K., 4279
Smith, Brian S., 4280, 4281
Smith, Clive, 4282
Smith, Demaris C., 4283
Smith, Eldred, 4284, 4285
Smith, Elizabeth H., 4286, 4287, 4288
Smith, Ellen, 4289
Smith, Frederick E., 4290, 4291
Smith, Joan C., 4292
Smith, John David, 4293
Smith, Keith A., 4294
Smith, Kelvin, 3582, 4295
Smith, L. E., 788
Smith, Leslie F., 4296, 4297
Smith, Margit J., 4298, 4299
Smith, Merrily A., 2824, 3074, 3348, 3406, 3605, 3928, 3953, 3977, 4300, 4301, 4302, 4303, 4304, 4305, 4356, 4362, 4363, 4375, 4862, 4863, 4864, 4884
Smith, Michael Clay, 4306
Smith, Perry, 1331, 2331, 3218, 3404, 5161
Smith, Richard D., 4307, 4308, 4309, 4310, 4311, 4312, 4313, 4314, 4315, 4316, 4317, 4318, 4319, 4320, 4321, 4363, 5351, 5352
Smith, Sheila A., 1523

Smith, Stephanie, 4322
Smith, Wendy, 3570, 4323, 4324,
    4325, 4326, 4327, 4328
Smithsonian Institution, 3715, 4329,
    4330, 5210, 5322
Smook, Gary A., 4331
Snider, Mike, 4332
Snow, E. F., 520
Snow, Michael R., 4333
Snyder, Eileen, 648
Sobota, Jan, 4334, 4335
Sobotka, Werner K., 424, 425, 426
Society of American Archivists, 1314,
    4336
Society of Archivists, London, 5266
Society of Mississippi Archivists
    Conservation Committee, 4337
Society of Motion Picture and
    Television Engineers, Inc., 3842,
    4338, 4339
Society of Photographic Scientists and
    Engineers, 4373
Soegren, Paul, 5357
Soest, H. A., 4340
Soete, George J., 3490
Soled, E. H., 4341
SOLINET (Southeast Library
    Network), 4351, 4352, 4353,
    4354, 4618
Solley, Thomas T., 4342
Soloviev, Andrei Yu, 4343
Sommer, Susan T., 4345
Sonnet-Azize, Rene G., 4346
Soon, Ang, 4347
Soteland, N. A., 4
South African Library, 659
South Australia State Library, 4348
South Carolina Department of
    Archives and History, 4349
South Carolina Historical Records
    Advisory Board, 4350
Spadoni, Carl, 4355
Sparks, Peter G., 4356, 4357, 4358,
    4359, 4360, 4361, 4362, 4363,
    5328
Sparks, William J., 543
Spatz, Richard E., 2523
Spawn, Carol M., 4364
Special Libraries Association, 4365
Speiser, Robert, 4228
Speller, Benjamin F., 4366
Spence, John, 4367
Spencer, Kathleen Moretto, 787
Spiers, Hilary, 800, 5047

Spindler, Robert P., 4368
Spitmuller, Pamela, 5249
Sprehe, J. Timothy, 4369
Spreitzer, Francis, 4370
Sprod, Dan, 4371
Srivastava, D. N., 4372
St. Laurent, Gilles, 4037, 4038, 4039
Stagnitto, Janice, 4374
Stainton, Sheila, 3625, 4051
Stam, David H., 4375, 4376, 4377,
    5224
Stambulov, T., 4340
Standiforth, Sarah, 4378
Stanfill, Nancy E., 4379
Stange, Eric, 4380
Stanley, Judith, 3714, 4381, 4382
Stanley, Ted, 4383, 4384
Stanley-Dunham, Janine, 1398
Stansfield, G., 4385
Starbird, Robert W., 3125
Stark, Alan, 4386
Starling, Kate, 3564
Starr, Mary Jane, 4387
State University of New York at Stony
    Brook, 4388
Stazicker, Elizabeth, 4389
Steckman, Elizabeth, 4390, 4391
Steel, Anne-Marie, 5110
Steele, Leslie, 3885
Steemers, Ted, 2105
Stehkaemper, Hugo, 4392
Sterlini, Philippa, 4393
Stern, Gail F., 343
Stern, Richard E., 628
Stevard, Bradley W., 4394
Stevens, Norman D., 4395, 4396, 4397
Stevenson, Condit Gaye, 4398
Stevenson, Mark, 4399
Stevenson, Rob, 4400
Stevik, Terry, 5228
Stewart, Deborah, 261, 4401
Stewart, Eleanore, 4402, 4403
Stewart, Robert W., 4404
Stiber, Linda, 4405
Stickells, Lloyd, 3907, 4224
Stielow, Frederick J., 4406, 4407,
    4408, 4409, 4410, 4411
Stinson, Stephen, 4412
Stirling, Isabel A., 4413
Stobie, Ian, 4414
Stockton, Scott A., 2582, 4415
Stokes, Daniel A., 4416
Stokes, Jan, 5265
Stolow, Nathan, 4417

Stone, Janet L., 4418
Stone, Susan, 2444
Stone, T. G., 2806
Storack, M. Speranza, 4419
Storch, Paul S., 4420
Storey, Richard, 4421
Storm, William D., 4422, 4423
Story, Keith C., 4424
Stover, Mark, 4425
Strang, Thomas J. K., 1373, 4426, 4427, 4428, 4429
Stranger, Carolla, 4430
Strassberg, Richard, 4431
Straub, Detmar, 224
Strauss, Robert J., 1775, 3411, 4432
Streit, Samual Allen, 4433, 4434
Strnadova, Jirina, 4435
Ströffer-Hua, Eckhard, 4437, 4438
Strohm, Robert F., 3971
Strong, Gary E., 4439
Stroud, James, 4440, 4441, 4442
Strüffer-Hua, Eckhard, 4436
Strzelczyk, Alieja B., 4443, 4444
Sturge, John, 4446
Sturges, Paul, 4447, 4448
Sturman, Shelly G., 4449
Styka, Wanda Magdaleine, 4450
Subt, Sylvia S. Y., 4451, 4452, 4453
Sugarman, Jane E., 4454
Sugaya, Hiroshi, 4455
Sugista, R., 2268
Sugnet, Chris, 677
Sullivan, John, 4456
Sullivan, Larry E., 4457
Sullivan, Mark, 4458
Sullivan, Peggy, 4459, 5338
Sun, Marjorie, 4460, 4461, 4462
Sundt, Christine L., 4463, 4464
Sung, Carolyn Hoover, 4465
Surprenant, Thomas T., 3159
Suryawanshi, D. G., 4466, 4467
Sutcliffe, Charles, 4468
Sutcliffe, Gary, 4469
Suthard, K. Peter, 4470
Suzuki, Toshiaki, 2425
Swan, Christopher, 4471
Swan, John, 4005
Swanson, Edward, 3441, 3442
Swartzburg, Susan G., 72, 2589, 4472, 4473, 4474, 4475, 4476, 4477, 4478, 4479, 4480, 4481, 4482, 4483, 4484, 4485, 4486, 4487, 4488, 4489, 4490, 4491, 4492, 4493, 4494, 4495, 4496, 4497,

4498, 4499, 4500, 4501, 4502, 4503
Swartzell, Ann, 2726, 4504, 4505, 4506, 4507, 4508, 4509, 4510, 4511, 4512, 4513, 4514, 4515, 4516, 4517
Swieszkowski, Linda, 4518
Swift, Katherine, 743, 902, 2312, 2936, 3491, 3628, 3669, 4519, 5059
Swora, Tamara, 2973, 4520
Sybulski, Walter, 5118
Sylvestre, Guy, 4522, 4523
Szczepanowska, Hanna Maria, 4524, 4525, 4526, 4527, 4528
Szermai, J. A., 4529
Szewczak, J. T., 4219
Szewezyk, David M., 4530
Szirmai, J. A., 1908
Szlabey, Gyorgyi, 567, 4531
Szyonczak, Ralph, 4532

Tahk, F. Christopher, 397
Talley, M. Kirby, Jr., 4533
Talwar, V. V., 4534
Tamada, Michael K., 4005
Tamblyn, Robert, 3052
Tamblyn, Robyn, 3052
Tanasi, Maria Teresa, 903, 1825
Tannenberg, Dieter, 4535
Tanselle, G. Thomas, 4536, 4537, 4538
Tarlton, Martha K., 2942
Taylor, Hugh A., 4539, 4540
Taylor, J. M., 4541
Taylor, Merrily E., 3159
Taylor, Thomas O., 4542, 4543
Technical Association of Pulp and Paper Industry (TAPPI), 4544
Teller, Alan, 4545
Templer, Julian, 4546
Tending, Antoine, 4547, 4548
Tennent, Norman H., 4549, 4619, 4620
Tennessee State Library and Archives, 4550
TenWolde, Anton, 4551
Teo, Elizabeth A., 4552
Teoman, Elizabeth Gay, 4553
Terris, Olwen, 4554
Terry, R. J., 4555
Tetreault, Jean, 1511
Tevetkova, J. P., 3343
Texas Association of Museums, 4557

Texas Associations for Higher
 Education of North Texas, 5341
Teygeler, Rene, 4558
Thackery, David, 4559
Thakre, R. P., 4560
Thibodeau, Kenneth, 4561
Thilakaratne, D. M., 1226
Thoma, George R., 4562, 4563, 4881
Thomas, Bill, 4564
Thomas, David L., 1080, 4565, 4566,
 4567, 4568, 4569, 4570
Thomas, James, 4571
Thomas, John B., 4572
Thomas, Julian, 4573, 4574
Thomas, Mark, 4575
Thomas, Sylvia, 4576
Thomas, Wendy, 4577
Thomasset, Annie, 4578
Thompson, Anthony Hugh, 4579
Thompson, Claudia G., 4580
Thompson, Frank, 4581
Thompson, Jack C., 4582, 4583, 4584,
 4585, 5034, 5220, 5221, 5222
Thompson, John A., 4586
Thompson, Lawrence S., 4587, 4588
Thomson, Garry, 4589, 4590, 4591
Thorburn, Georgine, 4592
Thorburn, Karen J., 4593
Thorp, Jennifer, 4595, 4596
Thorp, Valerie, 4594
Thurgood, Brian, 2145, 2146
Thurston, Anne C., 1085, 4597, 5218
Tibbits, Edie, 4598
Tibbo, Helen R., 4599
Tiedrich, Ellen, 1272
Tigelaar, Mary Peelen, 4600
Tilbrooke, David R. W., 4601
Tinsley, David J., 5291
Tisch, Thomas, 4602, 4603
Tissing, Robert W., 4604
Titus, Claire, 2037
Todd, Fred W., 3779
Todd, Victoria, 3356
Toigo, Jon William, 4605
Toll, Fred, 2145
Tomaiuolo, Nicholas, 4606
Tomazello, Maria, 4607
Tomer, Christinger, 4608, 4609
Toronto Area Archivists Group, 3452
Torraca, Giorgio, 4610
Torres, Amparo R. de, 3949, 4611,
 4612, 4613
Totka, Vincent A., Jr., 4614
Tottie, Thomas, 4615

Toulet, Jean, 4616
Towner, Lawrence W., 4617
Townsend, John, 4618, 4620, 4621
Townsend, Joyce H., 4619
Tozo-Waldmann, Suada, 4622
Tracy, Gay S., 3992, 4623, 4624
Trader, Margaret, 4625
Trainor, Julia, 4626
Traister, Daniel, 4627, 4628
Trant, Jennifer, 593
Traue, J. E., 4629
Travis, Jessica, 246
Trechsel, Heinz R., 4631
Tregarthen Jenkin, Ian, 4632
Tremain, Brian, 4633
Tremain, David, 4634, 4635
Trevitt, John, 4636, 4637
Trezza, Alphonse F., 4638
Trieb, Gilbert, 1536
Trinkaus-Randall, Gregor, 3618, 4639,
 4640, 4641, 4642, 4643, 4644,
 4645, 4646, 4647, 4648, 4649,
 4650, 4651
Trinkley, Michael, 4652, 4653, 4654,
 4655
Truelson, Stanley D., Jr., 4656
Trujillo, Rosanne, 4657
Truman, Carol, 4658
Trumpp, Thomas, 4659
Tsang, W. T., 4660
Tse, Season, 853, 4661, 4662
Tsuneshi, Warren M., 4991
Tuck, D. H., 4663
Tuffin, Brian, 4664
Tukovic-Kiseljev, Dubravka, 4668
Tumosa, Charles S., 1612, 3043
Turbusz, Mihaly, 1234
Turko, Karen, 4665, 4666, 4667
Turner, Anne M., 4669
Turner, Eric, 4670
Turner, Jeffrey H., 4671
Turner, John R., 4672, 4673, 4674
Turner, Judith A., 4675, 4676, 4677
Turner, Laura, 5327
Turner, Nancy, 4678
Turner, Patrick, 4679
Turner, Sandra, 4680
Tuttle, Craig A., 4681
Twomey, James E., 4683

Uginet, Marie Christine, 1379
Underhill, Karen, 4686
Ungarelli, Donald L., 4687, 4688,
 4689

Union Carbide, 4690, 4691
United Kingdom Public Record Office, 4692
United Nations Educational, Scientific and Cultural Organization, (UNESCO), 251, 1310, 3135, 3202, 4694, 4695
United States Advisory Committee on the Records of Congress, 4696
United States Advisory Council of Historic Preservation, 4697
United States Army Corps of Engineers, 4698
United States Congress, 4699, 4714, 4715, 4716, 4717
United States Congress, House, 4700, 4701, 4702, 4703, 4704, 4705, 4706, 4707, 4708, 4709, 4710, 4711, 4712, 4713
United States Congress, Senate, 4718, 4719, 4720, 4721
United States Department of Housing and Urban Development, 4725
United States Environmental Protection Agency, 4722, 4723, 4724, 5185
United States General Accounting Office, 4726, 4727, 4728
United States General Services Administration, 4730, 4731, 4697, 5184
United States Government Printing Office, 4732
United States National Agricultural Library, 4733
United States National Archives and Records Administration, 3683 3717 4734, 4735, 4736, 4737, 4738, 4739, 4740, 4741, 4742, 4743, 4744, 4745, 4746, 4747, 4748, 4749, 4750, 4751, 4752, 4753, 4754, 4755, 4756, 4757, 4758, 4973
United States National Bureau of Standards, 4759
United States National Commission of Libraries and Information Science, 4760
United States National Information Standards Organization, 4761, 4762, 4763
United States National Library of Medicine, 4764, 4765
United States National Parks Service, 4766, 47674768

Université du Québec á Montréal, 5187, 5188, 5190, 5191, 5192, 5193, 5194, 5195, 5196, 5197, 5198, 5199, 51200, 5201, 5202, 5203, 5204, 5205
University College, School of Library, Archives and Information Studies (London), 5218
University Microfilms, 5206, 5334
University of Arizona, College of Law Library, 4770
University of California at Berkeley Library, 4684
University of California, Los Angeles Libraries, 4771
University of California, San Diego Libraries, 4772
University of Delaware, 5229
University of Georgia Libraries, 4773, 4774, 4775, 4776, 4777
University of Iowa Center for the Book, 5282, 5283, 5284, 5354, 5355
University of Kansas Libraries, 4779
University of Kentucky Libraries, 4780
University of Missouri, Columbia Libraries, 4781, 4782
University of Missouri -St Louis. 5337
University of Oregon Library, 4783
University of Oxford Libraries, 4784
University of Pennsylvania Libraries, 4785
University of Pittsburgh University Libraries, 4786
University of Pittsburgh, School of Library and Information Science, 247
University of Rochester Library, 4787
University of Southern California University Libraries, 4788
University of Tennessee, Knoxville Library, 4789
University of Toronto Library, 4790
University of Virginia, 4344
University of Wales, 5315
University of Waterloo Library, 4791
University of Western Ontario, 4792
University Products, 1433
Unomah, J. I., 4793
Upham, Lois N., 4794, 5106
Uppgard, Jerannine, 2302
USA Teleproductions. 5271

Usmani, Muhamman Adil, 4796

Vagarov, Feodor M., 4797, 4798
Vaisey, David, 4799
Valauskas, Edward J., 4800, 4801, 4802
Valentin, Nieves, 4803, 4804, 4805, 4806, 4807, 4808
Valerie, Michèle, 1103
Vallas, Philippe, 4809
Vallejo, Rosa M., 4810
Van Artsdalen, Martha J., 4811
Van Bogart, John, 4812, 4813, 4814
Van Buskirk, James E., 4815
Van Dam, Theodore, 3838
van der Hoevan, Hans, 4816
van der Reyden, Dianne, 4078, 4817, 4818, 4819, 4820, 4821, 4822
Van der Wateren, Jan F., 4823
Van Deventer, Barbara, 881
Van Emden, H. F., 4824
Van Gulik, R., 4825
Van Haaften, Julia, 4826
Van Houton, Trudy, 2450
Van Hovweling, Douglas E., 4827
Van Vliet, Claire, 5264
Van Zelst, Lambertus, 4828
Vance, Jack, 4829
Vandiver, Frank, 4830
Vandiver, Pamela B., 4831
Varlamoff, Marie-Therese, 4832, 4833, 4834
Varlejs, Jana, 4835, 4836
Vaughan, Barbara, 4033, 4837
Veca, Eugenio, 273, 597
Vendl, Alfred, 426
Ventress, Alan, 860
Verheyen, Peter S., 4838
Verschoor, Hugo, 4839
Veverka, E. A., 4341
Viana, Cesar, 3929
Videnich, Jean, 4840
Villas, Philippe, 4841
Vinas, Ruth, 4842
Viñas, Vincente, 1264, 4842
Vincent, Tom, 614
Vincent-Daviss, Diana, 4843
Vine, Mark G., 4844, 4845
Vinod, Daniel, 4846
Virando, Jacqueline A., 4847
Virginia State Library & Archives, 5290
Visotskite, Vitaliya K., 1489
Visscher, William, 4848

Vitale, Cammie, 4849
Vitale, Timothy J., 3077, 4455, 4850, 4851, 4852
Vitiello, Giuseppe, 4853
Vnoucek, Jiri, 4854
Vober, John J., 4855
Vodopivec, Jedert, 4856, 4857, 4858, 4859
Vogelgesang, Peter, 4860
Volent, Paula, 3612
Volgyi, Peter, 4861
Von Endt, David, 1611
Voogt, L., 3305, 3665
Vossler, Janet L., 4862

Waechter, Otto, 4863, 4864, 4865
Waechter, Wolfgang, 4866, 4867, 4868, 4869
Wagner, Sarah, 4870, 4871, 4872, 4873
Wakeling, Ian, 4874
Wakeman, Geoffrey, 4875
Walch, Victoria Irons, 4876, 4877
Walckiers, M., 1076
Walia, R. K., 998
Walkden, Stephen A., 4878, 4879, 4880
Walker, Frank L., 4562, 4563
Walker, Franklin N., Jr., 4881, 4882
Walker, Gay, 3075, 4883, 4884, 4885, 4886, 4887, 4888, 4889, 4890
Wall, Carol, 342, 4891
Wallace, Jim, 4892
Wallace, Patricia E., 4893
Wallis, Terry Boone, 3044, 4894
Walne, Peter, 4895, 4896
Walsell Leather Museum, 4897
Walsh, Betty, 4898
Walsh, Joanna, 3865
Walsh, Judith C., 4899
Walston, Sue, 3010
Walter, Gerry, 4900
Walter, Katherine L., 4901
Walters, Tyler O., 4902, 4903
Walton, Bruce, 4904
Walworth, Vivian K., 4446, 4905
Wang, Kathryn H., 4906, 4907
Ward, Alan, 4908, 4909
Ward, Christine W., 4910, 4911
Ward, Philip R., 4912, 4913, 4914
Warden, Linda, 2475, 4915
Ware, Coral Mary, 4916
Ware, Mike, 4917
Warner, Glen, 4918

Warnow-Blewett, Joan, 4919
Warren, Morris, 2234
Warren, Richard, Jr., 4920, 4921
Warren, S. D. Company, 4922, 4923
Washington Research Library
    Consortium, 4924
Wasicky, M., 830
Wassell, J. L., 4925
Waterer, John, 4926
Waterhouse, John F., 4927
Waters, Donald J., 1327, 4928, 4929,
    4930, 4931, 4932
Waters, Peter, 3715, 4465, 4933, 4934,
    4935
Watkin, Alan, 4936, 4937
Watkins, Christine, 4939
Watkins, Stephanie, 4938
Watsky, Lance Ross, 4940
Watson, Adele L., 4941
Watson, Aldren A., 4942
Watson, Caroline F., 4943
Watson, Duane A., 4944
Watson, Tom, 4945, 4946
Watstein, Sarah Barbara, 4947
Watt, Marcia A., 4948, 4949, 4950
Watteeuw, Lieve, 5114, 5115
Wayne, John J., 4951, 4952
Weaver, Barbara, 4953
Weaver, Chuck, 4954
Weaver, Martin E., 4955
Weaver, Shari L., 4932, 4956
Weaver-Meyers, Pat L., 4957
Webb, Colin, 4958
Weber, David C., 4959, 4960
Weber, Harmut, 4961, 4962, 4963
Weber, Lisa, 4964
Weber, Mark, 4965
Weberg, Norman, 2149, 4187, 4189,
    4190
Webster, Duane E., 1352, 4005, 4966
Wedinger, Robert S., 4967, 4968,
    4969, 4970, 4971
Weeks, Linton, 4972
Wehrkamp, Tim, 4973
Wei T'o, 4992, 5351, 5352
Weidner, Marilyn Kemp, 4974, 4975
Weihs, Jean, 4976, 4977
Weinberg, Gerhard L., 4978
Weinstein, Frances Ruth, 4979
Weinstein, Neha, 4503
Weintraub, Steven, 364, 1903, 4980
Weir, Thomas E., Jr., 2114, 4981
Weiskel, Timothy, 4982
Weisman, Brenda, 4983

Weiss, Carla, 4984
Weiss, Dudley A., 4985, 4986, 4987,
    4988
Weiss, Philip, 4989
Weiss, R., 4990
Welch, Theodore F., 4991
Wellheiser, Johanna G., 490, 4993,
    4994
Wells, Ellen B., 4995
Wells, Rosemary, 4996, 4997
Wells, Rulon S., 808
Welsh, Elizabeth C., 4998
Welsh, Jane, 4034
Welsh, William J., 4063, 4999, 5000,
    5001, 5002, 5003, 5328
Weltman, Eric, 2639
Werner, A. E., 3010
West, Tim, 5004
Westbrook, Lynn, 5005, 5006
Westcott, David H., 5007, 5008
Western New York Library Resource
    Council, 5009
Westra, Pieter E., 5010
Weststrate, David F., 5011
Wettasingh, Saroja, 5012
Weyde, E., 5013
Wharram, Polly, 5014
Whealen, R. E., 5015
Wheeler, Daniel G., 5016
Wheeler, David L., 5017
Wheeler, George Segan, 4831
Wheeler, James, 5018, 5019, 5020
Wheeler, Tony, 5021
Wherry, A. M., 4421
Whiffen, Jean I., 4268, 5022
Whitaker, Albert H., 5023
White, David, 5024
White, John R., 5025
White, Kris A., 5026
White, Raymond, 3123
White, Robert M., 5027
White, William B., 456, 457, 459, 460,
    461, 462, 463, 464
White, William, 4005
Whitehurst, Anne, 2147, 2148, 2980
Whitfield, Susan, 5028
Whitmore, Paul M., 980, 5029, 5030
Whittman, Cynthia L., 980
Wick, Constance S., 5032
Wick, D. L., 892
Wicles, Schott, 3824
WiederKehr, Robert R. V., 5033
Wiegand, Wayne A., 1941
Wiendl, Frederico Maximiliano, 4607

Wiese, William H., 1583
Wiesner, Julius, 5034
Wilcox, Annie Tremmel, 5035
Wilcox, Michael, 5036, 5235, 5236
Wilhelm, Henry, 4137, 5037, 5038, 5039
Wiliam, Aled Rhys, 5040
Wilkinson, Frances C., 5041
Willard, Louis Charles, 5042
Willard, Vickie, 5043
Williams, Bernard, 5044, 5045, 5046
Williams, E. A., 5047
Williams, Edwin L., 5048, 5049, 5050
Williams, Gene, 5051, 5052
Williams, Joan, 4342
Williams, John C., 5054
Williams, Karen, 5053
Williams, Lisa B., 5055
Williams, Norman H., 5056
Williams, R. Scott, 1511, 1512
Williams, Richard S., Jr., 5057
Williams, Sara R., 608, 641, 1384
Williamson, C. J., 5058
Willis, Deborah, 5059
Willis, Don, 5060, 5061
Willis, R. Ellen, 2076
Wilman, Hugh, 5062, 5063, 5064
Wilson, A., 285
Wilson, Alexander, 5065
Wilson, David L., 5066
Wilson, J. Andrew, 5067, 5068
Wilson, J. F., 4421
Wilson, Paul, 5069, 5070
Wilson, William K., 4191, 5071, 5072, 5073, 5074, 5075, 5076
Wilt, M., 1678
Wilthew, Paul, 5077
Winkle, Becky, 5078
Winkler, Jean B., 2560
Winner, Seth, 2820
Winners, Karen, 5079
Winsor, Peter, 5080, 5081, 5082
Winston, Iris, 5083, 5084
Winterble, Peter G., 5085, 5086
Wisconsin, State Historical Society, 5087, 5227
Wise, Christine, 5088
Wisniewski, Ginny, 5089
Wisniewski-Klett, Virginia, 2549
Withnall, R, 594
Wittekind, Jürgen, 5090
Wodetzki, Jamie, 5091
Wojtczak, Miroslawa, 5092
Wold, Geoffrey H., 5093

Wolfe, Irmgard H., 1362, 5094
Wolff, Robin, 5095
Wolfinger, Matthew, 5096
Wolfson, Laurel Sturman, 2520
Wolven, Robert, 2068
Wood, Daniel B., 5097
Wood, Larry, 5098
Wood, Mary Lee, 5099, 5100
Wood, Steven L., 5101
Woodhouse, Mark, 5102
Woodman, Neville, 5103
Woods, Chris, 5104, 5105
Woods, Elaine W., 5106
Woods, Jennifer, 5107
Woodward, David, 5108
Woodward, Hazel, 5109
Woodworth, Loretta, 5332
Woolgar, Chris, 5110
Wootton, Mary, 3044
Worman, Eugene C., Jr., 5112
Wortman, William A., 5113
Wouters, Jan, 5114, 5115
Wray, Nick, 5116
Wright, Dorothy W., 5117, 5118, 5119
Wright, Gordon H., 5120
Wright, Logan S., 5121
Wright, Sandra, 5122, 5123, 5124
Wurzberger, Marilyn, 5125
Wust, Ruth, 5126
Wyly, Mary P., 5127, 5128
Wynen, Nancy, 5129
Wyoming University Laramie University Library, 5130

Xuejun Zou, 1989

Yaekel, Elizabeth, 5131
Yale University Libraries, 5132, 5209
Yamamoto, Nobuo, 5133
Yasue, Akio, 5134
Yasuzawa, Shuichi, 214
Yax, Maggie, 5135
Yee, Martha M., 5136
Yerburgh, Mark R., 5137
Yetter, George H., 5138
Yorke, Stephen, 5139
Young, Christine, 5140
Young, Laura S., 5141
Young, Patrick, 5142
Young, Philip H., 5143
Young, Raymond, 5144
Young, Richard F., 5145, 5146, 5147, 5148, 5291
Yurkiw, Peter, 5124

Yver, Carole, 1331

Zachary, Shannon, 4975
Zammit, Tony J., 4333
Zappala, Antonio, 5149, 5150, 5151
Zarubin, Michael Ya, 5152
Zedar, Judith, 1327
Zeidberg, David S., 5153, 5154
Zeier, Franz, 5155
Zeitschik, Marc, 5156
Zelinger, Jiri, 1461, 1547
Zeronian, S. Haig, 578, 863, 2217,
    2610, 3287, 3711, 4189, 5075,
    5157

Zimmerman, Carole, 5158, 5159
Zimmerman, Robert, 5160
Zinn, Edward, 3839, 5161, 5162
Zipkowitz, Fay, 5163
Zipp, Louise S., 5164
Zizhi, Feng, 5165
Zou, X., 5166
Zucker, Barbara, 5167, 5168
Zurawski, Elizabeth, 1853
Zwass, Vladimir, 2234
Zwinger, Ann H., 2367
Zycherman, Lynda A., 5169, 5170

Subject Index

academic libraries conservation, 2556, 3246, 3251, 4178, 4200

Academy of Natural Sciences Library, 4364

Academy of Sciences Library (Russia), 3022, 4934

accelerated aging, 212, 1609, 1611, 1675, 2291, 2826, 2910, 3714

acid paper, 491, 1039, 2069, 2213, 2893, 3247, 3304, 5112, 5342

Acme Bookbinding, 15

adhesives, 69, 89, 396, 543, 897, 1050, 1133, 1511, 1662, 2194, 3676; acrylic hot-melt, 543; EVA copolymer, 3676; heat set, 1647; hot melts, 3100; peel adhesion, 223; polyvinyl acetate, 4432; pressure-sensitive, 4305; PVA, 3794, 4360; removal of, 718; self-stick, 5276; stability, 1512; tapes, 2449

Africa, 3038, 3040, 3237, 3447

AKZO mass deacidification process, 2085, 4440

Alaska, 67

Albro, Tom, 4972

alethoscope image conservation, 3344

alkaline paper, 86–88, 1039, 1139, 1321, 2579, 2771, 2888, 3295, 3724, 4179, 4276, 4703, 4715, 4952; chemistry of, 2891; deterioration, 5171; in books, 1785; legislation for, 3355; manufacturers of, 1155; paper production of, 2597; printing with, 2831, 4732, 5103; recommendations for, 1787; uncoated, 182; use of, 331

American Association of Law Librarians, 123

American Institute for Conservation of Historic and Artistic Works, 133–36, 138, 140–41, 784

American Institute of Physics, 4919

American Library Association, 147–52, 155, 1348

American Museum of Natural History, 3875

American National Standards Institute (ANSI), 31, 148

ancient paper, ink, 1973

ANSI *See* American National Standards Institute

anthropological record preservation, 4229

approaches to preservation, 557

architectural records preservation, 4114, 4118–19, 4122

archives, 131, 352, 374, 552, 783, 834, 924, 956, 1124, 1230, 1368, 1848, 1861, 1917, 1992, 2516, 2544, 2616, 2805, 3009, 3573, 3900; access, 600; disinfecting, 2222; electronic, 1205, 4448; film, 1911; functions of, 833; fundamentals of, 2802; glossaries for, 1265; glossary for, 3349; infestation treatments, 2801; management, 247, 709, 709–10, 965, 1204, 1387, 1741, 2364, 4646; micro-environments for, 1992; museum dictionaries, 536; needs, 1196; organization of, 965; plastics in, 624, 919, 1725, 4412, 5058; procedures for, 738; standards, 4876; technology of, 835, 1991; tracking, 2114

Archives Nationales, 1777–79

Arizona, 2287, 2818

Arizona State Archives, 257

ARL *See* Association of Research Libraries

art conservation, 16, 240, 407, 906, 961, 980, 1042, 1338, 1611, 1649, 2459, 3113, 4042, 4073, 4498, 4831; analysis of, 1117; electronic imaging of, 2024; enzyme treatments, 3186; framing, 1648, 1696, 2792; fraud detection, 4541; history, 275; need for, 3291; restoration, 230, 545; standards, 1236; UV exposure, 3288

Asian Libraries, 2089

Association of Research Libraries (ARL), 314–20, 322–25, 327–28, 330, 988, 1909, 2168, 2865, 3071

Atkinson preservation typology, 786, 3580

audio conservation, 681, 773–74, 919, 978, 1022, 1375, 1477, 1557,

1559, 1830, 2274, 2305, 2317, 2625, 3012, 3082, 3547, 4037–38, 4053, 4126, 4908, 4920; bibliography for, 3545; CD media, 3125, 3755–56; de-accession, 785; editing, 92, 4123; formats for, 3937; literature, 1224, 2075; long-term storage, 5018; magnetic materials, 2112; methodology, 2075–76; optical disk and, 1225; overview, 1884; physical nature of, 4039; planning, 306; stability of, 3956; technologies for, 2491, 4224

audio preservation, 769, 788, 919, 2079, 3124, 3142, 3934, 4072

audio-visual conservation, 681, 1569, 2078, 2337, 2725, 3237, 3249, 3456, 3661, 3943, 4739; appraisals, 3660; bibliography, 3499; circulating collections care, 4579

Audubon's Birds of America, 5310

Australia, 351, 354, 1206, 1717, 1886–88, 2088, 2091, 2777, 2898, 3570, 3674, 4147–48, 4206, 4371, 4626, 4664, 4916, 4958

authenticity of printed material, 1930, 1932

Bangladesh, 2461

Banks, Paul, 1214

Barrow laminating process, 2366

Battelle mass deacidification process, 2699, 5090

Benchmark Book Repair system, 1371

bibles, 594, 5301

bibliographical evidence, 1092, 3549

bibliophlagous insects, organisms, 3504

Biblioteka Akademii Nauk preservation database, 4802

Bibliothèque Nationale de France, 265, 267, 688, 2281, 2623, 3586, 4809, 4841

binderies, 1784, 2302, 4478, 5271

binders, 606, 900, 2304

binding techniques, 1059, 1584, 1701, 2488, 2625, 3080, 3517, 4943

bindings, 102, 469, 669, 1953–54, 1974, 2062, 2238, 2358, 2415, 3060, 3804, 4195, 4205, 4233, 4875, 5141, 5242, 5249, 5251, 5255; adhesive, 562, 4360, 4943;

Byzantine, 3138; case type, 1785, 5260; cleat-laced, 4943; cloth, 102, 3131, 5239; durable, 4761; guidelines for, 1410; hard-board, laced-in, 392, 1617; history of, 1053; limp, 272; post type, 4090; round-backing, 245; sewn board, 654; structures, 1803, 1812; tape, 656; testing, 3411, 3510

bindings for preservation, 643, 1709, 1734, 1803, 2637, 2936, 3535, 3676, 3721, 3783

biodeterioration, 57, 109, 112, 531, 3129, 4525; control of, 4803, 4808; fungal organisms responsible for, 4560; micro-organisms in, 3389

bio-medical literature, 886, 1388–89, 2478, 3002, 4562, 4764

black bibliophiles and collectors, 4257

bleaching, 842, 1342, 2199, 2289, 2609, 4078, 4437; and conservation, 848; enzyme modification, 3343; hydrogen peroxide, 1060; kraft pulps, 2289; procedures for, 1547; yellowing, 3770

Blumberg Case, the, 103, 2251–52, 2882, 4849, 4989

book conservation, 78, 242, 245, 440, 623, 1111, 1331, 1480, 1514, 1818, 2434, 2442, 2547–49, 3101, 3201, 3240, 3873, 4207, 4380, 4529, 4560, 4676–77, 4907, 4995, 5135; cyclohexanol derivatives in, 830; decaying, 1653, 4534; handling of, 3952, 4298; special collections, 3627; treatments for, 242, 643, 1646, 1742; videos on, 5219–22

book covers, 201, 2361, 3785, 5229, 5232, 5234, 5237

Book of Cynog, 5040

book, paper de-accession, 4656

book preservation, 234, 1056, 1366, 1643, 1736, 2473, 2548, 3959, 4710; cost methodology, 1221; review of methods, 4838; structures for, 5089; techniques, 3126

Book Preservation Associates (BPA) mass deacidification process, 2234

book production, 471, 477, 3028, 3190, 3786, 5176, 5263, 5353 book repair, 319, 595, 636, 658, 777, 819, 1371, 1714, 1850, 2332, 2764, 3106, 3110, 3248, 4227; basic guides for, 1400, 1846; evaluation of treatments for, 3628; gamma rays treatment, 4795; manuals for, 4513; products for, 1444, 3422; self-adhesives for, 5276; techniques, 1627, 1854, 4098; varnishes for, 3010; VHS video on, 5309

book return robotics, 4397

bookbinding, 649, 1087, 1092, 1172–73, 1331, 1865, 3207, 3743, 4225, 5031, 5155; basics of, 2788, 5182; commercial, 388, 1650, 3147, 4287, 5209, 5292; evaluation of, 3793; introduction to, 1034, 2333; materials for, 899, 2630, 3204; structures of, 645, 3802–03; techniques, 896, 3803, 3849, 4601, 5210; technology in, 3797; training, 3121

book/document conservation, 795, 1381, 1807, 2046, 2416, 4132, 4799, 4828; bindings for, 646; literature, videos, 2979, 3589, 4476, 5178; management of, 2378, 2413; methodology of, 287, 1480, 2413, 2620, 4282; research, 4079; selecting for, 5082; vendors for, 3452

Bookkeeper deacidification process, 2217, 2523, 2686, 3559, 4699

BookLab, Inc., 647–48, 1925

book/paper restoration, 84, 250, 653, 665, 1052, 1415, 1506, 1604, 1630, 1651, 1814, 2648, 2744, 2769, 2809, 4193, 4253, 4413, 4850–51, 4950, 5315, 5335–36; disintegrating, 3429; in libraries, 1934; palm leaf, 2594; techniques, 421, 1935, 2809, 3107, 3390, 3524–26; VHS video on, 5220; wetted, 4192

books in peril, 445, 1382

Boolean Library, 4245, 4247

Bosnia/Herzegovina, 4622

Boston Library Consortium, 683

Boston Public Library, 684

Bowdoin College, 2650

boxmaking, 5263

BPA *See* Book Preservation Associates

Bradford's Law, 1457

Brahm, Walter, 714

Brahms Preservation Project, 2677

Brazil, 233, 243

breaking books for sale, 5112

Brigham Young University, 2566

British Columbia Provincial Museum, 4912

British Film Institute, 2346

British Library, 751–58, 1687, 1737, 2297, 2471, 2595

British Records Association, 2074

brittle book problem, 8, 41, 500, 508, 516, 802, 1237, 1469, 1876, 2020, 2031, 2083, 2106, 2557, 3183, 4460, 4700, 4958; congressional hearing on, 4700; national plan for, 4959; solutions for, 917, 1279, 1839, 3075

brittle book reformatting, 661, 1267, 1658, 1874, 3297, 3586, 4217, 5042

brittle journals, 8

Brooklyn Botanical Garden Library, 4983

buckram covers, 2361

buildings, 17, 2220, 3052, 3087, 4501, 4655, 4697, 5104, 5185; bibliography of materials, 4921; construction of, 3193; HVAC systems, 293, 3698; materials bibliography, 4921

Bulgaria, 2368

Burma, 1308

California State Library, 910–12

Cambodia, 253, 5017

Canada, 954, 1977, 3015, 4151, 4315, 4540, 4666–67

care and handling of books, 192, 524, 652, 1133, 1482, 1506, 1959–60, 2026, 5177; VHS video on, 5266–70

cartoon conservation, 2181

Case Western Reserve University Library, 1645

CD-ROM *See* compact disk, read only memory

chemical characteristics of books, 4, 27, 248, 623, 849, 1838, 4163

chemicals in conservation, 1105

chemicals in deacidification process, 3926

Chicago Historical Society flood, 2128

Chichester Cathedral Library, 2191
Child, Margaret S., 1047, 1212
China, 1762, 4002
Chinese white pigment, 2162
circus poster conservation, 1112
Clemson University Library, 1011
Cockerell, Sydney, 2080
collection management, 159, 381, 517,
    881, 1030, 1249, 1379, 1411,
    1449, 1735, 2546, 3340, 3759,
    4032, 4304, 4611, 4870, 5113;
    bibliography, 4612; handling of,
    124, 878, 1606, 4891; integration,
    4120; light protection, 3372;
    methodology, 389, 2306, 2324,
    3941, 4163, 5121; syllabus for
    serials, 4521; VHS videos on,
    5179, 5358
Colonial Williamsburg Foundation
    Library, 5138
Colorado, 2350–56, 2767
Colorado Libraries, 2353–56
Columbia University Libraries, 5311
commercial amylase, protease
    enzymes, 4661
Commission on Preservation and
    Access, 44, 1140, 1148, 2887,
    3916, 3997–99, 4004, 5085
Committee on the Records of
    Government, 1153
compact disk, read only memory (CD-
    ROM) technology, 85, 110, 217,
    224, 229, 961, 1207, 1413, 1441,
    1654–55, 2124, 2613, 3554, 4231,
    4948; aging tests, 687;
    introduction to, 2135; longevity,
    stability of, 2992, 2996, 4948;
    overview of, 2124; publishing,
    2134
Concordia University flood, 2990
Connecticut, 1168
connoisseur, 4225
Conservation Information Network,
    2284, 5080
conservation literature, videos, 3589,
    5178, 5258, 5285
Conservation Online, 4998
conservation techniques, methodology,
    345, 551, 730, 1344, 2347, 4600,
    4610, 4634, 5197, 5235–36, 5341;
    computer technology for, 950;
    filter paper analysis, 5029;
    microscopy, 2167, 2425; sling
    hygrometers, 4954; ultra violet
    filters, 2610; ultrasound
    humidification, 905; x-ray, 2167
conservation versus microfilm, 1367
conservation/preservation of library
    materials, 443, 1162, 1164
conservation/preservation supplies,
    suppliers, 3393
conservator concerns, 834, 1182, 2266,
    2413, 4438
conservator, selecting for, 138, 605,
    1023, 1411, 1872, 2532, 2985,
    3409, 3509, 3644, 4397, 4449,
    4609, 4755, 4398
conservators, curators guidelines, 172,
    175
Conserve O Gram series, 4766
conserving papers on nature, 2720
consultants (N.Y. metro area), 1431
contingency planning strategies, 864
cooperative bibliographic database,
    5080
cooperative conservation, 2311, 3596
cooperative microfilming, 1077
cooperative preservation, 499, 698,
    1435, 2000, 2013, 2122, 2175,
    2340, 2431, 2541, 2824, 2970,
    3191, 4929, 5118; basis for, 4608;
    considerations in, 4376;
    international program, 5000
Copying *See* photocopying
Core Agriculture Literature Project,
    2905
core literature, selecting, 264, 5119
Cornell University, 1311, 1380, 2201,
    2432, 2727, 3642, 4431
Cornell/Xerox project, 2436, 2442–44,
    2447
Cornell/Yale imaging projects, 4956
corporate records, 62, 262
costs of preservation, 4378
counter disaster manual, 3314
criteria for reversibility, 235, 4319
Croatia, 232
Cuba, 5022
Cullison, Bonnie Jo, 5127
cultural property conservation, 582,
    2275–76
Cunha, George, 3399
Czech Socialist Republic, 2052

daguerreotypes, 260, 454–57, 460,
    462–64, 3931
Dalhousie Law School Library fires,
    3020–21

damaged records recovery, 1166, 2208
de Arteni, Miriam, 5278
deacidification, 64, 424, 526, 547, 719,
    730, 792, 803, 932, 973, 1332–33,
    2075, 2651, 2669, 2698, 2886,
    3103, 3404, 3482, 4507, 5049,
    aqueous immersion, 424; effect of,
    2166; lithium process, 3310;
    myths, realities of, 4309; non-
    aqueous methods, 4317; non-
    gaseous, 1952; principles of,
    2203; retroactive approach, 3497;
    synopsis of methods, 4308; vapor
    phrase, 2675. *See also* mass
    deacidification
deacidification versus microfilming,
    2840
decomposition mechanisms, 422
decorative metals, 1285, 2506
delamination, 3031–32, 4405
deterioration of paper-based materials,
    239, 393–94, 792, 809, 842, 1496,
    1995, 2242, 2587, 2610, 3199,
    3540, 3712, 4793; biological,
    3391; environmental, 3539, 3543,
    3666, 5030; fungal organisms,
    4560; mass deacidification and,
    3484; starch degradation, 3919
Deutsche Bücherei, Leipzig, 4867–68
DEZ *See* diethyl zinc (DEZ)
    deacidification process
Dictionary of Paper, 2519
diethyl zinc (DEZ) deacidification
    facility, 2656
diethyl zinc (DEZ) deacidification
    process, 356, 723, 909, 1296,
    1298, 1392, 1599, 2073, 2105,
    2217, 2416, 2418, 2658–59, 2668,
    3120, 3387, 4309
digital imagery, 77, 590, 593, 792,
    1190–92, 1199, 1201, 1588,
    1618–19, 2318, 2432, 2438,
    2440–41, 2446, 2607, 2626, 2984,
    3837, 3861, 4749, 4930–31, 5044;
    preservation of, 2626; quality
    control, 4956
disaster management, 617, 745, 1069,
    1131, 1565, 1600, 1773, 2020,
    2422, 2737, 3026–27, 3223, 3267,
    3396, 3582, 3598, 4365, 4632,
    5123, 5277; employee trauma,
    4261, 4862; handbook for, 413;
    introduction to, 3395, 3980
disaster planning, 310, 367, 409, 416–

18, 553, 572, 630, 800, 814, 1038,
    1499, 1530, 1593, 1629, 1758,
    2334, 2711, 2774, 2919, 3333,
    3918, 3995, 5009, 5291; case
    studies, 1985, 4816, 4882, 4984;
    elements of, 1354, 4268, 4593,
    4595; hospital libraries, 130;
    template for, 2952
disaster preparedness, 344, 408, 779,
    815–16, 1062, 1450, 1455, 1767,
    2172, 2576, 2736, 3166, 3225;
    guidelines for, 1857, 3328, 3715,
    4772, 4840, 5148; VHS video on,
    5214; workbook for, 5147
disaster prevention, 490, 836, 1764,
    1781, 2172, 2592, 4133–34
disaster recovery, 310, 616, 836, 942,
    1434, 1484, 1757, 1808, 1897,
    1899, 1950, 2172, 2635, 2642,
    3085, 3506, 4134, 4984, 5079;
    bibliographies for, 2942, 4040;
    factors in, 958, 1498, 3844;
    guidance for, 1483, 3228; network
    development, 4033; network for,
    1369; salvage, 3646, 4592;
    technology for, 3231, 5093, 5097;
    training for, 871, 2257, 4639;
    vendors for, 1752; of vital records,
    4725, 4847
disaster response, 346, 377, 403, 1259,
    1415, 1437, 2334, 3395
disbinding, 1064, 1628
DistList for conservation, 2153
document conservation, 914, 1920,
    2948, 3240, 4207, 4881, 5044,
    5227, 5289; ancient, 5028;
    cultural, 913; encapsulation of,
    650; forensic examination of, 338,
    5043; forged documents, 707;
    repair of, 770, 2586–87; storage,
    1206; technology for, 4660;
    treatments in, 676; VHS video on,
    5343
document delivery technologies, 5064
document microphotography, 1986
document preservation, 4183
document restoration, 199, 1488, 2946,
    4254
document scanners, 4017
Domesday debate, 2451, 3735, 1978
Drake University, 5288
Drew University Library, 1209
drying procedures, 3, 421, 1415, 1551,
    1604, 1894, 2029, 2187, 2380,

2648, 2744, 2769, 2809, 3020–21, 3163, 3524–26, 4192, 4320, 4413, 4454, 4850–51
duplication for preservation, 1556, 1809, 3714
dust cloths, analysis of, 1091
Dwight Morrow paper project, 3468

earthquake, 48–49, 1640, 1673, 1707, 1754, 1945, 1988, 2758, 3238, 3480, 3652, 4941, 4960
East Carolina University, 4286, 4288
Eastern Africa, 2463
edge gilding, gauffering, 5233
education, training in conservation, 371, 412, 521, 2127, 2346, 2359, 2405, 3279, 3569, 3823, 3966, 3987, 4278, 4674, 5070, 5081, 5149
education, training in preservation, 437, 1072–73, 1078–79, 1094, 1098, 1186, 1213, 1215–16, 1377, 1579, 1652, 1669, 1743, 1776, 1783, 1813, 1835, 2081, 2165, 2176, 2202, 2276, 2282, 2286, 2404, 2602, 2746, 2790–91, 3042, 3057, 3065, 3173, 3490, 3887, 3948, 4252, 4325, 4477, 4489, 4835, 4902–03, 5070, 5338
El Salvador, 2618
electronic conversion of printed material, 1582, 2638, 2722, 3137, 4734
electronic document imaging, 4017–18
electronic formats recovery, 4605
electronic imaging, 1244, 1327, 1374, 1605, 4018–21, 4497, 4563
electronic incunabula, 2117
electronic preservation formats, 2319–20, 3957; CXP development, 2433
electronic publishing/resources, 739, 865, 1016
elementary school conservation, 5053
Elmira (NY) College, 5102
emergency preparedness, 335, 953, 3007, 3649–50, 4555, 4557; contingency planning of, 3278; federal assistance in, 3277; guide for site-specific plans, 4557; in art libraries, 2589
encapsulation, 488, 753
enclosures, 642, 2525, 2544, 2826, 5297–98; phase box construction, 2924; Phase-Box program

development, 2974; video on, 5259
encoding systems, 1931
encyclopedia of recorded sound, 4492
end sheets, 1785
endbands, 5245
endpaper, 625, 992, 3788, 5243
England, 1670–71, 1688, 1970, 4549, 4568, 4571, 4576, 4597, 4692, 4937, 5286
engravings, diagrams, 2096
environment, 236, 266, 375, 433, 711, 956, 1034, 1277, 1289, 1464, 1478, 1532, 1971, 1989, 1997, 2005, 2369, 2474, 2633, 2685, 3374, 3538, 4166, 4187, 4351–52, 4551, 4980; concerns of, 2762; guide for, 4051; home library, 2352; importance of, 46, 4552; material stress and, 3043; moisture control, 406; monitoring, 453, 2724, 4067; pollutants, 373
environmental controls, 363, 1331, 1765, 1867, 2006, 3174, 3329, 3647, 4330, 4389, 4392
enzyme removal, 221
enzymes in paper, 220–21, 1465, 2100
ephemeral materials, 2956
Estonia, 4673
ethical issues, 517, 527, 530, 4836
ethnographic materials care, 3768
ethylene oxide (EtO) fumigation, 1721, 2149, 2197, 4701
European Commission on Preservation and Access, 1141
European Register of Microfilm Masters, 4001, 4142
Everett Community College Library, 4945
exhibition, 361, 528, 895, 951, 1972, 1980, 2371, 2526, 3076, 3354, 3371, 3479, 3488, 3523, 3625, 4417, 5339; book cradles, 201, 415, 626; book supports, 951, 1044; case design, 981; micro-climates for, 390, 982, 1867; mounting techniques, 3354

facsimiles, 296, 343
family papers, 1118, 3901
Fawcett Library flood, 5088
film and video collections, 1446
film archiving, 1578
film conservation/preservation, 94,

183, 185, 209, 452, 458, 831, 1365, 1526, 1554, 1557, 1570, 1572, 1598, 1664, 2229, 2330, 2365, 2452, 2513, 2661, 2678, 2794, 3049–50, 3153, 3751, 4068, 5039, 5167; cellulose acetate, 3835; Cibachrome, 1750; color, 2185, 3221, 3347, 4529, 5037; deterioration, 1573–77; duplication, 2141, 2145, 2539, 3729; foxing, 1409; lantern slides, 3400; negatives, 2796, 3029, 5322; platinum, palladium, 1919; Polaroid, 3655; resin-coated, 3955; restoration, 2144, 2940; silver film, 3834; stability, 2139–40, 3833, 3840, 4297, 4620, 5038; storage, 716, 1408; sulfiding, 47

film supports, 24, 35, 37, 2348, 2999

fire, 2249, 4811, 5098; aftermath terminology, 4103; assessment method, 3565; detection systems, 3699; extinguishing methods, 4212; insurance options, 4689; safety introduction, 4652; VHS video on, 5212, 5225

fire protection, 115, 133, 279, 1686, 1765, 1824, 3165; guidelines for, 3268; recommended practices, 3269

fire suppression, 279–82, 1220, 2038, 2899, 3171; micromist, 278; minimum requirements, 3271; sprinkler systems, 4688, 5068; VHS video on, 5212

fixatives, 554

Florida, 1451, 1454–56

Florida State University, 1727, 4638

fluorescence imaging, 2019

FMC mass paper preservation system, 723, 1728, 4967, 4969

formaldehyde, 2099, 2631

foxing, 240–41, 1343, 1828–29, 2163–64, 2167, 2701–02, 4077

France, 18, 84, 332, 990, 1777–80, 3864, 4616, 4915

fraud, 2171

French books, 4006

fumigation methods, 83, 270, 410, 1020, 1602, 1721, 1867, 3129, 3385, 4050; carbon dioxide, 3564; disinfecting, 4993; ethylene oxide (EtO), 411; gamma radiation, 4607; orthophenyl phenol, 2017;

paraformaldehyde, 1990; safety standards of, 4310; sodium tetraborate, 1827; sulfuryl fluoride (Vikane), 1462; thymol, 376, 1990

funding, 1000, 1106, 1753, 2408, 3116, 3327, 3975, 4026, 4375, 4911

fungi, 111, 996, 1923, 3383, 3392, 3782, 3909, 4426; in books, 242, 1720; in stamp collections, 5011; on paper, 238; stains from, 4527

Gambia, 3348

Georgia State University, 3546

geoscience, 5164

Germany, 2528

Gettysburg address (preservation), 1842

glue, properties of, 1545–46, 3453

gold tooling, 5235–36

goldbeater's skin (video), 5302

Gore-Tex material, 3732

government records, 1153, 1560, 1751, 1819, 2204, 3272, 3293, 4070

Greenfield, Jane, 1210

Gregorian, Vartan, 3668

Guild of Book Workers Journal, 1627, 1982, 2550, 3215

Guildford College of Technology, 2789

Guyana, 3648

Haiti, 817

halons, 832, 3912, 4829, 5067

hand bookbinding, 1174, 1211, 1592, 1805, 1981, 4942, 5356

hand-made paper, 1274, 1683, 2759, 3044, 3505, 4191, 4467, 5216, 5244, 5280, 5306, 5318–19

Harold B. Lee Library, 2315

Harry Ransom Humanities Research Center, 1233, 1306, 1737

Harvard Book Depository, 1916

Hass, J. Warren, 5086

health concerns, 20, 127–28, 341, 406, 1154, 1955, 2288, 4236

Hebrew Union College, 2520

Help-Net Binding Preparation system, 2120

Helsinki University Library, 3633

Her Majesty's Stationers Office, 1745, 1946, 2482

heritage preservation, 59, 1353

historic, artistic works conservation, 132–33, 135–45

historical materials conservation, 32,
481, 733, 3917, 4010, 5131, 5230
historical materials preservation, 219,
733, 1017, 1036, 1595, 2937,
2998, 3093, 3118, 3316, 3850,
3895, 4559; access, 3325; binding
of, 1093, 1739, 1941, 3098; needs
assessment, 5004; records for,
3275, 3281; research in, 4978
history: of books, 360; of
papermaking, 4442
hot-stamping foils, 3808
Howard University, 2375
Hungary, 68–69, 1284, 1332, 1520,
1656, 1747, 2400–2403, 2921,
3662–63, 3968, 4234, 4573, 4861,
4866, 4961, 5092
Hunter, Dard, 1247
Huntington Library fire, 134, 3910
hurricanes: Andrew, 1452, 4138, 4623;
Gilbert, 2, 790; Hugo, 2853, 2900,
3594; Iwa, 3001; mitigation, 574;
preparedness primer, 4654

Idaho, 67, 3603, 3821
ILL *See* interlibrary loan
Illinois, 2373
Illinois State Library, 3581
illuminated manuscripts, 2614, 3218,
4678, 5303
Image Permanence Institute, 33
imaging technology, 591–92, 2574,
2734, 3004, 4446; bibliography,
602; glossary of terms, 297;
quality control in, 369
imitation leather, 4594, 4926
immovable cultural property, 3013
India, 52, 612, 1356, 2481, 4041, 4372
Indian Conservation Institute, 54
Indian libraries, 2554
Indiana University Libraries, 1510,
3149
indoor air quality, 60, 126, 2414, 2833,
3188, 4702, 4722–24, 4759, 5184;
air waste management, 1972;
industrial ventilation, 126;
particulate standards, 374
infestation, large-scale, 270
information and image management,
298
ink, 50, 731, 2975, 3289; composition
of, 3608, 3741; deinking
procedures, 4219; developments
in, 2684; iron gall, 1984, 4260;

testing of, 2584, 2975
insect control, 242, 406, 653, 778,
1276, 1334, 1372–73, 1638, 1722,
1724, 1892, 1904, 2169, 2462,
2500, 2502, 2580, 2608; freezing,
3303, 4307, 4320; history of,
3781; humidified nitrogen use,
3994; microwave radiation, 737;
molecular traps, 3848; non-
chemical methods, 4430, 4993;
non-toxic method, 4805; of stamp
collections, 5011; oxygen
replacement project, 4804;
sterilization, 4062
insect identification, 4979;
cockroaches, 3433; dry wood
termites, 4403; German
cockroach, 3434; powderpost
beetle, 1896; silverfish, firebrats,
book lice, 2580; smirnov beetle,
1549
Institute of Jazz Studies, 1964
Institute of Paper Conservation, 2793,
3883
institutional preservation programs,
1932, 2564
instruments used in conservation, 4420
insurance policies, coverage, options,
146, 1412, 2200, 4687
integrated pest management (IPM),
2054–55, 3368, 3433, 3435, 3445,
3528–29, 3531, 4424, 5190
interlibrary loan (ILL), 3292
International Federation of Library
Associations (IFLA), 4833
Internet, the, 1424, 1704, 2152, 3879,
3958, 4801
Iowa Cooperative Preservation
Consortium, 2524
Iowa flood, 203
Iowa State University, 2045
IPM *See* integrated pest management
Iran, 3341
Ireland, 1516–17
Iron Range Research Center, 5280
Islamic manuscripts, 4796
Israel, 1386
Italy, 207, 1141, 3145

Jam' al-Tawarikh conservation, 398
Jamaica, 1, 790, 2903, 3144, 4546
Japan, 63, 5003, 5133–34, 5186
Japanese book production, 340
Japanese machine-made paper, 3492

Japanese papermaking, 221, 2268, 2374, 2388, 2501, 5282–84, 5346, 5350
John F. Kennedy Library, 3402, 5015
Johns Hopkins University, 2694, 4251
Joliet Public Library fire, 2339
Journal of Academic Librarianship, 2109
Journal of Coatings Technology, 2155
Journal of Indian Museums, 58
Journal of Library and Science (India), 66
Juan Mandez photographic collection, 3467

Kansas, 2392
Kemp Public Library, 3932
Kentucky, 549, 3556
Kenya, 583, 720, 1109, 1525, 2262, 2423, 3030, 3236, 4548
knowledge preservation, 512, 1099, 1347, 1860, 3205, 3604, 3886, 4411, 4599
knowledge preservation considerations, 1233, 1240, 4536

Lada-Mocarski, Polly, 1215
Langholm Library Project, 1260
Langwell interleaf vapor phase, 2217
LAPNet, 2396, 2742–43
Large Electronic Imaging Project, 4404
laser removal of fungus stains, 4528
laser rot, 2419
Latin American materials, preservation of, 2108, 2110, 2619
law library conservation/preservation, 123, 226, 2987, 3659, 3688, 5172, 5174
LBJ Presidential Library, 4604
leafcasting process, 439, 447, 2036, 2624, 5114–15; attachment methods, 3062; imaging system to assist, 3209; leaf caster, 1258; leaf master, 1810; machines for, 2581; VHS, U-Matic video on, 5287
leather, 929, 1730, 1792, 2023, 2570, 3215, 3736, 4008, 4663; analyzing, 4340; deterioration of, 748, 2569; dressing, 2852; dyes, 3678; fungicides on, 931; hinges, 5243; literature on, 1723; methodology, 3616; nature of, 4630, 4926; praline-N use, 3871; skiving, paring of, 5220; spue on, 1459, 2938; sulphur content of, 2023; sulphur dioxide treatment, 1723; tanned, 929; vegetable-tanned, 3730
leather bindings, 118, 930, 1625, 2015–16, 2938, 2986; microbial degradation, 4443; restoration of, 3099; TALAS formula for, 3477
Lenin Library, 3128
Leningrad Library, 2673
letterforms, 5357
librarianship, 21, 105, 123, 155, 167, 206, 339, 507, 1103, 1391, 2225, 2357, 5052, 5217, 5293, 5327, 5341
libraries, 107–08, 149, 154, 166
Library at the Explorers Club, 801
Library Binding Institute, 3056, 3213, 3514, 3516, 3518–19, 3521
library bindings, 797, 3791, 3793, 3799, 3809, 4514, 4658, 4938, 4943, 4985–88; literature on, 3806; overview of, 3520; paper grain effect on, 3800; procedures, options, 3072, 3179, 3787; techniques for, 3610, 3802; testing of, 3807
Library Crime Research project, 2708
library management, 267, 763, 1104, 1302, 2710, 4139, 4510
library material conservation, 3150, 3502, 5333
Library of Congress, 76, 596, 2070, 2651, 2654, 2658–60, 2662–65, 2668–69, 2671, 2674, 2677, 2683–85, 2690, 2859, 2973, 4675, 4951; cellulose deterioration study, 4358; chemical process report, 4677, 4704; and deacidification, 2662, 2666, 3387, 3745, 4167, 4999; microfilming program, 3922; phased box program, 3210; preservation, conservation services, 3260, 4456; research at, 4185, 4187, 4267; thief from, 3852
Library of Parliament fire, 2029
library preservation, 1175
library research materials, 781, 2908, 3017–18
Linotype machines, 5223
literacy and access, 147
literature on conservation, 2237, 4913–

14

literature on preservation, 1847, 2237, 2395, 4949

Lithium Corporation of America, 4970

Los Angeles Public Library fire recovery, 3160, 3168–69, 3646, 4230, 4946

Los Angeles riots, 4668

Loughborough Polytech Library, 2102

Louisiana State University Library, 3461

machine-readable data, 120, 205, 1843, 1962, 2051, 2118, 2458, 2927, 2963, 2965; carriers, 3811

magnetic media, 1006, 1022, 1361, 1438, 2133, 4407–08; care and handling of, 4082; environment, 3458; permanence, 3591; shipping, handling of, 4338

Maine State Archives, 199

Malta, 4088

Mann Library, 1443

manuscripts, 18, 242, 1117, 1357, 1524, 1719, 2292, 2561, 2684, 3031, 3557, 4461; analysis of, 1440; aqueous deacidification of, 3763; bark type, 4558; bibliography of, 4678; borrowing of, 1538; bound paper, 550; Byzantine, 2477; cockled, 2747; composition of, 54, 1635; conservation of, 1635; damaged, 1506, 1656; decision-making process for, 3563; deterioration of, 1936; electronic preservation of, 3542; evaluation of treatments, 551; identification of, 675; illumination, 1815; illustrated, 1356; inks, 4583, 4856; palm leaf type, 4046, 4466; pigment identification, 3669; rare, 105, 157, 161, 163; resources for, 2321, 4168; restoration of, 1357; retention of structural evidence, 3548; security measures for, 3418; theft of, 177; treatment, 3626

map conservation, 75, 90, 892, 1281–83, 1660, 1937, 2493, 2571, 3876, 3967; bibliography of, 3597; CD-ROM technology for, 1207; chemical analysis, 2897; oversized, 1870

map librarianship, 2572

map preservation, 2150, 3597, 4215

MAPS *See* MicrogrAphic Preservation Service

maps in books, 1356

Marquette Electronic Archive system, 3542

Martinelli, David J., 1208

Maryland, 3003

mass conservation, 1733, 4869

mass deacidification, 268, 430, 638–39, 664, 721, 818, 847, 1096, 1297–98, 1331, 2819, 3332, 3991, 4104, 4144, 4359, 4584, 4665, 4667, 4970; Akzo process, 3330; bibliographies for, 3474, 5158; Book Preservation Associates (BPA) process, 2234; Bookkeeper process, 2217, 2523, 2686, 3359, 4699; diethyl zinc (DEZ) process, 356, 723, 909, 1296, 1298, 1392, 1599, 2073, 2105, 2217, 2416, 2418, 2658–59, 2668, 2918, 3120, 3387, 4309; evaluations, 1466, 1798, 2389, 2654, 2696, 2738, 2910, 2918, 3484, 3664, 4145, 4316, 4440, 4971, 4662; facility, 2665, 4704, 4720; magnesium butoxytriglycolate process, 2918; magnesium methyl carbonate process, 4145; techniques for, 1797, 2065, 3645; training, 4361; VHS video on, 5307; Wei T'o process, 723, 909, 1298, 1392, 2216–17, 4149–50, 4309, 4314, 4363, 4690

Massachusetts, 4641–42, 4644, 5023

matboards, 249

materials from Middle Ages, 4615

media librarianship, 1579, 1596

medieval book binding, 4419

medieval book restoration, 4854

Mekanotch bookbinding, 3795

Mellon Microfilming Project, 2475

Memory of the World project, 9, 1083, 1760, 4816, 4834

metal objects conservation, 5202

MicroChamber materials, 4845

microfiche, 993, 1799, 3095, 3143, 5008

microfilm, 302, 387, 690, 915, 1490; digitization, 772; permanence, 1193; reformatting, 2056; silver in, 301; substitution, 1004; technology, 588 microfilming, 167, 265, 303, 637, 662, 694, 789, 792, 880, 885, 1029, 1503, 1927, 2393, 2690; contracting for, 2235; costs of, 1874; diazo film, 184, 4671; future of, 349; guidelines for, 1589–90, 1998; history of, 694, 891; in-house microforms, 4664; redox blemishes, 4925;versus paper storage, 2133

microfilming for preservation, 670, 695, 860, 994, 1346, 1417, 2022, 2061, 2188, 2263, 2343, 2370, 2435, 2451, 2480, 2516, 2537, 2605, 2628, 2729, 2752, 2812, 2935, 2969, 2971, 2989, 3033, 3297, 3365, 3856, 3944, 4348, 4535, 4664, 5042, 5275; commercial microfilmer role in, 3291; cooperative efforts, 5001– 02; developments in, 2068, 5069; digitization and, 4885; future of, 4626, 5021, 5091; guidelines for, 3855; large collection, 1346; manual for, 3858; versus original paper, 4105; versus other technologies, 4005, 4284; planning for, 4887, 5007; production of, 169; risk factors, 4679; VHS video on, 5334

microfilming vendor selecting, 879, 882, 2726, 5101, 5156

microform publishing, 167, 968

microforms, 127, 164–65, 167, 283, 357, 366, 634, 696, 974, 1541, 1685, 1706, 1837, 2795, 5056, 5096; availability, 1403; cataloguing, 164; climate control, 5161–62; collection control, 2223; conversion, 563; evaluation of, 4370, 5323; future of, 5137; handling of, 5206; hypo limits of, 28; in-house, 4516; maintenance of, 3920, 4370; masters, 1422, 1928, 3859, 4626, 4853; processing of, 36; shipping, 165

micrographic management, 3125

MicrogrAphic Preservation Service (MAPS), 5304

micrographic restoration, 1868

microphotography manual, 1986

micropreservation project, 614

military records preservation, 4743

Mississippi Libraries, 3475–76, 5094

model preservation program, 3908

mold growth and damage, 531, 583, 587, 757, 1052, 1257, 1273, 1291, 1841, 2197, 2520, 3370, 3373, 3909, 4551, 4680; bibliography of, 5100; control of, 1867, 1887, 3175, 4806; health threat from, 794, 2863; identification of, 3705; malevolent mold growth, 3444; in stamp collections, 5011; structure, nature of molds, 5099

mold, mildew, fungi treatments, 259, 3384

Montreal, 2991

Mormon genealogy preservation project, 1245, 4218

Morrow, Carolyn Clark, 1436

motion picture conservation, 95–101, 106, 520, 1022, 1477, 1557, 2507, 2540; bibliographies, 3258, 3936; cleaning, 4602; digital mastering, 419; old films, 811, 4581; physical properties of, 908; silent films, 2679; simulated aging of film, 3750; storage, 4114, 4339; treatment for, 4127; UNESCO, 2077, 4694

multimedia materials preservation/access, 2156, 4977

Munster University Library, 3776, 4047

museums, 114, 121, 124–25, 859, 1231, 2341, 2912, 2958, 3942, 5196, 5213; art object handling, 4201; cases, 1335–36, 3460; climate control, 363, 790, 983–84, 2949, 3194, 3487; curatorship, 364, 2957, 4586; disaster planning, 367; disinfecting of, 1891; environment of, 3283, 4590, 5190; exhibitions, 548, 581, 4591, 5194; insect control, 1334; lighting, 228, 977, 1718, 3088, 4589, 5188; materials analysis, 3123; mounting techniques, 5312; pest management, 362, 3695, 5190; Solander boxes, 904; storage, 5193; terminology, 1385, 2224

museums conservation, 5187, 5192, 5195, 5198, 5205

music conservation, 1875, 2125, 2219, 4345, 4598

music librarianship, 2218

music preservation, 2220, 3939
mutilation, 39, 45, 82, 113, 342, 628, 2299, 2388, 2497, 3299; by bookmarks, 3212, 3914–15; by electronic security systems, 4947; by patrons, 5183; of popular journals, 4131; serials, of, 3212; VHS video on, 5300
Mylar, 2957, 4542

NAGARA *See* National Association of Government Archivists and Records Administrators
NAGARA GRASPP automated preservation planning system, 1312, 1315, 1316
NARA *See* National Archives and Records Administration
National Aeronautics and Space Administration (NASA) data, 4727–28
National Agricultural Text Digitizing Project, 215
National Archives Advisory Committee on Preservation, 927
National Archives and Records Administration (NARA), 269, 370, 612, 920, 934, 2293, 2398, 3876, 3898–99, 4743–44, 4746, 4748, 4750, 4752, 4755
National Archives of Canada, 945–47, 5122
National Association of Government Archivists and Records Administrators (NAGARA), 1316
National Book Trust India, 55
National Bureau of Standards on Materials for Archival Records, 5076
National Digital Library, 4332
National Endowment for the Humanities (NEH) Office of Preservation, 496, 1025, 1692–94, 2468, 2590, 3265
National Film Preservation Act, 2661, 3853
national goals for preservation, 4336
National Library of Australia, 61, 3691
National Library of Austria, 4864–65
National Library of Bhutan, 4196
National Library of Canada, 4992
National Library of Medicine, 2384, 4562
National Library of Venezuela, 622

National Library Services Board, 1226
National Manuscripts Conservation Trust, 2427, 4874
National Maritime Museum (UK), 1122
National Preservation Office, 1003
national preservation planning, 1163, 1178, 1351, 1666, 2981, 3181
National Preservation Program, 3059, 5324; for Agriculture, 1442
Nebraska, 3286, 4901
NEDCC *See* Northeast Document Conservation
NEH *See* National Endowment for the Humanities
Netherlands, 2508, 3305–07, 3665, 4810, 4817, 4839
New Bedford Whaling Museum, 22, 2101
New Jersey, 1216, 1447, 2750, 4391, 4488, 4503, 4953
New Plymouth school fire, 1789
New York, 59, 4910
New York Document Conservation Advisory Council, 59
New York Public Library, 400–401, 674, 3668
New York State Archives, 4910, 5289
New York State Library flood, 2821
New York Times, 3858, 5223
New York University, 3719, 4388; at Stoney Brook, 4387; rare books examination, 3719
New Zealand, 4629
Newark Public Library, 1740
Newberry Library (Chicago), 2603, 3334
newspaper clippings conservation, 1305
newspaper collection management, 6, 2766, 5106
Newspaper Preservation Act (1970), 4709
newspapers: conservation of, 6–7, 421, 424–25, 489, 1040, 1152, 1280, 2057, 2090, 2328; microfilming of, 615, 691, 1376, 2344, 2578, 2585, 2599, 2909, 3014, 3115; preservation of, 1882, 2189, 2210, 4160, 4387, 4794, 4996–97
Newsplan Program, 2328
Nigeria, 40, 65, 79–80, 231, 365, 1508, 1639, 1641–42, 1644, 2261, 3414, 3426, 4793

nitrate stock preservation, 251
non-paper materials conservation, 875–76, 923, 1053, 1885, 1906, 2130, 2596, 2825, 3498, 5203
non-standard collection management, 3567
North Carolina, 1956–57, 4366
Northeast Document Conservation Center, 70, 1300, 1674, 3367, 3398, 3412, 3415, 3417, 3623, 3978, 3982–83, 4458, 4471, 4768, 5163
Northern Arizona University, 4686
Northwestern University Library, 3035, 3375

Oberlin College Libraries, 4111–12
Oberlin Conference on thief, 4627
Ocker, Ralph, 1217
OCLC guidelines, 2314
OCR *See* optical character recognition
Ohio, 4445
Ohio State University Libraries, 672, 940, 2027, 2640, 3425, 3826
Oklahoma, 74
Oklahoma State Archives flood, 2058
Oklahoma State University Library, 3428
Old Sturbridge Village (MA), 3587
Omaha Project, 5314
Online Computer Library Center, Inc., 3451
optical character recognition (OCR), 2121, 4749
optical digital recording, 4860
optical disk, 28, 305, 540, 1700, 1711, 2116, 2161, 2436, 2641, 2664, 3047, 3645, 4757, 5027; and microfilm, 1479, 1698; as alternative, 1280, 2133, 4023, 4025; assessment of, 4900, 4963; equipment, review of, 4024; formats, 283; introduction to, 2135, 5025; legal issues, 91; permanence, 3591; review of technology, 4026–27; technology of, 3381; testing of disk system, 3825; use of, 3378, 3554; versus paper storage, 3656
Optical Disk Pilot program, 1711, 3701, 5000
Oregon, 67, 4585
original format preservation, 1074, 1786, 1804, 2785, 3102, 3135, 3408, 3893, 3968, 4382, 4537–38, 4923
out-of-print searching, acquisitions of, 465
oversized materials, 427, 960, 1902
overview of preservation, 3182, 4239, 4318, 4377, 4494, 4643
Ox Bow Conference, 4508
Oxford University, 4486, 4519, 4784
oxygen scavenger, 2558

Pakistan, 3657
pamphlet binding, 4226, 5296
paper, 47, 420, 426, 850, 1078, 1475, 2240, 2522, 3104, 4157, 4177, 5034, 5238; aging, 434, 3562, 3832; analysis of, 2167, 2425; archival, 248, 2817, 2832, 4186; artificial aging, 446; bibliography, 613; chemistry of, 4; chromatographic patterns in, 894; gelatin content, 4080; hemicellulose, 1677; kaolin-coated, 2918; lignin-containing paper, 1536; pigment-coated, 4822; pulp content, 1832; pure cellulose, 932; rag, 482; research in, 4819; surface cleaning, 1246, 4393; temperature effect, 1607–08; transparent, 1716; unstable, 509, 2595; untreated papers, 2910; verifax, 2362; wood pulp paper, 2894; xuan, 3214
paper collection management, 369
paper conservation, 139, 1264, 1383, 1399, 1625, 1938, 2020, 2039, 2103, 2177, 3602, 3607, 3710, 3764, 3883, 4188, 4256, 4842, 5157; acid deterioration, 4855; acid transfer, 4323; alkali reaction, 845; blistering, 1060; blue paper, 807; browning of, 2196; durable, 1062; methods for, 4255; morphology of, 1729; video on, 5246; wetting agents, 2926; yellowing, 578
paper conservation techniques, 730, 1337, 1822, 2462, 2837, 3353, 3780, 4227–28, 4248, 4435, 4444, 4454, 4858, 5144, 5316–17; acid-free glassine testing, 4328; aqueous immersion, 2892; graft copolymerization, 863, 1065, 2472; impregnating agents for,

1637; methyl cellulose impregnation, 3777; methylene blue testing, 4564; particle analysis, 609; proton milliprobe tool, 4136; raking light, 261; solvent treatments, 3951; videos on, 5254; washing, 2697, 2916

paper deterioration, 1679, 2487, 2768, 2775, 3494, 3507, 4094, 4661, 5200; biological factors of, 1826; causes of, 4191, 4255; cellulose deterioration, 1677; environmental factors, 4272; enzyme treatments effect, 4661; gamma irradiation and, 875, 2047; mechanism of, 4927; overview of causes, 4681

paper diffusion phenomena, 1487

paper grade finder, 1156

paper objects conservation, 216

paper preservation, 486, 631, 4880, 4974–75; aging effects, 189; conservator's role in, 4191; overview of, 4681

paper stabilization, 623, 1384, 1748, 3032, 5320

paper strengthening, 863, 1065, 1084, 1661, 2244, 2363, 2771; FMC mass paper preservation system, 4967–69; for newspapers, 4865; graft copolymerization, 1738; paper-splitting techniques, 423, 3472, 4962; with acrylics, 1064

paper testing methods, 1550

paperback books, 1278, 3693–94, 3798; albumen and salted type, 3827; mass market paperbacks, 1035; study of, 2192; versus hardbacks, 4228

papermaking, 47, 483–84, 599, 1127, 1917, 2048, 2183, 2486, 2645, 2943, 4044, 5186; acidity in, 909, 1397; alkaline paper, 2869, 4878–79; alkaline-neutral advantages in, 3711; chemical watermarking, 4939; complexity of, 3708; description of processes, 2532, 3709; fermentation, 483; fibers, 478, 1877; future of, 4156; lignin content effect, 3714; mineral fillers, 544; permanent-durable paper production, 4922–23; pigment-coated production, 3722; pulping, 47, 1247; technology of, 1126, 2759; terminology of, 4331;

videos on, 5345, 5354–55

papyrus, 380, 598, 1500, 2559, 4384

parchment, 568, 576, 896, 903, 987, 1057, 1357, 1461, 1594, 1825, 1908, 2816, 3607, 4848; historical overview, 3208; infilling of, 567; modern form, 1489; response to relative humidity, 4087; single leaf type, 3354

Parker Library, 2009–11

parylene, 1939, 2244–46

passive conservation concept, 4566

patrimony, 468, 4493

Patterson, Bob, 2749

Peabody Museum of Salem, 3618

pen ruling, 5321

Pennsylvania State University Libraries, 3585

People's Republic of Bulgaria, 1494

People's Republic of China, 1068, 2013

periodicals bindings, 3111

periodicals, preservation of, 2301, 3111

permanent paper, 148, 151, 255, 398, 909, 1473, 1782, 2383, 2386, 2400, 2470, 2751, 2771, 2834, 2845, 2856, 2860, 2867, 2870, 2872, 2878–79, 2885, 2928, 3471, 3592, 4165, 4283, 4703, 4852, 5054, 5074; argument for, 4637; concept of, 2137; effects of strengthening, deacidification on, 4164; EPA guidelines for, 3717; groundwood, 182, 1974; history of standards, 5073; legal issues, 2881; legislation for, 4292; lignin content effect, 2864, 5084, 5166; manufacturing processes, 3483; national policy on, 4716–18; production of, 4312; questionnaire data, 5150; standards for, 1183, 5151; testing of, 3083; U.S., U.K. progress report, 4636; use of, 3304, 3938

Permanent Paper Law, 2873

personal papers, preservation of, 257, 2391

pest management, 114, 362, 720, 735–36, 862, 1420, 1432, 1548–49, 1890, 1896, 2184, 2322; argon gas chamber, 1432; contracting services for, 3431; guide to, 5170; limitations of insecticides, 3639;

list of pests by material, damage, 4116; low oxygen atmospheres, 1890; modified atmospheres for, 4429, 4990; non-toxic methods for, 4311; passive control of, 4428; pesticide terminology, 3530; pesticide use checklist, 5169; summary of scientific research on, 5077; treatment strategies, 4385, 2055; vertebrate pests, 4427, 4439; VHS video on, 5329. *See also* integrated pest management (IPM)

pH, 182, 375, 483, 578–79, 717, 730, 2609, 3338; investigation, 870; measuring, 2830, 2875; neutral, 1785; VHS, U-Matic video on, 5351

phased conservation, concept of, 4934–35

philatelic conservation/preservation, 2947, 4109–10, 4543

phone directories preservation, 2663

photocopying, 153, 168, 193, 325, 352, 556, 643, 840, 1926, 2933, 3463, 3893, 4965

photocopying for preservation, 2849, 3361, 4506, 4886, 5063; bound volumes, 4299; guidelines for, 168; overhead photocopier development, 5062; quality of Xerographic copies, 4451–53; selecting photocopier, 4886, 5117

photographic album conservation, 837, 2180, 2226, 5168

photographic collection management, 2621

photographic conservation, 566, 580, 991, 1271, 1561, 2142, 2146–48, 2214, 2499, 2530–31, 3077, 3152, 4058, 4578; albumen prints, 3838; collection control, 4826; duplication, 3727–28; early photographs of, 4917; electrostatic copying, 4052, 4055, 4061; enclosures for, 4871; glossary of terms for, 3465; history of papermaking, 3345; in research libraries, 3831; instant photographs, 4905; manual for, 3904; need for standards, 3156; of early prints, 3828; overview of, 4258; photo CD format, 4049; picture aging, 209–10; print

framing, 4918; relative humidity (RH) affects, 2823; training in, 3830; treatments in, 3464

photographic preservation, 27, 56, 71–73, 2043, 2409, 2428, 4214; and access, 3734; archival, 2331; collection management, 2799, 3229; costs of preservation, 4125; glass plates, 2797; guidelines for, 3902; history of photography, 3457; image permanence, 4872; instant photographs, of, 4905; need for standards, 3156; optical disk project report, 4873; overview of, 3469; plate storage, 685; processing techniques, 405, 4337; storage methods, 4081; wet-plate negatives, 2822

photographic restoration, 3954

photographic terms, glossary of, 2591

photography, 211, 1113, 2138, 2430, 2604, 3154, 3843, 4541; biodeterioration, 450; care and handling of, 3935; chemistry, 186, 1558; collecting, 2994; deterioration, 1563; enclosures for, 3841; exhibition, 3930; gelatin silver, 3094; health concerns, 4197; history of, 826, 3940; industrial, 4057; microfiche for, 2803–04; negative print papers, 2119; old photographs, 3660; permanence of, 3346; processing standards, 187; slides, transparencies, 979, 1682; storage, 213, 3846–47

picture framing, 227

Pierpont Morgan Library, 3863

Pilkington Technology Center Fire, 1951

planning programs, 1081, 2285, 2290, 2757, 3069–71, 3073–74, 3140, 3148, 3177–78, 3198, 4888–89

plantain edition conservation, 2007

platinum print conservation, 1858

Plato's texts project, 808

playing cards conservation, 4334

polyester book bindings, 2358

pornography, 3551

Powell, Roger, 2080

preservation and access, 513–14, 698, 2786–87, 2972, 2983, 3008, 3114, 3117, 4827, 5139; art history, 1143, 1149; computer systems for,

3933; conflicts in, 3671;
electronic, 3963, 4713; hybrid
approach, 4348; hybrid systems
for, 5060–61; international
perspective, 4769; open access,
2728; opposition to, 3613;
technology, 4266

preservation concerns, 511, 668–69,
1028, 1238, 2109, 2360, 2634,
3192, 3880, 5274, 5279, 5308,
5347

preservation initiatives, 2091, 2300,
3151, 3342, 4302–03, 4509, 4523,
5290

preservation literature, 438, 523, 702,
793, 883, 888, 1522, 1667, 1772,
2448, 3537, 3681, 3700, 4262,
4949

preservation management, 156, 2176,
2567, 3025, 3561, 4096, 4327,
4511, 5208

preservation needs assessment, 666,
926, 1076, 1299, 2753–54, 2756,
3854, 4843; in government
records, 3257; in tropics, 3217;
methodology for, 989, 3410,
3812; versus commercial needs,
3004

preservation paradigm, 503

preservation planning programs, 4264

preservation problems, 444, 1924,
2173–74, 3241, 4493, 5006;
copyright laws, legislation issues,
3394; electronic formats, 5047;
history of, 3928; management
issues of, 4368

preservation programs, 386, 519, 660,
1235, 2773, 3605, 4415, 5024

preservation reformatting, 428, 1120,
1160, 3124, 3290, 4143, 4625

preservation techniques, 202, 476, 497,
627, 759, 966, 2014, 2327, 2968,
2997, 4625, 4756, 4813–14, 4982,
5328

preservation terms, glossary, 1458,
1906–07

preservation theory, 928

preservation trends, 2064

preservation verification, 2456–57

preservation versus access, 378, 564

preservation/conservation, 2329, 4026,
4353, 4474, 4567, 5065; concepts
for, 2165; concerns of, 3574;
manual for, 2329; of paper

records, 4906; options for, 3063;
principles of, 1544; technologies,
2165, 2782, 2929, 3848; VHS
video on, 5326

preventive conservation, 3744, 4176,
5187

Princeton University Library, 3534

principles of preservation, 429, 3947

printed music
conservation/preservation, 4598

printing, 3086, 4544, 5207, 5223,
5252, 5331

printmaking, papermaking,
bookbinding program, 5332

private archives, 522, 4180

problems in preservation, 147, 533,
701

Pro-Cite 2.02 software, 2107

Project Gutenberg, 5066

Project Open Book, 4932

Public Archives of Canada, 2136, 5124

Public library preservation, 4009

publishers' records, 1121

Puerto Rico, 3217

Purdue University Library, 3640

railway records, 4295

rare and fragile materials conservation,
898, 936, 2730, 2783, 2816, 3351,
3420, 4204, 4241, 5026

rare books, 105, 157, 161–63, 193,
233, 1101–02, 1626, 1960, 2066,
2515, 2629, 2783, 4624;
borrowing of, 1538; conservation
of, 1318, 2080, 3636; electronic
preservation of, 3542; handling of,
194; librarianship, 569;
microfilming, 233; reformatting to
CD-ROM, 3615; security for, 171,
177, 3418; thesaurus of, 162;
treatment of, 233, 441

Ratcliffe report, 1566, 1568, 3772,
4293

rebacking, 775, 5248, 5262

rebinding, 611, 1853, 2312, 5238

recasing, 3109, 5294

record album repair, 4056

recordkeeping, 136, 538, 610, 744,
1386, 1542, 4029, 4140–41, 4693,
4696, 4893, 5146

recordkeeping, electronic, 14, 42, 359,
601, 944, 1203, 1205, 1227, 2082,
3253–54, 3273–74, 4015, 4561,
4711, 4730–31, 4891, 4963;

archival questions, 4736–37; historical records, effects on, 4735; legal requirements of, 4270; long-term storage of, 4745; management of, 4740–42, 4747, 4893; research agenda development, 4964; technology for, 4748; VHS video on, 5218

recycled paper, 2232, 2527; effect of temperature, 3285; overview of production, advocation of standards, 4580; permanence of, 3630; quality of, 2843; strength of, 3284

regluing, 2485

relative humidity (RH), 25, 1157, 1256, 1607, 1610, 1612, 2828, 2884, 2995, 3089–91, 3632, 4846, 5189

Rentokil Bubble, 1020, 1602–03, 3564

reproduction of library material, 689, 692

reproduction technologies, 3243–44

Research Libraries Group (RLG) Digital Image Access Project, 47, 2534, 3643

resource sharing, 4377; versus preservation, 1922

resources for conservation, 336, 2152, 2336, 4102, 4500

responsibility for preservation, 4265, 4285, 4396, 4491, 4818

Rhode Island, 3866–67, 3869, 3986, 4066

Rhode Island College flood, 4984

RLG *See* Research Libraries Group

Rochester Institute of Technology, 3805

Roger, Rutherford D., 1218

Rogers and Hammerstein Archives of Recorded Sound, 2820

Romania, 2417

Russia, 1395, 1623–24, 2426, 2622, 2703, 3164, 4099, 4211, 4343, 4462, 4465, 4481, 4797, 5165

Russian, Soviet materials, 3023, 3139

Rutgers University, 4374, 4499

Rutimann, Hans, 5083

Sarajevo, 4622

scholarship and access, 129, 382, 501–02, 1141, 1621, 1786, 1930–32, 3118, 3491, 5349

school library preservation,

conservation, 4169, 4264

science, technology materials, 2521

scientific research, 11, 4267

scission, 2612

sci-tech material conservation/preservation, 1856, 3200

Scotland, 200, 2087, 2258–60, 2921–22, 3753, 4155, 4158

scrapbook preservation, 1425, 2044, 5168

scrolls, 1895

sculpture conservation, 5201

security, 10, 105, 107, 113, 150, 161, 231, 254, 559–60, 570, 678, 713, 800, 859, 969, 1008, 1250–51, 1272, 1802, 2034, 4277, 4406, 4421, 5125, 5156; bibliographies for, 4011–12; citation system, 4957; computer systems, 107, 344, 732, 890, 2126, 2705; enhancement, 1921; environmental issues and, 3478; equipment review, 935; fundamentals, 1681; guidelines, 767; handbook for, 2410; and human inspectors, 4290; keyways in, 2644; literature of, 404; marking, 1540; patrols, 2254; procedures, 2256; protocols, 4771, 5014, 5153; staff training, 4669; strategies, 4291; systems, 384, 1123, 1291, 2063, 4065

seismic disaster planning, 1158, 1229

seismoguard device, 2154

selling preservation, 1048

Senate Library Conservation Office, 5145

serials management, 1010, 4301, 5109

Shifu art, 5340

shrink-wrapping, 1390, 2040, 2420, 4374, 4738

silica gel, 2553, 3632, 3754

Simmons College, 703

sizing, 252, 395–96, 481, 485, 487, 597, 1877

Slavic books preservation, 1222

Slovenia, 4859

"Slow Fires: On the Preservation of the Human Record," 2944

small library conservation/preservation, 466, 5059, 5078

Smithsonian Institution, 117, 2001–02

softening agents, 903
SOLINET *See* Southeastern Library
     Network
sound recording and motion pictures
     preservation, 4940
South Africa, 659, 933, 1108–09
South Asian libraries, 51, 4190
South Carolina, 3140–41, 4350
South Texas College of Law Library,
     226
Southeast Asia, 53, 3601, 4324
Southeastern Library Network
     (SOLINET) 1018, 1770–71, 4618
Southern Africa, 2463, 3965, 5010
Soviet Library fire, 1623–24
Spain, 3218
special collections, 163, 173, 4434,
     4645, 4648
St. John's University, 5272
stack failure, 2758
stamping materials, 1202
standards, 4474; adhesives, 3794;
     administration, 3945; alkaline
     paper, 2876; architectural
     archives, 131; archival, 1755;
     archival materials, 5075; audio
     conservation, 4921; enforceable,
     255; environment, 372, 1034,
     2855, 4572; ethical conduct, 174,
     176; ethical conduct for, 176;
     Guild of Book Workers', 4089;
     imaging, 2377; industry versus
     preservation, 3053; ink, 4570;
     matboard, glazing terminology,
     893; methods to test paper, 723;
     microfilming, 2739; optical disk,
     2598; permanence, 23, 30, 2247,
     2841, 2861; permanent paper,
     475, 1788, 2868; preservation,
     504, 4512; recordkeeping, 3945;
     terminology, 166; USMARC
     terminology, 166
Stanford University, 813, 2467, 2988,
     4960
statistical methodologies for
     preservations, 1428
STEP leather project, 2569
storage, 60, 433, 1049, 1234, 1320,
     1463, 3222, 3252, 3319, 3621,
     3829, 3874, 3949, 4339, 4981,
     5071; archival, 25–26, 696, 1991,
     4484, 4843; book boxes, 963,
     1335, 4354, 4846, 4936; boxing
     material, 1992, 2050; electronic,

2735; environment, 3195, 5071;
     flat paper, 1848; long-term, 696;
     magnetic tape, 4812; maps, 1282,
     3967; microfilm, 29, 34, 36, 119;
     microforms, 3946; museum, 5193;
     of records, 4798; optical disk,
     1279–80, 3473; paper based, 67,
     69; photography, 3846–47; single-
     sheet, 2718; single-tier shelving,
     4763; systems for, 4754, 4757–58;
     techniques, 3758; thymol cabinets,
     1990; wheat starch paste, 3112,
     4418; works on paper, 726
strategies for preservation, 497, 3255
supplies, suppliers, 19, 796, 2591,
     2741
surrogate copies, 589, 1075, 2292,
     2967, 3386
surveys: analysis of, 1045; audio, film,
     video, 1883; brittle books, 5016;
     conservation, 1304; conservation
     time estimates, 158; education,
     training, 1072; library conditions,
     2288; methodology of, 640;
     micropublishers, 2455; motion
     picture conservation, 3202;
     museums, 237; NARS paper
     holding, 923; preservation and
     access, 3203, 4505; Pro-Cite 2.02
     software, 2107; RONDAC, 1047;
     sample of, 5033
Swartsburg, Susan, 1219
Sweden, 106, 3496
synthetic glues, 1546

tape cleaning, 222
techniques, 2582
television archives, 681, 3335, 4181,
     4682
Tennessee, 4550
Texas A&M University, 2003
Texas College of Law Library, 226
text storage and retrieval systems,
     4031
textbooks, 2186, 2562
textile conservation, 5204
theft, 39, 45, 66, 82, 104–05, 113, 150,
     154, 160, 285, 1331, 1509, 1580,
     1708, 1774, 1910, 2026, 2041,
     2171, 2254–55, 2293, 2706, 2835,
     3011, 3136, 4530, 5128, 5154; by
     employees, 4587, 4628; by
     patrons, 4614; by teenagers, 2097;
     case studies of, 1831, 2035;

literature on, 3969; Massachusetts
law on, 4275; prevention
guidelines, 3299; security
controls, 3447, 5154; thermal fax
paper, 2295, 2362
thermal papers, stability of, 353, 2190
theses, dissertation preservation, 705
Thin Layer Isoelectric Focusing, 3453
Time Weighted Preservation Index
(TWPI), 3839
transparent paper, 4821
trends in preservation/conservation,
2732
trimmer, character of, 466
Trinity College, Dublin, 901–02, 1013,
4198
TWPI *See* Time Weighted
Preservation Index
typefoundry, 5207, 5228

U. S. Advisory Committee on the
Records of Congress, 4696
ultra-thin tissues, 479
ultraviolet light, 2761
uncoated paperboard, 425
UNESCO, 9, 1085–86, 1299, 1537,
1635, 1760, 1790, 2179, 2411,
2776, 4522, 4565, 4569, 4816
Union Carbide, 4691
Universal Book Tester, 3801
University of California, 618, 2902,
3406, 4684; at Berkeley, 3953
University of Chicago, 5055
University of Columbia, 510, 2552
University of Connecticut, 518, 3055,
4532, 4658
University of Florida, 542
University of Georgia, 4773–77
University of Glasgow, 4778
University of Ibadan library, 78
University of Iowa library, 1614
University of Kansas, 4779
University of Kentucky, 4780
University of Malaya, 2537
University of Manitoba libraries, 565
University of Maryland, 2896
University of Michigan, 884
University of Missouri, 4781; St.
Louis, 5337
University of Oregon, 4783
University of Pennsylvania, 4785
University of Pittsburgh, 4786
University of Rochester, 4787
University of Southern California,
4788
University of Southhamption, England,
5110
University of Tennessee, 4789
University of Texas at Austin, 603,
2227
University of the South, 259
University of Toronto, 4790
University of Tulsa, 122
University of Waterloo, 4791
University of Western Ontario, 4792
University of West Indies, 1051
University of Wyoming, 5130
urban libraries, 375
U.S. Government Printing Office
(GPO), 2817, 2847, 3247, 4075,
4698, 4714
U.S. Machine-Readable Cataloging
(USMARC format), 5095
U.S. National Academy of Science, 32
U.S. Newspaper Project, 4457, 4495,
4794, 5106
USMARC *See* U.S. Machine-Readable
Cataloging
USSR Academy of Sciences, 561
Utah, 4035
Utah College Library Council, 2042
UV filtering materials, comparison of,
1268

vandalism, 800, 1123, 2706
vapor phase deacidification, 2675
varnishes, 3010
vellum, 12, 776, 896, 987, 1055, 1357,
1616, 1705, 2717, 3211–12, 3215,
3607, 4848; leaves binding, 5036
Victoria & Albert Museum, London,
4203
video acquisitions, cataloging, 4108
video format conservation, 985
video image preservation, 2964
videodiscs, 1242, 2135
videotape preservation, 632, 706, 921,
961, 1115, 1169–70, 2712–16,
3045, 3500, 4107, 5019–20, 5160
Virginia Historical Society, 3971

Wales, England, 3818–19, 4574
Walters Art Gallery, 3737
Washington Research Library
Consortium, 4924
waste disposal, 127
watermarks, 842
weeding, 749, 857, 1223, 1252–55,

2387, 3580
Wei T'o deacidification process, 723, 909, 1298, 1392, 2216–17, 4149–50, 4309, 4314, 4363, 4690; spray can system, 202, 5351–52
Weidner, Marilyn Kemp, 1213
Wesley (MA) Public Library, 3865
Western Africa, 4547
Western papers, production methods, 2374
Westport, Connecticut, 4063
Whatman paper, 1611
Wheaton College, 2157
whole-discipline preservation, 2854
Wide Area Information Server (WAIS) *See* Conservation Online
Widener Library, Harvard, 3629

William Salt Library Stafford, 3760
Wisconsin, 4614, 5087
wood, wood products, 577–78
World War I, 3617
World War II, 2053
WORM (write once, read many times) technology, 2124
wrappers, 1796, 4091
Wright, Frank Lloyd, 3220
writing paper, 2049

Yale University, 1210, 4883–84, 4890, 5132; Library, 4928
Young, Laura S., 1211

Zanzibar archives project, 4596
zero-span tensile strength, 47

About the Authors

Robert E. Schnare, Jr. (B.A., William Paterson University of New Jersey; M.L.S., University of Pittsburgh; M.A., University of Connecticut) is the director of the U.S. Naval War College Library, Newport, Rhode Island. He was formerly the director of the Special Collections Division at the U.S. Military Academy Library, West Point, New York. He also worked at the Connecticut State Library in Hartford, Connecticut, in the Archives, History, and Genealogy Division. He serves on the New England Library Network (NELINET) Board of Directors as chair of the Preservation Advisory Committee, cochair of the Federal Library Information Center Committee (FLICC) Preservation & Bindery Working Group, and chair of the Northeast Document Conservation Center's Advisory Committee. Schnare is the author of several articles on preservation management, disaster preparedness, and local history and genealogy, and he is active in numerous professional organizations. From 1979 to 1987, he compiled the publication column for *Conservation Administration News.*

Susan Garretson Swartzburg, 1938–1996 (B.A., Wells College; M.A.; New York University; M.L.S., Simmons College) was the assistant librarian for Collection Management, Rutgers University Libraries. She established the preservation programs at Yale and Rutgers and developed standard procedures for preservation planning and handling deteriorated library materials. She was active in IFLA, ALA, and the New Jersey Library Association and was a founder of the Princeton Preservation Group. She served on the Advisory Board of the Northeast Documents Conservation Center and the Wells College Book Arts Center. A prolific author, she served as associate editor of *Conservation Administration News* until 1994 and contributed regularly to library literature. Her publications include *Libraries and Archives: Design and Renovation with a Preservation Perspective* (Scarecrow Press, 1991) and *Preserving Library Materials: A Manual, 2nd edition* (Scarecrow Press, 1995).

George M. Cunha, 1914–1994 (Massachusetts Institute of Technology and the U.S. Naval War College), was a U.S. Navy captain with twenty-six years of service as a combat pilot in World War II and as an underwater weapons specialist. His military awards included the Distinguished Flying Cross, the Air Medal with star, and a Presidential Unit Citation. He worked as the Chief Conservator of the Boston Athenaeum in 1963 and later spearheaded the creation of the New England Documents Conservation Center in 1973. He retired to Kentucky in 1980. He was a fellow of the American Institute for Conservation, the Royal Society of Arts (London), the Society of American Archivists, the Guild of Book Workers, and the Pilgrim Society. In the field of preservation of library and archival materials he was a leader of great vision and a recognized international authority. His books are recognized as classics at the time they were written and filled a vacuum when there was no other literature on the subject of the conservation of library materials. He was tireless in spreading the word about preservation, and his legacy will live on in the countless students he mentored. Among his works are *Conservation of Library Materials* (Scarecrow Press, 1967) and *Library and Archives Conservation: 1980s and Beyond* (Scarecrow Press, 1983).